GUFFEY & LOEWY

Business Communication

Process & Product

9th Edition

Mary Ellen Guffey
Professor Emerita of Business
Los Angeles Pierce College

Dana Loewy
Business Communication Program
California State University, Fullerton

Australia • Brazil • Mexico • Singapore • United Kingdom • United States

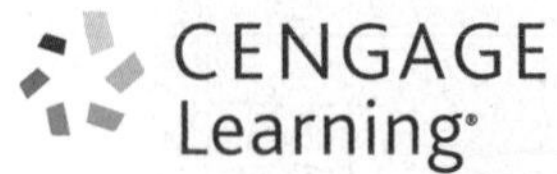

Business Communication: Process & Product, 9th Edition

Mary Ellen Guffey, Dana Loewy

Vice President, General Manager, Social Science & Qualitative Business: Erin Joyner

Product Director: Jason Fremder

Product Manager: Heather Mooney

Content Development Manager: John Rich

Product Assistant: Allie Janneck

Marketing Manager: Charisse Darin

Content Project Manager: Megan Guiliani

Manufacturing Planner: Ron Montgomery

Production Service: Cenveo Publisher Services

Sr. Art Director: Bethany Casey

Internal & Cover Designer: Tippy McIntosh

Cover Image: Donald Iain Smith/Blend Images/Getty Images

Intellectual Property

Analyst: Diane Garrity

Project Manager: Sarah Shainwald

Vector, Chapter Opener: A-R-T/Shutterstock.com

Zooming In Photo:Yeamake/Shutterstock.com

Career Coach Photo: wavebreakmedia/Shutterstock.com

Library of Congress Control Number: 2016958170

ISBN: 978-1-305-95796-1

Cengage Learning
20 Channel Center Street
Boston, MA 02210
USA

Printed in the United States of America
Print Number: 01 Print Year: 2016

Business Communication: Process & Product 9e

Dr. Mary Ellen Guffey
Emerita Professor of Business
Los Angeles Pierce College
m.e.guffey@cox.net

Dr. Dana Loewy
Business Communication Program
California State University, Fullerton
dloewy@fullerton.edu

Dear Business Communication Student:

Photographer: Barbara D'Allessandro

Dana Loewy and Mary Ellen Guffey

The Ninth Edition of ***Business Communication: Process & Product*** prepares you for a career in a complex mobile, social, and global workplace. To help you successfully navigate this vast networked environment, we have substantially revised our award-winning book. You will learn how social media networks and mobile technology function in the workplace and how you can strengthen your professional communication and critical thinking skills.

All of the features that have made this award-winning textbook so successful for nearly three decades have been updated in this edition. In addition to solid instruction in writing skills, which employers continue to demand, the Ninth Edition brings you numerous learning resources, a few of which are highlighted here:

- **MindTap.** This multimedia learning experience provides chapter quizzes, downloadable documents to revise, flashcards, and unparalleled resources to achieve success in the course.
- **"How-To" videos.** Helping you develop expert writing techniques, chapter how-to videos explain and illustrate many Ninth Edition concepts and model documents including bad-news, claim, adjustment, persuasive, and sales messages. These chapter-based videos build skills and develop confidence for both face-to-face and remote learners.
- **Integrated digital technologies.** The professional use of social media networks and mobile technology requires that you know best practices. This edition provides the latest advice to guide you in using these digital technologies safely and effectively in the workplace. You'll find best practices for texting, instant messaging, blogging, collaborating with wikis, and networking with social media in business today.
- **Latest trends in job searching.** Chapter 15 presents the most current trends, technologies, and practices affecting the job search, résumés, and cover letters in this digital age. You will learn how to build a personal brand, how to network, and how to write customized résumés plus create an effective LinkedIn profile.
- **Hottest trends in job interviewing.** Chapter 16 provides countless tips on how to interview successfully in today's highly competitive job market, including one-way and two-way video interviewing.
- **EtiquetteQ.** New communication platforms and casual workplace environments have blurred the lines of appropriateness, leaving workers wondering how to behave on the job. This edition delivers up-to-date guidance on acceptable workplace attire, professional behavior, and business etiquette for today's mobile and social workplace. Each chapter also provides a "Test Your Etiquette IQ" quiz with authentic questions and answers.

We wish you well in your course! As always, we welcome your comments and suggestions as you use the No. 1 business communication book in this country and abroad.

Cordially,

Mary Ellen Guffey and Dana Loewy

Business Communication: Process & Product, 9E

This book and this course may well be the most important in your entire college curriculum!

Why? This book and your course equip you with the skills you will most need in today's fast-paced information- and data-driven workplace.

MEETING EMPLOYER EXPECTATIONS

Survey after survey reveals that employers are seeking new hires with these key skills:

- Written and oral communication skills
- Critical thinking and analytical reasoning
- Ethical decision making
- Teamwork skills
- Professionalism

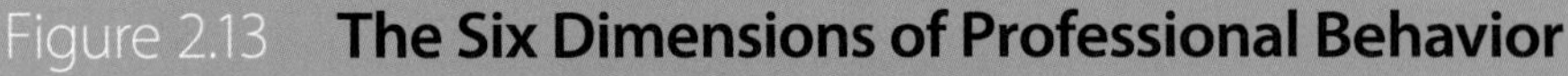

Figure 2.13 **The Six Dimensions of Professional Behavior**

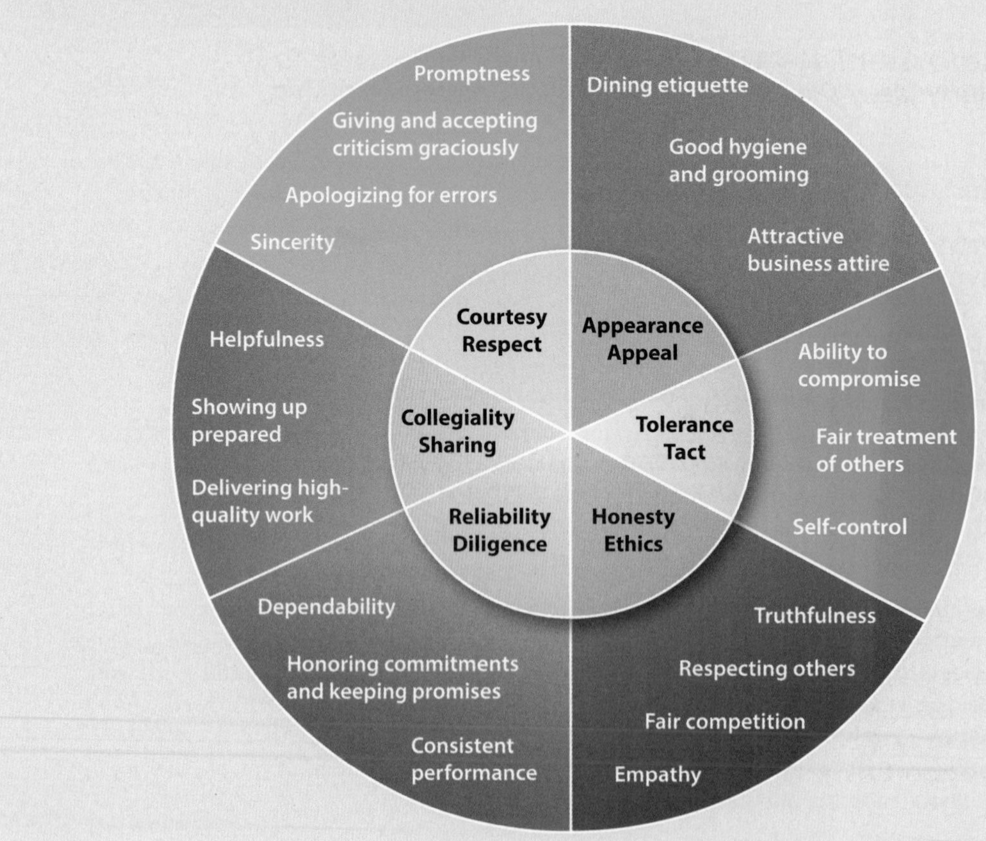

Business Communication: Process & Product, 9e

No other college course gives you training in all of these skills at once!

Business Communication: Process and Product, 9e, covers the following topics you will find indispensable in the digital-age workplace:

- Expert writing techniques geared to developing your writing skills plus interactive Documents for Analysis, authentic model documents, and engaging activities in which you apply your skills
- Presentation skills featuring contemporary examples including coverage of smartphone best practices to prepare you for the realities of workplace communication and technology
- Critical thinking questions and activities in every chapter to stimulate and develop skills
- Ethics Checks in addition to guidance and tools provided through discussion questions and ethical dilemma scenarios
- Teamwork skills with a heavy emphasis on professionalism and etiquette in the workplace so that you will know how to meet employer expectations
- Two employment chapters that present the latest trends in job searching, interviewing, and résumé writing, along with current, effective résumé models, tips for mobile devices and apps, and LinkedIn advice and illustrations
- Test Your Etiquette IQ, a recurring feature in each chapter, designed to shine a light on often blurry ideas about appropriateness and professionalism in the workplace.

PREMIUM ONLINE RESOURCES

- **MindTap, Your Personalized, Fully Online Digital Learning Platform.** This comprehensive learning platform guides you through readings, multimedia tools, and chapter-specific activities that increase learner involvement and produce significant learning outcomes. By being interactive, MindTap makes learning enjoyable and playful. You can deepen your understanding of business communication concepts at your own pace.
- **Aplia Homework.** Aplia helps you comprehend and remember chapter concepts in an engaging interactive format. You know immediately how well you are doing with immediate feedback on each problem set. You may even be able to repeat exercises to improve your score.
- **Grammar Review.** Grammar review exercises provide you with engaging online practice, covering key grammar concepts with interactive exercises that you can finish in your own time. Your unique needs are addressed through diagnostic assessments, pinpointing your areas of strength and potential remediation needs. A large and randomized pool of questions provides multiple opportunities to master each concept.

- **How-To Videos.** Appealing to visual learners, this edition provides about 32 short videos that explain and illustrate many Ninth Edition concepts and model documents including positive, bad-news, claim adjustment, persuasive, and sales messages. These videos are especially helpful to distance learners who are not able to benefit from in-class lectures.
- **Study Tools**
  - **PowerPoint Lectures.** Our totally new PowerPoint slides for the Ninth Edition review chapter concepts and highlight important points with contemporary, colorful images, and just enough animation.
  - **Interactive chapter quizzes** at the Student Companion Website enable you to test your knowledge of concepts with immediate feedback.
  - **Flashcards.** You can study with existing flashcards and make your own.

SOCIAL MEDIA NETWORKS AND MOBILE TECHNOLOGY

Trusted authors Mary Ellen Guffey and Dana Loewy understand social and mobile! The authors address workplace use of social media and communication technology in a chapter solely dedicated to best practices on the job. Because these skills are fundamental in the contemporary world of work, social media and communication technology are integrated in each chapter.

Every chapter reflects the pervasive influence of communication technology on business writing. This state-of-the-art coverage makes it clear that writing is more important than ever in the digital world. Careers are made or thwarted based on one's online digital persona.

Figure 1.8 **Traditional vs. Social Media Communication Between Businesses and Customers**

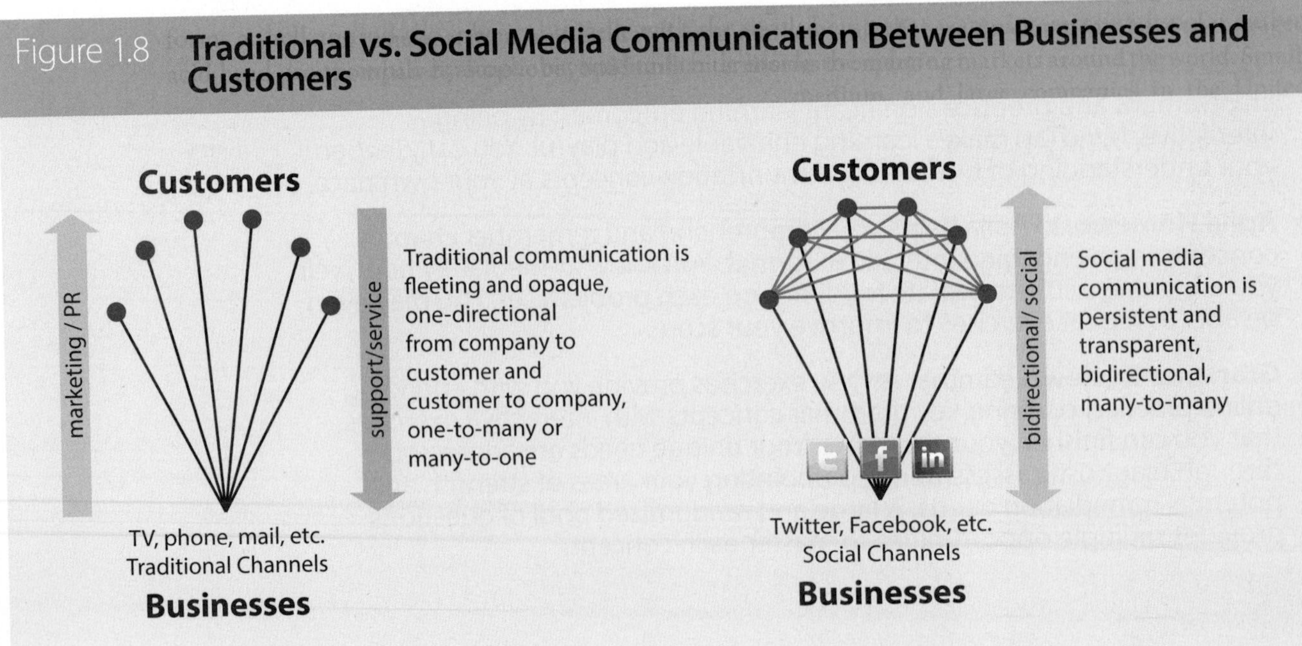

- New digital model documents throughout illustrate how social media networks are shaping today's communication and will help you understand professional social media applications.
- New activities, identified with the Social Media and Communication Technology icon, reflect the preeminence of writing in the digital workplace and prompt you to develop your professional social networking skills.

SOCIAL NETWORKS VS. OTHER U.S. WORKERS: COMPARING ATTITUDES TOWARDS QUESTIONABLE BEHAVIOR

Do you feel it is acceptable to...?	Active Social Networkers	Other U.S. Workers
"Friend" a client/customer on a social network	59%	28%
Blog or tweet negatively about your company or colleagues	42%	6%
Buy personal items with your company credit card as long as you pay it back	42%	8%
Do a little less work to compensate for cuts in benefits or pay	51%	10%
Keep a copy of confidential work documents in case you need them in your next job	50%	15%
Take a copy of work software home and use it on your personal computer	46%	7%
Upload vacation pictures to the company network or server so you can share them with co-workers	50%	17%
Use social networking to find out what my company's competitors are doing	54%	30%

Opening scenarios in each chapter illustrate social media and technology use, teamwork, meetings, persuasion, and more by companies that you know and interact with, such as Starbucks, Lyft, Walmart, Taco Bell, Sony, Royal Caribbean, olloclip, Pew Research, and JetBlue.

Nordstrom: A Fabulous Shopping Experience Goes Social

Yeamake/Shutterstock.com

Nordstrom's customer service is legendary. Like no other, the upscale fashion retailer empowers its employees to make their own decisions to best serve customers. Consider the Anchorage location once accepting returned tires that the retailer doesn't even sell. Another true story relates that an employee raced to deliver a scatterbrained customer's forgotten baggage to the airport prior to her departure. Both anecdotes exemplify the century-old company's motto: *to provide a fabulous customer experience by empowering customers and the employees who serve them.*

But Nordstrom's fabled devotion to customer service extends strategically into the virtual world to meet customers where they are. The retailer has invested heavily in technology; for example, to integrate its inventory management system with its website and the Nordstrom app—always with the clear purpose to enhance the customer experience. As a result, the company's online and offline worlds are seamlessly linked, and customers can find what they want in one place. Salespeople can track customer requests and needs online. This persistent effort to integrate digital capabilities has paid off. Nordstrom's revenue has grown by more than 50 percent in the last five years.[1] Its shares have jumped 120 percent.[2]

A strong social media engagement is key to Nordstrom's strategy to provide superb service and to drive traffic to its e-commerce site. As one of America's most connected companies,[3] it relies on crowdsourcing to learn which items to stock, and it responds rapidly to queries, in Spanish when needed. At currently 3.2 million likes, Nordstrom is a strong presence on Facebook. Pinterest, the popular online bulletin board, is a particular success story for early-adopter Nordstrom, which currently has some 4.4 million followers.[4]

With such public engagement, it's not surprising that Nordstrom has clearly defined social media use guidelines. Approved employees may connect with customers during working hours and even after hours, if allowed. They are admonished to use good judgment and abide by all corporate policies. They are told to be respectful, responsible, and ethical. Furthermore, Nordstrom's social media policy forbids the sharing of confidential corporate information as well as employees' and customers' private and personal information. Conflicts of interest are to be avoided, and compensated endorsements must be disclosed. The policy ends with this cheerful invitation: "Above all, remember to have fun and be yourself!"[5]

Nordstrom's digital strategy is making the company highly competitive. You will learn more about Nordstrom and be asked to complete a relevant task at the end of this chapter.

Critical Thinking

- After reading this case study, can you put into perspective the suggestion "have fun and be yourself"? What exactly does this invitation mean?
- Why does Nordstrom allow only certain employees to connect online with customers and other members of the public?
- Why do social media guidelines emphasize ethical behavior and ethical communication?

Brief Contents

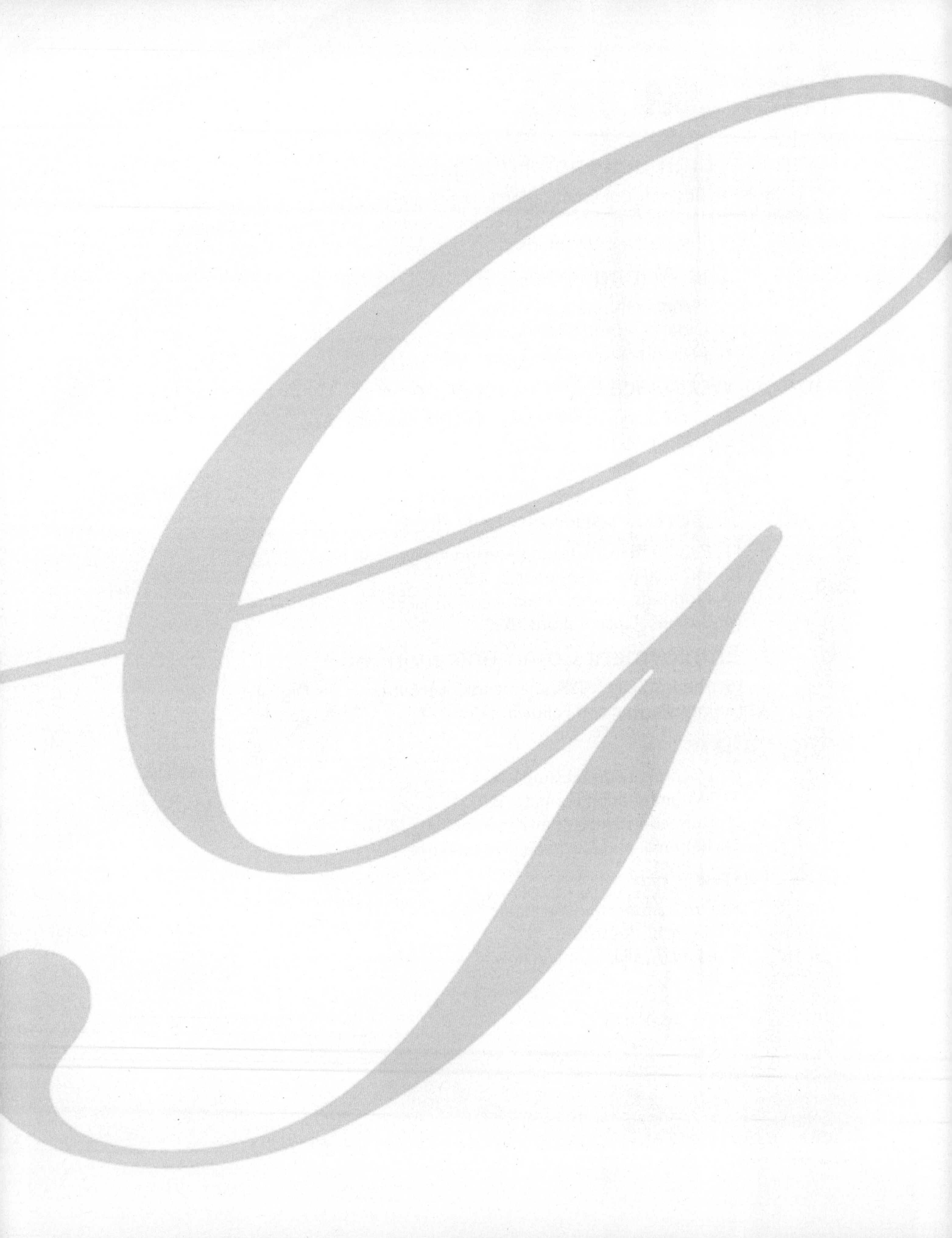

Contents

UNIT 1 Communication Foundations

Chapter 1
Business Communication in the Digital Age 2

AjFile/Shutterstock.com

Chapter 2
Professionalism: Team, Meeting, Listening, Nonverbal, and Etiquette Skills 42

Charlotte Purdy/Shutterstock.com

Dan Baciu/Shutterstock.com

racorn/Shutterstock.com

Chapter 5
Organizing and Drafting Business Messages 158

Darren Baker/Shutterstock.com

Chapter 6
Revising Business Messages 186

Monkey Business Images/Shutterstock.com

UNIT 3 Workplace Communication

Chapter 7
Short Workplace Messages and Digital Media 214

Bolyuk Rostyslav/Shutterstock.com

Chapter 8
Positive Messages 252

Stuart Jenner/Shutterstock.com

Chapter 9
Negative Messages 294

goodluz/Shutterstock.com

Chapter 10
Persuasive and Sales Messages 338

Phovoir/Shutterstock.com

UNIT 4 Reports, Proposals, and Presentations

Chapter 13 Proposals, Business Plans, and Formal Business Reports 482

Milles Studio/Shutterstock.com

Chapter 14 Business Presentations 520

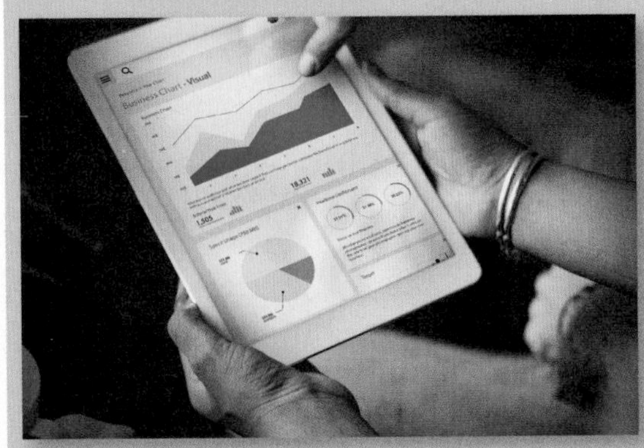
Rawpixel.com/Shutterstock.com

UNIT 5 Employment Communication

Chapter 15

The Job Search, Résumés, and Cover Letters in the Digital Age 564

Nicotombo/Shutterstock.com

Chapter 16

Interviewing and Following Up 612

goodluz/Shutterstock.com

Appendixes

End Matter

Appreciation for Support

No successful textbook reaches a No. 1 position without a great deal of help. We are exceedingly grateful to the reviewers and other experts who contributed their pedagogic and academic expertise in shaping *Business Communication: Process & Product.*

We extend sincere thanks to many professionals at Cengage Learning; Erin Joyner, Vice President, General Manager for Social Sciences, Humanities & Business; Michael Schenk, Executive Product Director for Business & Economics; John Rich, Content Development Manager; Megan Guiliani, Content Project Manager; Bethany Casey, Senior Art Director, and Diane Garrity, Intellectual Property Analyst.

Our heartfelt appreciation also goes to the following for their expertise in creating exceptional instructor and student support materials: Janet Mizrahi, University of California, Santa Barbara; Carolyn M. Seefer, Diablo Valley College; Thanakorn Kooptaporn, California State University, Fullerton; Michele Granger, Missouri State University; and Nicole Adams, University of Dayton.

Mary Ellen Guffey

Dana Loewy

Grateful Thanks to Reviewers

Janet G. Adams, *Minnesota State University,* Mankato

Leslie Adams, *Houston Baptist University*

Kehinde A. Adesina, *Contra Costa College*

Asberine Parnell Alford, *Suffolk Community College*

Virginia Allen, *Joliet Junior College*

Cynthia Anderson, *Youngstown State University*

Linda Landis Andrews, *University of Illinois, Chicago*

Vanessa D. Arnold, *University of Mississippi*

Lois J. Bachman, *Community College of Philadelphia*

Rebecca Barksdale, *University of Central Florida*

Sandra Berill, *Arkansas State University*

Teresa L. Beyer, *Sinclair Community College*

Cathie Bishop, *Parkland College*

Randi Blank, *Indiana University*

Elizabeth Bowers, *Orange Coast College and Golden West College*

Martha E. Bradshaw, *Southeastern Louisiana University*

Bernadine Branchaw, *Western Michigan University*

Maryanne Brandenburg, *Indiana University of Pennsylvania*

Charles P. Bretan, *Northwood University*

Paula E. Brown, *Northern Illinois University*

Vivian R. Brown, *Loredo Community College*

Domenic Bruni, *University of Wisconsin Oshkosh*

Phyllis C. Bunn, *Delta State University*

Mary Ann Burris, *Pueblo Community College*

Roosevelt D. Butler, *College of New Jersey*

Jane Campanizzi-Mook, *Franklin University*

James F. Carey, *Onondaga Community College*

Leila Chambers, *Cuesta College*

Patricia H. Chapman, *University of South Carolina*

Judie C. Cochran, *Grand Canyon University*

Marjorie Coffey, *Oregon State University*

Randy E. Cone, *University of New Orleans*

James Conley, *Eastern Michigan University*

Billie Miller Cooper, *Cosumnes River College*

Linda W. Cooper, *Macon State College*

Jane G. Corbly, *Sinclair Community College*

Martha Cross, *Delta State University*

Linda Cunningham, *Salt Lake Community College*

Lajuan Davis, *University of Wisconsin-Whitewater*

Fred DeCasperis, *Siena College*

Guy Devitt, *Herkimer County Community College*

Linda Di Desidero, *University of Maryland University College*

John Donnellan, *University of Texas at Austin*

J. Yellowless Douglas, *University of Florida*

Bertha Du-Babcock, *City University of Hong Kong*

Dorothy Drayton, *Texas Southern University*

Kay Durden, *University of Tennessee*

Anna Easton, *Indiana University*

Lorena B. Edwards, *Belmont University*

Donald E. English, *Texas A&M University*

Margaret Erthal, *Southern Illinois University*

Donna R. Everett, *Morehead State University*

Gwendolyn Bowie Ewing, *Southwest Tennessee Community College*

Anne Finestone, *Santa Monica Community College*

Peggy B. Fisher, *Ball State University*

Terry M. Frame, *University of South Carolina*

Gen Freese, *Harrisburg Area Community College*

Kerry J. Gambrill, *Florida Community College*

Judith L. Graham, *Holyoke Community College*

Carolyn G. Gray, *The University of Texas, Austin*

Diane Gruber, *Arizona State University West*

Susan Guzmán-Treviño, *Temple College*

David Hamilton, *Bemidji State University*

Bill Hargrave, *University of West Georgia*

Paul Hegele, *Elgin Community College*

Susan A. Heller, *Reading Area Community College*

K. Virginia Hemby, *Middle Tennessee State University*

Rovena L. Hillsman, *California State University, Sacramento*

Kenneth Hoffman, *Emporia State University*

Shirley Houston, *University of Nebraska*

Warren B. Humphrey, *University of Central Florida*

Robert G. Insley, *University of North Texas*

Edna Jellesed, *Lane Community College*

Glen J. Jenewein, *Portland Community College*

Kathy Jesiolowski, *Milwaukee Area Technical College*

Carolyn Spillers Jewell, *Pembroke State University*

Pamela R. Johnson, *California State University, Chico*

Eric Johnstone, *Montana State University*

Cheryl L. Kane, *University of North Carolina Charlotte*

Diana K. Kanoy, *Central Florida Community College*

Tina S. Kazan, *University of Illinois, Chicago*

Carolyn E. Kerr, *University of Pittsburgh*

Sonia Khatchadourian, *University of Wisconsin-Milwaukee*

Margaret S. Kilcoyne, *Northwestern State University*

G. Scott King, *Sinclair Community College*

Suzanne P. Krissler, *Orange County Community College*

Linda L. Labin, *Husson College*

Gary E. Lacefield, *University of Texas at Arlington*

Richard Lacy, *California State University, Fresno*

Suzanne Lambert, *Broward Community College*

Marilyn L. Lammers, *California State University, Northridge*

Lorita S. Langdon, *Columbus State Community College*

Joyce N. Larsen, *Front Range Community College*

Marianna Larsen, *Utah State University*

Barbara Lea, *West Valley College*

Claire E. Legowski, *North Dakota State University*

Mary E. Leslie, *Grossmont College*

Kathy Lynn Lewis-Adler, *University of North Alabama*

Kristie J. Loescher, *The University of Texas at Austin*

Jennifer Cook Loney, *Portland State University*

Mary Jean Lush, *Delta State University*

Sonia Maasik, *University of California, Los Angeles*

Bruce MacBeth, *Clarion University of Pennsylvania*

Georgia E. Mackh, *Cabrillo College*

Andrew Madson, *Milwaukee Area Technical College*

Anna Maheshwari, *Schoolcraft College*

Maureen L. Margolies, *University of Cincinnati*

Leon Markowicz, *Lebanon Valley College*

Thomas A. Marshall II, *Robert Morris College*

Jeanette Martin, *University of Mississippi*

John F. Mastriani, *El Paso Community College*

Cynthia H. Mayfield, *York Technical College*

Susan Smith McClaren, *Mt. Hood Community College*

Beryl C. McEwen, *North Carolina A&T State University*

Marya McFadden, *California State University Northridge*

Nancy McGee, *Davenport University*

Diana McKowen, *Indiana University*

Mary C. Miller, *Ashland University*

Marci Mitchell, *South Texas Community College*

Nancy B. Moody, *Sinclair Community College*

Danne Moore, *Shawnee State University*

Wayne A. Moore, *Indiana University of Pennsylvania*

Paul W. Murphey, *Southwest Wisconsin Technical College*

Lin Nassar, *Oakland Community College*

Beverly H. Nelson, *University of New Orleans*

Matt Newby, *Heald College*

John P. Nightingale, *Eastern Michigan University*

Ed Nagelhout, *University of Nevada*

Jeanne E. Newhall, *Middlesex Community College*

Alexa B. North, *State University of West Georgia*

Nancy Nygaard, *University of Wisconsin-Milwaukee*

Rosemary Olds, *Des Moines Area Community College*

James S. O'Rourke IV, *University of Notre Dame*

Smita Jain Oxford, *University of Mary Washington*

Ed Peters, *University of Texas at Arlington*

Melinda Phillabaum, *Indiana University*

Richard David Ramsey, *Southeastern Louisiana University, Hammond*

Betty Jane Robbins, *University of Oklahoma*

Janice Rowan, *Rowan University*

Calvin R. Parks, *Northern Illinois University*

Pamela A. Patey, *Riverside Community College*

Shara Toursh Pavlow, *University of Miami*

William Peirce, *Prince George's Community College and University of Maryland University College*

Joan Policano, *Onondaga Community College*

Paula J. Pomerenke, *Illinois State University*

Jean Anna Sellers, *Fort Hays State University*

Deborah Von Spreecken, *Anoka-Ramsey Community College*

Karen Sterkel Powell, *Colorado State University*

Gloria Power, *Delgado Community College*

Richard P. Profozich, *Prince George's Community College*

Carolyn Mae Rainey, *Southeast Missouri State University*

Richard David Ramsey, *Southeastern Louisiana University*

Richard G. Raspen, *Wilkes University*

Virginia L. Reynolds, *Cleveland State University*

Ruth D. Richardson, *University of North Alabama*

Joseph H. Roach, *Middlesex County College*

Terry D. Roach, *Arkansas State University*

Betty Jane Robbins, *University of Oklahoma*

Linda Sarlo, *Rock Valley College*

Christine A. Saxild, *Mt. Senario College*

Joseph Schaffner, *State University of New York at Alfred*

Annette Schley, *North Seattle Community College*

Betty L. Schroeder, *Northern Illinois University*

Carolyn M. Seefer, *Diablo Valley Community College*

Marilyn Simonson, *Lakewood Community College*

Sue C. Smith, *Palm Beach Community Collage*

Kathleen M. Sole, *University of Phoenix*

Charles L. Snowden, *Sinclair Community College*

Gayle A. Sobolik, *California State University, Fresno*

Jeanette Spender, *Arkansas State University*

Jan Starnes, *The University of Texas at Austin*

Judy Steiner-Williams, *Indiana University*

Ted D. Stoddard, *Brigham Young University*

Susan Switzer, *Central Michigan University*

Roni Szeliga, *Gateway Technical College*

Leslie S. Talley, *University of Central Florida*

Barbara P. Thompson, *Columbus State Community College*

Sally J. Tiffany, *Milwaukee Area Technical College*

Lori M. Townsend, *Niagara County Community College*

Mary L. Tucker, *Ohio University*

Richard F. Tyler, *Anne Arundel Community College*

Deborah Valentine, *Emory University*

Doris A. Van Horn Christopher, *California State University, Los Angeles*

David Victor, *Eastern Michigan University*

Lois Ann Wagner, *Southwest Wisconsin Technical College*

John L. Waltman, *Eastern Michigan University*

Marion Webb, *Cleveland State University*

Beverly A. Westbrook, *Delta College*

Carol Smith White, *Georgia State University*

Carol M. Williams, *Pima County Community College*

Debbie J. Williams, *Abilene Christian University*

Jane D. Williams, *J. Sargeant Reynolds Community College*

Rosemary B. Wilson, *Washtenaw Community College*

Beverly C. Wise, *State University of New York, Morrisville*

William E. Worth, *Georgia State University*

Myron D. Yeager, *Chapman University*

Karen Zempel, *Bryant and Stratton College*

About the Authors

Dr. Mary Ellen Guffey

A dedicated professional, Mary Ellen Guffey has taught business communication and business English topics for over thirty-five years. She received a bachelor's degree, summa cum laude, from Bowling Green State University; a master's degree from the University of Illinois, and a doctorate in business and economic education from the University of California, Los Angeles (UCLA). She has taught at the University of Illinois, Santa Monica College, and Los Angeles Pierce College.

Now recognized as the world's leading business communication author, Dr. Guffey corresponds with instructors around the globe who are using her books. She is the founding author of the award-winning *Business Communication: Process & Product*, the leading business communication textbook in this country. She also wrote *Business English*, which serves more students than any other book in its field; *Essentials of College English*; and *Essentials of Business Communication*, the leading text/workbook in its market. Dr. Guffey is active professionally, serving on the review boards of the *Business and Professional Communication Quarterly* and the *Journal of Business Communication*, publications of the Association for Business Communication. She participates in national meetings, sponsors business communication awards, and is committed to promoting excellence in business communication pedagogy and the development of student writing skills.

Dr. Dana Loewy

Dana Loewy has been teaching business communication at California State University, Fullerton since 1996. She enjoys introducing undergraduates to business writing and honing the skills of graduate students in managerial communication. Most recently, she has also taught various German courses and is a regular guest lecturer at Fach-hochschule Nürtingen, Germany. In addition to completing numerous brand-name consulting assignments, she is a certified business etiquette consultant. Dr. Loewy has collaborated with Dr. Guffey on recent editions of *Business Communication: Process & Product* as well as on *Essentials of Business Communication.*

Dr. Loewy holds a master's degree from Bonn University, Germany, and earned a PhD in English from the University of Southern California. Fluent in several languages, among them German and Czech, her two native languages, Dr. Loewy has authored critical articles in many areas of interest—literary criticism, translation, business communication, and business ethics. Before teaming up with Dr. Guffey, Dr. Loewy published various poetry and prose translations, most notably *The Early Poetry of Jaroslav Seifert* and *On the Waves of TSF.* Active in the Association for Business Communication, Dr. Loewy focuses on creating effective teaching/learning materials for undergraduate and graduate business communication students.

UNIT 1

Communication Foundations

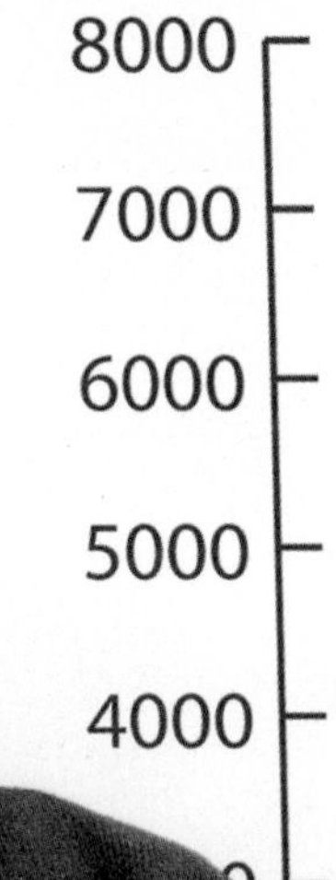

AjFile/Shutterstock.com

Chapter 1 Business Communication in the Digital Age

LEARNING OUTCOMES

After studying this chapter, you should be able to

1 Explain how communication skills fuel career success, and understand why writing skills are vital in a digital, mobile, and social-media-driven workplace.

2 Identify the tools for success in the hyperconnected 21st-century workplace; appreciate the importance of critical-thinking skills and personal credibility in the competitive job market of the digital age; and discuss how your education may determine your income.

3 Describe significant trends in today's dynamic, networked work environment, and recognize that social media and other communication technologies require excellent communication skills, in any economic climate.

4 Examine critically the internal and external flow of communication in organizations through formal and informal channels, explain the importance of effective media choices, and understand how to overcome typical barriers to organizational communication.

5 Analyze ethics in the workplace, understand the goals of ethical business communicators, and choose the tools for doing the right thing.

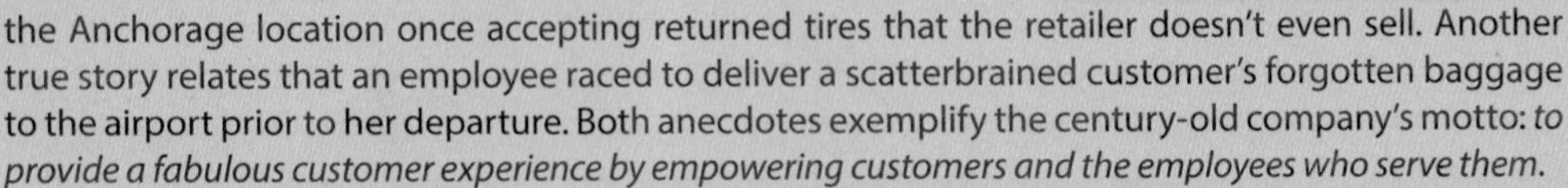

Yeamake/Shutterstock.com

Nordstrom: A Fabulous Shopping Experience Goes Social

Nordstrom's customer service is legendary. Like no other, the upscale fashion retailer empowers its employees to make their own decisions to best serve customers. Consider the Anchorage location once accepting returned tires that the retailer doesn't even sell. Another true story relates that an employee raced to deliver a scatterbrained customer's forgotten baggage to the airport prior to her departure. Both anecdotes exemplify the century-old company's motto: *to provide a fabulous customer experience by empowering customers and the employees who serve them.*

But Nordstrom's fabled devotion to customer service extends strategically into the virtual world to meet customers where they are. The retailer has invested heavily in technology; for example, to integrate its inventory management system with its website and the Nordstrom app—always with the clear purpose to enhance the customer experience. As a result, the company's online and offline worlds are seamlessly linked, and customers can find what they want in one place. Salespeople can track customer requests and needs online. This persistent effort to integrate digital capabilities has paid off. Nordstrom's revenue has grown by more than 50 percent in the last five years.[1] Its shares have jumped 120 percent.[2]

A strong social media engagement is key to Nordstrom's strategy to provide superb service and to drive traffic to its e-commerce site. As one of America's most connected companies,[3] it relies on crowdsourcing to learn which items to stock, and it responds rapidly to queries, in Spanish when needed. At currently 3.2 million likes, Nordstrom is a strong presence on Facebook. Pinterest, the popular online bulletin board, is a particular success story for early-adopter Nordstrom, which currently has some 4.4 million followers.[4]

With such public engagement, it's not surprising that Nordstrom has clearly defined social media use guidelines. Approved employees may connect with customers during working hours and even after hours, if allowed. They are admonished to use good judgment and abide by all corporate policies. They are told to be respectful, responsible, and ethical. Furthermore, Nordstrom's social media policy forbids the sharing of confidential corporate information as well as employees' and customers' private and personal information. Conflicts of interest are to be avoided, and compensated endorsements must be disclosed. The policy ends with this cheerful invitation: "Above all, remember to have fun and be yourself!"[5]

Nordstrom's digital strategy is making the company highly competitive. You will learn more about Nordstrom and be asked to complete a relevant task at the end of this chapter.

Critical Thinking

- After reading this case study, can you put into perspective the suggestion "have fun and be yourself"? What exactly does this invitation mean?
- Why does Nordstrom allow only certain employees to connect online with customers and other members of the public?
- Why do social media guidelines emphasize ethical behavior and ethical communication?

Communicating in the Digital World

LEARNING OUTCOME 1

Explain how communication skills fuel career success, and understand why writing skills are vital in a digital, mobile, and social-media-driven workplace.

What kind of workplace will you enter when you graduate, and which skills will you need to be successful in it? Expect a fast-paced, competitive, and highly connected digital environment. Communication technology provides unmatched mobility and connects individuals anytime and anywhere in the world. Today's communicators interact using multiple electronic devices and access information stored in remote locations, in the cloud.

This mobility and instant access explain why increasing numbers of workers must be available practically around the clock and respond quickly. Nordstrom and other technology-savvy businesses have recognized the power of social media networks and seek to engage their customers and other stakeholders where they meet online. Communication no longer flows one way; rather, electronic media have empowered the public to participate and be heard.

In this increasingly complex, networked, and mobile environment, communication skills matter more than ever.[6] Such skills are particularly significant when competition is keen. Job candidates with exceptional communication skills immediately stand out. In this chapter you will learn about communication skills in the digital era and about the contemporary world of work. Later you will study tools to help you negotiate ethical minefields and do the right thing. Each section covers the latest information about communicating in business while also providing tips to help you function effectively and ethically in today's fast-paced, information-driven workplace.

Communication Skills: Your Pass to Success

Over the last decade, employer surveys have consistently shown that strong communication skills are critical to effective job placement, work performance, career advancement, and organizational success.[7] In making hiring decisions, employers often rank communication skills among the most desirable competencies.[8]

Interviewers for defense contractor BAE Systems may request a writing sample to "literally see if the candidate can write," but also to find out whether the applicant can organize and share ideas, explains Curt Gray, senior vice president of human resources and administration. UPS requires its workers to write clear and concise messages and "to investigate, analyze and report their findings in a professional manner," says Matt Lavery, managing director of corporate talent acquisition.[9] In a poll, Fortune 1000 executives cited writing, critical-thinking, and problem-solving skills along with self-motivation and team skills as their top choices in new-hires.[10]

Writing skills can be your ticket to work—or your ticket out the door, according to a business executive responding to a significant survey. This much-quoted study of 120 American corporations by the National Commission on Writing found that two thirds of salaried employees have some writing responsibility. However, about one third of them do not meet the writing requirements for their positions.[11] "Businesses are crying out—they need to have people who write better," said Gaston Caperton, executive and College Board president.

Writing has been variously called a "career sifter," a "threshold skill," and "the price of admission,"[12] indicating that effective writing skills can be a stepping-stone to great job opportunities. Poorly developed writing skills, however, may derail a career. Writing is a marker of high-skill, high-wage, professional work, according to Bob Kerrey, former university president and chair of the National Commission on Writing. If you can't express yourself clearly, he says, you limit your opportunities for many positions.[13]

When we discuss communication skills, we generally mean reading, listening, nonverbal, speaking, and writing skills. In addition, workers today must be media savvy and exercise good judgment when posting messages on the Internet and writing e-mails. To be successful, they must guard their online image and protect the reputation of their employers. In this book we focus on the listening, nonverbal, speaking, and writing skills necessary in a digital workplace. Chapters are devoted to each of these skills. Special attention is given to writing skills because they are difficult to develop and increasingly significant in e-communication.

Writing in the Digital Age

Note: Because this is a well-researched textbook, you will find small superscript numbers in the text. These announce information sources. Full citations are located in the Notes section beginning on page 40 near the end of the book. This edition uses a modified American Psychological Association (APA) reference citation format.

If you are like many young adults, you may think that your daily texts, instant messages, Facebook posts, blog entries, and e-mails are not *real* writing. A Pew Internet & American Life study found that teens and young adults consider their frequent e-communication to be very different from the traditional writing they learn in school.[14] Perhaps young people understand that their digital writing is largely casual, but that employers expect more formal, thoughtful, informative, and error-free messages. In any case, the respondents in the study rightly believe that solid writing skills are a necessity in today's networked digital world.

Long gone are the days when business was mostly conducted face-to-face and when administrative assistants corrected spelling and grammar for their bosses. Although interpersonal skills still matter greatly, writing effectively is critical. Ever since the digital revolution swept the workplace, most workers write their own messages. New communication channels appeared, including the Web and e-mail, followed by instant messaging, blogs, and social media networks.

The mobile revolution is stimulating huge economic growth and has profoundly changed how we communicate; it has become the fastest-adopted technology of all time.[15] Figure 1.1 displays the emergence of new communication technology and the rapid growth of Internet users over the last two decades. So far, the number of Internet users has roughly doubled every five years.

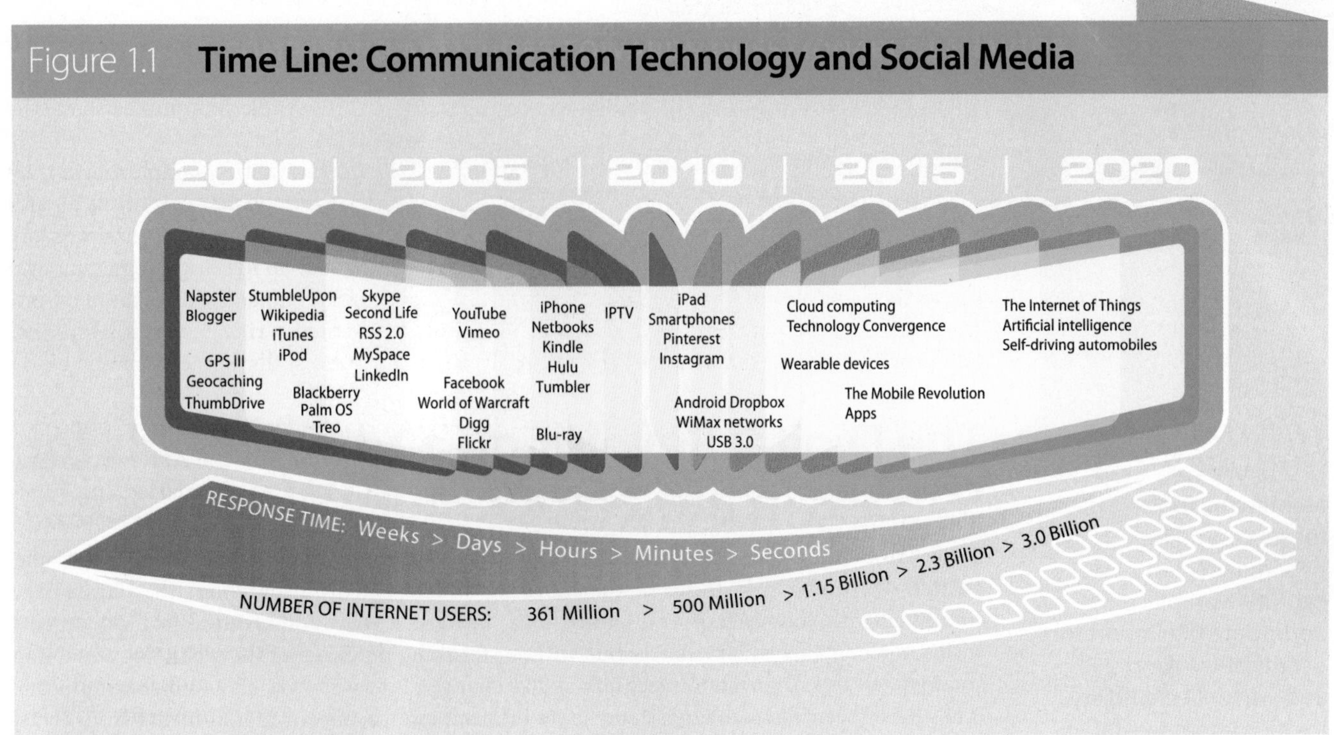

Figure 1.1 **Time Line: Communication Technology and Social Media**

Writing matters more than ever because the online media require more of it, not less.[16] An important poll by Hart Research Associates supports this view. The participating employers admitted that their expectations of employees have increased because the challenges on the job are more complex than in the past. The executives also said that employees today need a broader range of skills as well as higher levels of knowledge in their field.[17]

"Communicating clearly and effectively has NEVER been more important than it is today. Whether it's fair or not, life-changing critical judgments about you are being made based solely on your writing ability," says management consultant Victor Urbach. "Having excellent command of your online digital persona will enable you to quickly surpass those who present themselves weakly in the new competitive arena. Since you probably won't get a second chance, what kind of digital first impression will you choose to make?"[18] Developing these skills in this course will build your credibility and help you stand out.

It's Up to You: Communication Skills Can Be Learned

By enrolling in a business writing class, you have already taken the first step toward improving or polishing your communication skills. The goals of this course and this book include teaching you basic business communication skills, such as how to write an effective e-mail, a short message on a mobile device, or a clear business letter, and how to make a memorable presentation with various digital media.

Thriving in the challenging interconnected work world depends on many factors, some of which you cannot control. However, one factor that you do control is how well you communicate. You are not born with the abilities to read, listen, speak, and write effectively. These skills must be learned. This book and this course may well be the most important in your entire college curriculum because they will equip you with the skills most needed in today's fast-paced information- and data-driven workplace.

Reality Check

Digital Workplace Survival Skills

"To succeed in today's workplace, young people need more than basic reading and math skills. They need substantial content knowledge and information technology skills; advanced thinking skills, flexibility to adapt to change; and interpersonal skills to succeed in multi-cultural, cross-functional teams."[19]

—J. Willard Marriott, Jr., *chairman and CEO, Marriott International, Inc.*

photopixel/Shutterstock.com

LEARNING OUTCOME 2

Identify the tools for success in the hyperconnected 21st-century workplace; appreciate the importance of critical-thinking skills and personal credibility in the competitive job market of the digital age; and discuss how your education may determine your income.

The Digital Revolution and You: Tools for Success in the 21st-Century Workplace

If you are a young adult, chances are that you check Facebook, smartphone texts, Instagram, Twitter, or Tumblr first thing in the morning and repeatedly throughout the day to stay connected with your friends and family. Most likely you write and create digital documents with a notebook, tablet, or smartphone without thinking much about the technology enabling you to do all this. Information technology has changed how we work, play, and communicate. It has never been easier to access and share information via various digital media from a vast network of sources and to distribute it nearly instantly and to widespread audiences.[20] What hasn't changed is that communication skills need time and effort to develop.

To achieve literacy in the digital age means not only using multimedia applications and snazzy late-model gadgets but also thinking critically about new media. It means using technology thoughtfully and in a professional manner to achieve success in a hyperconnected world.

The 21st-century economy depends mainly on information and knowledge. Previously, in the Industrial Age, raw materials and physical labor were the key ingredients in the creation of wealth. Today, however, individuals in the workforce offer their knowledge, not their muscles. Knowledge workers (a term first coined by management guru Peter Drucker) get paid for their education and their ability to learn.[21]

Rachael Arnott/Shutterstock.com

More recently, we are hearing the term *information worker* to describe those who produce and consume information in the workplace.[22] Regardless of the terminology, knowledge and information workers engage in mind work. They must make sense of words, figures, and data. At the same time, the knowledge available in the "digital universe" is more than doubling every year, according to computing pioneer George Dyson.[23]

In this light it may not surprise you that jobs in the information technology sector are likely to jump 24 percent by 2020.[24] Mobile technology generated almost $3.3 trillion in revenue globally in one year alone and is responsible for 11 million jobs, according to Boston Consulting.[25] However, in a recovering but demanding U.S. labor market, hundreds of thousands of jobs in science, technology, engineering, and math remain unfilled.[26] Experts also worry about domestic talent shortages in skilled manufacturing.[27] In such a challenging environment, continuous, lifelong learning will make you more competitive and valuable to future employers. An adaptable, highly skilled workforce is well equipped to weather any economic climate as well as global competition.

Why Should You Care?

As a knowledge worker in the skills economy, you can expect to be generating, processing, and exchanging information. You will need to be able to transmit it effectively across various communication channels and multiple media. You might be called on to use e-mail, multimedia slide presentations, wikis, podcasts, or Facebook and other social media in a professional setting. With added job responsibilities, you will be expected to make sound decisions and solve complex problems. Interviewers at global giant Siemens probe job applicants for the ability "to quickly distill the key issues and relationships in complex situations," says Mike Panigel, senior vice president of human resources.[28]

In a recent PayScale study, writing proficiency is considered a hard skill; 44 percent of managers stated that it's the skill most lacking among recent college graduates. The respondents also criticized a lack of communication skills (46 percent) as well as critical thinking and problem solving skills (60 percent).[29] You are learning to think, read, and ask questions in a networked world, accessed with computers, tablets, smartphones, e-readers, wearable devices, and more. The avalanche of information that engulfs you daily requires you to evaluate all sources critically because information flows at a great speed, across various media, and in many directions. With potentially a global audience watching, you can choose to project a positive, professional image, or you can publish misinformation and embarrassing falsehoods.[30]

Courtesy of Karen Bruett

Reality Check

Wanted! 21st-Century Skills

In the media-driven world of the 21st century, workers must process vast amounts of information fast and judge accurately whether the information is reliable. "It's important that students know how to manage it, interpret it, validate it, and how to act on it."[31]

—Karen Bruett, *higher education expert, former Dell executive*

Thinking Critically in the Digital Age

Jobs that require thinking, brainpower, and decision-making skills are likely to remain plentiful. Whether you work in *m-commerce* (mobile technology businesses), *e-commerce* (Internet-based businesses), or *brick-and-mortar commerce*, nearly three out of four jobs involve some form of mind work. To be successful in these jobs, you will need to be able to think critically, make decisions, and communicate those decisions.

Management and employees work together in such areas as product development, quality control, and customer satisfaction. All workers, from executives to subordinates, need to think creatively and critically. Even in factory production lines, workers are part of the knowledge culture. Toyota's management philosophy of continuous improvement (*kaizen*) by engaged and empowered workers is much admired and emulated around the world.[32] When your boss or team leader says, "What do you think we ought to do?" you want to be able to supply good ideas and demonstrate that you can think critically. This means having opinions that are backed by reasons and evidence.

Faced with a problem or an issue, most of us do a lot of worrying before separating the issues or making a decision. Figure 1.2 provides a three-point plan to help you think critically and solve problems competently. As you can see, understanding the problem is essential and must come first. Generating and selecting the most feasible ideas is the intermediate step. Finally, the problem-solving model prompts you to refine, justify, and implement the solution. At the end of each chapter in this text, you will find activities and problems that will help you develop and apply your critical-thinking skills.

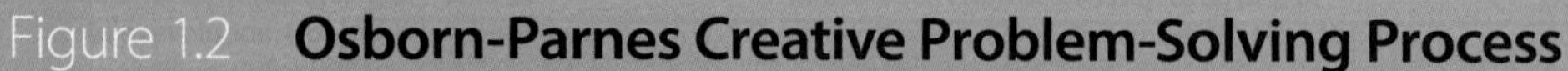
Figure 1.2 **Osborn-Parnes Creative Problem-Solving Process**

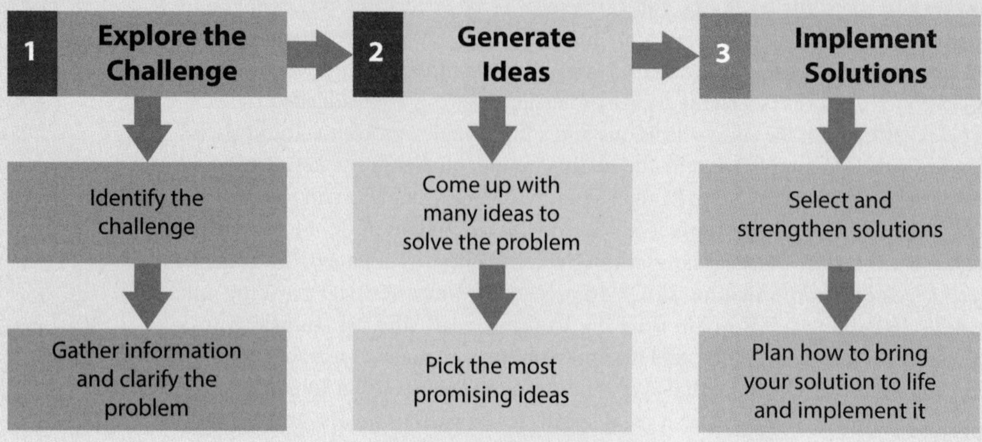
1 Explore the Challenge
2 Generate Ideas
3 Implement Solutions
Identify the challenge
Come up with many ideas to solve the problem
Select and strengthen solutions
Gather information and clarify the problem
Pick the most promising ideas
Plan how to bring your solution to life and implement it

Managing Your Career Well: Guarding Your Credibility

In a dynamic, highly competitive world of work, not even the most talented college graduate can afford to post or e-mail a résumé, kick back, and wait to be discovered. You will need to be proactive and exercise greater control over your career than college graduates before you did. Like most workers today, you will not find nine-to-five jobs, predictable pay increases, lifetime security, and even conventional workplaces.[33] Quite likely, your future employer may first observe your use of social networking tools before deciding to invite you for an interview.[34]

Don't presume that companies will provide you with a clearly defined career path or planned developmental experiences. In the private sector, you can expect to work for multiple employers, moving back and forth between work and education and between work and family responsibilities.[35] Increasingly, the workplace and your career will resemble not a vertical corporate ladder, but a more intricate, open, fluid, and interconnected framework—a *corporate lattice*.[36]

To keep up with evolving technologies and procedures, you can look forward to constant training and lifelong learning. Businesses are investing heavily in virtual training and social mobile learning. Such "everywhere" professional development is highly customized. It allows chief learning officers to track their employees' continued education needs as well as their progress while workers earn digital badges, similar to the Boy Scouts' tokens of achievement.[37] Whether you are currently employed or about to enter today's demanding workplace, you must be willing to continually learn new skills that supplement the strong foundation of basic skills you are acquiring in college.

Reality Check

retrorocket/ Shutterstock.com

Constant Career Readiness

"As work moves from climbing a career ladder to navigating a career lattice, people have to be in a mode of constant career readiness."[38]

—Jason Swanson, *futurist and director of strategic foresight at learning organization KnowledgeWorks*

In addition, in a hyperconnected professional environment, you must manage and guard your reputation—at the office and online. How you present yourself in the virtual world, meaning how well you communicate and protect your *brand,* may very well determine how successful your career will be. Your credibility is a precious asset. Thoughtful blog posts, well-crafted tweets, astute comments on LinkedIn and Facebook, as well as competent e-mails will help you continually make a positive impression. As one career advisor explains: "Every interaction—from how you greet your coworkers in the morning to how you summarize a status update in an email—contributes to how people view you."[39] In short, you will need to nurture and safeguard your professionalism online and off. You will learn more about soft skills and professionalism in Chapter 2.

Succeeding in an Improving but Competitive Job Market

Recent graduates will enter what economists say is the best job market for fresh-minted degree holders in nearly a decade. Still, about 1.5 unemployed workers will compete for each job opening.[40] What skills will make a difference for you? In one of its Job Outlook studies, the National Association of Colleges and Employers (NACE) recently asked employers what attributes they seek in new college graduates.

First, a prospective employee must meet the employer's fundamental criteria, including having the required major, course work, and GPA. By the way, many employers reported that they screened candidates by grade point average, with 3.0 (a B average) or higher favored strongly. If a candidate passes these hurdles, then employers look for leadership skills, the ability to work in a team, and written communication skills, as shown in Figure 1.3.[41]

Although employers seek these skills, they are not always pleased with what they find. The Association of American Colleges and Universities (AACU) asked groups of employers and college students a series of similar questions about career preparation. The results revealed a remarkable lack of agreement; students consistently ranked themselves as prepared in areas in which employers did not. In the key areas of written and oral communication and critical thinking, students were more than twice as likely as employers to think that they were well prepared.[42] To make sure you don't disappoint future employers, take advantage now of opportunities to strengthen your writing, presentation, and critical-thinking skills.

Figure 1.3 **Skills Jobs Seekers Should Offer**

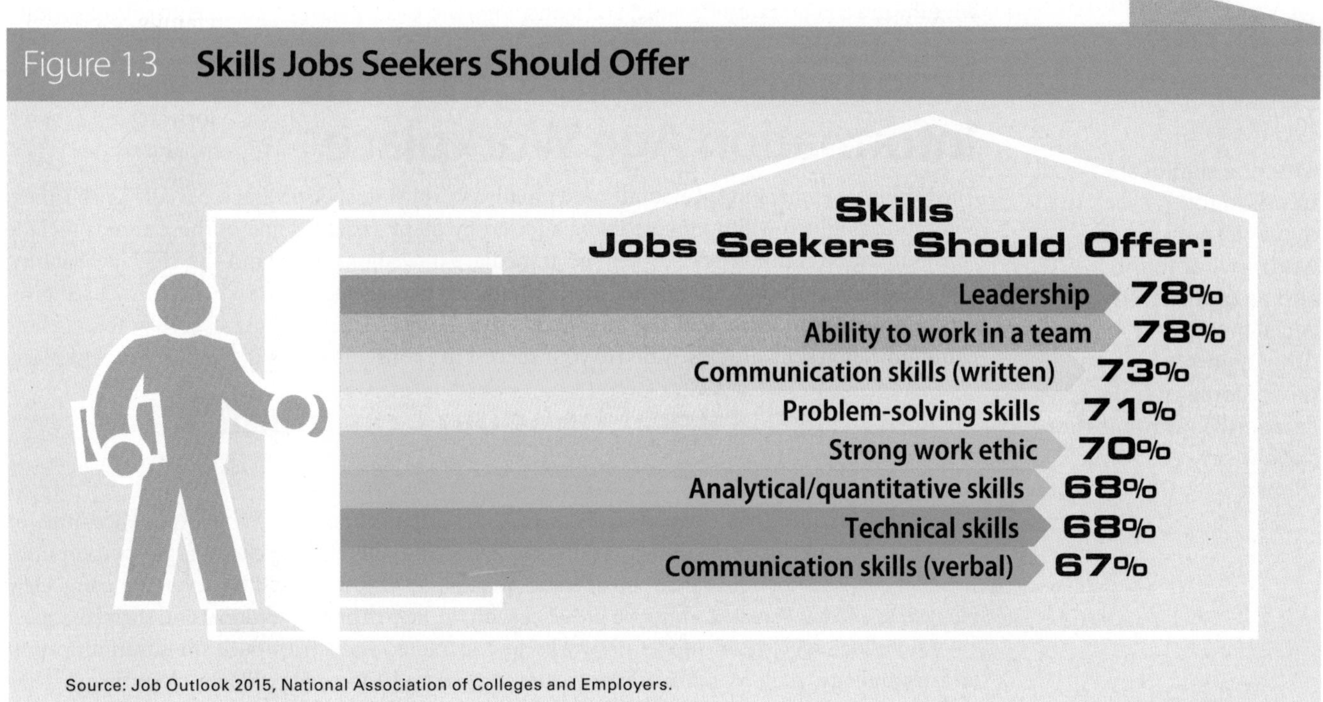

Source: Job Outlook 2015, National Association of Colleges and Employers.

Figure 1.4 The Education Bonus: Higher Income, Lower Unemployment

Education	Median Weekly Earnings	Unemployment Rate
High school dropout	$ 471	12.4%
High school diploma	652	8.3%
Some college, no degree	727	7.7%
Associate's degree	785	6.2%
Bachelor's degree or higher	1,367	4.5%

Source: U.S. Bureau of Labor Statistics. (2013, February 5). Labor force statistics from the current population survey; and U.S. Bureau of Labor Statistics (2013, May 22). Employment Projections: Earnings and unemployment rates by educational attachment.

How Your Education Drives Your Income

As college tuition rises steeply and student debt mounts, you may wonder whether going to college is worthwhile. Yet the effort and money you invest in earning your college degree will most likely pay off. College graduates earn more, suffer less unemployment, and can choose from a wider variety of career options than workers without a college education. Moreover, college graduates have access to the highest-paying and fastest-growing careers, many of which require a degree.[43]

As Figure 1.4 shows, graduates with bachelor's degrees earn nearly three times as much as high school dropouts and are almost three times less likely to be unemployed.[44]

Writing is one aspect of education that is particularly well rewarded. One corporate president explained that many job seekers present well. When he faced a hard choice between candidates, he used writing ability as the deciding factor. He said that sometimes writing is the only skill that separates a candidate from the competition. A survey of employers confirms that soft skills such as communication ability can tip the scales in favor of one job applicant over another.[45] Your ticket to winning in a competitive job market and launching a successful career is good communication skills.

LEARNING OUTCOME 3

Describe significant trends in today's dynamic, networked work environment, and recognize that social media and other communication technologies require excellent communication skills, in any economic climate.

Trends and Challenges in the Information Age Workplace

The workplace is changing profoundly and rapidly. As a businessperson and especially as a business communicator, you will undoubtedly be affected by many trends. Some of those trends include communication technologies such as social media, expectations of around-the-clock availability, and global competition. Other trends include flattened management hierarchies, team-based projects, a diverse workforce, and the mobile or virtual office. The following overview reveals how communication skills are closely tied to your success in a constantly evolving networked workplace.

Social Media and Changing Communication Technologies

Although interacting with others on Facebook, YouTube, Instagram, WhatsApp, FaceTime, or Twitter may seem a daily necessity to you, social media are still relatively new and untried communication channels for some small businesses. Most larger organizations, however, are completely plugged in and have created a positive presence with the help of both traditional and social media.

Quite logically, social media networks first attracted industries built on communication and technology, such as mainstream media outlets and information technology firms. New communication technologies also quickly took hold among marketers, in public relations, and

Figure 1.5 **Communication Technology in a Mobile and Social World— Costs and Benefits**

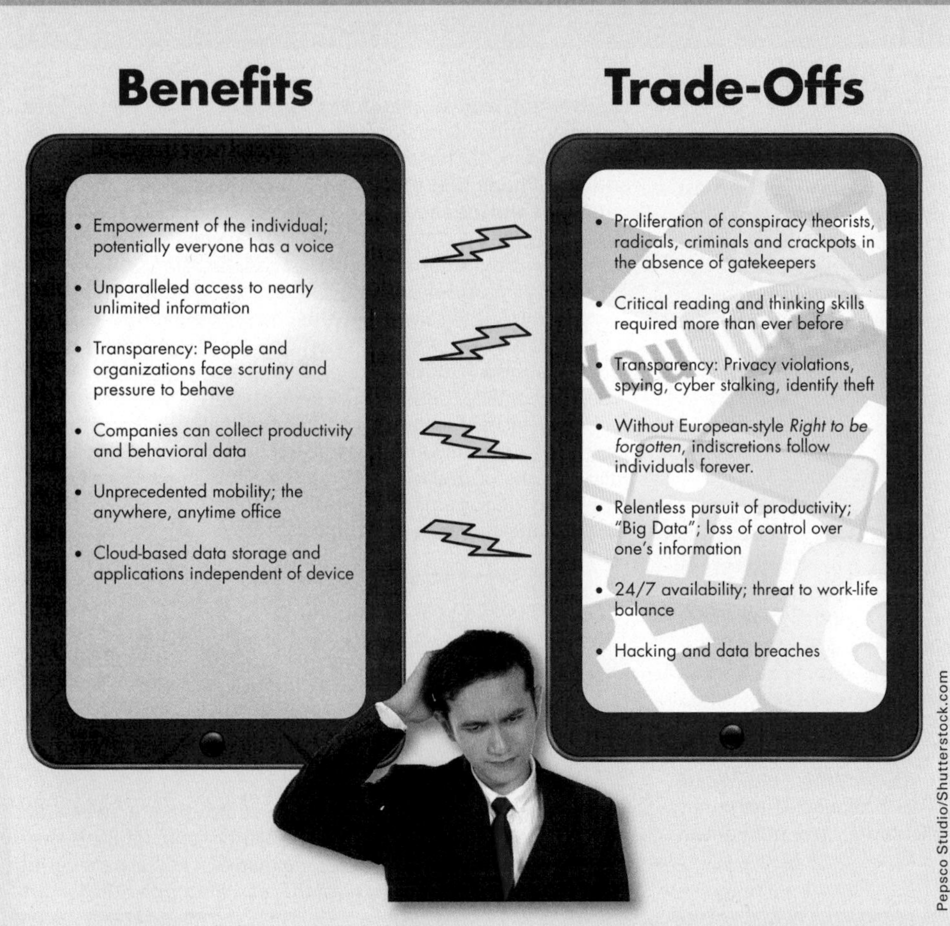

in advertising. Even so, many businesses relying on traditional media seem to be waiting to figure out how the new media might benefit them[46] to justify the investments.

Benefits
Trade-Offs
• Empowerment of the individual; potentially everyone has a voice
• Unparalleled access to nearly unlimited information
• Transparency: People and organizations face scrutiny and pressure to behave
• Companies can collect productivity and behavioral data
• Unprecedented mobility; the anywhere, anytime office
• Cloud-based data storage and applications independent of device
• Proliferation of conspiracy theorists, radicals, criminals and crackpots in the absence of gatekeepers
• Critical reading and thinking skills required more than ever before
• Transparency: Privacy violations, spying, cyber stalking, identify theft
• Without European-style Right to be forgotten, indiscretions follow individuals forever.
• Relentless pursuit of productivity; "Big Data"; loss of control over one's information
• 24/7 availability; threat to work-life balance
• Hacking and data breaches
Pepsco Studio/Shutterstock.com

However, even the most reluctant late adopters of technology eye the explosive growth of social media networks in the last decade with some interest. After all, online communities continue to draw huge numbers of people from all over the world. The 302 million active users of Twitter, the microblogging site, clock an average 500 million tweets per day.[47] Ordinary citizens can organize protests and boycotts within hours, even minutes. Bad customer service experiences can lead to lifelong grudges.[48] In short, word of mouth, positive and negative, can travel instantly at the speed of a few mouse clicks.

The various social media are maturing and yielding undeniable advantages. However, even their most avid users are learning that their favorite technologies also come with significant downsides—for example, data breeches and identify theft, as Figure 1.5 illustrates.

Tech-savvy companies are embracing digital tools to connect with consumers, invite feedback, and improve their products and services. They may announce promotions and events in blog posts, in tweets, on their company websites, and in online communities. Above all, plugged-in businesses realize that to manage public perceptions, they need to be proactive but also respond quickly and deftly within the social media when a crisis hits. They need to go where their customers are and attempt to establish and keep a loyal following online. It has never been easier to interact so fast with so many people at once.

At the very least, even if they still pass on social media, nearly all businesspeople today in some way rely on the Internet to collect information, serve customers, and sell products and services. Figure 1.6 on pages 12 and 13 illustrates many new office and communication

Figure 1.6 **Communication and Collaborative Technologies**

Communication Technologies at Work

Becoming familiar with communication technology can help you succeed on the job. Today's digital workplace is shaped by mobile devices, mobile apps, social media networks, superfast broadband and wireless access, and other technologies that allow workers to share information, work from remote locations, and be more productive in or away from the office. With today's tools you can exchange ideas, solve problems, develop products, forecast future performance, and complete team projects any time of the day or night and anywhere in the world.

Cloud Computing and Web 2.0

Increasingly, applications and data are stored in remote locations online, in the cloud.

Cloud computing means that businesses and individuals no longer need to maintain costly hardware and software in-house; instead, they can centralize data on their own remote servers or pay for digital storage space and software applications offered by providers online. Photo- and video-sharing sites such as Picasa and Flickr keep users' photos in the cloud. Similarly, Dropbox, a popular file-synchronization service, and online backup provider Carbonite allow users to edit and sync files online independent of the device used to access them. The term *Web 2.0* means that websites and Web applications have shifted from one-way, read-only communication to two-way, multidirectional, read-write communication. This profound change has allowed workers to participate, collaborate, and network in unprecedented ways.

Telephony: VoIP

Savvy businesses are switching from traditional phone service to voice over Internet protocol (VoIP). This technology allows callers to communicate using a broadband Internet connection, thus eliminating long-distance and local telephone charges. Higher-end VoIP systems now support unified voice mail, e-mail, click-to-call capabilities, and softphones (Web applications or mobile apps, such as Google Voice, for calling and messaging). Free or low-cost Internet telephony sites, such as the popular Skype and FaceTime, are also increasingly used by businesses, although their sound and image quality is often uneven.

Open Offices

The widespread use of laptops, tablets, and other smart devices, wireless technology, and VoIP has led to more fluid, flexible, and open workspaces. Smaller computers and flat-screen monitors enable designers to save space with boomerang-shaped workstations and cockpit-style work surfaces rather than space-hogging corner work areas. Smaller break-out areas for impromptu meetings are taking over some cubicle space, and digital databases are replacing file cabinets. Mobile technology allows workers to be fully connected and productive on the go.

Smart Mobile Devices and Digital Convergence

Lightweight, ever-smaller devices provide phone, e-mail, Web browsing, and calendar options anywhere there's a cellular or Wi-Fi network. Tablets and smartphones such as Android devices and the iPhone and iPad allow workers to tap into corporate databases and intranets from remote locations. Users can check customers' files, complete orders, collect payment, and send out receipts without returning to the office. Increasingly, businesses are issuing smartphones to their workers, abandoning landlines completely. At the same time, the need for separate electronic gadgets is waning as digital smart devices are becoming multi-functional and highly capable. With streaming video on the Web, connectivity between TVs and computers, and networked mobile devices, technology is converging, consolidating into increasingly powerful devices. Many smart devices today are fully capable of replacing digital point-and-shoot still photography and video cameras. Mobile smart devices are competing with TVs and computers for primacy.

Mobile Apps

Mobile apps are the software that enables smartphones to run and accomplish amazing feats. Despite their natural size limitations, mobile apps rival the capabilities of full-fledged software applications on laptops, on desktops, and in the cloud.

Wearable Devices

The most recent trend in mobile computing is wearable devices. Fitbit, Google Glass, Apple Watch, and similar accessories do more than track fitness activities. They are powerful mobile devices in their own right that can sync with other smart electronics.

Voice Recognition

Computers equipped with voice recognition software enable users to dictate up to 160 words a minute with accurate transcription. Voice recognition is particularly helpful to disabled workers and professionals with heavy dictation loads, such as physicians and attorneys. Users can create documents, enter data, compose and send e-mails, browse the Web, and control their notebooks, laptops, and desktops—all by voice. Smart devices can also execute tasks with voice command apps.

Electronic Presentations and Data Visualization

Business presentations in PowerPoint, Prezi, or Keynote can be projected from a laptop or tablet, or posted online. Sophisticated presentations may include animation, sound effects, digital photos, video clips, or hyperlinks to Internet sites. In some industries, PowerPoint slides (decks) are replacing or supplementing traditional hard-copy reports. Data visualization tools such as SAS can help businesses make sense of large amounts of complex data.

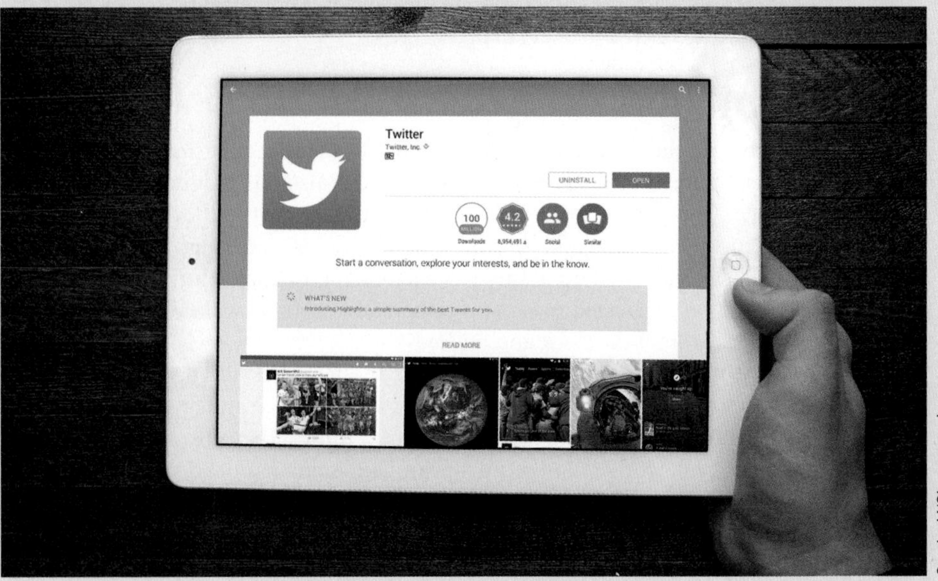

Castleski/Shutterstock.com

Social Media

Broadly speaking, the term *social media* describes technology that enables participants to connect and share in social networks online. For example, tech-savvy companies and individuals use Twitter to issue up-to-date news, link to their blogs and websites, or announce events and promotions. Microblogging services, such as Twitter and Tumblr, also allow businesses to track what is being said about them and their products. Similarly, businesses use social networks such as Facebook, Instagram, and others to interact with customers and build their brands. Companies may also prospect for talent using social media networks. Efforts to launch corporate social networks have seen mixed results. So far workers have been slow in embracing SharePoint, Jive, Yammer, Telligent, and similar enterprise-grade collaboration platforms, social networks, and community forums.

Collaboration With Blogs, Podcasts, and Wikis

Businesses use *blogs* to keep customers and employees informed and to receive feedback. Company news can be posted, updated, and categorized for easy cross-referencing. An audio or video file streamed online or downloaded to a digital music player is called a *podcast*. A *wiki* is an Internet or intranet site that allows multiple users to collaboratively create and edit digital files as well as media. Information can get lost in e-mails, but wikis provide an easy way to communicate and keep track of what's said. Wikis for business include Confluence, eXo Platform, Socialtext, and Jive.

Web Conferencing

With services such as GoToMeeting, WebEx, and Microsoft Live Meeting, all you need is a computer or a smart device and an Internet connection to hold a meeting (*webinar*) with customers or colleagues in real time. Although the functions are constantly evolving, Web conferencing currently incorporates screen sharing, chats, slide presentations, text messaging, and application sharing.

Videoconferencing

Videoconferencing allows participants to meet in special conference rooms equipped with cameras and television screens. Individuals or groups see each other and interact in real time, although they may be far apart. Faster computers, rapid Internet connections, and better cameras now enable 2 to 200 participants to sit at their computers or mobile devices and share applications, spreadsheets, presentations, and photos. The technology extends from the popular low-end Internet application Skype to sophisticated videoconferencing software that delivers HD-quality audio, video, and content sharing.

Gamification

Gamification is a trend that uses game design techniques to increase motivation and engagement. Much like exciting computer games, gamification platforms in business are designed to be fun and in turn increase productivity as well as revenue. Gamification techniques include using badges or points to tap into people's natural desires for competition, status, and achievement but also altruism, collaboration, and more. Gamification is used in marketing, sales, customer retention, training, and similar business applications.

technologies you will meet in today's workplace. To make the most of the new resources, you, as a skilled business communicator, must develop a tool kit of new communication skills. You will want to know how to select the best communication channel, how to use each channel safely and effectively, and how to incorporate the latest technologies and search tools efficiently. All of these topics are covered in later chapters.

Anytime, Anywhere: 24/7/365 Availability

Although the dizzyingly fast connectedness across time zones and vast distances offers businesses and individuals many advantages, it also has a darker side. As you rise on the career ladder, you may be expected to work long hours without extra compensation and be available practically anytime and anywhere should a crisis strike at work. In the last two decades, the line between work and leisure has become increasingly blurry. In many industries information workers are expected to remain tethered to their workplaces with laptops, tablets, and smartphones around the clock and on weekends.

The physical office is extending its reach, sometimes overreaching, perhaps. Compared to workers in other industrialized nations such as Japan and most European countries, Americans put in the longest hours (about 50 percent more). They also receive the shortest paid vacations. In contrast, workers in the European Union enjoy four to six weeks of paid time off per year. Most are also protected from overtime exceeding 48 hours per week.[49] A different picture emerges in the United States. As the digital revolution reached the masses in the 2000s, articles in major U.S. publications such as *The New York Times* decried the 24/7 work climate, citing its negative effects on workers' health and personal lives.[50] The perceived work-life imbalance became a hot topic. Be that as it may, the office today and in the future is mobile and always on.

In a global economy in which corporations own far-flung operations around the world, a networked information-driven workforce never goes off duty. Similarly, the organization essentially never sleeps, according to one expert. The 24/7 workplace operates around the clock, he says, with managers, staff, and teams always staying connected to share information when needed and address burning issues when they arise.[51] Managers exert power beyond the physical office. Moreover, work in the digital age demands that participants stay on until the project is finished, not when the clock strikes five or six at the end of the day. As your professional responsibilities grow, you can expect not only to be accessible 24/7 but also to feel the significant impact of globalization.

The Global Marketplace and Competition

The rise of new communication technologies, the removal of trade barriers, advanced forms of transportation, and saturated local markets—all of these developments have encouraged companies to move beyond familiar territories to emerging markets around the world. Small, medium, and large companies in the United States and abroad have expanded overseas. Teenagers in Singapore, Latvia, South Korea, Australia, and the United States alike flock in droves to popular store openings by Swedish clothing retailer H&M or its Spain-based rival Zara. Trader Joe's parent company, German discounter Aldi, is giving U.S. food retailers a run for their money by gaining ground in a crowded marketplace in the United States.[52]

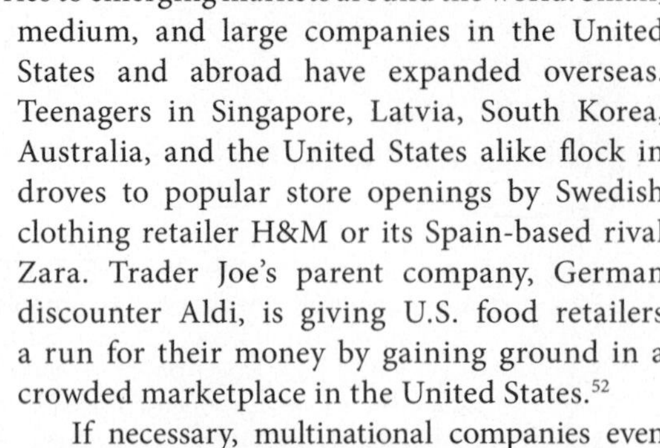

Betty LaRue/Alamy Stock Photo

If necessary, multinational companies even adjust their products to different palates. Because Indians are not crazy about doughnuts, Dunkin' Donuts radically reworked its menu in India and now rivals McDonald's with beef-free burger offerings.[53] After initial hiccups, Walmart has become hugely popular with Chinese shoppers who expect to bag unpackaged raw meat themselves and like to catch their own live frogs, fish, and turtles in open tanks.[54] Other adjustments to local preferences include payment modalities. McDonald's and KFC's parent Yum Brands are testing mobile ordering and mobile payment. They want to match Chinese consumers' digital connectedness to gain more fast-food business in China.[55] Many traditional U.S. companies are global players now and generate more profit abroad than at home.

Doing business in faraway countries means dealing with people who may be very different from you. They may practice different religions, follow different customs, have different lifestyles, and rely on different approaches in business. Now add the complications of multiple time zones, vast distances between offices, and different languages. No wonder global communicators can stumble. Take, for example, IKEA. Unprompted, the Swedish furniture giant took its accommodation of Saudi Arabia's strict religious rules so far that it caused a backlash at home and the company had to apologize for acting against its own values. IKEA had deleted women from some photos in its Saudi-targeted catalogs.[56]

Successful communication in new markets requires developing new skills and attitudes. These include cultural awareness, flexibility, and patience. Because these skills and attitudes may be difficult to achieve, you will receive special communication training to help you deal with intercultural business transactions.

Shrinking Management Layers

In traditional companies, information flows through many levels of managers. In response to intense global competition and other pressures, however, innovative businesses have for years been cutting costs and flattening their management hierarchies. This flattening means that fewer layers of managers separate decision makers from line workers. In flat organizations, in which the lines of communication are shorter, decision makers can react more quickly to market changes.

When GE Capital, General Electric's financial services arm, split into four business units, the reorganization spearheaded by the post–Jack Welch CEO, Jeffrey Immelt, met with skepticism. GE Capital's former chairman Denis Nayden exited, and the four unit heads started reporting directly to the CEO. The organization became flatter. Immelt reasoned that he wanted more immediate contact with the financial services teams.[57] He also believed that the greater number of direct reports would provide clarity for investors.

Despite this bold move, Immelt was forced to begin to shed GE Capital after the Great Recession, slim GE's operations, and return to the industrial conglomerate's core business in manufacturing.[58] Restructured companies generally slash divisions and shrink management layers to operate more efficiently.

Reality Check

intararit/
Shutterstock.com

Keeping the Organization Flat—A Core Value at Google

"I work with employees around the world to figure out ways to maintain and enhance and develop our culture and how to keep the core values we had in the very beginning—a flat organization, a lack of hierarchy, a collaborative environment—to keep these as we continue to grow and spread them and filtrate them into our new offices around the world."[59]

—Stacy Savides Sullivan, *VP, people operations & chief culture officer at Google*

An important factor in the flattening of management hierarchies was movement away from mainframe computing. As recognized by Thomas Friedman in his bestselling book *The World Is Flat*, the combination of the personal computer, the microprocessor, the Internet, fiber optics, and, more recently, wireless networks "flipped the playing field." Management moved away from command and control to connecting and collaborating horizontally.[60] This means that work is organized so that people can use their own talents more wisely.[61]

lightwavemedia/Shutterstock.com

Today's flatter organizations, however, also pose greater communication challenges. In the past, authoritarian and hierarchical management structures did not require that every employee be a skilled communicator. Managers simply passed along messages to the next level. Today, however, frontline employees as well as managers participate in critical thinking and decision making. Nearly everyone is a writer and a communicator.

Collaborative Environments and Teaming

Teamwork has become a reality in business. Many companies have created cross-functional teams to empower employees and boost their involvement in decision making. Such stable teams of people have learned to work well together over time. To generate new products, Johnson & Johnson started forming small teams and charged each with tackling a cosmetic problem. The acne team, composed of scientists along with marketing and production people, focused on finding ways to help teenagers zap zits. A pigmentation team struggled to create products that evened out skin tone.[62] Traditional teams helped turn around Simmons Bedding Company a decade ago by reducing waste in operations, boosting sales, and improving the relationships with dealers. Customer satisfaction and employee morale also soared.[63]

However, the complex and unpredictable challenges in today's workplace require rapid changes in course and greater flexibility, says Harvard management professor Amy Edmondson. She argues that the new era of business requires a new strategy she calls *teaming*: "Teaming is teamwork on the fly: a pickup basketball game rather than plays run by a team that has trained as a unit for years."[64] This means that instead of traditional standing teams, organizations are now forming ad hoc teams to solve particular problems. Such project-based teams disband once they have accomplished their objectives. Although the challenges of making such diverse and potentially dispersed teams function well are many, teaming is here to stay.

A sizable chunk of our future economy may rely on free agents who will be hired on a project basis. This practice is reminiscent of filmmaking, in which creative talent gathers to work on a feature film; after the wrap, the crew disperses to tackle the next movie, each with a whole new team. In one of its reports, accounting firm PricewaterhouseCoopers envisions a future workplace in which companies hire a network of independent contractors for short-term projects,[65] a far cry from today's full-time and relatively steady jobs.

Whether companies form standing or ad hoc teams, individuals must work together and share information. Working relationships can become strained when individuals don't share the same location, background, knowledge, or training. Some companies even hire communication coaches to help teams get along. Such experts work to develop interpersonal, negotiation, and collaboration techniques. However, companies would prefer to hire new workers who already possess these skills. That is why so many advertisements for new employees say "must possess good communication skills"—which you are learning in this book and this course.

> **Ethics Check**
>
> **Too Connected?**
>
> Office workers use smartphones, e-mail, voice mail, and text messaging. Many are literally always on call and feel overwhelmed. What are the limits of connectedness, and what is the expected response time for various media? Is it fair to dodge an unpleasant call by sending it to voice mail or to delay answering certain e-mail messages? How about text messages?

Growing Workforce Diversity

In addition to pervasive communication technology, advanced team management, and distant work environments, today's workplace is changing in yet another area. The U.S. workforce is becoming increasingly diverse. As shown in Figure 1.7, the white non-Hispanic population of the United States is expected to drop from 62 percent in 2015 to 53 percent in 2035. Hispanics will climb from 18 percent to 23 percent, while African Americans will hold steady at around 13 percent relative to the growing total U.S. population. Asians and Pacific Islanders will rise from 5 percent to 7 percent.[66]

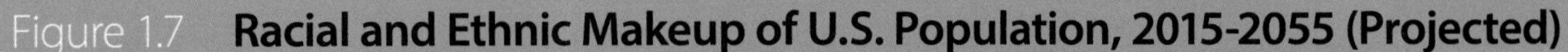

Figure 1.7 **Racial and Ethnic Makeup of U.S. Population, 2015-2055 (Projected)**

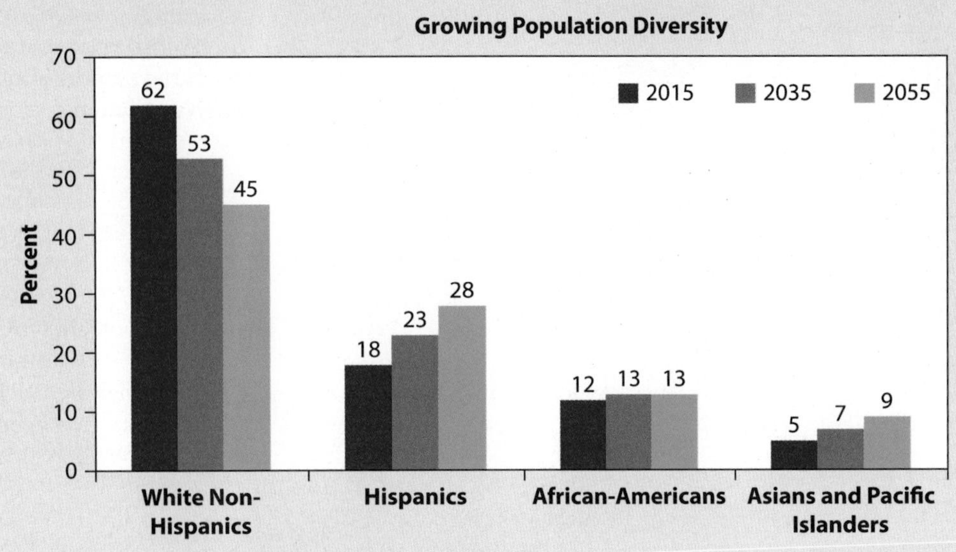

Source: U.S. Census Bureau, Population Division, December 2014.

Women attain higher education in greater numbers than men do; women ages twenty-five to thirty-four were 21 percent more likely than men to graduate from college and 48 percent more likely to have completed graduate school.[67] However, in many industries and in executive positions, they are still the minority. According to the National Science Foundation, the gender gap is most pronounced in business and industry, where women fill only 21 percent of jobs, followed by the high-tech industry (25 percent), and science and engineering (27 percent).[68] The U.S. Bureau of Labor Statistics projects that overall women will hold steady at 47 percent of the labor force by 2022, nearly unchanged from 2012.[69]

In addition to increasing numbers of minorities, the workforce will see a big jump in older workers. By 2022, the number of workers aged fifty-five and older will have grown to more than a quarter of the labor force, almost double the number in 2002.[70] To this competition for information-age jobs, add the influx of skilled immigrants. Despite barriers to immigration, some experts predict that by 2030 roughly 500 million people will legally work outside their home countries. This means that twice as many migrants, up from 250 million today, will seek economic opportunities abroad, displaced by armed conflict, natural disasters, and climate change.[71] As a result of these and other demographic trends, businesses must create work environments that value and support all people.

Communicating in this diverse work environment requires new attitudes and skills. Acquiring these new employment skills is certainly worth the effort because of the benefits diversity brings to consumers, work teams, and business organizations. A diverse staff is better able to read trends and respond to the increasingly diverse customer base in local and world markets.

In the workplace, diversity also makes good business sense. Teams made up of people with various experiences are more likely to create the products consumers demand. Customers also want to deal with companies that respect their values. They are more likely to say, “If you are a company whose ads do not include me, or whose workforce does not include me, I will not buy from you.” Learning to cooperate and communicate successfully with diverse coworkers should be a major priority for all businesspeople.

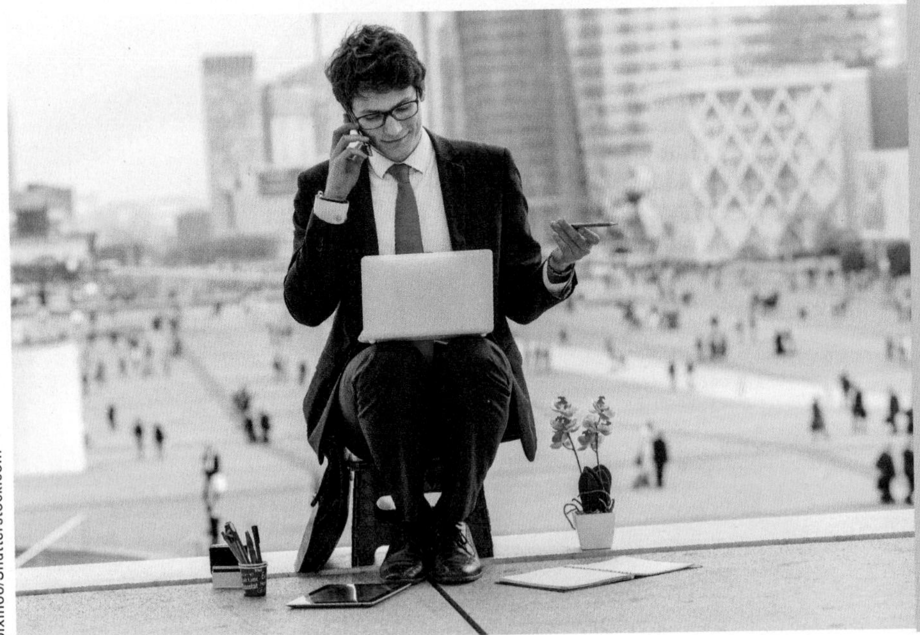

pixinoo/Shutterstock.com

Chances are if you go to work in the next five years, you may not have to leave home—you'll be one of the millions of mobile workers in the U.S. workforce.[72] The rising trend of these virtual workers is fueled by technological advances in smartphones, tablets, and BYOD programs, in which workers like you "bring your own devices" to use on the job. Studies show that virtual workers are happier and more productive. However, working without traditional offices creates unique challenges, including the lack of face-to-face communication with colleagues. What are some ways virtual workers can effectively communicate with stakeholders?

Virtual and Nonterritorial Offices

You may have heard people refer to the virtual office, a workspace that's mobile and decentralized. Today's physical work environments are changing profoundly. Thanks largely to advances in high-speed and wireless Internet access, millions of workers no longer report to nine-to-five jobs that confine them to offices. They have flexible working arrangements so they can work at home, on the road, and at the customer's place of business. Meet the work shifter, a new breed of telecommuter or, more broadly, teleworker, who remains outside the traditional office the majority of the time. The "anytime, anywhere" office the work shifter needs requires only a smartphone and a wireless connection.[73]

If the self-employed are factored in, teleworkers now represent almost 30 percent of the U.S. working adult population.[74] Reliable data tracking office road warriors are lacking, but as many as 52 million employees—nearly a third of the U.S. workforce—could likely be working from remote locations in the near future.[75] Yahoo under Marissa Mayer's leadership pulled the plug on telecommuting, but Anthem has a third of its staff work remotely. The health care provider claims that telework is a powerful recruitment incentive and that productivity has not suffered.[76]

To save on office real estate, a number of companies such as American Express and drug maker GlaxoSmithKline provide nonterritorial workspaces. Also known as mobile platforms and hot desks, these unassigned workspaces are up for grabs. The first to arrive gets the best desk and the corner window.[77] Increasingly, work shifters and home office workers resort to *coworking* as an alternative to holding business meetings at the local coffee shop or in the living room. Coworkers are professionals who share a communal office space on an as-needed basis. Although most coworking spaces provide monthly memberships, some offer day or hourly passes. Not just small businesses, but also major corporations, such as GE, KPMG, PepsiCo, and Merck, are moving workers into trendy shared offices.[78] WeWork and LiquidSpace are doing for office real estate what Uber has started for ride sharing—a platform for users to offer and seek flexible access to workspaces.

Open Office Rules

Rules for sharing open workspaces:

1. Don't hang around.
2. Limit chitchat.
3. Don't sneak up on anyone.
4. Don't eavesdrop or otherwise spy on others.
5. Speak in a soft voice.
6. Wear headphones.

Even in more traditional offices, employees work in open-plan spaces with flexible workstations, shared conference rooms, and boomerang-shaped desks that save space and discourage territorial behavior while encouraging casual interactions as well as spontaneous collaborations.

Information Flow and Media Choices in Today's Workplace

LEARNING OUTCOME 4

Examine critically the internal and external flow of communication in organizations through formal and informal channels, explain the importance of effective media choices, and understand how to overcome typical barriers to organizational communication.

You may want to connect with friends and family for a specific reason or just for fun. However, businesspeople almost always communicate strategically—that is, purposefully, hoping to achieve a particular outcome. Business communication functions can be summarized in three simple categories: (a) to inform, (b) to persuade, and/or (c) to promote goodwill. Most business messages have one of these functions as their purpose. Informing or sharing information is perhaps the most common communication function in all organizations today. On the job you will have a dizzying array of media to help you share information and stay connected both internally and externally. You will need to know which medium is most suitable to accomplish your goal and be able to distinguish between formal and informal channels.

The Networked Workplace in a Hyperconnected World

Social media and other information technology coupled with flatter hierarchies have greatly changed the way people communicate internally and externally at work. One major shift is away from one-sided, slow forms of communication such as hard-copy memos and letters to interactive, instant, less paper-based communication. Speeding up the flow of communication in organizations are e-mail, instant messaging (IM), texting, blogging, and interacting with social media such as Facebook, Twitter, and LinkedIn. Figure 1.8 shows a side-by-side comparison between the traditional one-directional business communication model and today's hyperconnected, many-to-many social media communication model.

Figure 1.8 **Traditional vs. Social Media Communication Between Businesses and Customers**

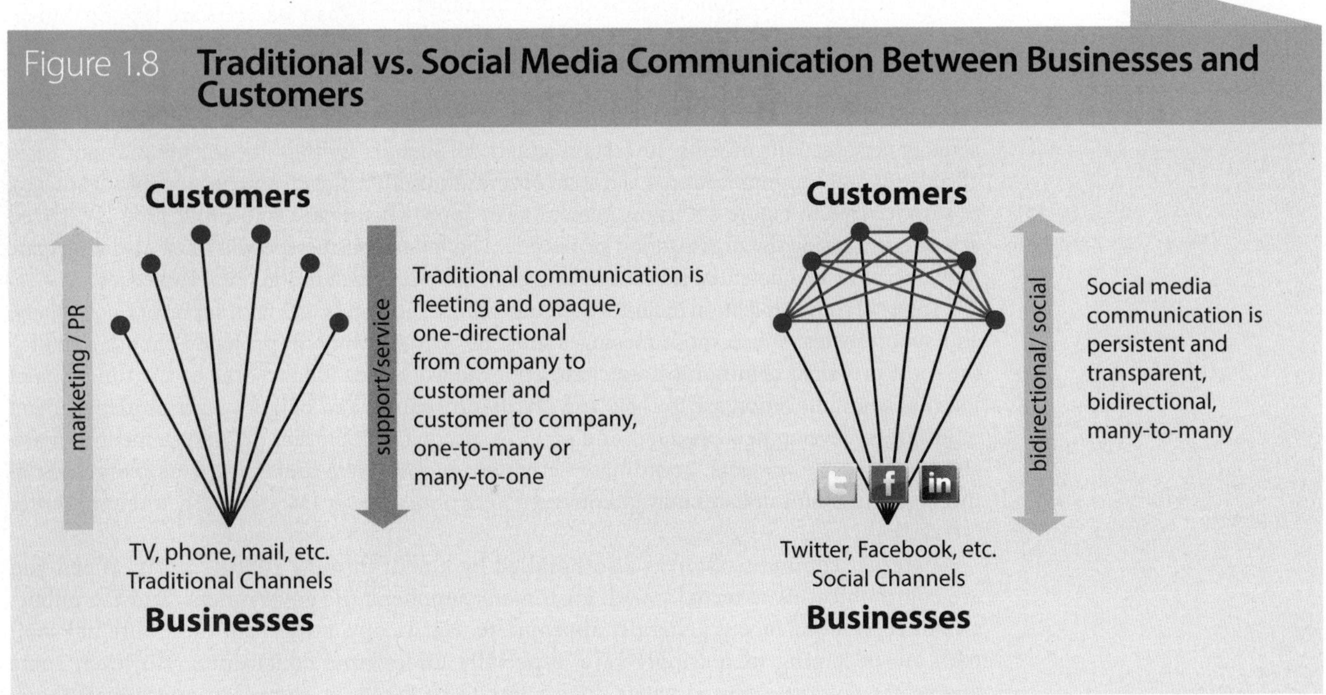

Fearing openly accessible social networks, many large organizations have developed their own internal social media platforms behind corporate firewalls. These enterprise social networks (e.g., Adobe's Unicom) combine e-mail, phone, chat, presence technology, and other communication tools, as you will learn in Chapter 7. To stay connected on the go, business communicators rely on mobile electronic devices and mobile apps that enhance work productivity.

Mobility and Interactivity. Mobility has revolutionized the way we communicate on the job. Internet access is ever present, whether provided by cell phone companies or wireless networks. Wireless access is increasingly blanketing entire office buildings, airports, hotels, restaurants, school and college campuses, cities, and other public spaces.

Other forms of interactive and mobile communication in the contemporary workplace are intranets (secured local area networks within organizations), corporate websites, audio and video podcasting, videoconferencing, and Web chats. The latter is rapidly becoming the preferred communication channel for online customer service. Consumers shopping online or inquiring about billing or technical support use the company website and chat with customer service representatives in real time by typing their questions. Live service agents respond with typed replies.

Smart Devices. The revolution in mobile communication technology that we have come to depend on is fueled by smart mobile electronics. They include smartphones, tablets, notebooks, and more recently, wearable technology such as Google Glass and the Apple Watch.

To understand the pervasiveness of mobile technology, consider that the world population now stands at 7.2 billion people; of those, 4.3 billion are mobile device users who own 7.5 billion smart electronic gadgets. By 2019, worldwide mobile users are expected to reach 5.2 billion with 11.5 billion mobile devices at their disposal.[79] Mobile access reached a tipping point in 2014, overtaking traditional stationary Internet access.[80] When Apple launched its phenomenally successful iPad, the gadget was hailed as a game changer. Although consumer sales of the most popular tablet have been eclipsed by phablets (large-screen smartphones), many businesses choose iPads on the go because they are lighter and cheaper than laptops.

Ahead of the popular iPhone, the Android platform has taken the smartphone market by storm worldwide. Android, primarily represented by Samsung devices, has grabbed a global market share of almost 80 percent; Apple iOS has captured over 18 percent.[81] Low-cost Android handsets also dominate the smartphone market in Africa, India, and China. Thus, millions of people access the Internet by mobile phone not only in industrialized nations but also in regions of the world where smartphones provide the only online access.

Internal and External Communication

Although most businesses rely on e-mail and digital files for communication, they still produce some paper-based documents. In certain situations, though, written documents may not be as effective as oral communication. Each form of communication has advantages and disadvantages, as summarized in Figure 1.9. These general rules apply whether the communication is directed at audiences inside the organization or outside. Digital-age businesspeople must also anticipate public scrutiny and potential leaks of information that may reach unintended audiences.

Internal communication includes exchanging ideas and messages with superiors, coworkers, and subordinates. When those messages must be written, you will probably choose e-mail—the most prevalent communication channel in the workplace today. Some of the functions of internal communication are to issue and clarify procedures and policies, inform management of progress, develop new products and services, persuade employees or management to make changes or improvements, coordinate activities, and evaluate and reward employees. Brief messages and status updates may be conveyed by text message or IM, especially when the writer is traveling.

External communication is also handled by e-mail in most routine cases. When you are communicating externally with customers, suppliers, the government, and the public, e-mail correspondence is generally appropriate. Hard-copy letters sent by traditional snail mail are becoming increasingly rare, especially under time constraints. However, some businesses do create signed paper documents to be faxed, or they scan and e-mail them.

Figure 1.9 **Comparing Forms of Organizational Communication**

Communication	Deliverables/Form	Advantages	Disadvantages
Paper based (hard copy)	Memos, letters, employee newsletters, brochures, performance appraisals, pay-packet enclosures, agendas and minutes, internal and external reports, questionnaires	Creates a permanent record, is convenient to distribute, may be economical, promotes comprehension and recall, allows precise and uniform expression, gives audience flexibility in when and how to receive content	Leaves a paper trail, requires skill and effort to produce, lacks verbal cues and warmth, cannot be immediately adjusted to audience feedback, may seem impersonal
Digital (soft copy)	E-mail, newsletters, brochures, instant messages, websites, intranets, blogs, social media posts, agendas and minutes, internal and external reports, questionnaires	In addition to all the advantages of paper output, is more economical than paper, can be mass produced and distributed, allows mobile access anytime and anywhere	Leaves a permanent digital footprint, can lead to public embarrassment on a massive scale, may be inaccessible to unplugged audiences, is subject to malfunctions
Oral	Telephone calls, face-to-face conversations, in-person meetings, conferences, team addresses, seminars, workshops, training sessions, roundtables, teleconferences	Provides immediate feedback, can be adjusted to the audience, can be delivered quickly, supplies nonverbal cues, may create warm feeling, can be powerful	Lacks a permanent record (unless recorded), may contain careless or imprecise expression, may be inappropriate for formal or complex ideas, does not promote easy recall

External functions involve answering inquiries about products or services, persuading customers to buy products or services, clarifying supplier specifications, issuing credit, collecting bills, responding to government agencies, and promoting a positive image of the organization.

When communicating with internal and external audiences, businesspeople must now also consider leaks and the backchannel. *Backchannel communication* is a simultaneous electronic background conversation during a conference presentation, lecture, or entertainment program. For example, when you live tweet or IM your friends while watching the latest episode of *The Walking Dead,* you are having a backchannel conversation.

In business, backchannel describes the synchronous digital interactions that run in the background parallel to a meeting or presentation. When AOL chief Tim Armstrong infamously fired a subordinate during an internal conference call in front 1,100 colleagues, the audio was leaked and instantly went viral. Business communicators must always anticipate unintended audiences and public criticism.

Media Richness and Social Presence

Business communicators must be able to choose from a wide range of communication channels the one most suitable to get the job done—that is, most likely to elicit the desired outcome. How to choose the appropriate medium to avoid ambiguity, confusing messages, and misunderstandings has long been studied by researchers. Media richness theory and the concept of social presence are particularly useful for evaluating the effectiveness of old and new media in a given situation.

Media Richness. Daft and Lengel's media richness theory attempts to classify media in organizations according to how much clarifying information they are able to convey from a sender to a recipient.[82] The more helpful cues and immediate feedback the medium provides, the richer it is; face-to-face and on the telephone, managers can best deal with complex organizational issues. For routine, unambiguous problems, however, media of lower richness, such as memos, reports, and other written communication, usually suffice. Figure 1.10 displays contemporary and traditional media based on their richness and, hence, their likely communication effectiveness.

Ideally, senders would choose the richest medium necessary to communicate the message to the recipient with as little ambiguity as possible. Because a rich medium (such as a face-to-face

Figure 1.10 **Media Richness and Communication Effectiveness**

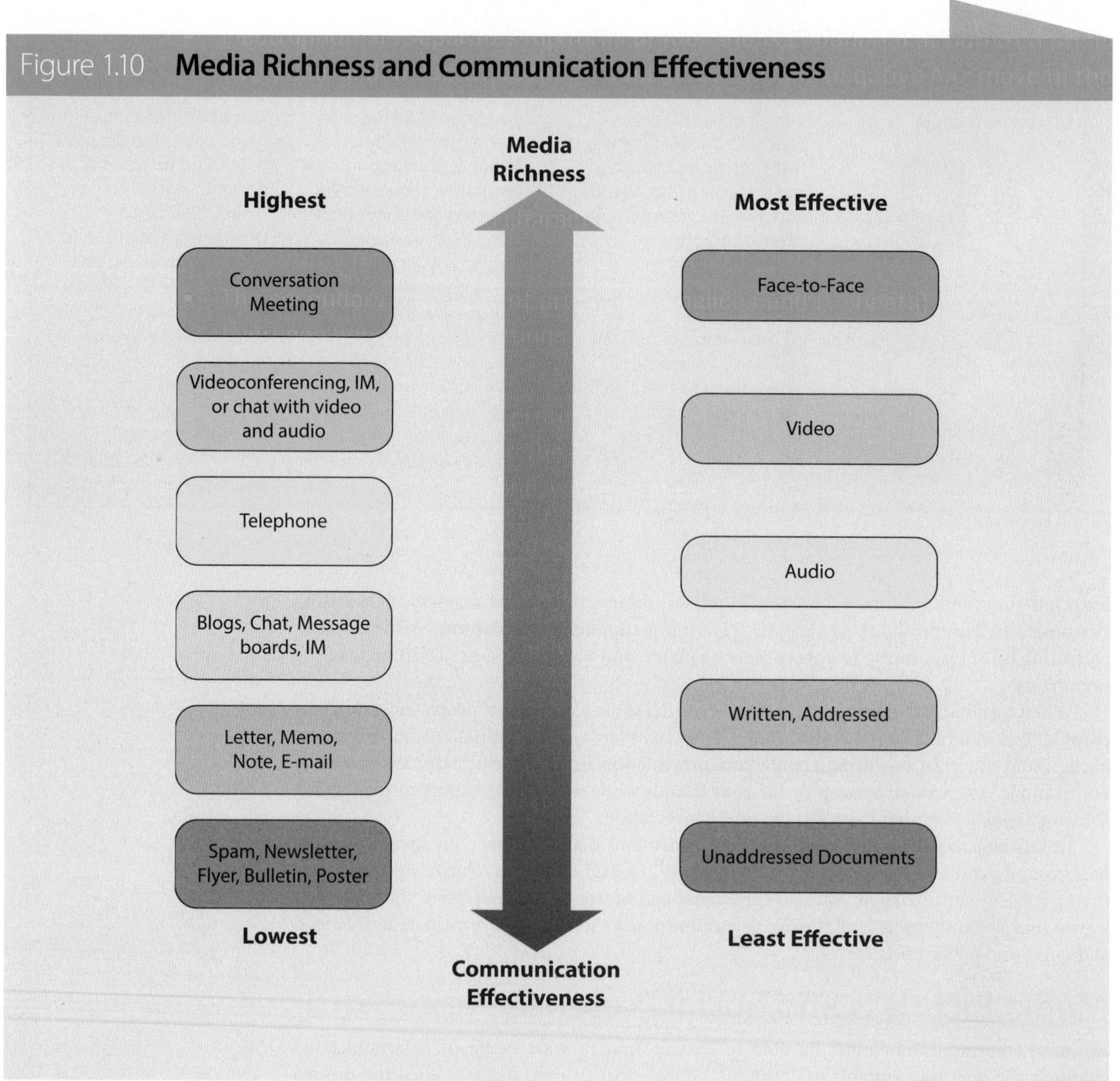

conversation) is not always available, communicators must often use leaner media (for example, e-mail) that may not be as effective in reducing ambiguity and decreasing the risk of miscommunication. Just think how hard it is to know whether a text or an e-mail is sarcastic.

Social Presence. *Social presence* has come to mean the degree to which people are engaged online and ready to connect with others. As proposed by Short, Williams, and Christie,[83] however, social presence is the degree of salience (being there) between a sender and receiver using a communication medium. Media with high social presence convey warmth and are personal. Social presence is greatest face-to-face, and less so in mediated and written communication, such as phone conversations and text messages. Likewise, social presence is greater in synchronous communication (live chat, IM) than in asynchronous communication (e-mail, forum post), which is rather impersonal.

Face-to-face we receive many more signals than just speech. For example, nonverbal cues, emotional disposition, and voice inflection help us interpret a message. In real time, we can ask the author of a message to clarify—something we cannot do as easily when the message arrives with a delay and is enabled by technology. You could say that social presence means how much awareness of the sender is conveyed along with the message. Communication can succeed as long as the chosen communication medium offers enough social presence to complete the task.[84]

Formal Communication Channels

Information within organizations flows through formal and informal communication channels. A free exchange of information helps organizations respond rapidly to changing markets, boost efficiency and productivity, build employee morale, serve the public, and take full advantage of the ideas of today's knowledge workers. Official information within an organization typically flows through formal channels in three directions: downward, upward, and horizontally, as shown in Figure 1.11.

Figure 1.11 **Information Flow in Organizations**

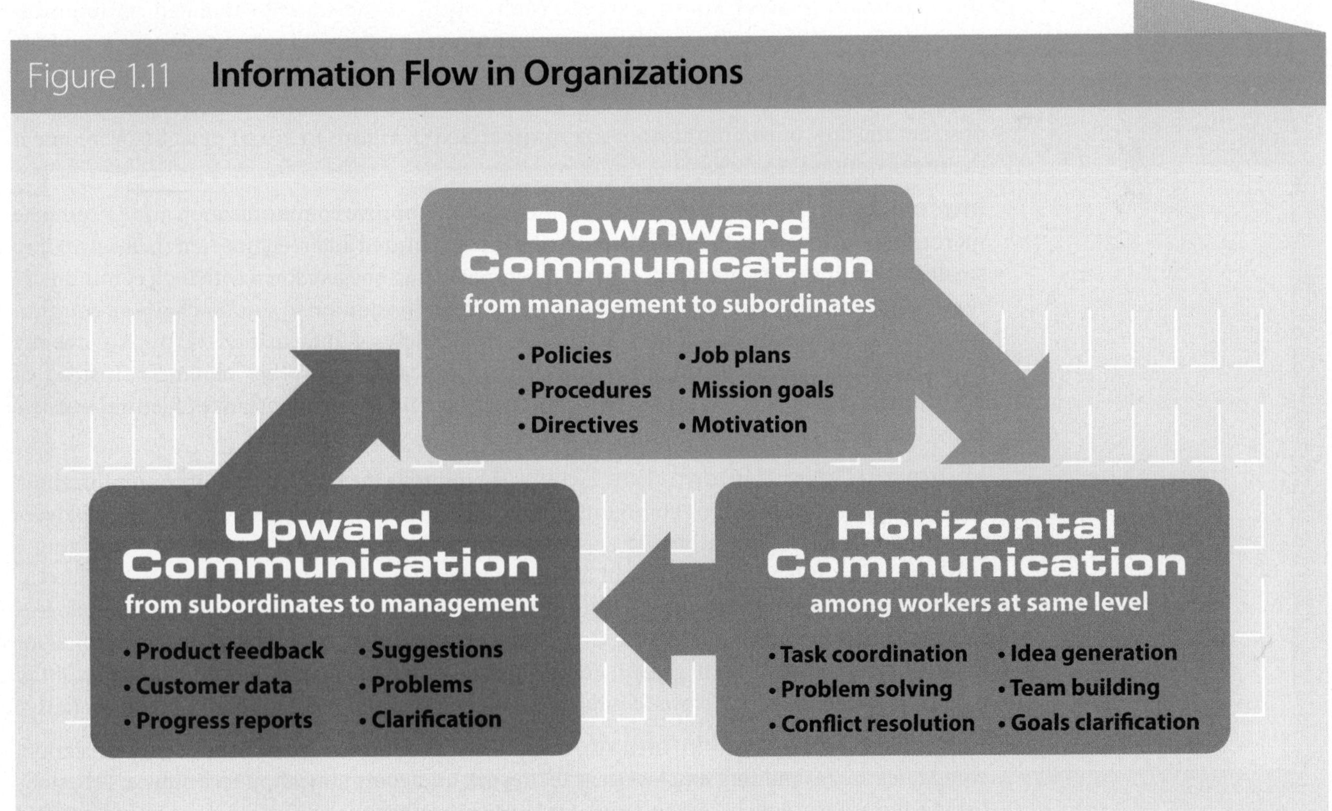

Figure 1.12 **Barriers Blocking the Flow of Communication in Organizations**

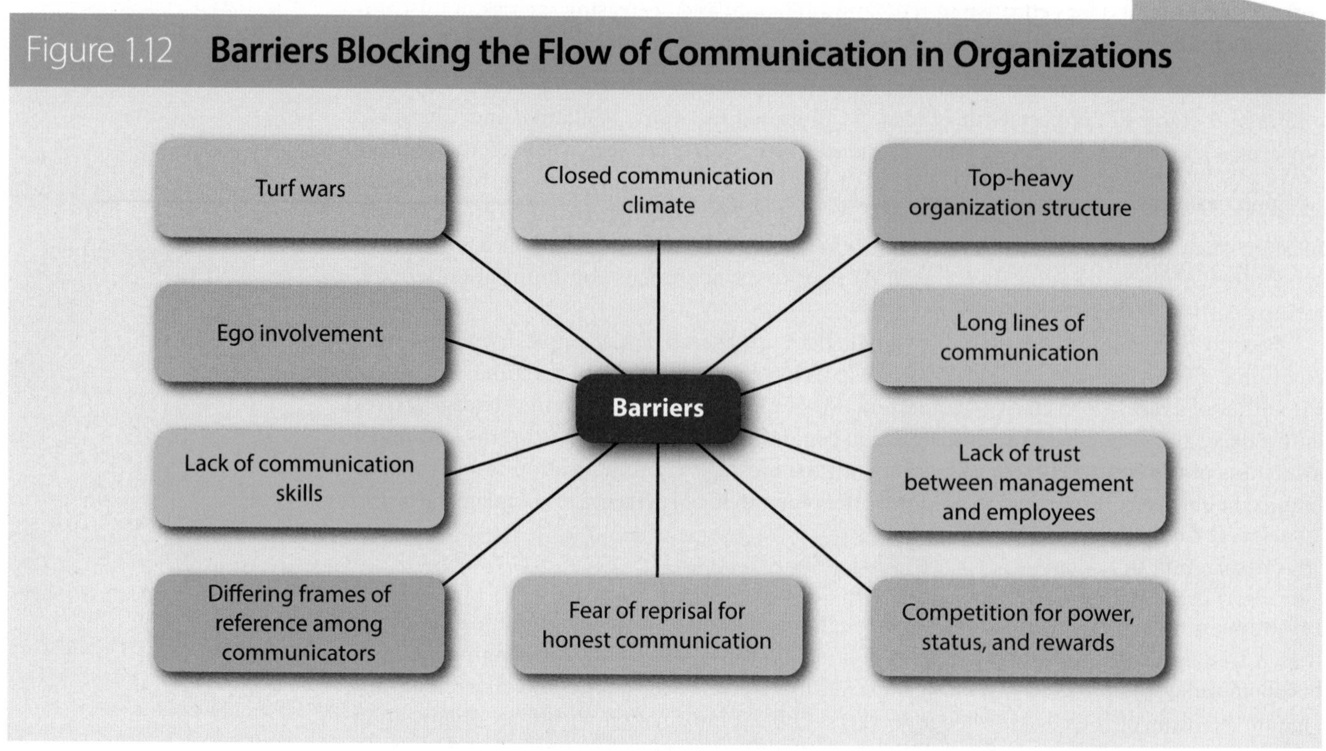

Formal channels of communication generally follow an organization's chain of command. That is, a message originates with executives and flows down through managers to supervisors and finally to lower-level employees. Many organizations have formulated communication policies that encourage regular open communication through newsletters, the corporate intranet, official messages, company-provided social networks, and blogs. Free-flowing, open communication invigorates organizations and makes them successful. Barriers, however, can obstruct the flow of communication, as summarized in Figure 1.12, and must be overcome if the organization is to thrive.

Improving Downward Information Flow. To improve communication and to compete more effectively, many of today's companies have restructured and reengineered themselves into smaller operating units and work teams. Rather than being bogged down with long communication chains, management speaks directly to employees. In addition to shorter chains of communication, management can improve the downward flow of information through company publications, announcements, meetings, videos, podcasts, and other channels. Instead of hoarding information at the top, today's managers recognize the importance of letting workers know how well the company is doing and what new projects are planned.

Improving Upward Information Flow. To improve the upward flow of communication, some companies are (a) hiring communication coaches to train employees, (b) asking employees to report customer complaints, (c) encouraging regular meetings with staff, (d) providing a trusting, nonthreatening environment in which employees can comfortably share their observations and ideas with management, and (e) offering incentive programs that encourage employees to collect and share valuable feedback. Companies are also building trust by setting up hotlines for anonymous feedback to management and by installing ombudsman programs. An *ombudsman* is a mediator who hears employee complaints, investigates, and seeks to resolve problems fairly.

Improving Horizontal Information Flow. To improve horizontal communication, companies are (a) training employees in teamwork and communication techniques, (b) establishing reward systems based on team achievement rather than individual achievement, and (c) encouraging full participation in team functions. However, employees must also realize that they are personally responsible for making themselves heard, for really understanding what other people say, and for getting the information they need. Developing those business communication skills is exactly what this book and this course will do for you.

Informal Communication Channels

Most organizations today share company news through consistent, formal channels such as e-mail, intranet posts, blogs, and staff meetings. Regardless, even within organizations with consistent formal channels, people still spread rumors about the company and gossip about each other.

The *grapevine* is an informal channel of communication that carries organizationally relevant gossip. This powerful but informal channel functions through social relationships; people talk about work when they are lunching, working out, golfing, and carpooling, as well as in e-mails, texts, and blogs. At one time gossip took place mostly around the water cooler. Today, however, gossip travels much more rapidly online.

Respecting the Power of the Grapevine. Researchers studying communication flow within organizations know that the grapevine can be a powerful, pervasive source of information. In some organizations it can account for as much as two thirds of an employee's information. Is this bad? Well, yes and no. The grapevine can be a fairly accurate and speedy source of organization information. Studies have demonstrated accuracy ratings of 75 to 80 percent for many grapevine transmissions.[85] The grapevine is often the fastest channel to disseminate information throughout an organization.[86] However, like a game of telephone, such messages can introduce falsehoods the longer the path that the news travels.

Psychotherapist Naomi Shragai blames typical workplace anxieties and executives' withholding of information for workers' reliance on the grapevine: "In the absence of adequate information from management, people naturally create narratives to fill the void."[87] But such disclosures carry risks. Sensitive rumors publicized online have cost many workers their jobs.

Understanding the Potential Benefits of the Grapevine. Sometimes office gossip can be downright positive. A Dutch university study found that up to 90 percent of office conversation consists of gossip. The authors believe that such chatter may foster group cohesion, strengthen the bonds among workers, and even improve productivity by making poor performers work harder.[88]

To many of us, gossip is fun and even entertaining. It encourages social bonding and makes us feel close to others who share our trust. We feel a part of the group and believe that we can influence others when we share a significant tidbit. We might even argue that gossip is good because it can help people learn how to behave and how to respond to social miscues faster and less awkwardly than if they made the mistakes themselves. For example, you're not likely to wear that new revealing camisole after hearing the scathing remarks being circulated about a similar one worn by Lacy in the Marketing Department.

As opposed to the offline grapevine, consumer-generated information online in social media, forums, Internet discussion boards, blogs, Facebook posts, and tweets provides an unsparing, revealing glimpse of what employees and the public are thinking. Social networking sites such as Glassdoor offer anonymous reviews that expose the inner workings of companies. Glassdoor also enables users to share typical interview questions with other job seekers and provides other invaluable insider information. High-profile leaks spread fast online, and their accuracy can be verified more easily than rumors in an offline grapevine.

Using the Grapevine Productively. Managers can use the grapevine productively by doing the following: (a) respecting employees' desire to know, (b) increasing the amount of information delivered through formal channels, (c) sharing bad as well as good news, (d) monitoring the grapevine, and (e) acting promptly to correct misinformation.[89] In addition, managers should model desirable behavior and not gossip themselves.[90]

As we have seen, office gossip online or off is complex and sometimes harmful. Productivity and morale may suffer as mistrust spreads. As a result, worker engagement plummets and turnover increases. If pervasive gossip qualifies as "malicious harassment," it may expose a company to legal liability.[91] Malicious gossip spread in e-mails, via text messages, or on social media

Ethics Check

Office Grapevine

Like a game of telephone, the grapevine can distort the original message because the news travels through many mouths and ears at the office. Knowing this, can you safely share with even a trusted colleague something you would not comfortably discuss with everyone?

sites can be used in defamation cases. It can become evidence against employers in supporting charges of harassment or maintaining a hostile work environment. Unfounded gossip can ruin careers and harm companies. In addition, employers look upon gossip as a productivity drain. The time spent gossiping reduces the time spent working.

Companies such as Nordstrom that actively monitor social media are better able to correct inaccuracies and misperceptions. To counter a negative YouTube video going viral with millions of views, Hewlett-Packard quickly responded on its blog and in Internet forums. The video alleged that HP face-tracking software was racist because it failed to recognize African-American faces. The company's excellent crisis communication reassured its audiences and won praise.[92] Through formal and informal channels of communication, smart companies keep employees and the public informed.

LEARNING OUTCOME 5

Analyze ethics in the workplace, understand the goals of ethical business communicators, and choose the tools for doing the right thing.

Ethics in the Workplace Needed More Than Ever

Ethics is once again a hot topic in business circles. On the heels of the banking crisis and the collapse of the real estate market, a calamitous recession followed, caused largely, some say, by greed and ethical lapses. With the passage of the Sarbanes-Oxley Act, the government required greater accountability. As a result, businesses are now eager to regain public trust by building ethical environments. Many have written ethical mission statements, installed hotlines, and appointed compliance officers to ensure strict adherence to their high standards and the law.

In addition, most individuals understand that lying is "corrosive," undermining trust in the workplace and destroying personal integrity.[93] Warren Buffett's much-quoted maxim applies here: "It takes 20 years to build a reputation and five minutes to ruin it."[94] More tangibly, lying in the form of fraud can cost a typical business about 5 percent of its revenue, leading, according to an association of investigators, to a projected global loss of nearly $3.7 trillion a year.[95] Figure 1.13 reveals the results of a workplace ethics survey showing a hopeful downward trend in unethical workplace behavior.

Figure 1.13 **Employees Reveal Office Dilemmas—Ethics Survey**

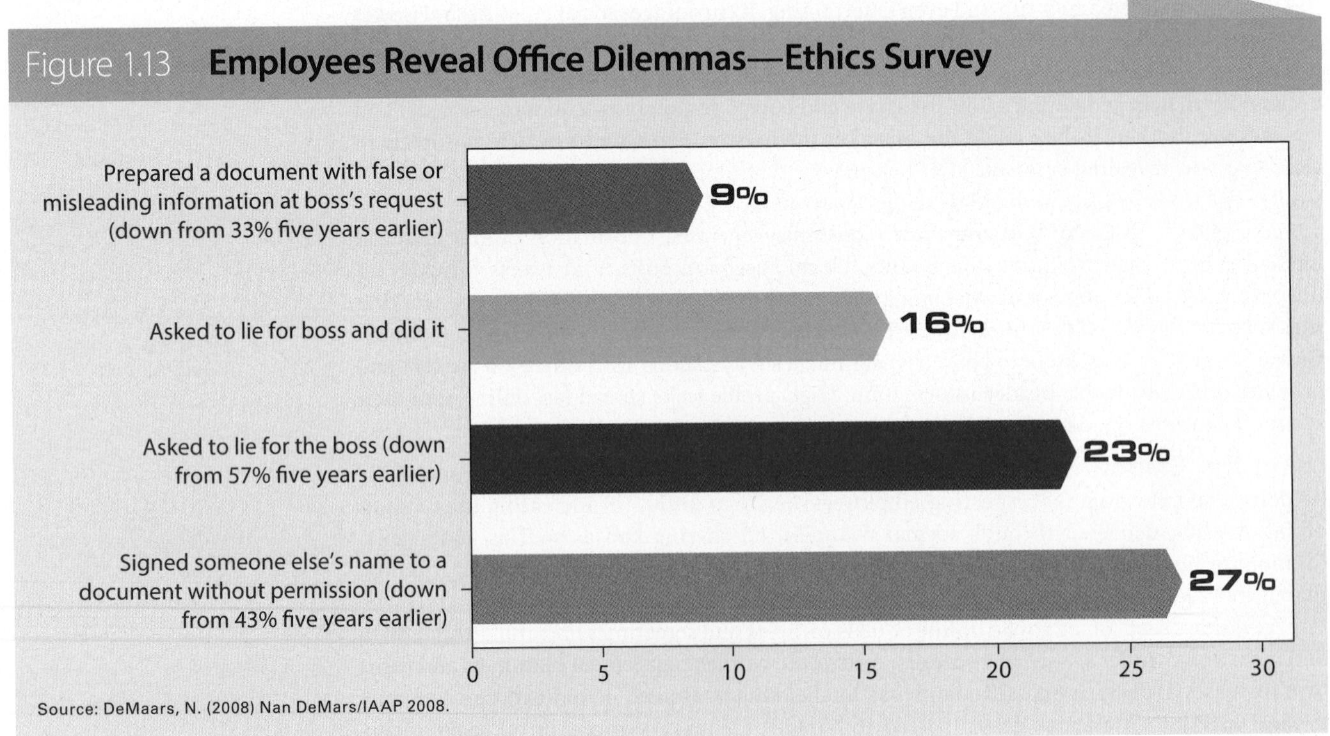

Source: DeMaars, N. (2008) Nan DeMars/IAAP 2008.

The financial mess and economic tailspin after 2007 forced many to wonder what caused the severe economic crisis. Who or what was to blame? Some observers claim that business organizations suffered from an ethics deficit; they were too intent on short-term profits and cared little about the dangerous risks they were taking. Executives and managers were so self-centered that they failed to see themselves as caretakers of their own institutions. Critics also extended their blame to business schools for not doing a better job of teaching ethics.[96] Still others complained that the financial debacle was caused by greedy individuals who were interested only in personal gain at all costs. Ethical lapses and a relaxed regulatory climate conspired to create the perfect storm that ripped through the economy.

Although the financial mess was not directly created by any single factor, many believe that it would not have occurred if those involved had acted less selfishly and more ethically. The entire topic of ethics in business has captured the spotlight as a result of the financial crisis and economic downturn. The topic of ethics could fill entire books. However, we will examine aspects that specifically concern you as a business communicator in today's workplace.

Defining Ethics

Ethics refers to conventional standards of right and wrong that prescribe what people should do. These standards usually consist of rights, obligations, and benefits to society. They also include virtues such as fairness, honesty, loyalty, and concern for others. Ethics is about having values and taking responsibility. Ethical individuals follow the law and refrain from theft, murder, assault, slander, and fraud. Figure 1.14 depicts some of the influences that form our awareness of ethics and help us develop a value system that guides our decisions. In the following discussion, we examine ethics in the workplace, study goals of ethical business communicators, and learn tools for doing the right thing.

Figure 1.14 **The Context of Ethical Decision Making**

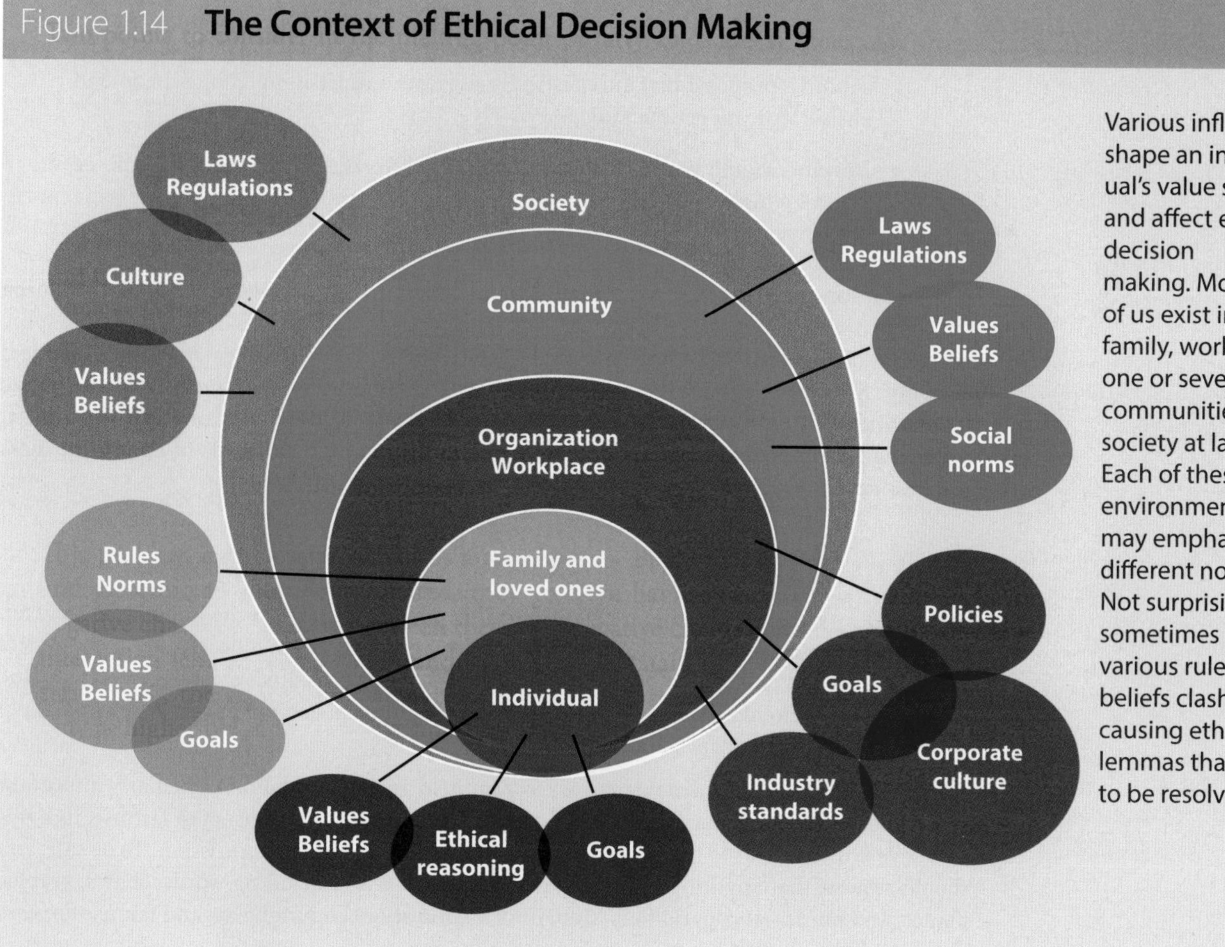

Various influences shape an individual's value system and affect ethical decision making. Most of us exist in a family, workplace, one or several communities, and society at large. Each of these environments may emphasize different norms. Not surprisingly, sometimes the various rules and beliefs clash, causing ethical dilemmas that need to be resolved.

As a business communicator, you should understand basic ethical principles so that you can make logical decisions when faced with dilemmas in the workplace. Professionals in any field deal with moral dilemmas on the job. However, just being a moral person and having sound personal or professional ethics may not be sufficient to handle the ethical issues you may face in the workplace. Consider the following ethical dilemmas:

- **E-mail message** You accidentally receive a message outlining your company's restructuring plan. You see that your coworker's job will be eliminated. He and his wife are about to purchase a new home. Should you tell him that his job is in danger?
- **Customer e-mail** You are replying to an e-mail from to a customer who is irate over a mistake you made. Should you blame it on a computer glitch, point the finger at another department, or take the blame and risk losing this customer's trust and possibly your job?
- **Progress report** Should you write a report that ignores problems in a project, as your boss asks? Your boss controls your performance evaluation.
- **Sales report** Should you inflate sales figures so that your team can meet its quarterly goal? Your team leader strongly urges you to do so, and you receive a healthy bonus if your team meets its goal.
- **Presentation** You are rushing to prepare a presentation. On the Web you find perfect wording and great graphics. Should you lift the graphics and wording but change a few words? You figure that if it is on the Web, it must be in the public domain.
- **Proposal** Your company urgently needs a revenue-producing project. Should you submit a proposal that unrealistically suggests a short completion schedule to ensure that you get the job?
- **Résumé** Should you inflate your grade point average or give yourself more experience or a higher job title than your experience warrants to make your résumé more attractive? The job market is very competitive.

On the job you will face many dilemmas, and you will want to react ethically. Determining the right thing to do, however, is not always an easy task. No solid rules guide us. For some people, following the law seems to be enough. They think that anything legal must also be ethical or moral. Most people, however, believe that ethical standards rise to a higher level. What are those standards? Although many ethical dilemmas have no right answer, one solution is often better than another. In deciding on that solution, keep in mind the goals of ethical business communicators.

Doing What Ethical Communicators Do

Taking ethics into consideration can be painful in the short term. In the long term, however, ethical behavior makes sense and pays off. Dealing honestly with colleagues and customers develops trust and builds strong relationships. The following guidelines can help you set specific ethical goals. Although these goals hardly constitute a formal code of conduct, they will help you maintain a high ethical standard.

Abiding by the Law. Know the laws in your field and follow them. Particularly important for business communicators are issues of copyright law. Under the concept of fair use, individuals have limited rights to use copyrighted material without seeking permission. To be safe, you should assume that anything produced privately after 1989—including words, charts, graphs, photos, and music—is copyrighted. More information about copyright law and fair use appears in Chapter 11 on page 421.

By the way, don't assume that Internet items are in the public domain and free to be used or shared. Files and media posted on the Internet are covered by copyright laws. The Recording Industry Association of America (RIAA) and the Motion Picture Association of America (MPAA) have sued individuals, website operators, and Internet service providers for allowing illicit downloading or sharing of music and movies. Tough penalties can include a felony conviction, up to five years in jail, and fines up to $250,000. If you are in accounting, financial management, investing, or corporate management, you should be aware of the restrictions set forth by the Sarbanes-Oxley Act or the provisions of the Dodd-Frank Act. Whatever your field, become familiar with its regulations.

Telling the Truth. Ethical business communicators do not intentionally make statements that are untrue or deceptive. Accused of selling stock based on insider information, businesswoman and TV personality Martha Stewart was actually jailed for lying about it. Hewlett-Packard CEO Mark Hurd was ousted in scandal after a probe into his relationship with a female contractor revealed that he had submitted inaccurate expense reports. Yahoo CEO Scott Thompson was forced to resign after only four months for padding his résumé. These big-time lies made headlines, and you may see no correlation to your life. On a personal level, however, we all may lie and deceive in various ways. We say things that are not so. We may exaggerate to swell the importance of our assertions.

Labeling Opinions. Sensitive communicators know the difference between facts and opinions. Facts are verifiable and often are quantifiable; opinions are beliefs held with confidence but without substantiation. It is a fact, for example, that women are starting businesses at two times the rate of men.[97] It is an opinion, though, that the so-called glass ceiling has held women back, forcing them to start their own businesses. Such a cause-and-effect claim would be difficult to prove. It is a fact that many corporations are spending billions of dollars to be socially responsible, including using ethically made products and developing eco-friendly technology. It is an opinion that consumers are willing to pay more for a pound of coffee if they believe that the seller followed ethical fair-trade production standards.[98] Assertions that cannot be proved are opinions, and stating opinions as if they were facts is unethical and, well, foolish.

Being Objective. Ethical business communicators recognize their own biases and strive to keep them from distorting a message. Suppose you are asked to investigate laptop computers and write a report recommending a brand for your office. As you visit stores, you discover that an old high school friend is selling Brand X. Because you always liked this individual and have faith in his judgment, you may be inclined to tilt your recommendation in his direction. However, it is unethical to misrepresent the facts in your report or to put a spin on your arguments based on friendship. To be ethical, you could note in your report that you have known the person for ten years and that you respect his opinion. In this way, you have disclosed your relationship as well as the reasons for your decision. Honest reporting means presenting the whole picture and relating all facts fairly.

Communicating Clearly. Ethical business communicators feel an obligation to write clearly so that receivers understand easily and quickly. Some states have even passed plain English (also called plain language) laws requiring businesses to write policies, warranties, and contracts in language comprehensible to average readers. Under former chairman Arthur Levitt, the Securities and Exchange Commission issued *A Plain English Handbook* explaining how to create clear SEC disclosure documents. Persistent lobbying efforts by plain-language advocacy groups at the federal level culminated in the Plain Writing Act. The law mandates that government agencies use unadorned prose in documents addressing the public. Plain English means short sentences, simple words, and clear organization. Communicators who intentionally obscure the meaning with long sentences and difficult words are being unethical.

Using Inclusive Language. Ethical business communicators use language that includes rather than excludes. They avoid expressions that discriminate against individuals or groups on the basis of their sex, ethnicity, disability, race, sexual orientation, or age. Language is discriminatory when it stereotypes, insults, or excludes people. You will learn more about how to use inclusive, bias-free language in Chapter 4.

Ethics Check

Blurt Out the Truth?

While serving as an interviewer on behalf of your organization, you are expected to tell prospective employees that the firm is a great place to work. However, you know that the work environment is bad, morale is low, and staff turnover is high. What should you do?

Giving Credit. Ethical communicators give credit for ideas by (a) referring to originators' names within the text; (b) using quotation marks; and (c) documenting sources with endnotes, footnotes, or internal references. You will learn how to do this in Chapter 11 and Appendix B. Don't suggest that you did all the work on a project if you had help. In school or on the job, stealing ideas, words, graphics, or any other original material is unethical.

In addition to legal and regulatory restrictions in their fields, many professionals uphold their own rigorous rules of conduct; for example, physicians, psychologists, and accountants follow standards of professional ethics much higher than the restrictions imposed by law. Similarly, members of the International Association of Business Communicators have developed a code of ethics with 12 guidelines (articles) that spell out criteria for determining what is right and wrong for members of its organization. Search for *IABC Code of Ethics for Professional Communicators* on the Web.

pathdoc/ Shutterstock.com

Reality Check

Explaining Ethical Blind Spots

"We have found that much unethical conduct that goes on, whether in social life or work life, happens because people are unconsciously fooling themselves. They overlook transgressions—bending a rule to help a colleague, overlooking information that might damage the reputation of a client—because it is in their interest to do so."[99]

—Max H. Bazerman and Ann E. Tenbrunsel, business ethicists, coauthors *of Blind Spots*

Choosing Tools for Doing the Right Thing

It's easy to commit ethical lapses because of natural self-interests and the desire to succeed. In composing messages or engaging in other activities on the job, business communicators can't help being torn by conflicting loyalties. Do we tell the truth and risk our jobs? Do we show loyalty to friends even if it means bending the rules? Should we be tactful or totally honest? Is it our duty to make a profit or to be socially responsible?

Acting ethically means doing the right thing given the circumstances. Each set of circumstances requires analyzing issues, evaluating choices, and acting responsibly. Resolving ethical issues is never easy, but the task can be made less difficult if you know how to identify key issues. The five questions in Figure 1.15 may help you resolve most ethical dilemmas. The checklist begins by asking whether an action is legal. You should go forward only if the action complies with the law. If it does, then test the ethical soundness of your plan by asking the remaining questions: Would you proceed if you were on the receiving end of the action, and can you rule out better options? Even if the answer is *yes*, consider then how a trusted mentor or your family, friends, and coworkers would view your decision.

Perhaps the best advice in ethical matters is contained in the Golden Rule: Treat others the way you wish to be treated. The principle of reciprocity has a long tradition and exists in most religions and cultures. This simple maxim can go a long way toward resolving conflict. The ultimate solution to all ethics problems is treating others fairly and doing what is right to achieve what is good. In succeeding chapters you will find additional discussions of ethical questions as they relate to relevant topics.

Figure 1.15 Five Questions to Guide Ethical Decisions

1. Is the action legal?
2. Would you do it if you were on the opposite side?
3. Can you rule out a better alternative?
4. Would a trusted advisor agree?
5. Would family, friends, employer, or coworkers approve?
If the action is illegal, STOP!
If yes, GO!
Even if it is legal, proceed with CAUTION

Ethics holds us to a higher standard than the law. Even when an action is legal, it may violate generally accepted principles of right and wrong.

Your Turn: Applying Your Skills at Nordstrom

Yeamake/Shutterstock.com

The upscale fashion retailer recognizes that customers expect speed and convenience, says Jamie Nordstrom, president of stores. The great-grandson of the company founder believes that "the retailers that deliver on those customers' expectations are the ones that are going to get their business."[100]

He grew up with the threat of new competitors unseating the family business, Jamie Nordstrom says, but he points to the company's longevity and continued success. Its secret? Engaging customers and listening to their needs: "We have to remind ourselves on a daily basis that if we're not listening to the customer, then we're probably not going to make a good decision—so that's our focus."

And listen Nordstrom does.

Your Task

You are an intern in the User Experience and Optimization division overseen by Erik Nordstrom, the current president of stores. You are learning about the "Nordie" ethos of truly believing in helping others and genuinely loving customer service. As the former chairman Bruce A. Nordstrom put it: "We can hire nice people and teach them to sell, but we can't hire salespeople and teach them to be nice."[101] Naturally, this means being kind online.

The intern supervisor wants you to study Facebook interactions among customers and Nordstrom representatives to learn about the friendly, casual tone employed in such virtual encounters. How are the Nordstrom posters helping their Facebook followers? What are some of their most prominent strategies? Read several days' worth of Facebook posts. Summarize your observations in an e-mail. Refer to Chapter 7 for information about how to draft an e-mail. Be sure to select two or three specific posts representing a pattern or strategy. For example, discuss particularly successful responses, whether they are prompted by an inquiry, complaint, or praise.

Summary of Learning Outcomes

1 Explain how communication skills fuel career success, and understand why writing skills are vital in a digital, mobile, and social-media-driven workplace.

- Communication skills matter more than ever before as communication technology has provided businesspeople with unprecedented mobility and workers write more, not less.
- Superior communication skills are critical to job placement, performance, career advancement, and organizational success; they can set you apart from other candidates.
- Workers must write their own messages and use fast communication channels such as social media that connect vast numbers of people.
- Writing skills can be learned; they are not inherent.

2 Identify the tools for success in the hyperconnected 21st-century workplace; appreciate the importance of critical-thinking skills and personal credibility in the competitive job market of the digital age; and discuss how your education may determine your income.

- Accessing and sharing various digital media from a vast network of sources and distributing them nearly instantly to widespread audiences have never been easier.
- Expect to be a knowledge worker who must think critically and develop opinions backed by evidence.
- You are learning to think, read, and ask questions in a networked world in which employers demand professionalism.
- Be prepared to take charge of your career as you work for multiple employers.
- Because technologies are constantly evolving, you must be flexible and engage in lifelong learning to be competitive, but your education will most likely cause your income to grow.

3 Describe significant trends in today's dynamic, networked work environment, and recognize that social media and other communication technologies require excellent communication skills, in any economic climate.

- The trends affecting today's workers include new communication technologies such as social media, expectations of around-the-clock availability, and global competition.
- Flattened management hierarchies, team-based projects, a diverse workforce, and the virtual office operating practically 24/7/365 are other significant trends.
- Workers need new skills and attitudes to collaborate successfully as team members in workplaces that are increasingly diverse and as potential telecommuters.
- Businesspeople need to have strong communication skills to make effective decisions and stay connected across time zones as well as vast distances.

4 Examine critically the internal and external flow of communication in organizations through formal and informal channels, explain the importance of effective media choices, and understand how to overcome typical barriers to organizational communication.

- Business communicators always seek to achieve a particular objective, aided by rapidly changing communication technologies.
- The mobile digital workplace is unthinkable without e-mail, IM, company intranets, corporate websites, audio and video podcasting, videoconferencing, and Web chats.

- Internal communication involves superiors, coworkers, and subordinates, whereas external communication includes customers, suppliers, government agencies, and the public.
- Media richness and social presence describe the communication media most suitable to avoid ambiguity in any workplace interaction.
- Formal channels of communication follow an organization's rank order; informal channels, such as the grapevine, deliver unofficial news among coworkers. Gossip can be damaging.

5 Analyze ethics in the workplace, understand the goals of ethical business communicators, and choose the tools for doing the right thing.

- Ethics describes standards of right and wrong prescribing what people should do and includes virtues such as fairness, honesty, and loyalty. Ethical standards are more rigorous than the law.
- The goals of ethical communicators include abiding by the law, telling the truth, labeling opinions, being objective, communicating clearly, using inclusive language, and giving credit.
- To do the right thing, ask these questions: (a) Is the action legal? (b) Would you do it if you were on the opposite side? (c) Can you rule out a better alternative? (d) Would a trusted advisor agree? and (e) Would your family, friends, employer, or coworkers approve?

Critical Thinking

1. What could be the career fallout for someone who is unwilling or unable to train to become a better communicator? Can workers today be successful if their writing is and remains poor? (L.O. 1)
2. Sharing various digital media impulsively can lead to embarrassment and worse. Have you or has someone you know ever regretted posting a comment, photo, or other media online? (L.O. 2)
3. How do you feel about the work-life balance in today's 24/7 "anytime, anywhere" digital workplace? Do you anticipate negative effects on your health and personal life? (L.O. 3)
4. Critics complain that texting and instant messaging lead to *textspeak,* poor writing characterized by acronyms, abbreviations, and emoticons. Others have claimed that emoji help supply important missing cues in lean media channels that are "toneless" otherwise.[102] What do you think? (L.O. 4)
5. **Ethical Issue:** Josh in the Accounting Department tells you that he heard from a reliable source that 15 percent of the staff will be fired within 120 days. You would love to share this juicy news with other department members, for their own defense and planning. Should you? Why or why not?

Activities

1.1 Social Media Inventory (L.O. 1–4)

Communication Technology | Social Media

Team

The millennials (those born after 1985) do not remember a time without computer technology and cell phones in wide use. People born in the 1990s have only known a society that depends on the Internet and mobile technology. Social media are second nature to most of these young people, who seem to be inseparably attached to their smart devices.

You too may live, learn, work, play, network, and shop in the digital world. Even if you are not crazy about the latest gadgets and gizmos, your daily life depends on technology because your cell phone, iPod, TV, DVD player, and other electronics wouldn't exist without it and are increasingly networked.

YOUR TASK Take stock of your Internet, social media, and other technology use. First establish useful criteria—for example, categories such as consumer electronics, social networking sites, preferred modes of communication with friends and family, and so forth. Within each category, list the technology you use most frequently. For instance, for social media networks, indicate your use of Facebook, Instagram, Snapchat, Twitter, Google+, YouTube, Hulu, LinkedIn, and more. How do you use each? Estimate how often you access these sites per day and indicate the tools you use (e.g., smartphone, tablet, laptop). How much do you text every day? Your instructor may ask you to create at least three categories such as the ones in the preceding list and record your responses in writing. Then compare your three lists within a group of five classmates or in assigned teams. Share your results individually or in teams, either verbally or in writing. Your instructor may ask you to summarize your observations about how plugged in you and your classmates are in a post on a discussion board or in an e-mail.

1.2 Collaborating on the Opening Case Study (L.O. 1–5)

Team

Each chapter contains a two-part case study of a well-known company. To help you develop collaboration and speaking skills as well as to learn about the target company and apply the chapter concepts, your instructor may ask you to do the following.

YOUR TASK Individually or as part of a three-student team during your course, work on one of the 16 case studies in the textbook. Answer the questions posed in both parts of the case study, look for additional information in articles or on websites, complete the application assignment, and then make a five- to ten-minute presentation to the class of your findings and reactions.

1.3 Introducing Yourself (L.O. 1, 2)

Communication Technology E-Mail

Social Media

Your instructor wants to know more about you, your motivation for taking this course, your career goals, and your writing skills.

YOUR TASK Send an e-mail or write a memo of introduction to your instructor. See Appendix A for memo formats and Chapters 7 and 8 for tips on preparing an e-mail message. In your message include the following:

a. Your reasons for taking this class

b. Your career goals (both temporary and long-term)

c. A brief description of your employment, if any, and your favorite activities

d. An assessment and discussion of your current communication skills, including your strengths and weaknesses Alternatively, your instructor may ask you to (a) create a profile for LinkedIn, the social networking site for professionals or (b) develop a profile within a learning-management system (e.g., Blackboard or Moodle) to introduce yourself to your classmates. Your instructor may challenge you to compose your introduction in 140 or fewer characters (see Chapter 6 for tips on writing tweets and other microblogging messages).

1.4 Small-Group Presentation: Introducing Team Members (L.O. 1, 2)

Team

Many business organizations today use teams to accomplish their goals. To help you develop speaking, listening, and teamwork skills, your instructor may assign team projects. One of the first jobs in any team is selecting members and becoming acquainted.

YOUR TASK Your instructor will divide your class into small groups or teams. At your instructor's direction, either (a) interview another group member and introduce that person to the group or (b) introduce yourself to the group. Think of this as an informal interview for a team assignment or a job. You will want to make notes from which to speak. Your introduction should include information such as the following:

a. Where did you grow up?

b. What work and extracurricular activities have you engaged in?

c. What are your interests and talents? What are you good at doing?

d. What have you achieved?

e. How familiar are you with various computer technologies?

f. What are your professional and personal goals? Where do you expect to be five years from now?

g. Name one thing about you that others might not guess when first meeting you.

To develop listening skills, team members should practice good listening techniques (see Chapter 2) and take notes. They should be prepared to discuss three important facts as well as remember details about each speaker.

Alternatively, expanding the task under (a), you could be asked to write a short professional biographical blurb after your interview of a group member. After feedback to ensure that it is correct, discuss with your partner or the whole group whether the bio would be attractive to employers looking for communication skills and other employability skills as presented in this chapter.

1.5 Communication Skills: Employer Wish List (L.O. 1)

Team Web

What do employers request when they list job openings in your field?

YOUR TASK Individually or in teams, check the listings at an online job board such as Monster, CollegeRecruiter, CareerBuilder, or CollegeGrad. Use your favorite search engine to locate their sites. Follow the instructions to search job categories and locations. Also check college resources and local newspaper listings of job openings (online). Find five or more job listings in your field. If possible, print the results of your search. If you cannot print, save the information on your smartphone or other mobile device. You could also go low-tech and simply make handwritten notes on what you find.

Examine the skills requested. How often do the job listings mention communication, teamwork, and computer skills? What tasks do the job listings mention? Discuss your findings with your team members. Prepare a list of the most frequently requested skills. Your instructor may ask you to submit your findings and/or report to the class.

1.6 Writing Skills: But My Job Won't Require Writing! (L.O. 1–3)

Team

Some job candidates experience a disconnect between what they expect to be doing in their career fields and what they actually will do.

YOUR TASK In teams or in class, discuss the accuracy of the following statements. Are they myths or facts?

a. No one really writes anymore. They just text and send e-mails.
b. Because I'm in a technical field, I will work with numbers, not words.
c. Secretaries will clean up my writing problems.
d. Technical writers do most of the real writing on the job.
e. Today's sophisticated software programs can fix any of my writing mistakes.
f. I can use forms and templates for most messages.

1.7 Exploring Work-Life Balance and Tweeting About It (L.O. 1–4)

Social Media Web

Work-life balance continues to be a hot-button topic. *The Huffington Post* website features dozens of articles on work-life balance. Some discuss the dangers of work encroaching on Americans' lives and families; others blame social media and mobile communication technology for the demise of work-life balance. A recent Bloomberg Business article declares: "Work-life balance is steadily becoming a unicorn in the working world."[103] Unicorns are mythic creatures of fantasy and as such truly rare! This statement suggests that work-life balance is unattainable.

If you feel adventurous, you could explore work-life balance in Europe and compare. The *Times* of London might be a good start. Most German publications provide complete English-language Web pages that you could search, too.

YOUR TASK Select your publication, for example, *The Huffington Post*. Input your search term *work-life balance*. Among the ten or so pages of articles, select one piece. Read it closely. Unless your instructor uses Twitter (or Tumblr) for this exercise, write a tweet in MS Word of no more than 130 characters out of the 140 allowed. Leave room for a comment in a retweet. Use a hashtag to start a conversation on the topic. Shorten long URLs (Web addresses) by visiting TinyURL. Your tweets should be teasers that induce the reader to click the link and read the article.

If directed, also write a social media post—think LinkedIn—of no more than 30 words. In addition, you could be asked to write a summary of the article of no more than 10 percent of the total word count. Do not copy from the original. Tweet, post, and summarize from memory. When submitting your work, indicate the character and word count of both the original article and your messages. Word count is easy once you select and copy the entire article and paste it into an empty MS Word page. Your instructor may show you Twitter examples.

1.8 Oral or Written Communication: How Rich Must the Media Be? (L.O. 4)

Communication Technology E-Mail Social Media

YOUR TASK First decide whether the following messages need to be communicated orally or in writing. After consulting the media richness diagram in Figure 1.10 on page 22, consider how rich the medium must be in each communication situation to convey the message most appropriately and reliably. You may want to choose channels such as e-mail, letter, report, texting, instant messaging, telephone call, live chat, teleconferencing, face-to-face conversation, or team meeting. Describe the advantages and disadvantages of each choice.

a. You are returning with the senior auditor from a client visit to company headquarters, where you must attend an important department meeting. It looks as though you will be at least 15 minutes late. What are your options?

b. Working at 8 a.m. in your Boston office, you need to get in touch with your counterpart at your company's West Coast office and ask a few clarifying formatting questions about a report on which the two of you are collaborating.

c. John, the information technology vice president, must tell employees about a new company social media policy. He has two employees in mind who particularly need this information.

d. As soon as possible, you need to learn from Daryle in Document Imaging whether she can make copies of a set of engineering blueprints. If she cannot, you need her advice on where you can get it done.

e. As a manager in your Human Resources department, you must terminate three employees in a companywide initiative to reduce costs.

f. It wasn't your fault, but an order for printed checks for a longtime customer was mishandled. The checks are not ready, and the customer is angry.

g. As chairman of the Employee Benefits Committee, you have worked with your committee for two months evaluating several health plan options. You are now ready to convey the recommendations of the committee to management.

1.9 Information Flow: What's Good and Bad About Gossip at Work? (L.O. 5)

E-Mail | Ethics | Team

Jon Bender, a managing partner at PrincetonOne, an executive search firm, was surprised to receive a nasty, gossipy e-mail about himself. He was obviously not the intended receiver. Instead of shooting back an equally incendiary message, he decided to talk with the sender. He said, "You're upset. Let's talk about it, but it's not appropriate in an e-mail."[104]

YOUR TASK In groups, discuss Mr. Bender's response to gossip about himself. Did he do the right thing? How would you have reacted? Although gossip is generally considered unacceptable and a negative force, it can be a tool for managers and employees. Make a list of at least four benefits and four negative consequences of workplace gossip. Be prepared to explain and defend each item.

1.10 Lax Attitudes Toward Ethics Among Active Social Networkers? (L.O. 5)

Communication Technology | Ethics | Social Media

Test yourself and see how your ethical decision making compares with the attitudes of other active social media users. The National Business Ethics Survey of 4,800 U.S. males ages nineteen to forty-five found that active social networkers showed a much greater acceptance of questionable workplace behavior than did other U.S. workers. Here are the survey questions:

Do you feel it is acceptable to...?		
"Friend" a client/customer on a social network	YES	NO
Blog or tweet negatively about your company or colleagues	YES	NO
Buy personal items with your company credit card as long as you pay it back	YES	NO
Do a little less work to compensate for cuts in benefits or pay	YES	NO
Keep a copy of confidential work documents in case you need them in your next job	YES	NO
Take a copy of work software home and use it on your personal computer	YES	NO
Upload vacation pictures to the company network or server so that you can share them with coworkers	YES	NO
Use social networking to find out what your company's competitors are doing	YES	NO

YOUR TASK Answer the survey questions. Then view the survey results on page 37. How do your responses stack up? In class share your impressions of the survey. What surprised you and why? With your classmates and your instructor, discuss the behaviors addressed in the study. Are some particularly egregious? Do some seem pretty harmless? Why or why not? Apply the tools for doing the right thing introduced in this chapter (see Figure 1.15, Five Questions to Guide Ethical Decisions). Your instructor may ask you to post your views on Blackboard, Moodle, or another discussion forum and to respond to your peers' posts.

SOCIAL NETWORKS VS. OTHER U.S. WORKERS: COMPARING ATTITUDES TOWARDS QUESTIONABLE BEHAVIOR		
Do you feel it is acceptable to...?	**Active Social Networkers**	**Other U.S. Workers**
"Friend" a client/customer on a social network	59%	28%
Blog or tweet negatively about your company or colleagues	42%	6%
Buy personal items with your company credit card as long as you pay it back	42%	8%
Do a little less work to compensate for cuts in benefits or pay	51%	10%
Keep a copy of confidential work documents in case you need them in your next job	50%	15%
Take a copy of work software home and use it on your personal computer	46%	7%
Upload vacation pictures to the company network or server so you can share them with co-workers	50%	17%
Use social networking to find out what my company's competitors are doing	54%	30%

Source: National Business Ethics Survey, Social Media Week.[105]

1.11 Ethical Dilemmas: Applying Tools for Doing the Right Thing (L.O. 5)

Ethics Team

As a business communicator, you may face various ethical dilemmas in your career. Many factors can determine your choice of an action to take.

YOUR TASK Study the seven dilemmas appearing on page 28. Select four of them and apply the tools for doing the right thing in Figure 1.15 on page 31 choosing an appropriate action. In a memo to your instructor or in a team discussion, explain the action you would take for each dilemma. Analyze your response to each question (Is the action you are considering legal? How would you see the problem if you were on the opposite side? and so forth).

Test Your Etiquette IQ

New communication platforms and casual workplace environments have blurred the lines of appropriateness, leaving workers wondering how to navigate uncharted waters. Indicate whether the following statements are true or false. Then see if you agree with the responses on p. R-1.

1. You're enjoying your weekend when you receive an e-mail from your boss asking for information. It's not urgent, so the best plan is to respond early on Monday.

   ________True ________False

2. Shawna is your go-to colleague with all the answers, but she's on vacation. You need to ask her a quick question that you're sure she could answer—if you could just reach her. Because she has a smartphone connected to work e-mail, it's perfectly acceptable to give her a quick phone call.

_______ True _______ False

3. You just returned to the office from a terrific lunch. Your spicy fish dish was tasty and enough for a second meal. Because everyone uses the office fridge to store food, it's appropriate to put it there so that you can warm it up for tomorrow's lunch.

_______ True _______ False

Chat About It

In each chapter you will find five discussion questions related to the chapter material. Your instructor may assign these topics for you to discuss in class, in an online chat room, or on an online discussion board. Some of the discussion topics may require outside research. You may also be asked to read and respond to postings made by your classmates.

TOPIC 1: Do you think that always being plugged in can erode performance, as some executives have claimed in a recent survey? One leader pointed out that major scientific breakthroughs occurred outside the laboratory when the scientist was engaged in a mundane task—or even asleep. How do you balance work (or school) and rest?

TOPIC 2: In your chosen career, what sorts of continuing education experiences do you think you might need to stay employed or be promoted?

TOPIC 3: Swedish furniture retailer IKEA removed women from photos to please Saudi Arabia's religious police and suffered a backlash in Sweden for it. British department store retailer Marks & Spencer felt compelled to hire all-female staff to attract Middle Eastern shoppers. How far should retailers and other businesses bend to conform to other cultures?

TOPIC 4: So far only 3 percent of young college graduates are unemployed, and they earn almost $1 million more over their lifetimes than their peers with high school diplomas; however, college grads graduate with an average debt of $25,000 to $30,000. Is college still a good investment?

TOPIC 5: Some experts believe that although computer technology is improving our lives in many ways, it might be impairing our ability to think critically by putting answers at our fingertips. What do you think?

Grammar and Mechanics | *Review 1*

Each chapter includes an exercise based on Appendix D, Grammar and Mechanics Guide. This appendix is a business communicator's condensed guide to language usage, covering 50 of the most used and abused language elements. It also includes a list of frequently misspelled words as well as a list of confusing words. In the first nine chapters, each exercise focuses on a specific set of grammar/mechanics guidelines. In the last seven chapters, exercises review all the guidelines plus spelling and confusing words.

Note: In addition to the exercises in the textbook, you will find similar exercises at **www.cengagebrain.com** under the Grammar/Mechanics tab. The online exercises parallel the sentences in this textbook and test the same principles. However, the online exercises provide feedback and explanations.

Sentence Structure

Study sentence structure in Guides 1 through 3 of Appendix D beginning on page D-1. Some of the following numbered word groups have sentence faults. On a sheet of paper, indicate whether the word group is (a) correctly punctuated (b) a fragment, (c) a comma splice, or (d) a run-on sentence. If incorrect, write a correct version. Also, identify the fault and the relevant guide. Avoid adding new phrases or rewriting in your own words. When finished, compare your responses with the key beginning on page Key-1.

EXAMPLE: The message was meant to inform, however it confused instead.

REVISION: The message was meant to **inform; however,** it confused instead. [c, Guide 3, Comma splice]

1. Although the recent job market for new college graduates is brighter. It's still highly competitive with 1.5 unemployed workers vying for every open position.
2. Economists say this is the best job market in nearly a decade, the improving U.S. economy and accelerating retirements of baby boomers are creating job openings across many fields.
3. Because you are entering a fast-paced, competitive, and highly connected digital environment. Communication and technology skills are critical to your career success.
4. Many qualified people will apply for openings, however candidates with exceptional communication skills will immediately stand out.
5. Nearly all potential employers said that being able to think critically, communicate clearly, and solve complex problems are more important than a candidate's undergraduate major.
6. The nine-to-five job may soon be a relic of the past. If millennials have their way.
7. Knowledge workers must be able to explain their decisions they must be critical thinkers.
8. Approximately 75 percent of the information gathered through the grapevine turns out to be true, however that means that at least 25 percent of the information is false.
9. Ethical companies experience less litigation, and they also are the target of less government regulation.
10. Even when an action is legal. It may violate generally accepted principles of right and wrong.

References

[1] Ross, J. W., Beath, C. M., & Sebastian, I. (2015, January 14). Why Nordstrom's digital strategy works (and yours probably doesn't). HBR.org. Retrieved from https://hbr.org/2015/01/why-nordstroms-digital-strategy-works-and-yours-probably-doesnt

[2] Lutz, A. (2014, December 30). How Nordstrom became the most successful retailer. Business Insider. Retrieved from http://www.businessinsider.com/nordstroms-business-strategy-is-working-2014-12

[3] Hatch, D. (2012, May 15). Nordstrom in fashion with social media, mobile tech. *U. S. News*. Retrieved from http://money.usnews.com/money/business-economy/articles/2012/05/15/nordstrom-in-fashion-with-social-media-mobile-tech

[4] Success story: Nordstrom. (2015). Pinterest for business. Retrieved from https://business.pinterest.com/en/success-stories/nordstrom

[5] Nordstrom. (2013, March 1). Social media employee guidelines. Retrieved from http://shop.nordstrom.com/c/social-networking-guidelines

[6] Satell, G. (2015, February 6). Why communication is today's most important skill. *Forbes*. Retrieved from http://www.forbes.com/sites/gregsatell/2015/02/06/why-communication-is-todays-most-important-skill; Canavor, N. (2012). *Business writing in the digital age*. Los Angeles: Sage; see also National Writing Project with DeVoss, D. N., Eidman-Aadahl, E., & Hicks, T. (2010). *Because digital writing matters*. San Francisco: Jossey-Bass.

[7] The National Leadership Council for Liberal Education & America's Promise. Association of American Colleges and Universities. (2007). College learning for the new global century. Retrieved from http://www.aacu.org/leap/documents/GlobalCentury_final.pdf; Casner-Lotto, J., Wright, M., & Barrington, L. (2006, October). Are they really ready to work? Employers' perspectives on the basic knowledge and applied skills of new entrants to the 21st century U.S. workforce. Retrieved from http://www.p21.org/storage/documents/FINAL_REPORT_PDF09-29-06.pdf

[8] 2016 workforce-skills preparedness report. (2016). PayScale. Retrieved from http://www.payscale.com/data-packages/job-skills; National Association of Colleges and Employers. (2014, November 18). Job outlook 2015: The skills/qualities employers want in new college graduate hires. Retrieved from https://www.naceweb.org/about-us/press/class-2015-skills-qualities-employers-want.aspx; The Association of American Colleges and Universities/Hart Research Associates. (2009, November). Raising the bar: Employers' views on college learning in the wake of the economic downturn. Retrieved from http://www.aacu.org/leap/documents/2009_EmployerSurvey.pdf

[9] Kay, A. (2011, May 30). What employers want: 5 more skills to cultivate. *USA Today*. Retrieved from http://www.usatoday.com/money/jobcenter/workplace/kay/2011-05-30-skills-employers-want-part-ii_N.htm

[10] The MetLife Survey of the American Teacher: Preparing students for college and careers. (2011, May). Retrieved from http://www.metlife.com/assets/cao/contributions/foundation/american-teacher/MetLife_Teacher_Survey_2010.pdf

[11] College Board: The National Commission on Writing. (2004, September). Writing: A ticket to work…Or a ticket out: A survey of business leaders. Retrieved from http://www.collegeboard.com/prod_downloads/writingcom/writing-ticket-to-work.pdf

[12] College Board: The National Commission on Writing. (2004, September). Writing: A ticket to work… Or a ticket out: A survey of business leaders, p. 3. Retrieved from http://www.collegeboard.com/prod_downloads/writingcom/writing-ticket-to-work.pdf; O'Rourke, IV, J. S. (2013). *Management communication: A case-analysis approach* (5th ed.). Boston: Prentice Hall, p. 9; Canavor, N. (2012). *Business writing in the digital age*. Los Angeles: Sage, p. 3.

[13] College Board: The National Commission on Writing. (2004, September). Writing: A ticket to work…Or a ticket out: A survey of business leaders. Retrieved from http://www.collegeboard.com/prod_downloads/writingcom/writing-ticket-to-work.pdf

[14] Pew/Internet & College Board: The National Commission on Writing. (2008, April 24). Writing, technology, and teens. Retrieved from http://www.collegeboard.com/prod_downloads/prof/community/PIP_Writing_Report_FINAL.pdf

15 Bezerra, J., Bock, W., Candelon, F., Chai, S., Choi, E., Corwin, J., DiGrande, S. Gulshan, R., Michael, D. C., & Varas, A. (2015, January 15). The mobile revolution: How mobile technologies drive a trillion-dollar impact. The Boston Consulting Group. Retrieved from https://www.bcgperspectives.com/content/articles/telecommunications_technology_business_transformation_mobile_revolution

16 Canavor, N. (2012). *Business writing in the digital age*. Los Angeles: Sage, pp. 1-3; National Writing Project with DeVoss, D. N., Eidman-Aadahl, E., & Hicks, T. (2010). *Because digital writing matters*. San Francisco: Jossey-Bass, pp. 1-5.

17 The Association of American Colleges and Universities/Hart Research Associates. (2009, November). Raising the bar: Employers' views on college learning in the wake of the economic downturn, p. 5-6. Retrieved from http://www.aacu.org/leap/documents/2009_EmployerSurvey.pdf

18 Quoted in Canavor, N. (2012). *Business writing in the digital age*. Los Angeles: Sage, p. 4.

19 Casner-Lotto, J., Wright, M., & Barrington, L. (2006, September). Are they really ready to work? Employers' perspectives on the basic knowledge and applied skills of new entrants to the 21st century U.S. workforce, p. 24. Retrieved from http://www.p21.org/storage/documents/FINAL_REPORT_PDF09-29-06.pdf

20 National Writing Project with DeVoss, D. N., Eidman-Aadahl, E., & Hicks, T. (2010). *Because digital writing matters*. San Francisco: Jossey-Bass, p. 7.

21 Drucker, P. (1989, May). New realities, new ways of managing. *Business Month*, pp. 50-51.

22 White, C. (2008, October 29). Knowledge and information workers: Who are they? Retrieved from http://www.b-eye-network.com/view/8897

23 Kelly, K. (2012, February 17). Q&A: Hacker historian George Dyson sits down with *Wired's* Kevin Kelly. *Wired Magazine* (March 2012). Retrieved from http://www.wired.com/magazine/2012/02/ff_dysonqa/all/1

24 Bennett, J. (2012). Surveys point to an improving job market. In: Employment trends 2012. Society for Human Resource Management and *The Wall Street Journal*, p. 9. Retrieved from http://www.shrm.org/research/documents/wsjbrochuresinglepages.pdf; Fox, A. (2010, January). At work in 2020. *HR Magazine*, p. 20.

25 Bezerra, J., Bock, W., Candelon, F., Chai, S., Choi, E., Corwin, J., DiGrande, S. Gulshan, R., Michael, D. C., & Varas, A. (2015, January 15). The mobile revolution: How mobile technologies drive a trillion-dollar impact. The Boston Consulting Group. Retrieved from https://www.bcgperspectives.com/content/articles/telecommunications_technology_business_transformation_mobile_revolution

26 Fox, A. (2010, January). At work in 2020. *HR Magazine*, p. 20.

27 Deloitte & Manufacturing Institute. (2011, September). Boiling point? The skills gap in U.S. manufacturing. National Association of Manufacturers. Retrieved from http://www.themanufacturinginstitute.org/~/media/A07730B2A798437D98501E798C2E13AA.ashx

28 Kay, A. (2011, May 30). What employers want: 5 more skills to cultivate. *USA Today*. Retrieved from http://www.usatoday.com/money/jobcenter/workplace/kay/2011-05-30-skills-employers-want-part-ii_N.htm

29 2016 workforce-skills preparedness report. (2016). PayScale. Retrieved from http://www.payscale.com/data-packages/job-skills

30 National Writing Project with DeVoss, D. N., Eidman-Aadahl, E., & Hicks, T. (2010). *Because digital writing matters*. San Francisco: Jossey-Bass, p. 150.

31 Quoted in Wallis, C. (2006, December 10). How to bring our schools out of the 20th century. *Time Magazine U.S.* Retrieved from http://www.time.com/time/magazine/article/0,9171,1568480,00.html

32 Maurer, R. (2014). *One small step can change your life the Kaizen way*. New York: Workman Publishing, pp. 8-11; Understanding Kaizen & the continuous improvement process. (2010). Process Improvement Japan. Retrieved from http://www.process-improvement-japan.com/continuous-improvement-process.html

33 Fox, A. (2010, January). At work in 2020. *HR Magazine*, p. 23. Retrieved from http://search.ebscohost.com

34 Meister, J. C., & Willyerd, K. (2010). *The 2020 workplace: How innovative companies attract, develop, and keep tomorrow's employees today*. New York: HarperCollins, p. 94.

35 O'Toole, J. & Lawler, E. E., III. (2006, July). *The new American workplace*. New York: Palgrave Macmillan, p. 17.

36 Benko, C., Anderson, M., & Vickberg, S. (2011). The corporate lattice: A strategic response to a changing world of work. Deloitte Review, Issue 8. Retrieved from http://latticemcc.com/downloads/PDFs/DeloitteReview_TheCorporateLattice.pdf

37 Everson, K. (2015, June 29). Be a Boy Scout: Prepare for digital badging. Chief Learning Officer. Retrieved from http://www.clomedia.com/articles/6346-be-a-boy-scout-prepare-for-digital-badging

38 Cited in Everson, K. (2015, June 29). Be a Boy Scout: Prepare for digital badging. Chief Learning Officer. Retrieved from http://www.clomedia.com/articles/6346-be-a-boy-scout-prepare-for-digital-badging

39 Morgan, H. (2014, September 3). How to be a better communicator in the workplace. *US News & World Report*. Retrieved from http://money.usnews.com/money/blogs/outside-voices-careers/2014/09/03/how-to-be-a-better-communicator-in-the-workplace

40 Jamrisko, M. (2015, June 18). It now takes almost twice as long to get hired as it did in 2010. Bloomberg Business. Retrieved from http://www.bloomberg.com/news/articles/2015-06-18/it-now-takes-almost-twice-as-long-to-get-hired-as-it-did-in-2010; Woolhouse, M. (2015, May 10). For new college grads, job market is best in a decade. Retrieved from *Boston Globe* at https://www.bostonglobe.com/business/2015/05/10/best-job-market-years-for-new-college-grads/MSx7hfTr5yRP7qKAyPAVUN/story.html

41 National Association of Colleges and Employers. (2014, November 18). Job outlook 2015: The skills/qualities employers want in new college graduate hires. Retrieved from https://www.naceweb.org/about-us/press/class-2015-skills-qualities-employers-want.aspx

42 Hart Research Associates. (2015, January 20). Falling short? College learning and career success. Selected findings from online surveys of employers and college students conducted on behalf of the Association of American Colleges & Universities. Retrieved from https://www.aacu.org/sites/default/files/files/LEAP/2015employerstudentsurvey.pdf

43 Rampell, C. (2013, February 19). College premium: Better pay, better prospects. Economix Blogs, New York Times. Retrieved from http://economix.blogs.nytimes.com/2013/02/19/college-premium-better-pay-better-prospects; Crosby, O., & Moncarz, R. (2006, Fall). The 2004-14 job outlook for college graduates. *Occupational Outlook Quarterly, 50*(3), 43. Retrieved from http://www.bls.gov/opub/ooq/2006/fall/art03.htm

44 Shah, N. (2013, April 2). College grads earn nearly three times more than high school dropouts. WSJ Blogs. Retrieved from http://blogs.wsj.com/economics/2013/04/02/college-grads-earn-nearly-three-times-more-than-high-school-dropouts

45 National Association of Colleges and Employers. (2012, October 24). The skills and qualities employers want in their class of 2013 recruits. Retrieved from http://www.naceweb.org/s10242012/skills-abilities-qualities-new-hires

46 Kaplan, A. M., & Haenlein, M. (2010). Users of the world, unite! The challenges and opportunities of social media. *Business Horizons*, *53*, 67-68. Retrieved from http://michaelhaenlein.com/Publications/publications.htm

47 Kietzman, J. H., Hermkens, K., McCarthy, I. P., & Silvestre, B. S. (2011). Social media? Get serious! Understanding the functional building blocks of social media. *Business Horizons*, *54*, 242. Retrieved from http://beedie.sfu.ca/profiles/JanKietzmann

48 Roberts, I. (2011, March 30). Consumer boycotts: How bad brand experience can turn into lifelong grudges. Retrieved from http://experiencematters.criticalmass.com

49 Cooper, C. L. (2011, May 25). America can learn from Europe on work-life balance. CNNOpinion. Retrieved from http://www.cnn.com/2011/OPINION/05/25/cooper.vacation.europe

50 Piazza, C. F. (2007, January 23). 24/7 workplace connectivity: A hidden ethical dilemma. SCU White Paper, p. 1. Retrieved from http://pdf.thepdfportal.net/?id=83369#

51 Ibid.

52 The Hartman Group. (2015, April 14). ALDI is a growing menace to American's grocery retailers. *Forbes*. Retrieved from http://www.forbes.com/sites/thehartmangroup/2015/04/14/aldi-is-a-growing-menace-to-americas-grocery-retailers

53 Rana, P. (2014, November 28). Dipping into India, Dunkin' Donuts changes menu. *The Wall Street Journal*. Retrieved from http://www.wsj.com/articles/dipping-into-india-dunkin-donuts-changes-menu-1417211158

54 10 Ways shopping at Wal-Mart in China is completely different from how it is in the US. (2014, January 5). Business Insider. Retrieved from http://en.rocketnews24.com/2014/01/05/10-ways-shopping-at-wal-mart-in-china-is-completely-different-from-how-it-is-in-the-us

55 Burkitt, L. (2015, July 5). McDonald's, KFC look to get faster in China by adding digital payment option. *The Wall Street Journal*. Retrieved from http://www.wsj.com/articles/mcdonalds-kfc-look-to-get-faster-in-china-by-adding-digital-options-1436120662

56 Jones, R. (2015, June 16). Foreign retailers bend to conform to Saudi religious rules. *The Wall Street Journal*. Retrieved from http://www.wsj.com/articles/foreign-retailers-bend-to-conform-to-saudi-religious-rules-1434421369

57 Rajan, R. G., & Wulf, J. (2006, November). The flattening firm: Evidence from panel data on the changing nature of corporate hierarchies. *Review of Economics and Statistics, 88*(4), 3. Retrieved from http://www.nber.org/papers/w9633

[58] Merced, J. de la, & Ross Sorkin, A. (2015, April 10). G.E. to retreat from finance in post-crisis reorganization. *The New York Times*. Retrieved from http://www.nytimes.com/2015/04/11/business/dealbook/general-electric-to-sell-bulk-of-its-finance-unit.html; Farrell, M. (2015, June 9). A look at GE's slim-down since the financial crisis. *The Wall Street Journal*. Retrieved from http://blogs.wsj.com/moneybeat/2015/06/09/a-look-at-ges-slim-down-since-the-financial-crisis

[59] Mills, E. (2007, April 27). Newsmaker: Meet Google's culture czar. Retrieved from http://news.cnet.com/Meet-Googles-culture-czar/2008-1023_3-6179897.html%5D

[60] Friedman, T. L. (2005). *The world is flat*. New York: Garrar, Straus and Giroux, pp. 178-179.

[61] Malone, T. W. (2004). *The future of work*. Cambridge, MA: Harvard Business School Press, p. 32.

[62] Weintraub, A. (2007, June 18). J & J's new baby. *BusinessWeek*, p. 48.

[63] Edmondson, A. C. (2012, April). Teamwork on the fly. *Harvard Business Review*. Retrieved from http://hbr.org/2012/04/teamwork-on-the-fly/ar/1

[64] Ibid.

[65] Fox, A. (2010, January). At work in 2020. *HR Magazine*, p. 21. Retrieved from http://search.ebscohost.com

[66] U.S. Census Bureau, Population Division. (2014, December). Percent of the projected population by Hispanic origin and race for the United States: 2015 to 2060 (NP2014-T11). Retrieved from http://www.census.gov/population/projections/data/national/2014/summarytables.html

[67] Council of Economic Advisers. (2014, October). Women's participation in education and in the workforce, p. 3. Retrieved from https://s3.amazonaws.com/s3.documentcloud.org/documents/1350163/women_education_workforce.pdf

[68] Fox, A. (2010, January). At work in 2020. *HR Magazine*, p. 22. Retrieved from http://search.ebscohost.com

[69] Toossi, M. (2013, December). Labor force projections to 2022: The labor force participation rate continues to fall. *Monthly Labor Review*. The Bureau of Labor Statistics Occupational Handbook. Retrieved from http://www.bls.gov/opub/mlr/2013/article/pdf/labor-force-projections-to-2022-the-labor-force-participation-rate-continues-to-fall.pdf

[70] Ibid.

[71] David Arkless, president of global corporate and government affairs at Manpower, Inc., in London quoted in Fox, A. (2010, January). At work in 2020. *HR Magazine*, p. 21. Retrieved from http://search.ebscohost.com

[72] Based on IDC forecasts U. S. mobile worker population to surpass 105 million by 2020. (2015, June 23). Business Wire. [Press release.] Retrieved from http://www.businesswire.com/news/home/20150623005073/en#.VYmhfEZB58m

[73] Holland, K. (2008, September 28). The anywhere, anytime office. *The New York Times*, p. 14 BU Y.

[74] Tugend, A. (2014, March 7). It's unclearly defined, but telecommuting is fast on the rise. *The New York Times*. Retrieved from http://www.nytimes.com/2014/03/08/your-money/when-working-in-your-pajamas-is-more-productive.html?_r=0

[75] Lister, K. (2010, February 21). How many people actually telecommute? Workshifting. Retrieved from http://www.workshifting.com/2010/02/how-many-people-actually-telecommute.html

[76] Whitney, E. (2015, July 28). Tired of the big city? Consider telecommuting from Montana. NPR.org. Retrieved from http://www.npr.org/2015/07/28/426858376/tired-of-the-big-city-consider-telecommuting-from-montana

[77] Silverman, R. E., & Sidel, R. (2012, April 17). Warming up to the officeless office. *The Wall Street Journal*. Retrieved from http://online.wsj.com/article/SB10001424052702304818404577349783161465976.html; Holland, K. (2008, September 28). The anywhere, anytime office. *The New York Times*, p. 14 BU Y.

[78] Clark, P. (2016, February 19). Co-working spaces are going corporate. *BloombergBusiness*. Retrieved from http://www.bloomberg.com/news/articles/2016-02-19/co-working-spaces-are-going-corporate

[79] Visual networking index (VNI). (2015, May). Cisco. Retrieved from http://www.cisco.com/c/en/us/solutions/service-provider/visual-networking-index-vni/index.html#~vniforecast

[80] Bosomworth, D. (2015, January 15). Mobile marketing statistics 2015. Smart Insights. Retrieved from http://www.smartinsights.com/mobile-marketing/mobile-marketing-analytics/mobile-marketing-statistics

[81] Smartphone OS market share, Q1 2015. (2015). International Data Corporation. Retrieved from http://www.idc.com/prodserv/smartphone-os-market-share.jsp

[82] Daft, R. L., & Lengel, R. H. (1983, May). Information richness: A new approach to managerial behavior and organization design. [Technical report], p. 13. Retrieved from http://www.dtic.mil/cgi-bin/GetTRDoc?AD=ADA128980; Daft, R. L. & Lengel, R. H. (1986). Organizational information requirements, media richness and structural design. *Management Science 32*(5), 560. Retrieved from http://search.ebscohost.com

[83] Short, J., Williams, E., & Christie, B. (1976). *The social psychology of telecommunications*. London: John Wiley.

[84] Discussion based in part on Kaplan, A., & Haenlein, M. (2010). Users of the world unite! The challenges and opportunities of social media. *Business Horizons, 53*, 59-69. Retrieved from http://michaelhaenlein.com/Publications/publications.htm

[85] Rozell, E. (2014, June 15). The office grapevine: Hurtful or helpful? *Springfield News-Leader*. Retrieved from http://www.news-leader.com/story/news/local/ozarks/2014/06/15/office-grapevine-hurtful-helpful/10550027; Steelcase Inc. (2007, August 9). Steelcase Workplace Index Survey examines 'water cooler' conversations at work. Retrieved from http://www.prnewswire.com. See also Wademan Dowling, D. (2009, April 24). The truth about office rumors. *Harvard Business Review*. Retrieved from http://blogs.hbr.org/dowling/2009/04/the-truth-about-office-rumors.html and DiFonzo, N. (2009). *The water cooler effect: An indispensable guide to understanding and harnessing the power of rumors*. New York: Penguin, pp. 151, 174-175, 180.

[86] Rozell, E. (2014, June 15). The office grapevine: Hurtful or helpful? *Springfield News-Leader*. Retrieved from http://www.news-leader.com/story/news/local/ozarks/2014/06/15/office-grapevine-hurtful-helpful/10550027

[87] Shragai, N. (2015, July 6). How rumour and gossip oil the wheels of office life. *Financial Times*. Retrieved from http://www.rit.edu/news/pdfs/shragai.pdf

[88] Drexler, P. (2014, February 14). The value of annoying co-workers. *The Wall Street Journal*. Retrieved from http://www.wsj.com/articles/SB10001424052702303704304579379431532672924

[89] Goman, C. K. (2006, June). I heard it through the grapevine. Paper presented at the International Association of Business Communicators, Vancouver, Canada.

[90] Quast, L. (2013, October 14). New managers: 5 ways to stop negative office gossip. *Forbes*. Retrieved from http://www.forbes.com/sites/lisaquast/2013/10/14/new-managers-5-ways-to-stop-negative-office-gossip

[91] Ibid.

[92] The *Marketing News* Staff. (2010, March 15). Digital dozen. Retrieved from http://www.marketingpower.com/resourceLibrary/Publications/MarketingNews/2010/3_15_10/Digital%20Dozen.pdf

[93] Green, A. (2014, June 5). Managing: I caught my employee in a lie. Now what? *The Business Journals*. Retrieved from http://www.bizjournals.com/bizjournals/how-to/human-resources/2014/06/managing-i-caught-my-employee-in-a-lie-now-what.html?page=all; Campbell, R. (2014, March 11). The surprisingly large cost of telling small lies. *The New York Times*. Retrieved from http://boss.blogs.nytimes.com/2014/03/11/the-surprisingly-large-cost-of-telling-small-lies/?_r=0

[94] DeMars, N. (2012, December 3). Business forum: When our leaders stray, we all pay. *Star Tribune*. Retrieved from http://www.startribune.com/business-forum-when-our-leaders-stray-we-all-pay/181623811

[95] 2014 Report to the nations on occupational fraud and abuse. (2014). Association of Certified Fraud Examiners. Retrieved from http://www.acfe.com/rttn-summary.aspx

[96] Gentile, M. C. (2009, February 5). Business schools: A failing grade on ethics. *BusinessWeek*. Retrieved from http://www.businessweek.com

[97] Women-owned businesses in the 21st century. (2010, October). U.S. Department of Commerce, Economics and Statistics Administration. Retrieved from http://www.esa.doc.gov/reports/women-owned-businesses-21st-century

[98] Trudel, R., & Cotte, J. (2008, May 12). Does being ethical pay? *The Wall Street Journal*, p. R4.

[99] Bazerman, M. H., & Tenbrunsel, A. E. (2011, April 20). Stumbling into bad behavior. *The New York Times*. Retrieved from http://www.nytimes.com/2011/04/21/opinion/21bazerman.html

[100] Hatch, D. (2012, May 15). Nordstrom in fashion with social media, mobile tech. U.S. News. Retrieved from http://money.usnews.com/money/business-economy/articles/2012/05/15/nordstrom-in-fashion-with-social-media-mobile-tech

[101] Spector, R., & McCarthy, P. (1999). The Nordstrom way, p. 6. Retrieved from http://cdn2.hubspot.net/hub/155473/file-375011712-pdf/nordstrom_way_pdf.pdf

[102] Will Schwalbe quoted in Lam, B. (2015, May 15). Why emoji are suddenly acceptable at work. *The Atlantic*. Retrieved from http://www.theatlantic.com/business/archive/2015/05/why-emoji-are-suddenly-acceptable-at-work/393191

[103] Otani, A. (2015, May 5). Five charts that show work-life balance is dead. *Bloomberg Business*. Retrieved from http://www.bloomberg.com/news/articles/2015-05-05/five-charts-that-show-work-life-balance-is-dead

[104] Armour, S. (2007, September 7). Did you hear the real story about office gossip? *USA Today*, p. 1B.

[105] Taylor, C. (2012, January 6). Study: Social networkers have more ethics problems at work. Gigaom. Retrieved from https://gigaom.com/2012/01/06/social-networking-employee-ethics

Chapter 2 Professionalism: Team, Meeting, Listening, Nonverbal, and Etiquette Skills

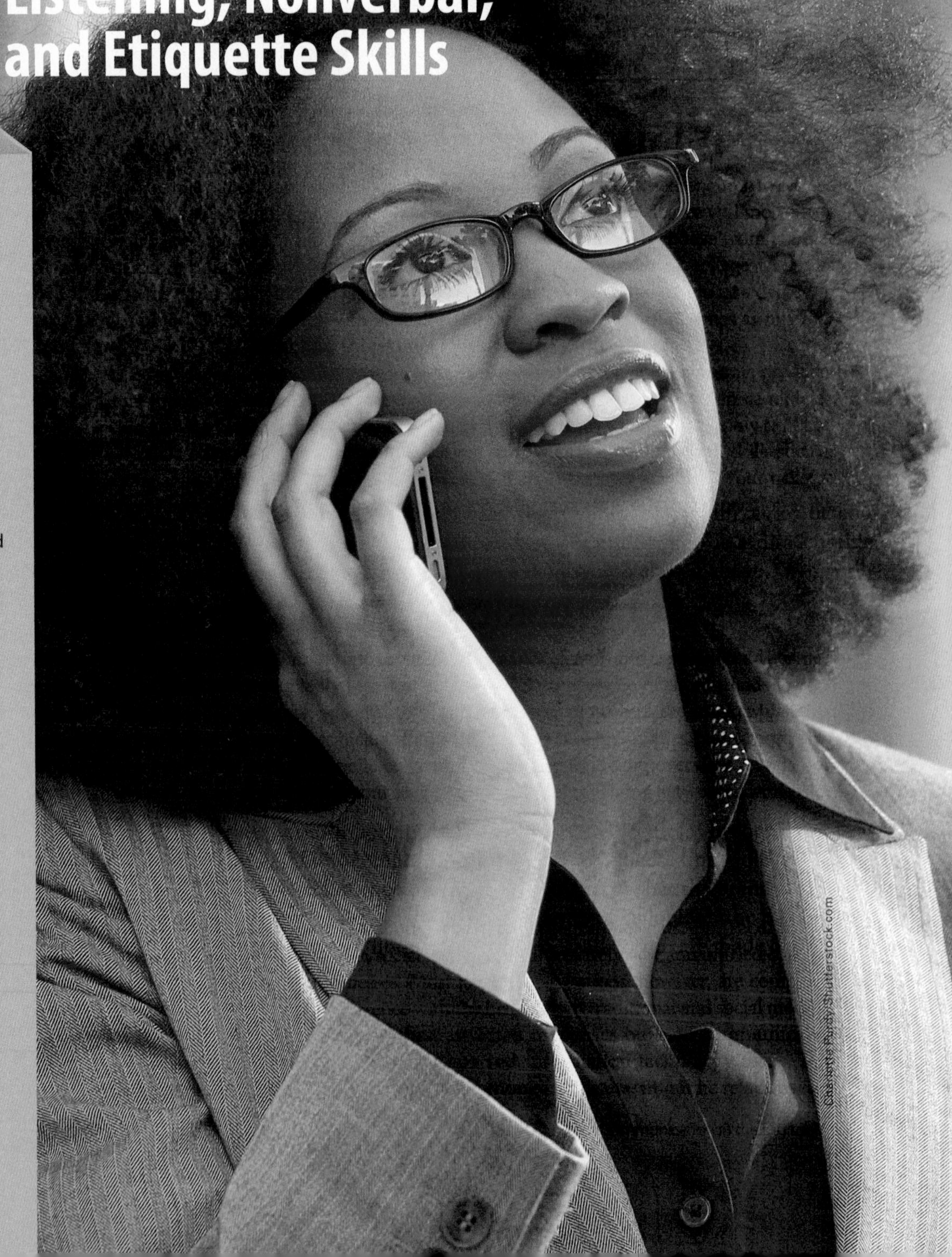

LEARNING OUTCOMES

After studying this chapter, you should be able to

1 Understand the importance of teamwork in the digital-era workplace, and explain how you can contribute positively to team performance.

2 Discuss effective practices and technologies for planning and participating in face-to-face meetings and virtual meetings.

3 Explain and apply active listening techniques.

4 Understand how effective nonverbal communication can help you advance your career.

5 Improve your competitive advantage by developing professionalism and business etiquette skills.

Lyft Epitomizes the Sharing Economy and Teamwork

Yeamake/Shutterstock.com

Today's sharing economy, an economic model in which individuals rent or borrow an asset owned by another, is upending entire industries, especially transportation. While Uber started the game-changing idea of ride sharing, the irreverent company Lyft, known for its magenta mustache branding, epitomizes the upheaval.

The high-tech, San Francisco–based business is itself a model of sharing. Consumers request a ride using the Lyft app, and minutes later a Lyft driver in the area appears. Riders avoid the hassle of driving, and drivers make some cash. The simple idea is working, as the company has enjoyed a fivefold growth in its first two years of existence and shows no signs of slowing down.[1] This success can be attributed in no small part to teamwork.

Lyft so values teamwork that part of the test new-hires must pass is a culture fit to determine whether they share the Lyft ethos of collaboration and mutual respect. Cofounder and CEO Logan Green says, "When we build a team, we look for incredibly smart, compassionate people who are all motivated by the same goal."[2]

In fact, Lyft's organizational structure is a series of teams instead of departments found in more traditional businesses. Team members regularly approach colleagues to solve problems. One software engineer talks about the rewards of being surrounded by "friendly people willing to help get things done."[3] A brand designer boasts, "All teams are very supportive and respectful to each other" and that Lyft's collaborative spirit fosters team "camaraderie, energy, and creativity."[4]

As Lyft grows, it has had to extend its relaxed yet professional workplace to virtual teams in other countries. When the company recently expanded to France, it helped employees get ready to bridge the distance gap by creating a presentation explaining effective communication in virtual teams.

Lyft and its ever-growing teams dedicated to a shared company vision embody the importance of teamwork in the digital workplace. Although Lyft may have a pink-fur-lined elevator and its employees may wear flip-flops and casual clothing, effective communication skills, respect for fellow workers, and professionalism are key to its growing success.

You will have a chance to complete a relevant task related to this case study at the end of this chapter.

Critical Thinking

- What is meant by the term *culture fit*, and why is it beneficial for both employer and employee?
- What individual behaviors lead to effective teams?
- What factors unique to virtual teams contribute to their success?

Adding Value to Professional Teams

Most businesses seek employees who can get along and deliver positive results that increase profits and boost their image. As a budding business professional, you have a stake in acquiring skills that will make you a strong job applicant and a valuable employee.

LEARNING OUTCOME 1

Understand the importance of teamwork in the digital-era workplace, and explain how you can contribute positively to team performance.

Impressing Digital-Age Employers

Employers are typically interested in four key areas: education, experience, hard skills, and soft skills. Hard skills refer to the technical skills in your field. Soft skills, however, are increasingly important in the knowledge-based economy of the digital era. Desirable competencies include not only oral and written communication skills but also active listening skills, appropriate nonverbal behavior, and proper business etiquette. In addition, employers such as Lyft want efficient and productive team members. They want managers and employees who are comfortable with diverse audiences, listen actively to customers and colleagues, make eye contact, and display good workplace manners. These soft skills are immensely important not only to be hired but also to be promoted.

Hiring managers naturally expect you to have technical expertise in your field and know the latest communication technology. Such skills and an impressive résumé may get you in the door. However, your long-term success depends on how well you communicate with your boss, coworkers, and customers and whether you can be an effective and contributing team member. Even in fields such as information technology, employers are looking for soft skills. Staffing firm Robert Half Technology surveyed chief information officers and found that IT (information technology) hiring managers "are seeking candidates who not only possess technical abilities, but can also meet deadlines and work well with customers and colleagues."[5]

Kiyoshi Ota/Bloomberg/Getty Images

Reality Check

Communication, a Baseline Skill at Evernote

"The most important baseline skill for any position is communication. We want you to be able to explain what you mean; we want you to be articulate. That cuts out a lot of people, because a lot of people are probably pretty good technically, but if you don't have excellent communication skills, it's going to be very frustrating for you and for other people."[6]

—Phil Libin, *former CEO of Evernote, the popular productivity app; now partner at General Catalyst*

As we discussed in Chapter 1, collaboration is the rule today, and an overwhelming majority of white-collar professionals (82 percent) need to partner with others to complete their work.[7] Research by design company Gensler shows that the 2,000 knowledge workers surveyed nationally spent on average about 20 percent of their time collaborating.[8] Workers collaborate not only at their desks, but also informally in hallways and flexible unassigned workspaces or in rooms equipped with the latest teleconferencing tools. Many connect remotely with their smart electronic devices. Major companies—for example, Google, Samsung, AT&T, Zappos, and ING DIRECT—have redesigned their workspaces to meet this growing need for collaboration.[9] Needless to say, solid soft skills rule in face-to-face and far-flung teams.

This chapter focuses on developing team, meeting, listening, nonverbal, and etiquette skills. These are some of the professional skills that employers seek in the hyperconnected, competitive work environment of the digital age.

Excelling in Teams

You will discover that the workplace is teeming with teams. You might find yourself a part of a work team, project team, customer support team, supplier team, design team, planning team, functional team, cross-functional team, or some other group. All of these teams are formed to accomplish specific goals.

It's no secret that one of the most important objectives of businesses is finding ways to do jobs better at less cost. This objective helps explain the popularity of teams, which are formed for the following reasons:

- **Better decisions.** Decisions are generally more accurate and effective because group and team members contribute different expertise and perspectives.
- **Faster responses.** When action is necessary to respond to competition or to solve a problem, small groups and teams can act rapidly.
- **Increased productivity.** Because they are often closer to the action and to the customer, team members can see opportunities for improving efficiency.
- **Greater buy-in.** Decisions arrived at jointly are usually better received because members are committed to the solution and are more willing to support it.
- **Less resistance to change.** People who have input into decisions are less hostile, aggressive, and resistant to change.
- **Improved employee morale.** Personal satisfaction and job morale increase when teams are successful.
- **Reduced risks.** Responsibility for a decision is diffused on a team, thus carrying less risk for any individual.

Jonathan Alcorn/Bloomberg/ Getty Images

Reality Check

Geeks Toil in Solitude

"Most inventors and engineers I've met are like me . . . they live in their heads. They're almost like artists. In fact, the very best of them are artists. And artists work best alone. . . . I'm going to give you some advice that might be hard to take. That advice is: Work alone . . . Not on a committee. Not on a team."[10]

—Steve Wozniak, *Apple cofounder*

Despite the current popularity of teams, however, they are not a solution for all workplace problems, particularly if such groups are dysfunctional. Harvard professor J. Richard Hackman claims that research "consistently shows that teams underperform despite all their extra resources."[11] This team expert and more recent studies suggest that organizations must strike a balance between solo effort—in highly creative endeavors—and collective action. "The most spectacularly creative people" are often introverted and prefer to work alone, which is when they do their best and most innovative work.[12] However, in most models of future organizations, teams—not individuals—function as the primary performance units.

Collaborating in Virtual Teams

In addition to working side by side in close proximity with potential teammates, you can expect to collaborate with coworkers in other cities and even in other countries. Such collaborations are referred to as *virtual teams*. This is a group of people who, aided by information technology, must accomplish shared tasks largely without face-to-face contact across geographic boundaries, sometimes on different continents and across time zones.[13]

Although Yahoo and Best Buy have reversed their acclaimed work-at-home policies, virtual teams are here to stay. Tech giant IBM "can't get enough people to move to emerging markets," says Bridget van Kralingen, North American general manager. Therefore, the company is "turning more often to virtual teams, who reach outcomes without ever meeting face to face."[14]

Many well-known German companies with a global reach maintain headquarters in picturesque small German towns (think Volkswagen, Adidas, Hugo Boss, and software corporation SAP). Virtual technology enables them to connect with their facilities in locations around the globe, wherever needed talent may reside.[15] SAP is headquartered in idyllic Walldorf, Germany, but it has established research and development centers in India, China, Israel, and the United States to save costs and take advantage of global know-how. Depending on the competence needed, employees from different locations form virtual teams that pool their expertise to complete particular assignments.[16] These teams must coordinate their work and complete their tasks across time and geographic zones. As you can see, work is increasingly viewed as what you do rather than a place you go.

In some organizations remote coworkers may be permanent employees from the same office or may be specialists called together for special projects. Regardless of the assignment, virtual teams can benefit from shared views, skills, and diversity.

Understanding the Four Phases of Team Development

Regardless of their specific purpose, teams normally go through predictable phases as they develop. The psychologist B. A. Tuckman identified four phases: *forming, storming, norming,* and *performing*, as Figure 2.1 illustrates.[17] Some groups get lucky and move

Figure 2.1 **Four Phases of Team Development in Decision Making**

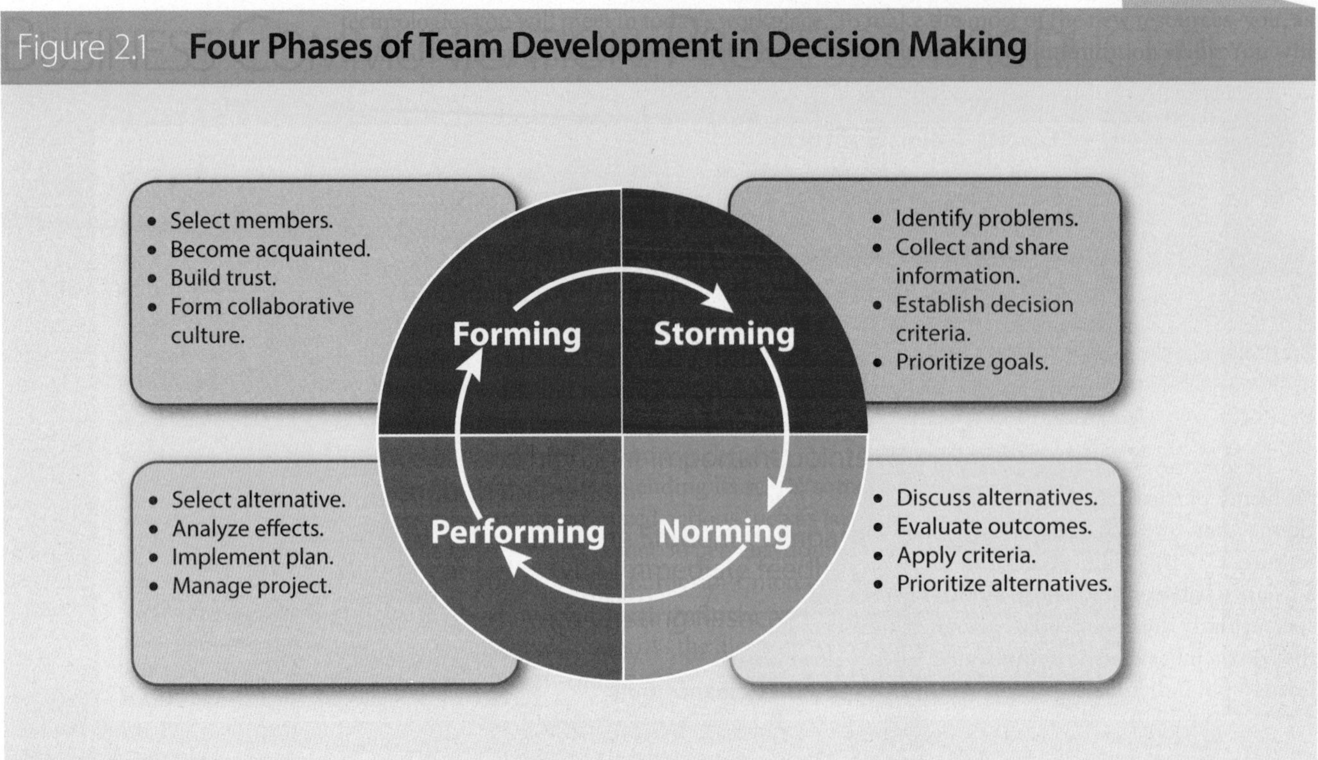

quickly from forming to performing. Other teams may never reach the final stage of performing. However, most struggle through disruptive, although ultimately constructive, team-building stages.

Forming. During the first stage, individuals get to know each other. They often are overly polite and feel a bit awkward. As they search for similarities and attempt to bond, they begin to develop trust in each other. Members discuss fundamental topics such as why the team is necessary, who "owns" the team, whether membership is mandatory, how large the team should be, and what talents members can contribute. A leader functions primarily as a traffic director. Groups and teams should resist the efforts of some members to dash through the first stages and race to the performing stage. Moving slowly through the stages is necessary to build a cohesive, productive unit.

Storming. During the second phase, members define their roles and responsibilities, decide how to reach their goals, and iron out the rules governing how they interact. Unfortunately, this stage often produces conflict, resulting in storming. A good leader, however, should step in to set limits, control the chaos, and offer suggestions. The leader will be most successful if she or he acts like a coach rather than a cop. Teams composed of dissimilar personality types may take longer to progress through the storming phase. Tempers may flare, sleep may be lost, leaders may be deposed. But most often the storm passes, and a cohesive group emerges.

Norming. Once the sun returns to the sky, teams and groups enter the norming stage. Tension subsides, roles are clarified, and information begins to flow among members. The group periodically checks its agenda to remind itself of its progress toward its goals. People are careful not to shake the hard-won camaraderie and formation of a single-minded purpose. Formal leadership is unnecessary because everyone takes on leadership functions. Important data are shared with the entire group, and mutual interdependence becomes typical. The group or team begins to move smoothly in one direction. Figure 2.1 shows how a team might proceed through the four phases while solving a problem and reaching a decision.

Performing. In Tuckman's team growth model, some groups never reach the final stage of performing. For those that survive the first three phases, however, the final stage is gratifying. Group members have established routines and a shared language. They develop loyalty and a willingness to resolve all problems. A can-do mentality pervades as they progress toward their goal. Fights are clean, and members continue working together without grudges. Best of all, information flows freely, deadlines are met, and production exceeds expectations.

Identifying Positive and Negative Team Behavior

Team members who are committed to achieving the group's purpose contribute by displaying positive behavior. How can you be a good team member? The most effective groups have members who are willing to establish rules and abide by them. Effective team members are able to analyze tasks and define problems so that they can work toward solutions. They offer information and try out their ideas on the group to stimulate discussion. They show interest in others' ideas by listening actively. Helpful team members also seek to involve silent members. They strive to resolve differences, and they encourage a warm, supportive climate by praising and agreeing with others. When they sense that agreement is near, they review significant points and move the group toward its goal by synthesizing points of understanding.

Not all groups, however, have members who contribute positively. Negative behavior is shown by those who constantly put down the ideas and suggestions of others. They insult, criticize, and aggress against others. They waste the group's time with unnecessary recounting of personal achievements or irrelevant topics. The team clown distracts the group with excessive joke-telling, inappropriate comments, and disruptive antics. Also disturbing are team members who withdraw and refuse to be drawn out. They have nothing to say, either for or against ideas being considered. To be a productive and welcome member of a group, be prepared to perform the positive tasks described in Figure 2.2. Avoid the negative behaviors.

Combating Groupthink

Conflict is normal in team interactions, and successful teams are able to resolve it using the methods you just learned. But some teams avoid conflict. They smooth things over and in doing so may fall victim to *groupthink*. This is a term coined by theorist Irving Janis to describe faulty decision-making processes by team members who are overly eager to agree with one another.[18] Apparently, when we deviate from a group, we fear rejection. Scientists variously call this natural reluctance "the pain of independence"[19] or describe it as "the hazards of courage."[20]

Figure 2.2 **Positive and Negative Group Behaviors**

Positive Group Behaviors	Negative Group Behaviors
✓ Setting rules and abiding by them	✗ Blocking the ideas of others
✓ Analyzing tasks and defining problems	✗ Insulting and criticizing others
✓ Contributing information and ideas	✗ Wasting the group's time
✓ Showing interest by listening actively	✗ Making improper jokes and comments
✓ Encouraging members to participate	✗ Failing to stay on task
	✗ Withdrawing, failing to participate

Several conditions can lead to groupthink: team members with similar backgrounds, a lack of systematic procedures, a demand for a quick decision, and a strong leader who favors a specific outcome. Symptoms of groupthink include pressure placed on any member who argues against the group's mutual beliefs, self-censorship of thoughts that stray from the group's agreement, collective efforts to rationalize, and an unquestioned belief in the group's moral authority. Teams suffering from groupthink fail to check alternatives, are biased in collecting and evaluating information, and ignore the risks of the preferred choice. They may also neglect to work out a contingency plan in case the preferred choice fails.[21]

Effective teams avoid groupthink by striving for team diversity—in age, gender, background, experience, and training. They encourage open discussion, search for relevant information, evaluate many alternatives, consider how a decision will be implemented, and plan for contingencies in case the decision doesn't work out.

Reaching Group Decisions

The way teams reach decisions greatly affects their morale and commitment, as well as the implementation of any team decision. In U.S. culture the majority usually rules, but other methods, five of which are discussed here, may be more effective. As you study these methods, think about which would be best for routine decisions and which would be best for dealing with emergencies.

- **Majority.** Group members vote and a majority wins. This method results in a quick decision but may leave an alienated minority uncommitted to implementation.
- **Consensus.** Discussion continues until all team members have aired their opinions and, ultimately, agree. This method is time consuming; however, it produces creative, high-quality discussion and generally elicits commitment by all members to implement the decision.
- **Minority.** Typically, a subcommittee investigates and makes a recommendation for action. This method is useful when the full group cannot get together to make a decision or when time is short.
- **Averaging.** Members haggle, bargain, wheedle, and negotiate to reach a middle position, which often requires compromise. With this method, the opinions of the least knowledgeable members may cancel the opinions of the most knowledgeable.
- **Authority rule with discussion.** The leader, boss, or manager listens to team members' ideas, but the final decision is his or hers. This method encourages lively discussion and results in participatory decision making. However, team members must have good communication skills. This method also requires a leader who is willing to make decisions.

Ethics Check

Members Riding Team's Coattails

Teamwork is a staple in college classes today and usually works well for students and their instructors. However, occasionally a rogue member will take advantage of a group and barely collaborate. How do you deal with a student who does sloppy work, misses team meetings, and fails to respond to calls or e-mails?

Defining Successful Teams

The use of teams has been called the solution to many ills in today's workplace.[22] Someone even observed that as an acronym TEAM means Together, Everyone Achieves More.[23] However, teams that do not work well together can actually increase frustration, lower productivity, and create employee dissatisfaction. Experts who have studied team dynamics and decisions have discovered that effective teams share some or all of the following characteristics.

Stay Small and Embrace Diversity. Teams may range from 2 to 25 members, although 4 or 5 is an optimal number for many projects. Teams smaller than ten members tend to agree more easily on a common objective and form more cohesive units.[24] For the most creative decisions, teams generally have male and female members who differ in age, ethnicity, social background, training, and experience. The key business advantage of diversity is the ability to view a project from multiple perspectives. Many organizations are finding that diverse teams can produce innovative solutions with broader applications than homogeneous teams can.

Agree on a Purpose. An effective team begins with a purpose. Working from a general purpose to specific goals typically requires a huge investment of time and effort. Meaningful discussions, however, motivate team members to buy in to the project. When the state of Montana decided to curb its traffic fatalities and serious injuries, the Montana Department of Transportation formed a broad coalition consisting of local, state, and federal agencies as well as traffic safety advocacy groups. Various stakeholders (e.g., insurance companies, local tribal leaders, Mothers Against Drunk Driving, and motorcycle safety representatives) joined in the effort to develop wide-ranging traffic safety programs. With input from all parties, a comprehensive highway safety plan was conceived that set targets and performance measures.[25]

Establish Procedures. The best teams develop procedures to guide them. They set up intermediate goals with deadlines. They assign roles and tasks, requiring all members to contribute equivalent amounts of real work. They decide how they will make decisions, whether by majority vote, consensus, or other methods discussed earlier. Procedures are continually evaluated to ensure movement toward the attainment of the team's goals.

Confront Conflict. Poorly functioning teams avoid conflict, preferring sulking, gossiping, or backstabbing. A better plan is to acknowledge conflict and address the root of the problem openly using the six-step plan outlined in Figure 2.3. Although it may feel emotionally risky, direct confrontation saves time and enhances team commitment in the long run. To be constructive, however, confrontation must be task oriented, not person oriented. An open airing of differences, in which all team members have a chance to speak their minds, should center on the strengths and weaknesses of the various positions and ideas—not on personalities. After hearing all sides, team members must negotiate a fair settlement, no matter how long it takes.

Communicate Effectively. The best teams exchange information and contribute ideas freely in an informal environment often facilitated by technology. Team members speak and

Figure 2.3 **Six Steps for Dealing With Conflict**

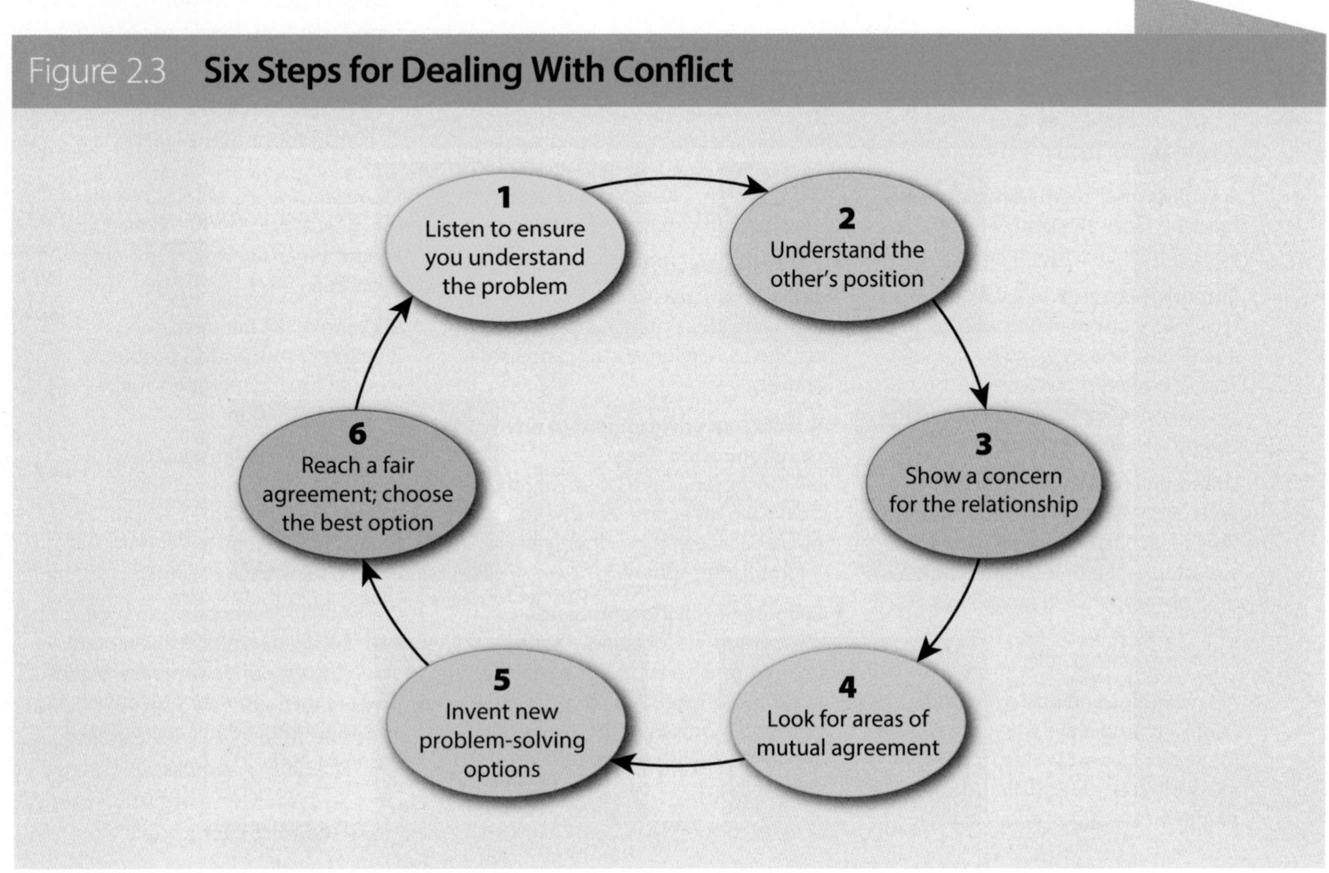

write clearly and concisely, avoiding generalities. They encourage feedback. Listeners become actively involved, read body language, and ask clarifying questions before responding. Tactful, constructive disagreement is encouraged. Although a team's task is taken seriously, successful teams are able to inject humor into their face-to-face interactions.

Collaborate Rather Than Compete. Effective team members are genuinely interested in achieving team goals instead of receiving individual recognition. They contribute ideas and feedback unselfishly. They monitor team progress, including what's going right, what's going wrong, and what to do about it. They celebrate individual and team accomplishments.

Accept Ethical Responsibilities. Teams as a whole have ethical responsibilities to their members, to their larger organizations, and to society. Members have a number of specific responsibilities to each other. As a whole, teams have a responsibility to represent the organization's view and respect its privileged information. They should not discuss with outsiders any sensitive issues without permission. In addition, teams have a broader obligation to avoid advocating actions that would endanger members of society at large.

Share Leadership. Effective teams often have no formal leader. Instead, leadership rotates to those with the appropriate expertise as the team evolves and moves from one phase to another. Many teams operate under a democratic approach. This approach can achieve buy-in to team decisions, boost morale, and create fewer hurt feelings and less resentment. In times of crisis, however, a strong team member may need to step up as a leader.

The following checklist summarizes effective techniques for developing successful teams.

Developing Team Effectiveness

- **Establish small teams.** Smaller teams function more efficiently and more effectively than larger teams.
- **Encourage diversity.** Innovative teams typically include members who differ in age, gender, ethnicity, and background. Team members should possess the necessary technical expertise, problem-solving skills, and interpersonal skills.
- **Determine the purpose, procedures, and roles.** Members must understand the task at hand and what is expected of them. Teams function best when operating procedures are ironed out early and each member assumes a specific role.
- **Acknowledge and manage conflict.** Conflict is productive when it motivates a team to search for new ideas, increase participation, delay premature decisions, or discuss disagreements. Keep conflict centered on issues rather than on people.
- **Cultivate effective communication skills.** Productive team members articulate ideas clearly and concisely, recognize nonverbal cues, and listen actively.
- **Advance an environment of open communication.** Teams are most productive when members trust each other and feel free to discuss all viewpoints openly in an informal atmosphere.
- **Encourage collaboration and discourage competition.** Sharing information in a cooperative effort to achieve the team purpose must be more important than competing with other members for individual achievement.
- **Share leadership.** Members with the most expertise should lead at various times during the project's evolution.
- **Strive to make fair decisions.** Effective teams resolve problems without forcing members into a win–lose situation.
- **Lighten up.** The most successful teams take their task seriously, but they are also able to laugh at themselves and interject humor to enliven team proceedings.
- **Continually assess performance.** Teams should establish checkpoints along the way to determine whether they are meeting their objectives and adjust procedures if progress is unsatisfactory.

Planning and Participating in Face-to-Face and Virtual Meetings

LEARNING OUTCOME 2

Discuss effective practices and technologies for planning and participating in face-to-face meetings and virtual meetings.

As you prepare to join the workforce, expect to attend meetings—lots of them! Estimates suggest that workers on average spend four hours a week in meetings and consider more than half of that time as wasted.[26] Managers spend even more time in meetings. Studies of executives in Europe and the United States reveal that nearly 60 percent of managers devote 21 to 60 percent of their workweeks to meetings with the average meeting lasting nearly three hours.[27] In one survey, managers considered over a third of meeting time unproductive and reported that two thirds of meetings fell short of their stated objectives.[28]

Business meetings consist of three or more people who assemble to pool information, solicit feedback, clarify policy, seek consensus, and solve problems. However, as growing numbers of employees work at distant locations, meetings have changed. Workers cannot always meet face-to-face. To be able to exchange information effectively and efficiently, you will need to know how to plan and participate in face-to-face as well as *virtual meetings.*

Reality Check

Monkey Business Images/Shutterstock.com

Managing Meetings That Matter

"'Mindful Meetings' are productive meetings with clear purpose and objectives, that involve the right people at the right time, and that use proven techniques to get the most out of the time invested. They don't happen by accident—key ingredients are preparation, good facilitation, balanced thinking, good recordkeeping, and appropriate follow-up."[29]

—Janice Francisco, *organizational development and innovation consultant*

Making Face-to-Face Meetings Productive

As inevitable and commonplace as meetings are, most workers dread them. Nearly 50 percent of respondents in a Salary.com survey named "too many meetings" as the biggest waste of time at work.[30] One business reporter complained that "long-winded colleagues consume all available oxygen, killing good ideas by asphyxiation."[31] Much to the dismay of managers, at Seagate Technology in Cupertino, California, some work groups were spending more than 20 hours a week in meetings.[32] However, if meetings are well run, workers actually desire more, not fewer, of them.[33] Your task, then, as a business communicator is to learn how to make them more efficient, satisfying, and productive.

Although meetings are disliked, they can be career-critical. At meetings, judgments are formed and careers are made or blunted.[34] Therefore, instead of treating them as thieves of your valuable time, try to see them as golden opportunities to demonstrate your leadership, communication, and problem-solving skills. To help you make the most of these opportunities, this section outlines best practices for running and contributing to meetings.

Determining the Purpose of a Meeting

A face-to-face meeting provides the most nonverbal cues and other signals that help us interpret the intended meaning of words. Thus, an in-person meeting is the richest of available media. No meeting should be called unless it is important, can't wait, and requires an exchange of ideas. If people are merely being informed, send an e-mail, text message, memo, or letter. Leave a phone or voice mail message, but don't call a costly meeting. Remember, the real expense of a meeting is the lost productivity of all the people attending. To decide whether the purpose of the meeting

Ethics Check

Unresponsive Team Member

Assume you are a member of a campus committee to organize a celebrity auction to raise funds for a local homeless shelter. Your friend Marika is committee chair, but she is carrying a heavy course load and is also working part time. As a result, she has taken no action. You call her, but she is evasive when you try to pin her down about committee plans. What should you do?

Figure 2.4 **Meeting Purpose and Number of Participants**

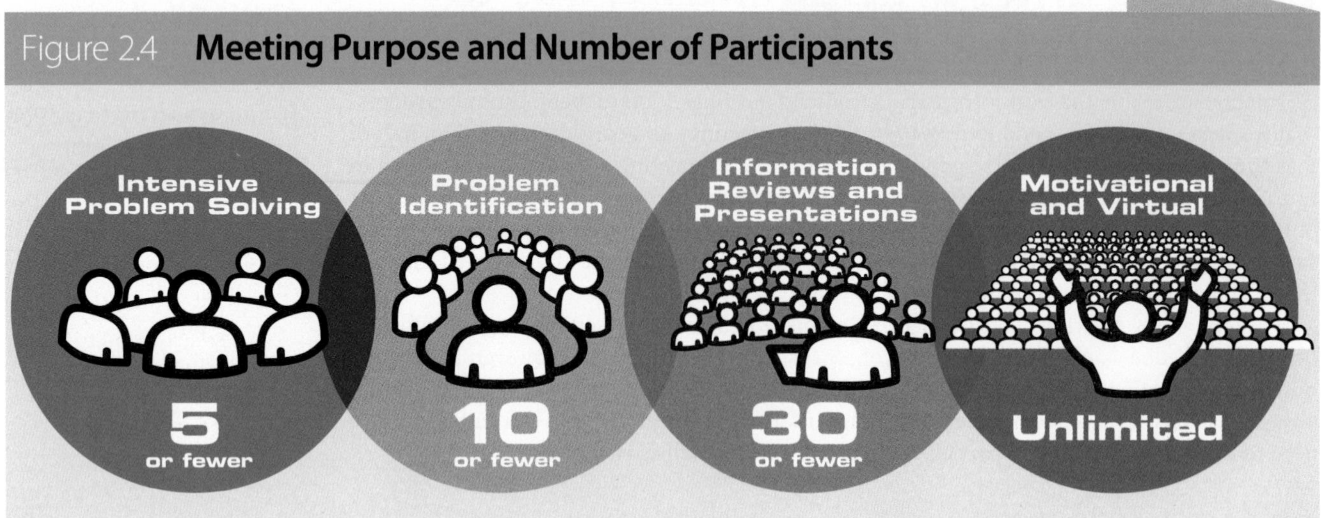

is valid, consult the key people who will be attending. Ask them what outcomes they desire and how to achieve those goals. This consultation also sets a collaborative tone and encourages full participation.

Selecting Meeting Participants. The purpose of the meeting determines the number of participants, as shown in Figure 2.4. If the meeting purpose is motivational, such as an awards ceremony for sales reps of cosmetics giant Avon or nutrition supplement seller Herbalife, then the number of participants is potentially unlimited. However, to make decisions, the best number is no more than eight participants, as studies suggest.[35] For high-stakes decisions, consultants recommend limiting the session to three to six key executives.[36]

Ideally, decision makers and people with the information necessary to make the decision should attend. Also attending should be people who will be responsible for implementing the decision and representatives of groups who will benefit from the decision. Let's consider Timberland and its signature employee volunteer program. Company leaders might meet with managers, employee representatives, and community leaders to decide how best to *green* a community center, improve school grounds, or frame houses for families of tornado victims.[37] Inviting key stakeholders who represent various interests, perspectives, and competencies ensures valuable input and, therefore, is more likely to lead to informed decisions.

Using Digital Calendars to Schedule Meetings. Finding a time when everyone can meet is often difficult. Fortunately, digital calendars make the task quick and efficient. Popular programs and mobile apps are Google Calendar, Apple Calendar, and the business favorite, Outlook Calendar (shown in Figure 2.5). Online calendars and mobile apps enable users to make appointments, schedule meetings, and keep track of daily activities.

To schedule meetings, you enter a meeting request and add the names of attendees. You select a date, enter a start and end time, and list the meeting subject and location. Then the meeting request goes to each attendee. Later you check the attendee availability tab to see a list of all meeting attendees. As the meeting time approaches, the program automatically sends reminders to attendees. The free Web-based meeting scheduler and mobile app Doodle is growing in popularity because it helps users poll participants to determine the best date and time for a meeting.

Distributing an Agenda and Other Information. At least two days before a meeting, distribute an agenda of topics to be discussed. Also include any reports or materials that participants should read in advance. For continuing groups, you might also include a copy of the minutes of the previous meeting. To keep meetings productive, limit the number of agenda

Figure 2.5 **Using Calendar Programs**

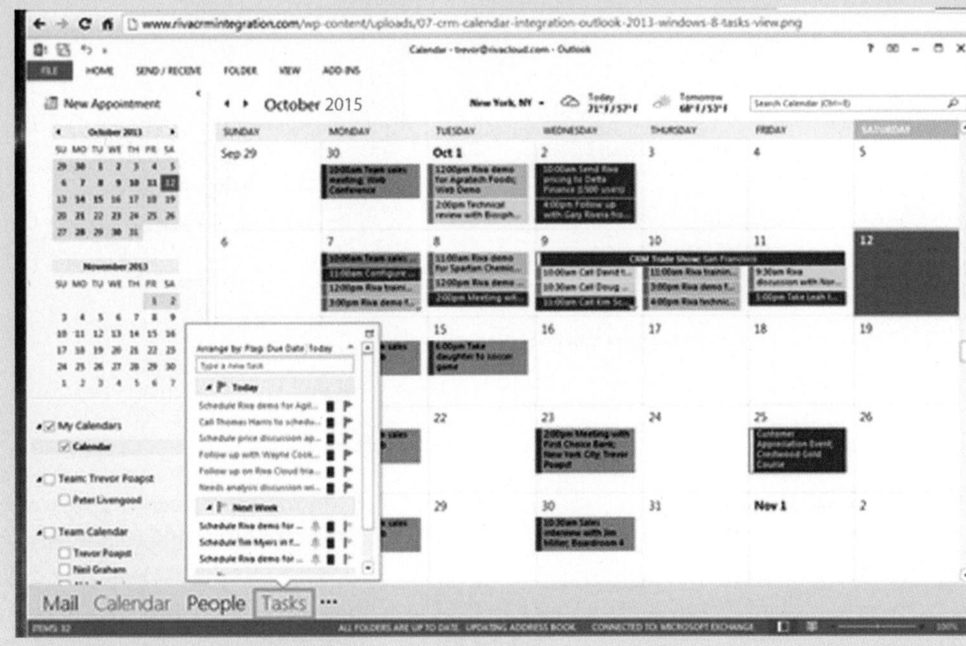

Calendar programs ease the frustration of scheduling meetings for busy people. The program allows you to check colleagues' calendars (if permission is given), locate a free time, schedule a meeting, send out an initial announcement, and follow up with reminders.

items. Remember, the narrower the focus, the greater the chances for success. A good agenda, as illustrated in Figure 2.6, covers the following information:

- Date and place of meeting
- Start time and end time
- Brief description of each topic, in order of priority, including the names of individuals who are responsible for performing some action
- Proposed allotment of time for each topic
- Any premeeting preparation expected of participants

Managing the Meeting

Whether you are the meeting leader or a participant, it is important to act professionally during the meeting. Meetings can be more efficient and productive if leaders and participants recognize how to get the meeting started, establish ground rules, move the meeting along, and handle conflict.

Getting Started and Establishing Ground Rules. Even if some participants are missing, start meetings promptly to avoid wasting time and irritating attendees. For the same reasons, don't give quick recaps to latecomers. Open the meeting with a three- to five-minute introduction that includes the following:

- Goal and length of the meeting
- Background of topics or problems
- Possible solutions and constraints
- Tentative agenda
- Ground rules to be followed

Figure 2.6 **Typical Meeting Agenda**

AGENDA
Quantum Travel International
Staff Meeting
September 4, 2018
10 to 11 a.m.
Conference Room

I. Call to order; roll call

II. Approval of agenda

III. Approval of minutes from previous meeting

	Person	Proposed Time
IV. Committee reports		
A. Social media news update	Jared	5 minutes
B. Tour packages	Lakisha	10 minutes
V. Old business		
A. Equipment maintenance	John	5 minutes
B. Client escrow accounts	Alicia	5 minutes
C. Internal newsletter	Adrienne	5 minutes
VI. New business		
A. New accounts	Garth	5 minutes
B. Pricing policy for Asian tours	Minh	15 minutes

VII. Announcements

VIII. Chair's summary, adjournment

Typical ground rules are communicating openly, being supportive, listening carefully, participating fully, confronting conflict frankly, silencing cell phones and other digital devices, and following the agenda. More formal groups follow parliamentary procedures based on Robert's Rules. The next step is to assign one attendee to take minutes and one to act as a recorder. The recorder uses a computer and projector or stands at a flipchart or whiteboard to list the main ideas being discussed and agreements reached.

Moving the Meeting Along. An effective leader lets others talk and tries to involve all participants. If the group has one member who dominates, the leader might say, *Thanks, Gary, for that perspective, but please hold your next point while we hear how Rachel would respond to that.* This technique also encourages quieter participants to speak up.

To avoid allowing digressions to sidetrack the group, try generating a parking lot list (a list of important but divergent issues that should be discussed later). Another way to handle digressions is to say, *Folks, we're drifting astray here. Please forgive me for pressing on, but let's return to the central issue of. . . .* It is important to adhere to the agenda and the schedule. Equally important, when the group seems to have reached a consensus, is to summarize the group's position and check to see whether everyone agrees.

Participating Actively and Productively. Meetings are an opportunity for you to showcase your abilities and boost your career. To get the most out of the meetings you attend, try these techniques:[38]

- **Arrive early.** You show respect and look well organized when you arrive a little early.
- **Come prepared.** Bring the agenda and any distributed materials. Study the topics and be ready with questions, comments, and good ideas.

- **Have a positive attitude.** Use positive body language; speak energetically.
- **Contribute respectfully.** Wait your turn to speak; raise your hand to be recognized.
- **Wait for others to finish.** Show respect and good manners by not interrupting.
- **Keep your voice calm and pleasant, yet energetic.** Avoid showing anger as this focuses attention on your behavior rather than on your ideas.
- **Give credit to others.** Gain allies and enhance your credibility by recognizing others in front of peers and superiors.
- **Use your cell phone, tablet, and laptop only for meeting-related tasks.** Focus your attention on the meeting, not on answering e-mails or working on your computer.

Pressmaster/Shutterstock.com

- **Help summarize.** Assist the meeting leader by reviewing points you have noted.
- **Express your views IN the meeting.** Build trust by not holding postmeeting sidebars that involve criticism and judgments.
- **Follow up.** Send the signal that you are efficient and caring by completing the actions assigned to you.

Reality Check

goodluz/Shutterstock.com

How Smart Are Smartphones and Tablets at Meetings?

During today's meetings attendees may bring smartphones and tablets to take notes. Because these devices are usually associated with gaming and texting, it's smart to explain. Matt Eventoff, founder of Princeton Public Speaking, gives this advice: "As soon as you take the device out, tell the other attendees, 'I use my iPad or phone to take notes.' That way, no one will question whether you're paying attention."

—Matt Eventoff, *owner, Princeton Public Speaking, a communication training business*

Handling Conflict in Meetings. As you learned earlier, conflict is natural and even desirable. However, it can also cause awkwardness and uneasiness. In meetings, conflict typically develops when people feel unheard or misunderstood. If two people clash, the best approach is to encourage each to make a complete case while group members give their full attention. Let each one question the other. Then, the leader should summarize what was said, and the participants should offer comments. The group may modify a recommendation or suggest alternatives before reaching consensus on a direction to follow.

Concluding and Following Up. End the meeting at the agreed time or sooner. The leader should summarize all decisions, assigned tasks, and deadlines. It may be necessary to ask attendees to volunteer for completing action items. All participants should understand what was accomplished. One effective technique that encourages full participation is a round-robin in which people take turns summarizing briefly their interpretations of what was decided and what happens next. Of course, this closure technique works best with smaller groups. The leader should conclude by asking the group to set a time for the next meeting. He or she should assure the group that a report will follow. Finally, the leader should thank participants for attending.

If minutes were taken, they should be distributed within a couple of days of the meeting. Meeting management programs and mobile apps offer a structured template such as that shown

Figure 2.7 E-Mail Meeting Minutes

Meeting proceedings are efficiently recorded in a summary distribution template that provides subject, date, time, participant names, absentee names, meeting documents and files, key points, decisions, and action items.

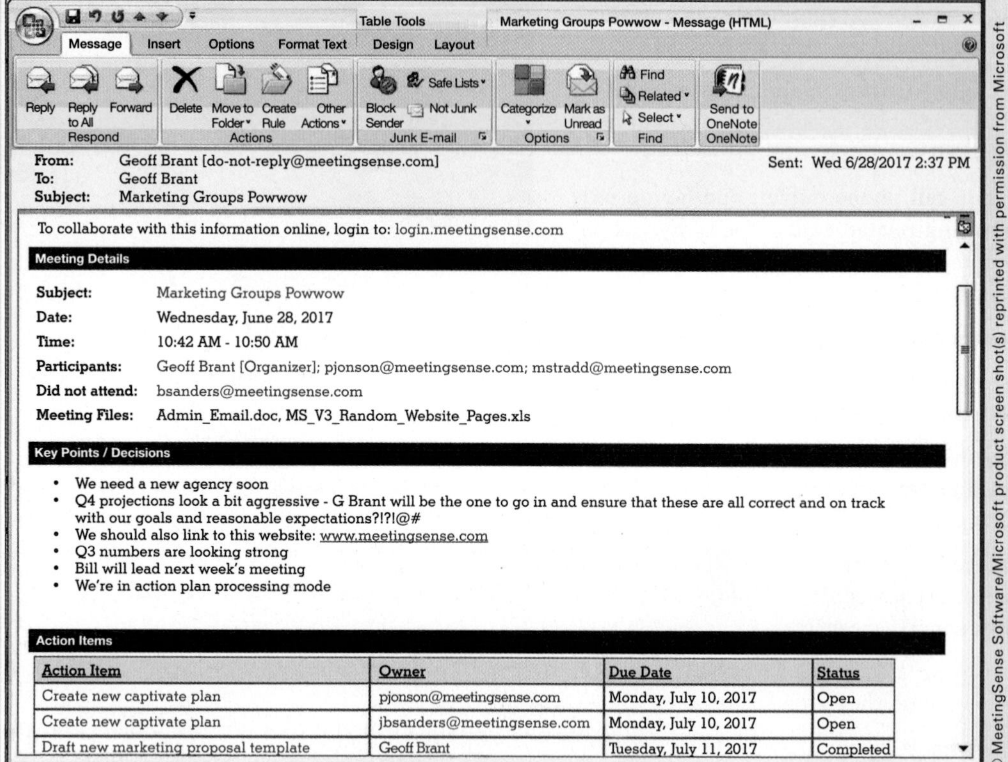

Table Tools | Marketing Groups Powwow - Message (HTML)

Message | Insert | Options | Format Text | Design | Layout

Reply | Reply to All | Forward | Respond | Delete | Move to Folder | Create Rule | Other Actions | Actions | Block Sender | Safe Lists | Not Junk | Junk E-mail | Categorize | Mark as Unread | Options | Find | Related | Select | Find | Send to OneNote | OneNote

From: Geoff Brant [do-not-reply@meetingsense.com] Sent: Wed 6/28/2017 2:37 PM
To: Geoff Brant
Subject: Marketing Groups Powwow

To collaborate with this information online, login to: login.meetingsense.com

Meeting Details

Subject: Marketing Groups Powwow
Date: Wednesday, June 28, 2017
Time: 10:42 AM - 10:50 AM
Participants: Geoff Brant [Organizer]; pjonson@meetingsense.com; mstradd@meetingsense.com
Did not attend: bsanders@meetingsense.com
Meeting Files: Admin_Email.doc, MS_V3_Random_Website_Pages.xls

Key Points / Decisions

- We need a new agency soon
- Q4 projections look a bit aggressive - G Brant will be the one to go in and ensure that these are all correct and on track with our goals and reasonable expectations?!?!@#
- We should also link to this website: www.meetingsense.com
- Q3 numbers are looking strong
- Bill will lead next week's meeting
- We're in action plan processing mode

Action Items

Action Item	Owner	Due Date	Status
Create new captivate plan	pjonson@meetingsense.com	Monday, July 10, 2017	Open
Create new captivate plan	jbsanders@meetingsense.com	Monday, July 10, 2017	Open
Draft new marketing proposal template	Geoff Brant	Tuesday, July 11, 2017	Completed

in Figure 2.7, which includes brief meeting minutes, key points and decisions, and action items. The leader needs to ensure that decisions are executed. The leader may need to contact participants to remind them of their assignments and to solicit help if necessary.

Preparing for Virtual Meetings

Virtual meetings are real-time gatherings of dispersed participants who connect with communication technology. As travel costs rise and companies slash budgets, many organizations are cutting back on meetings that require travel.[39] Instead, people may meet in audioconferences using telephones or in videoconferences using the Internet. Steady improvements in telecommunications networks, software applications, and bandwidth continue to fuel the shift to virtual meetings. These meetings have many purposes, including training employees, making sales presentations, coordinating team activities, and talking to customers.

Although the same good meeting management techniques discussed for face-to-face meetings prevail, additional skills and practices are important in virtual meetings. The following best practices recommended by experienced meeting facilitators will help you address premeeting issues such as technology glitches, scheduling across time zones, and language challenges.[40] Creating ground rules, anticipating limited media richness, managing turn-taking, and humanizing the interaction with remote members all achieve the best results during virtual meetings.

Andrey_Popov/Shutterstock.com

Videoconferencing at the enterprise level has changed the way employees at large organizations communicate. Increasingly, workers connect remotely using sophisticated communication technology. These virtual meetings take place in high-tech telepresence rooms—conference spaces with high-end equipment dedicated to videoconferencing—and enable employees at different locations to simulate face-to-face meetings. The benefits of videoconferencing are clear: less business travel saves time and money. However, such conferencing demands specific etiquette and behavior, including making eye contact with people on the screen, paying close attention, and not typing or eating. Experts also advise taking measures to avoid interruptions and avoid leaving suddenly.[41] Why does videoconferencing require distinct behavior and etiquette?

- **Select the most appropriate technology.** Decide whether audio- or videoconferencing is needed. Choose the appropriate program or application.
- **Ensure that all participants are able to use the technology.** Coach attendees who may need help before the session begins.
- **Encourage participants to log in 15 minutes early.** Some programs require downloads and installations that can cause immense frustration if not done early.
- **Be aware of different time zones.** Use Coordinated Universal Time (UTC) to minimize confusion resulting from mismatched local times. Avoid spanning a lunch hour or holding someone overtime.
- **Rotate your meeting time to be fair to all dispersed group members.** Ensure that everyone shares the burden of an inconvenient time.[42]
- **Decide what language to use.** If the meeting language may be difficult for some participants, think about using simple expressions and repeating major ideas. Always follow up in writing.
- **Explain how questions may be asked and answered.** Many meeting programs allow participants to virtually raise their hands using an icon on the computer screen and to type in their questions.
- **Ensure it is clear who is speaking in audioconferences.** Ask participants to always say their names before beginning to comment.
- **Remind the group to silence all electronic alerts and alarms.** Ask participants to mute ringers and buzzers and control background noise, or you may also hear dogs barking, telephones ringing, and toilets flushing.
- **Don't multitask.** Giving your full attention is critical. That includes texting and checking e-mail.
- **Anticipate the limitations of virtual technology.** Given the lack of nonverbal cues, be as precise as possible. Use simple language and summarize the discussion often. Confirm your understanding of the discussion. Project an upbeat, enthusiastic, and strong voice.
- **Manage turn-taking.** Ask questions of specific people. Invite each participant to speak for 30 seconds without interruption. Avoid asking vague questions such as, *Does everyone agree?*
- **Humanize virtual meetings.** Build camaraderie and trust. Leave time for small talk to establish a warm environment. Build trust and interest by logging in early and greeting others as they join in.

Some companies use teleconferencing informally to stimulate bonding and spontaneous collaboration between distant locations. Evernote, the company that provides a popular app for

Figure 2.8 Understanding Web Conferencing

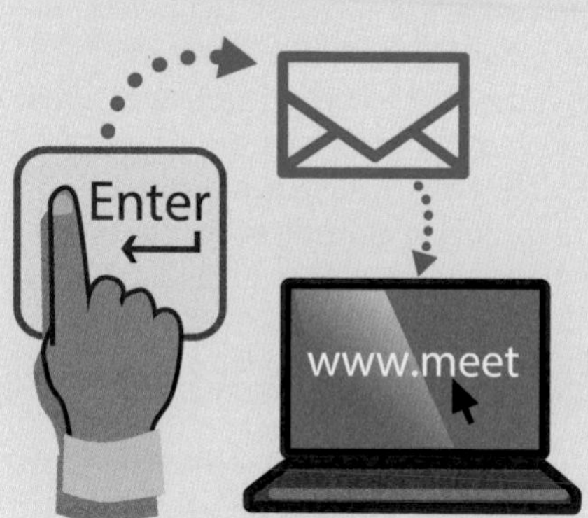

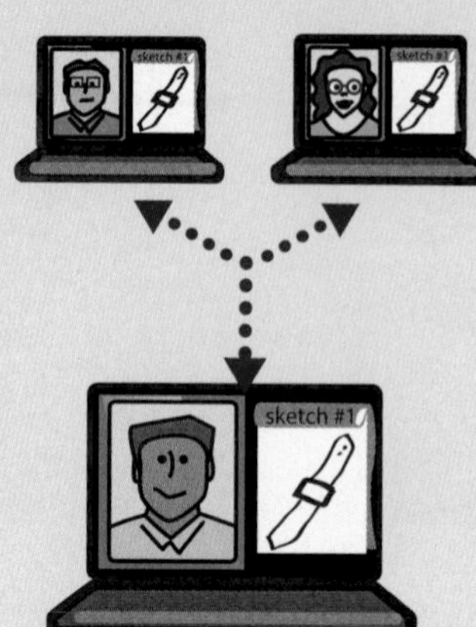

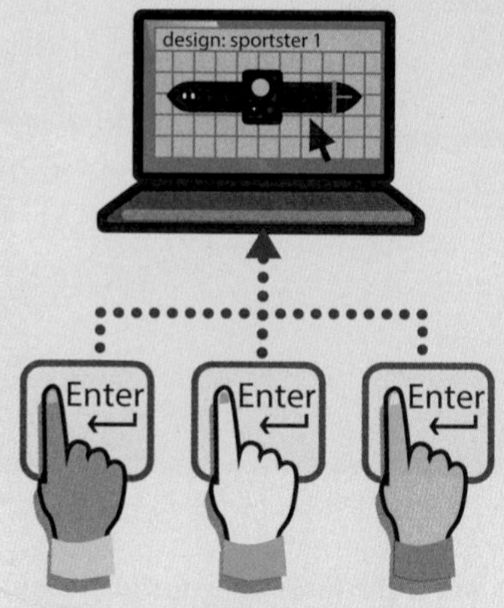

1. E-Mail Contact:
Alan T., president of Sportster Marketing, an athletic gear company in Seattle, WA, sends an email to Meghan R., chief designer at NexxtDesign in Venice, CA, to discuss a new sports watch. The e-mail includes meeting date and time and a link to launch the session.

2. Virtual Meeting:
When the Web conference begins, participants see live video of each other's faces on their screens. They look at photos of sports watches, share ideas, sketch designs on a shared "virtual whiteboard," and review contract terms.

3. Design Collaboration:
NexxtDesign artists and Sportster Marketing managers use peer-to-peer software that allows them to share spaces on each other's computers. The software enables them to take turns modifying the designs, and it also tracks all the changes.

notetaking and archiving, set up a virtual window between Mountain View, California, and its studio in Austin, Texas. A giant video screen connects the two offices in real time but not to facilitate meetings; rather, it invites workers simply to chat and exchange ideas.[43] Figure 2.8 shows how athletic gear company Sportster Marketing used Web conferencing to meet virtually and design a new sports watch.

Although many acknowledge that virtual meetings may not be as effective as face-to-face meetings,[44] virtual meetings are here to stay. Learning to plan and participate in them professionally will enhance your career as a business communicator. The following checklist summarizes helpful techniques for both face-to-face and virtual meetings.

Planning and Participating in Productive Meetings

Before the Meeting

- **Consider alternatives.** Unless a topic is important and pressing, avoid calling a meeting. Perhaps an e-mail message, telephone call, or intranet post would serve the purpose.
- **Invite the right people.** Invite people who have information and authority to make the decision and implement it.
- **Use a calendar program.** If available, use calendaring software to set a meeting date, issue invitations, and send the agenda.
- **Distribute an agenda.** Prepare an agenda that includes the date and place of the meeting, the starting and ending time, a brief description of each topic, the names of the people responsible for any action, and a proposed time allotment for each topic.

- **Train participants on technology.** Especially for virtual meetings, be sure participants are comfortable with the conferencing software.

During the Meeting

- **Start on time and introduce the agenda.** Discuss the goal and length of the meeting, provide backgrounds of topics for discussion, suggest possible solutions and constraints, propose a tentative agenda, and clarify the ground rules for the meeting.
- **Appoint a secretary and a recorder.** Ask one attendee to take notes of the proceedings, and ask another person to record discussion topics on a flipchart or whiteboard.
- **Encourage participation.** Ensure that all participants' views are heard and that no one monopolizes the discussion. Avoid digressions by steering the group back to the topics on the agenda. In virtual meetings be sure participants identify themselves before speaking.
- **Confront conflict frankly.** Encourage people who disagree to explain their positions completely. Then restate each position and ask for group comments. The group may modify a recommendation or suggest alternatives before agreeing on a plan of action.
- **Summarize along the way.** When the group seems to reach a consensus, summarize and see whether all members agree.

Ending the Meeting and Following Up

- **Review meeting decisions.** At the end of the meeting, consider using a round-robin to be sure everyone understands what has been decided. Discuss action items, and establish a schedule for completion.
- **Distribute minutes of the meeting.** A few days after the meeting, distribute the minutes. Use an e-mail template, if available.
- **Remind people of action items.** Follow up by calling people to see whether they are completing the actions recommended at the meeting.

Listening in the Workplace

LEARNING OUTCOME 3

Explain and apply active listening techniques.

The famous American entrepreneur and publisher Malcolm Forbes wrote, "The art of conversation lies in listening." Now, you may be thinking, everyone knows how to listen. Most of us believe that listening is an automatic response to noise. We do it without thinking. Perhaps that explains why so many of us are poor listeners. In this section we explore the importance of listening, the kinds of listening required in the workplace, and improving listening skills. Although many of the tips for improving your listening skills will be effective in your personal life, our discussion centers primarily on workplace and employment needs.

As you learned earlier, workers are communicating more than ever before, largely because of the Internet, social media, teamwork, global competition, and an emphasis on customer service. A vital ingredient in every successful workplace is high-quality communication, and three quarters of high-quality communication involves listening.[45]

Listening skills are important for career success, organization effectiveness, and worker satisfaction. Numerous studies and experts report that good listeners make good managers and that good listeners advance more rapidly in their organizations.[46] Studies of Fortune 500 companies report that soft skills such as listening, writing, and speaking are most likely to determine hiring and career success.[47] General Electric, a company known for grooming excellent leaders, counts listening among its most valuable leadership traits. GE Chairman and CEO Jeffrey R. Immelt considers "humble listening" to be one of four top characteristics in leaders.[48]

Reality Check

wavebreakmedia/Shutterstock.com

Listening and Career Success

"One of the best ways to gain a position and ensure success on a job is to exhibit that you are focused and understand what is going on. This is achieved through good listening skills."[49]

—Karen Sherman, *PhD, psychologist, New York*

iStockphoto.com/Nathan Gleave

Most of us can probably recall a situation in which smart portable electronics created a distraction, making listening difficult.

Poor Listening Habits

Although executives and employees devote the bulk of their communication time to listening, research suggests that they're not very good at it. In fact, most of us are poor listeners. Experts say that most people recall only between 25 and 50 percent of what they hear. Expect your boss, your coworkers, and your customers to retain only half or less of the conversation.[50]

Poor listening habits may result from several factors. Lack of training is one significant factor. Few schools give as much emphasis to listening as they do to the development of reading, speaking, and writing skills. In addition, our listening skills may be less than perfect because of the large number of competing sounds and stimuli in our lives that interfere with concentration. Finally, we are inefficient listeners because we are able to process speech much faster than others can speak. Although most speakers talk at about 125 to 175 words per minute, listeners can listen at 450 words per minute.[51] The resulting lag time fosters daydreaming, which clearly reduces listening efficiency.

Types of Workplace Listening

On the job you can expect to be involved in many types of listening. These include listening to supervisors, to colleagues, and to customers. If you are an entry-level employee, you will probably be most concerned with listening to superiors. But you also must develop skills for listening to colleagues and team members. As you advance in your career and enter the ranks of management, you will need skills for listening to subordinates. Finally, the entire organization must listen to customers, employees, government agencies, all stakeholders, and the public at large to compete in today's social and mobile business environment, in a service-oriented economy.

Listening to Supervisors. One of your most important tasks will be listening to instructions, assignments, and explanations about how to do your work. You will be listening to learn and to comprehend. To focus totally on the speaker, be sure you are not distracted by noisy surroundings or other tasks. Don't take phone calls, and don't try to complete another job while listening with one ear. Show your interest by leaning forward and striving for good eye contact.

Above all, take notes. Don't rely on your memory. Details are easy to forget. Taking selective notes also conveys to the speaker your seriousness about hearing accurately and completely. Don't interrupt. When the speaker finishes, paraphrase the instructions in your own words. Ask pertinent questions in a nonthreatening manner. Don't be afraid to ask "dumb" questions, if it means you won't have to do a job twice. Avoid criticizing or arguing when you are listening to a supervisor. Your goals should be to hear accurately and to convey an image of competence.

Listening to Colleagues and Teammates. Much of your listening will take place during interactions with coworkers and teammates. In these exchanges two kinds of listening are important. *Critical listening* enables you to judge and evaluate what you are hearing. You will be listening to decide whether the speaker's message is fact, fiction, or opinion. You will also be listening to decide whether an argument is based on logic or emotion. Critical listening requires an effort on your part. You must remain objective, particularly when you disagree with what you are hearing. Control your tendency to prejudge. Let the speaker complete the message before you evaluate it. *Discriminative listening* is necessary when you must discern, understand, and remember. It means you must identify main ideas, understand a logical argument, and recognize the purpose of the message.

Listening to Customers. The U.S. economy is heavily service oriented, and the new management mantra has become *Customers rule.* Many organizations know that listening to customers results in increased sales and profitability as well as improved customer acquisition and retention. The simple truth is that consumers feel better about companies that value their opinions—views that are amplified with unprecedented speed and reach by social media. Eighty-one percent of Twitter users now expect a response from companies to queries and complaints on the same day. Social media users prefer online help and want direct access to live support and experts; they want more than marketing and promotions.[52] Experts say that although 86 percent of companies are comfortable with social media, fewer than half of them seem to know how to engage customers in two-way communication with social media.[53]

How can organizations improve their customer listening techniques? Because employees are the eyes and ears of the organization, smart companies begin by hiring staff members who genuinely care about customers. Organizations intent on listening also train their employees to listen actively and to ask gentle, probing questions to ensure clear understanding. As you can see in Figure 2.9, employees trained in listening techniques are far more likely to elicit customer feedback and promote goodwill than untrained employees are.

Improving Workplace Listening

Listening on the job is more difficult than listening in college classes in which experienced professors present well-organized lectures and repeat important points. Workplace listening is more challenging because information is often exchanged casually or under time pressure. It may be disorganized, unclear, and cluttered with extraneous facts. Moreover, your fellow workers are usually friends. Because they are familiar with you, they may not be as polite and respectful as they are with strangers. Friends tend to interrupt, jump to conclusions, and take each other for granted.

Figure 2.9 **Listening to Customers: Comparing Trained and Untrained Listeners**

Untrained Listeners	Trained Listeners
✗ Tune out some of what the customer is saying because they know the answer	✓ Defer judgment; listen for the customer's feelings and assess the situation
✗ Focus on style; mentally dismiss grammar, voice tone, and speech mannerisms	✓ Pay most attention to content, not to appearances, form, or other surface issues
✗ Tend to listen mainly for facts and specific bits of information	✓ Listen completely, trying to really understand every nuance
✗ Attempt to take in everything being said, including exaggerations and errors ("fogging"), only to refute each comment	✓ Listen primarily for the main idea and avoid replying to everything, especially sidetracking issues
✗ Divide their attention among two or more tasks because listening is automatic	✓ Do one thing at a time, realizing that listening is a full-time job
✗ Tend to become distracted by emotional words, have difficulty controlling anger	✓ Control their anger and refuse to fight fire with fire
✗ Interrupt the customer	✓ Are silent for a few seconds after speakers finish to let them complete their thought
✗ Give few, if any, verbal responses	✓ Give affirming statements and invite additional comments

Listening in groups or listening to nonnative speakers further complicates the listening process. In groups, more than one person talks at once, and topics change rapidly. Group members are monitoring both verbal and nonverbal messages to learn what relates to their group roles. Listening to nonnative speakers often creates special challenges. Chapter 3 presents suggestions for communicating across cultures.

Ten Keys to Building Powerful Listening Skills

Despite the complexities and challenges of workplace listening, good listeners on the job must remember that their goal is to listen carefully and to *understand* what is being said so that they can do their work well. The following recommendations can help you improve your workplace listening effectiveness.

1. **Control external and internal distractions.** Move to an area where you can hear without conflicting noises or conversations. Block out surrounding physical distractions. Internally, try to focus totally on the speaker. If other projects are on your mind, put them on the back burner temporarily. When you are emotionally charged, whether angry or extremely happy, it is a good idea to postpone any serious listening.

2. **Become actively involved.** Show that you are listening closely by leaning forward and maintaining eye contact with the speaker. Don't fidget or try to complete another task at the same time you are listening. Listen to more than the spoken words. How are they said? What implied meaning, reasoning, and feelings do you hear behind the spoken words? Does the speaker's body language (eye contact, posture, movements) support or contradict the main message?

3. **Separate facts from opinions.** Facts are truths known to exist; for example, *Microsoft is located in Redmond, Washington.* Opinions are statements of personal judgments or preferences; for example, *Microsoft stock is always a good investment.* Some opinions are easy to recognize because speakers preface them with statements such as, *I think, It seems to me,* and *As far as I'm concerned.* Often, however, listeners must evaluate assertions to decide their validity. Good listeners consider whether speakers are credible and speaking within their areas of competence. They do not automatically accept assertions as facts.

4. **Identify important facts.** Speakers on the job often intersperse important information with casual conversation. Unrelated topics pop up—ball scores, a customer's weird request, a computer glitch, the boss's extravagant new sports car. Your task is to select what's crucial and register it mentally. What step is next in your project? Who does what? What is your role?

5. **Avoid interrupting.** When someone else has the floor, do not interrupt with a quick reply or opinion. Don't signal nonverbal disagreement such as negative head shaking, rolling eyes, sarcastic snorting, or audible sighs. Good listeners let speakers have their say. Interruptions are not only impolite, but also prevent you from hearing the speaker's complete thought. Listeners who interrupt with their opinions sidetrack discussions and cause hard feelings.

6. **Ask clarifying questions.** Good listeners wait for the proper moment and then ask questions that do not attack the speaker. Instead of saying, *But I don't understand how you can say that,* a good listener seeks clarification with statements such as, *Please help me understand by explaining more about . . . .* Because questions can put you in the driver's seat, think about them in advance. Use *open-ended questions* (those without set answers) to draw out feelings, motivations, ideas, and suggestions. Use *close-ended questions* (those that require a choice among set answers) to identify key factors in a discussion.[54] By the way, don't ask a question unless you are ready to be quiet and listen to the answer.

7. **Paraphrase to increase understanding.** To make sure you understand a speaker, rephrase and summarize a message in your own words. Be objective and nonjudgmental. Remember, your goal is to understand what the speaker has said—not to show how mindless the speaker's words sound when parroted. Remember, too, that other workplace listeners will also benefit from a clear summary of what was said.

Featureflash Photo Agency/ Shutterstock.com

Reality Check

Listen and Learn

Celebrated media proprietor and former talk show host Oprah Winfrey owes much of her success to the artful practice of listening and responding: "One of the greatest gifts you can give is your undivided attention," she says. Oprah's advice has inspired a devoted audience of followers: "Listen. Pay attention. Treasure every moment."[55]

—Oprah Winfrey, *media tycoon, former talk show host*

8. **Capitalize on lag time.** While you are waiting for a speaker's next idea, use the time to review what the speaker is saying. Separate the central idea, key points, and details. Sometimes you may have to supply the organization. Use lag time to silently rephrase and summarize the speaker's message. Another effective trick for keeping your mind from drifting is to try to guess what a speaker's next point will be. Most important, keep your mind focused on the speaker and his or her ideas—not on all the other work waiting for you.
9. **Take notes to ensure retention.** A wise person once said that he would rather have a short pencil than a long memory. If you have a hallway conversation with a colleague and don't have a pen or smart electronic device handy, make a mental note of the important items. Then write them down as soon as possible. Even with seemingly easily remembered facts or instructions, jot them down to ease your mind and also to be sure you understand them correctly. Two weeks later you will be glad you did. Be sure you have a good place to store notes about various projects, such as file folders, notebooks, digital files, or handy apps such as Evernote.
10. **Be aware of potential gender differences.** Men tend to listen for facts, whereas women tend to perceive listening as an opportunity to connect with the other person on a personal level.[56] Men tend to use interrupting behavior to control conversations, while women generally interrupt to communicate assent, to elaborate on an idea of another group member, or to participate in the topic of conversation. Female listeners tend to be attentive, provide steady eye contact, remain stationary, and nod their heads.[57] Male listeners are less attentive, provide sporadic eye contact, and move around. Of course, such generalizations about gender and communication risk becoming stereotypes as some authors point out.[58]

Being aware of these tendencies will make you a more sensitive and knowledgeable listener. To learn more about gender differences in communication, see the Career Coach box He Said, She Said in Chapter 3. The checklist that follows sums up useful tips for effective listening.

Improving Listening

- **Stop talking.** Accept the role of listener by concentrating on the speaker's words, not on your response.
- **Work hard at listening.** Become actively involved; expect to learn something.
- **Block out competing thoughts.** Concentrate on the message. Don't daydream during lag time.
- **Control the listening environment.** Move to a quiet area where you won't be interrupted by calls, texts, or visitors. Check to be certain that listeners can hear speakers.
- **Maintain an open mind.** Know your biases and try to correct for them. Be tolerant of less abled and different-looking speakers. Provide verbal and nonverbal feedback. Encourage the speaker with comments such as, *Yes*, *I see*, *OK*, and *Uh huh*. Ask polite questions, and look alert by leaning forward.
- **Paraphrase the speaker's ideas.** Silently repeat the message in your own words, sort out the main points, and identify supporting details. In conversation sum up the main points to confirm what was said.
- **Listen between the lines.** Observe nonverbal cues and interpret the feelings of the speaker: What is really being said?
- **Distinguish between facts and opinions.** Know the difference between factual statements and opinions stated as assertions.
- **Capitalize on lag time.** Use spare moments to organize, review, anticipate, challenge, and weigh the evidence.
- **Use memory devices.** If the information is important, develop acronyms, links, or rhymes to help you remember it.
- **Take selective notes.** If you are hearing instructions or important data, record the major points; then, revise your notes immediately or verify them with the speaker.

LEARNING OUTCOME 4

Understand how effective nonverbal communication can help you advance your career.

Communicating Nonverbally

Understanding messages often involves more than merely listening to spoken words. Nonverbal cues, in fact, can speak louder than words. These cues include eye contact, facial expression, body movements, time, space, territory, and appearance. All of these nonverbal cues affect how a message is interpreted, or decoded, by the receiver.

What Is Nonverbal Communication? Nonverbal communication includes all unwritten and unspoken messages, whether intended or not. These silent signals have a strong effect on receivers. However, understanding them is not simple. Does a downward glance indicate modesty? Fatigue? Does a constant stare reflect coldness? Dullness? Aggression? Do crossed arms mean defensiveness, withdrawal, or just that the person is shivering?

What If Words and Nonverbal Cues Clash? Messages are even harder to decipher when the verbal and nonverbal cues do not agree. What will you think if Scott says he is not angry, but he slams the door when he leaves? What if Alicia assures the hostess that the meal is excellent, but she eats very little? The nonverbal messages in these situations speak louder than the words. In fact, researchers believe that the bulk of any message we receive is nonverbal.

Nonverbal cues contradicting verbal messages speak louder than the words uttered. In one experiment speakers delivered a positive message but averted their eyes as they spoke. Listeners perceived the overall message to be negative. Moreover, listeners thought that gaze aversion suggested deception or lack of respect.[59] The lesson here is that effective communicators must be certain that all their nonverbal messages reinforce their spoken words and their professional goals. To make sure that you're on the right track to nonverbal communication competency, let's look at the silent nonverbal messages our bodies send.

Your Body Sends Silent Messages

Psychologist and philosopher Paul Watzlawick claimed that we cannot not communicate.

In other words, it's impossible to not communicate. This means that every behavior is sending a message even if we don't use words. The eyes, face, and body convey meaning without a single syllable being spoken. Although this discussion covers many forms of nonverbal communication, we are especially concerned with workplace applications. Think about how you can use the following nonverbal cues positively in your career.

Eye Contact. The eyes have been called the windows to the soul. Even if they don't reveal the soul, the eyes are often the best predictor of a speaker's true feelings and attitudes. Most of us cannot look another person straight in the eye and lie. As a result, in North American culture we tend to believe people who look directly at us. Sustained eye contact suggests trust and admiration; brief eye contact signals fear or stress. Prolonged eye contact or staring, though, can be intrusive and intimidating.

Good eye contact enables the message sender to see whether a receiver is paying attention, showing respect, responding favorably, or feeling distress. From the receiver's perspective, good eye contact, in North American culture, reveals the speaker's sincerity, confidence, and truthfulness. However, nonverbal cues, including eye contact, have different meanings in different cultures. Chapter 3 presents more information about cultural influences on nonverbal cues.

Facial Expression. The expression on a communicator's face can be almost as revealing of emotion as the eyes. Experts estimate that the human face can display over 250,000 expressions.[60] To hide their feelings, some people can control these expressions and maintain so-called poker faces. Most of us, however, display our emotions openly. Raising or lowering the eyebrows, squinting the eyes, swallowing nervously, clenching the jaw, smiling broadly—these voluntary and involuntary facial expressions can add to or entirely replace verbal messages.

Posture and Gestures. An individual's posture can convey anything from high status and self-confidence to shyness and submissiveness. Leaning toward a speaker suggests attentiveness and interest; pulling away or shrinking back denotes fear, distrust, anxiety, or disgust. Similarly, gestures can communicate entire thoughts via simple movements. However, the meanings of some of these movements differ in other cultures. In the United States and Canada, for example, forming the thumb and forefinger in a circle means everything is OK. But in parts of South America, the OK sign is obscene.

In the workplace you can make a good impression by controlling your posture and gestures. When speaking, make sure your upper body is aligned with the person to whom you're talking. Erect posture sends a message of confidence, competence, diligence, and strength. Women are advised to avoid tilting their heads to the side when making an important point. This gesture diminishes the main thrust of the message.[61]

Be careful, however, before attaching specific meanings to gestures or actions, because behavior and its interpretations strongly depend on context and on one's cultural background, as you will see in Chapter 3.

Ethics Check

Impressing Your Instructor

Projecting a professional image begins in your business communication classroom and in other courses in which your instructors evaluate your work and your participation. Imagine how a professor perceives students who skip classes, arrive late, forget homework, yawn with their tonsils showing, chew gum or eat, play with their electronic toys, and doodle during class. What message does such nonverbal behavior send?

Time, Space, and Territory Send Silent Messages

In addition to nonverbal messages transmitted by your body, three external elements convey information in the communication process: time, space, and territory.

Time. How we structure and use time tells observers about our personality and attitudes. For example, when Warren Buffett, industrialist, investor, and philanthropist, gives a visitor a prolonged interview, he signals his respect for, interest in, and approval of the visitor or the topic being discussed. By sharing his valuable time, he sends a clear nonverbal message. Likewise, when David Ing twice arrives late for a meeting, it could mean that the meeting has low priority to David, that he is a self-centered person, or that he has little self-discipline. These are assumptions that typical Americans might make. In other cultures and regions, though, punctuality is viewed differently. In the workplace you can send positive nonverbal messages by being on time for meetings and appointments, staying on task during meetings, and giving ample time to appropriate projects and individuals.

Space. How we order the space around us tells something about ourselves and our objectives. Whether the space is a bedroom, a dorm room, or an office, people reveal themselves in the design and grouping of their furniture. Generally, the more formal the arrangement, the more formal and closed the communication style. An executive who seats visitors in a row of chairs across from his desk sends a message of aloofness and a desire for separation. A team

Figure 2.10 **Four Space Zones for Social Interaction**

iStockphoto.com/lewkmiller

Intimate Zone
(1 to 1.5 feet)

iStockphoto.com/Dean Mitchell

Personal Zone
(1.5 to 4 feet)

iStockphoto.com/monkeybusinessimages

Social Zone
(4 to 12 feet)

© Kablonk Royalty-Free/Inmagine

Public Zone
(12 or more feet)

leader who arranges chairs informally in a circle rather than in straight rows or a rectangular pattern conveys her desire for a more open, egalitarian exchange of ideas. A manager who creates an open office space with few partitions separating workers' desks seeks to encourage an unrestricted flow of communication and work among departments.

Territory. Each of us has a certain area that we feel is our own territory, whether it is a specific spot or just the space around us. Your father may have a favorite chair in which he is most comfortable, a cook might not tolerate intruders in the kitchen, and veteran employees may feel that certain work areas and tools belong to them. We all maintain zones of privacy in which we feel comfortable. Figure 2.10 categorizes the four zones of social interaction among North Americans, as formulated by anthropologist Edward T. Hall.[62] Notice that North Americans are a bit standoffish; only intimate friends and family may stand closer than about 1.5 feet. If someone violates that territory, we may feel uncomfortable and step back to reestablish our space. In the workplace be aware of the territorial needs of others and don't invade their space.

Appearance Sends Silent Messages

Much like the personal appearance of an individual, the physical appearance of a business document transmits immediate and important nonverbal messages. Ideally, these messages should be pleasing to the eye.

Eye Appeal of Business Documents. The way an e-mail, letter, memo, or report looks can have either a positive or a negative effect on the receiver. Sloppy e-mails send a nonverbal message that you are in a terrific hurry or that you do not care about the receiver. Envelopes—through their postage, stationery, and printing—can suggest that the messages they carry are routine, important, or junk mail. Letters and reports can look neat, professional, well organized, and attractive—or just the opposite.

In succeeding chapters you will learn how to create documents that send positive nonverbal messages through their appearance, format, organization, readability, and correctness.

Personal Appearance. The way you look—your clothing, grooming, and posture—transmits an instant nonverbal message about you. Based on what they see, viewers make quick judgments about your status, credibility, personality, and potential. Business communicators who look the part are more likely to be successful in working with supervisors, colleagues, and customers. Because appearance is such a powerful force in business, some aspiring professionals are turning for help to image consultants (who charge up to $500 an hour!).

What do image consultants say? They suggest investing in appropriate, professional-looking clothing and accessories. Remember that quality is more important than quantity. Avoid flashy

One of the latest fads is body art in the form of tattoos and piercings. Once seen primarily on bikers, prisoners, and sailors, inked images increasingly adorn the bodies of Americans today. The Food and Drug Administration estimates that as many as 45 million Americans have at least one tattoo. Studies found the highest incidence of tattoos in eighteen- to twenty-nine-year-olds (38 percent).[63] Think twice, however, before displaying tats and piercings at work. Conspicuous body art may make you feel distinctive and slightly daring, but how might it affect your career?

Hero Images/Hero Images/Getty Images

garments, clunky jewelry, garish makeup, and overpowering colognes. Pay attention to good grooming, including a neat hairstyle, body cleanliness, polished shoes, and clean nails. Project confidence in your posture, both standing and sitting.

In recent years the trend is the movement toward one or more days per week of casual dress at work. Be aware, though, that casual clothes change the image you project and also may affect your work style. See the accompanying Career Coach box regarding the pros and cons of casual apparel.

In the preceding discussion of nonverbal communication, you learned that each of us sends and responds to thousands of nonverbal messages daily in our personal and work lives. You can harness the power of silent messages by reviewing Figure 2.11 and by studying the tips in the following checklist.

Figure 2.11 **Sending Positive Nonverbal Signals in the Workplace**

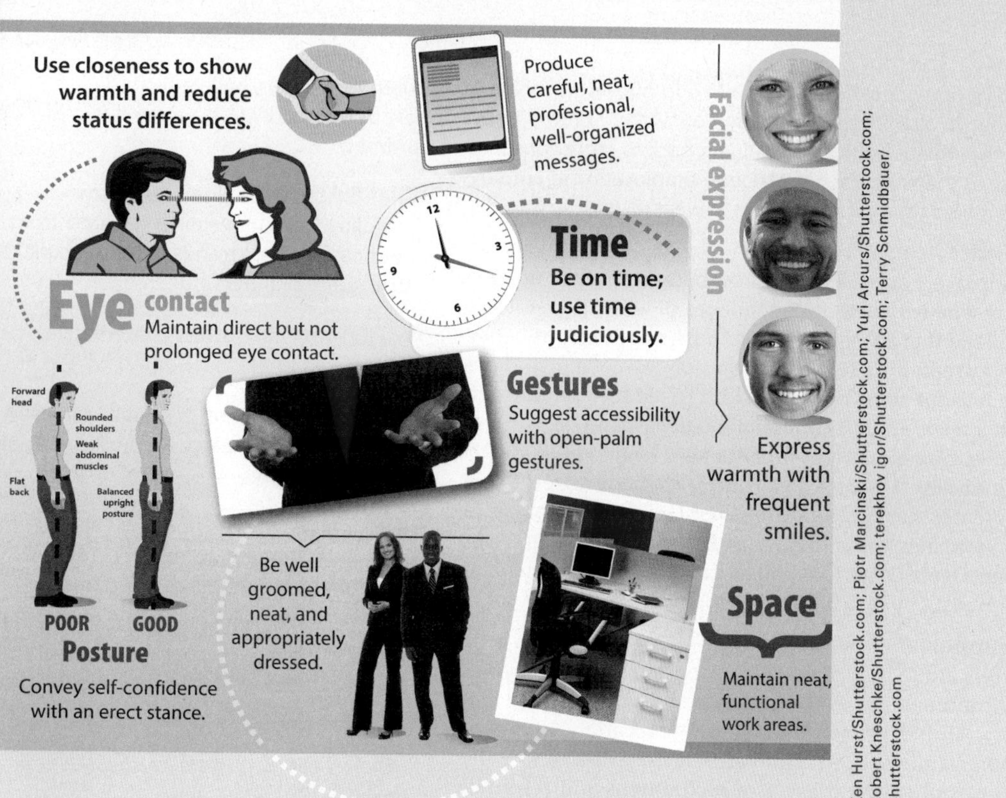

Ken Hurst/Shutterstock.com; Piotr Marcinski/Shutterstock.com; Yuri Arcurs/Shutterstock.com; Robert Kneschke/Shutterstock.com; terekhov igor/Shutterstock.com; Terry Schmidbauer/Shutterstock.com

Building Strong Nonverbal Communication Skills in the Workplace

- **Establish and maintain eye contact.** Remember that in North America appropriate eye contact signals interest, attentiveness, strength, and credibility.
- **Use posture to show interest.** Encourage interaction by leaning forward, sitting or standing erect, and looking alert.
- **Reduce or eliminate physical barriers.** Move out from behind a desk or lectern; arrange meeting chairs in a circle.
- **Improve your decoding skills.** Watch facial expressions and body language to understand the complete verbal and nonverbal message being communicated.
- **Probe for more information.** When you perceive nonverbal cues that contradict verbal meanings, politely seek additional clues (*I'm not sure I understand, Please tell me more about* . . ., or *Do you mean that . . . ?*).
- **Interpret nonverbal meanings in context.** Make nonverbal assessments only when you understand a situation or a culture.
- **Associate with people from diverse cultures.** Learn about other cultures to widen your knowledge and tolerance of intercultural nonverbal messages.
- **Appreciate the power of appearance.** Keep in mind that the appearance of your business documents, your business space, and yourself sends immediate positive or negative messages to others.
- **Observe yourself on video.** Ensure that your verbal and nonverbal messages are in sync by recording and evaluating yourself making a presentation.
- **Enlist friends and family.** Ask friends and family members to monitor your conscious and unconscious body movements and gestures to help you become a more effective communicator.

Career Coach

Perils of Casual Apparel in the Workplace

wavebreakmedia/Shutterstock.com

Your choice of work clothes sends a strong nonverbal message about you. It also affects the way you work. Some surveys suggest that the pendulum is swinging back to more conservative attire in the workplace,[64] although employers and employees have mixed feelings about what to wear to work.

What Critics Are Saying

Some employers oppose casual dress because, in their opinion, too many workers push the boundaries of what is acceptable. They contend that absenteeism, tardiness, and flirtatious behavior have increased since dress-down policies were first implemented. Relaxed dress codes also lead to reduced productivity and lax behavior.[65] Image counselor Judith Rasband claimed that the general casualization of America has resulted in an overall decline in civility. "Manners break down, you begin to feel down, and you're not as effective," she said.[66] Others fear that casual attire undermines the authority and credibility of executives, particularly females and minorities.[67] Moreover, customers are often turned off by casually attired employees.[68]

What Supporters Are Saying

Supporters argue that comfortable clothes and relaxed working environments lift employee morale, increase employee creativity, and improve internal communication.[69] Employees appreciate reduced clothing-related expenses, while employers use casual dress as a recruitment and retention tool. Because employees seem to love casual dress, nine out of ten employers have adopted casual-dress days for at least part of the workweek—even if it is just on Fridays during the summer.

What Employees Need to Know

The following suggestions, gleaned from surveys and articles about casual-dress trends in the workplace, can help you avoid casual-attire blunders.

- For job interviews, dress conservatively or call ahead to ask the interviewer or the receptionist what is appropriate.
- Find out what your company allows. Ask whether a dress-down policy is in place. Observe what others are wearing on casual-dress days.
- If your company has no casual-attire policy, volunteer to work with management to develop relevant guidelines, including illustrations of suitable casual attire.
- Avoid wearing the following items: T-shirts, sandals, flip-flops, shoes without socks, backless dresses, tank tops, shorts, miniskirts, spandex, athletic shoes, hiking boots, baseball caps, and visors.[70]
- When meeting customers, dress as well as or better than they do.

Developing Professionalism and Business Etiquette Skills at the Office and Online

LEARNING OUTCOME 5

Improve your competitive advantage by developing professionalism and business etiquette skills.

What exactly is professionalism? Your future employer will expect you to possess what are often referred to as soft skills in addition to your technical knowledge. Soft skills are the hallmark of a professional. They are essential career attributes that include the ability to communicate, work well with others, solve problems, make ethical decisions, and appreciate diversity.[71] Sometimes called employability skills or key competencies, these soft skills are desirable in all business sectors and job positions.[72] In the digital age, professionalism also means maintaining a positive online presence, a subject we discuss in Chapters 1 and 5.

Etiquette is more about attitude than about formal rules of behavior. Attitude is a desire to show others consideration and respect. It includes a desire to make others feel comfortable. Good manners and a businesslike, professional demeanor are among the top soft skills that employers seek in job candidates. Employers prefer courteous and professional job candidates over those who lack these skills and traits. But can you really learn how to be courteous, civil, and professional? Of course! This section gives you a few pointers.

Understanding Professionalism and the Cost of Incivility

Not everyone who seeks a job is aware of the employer's expectations. Some new-hires have no idea that excessive absenteeism or tardiness is grounds for termination. Others are surprised to learn that they are expected to devote their full attention to their duties when on the job. One young man wanted to read *Harry Potter* novels when things got slow. Many employees don't realize that they are sabotaging their careers when they sprinkle their conversation with *like, you know,* and uptalk (making declarative statements sound like questions).

Projecting and maintaining a professional image can make a real difference in helping you obtain the job of your dreams. Once you get that job, you are more likely to be taken seriously and much more likely to be promoted if you look and sound professional. Do not send the wrong message with unwitting or unprofessional behavior. Figure 2.12 reviews seven areas you will want to check to be sure you are projecting professionalism.

Gaining an Etiquette Edge in a Networked World

An awareness of courtesy and etiquette can give you a competitive edge in the job market. Etiquette, civility, and goodwill efforts may seem out of place in today's fast-paced offices. However, when two candidates have equal qualifications, the one who appears to be more polished and professional is more likely to be hired and promoted.

As workloads increase and face-to-face meetings decline, bad behavior is becoming alarmingly common in the American workplace and may exact a high cost "of whittling away at people's health, performance, and souls."[73] One survey showed that 71 percent of workers said they had been insulted, demeaned, ignored, or otherwise treated discourteously by their coworkers and supervisors.[74] Employers, of course, suffer from the resulting drop in productivity and exodus of talent. Employees, too, suffer. They worry about incidents, think about changing jobs, and cut back their efforts on the job. Workplace rudeness also turns customers away.[75] Businesses are responding to increasing incidents of *desk rage* and *cyberbullying* in American workplaces by establishing policies to enforce civility. In short, it is not hard to understand why employers are looking for people who are courteous, polite, respectful, and well mannered.

Figure 2.12 Projecting Professionalism When You Communicate

Unprofessional		Professional
Uptalk, a singsong speech pattern, making sentences sound like questions; *like* used as a filler; *go* for *said*; slang; poor grammar and profanity.	Speech habits	Recognizing that your credibility can be seriously damaged by sounding uneducated, crude, or adolescent.
Messages with incomplete sentences, misspelled words, exclamation points, IM slang, and mindless chatter; sloppy messages signal that you don't care, don't know, or aren't smart enough to know what is correct.	E-mail	Employers like to see subjects, verbs, and punctuation marks. They dislike IM abbreviations. They value conciseness and correct spelling, even in brief e-mail messages and texts.
E-mail addresses such as *hotbabe@outlook.com, supasnugglykitty@yahoo.com, or buffedguy@gmail.com.*	Internet	E-mail addresses should include a name or a positive, businesslike expression; they should not sound cute or like a chat room nickname.
An outgoing message with strident background music, weird sounds, or a joke message.	Voicemail	An outgoing message that states your name or phone number and provides instructions for leaving a message.
Soap operas, thunderous music, or a TV football game playing noisily in the background when you answer the phone.	Telephone presence	A quiet background when you answer the telephone, especially if you are expecting a prospective employer's call.
Using electronics during business meetings for unrelated purposes or during conversations with fellow employees; raising your voice (cell yell); forcing others to overhear your calls.	Cell phones, tablets	Turning off phone and message notification, both audible and vibrate, during meetings; using your smart devices only for meeting-related purposes.
Sending and receiving text messages during meetings, allowing texting to interrupt face-to-face conversations, or texting when driving.	Texting	Sending appropriate business text messages only when necessary (perhaps when a cell phone call would disturb others).

Figure 2.13 summarizes the many components of professional workplace behavior[76] and identifies six main dimensions that will ease your entry into the world of work.

Good manners, on the other hand, convey a positive image of an organization. People like to do business with those who show respect and treat others politely. Most of us also like to work in a pleasant environment. Considering how much time Americans spend at work, it makes sense that people prefer an agreeable environment to one that is rude and uncivil. Remember, too, that bad behavior can be recorded and posted for the world to see, practically forever!

You don't have to become an etiquette nut, but you might need to polish your social competencies a little to be an effective businessperson today. Here are a few simple pointers:

- **Use polite words.** Be generous with words and phrases such as *please, thank you*, and *you're welcome*.
- **Express sincere appreciation and praise.** Tell coworkers how much you appreciate their efforts. Remember that written and specific thank-you notes are even better than saying thanks.

Figure 2.13 **The Six Dimensions of Professional Behavior**

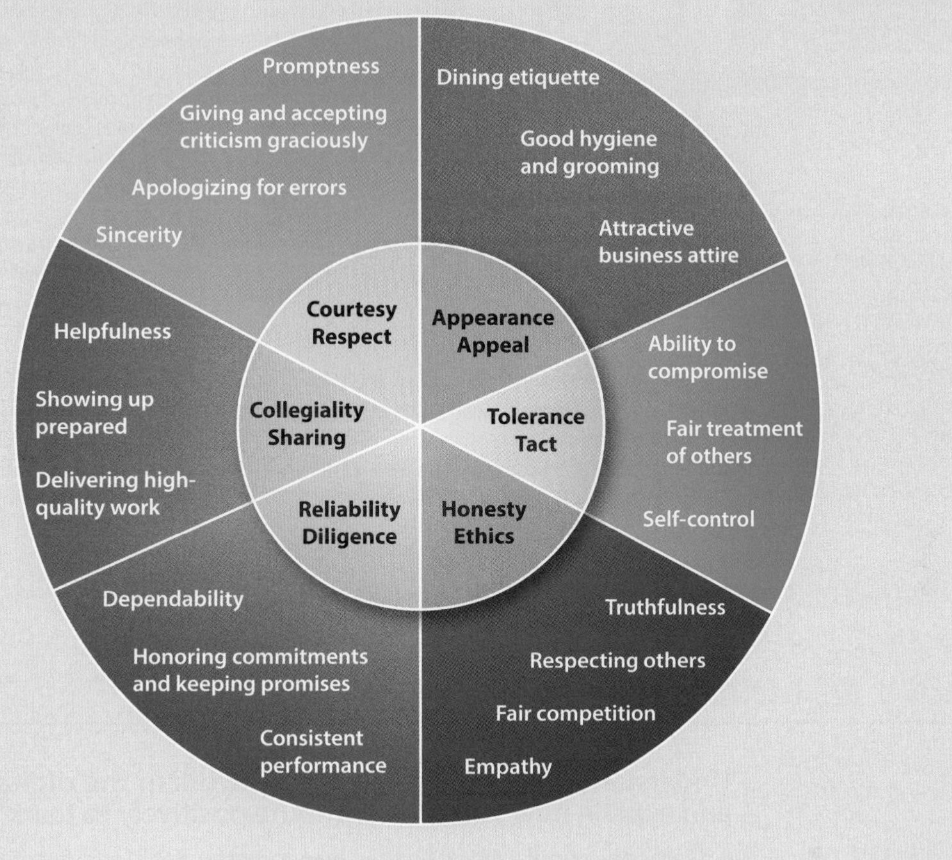

- **Be selective in sharing personal information.** Avoid talking about health concerns, personal relationships, or finances in the office.
- **Don't put people down.** If you have a reputation for criticizing people, your coworkers will begin to wonder what you are saying behind their backs.
- **Respect coworkers' space.** Turn down the ringer on your business phone, minimize the use of speakerphones, and turn your personal cell phone down or off during business hours. Avoid wearing heavy perfumes or bringing strong-smelling food.
- **Rise above others' rudeness.** Don't use profanity or participate in questionable joke-telling.
- **Be considerate when sharing space and equipment with others.** Clean up after yourself.
- **Choose the high road in conflict.** Avoid letting discussions degenerate into shouting matches. Keep a calm voice tone and focus on the work rather than on personality differences.
- **Disagree agreeably.** You may not agree with everyone, but you should respect their opinions.

Your Turn: Applying Your Skills at Lyft

An upstart in ride-sharing apps, Lyft and its youthful and energetic company culture can be seen in everything from its unique San Francisco headquarters to its organizational structure. With an open office space and relaxed atmosphere, Lyft is designed to encourage teamwork. Informal collaboration may occur when several employees gather over company-provided lunches. Shorter, planned meetings take place in small meeting rooms named after animals. However, as different as Lyft's culture is from traditional companies, its leaders know the importance of keeping employees informed *and* enthused. Sometimes that means large meetings.

Before beginning your task, take a moment to watch the six-minute video *Lyft's Fuzzy Pink Mission Headquarters* on YouTube, which illustrates Lyft's one-of-a-kind corporate headquarters.

Your Task

You are a new-hire at Lyft, and your boss, Priyanka, is calling a meeting that will involve approximately 50 staffers from several teams at Lyft headquarters. She would like your help with the preliminary steps of organizing the meeting and asks that you draft a list of tasks you'll perform to ensure that the meeting is productive. She also wants your ideas about adding an element of fun and humor to the meeting, as is typical at the company. Write an e-mail to Priyanka in which you outline the steps that lead to effective meetings, or discuss the steps with a teammate. Use your creativity and what you've learned about Lyft to devise an element that would bring levity to the meeting.

Summary of Learning Outcomes

1 Understand the importance of teamwork in the digital-era workplace, and explain how you can contribute positively to team performance.

- Teams are popular because they lead to better decisions, faster responses, increased productivity, greater buy-in, less resistance to change, improved morale, and reduced risks.
- Virtual teams are collaborations among remote coworkers connecting with technology.
- The four phases of team development are forming, storming, norming, and performing.
- Positive group behaviors include establishing and following rules, resolving differences, being supportive, praising others, and summarizing points of understanding.
- Negative behaviors include having contempt for others, wasting the team's time, and withdrawing.
- Successful teams are small and diverse, agree on a purpose and procedures, confront conflict, communicate well, don't compete but collaborate, are ethical, and share leadership.

2 Discuss effective practices and technologies for planning and participating in face-to-face meetings and virtual meetings.

- Before a meeting businesspeople determine its purpose and location, choose participants, use a digital calendar, and distribute an agenda.
- Experienced meeting leaders establish ground rules, move the meeting along, and confront any conflict; they end the meeting on time, make sure everyone is heard, and distribute meeting minutes promptly.

- Virtual meetings save travel costs but require attention to communication technology and to the needs of dispersed participants regarding issues such as different time zones and language barriers.
- Virtual meetings demand specific procedures to handle questions, noise, lack of media richness, and turn-taking. Because they are impersonal, virtual meetings benefit from building camaraderie and trust.

3 Explain and apply active listening techniques.

- Most of us are poor listeners; careers and organizational success depend on active listening.
- A fast processing speed allows us to let our minds wander; as untrained listeners, we are easily distracted.
- Listening to supervisors on the job, workers should take notes, avoid interrupting, ask pertinent questions, and paraphrase what they hear.
- When dealing with coworkers, good listeners identify facts, main ideas, and logical arguments.
- When listening to customers, employees should ask gentle, probing questions to ensure understanding.
- Effective listeners control distractions, show active involvement, separate facts from opinions, identify important facts, refrain from interrupting, ask clarifying questions, paraphrase, take advantage of lag time, take notes to ensure retention, and consider gender differences.

4 Understand how effective nonverbal communication can help you advance your career.

- Be aware of nonverbal cues such as eye contact, facial expression, and posture that send silent, highly believable messages.
- Understand that how you use time, space, and territory is interpreted by the receiver, who also reads the eye appeal of your business documents and your personal appearance.
- Build solid nonverbal skills by keeping eye contact, maintaining good posture, reducing physical barriers, improving your decoding skills, and probing for more information.
- Interpret nonverbal meanings in context, learn about other cultures, and understand the impact of appearance—of documents, your office space, and yourself.

5 Improve your competitive advantage by developing professionalism and business etiquette skills.

- Professionalism, good business etiquette, developed soft skills, social intelligence, polish, and civility are desirable workplace behaviors that are complemented by a positive online presence.
- Essential career attributes are the ability to communicate, working well with others, solving problems, making ethical decisions, and appreciating diversity.
- Practicing business etiquette on the job and online can put you ahead of others who lack polish.
- Good workplace behavior includes using polite words, giving sincere praise, respecting coworkers' space, rising above others' rudeness, taking the high road in conflict, and disagreeing agreeably.

Critical Thinking

1. Career expert Andrea Kay stresses that knowing oneself and showing empathy are important components of the soft skills that make people employable: "Many, many jobs are lost and careers derailed because of the way people act with each other, respond to stress, or deal with a conflict. . . . If you don't understand how you come across, or get swept away in your emotions, or don't recognize how others feel, how can you approach a difficult conversation with sensitivity to the other person?"[77] Have you ever been surprised at how you came across to others or misread another person's feelings? (L.O. 1)
2. Evaluate the following humorous analogy between the murder of a famous Roman emperor and the deadening effect of meetings: "This month is the 2,053rd anniversary of the death of Julius Caesar, who pronounced himself dictator for life before running the idea past the Roman Senate. On his way to a meeting, he was met by a group of senators who, wishing to express their unhappiness with his vocational aspirations, stabbed him to death. Moral of the story: Beware of meetings."[78] Is the comparison fitting? What might the author of the article have wanted to convey? (L.O. 2)
3. Why do executives and managers spend more time listening than do workers? (L.O. 3)
4. What arguments could you give for or against the idea that body language is a science with principles that specialists can interpret accurately? (L.O. 4)
5. **Ethical Issue:** After much discussion and even conflict, your workplace team has finally agreed on Plan B, but you are firmly convinced that Plan A is a much better option. Your team is presenting Plan B to the whole department, and company executives are present. A vice president asks you for your opinion. Should you (a) keep your mouth shut, (b) try to persuade the team to adopt Plan A, (c) explain why you believe Plan A is a better plan, (d) tell the VP and all present that Plan B is not your idea, or (e) discuss one or two points you can agree on in Plan B?[79]

Activities

2.1 Reaching Group Decisions: Majority, Consensus, or What? (L.O. 1)

Team

YOUR TASK In small groups decide which decision strategy is best for the following situations:

a. A logistics company needs to identify a more central, less expensive location for a distribution center.
b. A team of 15 employees must decide whether to choose the iPad or an Android tablet for their new equipment. Some team members dislike Apple's closed system and prefer the more open Android platform. However, Apple offers more apps.
c. Company employees numbering over 900 must decide whether to adopt a floating holiday plan proposed by management or stay with the current plan. A yes-or-no vote is required.
d. The owner of your company is meeting with all managers to decide which departments will be allowed to move into a new facility.
e. Appointed by management, an employee team is charged with making recommendations regarding casual Fridays. Management feels that too many employees are abusing the privilege.
f. Members of a business club must decide which members will become officers.
g. A group of town officials and volunteers must decide how to organize a town website and social media presence. Only a few members have technical expertise.
h. An employee committee of three members (two supervisors and the manager) must decide on promotions within a department.

2.2 Resolving Workplace Conflicts: Apply a Plan (L.O. 1)

Team

Although conflict is a normal part of every workplace, if unresolved, it can create hard feelings and reduce productivity.

YOUR TASK Analyze the following scenarios. In teams, discuss each scenario and apply the six-step procedure for dealing with conflict outlined in Figure 2.3. Choose two of the scenarios to role-play, with two of your team members taking roles.

a. During an important meeting, several agenda items deal with actions that are crucial to the success of a current project. They require that key decisions be made—fast! As usual, Gina is joking and telling entertaining anecdotes without regard for the meeting's urgency. Pete is becoming impatient and irritated. He doesn't understand why the other meeting participants, and the boss in particular, don't stop Gina's antics.

b. Zara, an accountant, cannot complete her report until Bailey, a salesman, provides her with all the necessary numbers and documentation. Zara thinks that Bailey is a procrastinator who forces her to deliver a rush job, thus causing her great stress and increasing the likelihood of error. Bailey believes that Zara is exerting pressure on both of them and setting unrealistic deadlines. As the conflict is intensifying, productivity decreases.

c. A company policy manual is posted and updated at the company intranet, an internal website. Employees must sign that they have read and understand the manual. A conflict arises when team member Xavier insists that employees should sign electronically. Fellow team member Luna thinks that a paper form should be signed by employees so that better records may be kept.

d. The author of a lengthy report refuses to collaborate with a colleague on future projects because she believes that her colleague's review of her document was superficial, short, and essentially useless. The report author is angry at the lack of attention her 25-page paper received.

e. Two management team members disagree about a new company social media policy. One wants to ban personal visits to Facebook and Twitter totally. The other believes that an outright ban is impossible to implement and might raise the ire of employees. He is more concerned with limiting Internet misuse, including visits to online game, pornography, and shopping sites. The management team members agree that they need a social media policy, but they disagree on what to allow and what to prohibit.

f. A manager and his assistant plan to attend a conference together at a resort location. Six weeks before the conference, the company announces a cutback and limits conference attendance to one person. The assistant, who has developed a presentation specifically for the conference, feels that he should be the one to attend. Travel arrangements must be made immediately.

2.3 Soft Skills: Personal Strengths Inventory (L.O. 1)

Web

When hiring future workers, employers look for hard skills (those we learn such as mastery of software applications or accountancy procedures) and soft skills. Soft skills are personal characteristics, strengths, and other assets. Studies have divided soft skills into four categories:

- Thinking and problem solving
- Oral and written communication
- Personal qualities and work ethic
- Interpersonal and teamwork

YOUR TASK Using the preceding categories to guide you, identify your own soft skills, paying attention to those you think a potential employer would value. Prepare lists of at least four items in each of the four categories. For example, as evidence of problem solving, you might list a specific workplace or student problem you recognized and solved. You will want to weave these words and phrases into cover letters and résumés, which are covered in Chapter 15.

2.4 Soft Skills: Which Competencies Are Most Desirable? (L.O. 1)

YOUR TASK Check job listings in your field at an online job board. Visit a job board such as Monster, CollegeRecruiter, CareerBuilder, or Indeed. Follow the instructions to search job categories and locations. Study many job listings in your field. Then prepare a list of the most frequently requested soft skills in your area of interest. Next to each item on the list, indicate the degree to which you believe you have the skill or trait mentioned. Your instructor may ask you to submit your findings and/or report to the class. If you are not satisfied with the selection at any job site, choose another.

2.5 Meeting Malaise: Beyond Contempt (L.O. 2)

Team | Web

"Meetings are indispensable when you don't want to do anything," observed the late economist John Kenneth Galbraith. This sentiment was echoed by Stanford professor Thomas Sowell, who declared: "People who enjoy meetings should not be in charge of anything." Finally, management guru Peter Drucker claimed: "Meetings are a symptom of a bad organization. The fewer meetings, the better."[80]

Much venomous ink has been spilled decrying meetings, but they won't go away because—despite their potential shortcomings—many workplace gatherings are necessary.

YOUR TASK Examine the preceding quotations and perhaps other statements deriding meetings. Are they exaggerations or accurate assessments? If the assertions of wastefulness are true, what does that mean for the health of organizations conducting large numbers of meetings? Individually or as a team, search the Web for information in defense of meetings. (a) Begin by discussing your own and classmates' experience with workplace meetings. (b) Interview your parents, other relatives, and friends about meetings. (c) Finding gripes is easy, but search the Web for advice on making meetings more effective. What information beyond the tips in this book can you find? In a class discussion or individually—perhaps in writing or in a slide presentation, such as PowerPoint, if your instructor directs—introduce your findings.

2.6 Stand-Up Meetings: Keeping Business Meetings Short and Sweet (L.O. 2)

Communication Technology | E-Mail | Team

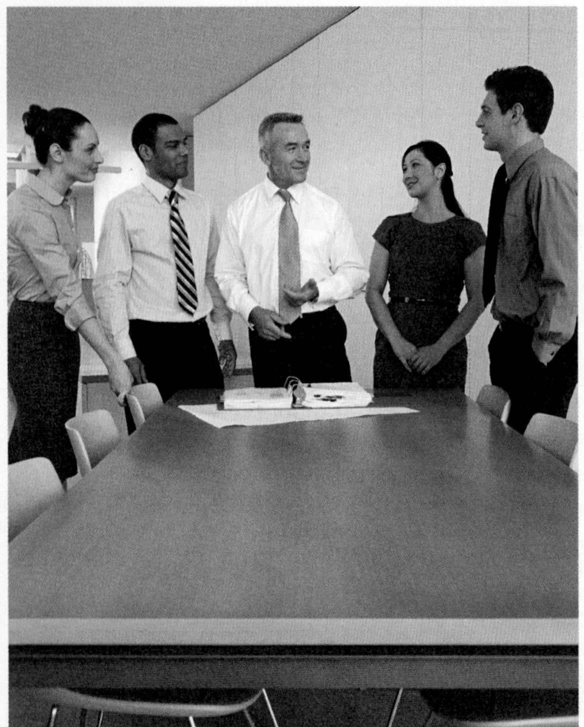

XiXinXing/Shutterstock.com

Here is an idea to shorten tedious meetings: Ban sitting down! A growing number of tech companies hold mandatory morning meetings in which nonwork chatter is frowned upon and all participants must stand. Called *the huddle* in one company and *a daily scrum* in another, these regular stand-up meetings last no longer than 15 minutes. At one company, if someone starts rambling, an employee holds up a rubber rat. A Microsoft development team determines the next speaker by tossing around a rubber chicken called Ralph. Other gimmicks include passing around a 10-pound medicine ball to literally keep the meeting moving. At one company, latecomers must pay a small fine, run a lap around the office building, or sing a nursery rhyme such as "I'm a Little Teapot." Other methods to speed up the proceedings include holding meetings just before lunch or gathering in cold stairwells.[81]

The idea of stand-up meetings is spreading in the wake of Agile, a method in software development that involves compressing lengthy projects into short segments. This approach also includes speedy daily updates from colleagues about three things: what was accomplished since the previous meeting, what will be done today, and what stands in the way of finishing the job. It turns out that the practice of holding meetings standing up dates back to some military commanders in World War I. A researcher who conducted a study of stand-up meetings found that they were about a third shorter than sit-down meetings, and the quality of decision making did not suffer at all. A recent survey of more than 6,000 global tech workers found that 78 percent held daily stand-up meetings.[82]

YOUR TASK As a team, brainstorm all possible applications of quick stand-up meetings. What types of businesses could benefit from such meetings? How would you ensure on-time arrival, participation and order during the meeting, and turn-taking? What type of sanctions would you impose for violations? If your instructor directs, write an e-mail (see Chapter 4) to persuade your current or past boss to adopt stand-up meetings.

2.7 Virtual Meetings: Improving Distance Meeting Buy-In (L.O. 2)

Communication Technology | Team | Web

Marina Elliot works at the headquarters for a large HMO that contracts with physicians across the nation. Her position requires her to impose organizational objectives and systems on smaller groups that often resist such interference. Marina recently needed to inform regional groups that the home office was instituting a systemwide change to hiring practices. To save costs, she set up a Web conference between her office in Charlotte and others in Chicago, Denver, and Seattle. Marina set the meeting for 10 a.m. Eastern Standard Time. At the designated date and hour, she found that the Seattle team was not logged in and she had to delay the session. When the Seattle team finally did log in, Marina launched into her presentation. She explained the reasons behind the change in a PowerPoint presentation that contained complex data she had not distributed prior to the conference. Marina heard cell phone ringtones and typing in the background as she spoke. Still, she pushed through her one-hour presentation without eliciting any feedback.

YOUR TASK In teams, discuss ways Marina might have improved the Web conference. Prepare a list of recommendations from your team.

2.8 Virtual Meetings: Connecting by Skype to Clarify an Order (L.O. 2)

Communication Technology | Social Media | Web

Paramount Fitness Corporation, a commercial strength equipment manufacturer in California, contracts with several distributors overseas who exclusively sell Paramount weight machines to gyms and fitness studios, not to the general public. The distributor in the UK, Mr. Rowan Been, has sent a confusing order by e-mail containing incorrect item numbers and product names as well as inconsistent quantities of items. Mr. Been doesn't respond to telephone calls or e-mail requests for clarification. You remember that you conversed with Mr. Been via Skype and notice to your delight that your distributor is online.

YOUR TASK Using Skype or FaceTime, call a classmate designated to play Mr. Been and request clarification of the rather large order. Improvise the details of the order in a Skype or FaceTime call to your peer (with or without a camera) applying the tips for virtual meetings in this chapter. Alternatively, your instructor may introduce a short background fact sheet or script for each participant, guiding your conversation and defining your roles and the particulars of the order. To use Skype with or without a camera, select a laptop, computer lab desktop computer, smartphone, iPod Touch, or iPad. This exchange can occur in the classroom or computer lab where the image can be projected onto a screen. The person playing the remote Skype partner should leave the room and connect from a quiet place outside. Fellow students and your instructor will evaluate your virtual meeting with Mr. Been.

2.9 Listening: An In-Person or Virtual Social Media Interview (L.O. 3)

Communication Technology Social Media Team

How much and to whom do businesspeople listen?

YOUR TASK Interview a businessperson about his or her workplace listening. Connect with a worker in your circle of friends, family, and acquaintances; in your campus network; at a prior or current job; or via LinkedIn or Facebook. Come up with questions to ask about listening—for example: (a) How much active listening do you practice daily? (b) To whom do you listen on the job? (c) How do you know that others are listening or not listening to you? (d) Can you share anecdotes of poor listening that led to negative outcomes? (e) Do you have tips for better listening?

2.10 Nonverbal Communication: Body Language (L.O. 4)

YOUR TASK What attitudes do the following body movements suggest to you? Do these movements always mean the same thing? What part does context play in your interpretations?

a. Whistling, wringing hands

b. Bowed posture, twiddling thumbs

c. Steepled hands, sprawling sitting position

d. Rubbing hand through hair

e. Open hands, unbuttoned coat

f. Wringing hands, tugging ears

2.11 Nonverbal Communication: Signals Sent by Casual Attire (L.O. 4)

Communication Technology E-Mail

Social Media Team 

Although many employers allow casual attire, not all employers and customers are happy with the results. To learn more about the implementation, acceptance, and effects of casual-dress programs, select one of the following activities, all of which involve some form of interviewing.

YOUR TASK

a. In teams, gather information from human resources directors to determine which companies allow casual-dress, or dress-down, days, how often, and under what conditions. The information may be collected by personal interviews, e-mail, telephone, or instant messaging.

b. In teams, conduct inquiring-reporter interviews. Ask individuals in the community how they react to casual dress in the workplace. Develop a set of standard interview questions.

c. In teams, visit local businesses on both casual-dress days and traditional business-dress days. Compare and contrast the effects of business-dress standards on such factors as the projected image of the company, the nature of the interactions with customers and with fellow employees, the morale of employees, and the productivity of employees. What generalizations can you draw from your findings?

2.12 The Silent Language of Tattoos: How Much Self-Expression on the Job? (L.O. 4)

Communication Technology E-Mail

Social Media Team

Tattoos and piercings have gained in popularity among young Americans over the last two decades. Recent findings by a Harris Poll and Pew Research Center suggest that nearly 40 percent of eighteen- to twenty-nine-year-olds and about one third of thirty- to forty-five-year-olds sport tattoos. Even so, body art is still not universally accepted.[83] Employment services firm Challenger, Gray & Christmas reports that job candidates among the millennials, also called Generation Y, do not particularly try to hide their body art. About 25 percent of this generation also show off piercings in places other than their earlobes.

CEO John Challenger suggests that a generational shift accounts for the changing mores: "Those making hiring decisions are younger and not as adherent to traditions about workplace appearance." Career expert Andrea Kay agrees, but she warns that acceptance among hiring managers varies by industry. She says that recruiters in the technology and retail fields may be more forgiving than those in banking and law. Tattoos and piercings send a strong message, and Kay cautions that if they make people at work uncomfortable, such decorations are detrimental. She has the following advice for job seekers: "People have adjusted their thinking in what is acceptable, but it still comes down to the impression you want to make on the people you're dealing with in your business."[84] Many workplaces today have policies covering body adornment, some requiring employees with customer contact to conceal such decorations.

YOUR TASK In teams or in class, discuss tattoos as a form of self-expression in the workplace. Gauge the attitudes toward tattoos and piercings in your class. Consider the limits to self-expression on the job. Think about casual clothing or blogging and tweeting about your employer. What is different? What are some of the similarities among these forms of self-expression? What types of nonverbal cues do body adornments send? Summarize your discussion orally or in an e-mail to your instructor. Alternatively, your instructor may ask you to post your responses to a Blackboard discussion board or some other forum that allows individual postings.

2.13 Nonverbal Communication Around the World (L.O. 4)

Intercultural | Web

Gestures play an important role when people communicate. Because culture shapes the meaning of gestures, miscommunication and misunderstanding can easily result in international situations.

YOUR TASK Use the Web to research the meanings of selected gestures. Make a list of ten gestures (other than those discussed in the text) that have different meanings in different countries. Consider the fingertip kiss, nose thumb, eyelid pull, nose tap, head shake, and other gestures. How are the meanings different in other countries?

2.14 Business Etiquette: Breaking the Smartphone Habit in Meetings (L.O. 5)

Communication Technology | Social Media | Team

Not long ago it was almost a status symbol for professionals to "lay [their] BlackBerrys or iPhones on a conference table before a meeting—like gunfighters placing their Colt revolvers on the card tables in a saloon."[85] Businesspeople would compulsively eyeball their smartphones and tablets to read e-mail, search Google, and check Facebook or Twitter during meetings. In fact, in a Robert Half Management survey, 85 percent of executives stated that meeting participants reading and responding to e-mails on their mobile devices is a common sight. However, the tide is turning. Increasingly, many professionals are tired of disruptions caused by electronic gadgets during meetings.

Etiquette consultants concur: "Electronic devices are like the smoking of the '90s," says Pamela Eyring, president of the Protocol School of Washington. "Companies are aggravated and losing productivity." Businesses hire her to enact formal policies and to teach workers "why it's not a good idea to be texting while your boss is speaking at the podium," Eyring says.[86] Nancy Flynn, executive director of the ePolicy Institute and author of *The Handbook of Social Media,* has this suggestion: "Require employees to turn off mobile devices during business-related meetings, seminars, conferences, luncheons and any other situation in which a ringing phone or tapping fingers are likely to disrupt proceedings or interrupt a speaker's or participant's train of thought."

Flynn notes that banning electronic devices in meetings is not just about interruptions: "You don't want employees shooting video via a smartphone during a meeting in which company secrets are discussed, then uploading the video to YouTube or sharing it with a competitor, reporter or other third party."[87]

YOUR TASK Organizations are only beginning to establish policies on smartphone use in meetings. Assume that your team has been asked to develop such a policy. Your boss can't decide whether to ask your team to develop a short policy or a more rigorous one. Unable to make a decision, he asks for two statements: (a) a short statement that treats employees as grown-ups who can exercise intelligent judgment and (b) a more complete set of guidelines that spell out exactly what should and should not be done.

Test Your Etiquette IQ

New communication platforms and casual workplace environments have blurred the lines of appropriateness, leaving workers wondering how to navigate uncharted waters. Indicate whether the following statements are true or false. Then see if you agree with the responses on p. R-1.

1. If a business meeting is long and you are not directly involved, it is acceptable for you to perform minor grooming tasks such as combing your hair, applying lipstick, or clipping your fingernails—as long as you do it discreetly.

   ________ True ________ False

2. At a business function designed to help people network and make contacts, you should plan to spend 15 to 20 minutes with each individual and then move on.

   ________ True ________ False

3. Even though you may be working on a team project together, you should not open the closed door of a coworker without knocking first.

   ________ True ________ False

Chat About It

In each chapter you will find five discussion questions related to the chapter material. Your instructor may assign these topics for you to discuss in class, in an online chat room, or on an online discussion board. Some of the discussion topics may require outside research. You may also be asked to read and respond to postings made by your classmates.

TOPIC 1: The Office of Disability Employment Policy in the U.S. Department of Labor provides information about employability skills—for example, enthusiasm and attitude. The agency concludes that a positive and enthusiastic attitude is critical to workplace success. How can you demonstrate a positive and enthusiastic attitude to your employer? What if you hate your job?

TOPIC 2: Suppose you are working on a team that has one or two dominant individuals who make most of the decisions and who sometimes don't consider your ideas. Instead of giving up and not participating, what could you do that would be more helpful to the team and to your career?

TOPIC 3: Psychologists say that we fear rejection when deviating from group consensus; we try to avoid the "hazards of courage" and may consequently fall victim to groupthink. Recall a past or present team experience. Can you relate to feeling "the pain of independence" when going against the majority opinion?

TOPIC 4: Consider a situation in your family, in your circle of friends, in high school, at college, during an internship, or at work that shows the potential risks of poor listening skills. How could the resulting misunderstandings or other negative consequences have been prevented? Which techniques would have helped avert the undesirable outcome?

TOPIC 5: A realtor who missed out on a $12,000 commission because he was serving on a sequestered jury that prohibited the use of cell phones has no regrets. He considers it rude to answer a phone during a meeting with a client and purposely leaves his phone in the car to avoid temptation.[88] What events would justify remaining permanently tethered to your mobile phone? What types of situations would warrant turning off or at least ignoring your electronic devices?

Grammar and Mechanics | *Review 2*

Verbs

Review Guides 4 through 9 in Appendix D, Grammar and Mechanics Guide, beginning on page D-2. On a separate sheet, revise the following sentences to correct any errors in verb use. For each error that you locate, write the guide number that reflects this usage. If a sentence is correct, write *C*.

EXAMPLE: If Rachel was in charge, she would have handled the matter differently.

REVISION: If Rachel were in charge, she would have handled the matter differently. [Guide 5]

1. Have you spoke with the other members of the virtual team?
2. During job interviews one of the most frequently requested soft skills are writing proficiency.
3. Meredith said she wished she was team leader for just one day.
4. Better decisions and faster response time explains why companies are using teams.
5. Neither the speaker nor members of the team was bothered by the technical mishap.
6. Conflict and disagreement is normal and should be expected in team interactions.
7. Every piece of information including e-mails and texts were made public during the trial.
8. A committee of faculty and students are examining strategies to improve campus conservation efforts.
9. Each of the employees was given the opportunity to chose a team to join.
10. When two candidates have equal qualifications, the one who appears to be more polished and professional is more likely to be hired and promoted.

References

[1] Nagy, E. (2015, January 22). The women leaders driving Lyft's impressive growth. Fastcompany.com. Retrieved from http://www.fastcompany.com/3041106/most-creative-people/the-women-leaders-driving-lyfts-impressive-growth

[2] Buhr, S. (2015, September 15). TC Cribs: A look inside Lyft's quirky, hot pink HQ. [Video file]. Video posted to http://techcrunch.com/2015/09/15/tc-cribs-a-look-inside-lyfts-quirky-hot-pink-hq

[3] Tjhayadi, H. (2015, June 5). What is it like to work for Lyft as a software engineer? Quora. Retrieved from https://www.quora.com/What-is-it-like-to-work-at-Lyft-as-a-software-engineer

[4] "Excellent culture!" (2015, May 26). Glassdoor. Retrieved from http://www.glassdoor.com/Reviews/Lyft-Reviews-E700614_P3.htm?filter.employmentStatus=REGULAR&filter.employmentStatus=PART_TIME&filter.employmentStatus=UNKNOWN

[5] Robert Half Technology. (2013, July 11). Workforce 101: More than one-third of CIOs plan to hire new IT graduates; lack of interpersonal skills greatest obstacle to success. Retrieved from http://rht.mediaroom.com/2013-07-11-Workforce-101-More-Than-One-Third-of-CIOs-Plan-to-Hire-New-IT-Graduates-Lack-of-Interpersonal-Skills-Greatest-Obstacle-to-Success?_ga=1.240489411.1712269979.1440284830

[6] Bryant, A. (2012, April 7). The phones are out, but the robot is in. *International New York Times*. Retrieved from http://www.nytimes.com/2012/04/08/business/phil-libin-of-evernote-on-its-unusual-corporate-culture.html

[7] Lechner, A. (2012, April 18). Better teamwork through better workplace design. *Harvard Business Review*. Retrieved from http://blogs.hbr.org/cs/2012/04/better_teamwork_through_office.html

[8] Gensler. (2013, June 26). Press release: Gensler releases 2013 U.S. workplace survey. Retrieved from www.gensler.com

[9] Waber, B., Mangolfi, J., & Lindsay, G. (2014, October). Workspaces that move people. *Harvard Business Review*. Retrieved from https://hbr.org/2014/10/workspaces-that-move-people; Spreitzer, G., Bacevice, P., & Garrett, L. (2015, September). Why people thrive in coworking spaces. *Harvard Business Review*. Retrieved from https://hbr.org/2015/05/why-people-thrive-in-coworking-spaces; Ritz, J. (2016, January 9). See how this 1930s building in Hollywood is transformed into the workplace of the future. *Los Angeles Times*. Retrieved from http://www.latimes.com/home/la-hm-neuehouse-20160109-story.html

[10] Cain, S. (2012, January 13). The rise of the new groupthink. *The New York Times*. Retrieved from http://www.nytimes.com/2012/01/15/opinion/sunday/the-rise-of-the-new-groupthink.html?pagewanted=all

[11] Coutu, D. (2009, May). Why teams don't work. *Harvard Business Review, 87*(5), 100. Retrieved from http://search.ebscohost.com

[12] Cain, S. (2012, January 13). The rise of the new groupthink. *The New York Times*. Retrieved from http://www.nytimes.com/2012/01/15/opinion/sunday/the-rise-of-the-new-groupthink.html?pagewanted=all

[13] Zofi, Y. S. (2012). *A manager's guide to virtual teams*. New York: American Management Association, p. 1.

[14] The Wall Street Journal & Society for Human Resource Management. (2012). Employment trends 2012. Retrieved from http://www.shrm.org/research/documents/wsjbrochuresinglepages.pdf

[15] Geiger, F. (2014, December 22). Germany's big firms pay price for small-town ties. *The Wall Street Journal*. Retrieved from http://www.wsj.com/articles/germanys-big-firms-pay-price-for-small-town-ties-1419305459

[16] Siebdrat, F., Hoegl, M., & Ernst, H. (2009, Summer). How to manage virtual teams. *MIT Sloan Management Review, 50*(4), p. 64. Retrieved from http://search.ebscohost.com

[17] Discussion of Tuckman's model based on Robbins, H. A., & Finley, M. (2000). *The new why teams don't work*. San Francisco: Berrett-Koehler, Chapter 29.

[18] Discussion of conflict and groupthink based on Toledo, R. (2008, June). Conflict is everywhere. *PM Network*. Retrieved from http://search.ebscohost.com; McNamara, P. (2003, August/September). Conflict resolution strategies. *OfficePro*, p. 25; Weiss, W. (2002, November). Building and managing teams. *SuperVision*, p. 19; Eisenhardt, K. (1997, July/August). How management teams can have a good fight. *Harvard Business Review*, pp. 77-85; Brockmann, E. (1996, May). Removing the paradox of conflict from group decisions. *Academy of Management Executives*, pp. 61-62; and Beebe, S., & Masterson, J. (1999). *Communicating in small groups*. New York: Longman, pp. 198-200.

[19] Emory University neuroscientist Gregory Berns quoted in Cain, S. (2012, January 13). The rise of the new groupthink. *The New York Times*. Retrieved from http://www.nytimes.com/2012/01/15/opinion/sunday/the-rise-of-the-new-groupthink.html?pagewanted=all

[20] J. Richard Hackman quoted in Coutu, D. (2009, May). Why teams don't work. *Harvard Business Review, 87*(5), 105. Retrieved from http://search.ebscohost.com

[21] Janis, I. L. (1982). *Groupthink: Psychological studies on policy decisions and fiascoes*. Boston: Houghton Mifflin. See also Miranda, S. M., & Saunders, C. (1995, Summer). Group support systems:

An organization development intervention to combat groupthink. *Public Administration Quarterly, 19*, 193-216. Retrieved from http://search.ebscohost.com

[22] Rey, J. (2010, June). Team building. *Inc., 32*(5), 68-71; Romando, R. (2006, November 9). Advantages of corporate team building. Ezine Articles. Retrieved from http://ezinearticles.com/?Advantages-of-Corporate-Team-Building&id=352961; Amason, A. C., Hochwarter, W. A., Thompson, K. R., & Harrison, A. W. (1995, Autumn). Conflict: An important dimension in successful management teams. *Organizational Dynamics, 24*, 1. Retrieved from http://search.ebscohost.com

[23] Ruffin, B. (2006, January). T.E.A.M. work: Technologists, educators, and media specialists collaborating. *Library Media Connection, 24*(4), 49. Retrieved from http://search.ebscohost.com; Parnell, C. (1996, November 1). Teamwork: Not a new idea, but it's transforming the workplace. *Executive Speeches, 63*, 46. Retrieved from http://search.ebscohost.com

[24] Ferrazzi, K. (2013, December 18). To make virtual teams succeed, pick the right players. HBR Blog Network. Retrieved from https://hbr.org/2013/12/to-make-virtual-teams-succeed-pick-the-right-players; Holtzman, Y., & Anderberg, J. (2011). Diversify your teams and collaborate: Because great minds don't think alike. *The Journal of Management Development, 30*(1), 79. doi: 10.1108/02621711111098389; Katzenbach, J., & Smith, D. (1994). *Wisdom of teams*. New York: HarperBusiness, p. 45.

[25] Montana Department of Transportation. (2015, June). Success through partnerships: Montana, Section 402. Retrieved from http://www.mdt.mt.gov/publications/docs/brochures/safety/safety_plan.pdf

[26] Austin, M. (2012, May 21). Wasted time in meetings costs businesses £26 billion. Techradar. Retrieved from http://www.techradar.com/us/news/world-of-tech/roundup/wasted-time-in-meetings-costs-businesses-26-billion-1081238; Herring, H. B. (2006, June 18). Endless meetings: The black holes of the workday. *The New York Times*. Retrieved from http://www.nytimes.com

[27] Loechner, J. (2009, May 12). Meeting optimization too. MediaPost. Retrieved from http://www.mediapost.com; Hollon, J. (2007, November 5). Meeting malaise. *Workforce Management, 68*(19). Retrieved from http://search.ebscohost.com

[28] Rogelberg, S. G., Shanock, L. R., & Scott, C. W. (2012). Wasted time and money in meetings: Increasing return on investment. *Small Group Research, 43*(2), 237. doi: 10.1177/1046496411429170

[29] Francisco, J. (2007, November/December). How to create and facilitate meetings that matter. *The Information Management Journal*, p. 54. Retrieved from http://search.ebscohost.com

[30] Gouveia, A. (2012). Wasting time at work 2012. Salary.com. Retrieved from http://www.salary.com/wasting-time-at-work-2012

[31] Shellenbarger, S. (2012, May 16). Meet the meeting killers—In the office, they strangle ideas, poison progress; how to fight back. *The Wall Street Journal*. Retrieved from http://search.proquest.com

[32] Shellenbarger, S. (2014, December 2). Stop wasting everyone's time. *The Wall Street Journal*. Retrieved from http://www.wsj.com/articles/how-to-stop-wasting-colleagues-time-1417562658

[33] Rogelberg, S. G., Shanock, L. R., & Scott, C. W. (2012). Wasted time and money in meetings: Increasing return on investment. *Small Group Research, 43*(2), 237. doi: 10.1177/1046496411429170

[34] Wuorio. J. (2010). 8 ways to show speaking skills in a meeting. Microsoft Business. Retrieved from http://webs.anokaramsey.edu/widdel/ftp/b1121/8%20ways%20to%20show%20speaking%20skills%20in%20a%20meeting.pdf

[35] Blenko, M. W., Rogers, P., & Mankins, M. C. (2010, September 27). *Decide and deliver: Five steps to breakthrough performance in your organization*. Boston, MA: HBR Press; Francisco, J. (2007, November/December). How to create and facilitate meetings that matter. *The Information Management Journal*, p. 54. Retrieved from http://search.ebscohost.com

[36] Frisch, B., & Peck, J. (2010, May 14). Meetings: How many people should be in the room? *Bloomberg Businessweek*. Retrieved from http://www.businessweek.com/managing/content/may2010/ca2010054_344173.htm

[37] Timberland responsibility. (2012). Retrieved from http://responsibility.timberland.com/service/?story=3; Marquis, C. (2003, July). Doing well and doing good. *The New York Times*, p. BU2.

[38] Based on Egan, M. (2006, March 13). Meetings can make or break your career. *Insurance Advocate, 117*, p. 24.

[39] Lohr, S. (2008, July 22). As travel costs rise, more meetings go virtual. *The New York Times*. Retrieved from http://www.nytimes.com

[40] Schlegel, J. (2012). Running effective meetings: Types of meetings. Salary.com. Retrieved from http://www.salary.com/running-effectivemeetings-6; Cohen, M. A., Rogelberg, S. G. Allen, J. A., & Luong, A. (2011). Meeting design characteristics and attendee perceptions of staff /team meeting quality. *Group Dynamics: Theory, Research, and Practice, 15*(1), 100–101; Schindler, E. (2008, February 15). Running an effective teleconference or virtual meeting. CIO. Retrieved from www.cio.com. See also Brenowitz, R. S. (2004, May). Virtual meeting etiquette. Article 601, Innovative Leader. Retrieved from http://www.winstonbrill.com

[41] Based on French, S. (2016, March 14.) Ten etiquette rules for videoconferencing. *The Wall Street Journal*, p. R4.

[42] Tips on meetings: Two rules for making global meetings work. (2011, April 11). *Harvard Business Review*. Retrieved from http://hbr.org/web/management-tip/tips-on-meetings

[43] Bryant, A. (2012, April 7). The phones are out, but the robot is in. *International New York Times*. Retrieved from http://www.nytimes.com/2012/04/08/business/phil-libin-of-evernote-on-its-unusual-corporate-culture.html

[44] Fox, J. (2014, October 8). Why virtual conferences will not replace face-to-face meetings. International Meetings Review. Retrieved from http://www.internationalmeetingsreview.com/research-education/why-virtual-conferences-will-not-replace-face-face-meetings-100145

[45] Rowh, M. (2006, April/May). Listen up! Tune out distractions, and tune in to people. Here's how listening skills help lead to success. *Career World, 34*(6), 22. Retrieved from http://search.ebscohost.com; Robbins, H., & Finley, M. (1995). *Why teams don't work*. Princeton, NJ: Peterson's/Pacesetter Books, p. 123.

[46] Pellet, J. (2003, April). Anatomy of a turnaround guru. *Chief Executive*, 41; Mounter, P. (2003). Global internal communication: A model. *Journal of Communication Management, 3*, 265; Feiertag, H. (2002, July 15). Listening skills, enthusiasm top list of salespeople's best traits. *Hotel and Motel Management*, 20; Goby, V. P., & Lewis, J. H. (2000, June). The key role of listening in business: A study of the Singapore insurance industry. *Business Communication Quarterly, 63*, 41-51; Cooper, L. O. (1997, December). Listening competency in the workplace: A model for training. *Business Communication Quarterly, 60*, 75-84; and Penley, L. E., Alexander, E. R., Jerigan, I. E., & Henwood, C. I. (1997). Communication abilities of managers: The relationship to performance. *Journal of Management, 17*, 57-76.

[47] Charan, R. (2012, June 21). The discipline of listening. HBR.org. Retrieved from https://hbr.org/2012/06/the-discipline-of-listening; Awang, F., Anderson, M. A., & Baker, C. J. (2003, Winter). Entry-level information services and support personnel: Needed workplace and technology skills. *The Delta Pi Epsilon Journal*, 48; and American Management Association. (1999, August). The challenges facing workers in the future. *HR Focus*, p. 6.

[48] Charan, R. (2012, June 21). The discipline of listening. HBR.org. Retrieved from https://hbr.org/2012/06/the-discipline-of-listening

[49] Rowh, M. (2006, April/May). Listen up! Tune out distractions, and tune in to people. Here's how listening skills help lead to success. *Career World, 34*(6), 22. Retrieved from http://search.ebscohost.com

[50] Crockett, R. O. (2011, March 14). Listening is critical in today's multicultural workplace. HBR.org. Retrieved from https://hbr.org/2011/03/shhh-listening-is-critical-in

[51] International Listening Association. (2009). Listening and speech rates. International Listening Association. Retrieved from http://www.listen.org

[52] Oracle. (2012, March). Consumer views of life help online 2012: A global perspective. Retrieved from http://www.oracle.com/us/products/applications/commerce/live-help-on-demand/oracle-live-help-wp-aamf-1624138.pdf

[53] Aberdeen Group. (2012, October). Social media and customer service: From listening to engagement. Oracle. Retrieved from http://www.oracle.com/us/products/applications/aberdeen-social-customer-svc-1902160.pdf

[54] Open and closed-ended questions. (2015). PewResearchCenter. Retrieved from http://www.people-press.org/methodology/questionnaire-design/open-and-closed-ended-questions; Effective communication. (1994, November). *Training Tomorrow*, 32-33.

[55] Winfrey, O. (2004, December). This month's mission. *O Magazine*, 28. Retrieved from http://www.oprah.com/omagazine/December-2004-What-Oprah-Knows-for-Sure; Oprah Winfrey Quotes. (n.d.). Goodreads.com. Retrieved from http://www.goodreads.com/author/quotes/3518.Oprah_Winfrey?page=4

[56] Wood, J. T. (2003). *Gendered lives: Communication, gender, and culture* (5th ed.). Belmont, CA: Wadsworth, pp. 119-120; Anderson, K. J., & Leaper, C. (1998, August). Meta-analyses of gender effects on conversational interruption: Who, what, when, where, and how. *Sex Roles: A*

Journal of Research, 225; and Booth-Butterfield, M. (1984). She hears: What they hear and why. *Personnel Journal*, *44*, 39.

[57] Tear. J. (1995, November 20). They just don't understand gender dynamics. *The Wall Street Journal*, p. A12; Wolfe, A. (1994, December 12). She just doesn't understand. *New Republic*, 26-34.

[58] Barker, L. L., & Watson, K. W. (2001). *Listen up: What you've never heard about the other half of every conversation: Mastering the art of listening*. New York: Macmillan, p. 138.

[59] Goudreau, J. (2012, March 22). Is your body language costing you a promotion? *Forbes*. Retrieved from http://www.forbes.com/sites/jennagoudreau/2012/03/22/will-your-body-language-mistakes-cost-you-a-promotion

[60] Birdwhistel, R. (1970). *Kinesics and context*. Philadelphia: University of Pennsylvania Press.

[61] Body speak: What are you saying? (2000, October). *Successful Meetings*, 49-51.

[62] Hall, E. T. (1966). *The hidden dimension*. Garden City, NY: Doubleday, pp. 107-122.

[63] Kluger, N. (2015). Epidemiology of tattoos in industrialized countries. In: Serup, J., Kluger, N., Bäumler, W., eds. *Tattooed skin and health*. Basel, Germany: Karger, p. 8.

[64] The tragic decline of business casual. (2010, October 6). Bloomberg Business. Retrieved from http://www.bloomberg.com/bw/stories/2010-10-06/the-tragic-decline-of-business-casual; Finney, P. (2007, October 23). Redefining business casual. *The New York Times*. Retrieved from http://search.ebscohost.com; see also Osterman, R. (2006, March 20). Casual loses its cool in business: More employers are trying to tighten up workplace clothing standards. *Sacramento Bee*. Retrieved from http://search.ebscohost.com; Business casual: Out of style? (2005, May). *HR Focus*, 9. Retrieved from http://search.ebscohost.com

[65] Cracking the dress code dilemma. (2015). Salary.com for Business. Retrieved from http://business.salary.com/cracking-the-dress-code-dilemma

[66] Wilkie, H. (2003, Fall). Professional presence. *The Canadian Manager*, 14; and Kaplan-Leiserson, L. (2000, November). Casual dress/back to business attire. *Training & Development*, 38-39.

[67] Kennedy, M. M. (1997, September-October). Is business casual here to stay? *Executive Female*, 31.

[68] Wood, N., & Benitez, T. (2003, April). Does the suit fit? *Incentive*, p. 31.

[69] Popick, J. (2012, September 21). 5 reasons to ditch your dress code. *Inc*. Retrieved from http://www.inc.com/janine-popick/5-reasons-to-ditch-your-dress-code.html

[70] Business casual out of style. (2005, May). *HR Focus*, *82*, 16. Retrieved from http://search.ebscohost.com; Egodigwe, L. (2003, March). Here come the suits. *Black Enterprise*, *33*, 59. Retrieved from http://search.ebscohost.com; and Summerson, C. (2002, November 18). The suit is back in business. *BusinessWeek*, p. 130.

[71] Mitchell, G. A., Skinner, L. B., & White, B. J. (2010). Essential soft skills for success in the twenty-first-century workforce as perceived by business educators. *The Delta Pi Epsilon Journal*, *52*(1). Retrieved from http://www.faqs.org/periodicals/201001/2036768821.html

[72] McEwen, B. C. (2010). Cross-cultural and international career exploration and employability skills. *National Business Education Association Yearbook 2010: Cross-Cultural and International Business Education*, *48*, 142.

[73] Porath, C. (2015, June 19). No time to be nice at work. *The New York Times*. Retrieved from http://www.nytimes.com/2015/06/21/opinion/sunday/is-your-boss-mean.html; Chao, L. (2006, January 17). Not-so-nice costs. *The Wall Street Journal*, p. B1.

[74] Rubin, C. (2010, July 12). The high cost of rudeness in the workplace. *Inc*. Retrieved from http://www.inc.com/news/articles/2010/07/how-rudeness-affects-the-workplace.html; Yu, W. (2012, January 3). Workplace rudeness has a ripple effect. *Scientific American*. Retrieved from http://www.scientificamerican.com/article.cfm?id=ripples-of-rudeness; Jayson, S. (2011, August 9). Incivility a growing problem at work, psychologists say. *USA Today*. Retrieved from http://www.usatoday.com/news/health/wellness/story/2011/08/Incivility-a-growing-problem-at-work-psychologists-say/49854130/1

[75] Porath, C., MacInnis, D., & Folkes, V. S. (2011, April 17). It's unfair: Why customers who merely observe an uncivil employee abandon the company. *Journal of Service Research*. doi: 10.1177/1094670511404393. Retrieved from http://jsr.sagepub.com/content/early/2011/04/15/1094670511404393

[76] Hughes, T. (2008). Being a professional. Wordconstructions.com. Retrieved from http://www.wordconstructions.com/articles/business/professional.html; Grove, C., & Hallowell, W. (2002). The seven balancing acts of professional behavior in the United States: A cultural values perspective. Grovewell.com. Retrieved from http://www.grovewell.com /pub-usa-professional.html

[77] Graves, J. A. (2013, January 15). 25 Career mistakes to banish for 2013. *U.S. News & World Report*. Retrieved from http://money.usnews.com/money/careers/slideshows/25-career-mistakes-to-banish-for-2013/17

[78] Gulley, P. (2009, March). 'Til we meet again: Nothing like a good old-fashioned business meeting to turn a crisis from bad to worse. *Indianapolis Monthly*, *32*(8). Retrieved from http://search.ebscohost.com

[79] Based on Ferguson. (2004). *Professional ethics and etiquette* (2nd ed.). New York: Ferguson.

[80] Hollon, J. (2007, November 13). Meeting malaise. *Workforce*. Retrieved from http://www.workforce.com/articles/6685-leading-the-way-in-hr-technology-january-2016

[81] Silverman, R. E. (2012, February 2). No more angling for the best seat; more meetings are stand-up jobs. *The Wall Street Journal*. Retrieved from http://www.wsj.com/articles/SB10001424052970204652904577193460472598378

[82] Ibid.

[83] Scenario based on Greenblatt, A. (2014, February 21). Job seekers still have to hide tattoos (from the neck up). National Public Radio. Retrieved from http://www.npr.org/2014/02/21/280213268/job-seekers-still-have-to-hide-tattoos-from-the-neck-up; Schepp, D. (2010, July 26). People@work: How to job hunt with tattoos. DailyFinance.com. Retrieved from http://www.dailyfinance.com/story/careers/tattoos-job-hunt-interviews-career/19566567

[84] Schepp, D. (2010, July 26). People@work: How to job hunt with tattoos. DailyFinance.com. Retrieved from http://www.dailyfinance.com/story/careers/tattoos-job-hunt-interviews-career/19566567

[85] Williams, A. (2008, June 24). At meetings, it's mind your BlackBerry or mind your manners. *The New York Times*, pp. A1, A3.

[86] O'Brien Coffey, J. (2011, September). How to manage smartphones at meetings. *Executive Travel Magazine*. Retrieved from http://www.executivetravelmagazine.com/articles/how-to-manage-smartphones-at-meetings

[87] Ibid.

[88] Ibid.

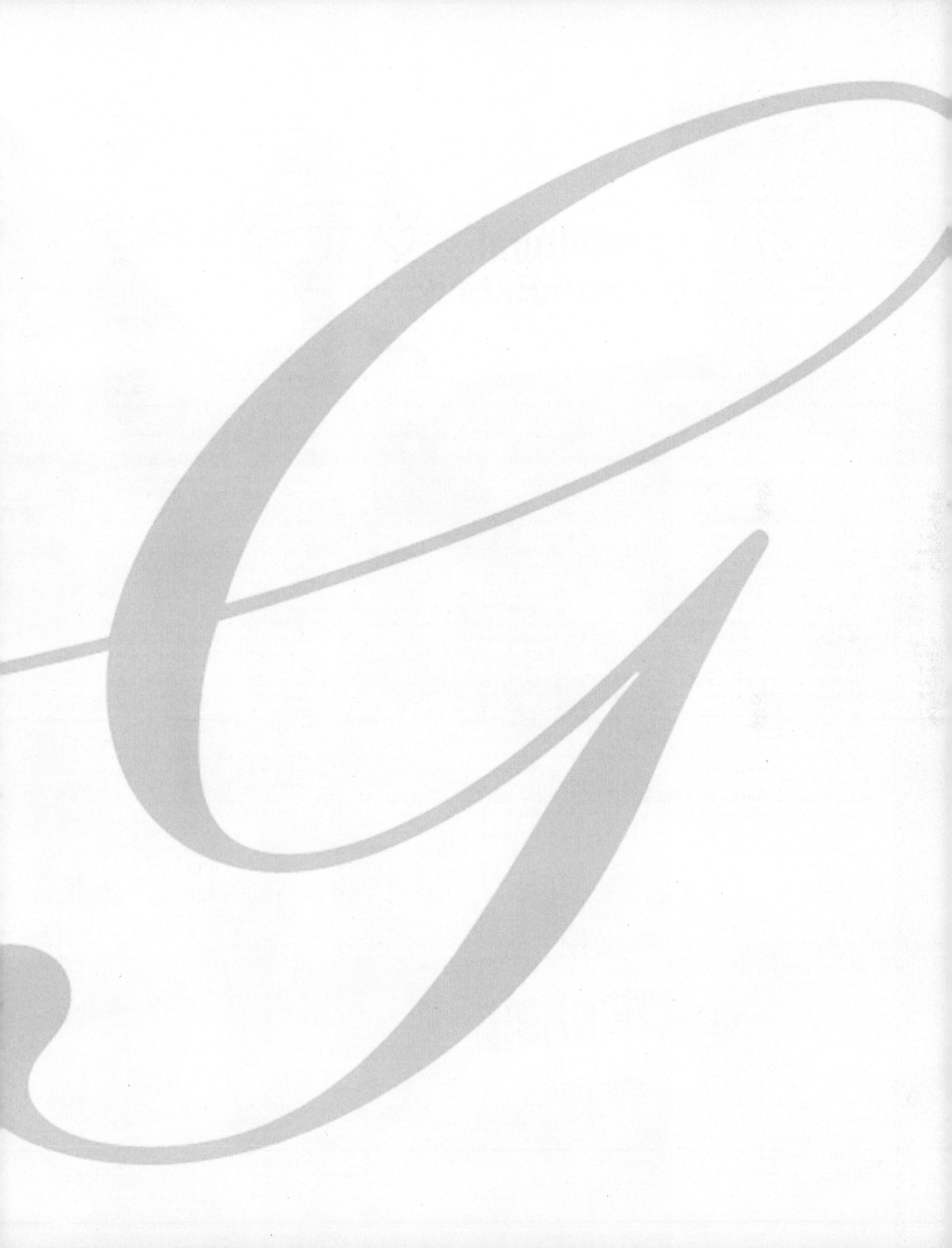

Chapter 3 Intercultural Communication

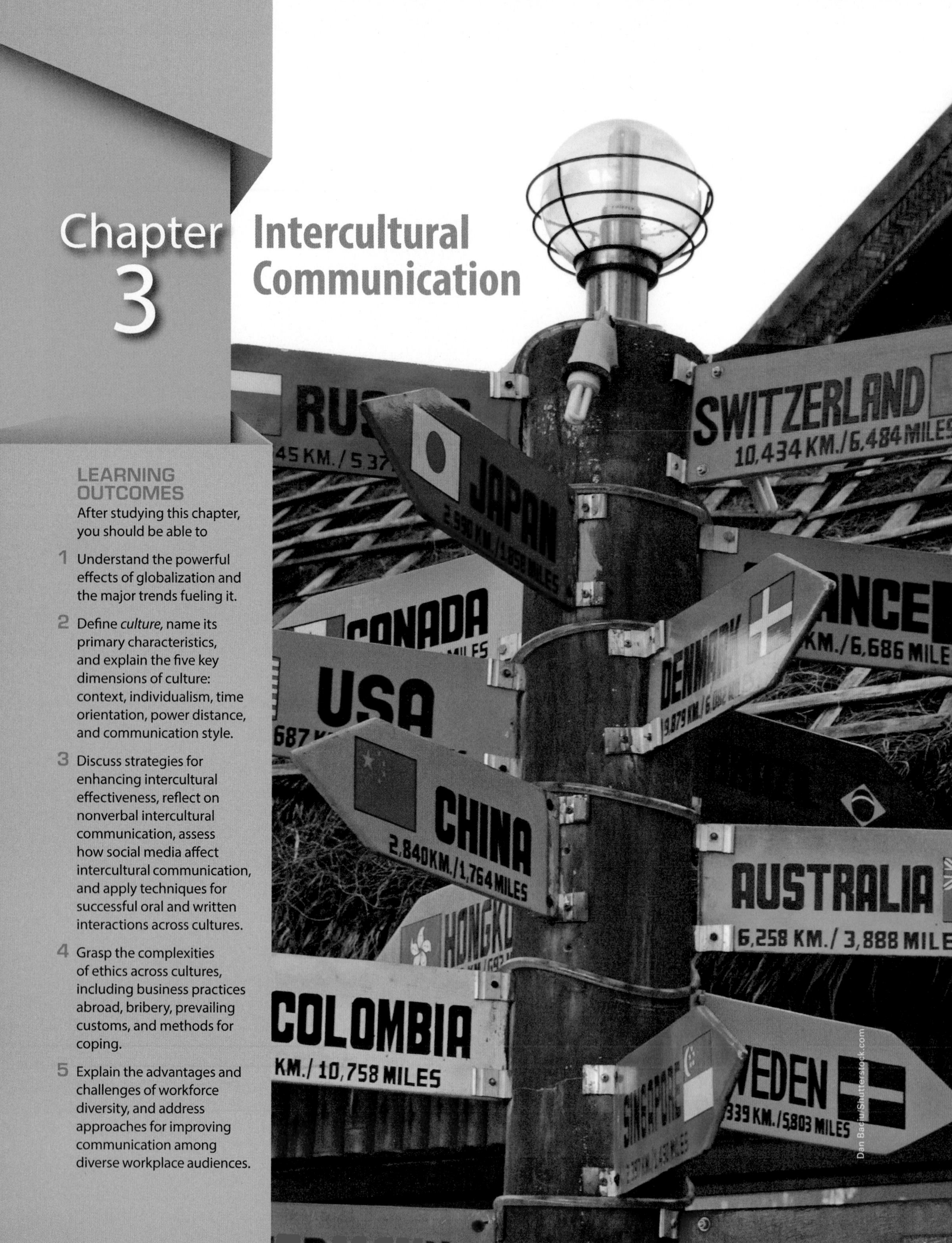

Dan Baciu/Shutterstock.com

LEARNING OUTCOMES

After studying this chapter, you should be able to

1 Understand the powerful effects of globalization and the major trends fueling it.

2 Define *culture,* name its primary characteristics, and explain the five key dimensions of culture: context, individualism, time orientation, power distance, and communication style.

3 Discuss strategies for enhancing intercultural effectiveness, reflect on nonverbal intercultural communication, assess how social media affect intercultural communication, and apply techniques for successful oral and written interactions across cultures.

4 Grasp the complexities of ethics across cultures, including business practices abroad, bribery, prevailing customs, and methods for coping.

5 Explain the advantages and challenges of workforce diversity, and address approaches for improving communication among diverse workplace audiences.

Intercultural and Ethics Challenges for the World's Largest Retailer

Yeamake/Shutterstock.com

Walmart's global intercultural blunders and occasional ethical lapses are well documented. In college business classes around the world, the giant retailer's missteps continue to serve as rich case studies of how not to expand abroad.[1] Walmart was forced to withdraw from its first European market, Germany, at a loss of $1 billion. Top executives didn't speak German; greeters with Midwestern folksiness were lost on German employees and shoppers. A court overturned Walmart's policy against dating coworkers, and the retailer's antiunion stance backfired in a country where unions and corporations collaborate closely.[2]

Walmart hasn't fared much better in Asia. Cultural differences and fierce local competition forced the world's largest retailer to exit South Korea. Consumers in this and other Asian countries don't buy in bulk. Koreans favor smaller packages and shop daily at a variety of stores.[3] In Japan Walmart recently shuttered 30 stores to cope with a fragmented market and brutal price competition,[4] but also because finicky Japanese consumers equate discounts with poor quality and don't trust a broad merchandise selection.[5] In India Walmart broke up with its local partner and was able to hold on only to its wholesale business without establishing superstores there. In addition, the Indian government investigated the company's foreign investment practices and other alleged misconduct.[6]

After entering China in 1996, Walmart failed to establish a strong presence in this lucrative market. Its key competitor, Sun Art, opted for a more localized approach and understood that Chinese shoppers prefer to buy groceries at outdoor markets, not in big-box stores. Also, more than everyday low prices, Chinese consumers desire quality and authenticity in products.[7] Says one analyst: "Instead of adjusting to the local competition by shrinking store sizes or selling higher margin products, Walmart is doing little to change its business model." He faults the retailer and other U.S. companies for not localizing their business models and management styles to keep up with new domestic players.[8] Another consultant concurs: "Companies can become complacent and arrogant and then they make mistakes when they expand overseas."[9]

In addition to adverse market forces and its intercultural slip-ups, Walmart has been the target of several bribery probes alleging possible violations of the Foreign Corrupt Practices Act in Mexico, India, China, and Brazil.[10] Can Walmart do better in its future international endeavors?

You will learn more about Walmart and be asked to complete a relevant task at the end of this chapter.

Critical Thinking

- When creating its international expansion policy, Walmart at first followed the advice of Harvard professor Theodore Levitt, who advocated standardization, not localization. "Gone are accustomed differences in national or regional preferences," Levitt wrote. Truly global firms sought to "force suitably standardized products and practices on the entire globe."[11] Should companies keep a standardized approach or adapt to local markets?
- What domestic and global changes prompt the international expansion of companies such as Walmart?
- What other U.S. businesses can you name that have merged with foreign companies or expanded to become multinational or global? Have you heard of any notable successes or failures?

The Growing Importance of Intercultural Communication

Learning Outcome 1

Understand the powerful effects of globalization and the major trends fueling it.

To drive profits, many organizations are expanding overseas. The global village predicted many years ago is here, making intercultural communication skills ever more important. Especially in North America, but also around the world, the movement toward a global economy has swelled to a torrent. If you visit a European or Asian city, you will see many familiar U.S. chains such as The Gap, Subway, Abercrombie & Fitch, Guess, Dunkin' Donuts, Apple, and KFC. To be immediately competitive, some companies formed multinational alliances. For example, Starbucks joined forces with Tata Global Beverages to form a joint venture called Tata Starbucks Limited, operating as Starbucks Coffee, A Tata Alliance.

However, as Walmart and many others learned, expanding companies sometimes stumble when they cross borders and are forced to surmount obstacles never before encountered. Confusion and clashes can result from intercultural differences. You may face such intercultural differences in your current or future jobs. Your employers, coworkers, or customers could very well be from other countries and cultures. You may travel abroad for your employer or on your own. Learning more about the powerful effect culture has on behavior will help you reduce friction and misunderstanding in your dealings with people from other cultures. Before examining strategies for helping you overcome intercultural obstacles, let's take a closer look at globalization and the trends fueling it.

Courtesy of Allen Adamson

Reality Check

Corporate Citizenship Always on Display

"In this new, transparent world, where everything a company does is seen by everybody and consumers are doing business with companies who 'do the right thing' in terms of treating their workers well, for the environment [and] sustainability, almost every company now has to connect corporate citizenship to their marketing and business much more than they did before."[12]

—Allen Adamson, *brand consultant and author*

Markets Go Global

Doing business beyond borders is now commonplace. Two South Korean conglomerates, LG and Samsung, rank as the most trusted brands in India, with Japanese Sony in third place.[13] Newell Rubbermaid offers stylish Pyrex cookware to European chefs; and McDonald's, KFC, and Starbucks serve hungry customers around the world. To compete in the lucrative health beverage industry in China, PepsiCo launched its first oats-based dairy drink. Another first was the exclusive distribution of the new product by the huge Chinese e-commerce site JD.com.[14]

Not only are familiar businesses expanding their markets beyond their borders, but acquisitions, mergers, alliances, and buyouts are obscuring the nationality of many companies. The iconic U.S. brand Frigidaire, founded in 1918, became a subsidiary of the Swedish appliance maker AB Electrolux.[15] The quirky Vermont ice cream purveyor Ben & Jerry's is a division of British-Dutch multinational Unilever. Last, "Your Neighborhood Grocery Store," Trader Joe's, is owned by Germany's discount grocer, Aldi, and now the parent company itself is aggressively expanding across the United States.[16]

Many home-grown companies with famous brands—such as Ford, Firestone, Coca-Cola, AT&T, Colgate, and JP Morgan—are now controlled by global enterprises. When the Japanese beverage empire Suntory bought Beam Inc., distiller of beloved whiskey brands Jim Beam and Maker's Mark, the deal caused a veritable social media storm, including calls for a boycott[17] Similarly, when Smithfield Farms, the 87-year-old Virginia-based purveyor of Smithfield hams and the Armour meat brand, was sold to a Chinese holding company, critics worried that another quintessentially American brand was lost. However, the hogs are still raised here, and the company is doing well financially and employment is growing locally.[18]

To succeed in today's interdependent global village, multinational companies try to capitalize on two seemingly opposite approaches.[19] On the one hand, they introduce new products in new territories—for example, suggesting that Italians forego their wine for American-style beer or awakening in Chinese consumers a penchant for potato chips and coffee. On the other hand, they localize their offerings to match each market. In China McDonald's and KFC highlight salads in response to the Chinese preference for grains, protein, and vegetables in each meal and have made rice more prominent than fries. In India McDonald's dropped beef and pork from its menu, instead substituting vegetarian options to suit the sizable proportion of Indians who don't eat meat.[20] As Figure 3.1 shows, Starbucks has established itself very successfully in China and India by adjusting its brand to the local market.

But not all overseas expansions succeed. Mattel's Barbie failed miserably in China. Even though the doll is quite popular there, the Barbie brand is not. Mattel opened the world's largest House of Barbie in Shanghai. The expensive six-story structure—complete with a restaurant, spa, hair and nail salon, and cocktail bar—featured all things Barbie in its Chinese incarnation (Ling) to appeal to Chinese shoppers. Why did Mattel fail? The store was too large and confusing, mixing adult pleasures, such as martinis and bust-firming treatments, with children's toys.[21]

Figure 3.1 Starbucks—A Global Brand That Understands Localization

As market researcher Shaun Rein puts it, Starbucks is a truly global brand because it has successfully adapted to a very different market and modified its model to fit China while remaining faithful to its core values. In India so far Starbucks has 76 outlets and plans to grow aggressively in a difficult market for cafés.

Sean Xu/Shutterstock.com

Starbucks' Triumph in China

Introduced flavors appealing to local tastes, such as green-tea flavored coffee drinks

Over 1,800 outlets in China: more profitable per store than the U.S.

Offers dine-in service and a comfortable environment with air conditioning

China: Starbucks' largest market outside the U.S.

$ premium pricing strategy

Superb service equal to 5-star hotels

Even consumers who prefer competing coffee products prefer Starbucks for its service.

Starbucks' annual turnover is much lower than the 30% common in China because of good benefits, work environments, and career options.

Outlets: meeting places for executives and gatherings of friends

Carrying a cup: a little personal luxury, a status symbol, a way to show sophistication

Coffee conquering tea cultures

Coffee consumption has nearly doubled over last 10 years.

Coffee, a "sexy" beverage to enjoy.

Neutral place to go and sit, hang out

Coffee has become the "in" thing.

Starbucks Growing in India

SAJJAD HUSSAIN/AFP/Getty Images

Competition

Growth of **café culture,** not so much of coffee

Instead of traditional coffee, young Indians favor Café Coffee Day's cold, sweet milkshakes and teas.

Indians prefer over-the-top, plush outlets.

Lavazza of Italy and Coffee Bean & Tea Leaf have outlets in India.

A small cappuccino costs $1.20 at Café Coffee Day, India's largest café chain, $1.85 at Starbucks

Rein, S. (2012, February 13). Why Starbucks succeeds in China. CNBC guest blog. Retrieved from http://www.cnbc.com/id/46186635/Rein_Why_Starbucks_Succeeds_in_China

Bailay, R. (2014, April 14). Coffee chain Starbucks expanding aggressively in India. *The Economic Times*. Retrieved from http://articles.economictimes.indiatimes.com/2014-04-14/news/49126396_1_costa-coffee-cafe-coffee-day-coffee-chain

Similarly, Home Depot, America's do-it-yourself center, closed all of its big-box China stores after years of losses. It failed to recognize that China, where cheap labor abounds, "is a do-it-for-me market, not a do-it-yourself market."[22]

Danish Siddiqui/REUTERS

Reality Check

Respect for Cultural Differences a Must

"One thing that struck me about Starbucks . . . was the respect it had for cultural differences, which is not always common with large companies. That respect now comes out in the way we design our stores, and treat our people."

—Avani Davda, *CEO, Tata Starbucks, India*

Major Trends Fuel Globalization

Although some companies fail, many domestic and international businesses are rushing to expand around the world. What is causing this dash toward the globalization of markets and blurring of national identities? Many companies, such as Walmart, are increasingly looking overseas as domestic markets mature. They can no longer expect double-digit sales growth at home. As summarized in Figure 3.2, aside from shrinking domestic markets, several trends

Figure 3.2 **Trends Fueling Globalization**

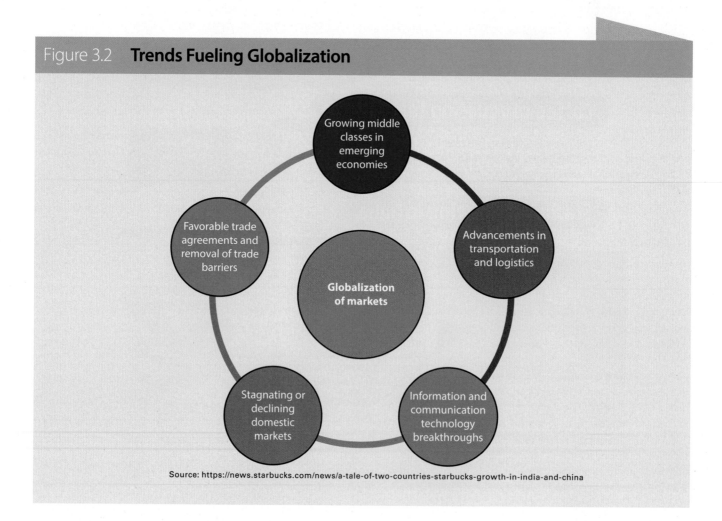

Source: https://news.starbucks.com/news/a-tale-of-two-countries-starbucks-growth-in-india-and-china

fuel global expansion including favorable trade agreements, growing numbers of middle-class consumers in emerging nations, transportation advancements, and increasingly sophisticated information and communication technologies.

Favorable Trade Agreements. A significant factor in the expansion of global markets is the passage of favorable trade agreements. The General Agreement on Tariffs and Trade (GATT) promotes open trade globally, and the North American Free Trade Agreement (NAFTA) expands free trade among Canada, the United States, and Mexico. NAFTA has created one of the largest and richest free-trade regions on earth. Additional trade agreements are causing markets to expand. At this writing the United States has 14 free trade agreements (FTAs) in force with 20 countries, with more to come, most prominently the Transatlantic Trade and Investment Partnership (TTIP) between the European Union and the United States.[23] These agreements significantly open global markets to imports and exports.

An Emerging Global Middle Class. Parts of the world formerly considered developing now boast robust middle classes. Once known only for cheap labor, many countries with emerging economies are now seen as promising markets. Estimates suggest that 70 percent of world growth over the next few years will come from emerging markets. The brightest spots are expected to be Brazil, Russia, India, and China—the so-called BRIC countries; however, lately political turmoil has slowed their growth.[24] By 2030 the global middle class will more than double, from 2 billion today to 4.9 billion, two thirds of whom will reside in the Asia-Pacific region.[25] Consumers in these emerging economies crave everything from cola to smartphones and high-definition TVs. What's more, many countries such as China and India have become less suspicious of foreign investment and free trade, thus fostering vigorous globalization.

Advancements in Transportation and Logistics. Of paramount importance in explaining the explosive growth of global markets are advancements in transportation and logistics. Supersonic planes carry goods and passengers to other continents overnight. Produce shoppers in Japan can choose from the finest artichokes, avocados, and apples only hours after they were picked in California. Americans enjoy bouquets of tulips, roses, and exotic lilies soon after harvesting in Holland and Colombia. Fruits and vegetables such as strawberries and asparagus, once available only in season, are now enjoyed nearly year-round.

Breakthroughs in transportation technology also push the drive toward globalization. For example, digital wireless sensor telemetry keeps shippers informed of vital information en route.[26] Senders can track the destination, the speed of movement, and even the temperature of a shipment's environment. This technology expands markets by enabling senders to monitor shipments and learn of delays or harmful conditions for the goods being shipped.

Growing Reach of Information and Communication Technologies. Probably the most significant factor fueling globalization is the development of information and communication technologies. These technologies have changed the way we live and do business with the help of the Internet, wireless networks, smartphones, mobile electronic devices, and other communication media. High-speed, high-capacity, and relatively low-cost communications have opened new global opportunities that make geographic location virtually irrelevant for many activities and services. Workers have access to company records, software programs, and colleagues whether they're working at home, in the office, or at the beach.

The world's new economic landscape enables companies to conduct business anytime, anywhere, and with any customer. As discussed in Chapters 1 and 2, technology is making a huge difference in the workplace. Wireless connectivity, portable electronic devices, teleconferencing, instant messaging, virtual private networks, and social media streamline business processes and improve access to critical company information. Managers in Miami or Milwaukee can use high-speed data systems to swap marketing plans instantly with their counterparts in Milan or Munich. Fashionistas can snap a digital photo of a garment on a runway in Europe and immediately transmit it to manufacturers in Hong Kong and Jakarta, Indonesia. Social media have delivered on the promise of a global village as we connect with our counterparts in all corners of the globe.

The changing landscape of business and society clearly demonstrates the need for technology savvy and connectedness around the world. Career success and personal wealth depend on the ability to use technology effectively.

JuliusKielaitis/Shutterstock.com

Reality Check

Do We Need Immigration?

Immigration to the United States has been decreasing, although the foreign-born population has grown 10 million over the last decade.[27] Some experts fear future labor shortages and a decline in U.S. competitiveness. According to the latest U.S. Census, 40 states have fewer children than in 2000, and states that don't—Texas, for example—owe their growth to immigrants: "The new engines of growth in America's population are Hispanics, Asians and other minorities."[28]

—William H. Frey, *demographer, senior fellow at the Brookings Institution*

Domestic Workforce Is Becoming Increasingly Diverse

As world commerce becomes more and more interconnected, another trend gives intercultural communication increasing importance: people are on the move. Lured by the prospects of peace, prosperity, education, or a fresh start, people from many cultures are moving to countries promising to fulfill their dreams. For generations the two most popular destinations have been the United States and Canada.

Because of increases in immigration over time, foreign-born people comprise an ever-growing portion of the total U.S. population. Over the next 40 years, the population of the United States is expected to grow by nearly 50 percent, from about 308.7 million in the year 2010 to as many as 458 million in 2050. Two thirds of that increase will be the result of higher fertility rates among immigrants and their offspring.[29]

This influx of immigrants is reshaping American and Canadian societies. Earlier immigrants were thought to be part of a melting pot of ethnic groups. Today, they are more like a tossed salad or spicy stew, with each group contributing its own unique flavor. Instead of the exception, cultural diversity is increasingly the norm. As we seek to accommodate multiethnic neighborhoods, multinational companies, and an intercultural workforce, we can expect some changes to happen smoothly. Other changes will involve conflict and resentment, especially for people losing their positions of power and privilege. Learning to accommodate and manage intercultural change is an important part of the education of any business communicator.

LEARNING OUTCOME 2

Define *culture*, name its primary characteristics, and explain the five key dimensions of culture: context, individualism, time orientation, power distance, and communication style.

Culture and Communication

Comprehending the verbal and nonverbal meanings of a message is difficult even when communicators share the same culture. When they come from different cultures, special sensitivity and skills are necessary. Although global business, new communication technologies, the Internet, and social media span the world, reducing distances, cultural differences still exist and can cause significant misunderstandings.

For our purposes, *culture* may be defined as the complex system of values, traits, morals, and customs shared by a society. Culture is a powerful operating force that molds the way we think, behave, and communicate. The objective of this chapter is to broaden your view of culture and open your mind to flexible attitudes so that you can avoid frustration when cultural adjustment is necessary.

The India Today Group/Getty Images

Today's global economy requires American businesspeople to be culturally aware. Even a simple greeting will differ by country. In Hong Kong, for example, it is customary to greet westerners with a handshake. However, unlike Americans, the Chinese lower their eyes to show respect while shaking hands. In India, visitors are greeted according to age, the eldest first. Italian businesspeople always shake hands first but may work up to a hug as a relationship grows. Learning the nuances of different cultures will make you a more effective and valuable representative of your organization. How can ignorance of a country's cultural norms affect global business dealings?[30]

Characteristics of Culture

Every country or region within a country has a unique common heritage, joint experience, or shared learning. This shared background creates its culture. Despite globalization, interculturalism, and extensive social networking, we should expect to have to make adjustments and adopt new attitudes. However, first we must understand some basic characteristics of culture.

Culture Is Learned. Rules, values, and attitudes of a culture are learned and passed down from generation to generation. For example, in many Middle Eastern and some Asian cultures, same-sex people may walk hand-in-hand in the street, but opposite-sex people may not do so. In Arab cultures conversations are sometimes held nose to nose. However, in Western cultures if a person stands too close, one may react as if violated: *He was all over me like a rash.* Cultural rules of behavior learned from your family and society are conditioned from early childhood.

Cultures Are Inherently Logical. The rules in any culture reinforce that culture's values and beliefs. They act as normative forces. For example, in China the localized black-haired Chinese Barbie doll called Ling was a failure for many reasons, one of which was the lack of understanding of what *feminine* means to the Chinese.[31] In China femininity means being sweet and soft, not smart and strong. Or it means being gentle rather than dazzling. Although current cultural behavior may seem silly and illogical to some people, nearly all serious rules and values originate in deep-seated beliefs. Acknowledging the inherent logic of a culture is extremely important when encountering behavior that differs from one's own cultural norms.

Culture Is the Basis of Self-Identity and Community. Culture is the basis for how we tell the world who we are and what we believe. People build their identities through cultural overlays to their primary culture. When North Americans make choices in education, career, place of employment, and life partner, they consider certain rules, manners, ceremonies, beliefs, languages, and values. These considerations add to their total cultural outlook and are major expressions of their self-identity.

Culture Combines the Visible and Invisible. To outsiders, the way we act—those things we do in daily life and work—are the most visible parts of our culture. On the surface, we recognize numerous signs of culture including the words we use, our body language and gestures, the way we dress, and our outward behavior. Under the surface, however, lie unspoken rules governing these outward signs. These unspoken and often unconscious rules are determined by our beliefs and values, attitudes and biases, feelings and fears, and upbringing. The elements of the invisible structure of culture vastly outnumber those of the visible structure, as illustrated by the iceberg concept shown in Figure 3.3.

Figure 3.3 **Culture Combines the Visible and Invisible**

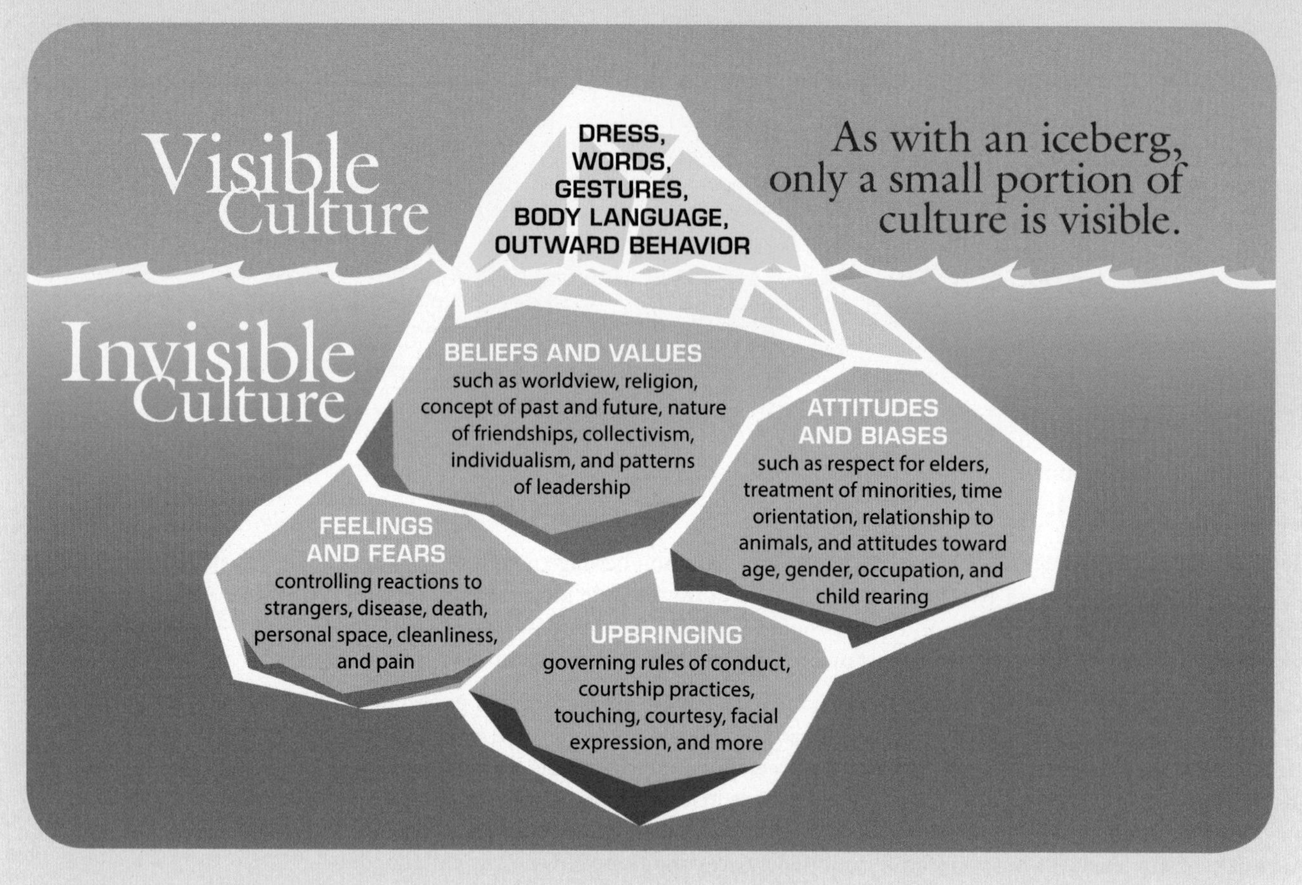
Visible Culture
DRESS,
WORDS,
GESTURES,
BODY LANGUAGE,
OUTWARD BEHAVIOR
As with an iceberg, only a small portion of culture is visible.
Invisible Culture
BELIEFS AND VALUES
such as worldview, religion, concept of past and future, nature of friendships, collectivism, individualism, and patterns of leadership
ATTITUDES AND BIASES
such as respect for elders, treatment of minorities, time orientation, relationship to animals, and attitudes toward age, gender, occupation, and child rearing
FEELINGS AND FEARS
controlling reactions to strangers, disease, death, personal space, cleanliness, and pain
UPBRINGING
governing rules of conduct, courtship practices, touching, courtesy, facial expression, and more

Culture Is Dynamic. Over time, cultures change. Changes are caused by advancements in technology and communication, as discussed earlier. Local differences are modified or slowly erased. Change is also caused by events such as migration, natural disasters, and wars. The American Civil War, for instance, produced far-reaching cultural changes for both the North and the South. Another major event in the United States was the exodus of people from farms. When families moved to cities, major changes occurred in the way family members interacted. Attitudes, behaviors, and beliefs change in open societies more quickly than in closed societies.

When social media networks emerged and added to the pull exerted by traditional mass media—for example, influential TV shows—deeply held cultural norms in the United States changed swiftly. In a 2001 study, Pew Research found that 57 percent of Americans opposed same-sex marriage versus 35 percent who supported it. Fifteen years later, 55 percent of Americans favored gay marriage, compared to 39 percent who opposed it. Generational change alone did not account for the shift; support was up in most segments of society, Pew showed.[32]

Dimensions of Culture

The more you know about culture in general and your own culture in particular, the better able you will be to adopt an intercultural perspective. In this book it is impossible to describe fully the infinite facets of culture, but we can outline some key dimensions identified by social scientists.

To help you better understand your culture and how it contrasts with other cultures, we describe five key dimensions of culture: context, individualism, time orientation, power distance, and communication style.

High and Low Context. Context is probably the most important cultural dimension and also the most difficult to define. It is a concept developed by cultural anthropologist Edward T. Hall. In his model, context refers to the stimuli, environment, or ambience surrounding an event. Communicators in low-context cultures (such as those in North America, Scandinavia, and Germany) depend little on the context of a situation and shared experience to convey their meaning. They assume that messages must be explicit, and listeners rely exclusively on the written or spoken word. In high-context cultures (such as those in Japan, China, and Middle Eastern countries), much is left unsaid because the listener is assumed to be already *contexted* and does not require much background information.[33] To identify low- and high-context countries, Hall arranged them on a continuum, as shown in Figure 3.4.[34]

Low-context cultures tend to be logical, analytical, and action oriented. Business communicators stress clearly articulated messages that they consider to be objective, professional, and efficient. High-context cultures are more likely to be intuitive and contemplative. Communicators in high-context cultures pay attention to more than the spoken or written words. They emphasize interpersonal relationships, nonverbal expression, physical setting, and social setting. For example, a Japanese communicator might say *yes* when he really means *no*. From the context of the situation, the Japanese speaker would indicate whether *yes* really means *yes* or whether it means *no*. The context, tone, time taken to answer, facial expression, and body cues convey the meaning of *yes*.[35] Thus, in high-context cultures, communication cues are transmitted by posture, voice inflection, gestures, and facial expression. Establishing relationships is an important part of communicating and interacting.

Ethics Check

Cultural Change: From Sexist to Gender-Neutral Language

Just a generation ago, businesspeople were *businessmen*, letter carriers were *postmen*, and flight attendants were *stewardesses*. A sea change in language now dictates gender neutrality to avoid typecasting. In business, the honorific *Ms.* is used for all women, regardless of their marital status. Does language reflect just the current culture, or does it have the power to effect change?

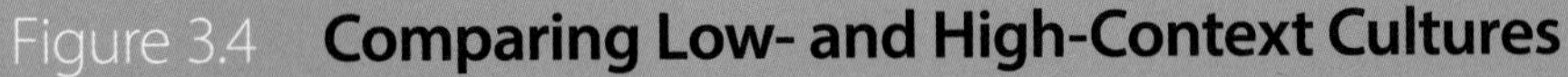

Figure 3.4 **Comparing Low- and High-Context Cultures**

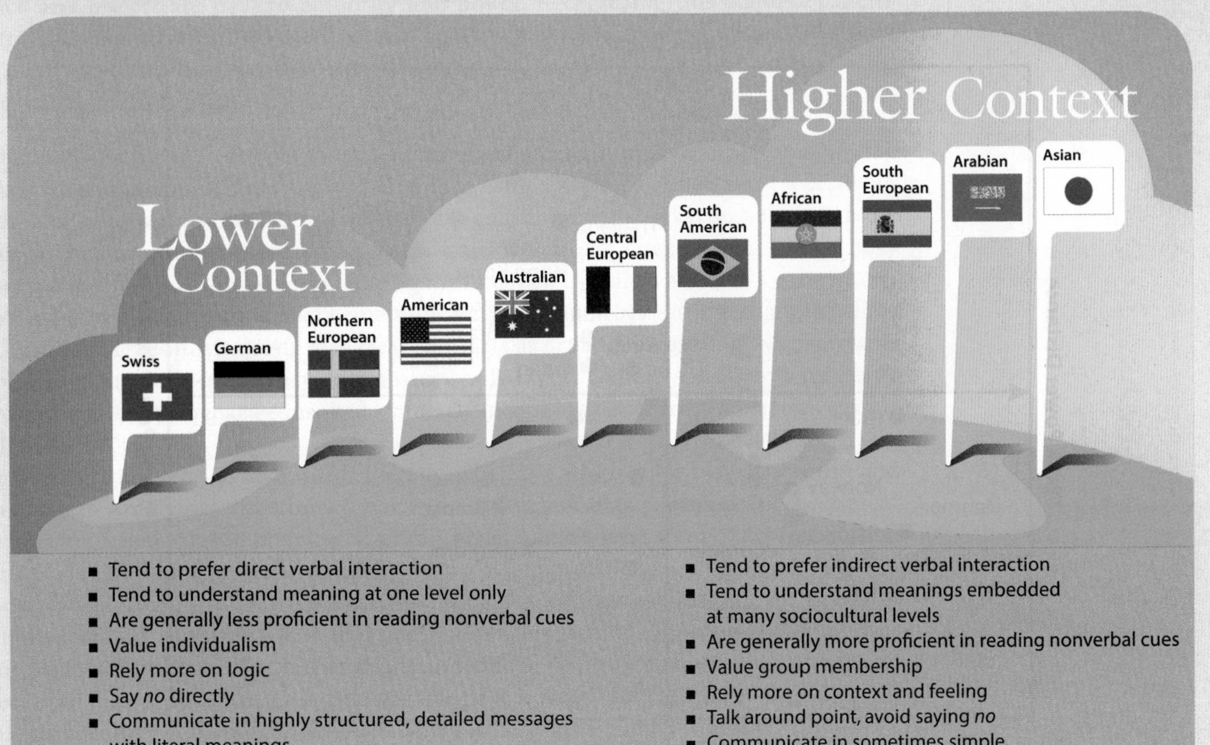

- Tend to prefer direct verbal interaction
- Tend to understand meaning at one level only
- Are generally less proficient in reading nonverbal cues
- Value individualism
- Rely more on logic
- Say *no* directly
- Communicate in highly structured, detailed messages with literal meanings
- Give authority to written information

- Tend to prefer indirect verbal interaction
- Tend to understand meanings embedded at many sociocultural levels
- Are generally more proficient in reading nonverbal cues
- Value group membership
- Rely more on context and feeling
- Talk around point, avoid saying *no*
- Communicate in sometimes simple, sometimes ambiguous messages
- Understand visual messages readily

LEARNING OUTCOME 3

Discuss strategies for enhancing intercultural effectiveness, reflect on nonverbal intercultural communication, assess how social media affect intercultural communication, and apply techniques for successful oral and written interactions across cultures.

Becoming Interculturally Proficient

Being aware of your own culture and how it contrasts with others is an important first step in achieving intercultural proficiency. Another step involves recognizing barriers to intercultural accommodation and striving to overcome them. Some of these barriers occur quite naturally and require conscious effort to surmount. You might be thinking, why bother? Probably the most important reasons for becoming interculturally competent are that your personal life will be more satisfying and your work life will be more productive, gratifying, and effective.

Strategies for Improving Intercultural Effectiveness

Remember that culture is learned. Developing cultural competence often involves changing attitudes. Through exposure to other cultures and through training, such as you are receiving in this course, you can learn new attitudes and behaviors that help bridge gaps between cultures. Following are some suggestions to help you boost your intercultural savvy.

Building Cultural Self-Awareness. Begin to think of yourself as a product of your culture, and understand that your culture is just one among many. Take any opportunity to travel or study abroad, if possible. You will learn much, not only about other cultures but also about your own. Try to stand outside and look at yourself. Do you see any reflex reactions and automatic thought patterns that are a result of your upbringing? These may be invisible to you until challenged by difference. Remember, your culture was designed to help you succeed and survive in a certain environment. Be sure to keep what works and yet be ready to adapt as environments change. Flexibility is an important survival skill.

Curbing Ethnocentrism. The belief in the superiority of one's own race is known as *ethnocentrism*, a natural attitude inherent in all cultures. If you were raised in North America, many of the dimensions of culture described previously probably seem right to you. For example, it is only logical to think that time is money and you should not waste it. Everyone knows that, right? That is why an American businessperson in an Arab or Asian country might feel irritated at time spent over coffee or other social rituals before any *real* business is transacted. In these cultures, however, time is viewed differently. Moreover, personal relationships must be established and nurtured before credible negotiations may proceed.

Ethnocentrism causes us to judge others by our own values. We expect others to react as we would, and they expect us to behave as they would. Misunderstandings naturally result. A North American smiling broadly, joking, and presenting excitedly a proposed project to German business partners may be perceived as lacking credibility. In turn, German businesspeople who respond soberly and ask direct, probing questions may appear rude and humorless. These knee-jerk ethnocentric judgments can be reduced through knowledge of other cultures and increased intercultural sensitivity.

Political conflict can reinforce ethnocentric gut-level reactions that are often fueled by ignorance and fear. Without a doubt, the fear of terrorism today is real and justified. Since the terrorist attacks on September 11, 2001, and the San Bernardino slaughter in 2015, Americans feel threatened on their own soil. Radical Islam, the wars in Iraq and Afghanistan, as well as terrorist attacks around the world have fueled anti-Arab and anti-Muslim sentiments in general. A recent poll found that half of Americans hold unfavorable views of Islam, and a majority of respondents aren't interested in, or certain whether they want to learn more about, the faith.[43] Battling prejudice and even hate may be a tall order for diversity training in the workplace, as the Ethical Insight box shows.

Understanding Generalizations and Stereotyping. Most experts recognize that it is impossible to talk about cultures without using mental categories, representations, and generalizations. These categories are sometimes considered stereotypes. Because the term *stereotype* has a negative meaning, intercultural authors Varner and Beamer suggested that we distinguish between *stereotype* and *prototype*.

Ethical Insights — Overcoming Prejudice: Negative Perceptions of Muslims in the United States

An assorted group of business professionals attending a diversity training class in Hartford, Connecticut, are asked for epithets they free-associate with the word *Muslim*. They call out *poor, uneducated immigrant, Arab, foreigner,* and *terrorist.*[44]

Goodwill Ambassadors

Aida Mansoor, wife of cardiologist Reza Mansoor, began teaching seminars explaining Islam immediately after September 11, 2001. Originally from Sri Lanka, the couple reluctantly embraced their role as ambassadors of their faith: "We were terrified, but we decided either we face this now or we pack up and leave," says Reza Mansoor. "If we were going to stay, we had to explain our faith. What was the other choice? To live in a country without self- respect or dignity?" Yet even in a diverse, tolerant city such as Hartford, Aida Mansoor has fielded jokes about her hijab, the Islamic head scarf she wears, and endured hate mail sent to her mosque.

Reacting to Discrimination

To illustrate the daily reality of Muslims in America, Mansoor shows her classes an experiment staged by a TV station. A bagel shop employee ostensibly refuses to serve a Muslim woman wearing a hijab. The camera reveals the other customers' reactions. Three people thank the clerk for standing up to "un-American terrorists." However, several customers leave in protest, and one man tells the clerk with tears in his eyes: "Every person deserves to be treated with respect, dignity."

Facts Versus Prejudice

A religious affiliation survey shows that 46 percent of Muslims in the United States boast a college education, nearly 70 percent are younger than forty, and 12.4 percent are engineers.[45] A majority of the world's Muslims are not Arabs; they live in India, many regions of Asia, Russia, and parts of Europe and Africa. Although the exact number is difficult to establish, experts generally agree that the United States is home to about 2 million Muslims, most of whom are U.S. citizens and oppose violence.

A *stereotype* is an oversimplified behavioral pattern applied uncritically to groups. Although they may be exaggerated and overgeneralized beliefs when applied to groups of people, stereotypes are not always entirely false.[46] Often they contain a grain of truth. When a stereotype develops into a rigid attitude and when it is based on erroneous beliefs or preconceptions, however, then it should be called a *prejudice.*

Varner and Beamer recommended using the term *prototype* to describe "mental representations based on general characteristics that are not fixed and rigid, but rather are open to new definitions."[47] Prototypes, then, are dynamic and change with fresh experience. Prototypes based on objective observations usually have a considerable amount of truth in them. That is why they can be helpful in studying culture. For example, South American businesspeople often talk about their families before getting down to business. This prototype is generally accurate, but it may not universally apply, and it may change over time.

Some people object to making any generalizations about cultures whatsoever. It is wise to remember, however, that whenever we are confronted with something new and unfamiliar, we naturally strive to categorize the data to make sense of them. In categorizing these new data, we are making generalizations. Significant intellectual discourse and science would be impossible without generalizations. Unfounded generalizations about people and cultures, of course, can lead to bias and prejudice. However, for our purposes, when we discuss cultures, it is important to be able to make generalizations and describe cultural prototypes.

Being Open-Minded. One desirable attitude in achieving intercultural proficiency is that of *tolerance.* Closed-minded people cannot look beyond their own ethnocentrism. But as global markets expand and as our own society becomes increasingly multiethnic, tolerance becomes especially significant. Some job descriptions now include statements such as *Must be able to interact with ethnically diverse personnel.*

To improve tolerance, you will want to practice *empathy.* This means trying to see the world through another's eyes. It means being less judgmental and more eager to seek common ground. One way to promote greater understanding is to work toward a common goal and, as a result, learn about each other. The Arava Institute, an environmental studies center at Kibbutz Ketura in Israel, brings together Jews, Muslims, and Christians to tackle water

Ethics Check

Who Are the World's Worst Tourists?

The demanding, ethnocentric traveler who finds fault with all that is different abroad and resorts to abominable behavior is no longer American—for now. An Expedia survey among 4,500 hotel owners ties the British and French as the most obnoxious tourists: the British top the most hated in Europe; the French, worldwide, for being "penny-pinching, rude, and terrible at languages."[49] As Chinese tourists travel the world in unprecedented numbers, Vice Premier Wang Yang decried "uncivilized behavior" among some Chinese travelers, including etching names on tourist sites, noise, and spitting.[50] On the plus side, the Japanese are the most favored guests.[51] What may account for such perceptions?

scarcity in the Middle East, home to 10 of the 15 most water-starved countries in the world. The diverse student body is Jewish Israeli, Arab, and non–Middle Eastern in almost three equal parts. Aside from learning to solve a common challenge in caring for the environment, the students attend peace-building forums in which they discuss race, religion, culture, and politics. For many, studying at Arava is the first encounter with counterparts of a different nationality or religion. The center develops one of the region's scarcest resources—trust.[48]

Being tolerant also involves patience. If a nonnative speaker is struggling to express an idea in English, Americans must avoid the temptation to finish the sentence and provide the word they presume is wanted. When we put words into their mouths, our foreign friends often smile and agree out of politeness, but our words may not express their thoughts. Remaining silent is another means of exhibiting tolerance. Instead of filling every lapse in conversation, North Americans, for example, should recognize that in Asian cultures people deliberately use periods of silence for reflection and contemplation.

Saving Face. In business transactions North Americans often assume that economic factors are the primary motivators of people. It is wise to remember, though, that strong cultural influences are also at work. *Saving face*, for example, is important in many parts of the world. *Face* refers to the image a person holds in his or her social network. Positive comments raise a person's social standing, but negative comments lower it.

People in low-context cultures are less concerned with face. Germans and North Americans, for instance, value honesty and directness; they generally come right to the point and tell it like it is. Mexicans, Asians, and members of other high-context cultures, on the other hand, are more concerned with preserving social harmony and saving face. They are indirect and go to great lengths to avoid offending by saying *no*. The Japanese, in fact, have 16 ways to avoid an outright *no*. The empathic listener recognizes the language of refusal and pushes no further. Accepting cultural differences and adapting to them with tolerance and empathy often results in a harmonious compromise.

Successful Nonverbal Intercultural Communication

Verbal skills in another culture can generally be mastered by studying hard enough. But nonverbal skills are much more difficult to learn. Nonverbal behavior includes the areas described in Chapter 2, such as eye contact, facial expression, posture, gestures, and the use of time, space, and territory. Fortunately, you can learn techniques to boost your intercultural competence.

How Nonverbal Cues Affect Communication. The messages sent by body language and the way we arrange time and space have always been open to interpretation. Does a raised eyebrow mean that your boss doubts your statement, or just that she is seriously considering it? Does that closed door to an office mean that your coworker is angry, or just that he is working on a project that requires concentration? Deciphering nonverbal communication is difficult for people who are culturally similar, and it is even more troublesome when cultures differ.

In Western cultures, for example, people perceive silence as negative. It suggests rejection, unhappiness, depression, regret, embarrassment, or ignorance. The English expression "The silence was deafening" conveys its oppressiveness. However, the Japanese admire silence and consider it a key to success. A Japanese proverb says, "Those who know do not speak; those who speak do not know." Silence is equated with respect and wisdom.[52]

Although nonverbal behavior is ambiguous within cultures and even more problematic between cultures, it nevertheless conveys meaning. If you've ever had to talk with someone who does not share your language, you probably learned quickly to use gestures to convey basic messages. Because gestures can create very different reactions in different cultures, one must be careful in using and interpreting them. In some societies it is extremely bad form to point one's finger, as in giving directions. Other hand gestures can also cause trouble. The thumbs-up symbol may be used to indicate approval in North America, but in Iran and Ghana it is a vulgar gesture.

As businesspeople increasingly interact with their counterparts from other cultures, they become more aware of these differences. Numerous lists of cultural dos and don'ts have been compiled. However, learning all the nuances of nonverbal behavior in other cultures is impossible; such lists are merely the tip of the cultural iceberg (see Figure 3.3). Striving to associate with people from different cultures can further broaden your intercultural savvy.

Techniques for Achieving Intercultural Competence. For improving effectiveness and achieving intercultural competence, one expert, M. R. Hammer, suggested that three processes or attitudes are effective. *Descriptiveness* refers to the use of concrete and specific feedback. As you will learn in Chapter 4 in regard to the process of communication, descriptive feedback is more effective than judgmental feedback. For example, using objective terms to describe the modest attire of Muslim women is more effective than describing it as unfeminine or motivated by the oppressive and unequal treatment of females.

A second attitude is what Hammer called *nonjudgmentalism.* This attitude goes a long way in preventing defensive reactions from communicators. Most important in achieving effective communication is *supportiveness.* This attitude requires us to support others positively with head nods, eye contact, facial expression, and physical proximity.[53]

From a practical standpoint, when interacting with businesspeople in other cultures, you would be wise to follow their lead. If they avoid intense eye contact, don't stare. If no one is putting elbows on a table, don't be the first to do so. Until you are knowledgeable about the meaning of gestures, it is probably a good idea to keep yours to a minimum. Learning the words for *please, yes,* and *thank you,* some of which are shown in Figure 3.6, is even better than relying on gestures.[54] Achieving intercultural competence in regard to nonverbal behavior may never be totally attained, but sensitivity, nonjudgmentalism, and tolerance go a long way toward improving interactions.

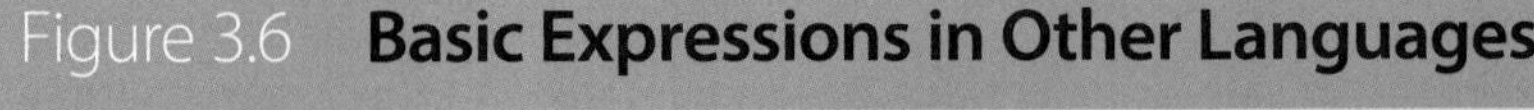

Figure 3.6 **Basic Expressions in Other Languages**

hello
please
thank you
yes
no
goodbye
sorry

as-salam alaykum
min fadhlik
shukran
aiwa/na'am
la
ma'a salama
asef(a)

guten Tag
bitte
danke
ja
nein
auf Wiedersehen
Entschuldigung

konnichiwa
onegai shimasu
arigato goizamasu
hai
iie [ee-yeh]
sayonara
sumimasen

zdravstvujte
požalujsta
spasiba
da
net [nyet]
do svidanija
izvinite

FRENCH

bonjour
s'il vous plaît
merci
oui
non
au revoir
pardon

buon giorno
per favore
grazie
sì
no
arrivederci
scusa

god dag
vær så snill
takk
ja
nei
ha det
beklager

buenos días
por favor
gracias
sí
no
adiós
perdón

Filip Bjorkman/Shutterstock.com

How Technology and Social Media Affect Intercultural Communication

Much has been made of the unprecedented hyperconnectivity facilitated by social media and communication technology today. Certainly, users can interact instantly across time zones and vast distances. With minimal resources, they can also potentially reach out to more individuals and groups all over the world than ever before in history. Not surprisingly, social media may potentially bridge cultural differences as well as reinforce them, depending on their users. New communication technology offers the potential for intercultural engagement. It is being adopted by global businesses at varying degrees, revealing each culture's values and norms.

Social Networking: Bridging Cultural Divides? What we make of the potential for connectedness and intercultural communication online is as much up to us as it would be at a dinner party at which we don't know any of the other guests. "Digital media is an amplifier. It tends to make extroverts more extroverted and introverts more introverted," says Clay Shirky, social media expert at New York University.[55] At the same time, the online environment may deepen feelings of isolation; it can make social presence and interpersonal contact more difficult because all contact is mediated electronically.[56]

In real life, as online, we instinctively tend to gravitate toward people who seem similar to us, believes Gaurav Mishra, a social media strategist from India: "[H]uman beings have a strong tendency to prefer the familiar, so we pay attention to people with a shared context and treat the rich Twitter public stream as background noise."[57] Twitter and other social media can boost intercultural communication; however, we must be willing to reach out across the boundaries that separate us. Shared causes can mobilize social media users halfway across the globe. The public around the world witnessed firsthand, real-time accounts of the Arab Spring and the Syrian uprising on Twitter and other social networks. The calls for regime change resonated in China, where unidentified Internet users started advocating for a Jasmine Revolution. Microblogging sites and other social media served as platforms for dissidents to call for gatherings in 13 major cities. When a large number of people congregated, they were arrested, one simply for placing a jasmine flower near a McDonald's in Beijing.[58]

The majority of social media pundits agree that Twitter in particular offers a rich opportunity for intercultural engagement. They credit the diversity of Twitter users and the open design of the microblogging platform for inviting intercultural exploration.[59] Zendesk customer advocate Justin Flitter says that Twitter makes it easier to connect with others across cultural divides: "Accents, tone, body language and other subtleties are reduced when it's just text on screen." Because people are sharing interests, they overcome potential barriers such as Twitter jargon and cultural context, Flitter believes.[60]

Social Networking: Erasing Cultural Differences or Deepening Them? Despite the equalizing influence of globalization, regional and cultural differences persist, as those who design media for markets in other countries know. Asian users may prefer muted pastel colors and anime-style graphics that North Americans would find unusual. Conversely, Korean and Japanese employees may balk at being compelled to post photos of themselves on company intranet pages. They opt for avatars or pictures of pets instead, possibly as an expression of personal modesty or expectations of privacy, whereas North Americans believe photos promote cohesion and make them seem accessible.[61]

Some have argued that social networks such as Facebook are predominantly infused by Anglo-Saxon culture (the United States, the UK, and Canada) and might not be as successful elsewhere.[62] However, 80 percent of Facebook users are located outside the United States and Canada. They converse in 70 languages on the site.[63] Aside from language, regional differences on Facebook and Twitter seem minor.

Improving Conversations in Intercultural Environments

Although speaking a foreign language fluently is best, many Americans lack that skill. Fortunately, global business transactions are increasingly conducted in English. English has become the language of technology, the language of Hollywood, and the language of business even in traditionally non-English-speaking countries. English is so dominant that when Korean, Russian, and Mexican officials recently met in Beijing at the Asia-Pacific Economic Cooperation (APEC) summit, they communicated in English. It's the only official language of APEC, even when that organization meets in China.[64] However, Americans and others who communicate with nonnative speakers are more likely to be understood if they observe a few polite and helpful suggestions.

Enhancing Oral Communication.

Americans abroad make a big mistake in thinking that nonnative speakers of English can always follow the conversation. Comprehension can be fairly superficial. Even though they speak English, foreign nationals appreciate your learning greetings and a few phrases in their language. It's also wise to speak slowly, use simple English, opt for short sentences, and avoid long, complex words. Following are additional suggestions to improve oral intercultural communication:

- **Observe eye messages.** Be alert to a glazed expression or wandering eyes. These tell you that the listener is lost.
- **Encourage accurate feedback.** Ask probing questions, and encourage the listener to paraphrase what you say. Do not assume that a *yes*, a nod, or a smile indicates comprehension.
- **Accept blame.** If a misunderstanding results, graciously accept the blame for not making your meaning clear.
- **Listen without interrupting.** Curb your desire to finish sentences or to fill out ideas for the speaker. Keep in mind that North Americans abroad are often accused of listening too little and talking too much.
- **Smile when appropriate.** The smile is often considered the single most understood and most useful form of communication. However, in some cultures excessive smiling may seem insincere.
- **Follow up in writing.** After conversations or oral negotiations, confirm the results and agreements with written messages. For proposals and contracts, hire a professional translator.

Improving Written Communication.

In sending letters, e-mails, and other documents to businesspeople in other cultures, try to adjust your writing style and tone. For example, in cultures in which formality and tradition are important, be scrupulously polite. Don't even think of sharing the latest joke. Humor translates very poorly and can cause misunderstanding and negative reactions. Familiarize yourself with customary channels of communication. Are letters, e-mails, and faxes common? Would a direct or indirect organizational pattern be more effective? What's more, forget about trying to cut through red tape: In some cultures bureaucracy is widely accepted. The following additional suggestions can help you prepare successful written messages for intercultural audiences.

- **Use short sentences and short paragraphs.** Sentences with fewer than 20 words and paragraphs with fewer than 8 lines are most readable.
- **Observe titles and rank.** Use last names, titles, and other signals of rank and status. Send messages to higher-status people and avoid sending copies to lower-rank people.
- **Avoid ambiguous expressions.** Include relative pronouns (*that, which, who*) for clarity in introducing clauses. Stay away from contractions (especially ones such as *Here's the*

problem). Avoid idioms and figurative clichés (*once in a blue moon*), slang (*my presentation really bombed*), acronyms (*ASAP*, for *as soon as possible*), abbreviations (*DBA*, for *doing business as*), jargon (*input, bottom line*), and sports references (*play ball, slam dunk, ballpark figure*). Use action-specific verbs (*purchase a printer* rather than *get a printer*).

- **Strive for clarity.** Avoid words that have many meanings (the word *light* has 18 meanings). If necessary, clarify words that may be confusing. Replace two-word verbs with clear single words (*return* instead of *bring back; delay* instead of *put off*; *maintain* instead of *keep up*).
- **Use correct grammar.** Be careful about misplaced modifiers, dangling participles, and sentence fragments. Use conventional punctuation.
- **Cite numbers carefully.** In international trade learn and use the metric system. In citing numbers use figures (*12*) instead of spelling them out (*twelve*). Always convert dollar figures into local currency. Avoid using figures to express the month of the year. In North America, for example, May 11, 2017, might be written as 5/11/17, whereas in Europe the same date might appear as 11.5.17. Figure 3.7 shows common international data formats.

Figure 3.7 **Typical Data Formats**

	United States	United Kingdom	France	Germany	Portugal
Dates	June 12, 2017 6/12/17	12 June 2017 12/6/17	12 juin 2017 12.06.17	12. Juni 2017 12.06.17	12 de Junho de 2017 12/06/2017
Time	9:45 p.m.	9:45 pm	21.45 21 h 45	21:45 Uhr 21.45	21h45 21.45h
Currency	$123.45 USD 123.45	£123.45 GBP 123.45	123,45 € EUR 123,45	123,45 € EUR 123,45	€ 123,45 EUR 123,45
Large numbers	1,234,567.89	1,234,567.89	1.234.567,89	1.234.567,89	1.234.567,89
Phone numbers	(302) 567-1234 302.567.1234	020 7734 8624 +44 20 7734 8624	01 43 36 17 00 +33 1 43 36 1700	(030) 2261 1004 +49 30 2261 1004	21 315 02 12 +351 21 315 02 12

An Intercultural E-Mail Message That Misses the Mark

Figure 3.8 illustrates an ineffective intercultural message. The writer uses a casual, breezy tone in a message to a Chinese company when a formal tone would be more appropriate. In addition, the e-mail includes slang and ambiguous expressions that would almost surely confuse a reader for whom English is not a first language.

In the effective version in Figure 3.9, the writer adopts a formal but pleasant, polite tone, striving for complete sentences and correct grammar. The effective e-mail message avoids slang (*on the up and up*), idioms, imprecise words (*I might do an order*), unclear abbreviations (*ASAP*), and confusing dates (5/8). To further aid comprehension, the writer organizes the message into a bulleted list with clear questions.

As the world economies continue to intermingle and globalization spreads, more businesspeople are adopting Western ways. Although Japanese writers may open letters with a seasonable greeting (*Cherry trees will soon be blooming*), it is unnecessary for a U.S. correspondent to do so.[65]

Figure 3.8 Ineffective Intercultural E-Mail Message – Model Document

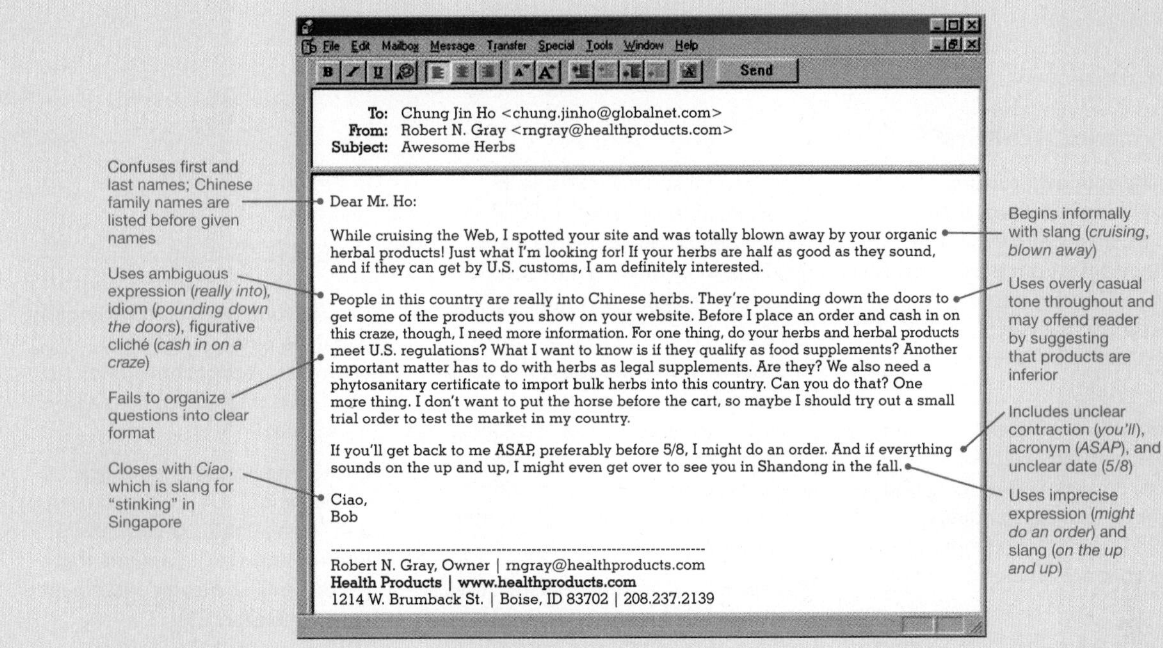

To: Chung Jin Ho <chung.jinho@globalnet.com>
From: Robert N. Gray <rngray@healthproducts.com>
Subject: Awesome Herbs

Dear Mr. Ho:

While cruising the Web, I spotted your site and was totally blown away by your organic herbal products! Just what I'm looking for! If your herbs are half as good as they sound, and if they can get by U.S. customs, I am definitely interested.

People in this country are really into Chinese herbs. They're pounding down the doors to get some of the products you show on your website. Before I place an order and cash in on this craze, though, I need more information. For one thing, do your herbs and herbal products meet U.S. regulations? What I want to know is if they qualify as food supplements? Another important matter has to do with herbs as legal supplements. Are they? We also need a phytosanitary certificate to import bulk herbs into this country. Can you do that? One more thing. I don't want to put the horse before the cart, so maybe I should try out a small trial order to test the market in my country.

If you'll get back to me ASAP, preferably before 5/8, I might do an order. And if everything sounds on the up and up, I might even get over to see you in Shandong in the fall.

Ciao,
Bob

Robert N. Gray, Owner | rngray@healthproducts.com
Health Products | www.healthproducts.com
1214 W. Brumback St. | Boise, ID 83702 | 208.237.2139

Confuses first and last names; Chinese family names are listed before given names
Uses ambiguous expression (*really into*), idiom (*pounding down the doors*), figurative cliché (*cash in on a craze*)
Fails to organize questions into clear format
Closes with *Ciao*, which is slang for "stinking" in Singapore
Begins informally with slang (*cruising, blown away*)
Uses overly casual tone throughout and may offend reader by suggesting that products are inferior
Includes unclear contraction (*you'll*), acronym (*ASAP*), and unclear date (5/8)
Uses imprecise expression (*might do an order*) and slang (*on the up and up*)

Figure 3.9 Effective Intercultural E-Mail Message – Model Document

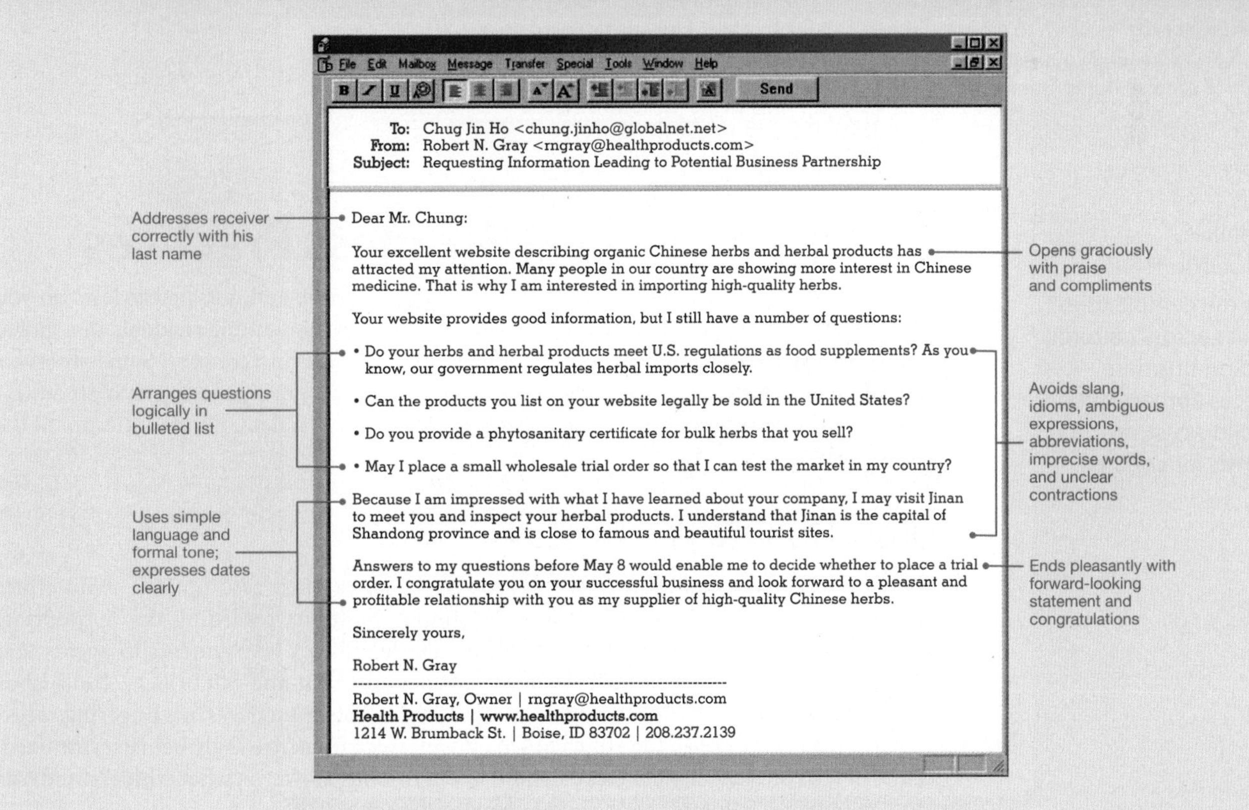

To: Chug Jin Ho <chung.jinho@globalnet.net>
From: Robert N. Gray <rngray@healthproducts.com>
Subject: Requesting Information Leading to Potential Business Partnership

Dear Mr. Chung:

Your excellent website describing organic Chinese herbs and herbal products has attracted my attention. Many people in our country are showing more interest in Chinese medicine. That is why I am interested in importing high-quality herbs.

Your website provides good information, but I still have a number of questions:

- Do your herbs and herbal products meet U.S. regulations as food supplements? As you know, our government regulates herbal imports closely.
- Can the products you list on your website legally be sold in the United States?
- Do you provide a phytosanitary certificate for bulk herbs that you sell?
- May I place a small wholesale trial order so that I can test the market in my country?

Because I am impressed with what I have learned about your company, I may visit Jinan to meet you and inspect your herbal products. I understand that Jinan is the capital of Shandong province and is close to famous and beautiful tourist sites.

Answers to my questions before May 8 would enable me to decide whether to place a trial order. I congratulate you on your successful business and look forward to a pleasant and profitable relationship with you as my supplier of high-quality Chinese herbs.

Sincerely yours,

Robert N. Gray

Robert N. Gray, Owner | rngray@healthproducts.com
Health Products | www.healthproducts.com
1214 W. Brumback St. | Boise, ID 83702 | 208.237.2139

Addresses receiver correctly with his last name
Arranges questions logically in bulleted list
Uses simple language and formal tone; expresses dates clearly
Opens graciously with praise and compliments
Avoids slang, idioms, ambiguous expressions, abbreviations, imprecise words, and unclear contractions
Ends pleasantly with forward-looking statement and congratulations

The following checklist summarizes suggestions for improving communication with intercultural audiences.

CHECKLIST

Achieving Intercultural Proficiency

- **Examine your own culture.** Culture is learned. Study your customs, biases, and views and how they differ from those in other societies. This may improve your understanding and acceptance of the values and behavior of people in other cultures.
- **Explore other cultures.** Education can help you alter cultural misconceptions, reduce fears, and minimize misunderstandings. Knowledge of other cultures opens your eyes and enriches your life.
- **Curb ethnocentrism.** Avoid judging others by your personal views. Overcome the view that other cultures are incorrect, defective, or primitive. Try to develop an open mind-set.
- **Treat each individual you meet as a *prototype*.** Be open to questioning and adjusting your perceptions of other cultures. Generalizations are natural and unavoidable, but beware of stereotypes and prejudice. Most people like to be treated as unique individuals, not typical representatives of an entire group.
- **Observe nonverbal cues in your culture.** Become more alert to the meanings of eye contact, facial expression, posture, gestures, and the use of time, space, and territory. How do they differ in other cultures?
- **Embrace nonjudgmentalism.** Strive to accept unfamiliar behavior as different, rather than as right or wrong. However, try not to be defensive in justifying your own culture. Strive for objectivity.
- **Be aware of culture when using communication technology.** Don't expect that individuals from other cultures think and act the same way you do; at the same time, try to reach out to others over common interests.
- **Use plain English.** Speak and write in short sentences using simple words and standard English. Eliminate puns, slang, jargon, acronyms, abbreviations, and any words that cannot be easily translated.
- **Encourage accurate feedback.** In conversations ask probing questions and listen attentively without interrupting. Do not assume that a *yes* or a smile indicates agreement or comprehension.
- **Adapt to local preferences.** Shape your writing to reflect the document styles of the reader's culture, if appropriate. Express currency in local figures. Write out months of the year for clarity.

LEARNING OUTCOME 4

Grasp the complexities of ethics across cultures, including business practices abroad, bribery, prevailing customs, and methods for coping.

Culture and Ethical Business Practices

When you do business around the world, whose values, culture, and, ultimately, laws do you follow? This perplexing problem faces conscientious organizations and individuals in a global economy. Do you heed the customs of your country or those of the host country? Some observers claim that when American businesspeople venture abroad, they're wandering into an ethical no-man's land, a murky world of payola where transactions often demand gratuities to oil the wheels of business.[66]

Doing Business Abroad

As companies do more and more business around the globe, their assumptions about ethics are put to the test. Businesspeople may face simple questions regarding the appropriate amount of money to spend on a business gift or the legitimacy of payments to agents and distributors to "expedite" business. They may also encounter out-and-out bribery, child-labor abuse, environment mistreatment, and unscrupulous business practices. In a lingering recession after the banking crisis, the ethics of U.S. businesses are increasingly being scrutinized. Violators of laws or company policies can land in big trouble. However, what ethical standards do these companies follow when they do business abroad?

Today most companies that are active in global markets have ethical codes of conduct. These codes are public documents and can usually be found on company websites. They are an accepted part of governance. The growing sophistication of these codes results in ethics training programs that often include complicated hypothetical questions. Ethics trainers teach employees to solve problems by reconciling legal requirements, company policies, and conflicting cultural norms.[67]

Businesses in other countries are also adopting ethics codes and helping employees live up to the standards. Alan Boeckmann, CEO of Fluor, the multinational construction firm, has worked very hard to rid his company of corruption. The battle against bribery in an industry in which corruption is rampant hasn't been easy. Yet the company experienced success after installing a company lawyer as head of compliance.[68] Enduring major tribulations, today IKEA is wildly successful in Russia.[69] However, after entering the market and investing $4 billion in Russia, the Swedish furniture powerhouse decided to halt further expansion. Safety inspectors, expecting bribes, were withholding permission for additional stores outside Moscow. The company cited "zero tolerance on corruption" and refused to pay up. Bribery in Russia serves the personal enrichment of law enforcement and other authorities to the tune of $300 billion annually.[70]

Transparency International, a Berlin-based watchdog group, compiled a ranking of corruption in many countries. Based on polls and surveys of businesspeople and journalists, the index shown in Figure 3.10 on page 106 presents a look at the perceptions of corruption.[71] Gauging corruption precisely is impossible. However, this graph reflects the feelings of individuals doing business in the countries shown. Of the countries selected for this graph, the least corrupt were Denmark, New Zealand, Finland, Sweden, Norway, and Singapore. The most corrupt were Somalia, North Korea, Afghanistan, and Iraq. Neck and neck with Uruguay, the United States ranked between Japan and Ireland at the bottom of the top 20. On a positive note, the United States has improved its ranking in recent years and advanced from rank 24 to rank 16.

Win McNamee/Getty Images

Reality Check

The Cost of Corruption

"[Corruption is] a cancer that steals from the poor, eats away at governance and moral fiber, and destroys trust."[72]

—Robert B. Zoellick, *former World Bank president*

Antibribery Laws

The United States is not highest on the index of least corrupt countries. However, it has taken the global lead in fighting corruption. In 1977 the U.S. government passed the Foreign Corrupt Practices Act. It prohibits payments to foreign officials for the purpose of obtaining or retaining business. But the law applies only to U.S. companies. Therefore, they are at a decided disadvantage when competing against less scrupulous companies from other nations. U.S. companies complained that they lost billions of dollars in contracts every year because they refused to bribe their way to success.

Most other industrialized countries looked the other way when their corporations used bribes. They considered the greasing of palms just a cost of doing business in certain cultures. The Germany-based multinational engineering giant Siemens was slapped with $800 million in fines in the United States for systematically paying off foreign officials around the world.[73] Similarly, French energy corporation Alstom had spent tens of millions of dollars in bribes to win contracts in Indonesia, Saudi Arabia, and other countries. In all,

Figure 3.10 **Corruption Perceptions Index: Highly Clean or Highly Corrupt?**

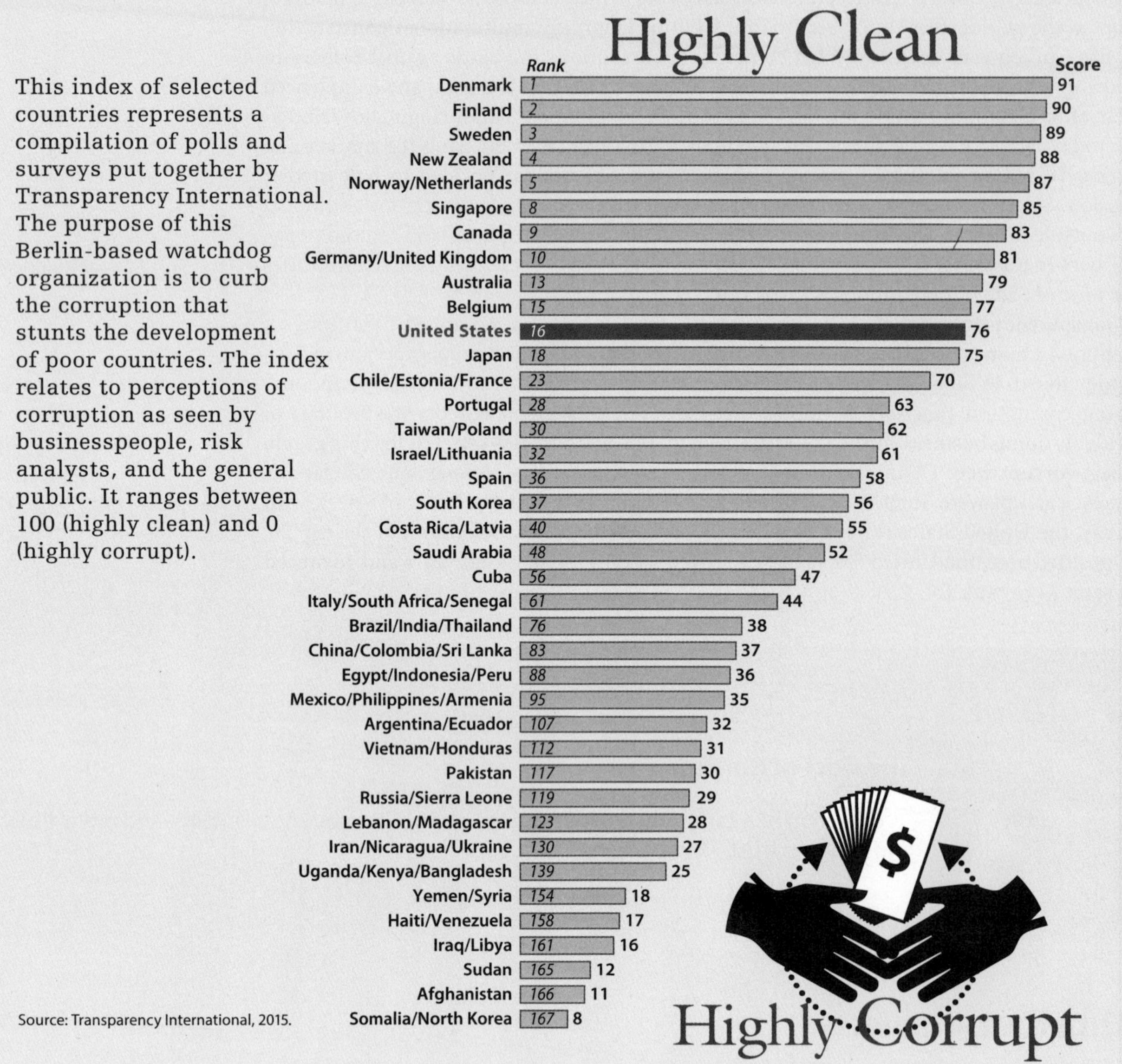

Alstom was forced to pay more than $770 million to settle the corruption charges,[74] hardly a mere slap on the wrist.

In the United States, bribery is a criminal offense, and American corporate officials found guilty are fined and sent to jail. For example, the U.S. government has launched a sweeping corruption investigation against FIFA, the international soccer federation. The Department of Justice has charged sports-marketing executives and soccer officials from the United States and South America with racketeering, wire fraud, money laundering, and additional offenses. Systemic corruption was allegedly rampant in the international soccer leadership for decades.[75]

Domestically, the Sarbanes-Oxley Act is a tool in the anticorruption battle. It forbids off-the-book bribes. However, American law does permit payments that may ease the way for routine government actions, such as expediting a visa request. Such payments are reportedly capped at about $500.[76]

More attention is now being paid to the problem of global corruption. With increased global interdependence, corruption is increasingly seen as costly as well as unethical. It has been estimated that moving from a clean government like that of Singapore to one as corrupt as Mexico's would have the same effect on foreign direct investment as an increase in the corporate tax rate of 50 percent.[77] Many of the world's industrialized countries formally agreed in 1999 to a new global treaty promoted by the Organization for Economic Cooperation and Development (OECD). This treaty bans the bribery of foreign government officials. Today, bribery is illegal almost everywhere in the world.[78]

Deciding Whose Ethics to Follow

Although world leaders seem to agree that bribing officials is wrong, many other shady areas persist. Drawing the lines of ethical behavior here at home is hard enough. When faced with a cultural filter, the picture becomes even murkier. Most people agree that mistreating children is wrong. But in some countries, child labor is not only condoned but also considered necessary for families to subsist. Although most countries want to respect the environment, they might also sanction the use of DDT because crops would be consumed by insects without it.

In some cultures, grease payments to customs officials may be part of their earnings—not blackmail. In parts of Africa, a *family* celebration at the conclusion of a business deal includes a party for which the foreign visitors are asked to pay. This payment is considered a sign of friendship and lasting business relationship, not a personal payoff. In some Third World countries, requests for assistance in developing technologies or reducing hunger may become part of a business package.[79]

The exchanging of gifts is another tricky subject. In many non-Western cultures, the gift exchange tradition has become a business ritual. Gifts not only are a sign of gratitude and hospitality but also generate a future obligation and trust. Americans, of course, become uneasy when gift giving seems to move beyond normal courtesy and friendliness. If it even remotely suggests influence peddling, they back off. Many companies suggest $50 as a top limit for gifts.

Whose ethics should prevail across borders? Unfortunately, no clear-cut answers can be found. Americans are sometimes criticized for being ethical fanatics, wishing to impose their moralistic views on the world. Also criticized are ethical relativists, who contend that no absolute values exist.[80]

Ethical Decision Making Across Borders

Instead of trying to distinguish *good* ethics and *bad* ethics, perhaps the best plan is to look for practical solutions to the cultural challenges of global business interaction. Following are suggestions that acknowledge different values but also respect the need for moral initiative.[81]

- **Broaden your view.** Become more sensitive to the values and customs of other cultures. Look especially at what they consider moral, traditional, practical, and effective.
- **Avoid reflex judgments.** Don't automatically judge the business customs of others as immoral, corrupt, or unworkable. Assume that they are legitimate and workable until proved otherwise.
- **Find alternatives.** Instead of caving in to government payoffs, perhaps offer nonmonetary public service benefits, technical expertise, or additional customer service.

- **Refuse business if options violate your basic values.** If an action seriously breaches your own code of ethics or that of your firm, give up the transaction.
- **Embrace transparency.** Conduct all relations and negotiations as openly as possible.
- **Don't rationalize shady decisions.** Avoid agreeing to actions that cause you to say, *This isn't really illegal or immoral*, *This is in the company's best interest*, or *No one will find out.*
- **Resist legalistic strategies.** Don't use tactics that are legally safe but ethically questionable. For example, don't call agents (who are accountable to employers) distributors (who are not).

When faced with an intercultural ethical dilemma, you can apply the same five-question test you learned in Chapter 1, Figure 1.15. Even in another culture, these questions can guide you to the best decision.

1. Is the action legal?
2. Would you do it if you were on the opposite side?
3. Can you rule out a better alternative?
4. Would a trusted advisor agree?
5. Would family, friends, an employer, or coworkers approve?

Michaeljung/Shutterstock.com

Reality Check

Diversity Encourages Unique Contributions That Benefit the Group

"Our research suggests that the mere presence of social diversity makes people with independent points of view more willing to voice those points of view, and others more willing to listen."[82]

—Katherine W. Phillips, *professor of leadership and ethics, Columbia Business School*

LEARNING OUTCOME 5

Explain the advantages and challenges of workforce diversity, and address approaches for improving communication among diverse workplace audiences.

Workforce Diversity: Benefits and Challenges

While North American companies are expanding global operations and adapting to a variety of emerging markets, the domestic workforce is also becoming more diverse. This diversity has many dimensions—race, ethnicity, age, religion, gender, national origin, physical ability, sexual orientation, and others. No longer, say the experts, will the workplace be predominantly Anglo oriented or male.

As discussed in Chapter 1, by 2020 many groups now considered minorities (African Americans, Hispanics, Asians, Native Americans) are projected to become 36 percent of the U.S. population. Between 2040 and 2050, these groups will reach the majority–minority crossover, the point at which they will represent the majority of the U.S. population.[83] Women will comprise nearly 50 percent of the workforce. Moreover, latest U.S. Census data suggest that the share of the population over sixty-five will jump from 13 percent now to almost 20 percent in 2030. Trends suggest that many of these older people will remain in the workforce. Because of technological advances, more physically challenged people are also joining the workforce.

Diversity and Its Advantages

As society and the workforce become more diverse, successful interactions and communication among identity groups bring distinct advantages in three areas.

Consumers. A diverse staff is better able to read trends and respond to the increasingly diverse customer base in local and world markets. Diverse consumers now want goods and services tailored to their needs. Teams made up of people with different experiences are better equipped to create products that these markets require. Consumers also want to deal with companies that respect their values and reflect themselves.

The CEO of PR firm Gravity, Yuriy Boykiv, speaks to this relationship between a diverse staff and customers: "My company's collective work calls for reaching consumers of multiple ethnicities, which is impossible to do without a deep understanding of a wide range of cultures. Our team consists of more than 40 people who collectively speak 20 different languages." Boykiv urges fellow executives to "Tap into the diversity of your workplace to gain a deep understanding of your workforce and your potential customer base."[84]

Work Teams. As you learned in Chapter 2, employees today often work in teams. Team members with different backgrounds may come up with more innovative and effective solutions than homogeneous teams. Leadership and ethics professor Katherine Phillips believes that "Diversity enhances creativity. It encourages the search for novel information and perspectives, leading to better decision making and problem solving. . . . Even simply being exposed to diversity can change the way you think," she says.[85] Aside from creativity, diverse teams tend to be good for the bottom line; they are 45 percent more likely to increase market share and 70 percent more likely to capture a new market.[86]

Business Organizations. Companies that set aside time and resources to cultivate and capitalize on diversity suffer fewer discrimination lawsuits, fewer union clashes, and less government regulatory action. Most important, though, is the growing realization among organizations that diversity is a critical bottom-line business strategy to improve employee relationships and increase productivity. Consultant Fred Miller points out that almost 80 percent of Fortune 500 companies have created some kind of diversity program because, among other things, diversity drives sales. The government and corporations increasingly contract only with suppliers who can show cultural readiness. "The world is changing," says Miller. "If it's not on your doorstep now, it will be soon. You can't wait. Reaction time must be instantaneous."[87] Developing a diverse staff that can work together is one of the biggest challenges facing business organizations today.

Diversity and Discord

Diversity can be a positive force within organizations. However, all too often it causes divisiveness, discontent, and clashes. Many of the identity groups, the so-called workforce disenfranchised, have legitimate gripes.

Women complain of the *glass ceiling*, that invisible barrier of attitudes, prejudices, and old boy networks blocking them from reaching important corporate positions. Some women feel that they are the victims of sexual harassment, unequal wages, sexism, and even their style of communication. See the Career Coach box on page 110 to learn more about gender talk and gender tension. On the other hand, men, too, have gender issues. A male HR professional complained that he was passed over for promotion because the hiring managers thought he was not warm enough, potentially a code for a female leadership style.[88]

Older employees feel that the deck is stacked in favor of younger employees. Minorities complain that they are discriminated against in hiring, retention, wages, and promotions. Physically challenged individuals feel that their limitations should not hold them back, and they fear that their potential is often prejudged. Religious affiliation too can lead to uneasy workplace relations. In fact, religion-based conflict in the American workplace is rising. "It's the fastest growth area in discrimination," says Robert E. Gregg, an attorney in Madison, Wisconsin. Religion has surpassed even sex and racial discrimination in the volume of litigation.[89]

wavebreakmedia/Shutterstock.com

Career Coach

He Said, She Said: Gender Talk and Gender Tension

Has the infiltration of gender rhetoric done great damage to the workplace? Are men and women throwing rotten tomatoes at each other as a result of misunderstandings caused by stereotypes of so-called masculine and feminine attitudes?[90] Judging from workplace surveys, gender differences are fading: 33 percent of American adults prefer a male boss and 20 percent prefer a female leader, but a whopping 46 percent have no preference. Some even believe that women make better bosses.[91]

Deborah Tannen's book *You Just Don't Understand: Women and Men in Conversation*, as well as John Gray's *Men Are From Mars, Women Are From Venus*, caused an avalanche of discussion (and some hostility) by comparing the communication styles of men and women.

Gender theorists suggest that one reason women can't climb above the glass ceiling is that their communication style is less authoritative than that of men. Compare the following observations (greatly simplified) from gender theorists:

	Women	**Men**
Object of talk	Establish rapport, make connections, negotiate inclusive relationships	Preserve independence, maintain status, exhibit skill and knowledge
Listening behavior	Attentive, steady eye contact; remain stationary; nod head	Less attentive, sporadic eye contact; move around
Pauses	Frequent pauses, giving chance for others to take turns	Infrequent pauses; interrupt each other to take turns
Small talk	Personal disclosure	Impersonal topics
Focus	Details first, pulled together at end	Big picture
Gestures	Small, confined	Expansive
Method	Questions, apologies; "we" statements; hesitant, indirect, soft speech	Assertions; "I" statements; clear, loud, take-charge speech

Improving Communication Among Diverse Workplace Audiences

Harmony and acceptance do not happen automatically when people who are dissimilar work together. This means that organizations must commit to diversity. Harnessed effectively, diversity can enhance productivity and propel a company to success. Mismanaged, it can become a tremendous drain on a company's time and resources. How companies deal with diversity will make all the difference in how they compete in an increasingly global environment. The following suggestions can help you and your organization find ways to improve communication and interaction.

- **Seek training.** Especially if an organization is experiencing diversity problems, awareness-raising sessions may be helpful. Spend time reading and learning about workforce diversity and how it can benefit organizations. Look upon diversity as an opportunity, not a threat. Intercultural communication, team building, and conflict resolution are skills that can be learned in diversity training programs.
- **Understand the value of differences.** Diversity makes an organization innovative and creative. Sameness fosters an absence of critical thinking called groupthink, discussed in Chapter 2. Case studies, for example, of the *Challenger* shuttle disaster suggest that groupthink prevented alternatives from being considered. Even smart people working collectively can make dumb decisions if they do not see the situation from different perspectives.[92] Diversity in problem-solving groups encourages independent and creative thinking.
- **Don't expect conformity.** Gone are the days when businesses could say, "This is our culture. Conform or leave."[93] Paul Fireman, former CEO of Reebok, stressed seeking people who have new and different stories to tell. "And then you have to make real room for them, you have to learn to listen, to listen closely, to their stories. It accomplishes next to nothing to employ those who are different from us if the condition of their employment

is that they become the same as us. For it is their differences that enrich us, expand us, provide us the competitive edge."[94]

- **Make fewer assumptions.** Be careful of seemingly insignificant, innocent workplace assumptions. For example, don't assume that everyone wants to observe the holidays with a Christmas party and a decorated tree. Celebrating only Christian holidays in December and January excludes those who honor Hanukkah, Kwanzaa, and the Lunar New Year. Moreover, in workplace discussions don't assume anything about others' sexual orientation or attitude toward marriage. For invitations, avoid phrases such as *managers and their wives. Spouses* or *partners* is more inclusive. Valuing diversity means making fewer assumptions that everyone is like you or wants to be like you.
- **Build on similarities.** Look for areas in which you and others not like you can agree or at least share opinions. Be prepared to consider issues from many perspectives, all of which may be valid. Accept that there is room for different points of view to coexist peacefully. Although you can always find differences, it is much harder to find similarities. Look for common ground in shared experiences, mutual goals, and similar values.[95] Concentrate on your objective even when you may disagree on how to reach it.

Your Turn: Applying Your Skills at Walmart

Yeamake/Shutterstock.com

Walmart may be one of the most vilified brands in America.[96] However, the company has launched significant efforts that may burnish its image and appeal to consumers who value good corporate citizenship.

Walmart announced that it would increase its minimum wage to $9 an hour, inching up to the federal rate of $10.10 for government contractors. Next the company decided to improve animal welfare in its supply chain, establishing anticruelty guidelines for food producers.[97] Then followed news that Walmart would stop selling A-15 military-style rifles, a move applauded by gun control advocates.[98] Finally, Walmart surprised critics and supporters alike by supporting gay rights in its home state of Arkansas and by refusing to sell products carrying the Confederate flag.[99]

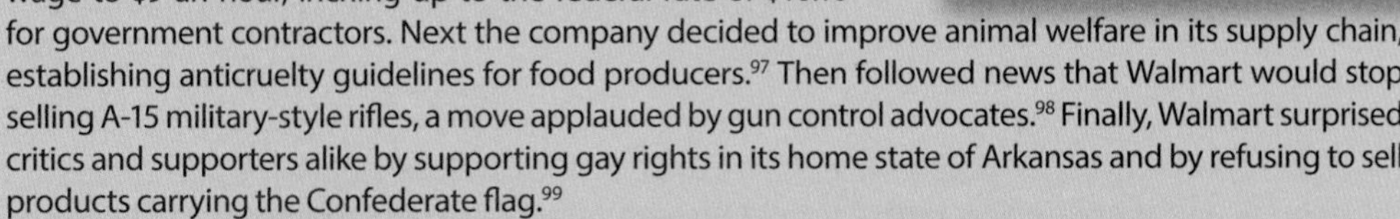

The retail giant has embraced three main strategies: global sustainability in its supply chain, women's economic empowerment, and nutrition initiatives.[100] Walmart challenged laundry manufacturers to reduce the water content in liquid laundry detergent 25 percent by 2018. In its global supply chain, the company also decided to decrease greenhouse gas by working with suppliers on optimizing agricultural production and training farmers in emerging markets.

Walmart's Women's Economic Empowerment initiative aims to increase sourcing from and training of women: One priority is to sell goods worth billions of dollars produced by women-owned businesses. A second priority is an educational effort through the Walmart Foundation, dedicated to training 1 million low-income women to help them find better jobs. Last, the retailer deployed a Great for You icon identifying healthier food options and pushed to reduce sodium and sugar in several national food brands.[101]

The closely watched bribery probes against Walmart in Mexico and India turned up little evidence of corporate malfeasance so far.[102]

Your Task

As a junior member of a joint task force at McKinsey & Co., a consulting firm advising Walmart, you are working to improve the image of the global retailer. Despite several praiseworthy initiatives, Walmart is still viewed by many with suspicion. Stories in the media detailing discrimination lawsuits, bribery investigations, and violations of labor practices have not been helpful. As a team, discuss the global impact of Walmart's sustainability effort. Create a communication plan that includes answers to questions such as the following: How should Walmart spread the news about its sustainability policies to reach the broader public and young people in particular? Consider the use of social media such as Facebook, Twitter, and Instagram. Your team may be asked to explain its decision to the class or to write a summary of the pros and cons of each option. Be prepared to support your choice.

Summary of Learning Outcomes

1 Understand the powerful effects of globalization and the major trends fueling it.

- Intercultural competency is needed to contend with several major trends. Shrinking domestic markets have prompted movement toward globalized markets free of trade barriers.
- Advanced transportation technology has made the world smaller and more intertwined.
- Communication and information technologies extend the global reach of business.
- In emerging economies the middle class is growing.
- The domestic workforce is becoming increasingly diverse as immigrants settle in North America, and their offspring outnumber the descendants of non-Hispanic whites.

2 Define *culture*, name its primary characteristics, and explain the five key dimensions of culture: context, individualism, time orientation, power distance, and communication style.

- Culture is the complex system of values, traits, morals, and customs shared by a society.
- Significant characteristics of culture include the following: (a) culture is learned, (b) cultures are inherently logical, (c) culture is the basis of self-identity and community, (d) culture combines the visible and invisible, and (e) culture is dynamic.
- Members of low-context cultures (e.g., North America, Scandinavia, and Germany) depend on words to express meaning.
- Members of high-context cultures (e.g., Japan, China, and Arab countries) rely more on context, such as social setting and a person's history, status, and position to convey meaning.
- Other key dimensions of culture include individualism, time orientation, power distance, and communication style.

3 Discuss strategies for enhancing intercultural effectiveness, reflect on nonverbal intercultural communication, assess how social media affect intercultural communication, and apply techniques for successful oral and written interactions across cultures.

- To function effectively in a global economy, we must learn about other cultures and be willing to change our attitudes once we become aware of our own cultural assumptions and biases.
- Ethnocentrism refers to the belief that one's own culture is superior to all others and holds all truths; to overcome stereotypes and become more tolerant, we need to practice empathy.
- Nonverbal miscommunication can be avoided by recognizing that body language, such as eye contact, posture, gestures, use of time, space, and territory, is largely culture dependent.
- Communicating in social media, people tend to seek out those who are like them; whether users reach out across boundaries depends on whether they are outgoing or introverted.
- To improve intercultural written messages, communicators accommodate the reader in organization, tone, and style; use short sentences and paragraphs; observe titles and rank; avoid ambiguous expressions; use correct grammar; and cite numbers carefully.

4 Grasp the complexities of ethics across cultures, including business practices abroad, bribery, prevailing customs, and methods for coping.

- Doing business abroad, businesspeople should expect differing views about ethical practices.
- To uphold sound ethical principles abroad, businesspeople should broaden their understanding of values and customs in other cultures and avoid reflex judgments regarding the morality or corruptness of actions.
- Seeking alternative solutions, refusing business if the options violate one's basic values, and conducting all relations as openly as possible are additional techniques for ethical dealings.
- Businesspeople who wish to uphold good business practices abroad should resist legalistic strategies, avoid rationalizing shady decisions, and apply a five-question ethics test when faced with a perplexing ethical dilemma.

5 Explain the advantages and challenges of workforce diversity, and address approaches for improving communication among diverse workplace audiences.

- A diverse workforce can benefit consumers, work teams, and business organizations.
- Diversity can also cause discord among identity groups.
- Business communicators should be aware of and sensitive to differences in the communication styles of men and women.
- To foster harmony and communication in diverse workplaces, many organizations develop diversity training programs.
- Workers are tasked with understanding and accepting the value of differences; they should not expect conformity, make fewer assumptions about others, and look for common ground.

Critical Thinking

1. When we travel or work abroad, we tend to be perceived not so much as individuals but as members of racial, ethnic, or national groups. For example, when visiting Europe, Americans can expect to be questioned on U. S. foreign policy, military actions, and economic influence. How can you ensure that you function as an effective ambassador of your country when working and traveling overseas? (L.O. 1, 3, and 5)
2. A stereotype is an oversimplified perception of a behavioral pattern or characteristic applied to entire groups. For example, the Swiss are hardworking, efficient, and neat; Germans are formal, reserved, and blunt; Americans are loud, friendly, and impatient; Canadians are polite, trusting, and tolerant; Asians are gracious, humble, and inscrutable. In what way are such stereotypes harmless or harmful? (L.O. 2, 3)
3. It is quite natural to favor one's own country over a foreign one. To what extent can ethnocentrism be considered a normal reaction, and when could it become destructive and unproductive? Provide examples to support your answer. (L.O. 2, 3)
4. Some economists and management scholars argue that statements such as *diversity is an economic asset* or *diversity is a new strategic imperative* are unproved and perhaps unprovable assertions. Should social responsibility or market forces determine whether an organization strives to create a diverse workforce? Why? (L.O. 5)
5. **Ethical Issue:** You know that it's not acceptable to make ethnic jokes, least of all in the workplace, but a colleague of yours keeps invoking the worst ethnic and racial stereotypes. How do you respond? Do you remain silent and change the subject, or do you speak up? What other options do you have in dealing with such a coworker? Consider whether your answer would change if the offender were your boss.

Activities

3.1 Minding One's Intercultural Social Media Manners (L.O. 1–3)

Intercultural Social Media

Consider your worst, most embarrassing intercultural blunder, and then imagine it amplified a thousandfold or millionfold for everyone to see. Social networking is instant and, once unleashed, it can't be throttled back. What follows is a partial list of extremely awkward social media slip-ups with intercultural implications.[103]

YOUR TASK Consider the gravity of each offense; then, individually or in groups, discuss each for its take-away, the lesson to be learned from it. Contribute your own intercultural blunders that you or someone you know has experienced. Explain lessons learned.

a. Lawyers are not immune to social media gaffes. They seem to be just as prone to oversharing as the rest of us, although they are bound by confidentiality and professional ethics in what often are sensitive cases. An Indiana state prosecutor tweeted "use live ammunition," and he meant using live rounds against peaceful protesters. The prosecutor was responding to the news that riot police were attempting to remove demonstrators from the state capitol in Madison, Wisconsin—public servants protesting budget cuts and threats to their collective bargaining rights.[104]

b. As if to prove that humor is not universally shared, nor is it always in good taste, comedian Gilbert Gottfried tweeted this lame joke in the wake of the tsunami in Japan: "Japan called me. They said 'maybe those jokes are a hit in the U.S., but over here, they're all sinking.'" At the time, Gottfried was the spokesperson for insurer Aflac.

c. Home improvement chain Lowe's allowed a discussion on its Facebook page to get out of hand after withdrawing its advertising from a TLC reality show about Muslim families. The 23,000 comments on Facebook that followed were mostly critical of the company, but some praised the home improvement giant. Only when the media picked up the story did the company respond to offensive and racist posts by deleting all the messages and explaining its late intervention as "respect for the transparency of social media."

d. Australian airline Qantas tried to lure its customers with gift packs to describe their "dream luxury in-flight experience." However, this promotion coincided with grounded flights in response to ongoing strikes, and the passengers took to venting and griping, not praising.

e. Red Cross social media specialist Gloria Huang sent out the following tweet from the organization's Twitter account *@RedCross*: "Ryan found two more 4 bottle packs of Dogfish Head's Midas Touch beer.... when we drink we do it right *#gettngslizzerd*." The late-night tweet stayed up for an hour. Huang's boss, Wendy Harman, fielded calls in the middle of the night and took the tweet down.

3.2 Analyzing Intercultural Gaffes (L.O. 1–3)

Intercultural

As business organizations become increasingly global in their structure and marketing, they face communication problems resulting from cultural misunderstandings.

YOUR TASK Based on what you have learned in this chapter, describe several broad principles that could be applied in helping the individuals involved understand what went wrong in the following events. What suggestions could you make for remedying the problems?

a. British transportation minister Susan Kramer faced embarrassment after presenting the mayor of Taipei, Taiwan, Ko Wen-je, with a watch—a taboo in Chinese culture. Ko remarked to reporters that he would "sell it to a scrap dealer" because a watch would be useless to him. *Giving a clock* and *attending an old person's funeral* sound very similar in Chinese.[105]

b. The owners of the British food company Sharwood spent millions of dollars launching a new curry sauce called Bundh. The firm was immediately deluged with calls from Punjabi speakers who said the new product sounded like their word for backside. How important is it for companies to test product names?[106]

c. During a festive dinner for a delegation from Singapore visiting the government of the Czech Republic, the conversation turned to the tasty main course they were eating. One of the Czech hosts explained to the inquiring foreign guests that they were enjoying a Czech specialty, rabbit, known for its light white meat. The Singaporeans' faces mirrored shock, embarrassment, and irritation. As inconspicuously as possible, they put down their silverware. Only later did the Czech delegation learn that rabbit is a pet in Singapore much like the house cat in European or North American households.[107]

d. The employees of a large U.S. pharmaceutical firm became angry over the e-mail messages they received from the firm's employees in Spain. The messages weren't offensive. Generally, these routine messages just explained ongoing projects. What riled the Americans was this: every Spanish message was copied to the hierarchy within its division. The Americans could not understand why e-mail messages had to be sent to people who had little or nothing to do with the issues being discussed. However, this was accepted practice in Spain.[108]

e. As China moves from a planned to a market economy, professionals suffer the same signs of job stress experienced in Western countries. Multinational companies have long offered counseling to their expatriate managers. Locals, however, frowned on any form of psychological therapy. When China's largest bank hired Chestnut Global Partners to offer employee counseling services, Chestnut learned immediately that it could not talk about such issues as conflict management. Instead, Chestnut stressed workplace harmony. Chestnut also found that Chinese workers refused one-on-one counseling. They preferred group sessions or online counseling.[109] What cultural elements were at work here?

3.3 Mastering International Time (L.O. 1–3)

Communication Technology | Intercultural | Web

Assume you are a virtual assistant working from your home. As part of your job, you schedule webcasts, online chats, and teleconference calls for businesspeople who are conducting business around the world.

YOUR TASK To broaden your knowledge of time zones, respond to the following questions.

a. What does the abbreviation UTC indicate? (Use Google and search for *UTC definition*.)

b. Internationally, time is shown with a 24-hour clock (sometimes called military time). What time does 13.00 indicate? (Use Google; search for *24-hour clock*.) How is a 12-hour clock different from a 24-hour clock? With which are you most familiar?

c. You must schedule an audioconference for a businessperson in Indianapolis, Indiana, who wants to talk with a person in Osaka, Japan. What are the best business hours (between 8 a.m. and 5 p.m.) for them to talk? (Many websites provide time zone converters. For example, try searching for *time and date*. Several websites display time and date in any time zone on Earth.)

d. What are the best business hours for an online chat between an executive in Atlanta and a vendor in Singapore?

e. When is a businessperson in Arizona most likely to reach a contact in Belgium on Skype during office hours? Your instructor may select other cities for you to search.

f. Why did your new business partner in Moscow, Russia, call you at 3 a.m. in the Eastern Standard Time zone (UTC-5) and was understandably shocked when he woke you up?

3.4 Twitter Opening up Countries and Cultures (L.O. 1, 3)

E-Mail | Intercultural | Social Media | Web

Perhaps you are one of a growing number of people who tweet regularly. Twitter and other social media have become primary news sources for many adults under age thirty. Apparently some millennials trust social media and each other more than anything said by government, business, or religious institutions.[110] Twitter feeds provide up-to-the-second news from war-torn regions, violent incidents, and sites of natural disasters at home and around the world. Twitter has also changed how public opinion of political events is formed and expressed. The so-called back channel, a running commentary on events still unfolding, often decides the winner of a debate even before the debate concludes.

Political blogger Chris Cillizza holds a dim view of the microblogging service: "There's no question that political Twitter reinforces a sort of groupthink—since everyone in the D.C. bubble is following everyone else on Twitter; it's an electronic echo chamber."[111] He points out that only 8 percent of Americans rely on Twitter for news and only 16 percent use Twitter at all. The influence of Twitter, however, defies these low figures.

Although government officials could technically cut both Internet connections and the SMS network, never again will a dictator be able to impose a complete information monopoly. Even if some of the information may be unreliable and unverifiable, tweets are the latest means of instant cross-border, globe-spanning communication and a high-speed alternative to traditional mainstream media.[112]

YOUR TASK Start by viewing *trending topics* on Twitter. Some may be business related. A few may be international. Use the search box to type any current international or business event to see what Twitter users are saying about it. For instance, check out the tweets of CNN's Christiane Amanpour or those of another well-known journalist; for example, Nick Gillespie or George Will. In the classroom, discuss the usefulness of Twitter as you see it. Your instructor may ask you to prepare an e-mail or memo identifying and summarizing three trending business topics. In your opinion, how accurately do the tweets convey the trend? Can trends be summarized in 140 characters? You will learn more about Twitter and other mobile media in Chapter 7.

3.5 Trek Bicycle Goes Global (L.O. 1, 3, and 5)

Intercultural Social Media 

Waterloo, Wisconsin, is the home of Trek Bicycle, manufacturer of super-lightweight carbon bikes. The small town (population 2,888) is about the last place you would expect to find the world's largest specialty bicycle maker. Trek started its global business in a red barn smack in the middle of Wisconsin farm country. It employs 1,500 people in Waterloo and serves 2,000 stores in the United States alone and 4,000 dealers worldwide in 65 countries. Even a huge recall of almost 1 million Trek bikes for problems with the quick-release lever on the front-wheel hub has not derailed the company.[113]

Nearly 50 percent of the sales of the high-tech bicycles come from international markets. Future sales abroad look promising as Trek expands into Chinese and Indian markets. In Asia bicycles are still a major means of transportation. To accommodate domestic and international consumers, Trek maintains a busy international website in 14 languages. Enter the search term *Trek Bikes*. Also, visit Trek Bicycles' Facebook fan page.

Like many companies, Trek encountered problems conducting intercultural transactions. For example, in Mexico, cargo was often pilfered while awaiting customs clearance. In Singapore a buyer balked at a green bike helmet, explaining that when a man wears green on his head, it means his wife is unfaithful. In Germany Trek had to redesign its packaging to reduce waste and meet environmental requirements. Actually, the changes required in Germany bolstered the company's overall image of environmental sensitivity.

YOUR TASK Based on principles you studied in this chapter, name several lessons other entrepreneurs can learn from Trek's international experiences.[114]

3.6 Negotiating Traps (L.O. 2, 3)

Intercultural

Businesspeople often have difficulty reaching agreement on the terms of contracts, proposals, and anything that involves bargaining. They have even more difficulty when the negotiators are from different cultures.

YOUR TASK Discuss the causes and implications of the following common mistakes made by North Americans in their negotiations with foreigners.

a. Assuming that a final agreement is set in stone
b. Lacking patience and insisting that matters progress more quickly than the pace preferred by the locals
c. Thinking that an interpreter is always completely accurate
d. Believing that individuals who speak English understand every nuance of your meaning
e. Ignoring or misunderstanding the significance of rank

3.7 Learn to Speak a Foreign Language or Just a Few Phrases With Livemocha or Busuu (L.O. 2, 3)

E-Mail Intercultural Social Media Web

Social media have taken the world by storm; therefore, it's not surprising that social networks have formed around various interests and pursuits. At least two major social networks have united people eager to learn or practice a foreign language online. The two major ones are Livemocha and busuu. Both offer free basic instruction and premium fee-based content in a number of popular languages.

YOUR TASK Compare the two online language learning communities. Consider these and similar questions: How many languages do they support? How do they operate, and how much do they cost? What features do they offer? How many users do they have? Learn a few phrases in a language that interests you and report back to class. Your instructor may ask you to summarize your findings in writing, in either an e-mail or an online post.

3.8 Checking in With Facebook (L.O. 1, 3)

Intercultural Social Media Team Web

With over 1.55 billion monthly active users, Facebook is currently the largest social networking site; it is available in 70 languages.[115] According to Pew Research Center, Facebook's growth in the United States has reached a plateau; in recent years the percentage of American adults on Facebook has flattened out at just above 70 percent.[116] A whopping 83 percent of daily active users are located outside the United States.[117] Facebook is focusing its efforts on fast-growing regions, Africa and India, where the social media site has reached the milestone of 100 million users.[118]

YOUR TASK As a team or alone, visit any of the Facebook tracking websites—for example, Facebook's own newsroom, Socialbakers, or Internet World Stats. Study the tables listing the top countries in various categories. Which country is currently the fastest-growing country in absolute numbers? Find out which country has the largest presence on Facebook outside the United States. Do not rely solely on absolute numbers, but compare population penetration rates; that is, the ratio between Facebook use and population.

Even if you don't speak another language, visit at last one non-English Facebook site and evaluate surface similarities and differences. Chances are that you will recognize some familiar features. Discuss similarities and differences in class. If you speak a foreign language, can you spot any customization that suggests adaptation to local preferences and customs?

As you will learn in Chapter 15, Facebook is also playing an increasing role in recruiting and other business applications.

3.9 Examining Cultural Stereotypes (L.O. 2, 3)

Intercultural Team 

As you have learned in this chapter, generalizations are necessary as we acquire and categorize new knowledge. As long as we remain open to new experiences, we won't be stymied by rigid, stereotypical perceptions of other cultures. Almost all of us at some point in our lives are subject to stereotyping by others, whether we are immigrants, minorities, women, members of certain professions, or Americans abroad. Generally speaking, negative stereotypes sting. However, even positive stereotypes can offend or embarrass because they fail to acknowledge the differences among individuals.

YOUR TASK Think about a nation or culture about which you have only a hazy idea. Jot down a few key traits that come to mind. For example, you may not know much about the Netherlands and the Dutch people. You can probably think of gouda cheese, wooden clogs, Heineken beer, tulips, and windmills. Anything else? Then consider a culture with which you are very familiar, whether it is yours or that of a country you have visited or studied. In one column, write down a few stereotypical perceptions that are positive. Then, in another column, record negative stereotypes you associate with that culture. Share your notes with your team or the whole class, as the instructor may direct. How do you respond to others' descriptions of your culture? Which stereotypes irk you and why? For a quick fact check and overview at the end of this exercise, google the *CIA World Factbook* or *BBC News Country Profiles.*

3.10 Analyzing a Problem International E-Mail (L.O. 3)

E-Mail Intercultural

American writers sometimes forget that people in other countries, even if they understand English, are not aware of the meanings of certain words and phrases.

YOUR TASK Study the following e-mail[119] to be sent by a U.S. firm to a potential supplier in another country. Identify specific weaknesses that may cause troubles for intercultural readers.

Dear Akira:

Because of the on-again/off-again haggling with one of our subcontractors, we have been putting off writing to you. We were royally turned off by their shoddy merchandise, the excuses they made up, and the way they put down some of our customers. Since we have our good name to keep up, we have decided to take the bull by the horns and see if you would be interested in bidding on the contract for spare parts.

By playing ball with us, you are sure to score big with your products. So please give it your best shot and fire off your price list ASAP. We will need it by 3/8 if you are to be in the running.

Yours,

3.11 Make Yourself at Home: Ambiguous Expressions Invite New Friends (L.O. 3)

Intercultural Team

To end conversations, North Americans often issue casual invitations to new acquaintances and even virtual strangers, such as *Visit me when you come to New York,* or *Come on over anytime.* However, nonnative speakers and visitors may misinterpret such casual remarks. They may embarrass their hosts and suffer disappointment by taking the offhand invitation literally and acting on it. Those interacting across cultures would be wise to avoid using expressions that have multiple meanings.

YOUR TASK Assume you are a businessperson engaged in exporting and importing. As such, you are in constant communication with suppliers and customers around the world. In messages sent abroad or in situations with nonnative speakers of English at home, what kinds of ambiguous expressions should you avoid? In teams or individually, list three to five original examples of idioms, slang, acronyms, sports references, abbreviations, jargon, and two-word verbs. Which phrases or behavior could be taken literally by a person from a different culture?

3.12 Greasing Palms Abroad: *Baksheesh, Mordida,* and *Kumshah* (L.O. 4)

Ethics Intercultural

In the Middle East, bribes are called *baksheesh*. In Mexico, they are *mordida*; and in Southeast Asia, *kumshah*. Although it takes place in many parts of the world, bribery is not officially sanctioned by any country. In the United States, the Foreign Corrupt Practices Act prohibits giving anything of value to a foreign official in an effort to win or retain business. However, this law does allow payments that may be necessary to expedite or secure "routine governmental action." For instance, a company could make small payments to obtain permits and licenses or to process visas or work orders. Also allowed are payments to secure telephone service and power and water supplies, as well as payments for the loading and unloading of cargo.

YOUR TASK In light of what you have learned in this chapter, how should you act in the following situations? Are the actions legal or illegal?[120]

a. Your company is moving toward final agreement on a contract in Pakistan to sell farm equipment. As the contract is prepared, officials ask that a large amount be included to enable the government to update its agriculture research. The extra amount is to be paid in cash to the three officials you have worked with. Should your company pay?

b. You have been negotiating with a government official in Niger regarding an airplane maintenance contract. The official asks to use your Diner's Club card to charge $2,028 in airplane tickets as a honeymoon present. Should you do it to win the contract?

c. You are trying to collect an overdue payment of $163,000 on a shipment of milk powder to the Dominican Republic. A senior government official asks for $20,000 as a collection service fee. Should you pay?

d. Your company is in the business of arranging hunting trips to East Africa. You are encouraged to give guns and travel allowances to officials in a wildlife agency that has authority to issue licenses to hunt big game. The officials have agreed to keep the gifts quiet. Should you make the gifts?

e. Your firm has just moved you to Malaysia, and your furniture is sitting on the dock. Cargo handlers won't unload it until you or your company pays off each local dock worker. Should you pay?

f. In Mexico your firm has been working hard to earn lucrative contracts with the national oil company, Pemex. One government official has hinted elaborately that his son would like to do marketing studies for your company. Should you hire the son?

3.13 Investigating Gifts, Gratuities, Kickbacks, and Entertainment Limits (L.O. 4)

Ethics | Intercultural | Team | Web

You are one of a group of interns at a large company. As part of your training, your director asks your team to investigate the codes of conduct of other companies. In particular, the manager asks you to find comparison information on gifts, gratuities, kickbacks, and entertainment limits.

YOUR TASK Search the Web for sections in codes of conduct that relate to gifts, gratuities, kickbacks, and entertainment. From three companies or organizations (such as Blue Cross Blue Shield, 3M Corporation, or a university), investigate specific restrictions. What do these organizations allow and restrict? Prepare a list summarizing your findings in your own words.

3.14 Investigating Gender Talk (L.O. 5)

Review the Career Coach feature on page 110 about gender talk and gender tension.

YOUR TASK In small groups or in a class discussion, consider these questions: Do men and women have different communication styles? Which style is more appropriate for today's team-based management? Do we need a kind of communicative affirmative action to give more recognition to women's ways of talking? Should men and women receive training encouraging the interchangeable use of these styles depending on the situation?

3.15 Encouraging Gender Diversity in Corporations (L.O. 5)

E-Mail | Intercultural | Team

Despite strides by some global companies toward greater diversity, the Alliance for Board Diversity (ABD) reports that women and minorities are still underrepresented in U.S. corporate boardrooms. The alliance, which includes the leadership organization Catalyst, found that white men still occupied nearly 70 percent of board seats at Fortune 100 companies. White males' share on boards in Fortune 500 companies was higher, at 73 percent.[121] The ABD believes that the pool of qualified women and minority executives is better than ever before for board positions at Fortune 500 companies.[122]

Diversity and inclusion seem to be good for business: A recent Catalyst study showed that boards with the highest representation of women performed significantly better than boards with the lowest representation. On average, the most diverse companies outperformed the least diverse organizations in returns on equity (53 percent), sales (42 percent), and invested capital (66 percent).[123] A McKinsey survey of 366 public companies ("Diversity Matters") produced similar results. Overall, businesses embracing racial and ethnic diversity were 35 percent more likely to do better than their industry rivals.[124]

How can greater gender diversity be accomplished? European countries such as Germany, the UK, France, Italy, and the Netherlands are taking radical measures. They are threatening to impose mandatory quotas within the next five years unless public companies increase the percentage of women on their corporate boards to as much as 40 percent. Critics counter that rigid quotas could jeopardize the very goal of greater diversity, unduly affect smaller companies, and encourage the appointment of token women just to satisfy the requirement. Rather, they suggest that politicians and business leaders pursue voluntary targets and appeal to investors to step up the pressure on companies to change.[125]

YOUR TASK Individually or in groups, discuss whether the United States should rely on the marketplace to effect change or whether the government should speed change along. If your instructor directs, summarize your thoughts in a concise e-mail message or a post on Blackboard, Moodle, or another online discussion board or in a chat room. Alternatively, plan a message to investors encouraging them to diversify their boards of directors to include more women and minorities.

Test Your Etiquette IQ

New communication platforms and casual workplace environments have blurred the lines of appropriateness, leaving workers wondering how to navigate uncharted waters. Indicate whether the following statements are true or false. Then see if you agree with the responses on p. R-1.

1. When representing your organization abroad on business, you should show your enthusiasm and friendliness with expansive gestures and first-name conversations.

_______ True _______ False

2. When traveling abroad, you should open doors and allow older businesspeople to enter a room and be seated before you.

_______ True _______ False

3. When greeting people in other countries, the best way to show confidence and friendliness is by shaking hands and making direct eye contact.

_______ True _______ False

Chat About It

In each chapter you will find five discussion questions related to the chapter material. Your instructor may assign these topics for you to discuss in class, in an online chat room, or on an online discussion board. Some of the discussion topics may require outside research. You may also be asked to read and respond to postings made by your classmates.

TOPIC 1: Discuss the dos and don'ts when traveling abroad, or establish criteria of appropriate behavior you would expect from tourists to your country. Be specific and give reasons.

TOPIC 2: Consider the social media you use daily. Could they help you connect with people outside your immediate circle of friends or family, people from other, perhaps unfamiliar cultures? Would you find it useful? Would you agree that people behave the same on social media networks as they do in real life and that some users are more outgoing than others? Give specific examples.

TOPIC 3: Identify a situation in which you were aware of ethnocentrism in your own actions or those of friends, family members, or colleagues. In general terms, describe what happened. What made you think the experience involved ethnocentrism?

TOPIC 4: Do some research to determine why Transparency International ranked Denmark, New Zealand, Finland, Sweden, Norway, and Switzerland as the least corrupt countries or why it ranked Iraq, Afghanistan, Sudan, North Korea, and Somalia as the most corrupt countries.

TOPIC 5: In your own experience, how accurate are characterizations that gender theorists make about differences between men and women? Support your views.

Grammar and Mechanics | *Review 3*

Nouns and Pronouns

Review Guides 10 through 18 about noun and pronoun usage in Appendix D, Grammar and Mechanics Guide, beginning on page D-4. On a separate sheet, revise the following sentences to correct errors in nouns and pronouns. For each error you locate, write the guide number that reflects this usage. Some sentences may have two errors. If the sentence is correct, write *C*. When you finish, check your answers on page Key-1.

EXAMPLE: My friend and me are both looking for jobs.

REVISION: My friend and I are both looking for jobs. [Guide 12]

1. During the investigation two attornies questioned all witnesses thoroughly.
2. Please send texts to my manager and I so that she and I both understand the situation.
3. Google encourages developers to create apps and games for families and children using it's new program.
4. Its a smart move on Google's part because it allows we consumers to select age-appropriate games for our children.
5. Send the report to the administrative assistant or myself when it's finished.
6. Every online sales rep must improve their writing skills to handle chat sessions.
7. The contract will be awarded to whomever submitted the lowest bid.
8. Most applications were made in time, but your's and her's missed the deadline.
9. Just between you and me, who do you think will be our new president?
10. It must have been her who sent the e-mail to Jason and me.

References

[1] Volk, A. (2014, November 9). Wal-Mart and workers' rights: A case study. *Harvard Political Review.* Retrieved from http://harvardpolitics.com/united-states/wal-mart-workers-rights-case-study; Jui, P. (2011, May 16). Walmart's downfall in Germany: A case study. *Journal of International Management*. Retrieved from https://journalofinternationalmanagement.wordpress.com/2011/05/16/walmarts-downfall-in-germany-a-case-study

[2] Macaray, D. (2011, August 29). Why did Walmart leave Germany? *The Huffington Post*. Retrieved from http://www.huffingtonpost.com/david-macaray/why-did-walmart-leave-ger_b_940542.html; Landler, M., & Barbaro, M. (2006, August 2). No, not always. *New York Times*, p. 1. Retrieved from http://www.nytimes.com

[3] Landler, M., & Barbaro, M. (2006, August 2). No, not always. *New York Times*, p. 1. Retrieved from http://www.nytimes.com

[4] Narayan, A., & Huang, G. (2014, October 30). *Bloomberg Business*. Retrieved from http://www.bloomberg.com/news/articles/2014-10-30/wal-mart-to-close-30-japan-stores-expand-in-fresh-food

[5] Pollock, L. (2014, October 30). Wal-Mart to close 30 underperforming stores in Japan. *The Wall Street Journal*. Retrieved from http://www.wsj.com/articles/wal-mart-to-close-30-underperforming-stores-in-japan-1414669827?alg=y

[6] Narayan, A. (2013, October). Wal-Mart faces setback to India retail foray. *Bloomberg Business*. Retrieved from http://www.bloomberg.com/news/articles/2013-10-10/wal-mart-faces-setback-to-india-retail-foray

[7] Trefis Team. (2014, April 2). Challenges Wal-Mart faces in Mexico and China. Forbes. Retrieved from http://www.forbes.com/sites/greatspeculations/2014/04/02/challenges-wal-mart-faces-in-mexico-and-china

[8] Rein, S. (2012, January 16). Why global brands fail in China. CNBC guest blog. Retrieved from http://www.cnbc.com/id/46009614; Soni, P. (2015, February 18). What are Walmart's growing pains in Asia? Market Realist. Retrieved from http://marketrealist.com/2015/02/walmart-isnt-heavyweight-china

[9] Gallant, P. (2014, April 10). 10 biggest overseas blunders: Mistakes international businesses can learn from. HSBC Global Connections. Retrieved from https://globalconnections.hsbc.com/brazil/en/articles/10-biggest-overseas-blunders-en

[10] Soni, P. (2015, February 18). Walmart's key challenges in its business environment. Market Realist. Retrieved from http://marketrealist.com/2015/02/walmarts-key-challenges-business-environment

[11] Smith, J. (2007). The perils of prediction. *World Trade*, *20*(1), 39-44. Retrieved from http://search.ebscohost.com

[12] Monllos, K. (2015, May 29). Is Walmart trying to brand itself as socially conscious? *Adweek*. Retrieved from http://www.adweek.com/news/advertising-branding/walmart-trying-brand-itself-socially-conscious-165034

[13] Kanekal, V. (2015, February 26). LG crowned the most trusted brand in India, Samsung second most: Report. Trak.in. Retrieved from http://trak.in/tags/business/2015/02/26/lg-most-trusted-brand-in-india-samsung

[14] Wang, Z. (2015, August 15). PepsiCo launches oats-based dairy drinks. *China Daily Europe*. Retrieved from http://europe.chinadaily.com.cn/business/2015-08/15/content_21608067.htm

[15] Frohlich, T. C., & Sauter, M. B. (2013, December 8). 10 classic USA brands that are foreign-owned. *USA Today*. Retrieved from http://www.usatoday.com/story/money/business/2013/12/08/10-classic-usa-brands-that-are-foreign-owned/3882739

[16] Chaudhuri, S. (2015, June 11). Aldi details U.S. expansion plan. *The Wall Street Journal*. Retrieved

from http://www.wsj.com/articles/aldi-details-u-s-expansion-plan-1434033903?alg=y

[17] Perlberg, S. (2014, January 14). Some Americans are threatening to stop drinking Jim Beam now that it's owned by a Japanese company. Business Insider. Retrieved from http://www.businessinsider.com/jim-beam-acquisition-jack-daniels-2014-1

[18] Randle, J. (2015, September 21). Little change at Virginia's China-owned Smithfield Foods. Retrieved from http://www.voanews.com/content/china-owned-smithfield-foods-growing-little-change/2972885.html

[19] Fleming, A. (2013, September 3). The geography of taste: How our food preferences are formed. *The Guardian*. Retrieved from http://www.theguardian.com/lifeandstyle/wordofmouth/2013/sep/03/geography-taste-how-food-preferences-formed

[20] Kannan, S. (2014, November 19). How McDonald's conquered India. BBC News. Retrieved from http://www.bbc.com/news/business-30115555

[21] Carlson, B. (2013, September 26). Why big American businesses fail in China. CNBC. Retrieved from http://www.cnbc.com/2013/09/26/why-big-american-businesses-fail-in-china.html

[22] Chou, K. (2015, September 25). Avoid its pitfalls and China is land of opportunity. *USA Today*. Retrieved from http://www.usatoday.com/story/tech/2015/09/25/avoid-its-pitfalls-and-china-land-opportunity/72821828; Carlson, B. (2013, September 26). Why big American businesses fail in China. CNBC. Retrieved from http://www.cnbc.com/2013/09/26/why-big-american-businesses-fail-in-china.html

[23] U.S. Free Trade Agreements. (2013, January 1). Export.gov. Retrieved from http://export.gov/FTA/index.asp; Free Trade Agreements; Office of the United States Trade Representative. (2015). Retrieved from http://www.ustr.gov/trade-agreements/free-trade-agreements; Walker, A. (2015, May 13). TTIP: Why the EU-US trade deal matters. BBC News. Retrieved from http://www.bbc.com/news/business-32691589

[24] Bremmer, I. (2015, January 22). The new world of business. *Fortune*. Retrieved from http://fortune.com/2015/01/22/the-new-world-of-business

[25] Ernst & Young. (2013, April 25). Entering the global middle class. Retrieved from http://www.ey.com/GL/en/Issues/Driving-growth/Middle-class-growth-in-emerging-markets—Entering-the-global-middle-class

[26] Vossos, T. (2011, April 3). The effect of advancements in transportation technology on global business. Retrieved from http://www.ehow.com/info_8160779_effects-transportation-technology-global-business.html

[27] More Mexicans leaving than coming to the U.S. (2015, November 19). Pew Research Center. Retrieved from http://www.pewhispanic.org/2015/11/19/more-mexicans-leaving-than-coming-to-the-u-s; Kotkin, J., & Ozuna, E. (2012, Winter). America's demographic future. *Cato Journal, 38*(1), 59. http://www.cato.org/pubs/journal/cj32n1/cj32n1-5.pdf

[28] William H. Frey cited in Kotkin, J., & Ozuna, E. (2012, Winter). America's demographic future. *Cato Journal, 38*(1), 60. http://www.cato.org/pubs/journal/cj32n1/cj32n1-5.pdf

[29] Kotkin, J., & Ozuna, E. (2012, Winter). America's demographic future. *Cato Journal, 38*(1), 59. http://www.cato.org/pubs/journal/cj32n1/cj32n1-5.pdf; Ortman, J. M., & Guarneri, C. E. (2009). United States population projections: 2000 to 2050. Retrieved from http://www.census.gov/population/projections; U.S. Census 2010. (2011, March 24). 2010 Census shows America's diversity. Retrieved from https://www.census.gov/newsroom/releases/archives/2010_census/cb11-cn125.html; U.S. Department of Labor. (2007). Futurework: Trends and challenges for work in the 21st century. Retrieved from http://www.dol.gov/oasam/programs/history/herman/reports/futurework/report.htm#.ULhdaWeQOWY

[30] Based on Wil. (2015, February 24.) Doing business in different cultures in English. EF English Live Blog. Retrieved from http://englishlive.ef.com/blog/doing-business-different-cultures/

[31] Wang, H. H. (2012, October 24). Why Barbie stumbled in China and how she could re-invent herself. *Forbes*. Retrieved from http://www.forbes.com/sites/helenwang/2012/10/24/why-barbie-stumbled-in-china-and-how-she-could-re-invent-herself

[32] Changing attitudes on gay marriage. (2015, July 29). Pew Research Center. Retrieved from http://www.pewforum.org/2015/07/29/graphics-slideshow-changing-attitudes-on-gay-marriage

[33] Hall E. T., & Hall, M. R. (2000). Key concepts: Underlying structures of culture. In Maryann H. Albrecht (Ed.), *International HRM: Managing diversity in the workplace*. Hoboken, NJ: Wiley-Blackwell, pp. 200-202; Hall, E. T., & Hall, M. R. (1990). *Understanding cultural differences*. Yarmouth, ME: Intercultural Press, pp. 183-184.

[34] Figure based on Chaney, L. H., & Martin, J. S. (2011). *Intercultural business communication* (5th ed.). Upper Saddle River, NJ: Prentice Hall, Chapter 5; J. Chung's analysis appearing in Chen, G. M., & Starosta, W. J. *Foundations of intercultural communication*. Boston: Allyn and Bacon, 1998, p. 51; and O'Hara-Devereaux, M. & Johansen, R. (1994). *Globalwork: Bridging distance, culture, and time*. San Francisco: Jossey-Bass, p. 55.

[35] Chaney, L. H., & Martin, J. S. (2011). *Intercultural business communication* (5th ed.). Upper Saddle River, NJ: Prentice Hall, p. 93.

[36] Chen, M.-J., & Miller, D. (2010, November). West meets East: Toward an ambicultural approach to management. *Academy of Management Perspectives, 24*(4), 19ff. Retrieved from http://search.ebscohost.com; Sheer, V. C., & Chen, L. (2003, January). Successful Sino-Western business negotiation: Participants' accounts of national and professional cultures. *The Journal of Business Communication, 40*(1), 62; see also Luk, L., Patel, M., & White, K. (1990, December). Personal attributes of American and Chinese business associates. *The Bulletin of the Association for Business Communication*, 67.

[37] Gallois, C., & Callan, V. (1997). *Communication and culture*. New York: Wiley, p. 24.

[38] Copeland, J. (1990, December 15). Stare less, listen more. American Airlines. *American Way*, p. 32.

[39] Gallois, C., & Callan, V. (1997). *Communication and culture*. New York: Wiley, p. 29.

[40] Copeland, L., & Griggs, L. (1985). *Going international*. New York: Penguin, p. 94.

[41] Ibid., p. 108.

[42] Ibid., p. 12.

[43] Poll results: Islam. (2015, April 10). Huff Post/YouGov. Retrieved from https://today.yougov.com/news/2015/03/09/poll-results-islam

[44] Ethical Insight based on Saslow, E. (2009, June 3). As the myths abound, so does Islamic outreach. *The Washington Post*, p. C1. Retrieved from http://www.dowjones.com/factiva

[45] Saslow, E. (2009, June 3). As the myths abound, so does Islamic outreach. *The Washington Post*, p. C1. Retrieved from http://www.dowjones.com/factiva

[46] Chen, G. M., & Starosta, W. J. (1998). *Foundations of intercultural communication*. Boston: Allyn and Bacon, p. 40.

[47] Varner, I., & Beamer, L. (2011). *Intercultural communication in the global workplace*. Boston: McGraw-Hill Irwin, p. 100.

[48] Blumberg, A. (2015, April 21). In the Middle East, Muslims and Jews work in unison to care for the environment. *The Huffington Post*. Retrieved from http://www.huffingtonpost.com/2015/04/21/arava-institute-muslim-jewish-dialogue_n_7105274.html

[49] Dale, R. (n.d.). British and French vie for "worst tourists" title. Center for Strategic & International Studies. Retrieved from http://csis.org/blog/british-and-french-vie-"worst-tourists"-title

[50] Hui, L., & Blanchard, B. (2013, July 29). Chinese tourists the focus of international scrutiny after several high-profile incidents. *The Huffington Post*. Retrieved from http://www.huffingtonpost.com/2013/05/30/chinese-tourists-behave-badly_n_3356988.html

[51] Dale, R. (n.d.). British and French vie for "worst tourists" title. Center for Strategic & International Studies. Retrieved from http://csis.org/blog/british-and-french-vie-"worst-tourists"-title

[52] Martin, J. S., & Chaney, L. H. (2006). *Global business etiquette*. Westport, CT: Praeger, p. 69.

[53] Hammer, M. R. quoted in Chen, H.-M., & Starosta, W. J. (1993). *Foundations of intercultural communication*. Boston: Allyn & Bacon, p. 247.

[54] Chaney, L. H., & Martin, J. S. (1995). *Intercultural business communication*. Englewood Cliffs, NJ: Prentice Hall Career and Technology, p. 67.

[55] Klass, P. (2012, January 9). Seeing social media more as portal than as pitfall. *The New York Times*. Retrieved from http://www.nytimes.com/2012/01/10/health/views/seeing-social-media-as-adolescent-portal-more-than-pitfall.html

[56] Konnikova, M. (2013, September 10). How Facebook makes us unhappy. *The New Yorker*. Retrieved from http://www.newyorker.com/tech/elements/how-facebook-makes-us-unhappy

[57] Carter, J. F. (2010, October 14). Why Twitter influences cross-cultural engagement. Mashable Social Media. Retrieved from http://mashable.com/2010/10/14/twitter-cross-cultural

[58] Kumar, V., & Svensson, J. (2015). *Promoting social change and democracy through information technology*. Hershey, PA: IGI Global, p. 149.

[59] Carter, J. F. (2010, October 14). Why Twitter influences cross-cultural engagement. Mashable Social Media. Retrieved from http://mashable.com/2010/10/14/twitter-cross-cultural

[60] Ibid.

[61] McGrath, C. (2009, August 5). Five lessons learned about cross-cultural social networking. ThoughtFarmer. Retrieved from http://www.thoughtfarmer.com/blog/2009/08/05/5-lessons-cross-cultural-social-networking/#comments

[62] Masterson, M. (2009, January 27). Can social software "work" in Germany? Enterprise 2.0 blog. Retrieved from http://enterprise20blog.com/2009/01/27/can-social-software-work-in-germany

[63] Market trends. (2012, January). Broadband strategies toolkit. Retrieved from http://broadbandtoolkit.org/1.4
[64] Martinez, A. (2014, November 14). Why Mandarin won't be a lingua franca. Retrieved from http://time.com/3585847/mandarin-lingua-franca
[65] Martin, J. S., & Chaney, L. H. (2006). *Global business etiquette*. Westport, CT: Praeger, p. 191.
[66] Finney, P. B. (2005, May 17). Shaking hands, greasing palms. *The New York Times*, p. C1.
[67] Berenbeim, R. (2000, May). Global ethics. *Executive Excellence*, p. 7.
[68] Kimes, M. (2009, February 16). Fluor's corporate crime fighter. *Fortune*, p. 26. Retrieved from http://search.ebscohost.com
[69] Kottasova, I. (2015, September 10). IKEA is making loads of money in Russia. Wait, what? CNNMoney London. Retrieved from http://money.cnn.com/2015/09/10/news/companies/ikea-russia-ruble
[70] Meyer, H. (2011, March 7). Corruption halts IKEA in Russia. *The Age*. Retrieved from http://www.theage.com.au/world/corruption-halts-ikea-in-russia-20110306-1bji5.html; see also Bush, J. (2009, July 2). Why IKEA is fed up with Russia. BusinessWeek.com. Retrieved from http://www.businessweek.com/magazine/content/09_28/b4139033326721.htm
[71] The 2013 Corruption Perceptions Index. Transparency International. Retrieved from http://www.transparency.org/policy_research/surveys_indices/cpi
[72] PricewaterhouseCoopers International. (2008, January). Confronting corruption: The business case for an effective anti-corruption programme. Retrieved from http://www.pwc.com/gx/en/forensic-accounting-dispute-consulting-services/business-case-anti-corruption-programme.jhtml
[73] Schubert, S., & Miller, T. C. (2008, December 21). Where bribery was just a line item. *New York Times*, p. BU1. Retrieved from http://search.proquest.com
[74] Viswanatha, A., & Barrett, D. (2015, October 19). Wal-Mart bribery probe finds few signs of major misconduct in Mexico. *The Wall Street Journal*. Retrieved from http://www.wsj.com/articles/wal-mart-bribery-probe-finds-little-misconduct-in-mexico-1445215737?tesla=y
[75] The FIFA investigation, explained. (2015, December 3). *The New York Times*. Retrieved from http://www.nytimes.com/2015/12/04/sports/soccer/fifa-investigation.html?action=click&contentCollection=Soccer&module=RelatedCoverage®ion=Marginalia&pgtype=article
[76] Finney, P. B. (2005, May 17). Shaking hands, greasing palms. *The New York Times*, p. C1.
[77] Wei, S-J. (2003, March 12). Corruption in developing countries. *Global Economics*. Retrieved from http://www.brookings.edu/research/speeches/2003/03/12development-wei
[78] Alvarez, S. (2006, December). Global integrity: Transparency International's David Nussbaum is fighting for a world that is free of bribery and corruption. *Internal Auditor, 63*(6), 53. Retrieved from http://www.dowjones.com/factiva
[79] Hodgson, K. (1992, May). Adapting ethical decisions to a global marketplace. *Management Review*, 56. Retrieved from http://www.dowjones.com/factiva. See also Digh, P. (1997, April). Shades of gray in the global marketplace. *HR Magazine*, p. 42. Retrieved from http://search.ebscohost.com
[80] Solomon, C. M. (1996, January). Put your ethics to a global test. *Personnel Journal*, 66-74. See also Smeltzer, L. R., & Jennings, M. M. (1998, January). Why an international code of business ethics would be good for business. *Journal of Business Ethics*, 57-66; Barker, T. S., & Cobb, S. L. (2000). A survey of ethics and cultural dimensions of MNCs [multinational companies]. *Competitiveness Review, 10*(2), 123. Retrieved from http://search.ebscohost.com
[81] Hodgson, K. (1992, May). Adapting ethical decisions to a global marketplace. *Management Review*, 54. Retrieved from http://www.dowjones.com/factiva; See also Franke, G. R. (2008, March). Culture, economic development, and national ethical attitudes. *Journal of Business Research, 61*(3). Retrieved from http://search.ebscohost.com
[82] Phillips, K. (2009, June 2). Diversity helps your business—But not the way you think. *Forbes*. Retrieved from http://www.forbes.com/2009/06/02/diversity-collaboration-teams-leadership-managing-creativity.html
[83] Colby, S. L., & Ortman, J. M. (2015, March). Projections of the size and composition of the U.S. population: 2014 to 2060. United States Census Bureau. Retrieved from http://www.census.gov/content/dam/Census/library/publications/2015/demo/p25-1143.pdf
[84] Boykiv, Y. (2015, June 3). How to build and sustain a diverse team. Fast Company. Retrieved from http://www.fastcompany.com/3046829/hit-the-ground-running/how-to-build-and-sustain-a-diverse-team
[85] Phillips, K. W. (2014, October 1). How diversity makes us smarter. *Scientific American*. Retrieved from http://www.scientificamerican.com/article/how-diversity-makes-us-smarter
[86] Boykiv, Y. (2015, June 3). How to build and sustain a diverse team. Fast Company. Retrieved from http://www.fastcompany.com/3046829/hit-the-ground-running/how-to-build-and-sustain-a-diverse-team
[87] Krotz, J. L. (2007). Diversity pays off for everyone of diversity. 21st Century Business Ideas. Retrieved from http://21st-century-business-ideas.blogspot.com/2007/06/diversity-pays-off-for-everyone.html
[88] Segal, J. A. (2015, October 1). How gender bias hurts men. Society for Human Resource Management. Retrieved from http://www.shrm.org/publications/hrmagazine/editorialcontent/2015/1015/pages/1015-discriminating-against-men.aspx
[89] Separation of church and cubicle: Religion in the workplace. (2015, April 30). Wharton, University of Pennsylvania. Retrieved from http://knowledge.wharton.upenn.edu/article/separation-of-church-and-cubicle-religion-in-the-modern-workplace
[90] Career Coach (He Said, She Said) based on Basow, S. A., & Rubenfeld, K. (2003, February). Troubles talk: Effects of gender and gender-typing. *Sex Roles: A Journal of Research*, 183. Retrieved from http://www.springerlink.com/content/rm75xx843786037q/fulltext.pdf; Wood, J. T. (2002). *Gendered lives*. Belmont, CA: Wadsworth, p. 119; Tear, J. (1995, November 20). They just don't understand gender dynamics. *The Wall Street Journal*, p. A12. Retrieved from http://www.dowjones.com/factiva; Roiphe, A. (1994, October). Talking trouble. *Working Woman*, pp. 28-31; Stuart, C. (1994, February). Why can't a woman be more like a man? *Training Tomorrow*, pp. 22-24; Wolfe, A. (1994, December 12). She just doesn't understand. *New Republic, 211*(24), pp. 26-34.
[91] Smith, J. (2015, April 3). Study finds women are better bosses than men—here's why. Business Insider. Retrieved from http://www.businessinsider.com/why-women-are-better-managers-than-men-2015-4
[92] Schwartz, J., & Wald, M. L. (2003, March 9). Smart people working collectively can be dumber than the sum of their brains. Appeared originally in *The New York Times*. Retrieved from http://www.mindfully.org/Reform/2003/Smart-People-Dumber9mar03.htm
[93] Capowski, G. (1996, June). Managing diversity. *Management Review*, p. 16.
[94] Makower, J. (1995, Winter). Managing diversity in the workplace. *Business and Society Review*, pp. 48-54.
[95] White, M. D. (2002). *A short course in international marketing blunders*. Novato, CA: World Trade Press, p. 46.
[96] Monllos, K. (2015, May 29). Is Walmart trying to brand itself as socially conscious? The value-focused chain seems to embrace corporate responsibility. *Adweek*. Retrieved from http://www.adweek.com/news/advertising-branding/walmart-trying-brand-itself-socially-conscious-165034; Hill, C. (2015, February 21). 4 reasons Walmart is the most-hated retailer in America. MarketWatch. Retrieved from http://www.marketwatch.com/story/4-reasons-walmart-is-the-most-hated-retailer-in-america-2015-02-18
[97] Monllos, K. (2015, May 29). Is Walmart trying to brand itself as socially conscious? The value-focused chain seems to embrace corporate responsibility. *Adweek*. Retrieved from http://www.adweek.com/news/advertising-branding/walmart-trying-brand-itself-socially-conscious-165034
[98] Pettypiece, S. (2015, August 26). Wal-Mart to stop selling military-style guns after demand drops. *Bloomberg Business*. Retrieved from http://www.bloomberg.com/news/articles/2015-08-26/wal-mart-to-stop-selling-military-style-guns-after-demand-drops
[99] Tabuchi, H. (2015, August 26). Walmart to end sales of assault-style rifles in U.S. stores. *The New York Times*. Retrieved from http://www.nytimes.com/2015/08/27/business/walmart-to-end-sales-of-assault-rifles-in-us-stores.html
[100] Kanani, R. (2014, July 7). How the world's largest company thinks about social responsibility. *Forbes*. Retrieved from http://www.forbes.com/sites/rahimkanani/2014/07/07/how-the-worlds-largest-company-thinks-about-social-responsibility
[101] Ibid.
[102] Viswanatha, A., & Barrett, D. (2015, October 19). Wal-Mart bribery probe finds few signs of major misconduct in Mexico. *The Wall Street Journal*. Retrieved from http://www.wsj.com/articles/wal-mart-bribery-probe-finds-little-misconduct-in-mexico-1445215737
[103] Scenario based on Marketing muck-ups: The biggest follies of 2011. (2011, December 12). *Advertising Age*. Retrieved from http://adage.com/article/special-report-book-of-tens-2011/marketing-muck-ups-biggest-follies-2011/231468; Marketing's biggest social-media blunders of 2011. (2011, December 12). *Advertising Age*. Retrieved from

http://adage.com/article/special-report-book-of-tens-2011/marketing-s-biggest-social-media-blunders-2011/231503; Wasserman, T. (2011, February 16). Red Cross does PR disaster recovery on rogue tweet. Mashable. Retrieved from http://mashable.com/2011/02/16/red-cross-tweet

[104] Jacobowitz, J. L. (2014, October 24). Lawyers beware: You are what you post! The case for cultural competence, legal ethics, and social media. *SMU Journal of Science & Technology Law Review*, p. 25. Retrieved from http://papers.ssrn.com/sol3/papers.cfm?abstract_id=2514678&download=yes

[105] British minister in cultural gaffe after giving Taipei mayor "taboo" watch. *The Guardian*. Retrieved from http://www.theguardian.com/world/2015/jan/27/british-minister-cultural-gaffe-taipei-mayor-taboo-watch

[106] Hookway, J. (2012, June 5). Ikea's products make shoppers blush in Thailand. *The Wall Street Journal*, p. A16.

[107] Špaček, L. (2008). *Nová velká kniha etikety.* Prague: Mladá Fronta, p. 260.

[108] Cottrill, K. (2000, November 6). The world according to Hollywood. *Traffic World*, p. 15.

[109] Conlin, M. (2007, April 23). Go-go-going to pieces in China. *BusinessWeek*, p. 88.

[110] Drexler, P. (2014, February 16). Millennials: Trust no one but Twitter. *Time*. Retrieved from http://ideas.time.com/2014/02/16/millennials-trust-no-one-but-twitter

[111] Cillizza, C. (2013, November 7). How Twitter has changed politics—and political journalism. *The Washington Post*. Retrieved from https://www.washingtonpost.com/news/the-fix/wp/2013/11/07/how-twitter-has-changed-politics-and-political-journalism

[112] Nasr, O. (2009, June 15). Tear gas and Twitter: Iranians take their protests online. CNN.com. Retrieved from http://edition.cnn.com/2009/WORLD/meast/06/14/iran.protests.twitter; Grossman, L. (2009, June 17). Iran protests: Twitter, the medium of the movement. *Time*. Retrieved from http://www.time.com/time/world/article/0,8599,1905125,00.html; Sarno, D. (2009, March 6). Twittergates: Twitter's @billgates isn't really Bill Gates. *Los Angeles Times*. Retrieved from http://latimesblogs.latimes.com/technology/2009/03/latest-twitter.html

[113] Trek riders: Here's what to do with your recalled bike. (2015, April 22). *USA Today*. Retrieved from http://www.usatoday.com/story/news/2015/04/22/trek-bicycle-recall-what-to-do/26172867

[114] Dawson, D. (2005, March 1). At the top and still climbing. High Performance Composites. CompositesWorld. Retrieved from http://www.compositesworld.com/articles/at-the-top-and-still-climbing.aspx; Wucker, M. (1998, December/January). Keep on trekking. *Working Woman*, pp. 32-36.

[115] Facebook statistics. (2015, September 20). Statistic Brain Research Institute. Retrieved from http://www.statisticbrain.com/facebook-statistics

[116] Duggan, M. (2015, August 19). Mobile messaging and social media 2015. Pew Research Center. Retrieved from http://www.pewinternet.org/2015/08/19/mobile-messaging-and-social-media-2015

[117] Stats. (n.d.). Facebook Newsroom. Retrieved from http://newsroom.fb.com/company-info

[118] Luckerson, V. (2014, October 4). Meet the woman heading Facebook's huge international growth. *Time*. Retrieved from http://time.com/3462041/facebook-growth

[119] Based on Knotts, R., & Thibodeaux, M. S. (1992). Verbal skills in cross-culture managerial communication. *European Business Review, 92*(2), v-vii.

[120] Martin, K., & Walsh, S. M. (1996, October). Beware the Foreign Corrupt Practices Act. *International Commercial Litigation*, 25-27; Lay-person's guide to Foreign Corrupt Practices Act (FCPA). (n.d.). United States Department of Justice. Retrieved from http://www.usdoj.gov/criminal/fraud/fcpa

[121] Alliance for Board Diversity. (2013, August 15). Missing pieces: Women and minorities on Fortune 500 boards. 2012 Alliance for Board Diversity census. Retrieved from http://theabd.org/ABD_Fact_Sheet_Final.pdf

[122] Alliance for Board Diversity. (2013, August 15). Board room diversity at a standstill in Fortune 500 companies. Retrieved from http://www.theabd.org/ABD_Missing_Pieces_Press_Release_Final_8_15.pdf

[123] Alliance for Board Diversity. (2013, August 15). Missing pieces: Women and minorities on Fortune 500 boards 2012 Alliance for Board Diversity census. Retrieved from http://theabd.org/ABD_Fact_Sheet_Final.pdf

[124] McKinsey & Company. (2015, January). Why diversity matters. Retrieved from http://www.mckinsey.com/insights/organization/why_diversity_matters

[125] Egan, M. (2015, March 24). Still missing: Female business leaders. CNN Money. Retrieved from http://money.cnn.com/2015/03/24/investing/female-ceo-pipeline-leadership; Ferrary, M. (2009, March 2). Why women managers shine in a downturn. *Financial Times*. Retrieved from http://www.ft.com/intl/cms/s/0/40bb00ac-06cb-11de-ab0f-000077b07658.html#axzz41KLxSIEG

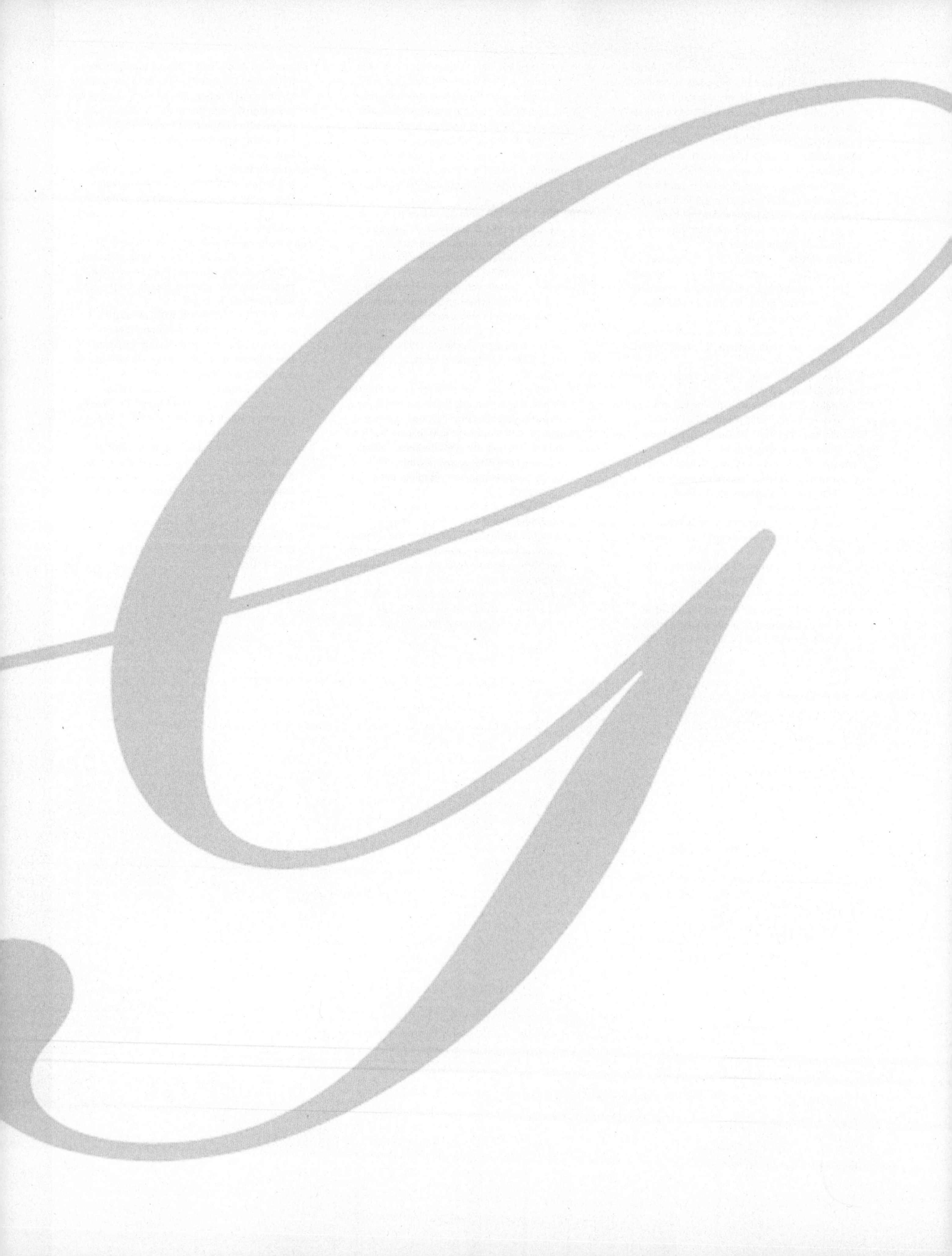

UNIT 2

The Writing Process in the Digital Era

Chapter 4
Planning Business Messages

Chapter 5
Organizing and Drafting Business Messages

Chapter 6
Revising Business Messages

racorn/Shutterstock.com

Chapter 4 Planning Business Messages

LEARNING OUTCOMES

After studying this chapter, you should be able to

1 Understand the nature of communication and its barriers in the digital era.

2 Summarize the 3-x-3 writing process and explain how it guides a writer.

3 Analyze the purpose of a message, anticipate its audience, and select the best communication channel.

4 Employ expert writing techniques such as incorporating audience benefits, the "you" view, conversational but professional language, a positive and courteous tone, bias-free language, plain language, and vigorous words.

5 Understand how teams approach collaborative writing projects and what collaboration tools support team writing.

TOMS Shoes Integrates For-Profit Entrepreneurship With Bleeding-Heart Philanthropy

Yeamake/Shutterstock.com

Zooming In

TOMS built a socially conscious movement into an amazingly profitable business. Initially, founder Blake Mycoskie had a simple idea: sell a pair of shoes today; give away a pair of shoes tomorrow. That message became a communication mantra for the entrepreneur, whose trademark canvas shoes propelled him, his ideas, and his brand into a global phenomenon. Since its founding in 2006, TOMS has provided over 35 million pairs of free shoes to people in developing countries. Expanding its philanthropic model beyond shoes, TOMS now helps provide eyeglasses, clean water, safe birthing techniques, and bullying prevention services to people in need.

Surprisingly, TOMS has created a fresh marketing model by "integrating old-fashioned for-profit entrepreneurship with new-wave, bleeding-heart philanthropy, bonding moneymaking and giving in an unprecedented manner."[1] TOMS' brand catapulted from humble beginnings into a sustainable cause independent of donations. And it made Blake Mycoskie a very rich entrepreneur.[2]

Vivien Killilea/Getty Images

Regardless of its success and good intentions, TOMS has its share of critics. They complain that in-kind donation programs are an inefficient means of helping people in need. Why not simply donate money to existing antipoverty programs? Critics also note that his shoes are made in China, Argentina, and Nigeria instead of in the countries where the shoes are being given. Rather than giving shoes, why not set up factories to make the shoes and give jobs?

Despite his critics, Mycoskie has created a powerful communication message that resonates with many consumers. To promote that message, TOMS has been savvy in using audience awareness and well-chosen media channels.

One of the company's most effective strategies has been its active engagement of college students through internships and campus programs. One intern in the TOMS online content department explained the importance of planning in creating Web content. "Content isn't just randomly pushed through at random times; it actually involves a lot of strategy and planning to maximize our efforts and our reach," intern Andrew Kirschner wrote in a blog post.[3]

Creating effective content certainly involves careful planning. It also requires the writer to be aware of the audience's needs, to write with a clear purpose, to hone words and phrases through careful editing, and to proofread to ensure the professionalism today's consumers demand. In short, from interns to managers, all professionals are more effective when they write using a process. You will learn more about TOMS and be asked to complete a relevant task at the end of this chapter.

Critical Thinking

- Do you remember the proverb declaring that if you give a man a fish, you feed him for a day; if you teach him how to fish, you feed him for a lifetime? Do you agree with critics who apply this proverb to TOMS' charity model?
- Beyond judging the charity work of TOMS, think about how its message and appeal have captured so much buy-in from young people. When you write business messages, how can you alter your writing to engage audiences of various ages or at various education levels?
- Why do even experienced writers actively follow a writing process?

Understanding the Communication Process

No one would argue that the digital revolution has not profoundly changed the way we live, the methods we use to conduct business, and especially the way we communicate. For instance, staff members and college interns (known as agents of change at TOMS) use videos, Facebook, Twitter, Pinterest, blogs, and e-mail to communicate with each other and create buzz with customers and fans.

As the world becomes increasingly interconnected, people are sending a staggering number of messages often delivered over social media platforms. However, even as we have accepted instant messaging, texting, Twitter, and other interactive media, the nature of communication remains unchanged. No matter how we create or send our messages, the basic communication process consists of the same elements. It starts with an idea that must be transmitted.

LEARNING OUTCOME 1

Understand the nature of communication and its barriers in the digital era.

In its simplest form, **communication** may be defined as the *transmission of information and meaning from a sender to a receiver.* The crucial element in this definition is *meaning.* The process is successful only when the receiver understands an idea as the sender intended it. How does an idea travel from one person to another? It involves a sensitive process, shown in Figure 4.1. This process can easily be sidetracked resulting in miscommunication. The process of communication, however, is successful when both the sender and receiver understand the process and how to make it work. In our discussion we are most concerned with professional communication in the workplace so that you can be successful as a business communicator in your career.

Sender Has Idea

The communication process begins when the sender has an idea. The form of the idea may be influenced by complex factors surrounding the sender. These factors include mood, frame of reference, background, culture, and physical makeup, as well as the context of the situation and many other factors. Senders shape their ideas based on their own experiences and assumptions. A manager sending an e-mail request to employees asking them to conserve energy assumes that they will be receptive. On the other hand, a direct-mail advertiser promoting a new life insurance plan assumes that receivers may give only a quick glance to something perceived as junk mail. To gain attention, the direct-mail piece must offer something special. What exactly

Figure 4.1 **The Communication Process**

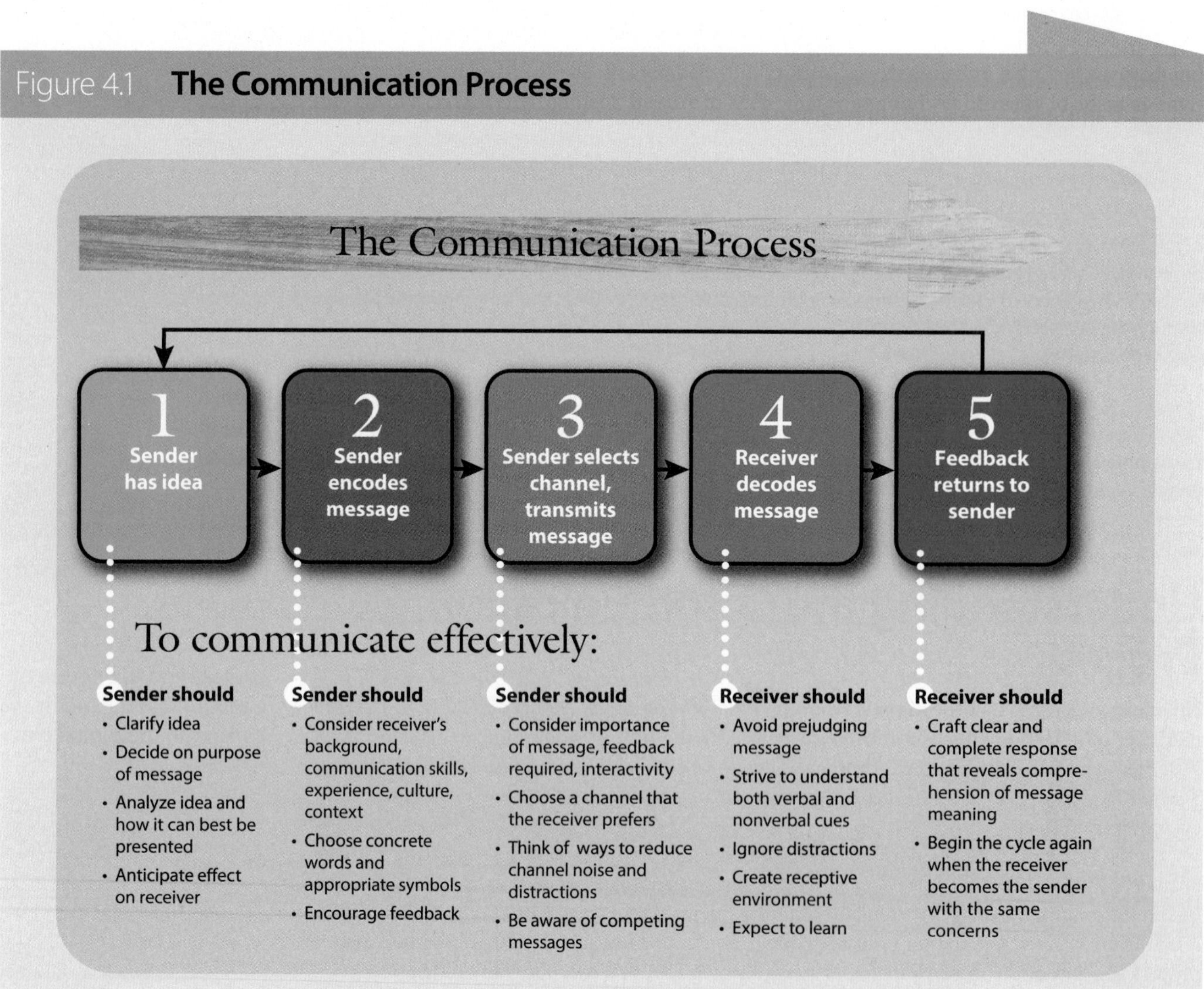
The Communication Process
1 Sender has idea
2 Sender encodes message
3 Sender selects channel, transmits message
4 Receiver decodes message
5 Feedback returns to sender
To communicate effectively:
Sender should
• Clarify idea
• Decide on purpose of message
• Analyze idea and how it can best be presented
• Anticipate effect on receiver
Sender should
• Consider receiver's background, communication skills, experience, culture, context
• Choose concrete words and appropriate symbols
• Encourage feedback
Sender should
• Consider importance of message, feedback required, interactivity
• Choose a channel that the receiver prefers
• Think of ways to reduce channel noise and distractions
• Be aware of competing messages
Receiver should
• Avoid prejudging message
• Strive to understand both verbal and nonverbal cues
• Ignore distractions
• Create receptive environment
• Expect to learn
Receiver should
• Craft clear and complete response that reveals compre-hension of message meaning
• Begin the cycle again when the receiver becomes the sender with the same concerns

does the sender want to achieve? How is the message likely to be received? When senders know their purpose and anticipate the expected response, they are better able to shape successful messages.

Sender Encodes Idea

The next step in the communication process involves *encoding*. This means converting the idea into words or gestures that will convey meaning. A major problem in communicating any message verbally is that words have different meanings for different people. Recognizing how easy it is to be misunderstood, skilled communicators choose familiar, concrete words. In choosing proper words and symbols, senders must be alert to the receiver's communication skills, attitudes, background, experiences, and culture. Including a smiley face in an e-mail announcement to stockholders may turn them off.

International messages require even more care. In Great Britain the press called a new recycling program a *scheme*, which seriously offended the New York–based sponsor of the program, RecycleBank. In the United States, *scheme* connotes deceit. In Britain, however, it carries no such negative meaning.[4] The most successful messages use appropriate words, gestures, and symbols selected specifically to match the situation. Good messages also encourage feedback and make it easy for the receiver to respond.

Sender Selects Channel and Transmits Message

The medium over which the message travels is the *channel*. Messages may be delivered by computer, wireless network, smartphone, social network, letter, memorandum, report, announcement, picture, spoken word, fax, Web page, or some other channel. Today's messages are increasingly carried over digital networks with much opportunity for distraction and breakdown. Receivers may be overloaded with incoming messages or unable to receive messages clearly on their devices. Only well-crafted messages may be accepted, understood, and acted on. Anything that interrupts the transmission of a message in the communication process is called *noise*. Channel noise may range from a weak Internet signal to sloppy formatting and typos in e-mail messages. Noise may even include the annoyance a receiver feels when the sender chooses an improper channel for transmission or when the receiver is overloaded with messages and information.

Receiver Decodes Message

The individual for whom the message is intended is the *receiver*. Translating the message from its symbol form into meaning involves *decoding*. Only when the receiver understands the meaning intended by the sender—that is, successfully decodes the message—does communication take place. Such success is often difficult to achieve because of a number of barriers that block the process.

No two people share the same life experiences or have the same skills. Decoding can be disrupted internally by the receiver's lack of attention, by bias against the sender, or by competing messages. It can be disrupted externally by loud sounds or illegible words. Decoding can also be sidetracked by semantic obstacles, such as misunderstood words or emotional reactions to certain terms. A memo that refers to women in the office as chicks or babes, for example, may disturb its receivers so much that they fail to focus on the total message. On the receiving end, successful decoding is more likely to be achieved when the receiver creates a receptive environment and ignores distractions. Alert receivers strive to understand both verbal and nonverbal cues, avoid prejudging the message, and expect to learn something.

Feedback Returns to Sender

The verbal and nonverbal responses of the receiver create *feedback*, a vital part of the communication process. Feedback helps the sender know that the message was received and understood. Senders can encourage feedback by asking questions such as, *Am I making myself clear?* and,

Ethics Check

Bypassing or False Advertising?

J. C. Penney produced a T-shirt emblazoned with a ferocious red and blue eagle beneath the words *American Made*. However, a small label inside revealed that the shirt was made in Mexico. In response to complaints that the slogan was deceptive, a Penney spokeswoman said that *American Made* referred to the person wearing the shirt, not to the manufacturer.[5]
Do you think this was a simple case of miscommunication?

The idea of sunglasses for cool dogs could receive both judgmental and evaluative feedback.

Is there anything you don't understand? Senders can further improve feedback by timing the delivery appropriately and by providing only as much information as the receiver can handle. Receivers improve the communication process by providing clear and complete feedback.

In the business world, one of the best ways to advance understanding is to paraphrase the sender's message with comments such as, *Let me try to explain that in my own words.* The best feedback tends to be descriptive rather than evaluative. Here's a descriptive response: *I understand you want to sell sunglasses for cool dogs, and you would call them Doggles.*[6] Here's an evaluative response: *Your business ideas are always wacky!* An evaluative response is judgmental and doesn't tell the sender whether the receiver actually understood the message. When the receiver returns feedback, this person then becomes the sender of a new cycle of communication with all of the same concerns as the original sender.

Barriers That Create Misunderstanding

The communication process is successful only when the receiver understands the message as intended by the sender. It sounds quite simple–yet it's not. How many times have you thought that you delivered a clear message, only to learn later that your intentions were misunderstood? Most messages that we send reach their destinations, but many are only partially understood.

You can improve your chances of communicating successfully by learning to recognize barriers that are known to disrupt the process. Some of the most significant barriers for individuals are bypassing, differing frames of reference, lack of language skill, and distractions.

Bypassing. An important barrier to clear communication involves words. Each of us attaches a little bundle of meanings to every word, and these meanings are not always similar. Bypassing happens when people miss each other with their meanings.[7] Let's say your boss asks you to help with a large customer mailing. When you arrive to do your share, you learn that you are expected to do the whole mailing yourself. You and your boss attached different meanings to the word *help.* Bypassing can lead to major miscommunication because people assume that meanings are contained in words. Actually, meanings are in people. For communication to be successful, the receiver and sender must attach the same symbolic meanings to their words. One study revealed a high likelihood of miscommunication when people use common but vague words such as *probably, always, never, usually, often, soon,* and *right away.* What do these words really mean?[8]

Differing Frames of Reference. Another barrier to clear communication is your *frame of reference.* Everything you see and feel in the world is translated through your individual frame of reference. Your unique frame is formed by a combination of your experiences, education, culture, expectations, personality, and other elements. As a result, you bring your own biases and expectations to any communication situation. Because your frame of reference is different from everyone else's, you will never see things exactly as others do. American managers eager to reach an agreement with a Chinese parts supplier, for example, were disappointed with the slow negotiation process. The Chinese managers, on the other hand, were pleased that so much time had been taken to build personal relationships with the American managers. Wise business communicators strive to prevent miscommunication by being alert to both their own frames of reference and those of others.

ESRI

Reality Check

Are You a 10?

When interviewing candidates for employment, this executive asks one important question: "How good of a writer are you, on a scale of 1 to 10?"[9]

—Jack Dangermond, *founder, Esri, geographic mapping software*

alphaspirit/Fotolia LLC

Does multitasking make you dumb? Neuroscientist Daniel Levitin asserts that multitasking is a misnomer. "What we're actually doing is rapidly shifting our attention from one thing to another." Such fast switching not only fatigues the brain, but just having the opportunity to multitask can lower your effective IQ by 10 points, says Levitin. When forced to switch tasks, multitaskers could not recall information or pay attention as well as single taskers. From loud conversations to near nonstop pings of incoming messages, multitasking and distractions are common communication obstacles in the workplace. How can employees in today's fast-paced digital workplace avoid and overcome distractions and barriers to effective communication?[11]

Lack of Language Skill. No matter how extraordinary the idea is, it won't be understood or fully appreciated unless the communicators involved have good language skills. Each individual needs an adequate vocabulary and skill in oral and written expression. Using unfamiliar words, jargon, and unrecognizable abbreviations can seriously impede the transmission of meaning. Consider the following message posted on LinkedIn regarding social media and search engines: *Although SEO is part of SEM, you can't just lump in SMM and PR under the SEO banner!* Translation: *Although search engine optimization (SEO) is part of search engine marketing (SMM), you can't just lump social media marketing (SMM) and public relations (PR) under the search engine optimization (SEO) banner!* You will learn more about using plain language and familiar words later in this chapter.

Distractions. Other communication barriers are emotional interference, physical distractions, and digital interruptions. Shaping an intelligent message is difficult when one is feeling joy, fear, resentment, hostility, sadness, or some other strong emotion. To reduce the influence of emotions on communication, both senders and receivers should focus on the content of the message and try to remain objective. Physical distractions such as faulty acoustics, noisy surroundings, or a poor mobile connection can disrupt oral communication. Similarly, sloppy appearance, poor printing, careless formatting, and typographical or spelling errors can disrupt written messages. What's more, technology doesn't seem to be helping. In this digital era, knowledge workers are increasingly distracted by multitasking, information overload, conflicting demands, and being constantly available digitally. Clear communication requires focusing on what is important and shutting out interruptions.[10]

Overcoming Communication Obstacles

Careful communicators can conquer barriers in a number of ways. Half the battle in communicating successfully is recognizing that the entire process is sensitive and susceptible to breakdown. Like a defensive driver anticipating problems on the road, a good communicator anticipates problems in encoding, transmitting, and decoding a message. Effective communicators also focus on the receiver's environment and frame of reference. They ask themselves questions such as, *How is that individual likely to react to my message?* or, *Does the receiver know as much about the subject as I do?*

Misunderstandings are less likely if you arrange your ideas logically and use words precisely. Mark Twain was right when he said, "The difference between an almost-right word and the right word is like the difference between lightning and the lightning bug." But communicating is more than expressing yourself well. A large part of successful communication is listening. Management advisor Peter Drucker observed that "too many executives think they are wonderful with people because they talk well. They don't realize that being wonderful with people means listening well."[12]

Effective communicators create an environment that encourages useful feedback. In oral communication this means asking questions such as, *Do you understand?* and, *What questions do you have?* as well as encouraging listeners to repeat instructions or paraphrase ideas. As a listener it means providing feedback that describes rather than evaluates. In written communication it means asking questions and providing access: *Do you have my phone numbers in case you have questions?* or, *Here's my e-mail address so that you can give me your response immediately.*

LEARNING OUTCOME 2

Summarize the 3-x-3 writing process and explain how it guides a writer.

Using the 3-x-3 Writing Process as a Guide

Today's new media and digital technologies enable you to choose from innumerable communication channels to create, transmit, and respond to messages. Nearly all communication, however, revolves around writing. Whether you are preparing a message that will be delivered digitally, orally, or in print, that message requires thinking and writing. Many of your messages will be digital. A **digital message** may be defined *as one that is generated, stored, processed, and transmitted electronically by computers using strings of positive and nonpositive binary code (0s and 1s).* That definition encompasses many messages, including e-mail, Facebook posts, tweets, videos, and other messages. For our purposes, we focus primarily on messages exchanged on the job. Because writing is central to all business communication, this chapter presents a systematic plan for preparing business messages in the digital era.

Defining Your Business Writing Goals

One thing you should immediately recognize about business writing is that it differs from other writing you have done. In preparing high school or college compositions and term papers, you probably focused on discussing your feelings or displaying your knowledge. Your instructors wanted to see your thought processes, and they wanted assurance that you had internalized the subject matter. You may have had to meet a minimum word count. Business writing is definitely not like that! It also differs from personal texts you may exchange with your friends and family. Those messages enabled you to stay connected and express your feelings. In the workplace, however, your writing should have the following characteristics:

- **Purposeful.** You will be writing to solve problems and convey information. You will have a definite strategy to fulfill in each message.
- **Economical.** You will try to present ideas clearly but concisely. Length is not rewarded.
- **Audience oriented.** You will concentrate on looking at a problem from the perspective of the audience instead of seeing it from your own.

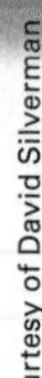

Courtesy of David Silverman

Reality Check

Why Is Business Writing So Bad?

Writing for the *Harvard Business Review,* David Silverman blasts "an educational system that rewards length over clarity." Students learn to overwrite, he says, in hopes that at least some of their sentences "hit the mark." Once on the job, they continue to act as if they were paid by the word, a perception that must be unlearned.[13]

—David Silverman, *entrepreneur and business teacher*

These distinctions actually ease your task. You won't be searching your imagination for creative topic ideas. You won't be stretching your ideas to make them appear longer. Writing consultants and businesspeople complain that many college graduates entering the workplace have a conscious—or perhaps unconscious—perception that quantity enhances quality. Wrong! Get over the notion that longer is better. Whether you are presenting your ideas in print, online, or in person, conciseness and clarity are what count in business.

The ability to prepare purposeful, concise, and audience-centered messages does not come naturally. Very few people, especially beginners, can sit down and draft an effective e-mail message, letter, or report without training. However, following a systematic process, studying model messages, and practicing the craft can make nearly anyone a successful business writer or speaker.

Introducing the 3-x-3 Writing Process

Regardless of what you are writing, the process will be easier if you follow a systematic plan. The 3-x-3 writing process breaks the entire task into three phases: *prewriting, drafting,* and *revising,* as shown in Figure 4.2.

To illustrate the writing process, let's say that you own a popular McDonald's franchise. At rush times, you face a problem. Customers complain about the chaotic multiple waiting lines to approach the service counter. You once saw two customers nearly get into a fistfight over cutting into a line. What's more, customers often are so intent on looking for ways to improve

Figure 4.2 **The 3-x-3 Writing Process**

1 Prewriting

Analyze
- What is your purpose?
- What do you want the receiver to do or believe?
- What channel should you choose: face-to-face conversation, group meeting, e-mail, memo, letter, report, blog, wiki, tweet, etc.?

Anticipate
- Profile the audience.
- What does the receiver already know?
- Will the receiver's response be neutral, positive, or negative? How will this affect your organizational strategy?

Adapt
- What techniques can you use to adapt your message to its audience?
- How can you promote feedback?
- Strive to use positive, conversational, and courteous language.

2 Drafting

Research
- Gather data to provide facts.
- Search company files, previous correspondence, and the Internet.
- What do you need to know to write this message?
- How much does the audience already know?

Organize
- Organize direct messages with the big idea first, followed by an explanation in the body and an action request in the closing.
- For persuasive or negative messages, use an indirect, problem-solving strategy.

Draft
- Prepare a first draft, usually quickly.
- Focus on short, clear sentences using the active voice.
- Build paragraph coherence by repeating key ideas, using pronouns, and incorporating appropriate transitional expressions.

3 Revising

Edit
- Edit your message to be sure it is clear, concise, conversational, readable.
- Revise to eliminate wordy fillers, long lead-ins, redundancies, and trite business phrases.
- Develop parallelism.
- Consider using headings and numbered and bulleted lists for quick reading.

Proofread
- Take the time to read every message carefully.
- Look for errors in spelling, grammar, punctuation, names, and numbers.
- Check to be sure the format is consistent.

Evaluate
- Will this message achieve your purpose?
- Does the tone sound pleasant and friendly rather than curt?
- Have you thought enough about the audience to be sure this message is appealing?
- Did you encourage feedback?

their positions in line that they fail to examine the menu. Then they are undecided when their turn arrives. You want to convince other franchise owners that a single-line (serpentine) system would work better. You could telephone the other owners. However, you want to present a serious argument with good points that they will remember and be willing to act on when they gather for their next district meeting. You decide to send a persuasive e-mail that you hope will win their support.

Prewriting. The first phase of the writing process prepares you to write. It involves *analyzing* the audience and your purpose for writing. The audience for your message will be other franchise owners, some highly educated and others not. Your purpose in writing is to convince them that a change in policy would improve customer service. You think that a single-line system, such as that used in banks, would reduce chaos and make customers happier because they would not have to worry about where they are in line.

Prewriting also involves *anticipating* how your audience will react to your message. You are sure that some of the other owners will agree with you, but others might fear that customers seeing a long single line might go elsewhere. In *adapting* your message to the audience, you try to think of the right words and the right tone that will win approval.

E.J. Baumeister Jr. / Alamy Stock Photo

Reality Check

Writing Matters

At investment banker Morgan Stanley, writing skills count. New-hires are often challenged when they have to adapt their writing for multiple audiences, says Keisha Smith. She points out that some tend to write long e-mails when only a short list is needed. Managers look over new-hires' e-mails before they are sent.[14]

—Keisha Smith, *global head of recruiting, Morgan Stanley*

Drafting. The second phase involves researching, organizing, and then drafting the message. In *researching* information for this message, you would probably investigate other kinds of businesses that use single lines for customers. You might check your competitors. What are Wendy's and Burger King doing? You might do some calling to see whether other franchise owners are concerned about chaotic lines. Before writing to the entire group, you might brainstorm with a few owners to see what ideas they have for solving the problem.

Once you have collected enough information, you would focus on *organizing* your message. Should you start out by offering your solution? Or should you work up to it slowly, describing the problem, presenting your evidence, and then ending with the solution? The final step in the second phase of the writing process is actually *drafting* the letter. At this point many writers write quickly, knowing that they will polish their ideas when they revise.

Revising. The third phase of the process involves editing, proofreading, and evaluating your message. After writing the first draft, you will spend considerable time *editing* the message for clarity, conciseness, tone, and readability. Could parts of it be rearranged to make your point more effectively? This is the time when you look for ways to improve the organization and tone of your message. Next, you will spend time *proofreading* carefully to ensure correct spelling, grammar, punctuation, and format. The final phase involves *evaluating* your message to decide whether it accomplishes your goal.

Figure 4.3 **Scheduling the Writing Process**

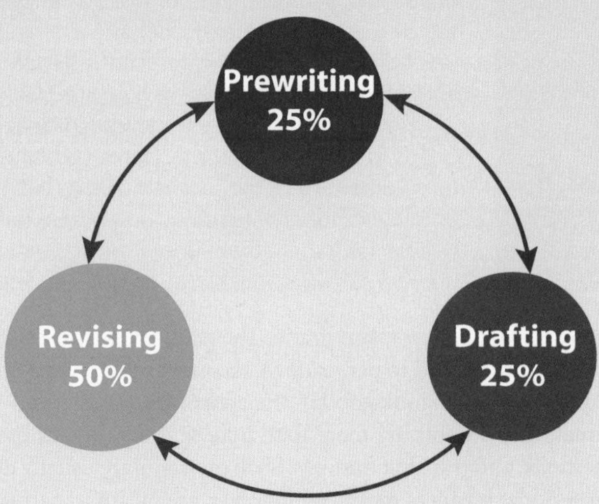

Although the writing process looks like a linear set of steps, it actually is recursive, enabling writers to revise their work continually as they progress. However, careful planning can avoid wasted time and frustration caused by rethinking and reorganizing during drafting.

Pacing the Writing Process

The time you spend on each phase of the writing process varies depending on the complexity of the problem, the purpose, the audience, and your schedule. On average, you should expect to spend about 25 percent of your time prewriting, 25 percent drafting, and 50 percent revising, as shown in Figure 4.3

These are rough guides, yet you can see that good writers spend most of their time on the final phase of revising and proofreading. Much depends, of course, on your project, its importance, and your familiarity with it. What is critical to remember, though, is that revising is a major component of the writing process even if the message is short.

It may appear that you perform one step and progress to the next, always following the same order. Most business writing, however, is not that rigid. Although writers perform the tasks described, the steps may be rearranged, abbreviated, or repeated. Some writers revise every sentence and paragraph as they go. Many find that new ideas occur after they have begun to write, causing them to back up, alter the organization, and rethink their plan. Beginning business writers often follow the writing process closely. With experience, though, they will become like other good writers and presenters who alter, compress, and rearrange the steps as needed.

Ethics Check

Busted for Buying Essays

Macquarie University in Australia revoked the degrees of two students and prevented others from graduating after learning that they had used an online ghost-writing service to complete assignments. A continuing national investigation revealed that up to 1,000 students from 16 universities had hired an online service to write their assignments.[15] Beyond lost degrees, what do students miss by buying essays?

Analyzing and Anticipating the Audience

Surprisingly, many people begin writing and discover only as they approach the end of a message what they are trying to accomplish. If you analyze your purpose before you begin, you can avoid having to backtrack and start over. The remainder of this chapter covers the first phase of the writing process: analyzing the purpose for writing, anticipating how the audience will react, and adapting the message to the audience.

Determining Your Purpose

LEARNING OUTCOME 3

Analyze the purpose of a message, anticipate its audience, and select the best communication channel.

As you begin to compose a workplace message, ask yourself two important questions: (a) Why am I sending this message? and (b) What do I hope to achieve? Your responses will determine how you organize and present your information.

Your message may have primary and secondary purposes. For college work your primary purpose may be merely to complete the assignment; secondary purposes might be to make

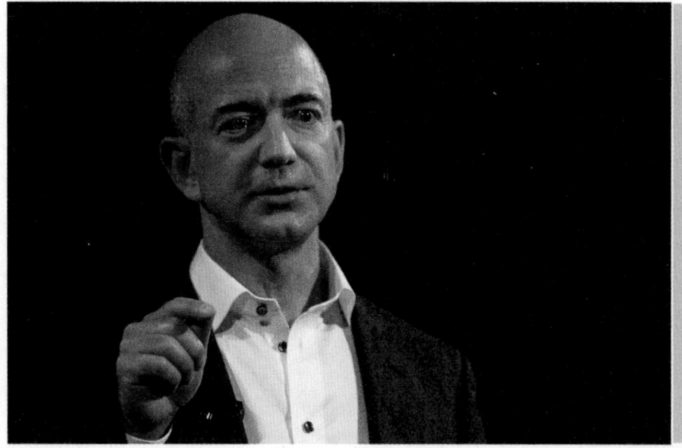
Bloomberg/Getty Images

After *The New York Times* published an article criticizing "callous management practices" at Amazon, CEO Jeff Bezos responded by quickly sending an e-mail to his staff of 180,000. Such damage control was imperative to buoy sagging employee morale. Bezos wrote an unambiguous reaction that illustrates careful consideration of the audience and the purpose of his purpose: "Even if it's rare or isolated, our tolerance for any such lack of empathy needs to be zero," he wrote. Demonstrating his personal involvement to fix the problem, Bezos even invited employees to respond directly to him. What questions do writers ask to help them understand their audiences?[16]

yourself look good and to earn an excellent grade. The primary purposes for sending business messages are typically to inform and to persuade. A secondary purpose is to promote goodwill. You and your organization want to look good in the eyes of your audience.

Many business messages do nothing more than *inform*. They explain procedures, announce meetings, answer questions, and transmit findings. Such messages are usually developed directly, as discussed in Chapter 5. Some business messages, however, are meant to *persuade*. These messages attempt to sell products, convince managers, motivate employees, and win over customers. Persuasive messages are often developed indirectly, as presented in Chapter 5 and subsequent chapters.

Anticipating and Profiling the Audience

A good writer anticipates the audience for a message: What is the reader or listener like? How will that person react to the message? Although one can't always know exactly who the receiver is, it is possible to imagine some of that person's characteristics. A copywriter at Lands' End, the shopping and Internet retailer, pictures his sister-in-law whenever he writes product descriptions for the catalog.

Profiling your audience is a pivotal step in the writing process. The questions in Figure 4.4 will help you profile your audience.

Figure 4.4 **Asking the Right Questions to Profile Your Audience**

Primary Audience

- Who is my primary reader or listener?
- What are my personal and professional relationships with this person?
- What position does this person hold in the organization?
- How much does this person know about the subject?
- What do I know about this person's education, beliefs, culture, and attitudes?
- Should I expect a neutral, positive, or negative response to my message?

Secondary Audience

- Who might see or hear this message in addition to the primary audience?
- How do these people differ from the primary audience?
- Do I need to include more background information?
- How must I reshape my message to make it understandable and acceptable to others to whom it might be forwarded?

How much time you devote to answering these questions depends on your message and its context. An analytical report that you compose for management or an oral presentation before a big group would, of course, demand considerable time profiling the audience. An e-mail message to a coworker or a message to a familiar supplier might require only a few moments of planning.

Preparing a blog on an important topic to be posted to a company website would require you to think about the local, national, and international audiences that might read that message. Similarly, posting brief personal messages at microblogging sites such as Facebook, Twitter, and Tumblr should make you think about who will read the messages. How much of your day and life do you want to share? Will customers and business partners be reading your posts?

No matter how short your message is, though, spend some time thinking about the people in your audience so that you can tailor your words to them. Remember that your receivers will be thinking, *What's in it for me?*(WIIFM). One of the most important writing tips you can take away from this book is remembering that every message you write should begin with the notion that your audience is thinking *WIIFM.*

Making Choices Based on the Audience Profile

Profiling your audience helps you make decisions about shaping the message. You will discover what language is appropriate, whether you are free to use specialized technical terms, whether you should explain the background, and so on. Profiling the audience helps you decide whether your tone should be formal or informal. Profiling helps you consider whether the receiver is likely to respond positively or negatively to your message, or be neutral about it.

Another consideration in profiling your audience is the possibility of a secondary audience. For example, let's say you start to write an e-mail message to your supervisor, Sheila, describing a problem you are having. Halfway through the message, you realize that Sheila will probably forward this message to her boss, the vice president. Sheila will probably not want to summarize what you said; instead, she may take the easy route and merely forward your e-mail. When you realize that the vice president may see this message, you decide to back up and use a more formal tone. You remove your inquiry about Sheila's family, you reduce your complaints, and you tone down your language about why things went wrong. Instead, you provide more background information, and you are more specific in identifying items the vice president might not recognize. Analyzing the task and anticipating the audience help you adapt your message so it will be effective for both primary and secondary receivers.

Selecting the Best Channel

After identifying the purpose of your message, you will want to select the most appropriate communication channel. In this digital era, the number of channels continues to expand, as shown in Figure 4.5. Your decision to send an e-mail message, schedule a videoconference, post a note on the company intranet, or use some other channel depends on some of the following factors:

- Importance of the message
- Amount and speed of feedback and interactivity required
- Necessity of a permanent record
- Cost of the channel
- Degree of formality desired
- Confidentiality and sensitivity of the message
- Receiver's preference and level of technical expertise

Figure 4.5 **Comparing Rich and Lean Communication Channels**

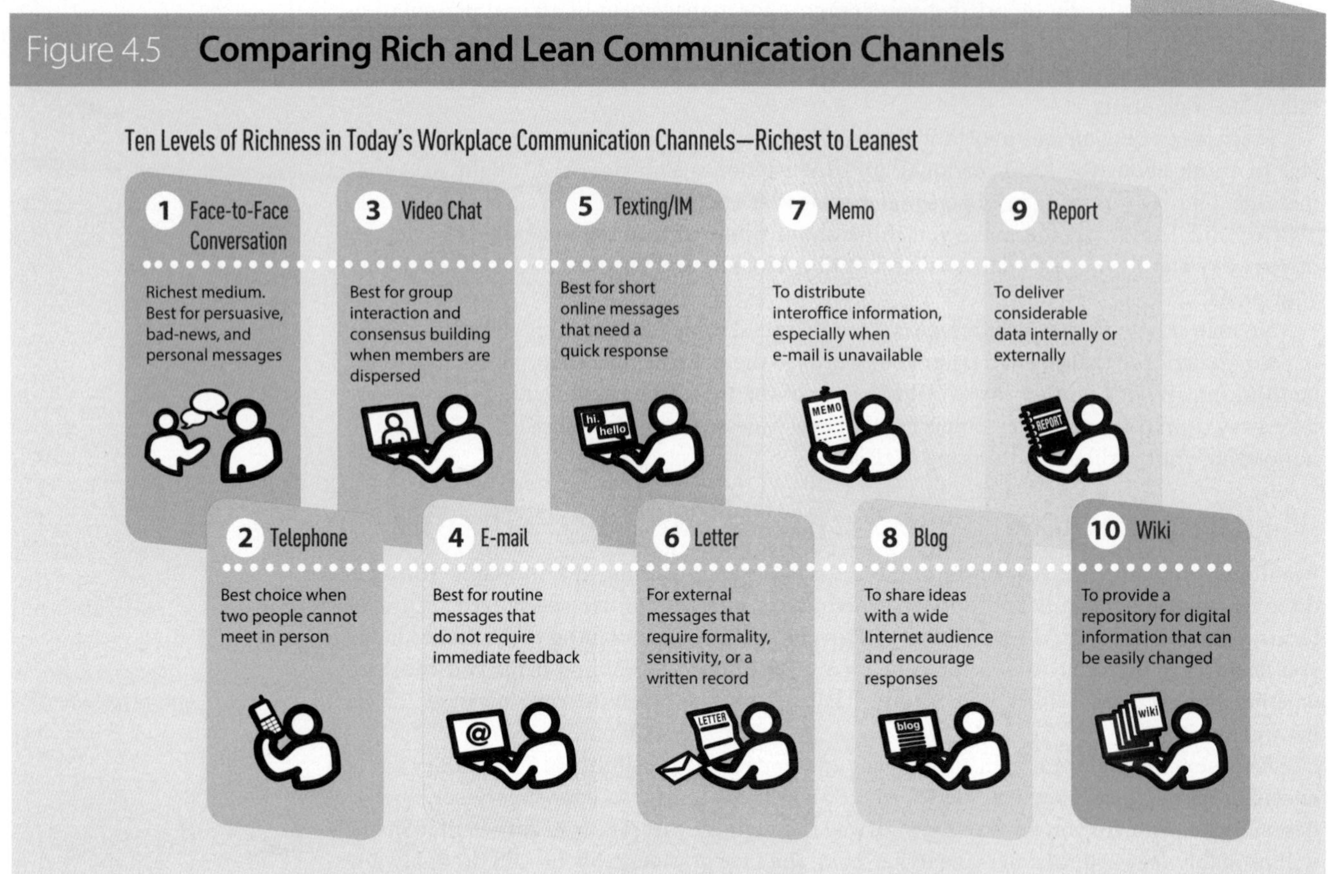

Ten Levels of Richness in Today's Workplace Communication Channels—Richest to Leanest
1 Face-to-Face Conversation
Richest medium. Best for persuasive, bad-news, and personal messages
3 Video Chat
Best for group interaction and consensus building when members are dispersed
5 Texting/IM
Best for short online messages that need a quick response
hi hello
7 Memo
To distribute interoffice information, especially when e-mail is unavailable
MEMO
9 Report
To deliver considerable data internally or externally
REPORT
2 Telephone
Best choice when two people cannot meet in person
4 E-mail
Best for routine messages that do not require immediate feedback
@
6 Letter
For external messages that require formality, sensitivity, or a written record
LETTER
8 Blog
To share ideas with a wide Internet audience and encourage responses
blog
10 Wiki
To provide a repository for digital information that can be easily changed
wiki

In addition to these practical issues, you will also consider how rich the channel is. As discussed in Chapter 1, the richness of a channel involves the extent to which a channel or medium recreates or represents all the information available in the original message. A richer medium, such as a face-to-face conversation, permits more interactivity and feedback. A leaner medium, such as a letter or an e-mail, presents a flat, one-dimensional message. Richer media enable the sender to provide more verbal and visual cues as well as to tailor the message to the audience.

Choosing the wrong medium can result in a message that is less effective or even misunderstood. If, for example, marketing manager Rodney must motivate the sales force to increase sales in the fourth quarter, he is unlikely to achieve his goal if he merely posts an announcement on the office bulletin board, writes a memo, or sends an e-mail. Rodney could be more persuasive with a richer channel, such as individual face-to-face conversations or a group meeting to stimulate sales. For sales reps on the road, a richer medium would be a videoconference. In choosing channels, keep in mind two tips: (a) Use the richest media available, and (b) employ richer media for more persuasive or personal communications.

LEARNING OUTCOME 4

Employ expert writing techniques such as incorporating audience benefits, the "you" view, conversational but professional language, a positive and courteous tone, bias-free language, plain language, and vigorous words.

Using Expert Writing Techniques to Adapt to Your Audience

After analyzing the purpose and anticipating the audience, writers begin to think about how to adapt a message to the task and the audience. Adaptation is the process of creating a message that suits the audience. Skilled communicators employ a number of expert writing techniques, such as those illustrated in the two versions of an e-mail in Figure 4.6. These techniques include featuring audience benefits, cultivating a "you" view, sounding conversational but professional, and using positive, courteous expression. Additional adaptive techniques include using bias-free language and preferring plain language with familiar but vigorous words.

Figure 4.6 **Applying Expert Writing Techniques to Improve an E-Mail Message**

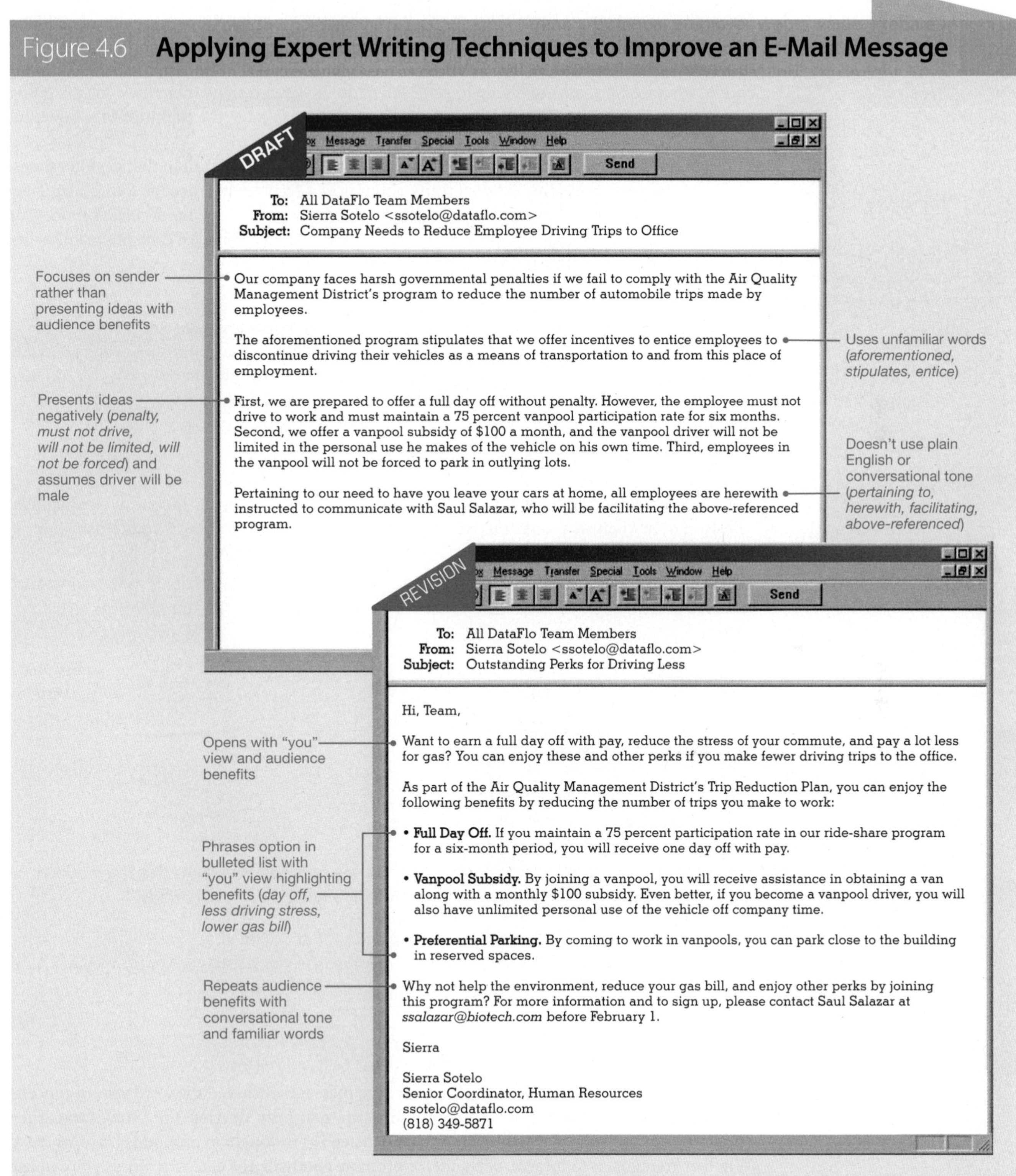

DRAFT
Message Transfer Special Tools Window Help
Send
To: All DataFlo Team Members
From: Sierra Sotelo <ssotelo@dataflo.com>
Subject: Company Needs to Reduce Employee Driving Trips to Office
Our company faces harsh governmental penalties if we fail to comply with the Air Quality Management District's program to reduce the number of automobile trips made by employees.
The aforementioned program stipulates that we offer incentives to entice employees to discontinue driving their vehicles as a means of transportation to and from this place of employment.
First, we are prepared to offer a full day off without penalty. However, the employee must not drive to work and must maintain a 75 percent vanpool participation rate for six months. Second, we offer a vanpool subsidy of $100 a month, and the vanpool driver will not be limited in the personal use he makes of the vehicle on his own time. Third, employees in the vanpool will not be forced to park in outlying lots.
Pertaining to our need to have you leave your cars at home, all employees are herewith instructed to communicate with Saul Salazar, who will be facilitating the above-referenced program.
Focuses on sender rather than presenting ideas with audience benefits
Uses unfamiliar words (aforementioned, stipulates, entice)
Presents ideas negatively (penalty, must not drive, will not be limited, will not be forced) and assumes driver will be male
Doesn't use plain English or conversational tone (pertaining to, herewith, facilitating, above-referenced)
REVISION
Message Transfer Special Tools Window Help
Send
To: All DataFlo Team Members
From: Sierra Sotelo <ssotelo@dataflo.com>
Subject: Outstanding Perks for Driving Less
Hi, Team,
Want to earn a full day off with pay, reduce the stress of your commute, and pay a lot less for gas? You can enjoy these and other perks if you make fewer driving trips to the office.
As part of the Air Quality Management District's Trip Reduction Plan, you can enjoy the following benefits by reducing the number of trips you make to work:
• Full Day Off. If you maintain a 75 percent participation rate in our ride-share program for a six-month period, you will receive one day off with pay.
• Vanpool Subsidy. By joining a vanpool, you will receive assistance in obtaining a van along with a monthly $100 subsidy. Even better, if you become a vanpool driver, you will also have unlimited personal use of the vehicle off company time.
• Preferential Parking. By coming to work in vanpools, you can park close to the building in reserved spaces.
Why not help the environment, reduce your gas bill, and enjoy other perks by joining this program? For more information and to sign up, please contact Saul Salazar at ssalazar@biotech.com before February 1.
Sierra
Sierra Sotelo
Senior Coordinator, Human Resources
ssotelo@dataflo.com
(818) 349-5871
Opens with "you" view and audience benefits
Phrases option in bulleted list with "you" view highlighting benefits (day off, less driving stress, lower gas bill)
Repeats audience benefits with conversational tone and familiar words

Spotlighting Audience Benefits

Focusing on the audience sounds like a modern idea, but actually one of America's early statesmen and authors recognized this fundamental writing principle over 200 years ago. In describing effective writing, Ben Franklin observed, "To be good, it ought to have a tendency to benefit the reader."[17] These wise words have become a fundamental guideline for today's business communicators. Expanding on Franklin's counsel, a contemporary communication consultant gives this solid advice to his business clients: "Always stress the benefit to the audience of whatever it is you are trying to get them to do. If you can show them how you are going to save them frustration or help them meet their goals, you have the makings of a powerful message."[18] Remember, WIIFM!

Adapting your message to the receiver's needs means putting yourself in that person's shoes. It's called *empathy.* Empathic senders think about how a receiver will decode a message. They try to give something to the receiver, solve the receiver's problems, save the receiver's money, or just understand the feelings and position of that person. Which version of each of the following messages is more appealing to the audience?

Sender Focus	Audience Focus
We are instructing herewith all employees to fill out the attached survey completely and immediately so that we can allocate our limited training resource funds appropriately.	By filling out the attached survey, you can be one of the first employees to sign up for our limited training resource funds.
Our warranty on our mobile device becomes effective only when we receive an owner's registration.	Your warranty on your mobile device begins working for you as soon as you return your owner's registration.
We are proud to announce our new real-time virus scanner that we think is the best on the market!	Now you can be sure that all your computers will be protected with our real-time virus scanner.

Reality Check

Matthias Pahl/Shutterstock.com

The Most Powerful Word in the Language

"When it comes to writing engaging content, 'you' is the most powerful word in the English language, because people are ultimately interested in fulfilling their own needs."[19]

—Brian Clark, *founder of leading marketing blog Copyblogger*

Developing the "You" View

Notice that many of the previous audience-focused messages included the word *you.* In concentrating on receiver benefits, skilled communicators naturally develop the "you" view. They emphasize second-person pronouns (*you, your*) instead of first-person pronouns (*I/we, us, our*). Whether your goal is to inform, persuade, or promote goodwill, the catchiest words you can use are *you* and *your.* Compare the following examples.

"I/We" View	"You" View
We are requiring all employees to respond to the attached company questionnaire about health benefits.	Because your ideas count, please complete the attached questionnaire about health benefits.
I need your account number before I can do anything about your claim.	Would you mind giving me your account number so that I can locate your records and help you solve this problem?
Our experienced staff has created a webinar that teaches how to promote your business on Pinterest.	Now you can get more Pinterest likes, repins, comments, and clicks by joining an upcoming webinar.

Although you want to focus on the reader or listener, don't overuse or misuse the second-person pronoun *you*. Readers and listeners appreciate genuine interest; on the other hand, they resent obvious attempts at manipulation. The authors of some sales messages, for example, are guilty of overkill when they include *you* dozens of times in a direct-mail promotion. What's more, the word can sometimes create the wrong impression. Consider this statement: *You cannot return merchandise until you receive written approval.* The word *you* appears twice, but the reader may feel singled out for criticism. In the following version, the message is less personal and more positive: *Customers may return merchandise with written approval.*

Another difficulty in emphasizing the "you" view and de-emphasizing *we/I* is that it may result in an overuse of the passive voice. For example, to avoid *We will give you* (active voice), you might write *You will be given* (passive voice). The active voice in writing is generally preferred because it identifies who is doing the acting. You will learn more about active and passive voice in Chapter 5.

In recognizing the value of the "you" attitude, however, you don't have to sterilize your writing and totally avoid any first-person pronouns or words that show your feelings. You can convey sincerity, warmth, and enthusiasm by the words you choose. Don't be afraid of phrases such as *I'm happy* or *We're delighted,* if you truly are. When speaking face-to-face, you can show sincerity and warmth with nonverbal cues such as a smile and a pleasant voice tone. In letters, e-mail messages, memos, and other digital messages, however, only expressive words and phrases can show your feelings. These phrases suggest hidden messages that say *You are important, I hear you,* and *I'm honestly trying to please you.*

Sounding Conversational but Professional

Most of the business messages you write replace conversation. Thus, they are most effective when they convey an informal, conversational tone instead of a formal, pretentious tone. Just how informal you can be depends greatly on the workplace. At Google, casual seems to be preferred. In a short message to users describing changes in its privacy policies, Google recently wrote, "We believe this stuff matters."[20] In more traditional organizations, that message probably would have been more formal. The dilemma for you, then, is knowing how casual to be in your writing. We suggest that you strive to be conversational but professional, especially until you learn what your organization prefers.

E-mail, instant messaging, chat, Twitter, and other short messaging channels enable you and your coworkers to have spontaneous conversations. Don't, however, let your messages become sloppy, unprofessional, or even dangerous. You will learn more about the dangers of e-mail and other digital channels later. At this point, though, we focus on the tone of the language.

To project a professional image, you want to sound educated and mature. The overuse of expressions such as *totally awesome, you know,* and *like,* as well as a reliance on unnecessary abbreviations (*BTW* for *by the way*), make a businessperson sound like a teenager. Professional messages do not include texting-style abbreviations, slang, sentence fragments, and chitchat. We urge you to strive for a warm, conversational tone that avoids low-level diction. Levels of diction, as shown in Figure 4.7, range from unprofessional to formal.

Figure 4.7 **Levels of Diction**

Unprofessional (Low-level diction)	Conversational (Middle-level diction)	Formal (High-level diction)
badmouth	criticize	denigrate
guts	nerve	courage
pecking order	line of command	dominance hierarchy
ticked off	upset	provoked
rat on	inform	betray
rip off	steal	expropriate
If we just hang in there, we'll snag the contract.	If we don't get discouraged, we'll win the contract.	If the principals persevere, they will secure the contract.

Your goal is a warm, friendly tone that sounds professional. Although some writers are too casual, others are overly formal. To impress readers and listeners, they use big words, long sentences, legal terminology, and third-person constructions. Stay away from expressions such as *the undersigned, the writer,* and *the affected party.* You will sound friendlier with familiar pronouns such as *I, we,* and *you.* The following examples illustrate a professional yet conversational tone:

Unprofessional	Professional
Hey, boss, Gr8 news! Firewall now installed!! BTW, check with me b4 announcing it.	Mr. Lopez, our new firewall software is now installed. Please check with me before announcing it.
Look, dude, this report is totally bogus. And the figures don't look kosher. Show me some real stats. Got sources?	Because the figures in this report seem inaccurate, please submit the source statistics.

Overly Formal	Conversational
All employees are herewith instructed to return the appropriately designated contracts to the undersigned.	Please return your contracts to me.
Pertaining to your order, we must verify the sizes that your organization requires prior to consignment of your order to our shipper.	We will send your order as soon as we confirm the sizes you need.

Being Positive Rather Than Negative

You can improve the clarity, tone, and effectiveness of a message by using positive rather than negative language. Positive language generally conveys more information than negative language does. Moreover, positive messages are uplifting and pleasant to read. Positive wording tells what *is* and what *can be done* rather than what *isn't* and what *can't be done.* For example,

Your order cannot be shipped by January 10 is not nearly as informative as *Your order will be shipped January 15.* An office supply store adjacent to an ice cream parlor in Maine posted a sign on its door that reads: *Please enjoy your ice cream before you enjoy our store.* That sounds much more positive and inviting than *No food allowed!*

Using positive language also involves avoiding negative words that create ill will. Some words appear to blame or accuse your audience. For example, opening a letter to a customer with *You claim that* suggests that you don't believe the customer. Other loaded words that can get you in trouble are *complaint, criticism, defective, failed, mistake,* and *neglected.* Also avoid phrases such as *you apparently are unaware of, you did not provide, you misunderstood,* and *you don't understand.* Often you may be unconscious of the effect of these words. Notice in the following examples how you can revise the negative tone to create a more positive impression.

Negative	Positive
This plan definitely cannot succeed if we don't obtain management approval.	This plan definitely can succeed if we obtain management approval.
You failed to include your credit card number, so we can't mail your order.	We look forward to completing your order as soon as we receive your credit card number.
Your letter of May 2 claims that you returned a defective headset.	Your May 2 letter describes a headset you returned.
Employees cannot park in Lot H until April 1.	Employees may park in Lot H starting April 1.
You apparently are unaware of our new mailing address for deposits because you used the old envelopes.	Enclosed are envelopes with our new mailing address for your deposits.

Expressing Courtesy

Maintaining a courteous tone involves not just guarding against rudeness but also avoiding words that sound demanding or preachy. Expressions such as *you should, you must,* and *you have to* cause people to instinctively react with *Oh, yeah?* One remedy is to turn these demands into rhetorical questions that begin with *Will you please* . . . . Giving reasons for a request also softens the tone.

Even when you feel justified in displaying anger, remember that losing your temper or being sarcastic will seldom accomplish your goals as a business communicator: to inform, to persuade, and to create goodwill. When you are irritated, frustrated, or infuriated, keep cool and try to defuse the situation. In dealing with customers in telephone conversations, use polite phrases such as *I would be happy to assist you with that, Thank you for being so patient,* and *It was a pleasure speaking with you.*

Less Courteous	More Courteous and Helpful
Can't you people get anything right? This is the second time I've notified you!	Please credit my account for $340. The latest update of my online account shows that the error noted in my e-mail of May 15 has not yet been corrected.
Claudia, you must complete all performance reviews by April 1.	Claudia, will you please complete all performance reviews by April 1.
You should organize a car pool in this department.	Organizing a car pool will reduce your transportation costs and help preserve the environment.
Am I the only one who can read the operating manual?	Let's review the operating manual together so that you can get your documents to print correctly next time.

If you are a new or young employee who wants to fit in, don't fail to be especially courteous to older employees (generally, those over thirty) and important people in superior positions.[21] To make a great impression and show respect, use good manners in person and in writing. For example, don't be presumptuous by issuing orders or setting the time for a meeting with a superior. Use first names only if given permission to do so. In your messages be sure to proofread meticulously even if the important person to whom you are writing sends careless, error-filled messages.[22]

Employing Bias-Free Language

In adapting a message to its audience, be sure your language is sensitive and bias free. Few writers set out to be offensive. Sometimes, though, we all say things that we never thought might be hurtful. The real problem is that we don't think about the words that stereotype groups of people, such as *the boys in tech support* or *the girls in the front office.* Be cautious about expressions that might be biased in terms of gender, race, ethnicity, age, or disability.

Generally, you can avoid gender-biased language by choosing alternate language for words involving *man* or *woman*, by using plural nouns and pronouns, or by changing to a gender-free word (*person* or *representative*). Avoid the *his or her* option whenever possible. It's wordy and conspicuous. With a little effort, you can usually find a construction that is graceful, grammatical, and unself-conscious.

Specify age only if it is relevant, and avoid expressions that are demeaning or subjective (such as *spry old codger*). To avoid disability bias, do not refer to an individual's disability unless it is relevant. When necessary, use terms that do not stigmatize disabled individuals. The following examples give you a quick look at a few problem expressions and possible replacements. The real key to bias-free communication, though, lies in your awareness and commitment. Be on the lookout to be sure that your messages do not exclude, stereotype, or offend people.

Gender Biased	Improved
female doctor, woman attorney, cleaning woman	doctor, attorney, cleaner
waiter/waitress, authoress, stewardess	server, author, flight attendant
mankind, man-hour, man-made	humanity, working hours, artificial
office girls	office workers
the doctor . . . he	doctors . . . they
the teacher . . . she	teachers . . . they
executives and their wives	executives and their spouses
foreman, flagman, workman, craftsman	lead worker, flagger, worker, artisan
businessman, salesman	businessperson, sales representative
Each employee had his picture taken.	Each employee had a picture taken. All employees had their pictures taken. Each employee had his or her picture taken.

Racially or Ethnically Biased	Improved
An Indian accountant was hired.	An accountant was hired.
James Lee, an African American, applied.	James Lee applied.

Age Biased	Improved
The law applied to old people.	The law applied to people over sixty-five.
Mildred Kay, 55, was transferred.	Mildred Kay was transferred.
a sprightly old gentleman	a man
a little old lady	a woman

Courtesy of IndependenceFirst/ Designer Clay Altman

Reality Check

Changing Perceptions With People-First Language

In a letter to the editor, a teacher criticized an article in *USA Today* on autism because it said "autistic child" rather than "child with autism." She championed "people-first" terminology, which avoids defining individuals by their ability or disability.[23] Can language change perceptions?

Disability Biased	Improved
afflicted with arthritis, suffering from arthritis, crippled by arthritis	has arthritis
confined to a wheelchair	uses a wheelchair
he's mentally retarded	he has a cognitive disability

Preferring Plain Language and Familiar Words

In adapting your message to your audience, use plain language and familiar words that you think audience members will recognize. Don't, however, avoid a big word that conveys your idea efficiently and is appropriate for the audience. Your goal is to shun pompous and pretentious language. Instead, use *go* words. If you mean *begin,* don't say *commence* or *initiate.* If you mean *pay,* don't write *compensate.* By substituting everyday, familiar words for unfamiliar ones, as shown here, you help your audience comprehend your ideas quickly.

Unfamiliar	Familiar
commensurate	equal
interrogate	question
materialize	appear
obfuscate	confuse
remuneration	pay, salary
terminate	end

At the same time, be selective in your use of jargon. *Jargon* describes technical or specialized terms within a field. These terms enable insiders to communicate complex ideas briefly, but to outsiders they mean nothing. Human resources professionals, for example, know precisely what's meant by *cafeteria plan* (a benefits option program), but most of us would be thinking about lunch. Geologists refer to *plate tectonics,* and physicians discuss *metastatic carcinomas.* These terms mean little to most of us. Use specialized language only when the audience will understand it. In addition, don't forget to consider secondary audiences: Will those potential receivers understand any technical terms used?

Using Precise, Vigorous Words

Strong verbs and concrete nouns give receivers more information and keep them interested. Don't overlook the thesaurus (or the thesaurus program on your computer) for expanding your word choices and vocabulary. Whenever possible, use specific words, as shown here.

Imprecise, Dull	More Precise
a change in profits	a 25 percent hike in profits a 10 percent plunge in profits
to say	to promise, confess, understand to allege, assert, assume, judge
to think about	to identify, diagnose, analyze to probe, examine, inspect

The following checklist reviews important elements in the first phase of the 3-x-3 writing process, prewriting. As you review these tips, remember the three basics of prewriting: analyzing, anticipating, and adapting.

CHECKLIST

Adapting a Message to Its Audience

- **Identify the message purpose.** Why are you writing, and what do you hope to achieve? Consider both primary and secondary audiences.
- **Select the most appropriate channel.** Consider the importance, feedback, interactivity, cost, formality, sensitivity, and richness of the options.
- **Profile the audience.** What is your relationship with the receiver? How much does the receiver know or need to know?
- **Focus on audience benefits.** Phrase your statements from the reader's view. Concentrate on the "you" view.
- **Avoid gender, racial, age, and disability bias.** Use bias-free words (*businessperson* rather than *businessman, manager* rather than *Hispanic manager, new employee* rather than *new twenty-two-year-old employee, uses a wheelchair* rather than *confined to a wheelchair*).
- **Be conversational but professional.** Strive for a warm, friendly tone that is not overly formal or familiar. Avoid slang and low-level diction.
- **Express ideas positively rather than negatively.** Instead of *We can't ship until June 1,* say *We can ship on June 1.*
- **Use short, familiar words.** Avoid big words and technical terms unless they are appropriate for the audience (*end* not *terminate*).
- **Search for precise, vigorous words.** Use a thesaurus if necessary to find strong verbs and concrete nouns (*announces* instead of *says, brokerage* instead of *business*).

LEARNING OUTCOME 5

Understand how teams approach collaborative writing projects and what collaboration tools support team writing.

Sharing the Writing in Teams

As you learned in Chapter 2, many of today's workers collaborate in teams to deliver services, develop products, and complete projects. It is almost assumed that today's progressive organizations will employ teams in some capacity to achieve their objectives. Because much of a team's work involves writing, you can expect to be putting your writing skills to work as part of a team.

When Is Team Writing Necessary?

Collaboration on team-written documents is necessary for projects that (a) are big, (b) have short deadlines, and (c) require the expertise or consensus of many people. Businesspeople sometimes also collaborate on short documents, such as memos, letters, information briefs, procedures, and policies. More often, however, teams work on big documents and presentations.

Why Are Team-Written Documents Better?

Team-written documents and presentations are standard in most organizations because collaboration has many advantages. Most important, collaboration usually produces a better product because many heads are better than one. In addition, team members and organizations benefit from team processes. Working together helps socialize members. They learn more about the organization's values and procedures. They are able to break down functional barriers, and they improve both formal and informal chains of communication. Additionally, they buy in to a project when they are part of its development. Members of effective teams are eager to implement their recommendations.

How Are Team-Written Documents Divided?

With big writing projects, teams may not actually function together for each phase of the writing process. Typically, team members gather at the beginning to brainstorm. They iron out answers to questions about the purpose, audience, content, organization, and design of their document or presentation. They develop procedures for team functioning, as you learned in Chapter 2. Then, they often assign segments of the project to individual members.

In Phase 1 of the writing process, teams work together closely as they discuss the project and establish their purpose. In Phase 2 members generally work separately when they conduct research, organize their findings, and compose a first draft. During Phase 3, some teams work together to synthesize their drafts and offer suggestions for revision. Other teams appoint one person to proofread and edit and another to prepare the final document. The revision and evaluation phase might be repeated several times before the final product is ready for presentation. Sharing the entire writing process, illustrated in Figure 4.8, means that all team members contribute their skills during the three phases.

Figure 4.8 **Sharing the Writing of Team Documents**

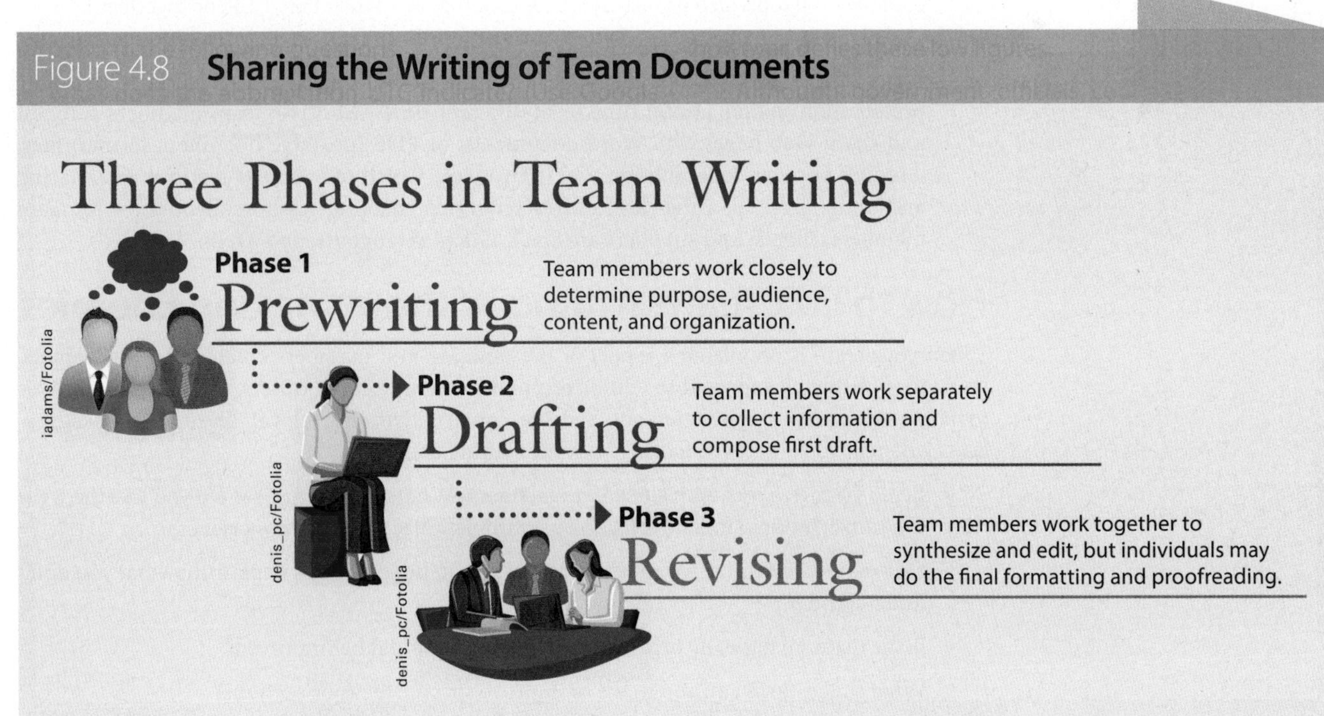

Three Phases in Team Writing
Phase 1
Prewriting
Team members work closely to determine purpose, audience, content, and organization.
Phase 2
Drafting
Team members work separately to collect information and compose first draft.
Phase 3
Revising
Team members work together to synthesize and edit, but individuals may do the final formatting and proofreading.
iadams/Fotolia
denis_pc/Fotolia
denis_pc/Fotolia

What Digital Collaboration Tools Support Team Writing?

One of the most frustrating tasks for teams is writing shared documents. Keeping the various versions straight and recognizing who made what comment can be difficult. Fortunately, digital collaboration tools are constantly being developed and improved. They range from simple to complex, inexpensive to expensive, locally installed to remotely hosted, commercial to open source, and small to large. Digital collaboration tools are especially necessary when team members are not physically in the same location. Even when members are nearby, they may use collaboration tools such as the following:

- **E-mail.** Despite its many drawbacks, e-mail remains a popular tool for online asynchronous (intermittent data transmission) collaboration. As projects grow more complex and involve more people who are not working near each other, however, e-mail becomes a clumsy, ineffective tool, especially for collaborative writing tasks.
- **Instant messaging and texting.** Because they ensure immediate availability, instant messaging and texting allow members to clear up minor matters immediately. They also may be helpful in initiating a quick group discussion.
- **Wikis.** A *wiki* is a website that allows multiple users to create, revise, and edit their own documents as well as contribute ideas to others'. A wiki facilitates teamwork because members can make comments and monitor the progress of a project. Perhaps the best part of a wiki is that it serves as an ongoing storehouse of information that can be used for reference. Wikis avoid the danger of losing track of information in e-mails and separate documents. You'll learn more about wikis in Chapter 7.
- **Track Changes and other tools.** MS Word includes **Track Changes** and **Comment** features that enable collaborators working on the same document to identify and approve edits made by team members. See the accompanying Plugged In box for more information about using these collaboration tools.
- **Web and telephone conferencing.** When teams need to share information and make decisions in real time, conferencing tools such as WebEx and GoToMeeting work well. Telephone conferencing tools also enable teams to work together when they can't be together.
- **Google Docs and other collaboration software.** For simple projects, collaboration software such as Google Docs permits teams to work on text documents, spreadsheets, and presentations either in real time or at different times. Multiple team members can edit and share Web pages, MS Word documents, or PDF (portable document format) files. Another popular collaboration tool is Dropbox, which offers cross-platform file sharing and online backup. Other useful, free programs enabling you to collaborate with team members, clients, and suppliers are Slack, Google Hangouts, and Trello.[24]

How to Edit Team Writing Without Making Enemies

When your team is preparing a report or presentation and members create different sections, you will probably be expected to edit or respond to the writing of others. Because no one likes to be criticized, make your statements specific, constructive, and helpful. The following suggestions will help you edit team writing without making enemies:

- Begin your remarks with a positive statement. What can you praise? Do you like the writer's conversational tone, word choice, examples, directness, or conciseness?
- Do you understand the writer's purpose? If not, be specific in explaining what you don't understand.
- Is the material logically organized? If not, how could it be improved?
- What suggestions can you make to improve specific ideas or sections?
- Make polite statements such as *I would suggest . . . , You might consider . . ., How about doing this . . . .*

PLUGGED IN

Using Track Changes and Other Editing Tools to Revise Collaborative Documents

Collaborative writing and editing projects are challenging. Fortunately, Microsoft Word offers useful tools to help team members edit and share documents electronically. Two simple but helpful editing tools are **Text Highlight Color** and **Font Color.** These tools, which are found on the **Home** tab in MS 2013 Office suite, enable reviewers to point out errors and explain problematic passages through the use of contrast. However, some projects require more advanced editing tools such as **Track Changes** and **Comment**.

Track Changes. To suggest specific editing changes to other team members, **Track Changes** is handy. The revised wording is visible on screen, and deletions show up in callout balloons that appear in the right-hand margin (see Figure 4.9). Various team members suggest revisions that are identified and dated. The original writer may accept or reject these changes. **Track Changes** is located on the **Review** tab.

Comment. Probably the most useful editing tool is the **Comment** function, also shown in Figure 4.9. This tool allows users to point out problematic passages or errors, ask or answer questions, and share ideas without changing or adding text. When more than one person adds comments, the comments appear in different colors and are identified by the writer's name and a date/time stamp. To use this tool in Word 2013, click **New Comment** from the drop-down **Review** tab. Then type your comment, which can be seen in the Web or print layout view (click **View** and **Print Layout** or **Web Layout**).

Completing a Document. When a document is finished, be sure to accept or reject all changes on the **Review** tab to remove tracking information. Also use the **Check for Properties** feature to inspect your document for hidden properties and personal information that you should remove.

Figure 4.9 Track Changes and Comment Feature in a Team Document

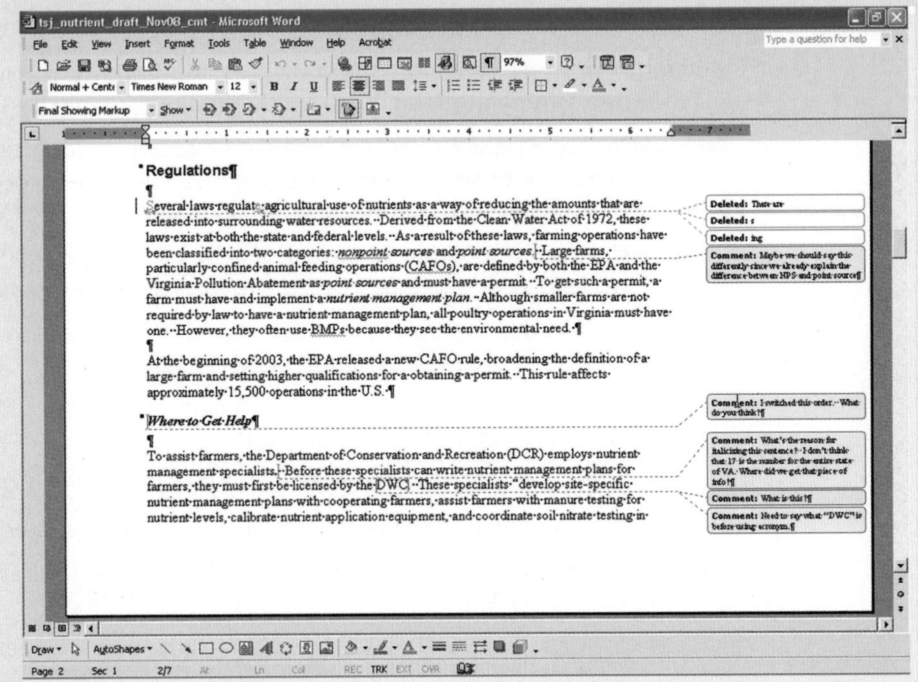

Team members can collaborate on shared documents with the **Track Changes** and **Comment** features in MS Word. Notice that **Track Changes** displays balloons to show deletions, comments, formatting changes, and the people who made the changes. See the Plugged In box for information on the usefulness of the **Track Changes** and **Comment** features when collaborating on team documents.

Your Turn: Applying Your Skills at TOMS

As a member of a group of agents of change (interns) at TOMS, you've read criticisms of the company. However, you genuinely believe that its one-for-one model is doing good in the world. You also enthusiastically support its One Day Without Shoes. The way it works is simple. Individuals go barefoot for one day. When asked why, they explain the impact of being shoeless on young children: diseases contracted from soil-transmitted germs, painful sores, infections, and absence from schools that require children to wear shoes.

Recently TOMS launched an additional special program. For every photo of bare feet tagged on Instagram in a two-week period, the company gave a new pair of shoes to a child in need. No purchase necessary! TOMS founder Blake Mycoskie said, "The best part is that even if someone is not a TOMS customer, he or she can simply take a photo and post *#withoutshoes* to make sure a child in need somewhere in the world will get a new pair."[25]

Conduct research to learn more about these initiatives at **www.toms.com**. With a group of three to five classmates, prepare a draft of a message that might be sent to fellow students encouraging them to participate in One Day Without Shoes. Pick a day for the event and provide information about where students can learn more about TOMS. Also encourage them to submit a photo of their bare feet tagged on Instagram. Choose a two-week period during which to submit.

Summary of Learning Outcomes

1 Understand the nature of communication and its barriers in the digital era.

- Although people are sending more messages and using new technologies in this digital era, the communication process still consists of the same basic elements.
- The sender encodes (selects) words or symbols to express an idea in a message. It travels verbally over a channel (such as e-mail, website, tweet, letter, text, or smartphone) or is expressed nonverbally with gestures or body language.
- *Noise,* such as loud sounds, misspelled words, poor reception, inattention, and information overload, may interfere with the transmission of a message.
- The receiver decodes (interprets) the message and may respond with feedback, informing the sender of the effectiveness of the message.
- Barriers that may create misunderstanding include bypassing, differing frames of reference, lack of language skill, and distractions.

2 Summarize the 3-x-3 writing process and explain how it guides a writer.

- Business writing should be purposeful, economical, and audience oriented.
- Following the 3-x-3 writing process helps writers create efficient and effective messages.
- Phase 1 of the 3-x-3 writing process (prewriting) involves analyzing the message, anticipating the audience, and considering ways to adapt the message to the audience.
- Phase 2 (drafting) involves researching the topic, organizing the material, and drafting the message.
- Phase 3 (revising) includes editing, proofreading, and evaluating the message. A writing process helps a writer by providing a systematic plan describing what to do in each step of the process.

3 **Analyze the purpose of a message, anticipate its audience, and select the best communication channel.**

- Before drafting, communicators must decide why they are creating a message and what they hope to achieve. Although many messages only inform, some must also persuade.
- After identifying the purpose, communicators visualize both the primary and secondary audiences, which helps them choose the most appropriate language, tone, and content for a message.
- Senders should remember that receivers will usually be thinking, *What's in it for me?* (WIIFM).
- Senders select the best channel by considering the importance of the message, the amount and speed of feedback required, the necessity of a permanent record, the cost of the channel, the degree of formality desired, the confidentiality and sensitivity of the message, and the receiver's preference and level of technical expertise.

4 **Employ expert writing techniques such as incorporating audience benefits, the "you" view, conversational but professional language, a positive and courteous tone, bias-free language, plain language, and vigorous words.**

- The term *audience benefits* suggests looking for ways to shape the message from the receiver's, not the sender's, view.
- Skilled communicators look at a message from the receiver's perspective, applying the "you" view without attempting to manipulate.
- Expert writing techniques also include using conversational but professional language along with positive language that tells what can be done rather than what can't be done. *(You can receive a discount with the proper code* rather than *We can't authorize a discount unless you include the proper code).*
- A courteous tone means guarding against rudeness and avoiding sounding preachy or demanding.
- Writers should also avoid language that excludes, stereotypes, or offends people (*lady lawyer, spry old gentleman,* and *confined to a wheelchair*).
- Plain language, familiar terms, strong verbs, and concrete nouns improve readability and effectiveness.

5 **Understand how teams approach collaborative writing projects and what collaboration tools support team writing.**

- Large projects or team efforts involving the expertise of many people often require team members to collaborate.
- During Phase 1 (prewriting) of the writing process, teams usually work together to brainstorm and work out their procedures and assignments.
- During Phase 2 (drafting), individual members research and write their portions of the project report or presentation.
- During Phase 3 (revising), teams may work together to combine and revise their drafts.
- Teams may use digital collaboration tools such as e-mail, instant messaging, texting, wikis, word processing functions such as **Track Changes**, Web conferencing, Google Docs, or other software to collaborate effectively.

Critical Thinking

1. The use of digital communication has overtaken face-to-face and voice-to-voice communication in the workplace. Has this shift changed the fundamental process of communication? (L.O. 1)

2. Why do you think employers prefer messages that are not written like high school and college essays? (L.O. 2)

3. Why should business writers strive to use short, familiar, simple words? Does this dumb down business messages? (L.O. 4)

4. A wise observer once said that bad writing makes smart people look dumb. Do you agree or disagree, and why? (L.O. 1–4)

5. Ethical Issue: After a workplace project was completed, you were rightfully upset. You and two other team members did all of the work, but two freeloaders are sharing in the credit. This probably wouldn't have happened in college team assignments. Should you report the freeloaders to the manager?

Activities

4.1 Audience Benefits and the "You" View (L.O. 4)

YOUR TASK Revise the following sentences to emphasize the perspective of the audience and the "you" view.

a. We are taking the proactive step of issuing all our customers new chip-enabled credit cards to replace expired or lost cards and prevent increasingly costly payouts we have suffered from fraud.

b. We take great pride in announcing our new schedule of low-cost, any-day flights to Hawaii.

c. Our strict safety policy forbids us from renting power equipment to anyone who cannot demonstrate proficiency in its use.

d. We're requesting that all employees complete the attached online survey by April 1 so that we may develop a master schedule for summer vacations more efficiently.

e. Our social media engineers are excited to announce a new free app called Fan Boosters that we believe will get fans to share, like, and subscribe to your content.

f. To save the expense of having team trainers set up your training classes in our limited office space, we suggest offering a customized class for your employees right in your own building.

g. Because we take pride in our national policy of selling name brands at discount prices, we can allow store credit but we cannot give cash refunds on returned merchandise.

4.2 Conversational but Professional (L.O. 4)

YOUR TASK Revise the following to make the tone conversational yet professional.

a. As per your recent request, the undersigned is happy to inform you that we are sending you forthwith the procedure manuals you requested.

b. Kindly be informed that it is necessary for you to designate the model number of the appliance before we can submit your order.

c. BTW, Angela went ballistic when the manager accused her of ripping off office supplies.

d. Pursuant to your e-mail of the 12th, please be advised that your shipment was sent April 15.

e. R head honcho wz like totally raggety kuz I wz sick n stuff n mist the team meet. Geez!

f. The undersigned respectfully reminds affected individuals that employees desirous of changing their health plans must do so before December 30.

4.3 Positive and Courteous Expression (L.O. 4)

YOUR TASK Revise the following statements to make them more positive and courteous.

a. Construction on your building is at a standstill because the contractor is unable to pour footings until the soil is no longer soggy.

b. A passport cannot be issued until an application is completed and a recent photo is included.

c. Your message of April 1 claims that the blade in your food processor malfunctioned. Although you apparently failed to read the operator's manual, we are sending you a replacement blade PLUS another manual. Next time read page 18 carefully so that you will know how to attach this blade.

d. Customers are ineligible for the 25 percent discount if they fail to provide the discount code at the time of purchase.

e. As team leader, you apparently failed to remember that you have already assigned me two gigantic and complex research tasks, and now you have dumped another big job on me—one that I can't possibly begin until after I finish the other two jobs.

f. We regret to announce that we can offer the 50 percent discount only to the the first 25 buyers, so act quickly!

4.4 Bias-Free Language (L.O. 4)

YOUR TASK Revise the following sentences to reduce bias (e.g., gender, racial, ethnic, age, disability).

a. In 18 or more states, an employee has the right to view his employee record.

b. Media Moguls hired Charissa Love, an African American, for the position of social media coordinator.

c. A skilled assistant proofreads her boss's documents and catches any errors he makes.

d. Curtis is crippled with arthritis, but his crippling rarely interferes with his work.

e. Recently appointed to the commission are a lady lawyer, a Nigerian CPA, and two businessmen.

f. The conference in the Bahamas offers special side trips for the wives of executives.

4.5 Plain Language and Familiar Words (L.O. 4)

YOUR TASK Revise the following sentences to use plain language and familiar words.

a. The writer tried to obfuscate the issue with extraneous and superfluous data.

b. To expedite ratification of the agreement, we beseech you to vote in the affirmative.

c. Although the remuneration seems low, it is commensurate with other pay packages.

d. Bank tellers were interrogated after the robbery, but no strong evidence materialized.

e. Researchers dialogued with individual students on campus, but subsequent group interviews proved fruitless.

4.6 Precise, Vigorous Words (L.O. 4)

YOUR TASK From the choices in parentheses, select the most precise, vigorous words.

a. If you find yourself (*having, doing, juggling*) many tasks, look for ways to reduce your involvement.

b. Rana's outstanding report contains (*a lot of, many, a warehouse of*) helpful data.

c. If necessary, we will (*review, change, reduce*) overtime hours to (*fix, balance, rework)* the budget.

d. The operations manager demanded a (*substantial, 20 percent, big*) reduction in staff travel expenditures.

e. In the courtroom the attorney (*said, alleged, thought*) that the car was stolen.

4.7 Document for Analysis: Improving a Negative, Discourteous, and Unprofessional Message (L.O. 4, 5)

Communication Technology | E-Mail | Team

YOUR TASK Analyze the following e-mail to be sent by the vice president to all supervisors and managers. In teams or individually, discuss the tone and writing faults in this message. Your instructor may ask you to revise the e-mail so that it reflects some of the writing techniques you learned in this chapter. How can you make this e-mail more courteous, positive, concise, precise, and audience oriented? Consider revising it as a collaboration project using Word's **Track Changes** and **Comment** features.

To: All Supervisors and Departmental Managers
From: Richard Mangrove, Vice President, Employee Relations
Subject: Dangerous Employee Performance Evaluations

All,

This is something I hate to do, but I must warn you that recently one of our employees filed a lawsuit against the company because of comments a supervisor made during a performance evaluation. This did not have to happen. Look, people, you must do better!

Because none of you are dense, here are suggestions you must share with all supervisors and managers regarding companywide evaluations:

- You cannot accurately evaluate an employee's performance unless you have a system to measure that performance. That's why the obvious very first step is developing performance standards and goals for each employee. To be effective, these standards and goals must be shared with the employee. However, don't do it orally. Do it in writing.
- The performance of each employee must be monitored throughout the year. Keep a log for each worker. Note memorable incidents or projects in which he was involved. But don't just keep favorable comments. I know that many of you are understandably averse to placing negative comments in an employee's file. However, MAN UP! Even negative comments must be included as part of the evaluation process.
- Once a year each employee must be formally evaluated in a written performance appraisal—yes, I do mean written! In a face-to-face meeting, let the employee know what you think they did well and what areas the employee may be able to improve. Be specific, give deadlines, be honest, and be realistic.

Giving evaluations can be difficult. With careful preparation, however, the process can be smooth and safe. Don't allow yourself or the company to get involved in any more legal ramifications.

Richard Mangrove
[Complete contact information]

4.8 Channel Selection: Various Business Scenarios (L.O. 3)

Communication Technology

YOUR TASK Using Figure 4.5 on page 138, suggest the best communication channels for the following messages. Assume that all channels shown are available, ranging from face-to-face conversations to instant messages, blogs, and wikis. Be prepared to justify your choices considering the richness of each channel.

a. You need to know whether Stephanie in Reprographics can produce a rush job for you in two days.

b. As part of a task force to investigate data breaches in financial institutions, you need to establish a central location where each team member can see general information about the task as well as add comments for others to see. Task force members are located throughout the country.

c. As an event planner, you have been engaged to research the sites for a celebrity golf tournament. What is the best channel for conveying your findings to your boss or planning committee?

d. You want to persuade your manager to change your assigned sales territory.

e. You're sitting on the couch in the evening streaming video on your laptop when you suddenly remember that you should have sent Michele details about a shared project. Should you text her right away before you forget?

f. As a sales manager, you want to know which of your sales reps in the field are available immediately for a quick teleconference meeting.

g. Your firm must respond to a notice from the Internal Revenue Service announcing that the company owes a penalty because it underreported its income in the previous fiscal year.

4.9 Analyzing Audiences (L.O. 3)

YOUR TASK Using the questions in Figure 4.4 on page 136, write a brief analysis of the audience for each of the following communication tasks. What kind of reaction should you expect from the primary reader and any secondary readers? What tone should you convey?

a. As an administrator at the municipal water department, you must write a letter to water users explaining that the tap water may taste and smell bad; however, it poses no threats to health.

b. As a new graduate, you are preparing a cover message to accompany your résumé for a job that you saw listed on a company website. You are confident that your qualifications match the job description.

c. You are about to send an e-mail to your regional sales manager describing your visit to a new customer who is demanding special discounts.

d. As a tech employee of TOMS, you have just returned from your first Giving Trip. You visited a small California town and worked with TOMS' sharing partner Save the Children to further its charity work. You were able to give free shoes and socks to needy, grateful children, some of whom lived in homes without electricity or plumbing. Now you are inspired to share what you learned about giving by writing a short article for the TOMS blog.

e. You are planning to write an e-mail to your manager to try to persuade her to allow you to attend a computer workshop that will require you to leave work early two days a week for ten weeks.

f. You are preparing an unsolicited sales message to a targeted group of executives promoting part-time ownership in a corporate jet plane.

4.10 How Annoying Is Business Jargon? (L.O. 4)

Business writing is most effective when writers avoid overused phrases that others find annoying, useless, and pretentious. Bloggers today are particularly fond of attacking business jargon. A quick Google search reveals such titles as "16 Business Jargon Words We Never, Ever Want to Hear Again" and "These 10 Office Phrases Need to Die a Swift Death." Writers at Forbes.com are especially unhappy about the spread of such jargon: "No longer solely the province of consultants, investors and business-school types, this annoying gobbledygook has mesmerized the rank and file around the globe."[26]

YOUR TASK Following are ten words or phrases that bloggers have found particularly egregious.

For each of these items, write your own definition. Use Google if you need help.

1. *thinking outside the box*
2. *circle back*
3. *peel back the layers of the onion*
4. *at the end of the day*
5. *drinking the Kool-Aid*
6. *right-sizing*
7. *blue-sky thinking*
8. *move the needle*
9. *tiger team*
10. *let's solution this*

4.11 Essays or Blogs: What Kinds of Writing Have You Done Previously? (L.O. 1–5)

Communication Technology | E-Mail | Social Media

What, no more term papers? Students blog instead? While employers are desperate to hire job seekers with solid communication skills, the debate over how best to prepare students for writing in the digital era is raging across the country. A professor at Duke University now wants to replace the old-style term paper with the blog. Cathy N. Davidson finds the academic paper requiring that the writer make a point, explain it, and defend it deeply offensive. She wants to make writing fun, practical, and relevant and believes that the blog is the ticket.[27]

Professor Davidson has plenty of detractors. "Writing term papers is a dying art, but those who do write them have a dramatic leg up in terms of critical thinking, argumentation and the sort of expression required not only in college, but in the job market," says Douglas B. Reeves, a columnist for the *American School Board Journal*. "It doesn't mean there aren't interesting blogs. But nobody would conflate interesting writing with premise, evidence, argument and conclusion," he says. The author of a recent survey of student engagement concurs with this criticism: "She's right," William H. Fitzhugh says of Professor Davidson. "Writing is being murdered. But the solution isn't blogs, the solution is more reading. We don't pay taxes so kids can talk about themselves and their home lives."

According to the National Survey of Student Engagement, 82 percent of college freshmen and more than half of seniors weren't asked to do a single paper of 20 pages or more. Most of their writing assignments were for papers of one to five pages. Another study estimated that 80 percent of high school students were not asked to write a history term paper of more than 15 pages. How much writing have you been asked to do in high school and college?

YOUR TASK In an e-mail or a memo to your instructor, reflect on your writing experience. See Appendix A for memo formats and Chapters 7 and 8 for tips on preparing a professional e-mail message. Consider the arguments in this controversy pitting what has been dubbed *old literacy* against *new literacy*. Explain to your instructor how much and what kind of writing you had to do in high school and in college. How long were typical assignments? What subjects did you discuss? What is your take on the controversy? Should term papers really be replaced by blog entries?

4.12 Using Track Changes and Comment Features to Edit a Document (L.O. 5)

Communication Technology | E-Mail | Team

YOUR TASK Organize into groups of three. Using the latest version of MS Word, copy and respond to the Document for Analysis in **Activity 4.7**. Set up a round-robin e-mail file exchange so that each member responds to the other group members' documents by using the **Comment** feature of Word to offer advice or suggestions for improvement. Submit a printout of the document with group comments, as well as a final edited document.

Test Your Etiquette IQ

New communication platforms and casual workplace environments have blurred the lines of appropriateness, leaving workers wondering how to navigate uncharted waters. Indicate whether the following statements are true or false. Then see if you agree with the responses on p. R-1.

1. At your office desk, it's easier to take notes from telephone calls when both hands are free. To be most efficient, you should set your phone to speaker so that your hands are always free to make notes either manually or on your computer.

   ________ True ________ False

2. In your office cubicle, you overhear Rick, who is two cubicles away, on the phone asking when the next management council meeting is scheduled. Because you know the date, you should shout it out so that Rick learns immediately the date of this critical meeting.

   ________ True ________ False

3. Your cell phone rings while you are at your desk. You see immediately that it's a personal call. If you think it's going to be a short call, you should go ahead and answer.

   ________ True ________ False

Chat About It

In each chapter you will find five discussion questions related to the chapter material. Your instructor may assign these topics for you to discuss in class, in an online chat room, or on an online discussion board. Some of the discussion topics may require outside research. You may also be asked to read and respond to postings made by your classmates.

TOPIC 1: After searching an alumni database, you decide to e-mail a professional who is working in the career you hope to enter. Your goal in writing this professional is to obtain firsthand information about this person's career and to receive career advice. However, you know nothing about this person. How could you profile the receiver to help you shape your message? What audience benefits could you use to persuade the receiver? What channel would you choose to deliver your message? What tone would you use?

TOPIC 2: Have you ever tried to make your writing longer than it needed to be? For example, did you count the words in what you wrote to meet a minimum word count? Do you agree with David Silverman (see the Reality Check on page 132) that students learn to overwrite in the hope that at least some of their sentences hit the mark?

TOPIC 3: Think about a time when someone had to reveal bad news to you. Did you feel that the best communication channel was used to deliver that news? What channels are richest? Should they always be used to reveal bad news or to be persuasive?

TOPIC 4: Think back to the last time you were involved in a team project. What did the team do that resulted in an efficient working process and a successful product, or an inefficient working process and an unsuccessful product?

TOPIC 5: Find a news article online that describes a company that used careless language in its communication with its customers, stockholders, or employees. Briefly explain what the company did and what it should have done instead.

Grammar and Mechanics | *Review 4*

Adjectives and Adverbs

Review Guides 19 and 20 about adjectives and adverbs in Appendix D, Grammar and Mechanics Guide, beginning on page D-8. On a separate sheet, revise the following sentences to correct errors in adjectives and adverbs. For each error you locate, write the guide number that reflects this usage. Some sentences may have two errors. If a sentence is correct, write *C*. When you finish, check your answers on page Key-1.

1. The ability to prepare a purposeful, concise, and audience-centered message does not come natural to most people.
2. Samantha thought she had done good when she wrote her part of the team report.
3. The team wiki enables everyone to see the most up to the minute status information.
4. All of our newly-created team documents can be posted quick to the wiki.
5. We all felt badly when one member lost her laptop and had no backup.
6. The 3-x-3 writing process provides step by step instructions for preparing messages.
7. Kevin found it difficult to pass up the once in a lifetime opportunity to travel worldwide.
8. Our project ran smooth after Jennifer reorganized the team.
9. Locally-installed online collaboration tools are easy-to-use and work well.
10. Well written business messages sound conversational but professional.

References

[1] Chu, J. (2013, June 17). Toms sets out to sell a lifestyle, not just shoes. Retrieved from http://www.fastcompany.com/3012568/blake-mycoskie-toms

[2] O'Connor, C. (2014, August 20). Bain deal makes TOMS shoes founder Blake Mycoskie a $300 million man. Retrieved from http://www.forbes.com/sites/clareoconnor/2014/08/20/bain-deal-makes-toms-shoes-founder-blake-mycoskie-a-300-million-man

[3] Kirschner, A. (2012, March 6). Intern adventures: Meet the interns, part II. [Blog post]. Retrieved from http://www.toms.com/blog/taxonomy/term/4

[4] Maltby. E. (2010, January 19). Expanding abroad? Avoid cultural gaffes. *The Wall Street Journal*, p. B5.

[5] Foderaro, L. (2009, May 18). Psst! Need the answer to no. 7? Just click here. *The New York Times*, p. A17.

[6] Li, L. (n.d.). 10 stupid business ideas that made millions. Retrieved from http://www.entrepreneursforachange.com/10-stupid-business-ideas-that-made-millions

[7] Sullivan, J., Karmeda, N., & Nobu, T. (1992, January/February). Bypassing in managerial communication. *Business Horizons, 34*(1), 72.

[8] Brewer, E., & Holmes, T. (2009, October). Obfuscating the obvious: Miscommunication issues in the interpretation of common terms. *Journal of Business Communication, 46*(4), 480-496.

[9] Quoted in Bryant, A. (2011, July 9). Cultivating his plants, and his company. *The New York Times*. Retrieved from http://www.nytimes.com/2011/07/10/business/esris-chief-on-tending-his-plants-and-his-company.html?pagewanted=all&_r=0

[10] McGirt, E. (2006, March 20). Getting out from under: Beset by interruptions, information overload, and irksome technology, knowledge workers need help: A survival guide. *Fortune*, p. 8. See also Evans, L. (2014, August 4). 4 ways to retrain your brain to handle information overload. Retrieved from http://www.fastcompany.com/3033845/the-future-of-work/4-ways-to-retrain-your-brain-to-handle-information-overload

[11] Levitin, D. J. (2015). *The organized mind: Thinking straight in the age of information overload*. New York: Plume/Penguin Random House, p. 97. See also Bradberry, T. (2015, January 6). The real harm in multitasking. *Inc.* Retrieved from http://www.inc.com/travis-bradberry/the-real-harm-in-multitasking.html

[12] Drucker, P. (1990). *Managing the non-profit organization: Practices and principles*. New York: HarperCollins, p. 46.

[13] Silverman, D. (2009, February 10). Why is business writing so bad? *Harvard Business Review*. Retrieved from https://hbrblogs.wordpress.com/david-silverman

[14] Quoted in Middleton, D. (2011, March 3). Students struggle for words. *The Wall Street Journal*. Retrieved from http://online.wsj.com/article/SB10001424052748703409904576174651780110970.html?mod=WSJ_hpp_sections_careerjournal

[15] Visentin, L. (2015, May 28). Macquarie University revokes degrees for students caught buying essays in MyMaster cheating racket. Retrieved from http://www.smh.com.au/national/education/macquarie-university-revokes-degrees-for-students-caught-buying-essays-in-mymaster-cheating-racket-20150528-ghba3z.html

[16] Based on Brennan, C. (2015, August 17). Daily Mail. Amazon CEO urges staff to 'email me directly about bullies' after investigation found people 'crying at their desks' because of cut-throat culture. DailyMail. Retrieved from http://www.dailymail.co.uk/news/article-3201617/Amazon-CEO-Jeff-Bezos-urges-staff-email-directly-bullies-investigation-people-crying-desks-cutthroat-culture.html

[17] Arnold, V. (1986, August). Benjamin Franklin on writing well. *Personnel Journal*, p. 17.

[18] Bacon, M. (1988, April). Quoted in Business writing: One-on-one speaks best to the masses. *Training*, p. 95.

[19] Clark, B. (n.d.). The two most important words in blogging. Retrieved from http://www.copyblogger.com/the-two-most-important-words-in-blogging

[20] Google. (2012, January 30). E-mail message to Mary Ellen Guffey.

[21] Canavor, N. (2012). *Business writing in the digital age*. Thousand Oaks, CA: Sage, p. 52.

[22] Ibid.

[23] Link, S. (2012, May 2). Use 'person first' language. [Letter to editor]. *USA Today*, p. 6A.

[24] Bulygin, D. (2015, May 27). 7 free easy-to-use online collaboration tools make teamwork simple. Retrieved from http://trendblog.net/6-easy-to-use-online-collaboration-tools-make-teamwork-simple

[25] Hoffman, E. (2015, May 5). Toms will give free shoes to children if you Instagram your bare feet. Retrieved from http://www.businessinsider.com/toms-one-day-without-shoes-2015-5#ixzz3esFptPTt

[26] Mallet, M., Nelson, B., & Steiner, C. (2012, January 26). The most annoying, pretentious and useless business jargon. Retrieved from http://www.forbes.com/sites/groupthink/2012/01/26/the-most-annoying-pretentious-and-useless-business-jargon

[27] Activity based on Richtel, M. (2012, January 20). Blogs vs. term papers. *The New York Times*. Retrieved from http://www.nytimes.com

Chapter 5

Organizing and Drafting Business Messages

LEARNING OUTCOMES

After studying this chapter, you should be able to

1 Apply Phase 2 of the 3-x-3 writing process, which begins with formal and informal research to collect background information.

2 Generate and organize ideas resulting from techniques such as brainstorming and brainwriting along with social media techniques such as crowdsourcing, crowdstorming, and crowdfunding.

3 Compose the first draft of a message using a variety of sentence types and avoiding sentence fragments, run-on sentences, and comma splices.

4 Improve your writing techniques by emphasizing important ideas, employing the active and passive voice effectively, using parallelism, and preventing dangling and misplaced modifiers.

5 Draft well-organized paragraphs using (a) the direct plan to define, classify, illustrate, or describe; (b) the pivoting plan to compare and contrast; or (c) the indirect plan to explain and persuade. Paragraphs should include (a) topic sentences, (b) support sentences, and (c) transitional expressions to build coherence.

Darren Baker/Shutterstock.com

MyEvent.com Moves From Weddings to Fundraising and Crowdsourcing

Yeamake/Shutterstock.com

Zooming In

"It all started about 15 years ago at a poker game when one of the guys announced that he was getting married, and we decided to make him a website to plan and organize the affair," said Rob Hirscheimer, cofounder of MyEvent.com.[1] What started as a one-time event eventually became one of the first wedding website builders on the Internet. Based on the idea that anyone can make a website with easy-to-use Web-based software, Rob and cofounder Mark Goldenberg brainstormed their wedding platform into a leading do-it-yourself event planning service.

Located in Montreal, MyEvent.com now provides complete Web packages that help individuals, businesses, and nonprofits organize such events as class and family reunions, personal and group fund-raisers, and corporate events. What's remarkable about its business success is that MyEvent.com has managed to remain relevant despite its small size (only 16 core employees) and despite seismic upheavals in Internet industries, including the dawn of Google, social networks, the mobile revolution, Web 2.0, and countless other game-changing technology and behavioral shifts.

One of the most popular MyEvent.com programs is MyFunRun, which provides a step-by-step, turnkey system for schools to raise funds. Students participate in a walk, run, or other activity, and donations arrive via e-mail, via social networks, and in person. Rather than selling candy, doughnuts, cookies, or other products, students engage in a healthy activity that raises funds for a good cause. MyFunRun is especially popular as a fund-raiser for parent–teacher associations at schools across the United States and Canada.

MyEvent.com has processed more than $85 million in e-commerce transactions through its customers' websites. Over 100,000 users have employed MyEvent.com sites for do-it-yourself fund-raising. Most recently it has entered the arena of crowdsourcing and crowdfunding. You can raise funds for any project or cause, such as financing a business startup, organizing a sporting event, or soliciting funds for a sick or disabled friend. Students even attempt to crowdfund their college tuition. You'll learn more about MyEvent.com and be asked to complete a relevant task at the end of this chapter.

istockphoto.com/kristian sekulic

Critical Thinking

- In what ways would research (gathering information) have helped the founders of MyEvent.com move beyond their original wedding platform and remain relevant in the rapidly changing world of Internet businesses?
- What techniques can business communicators at MyEvent.com and other companies use to generate ideas for new products as well as to improve business processes?
- Have you experienced any crowdsourcing or crowdfunding activity among your friends or relatives? Have you seen it in the news?

Beginning With Research

LEARNING OUTCOME 1

Apply Phase 2 of the 3-x-3 writing process, which begins with formal and informal research to collect background information.

Businesspeople must constantly make decisions, solve problems, and determine how to proceed. At MyEvent.com the owners faced significant challenges in adapting their business model to a rapidly changing social media world. Like other business leaders, the MyEvent.com owners strive to solve problems and make decisions by gathering information, generating ideas, and organizing those ideas into logical messages that guide their organizations. These activities are part of the second phase of the 3-x-3 writing process. You will recall that the 3-x-3 writing process, reviewed in Figure 5.1, involves three phases. This chapter focuses on the second phase of the process: researching, organizing, and drafting.

No smart businessperson would begin drafting a message before gathering background information. We call this process *research*, a rather formal-sounding term. For our purposes, however, *research* simply means collecting information about a certain topic. This is an important step in the writing process because that information helps the writer shape the

Figure 5.1 **The 3-x-3 Writing Process**

1 Prewriting

Analyze: Decide on the message purpose. What do you want the receiver to do or believe?

Anticipate: What does the audience already know? How will it receive this message?

Adapt: Think about techniques to present this message most effectively. Consider how to elicit feedback.

2 Drafting

Research: Gather background data by searching files and the Internet.

Organize: Arrange direct messages with the big idea first. For persuasive or negative messages, use an indirect, problem-solving strategy.

Draft: Prepare the first draft, using active-voice sentences, coherent paragraphs, and appropriate transitional expressions.

3 Revising

Edit: Eliminate wordy fillers, long lead-ins, redundancies, and trite business phrases. Strive for parallelism, clarity, conciseness, and readability.

Proofread: Check carefully for errors in spelling, grammar, punctuation, and format.

Evaluate: Will this message achieve your purpose? Is the tone pleasant? Did you encourage feedback?

message. Discovering significant information after a message is half completed often means having to start over and reorganize. To avoid frustration and inaccurate messages, writers collect information that answers several questions:

- What does the receiver need to know about this topic?
- What is the receiver to do?
- How is the receiver to do it?
- When must the receiver do it?
- What will happen if the receiver doesn't do it?

Whenever your communication problem requires more information than you have in your head or at your fingertips, you must conduct research. This research may be informal or formal.

What Are Informal Research Methods?

Many routine tasks—such as drafting e-mails, memos, letters, informational reports, and oral presentations—require information that you can collect informally. Where can you find information before starting a project? The following techniques are useful in informal research:

- **Search your company's files.** If you are responding to an inquiry or drafting a routine message, you often can find background information such as previous correspondence in your own files or those of the company. You might consult the company wiki or other digital and manual files. You might also consult colleagues.
- **Talk with the boss.** Get information from the individual making the assignment. What does that person know about the topic? What slant should you take? What other sources would that person suggest?
- **Interview the target audience.** Consider talking with individuals at whom the message is aimed. They can provide clarifying information that tells you what they want to know and how you should shape your remarks. Suggestions for conducting more formal interviews are presented in Chapter 11.

- **Conduct an informal survey.** Gather unscientific but helpful information through questionnaires, telephone surveys, or online surveys. In preparing a report predicting the success of a proposed company fitness center, for example, you might circulate a questionnaire asking for employee reactions.

What Are Formal Research Methods?

Long reports and complex business problems generally require formal research methods. Let's say you are part of the management team at MyEvent.com and you have been asked to help launch a new program that involves crowdsourcing. Or, let's assume you must write a term paper for a college class. Both tasks require more data than you have in your head or at your fingertips. To conduct formal research, consider the following research options:

- **Access digital sources.** Torrents of information are available online. A Google search for nearly any topic presents an overwhelming amount of information. Beyond Google, college and public libraries provide digital retrieval services that permit access to a wide array of books, scholarly journals, magazines, newspapers, and other online literature. With so much data drowning today's researchers, they struggle to decide what is current, relevant, and credible. Help is on the way, however! You'll learn more about researching and using electronic sources effectively in Chapter 11.
- **Search manually.** Valuable background and supplementary information is available through manual searching of resources in public and college libraries. These traditional sources include books and newspaper, magazine, and journal articles. Other sources are encyclopedias, reference books, handbooks, dictionaries, directories, and almanacs.
- **Investigate primary sources.** To develop firsthand, primary information for a project, go directly to the source. In helping to launch a crowdsourcing program at MyEvent.com, you might check out competing sites. You would check blogs, Twitter, Facebook, and newspapers to learn about circumstances leading to crowdsourcing. You could also use questionnaires, interviews, or focus groups. Big companies about to launch a new product such as an energy drink might conduct extensive market research, including scientific sampling methods that enable them to make accurate judgments and valid predictions.
- **Conduct scientific experiments.** Another source of primary data is experimentation. Instead of merely asking for the target audience's opinion, scientific researchers present choices with controlled variables. Assume, for example, that the management team at Jamba Juice wants to know at what price and under what circumstances consumers would purchase smoothies from Jamba Juice instead of from Blenders in the Grass. Instead of smoothies, let's say that Lands' End management wants to study the time of year and type of weather conditions that motivate consumers to begin purchasing sweaters, jackets, and cold weather gear. The results of such experimentation would provide valuable data for managerial decision making. Because formal research is particularly necessary for reports, you will study resources and techniques more extensively in Unit 4.

LEARNING OUTCOME 2

Generate and organize ideas resulting from techniques such as brainstorming and brainwriting along with social media techniques such as crowdsourcing, crowdstorming, and crowdfunding.

Generating Ideas and Organizing Information

Not all information for making decisions is available through research. Often fresh ideas to solve problems must be generated. For example, how can we expand our business into mobile technologies? How can we cut costs without losing market share? Should we radically reinvent our website? For years organizations have tried to solve problems and generate ideas in group discussions. Two methods have prevailed.

Brainstorming and Brainwriting

Traditionally, groups have generated ideas by **brainstorming,** which may be defined as the spontaneous contribution of ideas from members of a group. Here's how the technique works. A group gathers to solve a problem, and every member strives to present as many ideas as possible. The emphasis is on quantity, not quality. The ideas are then evaluated, and the best are selected. Critics, however, charge that brainstorming in this traditional format doesn't work. It results in the "loudmouth meeting-hog phenomenon," in which one extrovert dominates the conversation.[2] Not only can one person dominate the session, but early ideas tend to sway the group. "It's called anchoring, and it crushes originality," claimed Professor Leigh Thompson in a Fast Company interview.[3] Brainstorming favors first ideas, thus promoting groupthink and limiting fresh avenues of thought.

To overcome the shortcomings of traditional brainstorming, some critics champion **brainwriting.** This creativity technique involves writing out ideas rather than speaking them.[4] Supporters claim that brainwriting generates far more creative ideas than traditional brainstorming. Its emphasis is on writing first and discussing afterward. Notice in Figure 5.2 that brainstorming and brainwriting have much in common. The chief difference is in how the ideas are presented: orally or in writing. Brainstorming can be a wild affair with visionary off-the-wall suggestions, whereas brainwriting is quieter and more thoughtful. Both techniques, however, end in the same place—with the selection of the best ideas.

Crowdsourcing, Crowdstorming, and Crowdfunding

Closely related to brainstorming and brainwriting are three collaborative efforts with similar-sounding names that arose with the spread of social media networks. **Crowdsourcing** describes the practice of requesting ideas or services online from unknown crowd members rather than from traditional employees or contractors. Crowdsourcing has become an appealing and inexpensive method of tapping into the collective knowledge of consumers. Coca-Cola, for instance, invited its 50 million Facebook fans to offer ideas to "promote positivity both online and in the real world."[5] Toymaker Mattel asked what career its famous Barbie doll should pursue next. In conjunction with the University of Texas at Austin, computer giant Dell sponsored the Dell Social Innovation Challenge. This crowdsourcing program produced ideas such as recycling old tires to make rubber shoes for people in need. Another idea suggested a solar-powered food dehydrator to help farmers reduce food spoilage.

Figure 5.2 Comparing Brainstorming and Brainwriting to Solve Problems

Brainstorming

- Clarify the problem and explain its background.
- Establish a time limit for the session.
- Set a goal, such as 100 ideas.
- Require everyone to contribute or improve the ideas of others.
- Emphasize quantity, not quality. No criticism.
- Write ideas on flipcharts or on sheets of paper on the walls.
- Organize, classify, and rank the ideas.
- Choose the best ideas.

Brainwriting

- Define the problem and explain its background.
- Before or at the meeting, emphasize writing out ideas.
- In a group circle, present ideas. Or participants may write their ideas anonymously on sheets hung on walls.
- Classify the ideas into groups, deleting repetitions.
- Discuss the merits of each idea.
- Vote to select the best ideas.

LvNL/Shutterstock.com

Crowdstorming moves beyond crowdsourcing by requiring the crowd to evaluate and filter the ideas into a viable product or plan. Constantly evolving, crowdstorming patterns are moving from simple searches for ideas to more complex interactions in which internal or external groups take on specialized tasks. Consider the collaboration between the Japanese Cuusoo website community and The Lego Group. Cuusoo challenged its viewers to create a Lego model demonstrating an idea, such as a model of the big bang theory or a model illustrating the Wizard of Oz. Posted at the Cuusoo website, eligible projects had to be supported by 10,000 viewers by a certain deadline before the project could be approved for Lego production. The community could also suggest refinements to help submitters increase their chances of success. Surprisingly successful for Lego, 9 model sets have been produced, and 13 more have been announced.

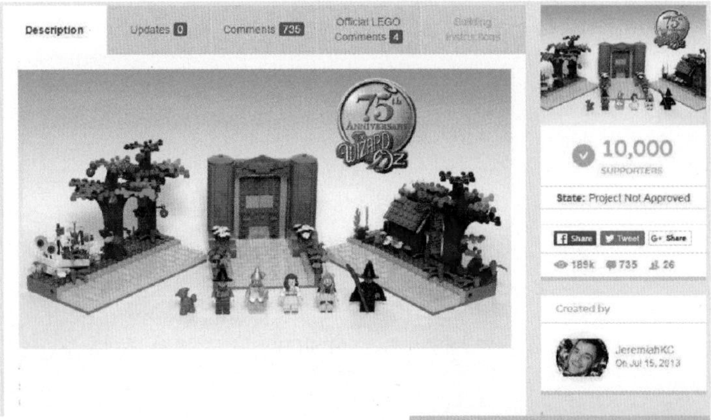

Source: ideas.lego.com

Produced through crowdstorming, this Wizard of Oz Lego set won support from 10,000 online commenters.

Crowdfunding is the practice of soliciting contributions, usually through the Internet, from a group of friends or strangers to finance a project, cause, or business venture. Capitalizing on the convenience of the Internet, the crowdfunding economy has exploded with requests to fund everything from fertility treatments to film projects and vacations.[6] Musicians, filmmakers, and artists have raised huge amounts that not only finance projects but also raise awareness of worthy causes. Jumping on the bandwagon, college students recognized crowdfunding as way to have their tuition paid. However, donation-based sites such as Campus Slice and Smartn.me aren't terribly successful. Like other experts, MyEvent.com founder Rob Hirscheimer agrees that it's usually futile to try to raise money for your education from strangers. A far better plan is to use crowdfunding to raise funds from your friends and relatives.[7]

Grouping Ideas to Show Relationships

After collecting data and generating ideas, writers must find some way to organize their information. Organizing includes two processes: grouping and strategizing. Skilled writers group similar items together. Then they place ideas in a strategic sequence that helps the reader understand relationships and accept the writer's views. Unorganized messages proceed free-form, jumping from one thought to another. Such messages fail to emphasize important points. Puzzled readers can't see how the pieces fit together, and they become frustrated and irritated. Many communication experts regard poor organization as the greatest failing of business writers. Two simple techniques can help writers organize data: the scratch list and the outline.

Using Lists and Outlines. In developing simple messages, some writers make a quick scratch list of the topics they wish to cover. Next they compose a message on their digital device directly from the scratch list. Most writers, though, need to organize their ideas—especially if the project is complex—into a hierarchy, such as an outline. The beauty of preparing an outline is that it gives writers a chance to organize their thoughts before becoming bogged down in word choice and sentence structure. Figure 5.3 shows the format for a typical outline.

Typical Document Components. How you group ideas into components depends on your topic and your channel of communication. Business documents usually contain typical components arranged in traditional strategies, as shown in Figure 5.4. Notice that an e-mail, memo, or letter generally is organized with an opening, body, and closing. Instructions for writing a procedure, such as how to use the company wiki, would proceed through a number of steps. The organizational plan for an informational report usually includes an introduction, facts, and a summary. However, the plan for an analytical report includes an introduction/

Figure 5.3 Format for an Outline

Title: Major Idea or Purpose

I. First major component
    A. First subpoint
        1. Detail, illustration, evidence
        2. Detail, illustration, evidence
        3. Detail, illustration, evidence
    B. Second subpoint
        1.
        2.
II. Second major component
    A. First subpoint
        1.
        2.
    B. Second subpoint
        1.
        2.
        3.

Tips for Making Outlines

- Define the main topic in the title.
- Divide the main topic into major components or classifications (preferably three to five).
- Break the components into subpoints.
- Don't put a single item under a major component; if you have only one subpoint, integrate it with the main item above it or reorganize.
- Strive to make each component exclusive (no overlapping).
- Use details, illustrations, and evidence to support subpoints.

Figure 5.4 Typical Major Components in Business Outlines

E-mail, Memo, Letter	Procedure	Informational Report	Analytical Report	Proposal
I. Opening II. Body III. Closing	I. Step 1 II. Step 2 III. Step 3 IV. Step 4	I. Introduction II. Facts III. Summary	I. Introduction/problem II. Facts/findings III. Conclusions IV. Recommendations (if requested)	I. Introduction II. Proposed solution III. Staffing IV. Schedule, costs V. Authorization

problem, facts/findings, conclusions, and recommendations (if requested). The plan for a proposal includes an introduction, a proposed solution, staffing, a schedule and/or costs, and authorization.

These document outlines may seem like a lot to absorb at this time. Later in this book, you will be introduced to all of the business documents outlined here, and you will learn how to expertly draft all of their parts.

Organizing Ideas Into Strategies

Thus far, you have seen how to collect information, generate ideas, and prepare an outline. How you order the information in your outline, though, depends on the strategy you choose. Two organizational strategies provide plans of action for typical business messages: the direct strategy and the indirect strategy. The primary difference between the two strategies is where the main idea is placed. In the direct strategy, the main idea comes first, followed by details, explanation, or evidence. In the indirect strategy, the main idea follows the details, explanation, and evidence. The strategy you select is determined by how you expect the audience to react to the message.

Direct Strategy for Receptive Audiences. In preparing to write any message, you need to anticipate the audience's reaction to your ideas and frame your message accordingly. When you expect the reader to be pleased, mildly interested, or neutral—use the direct strategy. That is, put your main point—the purpose of your message—in the first or second sentence. Dianna Booher, renowned writing consultant, pointed out that typical readers begin any message by saying, "So what am I supposed to do with this information?" In business writing you have to say, "Reader, here is my point!"[8] As quickly as possible, tell why you are writing. Compare the direct and indirect strategies in the following e-mail openings. Notice how long it takes to get to the main idea in the indirect opening.

Indirect Opening	Direct Opening
Our company has been concerned with attracting better-qualified prospective job candidates. For this reason, the Management Council has been gathering information about an internship program for college students. After considerable investigation, we have voted to begin a pilot program starting next fall. We are asking for your help in organizing it.	Please help us organize a college internship pilot program that the Management Council voted to begin next fall.

Explanations and details follow the direct opening. What's important is getting to the main idea quickly. This direct method, also called *frontloading*, has at least three advantages:

- **Saves the reader's time.** Many of today's businesspeople can devote only a few moments to each message. Messages that take too long to get to the point may lose their readers along the way.
- **Sets a proper frame of mind.** Learning the purpose up front helps the reader put the subsequent details and explanations in perspective. Without a clear opening, the reader may be thinking, "Why am I being told this?"
- **Reduces frustration.** Readers forced to struggle through excessive verbiage before reaching the main idea become frustrated. They resent the writer. Poorly organized messages create a negative impression of the writer.

Typical business messages that follow the direct strategy include routine requests and responses, orders and acknowledgments, nonsensitive memos, e-mails, informational reports, and informational oral presentations. All these tasks have one element in common: they do not address a sensitive subject that will upset the reader.

Indirect Strategy for Unreceptive Audiences. When you expect the audience to be uninterested, unwilling, displeased, or perhaps even hostile, the indirect strategy is more appropriate. In this strategy you reveal the main idea only after you have offered an explanation and evidence. This approach works well with three kinds of messages: (a) bad news, (b) ideas that

Ethics Check

How Sweet It Is

The makers of artificial sweetener Equal sued competitor Splenda because the latter claimed that Splenda was "made from sugar." In reality, Splenda's core ingredient is made from sucralose, a nonnutritive synthetic compound manufactured in laboratories. Although Splenda contains a sugar molecule, sucralose is not the same as sucrose, the technical name for pure table sugar, despite its similar-sounding name. Is it unethical for companies to intentionally advertise using wording that would confuse consumers?[9]

require persuasion, and (c) sensitive news, especially when being transmitted to superiors. The indirect strategy has these benefits:

- **Respects the feelings of the audience.** Bad news is always painful, but the trauma can be lessened by preparing the receiver for it.
- **Facilitates a fair hearing.** Messages that may upset the reader are more likely to be read when the main idea is delayed. Beginning immediately with a piece of bad news or a persuasive request, for example, may cause the receiver to stop reading or listening.
- **Minimizes a negative reaction.** A reader's overall reaction to a negative message is generally improved if the news is delivered gently.

Typical business messages that could be developed indirectly include e-mails, memos, and letters that refuse requests, deny claims, and disapprove credit. Persuasive requests, sales letters, sensitive messages, and some reports and oral presentations may also benefit from the indirect strategy. You will learn more about using the indirect strategy in Chapters 9 and 10.

In summary, business messages may be organized directly, with the main idea first, or indirectly, with the main idea delayed, as illustrated in Figure 5.5. Although these two strategies cover many communication problems, they should be considered neither universal nor inviolate. Every business transaction is distinct. Some messages are mixed: part good news, part bad; part goodwill, part persuasion. In upcoming chapters you will practice applying the direct and indirect strategies in typical situations. Then, you will have the skills and confidence to evaluate communication problems and vary these strategies depending on your goals.

Figure 5.5 **Audience Response Determines Direct or Indirect Strategy**

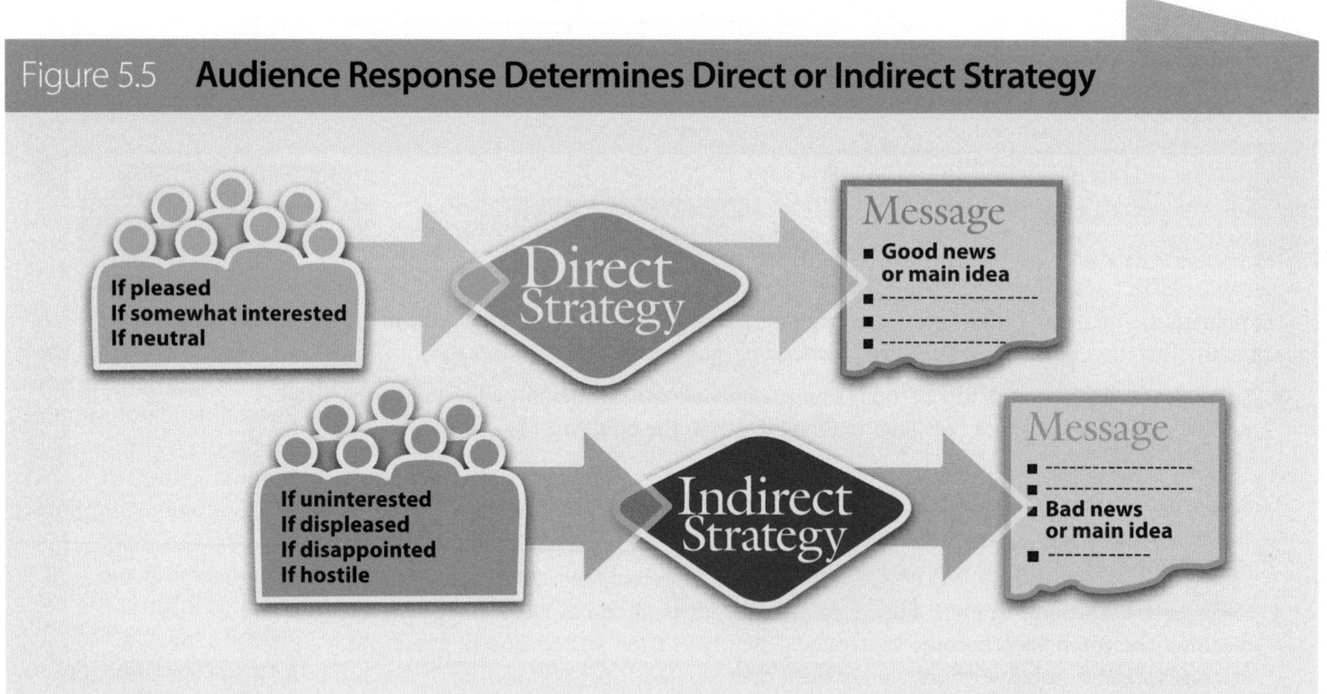

LEARNING OUTCOME 3

Compose the first draft of a message using a variety of sentence types and avoiding sentence fragments, run-on sentences, and comma splices.

Composing the First Draft With Effective Sentences

Once you have researched your topic, organized the data, and selected a strategy, you're ready to begin drafting. Many writers have trouble getting started, especially if they haven't completed the preparatory work. Organizing your ideas and working from an outline are very helpful in overcoming writer's block. Composition is also easier if you have a quiet environment in which to concentrate. Businesspeople with messages to compose set aside a given time and allow no calls, visitors, or other interruptions. This is a good technique for students as well.

As you begin writing, think about what style fits you best. Some experts suggest that you write quickly (*freewriting*). Get your thoughts down now and refine them in later versions. As you take up each idea, imagine that you are talking to the reader. Don't let yourself get bogged down. If you can't think of the right word, insert a substitute or type *find perfect word later.* Freewriting works well for some writers, but others prefer to move more slowly and think through their ideas more deliberately. Whether you are a speedy or a deliberate writer, keep in mind that you are writing the first draft. You will have time later to revise and polish your sentences.

Achieving Variety With Four Sentence Types

Messages that repeat the same sentence pattern soon become boring. To avoid monotony and to add spark to your writing, use a variety of sentence types. You have four sentence types from which to choose: simple, compound, complex, and compound-complex.

Simple Sentence

Contains one complete thought (an independent clause) with a subject and predicate verb:

The entrepreneur saw an opportunity.

Compound Sentence

Contains two complete but related thoughts. May be joined by (a) a conjunction such as *and, but,* or *or;* (b) a semicolon; or (c) a conjunctive adverb such as *however, consequently,* and *therefore*:

The entrepreneur saw an opportunity, and she responded immediately.
The entrepreneur saw an opportunity; she responded immediately.
The entrepreneur saw an opportunity; consequently, she responded immediately.

Complex Sentence

Contains an independent clause (a complete thought) and a dependent clause (a thought that cannot stand by itself). Dependent clauses are often introduced by words such as *although, since, because, when,* and *if.* When dependent clauses precede independent clauses, they always are followed by a comma:

When the entrepreneur saw the opportunity, she responded immediately.

Compound-Complex Sentence

Contains at least two independent clauses and one dependent clause:

When the entrepreneur saw the opportunity, she responded immediately; however, she needed capital.

Avoiding Three Common Sentence Faults

As you craft your sentences, beware of three common traps: fragments, run-on (fused) sentences, and comma-splice sentences. If any of these faults appears in a business message, the writer immediately loses credibility.

One of the most serious errors a writer can make is punctuating a **fragment** as if it were a complete sentence. A fragment is usually a broken-off part of a complex sentence. Fragments often can be identified by the words that introduce them—words such as *although, as, because, even, except, for example, if, instead of, since, such as, that, which,* and *when.* These words introduce dependent clauses. Make sure such clauses always connect to independent clauses.

Fragment	Revision
Because most transactions require a permanent record. Good writing skills are critical.	Because most transactions require a permanent record, good writing skills are critical.
The recruiter requested a writing sample. Even though the candidate seemed to communicate well.	The recruiter requested a writing sample even though the candidate seemed to communicate well.

A second serious writing fault is the **run-on (fused)** sentence. A sentence with two independent clauses must be joined by a coordinating conjunction (*and, or, nor, but*) or by a semicolon (;) or separated into two sentences. Without a conjunction or a semicolon, a run-on sentence results.

Run-On Sentence	Revision
Many job seekers prepare traditional résumés some also use digital portfolio websites.	Many job seekers prepare traditional résumés. Some also use digital portfolio websites.
One candidate sent an e-mail résumé another sent a link to her online portfolio.	One candidate sent an e-mail résumé; another sent a link to her online portfolio.

A third sentence fault is a **comma splice.** It results when a writer joins (splices together) two independent clauses with a comma. Independent clauses may be joined with a coordinating conjunction (*and, or, nor, but*) or a conjunctive adverb (*however, consequently, therefore,* and others). Notice that clauses joined by coordinating conjunctions require only a comma. Clauses joined by a coordinating adverb require a semicolon. To rectify a comma splice, try one of the possible revisions shown here:

Comma Splice	Revisions
Some employees prefer their desktop computers, others prefer their tablets.	Some employees prefer their desktop computers, but others prefer their tablets.
	Some employees prefer their desktop computers; however, others prefer their tablets.
	Some employees prefer their desktop computers; others prefer their tablets.

Courtesy of Lynn Gaertner-Johnston

Reality Check

What's the Appeal of Comma Splices?

On the topic of comma splices, one well-known writing coach says, "Why do intelligent people make the error? I think people worry that they will come across too informally or too plainly if they use [two] short sentences. They believe using 4-to-6-word sentences, especially two of them in a row, can't be professional. But two short, crisp, clear sentences in a row are professional and punchy."[10]

—Lynn Gaertner Johnson, *business writing trainer, coach, blogger*

Favoring Short Sentences

Because your goal is to communicate clearly, you should strive for sentences that average 20 words. Some sentences will be shorter; some will be longer. The American Press Institute reports that reader comprehension drops off markedly as sentences become longer.[11] Therefore, in crafting your sentences, think about the relationship between sentence length and comprehension.

Sentence Length	Comprehension Rate
8 words	100%
15 words	90%
19 words	80%
28 words	50%

Instead of stringing together clauses with *and, but,* and *however*, break some of those complex sentences into separate segments. Business readers want to grasp ideas immediately. They can do that best when thoughts are separated into short sentences. On the other hand, too many monotonous short sentences will sound grammar schoolish and may bore or even annoy the reader. Strive for a balance between longer sentences and shorter ones. Your grammar- and spell-checker can show you readability statistics that flag long sentences and give you an average sentence length.

Developing Business Writing Techniques

LEARNING OUTCOME 4

Improve your writing techniques by emphasizing important ideas, employing the active and passive voice effectively, using parallelism, and preventing dangling and misplaced modifiers.

Business writers can significantly improve their messages by working on a few writing techniques. In this section we focus on emphasizing and de-emphasizing ideas, using active and passive voice strategically, using parallelism, and avoiding dangling and misplaced modifiers.

Emphasizing Important Ideas

When you are talking with someone, you can emphasize your main ideas by saying them loudly or by repeating them slowly. You could even pound the table if you want to show real emphasis! Another way you could signal the relative importance of an idea is by raising your eyebrows, shaking your head, or whispering. But when you write, you must rely on other means to tell your readers which ideas are more important than others. Emphasis in writing can be achieved primarily in two ways: mechanically and stylistically.

Achieving Emphasis Through Mechanics. To emphasize an idea in print, a writer may use any of the following devices:

Underlining — Underlining draws the eye to a word.

Italics and boldface — Using *italics* or **boldface** conveys special meaning.

Font changes — Selecting a large, small, or *different* font draws interest.

All caps — Printing words in ALL CAPS is like shouting them.

Dashes — Dashes—used sparingly—can be effective.

Tabulation — Listing items vertically makes them stand out:

1. First item
2. Second item
3. Third item

Other means of achieving mechanical emphasis include the arrangement of space, color, lines, boxes, columns, titles, headings, and subheadings. Today's software and color printers provide a wonderful array of capabilities for setting off ideas. More tips on achieving emphasis are coming in Chapter 6, in which we cover document design.

Achieving Emphasis Through Style. Although mechanical devices are occasionally appropriate, more often a writer achieves emphasis stylistically. That is, the writer chooses words carefully and constructs sentences skillfully to emphasize main ideas and de-emphasize minor or negative ideas. Here are four suggestions for emphasizing ideas stylistically:

Use vivid, not general, words. Vivid words are emphatic because the reader can picture ideas clearly.

General	Vivid
The way we seek jobs has changed.	The Internet has dramatically changed how job hunters search for positions.
Someone will contact you as soon as possible.	Ms. Rivera will telephone you before 5 p.m. tomorrow, May 3.

Label the main idea. If an idea is significant, tell the reader.

Unlabeled	Labeled
Consider looking for a job online, but also focus on networking.	Consider looking for a job online; but, *most important*, focus on networking.
We shop here because of the customer service and low prices.	We like the customer service, but the *primary reason* for shopping here is the low prices.

Place the important idea first or last. Ideas have less competition from surrounding words when they appear first or last in a sentence. Observe how the concept of productivity can be emphasized by its position in the sentence:

Main Idea Lost	Main Idea Emphasized
Profit-sharing plans are more effective in increasing *productivity* when they are linked to individual performance rather than to group performance.	*Productivity* is more likely to be increased when profit-sharing plans are linked to individual performance rather than to group performance.

Give the important idea the spotlight. Don't dilute the effect of the main idea by making it share the stage with other words and clauses. Instead, put it in a simple sentence or in an independent clause.

Main Idea Lost	Main Idea Clear
Although you are the first trainee we have hired for this program, we had many candidates and expect to expand the program in the future. (The main idea is lost in a dependent clause.)	You are the first trainee we have hired for this program. (Simple sentence)

De-emphasizing When Necessary. To de-emphasize an idea, such as bad news, try one of the following stylistic devices:

Use general words.

Emphasizes Harsh Statement	De-emphasizes Harsh Statement
Our records indicate that you were recently fired.	Our records indicate that your employment status has recently changed.

Place the bad news in a dependent clause connected to an independent clause that contains something positive. In sentences with dependent clauses, the main emphasis is always on the independent clause.

Emphasizes Bad News	De-emphasizes Bad News
We cannot issue you credit at this time, but we have a special plan that will allow you to fill your immediate needs on a cash basis.	Although credit cannot be issued at this time, you can fill your immediate needs on a cash basis with our special plan.

Using the Active and Passive Voice Effectively

In active-voice sentences, the subject (the actor) performs the action. In passive-voice sentences, the subject receives the action. Active-voice sentences are more direct because they reveal the performer immediately. They are easier to understand and usually shorter. Most business writing should be in the active voice. However, passive voice is useful to (a) emphasize an action rather than a person, (b) de-emphasize negative news, and (c) conceal the doer of an action.

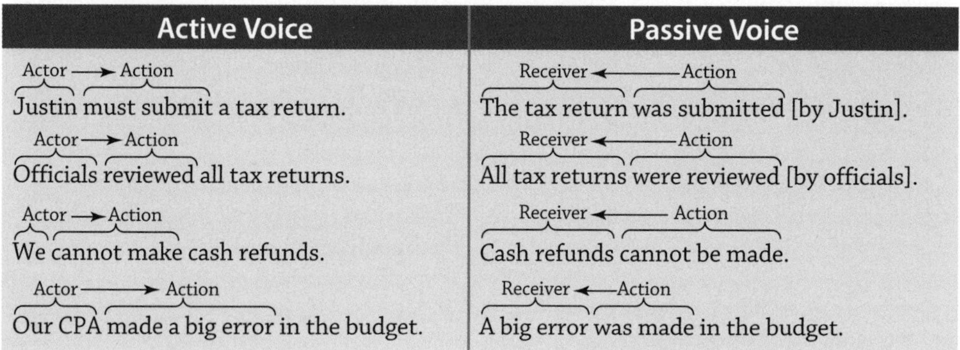

Active Voice	Passive Voice
Actor → Action Justin must submit a tax return.	Receiver ← Action The tax return was submitted [by Justin].
Actor → Action Officials reviewed all tax returns.	Receiver ← Action All tax returns were reviewed [by officials].
Actor → Action We cannot make cash refunds.	Receiver ← Action Cash refunds cannot be made.
Actor → Action Our CPA made a big error in the budget.	Receiver ← Action A big error was made in the budget.

Developing Parallelism

Parallelism is a skillful writing technique that creates balanced writing. Sentences written so that their parts are balanced, or parallel, are easy to read and understand. To achieve parallel

Daleen Loest/Shutterstock.com

When SeaWorld announced it was ending its controversial policy of breeding captive killer whales, the message needed to be clear and precise. Skillful writers emphasize major ideas by placing them front and center, and the blog post announcing the major policy turnaround at the marine theme park did just that: *We're making historic announcements at SeaWorld, including ending orca breeding, introducing new, inspiring and natural orca encounters, and launching new partnerships to protect oceans and marine animals.* The sentence structure highlights the main news immediately and uses the stylistic writing technique of parallelism to create balance and symmetry. What other strategies can you employ to improve your writing technique?[12]

construction, use similar structures to express similar ideas. For example, the words *computing, coding, recording,* and *storing* are parallel because the words all end in *-ing.* To express the list as *computing, coding, recording,* and *storage* is disturbing because the last item is not what the reader expects. Try to match nouns with nouns, verbs with verbs, and clauses with clauses. Avoid mixing active-voice verbs with passive-voice verbs. Your goal is to keep the wording balanced in expressing similar ideas.

Lacks Parallelism	Illustrates Parallelism
A wedding planner is in charge of arranging the venue, the flowers, and a person to take photographs.	A wedding planner is in charge of arranging the venue, the flowers, and a *photographer.* (Matches nouns.)
Our primary goals are to increase productivity, reduce costs, and the improvement of product quality.	Our primary goals are to increase productivity, reduce costs, and *improve product quality.* (Matches verbs.)
We are scheduled to meet in Tampa on January 5, we are meeting in Atlanta on the 15th of March, and in Columbus on June 3.	We are scheduled to meet in Tampa on January 5, *in Atlanta on March 15,* and in Columbus on June 3. (Matches phrases.)
Marcus audits accounts lettered A through L; accounts lettered M through Z are audited by Katherine.	Marcus audits accounts lettered A through L; *Katherine audits accounts lettered M through Z.* (Matches clauses.)
Our Super Bowl ads have three objectives: 1. We want to increase product use. 2. Introduce complementary products. 3. Our corporate image will be enhanced.	Our Super Bowl ads have three objectives: 1. *Increase* product use. 2. *Introduce* complementary products. 3. *Enhance* our corporate image. (Matches verbs in listed items.)

Photo by Dan Jacob

Reality Check

Good Writers Don't Let Their Modifiers Dangle in Public

"Always suspect an *-ing* word of dangling if it's near the front of a sentence; consider it guilty until proved innocent."[13]

—Patricia T. O'Conner, *author,* Woe Is I: The Grammarphobe's Guide to Better English in Plain English.

Avoiding Dangling and Misplaced Modifiers

For clarity, modifiers must be close to the words they describe or limit. A modifier dangles when the word or phrase it describes is missing from its sentence—for example, *Driving through Malibu Canyon, the ocean came into view.* This sentence says that the ocean was driving through Malibu Canyon. Revised, the sentence contains a logical subject: *Driving through Malibu Canyon, we saw the ocean come into view.*

A modifier is misplaced when the word or phrase it describes is not close enough to be clear—for example, *Firefighters rescued a dog from a burning car that had a broken leg.* Obviously, the car did not have a broken leg. The solution is to position the modifier closer to the word(s) it describes or limits: *Firefighters rescued a dog with a broken leg from a burning car.*

Introductory verbal phrases are particularly dangerous; be sure to follow them immediately with the words they logically describe or modify. Try this trick for detecting and remedying many dangling modifiers. Ask the question *Who*? or *What*? after any introductory phrase. The words immediately following should tell the reader who or what is performing the action. Try the *Who?* test on the first three danglers here:

Dangling or Misplaced Modifier	Clear Modification
Skilled at 3-D printing, the Disney character was easily copied by Jeff.	Skilled at 3-D printing, Jeff easily copied the Disney character.
Working together as a team, the project was finally completed.	Working together as a team, we finally completed the project.
After using two search engines, the website was finally found.	After using two search engines, I finally found the website.
The recruiter interviewed candidates who had excellent computer skills in the morning.	In the morning the recruiter interviewed candidates with excellent computer skills.
As a newbie in our office, we invite you to our Friday after-hours get-together.	As a newbie in our office, you are invited to our Friday after-hours get-together.

Drafting Effective Sentences

For Effective Sentences

- **Use a variety of sentence types.** To avoid monotony, include simple, compound, complex, and occasionally compound-complex sentences in your writing.
- **Avoid common sentence faults.** To avoid run-on sentences, do not join two clauses without appropriate punctuation. To avoid comma splices, do not join two clauses with a comma. To avoid fragments, be sure to use periods only after complete sentences.
- **Control sentence length.** Use longer sentences occasionally, but rely primarily on short and medium-length sentences.
- **Emphasize important ideas.** Place main ideas at the beginning of short sentences for emphasis.
- **Apply active- and passive-voice verbs strategically.** Use active-voice verbs (*She sent the text* instead of *The text was sent by her*) most frequently; they immediately identify the doer. Use passive-voice verbs to emphasize an action, to be tactful, or to conceal the performer.
- **Employ parallelism.** Balance similar ideas (*biking, jogging, and walking* instead of *biking, jogging, and to walk*).
- **Eliminate dangling and misplaced modifiers.** To avoid dangling modifiers, be sure that introductory verbal phrases are followed by the words that can logically be modified (*To win the lottery, you must purchase a ticket* rather than *To win the lottery, a ticket must be purchased*). To avoid misplaced modifiers, place them close to the words they modify (*With your family, please look over the brochure that is enclosed* rather than *Please look over the brochure that is enclosed with your family*).

LEARNING OUTCOME 5

Draft well-organized paragraphs using (a) the direct plan to define, classify, illustrate, or describe; (b) the pivoting plan to compare and contrast; or the (c) indirect plan to explain and persuade. Paragraphs should include (a) topic sentences, (b) support sentences, and (c) transitional expressions to build coherence.

Building Well-Organized Paragraphs

A paragraph is a group of sentences about one idea. To avoid muddled paragraphs, writers should be able to recognize basic paragraph elements, conventional sentence patterns, and three classic paragraph plans. They must also be able to polish their paragraphs by building coherence and using transitional expressions.

Well-constructed paragraphs discuss only one topic. A *topic sentence* reveals the primary idea in a paragraph and usually, but not always, appears first. Paragraphs may be composed of three kinds of sentences:

Topic sentence:	Expresses the primary idea of the paragraph.
Supporting sentence:	Illustrates, explains, or strengthens the primary idea.
Limiting sentence:	Opposes the primary idea by suggesting a negative or contrasting thought; may precede or follow the topic sentence.

These sentences may be arranged in any of three classic paragraph plans: direct, pivoting, and indirect.

Using the Direct Paragraph Plan to Define, Classify, Illustrate, or Describe

Paragraphs using the direct plan begin with the topic sentence, followed by supporting sentences. Most business messages use this paragraph plan because it clarifies the subject immediately. This plan is useful whenever you must define (a new product or procedure), classify (parts of a whole), illustrate (an idea), or describe (a process). Start with the topic sentence; then strengthen and amplify that idea with supporting ideas, as shown here:

Topic Sentence	A social audit is a report on the social performance of a company.
Supporting Sentences	Such an audit may be conducted by the company itself or by outsiders who evaluate the company's efforts to produce safe products, engage in socially responsible activities, and protect the environment. Many companies publish the results of their social audits in their annual reports. Ben & Jerry's Homemade, for example, devotes a major portion of its annual report to its social audit. The report discusses Ben & Jerry's efforts to support environmental restoration. Moreover, it describes workplace safety, employment equality, and peace programs.

You can alter the direct plan by adding a limiting sentence if necessary. Be sure, though, that you follow with sentences that return to the main idea and support it, as shown here:

Topic Sentence	Flexible work scheduling could immediately increase productivity and enhance employee satisfaction in our entire organization.
Limiting Sentences	Such scheduling, however, is impossible for all employees. Managers would be required to maintain their regular hours.
Supporting Sentences	For many other employees, though, flexible scheduling permits extra time to manage family responsibilities. Feeling less stress, employees are able to focus their attention better at work; hence they become more relaxed and more productive.

Using the Pivoting Paragraph Plan to Compare and Contrast

Paragraphs using the pivoting plan start with a limiting sentence that offers a contrasting or negative idea before delivering the topic sentence. Notice in the following example how two limiting sentences about drawbacks to foreign service careers open the paragraph; only then do the topic and supporting sentences describing rewards in foreign service appear. The pivoting plan is especially useful for comparing and contrasting ideas. In using the pivoting plan, be sure to emphasize the turn in direction with an obvious *but* or *however.*

Limiting Sentences Foreign service careers are certainly not for everyone. Many representatives are stationed in remote countries where harsh climates, health hazards, security risks, and other discomforts exist.

Topic Sentence However, careers in the foreign service offer special rewards for the special people who qualify.

Supporting Sentences Foreign service employees enjoy the pride and satisfaction of representing the United States abroad. They enjoy frequent travel, enriching cultural and social experiences in living abroad, and action-oriented work.

Using the Indirect Paragraph Plan to Explain and Persuade

Paragraphs using the indirect plan start with the supporting sentences and conclude with the topic sentence. This useful plan enables you to build a rationale, a foundation of reasons, before hitting the audience with a big idea—possibly one that is bad news. It enables you to explain your reasons and then in the final sentence draw a conclusion from them. In the following example, the vice president of a large accounting firm begins by describing the trend toward casual dress and concludes with a recommendation that his company alter its dress code. The indirect plan works well for describing causes followed by an effect.

Supporting Sentences According to a recent poll, more than half of all white-collar workers are now dressing casually at work. Many high-tech engineers and professional specialists have given up suits and ties, favoring khakis and sweaters instead. In our own business, our consultants say they stand out like sore thumbs because they are attired in traditional buttoned-down styles, while the businesspeople they visit are usually wearing comfortable, casual clothing.

Topic Sentence Therefore, I recommend that we establish an optional business casual policy allowing consultants to dress down, if they wish, as they perform their duties both in and out of the office.

In later chapters, you will learn more techniques for implementing direct and indirect writing strategies when you draft e-mails, memos, letters, reports, and other business messages as well as prepare oral presentations.

Ethics Check

Is It Ethical for Zappos to Fix the Grammar and Spelling in Its Customers' Reviews?

Estimates suggest that Zappos, the Internet's most popular site for quality footwear, has spent hundreds of thousands of dollars fixing more than a million of its customers' online reviews. Does this repair alter the authenticity of the reviews?[14]

Developing Paragraph Coherence

Paragraphs are coherent when ideas cohere—that is, when the ideas stick together and when one idea logically leads to the next. Well-written paragraphs take the reader through a number of steps. When the author skips from Step 1 to Step 3 and forgets Step 2, the reader is lost. Several techniques will help you keep the reader in step with your ideas.

Sustaining the Key Idea. Repeating a key expression or using a similar one throughout a paragraph helps sustain a key idea. In the following example, notice that the repetition of *guest* and *VIP* connects ideas.

> *Our philosophy holds that every customer is really a guest. All new employees are trained to treat guests in our theme parks as VIPs. We take great pride in respecting our guests. As VIPs, they are never told what they can or cannot do.*

Dovetailing Sentences. Sentences are dovetailed when an idea at the end of one connects with an idea at the beginning of the next. Dovetailing sentences is especially helpful with dense, difficult topics. It is also helpful with ordinary paragraphs, such as the following.

> *New hosts and hostesses learn about the theme park and its facilities. These facilities include telephones, food services, bathrooms, and attractions, as well as the location of offices. Knowledge of offices and the internal workings of the company is required of all staffers.*

Including Pronouns. Familiar pronouns, such as *we, they, he, she,* and *it,* help build continuity, as do demonstrative pronouns, such as *this, that, these,* and *those.* These words confirm that something under discussion is still being discussed. However, be careful with such pronouns. They often need a noun with them to make their meaning clear. In the following example, notice how confusing the pronoun *this* would be if the word *training* were omitted.

> *All new park employees receive a two-week orientation. They learn that every staffer has a vital role in preparing for the show. This training includes how to maintain enthusiasm.*

Employing Transitional Expressions. Transitional expressions are another excellent device for showing connections and achieving paragraph coherence. These words, some of which are shown in Figure 5.6, act as verbal road signs to readers and listeners. Transitional expressions enable the receiver to anticipate what's coming, reduce uncertainty, and speed comprehension. They signal that a train of thought is moving forward, being developed, possibly detouring, or ending. As Figure 5.6 shows, transitions can add or strengthen a thought, show time or order, clarify ideas, show cause and effect, contradict thoughts, and contrast ideas. Look back at the examples of direct, pivoting, and indirect paragraphs to see how transitional expressions and other techniques build paragraph coherence. Remember that coherence in communication rarely happens spontaneously; it requires effort and skill.

Controlling Paragraph Length

Although no rule regulates the length of paragraphs, business writers recognize that short paragraphs are more attractive and readable than longer ones. Paragraphs with eight or fewer lines look inviting. Long, solid chunks of print appear formidable. If a topic can't be covered in eight or fewer printed lines (not sentences), consider breaking it up into smaller segments.

Figure 5.6 **Transitional Expressions That Build Coherence**

To Add or Strengthen	To Show Time or Order	To Clarify	To Show Cause and Effect	To Contradict	To Contrast
additionally	after	for example	accordingly	actually	as opposed to
accordingly	before	for instance	as a result	but	at the same time
again	earlier	I mean	consequently	however	by contrast
also	finally	in other words	for this reason	in fact	conversely
beside	first	put another way	hence	instead	on the contrary
indeed	meanwhile	that is	so	rather	on the other hand
likewise	next	this means	therefore	still	previously
moreover	now	thus	thus	yet	similarly

The following checklist summarizes key points in preparing meaningful paragraphs.

Preparing Meaningful Paragraphs

- **Develop one idea.** Each paragraph should include a topic sentence plus supporting and limiting sentences to develop a single idea.
- **Use the direct plan.** To define, classify, illustrate, and describe, start with the topic sentence followed by supporting sentences.
- **Use the pivoting plan.** To compare and contrast ideas, start with a limiting sentence; then, present the topic sentence followed by supporting sentences.
- **Use the indirect plan.** To explain reasons or causes first, start with supporting sentences. Build to the conclusion with the topic sentence at the end of the paragraph.
- **Build coherence with linking techniques.** Hold ideas together by repeating key words, dovetailing sentences (beginning one sentence with an idea from the end of the previous sentence), and using appropriate pronouns.
- **Provide road signs with transitional expressions.** Use verbal signals to help the audience know where the idea is going. Words and phrases such as *moreover, accordingly, as a result,* and *therefore* function as idea pointers.
- **Limit paragraph length.** Remember that paragraphs with eight or fewer printed lines look inviting. Consider breaking up longer paragraphs if necessary.

Your Turn: Applying Your Skills at MyEvent.com

Yeamake/Shutterstock.com

As you learned at the beginning of this chapter, MyEvent.com is moving into crowdfunding, a trend that is firmly established across the country. It could generate a market for just the kind of do-it-yourself fund-raising programs offered by MyEvent.com. To capitalize on this trend, the cofounders of MyEvent.com would like to know how college students might make use of crowdfunding.

Your Task

As interns at MyEvent.com, you and your colleagues are in a unique position to provide useful information. You have been asked to generate ideas about how college and university students might employ crowdfunding. For what kinds of projects would crowdfunding make sense? To generate ideas, decide whether to use the brainstorming or the brainwriting technique illustrated in Figure 5.3. With three to five classmates, generate five or more solid ideas for crowdfunding. Ask your friends for their ideas. Organize your ideas into an e-mail message addressed to MyEvent.com in care of your instructor. See Appendix A for message formats and Chapters 7 and 8 for tips on preparing a professional e-mail message.

Writing Improvement Exercises

5.1 Sentence Types (L.O. 3)

YOUR TASK For each of the following sentences, select the letter that identifies its type:

1. Simple sentence
2. Compound sentence
3. Complex sentence
4. Compound-complex sentence

a. Bottled water consumption rose 2.2 percent in volume last year.

b. Because Americans are increasingly health conscious, they are drinking more bottled water than ever before.

c. Americans are drinking fewer soft drinks, and heavy-hitters Coca-Cola and PepsiCo are being hit hard.

d. Calorie-counting Americans are backing away from sugary soda, but they are also fleeing diet soda.

e. Sales volume across the entire beverage industry slid last year; however, smaller players such as Monster Beverage and Red Bull expanded their market share because they appealed to younger drinkers.

f. Water is hot, and diet soda is not.

5.2 Sentence Faults (L.O. 3)

YOUR TASK In the following, identify the sentence fault (fragment, run-on, comma splice). Then revise to remedy the fault.

a. Although PepsiCo signed Beyoncé to endorse its soft drinks. Sales continued to plummet.

b. In the beverage industry, the latest sales declines are astonishing. But not surprising.

c. Sugar-filled soft-drink sales have been declining for nine straight years, however diet drinks are not far behind.

d. Coca-Cola hired a creative director PepsiCo tried a new bottle design.

e. Health concerns are not the only problem, soft-drink makers are also facing a boom in alternative beverages.

f. PepsiCo and Coca-Cola are striving to return to profitability. Which explains why they are investing in energy drinks, sports drinks, and flavored water.

5.3 Emphasis (L.O. 4)

YOUR TASK For each of the following sentences, circle (1) or (2). Be prepared to justify your choice.

a. Which is more emphatic? Why?

   1. The new restaurant will attract foot traffic and also serve unique burgers.
   2. The new restaurant will attract foot traffic and, most important, will serve unique burgers.

b. Which is more emphatic? Why?

   1. For many reasons hamburgers are definitely American.
   2. Hot, fast, and affordable hamburgers are a uniquely American triumph.

c. Which is more emphatic? Why?

   1. Artisinal, small-batch burgers will compete well against the burger giants.
   2. Although many new burger restaurants are opening, ours will be unique because we plan to feature artisinal, small-batch burgers that we expect will compete well against the burger giants that have controlled the burger restaurant business for decades.

d. Which is more emphatic? Why?

   1. Because he has experience in the restaurant business, the new CEO comes highly recommended and is expected to appear at the next meeting of the management board on January 15, which has been rescheduled because of room conflicts.
   2. The new, experienced CEO comes highly recommended. He will appear at the next meeting of the management board on January 15.

e. Which emphasizes the writer of the report?

   1. Emma wrote a report about the emergence of fast casual restaurants such as Panera Bread and Chipotle Mexican Grill.
   2 A report about the emergence of fast casual resaurants such as Panera Bread and Chiptole Mexican Grill was written by Emma.

f. Which places more emphasis on the seminar?

   1. A training seminar for all new managers starts June 1.
   2. We are pleased to announce that starting June 1 a training seminar for all new managers will include four prominent speakers who own famous restaurants.

g. Which is more emphatic? Why?

   1. Three burger restaurants compete for business: (a) McDonald's, (b) Burger King, and (c) Shake Shack.
   2. Three burger restaurants compete for business:

      a. McDonald's

      b. Burger King

      c. Shake Shack

5.4 Active Voice (L.O. 4)

YOUR TASK Business writing is more forceful when it uses active-voice verbs. Revise the following sentences so that verbs are in the active voice. Put the emphasis on the doer of the action. Add subjects if necessary.

- **Example:** Laws were passed to protect homeowners from scams.
- **Revision:** Governments passed laws to protect homeowners from scams.

a. Workers were asked to wear badges with tiny sensors to monitor their communication and activity patterns at Bank of America.

b. Tracking devices are being installed by many companies to gather real-time information on how employees interact.

c. Reliable data about how workers do their jobs are difficult to collect.

d. Concern was expressed by some workers about the difference between Big Data and Big Brother.

e. Companies were warned by managers that privacy issues and making sense of the data were equally perplexing issues.

f. Laws are being considered to restrict gathering worker data without their knowledge.

5.5 Passive Voice (L.O. 4)

YOUR TASK When indirectness or tact is required, use passive-voice verbs. Revise the following active-voice sentences so that they are in the passive voice.

- **Example:** Michelle did not submit the proposal before the deadline.
- **Revision:** The proposal was not submitted before the deadline.

a. Michelle made a serious error in our annual tax figures.

b. We discovered the error too late to correct the annual report.

c. The Federal Trade Commission targeted deceptive diet advertisements by weight-loss marketers.

d. We issue refunds only for the amount of the purchase; we are unable to include shipping and handling charges.

e. An embarrassing mishap was caused because someone misinterpreted the procedures somehow.

5.6 Parallelism (L.O. 4)

YOUR TASK Revise the following sentences so that their parts are balanced.

a. (**Hint:** Match verbs.) Critics complain that young people today are obsessed with playing video games, taking selfies, and they are constantly checking their Facebook pages.

b. (**Hint:** Match adjectives.) To be hired, an applicant must be reliable, creative, and show enthusiasm.

c. (**Hint:** Match verb phrases.) Job seekers use the Internet to find job opportunities, market themselves to companies, showcase their skills, and they hope to be able to land that dream job.

d. (**Hint:** Match adjectives.) Recent graduates are seeking jobs that are stimulating and a challenge.

e. LinkedIn can help college students by sending job alerts, by leveraging their networks, they can research a company, and LinkedIn can take the awkwardness out of asking for recommendations.

f. A company's website might contain valuable information such as you might find current job openings, the company's mission statement might be there, and the names of key hiring managers could be available.

g. When you want to complain about something, sending an e-mail or a letter is better than to make a telephone call.

h. The NSF application for a grant requires this information: proposed funds required for staff salaries, how much we expect to spend on equipment, and what is the length of the project.

5.7 Dangling and Misplaced Modifiers (L.O. 4)

YOUR TASK Revise the following sentences to avoid dangling and misplaced modifiers.

a. While interviewing applicants, questions are often asked by recruiters about qualifications.

b. To be reimbursed, the enclosed application must be filled out and returned.

c. Skilled at social networking, the marketing contract was won by ReachOut.

d. Susan made a presentation about workplace drug problems in our boardroom.

e. Angered by autodialed and prerecorded calls and texts, complaints deluged PayPal.

5.8 Organizing Paragraph Sentences (L.O. 5)

In a memo to the college president, the athletic director argues for a new stadium scoreboard. One paragraph will describe the old scoreboard and why it needs to be replaced. Study the following list of ideas for that paragraph.

1. The old scoreboard is a tired warhorse that was originally constructed in the 1970s.

2. It is now hard to find replacement parts when something breaks.
3. The old scoreboard is not energy efficient.
4. Coca-Cola has offered to buy a new sports scoreboard in return for exclusive rights to sell soda pop on campus.
5. The old scoreboard should be replaced for many reasons.
6. It shows only scores for football games.
7. When we have soccer games or track meets, we are without a functioning scoreboard.

a. Which sentence should be the topic sentence?_____

b. Which sentence(s) should be developed in a separate paragraph?_____

c. Which sentences should become support sentences? _____

5.9 Helping Costco Word an Important Sign (L.O. 4) **Team**

The giant superstore Costco makes several requirements of its customers. Children must be kept with their parents at all times. They can't wander around to the various food stations of the warehouse on their own. Costco also asks that its customers not show up looking as if they just came from the beach. Hey, it's not too much to ask that they wear shoes and shirts while shopping. Lastly, Costco wants permission to look in the briefcases, backpacks, and packages of those entering its warehouse. It's too easy to slip items into big bags. Unlike other supermarkets, Costco is a private membership store and thus can make reasonable demands of its customers. But it needs help. How can it fit all of these restrictions on a concise sign at its entrance?

YOUR TASK Assume you are a staff member of a consultancy hired by Costco to draft a sign for the entrance. Individually or in teams, prepare two versions of an entrance sign—one written from a negative point of view (*don't do this, don't do that*) and one from a positive point of view. Keep your sign brief, and be sure the items are parallel. Your instructor may have you present your versions in class for discussion. Then your instructor may show you the actual entrance sign.

5.10 Building Coherent Paragraphs (L.O. 5)

YOUR TASK Use the information from the sentences in **Activity 5.8** to write a coherent paragraph about replacing the sports scoreboard. Strive to use three devices to build coherence: (a) repetition of key words, (b) pronouns that clearly refer to previous nouns, and (c) transitional expressions.

5.11 Revising an Incoherent Paragraph (L.O. 5)

YOUR TASK Revise the following wordy and poorly organized paragraph. Add a topic sentence. Correct problems with pronouns, parallelism, and misplaced or dangling modifiers. Add transitional expressions if appropriate.

You may be interested in applying for a new position within the company. The Human Resources Department maintains these lists, and you may see which jobs are available immediately. The positions are at a high level. Current employees may apply immediately for open positions in production, for some in marketing, and jobs in administrative support are also available. To make application, these positions require immediate action. Come to the Human Resources Department. On the company intranet you can see the lists showing the open positions, what the qualifications are, and job descriptions are shown. Many of the jobs are now open. That's why we are sending this now. To be hired, an interview must be scheduled within the next two weeks.

5.12 Revising a Wordy Paragraph (L.O. 5)

YOUR TASK Revise the following poorly written paragraph. Add a topic sentence and improve the organization. Correct problems with pronouns, parallelism, wordiness, and misplaced or dangling modifiers.

As you probably already know, this company (Lasertronics) will be installing new computer software shortly. There will be a demonstration April 18, which is a Tuesday. You are invited. We felt this was necessary because this new software is so different from our previous software. It will be from 9 to 12 a.m. in the morning. This will show employees how the software programs work. They will learn about the operating system, and this should be helpful to nearly everyone. There will be information about the new word processing program, which should be helpful to administrative assistants and product managers. For all you people who work with payroll, there will be information about the new database program. We can't show everything the software will do at this one demo, but for these three areas there will be some help at the Tuesday demo. Presenting the software, the demo will feature Joshua Travis. He is the representative from Quantum Software.

5.13. Building a Coherent Paragraph (L.O. 5)

From the following information, develop a coherent paragraph with a topic and support sentences. Strive for conciseness and coherence.

- Car dealers and lenders offer a variety of loan terms.
- To get the best deal, shop around when buying a new or used car.

- You have two payment options: you may pay in full or finance over time.
- You should compare offers and be willing to negotiate the best deal.
- If you are a first-time buyer—or if your credit isn't great—be cautious about special financing offers.
- Buying a new or used car can be challenging.
- Financing increases the total cost of the car because you are also paying for the cost of credit.
- If you agree to financing that carries a high interest rate, you may be taking a big risk. If you decide to sell the car before the loan expires, the amount you get from the sale may be far less than the amount you need to pay off the loan.
- If money is tight, you might consider paying cash for a less expensive car than you originally had in mind.

Activities

Note: All Documents for Analysis are provided at **www.cengagebrain.com** for you to download and revise.

5.14 Document for Analysis: Faulty E-Mail Message (L.O. 3–5)

E-Mail Team

YOUR TASK Study the numbered sentences in the following poorly written e-mail message. In teams or in a class discussion, identify specific sentence faults. **Hint:** You should find five sentence fragments, one dangling modifier, one passive-voice sentence, and one parallelism fault. Your instructor may ask you to revise the message to remedy these writing faults.

To: Sierra.Maldonado@gmail.com
From: Justin.Corona@premierefinances.com
Subject: Responding to Your Question About eBay Profits

Hi, Sierra,

[1]As your CPA, I'm happy to respond to your request for clarification of the tax status of profits from eBay. [2]Or one of the other online sellers such as Etsy, Amazon, and Bonanza.

[3]As you are probably already aware, you can use eBay or one of the other sellers to clean out your closets or to run a small business. [4]Tax liabilities should definitely be clarified. [5]Although no clear line separates fun from profit or a hobby from a business. [6]One thing is certain: the IRS taxes all income.

[7]A number of factors will help you determine whether your hobby is a business. [8]To use eBay safely, the following questions should be considered:

- [9]Do you run the operation in a businesslike manner? [10]That is, do you keep records, is your profit and loss tracked, and how about keeping a separate checking account?
- [11]Do you devote considerable time and effort to your selling? [12]If you spend eight or more hours a day trading on eBay. [13]The IRS would tend to think you are in a business.
- [14]Some people depend on the income from their eBay activities for their livelihood. [15]Do you?
- [16]Are you selling items for more than they cost you? [17]If you spend $5 for a garage sale vase and sell it for $50. [18]The IRS would probably consider this a business transaction.
- [19]All profits are taxable. [20]Even for eBay sellers who are just playing around. [21]If you wish to discuss this further, please call me at 213-456-8901.

Justin Corona
[Full contact information]

5.15 Brainstorming: Solving a Problem on Campus (L.O. 1, 2)

Team

YOUR TASK In teams of three to five, analyze a problem on your campus such as the following: insufficient parking on campus, unavailable classes, closed campus facilities for students taking evening or weekend classes, unrealistic degree requirements, a lack of student intern programs, an inadequate registration process, too few healthy and affordable food choices, a lack of charging stations for electric vehicles, and so forth. Use brainstorming techniques to generate ideas that clarify the problem, and explore its solutions. Either individually or as a team, organize the ideas into an outline with three to five main points and numerous subpoints. Assume that your ideas will become part of a message to be sent to an appropriate campus official or to your campus newspaper. Remember, however, your role as a student. Be polite, positive, and constructive—not negative, hostile, or aggressive.

5.16 Brainstorming: Solving a Problem at Work (L.O. 1, 2)

E-Mail

YOUR TASK Analyze a problem that exists where you work or go to school such as noisy work areas, an overuse of express mail services, understaffing during peak customer service hours, poor scheduling of employees, inappropriate cell phone use, an inferior or inflexible benefits package, outdated equipment, wasting time on social media instead of working, or one of the campus problems listed in **Activity 5.15.** Select a problem about which you have some knowledge. Organize the ideas into an outline with three to five main points and numerous subpoints. Be polite, positive, and constructive. E-mail the outline to your boss (your instructor). Include an introduction (such as, *Here is the outline you requested in regard to . . .*). Include a closing that offers to share your outline if your boss would like to see it.

Test Your Etiquette IQ

New communication platforms and casual workplace environments have blurred the lines of appropriateness, leaving workers wondering how to navigate uncharted waters. Indicate whether the following statements are true or false. Then see if you agree with the responses on p. R-1.

1. You're late for a meeting. The best thing to do is text a message saying, "Sorry, I'm running 20 minutes late."

   ________ True ________ False

2. You're talking with a coworker when you see an incoming text. To show your efficiency, you should answer it immediately.

   ________ True ________ False

3. As you are talking on your cell, you can't hear the other person very well. The best response is to speak more loudly so that you can be heard.

   ________ True ________ False

Chat About It

In each chapter you will find five discussion questions related to the chapter material. Your instructor may assign these topics for you to discuss in class, in an online chat room, or on an online discussion board. Some of the discussion topics may require outside research. You may also be asked to read and respond to postings made by your classmates.

TOPIC 1: Some critics complain that crowdfunding projects, such as requesting funds to pay college tuition, are essentially begging. How do you see it? Would you do it?

TOPIC 2: This chapter describes brainstorming and brainwriting as techniques for generating ideas. Explore the Internet for other methods such as *freewriting, looping, listing, clustering,* and *reporters' questions.* Select a method that appeals to you, and explain why it would be effective.

TOPIC 3: Some writers have trouble writing the opening sentence of a message. Occasionally, a quotation makes for an appropriate opening. Assume that you need to motivate an employee to achieve more at work. Find a famous quotation online about motivation that might be an appropriate opening for such a message. In addition, write a sentence that would effectively transition from this opening.

TOPIC 4: In your opinion, how many business managers know what a comma splice is? If some managers don't know what a comma splice is, then is it critical that you avoid comma splices in your writing?

TOPIC 5: Why is it important for writers to think about the length of their sentences? Learn how to display the average sentence length in a document using Microsoft Word. Explain the process briefly.

Grammar and Mechanics | *Review 5*

Commas

Review Guides 21 through 26 about commas in Appendix D, Grammar and Mechanics Guide, beginning on page D-8. On a separate sheet, revise the following sentences to correct errors in comma usage. For each error that you locate, write the guide number that reflects this usage. The more you recognize the reasons, the better you will learn these punctuation guidelines. If a sentence is correct, write *C*. When you finish, check your answers on page Key-1.

EXAMPLE: When you prepare to write any message you need to anticipate the audience's reaction.

REVISION: When you prepare to write any **message,** you need to anticipate the audience's reaction.

1. Informal research methods include looking in the files talking with your boss and interviewing the target audience.
2. When we use company e-mail we realize that our messages are monitored.
3. By learning to distinguish between dependent and independent clauses you will be able to avoid serious sentence faults.
4. Active-voice verbs are best in most business messages but passive-voice verbs are useful when sensitivity is required.
5. We hired Gabriella Lugo who was the applicant with the best qualifications as our new social media manager.
6. Although the letter was written on April 15 2014 it was not delivered until June 30 2018.
7. The new social media business by the way is flourishing and is expected to show a profit soon.
8. After he graduates Luke plans to move to Austin and find work there.
9. Last fall our company introduced policies regulating the use of cell phones texting and e-mail on the job.
10. The problem with many company telecommunication policies is that the policies are self-policed and never enforced.

References

[1] Hirscheimer, R., cofounder, MyEvent.com (interview with Mary Ellen Guffey, July 21, 2015).

[2] Greenfield, R. (2014, July 29). Brainstorming doesn't work; try this technique instead. Fast Company. Retrieved from http://www.fastcompany.com/3033567/agendas/brainstorming-doesnt-work-try-this-technique-instead

[3] Ibid.

[4] Russell, M. (2013). Brainwriting: A more perfect brainstorm. InnovationManagement.se. Retrieved from http://www.innovationmanagement.se/imtool-articles/brainwriting-a-more-perfect-brainstorm

[5] Moye, J. (2015, January 26). #MakeItHappy: Coca-Cola's big game ad to champion online positivity. Coca-Cola Journey. [Blog post]. Retrieved from http://www.coca-colacompany.com/stories/makeithappy-coca-colas-big-game-ad-to-champion-online-positivity

[6] Press, G. (2015, February 16). 15 Most-funded crowdfunding projects on Kickstarter and Indiegogo. Forbes. Retrieved from http://www.forbes.com/sites/gilpress/2015/02/16/15-most-funded-crowdfunding-projects-on-kickstarter-and-indiegogo. See also Briody, G. (2013, May 14). Crowdfunding: Why strangers will pay your tuition. *The Fiscal Times*. Retrieved from http://www.thefiscaltimes.com/Articles/2013/05/14/Crowdfunding-Why-Strangers-Will-Pay-Your-Tuition

[7] Hirscheimer, R., cofounder, MyEvent.com (interview with Mary Ellen Guffey, July 21, 2015).

[8] Rindegard, J. (1999, November 22). Use clear writing to show you mean business. *InfoWorld*, p. 78.

[9] Hull, J. S. (2007). Splenda hearings. Retrieved from http://www.janethull.com/newsletter/0607/splenda_hearings.php

[10] Johnson, L. G. (2011, January 12). Avoid this simple comma splice error. Business Writing. Retrieved from http://www.businesswritingblog.com/business_writing/2011/01/avoid-this-simple-comma-splice-error.html

[11] Goddard, R. W. (1989, April). Communication: Use language effectively. *Personnel Journal*, 32.

[12] A message to our fans. (2016, March 17.) SeaWorld cares. Blog. Retrieved from https://seaworldcares.com/2016/03/A-Message-To-Our-Fans

[13] O'Connor, P. (1996). *Woe is I*. New York: Putnam, p. 161.

[14] Agger, M. (2011, May 10). Awsum shoes! Slate. Retrieved from http://www.slate.com/articles/technology/technology/2011/05/awsum_shoes.html

[15] Booher, D. (2007). *The voice of authority*. New York: McGraw-Hill, p. 93.

Chapter 6 Revising Business Messages

Monkey Business Images/ Shutterstock.com

LEARNING OUTCOMES

After studying this chapter, you should be able to

1 Polish business messages by revising for conciseness, which includes eliminating flabby expressions, long lead-ins, *there is/are* and *it is/was* fillers, redundancies, and empty words, as well as condensing for microblogging.

2 Improve clarity in business messages by keeping the ideas simple, slashing trite business phrases, dropping clichés, scrapping slang and buzzwords, rescuing buried verbs, and restraining exuberance.

3 Enhance readability by understanding document design including the use of white space, margins, typefaces, fonts, numbered and bulleted lists, and headings.

4 Recognize proofreading problem areas, and apply effective techniques to catch mistakes in both routine and complex documents.

5 Evaluate a message to judge its effectiveness.

Yeamake/Shutterstock.com

Zooming In

Taco Bell Seeks to Shatter Sea of Sameness

Like many fast-food restaurants, Taco Bell searches for innovations that will make it stand out and avoid a "sea of sameness." It's been tinkering with its menu for years as it strives to boost sales and grab market share. A few years back, it rolled out its Cantina Bell menu, offering a gourmet selection of dishes made with upscale ingredients and fewer calories, which seemed to appeal to anti-obesity demands. Customers, however, snubbed its fancy meals and low-calorie, low-fat dishes.

"People are not looking for diet food," said new Taco Bell CEO Brian Niccol. "What they are looking for is food that gives them energy."[1] Niccol hopes to inspire a youthful spirit that he thinks is "ripe to unlock." He has already changed the company's slogan from *Think outside the bun* to *Live mas*. Striving to marry the ideas that "food is fuel" and "food is an experience," he champions innovation. His goal is to attract even more millennials, a profitable demographic sought by many fast-food chains.

Striving to compete with fast casual restaurants such as arch-rival Chipotle Mexican Grill, Taco Bell tried another new menu concept centered on "American-inspired" tacos, craft beers, and alcoholic milkshakes. It tested this concept in a glitzy pilot restaurant in southern California called U.S. Taco Company. Unable to secure a liquor license or many customers, it quietly closed its doors after a year.[2]

Yum brands (owner of Taco Bell, Pizza Hut, and KFC) is one of the world's largest restaurant companies with over 41,000 restaurants in more than 125 countries. Although Taco Bell has the most restaurants, it continues to suffer from a limited menu and bad publicity resulting from situations such as a lawsuit falsely accusing it of adulterating its beef with binders and extenders.[3] It survived this bad publicity and emerged with a gigantic hit: Doritos Locos, a cheese-flavored shell stuffed with spicy beef filling. Even this breakout menu stunner, however, could take Taco Bell only so far.

Rob Wilson/Shutterstock.com

In the increasingly crowded fast-food market, customers are shifting away from the traditional burger and chicken fast foods. Poised to capitalize on this movement, Taco Bell must create new appealing products and respond to market trends.

You will learn more about Taco Bell and be asked to complete a relevant task at the end of this chapter.

Critical Thinking

- Assume that a recently hired culinary product manager is charged with generating and implementing new menu suggestions. What role does communication skill play in this person's effectiveness in completing this task?
- Do you think a culinary product manager would make an oral or a written presentation of new menu ideas?
- Why is a writing process helpful in developing a presentation of new ideas?

Stopping to Revise: Applying Phase 3 of the Writing Process

In this fast-paced era of e-mailing, texting, and tweeting, the idea of stopping to revise a message seems almost alien to productivity. What? Stop to proofread? Crazy idea! No time! However, sending quick but sloppy business messages not only fails to enhance productivity but also often produces the opposite result. Those hurried messages can be confusing and frustrating. They often set into motion a maddening ping-pong series of back-and-forth queries and responses seeking clarification. To avoid messages that waste time, create confusion, and reduce your credibility, take time to slow down and revise—even for short messages.

The final phase of the 3-x-3 writing process focuses on editing, proofreading, and evaluating. Editing means improving the content and sentence structure of your message. Proofreading involves correcting its grammar, spelling, punctuation, format, and mechanics. Evaluating is the process of analyzing whether your message achieves its purpose. One may not expect the restaurant business to require these kinds of skills. However, the new culinary product manager at Taco Bell—and many similar businesspeople—realize that bright ideas are worth little unless they can be communicated effectively to fellow workers and to management. In the communication process, revision can often mean the difference between the acceptance or rejection of ideas.

LEARNING OUTCOME 1

Polish business messages by revising for conciseness, which includes cutting flabby expressions, long lead-ins, *there is/are* and *it is/was* fillers, redundancies, and empty words, as well as condensing for microblogging.

Although the drafting process differs depending on the person and the situation, this final phase should occupy a significant share of the total time you spend on a message. As you learned earlier, some experts recommend devoting about half the total writing time to the third phase of the writing process.[4]

Rarely is the first or even second version of a message satisfactory. Only amateurs expect writing perfection on the first try. The revision stage is your chance to make sure your message says what you mean and makes you look good. Many professional writers compose the first draft quickly without worrying about language, precision, or correctness. Then they revise and polish extensively. Other writers, however, prefer to revise as they go—particularly for shorter business documents.

Whether you revise immediately or after a break, you will want to examine your message critically. You should be especially concerned with improving its conciseness, clarity, and readability.

Polishing Your Messages by Revising for Conciseness

In business, time is indeed money. Translated into writing, this means that concise messages save reading time and, thus, money. In addition, messages that are written directly and efficiently are easier to read and comprehend. In the revision process, look for shorter ways to say what you mean. Examine every sentence you write. Could the thought be conveyed in fewer words? Your writing will be more concise if you eliminate flabby expressions, drop unnecessary introductory words, get rid of redundancies, and purge empty words.

Cutting Flabby Expressions

As you revise, focus on eliminating flabby expressions. This takes conscious effort. As one expert copyeditor observed, "Trim sentences, like trim bodies, usually require far more effort than flabby ones."[5] Turning out slim sentences and lean messages means that you will strive to trim the fat. For example, notice the flabbiness in this sentence: *Due to the fact that sales are booming, profits are good.* It could be said more concisely: *Because sales are booming, profits are good.* Many flabby expressions can be shortened to one concise word, as shown here and illustrated in Figure 6.1. Notice in this figure how you can revise digital documents with strikethrough formatting and color. If you are revising print documents, use popular proofreading marks.

Flabby	Concise
as a general rule	generally
at a later date	later
at this point in time	now, presently
despite the fact that	although
due to the fact that, inasmuch as, in view of the fact that	because
feel free to	please
for the period of	for
in addition to the above	also
in all probability	probably
in the event that	if
in the near future	soon
in very few cases	seldom
until such time as	until
with regard to	about

Figure 6.1 Revising Digital and Print Documents

Revising Digital Documents Using Strikethrough and Color

~~This is a short note to let you know that, as~~ As you requested, I ~~made an investigation of~~ investigated several of our competitors' websites. Attached ~~hereto~~ is a summary of my findings. ~~of my investigation.~~ I was ~~really~~ most interested in ~~making a comparison of the employment of strategies for~~ comparing marketing strategies as well as ~~the use of~~ navigational graphics ~~used~~ to guide visitors through the sites. ~~In view of the fact that~~ Because we will be revising our own website ~~in the near future~~ soon, I was ~~extremely~~ intrigued by the organization, ~~kind of~~ marketing tactics, and navigation at each ~~and every~~ site I visited.

When revising digital documents, you can use simple word processing tools such as strikethrough and color. In this example, strikethroughs in red identify passages to be deleted. The strikethrough function is located on the **Font** tab. We used blue to show inserted words, but you may choose any color you prefer.

Revising Printed Documents Using Proofreading Symbols

When revising printed documents, use standard symbols to manually show your revisions.

~~This is a short note to let you know that,~~ as you requested, I ~~made an~~ investigat[ed]~~ion of~~ several of our competitors' websites. Attached ~~hereto~~ is a summary of my findings. ~~of my investigation.~~ I was ~~really~~ most interested in [comparing] ~~making a comparison of the employment of~~ [marketing] strategies ~~for marketing~~ as well as ~~the use of~~ navigational graphics ~~used~~ to guide visitors through the sites. ~~In view of the fact that~~ [Because] we will be revising our own website [soon] ~~in the near future,~~ I was ~~extremely~~ intrigued by the organization, ~~kind of~~ marketing tactics, and navigation at each ~~and every~~ site I visited.

Popular Proofreading Symbols

- Delete
- Capitalize
- Insert
- Insert comma
- Insert period
- Start paragraph

More symbols are in Appendix C on page C-1.

Ditching Long Lead-Ins

Concise sentences avoid long lead-ins with unnecessary introductory words. Consider this sentence: *I am sending you this e-mail to announce that we have hired a new manager.* It's more concise and direct without the long lead-in: *We have hired a new manager.* The meat of the sentence often follows the words *that* or *because,* as shown in the following:

Wordy	Concise
Human Resources is sending this announcement to let everyone know that Monday is an official holiday.	Monday is an official holiday.
This is to inform you that you may find lower airfares at our website.	You may find lower airfares at our website.
I am writing this letter because Dr. Melody Alexander suggested that your organization was hiring trainees.	Dr. Melody Alexander suggested that your organization was hiring trainees.

Purging *there is/are* and *it is/was* Fillers

In many sentences the expressions *there is/are* and *it is/was* function as unnecessary fillers. In addition to taking up space, these fillers delay getting to the point of the sentence. Eliminate them by recasting the sentence. Many—but not all—sentences can be revised so that fillers are unnecessary.

Wordy	Concise
There are more women than men enrolled in college today.	More women than men are enrolled in college today.
There is an aggregator that collects and organizes blogs.	An aggregator collects and organizes blogs.
It was a Facebook post that revealed the news.	A Facebook post revealed the news.

Rejecting Redundancies

Expressions that repeat meaning or include unnecessary words are redundant. Saying *unexpected surprise* is like saying *surprise surprise* because *unexpected* carries the same meaning as *surprise.* Excessive adjectives, adverbs, and phrases often create redundancies and wordiness. Redundancies do not add emphasis, as some people think. Instead, they identify a writer as careless. As you revise, look for redundant expressions such as the following:

Redundant	Concise
absolutely essential	essential
adequate enough	adequate
basic fundamentals	fundamentals *or* basics
big in size	big
combine together	combine
exactly identical	identical
each and every	each *or* every
necessary prerequisite	prerequisite
new beginning	beginning
PIN number	PIN
refer back	refer
repeat again	repeat
true facts	facts

Editing Empty Words

Familiar phrases roll off the tongue easily, but many contain expendable parts. Be alert to these empty words and phrases: *case, degree, the fact that, factor, instance, nature,* and *quality.* Notice how much better the following sentences sound when we remove all the empty words:

> ~~In the case of~~ Twitter~~, it~~ increased users but lost share value.
>
> Because of the ~~degree of~~ research required, the budget was increased.
>
> We are aware ~~of the fact~~ that sales soared when pushed by social networking.
>
> Except for ~~the instance of~~ Toyota, Japanese imports sagged.

She chose a career in a field that was analytical ~~in nature~~. [OR: She chose a career in an analytical field.]

Student writing in that class is excellent ~~in quality~~.

Also avoid saying the obvious. In the following examples, notice how many unnecessary words we can omit through revision:

~~When it arrived~~, I cashed your check immediately. *(Announcing the check's arrival is unnecessary. That fact is assumed in its cashing.)*

As consumers learn more about ingredients ~~and as they become more knowledgeable~~, they are demanding fresher foods. *(Avoid repeating information.)*

Look carefully at clauses beginning with *that, which*, and *who*. They can often be shortened without loss of clarity. Search for phrases such as *it appears that*. These phrases often can be reduced to a single adjective or adverb, such as *apparently*.

successful
Changing the name of a ∧ company ~~that is successful~~ is always risky.

All employees ~~who are among those~~ completing the course will be reimbursed.

final
Our ∧ proposal, ~~which was~~ slightly altered ~~in its final form~~, won approval.

weekly
We plan to schedule ∧ meetings ~~on a weekly basis~~.

Stuart Conway/Camera Press/Redux

Reality Check

How to Lose a Customer Fast

"Good writing is brevity, and brevity is marketing. Want to lose me as a customer, forever, guaranteed? Have a grammar error on any form of outward communication."[6]

—Peter Shankman, *founder of Geek Factory, blogger, angel investor, author*

Microblogging and Conciseness

Microblogging is a term you probably haven't heard very often, but chances are you have posted a microblog message today. As its name suggests, *microblogging* consists of short messages exchanged on social media networks such as Twitter, Facebook, and Tumblr. Businesses are eagerly joining these microblogging networks to hear what's being said about them and their products. When they hear complaints, they can respond immediately and often solve customer problems. Companies are also using microblogging to make announcements, promote goodwill, and sell their products.

Microblogging may be public or private. Twitter and similar social networks are public channels with messages broadcast to the world. Twitter initially limited each tweet to 140 characters, but more recently it has allowed longer messages. Still, brevity is the hallmark of Twitter.

IanC66/Shutterstock.com

Corporations from Italian auto manufacturer Fiat to ice cream icon Ben & Jerry's have jumped on the Twitter bandwagon to reach and influence their customers—most of the time in 140 characters or less. American Airlines notably excels in the social media *Twittersphere* where it engages with followers on many fronts. Whether the social media staff is informing customers of an airport traffic jam using just 64 characters or empathizing with frustrated travelers in only 74 characters, American's tweets illustrate the tightly worded but natural style that characterizes microblogging. What other elements make tweets most effective?[7]

Enterprise Microblogging. Recognizing the usefulness of microblogging but desiring more confidentiality and security, some companies prefer to keep their messages internal. *Enterprise microblogging* enables companies using special platforms to collaborate, share information, and communicate privately within their organizations. Popular enterprise microblogging platforms are Yammer, Socialcast, and Rypple. Yammer promotes itself as a productivity tool. Instead of replying to the standard Twitter question, "What are you doing?", Yammerers ask, "What are you working on?" When employees answer, a feed is created in a central location enabling coworkers to discuss ideas, post news, ask questions, and share links.

Examples of Company Twitter Messages. Regardless of the microblogging platform, conciseness is critical. Your messages must be short—without straying too far from conventional spelling, grammar, and punctuation. Sound difficult? It is, but it can be done, as shown in the following 140-character examples of workplace tweets:

Source: Twitter

Replying to Customer

@walmart

@PhilMiller We appreciate your sharing your feedback with us. We're very sorry for the inconvenience and understand your frustration. Ani

Source: Twitter

Sending Helpful Information

@continentalgas

@CleverMom Some boilers can be confusing. Please check our boiler manual to help you figure it out. Try http://po.st/BoilerManual Sarah

FloridaStock/Shutterstock.com

Promoting Service Concisely

@ABCbirdandpest

We manage conflict with birds, wildlife, and urban pests proactively and responsibly to ensure our customers' business continuity. bit.ly/feedback2017

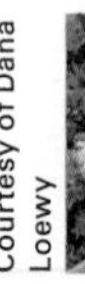

Courtesy of Dana Loewy

Sharing Information

@danaloewy

A new study presents millennials' workplace readiness in a more favorable light. http://fb.me/3suV9QOqL

Announcing Closure for Company Party

@Zappos

Hi all! We are closed for our annual Vendor Party! We will reopen at 7am PST tomorrow. We can still be reached at cs@zappos.com if needed.

Tips for Writing Concise, Effective Tweets. Your microblogging messages will be most effective if you follow these tips:

- Include only main ideas focused on useful information.
- Choose descriptive but short words.
- Personalize your message if possible.
- Be prepared to draft several versions striving for conciseness, clarity, and, yes, even correctness.

It's like playing a game: can you get your message across in only 140 characters? You'll learn more about blogging in Chapter 7.

AP Photo/Marcio Jose Sanchez

Reality Check

Even a Cartoonist Must Learn to Write Directly and Simply

Scott Adams, creator of the Dilbert cartoon, knows that even cartoonists must learn to write directly and simply. "I took a two-day class in business writing that taught me how to write direct sentences and to avoid extra words. Simplicity makes ideas powerful. Want examples? Read anything by Steve Jobs or Warren Buffet."[8]

—Scott Adams, *Dilbert cartoonist*

Improving Message Clarity

LEARNING OUTCOME 2

Improve clarity in business messages by keeping the ideas simple, slashing trite business phrases, dropping clichés, scrapping slang and buzzwords, rescuing buried verbs, and restraining exuberance.

One of the most important tasks in revising is assessing the clarity of your message. A clear message is one that is immediately understood. Employees, customers, and investors increasingly want to be addressed in a clear and genuine way. Fuzzy, long-winded, and unclear writing prevents comprehension. Readers understand better when information is presented clearly and concisely, as a Dartmouth study illustrates in Figure 6.2. Numerous techniques can improve the clarity of your writing including applying the KISS formula (Keep It Short and Simple), dumping trite business phrases, scrapping clichés and buzzwords, rescuing buried verbs, and restraining exuberance.

Keep It Short and Simple

To achieve clarity, resist the urge to show off or be fancy. Remember that your goal is not to impress a reader. As a business writer, your goal is to *express*, not *impress*. One way to achieve clear writing is to apply the familiar KISS formula. Use active-voice sentences that avoid indirect, pompous language.

Wordy and Unclear	Improved
High-quality learning environments for children are a necessary precondition for facilitation and enhancement of the ongoing learning process.	To learn properly, children need good schools.
In regard to the matter of obtaining optimal results, it is essential that employees be given the implements that are necessary for jobs to be completed satisfactorily.	For best results give employees the tools they need to do the job.

Figure 6.2 Conciseness Aids Clarity in Understanding Drug Facts

People who correctly quantified a heart drug's benefits after reading concise fact box.

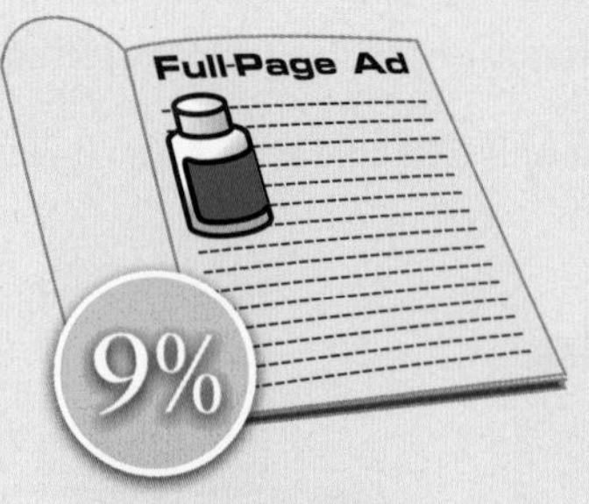

People who correctly quantified a heart drug's benefits after reading the company's long ad.

Consumers understand drug effects better when the information is presented concisely and clearly. A Dartmouth University study revealed that concise fact boxes were superior to the tiny-type, full-page DTC (direct-to-consumer) advertisements that drug manufacturers usually publish.

Slashing Trite Business Phrases

In an attempt to sound businesslike, some business writers repeat the same stale expressions that others have used over the years. Your writing will sound fresher and more vigorous if you eliminate these trite phrases or find more original ways to convey the idea.

Trite Phrase	Improved
as per your request	as you request
pursuant to your request	at your request
enclosed please find	enclosed is
every effort will be made	we'll try
in accordance with your wishes	as you wish
in receipt of	have received
please do not hesitate to	please
respond forthwith	respond immediately
thank you in advance	thank you
under separate cover	separately
with reference to	about

Cutting Clichés

Clichés are expressions that have become exhausted by overuse. Many cannot be explained, especially to those who are new to our culture. Clichés lack not only freshness but also clarity. Instead of repeating clichés such as the following, try to find another way to say what you mean.

below the belt
better than new
beyond a shadow of a doubt
easier said than done
exception to the rule
fill the bill
first and foremost
good to go
last but not least
make a bundle
pass with flying colors
quick as a flash
shoot from the hip
stand your ground
think outside the box
true to form

mmkarabella/ Shutterstock.com

Reality Check

What's Bad, Boring, and Barely Read All Over?

"If you could taste words, most corporate websites, brochures, and sales materials would remind you of stale, soggy rice cakes: nearly calorie free, devoid of nutrition, and completely unsatisfying. . . . Unfortunately, years of language dilution by lawyers, marketers, executives, and HR departments have turned the powerful, descriptive sentence into an empty vessel optimized for buzzwords, jargon, and vapid expressions."[9]

—Jason Fried, *software developer and cofounder of 37 signals*

Scrapping Slang and Buzzwords

Slang is composed of informal words with arbitrary and extravagantly changed meanings. Slang words quickly go out of fashion because they are no longer appealing when everyone begins to understand them. If you want to sound professional, avoid expressions such as *snarky, lousy, blowing the budget, bombed, getting burned,* and Twitter slang such as *b/c* (because), *FOMO* (fear of missing out), *ICYMI* (in case you missed it), and *br* (best regards).

Equally unprofessional and imprecise are business buzzwords. These are technical expressions that have become fashionable and often are meant to impress rather than express. Business buzzwords include empty terms such as *optimize, incentivize, impactful, leveraging, right-size,* and *paradigm shift.* Countless businesses today use vague rhetoric such as *cost effective, positioned to perform, solutions-oriented,* and *value-added services with end-to-end fulfillment.*

Consider the following statement of a government official who had been asked why his department was dropping a proposal to lease offshore oil lands: *The Administration has an awful lot of other things in the pipeline, and this has more wiggle room so they just moved it down the totem pole.* He added, however, that the proposal might be offered again since *there is no pulling back because of hot-potato factors.* What exactly does this mean?

Rescuing Buried Verbs

Buried verbs are those that are needlessly converted to wordy noun expressions. This happens when verbs such as *acquire, establish,* and *develop* are made into nouns such as *acquisition, establishment,* and *development.* Such nouns often end in *-tion, -ment,* and *-ance.* Sometimes called *zombie nouns* because they cannibalize and suck the life out of active verbs,[10] these nouns increase sentence length, slow the reader, and muddy the thought. Notice how you can make your writing cleaner and more forceful by avoiding buried verbs and zombie nouns:

Buried Verbs	Unburied Verbs
conduct a discussion of	discuss
create a reduction in	reduce
engage in the preparation of	prepare
give consideration to	consider
make an assumption of	assume
make a discovery of	discover
perform an analysis of	analyze
reach a conclusion that	conclude
take action on	act

Restraining Exuberance

Occasionally, we show our exuberance with words such as *very, definitely, quite, completely, extremely, really, actually,* and *totally.* These intensifiers can emphasize and strengthen your meaning. Overuse, however, sounds unbusinesslike. Control your enthusiasm and guard against excessive use.

Excessive Exuberance	Businesslike
The manufacturer was *extremely* upset to learn that its smartphones were *definitely* being counterfeited.	The manufacturer was upset to learn that its smartphones were being counterfeited.
We *totally* agree that we *actually* did not give his proposal a *very* fair trial.	We agree that we did not give his proposal a fair trial.

LEARNING OUTCOME 3

Enhance readability by applying document design including the use of white space, margins, typefaces, fonts, numbered and bulleted lists, and headings.

Applying Document Design to Enhance Readability

Want to make your readers think you are well-organized and intelligent? You can accomplish this by cleverly using document design! Doing so will also enhance the readability of your messages.

In the revision process, you have a chance to adjust formatting and make other changes so that readers grasp your main points quickly. Significant design techniques to improve readability include the appropriate use of white space, margins, typefaces, numbered and bulleted lists, and headings for visual impact.

Employing White Space

Empty space on a page is called *white space.* A page crammed full of text or graphics appears busy, cluttered, and unreadable. To increase white space, use headings, bulleted or numbered lists, and effective margins. Remember that short sentences (20 or fewer words) and short paragraphs (eight or fewer printed lines) improve readability and comprehension. As you revise, think about shortening long sentences. Consider breaking up long paragraphs into shorter chunks.

Understanding Margins and Text Alignment

Margins determine the white space on the left, right, top, and bottom of a block of type. They define the reading area and provide important visual relief. Business letters and memos usually have side margins of 1 to 1.5 inches.

Your word processing program probably offers four forms of margin alignment: (a) lines align only at the left, (b) lines align only at the right, (c) lines align at both left and right (*justified*), and (d) lines are centered. Nearly all text in Western cultures is aligned at the left and reads from left to right. The right margin may be either *justified* or *ragged right.* The text in books, magazines, and other long works is often justified on the left and right for a formal appearance.

Justified text, however, may require more attention to word spacing and hyphenation to avoid awkward empty spaces or rivers of spaces running through a document. When right margins are *ragged*—that is, without alignment or justification—they provide more white space and improve readability. Therefore, you are best served by using left-justified text and ragged-right margins without justification. Centered text is appropriate for headings and short announcements, but not for complete messages.

Figure 6.3 **Typefaces With Different Personalities for Different Purposes**

All-Purpose Sans Serif	Traditional Serif	Happy, Creative Script/Funny	Assertive, Bold Modern Display	Plain Monospaced
Arial	Century	Brush Script	Britannic Bold	Courier
Calibri	Garamond	Comic Sans	Broadway	Letter Gothic
Helvetica	Georgia	Gigi	Elephant	Monaco
Tahoma	Goudy	Jokerman	Impact	Prestige Elite
Univers	Palatino	Lucinda	Bauhaus 93	
Verdana	Times New Roman	Kristen	SHOWCARD	

Choosing Appropriate Typefaces

Business writers today may choose from a number of typefaces on their word processors. A typeface defines the shape of text characters. A wide range of typefaces, as shown in Figure 6.3, is available for various purposes. Some are decorative and useful for special purposes. For most business messages, however, you should choose from *serif* or *sans serif* categories.

Serif typefaces have small features at the ends of strokes. The most common serif typeface is Times New Roman. Other popular serif typefaces are Century, Georgia, and Palatino. Serif typefaces suggest tradition, maturity, and formality. They are frequently used for body text in business messages and longer documents. Because books, newspapers, and magazines favor serif typefaces, readers are familiar with them.

Sans serif typefaces include Arial, Calibri, Gothic, Tahoma, Helvetica, and Univers. These clean characters are widely used for headings, signs, and material that does not require continuous reading. Web designers often prefer sans serif typefaces for simple, pure pages. For longer documents, however, sans serif typefaces may seem colder and less accessible than familiar serif typefaces.

For less formal messages or special decorative effects, you might choose one of the happy fonts such as Comic Sans or a bold typeface such as Impact. You can simulate handwriting with a script typeface. Despite the wonderful possibilities available on your word processor, don't get carried away with fancy typefaces. All-purpose sans serif and traditional serif typefaces are most appropriate for your business messages. Generally, use no more than two typefaces within one document.

Understanding Type Fonts, Sizes, and Listing Techniques

Font refers to a specific style (such as *italic*) within a typeface family (such as Times New Roman). Most typeface families offer various fonts such as CAPITALIZATION, SMALL CAPS, **boldface**, *italic*, and underline, as well as less common fonts such as outline and shadow.

Font styles are a mechanical means of adding emphasis to your words. ALL CAPS, SMALL CAPS, and **bold** are useful for headings, subheadings, and single words or short phrases in the text. ALL CAPS, HOWEVER, SHOULD NEVER BE USED FOR LONG STRETCHES OF TEXT BECAUSE ALL THE LETTERS ARE THE SAME HEIGHT, MAKING IT DIFFICULT FOR READERS TO DIFFERENTIATE WORDS. In addition, excessive use of all caps feels like shouting and irritates readers. **Boldface,** *italics*, and underlining are effective for calling attention to important points and terms. Be cautious, however, when using fancy or an excessive number of font styles. Don't use them if they will confuse, annoy, or delay readers.

During the revision process, think about type size. Readers are generally most comfortable with 10- to 12-point type for body text. Smaller type enables you to fit more words into a space. Tiny type, however, makes text look dense and unappealing. Slightly larger type makes material more readable. Overly large type (14 points or more) looks amateurish and out of place for body text in business messages. Larger type, however, is appropriate for headings.

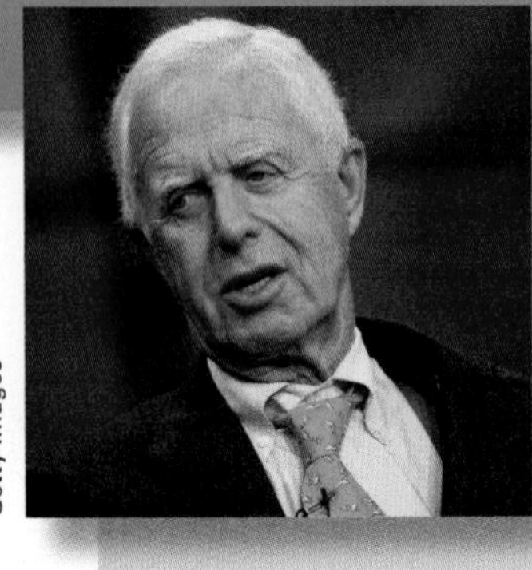

Bloomberg/Contributor/ Getty Images

Reality Check

Complaining of an Avalanche of Impenetrable Verbiage

An advocate for plain English, Arthur Levitt champions readability in investor documents. He advocates using the active voice, familiar words, and graphic techniques such as boldface, headings, and lists. However, he has been only partially successful, he complains, because such efforts "get tugged into the ditch by the irresistible pull of legal jargon" with documents "buried in an avalanche of impenetrable verbiage."[11]

—Arthur Levitt, *former chair, U.S. Securities and Exchange Commission*

Numbering and Bulleting Lists for Quick Comprehension

One of the best ways to ensure rapid comprehension of ideas is through the use of numbered or bulleted lists. Lists provide high *skim value*. This means that readers can browse quickly and grasp main ideas. By breaking up complex information into smaller chunks, lists improve readability, understanding, and retention. They also force the writer to organize ideas and write efficiently.

In the revision process, look for ideas that could be converted to lists, and follow these techniques to make your lists look professional:

- **Numbered lists.** Use for items that represent a sequence or reflect a numbering system.
- **Bulleted lists.** Use to highlight items that don't necessarily show a chronology.
- **Capitalization.** Capitalize the initial word of each line.
- **Punctuation.** Add end punctuation only if the listed items are complete sentences.
- **Parallelism.** Make all the lines consistent; for example, start each with a verb.

In the following examples, notice that the list on the left presents a sequence of steps with numbers. The bulleted list does not show a sequence of ideas; therefore, bullets are appropriate. Also notice the parallelism in each example. In the numbered list, each item begins with a verb. In the bulleted list, each item follows an adjective/noun sequence. Business readers appreciate lists because they focus attention. Be careful, however, not to use so many that your messages look like grocery lists.

Numbered List	Bulleted List
Our recruiters follow these steps when hiring applicants:	To attract upscale customers, we feature the following:
1. Examine the application.	• Quality fashions
2. Interview the applicant.	• Personalized service
3. Check the applicant's references.	• Generous return policy

Adding Headings for Visual Impact

Headings are an effective tool for highlighting information and improving readability. They encourage the writer to group similar material together. Headings help the reader separate major ideas from details. They enable a busy reader to skim familiar or less important information. They also provide a quick preview or review. Headings appear most often in reports, which you will study in greater detail in Chapters 11, 12, and 13. However, main headings, subheadings, and category headings can also improve readability in e-mails, memos, and letters. In the following example, they are used with bullets to summarize categories:

Category Headings
Our company focuses on the following areas in the employment process:

- **Attracting applicants.** We advertise for qualified applicants, and we also encourage current employees to recommend good people.
- **Interviewing applicants.** Our specialized interviews include simulated customer encounters as well as scrutiny by supervisors.
- **Checking references**. We investigate every applicant thoroughly. We contact former employers and all listed references.

In Figure 6.4 the writer was able to convert a dense, unappealing e-mail into an easier-to-read version by applying document design. Notice that the all-caps font in the first paragraph makes its meaning difficult to decipher. Justified margins and lack of white space further reduce readability. In the revised version, the writer changed the all-caps font to upper- and lowercase and also used ragged-right margins to enhance visual appeal. One of the best document design techniques in this message is the use of headings and bullets to help the reader see chunks of information in similar groups. All of these improvements are made in the revision process. You can make any message more readable by applying the document design techniques presented here.

Ethics Check

Costly Writing

Bad writing can be expensive: A Philadelphia lawyer was charged with malpractice to the tune of $6.6 million for drafting a poor commercial lease. The judge in Los Angeles said the draft was "inartfully written and done so in a confusing fashion, which lends itself to ambiguities and disagreements."[12] Can you think of other situations in which writing can be deliberately or accidentally misleading and expensive?

Proofreading to Catch Errors

LEARNING OUTCOME 4

Recognize proofreading problem areas, and apply effective techniques to catch mistakes in both routine and complex documents.

Alas, none of us is perfect, and even the best writers sometimes make mistakes. The problem, however, is not making the mistakes; the real problem is not finding and correcting them. Documents with errors affect your credibility and the success of your organization, as illustrated in Figure 6.5.

Once you have the message in its final form, it's time to proofread. Don't proofread earlier because you may waste time checking items that eventually are changed or omitted. Important messages—such as those you send to management or to customers or turn in to instructors for grades—deserve careful revision and proofreading. Even messages you post at dating sites deserve careful proofing. A survey of 5,000 singles by dating site Match revealed that 80 percent of women and 75 percent of men said they valued correct grammar highly, putting it ahead of a person's confidence and even ahead of good-looking teeth.[13]

When you finish a first draft, plan for a cooling-off period. Put the document aside and return to it after a break, preferably after 24 hours or longer. Proofreading is especially difficult because most of us read what we thought we wrote. That's why it's important to look for specific problem areas.

What to Watch for in Proofreading

Careful proofreaders check for problems in the following areas:

- **Spelling.** Now is the time to consult the dictionary. Is *recommend* spelled with one or two *c*'s? Do you mean *affect* or *effect*? Use your computer spell-checker, but don't rely on it totally.

Figure 6.4 Document Design Improves Readability

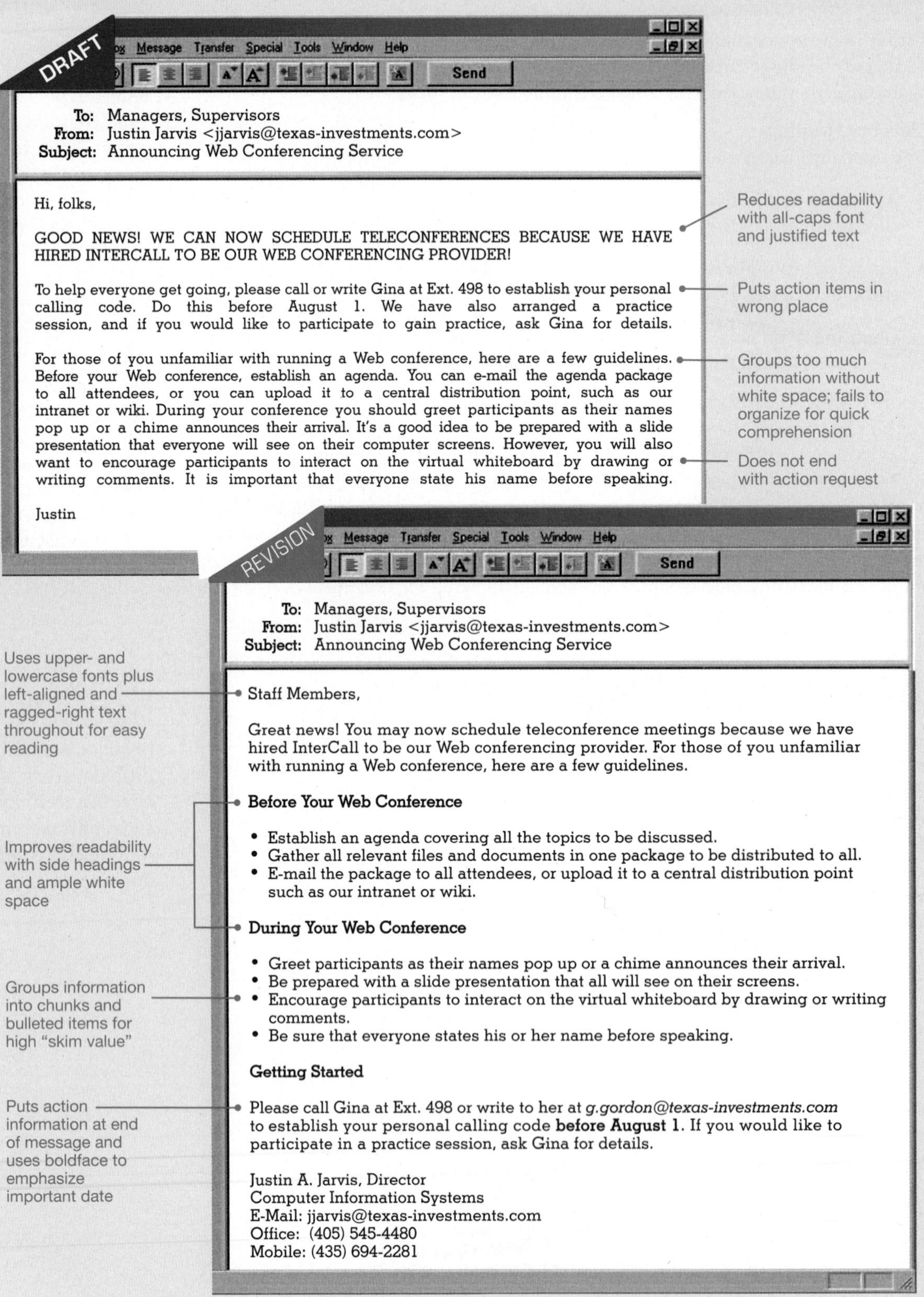

DRAFT
Message Transfer Special Tools Window Help
Send
To: Managers, Supervisors
From: Justin Jarvis <jjarvis@texas-investments.com>
Subject: Announcing Web Conferencing Service
Hi, folks,
GOOD NEWS! WE CAN NOW SCHEDULE TELECONFERENCES BECAUSE WE HAVE HIRED INTERCALL TO BE OUR WEB CONFERENCING PROVIDER!
To help everyone get going, please call or write Gina at Ext. 498 to establish your personal calling code. Do this before August 1. We have also arranged a practice session, and if you would like to participate to gain practice, ask Gina for details.
For those of you unfamiliar with running a Web conference, here are a few guidelines. Before your Web conference, establish an agenda. You can e-mail the agenda package to all attendees, or you can upload it to a central distribution point, such as our intranet or wiki. During your conference you should greet participants as their names pop up or a chime announces their arrival. It's a good idea to be prepared with a slide presentation that everyone will see on their computer screens. However, you will also want to encourage participants to interact on the virtual whiteboard by drawing or writing comments. It is important that everyone state his name before speaking.
Justin
Reduces readability with all-caps font and justified text
Puts action items in wrong place
Groups too much information without white space; fails to organize for quick comprehension
Does not end with action request
REVISION
Message Transfer Special Tools Window Help
Send
To: Managers, Supervisors
From: Justin Jarvis <jjarvis@texas-investments.com>
Subject: Announcing Web Conferencing Service
Staff Members,
Great news! You may now schedule teleconference meetings because we have hired InterCall to be our Web conferencing provider. For those of you unfamiliar with running a Web conference, here are a few guidelines.
Before Your Web Conference
• Establish an agenda covering all the topics to be discussed.
• Gather all relevant files and documents in one package to be distributed to all.
• E-mail the package to all attendees, or upload it to a central distribution point such as our intranet or wiki.
During Your Web Conference
• Greet participants as their names pop up or a chime announces their arrival.
• Be prepared with a slide presentation that all will see on their screens.
• Encourage participants to interact on the virtual whiteboard by drawing or writing comments.
• Be sure that everyone states his or her name before speaking.
Getting Started
Please call Gina at Ext. 498 or write to her at *g.gordon@texas-investments.com* to establish your personal calling code **before August 1**. If you would like to participate in a practice session, ask Gina for details.
Justin A. Jarvis, Director
Computer Information Systems
E-Mail: jjarvis@texas-investments.com
Office: (405) 545-4480
Mobile: (435) 694-2281
Uses upper- and lowercase fonts plus left-aligned and ragged-right text throughout for easy reading
Improves readability with side headings and ample white space
Groups information into chunks and bulleted items for high "skim value"
Puts action information at end of message and uses boldface to emphasize important date

- **Grammar.** Locate sentence subjects; do their verbs agree with them? Do pronouns agree with their antecedents? Review the grammar and mechanics principles in Appendix D if necessary. Use your computer's grammar-checker, but be suspicious; sometimes it's flat-out wrong.
- **Punctuation.** Make sure that introductory clauses are followed by commas. In compound sentences put commas before coordinating conjunctions (*and, or, but, nor*). Double-check your use of semicolons and colons.
- **Names and numbers.** Compare all names and numbers with their sources because inaccuracies are not always visible. Especially verify the spelling of the names of individuals receiving the message. Most of us immediately dislike someone who misspells our name.
- **Format.** Be sure that your document looks balanced on the page. Compare its parts with those of the standard document formats shown in Appendix A. If you indent paragraphs, be certain that all are indented.

Figure 6.5 **Why Proofread?**

WHY PROOFREAD? IN BUSINESS, ACCURACY MATTERS
A survey of business professionals revealed the following:
100% said that writing errors influenced their opinions about a business.
57% will stop considering a company if its print brochure has one writing error.
77% have eliminated a prospective company from consideration in part because of writing errors.
75% thought misspelled words were inexcusable.
30% of Web visitors will leave if a website contains writing errors.
Goodluz/Shutterstock.com

How to Proofread Routine Documents

Most routine documents require a light proofreading. If you read on screen, use the down arrow to reveal one line at a time. This focuses your attention at the bottom of the screen. A safer proofreading method, however, is reading from a printed copy. Regardless of which method you use, look for typos and misspellings. Search for easily confused words, such as *to* for *too* and *then* for *than*. Read for missing words and inconsistencies. For handwritten or printed messages, use standard proofreading marks, shown briefly in Figure 6.1 or completely in Appendix C. For digital documents and collaborative projects, use the simple word processing tools such as strikethrough and color shown in Figure 6.1. You can also use the **Comment** and **Track Changes** functions described in Chapter 4, Figure 4.9.

How to Proofread Complex Documents

Long, complex, or important documents demand careful proofreading. Apply the previous suggestions but also add the following techniques:

- Print a copy, preferably double-spaced, and set it aside for at least a day. You will be more alert after a breather.
- Allow adequate time to proofread carefully. A common excuse for sloppy proofreading is lack of time.

Ethics Check

Overly Helpful

Students sometimes visit writing centers to receive useful advice and help. However, some well-meaning tutors take over, revising documents until they don't resemble the original student work. Instructors worry that the resulting documents amount to cheating. Yet in the workplace today, writers must collaborate, and drafts go through multiple revisions. Individual authorship is often not relevant. How much revision is acceptable in a college setting? How much is acceptable in the workplace?

- Be prepared to find errors. One student confessed, "I can find other people's errors, but I can't seem to locate my own." Psychologically, we don't expect to find errors, and we don't want to find them. You can overcome this obstacle by anticipating errors and congratulating, not criticizing, yourself each time you find one.
- Read the message at least twice—once for word meanings and once for grammar and mechanics. For very long documents (book chapters and long articles or reports), read a third time to verify consistency in formatting.
- Reduce your reading speed. Concentrate on individual words rather than ideas.
- For documents that must be perfect, enlist a proofreading buddy. Have someone read the message aloud. Spell names and difficult words, note capitalization, and read punctuation.
- Use the standard proofreading marks shown in Appendix C to indicate changes.

Many of us struggle with proofreading our own writing because we are seeing the same information over and over. We tend to see what we expect to see as our eyes race over the words without looking at each one carefully. We tend to know what is coming next and glide over it. To change the appearance of what you are reading, you might print it on a different-colored paper or change the font. If you are proofing on screen, enlarge the page view or change the background color of the screen.

Evaluating the Effectiveness of Your Message

LEARNING OUTCOME 5

Evaluate a message to judge its effectiveness.

As part of applying finishing touches, take a moment to evaluate your writing. Remember that everything you write, whether for yourself or someone else, takes the place of a personal appearance. If you were meeting in person, you would be certain to dress appropriately and professionally. The same standard applies to your writing. Evaluate what you have written to be certain that it attracts the reader's attention. Is it polished and clear enough to convince the reader that you are worth listening to? How successful will this message be? Does it say what you want it to? Will it achieve your purpose? How will you know whether it succeeds?

The best way to judge the success of your communication is through feedback. For this reason you should encourage the receiver to respond to your message. This feedback will tell you how to modify future efforts to improve your communication technique.

Your instructor will also be evaluating some of your writing. Although any criticism is painful, try not to be defensive. Look on these comments as valuable advice tailored to your specific writing weaknesses—and strengths. Many businesses today spend thousands of dollars bringing in communication consultants to improve employee writing skills. You are getting the same training in this course. Take advantage of this chance—one of the few you may have—to improve your skills. The best way to improve your skills, of course, is through instruction, practice, and evaluation.

In this class you have all three elements: instruction in the writing process, practice materials, and someone to guide you and evaluate your efforts. Those three elements are the reasons this book and this course may be the most valuable in your entire curriculum. Because it's almost impossible to improve your communication skills alone, take advantage of this opportunity.

The task of editing, proofreading, and evaluating, summarized in the following checklist, is hard work. It demands objectivity and a willingness to cut, cut, cut. Though painful, the process is also gratifying. It's a great feeling when you realize your finished message is clear, concise, and effective.

CHECKLIST

Editing, Proofreading, and Evaluating

- **Cut flabby expressions.** Strive to reduce wordy phrases to single words (*as a general rule* becomes *generally*; *at this point in time* becomes *now*).
- **Ditch opening fillers and long lead-ins.** Revise sentences so that they don't start with fillers (*there is, there are, it is, it was*) and long lead-ins (*this is to inform you that*).
- **Reject redundancies.** Eliminate words that repeat meanings, such as *refer back*. Watch for repetitious adjectives, adverbs, and phrases.
- **Eliminate empty writing.** Check phrases that include *case, degree, the fact that, factor*, and other words and phrases that unnecessarily increase wordiness. Avoid saying the obvious.
- **Write concisely for microblogging.** Keep your messages short without sacrificing proper spelling, grammar, and punctuation.
- **Keep the message simple.** Express ideas directly. Don't show off or use fancy language.
- **Slash trite business phrases.** Keep your writing fresh, direct, and contemporary by skipping such expressions as *enclosed please find* and *pursuant to your request.*
- **Scrap clichés and slang.** Avoid expressions that are overused and unclear (*below the belt, shoot from the hip*). Don't use slang, which is not only unprofessional but also often unclear to a wide audience.
- **Rescue buried verbs.** Keep your writing vigorous by not converting verbs to nouns (*analyze* not *make an analysis of*).
- **Restrain exuberance.** Avoid overusing intensifiers such as *really, very, definitely, quite, completely, extremely, actually,* and *totally.*
- **Improve readability through document design.** Use bullets, lists, headings, capital letters, underlining, boldface, italics, and blank space to spotlight ideas and organize them.
- **Proofread for correctness.** Check spelling, grammar, and punctuation. Compare names and numbers with their sources. Double-check the format to be sure you have been consistent.
- **Evaluate your final product.** Will your message achieve its purpose? Could it be improved? How will you know whether it is successful?

Your Turn: Applying Your Skills at Taco Bell

Yeamake/Shutterstock.com

As an assistant in the communications division of Taco Bell, you have been asked to help Dustin, the newly hired culinary product manager, revise a memo he has written. Assume that CEO Brian Niccol has asked all managers for innovative ideas. Niccol is interested in current food trends and in creating exciting new menu items responding to those food trends. The CEO emphasized this when he said, "If you let the brand grow old, you will die. That means you deliver experiences that really matter to the current generation."[14] In his new position as culinary manager, Dustin wants very much to suggest new items for Taco Bell that are in keeping with management's push for innovation and that also reflect current food trends.

Dustin has prepared a rough draft of a memo summarizing his longer report, which he will present at a management meeting next week. Although exceptionally talented in cuisine, he realizes that his writing skills are not as well developed as his cooking skills. He comes to the corporate communication department and shows your boss the first draft of his memo. Your boss is a nice guy, and, as a favor, he revises the first two paragraphs, shown in Figure 6.6.

Your Task

The head of corporate communication has many important tasks to oversee. He hands Dustin's memo to you, his assistant, and tells you to finish cleaning it up. He adds, "His ideas are right on target, but the main points are totally lost in wordy sentences and solid paragraphs. Revise this and concentrate on conciseness, clarity, and readability. Do you think some bulleted lists would help this memo?" Revise the remaining four paragraphs of the memo using the techniques you learned in this chapter. Prepare a copy of the complete memo, incorporating the edits shown, to submit to your boss (your instructor).

Figure 6.6 **Partially Revised First Draft**

DRAFT

Date: May 9, 2018
To: Taco Bell Management Council
From: Dustin Ortiz, Culinary Product Manager
Subject: ~~New Ideas~~ Eating Trends and New Menu Options

As ~~per your~~ you requested, ~~the writer is~~ I am submitting the following ideas based on ~~his~~ my ~~personal~~ observation and research ~~in regard to~~ about eating trends in fast-food restaurants ~~that serve fast-food. As you suggested, I am also offering b~~Below is a rough outline of possible concepts to ~~enlarge and~~ expand Taco Bell's menu reflecting ~~these aforementioned~~ current eating trends. ~~This is to inform you that t~~This memo ~~represents a summary of~~ summarizes the findings ~~that I have extracted~~ from my longer report to be presented at your next Management Council meeting.

First ~~and foremost~~, I ~~would like to~~ will focus on new menu items that are ~~more~~ fresher, ~~and much~~ more sophisticated, ~~And~~ and ~~with more~~ locally grown ~~items~~. However, I know that these items must also meet ~~Taco Bells~~ Bell's strict criteria: high-quality flavor, ~~they must be portable~~ portability, and ~~they must be easily produced~~ ease of production. In ~~an~~ a recovering economy ~~that is recovering~~, our restaurant ~~can and most certainly~~ should offer value as well as tasty food ~~that tastes very good~~. From my ~~personal~~ firsthand experience ~~that I gained firsthand~~ as a chef and from current reading and research, I have ~~made an observation of~~ observed numerous eating trends.

Taking a Look at Trends in Fast-Food Eating Preferences

As you probably know, Mexican cuisine is increasingly popular from coast to coast, but today's customers—especially millennials—want much more intense flavors. With locally sourced ingredients. There are four trends that are most appropriate for us to take action on as we revamp the Taco Bell menu.

The first deals with the matter of **high-protein items**. A lot of recent research reveals that 42 percent of all millennials as well as more then half of all adults think that it is important to eat more protein. A second trend deals with **spices**. Consumers are appreciating much more highly spiced foods and hot sauces. Spicy Thai and other ethnic dishes are growing in popularity. A third trend has to do with **freshness**. As consumers become more knowledgeable and more discriminating they are making a demand for fresher ingredients. Which are often locally grown. A fourth trend has to do with **small portions**. Trend watchers say that 35 percent of all meals that are eaten by millennials are snacks, thus suggesting small portions.

A Few Ideas for New Menu Options

Despite the fact that my full report contains a number of additional trends and menu ideas, here are three significant menu concepts that are significant and important:

First, I am totally of the opinion that we should add a **PowerProtein Menu**. Reflecting the trend toward more protein, I suggest that we could be offering high-protein breakfast items such as steak burritos and Greek yogurt with granola. Second, I would like to recommend a **Fresh-Flavored Salsa Bar**. To appeal to those desiring fresh flavors, we could offer homemade exotic salsas. With locally sourced ingredients for bold flavors and textures. Third, to cater to snackers, I suggest **Small Plate** items. We could offer grilled sweet potato nachos with crumbled cojito and gooey cheese sauce on top. Other small plates might offer jalapeno pepper quinoa bites that are cheesy and spicy along with sharable snacks such as rolled chicken tacos.

I would be more than delighted and happy to have a discussion of these ideas with you in greater detail and have a demonstration of them in the kitchen. Please accept my humble thanks for this opportunity to work with you in expanding our menu to ensure that Taco Bell remains tops in Mexican cuisine.

Reduces wordiness throughout

Revises trite expression (*as per your request*) and uses first-person pronoun

Shortens wordy noun phrase (*represents a summary*) to more efficient verb (*summarizes*)

Deletes *and foremost* to avoid cliché; reduces excessive exuberance (*much more*)

In the remaining report, edit to reduce wordiness and correct errors

Use bulleted list with headings to improve readability in this paragraph

Revise wordy phrases (*Despite the fact that*)

Consider a bulleted or numbered list to improve this dense paragraph

Convert buried verbs (*have a discussion*) and reduce other wordiness

The first two paragraphs show revisions. Your task is to finish the revision.

Improves subject line

Converts four-word phrase (*that serve fast food*) to adjective (*fast-food*)

Develops parallelism (*flavor, portability, ease of production*)

Unburies verb by changing *made an observation* to *observed*

Summary of Learning Outcomes

1 Polish business messages by revising for conciseness, which includes eliminating flabby expressions, long lead-ins, *there is/are* and *it is/was* fillers, redundancies, and empty words, as well as condensing for microblogging.

- Revise for conciseness by eliminating flabby expressions (*as a general rule, at a later date, at this point in time*).
- Eliminate long lead-ins (*this is to inform you that*), fillers (*there is, there are*), redundancies (*basic essentials*), and empty words (*in the case of, the fact that*).
- Revise microblogging messages rigorously to convey meaning in as few as 140 characters.

2 Improve clarity in business messages by keeping the ideas simple, slashing trite business phrases, dropping clichés, scrapping slang and buzzwords, rescuing buried verbs, and restraining exuberance.

- Apply the KISS formula (Keep It Short and Simple) to improve message clarity.
- Slash trite business phrases (*as per your request, enclosed please find, pursuant to your request*).
- Cut clichés (*better than new, beyond a shadow of a doubt, easier said than done*).
- Scrap slang (*snarky, lousy, bombed*) and buzzwords (*paradigm shift, incentivize*).
- Rescue buried nouns (*to investigate* rather than *to conduct an investigation* and *to analyze* rather than *to perform an analysis*).
- Avoid overusing intensifiers that show exuberance (*totally, actually, very, definitely*).

3 Enhance readability by understanding document design including the use of white space, margins, typefaces, fonts, numbered and bulleted lists, and headings.

- To improve message readability and comprehension, provide ample white space, appropriate side margins, and ragged-right (not justified) margins.
- For body text use serif typefaces (fonts with small features at the ends of strokes, such as Times New Roman, Century, and Palatino); for headings and signs, use sans serif typefaces (clean fonts without small features, such as Arial, Helvetica, and Tahoma).
- Create numbered and bulleted lists to provide high skim value in messages.
- Boost visual impact and readability with headings in business messages and reports.

4 Recognize proofreading problem areas, and apply effective techniques to catch mistakes in both routine and complex documents.

- When proofreading, be especially alert to spelling, grammar, punctuation, names, numbers, and document format.
- Proofread routine documents line by line on the computer screen or from a printed draft copy immediately after finishing.
- Proofread complex documents after a breather. Read from a printed copy, allow adequate time, reduce your reading speed, and read the document at least three times—for word meanings, grammar and mechanics, and formatting.

5 Evaluate a message to judge its effectiveness.

- Encourage feedback from the receiver of your message so that you can determine whether your communication achieved its goal.
- Be open to any advice from your instructor on how to improve your writing skills.

Critical Thinking

1. A blogger recently asserted that "the pervasive use of email for business has made the work of writing well even more difficult because it invites—relentlessly—hitting Send before you have thought through, organized, reviewed, and even rewritten your message."[15] Do you agree that the process of writing has become more difficult with e-mail? (L.O. 1)

2. In this digital era of rapid communication, how can you justify the time it takes to stop and revise a message? (L.O. 1–5)

3. Assume you have started a new job in which you respond to customers by using boilerplate (previously constructed) paragraphs. Some of them contain clichés such as *pursuant to your request* and *in accordance with your wishes*. Other paragraphs are wordy and violate the principle of using concise and clear writing that you have learned. What should you do? (L.O. 2)

4. Because business writing should have high skim value, why not write everything in bulleted lists? (L.O. 3)

5. Ethical Issue: Consider the case of Sage, who is serving as interim editor of the company newsletter. She receives an article written by the company president describing, in abstract and pompous language, the company's goals for the coming year. Sage believes the article will need considerable revising to make it readable. Attached to the president's article are complimentary comments by two of the company vice presidents. What action should Sage take?

Writing Improvement Exercises

6.1 Flabby Expressions (L.O. 1)

YOUR TASK Revise the following sentences to eliminate flabby expressions.

a. Despite the fact that we lost the contract, we must at this point in time move forward.

b. In the event that interest rates increase, we will begin investing in the very near future.

c. We cannot fill the order until such time as payment is received for previous shipments.

d. As a general rule, we would not accept the return; however, we will in all probability make an exception in this case.

e. In very few cases will investors buy stocks that fail to pay dividends or increase in value.

6.2 Long Lead-Ins (L.O. 1)

YOUR TASK Revise the following to eliminate long lead-ins and wordiness.

a. This message is to let you know that I received your e-mail and its attachments.

b. This memo is to notify everyone that we will observe Monday as a holiday.

c. I am writing this letter to inform you that your homeowner's coverage expires soon.

d. This is to warn everyone that the loss of laptops endangers company security.

e. In the majority of instances, most of the shipping errors can be attributed to mistakes in the preparation of the address label.

6.3 *There is/are* and *it is/was* Fillers (L.O. 1)

YOUR TASK Revise the following to avoid wordy fillers.

a. There are many businesses that are implementing strict e-mail policies for employees.

b. It is the CEO who must approve the plan.

c. There are several Web pages you must update.

d. The manager says that there are many employees who did not return the health surveys.

e. It is my personal opinion that there are too many people dying while taking dangerous selfies.

6.4 Redundancies (L.O. 1)

YOUR TASK Revise the following to avoid redundancies.

a. Because the proposals are exactly identical, we need not check each and every item.

b. Some of the funniest animated gifs on Twitter, Tumblr, and Reddit combine together clips from movies or TV to produce comedic masterpieces.

c. It was the consensus of opinion that all office walls be painted beige in color.

d. Our supervisor requested that team members return back to the office.

6.5 Empty Words (L.O. 1)

YOUR TASK Revise the following to eliminate empty words and obvious meanings.

a. He scheduled the meeting for 11 a.m. in the morning.

b. Because of the surprising degree of response, the company expanded its free gift program.

c. I have before me your proposal sent by FedEx, and I will distribute it immediately.

d. Are you aware of the fact that our budget has a deficit in the amount of approximately $100,000?

e. In the normal course of events, we try to write to all of our clients with regard to their investments irregardless of the amount invested.

6.6 Condensing for Microblogging: Tweets With Replies (L.O. 1)

YOUR TASK Read the following Twitter messages and write a 140-character tweet reply to each. Be selective in what you include. Your instructor may show you the actual responses that the company wrote.

a. ***@DustinB* to *@Walmart*: Having a terrible time with savings catcher losing my money! Will someone help?** Prepare a response that explains that Walmart can't really fix this problem. But we can refer the customer to our Savings Catcher team at 866-224-1663. Or the customer could e-mail *SavCatch@wal-mart.com* for assistance.

b. ***@NicoleD* to *@Whole Foods Market*: Did you guys discontinue the heavenly super stars gummies ?!?!?!** Prepare a response explaining that you had to check with WFM's private label team to see whether this was a WFM item or a private brand. Unfortunately, you learned that this private brand of gummy candy has been discontinued at Whole Foods Market. However, you will pass along the suggestion in an effort to get this customer's favorite gummies back in the store!

c. ***@Courtney88* to *@Southwest Air*: Absolutely floored by *@SouthwestAir.* No wonder your bags fly free, there's a chance they'll lose it & can't give you a clue where it is.** Prepare a response that explains that Southwest takes all baggage issues absolutely seriously. Request that the customer send a direct message (DM) with the customer's flight confirmation number. This action will help with the baggage search.

d. ***@Tucson79* to *@VW*: Sunroof on wife's Bug is noisy to the point that may not get VW for next car. Mentioned this at service, still whistles constantly.** Prepare a response based on the following. We can't immediately know the problem, but we do very much want to learn how we may be able to help. We will need you to DM us with the following information: your VIN number and your e-mail address. These pieces of information will enable us to reach out to you.

e. ***@RachelD* to *@CapitalOne*. Shout out to *@CapitalOne* for immediately catching fraudulent activity on my account and resolving it in a 7-minute phone call!** Prepare a response that acknowledges receipt of the tweet but also conveys the goal of CapitalOne to make the lives of customers easier so they can catch up on things like shopping, TV, and movies. Include a winking happy face ☺

6.7 Trite Business Phrases (L.O. 2)

YOUR TASK Revise the following sentences to eliminate trite business phrases.

a. As per your request, we will no longer send you e-mail offers.

b. Thank you in advance for considering our plea for community support.

c. Every effort will be made to send the original copies under separate cover.

d. Enclosed please find a check in the amount of $700.

e. In accordance with your wishes, we are responding forthwith to return your funds.

6.8 Clichés, Slang, Buzzwords, and Wordiness (L.O. 2)

YOUR TASK Revise the following sentences to avoid confusing clichés, slang, buzzwords, and wordiness.

a. Although our last presentation bombed, we think that beyond the shadow of a doubt our new presentation will fly.

b. Our team must be willing to think outside the box in coming up with marketing ideas that pop.

c. True to form, our competitor has made a snarky claim that we think is way below the belt.

d. If you will refer back to the budget, you will see that there are provisions that prevent blowing the budget.

e. The team leader didn't know that we were literally starving and getting very hangry b/c someone 4got to order lunch.

6.9 Buried Verbs (L.O. 2)

YOUR TASK Revise the following to recover buried verbs.

a. Ms. Rivera gave an official appraisal of the home's value.

b. Web-based customer service certainly causes a reduction in overall costs.

c. Management made a recommendation affirming abandonment of the pilot project.

d. The board of directors will give consideration to the contract at the next meeting.

e. We must reach an agreement in the affirmative regarding location before we can make an authorization to commit to a property purchase.

6.10 Lists, Bullets, and Headings (L.O. 3)

YOUR TASK Revise the following sentences and paragraphs using lists, bullets, and category headings, if appropriate. Improve parallel construction and readability while reducing wordiness.

a. Create an introductory sentence and a list from the following wordy paragraph.

This information is to let you know that a high-powered MBA program costs hundreds of dollars an hour. However, our program covers the same information. That information includes entrepreneurship tips as well as how to start a business. You will also learn information about writing a business plan and understanding taxes. In addition, our MBA program covers how to go about writing a marketing feasibility study. Another important topic that our program covers is employment benefits plans.

b. From the following paragraph, prepare a concise introduction plus a bulleted list of tips.

Unadvertised, or hidden, jobs may make up as much as 80 percent of unfilled openings, according to Fred Coon, a licensed employment agent. To uncover hidden jobs, Coon suggests that those entering the workforce think about joining industry groups. Associations, chambers of commerce, and Toastmasters are excellent ways to make contacts before you need them. Coon also suggests talking to insiders. Insights from those already in the industry can help new workers learn how to best chart their career paths. Another way to find hidden jobs is to search company websites. Many companies post openings only on their corporate websites.

c. Revise the following dense, wordy paragraph to create an introductory sentence plus a bulleted list.

We all know that withdrawing money from an ATM is a quick and convenient way to access your money, especially if you are having a cash emergency. But not everyone uses an ATM safely. To do so, there are a few procedures that you can follow to feel safe. First, don't use an ATM unless it is located in a well-lit area that is also busy. This is especially important after nightfall. Next, a careful person will look around to see if there are any suspicious people loitering about. It's always wise to use a challenging PIN, which should have more than four letters or numbers. When you approach the ATM machine, check it out. Do you see any false fronts or anything doubtful? Finally, you must always protect your PIN. One way to do that is by placing your hand over the keypad to act as a shield.

d. From the following wordy paragraph, create a concise introductory statement plus a bulleted list with category headings.

This is to inform you that our on-site GuruGeek computer technicians can provide you with fast, affordable solutions to residential and also to small business clients. Our most popular offerings include antivirus security. This service involves having our GuruGeek protect your computer against viruses, worms, and spyware as well as help you avoid e-mail attacks, identity theft, and malicious hacker programs. Our wireless networking service enables you to share Internet access through a single wireless router so that many computer users use one network at the same time. They are all using the same network. Another popular service is data backup and recovery. Our technicians focus on helping small businesses and home users protect their data without making an investment of a lot of time and energy.

Activities

Note: All Documents for Analysis may be downloaded from **www.cengagebrain.com** so that you do not have to rekey the entire message.

6.11 Document for Analysis: Wretched E-Mail Invitation (L.O. 1–5)

E-Mail

YOUR TASK The following wordy, inefficient, and disorganized message invites department managers to three interviewing sessions to select student interns. However, to be effective, this message desperately needs revision. Study the message and list at least five weaknesses. Then revise to avoid excessive wordiness and repetition. Also think about how to develop an upbeat tone and improve readability. Can you reduce this sloppy 15-sentence message to six efficient sentences plus a list—and still convey all the necessary information?

To: Department Managers List
From: Aaron Alexander <aalexander@vasco.com>
Subject: Upcoming Interviews

For some time our management team has been thinking about hiring several interns. We decided to offer compensation to the interns in our internship program because in two fields (computer science and information systems) interns are usually paid, which is the norm. However, you may be disappointed to learn that we can offer only three internships.

In working with our nearby state university, we have narrowed the field to six excellent candidates. These six candidates will be interviewed. This is to inform you that you are invited to attend three interviewing sessions for these student candidates. Your presence is required at these sessions to help us avoid making poor selections.

Mark your calendars for the following three times. The first meeting is May 3 in the conference room. The second meeting is May 5 in Office 22 (the conference room was scheduled). On May 9 we can finish up in the conference room. All of the meetings will start at 2 p.m. In view of the fact that your projects need fresh ideas and talented new team members, I should not have to urge you to attend and be well prepared.

Please examine all the candidates' résumés at the company wiki and send me your ranking lists.

Aaron Alexander

[Full contact information]

6.12 Document for Analysis: Weak Employee Suggestion to Boss (L.O. 1–5)

E-Mail Team

YOUR TASK Study the following weak message from an employee to her boss. In teams or in a class discussion, list at least five weaknesses. If your instructor directs, revise to eliminate flabby expressions, long lead-ins, *there is/there are* fillers, trite business expressions, clichés, and buried verbs, and to address lack of parallelism, lack of plain English, and other problems.

To: Daniel Kalanek <dkalanek@fidelityfirst.com>
From: Cheryl Madzar<cmadzar@fidelityfirst.com>
Subject: My Suggestion

Mr. Kalanek,

Pursuant to the fact that you asked for suggestions on how to improve customer relations, I am submitting my idea. I am writing you this message to let you know that I think we can improve customer satisfaction easy by making a change in our counters.

Last December glass barriers were installed at our branch. There are tellers on one side and customers on the other. The barriers have air vents to be able to allow us tellers to carry on communication with our customers. Management thought that these barriers that are bullet proof would prevent and stop thieves from catapulting over the counter.

However, there were customers who were surprised by these large glass partitions. Communication through them is really extremely difficult and hard. Both the customer and the teller have to raise their voices to be heard. It's even more of an inconvenience when you are dealing with a person that is elderly or someone who happens to be from another country. Beyond a shadow of a doubt, these new barriers make customers feel that they are being treated impersonal.

I did research into the matter of these barriers and made the discovery that we are the only bank in town with them. There are many other banks that are trying casual kiosks and open counters to make customers feel that they are more at home.

Although it may be easier said than done, I suggest that we actually give serious consideration to the removal of these barriers as a beginning and initial step toward improving customer relations.

Cheryl Madzar

[Full contact information]

6.13 Document for Analysis: Deficient Report on Use of PowerPoint (L.O. 1–5)

E-Mail Team

YOUR TASK Study the following poorly expressed message from a manager to her team leader. In teams or in a class discussion, list at least five weaknesses. If your instructor directs, revise to remedy these weaknesses. Look for ways to improve readability with bulleted or numbered points.

To: Danika Thorson <dthorson @pinnacle.com>
From: Marcelo Lopez <mlopez@pinnacle.com>
Subject: PowerPoint Tips

Danika,

This message is being written because, pursuant to your request, I attended a seminar about the use of PowerPoint in business presentations. You suggested that there might be tips that I would learn that we could share with other staff members, many of whom make presentations that almost always include PowerPoint. The speaker, Deb Grousbeck, made some very good points on the subject of PowerPoint. There were several points of an important nature that are useful in avoiding what she called "Death by PowerPoint." Our staff members should give consideration to the following:

Create first the message, not the slide. Only after preparing the entire script should you think about how to make an illustration of it.

You should prepare slides with short lines. Your slides should have only four to six words per line. Short lines act as an encouragement to people to listen to you and not read the slide.

Don't put each and every thing on the slide. If you put too much on the slide, your audience will be reading Item C while you are still talking about Item A. As a last and final point, she suggested that presenters think in terms of headlines. What is the main point? What does it mean to the audience?

Please do not hesitate to let me know whether you want me to elaborate and expand on these presentation techniques subsequent to the next staff meeting.

Marcelo

[Full contact information]

6.14 Document for Analysis: Poor Response to Customer Inquiry About Social Media (L.O. 1–5)

E-Mail Team

YOUR TASK Study the following message. In teams or in a class discussion, list at least five weaknesses. If your instructor directs, revise to remedy those weaknesses. Look for ways to improve readability with bulleted or numbered points.

To: Blanca Nunez <bnunez@nunezassociates.com>
From: Tor Macinnis <tmacinnis@allmattersmedia.com>
Subject: Hopping on the Social Media Buzz

Dear Ms. Nunez:

This is a message to thank you for your inquiry regarding All Matters Media! Due to the fact that the buzz around social media is so loud, you're exceedingly smart to want to understand the paths to success before you jump in so that you can avoid mistakes.

Using social media tools and networks involves connecting people, it involves interacting, and being able to share online. There is hardly a day that goes by without hearing about success stories that are truly remarkable coming from businesses getting active on social media sites such as Facebook, Twitter, and LinkedIn.

How can social media help your business? It can drive brand awareness and build customer loyalty. It can make it easy for you to listen to what consumers are saying. In addition to the above, it can create referral business for you. It provides you with an audience that is built in. Social media such as we see on the Web today is a logical extension of what people have been doing for centuries: communicating! Whether you are in the act of building a community to support your customers or whether you are thinking outside the box and want to create a blog to keep the public informed, All Matters Media can put your company in a position at the forefront of this fabulous marketing opportunity.

Thanking you in advance, please drop an e-mail or let me call you to schedule an appointment. Let us give your company the human touch with the creation of an online voice and personality just for you.

Socially yours,

Tor Macinnis

[Full contact information]

6.15 Investigating Writing in Your Field (L.O. 1–5)

How much writing is required by people working in your career area? The best way to learn about on-the-job writing is to talk with someone who has a job similar to the one you hope to have one day.

YOUR TASK Interview someone working in your field of study. Your instructor may ask you to present your findings orally or in a written report. Ask questions such as these: What kind of writing do you do? What kind of planning do you do before writing? Where do you get information? Do you brainstorm? Make lists? Do you compose on a computer or on your iPad? How many e-mail messages do you typically write in a day? How long does it take you to compose a routine one- or two-page memo, e-mail, or letter? Do you revise? How often? Do you have a preferred method for proofreading? When you have questions about grammar and mechanics, what or whom do you consult? Does anyone read your drafts and make suggestions? Can you describe your entire composition process? Do you ever work with others to produce a document? How does this process work? What makes writing easier or harder for you? Have your writing methods and skills changed since you left school?

6.16 How Readable Is Your Apartment Lease? (L.O. 1–3)

E-Mail Ethics Team

Have you read your apartment lease carefully? Did you understand it? Many students—and their friends and family members—are intimidated, frustrated, or just plain lost when they try to comprehend an apartment lease.

YOUR TASK Locate an apartment lease—yours, a friend's, or a family member's. In teams, analyze its format and readability. What size is the paper? How large are the margins? Is the type large or small? How much white space appears on the page? Are paragraphs and sentences long or short? Does the lease contain legalese or obscure language? What makes it difficult to understand? In an e-mail message to your instructor, summarize your team's reaction to the lease. Your instructor may ask you to revise sections or the entire lease to make it more readable. In class, discuss how ethical it is for an apartment owner to expect a renter to read and comprehend a lease while sitting in the rental office.

Test Your Etiquette IQ

New communication platforms and casual workplace environments have blurred the lines of appropriateness, leaving workers wondering how to navigate uncharted waters. Indicate whether the following statements are true or false. Then see if you agree with the responses on p. R-1.

1. Although you would not enter an office with a closed door without knocking, cubicles have no doors. Therefore, it's ridiculous to consider knocking before entering.

   ________ True ________ False

2. As a manager, you learn that your employee Barbara is having exploratory surgery. Other employees ask you why Barbara is missing work. Although you would like to show concern and sympathy, it's better that you not disclose personal information about employees.

   ________ True ________ False

3. In a new position, you are pleasantly surprised to find that your boss is about your age and seems very friendly. The best strategy for your career is to strive to become good buddies with your boss.

   ________ True ________ False

Chat About It

In each chapter you will find five discussion questions related to the chapter material. Your instructor may assign these topics for you to discuss in class, in an online chat room, or on an online discussion board. Some of the discussion topics may require outside research. You may also be asked to read and respond to postings made by your classmates.

TOPIC 1: Many years ago renowned writing expert William Zinsser declared, "Clutter is the disease of American writing. We are a society strangling in unnecessary words, circular constructions, pompous frills and meaningless jargon."[16] Do you think he was too harsh? Do you believe he might feel differently about today's business writing?

TOPIC 2: When you tackle a serious writing project, do you prefer freewriting, in which you rapidly record your thoughts, or do you prefer to polish and revise as you go? What are the advantages and disadvantages of each method for you? Do you use the same method for both short and long messages?

TOPIC 3: Think about your own speaking and writing. Do you have some favorite redundancies that you use in spoken or written messages? What could you say that would be more precise?

TOPIC 4: What proofreading tasks can you safely ask a proofreading buddy to perform? What if that person is not a skilled writer?

TOPIC 5: Are you a good proofreader? Is it easier to find other people's errors than your own? Why? What are you good at finding? What do you frequently miss?

Grammar and Mechanics | *Review 6*

Semicolons and Colons

Review Guides 27 through 30 about semicolons and colons in Appendix D, Grammar and Mechanics Guide, beginning on page D-10. On a separate sheet, revise the following sentences to correct errors in semicolon and colon usage. Do not start new sentences. For each error that you locate, write the guide number that reflects this usage. The more you recognize the reasons, the better you will learn these punctuation guidelines. If a sentence is correct, write *C.* When you finish, check your answers on page Key-2.

EXAMPLE: Companies find it difficult to name new products consequently they often hire specialists.

REVISION: Companies find it difficult to name new **products; consequently,** they often hire specialists.

1. Tech specialists created a snazzy new app, however it lacked an exciting name.
2. Companies find it difficult to name new products consequently they often hire specialists.
3. New product names must be interesting however many of the best names are already taken.
4. Branding a product is a creative endeavor, the name becomes a product's shorthand.
5. Global names must be appealing in such faraway places as Beijing China Toronto Canada and Dubai City United Arab Emirates.
6. One naming expert warned companies with the following comment "Be aware of global consequences. For example, Bimbo is the name of a Mexican baking conglomerate. However, the word in English has an unsavory meaning."
7. Product and company names are developed by combining the following three linguistic elements morphemes, phonemes, and syntax.
8. One of the reasons company names such as Google and Apple work is that they are catchy, however they are also backed by high-quality products.
9. Some English sounds (such as L, V, F, and W) are considered feminine, others (such as X, M, and Z) are viewed as masculine.
10. Among the company officers judging new names were Sierra Love, vice president, Rachel Lohr, CFO, and Megan Cervantes, manager.

References

[1] Sacks, B. (2014, July 11). Taco Bell's health goal: Power protein menu, zero-calorie drinks. *Los Angeles Times*. Retrieved from http://www.latimes.com/business/la-fi-taco-bell-protein-power-menu-20140711-story.html. See also Jargon, J. (2016, March 11). Taco Bell rolls out new $1 menu as battle for breakfast heats up. *The Wall Street Journal*, p. B6.

[2] Northrup, L. (2015, September 15). Taco Bell abruptly closes its upscale 'American-inspired' Taco Restaurant. Consumerist. Retrieved from http://consumerist.com/2015/09/18/taco-bell-abruptly-closes-its-upscale-american-inspired-taco-restaurant

[3] Horovitz, B. (2012, February 20). Taco Bell + Doritos = success? *USA Today*, p. B1.

[4] Elbow, P. (1998). *Writing with power: Techniques for mastering the writing process.* Oxford, UK: Oxford University Press, p. 30.

[5] Cook, C. K. (1985). *Line by line*. Boston: Houghton Mifflin, p. 17.

[6] Shankman, P. (2011, May 20). I will never hire a "social media expert," and neither should you. Retrieved from http://shankman.com/i-will-never-hire-a-social-media-expert-and-neither-should-you

[7] Based on Parmar, B. (2015, April 27). 50 companies that get Twitter – and 50 that don't. *Harvard Business Review*. Retrieved from https://hbr.org/2015/04/the-best-and-worst-corporate-tweeters

[8] Adams, S. (2011, April 9-10). How to get a real education. *The Wall Street Journal*, pp. C1-C2.

[9] Fried, J. (2010, May 1). Why is business writing so awful? *Inc.* magazine. Retrieved from http://www.inc.com/magazine/20100501/why-is-business-writing-so-awful.html

[10] Sword, H. (2012, July 25). Zombie nouns. 3 Quarks Daily. Retrieved from http://www.3quarksdaily.com/3quarksdaily/2012/07/zombie-nouns.html

[11] Levitt, A. (2011, April 2). A word to Wall Street: 'Plain English,' please. *The Wall Street Journal*. Retrieved from http://online.wsj.com/article/SB10001424052748704471904576231002037599510.html

[12] Duffy, S. P. (2007, April 23). Attorney hit with $6.6 million malpractice verdict. Corporate Counsel. Retrieved from http://www.corpcounsel.com/id=900005479447/Attorney-Hit-With-66-Million-Malpractice-Verdict?slreturn=20160203175336 [Inserted new link]

[13] Wells, G. (2015, October 8). How grammar snobs no u ain't mr rite. *The Wall Street Journal*, p. A1.

[14] Masunaga, S. (2015, July 19). How I made it: Taco Bell CEO Brian Niccol. *Los Angeles Times*. Retrieved from http://www.latimes.com/business/la-fi-himi-niccol-20150719-story.html

[15] The trouble with email. (2015, September 13). Business Today. Retrieved from http://businesstodaync.com/the-trouble-with-email

[16] Zinsser, W. (1976). *On writing well*. New York: HarperCollins.

UNIT
3
Workplace Communication
Chapter 7
Short Workplace Messages and Digital Media
Chapter 8
Positive Messages
Chapter 9
Negative Messages
Chapter 10
Persuasive and Sales Messages
Bolyuk Rostyslav/Shutterstock.com

Chapter 7 Short Workplace Messages and Digital Media

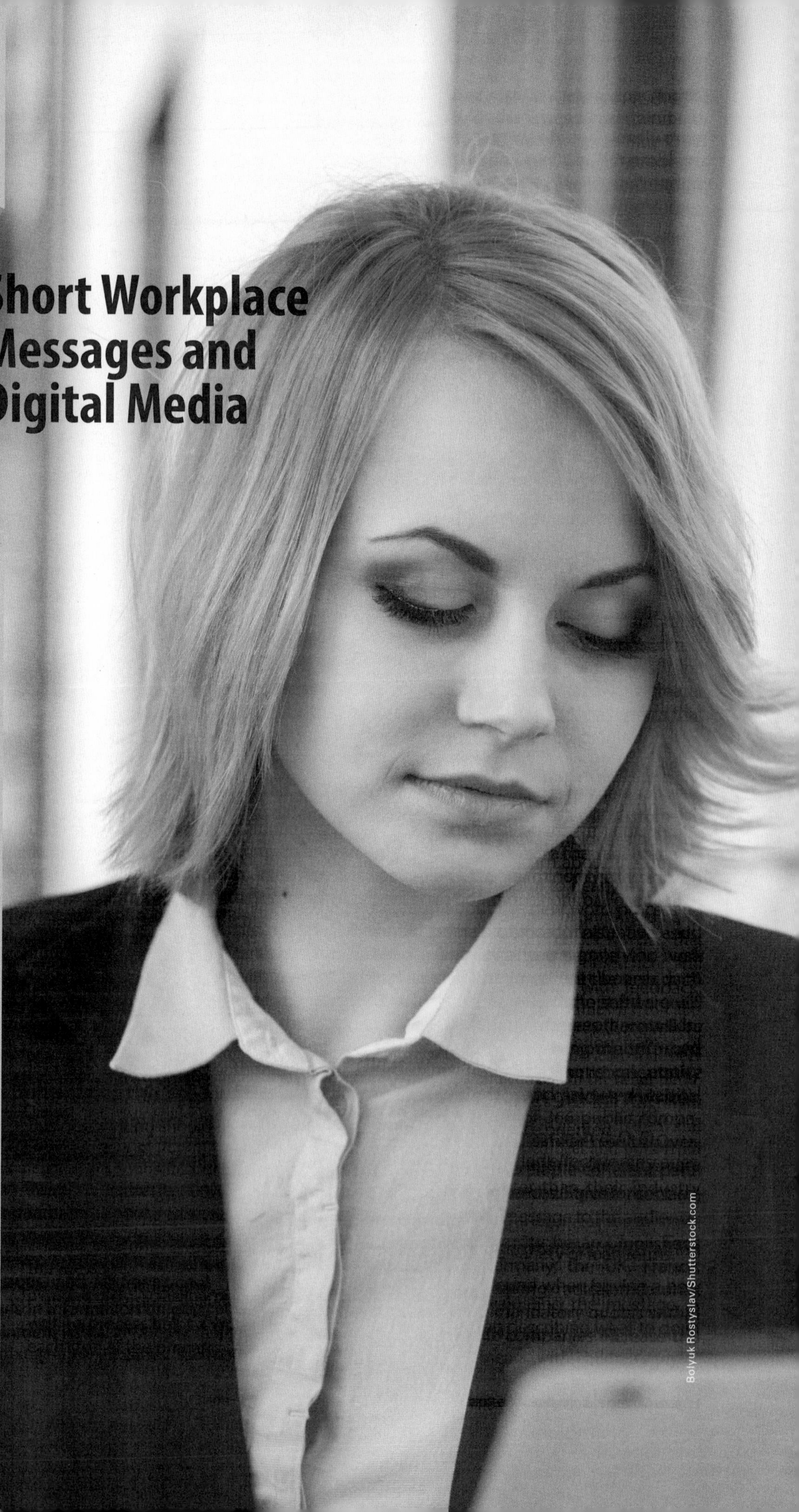

Bolyuk Rostyslav/Shutterstock.com

LEARNING OUTCOMES

After studying this chapter, you should be able to

1 Understand e-mail, memos, and the professional standards for their usage, structure, and format in the digital era workplace.

2 Explain workplace instant messaging and texting as well as their liabilities and best practices.

3 Identify professional applications of podcasts and wikis, and describe guidelines for their use.

4 Describe how businesses use blogs to connect with internal and external audiences, and list best practices for professional blogging.

5 Define business uses of social networking.

Yeamake/Shutterstock.com

Sony Hack Signals the End of Privacy

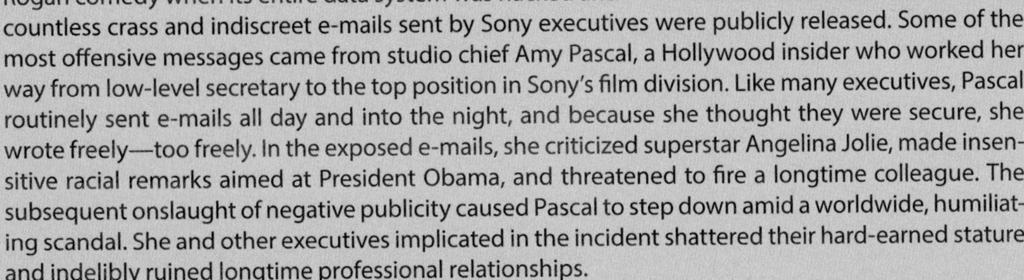

Sony Pictures Entertainment—the global conglomerate headquartered in Los Angeles—has delighted movie viewers with blockbuster film franchises such as *Men in Black* and *Spider-Man*. Recently Sony was about to release a Seth Rogan comedy when its entire data system was hacked and countless crass and indiscreet e-mails sent by Sony executives were publicly released. Some of the most offensive messages came from studio chief Amy Pascal, a Hollywood insider who worked her way from low-level secretary to the top position in Sony's film division. Like many executives, Pascal routinely sent e-mails all day and into the night, and because she thought they were secure, she wrote freely—too freely. In the exposed e-mails, she criticized superstar Angelina Jolie, made insensitive racial remarks aimed at President Obama, and threatened to fire a longtime colleague. The subsequent onslaught of negative publicity caused Pascal to step down amid a worldwide, humiliating scandal. She and other executives implicated in the incident shattered their hard-earned stature and indelibly ruined longtime professional relationships.

E-mail is not the only form of electronic media that has caused people from all walks of life to be shamed. Tasteless text messages have forced members of Congress to resign. An inappropriate e-mail cost a young investment banker not one but two prestigious jobs and is making the rounds on Wall Street.[1] The take-away is clear: Nothing written and sent over digital media is private or confidential simply because any message can be monitored, forwarded, or printed out. The savvy business professional treats every text, instant message, e-mail, and social media post as if it will be seen by the world.

Critical Thinking

- Why should you be prudent when sending or forwarding insensitive comments, even from your personal device?
- How might sending tactless messages affect a career?
- How effective is an apology given after an indiscreet message is revealed?

Writing Digital Age E-Mail Messages and Memos

LEARNING OUTCOME 1

Understand e-mail, memos, and the professional standards for their usage, structure, and format in the digital era workplace.

Communication is rapidly changing in this digital era. The Web has evolved from a mere repository of passively consumed information to Web 2.0 and beyond—a dynamic, interactive, and highly networked environment. Users are empowered, active participants who create content, review products, and edit and share information. As discussed in previous chapters, communicators are increasingly relying on mobile devices. Messages are shorter and more frequent, and response time is much speedier. Social media networks such as Twitter have transformed communication from one-on-one conversations to one-to-many transmissions. For better or worse, citizen journalists have the power to distribute news items and media links to multitudes on the fly. In addition, social networking sites such as Facebook, Pinterest, and Instagram have revolutionized the way we keep in touch with friends and family.

Similarly, in the workplace new devices and technologies are transforming the way we exchange information and conduct business. Ever more data are stored on and accessed from remote networks, not individual computers. This storing and accessing of data along with software applications in remote networks (the cloud) is called *cloud computing.* In many businesses desktop computers, once the mainstay of the office, are becoming obsolete. They're being replaced with ever-smaller laptops, smartphones, tablets, and other powerful mobile devices. Virtual private networks (VPNs) offer secure access to organizations' information from any location in the world that provides an Internet connection. Whether they like it or not, businesspeople are increasingly connected 24/7.

Doubtless you are already connecting digitally with your friends, family, and Internet pals. However, chances are that you need to understand how businesses transmit information electronically and how they use communication technologies. This chapter explores short forms of workplace communication, beginning with e-mail, which many workers love to hate, and memos, which are disappearing but still necessary in many organizations. Moving on to newer media, you will learn about workplace text messaging and interoffice chat applications, corporate blogs, podcasts, wikis, and social networking sites. Learning these workplace technologies and best practices can save you time, reduce blunders, and help you excel as a professional.

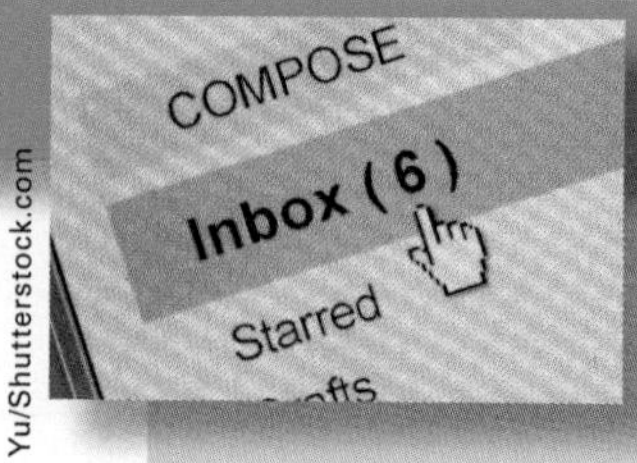

Feng Yu/Shutterstock.com

Reality Check

E-Mail Is Still King at the Office

Predictions of e-mail's demise are premature despite fast-growing communication tools such as Slack and Asana: "People use email because it's the best, most reliable way to get anybody on the planet and none of these other tools let you do that; none of them."[2]

—Ted Schadler, *VP, senior technology analyst with Forrester Research*

E-Mail: Love It or Hate It—But It's Here to Stay

Critics say that e-mail is outdated, inefficient, and slowly dying. They complain that it takes too much time, increases stress, and leaves a dangerous permanent record admissible in a court of law. However, e-mail in the workplace is unlikely to go away. Despite the attention that social media and new messaging software receive in the news, most business messages are still sent by e-mail.[3] Office workers send or receive on average 122 messages a day; that means an e-mail exchange every four minutes, says research firm Radicati Group.[4]

Neither social media, texting, and video chatting, nor phishing, hacking, and spam have diminished the high importance of e-mail in the workplace. Not even fast-growing popular applications such as the interoffice chat program Slack are likely to replace e-mail anytime soon, although Slack is an ideal collaboration tool.[5] E-mail use among American workers has held steady at 61 percent since 2002, according to Pew Research.[6]

E-mail has replaced paper memos for many messages inside organizations and some letters to external audiences. A majority of businesspeople (as high as 70 percent) now first open their e-mail on mobile devices.[7] Because you can expect to use e-mail extensively to communicate at work, it's smart to learn how to do it efficiently and expertly. You may have to adjust your current texting and Facebook posting practices, but turning out professional e-mails is an easily attainable goal.

Why People Complain About E-Mail

Although e-mail is recognized as the mainstay of business communication, it's not always done well. Businesspeople are tired of "untangling a snarl of email threads" and resent "that most people don't take the time to reflect on what they have written or to proofread it before hitting SEND."[8] A *Wall Street Journal* article reported that many business schools were ramping up their writing programs or hiring writing coaches because of complaints about their graduates' skills.[9] Adding to the complaints, Christopher Carlson, recruiting officer at the Tennessee Valley Authority, said that new MBA graduates exchange more than 200 e-mails a day, and some read like text messages. "They're not [even] in complete sentences," he said.[10]

In addition to the complaints about confusing and poorly written e-mails, many people are overwhelmed with too many messages. Social computing expert Gloria Mark says that e-mail use is "out of control," stressing out workers who battle clogged inboxes and check their e-mail 74 times a day on average.[11] Some of those messages are unnecessary, such as those that merely confirm receipt of a message or ones that express thanks. The use of *Reply All* adds to the inbox, irritating those who have to plow through dozens of messages that barely relate to them. Others blame e-mail for eliminating the distinction between work life and home life. They feel an urgency to be available 24/7 and respond immediately.

Ethics Check

Hiding Blind Copies

Some workers use *Bcc* (*blind carbon copy*) to copy their friends and colleagues on e-mails when they don't want the recipient to know that a third party will also read the message. Do you believe that hiding copies from the recipient is harmless and acceptable?

michaeljung/Shutterstock.com

Reality Check

Every Electronic Message Leaves a Trail

"A basic guideline is to assume that others will see what you write, so don't write anything you wouldn't want everyone to see. Don't write anything that would be ruinous to you or hurtful to others. After all, email is dangerously easy to forward, and it's better to be safe than sorry."[12]

—Barbara Pachter, *business etiquette expert and career coach*

Still other e-mail senders fail to recognize how dangerous e-mail can be. After deletion, e-mail files still leave trails on servers within and outside organizations. Messages are also backed up on other servers, making them traceable and recoverable by forensic experts. Long-forgotten messages may turn up in court cases as damaging and sometimes costly evidence. BP engineer Brian Morel e-mailed the following note to a colleague six days before the disastrous explosion of the Deepwater Horizon oil platform off the coast of Louisiana. He said, "This has been a nightmare well which has everyone all over the place." This and other incriminating e-mails prompted BP to agree to an ongoing settlement currently at $28 billion.[13]

Organizations can legally monitor their staff's personal e-mail accounts too if the workers access them on the company's computer network. Moreover, if employees set up their company's e-mail on their smartphones, they have given their employer the right to remotely delete all personal data on that mobile device.[14] Even writers with nothing to hide should be concerned about what may come back to haunt them. Your best bet is to put nothing in an e-mail message that you wouldn't post on your office door. Also be sure that you know your organization's e-mail policy before sending personal messages or forwarding work-related information to your personal e-mail account. Estimates suggest that as many as a third of bosses have fired an employee for an e-mail or Internet-related violation.[15]

Despite its dark side, e-mail has many advantages and remains a prime communication channel. Therefore, it's to your advantage to learn when and how to use it efficiently and safely.

Knowing When E-Mail Is Appropriate

E-mail is appropriate for short, informal messages that request information and respond to inquiries. It is especially effective for messages to multiple receivers and messages that must be archived (saved). An e-mail is also appropriate as a cover document when sending longer attachments.

E-mail, however, is not a substitute for face-to-face conversations or telephone calls. These channels are much more successful if your goal is to convey enthusiasm or warmth, explain a complex situation, present a persuasive argument, or smooth over disagreements. One expert advises delivering messages in person when they "require a human moment"—that is, when they are emotional, require negotiation, and relate to personnel.[16] Managers and employees echo this advice, as revealed in workplace surveys. They were adamant about using face-to-face contact, rather than e-mail, for critical work situations such as human resources annual reviews, discipline, and promotions.[17]

Composing Professional E-Mails

Professional e-mails are quite different from messages you may send to friends. Instead of casual words tossed off in haste, professional e-mails are well-considered messages that involve all three stages of the writing process. They have compelling subject lines, appropriate greetings, well-organized bodies, and complete closing information.

Draft a Compelling but Concise Subject Line. The most important part of an e-mail is its subject line—not surprising when writers can expect that their messages will be viewed on mobile devices. To improve your chances that your e-mails will actually be read, avoid meaningless statements such as *Help, Important,* or *Meeting.* Summarize the purpose of the message clearly and make the receiver want to open the message. Try to include a verb (*Need You to Attend Las Vegas Trade Show*). In some instances the subject line can be the entire message (*Meeting Changed From May 3 to May 10*). Also be sure to adjust the subject line if the topic changes after a thread of replies emerges.

Include a Greeting. To help receivers see the beginning of a message and to help them recognize whether they are the primary or secondary receiver, include a greeting. The greeting sets the tone for the message and reflects your audience analysis. For friends and colleagues, try friendly greetings (*Hi, Sandra, Thanks, Sandra, Good morning, Sandra,* or *Greetings, Sandra*). For more formal messages and those to outsiders, include an honorific and last name (*Dear Ms. Stevens*).

Organize the Body for Readability and Tone. In the revision phase, ask yourself how you could make your message more readable. Did you start directly? Did you group similar topics together? Could some information be presented with bulleted or numbered lists? Could you add headings—especially if the message contains more than a few paragraphs? Do you see any phrases or sentences that could be condensed? Get rid of wordiness, but don't sacrifice clarity. If a longer sentence is necessary for comprehension, then keep it. To convey the best tone, read the message aloud. If it sounds curt, it probably is.

Close Effectively. At the end of your message, include an action statement with due dates and requests. Although complimentary closes are unnecessary, you might include a friendly closing such as *Many thanks* or *Warm regards.* Do include your name because messages without names become confusing when forwarded or when they are part of a long string of responses.

For most messages, include full contact information in a signature block that can be inserted automatically. Figure 7.1 illustrates a typical e-mail with proper formatting.

Controlling Your Inbox

Business communicators love to complain about e-mail, and some young people even deny its existence. In the business world, however, e-mail writing IS business writing.[18] Instead of letting your inbox consume your time and crimp your productivity, you can control it by observing a few time-management strategies.

The most important strategy is checking your e-mail at set times, such as first thing in the morning and again after lunch or at 4 p.m. To avoid being distracted, be sure to turn off your audio and visual alerts. No fair peeking! If mornings are your best working times, check your e-mail later in the day. Let your boss and colleagues know about your schedule for responding.

Another excellent time-saver is the two-minute rule. If you can read and respond to a message within two minutes, then take care of it immediately. For messages that require more time, add them to your to-do list or schedule them on your calendar. To be polite, send a quick note telling the sender when you plan to respond. Google chairman Eric Schmidt offers this advice: "Remember the old OHIO acronym: Only Hold It Once. If you read the note and know what needs doing, do it right away. Otherwise you are dooming yourself to rereading it, which is 100 percent wasted time."[19]

Replying Efficiently With Down-Editing

When answering e-mail, a neat skill to develop is *down-editing.* This involves inserting your responses to parts of the incoming message. After a courteous opening, your reply message will include only the parts of the incoming message to which you are responding. Delete the sender's message headers, signature, and all unnecessary parts. Your responses can be identified with your initials, if more than one person will be seeing the response. Another efficient trick is to use a different color for your down-edits. It takes a little practice to develop this skill, but the down-edited reply reduces confusion, saves writing and reading time, and makes you look super savvy.

Figure 7.2 shows a number of additional best practices for managing your e-mail.

Figure 7.1 Formatting an E-Mail Request

1 Prewriting

Analyze: The purpose of this e-mail is to solicit feedback regarding a casual-dress policy.

Anticipate: The message is going to a subordinate who is busy but probably eager to be consulted in this policy matter.

Adapt: Use a direct approach beginning with the main idea. Strive for a positive, professional tone rather than an autocratic, authoritative tone.

2 Drafting

Research: Collect secondary information about dress-down days in other organizations. Collect primary information by talking with company managers.

Organize: Begin with the main idea followed by a brief explanation and questions. Conclude with an end date and a reason.

Draft: Prepare the first draft remembering that the receiver is busy and appreciates brevity.

3 Revising

Edit: Rewrite questions to ensure that they are parallel and readable.

Proofread: Decide whether to hyphenate *casual-dress policy* and *dress-down days*. Be sure commas follow introductory clauses. Check question marks.

Evaluate: Does this message encourage participatory management? Will the receiver be able to answer the questions and provide feedback as requested?

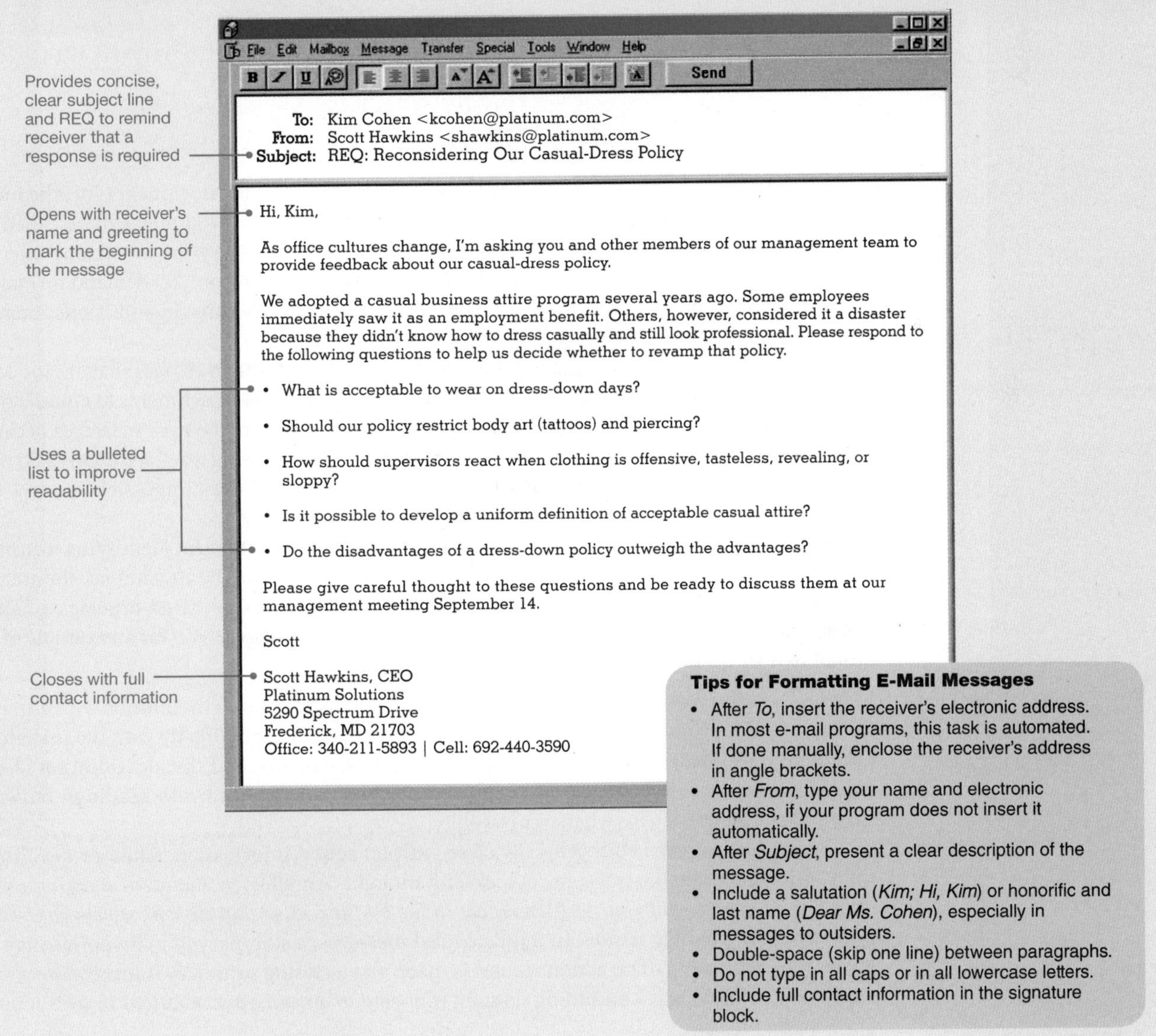

File Edit Mailbox Message Transfer Special Tools Window Help
Send
Provides concise, clear subject line and REQ to remind receiver that a response is required
Opens with receiver's name and greeting to mark the beginning of the message
Uses a bulleted list to improve readability
Closes with full contact information

To: Kim Cohen <kcohen@platinum.com>
From: Scott Hawkins <shawkins@platinum.com>
Subject: REQ: Reconsidering Our Casual-Dress Policy

Hi, Kim,

As office cultures change, I'm asking you and other members of our management team to provide feedback about our casual-dress policy.

We adopted a casual business attire program several years ago. Some employees immediately saw it as an employment benefit. Others, however, considered it a disaster because they didn't know how to dress casually and still look professional. Please respond to the following questions to help us decide whether to revamp that policy.

- What is acceptable to wear on dress-down days?
- Should our policy restrict body art (tattoos) and piercing?
- How should supervisors react when clothing is offensive, tasteless, revealing, or sloppy?
- Is it possible to develop a uniform definition of acceptable casual attire?
- Do the disadvantages of a dress-down policy outweigh the advantages?

Please give careful thought to these questions and be ready to discuss them at our management meeting September 14.

Scott

Scott Hawkins, CEO
Platinum Solutions
5290 Spectrum Drive
Frederick, MD 21703
Office: 340-211-5893 | Cell: 692-440-3590

Tips for Formatting E-Mail Messages

- After *To*, insert the receiver's electronic address. In most e-mail programs, this task is automated. If done manually, enclose the receiver's address in angle brackets.
- After *From*, type your name and electronic address, if your program does not insert it automatically.
- After *Subject*, present a clear description of the message.
- Include a salutation (*Kim; Hi, Kim*) or honorific and last name (*Dear Ms. Cohen*), especially in messages to outsiders.
- Double-space (skip one line) between paragraphs.
- Do not type in all caps or in all lowercase letters.
- Include full contact information in the signature block.

Figure 7.2 **Best Practices for Better E-Mail**

Getting Started

- Don't write if another channel—such as IM, social media, or a phone call—might work better.
- Send only content you would want published.
- Write compelling subject lines, possibly with names and dates: *Jake: Can You Present at January 10 Staff Meeting?*

Replying

- Scan all e-mails, especially those from the same person. Answer within 24 hours or say when you will.
- Change the subject line if the topic changes. Check the threaded messages below yours.
- Practice down-editing; include only the parts from the incoming e-mail to which you are responding.
- Start with the main idea.
- Use headings and lists.

Observing Etiquette

- Obtain approval before forwarding.
- Soften the tone by including a friendly opening and closing.
- Resist humor and sarcasm. Absent facial expression and tone of voice, humor can be misunderstood.
- Avoid writing in all caps, which is like SHOUTING.

Closing Effectively

- End with due dates, next steps to be taken, or a friendly remark.
- Add your full contact information including social media addresses.
- Edit your text for readability. Proofread for typos or unwanted auto-corrections.
- Double-check before hitting **Send.**

Writing Interoffice Memos

In addition to e-mail, you should be familiar with another workplace document type, the interoffice memorandum. Although e-mail has largely replaced memos, you may still be called on to use the memo format in specific instances. Memos are necessary for important internal messages that (a) are too long for e-mail, (b) require a permanent record, (c) demand formality, or (d) inform employees who may not have access to e-mail. Within organizations, memos deliver changes in procedures, official instructions, and reports.

The memo format is particularly necessary for complex internal messages that are too long for e-mail. Prepared as memos, long messages are then delivered as attachments to e-mail cover messages. Memos seem to function better as permanent records than e-mail messages because the latter may be difficult to locate and may contain a trail of confusing replies. E-mails also may change the origination date whenever the file is accessed, thus making it impossible to know the original date of the message.

When preparing e-mail attachments, be sure that they carry sufficient identifying information. Because the cover e-mail message may become separated from the attachment, the attachment must be fully identified. Preparing the e-mail attachment as a memo provides a handy format that identifies the date, sender, receiver, and subject. See Figure 10.9 for an example of an e-mail sent with a memo attachment.

Similarities Between Memos and E-Mails. Memos have much in common with e-mails. Both usually carry nonsensitive information that may be organized directly with the main idea first. Both have guide words calling for a subject line, a dateline, and the identification of the sender and receiver. To enhance readability, both should be organized with headings, bulleted lists, and enumerated items whenever possible.

E-mails and memos both generally close with (a) action information, dates, or deadlines; (b) a summary of the message; or (c) a closing thought. An effective memo or e-mail closing might be, *Please submit your written report to me by June 15 so that we can review your data before our July planning session.* In more detailed messages, a summary of main points may be an appropriate closing. If no action request is made and a closing summary is unnecessary, you might end with a simple concluding thought (*I'm glad to answer your questions* or *This sounds like a useful project*).

You need not close messages to coworkers with goodwill statements such as those found in letters to customers or clients. However, some closing thought is often necessary to avoid sounding abrupt. Closings can show gratitude or encourage feedback with remarks such as *I sincerely appreciate your help* or *What are your ideas on this proposal?* Other closings look forward to what's next, such as *How would you like to proceed?* Avoid closing with overused expressions such as *Please let me know if I may be of further assistance.* This ending sounds mechanical and insincere.

In Figure 7.3, notice how interoffice memos are formatted and how they can be created to improve readability with lists and white space. The accompanying checklist offers tips for creating professional e-mail messages and memos.

Figure 7.3 **Formatting an Interoffice Memo**

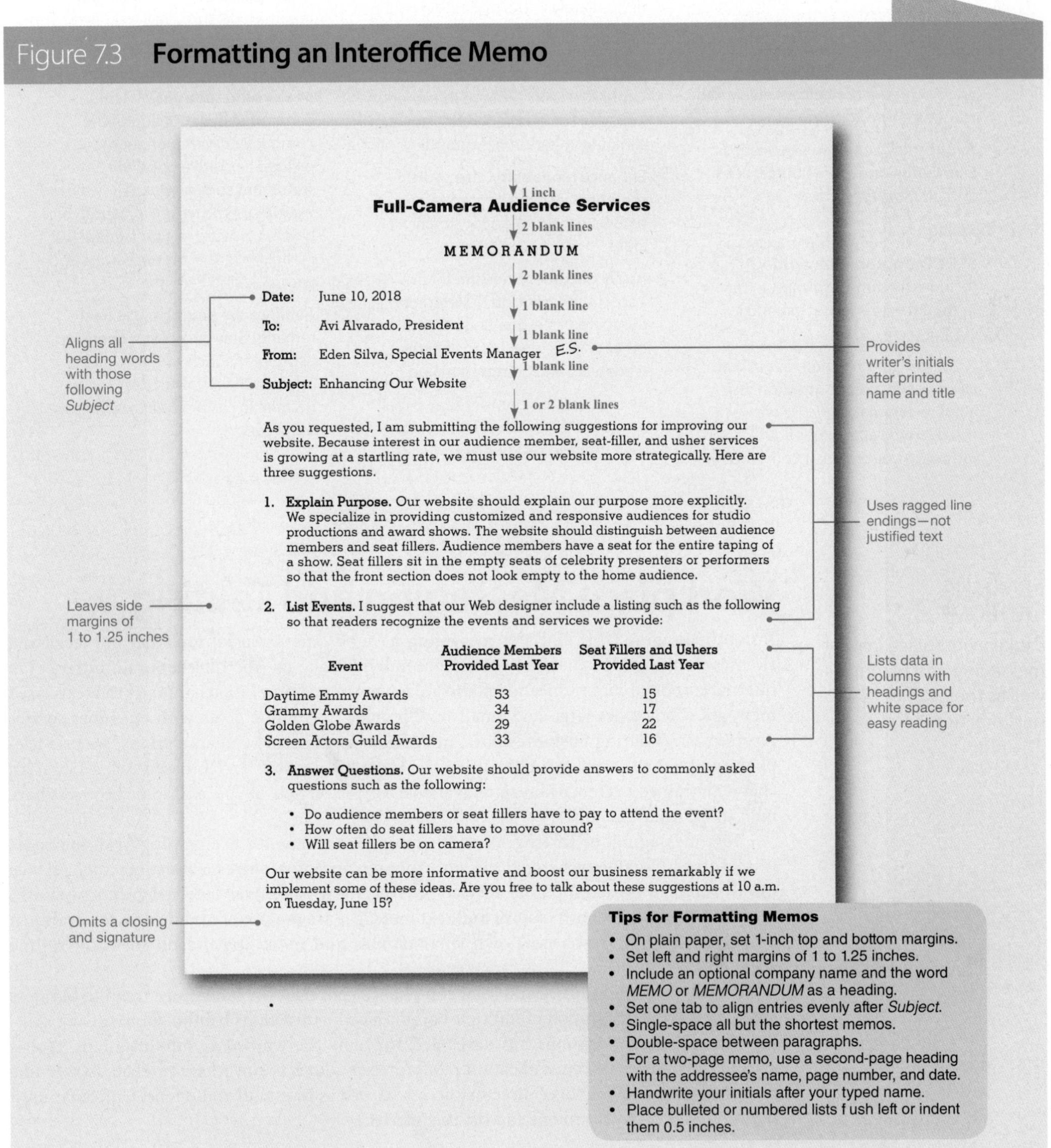

Full-Camera Audience Services

MEMORANDUM

Date: June 10, 2018

To: Avi Alvarado, President

From: Eden Silva, Special Events Manager *E.S.*

Subject: Enhancing Our Website

As you requested, I am submitting the following suggestions for improving our website. Because interest in our audience member, seat-filler, and usher services is growing at a startling rate, we must use our website more strategically. Here are three suggestions.

1. **Explain Purpose.** Our website should explain our purpose more explicitly. We specialize in providing customized and responsive audiences for studio productions and award shows. The website should distinguish between audience members and seat fillers. Audience members have a seat for the entire taping of a show. Seat fillers sit in the empty seats of celebrity presenters or performers so that the front section does not look empty to the home audience.

2. **List Events.** I suggest that our Web designer include a listing such as the following so that readers recognize the events and services we provide:

Event	Audience Members Provided Last Year	Seat Fillers and Ushers Provided Last Year
Daytime Emmy Awards	53	15
Grammy Awards	34	17
Golden Globe Awards	29	22
Screen Actors Guild Awards	33	16

3. **Answer Questions.** Our website should provide answers to commonly asked questions such as the following:

   - Do audience members or seat fillers have to pay to attend the event?
   - How often do seat fillers have to move around?
   - Will seat fillers be on camera?

Our website can be more informative and boost our business remarkably if we implement some of these ideas. Are you free to talk about these suggestions at 10 a.m. on Tuesday, June 15?

1 inch
2 blank lines
2 blank lines
1 blank line
1 blank line
1 blank line
1 or 2 blank lines
Aligns all heading words with those following *Subject*
Provides writer's initials after printed name and title
Uses ragged line endings—not justified text
Leaves side margins of 1 to 1.25 inches
Lists data in columns with headings and white space for easy reading
Omits a closing and signature

Tips for Formatting Memos

- On plain paper, set 1-inch top and bottom margins.
- Set left and right margins of 1 to 1.25 inches.
- Include an optional company name and the word *MEMO* or *MEMORANDUM* as a heading.
- Set one tab to align entries evenly after *Subject.*
- Single-space all but the shortest memos.
- Double-space between paragraphs.
- For a two-page memo, use a second-page heading with the addressee's name, page number, and date.
- Handwrite your initials after your typed name.
- Place bulleted or numbered lists f ush left or indent them 0.5 inches.

CHECKLIST

Professional E-Mail and Memos

Subject Line

- **Summarize the central idea.** Express concisely what the message is about and how it relates to the reader.
- **Include labels if appropriate.** Labels such as *FYI* (*for your information*) and *REQ* (*required*) help receivers recognize how to respond.
- **Avoid empty or dangerous words.** Don't write one-word subject lines such as *Help, Problem*, or *Free.*

Opening

- **State the purpose for writing.** Include the same information that is in the subject line, but expand it.
- **Highlight questions.** If you are requesting information, begin with the most important question, use a polite command (*Please answer the following questions about*...), or introduce your request courteously.
- **Supply information directly.** If responding to a request, give the reader the requested information immediately in the opening. Explain later.

Body

- **Explain details.** Arrange information logically. For detailed topics develop separate coherent paragraphs.
- **Enhance readability.** Use short sentences, short paragraphs, and parallel construction for similar ideas.
- **Apply document design.** If appropriate, provide bulleted or numbered lists, headings, tables, or other graphic devices to improve readability and comprehension.
- **Be cautious.** Remember that e-mail messages often travel far beyond their intended audiences.

Closing

- **Request action.** If appropriate, state specifically what you want the reader to do. Include a deadline, with reasons, if possible.
- **Provide a goodwill statement or a closing thought.** When communicating outside of the company or with management, include a positive goodwill statement such as *Our team enjoyed working on the feasibility report, and we look forward to your feedback*. If no action request is necessary, end with a closing thought.
- **Avoid cliché endings.** Use fresh remarks. Stay away from overused expressions such as *If you have additional questions, please do not hesitate to call* or *Thank you for your cooperation.*

LEARNING OUTCOME 2

Explain workplace instant messaging and texting as well as their liabilities and best practices.

Workplace Messaging and Texting

Instant messaging (IM) and text messaging have become powerful tools beyond teens and twentysomethings. IM enables two or more individuals to use the Internet or an intranet (an internal corporate communication platform) to chat in real time by exchanging brief text-based messages. Companies large and small now provide live online chats with customer service representatives during business hours, in addition to the usual contact options, such as telephone and e-mail. Academic libraries in the United States staff a Web-based Ask a Librarian chat with trained reference librarians available 24/7. Facebook, Skype, and some browsers have built-in IM (chat) functions.

Text messaging, or texting, is another popular means for exchanging brief messages in real time. Usually exchanged via smartphone, texting requires a short message service (SMS) supplied by a cell phone service provider or a voice over Internet protocol (VoIP) service. Increasingly, both instant and text messages are sent from mobile devices as almost 64 percent of Americans now own smartphones and many depend on them for online access.[20]

Fueled by online security and legal compliance concerns, the other huge trend in business enterprises is the integration of multiple communication functions behind corporate firewalls. For example, Adobe Systems has developed Unicom. The Unified Communications Tool is an all-in-one internal communication platform that connects coworkers by chat, Twitter-like microblogging, and employee directory access, as well as by e-mail and phone. Unicom is used in the office or remotely, in one easy-to-use interface.

Maxal Tamor/Shutterstock.com

Our reliance on our smartphones is undeniable—but not for making calls. The average American makes or answers only six phone calls a day. However, smartphones (and thumbs!) get a workout from sending and responding to text messages. The average American receives 30 texts a day and spends 26 minutes texting. Because many send the messages on the fly, texting in work contexts can be fraught with pitfalls. Sending a text to the wrong person can lead to misunderstandings and embarrassment. The autocorrect feature often creates awkward and bizarre statements that require apologies and do-overs. In which situations would a text message be more effective than a phone call?[21]

Web 2.0 social media campaigns are also usually integrated, meaning that they employ several social networks at once to increase the effectiveness of an appeal. For the sake of simplicity, however, we will examine the short-form functions separately.

The Technology Behind Instant Messaging and Texting

Many large companies provide enterprise-grade IM secured by a firewall. However, smaller companies and most of us might use a popular smartphone app such as WhatsApp, Facebook Messenger, QQ, or WeChat. Apps enable people to use IM on their handheld devices such as the iPhone, the Android smartphone, or a tablet. Smartphones and tablets require a 3G or 4G cell phone network, but they also allow generally free Wi-Fi access where available.

Originally, IM communication was primarily exchanged between two computers that were linked by servers. To chat, each party needed to download a piece of software called a client. Increasingly, though, IM services are Web-based and mobile. They have evolved from text chat to allow voice and video chat (e.g., Google Hangouts, FaceTime, Snapchat, AIM, and Skype) with no need to install an IM client. You can then exchange messages such as those shown in Figure 7.4.

Texting, on the other hand, usually requires a smartphone, and users pay for the service, often a flat rate for a certain number of text or media messages per month. Some VoIP providers such as RingCentral and Skype offer texting. For a small fee, Skype subscribers can send text messages to SMS-enabled phones in the United States and instant messages both domestically and internationally. Again, Skype and other formerly computer-based applications are simultaneously available on mobile devices and are making communication on the go more convenient than ever before.

Impact of Instant Messaging and Texting

Text messaging and IM are convenient alternatives to the telephone and are replacing e-mail for short internal communication. French IT giant Atos switched its in-house communication entirely from e-mail to a Facebook-style interface and instant messaging called blueKiwi.[22] More than 3.2 billion IM accounts worldwide[23] attest to IM's popularity. As many as 67 percent of business professionals use text and instant messaging.[24]

Benefits of IM and Texting. The major attraction of instant messaging is real-time communication with colleagues anywhere in the world—as long as a cell phone signal or a Wi-Fi

Figure 7.4 Instant Messaging for Brief, Fast Communication

Figure 7.4 shows a brief IM exchange between a supervisor and a subordinate. Both are using a secure enterprise-grade IM program.

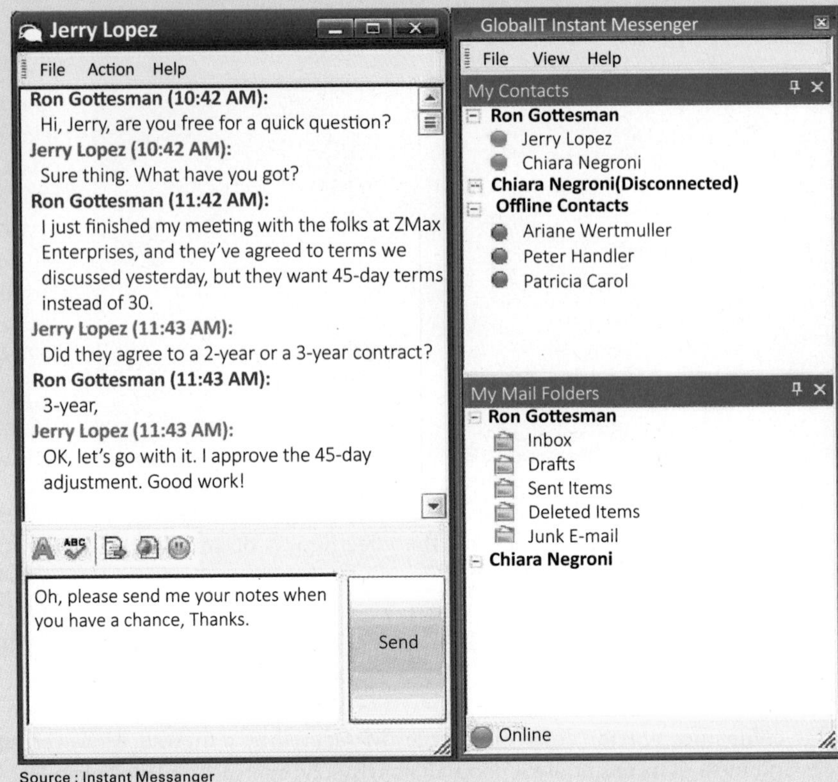

Source : Instant Messanger

connection is available. Because IM allows people to share information immediately and make decisions quickly, its impact on business communication has been dramatic. Group online chat capabilities in enterprise-grade IM applications allow coworkers on far-flung project teams to communicate instantly. An application such as Slack can replace e-mail for collaboration and real-time messaging.

Like IM, texting can be a low-cost substitute for voice calls, delivering a message between private mobile phone users fast, quietly, and discreetly. Organizations around the world provide news alerts, financial information, and promotions to customers via text. Credit card accounts can be set up to notify account holders by text or e-mail of approaching payment deadlines. Verizon Wireless sends automated texts helping customers track their data usage. Aeropostale, Best Buy, Pizza Hut, Staples, Vans, and hundreds of other businesses connect with consumers by opt-in text messaging. Text alerts sent by Old Navy are shown in Figure 7.5.

The immediacy of instant and text messaging has created many fans. A user knows right away whether a message was delivered. Messaging avoids phone tag and eliminates the downtime associated with personal telephone conversations. Another benefit includes *presence functionality*. Coworkers can locate each other online, thus avoiding wild goose chases hunting someone who is out of the office. Many people consider instant messaging and texting productivity boosters because they enable users to get answers quickly and allow multitasking.

Risks of IM and Texting. Despite their popularity among workers, some organizations forbid employees to use instant and text messaging for a number of reasons. Employers consider instant messaging yet another distraction in addition to the telephone, e-mail, and the Internet. Some organizations also fear that employees using free consumer-grade instant

Figure 7.5 Old Navy Uses SMS Marketing

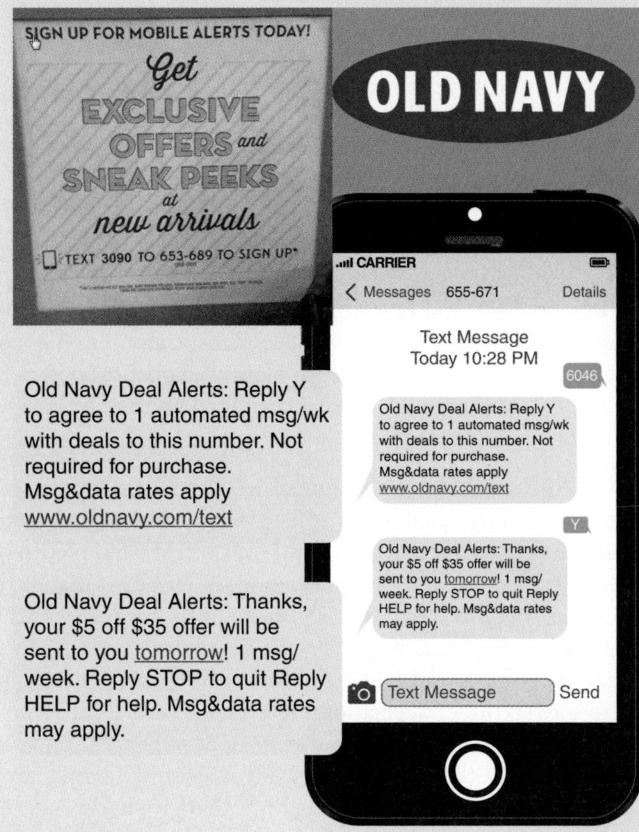
SIGN UP FOR MOBILE ALERTS TODAY!
Get EXCLUSIVE OFFERS and SNEAK PEEKS at new arrivals
TEXT 3090 TO 653-689 TO SIGN UP*
OLD NAVY
CARRIER
Messages 655-671
Details
Text Message
Today 10:28 PM
6046
Old Navy Deal Alerts: Reply Y to agree to 1 automated msg/wk with deals to this number. Not required for purchase. Msg&data rates apply www.oldnavy.com/text
Y
Old Navy Deal Alerts: Thanks, your $5 off $35 offer will be sent to you tomorrow! 1 msg/ week. Reply STOP to quit Reply HELP for help. Msg&data rates may apply.
Text Message
Send

Source : Tatango

Old Navy encourages consumers to sign up for its mobile alert program. Once customers opt in by texting their nearest store's number to the dedicated short code 653-689 (old-navy), they receive text messages announcing sneak peeks at new merchandise, rebates, and exclusive offers.

messaging systems will reveal privileged information and company records. The financial sector is particularly vulnerable to charges of impropriety such as insider trading; firms ranging from JPMorgan Chase, Barclays, and Citigroup to RBS have banned instant messaging for external use.[25] Large corporations are protecting themselves by taking instant messaging behind the firewall where they can log and archive traffic. They are also warning employees to avoid clicking links within messages—even when those messages appear to be from high-ranking company officials.

MALWARE ALERT

Rawpixel.com/Shutterstock.com

Reality Check

Waltzing Right Past the Firewall

"If the bad guys can get an employee to give up his or her user credentials or download some malware, they can likely waltz right past the technological controls looking for all intents and purposes as if they belong there."[26]

—Dirk Anderson, *regional vice president, security firm, Coalfire Systems, Inc.*

Liability Burden. A worker's improper use of mobile devices while on company business can expose the organization to staggering legal liability. A jury awarded $18 million to a victim struck by a transportation company's big rig whose driver had been checking text messages. Another case resulted in a $21 million verdict to a woman injured by a trucker who had used a cell phone while driving a company truck. A construction firm had to pay $4.75 million to a man injured by a driver using a company-provided cell phone.[27] Overall, as many as 34 percent of Americans admit to having texted while driving. Such DWI (driving while intexticated) is rampant. In one year alone, 1.3 million crashes, or 23 percent of all collisions, involved cell phones.[28] Unfortunately, 77 percent of young adults are confident that they can safely text and drive.[29]

Organizations are fighting back to raise awareness and diminish liability. They are instituting detailed digital age e-policies, offering formal employee training, and using technology tools such as monitoring, filtering, and blocking. In one survey, more than half of employers stated that they monitor the Internet (66 percent); 43 percent monitored e-mail, 36 percent monitored social media, and 12 percent monitored blogs. Personal use restrictions of e-mail are enforced by a full 83 percent of organizations; more than a third of businesses also enforce personal use rules for company IM and texting.[30]

Security and Legal Requirements. Companies also worry about phishing (fraudulent schemes), viruses, malware (malicious software programs), and spim (IM spam). Like e-mail, instant and text messages as well as all other electronic records are subject to discovery (disclosure); that is, they can become evidence in lawsuits. Wall Street regulatory agencies NASD, SEC, and NYSE require that IM exchanged between brokers and clients be retained for three to six years, much like e-mail and printed documents.[31] Moreover, companies fear instant messaging and texting because the services necessitate that businesses track and store messaging conversations to comply with legal requirements. This task may be overwhelming. In addition, IM and texting have been implicated in inappropriate uses such as bullying and the notorious sexting. Currently, banks are terrified that employees will fall prey to spear phishing (clicking links that give hackers access to sensitive information).[32]

Best Practices for Instant Messaging and Texting

The effectiveness of short messaging for marketing is impressive if the appeal is done right. When UPS needed to hire 50,000 seasonal workers at the end of the year, its integrated social media effort drove over a million potential job candidates to view online videos about the shipping company, resulting in 150,000 applications. The SMS text campaign alone attracted more than 31,000 applicants and cost just $30,000, a respectable return on investment.[33]

Aside from digital marketing, instant messaging and texting can save time and simplify communication with coworkers and customers. Before using IM or text messaging on the job, be sure you have permission. Do not download and use software without checking with your supervisor. If your organization does allow IM or texting, you can use it efficiently and professionally by following these guidelines:

- Adhere to company policies at all times: netiquette rules, code of conduct, ethics guidelines, as well as harassment and discrimination policies.[34]
- Don't use IM or text messages to disclose sensitive information: financial, company, customer, employee, or executive data.
- Steer clear of harassment and discriminatory content against classes protected by law (race, color, religion, sex, sexual orientation, national origin, age, and disability).
- Be vigilant about the appropriateness of photos, videos, and art that you link to or forward.

- As with e-mail, don't say anything that would damage your reputation or that of your organization.
- Don't text or IM while driving a car. Pull over if you must read or send a message.
- Organize your contact lists to separate business contacts from family and friends.
- Avoid unnecessary chitchat, and know when to say goodbye. If personal messaging is allowed, keep it to a minimum.
- Keep your presence status up-to-date so that people trying to reach you don't waste their time. Make yourself unavailable when you need to meet a deadline.
- Beware of jargon, slang, and abbreviations; although they may reduce keystrokes, they can be confusing and appear unprofessional.
- Use good grammar and proper spelling.

Text Messaging and Business Etiquette

Texting is quick and unobtrusive, and for routine messages it is often the best alternative to a phone call or e-mail. Given the popularity of text messaging, etiquette experts are taking note.[35] Figure 7.6 summarizes the suggestions they offer for the considerate and professional use of texting.

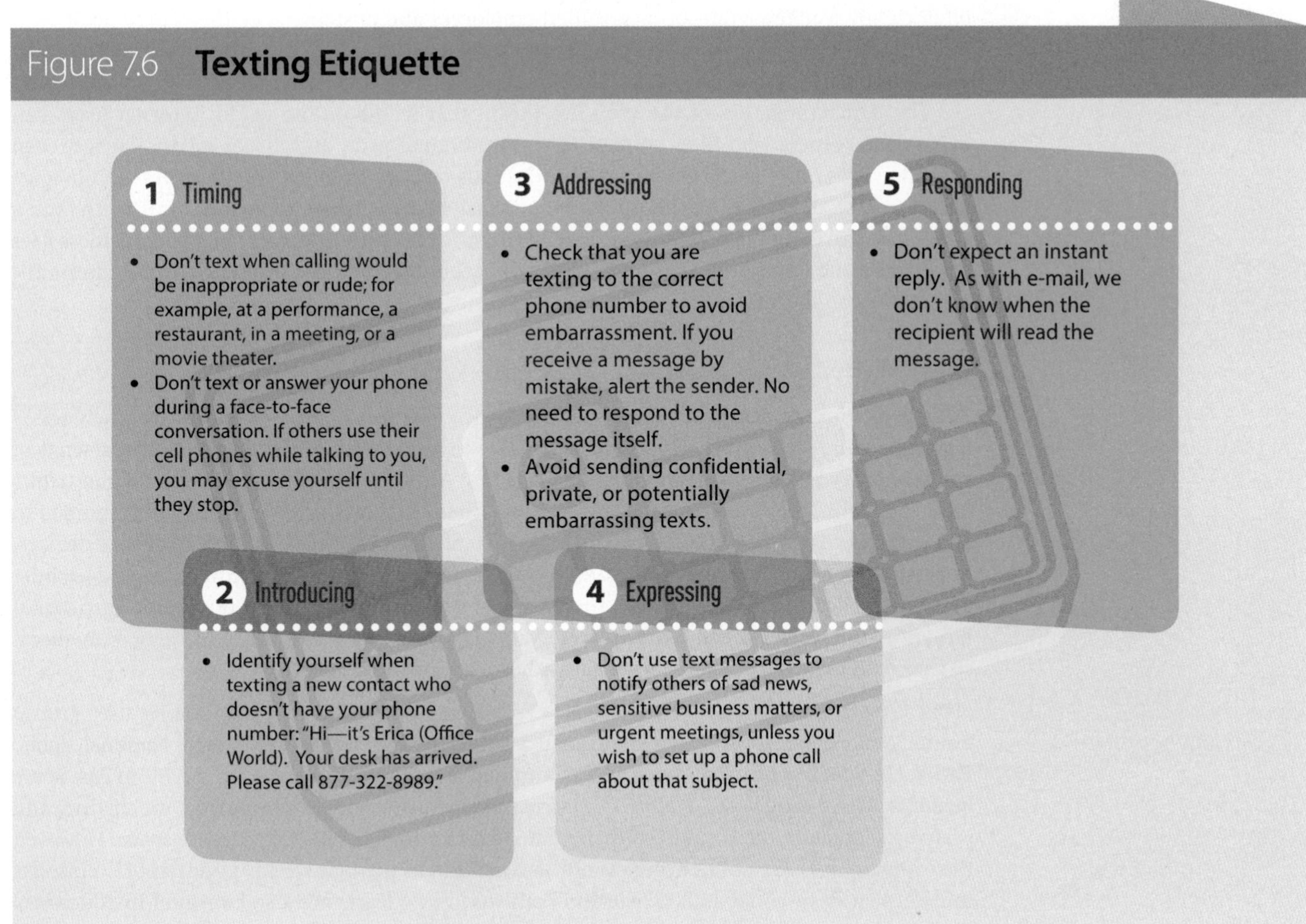
Figure 7.6 **Texting Etiquette**

1 Timing
• Don't text when calling would be inappropriate or rude; for example, at a performance, a restaurant, in a meeting, or a movie theater.
• Don't text or answer your phone during a face-to-face conversation. If others use their cell phones while talking to you, you may excuse yourself until they stop.
2 Introducing
• Identify yourself when texting a new contact who doesn't have your phone number: "Hi—it's Erica (Office World). Your desk has arrived. Please call 877-322-8989."
3 Addressing
• Check that you are texting to the correct phone number to avoid embarrassment. If you receive a message by mistake, alert the sender. No need to respond to the message itself.
• Avoid sending confidential, private, or potentially embarrassing texts.
4 Expressing
• Don't use text messages to notify others of sad news, sensitive business matters, or urgent meetings, unless you wish to set up a phone call about that subject.
5 Responding
• Don't expect an instant reply. As with e-mail, we don't know when the recipient will read the message.

Bloomicon/Shutterstock.com

Reality Check

Jump Starting Collaboration With Wikis

"Wikis are where work gets done. A blog can disseminate information to a wider audience, but to get work done, you go to a wiki, where you collaborate, iterate, pull information together from disparate sources and then hammer something into actionable information."[36]

—Aaron Fulkerson, *cofounder and CEO of software provider MindTouch*

LEARNING OUTCOME 3

Identify professional applications of podcasts and wikis, and describe guidelines for their use.

Making Podcasts and Wikis Work for Business

In the digital era, empowered by interactivity, individuals wield enormous influence because they can potentially reach huge audiences. Far from being passive consumers, today's Internet users have the power to create Web content; interact with businesses and each other; review products, self-publish, or blog; contribute to wikis; and tag and share images and other files. Businesses often rightly fear the wrath of disgruntled employees and customers, or they curry favor with influential plugged-in opinion leaders, the so-called influencers. Like Twitter, other communication technologies such as podcasts and wikis are part of the user-centered virtual environment.

The democratization of the Web has meant that in the online world, Internet users can bypass gatekeepers who filter content in the traditional print and visual media. Hence, even extreme views often reach audiences of thousands or even millions. The dangers are obvious. Fact checking often falls by the wayside, buzz may become more important than truth, and a single keystroke can make or destroy a reputation. This section addresses prudent business uses of podcasts and wikis because you are likely to encounter these and other electronic communication tools on the job.

Business Podcasts or Webcasts

Perhaps because podcasts are elaborate to produce and require quality hardware, their use is lagging behind that of other digital media. However, they have their place in the arsenal of contemporary business communication strategies. Although the terms *podcast* and *podcasting* have caught on, they are somewhat misleading. The words *broadcasting* and *iPod* combined to create the word *podcast*; however, audio and video files can be played on any number of devices, not just Apple's iPod. *Webcasting* for audio content and *vcasting* for video content would be more accurate. Podcasts can extend from short clips of a few minutes to 30-minute or longer digital files. Most are recorded, but some are live. Naturally, large video files gobble up a lot of memory, so they tend to be streamed on a website rather than downloaded.

How Organizations Use Podcasts. Podcasting has found its place among user groups online. Major news organizations and media outlets podcast radio shows (e.g., National Public Radio, *Harvard Business Review*) as well as commentaries about TV shows, from ABC to Fox. Some businesses have caught on. WEBS, the largest independent retailer of knitting, crocheting, and weaving supplies in the United States, operates out of a 16,000-square-foot store space. However, the company sells most of its products online thanks to its popular weekly podcasts (427 episodes to date) that draw about 13,000 listeners each week.[37] Podcasts are also common in education. Students can access instructors' lectures, interviews, sporting events, and other content. Apple's iTunes U is perhaps the best-known example of free educational podcasts from Berkeley, Stanford, and other universities. Podcasts encoded as MP3 files can be downloaded to a computer, a smartphone, a tablet, or an MP3 player to be enjoyed on the go, often without Web access.

Delivering and Accessing Podcasts. Businesses have embraced podcasting for audio and video messages that do not require a live presence yet offer a friendly human face. Because they can broadcast repetitive information that does not require interaction, podcasts can replace costlier live teleconferences. IBM is training its sales force with podcasts that are available anytime. The company also provides developerWorks video podcasts for software engineers and others. Real estate agents create podcasts to enable buyers to take virtual walking tours of available homes at their leisure. For example, The Corcoran Group's channel on YouTube features professionally produced videos of luxurious real estate properties in New York. Human resources policies can also be presented in the form of podcasts for unlimited viewing on demand.

Podcasts are featured on media websites and company portals or shared on blogs and social networking sites, often with links to YouTube and Vimeo. They can usually be streamed or downloaded as media files. Entrepreneur on Fire, shown in Figure 7.7, provides popular podcasts on many business topics of particular interest to entrepreneurs. The growth in smartphone use and other technological advances have boosted the reach and popularity of podcasting: a Pew survey found that 33 percent of Americans 12 years of age and older had listened to at least one podcast. The percentage of those who had listened to a podcast in the past month has almost doubled within one decade, from 9 to 17 percent. Roughly half of Americans stated they are aware of podcasting.[38]

Experts advise business podcasters first to provide quality content with an authentic voice to build value, and to consider money making second.[39] To browse and learn from popular favorites, search for *iTunes Charts*, a site displaying the top 100 most popular podcasts, some business-related (e.g., Freakonomics Radio, Planet Money, and audio versions of TED talks). Podcast Awards, an annual ranking of favorites selected by listeners and podcasters, is another resource for finding valuable podcasts in various categories, including business, science, and technology.

Collaborating With Wikis

Wikis are another feature of the interactive, participatory Web 2.0 environment. As discussed in Chapter 4, a wiki is a Web-based tool that employs easy-to-use collaborative software to allow multiple users collectively to create, access, and modify documents. Think Wikipedia, the well-known online encyclopedia. You will find wikis in numerous subject categories on the Internet.

Figure 7.7 **Entrepreneur on Fire Podcasts**

With its engaging daily episodes, John Lee Dumas' Entrepreneur on Fire is among the most popular business podcasts today. Dumas hosts various experts discussing topics relevant to entrepreneurs. A tally of Dumas' monthly earnings may be a potentially noteworthy and motivating feature for aspiring business tycoons who visit the EOFire podcast portal.

Wiki editors may be given varying access privileges and control over the cloud-based material; however, many public wikis are open to anyone. Not surprisingly, some organizations with a top-down culture fear the openness of wikis, and adoption rates have slowed despite the need of larger businesses for rigorous *knowledge management*.[40]

Two major advantages of wikis come to mind. First, wikis capitalize on *crowdsourcing*, which can be defined as the practice of tapping into the combined knowledge of a large community to solve problems and complete assignments. Second, working on the same content jointly eliminates the infamous problem of version confusion. Most wikis store all changes and intermediate versions of files, so that users can return to previous stages if necessary.

Benefits of corporate wikis include enhancing the reputation of expert contributors, making work flow more easily, and improving an organization's processes.[41] Tech companies tend to adopt new collaboration tools faster than more traditional organizations do. IBM, for example, uses 14 wikis to share documentation for its IBM Collaboration Solutions software and WebSphere products and to interact with the community of adopters. Networking giant Cisco Systems also encourages the free flow of information facilitated by wikis.

How Businesses Use Wikis. Enterprises using wikis usually store their internal data on an intranet, a private network. An enterprise-level wiki serves as an easy-to-navigate, efficient central repository of company information, complete with hyperlinks and keywords pointing to related subjects and media. The four main uses of wikis in business, shown in Figure 7.8,[42] range from providing a shared internal knowledge base to storing templates for business documents.

Popular simple-to-use wiki hosting services, called *wiki farms*, are PBworks, Wikia, Wikidot, Ourproject.org, eXo Cloud, and Wikispaces. Some are noncommercial. Consider starting a wiki for your next classroom project requiring teamwork. Alternatively, explore Google Docs and Google Sites, both now categorized with other applications under the new general label Google Apps for Work.

Figure 7.8 **Four Main Uses for Business Wikis**

The global wiki

For companies with a global reach, a wiki is an ideal tool for information sharing between headquarters and satellite offices. Far-flung team members can easily edit their work and provide input to the home office and each other.

The wiki knowledge base

Teams or departments use wikis to collect and disseminate information to large audiences creating a database for knowledge management. For example, human resources managers may update employee policies, make announcements, and convey information about benefits.

Wikis for meetings

Wikis can facilitate feedback from employees before and after meetings and serve as repositories of meeting minutes. In fact, wikis may replace some meetings, yet still keep a project on track.

Wikis for project management

Wikis offer a highly interactive environment for project information with easy access and user input. All participants have the same information, templates, and documentation readily available.

© Adam Houlahan

Reality Check

The Importance of Blogging

"Blogging on a regular basis represents an enormous opportunity for growth, creating a more powerful and far-reaching online presence. There is no better or simpler way to add content to your website that is unique, relevant and of interest to your target audience."[43]

—Adam Houlahan, *social entrepreneur and author*

Blogging for Business

LEARNING OUTCOME 4

Describe how businesses use blogs to connect with internal and external audiences, and list best practices for professional blogging.

The biggest advantage of business blogs is that they potentially reach a far-flung, vast audience. A blog is a website or social media platform with journal entries on any imaginable topic usually written by one person, although most corporate blogs feature multiple contributors. Typically, readers leave comments. Businesses use blogs to keep customers, employees, and the public at large informed and to interact with them.

Marketing firms and their clients are looking closely at blogs because blogs can invite spontaneous consumer feedback faster and more cheaply than such staples of consumer research as focus groups and surveys. Employees and executives at companies as varied as Exxon Mobil, Target, General Motors, Patagonia, and Whole Foods Market maintain blogs. They use blogs to communicate internally with employees and externally with the public. Currently, 103 Fortune 500 companies (21 percent) are blogging, but a decline in blog use may have begun. Researchers note "some movement towards visually rich platforms such as Instagram," which most recently enjoyed a double-digit growth in usage among the Fortune 500.[44]

Blog adoption varies across industries. Predictably, semiconductor and electronics makers (56 percent), entertainment firms (50 percent), and general merchandisers (40 percent) are most likely to embrace blogs, followed by telecommunications firms (36 percent) and commercial banks (22 percent).[45] Popular social media platforms such as Instagram and LinkedIn have added a blogging feature, a move that may precipitate the decrease of stand-alone blogs. Instead, corporate Twitter use is high in a field dominated by Facebook, as we will see in the last section of this chapter.

Cate Costa

Business blogs have become a staple of the public relations mix for both large and small organizations. With their casual tone and immediacy, blogs are a great way for businesses to connect with their stakeholders. Cate Costa's New Venture Mentor blog targets entrepreneurs, and the site contains advice for planning, launching, and growing a new business. The posts cover a wide range of topics, from how to price a product to what not to do when courting investors. Costa also uses the blog to promote her own services as a consultant to first-time entrepreneurs. How does a blog differ from a news article?[46]

How Companies Blog

Like other social networking tools, corporate blogs create virtual communities, build brands, and develop relationships. Specifically, companies use blogs for public relations, customer relations, crisis communication, market research, viral marketing, internal communication, online communities, and recruiting.

Public Relations, Customer Relations, and Crisis Communication. One of the prominent uses of blogs is to provide up-to-date company information to the press and the public. Blogs can be written by rank-and-file employees or by top managers. Executive chairman Bill Marriott is an avid and astute blogger. He writes about his volunteer work, leadership, family history, and more. His Marriott on the Move blog feels personal and honest:

> Five years ago, when I started this blog I wasn't sure what to expect. I love writing and sharing my thoughts with family, friends and talking to associates and customers. So I figured, well I guess so, why not? Through the years it's been a great outlet for me and I look forward to hearing from you every time I hit the "publish" button.[47]

Just one of several General Electric blogs, Edison's Desk, operated by GE Global Research, addresses industry insiders and the interested public. In its Best Buy Blogger Network, the electronics retailer gives a voice to average Joes and Janes who review all kinds of gizmos as brand ambassadors. The Best Buy blog acts as a forum actively soliciting customer input. Again, engaging customers in this way by tapping into their collective wisdom is called crowdsourcing. Many companies now use crowdsourcing promotions to connect with their customers and generate buzz that they hope will go viral on the Internet. For ten years Frito-Lay's Crash the Superbowl contest lured fans to create a humorous Doritos commercial. Nearly 4,500 consumer-generated submissions from 28 countries competed for a $1 million prize. Finalists were subjected to a fan vote on Doritos.com, and the winning ad ran during the Super Bowl.[48]

A company blog is a natural forum for late-breaking news, especially when disaster strikes. Business bloggers can address rumors, combat misinformation, and initiate damage control. Tony "Frosty" Welch, top social media strategist at Hewlett-Packard, averted a crisis before a video tagged "HP Computers Are Racist" would explode on the Internet (currently at over 3 million YouTube views). The now infamous webcam-made video demonstrated that HP's face-tracking software registered only light-skinned faces. In a model blog response, Welch thanked the video creators, addressed the design flaw, and promised a remedy.[49]

Although a blog cannot replace other communication channels in a PR crisis or an emergency, it should be part of the overall effort to soothe the public's emotional reaction with a human voice of reason.

Market Research and Viral Marketing. Because most blogs invite feedback, they can be invaluable sources of opinion and bright ideas from customers as well as industry experts. Starbucks is a Fortune 500 company that understands blogging and crowdsourcing in particular. My Starbucks Idea blog, depicted in Figure 7.9, is a public forum for the sharing of product ideas. Members vote and comment on the suggestions and eliminate poor ideas.

In addition to monitoring visitor comments on their corporate blogs, large companies employ teams of social media experts and marketers who scrutinize the blogosphere for buzz and positive or negative postings about their organizations and products. The term *viral marketing* refers to the rapid spread of messages online, much like infectious diseases that pass from person to person. Marketers realize the potential of getting the word out about their products and services in the blogosphere, where their messages are often picked up by well-connected bloggers, the so-called influencers, who boast large audiences. Viral messages must be authentic and elicit an emotional response, but for that very reason they are difficult to orchestrate. Online opinion leaders resent being co-opted by companies using overt hard-sell tactics.

Online Communities. Like Twitter, which is now drawing a loyal core following to businesses and brands, company blogs can attract a devoted community of participants. Such followers want to keep informed about company events, product updates, and other news. In

Figure 7.9 Starbucks Blog Specializes in Crowdsourcing

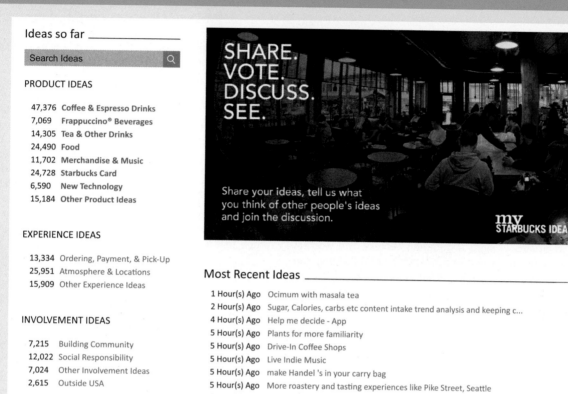

Ideas so far

Search Ideas

PRODUCT IDEAS

47,376 Coffee & Espresso Drinks
7,069 Frappuccino® Beverages
14,305 Tea & Other Drinks
24,490 Food
11,702 Merchandise & Music
24,728 Starbucks Card
6,590 New Technology
15,184 Other Product Ideas

EXPERIENCE IDEAS

13,334 Ordering, Payment, & Pick-Up
25,951 Atmosphere & Locations
15,909 Other Experience Ideas

INVOLVEMENT IDEAS

7,215 Building Community
12,022 Social Responsibility
7,024 Other Involvement Ideas
2,615 Outside USA

SHARE.
VOTE.
DISCUSS.
SEE.
Share your ideas, tell us what you think of other people's ideas and join the discussion.
my STARBUCKS IDEA

Most Recent Ideas

1 Hour(s) Ago Ocimum with masala tea
2 Hour(s) Ago Sugar, Calories, carbs etc content intake trend analysis and keeping c...
4 Hour(s) Ago Help me decide - App
5 Hour(s) Ago Plants for more familiarity
5 Hour(s) Ago Drive-In Coffee Shops
5 Hour(s) Ago Live Indie Music
5 Hour(s) Ago make Handel 's in your carry bag
5 Hour(s) Ago More roastery and tasting experiences like Pike Street, Seattle
6 Hour(s) Ago Joint Venture with Chocolate companies
6 Hour(s) Ago Apple Jacks Cereal Bars

turn, they can contribute new ideas. Few companies enjoy the brand awareness and customer loyalty of Coca-Cola. With its colorful blog Coca-Cola Conversations, the soft drink maker shares its rich past ("Coke Bottle 100") and thus deepens Coke fans' loyalty. Coke's marketing is subtle; the blog is designed to provide a "unique experience" to fans.

Internal Communication and Recruiting. Blogs can be used to keep virtual teams on track and share updates on the road. Members in remote locations can stay in touch by smartphone and other devices, exchanging text, images, sound, and video clips. In many companies, blogs have replaced hard-copy publications in offering late-breaking news or tidbits of interest to employees. Blogs can create a sense of community and stimulate employee participation.

Blogs mirror the company culture and present an invaluable opportunity for job candidates to size up a potential employer and the people working there.

Reality Check

Internal Blogging: Capitalizing on Knowledge

"Sharing information with others is a way of learning, and . . . especially in written form, helps people build up expertise on the subject. Blogging internally in your company is a great way to clarify your knowledge and expertise in a way that helps you understand it better."[50]

—Bill Cushard, *training lead at ServiceRocket, a software training company*

PLUGGED IN

Are You Ready for Gamification and Wearables?

Employers worry about a lack of engagement in workers, particularly in millennials, the least engaged age group in the workplace (29 percent)—less so than Generation X and baby boomers (33 percent), according to Gallup.[51]

Gamification. To boost worker engagement, companies are experimenting with *gamification*. From recruiting to training and development, organizations are adopting gaming concepts to introduce fun, play, competition, transparency, and persistence (some say addiction) to basic human resources functions.[52]

PwC Hungary challenges job applicants with a Monopoly-like game called Multipoly to test their readiness for teamwork and their ability to solve real-world business problems. Walmart has used gamification to deliver safety training to 5,000 associates in eight distribution centers. The workers competed for points and rankings and, as they connected emotionally with the game, became more likely to discuss and adhere to safety protocols. Much like Boy Scouts, participants earn badges if they exceed expectations. Like computer game points, scores in gamelike workplace processes appear on digital leaderboards for all to see; players compete against themselves and other participants.

Wearables. Wearable technology—such as heart rate monitors and skin response sensors—enables companies to monitor worker productivity and lifestyle by outfitting them with wearable technological devices. Much like fitness devices worn by athletes, wearables can measure brain activity, record movement, and even monitor posture.[53] Bio-sensing wearables are entering the mining, construction, and oil and gas industries, mainly to monitor workers' health and safety.

Employers love wearables because they believe the devices can help them save on health-care costs. They feel justified in tracking workers' behavior even outside the workplace. They argue that lifestyle choices—including alcohol and caffeine intake, exercise, sleep, eating habits, and smoking—affect job performance. They want to measure stress levels and productivity. Critics fear poor morale and pushback if workers don't know how information is used and fear that their data are not private and secure.

Blogging Best Practices: Seven Tips for Master Bloggers

Much advice is freely accessible on the Web, but this section offers guidelines culled from experienced bloggers and communication experts that will lead you to successful online writing. As with any public writing, your posts will be scrutinized; therefore, you want to make the best impression.

Craft a Catchy but Concise Title. The headline is what draws online readers to even click to go to your post. Some are intriguing questions or promises. Bloggers often use numbers to structure their posts. Here are some examples of blog post titles: *Six Apps You Don't Want to Miss; 5 Tips to Keep Spear Phishers Out of Your Inbox; Create Powerful Imagery in Your Writing; How Financially Sexy is Your Household?; The False Choice of Mediocrity.*

Ace the Opening Paragraph. The lead must deliver on the promise of the headline. Identify a need and propose to solve the problem. Ask a relevant question. Say something startling. Tell an anecdote or use an analogy to connect with the reader. The author of "How Many Lives Does a Brand Have?" opened with this:

> It's said that cats have nine lives, but how many lives does a brand have? The answer, it seems, is definitely more than one. Recently, in Shanghai, a friend took me to one of the city's most sophisticated luxury malls . . . .[54]

Provide Details in the Body. Mind the *So what?* and *What's in it for me?* questions. Use vivid examples, quotations and testimonials, or statistics. Structure the body with numbers, bullets, and subheadings. Use expressive action verbs (*buy* for *get*; *own* for *have*; *travel* or *jet* for *go*). Use conversational language to sound warm and authentic. Use contractions (*can't* for *cannot*; *doesn't* for *does not*; *isn't* for *is not*).

Consider Visuals. Add visual interest with relevant images and diagrams. Keep paragraphs short and use plenty of white space around them. Aim to make the look simple and easy to scan.

Include Calls to Action. Call on readers in the title to do something or provide a take-away and gentle nudge at the end. Chris Brogan, writing in his blog Become a Dream Feeder, said the following: "So, how will you make your blog into a dream feeder? Or do you do that already? What dreams do your readers have?"[55] Brogan advises asking open-ended questions or telling the reader what to do: "So, be sure to ask about 360-degree security tactics that aim to stop inbound attacks, but also to block outbound data theft attempts."

Edit and Proofread. Follow the revision tips in Chapter 6 of this book. Cut any unneeded words, superfluous sentences, and irrelevant ideas. Fix awkward, wordy, and repetitious sentences. Edit and proofread as if your life depended on it—your reputation might. The best blogs are error free.

Respond to Posts Respectfully. Build a positive image by posting compelling comments on other bloggers' posts. Politely and promptly reply to comments on your site. This reply to Guy Kawasaki's infographic makes a positive observation about the post and adds a valuable thought, albeit with a glaring spelling error and missing commas:

> Great graphic portrayal of the human connection. Three other areas might include 1) use people's first name (something pretty basic but often forgotten) 2) listen before you talk (a great one for bosses when meeting with employees) and 3) don't be afraid to pay complements [sic] when they are warranted.[56]

If you disagree with a post, do so respectfully. Don't ramble.

Your blog posts can benefit from the journalistic pattern shown in Figure 7.10 by emphasizing the big news up front, supported with specifics and background information.

Figure 7.10 **Writing a Captivating Blog**

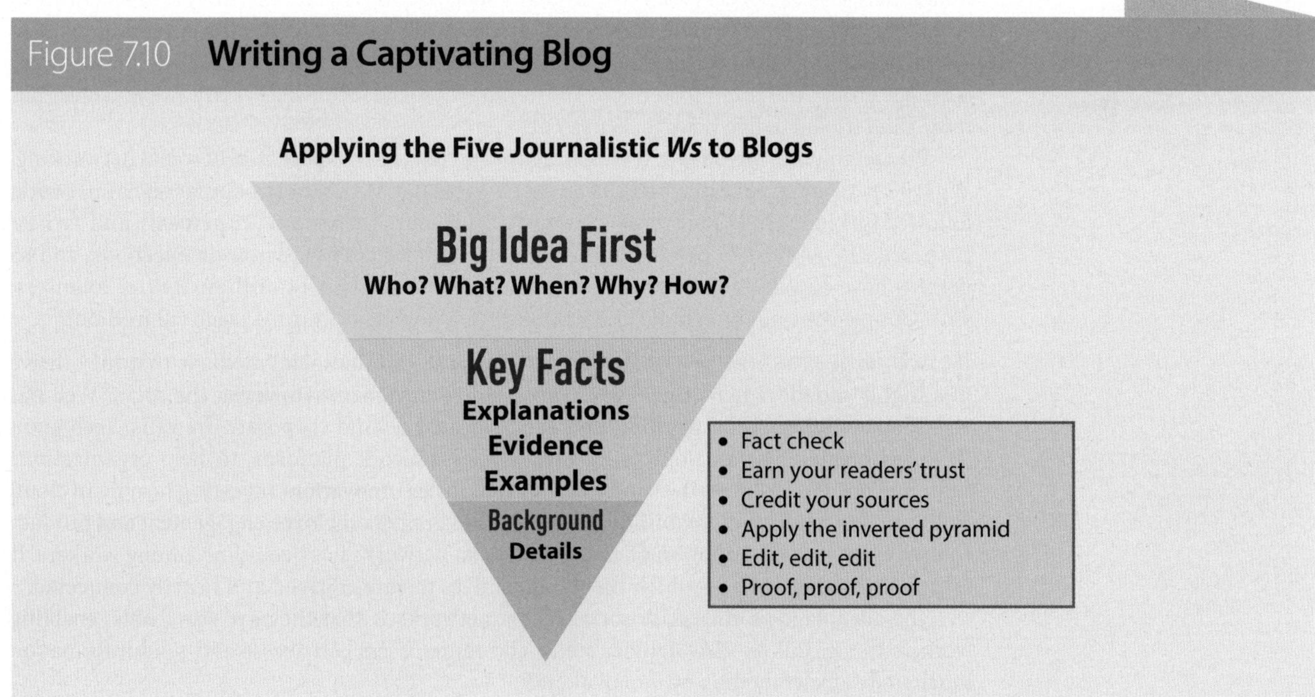

Reality Check

Social Media as Part of a Multichannel Strategy

"I soon learned that digital marketing is a lot more complicated than I thought. Although social media is ideal for promotion and building awareness, it does not always work well to get customers to act. For many digital businesses like ours, email remains the most powerful tool to close the sale and gain paying customers."[57]

—Jeff Cornwall, *entrepreneurship professor,* Forbes *contributor*

LEARNING OUTCOME 5

Define business uses of social networking.

Social Networking for Business

Popular social networking sites such as Facebook and Twitter are used by businesses for similar reasons and in much the same way as podcasts, blogs, and wikis. Social networking sites enable businesses to connect with customers and employees, share company news, and exchange ideas. Social online communities for professional audiences (e.g., LinkedIn), discussed in Chapter 15, help recruiters find talent and encounter potential employees before hiring them. Today, about 94 percent of hiring managers use social media as part of their screening processes.[58]

Tapping Into Social Media

A full 90 percent of organizations now use social media for business.[59] At the same time, workers report that social media play a very small role (4 percent) in their day-to-day job tasks. They list e-mail (61 percent) and the Internet (54 percent) as their most important work tools.[60] However, business interest in social networking sites is not surprising if we consider that 90 percent of millennials, also called Generation Y, regularly socialize and chat online. They are most likely to access the Internet with smartphones and laptops. Millennials lead in instant messaging, blog reading, listening to music, playing online games, and participating in virtual worlds. However, older age groups are gaining on them. The number of social media users sixty-five and older has more than tripled in five years to 35 percent.[61]

Predictably, businesses are trying to adapt and tap the vast potential of social networking. With 58 percent of American adults as users, Facebook is the most popular social network, followed by LinkedIn (23 percent), Pinterest (22 percent), Instagram (21 percent), and Twitter (19 percent).[62] Almost 75 percent of the Fortune 500 companies are now on Facebook, and 85 percent have corporate Twitter accounts. Facebook leads with 14 million Twitter followers, with Google coming in second (12.5 million), and Starbucks in third place (10 million).[63]

How Businesses Use Social Media. The key to all the social media is that they thrive in a highly mobile, interactive, hyperconnected environment. However, the social Web has also spawned internal networking sites safely located behind corporate firewalls. Tech giant IBM has created Connections, a business social network platform, to help organizations share knowledge, improve decision making, and foster innovation. Investing heavily in cloud computing to the tune of $16 billion, IBM promises greater employee engagement and productivity.[64] However, the adoption of enterprise social networks has been slow among workers. It is highest in companies in which the top executives too are engaged and heavily connected.[65]

The advantage of enterprise social media networks is that they are searchable, enabling workers to tag, follow, view activity feeds, and more. Users can access and send information much more efficiently than by e-mail alone.[66]

Adopting the Facebook Model. Some companies have found that the Facebook model can be adapted to internal networks, many of which run on the Chatter or Yammer enterprise social networking platforms. For one thing, staff members already intuitively understand how a corporate social network operates because they are familiar with Facebook. Red Robin's Yammer-based corporate social network, dubbed Yummer, gave a voice to frontline staff and other employees who normally don't have a say. It led to a better burger recipe and became a mine for creative ideas.[67]

Connecting Far-Flung Workers. Because social networks are about connections, they also enable companies to match up and connect dispersed employees. Rosemary Turner, the president of UPS in northern California, manages a far-flung team of 17,000 workers who drive delivery trucks, work the loading docks, or make sales calls. She uses Twitter to update her team about road conditions but also to highlight employee accomplishments, posing with them in photos and sharing them online. UPS employees are comfortable with Twitter; its open dialogue mirrors the transparent company culture and fosters trust.[68]

Crowdsourcing Customers. Social networks and blogs also help companies to invite customer input at the product design stage. On its IdeaStorm site, Dell has solicited almost 25,000 new product ideas and suggested improvements, including glossy 4K monitors, better power cords, and an improved trackball mouse. As Figure 7.11 shows, large companies have established successful social media presences.

Experts predict that social media will become as important for the economy as mobile phones and cloud computing: "Mobile is an extension of the cloud, because it lets you get your data wherever you are. And social is the layer on top of that, making it easier to cross-communicate," says California-based venture capitalist Stacey Bishop.[69] IBM CEO Ginni Rometty likened social media to the "new manufacturing plant, not just the new water cooler." She believes in social engagement, in a workforce that is "powered by a network, enriched by knowledge."[70]

Potential Risks of Social Media for Businesses. Online public social networks hold great promise for businesses while also presenting some risk. Most managers want plugged-in employees with strong tech skills. They like to imagine their workers as brand evangelists. They fantasize about their products becoming overnight sensations thanks to viral marketing.

Figure 7.11 Most Popular Brands on Facebook

Facebook has reached 1.55 billion users. For comparison, LinkedIn has 400 million members, Twitter claims 307 million active users, and Google Plus has 418 million active users. Facebook allows registered users to create individual home pages as well as group pages based on their interests. The top three brands with the most fans are Coca-Cola (96.1 million), YouTube (81.4 million), and Red Bull (44.7 million).

Source : Facebook

Ethics Check

Pricing Blunder Broadcast Far and Wide via Social Media

Because of a software glitch, Tesco, the world's third-largest retailer based in the United Kingdom, offered a new iPad worth £659 ($1,021) for £49.99 ($77) on its website. Within hours the news exploded on Facebook and Twitter. Some customers ordered as many as 20 iPads and insisted that Tesco honor the advertised price. The company quickly corrected the online pricing error and would not accept orders at the incorrect price. Was Tesco obligated to honor the offer?

However, they also fret about incurring productivity losses, compromising trade secrets, attracting the wrath of huge Internet audiences, and facing embarrassment over inappropriate and damaging employee posts.[71]

Businesses take different approaches to the dark side of social networking. Some, such as Zappos, take a hands-off approach and encourage employee online activity. Others, such as IBM, have drafted detailed policies to cover all forms of self-expression online. According to one survey, a full 80 percent of businesses have social media policies; 36 percent of businesses block access to social networking sites, and in most countries, they are well within their legal rights in doing so.[72] Other studies peg the percentage of employers who block certain websites higher, at 46 percent.[73] Several top German corporations, including Volkswagen and Porsche, have banned social media outright, fearing a loss of productivity and industrial espionage.[74] However, experts believe that organizations should embrace positive word-of-mouth testimonials from employees about their jobs, not quash them with rigid policies.[75] In the United States and some other countries, social media policies need to be guidelines, not rules, or they could violate labor laws under certain circumstances.[76]

Because the lines between work time and personal time are increasingly blurry, some organizations allow partial access by limiting what employees can do online. They may disable file sharing to protect sensitive information.

Using Social Networking and Keeping Your Job

Experts agree that, as with any public online activity, users of social networking sites would do well to exercise caution. Privacy is a myth, and sensitive information should not be shared lightly, least of all risqué photographs. Furthermore, refusing friend requests or unfriending individuals could jeopardize professional relationships. Consider the tips in Figure 7.12 provided by career counselor Julie Powell[77] if you like to visit social networking sites and want to keep your job.

Figure 7.12 **Guidelines for Safe Social Networking**

Establish boundaries

Don't share information, images, and media online that you would not be comfortable sharing openly in the office.

Distrust privacy settings

Privacy settings don't guarantee complete protection from prying eyes. Facebook has come under fire for changing privacy settings and opening unwitting user's profiles for the world to see.

Rein in your friends

One of your 500 Facebook friends may tag you in an inappropriate photograph. Tags make pictures searchable; an embarrassing college incident may resurface years later. Always ask before tagging someone.

Beware *"friending"*

Don't reject friend requests from some coworkers while accepting them from others. Snubbed colleagues may harbor ill feelings. Don't friend your boss unless he or she friends you first. Send friend requests only once.

Expect the unexpected

Recruiters now routinely check applicants' online presence. Some employers have gone so far as to demand that candidates disclose their Facebook log-in information. Facebook and lawmakers have criticized the practice.

The checklist that follows highlights some employee dos and don'ts that you should abide by to keep out of trouble on the job.

Using Digital Media Like a Pro

Dos: Know Workplace Policies and Avoid Private Use of Media at Work

- **Learn your company's rules.** Some companies require workers to sign that they have read and understand Internet and digital media use policies. Being informed is your best protection.
- **Avoid sending personal e-mail, IMs, or texts from work machines and devices.** Even if your company allows personal use during lunch or after hours, keep it to a minimum. Better yet, wait to use your own electronic devices away from work.
- **Separate work and personal data.** Keep information that could embarrass you or expose you to legal liability on your personal storage devices, on hard drives, or in the cloud, never on your office computer.
- **Be careful when blogging, tweeting, or posting on social networking sites.** Unhappy about not receiving a tip, a Beverly Hills waiter lost his job for tweeting disparaging remarks about an actress. Forgetting that his boss was his Facebook friend, a British employee was fired after posting "OMG, I HATE MY JOB!" and calling his supervisor names.[78]
- **Keep sensitive information private.** Use privacy settings, but don't trust the private areas on Facebook, Twitter, Flickr, and other social networks.
- **Stay away from pornography, sexually explicit jokes, and inappropriate screen savers.** Anything that might poison the work environment is a harassment risk and, therefore, prohibited.

Don'ts: Avoid Questionable Content, Personal Documents, and File Sharing

- **Don't spread rumors, gossip, and negative, defamatory comments.** Because all digital information is subject to discovery in court, avoid unprofessional content and conduct, including complaints about your employer, customers, and employees.[79]
- **Don't download and share cartoons, video clips, photos, and art.** Businesses are liable for any recorded digital content regardless of the medium used.[80]
- **Don't open attachments sent by e-mail.** Attachments with executable files or video files may carry viruses, spyware, or other malware (malicious programs).
- **Don't download free software and utilities to company machines.** Employees can unwittingly introduce viruses, phishing schemes, and other cyber bugs.
- **Don't store your music and photos on a company machine (or server), and don't watch streaming videos.** Capturing precious company bandwidth for personal use is a sure way to be shown the door.
- **Don't share files, and avoid file-sharing services.** Clarify whether you may use Google Docs and other services that offer optional file sharing. Stay away from distributors of pirated files such as Torrentz or clones and offshoots of the notorious Pirate Bay site.

Your Turn: Applying Your Skills at Sony

Yeamake/Shutterstock.com

You are thrilled that you've been hired as a development intern at Sony Picture's online network Crackle, where you will read and review scripts. On your first day, your supervisor, Marty Frankel, asks that you jot down a list of the kinds of information you would never include in any Sony-related correspondence before you tackle your first stack of scripts.

Your Task

In groups of two or three, decide whether to send Marty an e-mail or give her a hard-copy memo. After you choose the channel, choose the organizing strategy you will use. Write the e-mail or memo and include eight to ten taboo topics.

Summary of Learning Outcomes

1 Understand e-mail, memos, and the professional standards for their usage, structure, and format in the digital era workplace.

- The exchange of information in organizations today is increasingly digital and mobile.
- Office workers still send paper-based messages when they need a permanent record; wish to maintain confidentiality; and need to convey formal, long, and important messages.
- E-mail is still the lifeblood of businesses, but instant messaging is gaining popularity.
- E-mail and memo subject lines summarize the central idea, which is restated in the opening. The body provides details. The closing includes (a) action information and deadlines, (b) a summary, or (c) a closing thought.
- Skilled e-mail writers take advantage of down-editing. In a reply they delete the unnecessary parts of the sender's message and insert their responses.
- Careful e-mail users write concisely and don't send content they wouldn't want published.

2 Explain workplace instant messaging and texting as well as their liabilities and best practices.

- Instant messaging (IM) and text messaging with customers, employees, and suppliers are fast, discreet, and inexpensive.
- Risks include productivity losses, leaked trade secrets, and legal liability from workers' improper use of digital media; fraud, malware, and spam pose additional risks.
- Best practices include following company policies, avoiding sensitive information, not sending inappropriate digital content, and using correct grammar and spelling.
- Text messages should observe proper timing, be addressed to the correct person, and identify the sender; savvy workers don't send sensitive news or expect an instant reply.

3 Identify professional applications of podcasts and wikis, and describe guidelines for their use.

- Business podcasts are digital audio or video files ranging from short clips to long media files.
- Applications that do not require a human presence (e.g., training videos) lend themselves to podcast recordings that users can stream or download on the go.
- Wikis enable far-flung team members to share information and build a knowledge base.
- Wikis can be used to replace meetings, manage projects, and document projects large and small.

4 Describe how businesses use blogs to connect with internal and external audiences, and list best practices for professional blogging.

- Blogs help businesses to keep customers, employees, and suppliers informed and to receive feedback.
- Online communities can form around blogs.
- Companies employ blogs for public relations and crisis communication, market research and viral marketing, internal communication, and recruiting.

5 Define business uses of social networking.

- Social media such as Facebook and Twitter allow firms to share company news; exchange ideas; and connect with customers, employees, other stakeholders, and the public.
- Companies boost their brand recognition, troubleshoot customer problems, and engage customers by using established social media; they may create enterprise social networks in house to promote internal communication.
- Productivity losses, legal liability, leaking of trade secrets, and angry Internet users are potential risks of social media use at work.
- Workers should share only appropriate, work-related information, not post questionable content; they should activate and monitor their privacy options on social media sites.

Critical Thinking

1. According to surveys, millennials voice the strongest opposition to government surveillance. The Pew Research Center found that almost three quarters of millennials adjust their privacy settings to limit access to their information.[81] Millennials seem to be willing to trade privacy for security online. In other words, they safeguard their data for fear of identity theft even if the process is cumbersome, but they worry much less about their privacy, for example, when companies sell their personal information. If facing the choice between safety and privacy, which would you choose? How concerned are you about privacy and security online? Do you watch your own privacy settings? (L.O. 1–5)

2. In her book *Alone Together,* MIT professor Sherry Turkle argued that increasing dependence on technology leads to a consequent diminution in personal connections. "Technology is seductive when what it offers meets our human vulnerabilities. And as it turns out, we are very vulnerable indeed. We are lonely but fearful of intimacy. Digital connections . . . may offer the illusion of companionship without the demands of friendship."[82] Do you agree that technology diminishes personal relationships rather than bringing us closer together? Do social media fool us into thinking that we are connected when in reality we bear none of the commitments and burdens of true friendship? (L.O. 1–5)

3. Consider the potential impact of gamification and wearable devices on your career. How do you feel about the tracking of employees and the monitoring of your vital functions on the job and outside the workplace? Can you think of other vulnerable technologies? What advice would you give someone who is not sure how to handle invasive technologies that may threaten privacy and security? As one expert put it: "We are living in the digital equivalent of the Wild Wild West and big data is a wide open frontier full of opportunity but fraught with unknown hazards and potentially deadly pitfalls."[83] (L.O. 1–5)

4. Computer antivirus expert John McAfee claims that technological intrusions into our privacy degrade our humanity. "Google, or at least certain people at Google . . . would like us to believe that if we have nothing to hide, we should not mind if everybody knows everything that we do," McAfee stated at the annual DEF CON hacking conference in Las Vegas. "We cannot have intrusions into our lives and still have freedom," he said.[84] Do you agree with McAfee? Why or why not? (L.O. 1–5)

5. Ethical Issue: Although they don't actually pay people to act as fans on social networks and entice their friends to do so as well, some marketers employ machines, called bots, to inflate the number of their fans and followers online. In third world countries, businesses trafficking in fake profiles, the so-called click farms, are selling 1,000 followers for $10. Social networks try to respond by deleting fake accounts, and the likes earned in the process vanish too. Google has introduced an algorithm to eliminate spammers and other abusers of its systems, and Facebook and Twitter will probably follow suit.[85] Why do some businesses resort to such measures? What might be the consequences of faking fans? How do you feel about companies and their brands pretending that they have actual traffic on their sites?

Activities

Note: All Documents for Analysis are provided at **www.cengagebrain.com** for you to download and revise.

7.1 Document for Analysis: Hastily Written E-Mail Needs Drastic Revision (L.O. 1)

E-Mail

Polychron, Inc., is considering launching an internship program, and Camille Montano, manager of Human Resources, seeks information from members of the management team.

YOUR TASK Study the first draft of her hastily written message and list its weaknesses. Then revise it to create a concise, clear message. Consider patterning your revision on Figure 7.1 in this chapter.

To: Jackson Prewarski <jprewarski@polychron.com>
From: Camille Montano <cmontano@polychron.com>
Subject: Interns?

Hi, Jackson,

You may remember that some time ago our management team here at Polychron talked about an internship program. The topic has come up again at this time, and I'm taking this opportunity to ask you to please answer some questions about whether this is a good idea or not. As our organization continues to expand, interns might make sense. But there are many points that we need to discuss, and I've put together a few questions that I think we should cover at the next management meeting. Please mark your calendar to meet on March 14 at 9 a.m. in the morning.

First, we really need to discuss whether an internship program is advantageous to us here at Polychron. In addition, what are the disadvantages? Next, what are some of the ramifications legally of hosting an internship program here in our state? Another question that enters my mind is whether we should pay interns. Do they receive college credit instead? I wonder if that serves as satisfactory compensation. Finally, we need to discuss where this program would be launched within Polychron. What departments to pilot such a program?

I hope you will give careful thought to these questions and come prepared to discuss.

Camille

[Full contact information]

7.2 Document for Analysis: Web Conferencing Made Simple (L.O. 1)

E-Mail

Jeremy Harper, a blogger and Web conferencing expert, responds to a request from Christina Cruz, who wants advice for an article she is writing. His advice is good, but his message is poorly organized, contains grammar and other errors, and is hard to read.

YOUR TASK Analyze the following message and note five weaknesses with examples. Then revise if your instructor advises. Remember that you can download these documents at **www.cengagebrain.com.**

To: Christina Cruz <ccruz@sagepublications.com>
From: Jeremy Harper <jeremy.harper@pcs.com>
Subject: Replying to Your Request

Dear Christina Cruz:

Hey, thanks for asking me to make a contribution to the article you are preparing and working up for *Networking Voices*. Appreciate this opportunity! Although you asked me to keep it brief, I could give you an extensive, comprehensive list of dos and don'ts for Web conferencing. If you want this, let me know.

As an alternative to in-person meetings, Web conferencing is increasingly popular. Here's five tips for your article. First and foremost, plan ahead. All participants should be notified of things like the date, time, and duration. It's your job to send log-ins, passwords, and printed documents by e-mail. My next advise is about identifying yourself. Don't assume that attendees will automatically recognize your voice. The first few times you speak, its good to state your name.

Another tip has to do with muting (turning off) your phone. Believe me, there's nothing worse than barking dogs, side conversations. And worst of all is the sound of toilets flushing during a conference. Ick!

You should play with your microphone and speakers until you sound good. And of course, don't shuffle papers. Don't eat. Don't move things while your speaking.

My final tip involves using a lobby slide to open. This is a slide that tells the meeting details. Such as the start time, audio information, and the agenda. This lobby slide should go up about 10 to 15 minutes before the meeting begins.

Hope this helps!

Jeremy Harper

[Full contact information]

7.3 Document for Analysis: Lost in the Cloud (L.O. 1)

In the following interoffice memo, product manager Alexandra Amato reports to CEO Mason Razipour the high points of a workshop he asked her to attend. Alexandra's jumbled memo offers solid information, but it is so poorly written that it fails to achieve its purpose.

YOUR TASK Analyze the message and list at least five weaknesses. Revise if directed.

Date: July 10, 2018
To: Mason Razipour, CEO
From: Alexandra Amato, Product Manager
Subject: Cloud Computing

Some time ago you signed me up to attend The Promise of Cloud Computing workshop. I did attend it on July 8. Herewith is a short report, as you requested. If you prefer, I could give a presentation about what I learned at the next management council meeting. Is that meeting coming up in August?

Okay, here's my report. I know you asked that it be brief, so will do! Lisa Moritz, the workshop leader told the group that the big problem today is that in this anytime/anywhere workplace employees are working with tons of devices from various locations. With employees scattered around, software and file storage must be accessible anywhere, anytime. It can't be on one type of device, and it can no longer be stuck in one place to be accessed with incompatible devices. Lisa told us that there are three main ways that cloud computing can improve the workplace. No. 1. Cloud computing makes it possible to access nearly all types of applications or software. A vast number of cloud-based services (e-mail, online storage, online file transfer) can be made available to lots of users—without the problem of compatibility. Another big benefit is the promise of making employees more efficient. How? Free access to unlimited ways to provide on-the-spot solutions eliminates searching and downtime. Cloud computing is also a way to improve communications. It completely transforms the way work is performed. Lisa didn't tell us exactly how this was accomplished, but she said that cloud computing makes for a happier, mentally healthy atmosphere all around.

This is just a bare-bones summary of what I learned. If you want to hear more, please do not hesitate to call.

Note: This message is formatted as an interoffice memo.

7.4 Document for Analysis: Instant Messaging at a Local Auto Dealer (L.O. 2)

Communication Technology | Social Media | Web

Read the following log of a live IM chat between a customer service representative and a visitor to a Chicago car dealership's website.

YOUR TASK In class discuss how Ethan could have made this interaction with a customer more effective. Is his IM chat with Mr. Ree professional, polite, and respectful? If your instructor directs, rewrite Ethan's responses to Mr. Ree's queries.

Dealer rep: Hey, I'm Ethan. How's it goin? Welcome to Perillo BMW the best dealer in Chicago!

Customer: ??

Dealer rep: Im supposed to provid live assistance. What can I do you for?

Customer: I want buy car.

Dealer rep: May I have your name fist?

Customer: Ree Min-jun.

Dealer rep: Whoa! Is that a dude's name? Okay. What kind? New inventory or preowned?

Customer: BMW. 2018 model. for family, for business.

Dealer rep: New, then, huh? Where are you from, Ree?

Customer: What car you have?

Dealer rep: We got some that will knock your socks off.

Customer: I want green car, no high gasoline burn.

Dealer rep: My man, if you can't afford the gas on these puppies, you shouldn't buy a Beemer, you know what I mean? Or ya want green color?

Customer: ?

Dealer rep: Okeydoke, we got a full lineup. Which series, 1, 2, 3, 4, 5, 6, or 7? Or an X1, X3, X4, X5, or X6? A Z4 convertible?

Customer: BMW i3?

Dealer rep: Nope. That's the electric car! Oh I dont recommend those. We got two i3, one for $44,200 and one for $47,700.

Customer: Eurepean delivery?

Dealer rep: Oh, I know zip about that. Let me find someone who does. Can I have your phone number and e-mail?

Customer: i prefer not get a phone call yet... but 312-484-6356 is phone numer and minjunree@t-tech.net email

Dealer rep: Awsome. Well give you a jingle back or shoot you an email pronto! Bye.

7.5 Chatting With Citynet Mobile Customer Service (L.O. 2)

Communication Technology | Social Media | Team | Web

Read the following log of a live IM chat between a Citynet Mobile customer service representative and a customer inquiring about an unexpected fee.

YOUR TASK Evaluate the exchange based on word choice, grammar, tone, and professionalism. How well does the customer service representative handle the customer's inquiry? Is it resolved fairly, and is it likely to foster a good business relationship? Individually or in small groups, discuss alternative strategies for this online chat, if applicable. Consider the organization's goals in providing live chat representatives; were those goals met? If your instructor directs, revise the dialogue.

Please hold for a Citynet Mobile sales representative to assist you with your order. Thank you for your patience. You are now chatting with *Wendy K.*

Wendy K.: Hello. Thank you for visiting our chat service. May I help you with your order today?

Customer: Yes, I'm about to finish my order, but suddenly there's a $30 upgrade fee? What's that? I'm surprised. I thought I'm getting an upgrade discount.

Wendy K.: Citynet Mobile implemented a $30 upgrade fee for existing customers purchasing new mobile equipment at a discounted price with a two-year contract. This fee will help us continue to provide customers with the level of service and support they have come to expect, which includes Wireless Workshops, online educational tools, and consultations with experts who provide advice and guidance on devices that are more sophisticated than ever.

Customer: Okay, so that means the phone advertised at $149.99 is really going to cost me $30 more? Other companies don't have 2-year contracts anymore.

Wendy K.: Are you an existing customer?

Wendy K.: You have the option to apply the $30 to your account.

Customer: Yes, I am. I have been for many years and each month I'm paying $140 for my service. I'm a bit taken aback by this last-minute charge. I have just chatted with another representative and that wasn't brought up.

Customer: It's not the additional charge, it's how "sneakily" it pops up at the end just as the customer is about to click "BUY."

Wendy K.: Yes, I understand, it was just implemented last week on the 22nd.

Customer: Just my luck. Okay, I don't really need an upgrade. My Samsung Galaxy 6 is doing its work nicely and I have unlimited data. So I won't go through with it. You are losing my $180 business today.

Wendy K.: I understand how you feel and appreciate your loyalty. In addition to receiving discounts on device prices when upgrading, we do from time to time send our loyal customers specials, offers and updates on new equipment, products, and price plans.

Customer: I know. I did get one such ad for Mother's Day, the Galaxy 7 for $149.99. Okay, I'll wait until the price drops. No problem. Thank you.

Wendy K.: Is there anything else I can help you with today?

Customer: No, thanks. Your customer service is getting worse.

Customer: Not you personally, but the "perks." Your company is adding hidden fees. Not cool. — Have a good day.

7.6 Instant Messaging: Practicing Your Professional IM Skills (L.O. 2)

Communication Technology | Social Media | Team | Web

Your instructor will direct this role-playing group activity. Using instant messaging, you will simulate one of several typical business scenarios—for example, responding to a product inquiry, training a new-hire, troubleshooting with a customer, or making an appointment. For each scenario, two or more students chat professionally with only a minimal script to practice on-the-spot, yet courteous professional interactions by IM. Your instructor will determine which client software or app you will need and provide brief instructions to prepare you for your role.

If you don't have instant messaging software on your computer or smart device yet, download the application first—for example, AIM, Google Hangouts, Skype, or IM aggregators such as Trillian or Pidgin that allow you to chat with people using various IM clients or apps. All IM software enables users to share photos and large media files. You can make voice calls and use webcam video as well. These advanced features turn IM software into a simple conferencing tool and video phone. You can connect with users who have the same software all around the world. Contrary to calling landlines or cell phones, peer-to-peer voice calls are free. Most IM clients also offer mobile apps for your smartphone, so that you can IM or call other users while you are away from a computer. WhatsApp, Facebook Messenger, QQ, WeChat, and Skype are just a few of the most popular apps. You may want to use a computer because downloading chat sessions is easier on a computer than on a smartphone.

YOUR TASK Open the IM or chat program your instructor chooses. Follow your instructor's directions closely as you role-play the business situation you were assigned with your partner or team. The scenario involves two or more people who communicate by instant messaging in real time.

7.7 Analyzing a Podcast (L.O. 3)

Communication Technology | E-Mail | Social Media | Web

Browsing the podcasts at iTunes, you stumble across the Quick and Dirty Tips series, specifically Money Girl, who dispenses financial advice. You sign up for the free podcasts that cover a variety of business topics. You can also visit the website Quick and Dirty Tips or interact with Laura D. Adams on her Money Girl Facebook page. Alternatively, examine the advice conveyed via podcast, the Web, Facebook, and Twitter by clever Grammar Girl Mignon Fogarty.

YOUR TASK Pick a Money Girl podcast that interests you. Listen to it or obtain a transcript on the website and study it for its structure. Is it direct or indirect? How is it presented? What style does the speaker adopt? How useful is the information provided? At your instructor's request, write an e-mail that discusses the podcast you analyzed. Alternatively, if your instructor allows, you could also send a very concise summary of the podcast by text message from your cell phone or tweet to your instructor. Try limiting yourself to 140 characters to practice conciseness, although Twitter now allows longer messages.

7.8 Creating a Simple Business Podcast (L.O. 3)

Communication Technology | Social Media | Web

Do you want to try your hand at producing a podcast? Businesses rely on a host of social media and communication technologies when reaching out to the public or internally to their workers. As you have seen, some companies produce such short audio or video clips on focused, poignant subjects. The following process describes how to create a simple podcast.

Select software. Aside from popular software such as Propaganda, Audacity, and GarageBand (Mac only), newer podcast creation software such as Hipcast, Yodio, and Podbean work in the cloud. They allow recordings within a Web browser or from a smartphone. Most can also be accessed as mobile apps.

Obtain hardware. For high sound quality, you may need a sophisticated microphone and other equipment. The recording room must be properly shielded against noise, echo, and other interference. Many universities and some libraries provide recording booths.

Organize the message. Make sure your broadcast has a beginning, middle, and end. Build in some redundancy. Previews, summaries, and transitions are important to help your audience follow the message.

Choose an extemporaneous or scripted delivery. Extemporaneous delivery means that you prepare, but you use only brief notes. It usually sounds more spontaneous and natural than reading from a script, but it can also lead to redundancy, repetition, and flubbed lines.

Prepare and practice. Practice before recording. Editing audio or video is difficult and time consuming. Try to get your recording right, so that you won't have to edit much.

Publish your message. Once you post the MP3 podcast to your course website or blog, you can introduce it and request feedback.

YOUR TASK Create a short podcast about a business-related subject you care about. Producing a simple podcast does not require sophisticated equipment. With free or inexpensive recording, editing, and publishing software such as Propaganda or Audacity, you can inform customers, mix your own music, or host interviews. Any digital recorder can be used to create a no-frills podcast if the material is scripted and well rehearsed.

7.9 Reviewing Corporate Blogs (L.O. 4)

Communication Technology | E-Mail | Social Media | Web

Here is your opportunity to view and evaluate a corporate blog. As we have seen, about 21 percent of the Fortune 500 companies, or 103 of them, have public blogs, and their use has been declining lately, mainly because businesses fear missteps and legal liability. The other reason for the dwindling use of blogs is the skyrocketing popularity of Instagram, which in many ways has replaced standalone corporate blogs. However, the companies and their CEOs who do blog can impart valuable lessons.

YOUR TASK Within your favorite browser, search for *CEO blogs, index of corporate blogs, index of CEO blogs,* and similar phrases. You will likely end up at CEO.com and at other sites that may list the top ten or so most popular corporate blogs (e.g., Whole Foods, Caterpillar, Coca-Cola, Walmart, and Allstate). You can also find blogs penned by chief executives. Select a corporate or CEO blog you find interesting, browse the posts, and read some of the content. Furthermore, note how many of the points the blog makes match the guidelines in this book. If your instructor directs, write a brief informational memo or e-mail summarizing your observations about the business blog, its style, the subjects covered, and so forth.

7.10 Composing a Personal Blog Entry (L.O. 4)

Communication Technology | E-Mail | Social Media | Web

Review the guidelines for professional blogging in this chapter. Find a recent social media–related study or survey, and target an audience of business professionals who may wish to know more about social networking. Search for studies conducted by respected organizations and businesses such as Pew Internet, Robert Half International, Burson-Marsteller, ePolicy Institute, and U.S. government agencies, as applicable. As you plan and outline your post, follow the advice provided in this chapter. Although the goal is usually to offer advice, you could also weigh in with your opinion regarding a controversy. For example, do you agree with companies that forbid employees to use company-owned devices and networks for social media access? Do you agree that millennials are losing social skills because of excessive online connectivity?

YOUR TASK Compose a one-page blog entry in MS Word and submit it in hard copy. Alternatively, post it to the discussion board on the class course-management platform, or e-mail it to your instructor, as appropriate. Because you will be using outside sources, be careful to paraphrase correctly. Visit Chapter 11 to review how to put ideas into your own words with integrity.

7.11 Writing Superefficient Tweets (L.O. 5)

Communication Technology | Social Media

As you have seen in Chapter 6, Twitter has forced its users to practice extreme conciseness by limiting tweets to 140 characters. Now the microblogging platform plans to offer a long-form service, although users can already take screenshots of text and post them to bypass the restriction. Twitter CEO Jack Dorsey tweeted that he loves the "beautiful constraint" of short messaging and that "the majority of tweets will always be short and sweet and conversational."[86]

Some music reviewers have risen to the challenge and reviewed whole albums in no more than 140 characters. National Public Radio put Stephen Thompson, one of its music editors, to the test. "I approach Twitter as a science," Thompson says.[87] He sees well-designed tweets as online equivalents of haiku, a highly structured type of Japanese poetry. Thompson believes that tweets should be properly punctuated, be written in complete sentences, and of course, not exceed the 140-character limit. His rules also exclude abbreviations.

Here are two samples of Thompson's mini reviews: "Mos Def is a hip-hop renaissance man on smart songs that look to the whole world and its conflicts. Slick Rick's guest spot is a nice touch." The second one reads: "The Phenomenal Handclap Band: Chugging, timeless, jammy throwback from eight shaggy Brooklyn hipsters. Starts slowly, gets hypnotically fun."[88]

YOUR TASK As an intern in Stephen Thompson's office, review your favorite album in 140 characters or fewer, following your boss's rules. After you have warmed up, your instructor may direct you to other concise writing tasks. Send a tweet to your instructor, if appropriate. Alternatively, practice writing Twitter posts in MS Word or on an online discussion board. The best tweets could be shared with the class.

7.12 What? You Tweeted THAT? (L.O. 5)

Communication Technology | E-Mail | Social Media

The modern workplace is a potential digital minefield. The imprudent use of practically any online tool—whether e-mail, IM, texting, tweeting, blogging, or posting to Facebook—can land workers in hot water and even lead to dismissal. Here are five ways Twitter can get you canned for showing poor judgment:[89]

a. **Sending hate tweets about the boss.** Example: *My idiot boss said he put in for raises. I think he lies. He is known for that. His daddy owns the company.*

b. **Lying to the boss and bragging about it.** Example: *I so lied to my boss . . . I was late but I said I forgot my badge and got away with it.*

c. **Romancing the boss (kissing and telling).** Example: *I give the boss what he wants, and the fringe benefits are amazing.*

d. **Announcing the desire to quit.** Example: *So close to quitting my job right now. Sometimes I can't [expletive] stand this place [expletive] moron assistant plant manager I'm about to deck him.*

e. **Blocking your boss.** Example: *i kept my promise . . . my boss thought she was gonna follow me on here . . . i BLOCKED her [expletive] ASAP.*

YOUR TASK Discuss each violation of Twitter best practices, or summarize in general why these tweets are potentially damaging to their authors. How could the Twitter users have handled their grievances more professionally? Comment on the style of these questionable tweets. If your instructor requests, summarize your observations in an e-mail message or an online post.

7.13 Creating a Twitter List (L.O. 5)

Communication Technology | Social Media | Web

Twitter lists make microblogging useful for private individuals and businesses. A Twitter list is based on the premise that people like to talk with other like-minded people. Users come together in communities around topics (politics, sports, art, business, and so on). List members can tweet about the big news stories of the day, bounce ideas off other participants online, or just join the conversation—all in no more than 140 characters at this time. Your instructor may create a public or private group for the class and ask you to complete short assignments in the form of tweets. Posts in a private group are not shared with other general users, yet they should be relevant to the class content and professional.

YOUR TASK Sign into Twitter and follow the group designated by your instructor. Your instructor may ask you to comment on an assigned topic or encourage you to enter into a freewheeling discussion with other members of your class online. Your instructor may act as a group moderator evaluating the frequency and quality of your contributions.

7.14 The Dark Side: Hooked on Social Media? (L.O. 5)

Social Media

Could you give up your electronic toys for 24 hours without withdrawal symptoms? Would you be able to survive a full day unplugged from all media? For a few years now, articles have been appearing about unplugging from social media at least temporarily and trying a digital detox or conducting a Facebook cleanse.[90] Most authors describe their experiments in the language of addiction, complete with cravings and withdrawal symptoms. A class of 200 students at the University of Maryland, College Park, went media free for 24 hours and then blogged about the experience.[91]

Some sounded like addicts going cold turkey, "In withdrawal. Frantically craving. Very anxious. Extremely antsy. Miserable. Jittery. Crazy." One student lamented: "I clearly am addicted and the dependency is sickening." In the absence of technology that anchors them to friends and family, students felt bored and isolated. One wrote: "I felt quite alone and secluded from my life. Although I go to a school with thousands of students, the fact that I was not able to communicate with anyone via technology was almost unbearable."

The study reveals a paradigm shift in human interaction. A completely digital generation is viscerally wedded to electronic toys, so much so that technology has become an indispensable part of young people's lives.

Perceived advantages: Electronically abstinent students stated that they spent more time on course work, took better notes, and were more focused. As a result, they said they learned more and became more productive. They also reported that they spent more time with loved ones and friends face-to-face. Life slowed down and the day seemed much longer to some.

YOUR TASK Discuss in class, in a chat, or in an online post the following questions: Have you ever unplugged? What was that experience like? Could you give up your cell phone, iPod, TV, car radio, magazines, newspapers, and computer (no texting, Facebook, or IM) for a day or longer? What would you do instead? Is there any harm in not being able to unplug?

7.15 Entrusting Your Data to the Cloud (L.O. 5)

Communication Technology | E-Mail | Social Media | Web

For businesses, cloud computing might as well mean cloud nine,[92] and businesses are investing heavily to migrate to the cloud.[93] Companies are increasingly relying on cloud-based computer applications that can be accessed by mobile phones, tablets, and computers anytime and anywhere. If you use Amazon, Flickr, Gmail, Facebook, or Dropbox, to name a few, you are already participating in cloud computing. Your photos and other data are stored in remote locations, and you can access them with your laptop, netbook, smartphone, or tablet.

Companies are lured to cloud computing by the promise of greater efficiency and higher profits. Blue Cross of Pennsylvania has enabled its 300,000 members to access medical histories and claims information with their smartphones. Like other tech companies, Serena Software has fully embraced the cloud, even using Facebook as the primary source of internal communication. Coca-Cola Enterprises has provided 40,000 sales reps, truck drivers, and other workers in the field with portable devices to connect with the home office instantly, allowing them to respond to changing customer needs and problems.

However, skeptics warn that convenience carries risks, and that caution is in order. For one thing, once the information leaves our electronic device for the cloud, we don't know who may intercept it. In addition to data security, networks must be reliable, so that users can access them anytime. Amazon's service outages, while rare, tend to lead to far-reaching cascading disruptions in other cloud services.[94] In the past such outages knocked out the websites of several organizations, including Reddit, Foursquare, Pfizer, Netflix, and Nasdaq, all of which were using Amazon's cloud-based technology.[95] The other major risk has to do with data security and digital privacy. The hacking of sites containing risqué celebrity photos outraged Hollywood[96] and illustrates the dangers of entrusting files and data to the cloud.

YOUR TASK Which cloud services or applications are you already using? What are their advantages and disadvantages? Can you identify security risks that the desire for convenience may invite? Which data types are potentially most sensitive? Is convenience worth the risk? Should sensitive data and revealing information be entrusted to the cloud? If your instructor directs, write an e-mail briefly discussing the benefits and drawbacks of cloud storage, or post a short response to the discussion board of your learning-management system (e.g., Blackboard, Moodle).

Test Your Etiquette IQ

New communication platforms and casual workplace environments have blurred the lines of appropriateness, leaving workers wondering how to navigate uncharted waters. Indicate whether the following statements are true or false. Then see if you agree with the responses on p. R-1.

1. Because e-mail is not transmitted on letterhead stationery and is rather casual, it doesn't require you to apply the same formal standards that you use for other office correspondence.

   ________ True ________ False

2. If you receive an e-mail from Kevin that contains important information that Lisa should know, you should take advantage of the forwarding function by sending the message on to Lisa, thus saving you the trouble of rekeying the important parts.

   ________ True ________ False

3. At a business lunch in a restaurant, you should place your cell phone on the table so that you can answer it quickly without bothering patrons at other tables.

   ________ True ________ False

Chat About It

In each chapter you will find five discussion questions related to the chapter material. Your instructor may assign these topics for you to discuss in class, in an online chat room, or on an online discussion board. Some of the discussion topics may require outside research. You may also be asked to read and respond to postings made by your classmates.

TOPIC 1: Why is clear and correct writing still needed, even in short posts, IM, and text messages?

TOPIC 2: Describe a time when you should have had a face-to-face meeting instead of sending an electronic message. Why would the face-to-face meeting have been better?

TOPIC 3: Find an example of an e-mail or text that caused a problem for the sender because the message found its way to an unintended recipient. What problem did the situation cause?

TOPIC 4: What is your strategy to avoid sending an IM, tweet, or text message that you might regret later?

TOPIC 5: The Telephone Consumer Protection Act of 1991 has also been applied to unsolicited SMS messages, limiting them severely and potentially costing spammers $500 per violation. What are the conflicting interests from the point of view of smartphone owners, the SMS marketing industry, and companies that want to get their messages out to consumers?

Grammar and Mechanics | *Review 7*

Apostrophes and Other Punctuation

Review Guides 31 through 38 about apostrophes and other punctuation in Appendix D, Grammar and Mechanics Guide, beginning on page D-12. On a separate sheet or on your computer, revise the following sentences to correct errors in the use of apostrophes and other punctuation. For each error you locate, write the guide number that reflects this usage. The more you recognize the reasons, the better you will learn these punctuation guidelines. If a sentence is correct, write *C*. When you finish, check your answers on page Key-2.

EXAMPLE: Employees were asked not to use the companys computers to stream video.

REVISION: Employees were asked not to use the **company's** computers to stream video. [Guide 32]

1. In just one years time, James increased the number of his blog followers by 50 percent.
2. Many followers of James blog commented on the overuse of the Reply All button.
3. Even her friends resented Rebecca smoking in the hallways.
4. Our three top sales reps, Sam, Ashley, and Noah received substantial bonuses.
5. Success often depends on an individuals ability to adapt to change.
6. You must replace the ink cartridge see page 8 in the manual, before printing.
7. Zeke wondered whether all sales managers databases needed to be updated.
8. (Direct quotation) The death of e-mail, said Mike Song, has been greatly exaggerated.
9. My friend recommended an article titled Ten Tools for Building Your Own Mobile App.
10. The staffing meeting starts at 10 a.m. sharp, doesn't it.

References

[1] Huang, D. (2015, June 3). The ten commandments for Wall Street interns. *The Wall Street Journal.* Retrieved from http://blogs.wsj.com/moneybeat/2015/06/03/the-ten-commandments-for-wall-street-interns

[2] Feintzeig, R. (2014, June 17). A company without email? Not so fast. *The Wall Street Journal.* Retrieved from http://www.wsj.com/articles/a-company-without-email-not-so-fast-1403048134

[3] Cardon, P. W., & Marshall, B. (2015). The hype and reality of social media use for work collaboration and team communication. *International Journal of Business Communication, 52*(3), 286. doi:10.1177/2329488414525446; Purcell, K., & Rainie, L. (2014, December 30). Email and the Internet are the dominant technological tools in American workplaces. Pew Research Center. Retrieved from http://www.wsj.com/articles/a-company-without-email-not-so-fast-1403048134

[4] Jacobs, S. P. (2015, October 29). How e-mail killer Slack will change the future of work. *Time.* Retrieved from http://time.com/4092354/how-e-mail-killer-slack-will-change-the-future-of-work

[5] Feintzeig, R. (2014, June 17). A company without email? Not so fast. *The Wall Street Journal.* Retrieved from http://www.wsj.com/articles/a-company-without-email-not-so-fast-1403048134

[6] Purcell, K., & Rainie, L. (2014, December 30). Email and the Internet are the dominant technological tools in American workplaces. Pew Research Center. Retrieved from http://www.wsj.com/articles/a-company-without-email-not-so-fast-1403048134

[7] van Rijn, J. (2016, February). The ultimate mobile email stats overview. eMailmonday. Retrieved from http://www.emailmonday.com/mobile-email-usage-statistics; O'Dell, J. (2014, January 22). 65% of all email gets opened first on a mobile device—and that's great news for marketers. Venturebeat. Retrieved from http://venturebeat.com/2014/01/22/65-of-all-email-gets-opened-first-on-a-mobile-device-and-thats-great-news-for-marketers

[8] Lamb, S. E. (2015). *Writing well for business success.* New York: St. Martin's Griffin, p. 138.

[9] Middleton, D. (2011, March 3). Students struggle for words. *The Wall Street Journal,* Executive edition. Retrieved from http://online.wsj.com/article/SB10001424052748703409904576174651780110970.html

[10] Ibid.

[11] Feintzeig, R. (2014, June 17). A company without email? Not so fast. *The Wall Street Journal.* Retrieved from http://www.wsj.com/articles/a-company-without-email-not-so-fast-1403048134

[12] Smith, J., & Sugar, R. (2015, June 29). 14 email etiquette rules every professional should know. Business Insider. Retrieved from http://www.businessinsider.com/email-etiquette-rules-every-professional-should-know-2015-6

[13] Vance, A. (2014, December 4). The eight most expensive e-mail snafus in corporate history. *Bloomberg Business.* Retrieved from http://www.bloomberg.com/bw/articles/2014-12-04/e-mail-the-eight-most-expensive-snafus-in-corporate-history

[14] Brandeisky, K. (2015, March 3). 5 things you didn't know about using personal email at work. *Money.* Retrieved from http://time.com/money/3729939/work-personal-email-hillary-clinton-byod

[15] American Management Association. (2014, November 17). The latest on workplace monitoring and surveillance. American Management Association. Retrieved from http://www.amanet.org/training/articles/The-Latest-on-Workplace-Monitoring-and-Surveillance.aspx; Tugend, A. (2012, April 21). What to think about before you hit 'Send.' *The New York Times,* p. B5.

[16] Lamb, S. E. (2015). *Writing well for business success.* New York: St. Martin's Griffin, p. 139.

[17] Kupritz, V. W., & Cowell, E. (2011, January). Productive management communication: Online and face-to-face. *Journal of Business Communication, 48*(1), 70-71.

[18] Terk, N. (2012, January 18). E-mail education: Global headaches and universal best practices. Newswire Today. Retrieved from http://www.newswiretoday.com/news/104276

[19] Schmidt, E., & Rosenberg, J. (2014, September 24). 9 rules for emailing from Google exec Eric Schmidt. *Time.* Retrieved from http://time.com/3425368/google-email-rules

[20] Smith, A. (2015, April 1). U.S. smartphone use in 2015. Pew Research Center. Retrieved from http://www.pewinternet.org/2015/04/01/us-smartphone-use-in-2015

[21] Based on Rawes, E. (2015, February 13.) 5 of the funniest autocorrect fails in work text messages. CheatSheet. Retrieved from http://www.cheatsheet.com/personal-finance/5-of-the-funniest-autocorrect-fails-in-work-text-messages.html/?a=viewall

[22] Matlack, C. (2015, October 8). One company tries life without (much) e-mail. *Bloomberg Business.* Retrieved from http://www.bloomberg.com/news/articles/2015-10-08/one-company-tries-life-without-much-e-mail

[23] The Radicati Group. (2015, March). Instant messaging statistics report, 2015-2019. Radicati Group. Retrieved from http://www.radicati.com/wp/wp-content/uploads/2015/02/Instant_Messaging_Statistics_Report_2015-2019_Executive_Summary.pdf

[24] Baldwin, H. (2014, February 17). Instant messaging is going corporate. *Forbes.* Retrieved from http://www.forbes.com/sites/howardbaldwin/2014/02/17/instant-messaging-is-going-corporate

[25] Bit, K. (2014, June 9). Cohen's Point72 bans instant messaging for some managers. *Bloomberg Business.* Retrieved from http://www.bloomberg.com/news/articles/2014-06-09/cohen-s-point72-bans-instant-messaging-for-some-managers; Finnegan, M. (2013, December 6). JPMorgan plans instant messaging ban for traders. *Computerworld UK.* Retrieved from http://www.computerworlduk.com/news/it-business/jp-morgan-plans-instant-messaging-ban-for-traders-3493907

[26] Anderson, D. (2014). Best practices for employees to protect the company from hackers. *Entrepreneur.* Retrieved from https://www.entrepreneur.com/article/237174.

[27] Flynn, N. (2012, March). *The social media handbook: Rules, policies, and best practices to successfully manage your organization's social media presence, posts, and potential.* San Francisco: Pfeiffer/Wiley.

[28] Marino, K. (2012, June 22). DWI: Driving while intexticated—infographic. OnlineSchools.com. Retrieved from http://www.onlineschools.com/in-focus/driving-while-intexticated

[29] Driving while intexticated: The new DWI. (2014). Retrieved from http://vehiclemd.com/driving-while-intexticated-the-new-dwi

[30] Flynn, N. (2012, March). *The social media handbook: Rules, policies, and best practices to successfully manage your organization's social media presence, posts, and potential*. San Francisco: Pfeiffer/Wiley.

[31] Malito, A. (2015, November 19). Here's the price advisers pay for ignoring boring email archives. *Investment News*. Retrieved from http://www.investmentnews.com/article/20151119/FREE/151119923/heres-the-price-advisers-pay-for-ignoring-boring-email-archives

[32] Sidel, R. (2015, December 21). Hackers exploit staffers at banks. *The Wall Street Journal*, p. C1.

[33] Marketing News Staff. (2010, March 15). Digital dozen. AMA.org. Retrieved from http://www.marketingpower.com/resourceLibrary/Publications/MarketingNews/2010/3_15_10/Digital%20Dozen.pdf

[34] Flynn, N. (2012, March). *The social media handbook: Rules, policies, and best practices to successfully manage your organization's social media presence, posts, and potential*. San Francisco: Pfeiffer/Wiley.

[35] Based on The Emily Post Institute. (2011, April 15). Text messaging anarchy. Retrieved from http://emilypost.com/2011/04/text-messaging-anarchy

[36] All, A. (2009, October 6). Wikis: Where work gets done. IT Business Edge. Retrieved from http://www.itbusinessedge.com/cm/blogs/all/wikis-where-work-gets-done/?cs=36409

[37] WEBS Yarn Store. (n.d.). Ready, set, Knit! Retrieved from http://blog.yarn.com/ready-set-knit-427-kathy-talks-with-carol-sulcoski; Kessler, S. (2011, February 28). 3 podcast success stories from creative small businesses. Mashable. Retrieved from http://mashable.com/2011/02/28/podcast-small-business/#3yKs0.MbfGqd

[38] Smith, A. (2015, April 1). U.S. smartphone use in 2015. Pew Research Center. Retrieved from http://www.pewinternet.org/2015/04/01/us-smartphone-use-in-2015

[39] Clark, D. (2014, October 28). How to launch a successful podcast – fast. *Forbes*. Retrieved from http://www.forbes.com/sites/dorieclark/2014/10/28/how-to-launch-a-successful-podcast-fast; Casel, B. (2011, March 25). 7 Tips for launching a successful podcast. Mashable. http://mashable.com/2011/03/25/podcasting-tips

[40] Jackson, P., & Klobas, J. (2012, July 23). Deciding to use an enterprise wiki: The role of social institutions and scripts. *Knowledge Management Research & Practice, 11*, 323-333. doi:10.1057/kmrp.2012.20; Behringer, N., & Sassenberg, K. (2015, February 19). Introducing social media for knowledge management: Determinants of employees' intentions to adopt new tools. *Computers in Human Behavior, 48*, 290-296. Retrieved from http://www.sciencedirect.com

[41] Brichni, M., Mandran, N., Gzara, L., Dupuy-Chessa, S., & Rozier, D. (2014). Wiki for knowledge sharing, a user-centered evaluation approach: A case study at STMicroelectronics. *Journal of Knowledge Management, 18*(6), 1232-1217. Retrieved from http://www.emeraldinsight.com; Majchrzak, A., Wagner, C., & Yates, D. (2006). Corporate wiki users: Results of a survey. CiteSeer. Retrieved from http://citeseerx.ist.psu.edu/viewdoc/summary?doi=10.1.1.97.407

[42] The five main uses of wikis based on Nations, D. (2009). The business wiki: Wiki in the workplace. About.com: Web Trends. Retrieved from http://webtrends.about.com/od/wiki/a/business-wiki.htm

[43] Houlahan, A. (2015, September 28). The importance of blogging for your brand. Retrieved from https://www.adamhoulahan.com/the-importance-of-blogging-for-your-brand

[44] Barnes, N. G., Lescault, A. M., & Holmes, G. (2015). The 2015 Fortune 500 and social media: Instagram gains, blogs lose. Center for Marketing Research, University of Massachusetts Dartmouth. Retrieved from http://www.umassd.edu/cmr/socialmediaresearch/2015fortune500andsocialmedia

[45] Barnes, N. G., Lescault, A. M., & Holmes, G. (2015, November). The 2015 Fortune 500 and social media: Instagram gains, blogs lose. The Conference Board. Retrieved from https://www.conference-board.org/topics/publicationdetail.cfm?publicationid=7113&topicid=30&subtopicid=220

[46] Based on Waring, D. (2015, June 30.) Best small business blogs of 2015. FitSmallBusiness. Retrieved from http://fitsmallbusiness.com/small-business-blogs/#

[47] Marriott, Jr., J. W. "Bill." (2012, June 11). Five years blogging—Pen pals, pilates and hitting publish. Retrieved from http://www.blogs.marriott.com/marriott-on-the-move/2012/06/5-years-as-a-blogger.html

[48] Schultz, E. J. (2016, January 4). See the "Crash the Super Bowl" finalists' ads. *Advertising Age*. Retrieved from http://adage.com/article/special-report-super-bowl/crash-super-bowl-finalist-ads/301978

[49] Coursey, D. (n.d.). What racist webcams? HP handled issue well. *PC World*. Retrieved from http://www.pcworld.com/article/185270/What_Racist_Webcams_HP_Handled_Issue_Well.html

[50] Coy, C. (2014, February 27). The future of corporate learning: Internal blogging. Cornerstone Blog. Retrieved from https://www.cornerstoneondemand.com/blog/future-corporate-learning-internal-blogging#.VpJWYvkrJhE

[51] Meister, J. (2015, March 30). Future of work: Using gamification for human resources. *Forbes*. Retrieved from http://www.forbes.com/sites/jeannemeister/2015/03/30/future-of-work-using-gamification-for-human-resources/#2715e4857a0b570f838432ba

[52] Ibid.

[53] Ibid.

[54] Lindstrom, M. (2012, July 3). How many lives does a brand have? Fast Company. Retrieved from http://www.fastcompany.com/1841927/buyology-martin-lindstrom-lives-of-brands-china-marketing

[55] Brogan, C. (2012, July 13). Become a dream feeder. Retrieved from http:// www.chrisbrogan.com/dreamfeeder

[56] Cairns, B. (2012, January 24). Blog comment. Retrieved from http://blog.guykawasaki.com/2011/06/how-to-increase-your-likability.html#axzz20dk8CnTk

[57] Cornwall, J. (2015, October 24). Why email marketing is more effective than social media. *Forbes*. Retrieved from http://www.forbes.com/sites/jeffcornwall/2015/10/24/why-email-marketing-is-more-effective-than-social-media

[58] Pozin, I. (2014, July 12). Productivity vs. distraction: Should you block social media at work? TNW News. Retrieved from http://thenextweb.com/entrepreneur/2014/07/12/productivity-vs-distraction-block-social-media-work/#gref

[59] Proskauer Rose LLP. (2014). Social media in the workplace around the world 3.0. 2013/14 survey, p. 2. Retrieved from http://www.proskauer.com/files/uploads/social-media-in-the-workplace-2014.pdf

[60] Purcell, K., & Rainie, L. (2014, December 30). Technology's impact on workers. Pew Research Center. Retrieved from http://www.pewinternet.org/2014/12/30/technologys-impact-on-workers

[61] Perrin, A. (2015, October 18). Social media usage: 2005-2015. Pew Research Center, p. 4. Retrieved from http://www.pewinternet.org/files/2015/10/PI_2015-10-08_Social-Networking-Usage-2005-2015_FINAL.pdf

[62] Duggan, M., Ellison, N. B., Lampe, C., Lenhart, A., & Madden, M. (2015, January 9). Social media update 2014. Pew Research Center. Retrieved from http://www.pewinternet.org/2015/01/09/social-media-update-2014

[63] Barnes, N. G., Lescault, A. M., & Holmes, G. (2015). The 2015 Fortune 500 and social media: Instagram gains, blogs lose. Center for Marketing Research, University of Massachusetts Dartmouth. Retrieved from http://www.umassd.edu/cmr/socialmediaresearch/2015fortune500andsocialmedia

[64] Schaefer, M. (2014, February 11). IBM CEO Ginni Rometty points to social strategy with a twist. Grow. Retrieved from http://www.businessesgrow.com/2014/02/11/ginni-rometty

[65] Li, C. (2015, April 7). Why no one uses the corporate social network. *Harvard Business Review*. Retrieved from https://hbr.org/2015/04/why-no-one-uses-the-corporate-social-network

[66] Cardon, P. (2015). Enterprise social networks (Internal social media platforms). *NBEA 2015 Yearbook: Recent and Projected Technology Trends Affecting Business Education*, p. 37.

[67] Lavenda, D. (2014, February 6). How Red Robin transformed its business with Yammer. Fast Company. Retrieved from http://www.fastcompany.com/3025396/work-smart/how-red-robin-burgers-got-yummier-with-yammer; Mullaney, T. (2012, May 16). Social media is reinventing how business is done. *USA Today*. Retrieved from http://www.usatoday.com/money/economy/story/2012-05-14/social-media-economy-companies/55029088/1

[68] Li, C. (2015, April 7). Why no one uses the corporate social network. *Harvard Business Review*. Retrieved from https://hbr.org/2015/04/why-no-one-uses-the-corporate-social-network

[69] Mullaney, T. (2012, May 16). Social media is reinventing how business is done. *USA Today*. Retrieved from http://www.usatoday.com/money/economy/story/2012-05-14/social-media-economy-companies/55029088/1

[70] Schaefer, M. (2014, February 11). IBM CEO Ginni Rometty points to social strategy with a twist. Grow. Retrieved from http://www.businessesgrow.com/2014/02/11/ginni-rometty

[71] Ciccatelli, A. (2014, April 14). The reality of managing social media risk in business. Inside Counsel. Retrieved from http://www.insidecounsel.com/2014/04/24/the-reality-of-managing-social-media-risk-in-busin

[72] Proskauer Rose LLP. (2014). Social media in the workplace around the world 3.0. 2013/14 survey, p. 2. Retrieved from http://www.proskauer.com/files/uploads/social-media-in-the-workplace-2014.pdf

[73] Purcell, K., & Rainie, L. (2014, December 30). Technology's impact on workers. Pew Research Center. Retrieved from http://www.pewinternet.org/2014/12/30/technologys-impact-on-workers

[74] Flynn, N. (2012, March). *The social media handbook: Rules, policies, and best practices to successfully manage your organization's social media presence, posts, and potential.* San Francisco: Pfeiffer/Wiley.

[75] Pozin, I. (2014, July 12). Productivity vs. distraction: Should you block social media at work? TNW News. Retrieved from http://thenextweb.com/entrepreneur/2014/07/12/productivity-vs-distraction-block-social-media-work/#gref; Wright, A. D. (2012, February 3). Social media policies slowly catch on worldwide. Society for Human Resource Management. Retrieved from http://www.shrm.org/hrdisciplines/global/Articles/Pages/WorldwidePolicies.aspx

[76] Proskauer Rose LLP. (2014). Social media in the workplace around the world 3.0. 2013/14 survey, p. 2. Retrieved from http://www.proskauer.com/files/uploads/social-media-in-the-workplace-2014.pdf

[77] Villano, M. (2009, April 26). The online divide between work and play. *The New York Times*. Retrieved from http://www.nytimes.com

[78] Flynn, N. (2012, March). *The social media handbook: Rules, policies, and best practices to successfully manage your organization's social media presence, posts, and potential.* San Francisco: Pfeiffer/Wiley.

[79] Ibid.

[80] Ibid.

[81] Bryan, B. (2015, June 24). Millennials are more than happy to trade privacy for security. Business Insider. Retrieved from http://www.businessinsider.com/millennials-willing-to-trade-privacy-for-safety-online-2015-6

[82] Turkle. S. (2011). *Alone together: Why we expect more from technology and less from each other.* New York: Basic Books, p. 1.

[83] Burns-McBeth, C. (2015, March 3). What is the real use of big data technology in our society? *Forbes*. Retrieved from http://www.forbes.com/sites/sungardas/2015/03/03/big-data-or-big-brother/#2715e4857a0b48ae89467a43

[84] Clifford, C. (2014, October 3). Marissa Mayer: Privacy fanatic will have a less awesome life online. *Entrepreneur.* Retrieved from http://www.entrepreneur.com/article/238084

[85] Hutchinson, A. (2014, January 21). The inevitable bite of buying followers and likes. Social Media Today. Retrieved from http://www.socialmediatoday.com/content/inevitable-bite-buying-followers-and-likes

[86] Dorsey, J. (2016, January 5). Twitter post. Retrieved from https://mobile.twitter.com/jack/status/684496529621557248

[87] Greene, D. (Host). (2009, July 2). Twitter music reviews: Criticism as haiku. *Morning Edition.* Washington, DC: National Public Radio. Retrieved from http://www.npr.org/templates/story/story.php?storyId=106178234

[88] Ibid.

[89] Montoya, M. (2012, October 16.) 5 ways Twitter can get you fired. Examiner.com. Retrieved from http://www.examiner.com/article/5-ways-twitter-can-get-you-fired

[90] Hempel, J. (2015, August 2). I'm quitting social media to learn what I actually like. *Wired.* Retrieved from http://www.wired.com/2015/08/im-quitting-social-media-learn-actually-like

[91] Moeller, S. D. (2010). 24 hours: Unplugged. Retrieved from http://withoutmedia.wordpress.com; The Associated Press. (2009, September 6). Center tries to treat Web addicts. *The New York Times*. Retrieved from http://www.nytimes.com

[92] Activity based on based on Hamm, S. (2009, June 15). Cloud computing's big bang for business. *Businessweek*, pp. 43-44; Wildstrom, S. H. (2009, April 6). What to entrust to the cloud. *Businessweek*, pp. 89-90; Burrows, P. (2009, August 17). Apple and Google: Another step apart. *Businessweek*, pp. 24-25; and Hamm, S. (2009, April 6). IBM reaches for the clouds. *Businessweek*, p. 34.

[93] Columbus, L. (2015, June 8). 55% of enterprises predict cloud computing will enable new business models in three years. *Forbes*. Retrieved from http://www.forbes.com/sites/louiscolumbus/2015/06/08/55-of-enterprises-predict-cloud-computing-will-enable-new-business-models-in-three-years/#2715e4857a0b158d8cb7c0b2

[94] Babcock, C. (2015, September 22). Amazon disruption produces cloud outage spiral. Information Week. Retrieved from www.informationweek.com/cloud/infrastructure-as-a-service/amazon-disruption-produces-cloud-outage-spiral/d/d-id/1322279

[95] Weissberger, A. (2011, April 22). Amazon's EC2 outage proves cloud failure recovery is a myth! The Viodi View. Retrieved from http://viodi.com/2011/04/22/amazons-ec2-outage-proves-cloud-failure-recovery-is-a-myth

[96] Burns, J. M. (2015, September 1). A massive leak of risqué and nude celebrity photos sparks outrage in Hollywood. *Huffington Post.* Retrieved from http://www.huffingtonpost.com/john-m-burns/a-massive-leak-of-risque-_b_5747734.html

Chapter 8 Positive Messages

LEARNING OUTCOMES

After studying this chapter, you should be able to

1 Understand the channels through which typical positive messages travel in the digital era—e-mails, memos, and business letters—and apply the 3-x-3 writing process.

2 Compose direct messages that make requests, respond to inquiries online and offline, and deliver step-by-step instructions.

3 Prepare contemporary messages that make direct claims and voice complaints, including those posted online.

4 Create adjustment messages that salvage customers' trust and promote further business.

5 Write special messages that convey kindness and goodwill.

Stuart Jenner/Shutterstock.com

JetBlue: Speedy Customer Service with Humor

Yeamake/Shutterstock.com

JetBlue, the low-cost airline renowned for its superior customer service, handles thousands of routine messages each day. Because the company's on-the-go travelers need real-time answers, one of JetBlue's primary channels for communicating with them is Twitter. The social media site allows the airline to quickly engage with customers who tweet typical business messages, from neutral inquiries about airline policies to positive messages about JetBlue's service—and the occasional complaint. How companies engage with negative messages is discussed in Chapter 9.

Responses to routine messages use the direct strategy, which is well suited for brief tweets. JetBlue's 25 Twitter customer service reps analyze each situation, organize their ideas for coherence, and frame replies to yield positive outcomes. What's more, the goal is to do all that within ten minutes of receiving a tweet!

One of the reasons social media work so well for JetBlue's routine communication is that the one-on-one conversations are an excellent way to build goodwill. One happy customer recently wrote, "Great customer service and comfortable plane. I like the added space between seats," to which a JetBlue employee responded, "Thanks, Keara! Sit back, relax, and enjoy!"[1] The cheerful response helps the customer connect with the airline and reinforces its reputation for superior customer service. JetBlue responders are also known for their humor. A customer about to take off recently sent a tweet emulating the flight attendant's distinctive Boston accent, "Ladies and gentlemen, we've now closed the *boahrdin' doorah* now *depahting'* off to Boston."[2] The customer service rep continued the joke with the reply, "Wicked good. You got that accent down! Enjoy your flight to Boston!"[3] Sprinkling in such informal dashes of humor reinforces JetBlue's strategy of using Twitter to build goodwill with its customers.

Tweets are also an effective way to respond to routine inquiries. A customer who asks a question about changing flights receives factual information written in a direct and concise manner: "The $50 is for a confirmed seat for our same day change policy. Standby is only allowed for the flight prior to yours."[4] Such a straightforward answer fits JetBlue's ethos of complete transparency with its customers.

The airline's Customer Bill of Rights states "JetBlue is dedicated to bringing humanity back to air travel." This organizational mission is apparent in many of the customer service representatives' direct communications. A rep recently responded to a grateful customer whose fees were waived on a flight to attend a family funeral: "We're happy to do what we can to assist families during this difficult time. All the best."[5] The respectful and empathic reply reflects the airline's singular approach to serving customers and sheds the best possible light on the organization. Such communication is one of the reasons JetBlue has repeatedly won the J. D. Power & Associates award for *Highest Customer Satisfaction Among Low-Cost Carriers in North America*.[6]

Critical Thinking

- Why are tweets particularly effective for composing direct responses to routine inquiries?
- When JetBlue customer service representatives engage with customers who have inquired about the airline's products or services, is it appropriate to do more than just answer the question?
- Why do organizations such as JetBlue, Walmart, and Amazon embrace customer comments, some of which may not be positive?

Neutral and Positive Messages: The Writing Process

LEARNING OUTCOME 1

Understand the channels through which typical positive messages travel in the digital era—e-mails, memos, and business letters—and apply the 3-x-3 writing process.

In the workplace most messages are positive or neutral and, therefore, direct. Positive messages are routine and straightforward; they help workers conduct everyday business. Such routine messages include simple requests for information or action, replies to customers, and explanations to coworkers. Other types of positive messages are instructions, direct claims, and complaints.

E-mails, memos, and letters are the channels most frequently used. In addition, businesses today must listen and respond to social media. At the same time, in some industries, memos continue to be an important channel of communication within organizations, whereas letters are a vital paper-based external channel. As discussed in Chapter 7, e-mail and social media are used to communicate within organizations as well as with outside audiences. What do all these channels have in common? As shown in Chapter 1, they all require solid writing skills. In the glaring light of social media, writing skills—or the lack of them—are amplified mercilessly and can sink careers.

In this book we divide business messages into three content areas: (a) **positive** messages communicating straightforward requests, replies, and goodwill, covered in this chapter; (b) **negative** messages delivering refusals and bad news, covered in Chapter 9; and (c) **persuasive** messages, including sales pitches, covered in Chapter 10. This chapter focuses on routine, positive messages. These will make up the bulk of your workplace communication. Here is a quick review of the 3-x-3 writing process to help you apply it to positive messages. You will also learn when to respond by business letter and how to format it.

Phase 1: Analyzing, Anticipating, and Adapting

In Phase 1, prewriting, you will need to spend some time analyzing your task. It is amazing how many of us are ready to put our pens or computers into gear before engaging our minds. Too often, writers start messages without enough preparation. As you begin the writing process, ask yourself these important questions:

- **Do I really need to write this e-mail, memo, or letter?** A phone call, an IM inquiry, or a quick visit to a nearby coworker might solve the problem—and save the time and expense of a written message. On the other hand, some written messages are needed to provide a permanent record or to develop a thoughtful plan.
- **Why am I writing?** Know why you are writing and what you hope to achieve. This will help you recognize the important points and decide where to place them.
- **How will the reader react?** Visualize the reader and the effect your message will have. Imagine that you are sitting and talking with your reader. Avoid speaking bluntly, failing to explain, or ignoring your reader's needs. Shape the message to benefit the reader. Remember that e-mails may very well be forwarded to someone else and that ill-conceived social media posts can trigger very public reactions.
- **What channel should I use?** It's tempting to use e-mail for much of your correspondence. However, a phone call or face-to-face visit is a better channel choice if you need to (a) convey enthusiasm, warmth, or another emotion; (b) supply a context; or (c) smooth over disagreements. A business letter is better when the matter requires (a) a permanent record, (b) confidentiality, or (c) formality. A social media response is needed to reply to certain public posts whenever time is of the essence.
- **How can I save my reader's time?** Think of ways that you can make your message easier to comprehend at a glance. Use bullets, asterisks, lists, headings, and white space to improve readability.

Understanding Business Letters. Despite the advent of e-mail, social networking, and other digital communication technologies, in certain situations letters are still the preferred channel of communication for delivering messages *outside* an organization. Such letters go to suppliers, government agencies, other businesses, and, most important, customers. You may think that everybody is online, but at an Internet penetration rate in North America of 88 percent,[7] a portion of the U.S. population is still unplugged. Just as they are eager to connect with a majority of consumers online, businesses continue to give letters to customers a high priority because these messages, too, encourage product feedback, project a favorable image of the organization, promote future business, and signal greater formality.

Whether you send a business letter will depend on the situation and the preference of your organization. Business letters are necessary when the situation calls for a permanent record. For example, when a company enters into an agreement with another company, business letters introduce the agreement and record decisions and points of understanding. Business letters deliver contracts, explain terms, exchange ideas, negotiate agreements, answer vendor questions, and maintain customer relations.

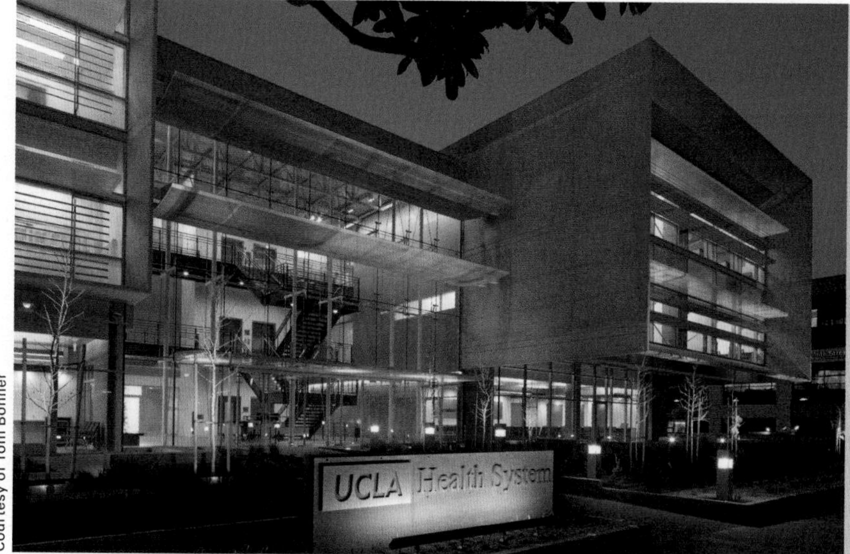

Courtesy of Tom Bonner

Despite the popularity of e-mail and other digital communication channels, certain situations call for a more permanent and confidential record that requires a letter. Businesses may mail letters to vendors, other businesses, the government, or customers. Such was the case recently when the UCLA Health network fell victim to a cyberattack that put thousands of patients' private information at risk. Sent by the organization's chief compliance officer, the letter clearly laid out the types of information that may have been affected as well as UCLA's response to the attack. It offered those affected with free credit monitoring and ended with a sincere apology. Why do you think UCLA sent a letter to its patients?

Business letters are confidential. They are less likely than electronic media to be intercepted, misdirected, forwarded, retrieved, or otherwise inspected by unintended recipients. Also, business letters presented on company stationery carry a sense of formality and importance not possible with e-mail. They look important, as illustrated in Figure 8.1, a customer-welcoming letter in the popular block format.

Finally, business letters deliver persuasive, well-considered messages. Letters can persuade people to change their actions, adopt new beliefs, make donations, contribute their time, and try new products. Direct-mail letters remain a powerful tool to promote services and products, boost online and retail traffic, and enhance customer relations. You will learn more about writing persuasive and sales messages in Chapter 10.

Phase 2: Researching, Organizing, and Drafting

In Phase 2, drafting, you will first want to check the files, gather documentation, and prepare your message. Make an outline of the points you wish to cover. For short messages jot down notes on the document you are answering or make a scratch list on your computer or handheld device.

For longer documents that require formal research, use the outlining techniques discussed in Chapter 5. As you compose your message, avoid amassing huge blocks of text. No one wants to read endless lines of type. Instead, group related information into paragraphs, preferably short ones. Paragraphs separated by white space look inviting. Be sure that each paragraph includes a topic sentence backed up by details and evidence. If you bury your main point in the middle of a paragraph, the reader may miss it. Also plan for revision, because excellence is rarely achieved on the first effort.

Peter DaSilva/The New York Time/Redux

Reality Check

Thoughtful Writing Requires Revising

"Writing thoughtfully crafted correspondence and communication takes time. More time than people care enough to spend. Writing thoughtfully takes time, and several refinement cycles. But we've become a first-draft culture. Write an e-mail. Send. Write a blog post. Publish. Write a presentation. Present. The art of crafting something well is [lost] in communications."[8]

—Nancy Duarte, *writer and graphic designer*

Figure 8.1 **Direct Letter Welcoming Customer—Block Style**

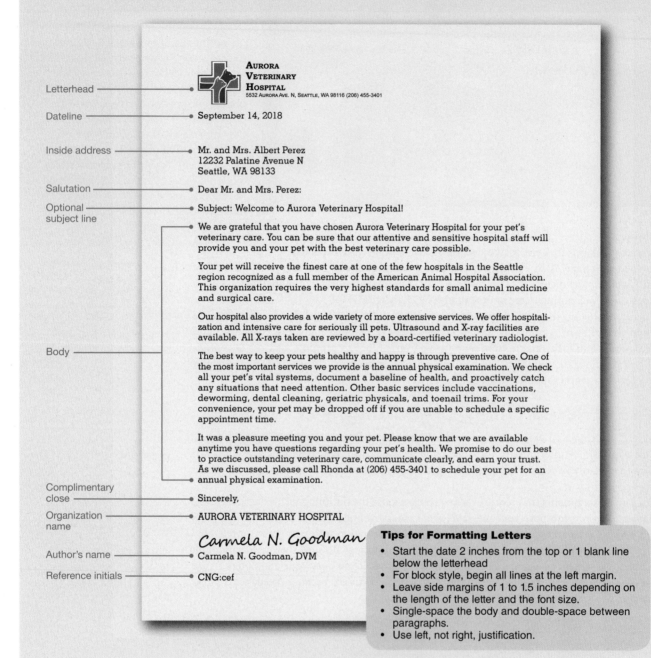

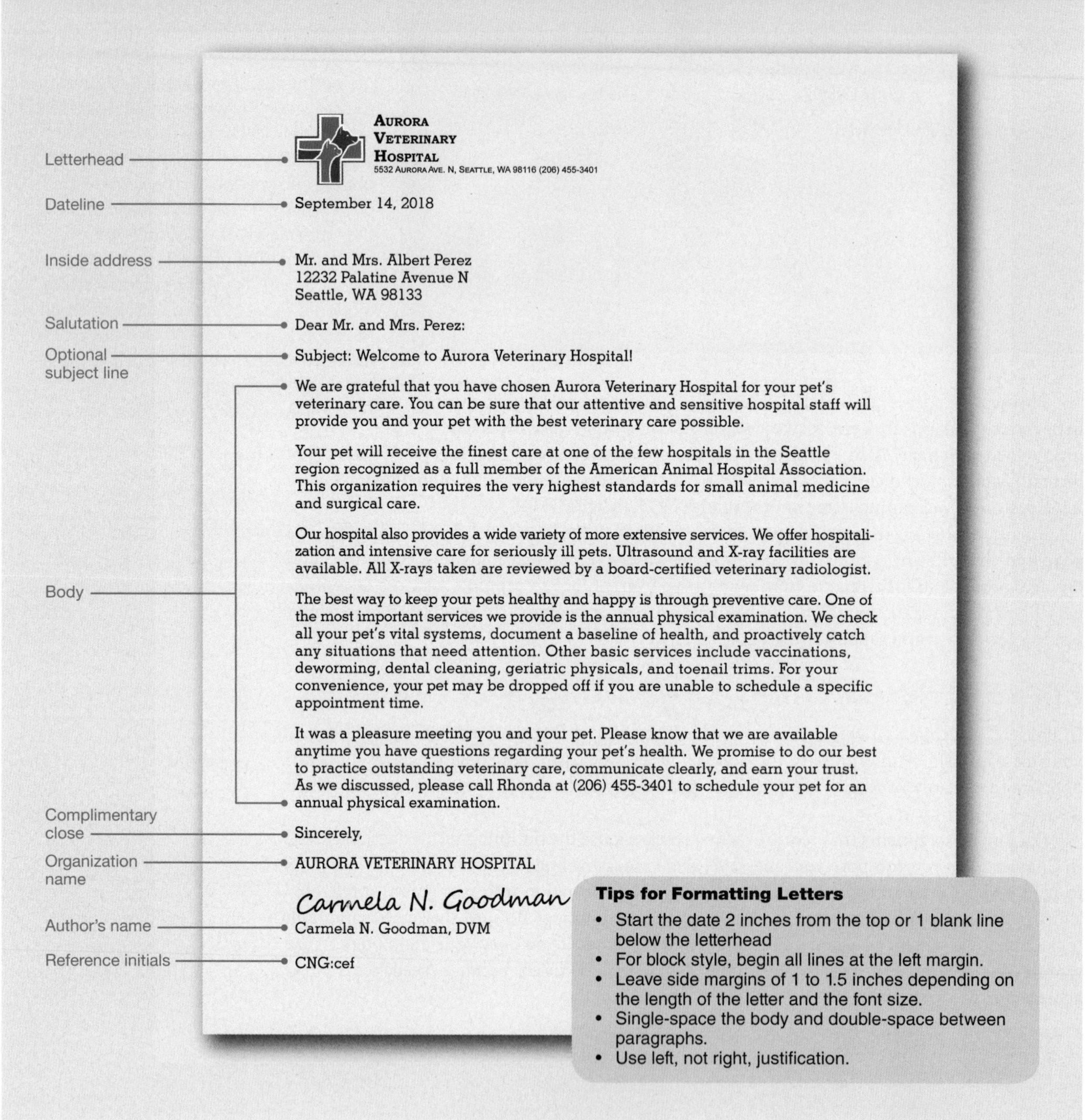

Letterhead — **Aurora Veterinary Hospital**
5532 Aurora Ave. N, Seattle, WA 98116 (206) 455-3401

Dateline — September 14, 2018

Inside address — Mr. and Mrs. Albert Perez
12232 Palatine Avenue N
Seattle, WA 98133

Salutation — Dear Mr. and Mrs. Perez:

Optional subject line — Subject: Welcome to Aurora Veterinary Hospital!

Body —

We are grateful that you have chosen Aurora Veterinary Hospital for your pet's veterinary care. You can be sure that our attentive and sensitive hospital staff will provide you and your pet with the best veterinary care possible.

Your pet will receive the finest care at one of the few hospitals in the Seattle region recognized as a full member of the American Animal Hospital Association. This organization requires the very highest standards for small animal medicine and surgical care.

Our hospital also provides a wide variety of more extensive services. We offer hospitalization and intensive care for seriously ill pets. Ultrasound and X-ray facilities are available. All X-rays taken are reviewed by a board-certified veterinary radiologist.

The best way to keep your pets healthy and happy is through preventive care. One of the most important services we provide is the annual physical examination. We check all your pet's vital systems, document a baseline of health, and proactively catch any situations that need attention. Other basic services include vaccinations, deworming, dental cleaning, geriatric physicals, and toenail trims. For your convenience, your pet may be dropped off if you are unable to schedule a specific appointment time.

It was a pleasure meeting you and your pet. Please know that we are available anytime you have questions regarding your pet's health. We promise to do our best to practice outstanding veterinary care, communicate clearly, and earn your trust. As we discussed, please call Rhonda at (206) 455-3401 to schedule your pet for an annual physical examination.

Complimentary close — Sincerely,

Organization name — AURORA VETERINARY HOSPITAL

Carmela N. Goodman

Author's name — Carmela N. Goodman, DVM

Reference initials — CNG:cef

Tips for Formatting Letters

- Start the date 2 inches from the top or 1 blank line below the letterhead
- For block style, begin all lines at the left margin.
- Leave side margins of 1 to 1.5 inches depending on the length of the letter and the font size.
- Single-space the body and double-space between paragraphs.
- Use left, not right, justification.

Phase 3: Editing, Proofreading, and Evaluating

Phase 3, revising, involves putting the final touches on your message. Careful and caring writers ask themselves the following questions:

- **Is the message clear?** Viewed from the receiver's perspective, are the ideas clear? Did you use plain English? If the message is passed on to others, will they need further explanation? Consider having a colleague critique your message if it is an important one.

- **Is the message correct?** Are the sentences complete and punctuated properly? Did you overlook any typos or misspelled words? Remember to use your spell-checker and grammar-checker to proofread your message before sending it.
- **Did you plan for feedback?** How will you know whether this message is successful? You can improve feedback by asking questions (such as *Are you comfortable with these suggestions?* or *What do you think?*). Remember to make it easy for the receiver to respond.
- **Will this message achieve its purpose?** The last step in the 3-x-3 writing process is evaluating the product.

Ethics Check

Surprising the Boss

Kyra Montes uses e-mail for nearly all messages. She is ecstatic over a new job offer and quickly sends an e-mail to her manager announcing that she is leaving. He did not know she was looking for a new position. Is this an appropriate use of e-mail?

Routine Request, Response, and Instruction Messages

In the workplace positive messages take the form of e-mails, memos, and letters. Brief positive messages are also delivered by instant messaging, texting, and social media. When you need information from a team member in another office, you might send an e-mail or use IM. If you must explain to employees a new procedure for ordering supplies and rank-and-file workers do not have company e-mail, you would write an interoffice memo. When you welcome a new customer or respond to a customer letter asking about your products, you would prepare a letter.

The majority of your business messages will involve routine requests and responses to requests, which are organized directly. Requests and replies may be transmitted in e-mails, memos, letters, or social media posts. You might, for example, receive an inquiry via Twitter or Facebook about an upcoming product launch. You may need to request information from a hotel as you plan a company conference. You might be answering an inquiry by e-mail from a customer about your services or products. These kinds of routine requests and replies follow a similar pattern.

LEARNING OUTCOME 2

Compose direct messages that make requests, respond to inquiries online and offline, and deliver step-by-step instructions.

Writing Requests

When you write messages that request information or action and you think your request will be received positively, start with the main idea. The most emphatic positions in a message are the opening and closing. Readers tend to look at them first. You should capitalize on this tendency by putting the most significant statement first. The first sentence of an information request is usually a question or a polite command. It should not be an explanation or justification, unless resistance to the request is expected. When the information or action requested is likely to be forthcoming, immediately tell the reader what you want.

The e-mail in Figure 8.2 inquiring about hotel accommodations begins immediately with the most important idea: Can the hotel provide meeting rooms and accommodations for 250 people? Instead of opening with an explanation of who the writer is or why the writer happens to be writing this message, the e-mail begins directly.

If several questions must be asked, you have two choices. You can ask the most important question first, as shown in Figure 8.2, or you can begin with a summary statement, such as *Please answer the following questions about providing meeting rooms and accommodations for 250 people from September 23 through September 26.* Avoid beginning with *Will you please. . . .* Although such a statement sounds like a question, it is actually a disguised command. Because you expect an action rather than a reply, you should punctuate this polite command with a period instead of a question mark. To avoid having to choose between a period and a question mark, just omit *Will you* and start with *Please answer.*

Ethics Check

Stretching the Truth

A magazine publisher sends you a letter saying that you should renew your subscription immediately to ensure continued delivery. Your subscription is paid for at least a year in advance, but nowhere in the letter or magazine label does your subscription end date appear. How far can a writer go in stretching the truth to achieve a purpose?

Providing Details. The body of a message that requests information or action provides necessary details. Remember that the quality of the information obtained from a request depends on the clarity of the inquiry. If you analyze your needs, organize your ideas, and

Figure 8.2 **Applying the Writing Process to a Direct Request E-Mail**

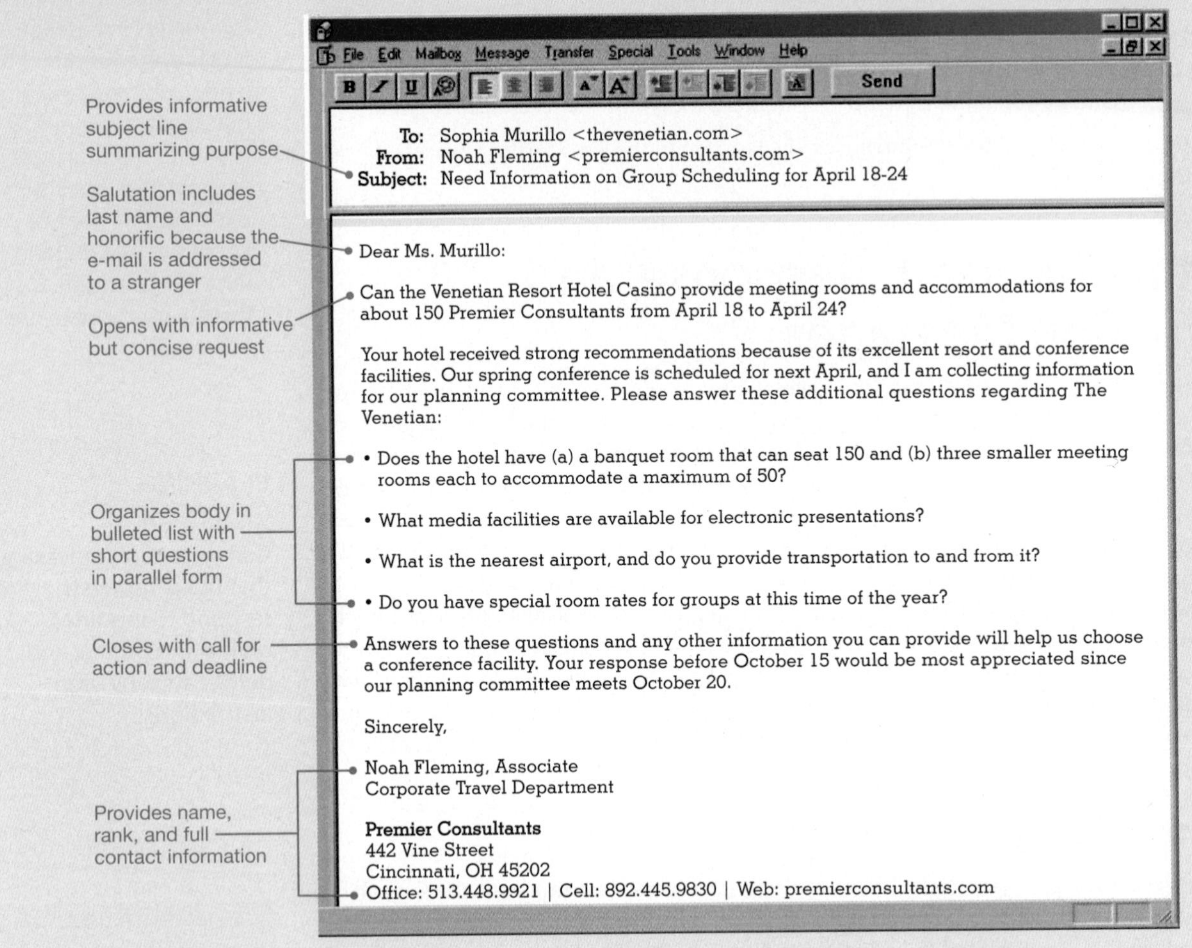
File Edit Mailbox Message Transfer Special Tools Window Help
Send
Provides informative subject line summarizing purpose
Salutation includes last name and honorific because the e-mail is addressed to a stranger
Opens with informative but concise request
Organizes body in bulleted list with short questions in parallel form
Closes with call for action and deadline
Provides name, rank, and full contact information

To: Sophia Murillo <thevenetian.com>
From: Noah Fleming <premierconsultants.com>
Subject: Need Information on Group Scheduling for April 18-24

Dear Ms. Murillo:

Can the Venetian Resort Hotel Casino provide meeting rooms and accommodations for about 150 Premier Consultants from April 18 to April 24?

Your hotel received strong recommendations because of its excellent resort and conference facilities. Our spring conference is scheduled for next April, and I am collecting information for our planning committee. Please answer these additional questions regarding The Venetian:

- Does the hotel have (a) a banquet room that can seat 150 and (b) three smaller meeting rooms each to accommodate a maximum of 50?
- What media facilities are available for electronic presentations?
- What is the nearest airport, and do you provide transportation to and from it?
- Do you have special room rates for groups at this time of the year?

Answers to these questions and any other information you can provide will help us choose a conference facility. Your response before October 15 would be most appreciated since our planning committee meets October 20.

Sincerely,

Noah Fleming, Associate
Corporate Travel Department

Premier Consultants
442 Vine Street
Cincinnati, OH 45202
Office: 513.448.9921 | Cell: 892.445.9830 | Web: premierconsultants.com

frame your request logically, you are likely to receive a meaningful answer that doesn't require a follow-up message. Whenever possible, focus on benefits to the reader (*To ensure that you receive the exact sweater you want, send us your color choice*). To improve readability, itemize appropriate information in bulleted or numbered lists. Notice that the questions in Figure 8.2 are bulleted, and they are parallel. That is, they use the same balanced construction.

Closing With Appreciation and an Action Request. In the closing of your message, tell the reader courteously what is to be done. If a date is important, set an end date to take action and explain why. Some careless writers end request messages simply with *Thank you*, forcing the reader to review the contents to determine what is expected and when. You can save the reader's time by spelling out the action to be taken. Avoid other overused endings such as *Thank you for your cooperation* (trite), *Thank you in advance for . . .* (trite and presumptuous), and *If you have any questions, do not hesitate to call me* (suggests that you didn't make yourself clear).

Showing appreciation is always appropriate, but try to do so in a fresh and efficient manner. For example, you could hook your thanks to the end date (*Thanks for returning the* questionnaire before May 5, when we will begin tabulation*). You might connect your appreciation to a statement developing reader benefits (*We are grateful for the information you will provide because it will help us serve you better*). You could briefly describe how the information will help you (*I appreciate this information, which will enable me to . . .*). When possible, make it easy for the reader to comply with your request (*Note your answers on this sheet and return it in the postage-paid envelope* or *Here is my e-mail address so that you can reach me quickly*).

Responding to Requests

Often, your messages will respond directly and favorably to requests for information or action. A customer wants information about a product, a supplier asks to arrange a meeting, an employee inquires about a procedure, or a manager requests your input on a marketing campaign. In complying with such requests, you will want to apply the same direct strategy you used in making requests.

A customer reply e-mail that starts with an effective subject line, as shown in Figure 8.3, helps the reader recognize the topic immediately. The subject line refers in abbreviated form to

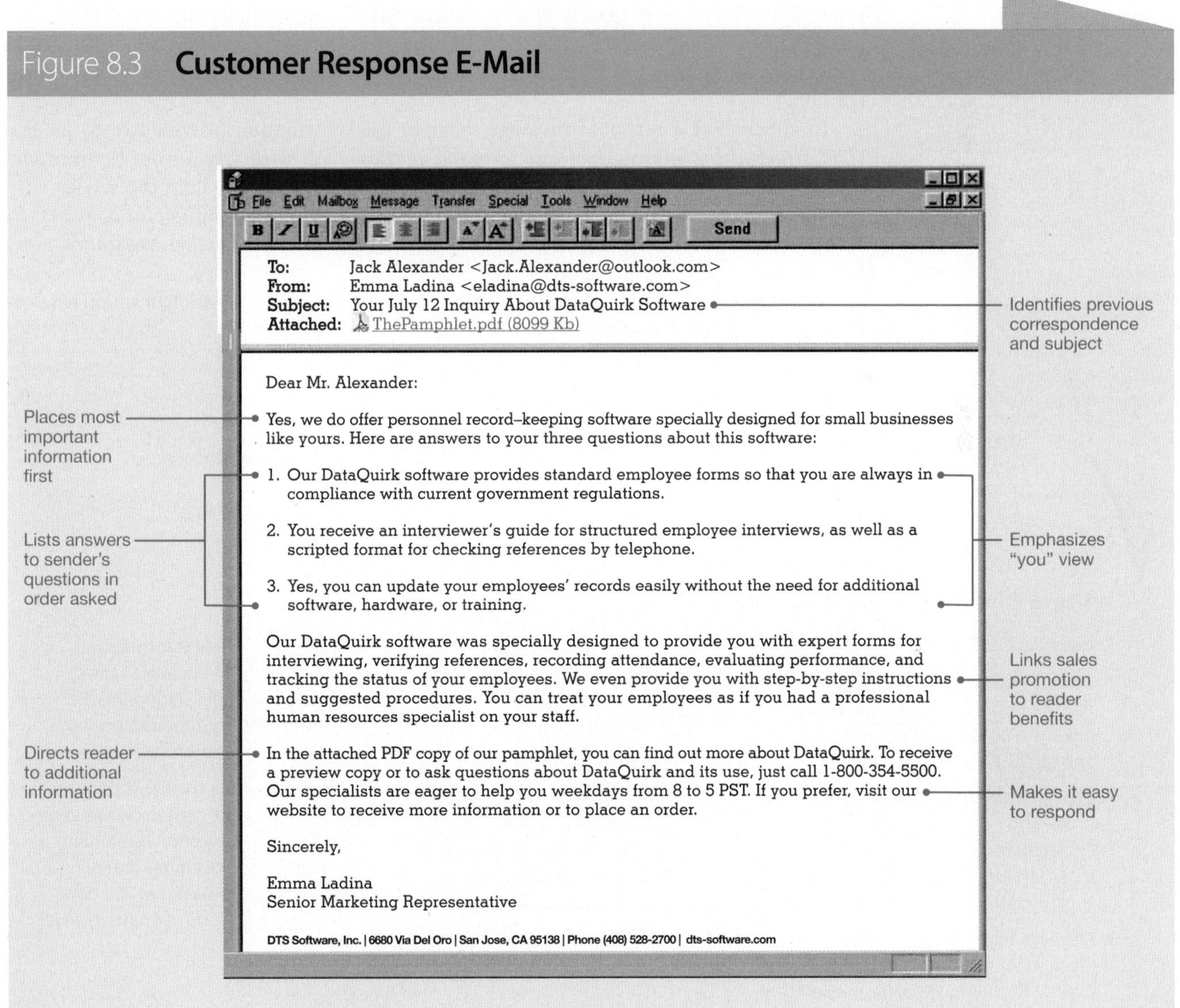

To: Jack Alexander <Jack.Alexander@outlook.com>
From: Emma Ladina <eladina@dts-software.com>
Subject: Your July 12 Inquiry About DataQuirk Software
Attached: ThePamphlet.pdf (8099 Kb)

Dear Mr. Alexander:

Yes, we do offer personnel record-keeping software specially designed for small businesses like yours. Here are answers to your three questions about this software:

1. Our DataQuirk software provides standard employee forms so that you are always in compliance with current government regulations.

2. You receive an interviewer's guide for structured employee interviews, as well as a scripted format for checking references by telephone.

3. Yes, you can update your employees' records easily without the need for additional software, hardware, or training.

Our DataQuirk software was specially designed to provide you with expert forms for interviewing, verifying references, recording attendance, evaluating performance, and tracking the status of your employees. We even provide you with step-by-step instructions and suggested procedures. You can treat your employees as if you had a professional human resources specialist on your staff.

In the attached PDF copy of our pamphlet, you can find out more about DataQuirk. To receive a preview copy or to ask questions about DataQuirk and its use, just call 1-800-354-5500. Our specialists are eager to help you weekdays from 8 to 5 PST. If you prefer, visit our website to receive more information or to place an order.

Sincerely,

Emma Ladina
Senior Marketing Representative

DTS Software, Inc. | 6680 Via Del Oro | San Jose, CA 95138 | Phone (408) 528-2700 | dts-software.com

Figure 8.3 **Customer Response E-Mail**

previous correspondence and/or summarizes a message (*Subject: Your July 12 Inquiry About DataQuirk Software*). Knowledgeable business communicators use a subject line to refer to earlier correspondence so that in the first sentence, the most emphatic spot in a letter, they are free to emphasize the main idea.

In the first sentence of a direct reply e-mail, deliver the information the reader wants. Avoid wordy, drawn-out openings (*I am responding to your e-mail of December 1, in which you request information about . . .*). More forceful and more efficient is an opener that answers the inquiry (*Here is the information you wanted about . . .*). When agreeing to a request for action, announce the good news promptly (*Yes, I will be happy to speak to your business communication class on the topic of . . .*).

In the body of your response, supply explanations and additional information. Because an e-mail, like any other document written for your company, may be considered a legally binding contract, be sure to check facts and figures carefully. Under certain circumstances in some U.S. states, an e-mail can also become an enforceable document; therefore, exercise caution when using a company e-mail address or anytime you are writing for your employer online. If a policy or procedure needs authorization, seek approval from a supervisor or executive before writing the message.

When customers or prospective customers inquire about products or services, your response should do more than merely supply answers. Try to promote your organization and products. Be sure to present the promotional material with attention to the "you" view and to reader benefits (*You can use our standardized tests to free you from time-consuming employment screening*).

In concluding a response message, refer to the information provided or to its use. (*The attached list summarizes our recommendations. We wish you all the best in redesigning your social media presence.*) If further action is required, help the reader with specifics (*The Small Business Administration publishes a number of helpful booklets. Its Web address is . . .*). Avoid signing off with clichés (*If I may be of further assistance, don't hesitate to . . .*).

The following checklist reviews the direct strategy for writing information or action requests and replying to such messages.

Writing Direct Requests and Responses

Requesting Information or Action

- **Open by stating the main idea.** To elicit information, ask a question or issue a polite command (*Please answer the following questions . . .*).
- **Explain and justify the request.** In the body arrange questions or information logically in parallel, balanced form. Clarify and substantiate your request.
- **Request action in the closing.** Close a request by summarizing exactly what is to be done, including dates or deadlines. Express appreciation. Avoid clichés (*Thank you for your cooperation, Thanking you in advance*).

Responding to Requests

- **Open directly.** Immediately deliver the information the receiver wants. Avoid wordy, drawn-out openings (*I have before me your request of August 5*). When agreeing to a request, announce the good news immediately.
- **Supply additional information.** In the body provide explanations and expand initial statements. For customer letters, promote products and the organization.
- **Conclude with a cordial statement.** Refer to the information provided or its use. If further action is required, describe the procedures and give specifics. Avoid clichés (*If you have questions, please do not hesitate to let me know*).

PLUGGED IN

The Right to Be Forgotten: Protecting Digital Privacy or Muzzling Free Speech?

Have you ever posted anything online you later regretted? Or have you googled yourself and didn't like some of the results? If yes, you might want to consider the *right to be forgotten* law passed to offset an Internet that never forgets.

The European Court of Justice recently enacted this novel right by compelling corporations such as Google to remove inappropriate posts, images, and other compromising online information from search results if EU residents requested they do so.

Advocates believe that the right to be forgotten allows users to control their personal data that are posted, bought, and sold by third parties most often without consent. Moreover, the proponents of the law dispute that free speech may be compromised if links to legitimate news stories containing information someone may deem offensive are removed.

Critics, however, argue that removing objectionable search results may amount to the suppression of information that the public has a right to know.[9] Detractors worry that the definition of *private information* is imprecise and the right to be forgotten could be abused if it were asserted worldwide, not just in the European regional versions of global search engines.

It all started with a Spaniard who was upset that 12 years after his home had been repossessed, this negative information was still available online.[10] In a lawsuit that went all the way to the highest European court, the right to be forgotten was asserted and the plaintiff won.

Google, the largest search engine worldwide, was ordered to delink pages containing information distasteful to the requesting party. The expected onslaught of requests has not materialized, however. Out of billions of pages, so far the removal of only about a million Web links was requested, 40 percent of which have been delinked. This means that the pages, although not literally removed, no longer show up in search results. The vast majority, more than 99 percent of the offensive links, turned up personal details about private individuals, not public figures or news stories about serious crimes.[11]

Google already has a policy of delisting sites that violate copyright or contain identifiable private information, such as social security numbers, bank account numbers, and risqué images posted without the subject's consent.[12]

Americans do worry about government surveillance and information sharing by business organizations. In a recent poll, more than 80 percent of respondents expressed great concern and stated that they supported proposals to strengthen online privacy. Over 90 percent called on businesses to safeguard and not share customers' private information, and almost 80 percent believe that the federal government should actively protect their financial and other personal information online.[13] Republicans and Democrats alike back laws that would empower Americans to take control of their personal privacy.[14]

ra2studio/Shutterstock.com

Reality Check

Developing a Comment Monitoring Policy

"If you're going to use social media, then embrace commenting. Don't just tolerate comments. Don't just accept comments. Interact. Comment back. If you are a company of one person, you may not need a policy for responding. Otherwise, before answering comments, develop some rules to live by."[15]

—Amanda Ford, *Tymado Multimedia Solutions*

Reacting to Customer Comments Online

We live in an age when vocal individuals can start a firestorm of criticism online or become powerful *brand ambassadors* who champion certain products. Therefore, businesses must listen to social media comments about themselves and, if necessary, respond. You may ask, how do companies know when to respond, and how? This invaluable knowledge is an evolving field and, some would say, a minefield littered with disastrous missteps and missed opportunities.

Figure 8.4 Social Media Response Flowchart

To help their employees make a prudent decision about whether and how to respond to online posts, companies are creating decision trees and diagrams such as the one shown here.[16]

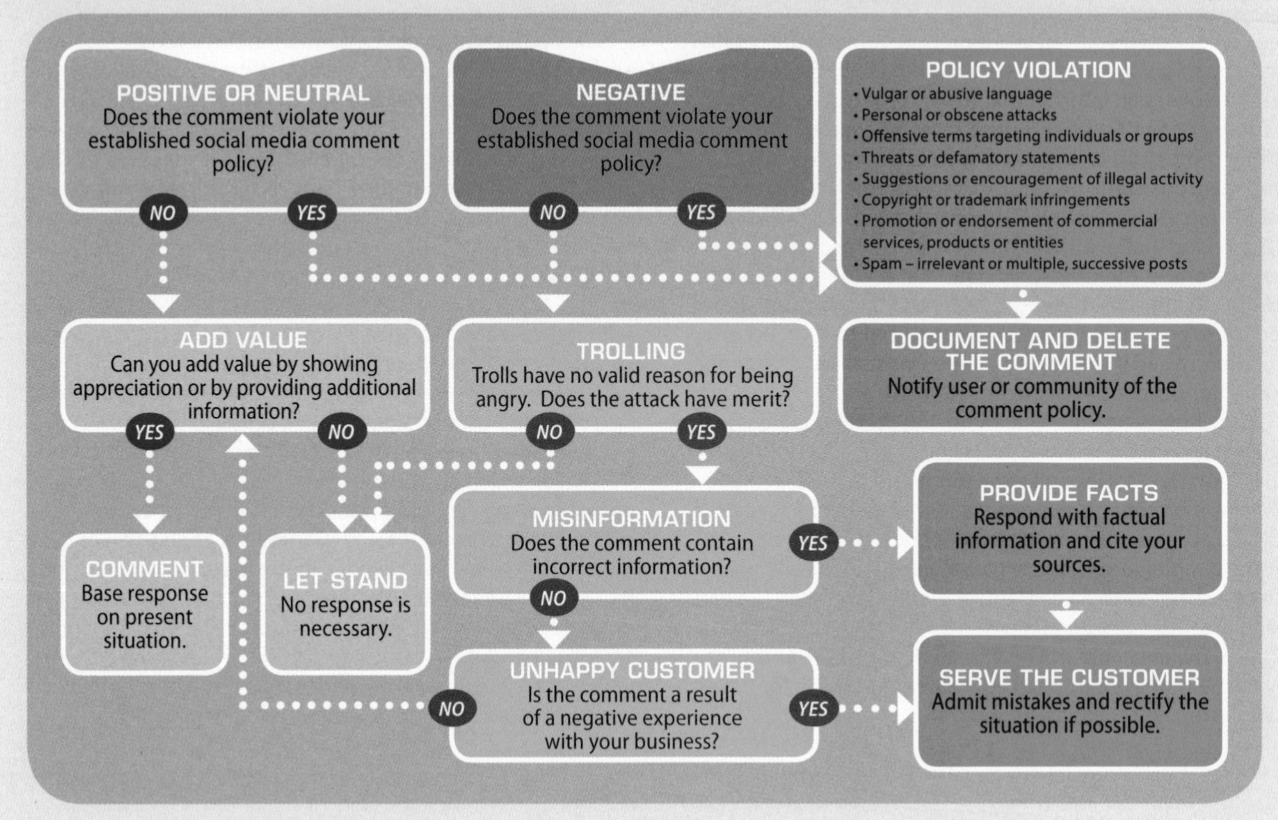

However, social media marketing experts are developing guidelines to provide organizations with tools for strategic decision making in various situations. Figure 8.4 shows a social media response flowchart, now increasingly common in for-profit and nonprofit organizations alike. Businesses can't control the conversation without disabling fans' comments on their Facebook walls or blogs, but they can respond in a way that benefits customers, prevents the problem from snowballing, and shines a positive light on the organization.

Embracing Customer Comments. Customer reviews online are opportunities for savvy businesses to improve their products or services and may serve as a free and efficient crowdsourced quality-control system. Retailers such as Walmart, Amazon, and L.L. Bean use powerful software to sift through billions of social media posts and product reviews. The data offer real-time feedback that may help clear up supply chain bottlenecks, expose product flaws, and improve operating instructions.[17] For example, angry reviews on its website alerted Walmart to a problem with a prepaid wireless Internet stick that Walmart was selling and prompted a remedy within two days.

Adopting Best Practices for Replying to Online Posts. Social media experts say that not every comment on the Web merits a response. They recommend responding to posts only when you can add value—for example, by correcting false information or providing customer service. Additional guidelines for professional responses to customer comments are summarized in Figure 8.5.

Figure 8.5 Responding to Customers Online

As businesses increasingly interact with their customers and the public online, they are developing rules of engagement and best practices.[18]

Be positive.

- Respond in a friendly, upbeat, yet professional tone.
- Correct mistakes politely.
- Do not argue, insult, or blame others.

Be honest.

- Own up to problems and mistakes.
- Inform customers when and how you will improve the situation.

Be transparent.

- State your name and position with the business.
- Personalize and humanize your business.

Be helpful.

- Point users to valuable information on your website or other approved websites.
- Follow up with users when new information is available.

Composing Instruction Messages

Instruction messages describe how to complete a task. You may be asked to write instructions about how to repair a paper jam in the photocopier, order supplies, file a grievance, or hire new employees. Instructions are different from policies and official procedures, which establish rules of conduct to be followed within an organization. We are most concerned with creating messages that clearly explain how to complete a task.

Like requests and responses, instruction messages follow a straightforward, direct approach. Before writing instructions for a process, be sure you understand the process completely. Practice doing it yourself. A message that delivers instructions should open with an explanation of why the procedure or set of instructions is necessary.

Creating Step-by-Step Instructions. The body of an instruction message should use plain English and familiar words to describe the process. Your messages explaining instructions will be most readable if you follow these guidelines:

- Divide the instructions into steps.
- List the steps in the order in which they are to be carried out.

Ethics Check

How Authentic Are Customer Reviews Online?

As the value of social media buzz is steadily increasing, so are efforts to rig the system. Not all customer critiques on the Web can be trusted, particularly when so many are anonymous. Some businesses pay for positive online reviews or encourage their employees to sing the praises of their own products while knocking the competition.[19] How seriously should companies take the threat of potentially fraudulent reviews?

Courtesy of Chris Campbell

Reality Check

The Power of Responding Well to Online Reviews

"For any business owner, it can be a scary thought that reviews can so significantly affect one's reputation. But responding to a review can be equally powerful. A response to a bad review can protect online business reputation and minimize the review's negative impact, while a response to a five-star review can reinforce customer satisfaction and drive positive word of mouth."[20]

—Chris Campbell, CEO, *Review Trackers*

- Arrange the items vertically with numbers.
- Begin each step with an action verb using the imperative (command) mood rather than the indicative mood.

Indicative Mood	Imperative Mood
The contract should be sent immediately.	Send the contract immediately.
The first step involves downloading the app.	Download the app first.
A survey of employees is necessary to learn what options they prefer.	Survey employees to learn the options they prefer.

In the closing of a message issuing instructions, try to tie following the instructions to benefits to the organization or individual.

If you are asked to prepare a list of instructions that is not part of a message, include a title such as *How to Clear Paper Jams*. Include an opening paragraph explaining why the instructions are needed.

Revising a Message Delivering Instructions. Figure 8.6 shows the first draft of an interoffice memo written by Brian Belmont. His memo was meant to announce a new method for employees to follow in requesting equipment repairs. However, the tone was negative, the explanation of the problem rambled, and the new method was unclear. Finally, Brian's first memo was wordy and filled with clichés (*do not hesitate to call*).

In the revision Brian improved the tone considerably. The frontloaded main idea is introduced with a *please*, which softens an order. The subject line specifies the purpose of the memo. Instead of dwelling on past procedures and failures (*we are no longer using* and *many mix-ups in the past*), Brian revised his message to explain constructively how reporting should be handled.

Brian realized that his original explanation of the new procedure was confusing. To clarify the instructions, he itemized and numbered the steps. Each step begins with an action verb in the imperative (command) mood (*Log in, Indicate, Select, Identify,* and *Print*). It is sometimes difficult to force all the steps in a list into this kind of command language. Brian struggled, but he finally found verbs that worked.

Why should you go to so much trouble to make lists and achieve parallelism? Because readers can comprehend what you have said much more quickly. Parallel language also makes you look professional and efficient.

In writing messages that deliver instructions, be careful of tone. Today's managers and team leaders seek employee participation and cooperation. These goals can't be achieved, though, if the writer sounds like a dictator or an autocrat. Avoid making accusations and fixing blame. Rather, explain changes, give reasons, and suggest benefits to the reader. Assume that employees want to contribute to the success of the organization and to their own achievement. Notice in the Figure 8.6 revision that Brian tells readers that they will save time and reduce mix-ups if they follow the new method.

LEARNING OUTCOME 3

Prepare contemporary messages that make direct claims and voice complaints, including those posted online.

Direct Claims and Complaints

In business, things can and do go wrong—promised shipments are late, warrantied goods fail, and service is disappointing. When you as a customer must write to identify or correct a wrong, the message is called a *claim*. Straightforward claims are those to which you expect the receiver to agree readily.

Increasingly, consumers resort to telephone calls, they e-mail their claims, or—as we have seen—they vent their peeves in online posts. Large companies can afford to employ social media specialists who monitor and respond to comments. However, small and midsized businesses often have few options other than Google Alerts and their own limited forays into social networking.

Figure 8.6 Memo Explaining Instructions

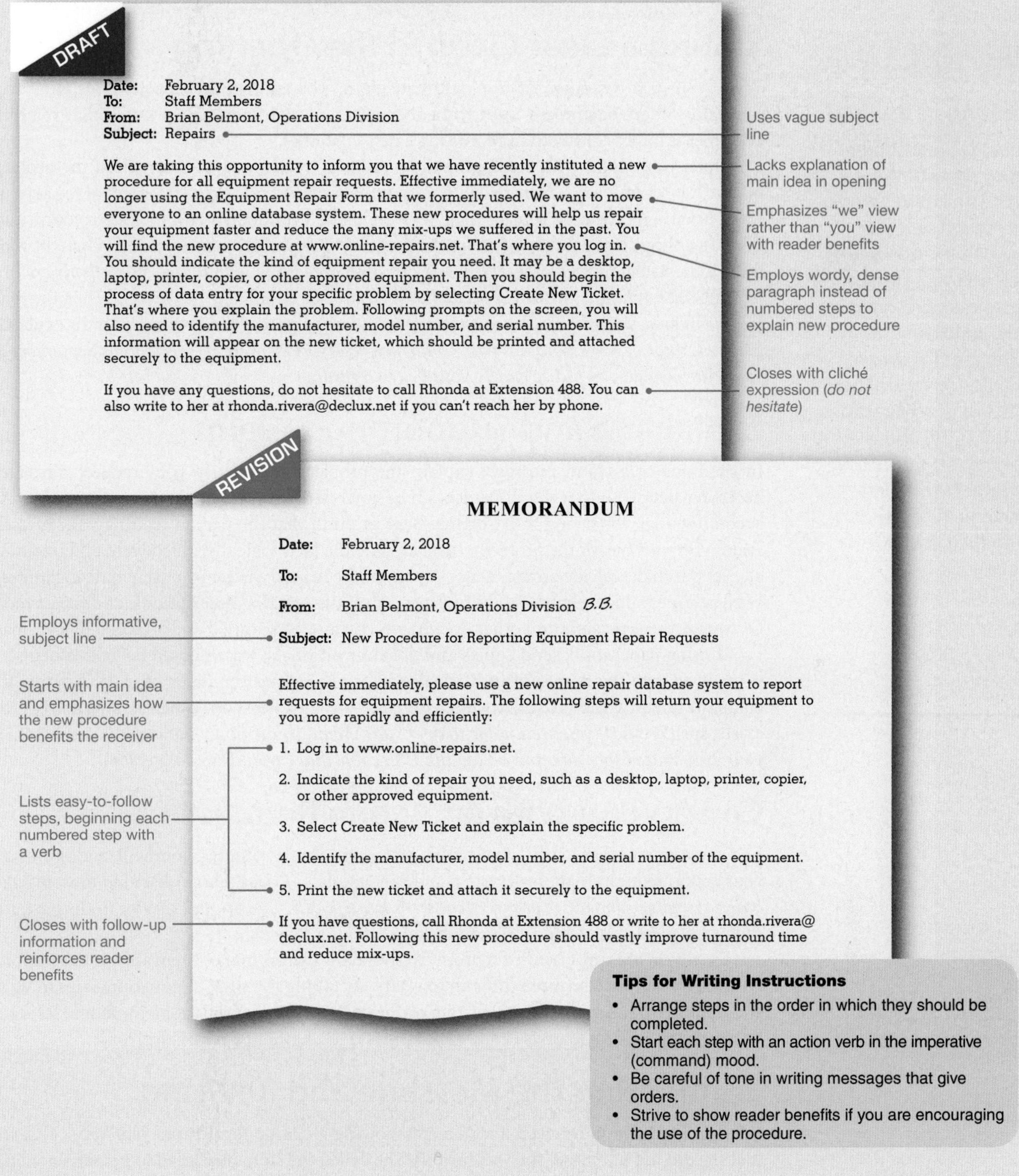

DRAFT

Date: February 2, 2018
To: Staff Members
From: Brian Belmont, Operations Division
Subject: Repairs

We are taking this opportunity to inform you that we have recently instituted a new procedure for all equipment repair requests. Effective immediately, we are no longer using the Equipment Repair Form that we formerly used. We want to move everyone to an online database system. These new procedures will help us repair your equipment faster and reduce the many mix-ups we suffered in the past. You will find the new procedure at www.online-repairs.net. That's where you log in. You should indicate the kind of equipment repair you need. It may be a desktop, laptop, printer, copier, or other approved equipment. Then you should begin the process of data entry for your specific problem by selecting Create New Ticket. That's where you explain the problem. Following prompts on the screen, you will also need to identify the manufacturer, model number, and serial number. This information will appear on the new ticket, which should be printed and attached securely to the equipment.

If you have any questions, do not hesitate to call Rhonda at Extension 488. You can also write to her at rhonda.rivera@declux.net if you can't reach her by phone.

Uses vague subject line
Lacks explanation of main idea in opening
Emphasizes "we" view rather than "you" view with reader benefits
Employs wordy, dense paragraph instead of numbered steps to explain new procedure
Closes with cliché expression (*do not hesitate*)

REVISION

MEMORANDUM

Date: February 2, 2018

To: Staff Members

From: Brian Belmont, Operations Division *B.B.*

Subject: New Procedure for Reporting Equipment Repair Requests

Effective immediately, please use a new online repair database system to report requests for equipment repairs. The following steps will return your equipment to you more rapidly and efficiently:

1. Log in to www.online-repairs.net.
2. Indicate the kind of repair you need, such as a desktop, laptop, printer, copier, or other approved equipment.
3. Select Create New Ticket and explain the specific problem.
4. Identify the manufacturer, model number, and serial number of the equipment.
5. Print the new ticket and attach it securely to the equipment.

If you have questions, call Rhonda at Extension 488 or write to her at rhonda.rivera@declux.net. Following this new procedure should vastly improve turnaround time and reduce mix-ups.

Employs informative, subject line
Starts with main idea and emphasizes how the new procedure benefits the receiver
Lists easy-to-follow steps, beginning each numbered step with a verb
Closes with follow-up information and reinforces reader benefits

Tips for Writing Instructions

- Arrange steps in the order in which they should be completed.
- Start each step with an action verb in the imperative (command) mood.
- Be careful of tone in writing messages that give orders.
- Strive to show reader benefits if you are encouraging the use of the procedure.

This is why in an age of digital communication, claims written as letters still play an important role even as they are being replaced by telephone calls, e-mails, and social media posts. Depending on the circumstances, letters more convincingly establish a record of what happened. Some business communicators opt for letters they can either attach to e-mail messages or fax. Regardless of the channel, straightforward claims use a direct approach. Claims that require a persuasive response are presented in Chapter 10.

Ethics Check

Renting or Buying?

Lucky U.S. consumers enjoy some of the world's most generous merchandise return policies. It is no wonder, perhaps, that some customers presumably buy video cameras or dresses for special events and return them afterward, no questions asked. Is this so-called renting, or wardrobing, wrong? Do retailers invite such behavior with their liberal policies?[21]

Stating a Clear Claim in the Opening

When you, as a customer, have a legitimate claim, you can expect a positive response from a company. Smart businesses want to hear from their customers. They know that retaining a customer is far less costly than recruiting a new customer.

Open your claim with a compliment, a point of agreement, a statement of the problem, a brief review of action you have taken to resolve the problem, or a clear statement of the action you want. You might expect a replacement, a refund, a new product, credit to your account, correction of a billing error, free repairs, a free inspection, or cancellation of an order. When the remedy is obvious, state it immediately (*Please correct an erroneous double charge of $59 to my credit card for LapLink migration software. I accidentally clicked the Submit button twice*). When the remedy is less obvious, you might ask for a change in policy or procedure or simply for an explanation (*Because three of our employees with confirmed reservations were refused rooms September 16 in your hotel, would you please clarify your policy regarding reservations and late arrivals*).

Explaining and Supporting a Claim

In the body of a claim message, explain the problem and justify your request. Provide the necessary details so that the difficulty can be corrected without further correspondence. Avoid becoming angry or trying to fix blame. Bear in mind that the person reading your message is seldom responsible for the problem. Instead, state the facts logically, objectively, and unemotionally; let the reader decide on the causes. If you choose to send a letter by postal mail, include copies of all pertinent documents such as invoices, sales slips, catalog descriptions, and repair records. Of course, those receipts and other documents can also be scanned and attached to an e-mail.

If using paper mail, send copies and *not* your originals, which could be lost. When service is involved, cite the names of individuals you spoke to and the dates of calls. Assume that a company honestly wants to satisfy its customers—because most do. When an alternative remedy exists, spell it out (*If you are unable to offer store credit, please apply the second amount of $59 to your TurboSpeed software and a LapLink USB cable that I would like to buy too*).

Concluding With an Action Request

End a claim message with a courteous statement that promotes goodwill and summarizes your action request. If appropriate, include an end date (*I hope you understand that mistakes in ordering online sometimes occur. Because I have enjoyed your prompt service in the past, I hope that you will be able to issue a refund or store credit by May 2*).

Finally, in making claims, act promptly. Delaying claims makes them appear less important. Delayed claims are also more difficult to verify. By taking the time to put your claim in writing, you indicate your seriousness. A written claim starts a record of the problem, should later action be necessary. Be sure to save a copy of your message whether paper or electronic.

Completing the Message and Revising

When Jade Huggins received a statement showing a charge for a three-year service warranty that she did not purchase, she was furious. She called the store but failed to get satisfaction. She decided against voicing her complaint online because she wished for a quick resolution and doubted that a social media post would be noticed by the small business. She chose to write an e-mail to the customer service address featured prominently on the MegaMedia website. You can see the first draft of her direct claim e-mail in Figure 8.7. This draft gave her a chance to vent her anger, but it accomplished little else. The tone was belligerent, and it assumed that the company intentionally mischarged her. Furthermore, it failed to tell the reader how to remedy the problem. The revision, also shown in Figure 8.7, tempered the tone, described the problem objectively, and provided facts and figures. Most important, it specified exactly what Jade wanted to be done.

Figure 8.7 **Direct Claim E-Mail**

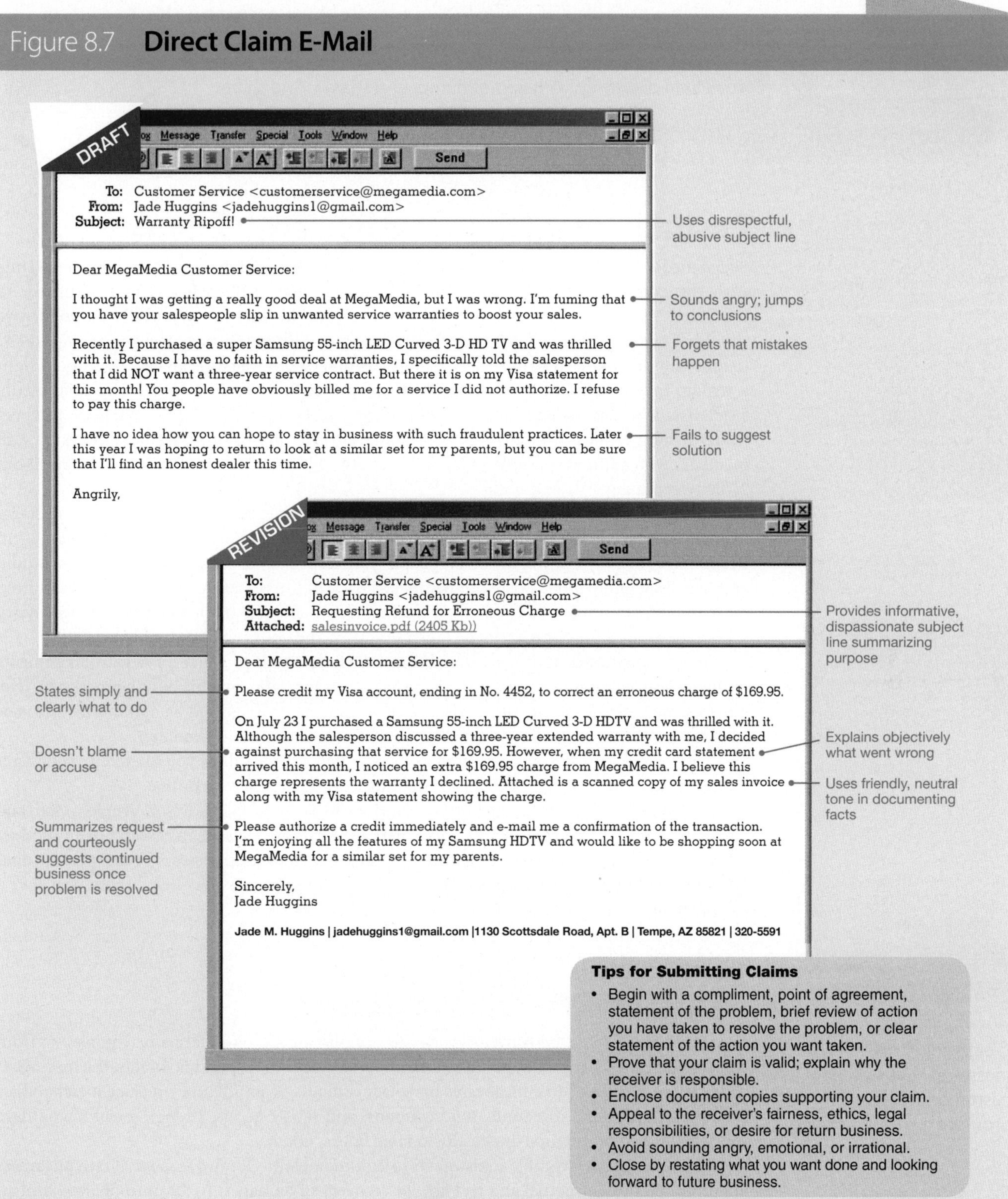

DRAFT
Send
To: Customer Service <customerservice@megamedia.com>
From: Jade Huggins <jadehuggins1@gmail.com>
Subject: Warranty Ripoff!
Uses disrespectful, abusive subject line
Dear MegaMedia Customer Service:
I thought I was getting a really good deal at MegaMedia, but I was wrong. I'm fuming that you have your salespeople slip in unwanted service warranties to boost your sales.
Sounds angry; jumps to conclusions
Recently I purchased a super Samsung 55-inch LED Curved 3-D HD TV and was thrilled with it. Because I have no faith in service warranties, I specifically told the salesperson that I did NOT want a three-year service contract. But there it is on my Visa statement for this month! You people have obviously billed me for a service I did not authorize. I refuse to pay this charge.
Forgets that mistakes happen
I have no idea how you can hope to stay in business with such fraudulent practices. Later this year I was hoping to return to look at a similar set for my parents, but you can be sure that I'll find an honest dealer this time.
Fails to suggest solution
Angrily,
REVISION
Send
To: Customer Service <customerservice@megamedia.com>
From: Jade Huggins <jadehuggins1@gmail.com>
Subject: Requesting Refund for Erroneous Charge
Attached: salesinvoice.pdf (2405 Kb))
Provides informative, dispassionate subject line summarizing purpose
Dear MegaMedia Customer Service:
States simply and clearly what to do
Please credit my Visa account, ending in No. 4452, to correct an erroneous charge of $169.95.
On July 23 I purchased a Samsung 55-inch LED Curved 3-D HDTV and was thrilled with it. Although the salesperson discussed a three-year extended warranty with me, I decided against purchasing that service for $169.95. However, when my credit card statement arrived this month, I noticed an extra $169.95 charge from MegaMedia. I believe this charge represents the warranty I declined. Attached is a scanned copy of my sales invoice along with my Visa statement showing the charge.
Doesn't blame or accuse
Explains objectively what went wrong
Uses friendly, neutral tone in documenting facts
Please authorize a credit immediately and e-mail me a confirmation of the transaction. I'm enjoying all the features of my Samsung HDTV and would like to be shopping soon at MegaMedia for a similar set for my parents.
Summarizes request and courteously suggests continued business once problem is resolved
Sincerely,
Jade Huggins
Jade M. Huggins | jadehuggins1@gmail.com |1130 Scottsdale Road, Apt. B | Tempe, AZ 85821 | 320-5591
Tips for Submitting Claims
• Begin with a compliment, point of agreement, statement of the problem, brief review of action you have taken to resolve the problem, or clear statement of the action you want taken.
• Prove that your claim is valid; explain why the receiver is responsible.
• Enclose document copies supporting your claim.
• Appeal to the receiver's fairness, ethics, legal responsibilities, or desire for return business.
• Avoid sounding angry, emotional, or irrational.
• Close by restating what you want done and looking forward to future business.

wavebreakmedia/Shutterstock.com

Reality Check

Count to a Hundred!

"E-venting is particularly risky. We think it's private because we can do it in a secluded place, like our bed while we're in our pajamas. We have our phones with us all the time so we often e-vent before we've had a chance to calm down. A rant put out via the Internet is a click away from being shared. And shared. And shared."[22]

—Elizabeth Bernstein, columnist, *The Wall Street Journal*

Posting Complaints and Reviews Online

Social media experts advise consumers to exhaust all other options for claims and complaints with the company before venting online.[23] Just as you probably wouldn't complain to the Better Business Bureau without giving a business at least one chance to respond, you shouldn't express dissatisfaction just to let off steam. Although it may feel good temporarily to rant, most businesses want to please their customers and welcome an opportunity to right a wrong. Increasingly, businesses are beefing up their customer service with social media specialists who field complaints on Twitter and Facebook.[24] Travelers in particular expect nearly instant replies from airlines to their gripes, even minor ones. Delta employs 40 staff members who address roughly 3,000 daily tweets. At Southwest, 29 employees tackle about 2,700 tweets a day.[25]

Letting loose in ill-conceived online comments is a bad idea for two reasons. First, social media posts have a way of ending up in the wrong hands, making vicious complainers seem irrational. As always, think whether people you respect and prospective employers would approve. Even anonymous posts can be tracked back to the writer. An Ohio waitress was fired for schooling a customer—a Facebook acquaintance—on how to tip properly.[26] Moreover, nasty "cyber chest-pounding" might not be taken seriously, and your remarks could be deleted.[27]

Second, businesses and professionals can take individuals to court for negative comments online. A chiropractor in San Francisco sued a patient for criticizing his billing process on Yelp. The case was settled out of court. Also, libelous statements disguised as opinion (*In my view attorney Jack Miller is stealing $4,000 from his clients*) can get you in trouble.[28]

The tips in Figure 8.8, gleaned from *Consumer Reports,* will allow you to exercise your right to free speech while staying safe when critiquing a product or service online.

Shoppers read online comments on sites such as Yelp, TripAdvisor, Angie's List, and Amazon. A solid 74 percent of U.S. consumers read user reviews when researching a product category, and a whopping 88 percent check out reviews of local businesses.[29] Even if posting does not achieve your objective, your well-written complaint or review may help others. You have a responsibility. Use it wisely.

LEARNING OUTCOME 4

Create adjustment messages that salvage customers' trust and promote further business.

Adjustment Messages

Even the best-run and best-loved businesses occasionally receive claims or complaints from consumers. When a company receives a claim and decides to respond favorably, the message is called an *adjustment.* Most businesses make adjustments promptly: they replace merchandise, refund money, extend discounts, send coupons, and repair goods. In fact, social media have shortened the response time drastically to mere hours, not days.

Businesses make favorable adjustments to legitimate claims for two reasons. First, consumers are protected by contractual and tort law for recovery of damages. If, for example, you find an insect in a package of frozen peas, the food processor of that package is bound by contractual

Figure 8.8 Guidelines for Writing Online Reviews and Complaints

Establish your credibility.

- Zero in on your objective and make your comment as concise as possible.
- Focus only on the facts and be able to support them.

Consider the Web's permanence.

- Know that your review may be posted indefinitely, even if you change your mind and modify a post later.

Check posting rules.

- Understand what's allowed by reading the terms and conditions on the site.
- Keep your complaint clean, polite, and to the point.

Accept offers to help.

- Reply if a business offers to help or discuss the problem; update your original post as necessary.

Provide balanced reviews.

- To be fair, offset criticism with positives to show that you are a legitimate consumer.
- Suggest improvements even in glowing reviews; all-out gushing is suspicious and not helpful.

Refuse payment for favorable critiques.

- Never accept payment to change your opinion or your account of the facts.
- Comply with requests for a review if you are a satisfied customer.

law to replace it. If you suffer injury, the processor may be liable for damages. Second, and more obviously, most organizations genuinely want to satisfy their customers and retain their business.

In responding to customer claims, you must first decide whether to grant the claim. Unless the claim is obviously fraudulent or excessive, you will probably grant it. When you say *yes*, your adjustment message will be good news to the reader. Deliver that good news by using the direct strategy. When your response is *no*, the indirect strategy might be more appropriate. Chapter 9 discusses the indirect strategy for conveying negative news. You have three goals in adjustment messages:

- Rectifying the wrong, if one exists
- Regaining the confidence of the customer
- Promoting further business

Revealing Good News Up Front

Instead of beginning with a review of what went wrong, present the good news in an adjustment message immediately. When Kimberly Lu responded to the claim letter from customer Optima Ventures about a missing shipment, her first draft, shown at the top of Figure 8.9, was angry. No wonder. Optima Ventures apparently had provided the wrong shipping address, and the goods were returned. Once Kimberly and her company decided to send a second shipment and comply with the customer's claim, however, she had to give up the anger. Her goal was to regain the goodwill and the business of this customer. The improved version of her letter announces that a new shipment will arrive shortly.

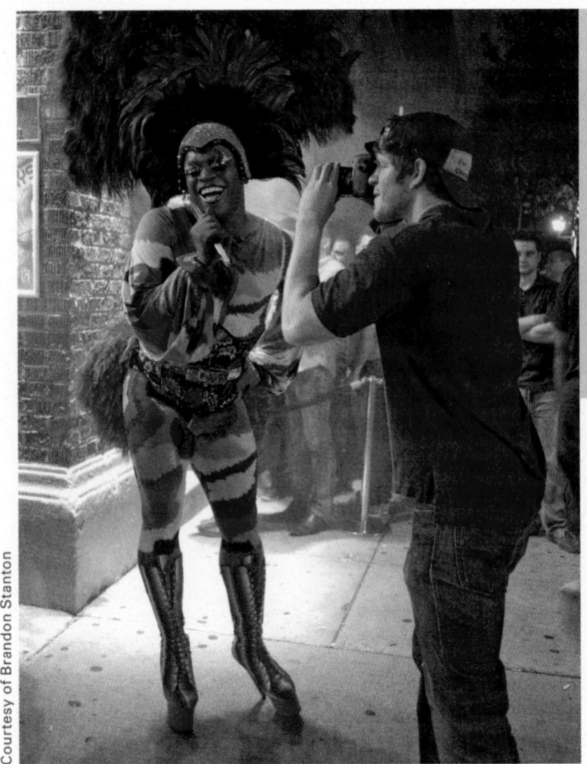
Courtesy of Brandon Stanton

Brandon Stanton's photo project "Humans of New York" has gone viral and earned rave reviews in *The Wall Street Journal* and *The Atlantic*. But when fashion-apparel label DKNY featured the photos in an in-store display without obtaining permission or offering compensation, Stanton's half-million Facebook followers protested through social media and on DKNY's Facebook site. Within hours of the stir, DKNY responded online saying, "We deeply regret this mistake. Accordingly, we are making a charitable donation of $25,000 to the YMCA in Bedford-Stuyvesant, Brooklyn, in Mr. Stanton's name." How do businesses generally handle consumer complaints?[21]

If you decide to comply with a customer's claim, let the receiver know immediately. Don't begin your letter with a negative statement (*We are very sorry to hear that you are having trouble with your dishwasher*). This approach reminds the reader of the problem and may rekindle the heated emotions or unhappy feelings experienced when the claim was written. Instead, focus on the good news. The following openings for various letters illustrate how to begin a message with good news:

You're right! We agree that the warranty on your American Standard Model UC600 dishwasher should be extended for six months.

You will be receiving shortly a new Samsung smartphone to replace the one that shattered when dropped recently.

Please take your portable Admiral microwave oven to A-1 Appliance Service, 200 Orange Street, Pasadena, where it will be repaired at no cost to you.

The enclosed check for $325 demonstrates our desire to satisfy our customers and earn their confidence.

In announcing that you will make an adjustment, do so without a grudging tone—even if you have reservations about whether the claim is legitimate. Once you decide to comply with the customer's request, do so happily. Avoid halfhearted or reluctant responses (*Although the American Standard dishwasher works well when used properly, we have decided to allow you to take yours to A-1 Appliance Service for repair at our expense*).

Explaining Compliance in the Body of an Adjustment Message

In responding to claims, most organizations sincerely want to correct a wrong. They want to do more than just make the customer happy. They want to stand behind their products and services; they want to do what is right.

In the body of the message, explain how you are complying with the claim. In all but the most routine claims, you should seek to regain the confidence of the customer. You might reasonably expect that a customer who has experienced difficulty with a product, with delivery, with billing, or with service has lost faith in your organization. Rebuilding that faith is important for future business.

How to rebuild lost confidence depends on the situation and the claim. If procedures need to be revised, explain what changes will be made. If a product has defective parts, tell how the product is being improved. If service is faulty, describe genuine efforts to improve it. Notice in

Figure 8.9 Customer Adjustment Letter

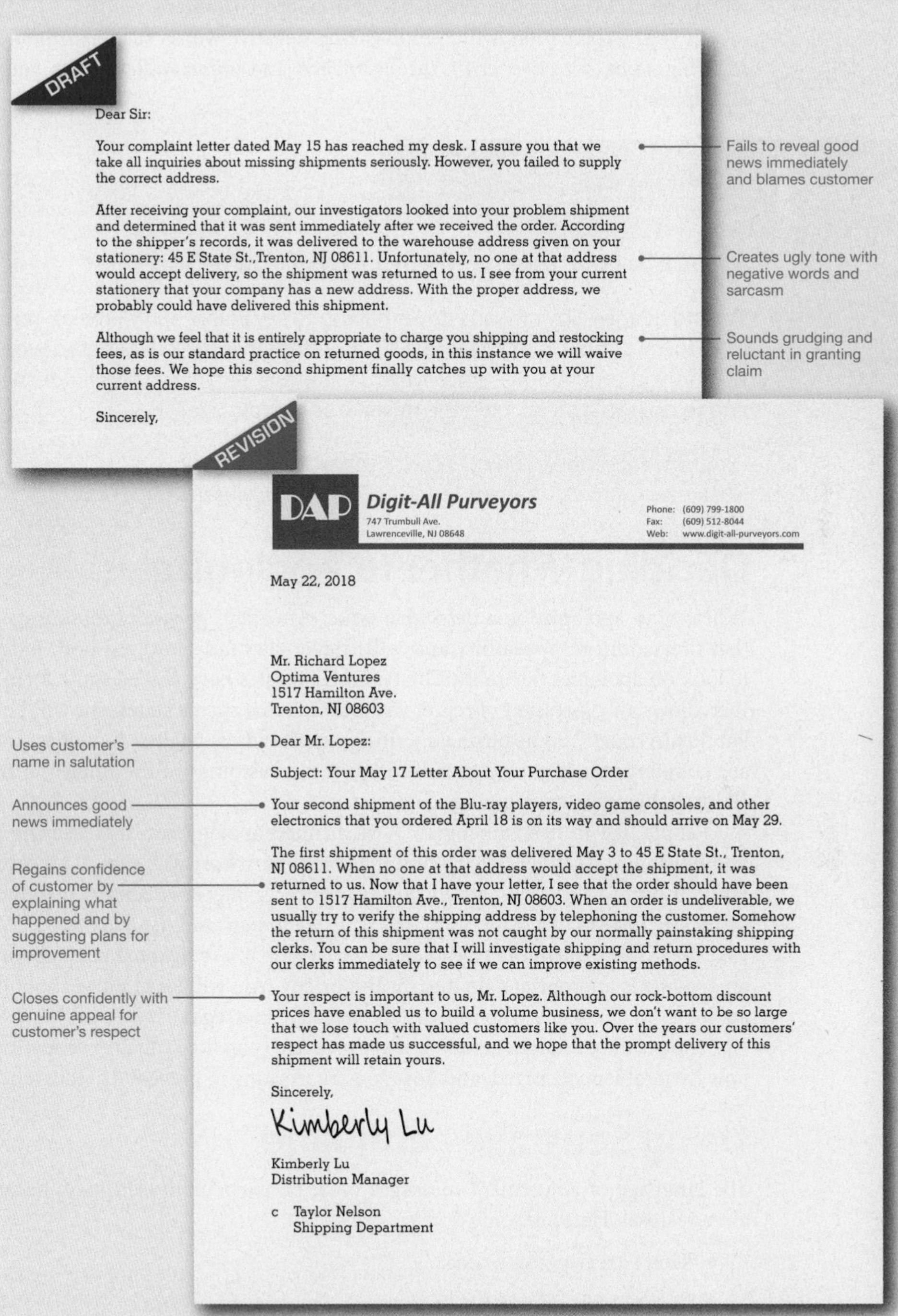

DRAFT

Dear Sir:

Your complaint letter dated May 15 has reached my desk. I assure you that we take all inquiries about missing shipments seriously. However, you failed to supply the correct address.

After receiving your complaint, our investigators looked into your problem shipment and determined that it was sent immediately after we received the order. According to the shipper's records, it was delivered to the warehouse address given on your stationery: 45 E State St.,Trenton, NJ 08611. Unfortunately, no one at that address would accept delivery, so the shipment was returned to us. I see from your current stationery that your company has a new address. With the proper address, we probably could have delivered this shipment.

Although we feel that it is entirely appropriate to charge you shipping and restocking fees, as is our standard practice on returned goods, in this instance we will waive those fees. We hope this second shipment finally catches up with you at your current address.

Sincerely,

Fails to reveal good news immediately and blames customer
Creates ugly tone with negative words and sarcasm
Sounds grudging and reluctant in granting claim
REVISION

DAP Digit-All Purveyors
747 Trumbull Ave.
Lawrenceville, NJ 08648
Phone: (609) 799-1800
Fax: (609) 512-8044
Web: www.digit-all-purveyors.com

May 22, 2018

Mr. Richard Lopez
Optima Ventures
1517 Hamilton Ave.
Trenton, NJ 08603

Dear Mr. Lopez:

Subject: Your May 17 Letter About Your Purchase Order

Your second shipment of the Blu-ray players, video game consoles, and other electronics that you ordered April 18 is on its way and should arrive on May 29.

The first shipment of this order was delivered May 3 to 45 E State St., Trenton, NJ 08611. When no one at that address would accept the shipment, it was returned to us. Now that I have your letter, I see that the order should have been sent to 1517 Hamilton Ave., Trenton, NJ 08603. When an order is undeliverable, we usually try to verify the shipping address by telephoning the customer. Somehow the return of this shipment was not caught by our normally painstaking shipping clerks. You can be sure that I will investigate shipping and return procedures with our clerks immediately to see if we can improve existing methods.

Your respect is important to us, Mr. Lopez. Although our rock-bottom discount prices have enabled us to build a volume business, we don't want to be so large that we lose touch with valued customers like you. Over the years our customers' respect has made us successful, and we hope that the prompt delivery of this shipment will retain yours.

Sincerely,

Kimberly Lu

Kimberly Lu
Distribution Manager

c Taylor Nelson
Shipping Department

Uses customer's name in salutation
Announces good news immediately
Regains confidence of customer by explaining what happened and by suggesting plans for improvement
Closes confidently with genuine appeal for customer's respect

Figure 8.9 that the writer promises to investigate shipping procedures to see whether improvements might prevent future mishaps.

Sometimes the problem is not with the product but with the way it is being used. In other instances customers misunderstand warranties or inadvertently cause delivery and billing mix-ups by supplying incorrect information. Remember that rational and sincere explanations will do much to regain the confidence of unhappy customers.

In your explanation avoid emphasizing negative words such as *trouble, regret, misunderstanding, fault, defective, error, inconvenience,* and *unfortunately.* Keep your message positive and upbeat.

Bloomberg/Getty Images

Reality Check

Intuit CEO: Love Means Having to Say You're Sorry

"The old adage—love means never having to say you're sorry—never rang true for me. It doesn't apply in my personal life, nor does it apply in business. If you disappoint the ones you care about—employees, customers, partners, shareholders—the right thing to do is to step up, own the mistake and apologize."[30]

—Brad Smith, *president and chief executive officer, Intuit*

Deciding Whether to Apologize

Whether to apologize is a debatable issue. Attorneys generally discourage apologies fearing that they admit responsibility and will trigger lawsuits. However, both judges and juries tend to look on apologies favorably. Thirty-six U.S. states have passed some form of an apology law that allows an expression of regret without fear that such a statement will be used as a basis for liability in court.[31] Some business writing experts advise against apologies, contending that they are counterproductive and merely remind the customer of the unpleasantness related to the claim. If, however, apologizing seems natural, do so.

People like to hear apologies. A well-timed apology can increase the culprits' influence and likeability. They will be perceived as more trustworthy.[32] Don't, however, fall back on the familiar phrase, *I'm sorry for any inconvenience we may have caused.* It sounds mechanical and insincere. Instead, try something like this: *We understand the frustration our delay has caused you, We're sorry you didn't receive better service,* or *You're right to be disappointed.* If you feel that an apology is appropriate, do it early and briefly. You will learn more about delivering effective apologies in Chapter 9 when we discuss negative messages.

The primary focus of an adjustment message is on how you are complying with the request, how the problem occurred, and how you are working to prevent its recurrence.

Using Sensitive Language

The language of adjustment messages must be particularly sensitive, because customers are already upset. Here are some don'ts:

- Don't use negative words.
- Don't blame customers—even when they may be at fault.
- Don't blame individuals or departments within your organization; it's unprofessional.
- Don't make unrealistic promises; you can't guarantee that the situation will never recur.

To regain the confidence of your reader, consider including resale information. Describe a product's features and any special applications that might appeal to the reader. Promote a new product if it seems appropriate.

Showing Confidence in the Closing

End positively by expressing confidence that the problem has been resolved and that continued business relations will result. You might mention the product in a favorable light, suggest a new product, express your appreciation for the customer's business, or anticipate future business. It's often appropriate to refer to the desire to be of service and to satisfy customers. Notice how the following closings illustrate a positive, confident tone:

> *You were most helpful in informing us of this situation and permitting us to correct it. We appreciate your thoughtfulness in writing to us.*
>
> *Thanks for writing. Your satisfaction is important to us. We hope that this refund check convinces you that service to our customers is our No. 1 priority. Our goals are to earn your confidence and continue to justify that confidence with quality products and excellent service.*
>
> *For your patience and patronage, we are truly grateful.*
>
> *Your Asus Netbook will come in handy whether you are connecting with friends, surfing the net, listening to music, watching movies, or playing games. What's more, you can add a Total Defense Premium Security package and a deluxe carrying bag for a little more. Take a look at the enclosed booklet detailing the big savings for essential technology on a budget. We value your business and look forward to your future orders.*

Although the direct strategy works for many requests and replies, it obviously won't work for every situation. With more practice and experience, you will be able to alter the pattern and apply the writing process to other communication problems. See the accompanying checklist for a summary of what to do when you must write claim and adjustment messages.

CHECKLIST

Direct Claim, Complaint, and Adjustment Messages

- **Begin directly with the purpose.** Present a clear statement of the problem or the action requested such as a refund, a replacement, credit, an explanation, or the correction of an error. Add a compliment if you have been pleased in other respects.
- **Explain objectively.** In the body tell the specifics of the claim. Consider reminding the receiver of ethical and legal responsibilities, fairness, and a desire for return business. Provide copies of necessary documents.
- **Conclude by requesting action.** Include an end date, if important. Add a pleasant, forward-looking statement. Keep a copy of the message.
- **Exercise good judgment.** Online postings are permanent. Make your comments concise and focus only on the facts. Respect posting rules and be polite. Provide balanced reviews. Shun anonymity.

Messages That Make Adjustments

- **Open with approval.** Comply with the customer's claim immediately. Avoid sounding grudging or reluctant.
- **In the body win back the customer's confidence.** Explain the cause of the problem, or describe your ongoing efforts to avoid such difficulties. Apologize if you feel that you should, but do so early and briefly. Avoid negative words, accusations, and unrealistic promises. Consider including resale and sales promotion information.
- **Close positively.** Express appreciation to the customer for writing, extend thanks for past business, anticipate continued patronage, refer to your desire to be of service, and/or mention a new product if it seems appropriate.

LEARNING OUTCOME 5

Write special messages that convey kindness and goodwill.

Goodwill Messages

Many communicators are intimidated when they must write goodwill messages expressing thanks, recognition, and sympathy. Finding the right words to express feelings is often more difficult than writing ordinary business documents. That is why writers tend to procrastinate when it comes to goodwill messages. Sending a ready-made card or picking up the telephone is easier than writing a message. Remember, though, that the personal sentiments of the sender are always more expressive and more meaningful to readers than are printed cards or oral messages. Taking the time to write gives more importance to our well-wishing. Personal notes also provide a record that can be reread, savored, and treasured.

In expressing thanks, recognition, or sympathy, you should always do so promptly. These messages are easier to write when the situation is fresh in your mind. They also mean more to the recipient. Don't forget that a prompt thank-you note carries the hidden message that you care and that you consider the event to be important. The best goodwill messages—whether thanks, congratulations, praise, or sympathy—concentrate on the five Ss. Goodwill messages should be

- **Selfless.** Focus the message solely on the receiver, not the sender. Don't talk about yourself; avoid such comments as *I remember when I . . . .*
- **Specific.** Personalize the message by mentioning specific incidents or characteristics of the receiver. Telling a colleague *Great speech* is much less effective than *Great story about McDonald's marketing in Moscow.* Take care to verify names and other facts.
- **Sincere.** Let your words show genuine feelings. Rehearse in your mind how you would express the message to the receiver orally. Then transform that conversational language to your written message. Avoid pretentious, formal, or flowery language (*It gives me great pleasure to extend felicitations on the occasion of your firm's twentieth anniversary*).
- **Spontaneous.** Keep the message fresh and enthusiastic. Avoid canned phrases (*Congratulations on your promotion, Good luck in the future*). Strive for directness and naturalness, not creative brilliance.
- **Short.** Although goodwill messages can be as long as needed, try to accomplish your purpose in only a few sentences. What is most important is remembering an individual. Such caring does not require documentation or wordiness. Individuals and business organizations often use special note cards or stationery for brief messages.

Saying Thank You

When someone has done you a favor or when an action merits praise, you need to extend thanks or show appreciation. Letters of appreciation may be written to customers for their orders, to hosts for their hospitality, to individuals for kindnesses performed, to employees for a job well done, and especially to customers who complain. After all, whether in social media posts, by e-mail, or on paper, complaints are actually providing you with "free consulting reports from the field." Complainers who feel that their complaints were heard often become the greatest promoters of an organization.[33]

Because the receiver will be pleased to hear from you, you can open directly with the purpose of your message. The letter in Figure 8.10 thanks a speaker who addressed a group of marketing professionals. Although such thank-you notes can be quite short, this one is a little longer because the writer wants to lend importance to the receiver's efforts. Notice that every sentence relates to the receiver and offers enthusiastic praise. By using the receiver's name along with contractions and positive words, the writer makes the letter sound warm and conversational.

Written notes that show appreciation and express thanks are significant to their receivers.

Figure 8.10 **Thank-You Letter for a Favor**

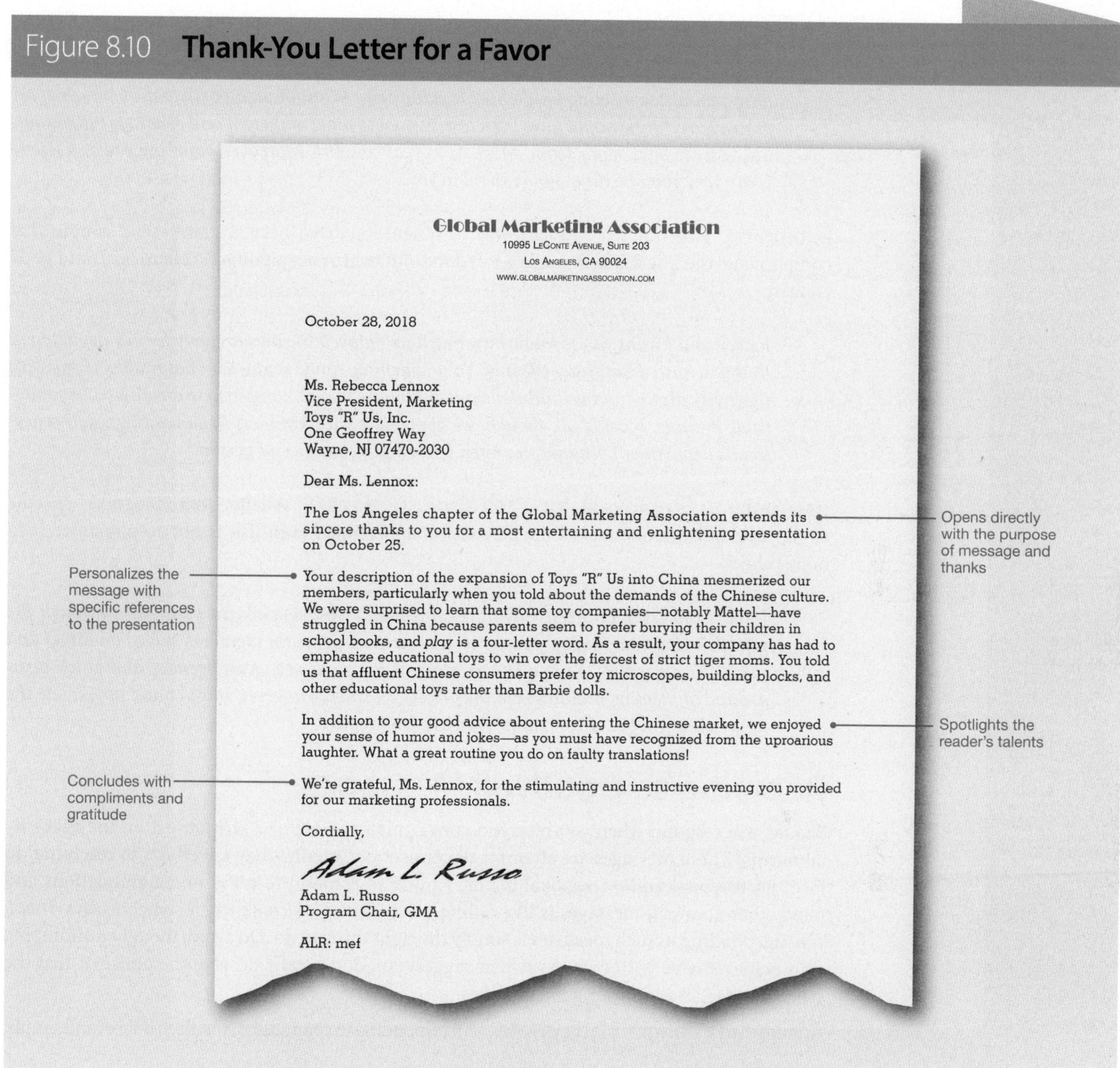

Global Marketing Association
10995 LeConte Avenue, Suite 203
Los Angeles, CA 90024
www.globalmarketingassociation.com

October 28, 2018

Ms. Rebecca Lennox
Vice President, Marketing
Toys "R" Us, Inc.
One Geoffrey Way
Wayne, NJ 07470-2030

Dear Ms. Lennox:

The Los Angeles chapter of the Global Marketing Association extends its sincere thanks to you for a most entertaining and enlightening presentation on October 25.

Your description of the expansion of Toys "R" Us into China mesmerized our members, particularly when you told about the demands of the Chinese culture. We were surprised to learn that some toy companies—notably Mattel—have struggled in China because parents seem to prefer burying their children in school books, and *play* is a four-letter word. As a result, your company has had to emphasize educational toys to win over the fiercest of strict tiger moms. You told us that affluent Chinese consumers prefer toy microscopes, building blocks, and other educational toys rather than Barbie dolls.

In addition to your good advice about entering the Chinese market, we enjoyed your sense of humor and jokes—as you must have recognized from the uproarious laughter. What a great routine you do on faulty translations!

We're grateful, Ms. Lennox, for the stimulating and instructive evening you provided for our marketing professionals.

Cordially,

Adam L. Russo

Adam L. Russo
Program Chair, GMA

ALR: mef

Opens directly with the purpose of message and thanks
Personalizes the message with specific references to the presentation
Spotlights the reader's talents
Concludes with compliments and gratitude

Although messages that express thanks may be as long as the letter shown above in Figure 8.10, you generally write a short note on special notepaper or heavy card stock. The following messages provide models for expressing thanks for a gift, for a favor, and for hospitality.

Expressing Thanks for a Gift. When expressing thanks, tell what the gift means to you. Use sincere, simple statements.

> *Thanks, Laura, to you and the other members of the department for honoring me with the elegant Waterford crystal vase at the party celebrating my twentieth anniversary with the company. The height and shape of the vase are perfect to hold roses and other bouquets from my garden. Each time I fill it, I'll remember your thoughtfulness in choosing this lovely gift for me.*

Sending Thanks for a Favor. In showing appreciation for a favor, explain the importance of the gesture to you.

I sincerely appreciate your filling in for me last week when I was too ill to attend the planning committee meeting for the spring exhibition. Without your participation, much of my preparatory work would have been lost. Knowing that competent and generous individuals like you are part of our team, Mark, is a great comfort. Moreover, counting you as a friend is my very good fortune. I'm grateful to you.

Extending Thanks for Hospitality. When you have been a guest, send a note that compliments the fine food, charming surroundings, warm hospitality, excellent host, and good company.

Jeffrey and I want you to know how much we enjoyed the dinner party for our department that you hosted Saturday evening. Your charming home and warm hospitality, along with the lovely dinner and sinfully delicious chocolate dessert, combined to create a truly memorable evening. Most of all, though, we appreciate your kindness in cultivating togetherness in our department. Thanks, Jennifer, for being such a special person.

Recognizing Employees for Their Contributions. A letter that recognizes specific employee contributions makes the person feel appreciated even if it is not accompanied by a bonus check.

Jerry, I am truly impressed by how competently you shepherded your team through the complex Horizon project. Thanks to your leadership, team members stayed on target and met their objectives. Your adept meeting facilitation, use of an agenda, and quick turnaround of meeting minutes kept the project on track. However, most of all I appreciate the long hours you put in to hammer out the final report.

Replying to Goodwill Messages

Should you respond when you receive a congratulatory note or a written pat on the back? By all means! These messages are attempts to connect personally; they are efforts to reach out, to form professional and/or personal bonds. Failing to respond to notes of congratulations and most other goodwill messages is like failing to say *You're welcome* when someone says *Thank you.* Responding to such messages is simply the right thing to do. Do avoid, though, minimizing your achievements with comments that suggest you don't really deserve the praise or that the sender is exaggerating your good qualities.

Answering a Congratulatory Note. In responding to congratulations, keep it short and simple.

Thanks for your kind words regarding my award, and thanks, too, for forwarding me the link to the article online. I truly appreciate your warm wishes.

Responding to Praise. When acknowledging a pat-on-the-back note, use simple words in conveying your appreciation.

Your note about my work made me feel good. I'm grateful for your thoughtfulness.

Expressing Sympathy and Sending Condolences

Most of us can bear misfortune and grief more easily when we know that others care. Notes expressing sympathy, though, are probably more difficult to write than any other kind of message. Commercial sympathy cards make the task easier—but they are far less meaningful than personal notes. Grieving friends want to know what you think—not what Hallmark's card writers think.

To help you get started, you can always glance through cards expressing sympathy. They will supply ideas about the kinds of thoughts you might wish to convey in your own words. In writing a sympathy note, (a) refer to the death or misfortune sensitively, using words that show you understand what a crushing blow it is; (b) in the case of a death, praise the deceased in a personal way; (c) offer assistance without going into excessive detail; and (d) end on a reassuring, forward-looking note. Sympathy messages may be typed, although handwriting seems more personal. In either case, use notepaper or personal stationery.

As you write your condolence note, mention the loss tactfully, recognize good qualities of the deceased, assure the receiver of your concern, offer assistance, and conclude on a reassuring note.

> *We are deeply saddened, Vanessa, to learn of the death of your husband. Will's kind nature and friendly spirit endeared him to all who knew him. He will be missed. Although words seem empty in expressing our grief, we want you to know that your friends at QuadCom extend their profound sympathy to you. If we may help you or lighten your load in any way, you have but to call.*
>
> *We know that the treasured memories of your many happy years together, along with the support of your family and many friends, will provide strength and comfort in the months ahead.*

Using E-Mail for Goodwill Messages

In expressing thanks or responding to goodwill messages, handwritten notes are most impressive. However, if you frequently communicate with the receiver by e-mail and if you are sure your note will not get lost, then sending an e-mail goodwill message is acceptable, according to the Emily Post Institute.[34]

To express sympathy immediately after learning of a death or accident, you might precede a phone call or a written condolence message with an e-mail. E-mail is a fast and nonintrusive way to show your feelings. However, advises the Emily Post Institute, immediately follow with a handwritten note. Remember that e-mail messages are quickly gone and forgotten. Handwritten or printed messages remain and can be savored. Your thoughtfulness is more lasting if you take the time to prepare a handwritten or printed message on notepaper or personal stationery.

Goodwill Messages

General Guidelines: The Five Ss

- **Be selfless.** Discuss the receiver, not the sender.
- **Be specific.** Instead of generic statements (*You did a good job*), include special details (*Your marketing strategy to target key customers proved to be outstanding*).
- **Be sincere.** Show your honest feelings with conversational, unpretentious language (*We are all very proud of your award*).
- **Be spontaneous.** Strive to make the message natural, fresh, and direct. Avoid canned phrases (*If I may be of service, please do not hesitate . . .*).
- **Keep the message short.** Remember that, although they may be as long as needed, most goodwill messages are fairly short.

(Continued)

Giving Thanks

- **Cover three points in gift thank-yous.** (a) Identify the gift, (b) tell why you appreciate it, and (c) explain how you will use it.
- **Be sincere in sending thanks for a favor.** Tell what the favor means to you. Avoid superlatives and gushiness. Maintain credibility with sincere, simple statements.
- **Offer praise in expressing thanks for hospitality.** Compliment, as appropriate, the (a) fine food, (b) charming surroundings, (c) warm hospitality, (d) excellent host, and (e) good company.
- **Be specific when recognizing employees.** To make a note of appreciation meaningful, succinctly sum up the accomplishments for which you are grateful.

Responding to Goodwill Messages

- **Respond to congratulations.** Send a brief note expressing your appreciation. Tell how good the message made you feel.
- **Accept praise gracefully.** Don't make belittling comments (*I'm not really all that good!*) to reduce awkwardness or embarrassment.

Extending Sympathy

- **Refer to the loss or tragedy directly but sensitively.** In the first sentence, mention the loss and your personal reaction.
- **For deaths, praise the deceased.** Describe positive personal characteristics (*Howard was a forceful but caring leader*).
- **Offer assistance.** Suggest your availability, especially if you can do something specific.
- **End on a reassuring, positive note.** Perhaps refer to the strength the receiver finds in friends, family, colleagues, or faith.

Your Turn: Applying Your Skills at JetBlue

JetBlue customers regularly share their experiences with the airline on social media, especially Twitter. It's common, for example, that a first-time JetBlue customer tweets a message such as *My first time on JetBlue. Wonder if the hype about great service is true.* Although the comment is not a question or a complaint, a response designed to build goodwill will come within ten minutes.

Familiarize yourself with JetBlue's company focus at **https://www.jetblue.com/corporate-social-responsibility** and its Customer Bill of Rights at **https://www.jetblue.com/about**. You might want to look at some recent tweets on Twitter *@jetblue*.

Your Task

In teams of four to six, divide your group into JetBlue travelers and JetBlue customer service agents. Travelers brainstorm to come up with several positive or negative customer comments about air travel and write them as tweets sent to *@jetblue*. Students impersonating customer service representatives reply to the tweets with direct, concise responses that promote a positive feeling about the organization. Reviewing JetBlue's customer service philosophy carefully will make replying to posts as a JetBlue social media agent easier.

Summary of Learning Outcomes

1 Understand the channels through which typical positive messages travel in the digital era—e-mails, memos, and business letters—and apply the 3-x-3 writing process.

- When writing neutral and positive messages—e-mails, interoffice memos, or business letters—you can be direct because they convey routine, nonsensitive information.
- In Phase 1 of the writing process, determine your purpose, visualize your audience, and anticipate the reader's reaction.
- In Phase 2 collect information, make an outline, and write the first draft.
- In Phase 3 edit for clarity, proofread, and ensure skim value. Decide whether the message accomplishes its goal.
- Use business letters when a permanent record is required; when confidentiality is critical; when formality and sensitivity are essential; and when a persuasive, well-considered presentation is important.
- Write business letters on company stationery in block style with all lines starting at the left margin.

2 Compose direct messages that make requests, respond to inquiries online and offline, and deliver step-by-step instructions.

- In messages requesting information or action, state the purpose in the opening; explain the request in the body; express any questions in a parallel and grammatically balanced form; and close by telling the reader courteously what to do while showing appreciation.
- In complying with requests, deliver the good news in the opening; explain and provide additional information in the body; and write a cordial, personalized closing that tells the reader how to proceed if action is needed.
- When writing instruction messages, divide the instructions into steps; list steps in the correct order; arrange the items vertically with bullets or numbers; begin each step with an action verb using the imperative; and ensure that the instructions don't sound dictatorial.
- When responding online, follow the example of businesses that strive to be positive, transparent, honest, timely, and helpful.

3 Prepare contemporary messages that make direct claims and voice complaints, including those posted online.

- When you compose a message to identify a wrong and request a correction, you are writing a *claim*; direct claims are requests to which receivers are expected to readily agree.
- Begin by describing the problem or action to be taken; in the message body explain the request without emotion; in the closing summarize the request or action to be taken. Include an end date, if applicable, and express faith in future business if the problem is resolved.
- Include copies of relevant documents to support your claim.
- Take your complaint online only after exhausting all other options with the business in question; keep your post concise and clean; focus on your objective; and be prepared to support the facts.

4 Create adjustment messages that salvage customers' trust and promote further business.

- When granting a customer's claim, you are providing an *adjustment*, which has three goals: (a) rectifying the wrong, if one exists; (b) regaining the confidence of the customer; and (c) promoting further business.
- In the opening immediately grant the claim without sounding grudging. To regain the customer's trust, in the body explain what went wrong and how the problem will be corrected. However, you may want to avoid acknowledging liability for any problems.
- In the closing express appreciation; extend thanks for past business; refer to a desire to be of service; and mention a new product, if appropriate.
- If you believe that an apology should be offered, present it early and briefly.

5 Write special messages that convey kindness and goodwill.

- Make sure that messages that deliver thanks, praise, or sympathy are selfless, specific, sincere, spontaneous, and short.
- When thanking someone for a gift, tell why you appreciate it, and explain how you will use it.
- When thanking someone for a favor, convey what the favor means to you, but don't gush.
- In expressions of sympathy, mention the loss tactfully; recognize good qualities in the deceased (in the case of a death); sincerely offer assistance; and conclude on a positive, reassuring note.

Critical Thinking

1. A writer compared letters and social media posts: "What is special about a letter is the time that is taken in creating a letter—that someone went to the trouble of finding a piece of paper, sitting down, crafting their thoughts, putting them on paper, and that they created this document really just for me. A letter is a very singular expression, it's a unique document, and for that reason, to get it in the mail feels almost like a gift. . . . It's a piece of paper that I can feel. . . . There's a physical connection."[35] How might these observations apply to business letters? What other special traits can you identify? (L.O. 1)
2. A Pew Research Center study found that 89 percent of cell phone owners had used their phones during the last social gathering they attended, but they weren't happy about it; 82 percent of respondents said their use of smartphones in social settings hurt the conversation. Do you split your attention between your screen and face-to-face conversations? Do you believe it's possible to be sufficiently present while texting? (L.O. 2)
3. Why is it smart to keep your cool when making a claim, and how should you go about it? (L.O. 3)
4. Why is it important to regain the confidence of a customer in an adjustment message? How can it be done? (L.O. 4)
5. **Ethical Issue:** Credit repair companies are notorious for making grand promises that they can't legally fulfill. The Federal Trade Commission has warned that none of those companies are legitimate. Experts say that people with credit blemishes would be better off saving their money and trying to repair their bad credit themselves. One path to better credit involves the writing of so-called goodwill letters. A goodwill letter in this context is a formal message to individual creditors asking them for compassion and requesting that they stop reporting negative information such as late payments on one's credit report. Discuss why writing such goodwill letters instead of calling or sending an e-mail might be a good strategy.

Writing Improvement Exercises

8.1 Short Responses to Online Comments
(L.O. 1–5)

Social Media 

YOUR TASK Explain the positive and negative attributes of the following online posts.[36] Examine the companies' responses to them. Do they follow the guidelines in this chapter? How do the consumers' posts measure up?

a.

Alfredo Gomez Fausto Genovese **im trying to book my room through your facebook at the book now and save 30% off but its telling me the offer expired! ? what do i do?**
Yesterday at 4:38 am • Like • Comment

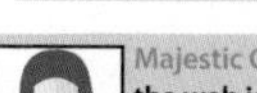

View all 7 comments

Majestic Club Resort & Casino-Las Vegas **Alberto – the sale on the web is booking okay. We are solving the page error on the Facebook exclusive offer at this time. It will be bookable shortly. :)**
16 hours ago • Like • Flag

Alfredo Gomez Fausto Genovese **thank you so much MC...know i know when i go in January i will be taken care of..Definitely AAAA diamond hospitality and service**
7 hours ago • Like • Flag

Kochkanyan Juliya/Shutterstock.com

b.

JD Lopez **when is the LG BANTER coming out?**
11 hours ago • Like • Comment

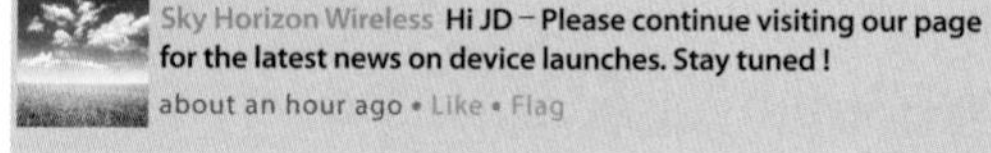

Sky Horizon Wireless Hi JD – Please continue visiting our page for the latest news on device launches. Stay tuned !
about an hour ago • Like • Flag
Write a comment...

pkchai/Shutterstock.com; gillmar/Shutterstock.com

c.

Maria Daley **You should extend your 15% off since I tried to order things off the website and it crashed. Then I tried calling the 1 800 number and it is constantly busy. Very disappointed that I can not place my order!**
Monday at 11:09 pm • Like • Comment

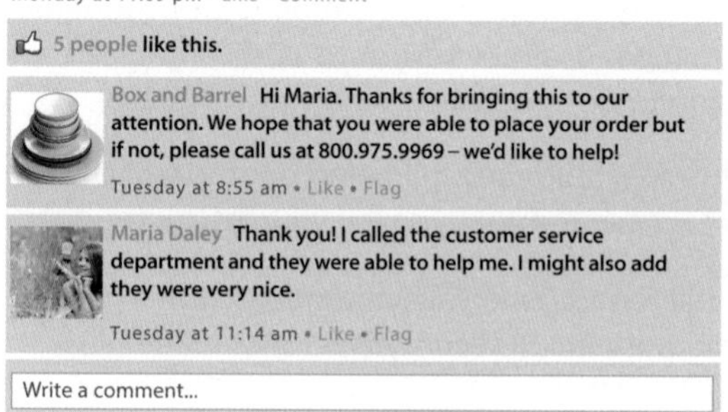

5 people like this.
Box and Barrel Hi Maria. Thanks for bringing this to our attention. We hope that you were able to place your order but if not, please call us at 800.975.9969 – we'd like to help!
Tuesday at 8:55 am • Like • Flag
Maria Daley Thank you! I called the customer service department and they were able to help me. I might also add they were very nice.
Tuesday at 11:14 am • Like • Flag
Write a comment...

BestPhotoStudio/Shutterstock.com; Africa Studio/Shutterstock.com;

d.

Dee Innes **Is there any hope that Turbotax could be written for Ubuntu Linux? It would be really great. I know I would appreciate it because I am moving away from windows and I am sure other Ubuntu users would like it too!**
October 28 at 11:57 pm • Like • Comment

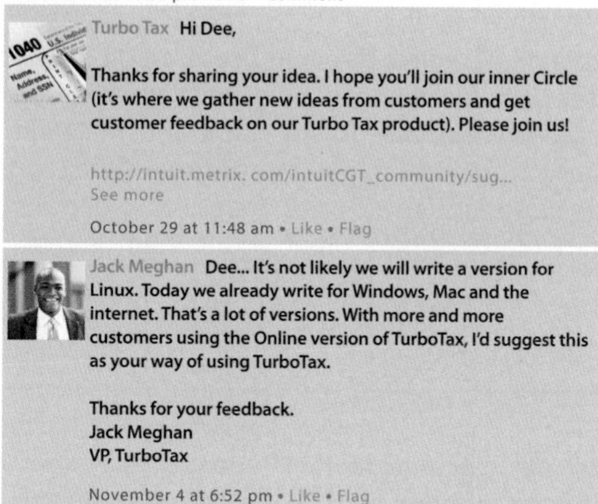

Turbo Tax Hi Dee,
Thanks for sharing your idea. I hope you'll join our inner Circle (it's where we gather new ideas from customers and get customer feedback on our Turbo Tax product). Please join us!
http://intuit.metrix. com/intuitCGT_community/sug...
See more
October 29 at 11:48 am • Like • Flag
Jack Meghan Dee... It's not likely we will write a version for Linux. Today we already write for Windows, Mac and the internet. That's a lot of versions. With more and more customers using the Online version of TurboTax, I'd suggest this as your way of using TurboTax.
Thanks for your feedback.
Jack Meghan
VP, TurboTax
November 4 at 6:52 pm • Like • Flag
Write a comment...

Cheryl Savan/Shutterstock.com; michaeljung/Shutterstock.com; Garry L./Shutterstock.com

8.2 Writing Instructions (L.O. 2)

YOUR TASK Revise each of the following wordy, dense paragraphs into a set of concise instructions. Include an introductory statement or title.

a. Making YouTube Videos

More and more amateurs are making YouTube videos, but if you have never done it before, here are some important tips. First, of course, you will need some kind of video recording device such as a smartphone, webcam, or camcorder. Another thing you will have to do is make a decision on whether or not to make a video blog, comedy skit, how-to video, or video about travel. Because nothing is perfect the first time, you should record several takes, which you can stitch together later. Next you must transfer the video files to your computer. Finally, be sure to use computer editing software to delete, improve, or change anything in your footage.

b. Submitting a Catalog Order

As a visitor and customer to our catalog website, you can place an order by following certain steps. Let me explain those steps. One of the first things you will want to do is look over everything and find the items you want from our catalog. Then your shopping cart is important. You will add items to your shopping cart. When you are finished adding things to your shopping cart, the next step is to proceed to checkout. But wait! Have you created a new account? After creating a new account, we next need to know what shipping address to ship your items to. We will also need to have you choose a shipping method. Then you will be expected to provide payment information. Finally, you are nearly done! Payment information must be provided, and then you are ready to review your order and submit it.

c. Obtaining Credit

Obtaining credit and keeping good credit can be difficult, especially for young people. Here are five suggestions that will help you obtain credit and maintain a good credit score. One thing I like to suggest first is getting a gas store card. These cards are easier to get than regular credit cards. What's great about them is that you can establish a credit history by making small payments in full and on time. To maintain good credit, you should always pay your bills on time. Delinquencies are terrible. They create the biggest negative effect on a credit score. If you already have credit cards, your balance should be paid down. If you can't afford to do that, you might take a loan from a family member or friend. If you have unused credit card accounts, don't close them. I know it sounds as if you should, but actually, canceling a card can lower your score. Don't do it! Finally, never max out your credit cards. A good rule of thumb to follow is keeping your balance below 30 percent of your credit limit.

Activities

Note: All Documents for Analysis are provided at **www.cengagebrain.com** for you to download and revise.

8.3 Document for Analysis: Direct Request—Patient Privacy Breach at Medical Office (L.O. 2)

E-Mail

The following serious message requests information, but its poor organization and other writing faults prevent it from accomplishing its goal.

YOUR TASK Analyze this message and list at least five writing weaknesses. If your instructor directs, revise the message using the suggestions you learned in this and previous chapters.

To: w.e.vance@securityspecialists.com
From: dr.jeremy.chen@valleyinternists.com
Subject: Inquiry

Dear Sir:

I am a physician in a small medical practice, and I am worried about protecting patients' medical information. Your website (SecuritySpecialists.com) looks quite promising but I found it overwhelming. I could not find answers to my specific questions, so I am writing this message to ask them. Could you call me within the next two days? I'm usually in surgery until 4 p.m. most days and try to leave at 6 p.m.

First, as I mentioned heretofore, my practice is small. Do you have experience in working with small medical practices? We may already have experienced a security breach. When you investigate, if you find out that privacy laws have been broken, do you report them to government agencies immediately?

We're really extremely interested in how you investigate an incident that may have taken place. If you discover a privacy breach, do you help your client make notification to his patients who are affected? Additionally, are you discreet about it?

I look forward to hearing from you.

Jeremy Chen, M.D.

8.4 Document for Analysis: Direct Response—Sending Answers to Data Breach Questions (L.O. 2)

E-Mail

The following message responds to the inquiry in **Activity 8.3.** Dr. Chen asks for information about dealing with a data breach at his medical firm. Mr. Vance, from Security Specialists, wants to respond briefly and answer more fully in a telephone conversation with Dr. Chen. However, the following direct response is disorganized and needs revision to be effective in achieving its goal.

YOUR TASK Study the following poorly written message, list its weaknesses, and revise it if your instructor directs.

To: dr.jeremy.chen@valleyinternists.com
From: w.e.vance@securityspecialists.com
Subject: Data Breaches

Dear Dr. Chen:

We have received your inquiry, which has been directed to me for response. I can assure you that our company can do what you want in the way of cyber security, data breach response, and incident analysis solutions. We are specialists. You asked some specific questions, such as having experience with smaller medical establishments. I can assure you that, yes, we certainly do have such experience. Even with limited resources, smaller companies will benefit from basic security awareness training in a manner related to how to properly handle, store, and the processing of patient health information.

In regard to any incident that may have already occurred, we are experienced at investigating incidents, we analyze clues, and we can quickly and defensively uncover critical information. In regard to notifying patients of any breach, we assure you that we can give discreet breach notification that is prompt and we also customize it for your business. However, I must warn you in advance that if we become aware of any wrongdoing, we must notify any applicable government or law enforcement agencies because we are obligated to do so. But I can assure you that such notification is hardly ever necessary. We can discuss your concerns more extensively by telephone. Thank you for your interest in Security Specialists.

Warren E. Vance

[Full contact information]

8.5 Document for Analysis: Instruction E-Mail (L.O. 2)

E-Mail

The following wordy and poorly expressed e-mail from a CEO discusses a growing problem for organizations: how to avoid the loss of valuable company data to hackers.

YOUR TASK Study the message, list its weaknesses, and then rewrite it in the form of an instruction message. Is it better to use bullets or numbers for an internal list?

To: Staff Members
From: G. B. Goldman <gbgoldman@firstfederal.com>
Subject: Hackers!

Staff Members:

This is to inform you that, like other banks, we are afraid of hackers. We fear that employees will expose valuable information to hackers without realizing what they are doing. Because of our fear, we have consulted cybersecurity experts, and they gave us much good advice with new procedures to be followed. Here are the procedures suggested by experts:

1. We don't want you to leave out-of-office messages. These voice mail or e-mails might explain when you will be away. Such messages are a red flag to hackers telling them that your computer is vacant and not being monitored.
2. Because smartphones can be lost or stolen, don't snap photos of company documents. Phones may be lost or stolen, and our data might be compromised.
3. Although small memory devices (thumb drives) are handy and easy to use, you may be inclined to store company files or information on these drives. Don't do it. They can easily be lost, thus exposing our company information.
4. Using work e-mail addresses for social media is another problem area. When you post details about your job, hackers can figure out an organization's best target.
5. Phishing links are the worst problem. Any request for password information or any requests to click links should be viewed with suspicion. Never click them. Even messages that seem to be from high-level officials or the human resources department within our own company can be sophisticated, realistic fakes. Examples include a request to click a link to receive a package or to download a form from within the company.

We want to let you all know that within the next two months, we plan to begin implementing a program that will educate and train employees with regard to what to avoid. The program will include fake phishing messages. The program will be explained and you will learn more from your managers in training workshops that are scheduled to begin September 1.

G. B. Goldman, CEO

[Full contact information]

8.6 Document for Analysis: Direct Claim—Very Unhappy Customer (L.O. 3)

The writer of the following letter is too angry to compose a logical and rational claim. Her message is more suited to venting than to achieving the goal of receiving a refund.

YOUR TASK Analyze this message, list at least five weaknesses, and revise it if your instructor directs.

Current date

Mr. Joseph A. Morgan
Regional General Manager
ProCar Rentals
304 South Powell Road
Mesa, AZ 85275

Dear Regional General Manager Joseph Morgen:

You're not going to believe this horror story I have to relate to you about how incompetent the amateurish bozos are that work for you! You should fire the whole bunch at the Phoenix-Mesa Gateway Airport branch. I'm tired of lousy service and of being charged an arm and a leg for extras that end up not functioning properly. Calling your company is useless because no one answers the phone or returns calls!

In view of the fact that my colleague and I were forced to wait for an hour for a car at Phoenix-Mesa Gateway Airport on July 7, your local branch people gave us a free navigation device. That would have been really nice in the event that the thing had actually worked, which it didn't. We advised the counter person that the GPS was broken, but it took another half hour to receive a new one and to finally start our business trip.

Imagine our surprise when the "free" GPS showed up on our bill apparently costing a whopping $180, plus tax! What came next would qualify as some dark Kafkaesque nightmare. I spent hours over the next three weeks talking to various employees of your questionable organization who swore that only "the manager" could help me, but this mysterious person was never available to talk. At this point in time, I called your Phoenix central location again and refused to get off the phone until I spoke to "the manager," and, lo and behold, he promised to credit the cost of the GPS to our corporate account. Was my nightmare over? No!

When we checked the status of the refund on our credit card statement, we noticed that he had forgotten to refund about $60 in taxes and surcharges that had also been assessed. So much for a full refund!

Inasmuch as my company is a new customer and inasmuch as we had hoped to use your agency for our future car rentals because of your competitive rates, I trust that you will give this matter your prompt attention.

Your very upset customer,

8.7 Responding to Posts Online (L.O. 2)

Social Media 

YOUR TASK Decide whether to respond to the following online posts.[37] If you believe you should respond, compose a concise Facebook reply following the guidelines in this chapter. Your instructor may also direct that you rewrite some of the posts themselves, if necessary.

a. Dani posted this to the Box and Barrel Facebook site: *So sad!! Ran to my store to pick up Pumpkin Yippee Pie mix and it's all sold out. :(And all sold out online also! Bummer. I knew I should've bought more! LOL….*

b. Carrie posted this comment on the Zappos Facebook site: *I ordered a few things on the 20th and opted for next day shipping…but UPS says expected delivery date is the 30th! -:-(*

c. Steve wrote the following to upscale men's clothing purveyor Brooks Brothers: *I first began shopping at Brooks Brothers about six years ago. I had read a book on menswear called "Style" by Russell Smith. He made mention to brass collar stays. I could not find them in Canada. I wandered into a Brooks Brothers store in Michigan and asked, "You don't sell brass collar stays do you?" The salesman said, "Of course." I bought collar stays, shirts and pajamas that day. A devoted customer I became. You can imagine how happy I am that Brooks Brothers has come to Canada. Bienvenue! Welcome!*

d. Allison posted this message on Geico's Facebook page: *I just wanted to thank Geico for all your support on a claim I filed. The service was excellent at one of your body repair shops and also, your customer service is top notch: calls, emails, and not to mention the site which gives you all details possible like pictures, status of the claim, easy contact us section, upload of files. GREAT WEBSITE and SERVICE. Geico has me in GOOD HANDS, not Allstate :-)*

e. Mikaela posted this request for information on the Facebook page of her favorite resort hotel, Monte Carlo Resort & Casino in Las Vegas: *Will the pool still be opened this weekend?*

8.8 Direct Request: Seeking a Social Media Specialist (L.O. 2)

E-Mail Social Media

As the director of corporate communication for Home Center, a large home supply store, you are charged with looking into the possible hiring of a social media specialist. You know that other companies have both profited from and been hurt by fast-moving viral news. Social media experts, companies hope, can monitor cyberspace and be ready to respond to both negative and positive messages. They can help build a company's brand and promote its online reputation. They can also develop company guidelines for employee use and encourage staffers to spread the good word about the organization.

To learn more about social media jobs, you decide to go to Doug Goodwin, who was recommended as a social media consultant by your CEO John Brauburger. You understand that Mr. Goodwin has agreed to provide information and will be paid by HomeCenter. The CEO wants you to explore the possibilities. You decide that this is not a matter that can be handled quickly by a phone call. You want to get answers in writing.

Many issues concern you. For one thing, you are worried about the hiring process. You are not sure about a reasonable salary for a social media expert. You don't know where to place that person within your structure. Would the media expert operate out of corporate communications, marketing, customer service, or exactly where? Another thing that disturbs you is how to judge a candidate. What background would you require? How will you identify the best candidate? And what about salary? Should you be promising a full-time salary for doing what most people consider to be fun?[38]

YOUR TASK Compose an e-mail inquiry to *doug.goodwin@mediaresources.com.* Explain your situation and list specific questions. Mr. Goodwin is not an employment source; he is a consultant who charges for his information and advice. Make your questions clear and concise. You realize that Mr. Goodwin would probably like to talk on the phone or visit you, but make clear that you want a written response so that you can have a record of his information to share when you report to the CEO.

8.9 Direct Request: Planning a Winter Retreat in Jackson Hole, Wyoming (L.O. 2)

E-Mail Web

Your employer, Pointer Media Group of Chicago, Illinois, has had an excellent year, and the CEO, Jeremy Pointer, would like to reward the troops for their hard work with a rustic yet plush winter retreat. The CEO wants his company to host a four-day combination conference/retreat/vacation for his 55 marketing and media professionals and their spouses or significant others at some spectacular winter resort.

One of the choices is Jackson Hole, Wyoming, a famous ski resort town with steep slopes and dramatic mountain views. The location is popular for its proximity to Grand Teton National Park, Yellowstone, and the National Elk Refuge. As the marketing manager, you will also look into winter resorts in Utah and Colorado. As you search the Web and investigate the options in Jackson Hole, you are captivated by the Four Seasons Resort, a five-star facility with outdoor pool, spa tub, ski in/ski out access, and an amply equipped gym and fitness room. Other amenities include an on-site spa with massage and treatment rooms, a sauna, and facial and body treatments.

The website of the Four Seasons Jackson Hole is not very explicit on the subject of business and event facilities, so you decide to jot down a few key questions. You estimate that your company will require about 50 rooms. You will also need two conference rooms (to accommodate 25 participants or more) for one and a half days. You want to know about room rates, conference facilities, A/V equipment in the conference rooms, and entertainment options for families. You have two periods that would be possible: December 10-14 or January 14-18. You realize that both are peak times, but you wonder whether you can get a discounted group rate. You are interested in entertainment on site, Jackson Hole, and tours to the nearby national parks. Jackson Hole airport is 4.5 miles away, and you would like to know whether the hotel operates a shuttle. Also, one evening the CEO will want to host a banquet for about 85 people. Mr. Pointer wants a report from you by September 14.

YOUR TASK Write a well-organized direct request e-mail to Jackie Sullivan, Sales Manager, Four Seasons Resort. You might like to take a look at the Four Seasons Resort website at and search for general information about Jackson, Wyoming.

8.10 Direct Response: Chesapeake Sail & Canvas Receives a Poor Customer Rating on Yelp (L.O. 2)

Social Media Web

Yelp, the social network for consumer reviews and local searches, logs approximately 89 million monthly unique visitors and has listed 90 million reviews at this time.[39] Many users rely on what they hope to be real reviews by real people, as the company claims. They wish to make more informed buying decisions based on Yelp reviews. Businesses would do well to monitor their status on Yelp because anything less than a four- or five-star rating might be a blemish costing them sales.

Barry Gregg, owner of Chesapeake Sail & Canvas in Annapolis, Maryland, watches his Yelp reviews. Currently, he has six reviews, all five stars. Imagine his surprise when he recently received a rating of one star from Angela K.:

> Chesapeake Canvas does good work, but it seems to have become a casualty of its own success. The company is unresponsive when you call and e-mail. I will take my business elsewhere because after 3 weeks, I still haven't heard about that estimate for my marine canvas. I had left a voice mail message and sent an e-mail. No response. I called again and was received as if my request were outlandish when I expressed the hope of getting a quote that same week. Since then, silence. Not cool. And I am a repeat customer. . . . People, fortunately there are other businesses out there!

The writer says she is a returning customer. Barry sighs because he is really shorthanded. His administrative assistant has been sick a lot lately, and inquiries have gone unanswered; communication has not been flowing well. Business is booming, and he does not have enough qualified installers; as a result, weeks elapse before his small crew gets around to completing a job. Barry searches his files and finds the job the company completed for Angela four years ago. Chesapeake had made a dodger, sail cover, and other smaller canvas items for Angela's 30-foot Catalina sailboat.

YOUR TASK Consider Barry's options. Should he respond to the one negative review? What could be the consequences of ignoring it? If you believe that Barry should respond, discuss first how. He has the disgruntled customer's e-mail, phone number, and street address. He could post a reply on Yelp to provide a commentary to the bad review. If your instructor directs, plan a strategy for Barry and respond to the customer in the way you believe is best for Barry and his business.

8.11 Direct Response: The Right to Be Forgotten (L.O. 1–5)

Communication Technology E-Mail

Team Web

As the Plugged In feature in this chapter demonstrates, Americans strongly dislike government surveillance and information sharing by businesses. In an opinion poll, 80 percent of respondents expressed great concern and stated that they support proposals to strengthen online privacy. More than 90 percent demanded that businesses safeguard and not share customers' private information, and almost 80 percent believe the federal government should actively protect their financial and other personal information in cyberspace.[40] Republicans and Democrats alike back laws that would empower Americans to take control of their personal privacy.[41] However, *the right to be forgotten* does not exist in the United States and has not yet inspired much public debate.

YOUR TASK As a group or individually, research the right to be forgotten as it applies to the specific court decision by the highest European court. If directed to do so, look for discussions of this complex issue in the United States. Then consider the questions posed in the Plugged In feature. Are you a cautious social media user, or have you posted information online that you wished you hadn't shared? Do you have friends who overshare and might damage their reputation and job prospects? Would you back efforts to force search engines to make embarrassing content disappear from searches? After a full discussion face-to-face or facilitated by an online discussion board—if directed to do so—write a direct memo or e-mail to your instructor explaining your individual or group opinion on the right to be forgotten and online privacy.

8.12 Direct Response: Interviewing at Marmont & Associates (L.O. 2)

E-Mail

Carl Mekeel, founder and CEO of Marmont & Associates, is a busy architect. As he expands his business, he is looking for ecologically conscious designers who can develop sustainable architecture that minimizes the negative environmental impact of buildings. His company has an open position for an environmental architect/designer. Three candidates were scheduled to be interviewed on March 14. However, Mr. Mekeel now finds he must be in Dallas during that week to consult with the builders of a 112-unit planned golf course community. He asks you, his office manager, to call the candidates, reschedule for March 28 or March 29, and prepare a memo with the new times as well as a brief summary of the candidates' backgrounds.

Fortunately, you were able to reschedule all three candidates. Scott Hogarth will come on March 29 at 11 a.m. Mr. Hogarth specializes in passive solar energy and has two years of experience with SolarPlus, Inc. He has a bachelor's degree from the University of Southern California. Christine Lindt has a master's degree from Boise State University and worked for five years as an architect planner for Boise Builders, with expertise in sustainable building materials. She will come on March 28 at 2 p.m. Without a degree but with ten years of building experience, Jerry Rodriguez is scheduled for March 28 at 10 a.m. He is the owner of Green Building Consulting and has experience with energy efficiency, sustainable materials, domes, and earth-friendly design. You are wondering whether Mr. Mekeel forgot to include Phil Barker, his partner, who usually helps make personnel selections.

YOUR TASK Prepare a memo (or e-mail if your instructor directs) to Mr. Mekeel with all the information he needs in the most readable format. Consider using a three-column table format for the candidate information.

8.13 Instruction Message: How to Copy Pictures and Text from PDF Documents (L.O. 2)

As a summer intern in the Marketing Department at Jovanovic Laboratory Supply, Inc., in Bozeman, Montana, you have been working on the company's annual catalog. You notice that staffers could save a lot of valuable time by copying and inserting images and text from the old edition into the new document. Your boss, Marketing Director Jenny Zhang, has received numerous inquiries from staffers asking how to copy text and images from previous editions. You know that this can be done, and you show a fellow worker how to do it using a PDF feature called **Take a Snapshot**. Marketing Director Zhang decides that you are quite a tech-savvy student. Because she has so much confidence in you, she asks you to draft a memo detailing the steps for copying images and text passages from portable document format (PDF) files.

You start by viewing the **Edit** pull-down menu in an open PDF document. Depending on the Acrobat version, a feature called **Take a Snapshot** can be seen. It is preceded by a tiny camera icon and a check mark when the tool is activated. To copy content, you need to select the part of the PDF document that you want to capture. The cursor will change its shape once the feature is activated. Check what shape it acquires. With the left mouse button, click the location where you want to copy a passage or image.

At the same time, you need to drag the mouse over the page in the direction you want. A selected area appears that you can expand and reduce, but you can't let go of the left mouse button. Once you release the left mouse button, a copy of the selected area will be made. You can then paste the selected area into a blank Microsoft Office document, whether Word, Excel, or PowerPoint. You can also take a picture of an entire page.

YOUR TASK Prepare a memo addressed to Marketing Department staff members for the signature of Jenny Zhang. Practice the steps described here in abbreviated form, and arrange all necessary instructions in a logical sequence. You may need to add steps not noted here. Remember, too, that your audience may not be as computer literate as you are, so ensure that the steps are clear and easy to follow.

8.14 Instruction E-Mail Inviting Down-Editing Needs Revision (L.O. 2)

E-Mail

The following message, which originated in an international technology company, was intended to inform new team members about their upcoming move to a different office location. But its stream-of-consciousness thinking and jumbled connections leave the receiver confused as to what is expected and how to respond.

YOUR TASK Study the complete message. Then revise it with (a) a clear introduction that states the purpose of the message, (b) a body with properly announced lists, and (c) a conclusion that includes a call to action and a deadline. Improve the organization by chunking similar material together. What questions must be answered? What tasks should be performed? Should this message show more of a "you" view? In addition, make it easy for receivers to respond. Receivers will be down-editing—that is, returning the message with their responses (in another color) interspersed among the listed items.

Hello everyone,

We'll be moving new team members into a new location next week so there are things we need you to do to be ready for the move. For one thing, let me know which Friday you want your personal items moved. The possibilities are November 9 and 16. Also, if you have an ergonomic desk or chair you want moved, let me know. By the way, we'll be sending boxes, labels, tape and a move map four or five days before the move date you choose, so let me know if this timeframe allows you enough time to pack your belongings. And if you are bringing office equipment from your current team to the new team, let me know. Remember that company policy allows you to take a workstation/laptop from your current team to the new workstation. So check with your admin and let me know what office equipment you will be bringing. Incidentally, your new workstation will have a monitor and peripherals.

You'll need to do some things before the movers arrive. Make sure you put foam pads around your valuable, fragile items and then box them up. This includes things such as IT plaques, glass, or anniversary glass sculptures. If the glass things break, replacing them is expensive and the cost center is responsible for replacement. You may want to move them yourself and not have the movers do it.

Another thing—make sure you pack up the contents of all gray filing cabinets because movers do not move those. Also, write on the move map the number and delivery location of whiteboards, corkboards, and rolling cabinets. Most important, make sure you add a name label to all your belongings, such as desk phones, docking stations, peripherals, monitors, tables, ergonomic desks, ergonomic chairs, etc. If you see old move labels on recycled boxes, remove them or cross them out.

Get back to me ASAP. And by the way, the movers will arrive between 4 p.m. and midnight on the move date.

Thank you

8.15 Direct Claim: New Iron Gate Needs Work (L.O. 3)

You work for NCP, New Century Properties, in Portland, Oregon. Your employer specializes in commercial real estate. Yesterday one of your business tenants in the trendy NW 23rd neighborhood complained about problems with an iron gate you had installed by Castle Iron Works just six months earlier, on August 20. Apparently, the two doors of the gate have settled and don't match in height. The gate gets stuck. It takes much force to open, close, and lock the gate. The iron gate was painted, and in some spots rust is bleeding onto the previously pristine white paint. The tenant at 921 NW 23rd Ave., Portland, OR 97210 is a petite shop owner, who complained to you about struggling with the gate at least twice a day when opening and closing her store.

You realize that you will have to contact the installer, Castle Iron Works, and request that the company inspect the gate and remedy the problem. Only six months have passed, and you recall that the warranty for the gate was for one year. To have a formal record of the claim, and because Castle Iron Works does not use e-mail, you decide to write a claim letter.

YOUR TASK Address your letter to Van Phan Luong at Castle Iron Works, 2255 NW Yeon Avenue in Portland, OR 97210. To jog his memory, you will enclose a copy of the company's proposal/invoice. Your business address is 1960 NE Irving Street, Portland, OR 97209, phone (503) 335-5443 and fax (503) 335-5001.

8.16 Direct Claim: The Real Thing (L.O. 3)

Like most consumers, you have probably occasionally been unhappy with service or with products you have used.

YOUR TASK Select a product or service that has disappointed you. Write a claim letter requesting a refund, replacement, explanation, or whatever seems reasonable. Generally, such letters are addressed to customer service departments. For claims about food products, be sure to include bar code identification from the package, if possible. Your instructor may ask you to mail this letter. Remember that smart companies want to know what their customers think, especially if a product could be improved. Give your ideas for improvement. When you receive a response, share it with your class.

8.17 Direct Claim: But It Doesn't Work! (L.O. 3)

E-Mail

After you receive an unexpected bonus, you decide to indulge and buy a new ultra HD 4K TV. You conduct research to compare prices and decide on a Sony 65-inch ultra HD 4K TV Model KD-75X9405C. You spot the TV at Digital Depot for $2,798.00 plus tax, the lowest price you could find. Although the closest store is a 45-minute drive, the price is so good you decide it's worth the trip. You sell your old TV to make room for the Sony and spend several hours installing the new set. It works perfectly, but the next day when you go to turn it on, nothing happens. You check everything, but no matter what you do, you can't get a picture. You're irritated! You are without a TV and have wasted hours hooking up the Sony. Assuming it's just a faulty set, you pack up the TV and drive back to Digital Depot. You have no trouble returning the item and come home with a second Sony.

Again you install the TV, and again you enjoy your new purchase. But the next day, you have no picture for a second time. Now you are fuming! Not looking forward to your third trip to Digital Depot, you repack the Sony and return it. The customer service representative tries to offer you another Sony TV, but you decline. You point out all the trouble you have been through and say you would prefer a more reliable TV from a different manufacturer that is the same size and in the same price range as the Sony. Digital Depot carries a Panasonic (Model TX-65CZ952) that fits your criteria, but at $4,997.95, it is much more than you had budgeted. You feel that after all the problems you have endured, Digital Depot should sell you the Panasonic at the same price as the Sony. However, when you call to discuss the matter, you are told to submit a written request.

YOUR TASK Write a direct claim letter to Dennis Garcia, Manager, Digital Depot, 2300 Austin Street, Houston, TX 77074, asking him to sell you the TV for less than the advertised price. Alternatively, if your instructor directs, write this message as an e-mail.

8.18 Adjustment: Erroneous Charge for GPS Reversed (L.O. 4)

As assistant to Joseph A. Morgan, Regional General Manager at ProCar Rentals, you read a shockingly irate complaint letter from a corporate customer (See **Activity 8.6**) addressed to your boss. Amanda Greene-Hedwig, Sales Manager for Greene Engineering Solutions, Inc., in Phoenix, Arizona, has angrily detailed her tribulations with your company's Phoenix-Mesa Gateway Airport branch.

Apparently, she and a colleague suffered long delays in obtaining their rental car. To compensate for the late car delivery, the customers received complimentary use of a navigation device, a $180 value plus taxes and surcharges that added up to another $60. However, at the end of their rental period, their bill reflected the full cost of the GPS. After multiple phone calls to the Phoenix-Mesa Gateway Airport branch as well as to the ProCar Rentals corporate offices, Ms. Greene-Hedwig apparently was finally able to have the $180 credited to Greene Engineering Solutions' business account. However, soon she realized that the $60 levy had not been credited. She now wants the remainder of the refund. Ms. Greene-Hedwig has no confidence in the Phoenix-Mesa branch and is asking your boss to intervene on her behalf and reverse the remaining $60 charge.

Mr. Morgan asks you to investigate what has gone so terribly wrong at the Phoenix-Mesa Gateway Airport location. You learn that the branch is an independent franchisee, which may explain such a laxness in customer service that is unacceptable under corporate rules. In addition, you find out that the branch manager, Frank Anderson, was traveling on company business during Ms. Greene-Hedwig's rental period and then left town to attend two management training seminars. Mr. Morgan is concerned that ProCar might lose this disappointed customer and decides to offer 20 percent discount vouchers for the engineering company's next three rentals, valid at any U.S. branch. He wants you to draft the letter and enclose the discount vouchers.

YOUR TASK Write a polite adjustment letter to Amanda Greene-Hedwig, Greene Engineering Solutions, Inc., 2328 East Van Buren St., Phoenix, AZ 85006, to secure the customer's goodwill and future business.

8.19 Adjustment: We Can Restretch but Not Replace (L.O. 4)

E-Mail

Your company, Masterpiece International, sells paintings through its website and catalogs. It specializes in workplace art intended for offices, executive suites, conference rooms, and common areas. To make shopping for office art easy, your art consultants preselect art, making sure that the finished product is framed and delivered in perfect shape. You are proud that Masterpiece International can offer fine works of original art at incredibly low prices.

Recently, you received an e-mail from Heinz Property Management claiming that a large oil painting that your company sent had arrived in damaged condition. The e-mail said, "This painting sags, and we can't possibly hang it in our executive offices." You were surprised at this message because the customer had signed for delivery and not mentioned any damage. The e-mail went on to demand a replacement.

You find it difficult to believe that the painting is damaged because you are so careful about shipping. You give explicit instructions to shippers that large paintings must be shipped standing up, not lying down. You also make sure that every painting is wrapped in two layers of convoluted foam and one layer of Perf-Pack foam, which should be sufficient to withstand any bumps and scrapes that negligent shipping may cause. Nevertheless, you decide to immediately review your packing requirements with your shippers.

It's against your company policy to give refunds or replace paintings that the receiver found acceptable when delivered. However, you could offer Heinz Property Management the opportunity to take the painting to a local framing shop for restretching at your expense. The company could send the restretching bill to Masterpiece International at 438 West 84th Street, New York, NY 10024.

YOUR TASK Compose an e-mail adjustment message that regains the customer's confidence. Send it to Henry M. Heinz at *hmheinz@heinzproperty.com.*

8.20 Thanks for a Favor: Glowing Letter of Recommendation (L.O. 5)

E-Mail

One of your instructors has complied with your urgent request for a letter of recommendation and has given you an enthusiastic endorsement. Regardless of the outcome of your application, you owe thanks to all your supporters. Respond promptly after receiving this favor. Also, you can assume that your instructor is interested in your progress. Let him or her know whether your application was successful.

YOUR TASK Write an e-mail or, better yet, a letter thanking your instructor. Remember to make your thanks specific so that your words are meaningful. Once you know the outcome of your application, use the opportunity to build more goodwill by writing to your recommender again.

8.21 Thanks for a Favor: Business Etiquette Training Session (L.O. 5)

Team Web

Your business communication class was fortunate to have the etiquette and protocol expert Pamela Eyring speak to you. A sought-after TV commentator and media personality, she runs The Protocol School of Washington, a training center for etiquette consultants and protocol officers. Ms. Eyring emphasized the importance of soft skills. She talked about outclassing the competition and dining like a diplomat. She addressed topics such as business entertaining, invitations, introductions, greetings, seating arrangements, toasting, eye contact, remembering names, and conversation skills. In the table manners segment, among other topics, she discussed dining dos and don'ts, host and guest duties, seating and napkin placement, place settings and silverware savvy, eating various foods gracefully, and tipping. With characteristic poise but also humor, Ms. Eyring brought utensils, plates, and napkins to demonstrate correct table manners.

The class was thrilled to receive hands-on training from a nationally known business etiquette expert who was able to lessen their fears of making fools of themselves during business meals or at business mixers.

YOUR TASK Individually or in groups, draft a thank-you letter to Pamela Eyring, president of The Protocol School of Washington, P.O. Box 676, Columbia, SC 29202. Check out the company's website **http://www.psow.edu**, or find The Protocol School of Washington on Facebook, where you can follow Ms. Eyring's frequent media appearances, interviews, and etiquette advice.

8.22 Responding to Good Wishes: Saying Thank You (L.O. 5)

YOUR TASK Write a short note thanking a friend who sent you good wishes when you recently completed your degree.

8.23 Extending Sympathy: To a Spouse (L.O. 5)

YOUR TASK Imagine that the spouse of a coworker recently died in an automobile accident. Write the coworker a letter of sympathy.

Test Your Etiquette IQ

New communication platforms and casual workplace environments have blurred the lines of appropriateness, leaving workers wondering how to navigate uncharted waters. Indicate whether the following statements are true or false. Then see if you agree with the responses on p. R-1.

1. After completing a successful deal, you want to send a gift but the client's company has a no-gifts policy. You think, however, that it is acceptable for you to send a gourmet food basket or a subscription to a trade magazine for the entire office.

   _______ True _______ False

2. When receiving a business card, you should treat it as a gift. Take a moment to study the card and perhaps remark on its distinctive design.

   _______ True _______ False

3. If you have caller ID and you recognize an incoming call, you should consider carefully before picking up the phone and greeting the caller with his first name.

   _______ True _______ False

Chat About It

In each chapter you will find five discussion questions related to the chapter material. Your instructor may assign these topics for you to discuss in class, in an online chat room, or on an online discussion board. Some of the discussion topics may require outside research. You may also be asked to read and respond to postings made by your classmates.

TOPIC 1: Airbnb used a reciprocal review system: the hosts would review their guests and the guests would then review their hosts. The social network, which relies on reputational data to function properly, found that most reviews were dishonest, too rosy. What could explain that positive bias? How do you feel about overly glowing online reviews?

TOPIC 2: Do you agree that saying sorry for a mishap in doing business is difficult? Even aside from fears of litigation, some businesspeople struggle with apologizing properly. Have you experienced situations in which saying sorry was difficult? What makes an apology effective?

TOPIC 3: When responding favorably to a request that you are not thrilled to grant, why is it important in business to nevertheless sound gracious or even agreeable?

TOPIC 4: Conduct research regarding costly mistakes that resulted from unclear instructions. What is the most costly mistake you discovered?

TOPIC 5: Describe an occasion in which you should have written a goodwill message but failed to do so. Why was it difficult to write that message? What would make it easier for you to do so?

Grammar and Mechanics | *Review 8*

Capitalization

Review Guides 39 through 46 about capitalization in Appendix D, Grammar and Mechanics Guide, beginning on page D-14. On a separate sheet, revise the following sentences to correct capitalization errors. For each error you locate, write the guide number that reflects this usage. Sentences may have more than one error. If a sentence is correct, write *C*. When you finish, check your answers on page Key-2.

EXAMPLE: Neither the Manager nor the Vice President would address hiring in the south.

REVISION: Neither the **manager** nor the **vice president** would address hiring in the **South**. [Guides 41, 43]

1. Our Sales Manager and Director of Operations thought that the Company should purchase a new nordictrack treadmill for the Fitness room.
2. All american airlines passengers must exit the plane at gate 2B in terminal 4 when they reach seattle-tacoma international airport.
3. The secretary of state of the united states urged members of the european union to continue to seek peace in the middle east.
4. My Uncle, who lives in the midwest, has a big mac and a diet coke for Lunch nearly every day.
5. Our corporate Vice President and President met with several Directors on the west coast to discuss how to develop Apps for facebook.
6. The World's Highest Tax Rate is in belgium, said professor du-babcock, who teaches at the city university of hong kong.
7. Alyson Davis, who heads our consumer services division, has a Master's Degree in Marketing from california state university.
8. Please consult figure 2.3 in chapter 2 to obtain u.s. census bureau population figures for the northeast.
9. Last Summer did you see the article titled "the global consequences of using crops for fuel"?
10. Kahee plans to take courses in Management, Economics, and History in the Spring.

References

[1] Whipple, K. [keara_whipple]. (2016. February 9.) Great customer service and comfortable plane. [Tweet]. Retrieved from https://mobile.twitter.com/JetBlue/status/697178433974042624

[2] Jeffrey. [BravoJeffrey]. (2016, February 9). Ladies and gentlemen. [Tweet]. Retrieved from https://mobile.twitter.com/BravoJeffrey/status/697118794343411713

[3] JetBlue Airways. [JetBlue]. (2016, February 9.) Wicked good. [Tweet]. Retrieved from https://mobile.twitter.com/JetBlue/status/697120242749800451

[4] Kolowich, L. (2014, July 28). Delighting people in 140 characters: An inside look at JetBlue's customer service success. Retrieved from http://blog.hubspot.com/marketing/jetblue-customer-service-twitter

[5] JetBlue Airways. [JetBlue]. (2016, February 9.) We're happy to do what we can to assist families during this difficult time. [Tweet]. Retrieved from https://mobile.twitter.com/JetBlue/status/697182302565240832

[6] Kolowich, L. (2014, July 28). Delighting people in 140 characters: An inside look at JetBlue's customer service success. Retrieved from http://blog.hubspot.com/marketing/jetblue-customer-service-twitter

[7] Global Internet penetration rates as of January 2015, by region. (2016). Statista. Retrieved from http://www.statista.com/statistics/269329/penetration-rate-of-the-internet-by-region

[8] Duarte, N. (2010, April 27). What's in the president's briefing book anyway? Retrieved from http://www.duarte.com/blog/whats-in-the-presidents-briefing-book-anyway

[9] NPR Staff. (2015, August 18). Debate: Should the U.S. adopt the "Right to Be Forgotten" online? NPR.org. Retrieved from http://www.npr.org/2015/03/18/393643901/debate-should-the-u-s-adopt-the-right-to-be-forgotten-online

[10] Rosoff, M. (2015, August 20). This ruling shows the absurdity of Europe's "right to be forgotten" law. *Business Insider*. Retrieved from http://www.businessinsider.com/eu-right-to-be-forgotten-law-is-idiotic-2015-8

[11] Manjoo, F. (2015, August 5). "Right to Be Forgotten" online could spread. *The New York Times*. Retrieved from http://www.nytimes.com/2015/08/06/technology/personaltech/right-to-be-forgotten-online-is-poised-to-spread.html

[12] Ibid.

[13] Anzalone, Liszt, Grove Research, & Freedman Consulting. (2015, November 23). Poll finds strong support for expanding online privacy protections and Internet access. Retrieved from http://tfreedmanconsulting.com/documents/PrivacyandAccessResearchFindings_151123.pdf

[14] Romero, A. D., & Boldin, M. (2016, January 20). How Americans can take back online privacy. *Time*. Retrieved from http://time.com/4185320/personal-privacy

[15] Ford, A. (2011, June 28). Develop a comment monitoring policy… Or use this one. Tymado Multimedia Solutions. Retrieved from http://tymado.com/2011/06/develop-a-comment-monitoring-policy-or-use-this-one

[16] Ibid.

[17] Banjo, S. (2012, July 29). Firms take online reviews to heart. *The Wall Street Journal*. Retrieved from http://online.wsj.com/article/SB10001424052702303292204577517394043189230.html

[18] Cited by permission from Ford, A. (2011, June 28). Develop a comment monitoring policy… Or use this one. Tymado Multimedia Solutions. Retrieved from http://tymado.com/2011/06/develop-a-comment-monitoring-policy-or-use-this-one

[19] Banjo, S. (2012, July 29). Firm take online reviews to heart. *The Wall Street Journal*. Retrieved from http://online.wsj.com/article/SB10001424052702303292204577517394043189230.html

[20] Campbell, C. (2015, February 15). 7 tips for listening—and responding—to your customers. *Inc*. Retrieved from http://www.inc.com/chris-campbell/7-tips-to-use-customer-reviews-to-your-advantage.html

[21] Based on Many unhappy returns: Retailers combat "wardrobing." (2014, December 26). NBC News. Retrieved from http://www.nbcnews.com/storyline/business-of-the-holidays/many-unhappy-returns-retailers-combat-wardrobing-n275046; Stock, K. (2013, September 18). Bloomingdale's will no longer lend you a party dress. *Bloomberg Business*. Retrieved from http://www.bloomberg.com/bw/articles/2013-09-18/bloomingdales-will-no-longer-lend-you-a-party-dress; An eagle eye on retail scams. (2005, August 8). *Businessweek*. Retrieved from http://www.businessweek.com

[22] Bernstein, E. (2015, August 10). Don't hit send: Angry emails just make you angrier. *The Wall Street Journal*. Retrieved from http://www.wsj.com/articles/dont-hit-send-angry-emails-just-make-you-angrier-1439227360

[23] Torabi, F. (2011, July 28). Bad customer service? 3 smarter ways to complain. CBS News. Retrieved from http://www.cbsnews.com/8301-505144_162-41542345/bad-customer-service-3-smarter-ways-to-complain; Pilon, M. (2009, August 5). How to complain about a company.

The Wall Street Journal. Retrieved from http://blogs.wsj.com/wallet/2009/08/05/how-to-complain-about-a-company/tab/print

[24] White, M. (2015, October 19). Lost bags, at 140 characters, and airlines respond. *The New York Times*. Retrieved from http://www.nytimes.com/2015/10/20/business/lost-bags-at-140-characters-and-airlines-respond.html

[25] Ibid.

[26] Tuey, H. (2014, July 2). Findlay waitress fired for Facebook post about tipping. WTOL 11. Retrieved from http://www.wtol.com/story/25918895/findlay-waitress-fired-for-facebook-post-about-tipping?hpt=us_bn9

[27] New ways to complain: Airing your gripes can get you satisfaction—or trouble. (2011, August). Consumer Reports.org. Retrieved from http://www.consumerreports.org/cro/money/consumer-protection/new-ways-to-complain/overview/index.htm

[28] Ibid.

[29] Campbell, C. (2015, February 15). 7 tips for listening—and responding—to your customers. Inc. Retrieved from http://www.inc.com/chris-campbell/7-tips-to-use-customer-reviews-to-your-advantage.html

[30] Smith, B. (2015, January 23). In business, love means having to say you're sorry. LinkedIn. Retrieved from https://www.linkedin.com/pulse/business-love-means-having-say-youre-sorry-brad-smith

[31] States with apology laws. (n.d.). Sorry Works! Retrieved from http://www.sorryworks.net/apology-laws-cms-143; Daicoff, S. (2013, February 15). Apology, forgiveness, reconciliation and therapeutic jurisprudence. *Pepperdine Dispute Resolution Law Journal, 13*(1), 2. Retrieved from http://digitalcommons.pepperdine.edu/cgi/viewcontent.cgi?article=1240&context=drlj

[32] Hollis, L. (2014, February 27). Sorry seems to be the hardest word. *Management Today*. Retrieved from http://www.managementtoday.co.uk/news/1281578/sorry-seems-hardest-word

[33] Baer, J. (2015, June 24). How asking for help can turn haters into brand advocates. *Inc*. Retrieved from http://www.inc.com/jay-baer/how-asking-for-help-can-turn-haters-into-brand-advocates.html; Ho, M. (2014, September 29). How to deal with negative Facebook comments on your brand's page. *Adweek: Social Times*. Retrieved from http://www.adweek.com/socialtimes/how-to-deal-with-negative-facebook-comments/301063

[34] Emily Post Institute. (2016). Advice: Sympathy notes and letters. Retrieved from http://emilypost.com/advice/sympathy-notes-and-letters

[35] A case for the dwindling art of letter writing in the 21st century. (2014, June 5). Radio Boston WBUR. Retrieved from http://radioboston.wbur.org/2014/06/05/letter-writing-century

[36] Based on Buddy Media. (2011). How do I respond to that? The definitive guide to Facebook publishing & moderation. Retrieved from https://www.hashdoc.com/documents/3504/the-definitive-guide-to-facebook-publishing-and-moderation

[37] Based on Buddy Media. (2011). How do I respond to that? The definitive guide to Facebook publishing & moderation. Retrieved from https://www.hashdoc.com/documents/3504/the-definitive-guide-to-facebook-publishing-and-moderation

[38] Portions based on Gillette, F. (2010, July 19-25). Twitter, twitter, little stars. *Bloomberg Businessweek*, pp. 64-67.

[39] 10 Things you should know about Yelp. (2016). Retrieved from http://www.yelp.com/about

[40] Anzalone, Liszt, Grove Research, & Freedman Consulting. (2015, November 23). Poll finds strong support for expanding online privacy protections and Internet access. Retrieved from http://tfreedmanconsulting.com/documents/PrivacyandAccessResearchFindings_151123.pdf

[41] Romero, A. D., & Boldin, M. (2016, January 20). How Americans can take back online privacy. *Time*. Retrieved from http://time.com/4185320/personal-privacy

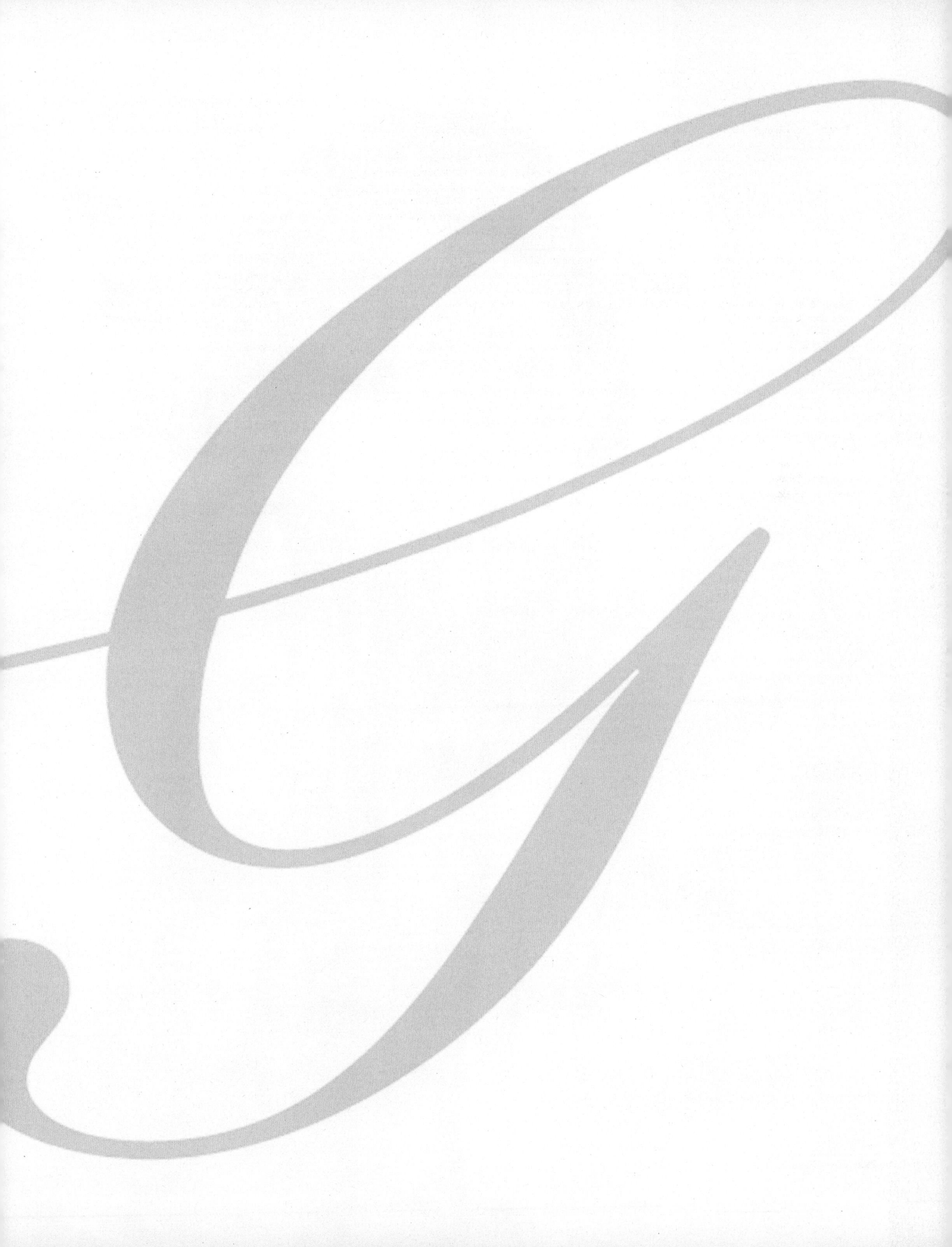

Chapter 9 Negative Messages

LEARNING OUTCOMES

After studying this chapter, you should be able to

1 Understand the strategies of business communicators in conveying negative news, apply the 3-x-3 writing process, and avoid legal liability.

2 Distinguish between the direct and indirect strategies in conveying unfavorable news.

3 Explain the components of effective negative messages, including opening with a buffer, apologizing, showing empathy, presenting the reasons, cushioning the bad news, and closing pleasantly.

4 Apply effective techniques for refusing typical requests or claims as well as for presenting bad news to customers in print or online.

5 Describe and apply effective techniques for delivering bad news within organizations.

Crises Rock the Cruise Industry and Rattle Cruise Passengers

"We have been stuck in 125+ mph winds, 30+ foot waves for 4 hours . . . At the height of the storm waves breaking above the top of the lifeboats and ship listing almost 45 degrees, with wind looked like a total white out."[1] This tweet by *Jjohnb* sums up the situation aboard Royal Caribbean's *Anthem of the Seas*. With 4,529 passengers and 1,616 crew members, the world's third-largest cruise ship ran into severe weather in the Atlantic and was forced to return to New Jersey. Four passengers were injured, and a class action lawsuit has been filed by terrified survivors of the ordeal, during which all guests were confined to their cabins for 12 hours, many fearing for their lives. The National Transportation Safety Board launched an investigation into whether the cruise line had recklessly ignored dire weather warnings by the National Oceanic and Atmospheric Administration.[2]

The global cruise industry continues to grow, generating $40 billion a year in revenues, and is expected to carry 25 million annual passengers by 2019, more than half of them Americans.[3] Engine fires and resulting power failures; outbreaks of norovirus; rowdy, inebriated passengers; petty and serious crimes; people lost at sea; crew labor issues; and a growing awareness of gross pollution stemming from the behemoths of the sea—these serious negatives don't seem to deter many Americans from booking sea voyages. Most travelers use Royal Caribbean and Carnival Cruise Lines, the world's largest. The well-publicized incidents forced the companies to develop an almost routine procedure for apologies and remedies. The cruise lines typically apologize and offer refunds for days cut short during a voyage. In egregious cases the companies give full refunds. In addition, they usually offer 50 percent off future cruises.

Cruise lines have had much to apologize for. Cruise Junkie, a site run by sociologist Ross Klein, and Cruise Minus keep a running tally of incidents at sea.[4] After an engine fire aboard the *Carnival Splendor,* nearly 3,300 passengers subsisted for three days on Spam, Pop-Tarts, and canned food flown in by navy helicopters as the disabled ship was towed to San Diego.[5] Then president and CEO of Carnival Cruise Lines, Gerry Cahill, won praise for sincerely apologizing at an early press conference. The cruise line posted frequent updates on Twitter, Facebook, a popular blog, and its website. Adroit communication with distressed passengers was needed again when another Carnival ship, *Costa Allegra,* experienced an engine room fire and power blackout off the Seychelles Islands.[6] However, the *Costa Concordia* accident in Italy that killed 32 passengers reached a different scale, and caused much negative publicity. Lately, Americans' enthusiasm for cruises appears to be waning; 44 percent of cruise passengers said they were less likely to take a cruise again compared to the previous year; the percentage rose to 58 among people who have never taken a cruise.[7] You will learn more about this case later in this chapter.

Critical Thinking

- Suppose you made an honest mistake that could prove expensive for your employer or internship provider. Would you blurt out the bad news immediately, or consider strategies to soften the blow somewhat?
- What are some of the techniques you could use if you had to deliver a bad-news message in print or online for a company such as Royal Caribbean or Carnival Cruise Lines?
- In its communication during the *Anthem of the Seas* incident, Royal Caribbean first tried to reassure the public on Twitter and downplay the severity of the storm. Meanwhile, passengers had full Internet access throughout the crisis. Initially after the incident, the company stated that the captain had sole discretion in deciding whether to sail. Two days later the company issued an apology on its Press Center website and in e-mails to customers, claiming the storm had been more severe than anticipated. The cruise line admitted that it must improve its storm avoidance policy and guidance to sea captains. The now customary refunds were offered, too. Based on the information presented here, how would you evaluate Royal Caribbean's crisis management and communication skills?

Communicating Negative News Effectively

Bad things happen in all businesses. At Royal Caribbean, bad weather, virus outbreaks on board, and technical trouble can ruin cruises. In other businesses, goods are not delivered, products fail to perform as expected, service is poor, billing gets fouled up, or customers are misunderstood. You may have to write messages ending business relationships, declining proposals, explaining service outages, describing data breaches, announcing price increases, refusing requests for donations, terminating employees, turning down invitations, or responding to unhappy customers. You might have to apologize for mistakes in orders or pricing, the rudeness of employees, overlooked appointments, substandard service, faulty accounting, defective products, or jumbled instructions. As a company representative, you may have to respond to complaints posted for the world to see on Twitter, Facebook, or complaint websites.

The truth is that everyone occasionally must deliver bad news in business. Because bad news disappoints, irritates, and sometimes angers the receiver, such messages must be written carefully. The bad feelings associated with disappointing news can generally be reduced if the

Bloomberg/Getty Images

Mexican fast-food chain Chipotle was slammed with bad news when the CDC declared an *E. coli* outbreak among people who had dined at the eatery. From California to Delaware, the outbreak spread across 11 states and sickened 60 people. Because Chipotle boasts about the quality of its food, the scandal was especially damaging. CEO Steve Ells issued a statement declaring the company would "enhance our already high standards for food safety" and offered "deepest sympathies to those affected." Nevertheless, Chipotle stock took a nosedive. Which communication goals for conveying unfavorable news did Ells's statement attempt to address?[8]

receiver (a) knows the reasons for the rejection, (b) feels that the news was revealed sensitively, and (c) believes the matter was treated seriously and fairly.

In this chapter you will learn when to use the direct strategy and when to use the indirect strategy to deliver bad news. You will study the goals of business communicators in working with unfavorable news and learn techniques for achieving those goals.

LEARNING OUTCOME 1

Understand the strategies of business communicators in conveying negative news, apply the 3-x-3 writing process, and avoid legal liability.

Articulating Goals in Communicating Negative News

Delivering negative news is not the happiest communication task you may have, but it can be gratifying if you do it effectively. As a business communicator working with bad news, you will have many goals, the most important of which are summarized in Figure 9.1.

Figure 9.1 Goals in Conveying Unfavorable News

Explaining clearly and completely

- Readers understand and, in the best case, accept the bad news.
- Recipients do not have to call or write to clarify the message.

Conveying empathy and sensitivity

- Writers use language that respects the reader and attempts to reduce bad feelings.
- When appropriate, writers accept blame and apologize without creating legal liability for the organization or themselves.

Projecting a professional image

Writers stay calm, use polite language, and respond with clear explanations of why a negative message was necessary even when irate customers sound threatening and overstate their claims.

Maintaining friendly relations

Writers demonstrate their desire to continue pleasant relations with the receivers and to regain their confidence.

Being fair

Writers show that the decision was fair, impartial, and rational.

The goals outlined in Figure 9.1 are ambitious, and we are not always successful in achieving them all. However, many senders have found the strategies and techniques you are about to learn helpful in conveying disappointing news sensitively and safely. With experience, you will be able to vary these strategies and adapt them to your organization's specific communication tasks.

Applying the 3-x-3 Writing Process

Thinking through the entire writing process is especially important when writing bad-news messages because the way bad news is revealed often determines how it is accepted. You have probably heard people say, "I didn't mind the news so much, but I resented the way I was told!" Certain techniques can help you deliver bad news sensitively, beginning with the familiar 3-x-3 writing process.

Analyzing, Anticipating, and Adapting. In Phase 1 (prewriting), you need to analyze the bad news and anticipate its effect on the receiver. When Intuit decided to modify its popular TurboTax desktop software, the company underestimated the impact of the change. The Internet exploded with negative comments about Intuit for upselling and crippling the older version of the software. The company apologized, but apparently, lacking adequate remedies, Intuit's apologies didn't appease TurboTax users. CEO Brad Smith then turned to the public in a three-minute video, in which he offered another heartfelt apology and explained how Intuit would fix the problem. Smith admitted that he had failed to anticipate the displeasure over the product change as well as the firestorm that ensued. In his video, the contrite CEO even read angry social media posts on camera.[9] In a remorseful blog post, the head of the TurboTax team apologized as well.[10] However, the entire situation might have been handled better if Intuit had given more thought to analyzing the situation and anticipating its effect.

When you have bad news to convey, one of your first considerations is how that message will affect its receiver. If the disappointment will be mild, announce it directly. For example, a small rate increase in a newspaper or Web subscription can be announced directly. If the bad news is serious or personal, consider techniques to reduce the pain. In the Intuit situation, a bad-news message should have prepared the TurboTax user, given reasons for omitting customary forms and upselling to more expensive products, possibly offered alternatives, and sought the goodwill of the receiver.

Choose words that show that you respect the reader as a responsible, valuable person. Select the best channel to deliver the bad news. In many negative situations, you will be dealing with a customer. If your goal is retaining the goodwill of a customer, a letter on company stationery will be more impressive than an e-mail.

Researching, Organizing, and Drafting. In Phase 2 (drafting), you will gather information and brainstorm for ideas. Jot down all the reasons you have that explain the bad news. If four or five reasons prompted your negative decision, concentrate on the strongest and safest ones. Avoid presenting any weak reasons; readers may seize on them to reject the entire message. Include an ample explanation of the negative situation, and avoid fixing blame.

When the U.S. Postal Service has to deliver damaged mail, it includes an explanation, such as the following: *Because the Post Office handles millions of pieces of mail daily, we must use mechanical methods to ensure prompt delivery. Damage can occur if mail is insecurely enveloped or bulky contents are enclosed. When this occurs and the machinery jams, it often damages other mail that was properly prepared.* Notice that the message offers the strongest reason for the problem, although other reasons may have been possible. Notice, too, that the explanation tactfully skirts the issue of who caused the problem.

In composing any negative message, conduct research if necessary to help you explain what went wrong and why a decision or action is necessary.

Editing, Proofreading, and Evaluating. In Phase 3 (revising), you will read over your message carefully to ensure that it says what you intend. Check your wording to be sure you are concise without being gruff. If you find that you have overused certain words, use a thesaurus to find synonyms. Read your sentences to see if they sound like conversation and flow smoothly. This is the time to edit and improve coherence and tone. In bad-news messages, the tone is especially important. Readers are more likely to accept negative messages if the tone is friendly and respectful. Even when the bad news can't be changed, its effect can be reduced somewhat by the way it is presented.

In the last phase of the writing process, proofread to make sure your verbs agree with their subjects, your sentences are properly punctuated, and all words are spelled correctly. Pay attention to common mistakes (*its/it's; than/then; their/there*). If your word processing application checks grammar, be sure to investigate those squiggly underscores. Finally, evaluate your message. Is it too blunt? Too subtle? Have you delivered the bad news clearly but professionally?

Conveying Negative News Without Incurring Legal Liability

Before we examine the components of a negative message, let's look more closely at how you can avoid exposing yourself and your employer to legal liability in writing negative messages. Although we can't always anticipate the consequences of our words, we should be alert to three causes of legal difficulties: (a) abusive language, (b) careless language, and (c) the good-guy syndrome.

Abusive Language. Calling people names (such as *deadbeat, crook*, or *quack*) can get you into trouble. *Defamation* is the legal term for any false statement that harms an individual's reputation. When the abusive language is written, it is called *libel*; when spoken, it is *slander.*

To be actionable (likely to result in a lawsuit), abusive language must be (a) false, (b) damaging to one's good name, and (c) published—that is, written or spoken within the presence of others. Therefore, if you were alone with Jane Doe and accused her of accepting bribes and selling company secrets to competitors, she couldn't sue because the defamation wasn't published. Her reputation was not damaged. However, if anyone heard the words or if they were written, you might be legally liable.

Similarly, you may be prosecuted if you transmit a harassing or libelous message by e-mail or post it on Facebook, Twitter, or other social networking sites. In what was dubbed a *Twibel* case, singer Courtney Love's attorney sued the performer for defamation after Love's Twitter posts alleged that her lawyer was corruptible. Although Love won, the court battle dragged on for years.[11] The musician was not so lucky when Dawn Simorangkir sued her twice over tweets that accused the designer of criminal behavior. Singer Love lost and had to fork over almost $800,000.[12] Tweets and other electronic transmissions are considered to be published.

Moreover, a company may incur liability for messages sent through its computer network by employees. That's why most organizations are monitoring outgoing and internal messages. "When inappropriate e-mail is sent using the company's e-mail address, the employer's identity is associated with the e-mail, which could seriously harm the employer's reputation," warn attorneys Barbara J. Stratton and Sarah J. Becker. Also, employers who don't prevent misconduct can face harassment lawsuits, the lawyers caution.[13] Instant messaging and texting add another danger for companies. Whether your message is in print or electronic, avoid making unproven charges or letting your emotions prompt abusive language.

Careless Language. As the marketplace becomes increasingly litigious, we must be certain that our words communicate only what we intend. Take the case of a factory worker injured on the job. His attorney subpoenaed company documents and discovered a seemingly harmless letter sent to a group regarding a plant tour. These words appeared in the letter: "Although we are honored at your interest in our company, we cannot give your group a tour of the plant operations as it would be too noisy and dangerous." The court found in favor of the worker, inferring from the letter that working conditions were indeed hazardous.[14] The letter writer did not intend to convey the impression of dangerous working conditions, but the court accepted that interpretation.

The Good-Guy Syndrome. Most of us hate to have to reveal bad news—that is, to be the bad guy. To make ourselves look better, to make the receiver feel better, and to maintain good relations, we are tempted to make statements that are legally dangerous. Consider the case of a law firm interviewing job candidates. One of the firm's partners was asked to inform a candidate that she was not selected. The partner's letter said, "Although you were by far the most qualified candidate we interviewed, unfortunately, we have decided we do not have a position for a person of your talents at this time." To show that he personally had no reservations about this candidate and to bolster the candidate, the partner offered his own opinion. However, he differed from the majority of the recruiting committee. When the rejected interviewee learned later that the law firm had hired two male attorneys, she sued, charging sexual discrimination. The court found in favor of the rejected candidate. It agreed that a reasonable inference could be made from the partner's letter that she was the most qualified candidate.[15]

Two important lessons emerge. First, business communicators act as agents of their organizations. Their words, decisions, and opinions are assumed to represent those of the organization. If you want to communicate your personal feelings or opinions, use your home computer or write on plain paper (rather than company letterhead) and sign your name without title or affiliation. Second, volunteering extra information can lead to trouble. Therefore, avoid supplying data that could be misused, and avoid making promises that can't be fulfilled. Don't admit or imply responsibility for conditions that caused damage or injury. Even some apologies (*We're sorry that a faulty bottle cap caused damage to your carpet*) may suggest liability.

Analyzing Negative-News Strategies

LEARNING OUTCOME 2

Distinguish between the direct and indirect strategies in conveying unfavorable news.

Unfavorable news in business doesn't always fall into neat categories. To successfully convey bad news, writers must carefully consider the audience, purpose, and context. Experienced business communicators understand that their approaches to negative news must be flexible.[16] However, as a business writer in training, you have at your disposal two basic strategies for delivering negative news: direct and indirect.

Which approach is better suited for your particular message? One of the first steps you will take before delivering negative news is analyzing how your receiver will react to this news. In earlier chapters we discussed applying the direct strategy to positive messages. We suggested using the indirect strategy when the audience might be unwilling, uninterested, displeased, disappointed, or hostile. In this chapter we expand on that advice and suggest additional considerations that can help you decide which strategy to use.

When to Use the Direct Strategy

The direct strategy saves time and is preferred by some who consider it to be more professional and even more ethical than the indirect strategy. The direct strategy may be more effective in situations such as the following:

- **When the bad news is not damaging.** If the bad news is insignificant (such as a small increase in cost) and doesn't personally affect the receiver, then the direct strategy makes sense.
- **When the receiver may overlook the bad news.** Changes in service, new policy requirements, legal announcements—these critical messages may require boldness to ensure attention.

- **When the organization or receiver prefers directness.** Some companies and individuals expect all internal messages and announcements—even bad news—to be straightforward and presented without frills.
- **When firmness is necessary.** Messages that must demonstrate determination and strength should not use delaying techniques. For example, the last in a series of collection letters that seek payment on an overdue account may require a direct opener.

Security breach messages provide a good example of how to employ the direct strategy in delivering bad news. Notice in Figure 9.2 that the writer, Garrett Blake, is fairly direct in announcing that consumer identity information was lost at Well Point Federal Credit Union.

Figure 9.2 **Announcing Bad News Directly: Security Breach Letter**

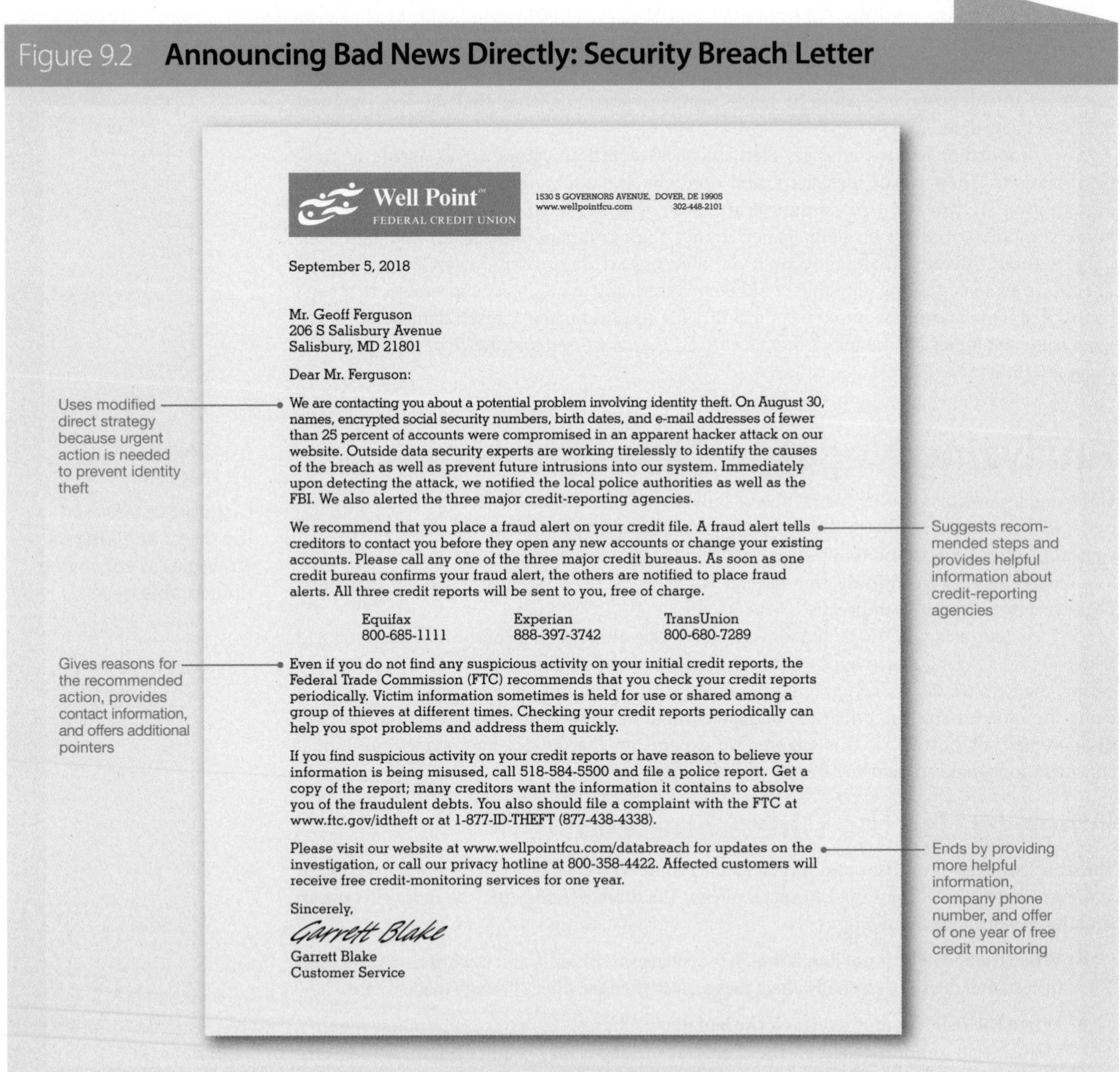

Well Point℠ FEDERAL CREDIT UNION
1530 S GOVERNORS AVENUE, DOVER, DE 19905
www.wellpointfcu.com 302-448-2101

September 5, 2018

Mr. Geoff Ferguson
206 S Salisbury Avenue
Salisbury, MD 21801

Dear Mr. Ferguson:

We are contacting you about a potential problem involving identity theft. On August 30, names, encrypted social security numbers, birth dates, and e-mail addresses of fewer than 25 percent of accounts were compromised in an apparent hacker attack on our website. Outside data security experts are working tirelessly to identify the causes of the breach as well as prevent future intrusions into our system. Immediately upon detecting the attack, we notified the local police authorities as well as the FBI. We also alerted the three major credit-reporting agencies.

We recommend that you place a fraud alert on your credit file. A fraud alert tells creditors to contact you before they open any new accounts or change your existing accounts. Please call any one of the three major credit bureaus. As soon as one credit bureau confirms your fraud alert, the others are notified to place fraud alerts. All three credit reports will be sent to you, free of charge.

Equifax	Experian	TransUnion
800-685-1111	888-397-3742	800-680-7289

Even if you do not find any suspicious activity on your initial credit reports, the Federal Trade Commission (FTC) recommends that you check your credit reports periodically. Victim information sometimes is held for use or shared among a group of thieves at different times. Checking your credit reports periodically can help you spot problems and address them quickly.

If you find suspicious activity on your credit reports or have reason to believe your information is being misused, call 518-584-5500 and file a police report. Get a copy of the report; many creditors want the information it contains to absolve you of the fraudulent debts. You also should file a complaint with the FTC at www.ftc.gov/idtheft or at 1-877-ID-THEFT (877-438-4338).

Please visit our website at www.wellpointfcu.com/databreach for updates on the investigation, or call our privacy hotline at 800-358-4422. Affected customers will receive free credit-monitoring services for one year.

Sincerely,

Garrett Blake

Garrett Blake
Customer Service

Uses modified direct strategy because urgent action is needed to prevent identity theft
Suggests recommended steps and provides helpful information about credit-reporting agencies
Gives reasons for the recommended action, provides contact information, and offers additional pointers
Ends by providing more helpful information, company phone number, and offer of one year of free credit monitoring

Although he does not blurt out "your information has been compromised," the writer does announce a potential identity theft problem in the first sentence. He then explains that a hacker attack has compromised roughly a quarter of customer accounts. In the second paragraph, he recommends that credit union customer Geoff Ferguson take specific corrective action to protect his identity and offers helpful contact information. The tone is respectful and serious. The credit union's letter is modeled on an FTC template that was praised for achieving a balance between a direct and indirect opening.[17]

If you must write a security breach message, describe clearly what information was compromised, if known. Explain how the breach occurred, what data were stolen, and, if you know, how the thieves have used the information. Next, disclose what your company has done to repair the damage. Then list the recommended responses most appropriate for the type of data compromised. For instance, if social security numbers were stolen, urge victims to place fraud alerts on their credit reports; include the agencies' addresses. Designate a contact person in your organization, and work with law enforcement to ensure that your notification does not jeopardize the investigation in any way.

When to Use the Indirect Strategy

The indirect strategy does not reveal the bad news immediately. This strategy, at least theoretically, enables you to keep the reader's attention until you have been able to explain the reasons for the bad news. Some writing experts suggest that the indirect strategy "ill suits today's skeptical, impatient, even cynical audience."[18] Others have argued the relative merits of both approaches and their effects on the receiver.[19] To be sure, in social media, bluntness seems to dominate the public debate. Directness is equated with honesty; hedging, with deceit.

Regardless, many communicators prefer to use the indirect strategy to soften negative news. Whereas good news can be revealed quickly, bad news may be easier to accept when broken gradually. Even a direct bad-news message can benefit from sandwiching the negative news between positive statements.[20] Here are typical instances in which the indirect strategy works well:

- **When the bad news is personally upsetting.** If the negative news involves the receiver personally, such as a layoff notice, the indirect strategy makes sense. Telling an employee that he or she no longer has a job is probably best done in person and by starting indirectly and giving reasons first. When a company has made a mistake that inconveniences or disadvantages a customer, the indirect strategy also makes sense.
- **When the bad news will provoke a hostile reaction.** When your message will irritate or infuriate the recipient, the indirect method may be best. It begins with a buffer and reasons, thus encouraging the reader to finish reading or hearing the message. A blunt announcement may make the receiver stop reading.

Jeanette Dietl/Shutterstock.com

Reality Check

When Saying No, Be Gentle

"It's important to be real and upfront with your customers but in a gentle manner. They are the most valuable part of your business, and you need to be transparent if you want them to use your product or service again. When saying no, inform them of your company policies and always offer a solution or next step, as this will show what you're doing to better the situation."[21]

—George Bousis, *founder and CEO, Raise Marketplace, Inc.*

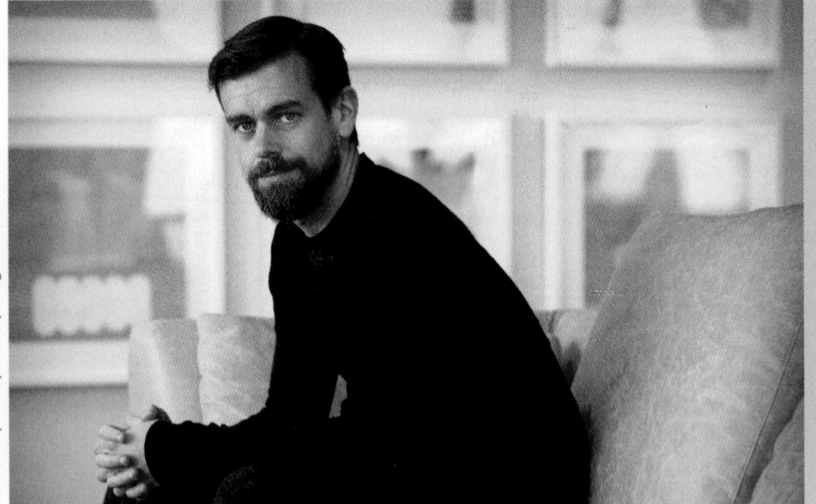

Jack Dorsey/Newspix/Getty Images

When Twitter CEO Jack Dorsey sent an e-mail to staffers informing them of a restructuring plan, he used writing strategies to ensure that his audience would understand and accept the bad news. In a first-sentence buffer statement, Dorsey mentioned the organization's need to be "on a stronger path to grow." He followed with reasons for the restructuring, including the need for a "nimbler team." Finally, in the e-mail's fourth paragraph, Dorsey slipped in the bad news: "We plan to part ways with 336 people from across the company." What helps determine the choice to use the indirect method to deliver bad news?[22]

- **When the bad news threatens the customer relationship.** If the negative message may damage a customer relationship, the indirect strategy may help salvage the customer bond. Beginning slowly and presenting reasons that explain what happened can be more helpful than directly announcing bad news or failing to adequately explain the reasons.
- **When the bad news is unexpected.** Readers who are totally surprised by bad news tend to have a more negative reaction than those who expected it. If a company suddenly closes an office or a plant and employees had no inkling of the closure, that bad news would be better received if it were revealed cautiously with reasons first.

Whether to use the direct or indirect strategy depends largely on the situation, the reaction you expect from the audience, and your goals. The direct method saves time and is preferred by some who consider it more professional and even more ethical than the indirect method. Others think that revealing bad news slowly and indirectly shows sensitivity to the receiver. By preparing the receiver, you tend to soften the impact. Moreover, although social media users may favor the direct approach, the majority of negative messages are still conveyed indirectly. As you can see in Figure 9.3, the major differences between the two strategies are whether you start with a buffer and how early you explain the reasons for the negative news.

Keeping the Indirect Strategy Ethical

You may worry that the indirect organizational strategy is unethical or manipulative because the writer deliberately delays the main idea. Now, consider the alternative. Breaking bad news bluntly can cause pain and hard feelings. By delaying bad news, you soften the blow somewhat, as well as ensure that your reasoning will be read while the receiver is still receptive. One psychologist recognized the significance of the indirect strategy when she stated, "If the *why* of my *no* is clear and understandable, it's less likely that the other person will take it as being a *no* to them."[23] In using the indirect strategy, your motives are not to deceive the reader or to hide the news. Rather, your goal is to be a compassionate, yet effective communicator.

The key to ethical communication lies in the motives of the sender. Unethical communicators *intend to deceive*. Although the indirect strategy provides a setting in which to announce bad news, it should not be used to avoid or misrepresent the truth. For example, the Internet is rife with bogus offers such as skin care products promising to deliver the fountain of youth. Some offer miraculous weight loss with the help of green coffee bean extract or raspberry

Figure 9.3 **Comparing the Direct and Indirect Strategies for Negative Messages**

ketone supplements, to name just two of the current scams. Unscrupulous marketers advertise on trusted websites of national news organizations and falsely claim endorsements by Oprah Winfrey and Dr. Oz, says Truth in Advertising, a nonprofit dedicated to stamping out deceptive advertising.[24] As you will see in Chapter 10, misleading, deceptive, and unethical claims are never acceptable. In fact, many of them are simply illegal.

Composing Effective Negative Messages

LEARNING OUTCOME 3

Explain the components of effective negative messages, including opening with a buffer, apologizing, showing empathy, presenting the reasons, cushioning the bad news, and closing pleasantly.

Even though it may be impossible to make the receiver happy when delivering negative news, you can reduce bad feelings and resentment by structuring your message sensitively. Most negative messages contain some or all of these parts: buffer, reasons, bad news, and closing. This section also discusses apologies and how to convey empathy in delivering bad news.

Opening Indirect Messages With a Buffer

A buffer is a device to reduce shock or pain. To buffer the pain of bad news, begin with a neutral but meaningful statement that makes the reader continue reading. The buffer should be relevant and concise and provide a natural transition to the explanation that follows. The individual situation, of course, will help determine what you should put in the buffer. Avoid trite buffers such as *Thank you for your letter.*

Not all business communication authors agree that buffers increase the effectiveness of negative messages. However, in many cultures softening bad news is appreciated. Following are buffer possibilities.

Best News. Start with the part of the message that represents the best news. For example, a message to customers who purchased mobile device insurance announced a progressive rate increase that was tied to the replacement value of each smart device. Only customers with very expensive handsets will experience price increases. You might start by reminding customers about the value of insuring a mobile device, *As a reminder, your Premium Electronics Protection provides the benefit of a replacement device when your smartphone is accidentally damaged, including liquid damage, loss, theft, and malfunction. Although devices are becoming increasingly expensive, no changes will be made to your deductible amount or coverage.*

Compliment. Praise the receiver's accomplishments, organization, or efforts, but do so with honesty and sincerity. For instance, in a letter declining an invitation to speak, you could write, *The Thalians have my sincere admiration for their fund-raising projects on behalf of hungry children. I am honored that you asked me to speak Monday, November 5.*

Appreciation. Convey thanks for doing business, for sending something, for showing confidence in your organization, for expressing feelings, or simply for providing feedback. Suppose you had to draft a letter that refuses employment. You could say, *I appreciated learning about the hospitality management program at Cornell and about your qualifications in our interview last Friday.* Avoid thanking the reader, however, for something you are about to refuse.

Agreement. Make a relevant statement with which both reader and receiver can agree. A letter that rejects a business loan application might read, *We both realize how much falling crude oil prices on the world market have devastated domestic oil production.*

Facts. Provide objective information that introduces the bad news. For example, in a memo announcing cutbacks in the hours of the employees' cafeteria, you might say, *During the past five years, the number of employees eating breakfast in our cafeteria has dropped from 32 percent to 12 percent.*

Understanding. Show that you care about the reader. Notice how in this letter to customers announcing a product defect, the writer expresses concern: *We know that you expect superior performance from all the products you purchase from OfficeCity. That's why we're writing personally about the Omega printer cartridges you recently ordered.*

Blueguy/Shutterstock.com

Reality Check

Apologies Foster a Culture of Improvement and Innovation

"I often say sorry to employees. I flag up when something isn't working and tell them not to worry because it has shown how not to do things. Then we look at how we can do it better. Feeling comfortable with apologies and admitting things aren't working, especially when you are the CEO, is vital if you want a culture where staff aren't afraid to fail and can look for ways to improve the business."[25]

—Anne Lise Kjaer, *futurist and CEO, Kjaer Global*

Apologizing

You learned about making apologies in adjustment messages in Chapter 8. We expand that discussion here because apologies are often part of negative-news messages. An apology is defined as an "admission of blameworthiness and regret for an undesirable event."[26] Apologies to customers are especially important if you or your company erred. They cost nothing, and they go a long way in soothing hard feelings.

The truth is that sincere apologies work and affect the bottom line. A study of 130 press releases shows that companies are twice as likely to pass the buck than to own up to their mistakes; however, businesses blaming external factors instead of taking responsibility for their failings tend to experience ongoing financial decline. Those who own up to their poor performance see their finances recover and improve.[27] Another study suggested that CEOs who appeared genuinely sad, not merely contrite, in videos saw their companies' stock prices rise after an apology. Conversely, leaders who smiled while apologizing were perceived as insincere, and their companies' stock prices dropped.[28]

Professional writer John Kador recommends what he calls the Five Rs model for effective apologies in business messages[29] summarized in Figure 9.4.

Consider these poor and improved apologies:

Poor apology: We regret that you are unhappy with the price of frozen yogurt purchased at one of our self-serve scoop shops.

Improved apology: We are genuinely sorry that you were disappointed in the price of frozen yogurt recently purchased at one of our self-serve scoop shops. Your opinion is important to us, and we appreciate your giving us the opportunity to look into the problem you describe.

Figure 9.4 **Apologizing Effectively in the Digital Age: The Five Rs**

Recognition
Acknowledge the specific offense.

- Organizations that apologize have better outcomes.
- Individuals who apologize well rise higher in management and have better relationships.

Responsibility
Accept personal responsibility.

- Accountability means taking reponsibility and rejecting defensiveness.
- Accountability is an important skill.
- The cover-up is always worse than the crime.

Restitution
Explain exactly how you will fix it.

- A concrete explanation of what you will do to make things right is best.
- The remedy should be appropriate, adequate, and satisfying.

Remorse
Embrace *I apologize* and *I am sorry*.

- Apologies may become necessary unexpectedly.
- We can prevent automatic defensiveness by being prepared to apologize when the need arises.
- Apologies should be honest, sincere, and authentic.

Repeating
Say it won't happen again and mean it.

- Written apologies are more formal than spoken but work about the same.
- By communicating effectively over the long term, businesses gain the trust of employees, the public, as well as the media and are therefore better equipped to weather crises successfully.

Ethics Check

Volkswagen CEO's Sputtering Apology

Volkswagen CEO Matthias Müller was criticized for his nonapology during the emission-cheating scandal involving 480,000 diesel cars. In a National Public Radio interview, Müller insisted the carmaker "didn't lie" to U.S. regulators. Instead he blamed a technical problem and a misinterpretation of U.S. law. When pressed on ethical problems at VW, Müller retorted: "I cannot understand why you say that." However, later that day, Müller blamed noise and chaos for the poor first interview. He said: "We fully accept the violation. There is no doubt about it." He promised that VW would do its "utmost" to resolve the problem.[30]

Poor apology: We apologize if anyone was affected.

Improved apology: I apologize for the frustration our delay caused you. As soon as I received your message, I began looking into the cause of the delay and realized that our delivery tracking system must be improved.

Poor apology: We are sorry that mistakes were made in filling your order.

Improved apology: You are right to be concerned. We sincerely apologize for the mistakes we made in filling your order. To prevent recurrence of this problem, we are . . . .

Showing Empathy

One of the hardest things to do in negative messages is to convey sympathy and empathy. As discussed in Chapter 3, *empathy* is the ability to understand and enter into the feelings of another. Researchers have established a so-called empathy quotient and ranked 100 companies on their ability to respond to customers' needs promptly and sincerely. LinkedIn took first place and was praised for its strong presence on rival social media network Twitter—for going where its customers are, even at the risk of appearing to endorse a competing product.[31] The researchers insisted that businesses "must demonstrate empathy across three channels: internally, to their own employees, externally, to their customers, and finally to the public via social media." Although some companies may fear appearing weak and vulnerable, authentic dialogue is expected in today's transparent social media environment.[32]

Here are examples of ways to express empathy in written messages:

- In writing to an unhappy customer: *We did not intentionally delay the shipment, and we sincerely regret the disappointment and frustration you must have suffered.*
- In laying off employees: *It is with great regret that we must take this step. Rest assured that I will be more than happy to write letters of recommendation for anyone who asks.*
- In responding to a complaint: *I am deeply saddened that our service failure disrupted your sale, and we will do everything in our power to . . . .*
- In showing genuine feelings: *You have every right to be disappointed. I am truly sorry that . . . .*

Presenting the Reasons

Providing an explanation reduces feelings of ill will and improves the chances that readers will accept the bad news. Without sound reasons for denying a request, refusing a claim, or revealing other bad news, a message will fail, no matter how cleverly it is organized or written.

Jens Schwarz/laif/Redux Pictures

Reality Check

Empathy Pays

"Empathy is not a soft nurturing value but a hard commercial tool that every business needs as part of their DNA. Our aim is to make every interaction our customers have with us an individual one."[33]

—René Schuster, *chief operating officer, VimpelCom, formerly CEO of Telefónica Germany*

For example, if you must deny a customer's request, as part of your planning before writing, you analyze the request and decide to refuse it for specific reasons. Where do you place your reasons? In the indirect strategy, the reasons appear before the bad news. In the direct strategy, the reasons appear immediately after the bad news.

Explaining Clearly. If the reasons are not confidential and if they will not create legal liability, you can be specific: *Growers supplied us with a limited number of patio roses, and our demand this year was twice that of last year.* In responding to a billing error, explain what happened: *After you informed us of an error on your January bill, we investigated the matter and admit the mistake was ours. Until our new automated system is fully online, we are still subject to the frailties of human error. Rest assured that your account has been credited, as you will see on your next bill.* In refusing a speaking engagement, tell why the date is impossible: *On January 17 we have a board of directors meeting that I must attend.* Don't, however, make unrealistic or dangerous statements in an effort to be the good guy.

Citing Reader or Other Benefits, if Plausible. Readers are more open to bad news if in some way, even indirectly, it may help them. In refusing a customer's request for free hemming of skirts and slacks, Lands' End wrote: "We tested our ability to hem skirts a few months ago. This process proved to be very time-consuming. We have decided not to offer this service because the additional cost would have increased the selling price of our skirts substantially, and we did not want to impose that cost on all our customers."[34] Readers also accept bad news more readily if they recognize that someone or something else benefits, such as other workers or the environment: *Although we would like to consider your application, we prefer to fill managerial positions from within.* Avoid trying to show reader benefits, though, if they appear insincere: *To improve our service to you, we are increasing our brokerage fees.*

Explaining Company Policy. Readers resent blanket policy statements prohibiting something: *Company policy prevents us from making cash refunds* or *Contract bids may be accepted from local companies only* or *Company policy requires us to promote from within.* Instead of hiding behind company policy, gently explain why the policy makes sense: *We prefer to promote from within because it rewards the loyalty of our employees. In addition, we have found that people familiar with our organization make the quickest contribution to our team effort.* By offering explanations, you demonstrate that you care about readers and are treating them as important individuals.

Choosing Positive Words. Because the words you use can affect a reader's response, choose carefully. Remember that the objective of the indirect strategy is holding the reader's attention until you have had a chance to explain the reasons justifying the bad news. To keep the reader in a receptive mood, avoid expressions with punitive, demoralizing, or otherwise negative connotations. Stay away from such words as *cannot, claim, denied, error, failure, fault, impossible, mistaken, misunderstand, never, regret, rejected, unable, unwilling, unfortunately,* and *violate.*

Showing Fairness and Serious Intent. In explaining reasons, show the reader that you take the matter seriously, have investigated carefully, and are making an unbiased decision. Receivers are more accepting of disappointing news when they feel that their requests have been heard and that they have been treated fairly. In canceling funding for a program, board members provided this explanation: *As you know, the publication of* Urban Artist *was funded by a renewable annual grant from the National Endowment for the Arts. Recent cutbacks in federally sponsored city arts programs have left us with few funds. Because our grant has been discontinued, we have no alternative but to cease publication of* Urban Artist. *You have my assurance that the board has searched long and hard for some other viable funding, but every avenue of recourse has been closed before us. Accordingly, June's issue will be our last.*

Cushioning the Bad News

Although you can't prevent the disappointment that bad news brings, you can reduce the pain somewhat by breaking the news sensitively. Be especially considerate when the reader will suffer personally from the bad news. A number of thoughtful techniques can cushion the blow.

Positioning the Bad News Strategically. Instead of spotlighting it, sandwich the bad news between other sentences, perhaps among your reasons. Don't let the refusal begin or end a paragraph; the reader's eye will linger on these high-visibility spots. Another technique that reduces shock is putting a painful idea in a subordinate clause: *Although another candidate was hired, we appreciate your interest in our organization and wish you every success in your job search.* Subordinate clauses often begin with words such as *although, as, because, if,* and *since.*

Using the Passive Voice. Passive-voice verbs enable you to depersonalize an action. Whereas the active voice focuses attention on a person (*We don't give cash refunds*), the passive voice highlights the action (*Cash refunds are not given because . . .*). Use the passive voice for the bad news. In some instances you can combine passive-voice verbs and a subordinate clause: *Although franchise scoop shop owners cannot be required to lower their frozen yogurt prices, we are happy to pass along your comments for their consideration.*

Highlighting the Positive. As you learned earlier, messages are far more effective when you describe what you can do instead of what you can't do. Rather than *We will no longer allow credit card purchases,* try a more positive appeal: *We are now selling gasoline at discount cash prices.*

Implying the Refusal. It is sometimes possible to avoid a direct statement of refusal. Often, your reasons and explanations leave no doubt that a request has been denied. Explicit refusals may be unnecessary and at times cruel. In this refusal to contribute to a charity, for example, the writer never actually says *no*: *Because we will soon be moving into new offices in Glendale, all our funds are earmarked for relocation costs. We hope that next year we will be able to support your worthwhile charity.* The danger of an implied refusal, of course, is that it is so subtle that the reader misses it. Be certain that you make the bad news clear, thus preventing the need for further correspondence.

Suggesting a Compromise or an Alternative. A refusal is not so depressing—for the sender or the receiver—if a suitable compromise, substitute, or alternative is available. In denying permission to a group of students to visit a historical private residence, for instance, this writer softens the bad news by proposing an alternative: *Although private tours of the grounds are not given, we do open the house and its gardens for one charitable event in the fall.* You can further reduce the impact of the bad news by refusing to dwell on it. Present it briefly (or imply it), and move on to your closing.

Closing Pleasantly

After explaining the bad news sensitively, close the message with a pleasant statement that promotes goodwill. The closing should be personalized and may include a forward look, an alternative, good wishes, freebies, resale information, or a sales promotion. *Resale* refers to mentioning a product or service favorably to reinforce the customer's choice. For example, *you chose our best-selling model.*

Forward Look. Anticipate future relations or business. A letter that refuses a contract proposal might read: *Thanks for your bid. We look forward to working with your talented staff when future projects demand your special expertise.*

Alternative Follow-Up. If an alternative exists, end your letter with follow-through advice. For example, in a letter rejecting a customer's demand for replacement of landscaping plants, you might say: *I will be happy to give you a free inspection and consultation. Please call 301-746-8112 to arrange a date for my visit.* In a message to a prospective home buyer: *Although the lot you saw last week is now sold, we do have two excellent lots available at a slightly higher price.* In reacting to an Internet misprint: *Please note that our website contained an unfortunate misprint*

Figure 9.5 **Delivering Bad News Sensitively**

1 Buffer
- Best news
- Compliment
- Appreciation
- Agreement
- Facts
- Understanding
- Apology

2 Reasons
- Cautious explanation
- Reader or other benefits
- Company policy explanation
- Positive words
- Evidence that matter was considered fairly and seriously

3 Bad News
- Embedded placement
- Passive voice
- Implied refusal
- Compromise
- Alternative

4 Closing
- Forward look
- Information about alternative
- Good wishes
- Freebies
- Resale
- Sales promotion

offering $850-per-night Bora Bora bungalows at $85. Although we cannot honor that rate, we are offering a special half-price rate of $425 to those who responded.

Good Wishes. A letter rejecting a job candidate might read: *We appreciate your interest in our company, and we extend to you our best wishes in your search to find the perfect match between your skills and job requirements.*

Freebies. When customers complain—primarily about food products or small consumer items—companies often send coupons, samples, or gifts to restore confidence and to promote future business. In response to a customer's complaint about a frozen dinner, you could write: *Your loyalty and your concern about our frozen entrées are genuinely appreciated. Because we want you to continue enjoying our healthy and convenient dinners, we are enclosing a coupon that you can take to your local market to select your next Green Valley entrée.*

Resale or Sales Promotion. When the bad news is not devastating or personal, references to resale information or promotion may be appropriate: *The computer workstations you ordered are unusually popular because of their stain-, heat-, and scratch-resistant finishes. To help you locate hard-to-find accessories for these workstations, we invite you to visit our website where our online catalog provides a huge selection of surge suppressors, multiple outlet strips, security devices, and PC tool kits.*

Avoid endings that sound canned, insincere, inappropriate, or self-serving. Don't invite further correspondence (*If you have any questions, do not hesitate . . .*), and don't refer to the bad news. Figure 9.5 reviews suggestions for delivering bad news sensitively.

Refusing Typical Requests and Claims

LEARNING OUTCOME 4

Apply effective techniques for refusing typical requests or claims as well as for presenting bad news to customers in print or online.

When you must refuse typical requests, you will first think about how the receiver will react to your refusal and decide whether to use the direct or the indirect strategy. If you have any doubt, use the indirect strategy. As you move forward in your career and become a professional or a representative of an organization, you may receive requests for favors or contributions. You may also be invited to speak or give presentations.

Businesses must occasionally respond to disappointed customers in print and online. In many instances disappointed customers are turning to the Internet to air their grievances. Complaints about products and services now appear on sites such as Complaints.com, and ShamScam as well as on Facebook, Twitter, and other social networks. Large companies have social media staff members who monitor negative messages online and solve problems whenever customers voice their discontent.

Rejecting Requests for Favors, Money, Information, and Action

Requests for favors, money, information, and action may come from charities, friends, or business partners. Many are from people representing commendable causes, and you may wish you could comply. However, resources are usually limited. In a letter from Delta Management Associates, shown in Figure 9.6, the company must refuse a request for a donation to a charity. Following the indirect strategy, the letter begins with a buffer acknowledging the request. It also praises the good works of the charity and uses those words as a transition to the second paragraph. In the second paragraph, the writer explains why the company cannot donate. Notice that the writer reveals the refusal without actually stating it (*Because of internal restructuring*

Figure 9.6 **Refusing Donation Request**

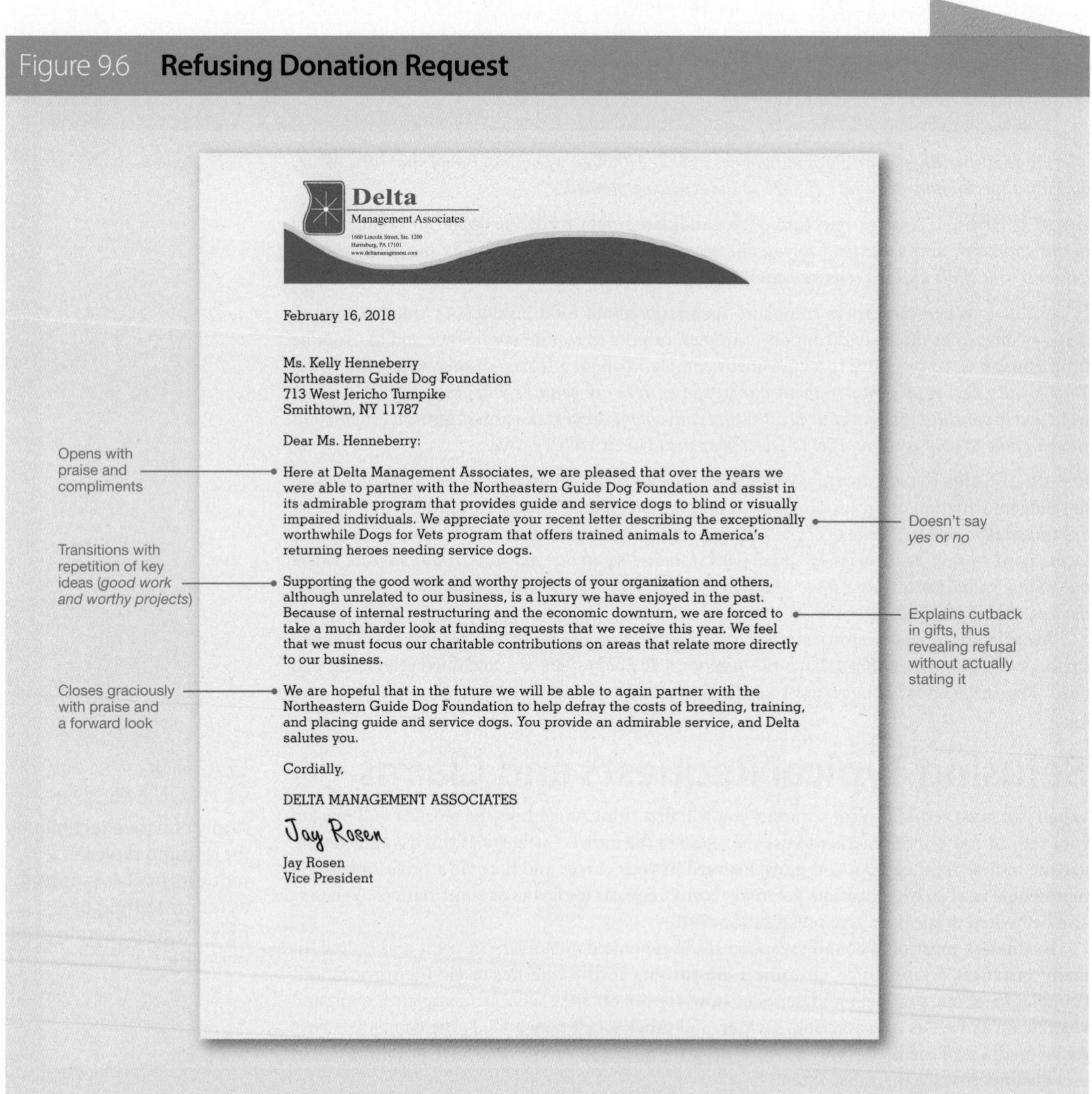

Delta
Management Associates

February 16, 2018

Ms. Kelly Henneberry
Northeastern Guide Dog Foundation
713 West Jericho Turnpike
Smithtown, NY 11787

Dear Ms. Henneberry:

Here at Delta Management Associates, we are pleased that over the years we were able to partner with the Northeastern Guide Dog Foundation and assist in its admirable program that provides guide and service dogs to blind or visually impaired individuals. We appreciate your recent letter describing the exceptionally worthwhile Dogs for Vets program that offers trained animals to America's returning heroes needing service dogs.

Supporting the good work and worthy projects of your organization and others, although unrelated to our business, is a luxury we have enjoyed in the past. Because of internal restructuring and the economic downturn, we are forced to take a much harder look at funding requests that we receive this year. We feel that we must focus our charitable contributions on areas that relate more directly to our business.

We are hopeful that in the future we will be able to again partner with the Northeastern Guide Dog Foundation to help defray the costs of breeding, training, and placing guide and service dogs. You provide an admirable service, and Delta salutes you.

Cordially,

DELTA MANAGEMENT ASSOCIATES

Jay Rosen

Jay Rosen
Vice President

Opens with praise and compliments
Transitions with repetition of key ideas (*good work and worthy projects*)
Closes graciously with praise and a forward look
Doesn't say *yes* or *no*
Explains cutback in gifts, thus revealing refusal without actually stating it

and the economic downturn, we are forced to take a much harder look at funding requests that we receive this year). This gentle refusal makes it unnecessary to be blunter in stating the denial.

In some donation refusal letters, the reasons may not be fully explained: *Although we can't provide financial support at this time, we all unanimously agree that the Make-A-Wish Foundation contributes a valuable service to sick children.* The emphasis is on the foundation's good deeds rather than on an explanation for the refusal.

Messages that refuse requests for favors, money, information, and action can often be tactfully handled by showing appreciation for the inquiry and respect for the writer. Businesses that are required to write frequent refusals might prepare a form letter, changing a few variables as needed.

Declining Invitations

When you must decline an invitation to speak or make a presentation, you generally try to provide a response that says more than *I can't* or *I don't want to.* Unless the reasons are confidential or business secrets, try to explain them. Because responses to invitations are often taken personally, make a special effort to soften the refusal. In the e-mail shown in Figure 9.7, an accountant must say *no* to the invitation from a friend's son to speak before the young man's college business club. This refusal starts with conviviality and compliments.

The writer then explains why she cannot accept. The refusal is embedded in a long paragraph and de-emphasized in a subordinate clause (*Although your invitation must be declined*). The reader naturally concentrates on the main clause that follows (*I would like to recommend*...). If no alternative is available, focus on something positive about the situation (*Although I'm not an expert, I commend your organization for selecting this topic*). Overall, the tone of this refusal is warm, upbeat, and positive.

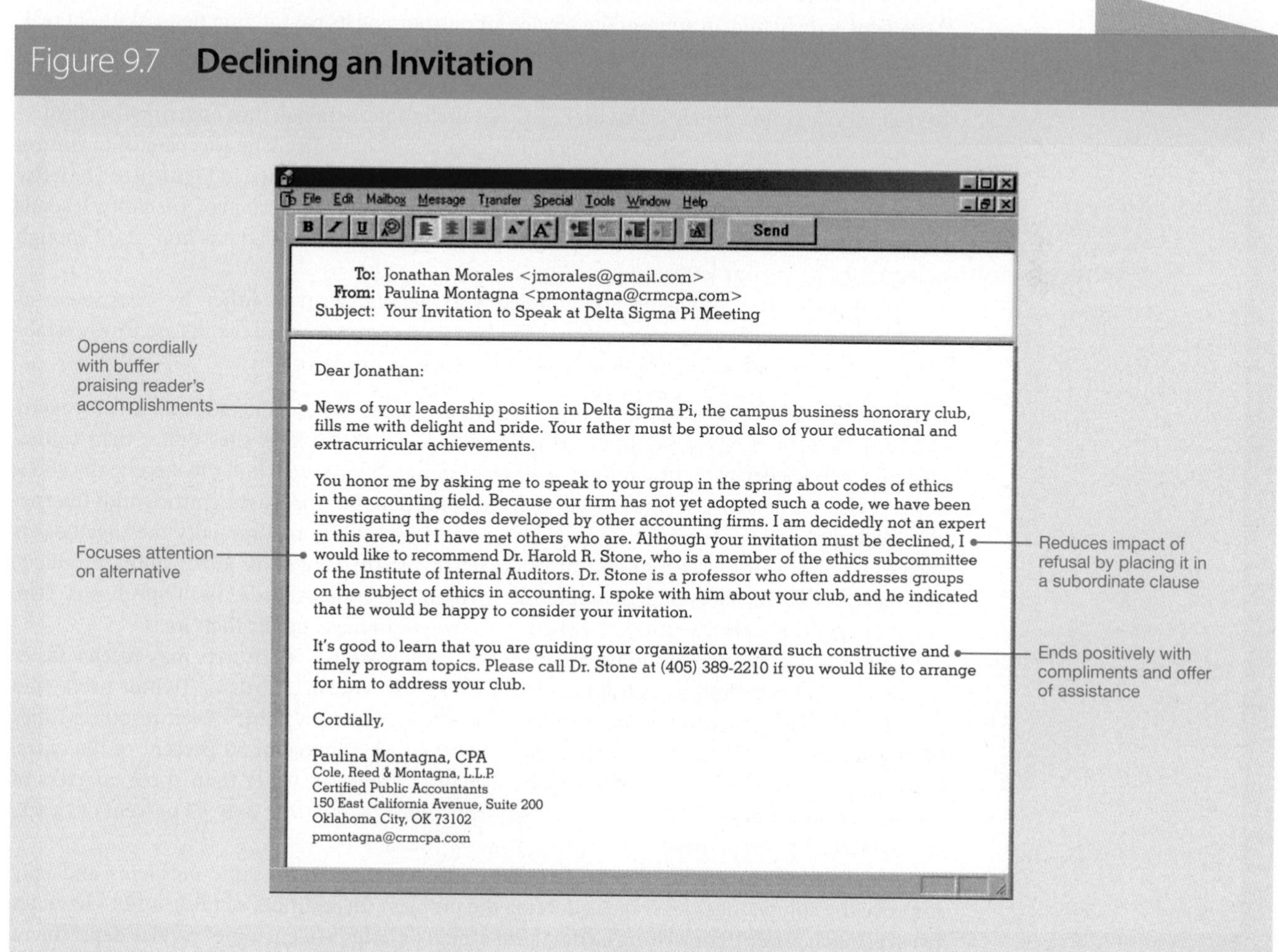

Figure 9.7 **Declining an Invitation**

File Edit Mailbox Message Transfer Special Tools Window Help
Send
Opens cordially with buffer praising reader's accomplishments
Focuses attention on alternative
Reduces impact of refusal by placing it in a subordinate clause
Ends positively with compliments and offer of assistance

To: Jonathan Morales <jmorales@gmail.com>
From: Paulina Montagna <pmontagna@crmcpa.com>
Subject: Your Invitation to Speak at Delta Sigma Pi Meeting

Dear Jonathan:

News of your leadership position in Delta Sigma Pi, the campus business honorary club, fills me with delight and pride. Your father must be proud also of your educational and extracurricular achievements.

You honor me by asking me to speak to your group in the spring about codes of ethics in the accounting field. Because our firm has not yet adopted such a code, we have been investigating the codes developed by other accounting firms. I am decidedly not an expert in this area, but I have met others who are. Although your invitation must be declined, I would like to recommend Dr. Harold R. Stone, who is a member of the ethics subcommittee of the Institute of Internal Auditors. Dr. Stone is a professor who often addresses groups on the subject of ethics in accounting. I spoke with him about your club, and he indicated that he would be happy to consider your invitation.

It's good to learn that you are guiding your organization toward such constructive and timely program topics. Please call Dr. Stone at (405) 389-2210 if you would like to arrange for him to address your club.

Cordially,

Paulina Montagna, CPA
Cole, Reed & Montagna, L.L.P.
Certified Public Accountants
150 East California Avenue, Suite 200
Oklahoma City, OK 73102
pmontagna@crmcpa.com

Dealing With Disappointed Customers in Print and Online

All businesses offering products or services must sometimes deal with troublesome situations that cause unhappiness to customers. Merchandise is not delivered on time, a product fails to perform as expected, service is deficient, charges are erroneous, or customers are misunderstood. Whenever possible, these problems should be dealt with immediately and personally. Most business professionals strive to control the damage and resolve such problems in the following manner:[35]

- Call or e-mail the individual or reply to his or her online post within 24 hours.
- Describe the problem and apologize.
- Explain why the problem occurred, what you are doing to resolve it, and how you will prevent it from happening again.
- Promote goodwill by following up with a message that documents the phone call or acknowledges the online exchange of posts.

Responding by E-Mail and in Hard Copy. Written messages are important (a) when personal contact is impossible, (b) to establish a record of the incident, (c) to formally confirm follow-up procedures, and (d) to promote good relations. Dealing with problems immediately is very important in resolving conflict and retaining goodwill.

A bad-news follow-up letter is shown in Figure 9.8. Consultant Kimberly Haydn found herself in the embarrassing position of explaining why she had given out the name of her client to a salesperson. The client, C & C Resources International, had hired her firm, MKM Consulting Associates, to help find an appropriate service for outsourcing its payroll functions. Without realizing it, Kimberly had mentioned to a potential vendor (ABS Payroll Services, Inc.) that her client was considering hiring an outside service to handle its payroll. An overeager salesperson from ABS Payroll Services immediately called on C & C Resources International, thus angering the client.

Kimberly Haydn first called her client to explain and apologize. She was careful to control her voice and rate of speaking. She also followed up with the letter shown in Figure 9.8. The letter not only confirms the telephone conversation but also adds the right touch of formality. It sends the nonverbal message that the writer takes the matter seriously and that it is important enough to warrant a hard-copy letter.

Many consumer problems are handled with letters, written either by consumers as complaints or by companies in response. However, e-mail and social networks are firmly established as channels for delivering complaints and negative messages.

Managing Negative News Online. Today's impatient, hyperconnected consumers eagerly embrace the idea of delivering their complaints to social networking sites rather than calling customer service departments. Why rely on word of mouth or send a letter to a company about poor service or a defective product when you can shout your grievance to the entire world? Internet sites such as Complaints.com, Ripoff Report, and MeasuredUp, and specialty message boards such as Cruise Critic, encourage consumers to quickly share complaints about stores, products, and services that fall short of their standards. Twitter, Facebook, Angie's List, TripAdvisor, Yelp, and many more are also favorite sites where consumers can make public their ire.

Complaint sites are gaining momentum for many reasons. Consumers may receive faster responses to tweets than to customer service calls.[36] Nearly two thirds of Twitter users who complain on Twitter expect an answer from brands in under an hour.[37] Even response times to grievances sent by e-mail have shrunk to less than 60 minutes in 50 percent of the cases, according to a recent analysis of 16 billion e-mails.[38] However, fewer than three quarters of retailers bothered to answer e-mail messages from consumers, while only 43 percent of tweets are answered by companies.[39]

Airing gripes in public also helps other consumers avoid the same problems and may improve the complainer's leverage in solving the problem. In addition, sending a 140-character tweet is much easier than writing a complaint e-mail or letter to a customer service department

Figure 9.8 Bad-News Follow-Up Message

MKM CONSULTING ASSOCIATES

350 Tijeras Avenue NW
Albuquerque, NM 87102

(505) 842-0971
www.mkmconsulting.com

May 7, 2018

Mr. Roger Martinez
Director, Administrative Operations
C & C Resources International
2740 Harper Drive NE, Ste. 310
Santa Fe, NM 87506

Dear Mr. Martinez:

You have every right to expect complete confidentiality in your transactions with an independent consultant. As I explained in yesterday's telephone call, I am very distressed that you were called by a salesperson from ABS Payroll Services, Inc. This should not have happened, and I apologize to you again for inadvertently mentioning your company's name in a conversation with a potential vendor, ABS Payroll Services, Inc.

All clients of MKM Consulting are assured that their dealings with our firm are held in the strictest confidence. Because your company's payroll needs are so individual and because you have so many contract workers, I was forced to explain how your employees differed from those of other companies. Revealing your company name was my error, and I take full responsibility for the lapse. I can assure you that it will not happen again. I have informed ABS Payroll Services that it had no authorization to call you directly and that its actions have forced me to reconsider using its services for my future clients.

A number of other payroll services offer outstanding programs. I'm sure we can find the perfect partner to enable you to outsource your payroll responsibilities, thus allowing your company to focus its financial and human resources on its core business. I look forward to our next appointment when you may choose from a number of excellent payroll outsourcing firms.

Sincerely,

Kimberly Haydn

Kimberly Haydn
Partner

Opens with agreement and apology

Takes responsibility and promises to prevent recurrence

Closes with forward look

Explains what caused the problem and how it was resolved

Tips for Resolving Problems and Following Up

- Whenever possible, call or see the individual involved.
- Describe the problem and apologize.
- Explain why the problem occurred.
- Take responsibility, if appropriate.
- Explain what you are doing to resolve it.
- Explain what you are doing to prevent recurrence.
- Follow up with a message that documents the personal contact.
- Look forward to positive future relations.

or navigating endless telephone menus to reach an agent. Businesses can employ some of the following effective strategies to manage negative news on social networking sites and blogs:

- **Recognize social networks as an important communication channel.** Instead of fearing social networks as a disruptive force, smart companies greet these channels as opportunities to look into the true mind-set of customers and receive free advice on how to improve.
- **Become proactive.** Company blogs and active websites with community forums help companies listen to their customers as well as spread the word about their own good deeds. Home Depot's site describing its foundation, workshops, and careers now outranks HomeDepotSucks.com, which used to rank No. 1 for searches on the keywords *home depot.*

- **Join the fun.** Wise companies have joined Twitter, Facebook, Instagram, Flickr, YouTube, and LinkedIn so they can benefit from interacting with their customers and the public.
- **Monitor comments.** Many large companies employ social media managers and other digital media staff to monitor online traffic and respond immediately whenever possible. At Southwest Airlines and other carriers, teams listen online to what people are saying about their companies. Their policy is to engage the positive and address the negative—all within 24 hours.

When domain registrar and Internet hosting provider GoDaddy experienced a nearly six-hour service disruption that affected the websites of more than 10 million customers, the company responded swiftly. It took to social media and used multiple channels to reassure its users. Figure 9.9 shows a blog post by GoDaddy CEO Scott Wagner addressing the bad news head-on and apologizing to customers.[40]

Figure 9.9 **GoDaddy Blog Delivers Bad News About Service Disruption Directly**

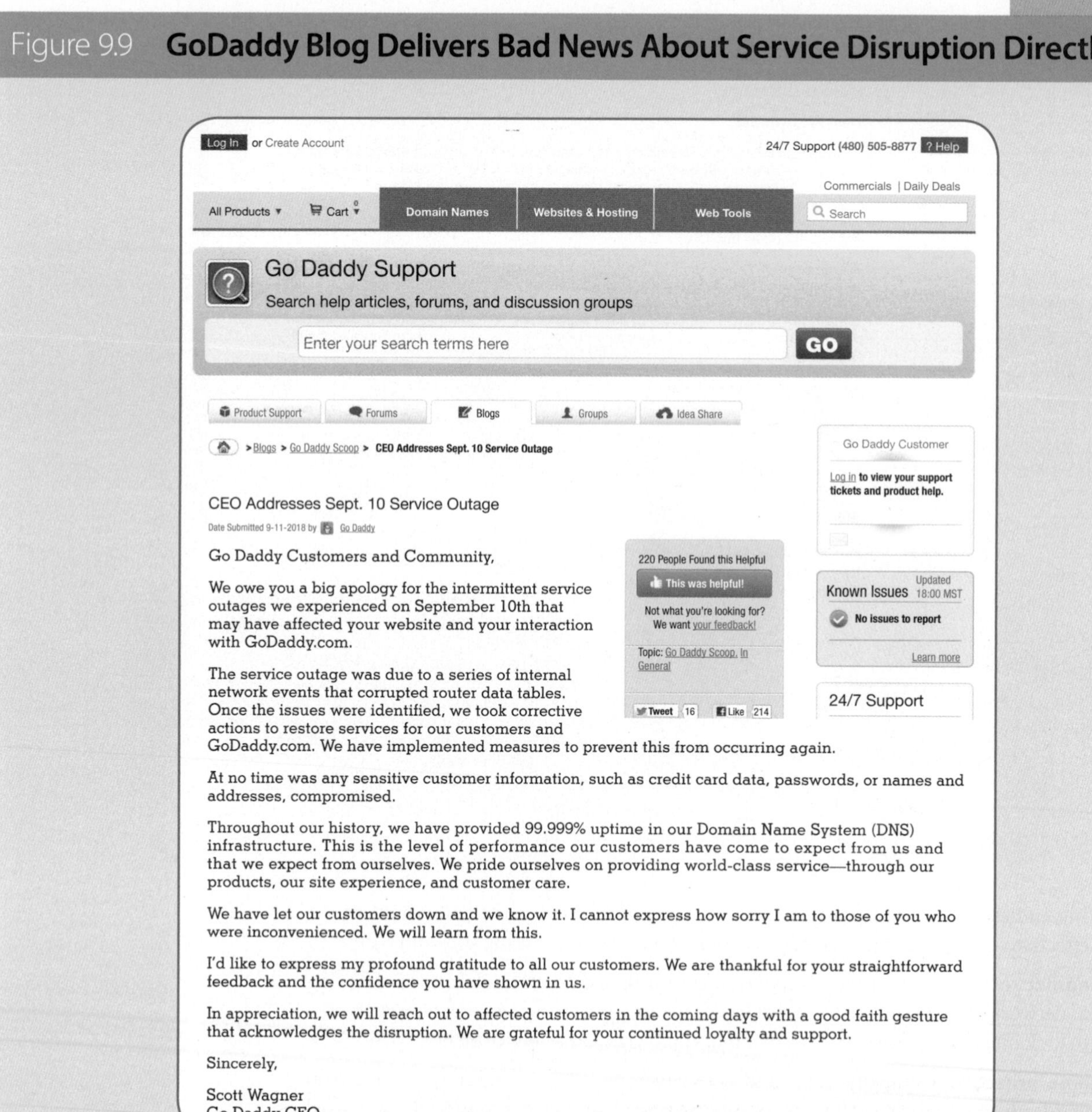

CEO Addresses Sept. 10 Service Outage

Date Submitted 9-11-2018 by Go Daddy

Go Daddy Customers and Community,

We owe you a big apology for the intermittent service outages we experienced on September 10th that may have affected your website and your interaction with GoDaddy.com.

The service outage was due to a series of internal network events that corrupted router data tables. Once the issues were identified, we took corrective actions to restore services for our customers and GoDaddy.com. We have implemented measures to prevent this from occurring again.

At no time was any sensitive customer information, such as credit card data, passwords, or names and addresses, compromised.

Throughout our history, we have provided 99.999% uptime in our Domain Name System (DNS) infrastructure. This is the level of performance our customers have come to expect from us and that we expect from ourselves. We pride ourselves on providing world-class service—through our products, our site experience, and customer care.

We have let our customers down and we know it. I cannot express how sorry I am to those of you who were inconvenienced. We will learn from this.

I'd like to express my profound gratitude to all our customers. We are thankful for your straightforward feedback and the confidence you have shown in us.

In appreciation, we will reach out to affected customers in the coming days with a good faith gesture that acknowledges the disruption. We are grateful for your continued loyalty and support.

Sincerely,

Scott Wagner
Go Daddy CEO

An almost identical message went out by e-mail to all GoDaddy users offering a 30 percent discount on any new product or renewal to compensate for the loss of service. In addition, the company provided frequent Twitter updates. "Status Alert: Hey, all. We're aware of the trouble people are having with our site. We're working on it." Subsequently, *@GoDaddy* tweeted: "Update: Still working on it, but we're making progress. Some service has already been restored. Stick with us."[41] In a 24/7 news cycle and facing an Internet that never sleeps, companies lose if they snooze. Because the bad news didn't injure people's feelings, the company could afford to state the unfavorable news directly.

Handling Problems With Orders

Not all customer orders can be filled as received. Suppliers may be able to send only part of an order or none at all. Substitutions may be necessary, or the delivery date may be delayed. Suppliers may suspect that all or part of the order is a mistake; the customer may actually want something else. In writing to customers about problem orders, it is generally wise to use the direct strategy if the message has some good-news elements. However, when the message is disappointing, the indirect strategy may be more appropriate.

Let's say you represent Live and Learn Toys, a large West Coast toy manufacturer, and you are scrambling for business in a slow year. A big customer, Child Land, calls in August and asks you to hold a block of your best-selling toy, the Space Station. Like most vendors, you require a deposit on large orders. September rolls around, and you still haven't received any money from Child Land. You must now write a tactful e-mail asking for the deposit—or else you will release the toy to other buyers. The problem, of course, is delivering the bad news without losing the customer's order and goodwill. Another challenge is making sure the reader understands the bad news. An effective message might begin with a positive statement that also reveals the facts:

> *You were smart to reserve a block of 500 Space Stations, which we have been holding for you since August. As the holidays approach, the demand for all our learning toys, including the Space Station, is rapidly increasing.*

Next, the message should explain why the payment is needed and what will happen if it is not received:

> *Toy stores from Florida to California are asking us to ship these Space Stations. One reason the Space Station is moving out of our warehouses so quickly is its assortment of gizmos that children love, including a land rover vehicle, a shuttle craft, a hovercraft, astronauts, and even a robotic arm. As soon as we receive your deposit of $4,000, we will have this popular item on its way to your stores. Without a deposit by September 20, though, we must release this block to other retailers.*

The closing makes it easy to respond and motivates action:

> *For expedited service, please call our sales department at 800-358-4488 and authorize the deposit using your business credit card. You can begin showing the fascinating Live and Learn toy in your stores by November 1.*

Announcing Rate Increases and Price Hikes

Informing customers and clients of rate increases or price hikes can be like handling a live grenade. These messages necessarily cause consumers to recoil. With skill, however, you can help your customers understand why the rate or price increase is necessary.

The important steps in these negative messages are explaining the reasons and hooking the increase to benefits. For example, a price increase might be necessitated by higher material costs, rising taxes, escalating insurance, a driver pay increase—all reasons you cannot control. You might cite changing industry trends or technology innovations as causes of increased costs.

In developing audience benefits and building goodwill, think about how the increase will add new value or better features, make use more efficient, or make customers' lives easier. Whenever possible, give advance warning of rate increases—for example: *Because you are an important customer to us, I wanted to inform you about this right away. Our energy costs have almost doubled over the last year, forcing us to put through a 10 percent price increase effective July 1. You order these items regularly, so I thought I'd better check with you to see if it would make sense to reorder now to save you money and prevent last-minute surprises.*

In today's digital environment, rate and price increases may be announced by e-mail or online, as shown in Figure 9.10. Despite the increasing popularity of its streaming video service, CineFile's profitable disc-delivery division has kept a core of customers in rural areas with spotty Internet service and among people who want a greater selection of titles. However, CineFile had to increase the charge for access to Blu-ray movies by mail. In its blog it explained how Blu-ray discs are not only superior to DVDs but also more expensive. To provide its customers with a comprehensive library of Blu-ray movies, CineFile has to raise its rates. Notice that the rate increase is tied to benefits to customers.

Figure 9.10 **E-Mail Announcing Price Increase With Audience Benefits**

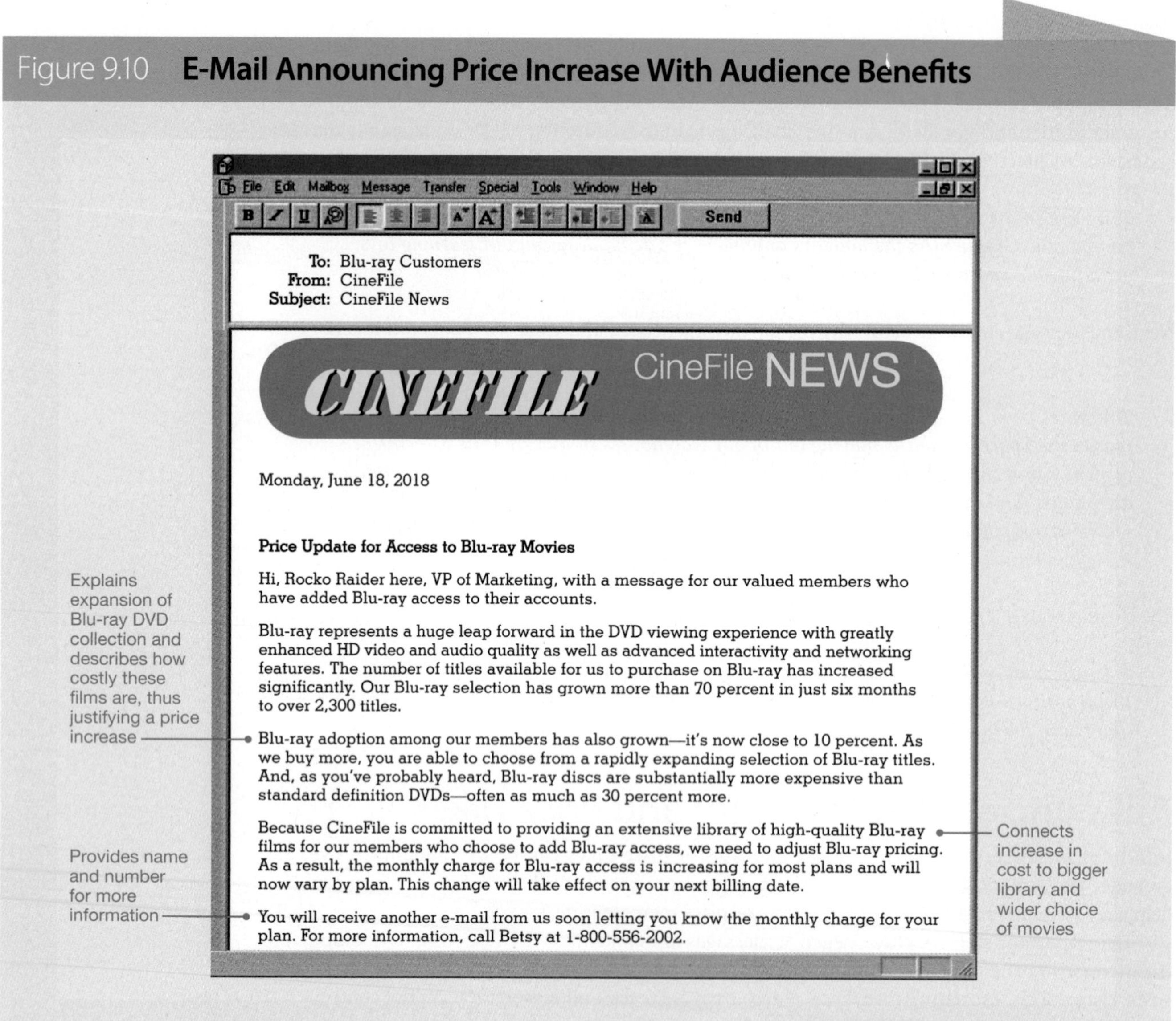

To: Blu-ray Customers
From: CineFile
Subject: CineFile News

CINEFILE CineFile NEWS

Monday, June 18, 2018

Price Update for Access to Blu-ray Movies

Hi, Rocko Raider here, VP of Marketing, with a message for our valued members who have added Blu-ray access to their accounts.

Blu-ray represents a huge leap forward in the DVD viewing experience with greatly enhanced HD video and audio quality as well as advanced interactivity and networking features. The number of titles available for us to purchase on Blu-ray has increased significantly. Our Blu-ray selection has grown more than 70 percent in just six months to over 2,300 titles.

Blu-ray adoption among our members has also grown—it's now close to 10 percent. As we buy more, you are able to choose from a rapidly expanding selection of Blu-ray titles. And, as you've probably heard, Blu-ray discs are substantially more expensive than standard definition DVDs—often as much as 30 percent more.

Because CineFile is committed to providing an extensive library of high-quality Blu-ray films for our members who choose to add Blu-ray access, we need to adjust Blu-ray pricing. As a result, the monthly charge for Blu-ray access is increasing for most plans and will now vary by plan. This change will take effect on your next billing date.

You will receive another e-mail from us soon letting you know the monthly charge for your plan. For more information, call Betsy at 1-800-556-2002.

File Edit Mailbox Message Transfer Special Tools Window Help
Send
Explains expansion of Blu-ray DVD collection and describes how costly these films are, thus justifying a price increase
Provides name and number for more information
Connects increase in cost to bigger library and wider choice of movies

Denying Claims

Customers occasionally want something they are not entitled to or that you can't grant. They may misunderstand warranties or make unreasonable demands. Because these customers are often unhappy with a product or service, they are emotionally involved. Messages that say *no* to emotionally involved receivers will probably be your most challenging communication task. As publisher Malcolm Forbes observed, "To be agreeable while disagreeing—that's an art."[42]

Fortunately, the reasons-before-refusal plan helps you be empathic and artful in breaking bad news. Obviously, in denial letters you will need to adopt the proper tone. Don't blame customers, even if they are at fault. Avoid *you* statements that sound preachy (*You would have known that cash refunds are impossible if you had read your contract*). Use neutral, objective language to explain why the claim must be refused. Consider offering resale information to rebuild the customer's confidence in your products or organization. In Figure 9.11 the writer denies a customer's claim for the difference between the price the customer paid for speakers and the price he saw advertised locally (which would have resulted in a cash refund of $100). Although the catalog service does match any advertised lower price, the price-matching policy applies only to exact models. This claim must be rejected because the advertisement the customer submitted showed a different, older speaker model.

Figure 9.11 **E-Mail Denying a Claim**

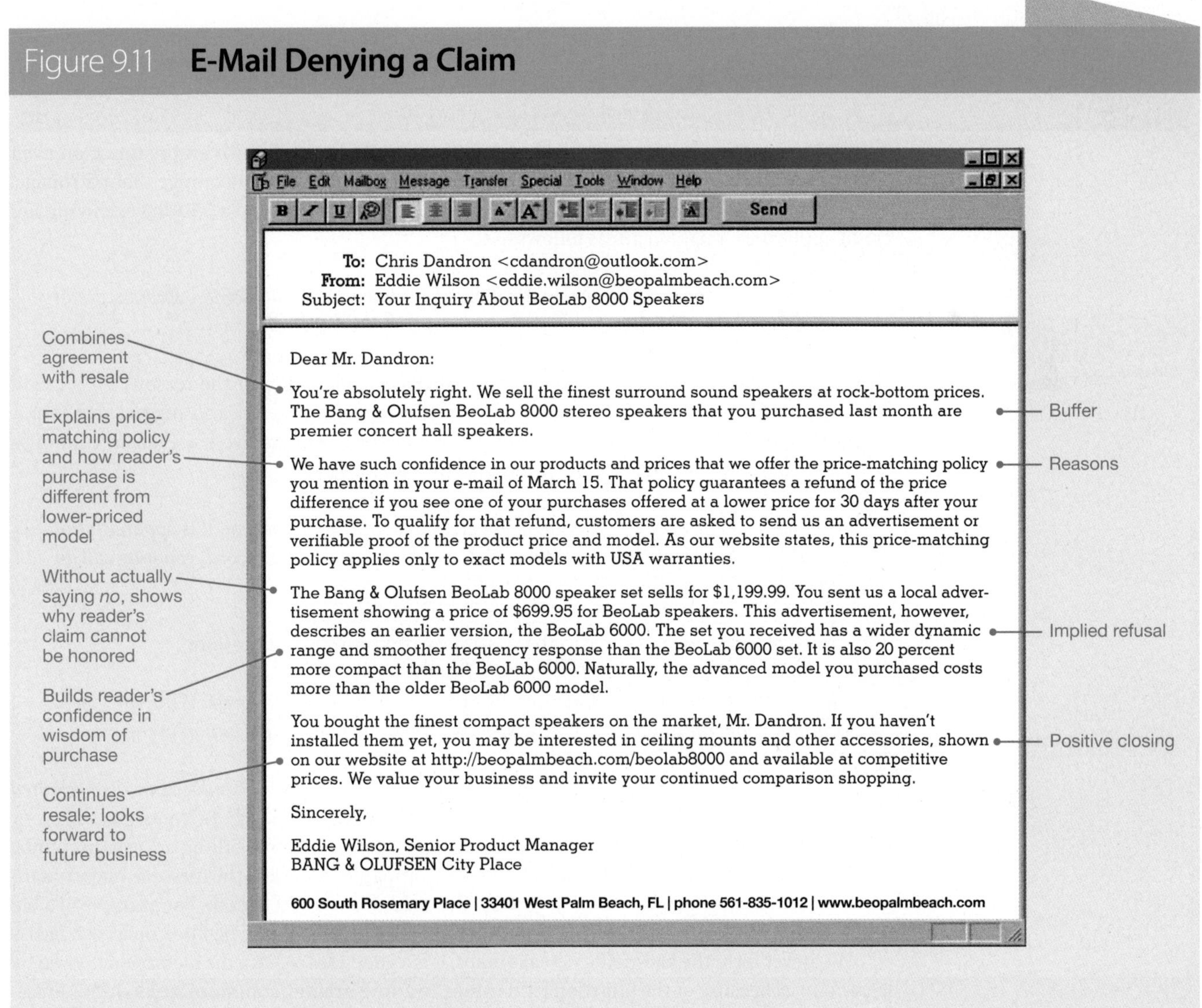

File Edit Mailbox Message Transfer Special Tools Window Help
Send
To: Chris Dandron <cdandron@outlook.com>
From: Eddie Wilson <eddie.wilson@beopalmbeach.com>
Subject: Your Inquiry About BeoLab 8000 Speakers
Dear Mr. Dandron:
You're absolutely right. We sell the finest surround sound speakers at rock-bottom prices. The Bang & Olufsen BeoLab 8000 stereo speakers that you purchased last month are premier concert hall speakers.
We have such confidence in our products and prices that we offer the price-matching policy you mention in your e-mail of March 15. That policy guarantees a refund of the price difference if you see one of your purchases offered at a lower price for 30 days after your purchase. To qualify for that refund, customers are asked to send us an advertisement or verifiable proof of the product price and model. As our website states, this price-matching policy applies only to exact models with USA warranties.
The Bang & Olufsen BeoLab 8000 speaker set sells for $1,199.99. You sent us a local advertisement showing a price of $699.95 for BeoLab speakers. This advertisement, however, describes an earlier version, the BeoLab 6000. The set you received has a wider dynamic range and smoother frequency response than the BeoLab 6000 set. It is also 20 percent more compact than the BeoLab 6000. Naturally, the advanced model you purchased costs more than the older BeoLab 6000 model.
You bought the finest compact speakers on the market, Mr. Dandron. If you haven't installed them yet, you may be interested in ceiling mounts and other accessories, shown on our website at http://beopalmbeach.com/beolab8000 and available at competitive prices. We value your business and invite your continued comparison shopping.
Sincerely,
Eddie Wilson, Senior Product Manager
BANG & OLUFSEN City Place
600 South Rosemary Place | 33401 West Palm Beach, FL | phone 561-835-1012 | www.beopalmbeach.com
Combines agreement with resale
Explains price-matching policy and how reader's purchase is different from lower-priced model
Without actually saying *no*, shows why reader's claim cannot be honored
Builds reader's confidence in wisdom of purchase
Continues resale; looks forward to future business
Buffer
Reasons
Implied refusal
Positive closing

The e-mail to Chris Dandron opens with a buffer that agrees with a statement in the customer's e-mail. It repeats the key idea of product confidence as a transition to the second paragraph. Next comes an explanation of the price-matching policy. The writer does not assume that the customer is trying to pull a fast one. Nor does he suggest that the customer is a dummy who didn't read or understand the price-matching policy. The safest path is a neutral explanation of the policy along with precise distinctions between the customer's speakers and the older ones. The writer also gets a chance to resell the customer's speakers and demonstrate what a quality product they are. By the end of the third paragraph, it is evident to the reader that his claim is unjustified.

Refusing Credit

When customers apply for credit, they must be notified within 30 days if that application is rejected. The Fair Credit Reporting Act and Equal Credit Opportunity Act state that consumers who are denied loans must receive a notice of adverse action from the business explaining the decision. The business can refer the applicant to the credit-reporting agency, whether Experian, Equifax, or TransUnion, that provided the information upon which the negative decision was based. If you must write a letter to a customer denying credit, you have four goals in conveying the refusal:

- Avoiding language that causes hard feelings
- Retaining the customer on a cash basis
- Preparing for possible future credit without raising false expectations
- Avoiding disclosures that could cause a lawsuit

Because credit applicants are likely to continue to do business with an organization even if they are denied credit, you will want to do everything possible to encourage that patronage. Therefore, keep the refusal respectful, sensitive, and upbeat. A letter to a customer denying her credit application might begin as follows:

> *We genuinely appreciate your application of January 12 for a Fashion Express credit account.*

To avoid possible litigation, many companies offer no explanation of the reasons for a credit refusal. Instead, they provide the name of the credit-reporting agency and suggest that inquiries be directed to it. In the following example, notice the use of passive voice (*credit cannot be extended*) and a long sentence to de-emphasize the bad news:

> *After we received a report of your current credit record from Experian, it is apparent that credit cannot be extended at this time. To learn more about your record, you may call an Experian credit counselor at (212) 356-0922.*

The cordial closing looks forward to the possibility of a future reapplication:

> *Thanks, Ms. Love, for the confidence you have shown in Fashion Express. We invite you to continue shopping at our stores, and we look forward to your reapplication in the future.*

Some businesses do provide reasons explaining credit denials (*Credit cannot be granted because your firm's current and long-term credit obligations are nearly twice as great as your firm's total assets*). They may also provide alternatives, such as deferred billing or cash discounts. When the letter denies a credit application that accompanies an order, the message may contain resale information. The writer tries to convert the order from credit to cash. For example, if a big order cannot be filled on a credit basis, perhaps part of the order could be filled on a cash basis.

Whatever form the bad-news message takes, it is a good idea to have the message reviewed by legal counsel because of the litigation land mines awaiting unwary communicators in this area.

Managing Bad News Within Organizations

LEARNING OUTCOME 5

Describe and apply effective techniques for delivering bad news within organizations.

A tactful tone and a reasons-first approach help preserve friendly relations with customers. These same techniques are useful when delivering bad news within organizations. Interpersonal bad news might involve telling the boss that something went wrong or confronting an employee about poor performance. Organizational bad news might involve declining profits, lost contracts, harmful lawsuits, public relations controversies, and changes in policy. Whether you use a direct or an indirect strategy in delivering that news depends primarily on the anticipated reaction of the audience. Generally, bad news is better received when reasons are given first. Within organizations, you may find yourself giving bad news in person or in writing.

Delivering Bad News in Person

Whether you are an employee or a supervisor, you may have the unhappy responsibility of delivering bad news. First, decide whether the negative information is newsworthy. For example, trivial, noncriminal mistakes or one-time bad behaviors are best left alone. However, fraudulent travel claims, consistent hostile behavior, or failing projects must be reported.[43] For example, you might have to tell the boss that the team's computer picked up a virus that caused it to lose all its important files. Similarly, as a team leader or supervisor, you might be required to confront an underperforming employee. If you know that the news will upset the receiver, the reasons-first strategy is most effective. When the bad news involves one person or a small group nearby, you should generally deliver that news in person. Here are pointers on how to do so tactfully, professionally, and safely:[44]

- **Gather all the information.** Cool down and have all the facts before marching in on the boss or confronting someone. Remember that every story has two sides.
- **Prepare and rehearse.** Outline what you plan to say so that you are confident, coherent, and dispassionate.
- **Explain: past, present, future.** If you are telling the boss about a problem such as the computer crash, explain what caused the crash, the current situation, and how and when you plan to fix it.
- **Consider taking a partner.** If you fear a shoot-the-messenger reaction, especially from your boss, bring a colleague with you. Each person should have a consistent and credible part in the presentation. If possible, take advantage of your organization's internal resources. To lend credibility to your view, call on auditors, inspectors, or human resources experts.
- **Think about timing.** Don't deliver bad news when someone is already stressed or grumpy. Experts also advise against giving bad news on Friday afternoon when people have the weekend to dwell on it.
- **Be patient with the reaction.** Give the receiver time to vent, think, recover, and act wisely.

Refusing Workplace Requests

Occasionally, managers must refuse requests from employees. In Figure 9.12 you see the first draft and revision of a message responding to a request from a key specialist, Luke Carson. He wants permission to attend a conference. However, he can't attend the conference because the timing is bad; he must be present at budget planning meetings scheduled for the same two weeks. Normally, this matter would be discussed in person. However, Luke has been traveling among branch offices, and he just hasn't been in the office recently.

Figure 9.12 Refusing an Internal Request

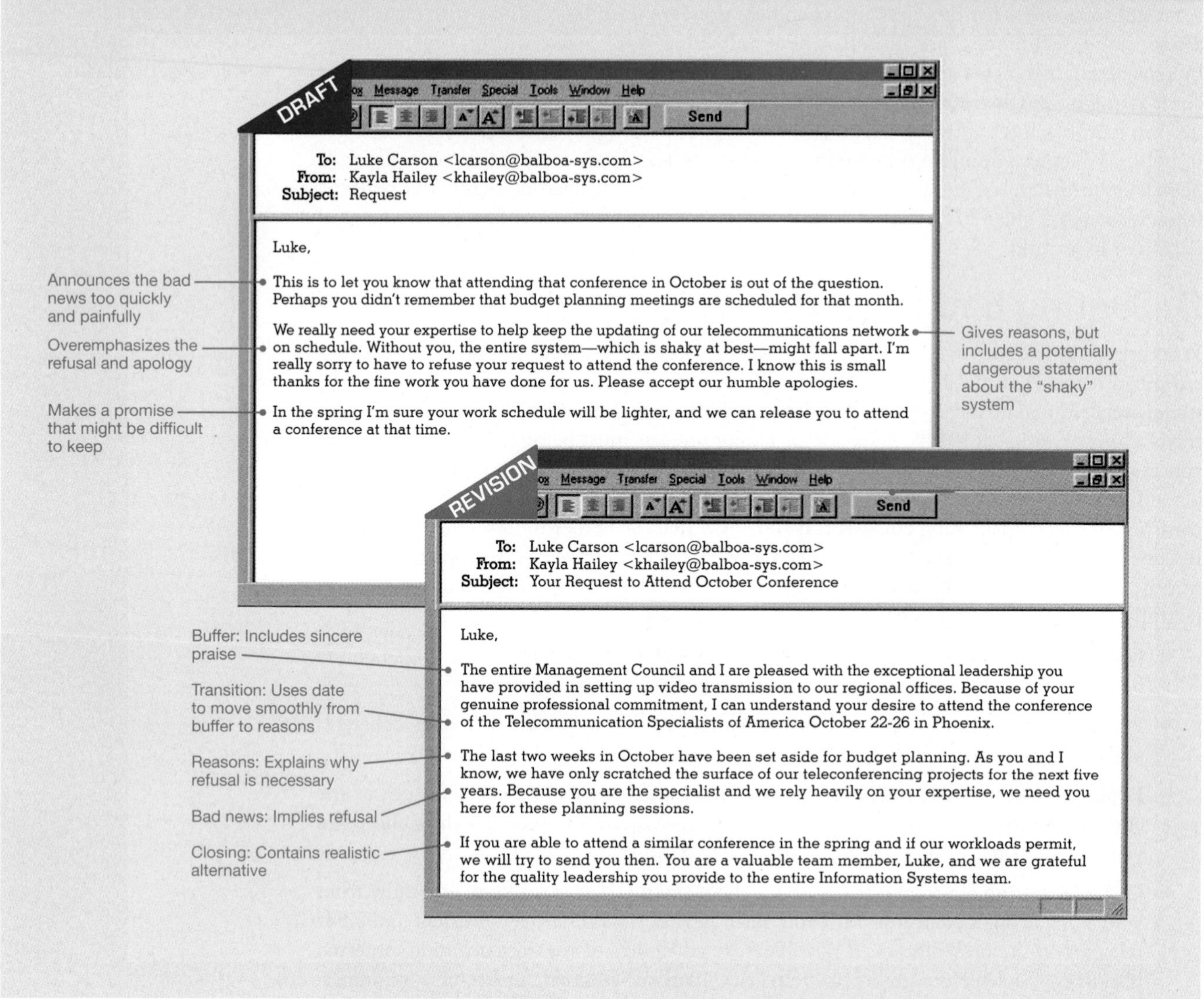

DRAFT

To: Luke Carson <lcarson@balboa-sys.com>
From: Kayla Hailey <khailey@balboa-sys.com>
Subject: Request

Luke,

This is to let you know that attending that conference in October is out of the question. Perhaps you didn't remember that budget planning meetings are scheduled for that month.

We really need your expertise to help keep the updating of our telecommunications network on schedule. Without you, the entire system—which is shaky at best—might fall apart. I'm really sorry to have to refuse your request to attend the conference. I know this is small thanks for the fine work you have done for us. Please accept our humble apologies.

In the spring I'm sure your work schedule will be lighter, and we can release you to attend a conference at that time.

Announces the bad news too quickly and painfully

Overemphasizes the refusal and apology

Makes a promise that might be difficult to keep

Gives reasons, but includes a potentially dangerous statement about the "shaky" system

REVISION

To: Luke Carson <lcarson@balboa-sys.com>
From: Kayla Hailey <khailey@balboa-sys.com>
Subject: Your Request to Attend October Conference

Luke,

The entire Management Council and I are pleased with the exceptional leadership you have provided in setting up video transmission to our regional offices. Because of your genuine professional commitment, I can understand your desire to attend the conference of the Telecommunication Specialists of America October 22-26 in Phoenix.

The last two weeks in October have been set aside for budget planning. As you and I know, we have only scratched the surface of our teleconferencing projects for the next five years. Because you are the specialist and we rely heavily on your expertise, we need you here for these planning sessions.

If you are able to attend a similar conference in the spring and if our workloads permit, we will try to send you then. You are a valuable team member, Luke, and we are grateful for the quality leadership you provide to the entire Information Systems team.

Buffer: Includes sincere praise

Transition: Uses date to move smoothly from buffer to reasons

Reasons: Explains why refusal is necessary

Bad news: Implies refusal

Closing: Contains realistic alternative

The vice president's first inclination was to dash off a quick e-mail, as shown in Figure 9.12, and tell it like it is. However, the vice president realized that this message was going to hurt and that it had possible danger areas. Moreover, the message misses a chance to give Luke positive feedback. An improved version of the e-mail starts with a buffer that delivers honest praise (*pleased with the exceptional leadership you have provided* and *your genuine professional commitment*). By the way, don't be stingy with compliments; they cost you nothing. To paraphrase the motivational speaker Zig Ziglar, we don't live by bread alone. We need buttering up once in a while.[45] The buffer also includes the date of the meeting, used strategically to connect the reasons that follow.

The middle paragraph provides reasons for the refusal. Notice that they focus on positive elements: Luke is the specialist; the company relies on his expertise; and everyone will benefit if he passes up the conference. In this section it becomes obvious that the request is being refused. The writer is not forced to say, *No, you may not attend.* Although the refusal is implied, the reader gets the message.

The closing suggests a qualified alternative (*if our workloads permit, we will try to send you then*). It also ends positively with gratitude for Luke's contributions to the organization and with another compliment (*you're a valuable player*). The improved version focuses on explanations and praise rather than on refusals and apologies. The success of this message depends on attention to the entire writing process, not just on using a buffer or scattering a few compliments throughout.

Reality Check

Roman Samborskyi/ Shutterstock.com

Tackling Tough Workplace Talks

"In difficult conversation, the keys to success are good strategy and tactics for handling the hard parts well; balance between extremes; and self-respect, respect for your counterpart and respect for the problem between you. That means breaking habits of mistaking tough conversations for warfare, getting caught up in emotional reactions and assuming that we know the unpredictable. It's not always easy, but it's better."[46]

—Holly Weeks, *author of* Failure to Communicate: How Conversations Go Wrong and What You Can Do to Right Them

Announcing Bad News to Employees and the Public

In an age of social media, damaging information can rarely be contained for long. Executives can almost count on it to be leaked. Corporate officers who fail to communicate effectively and proactively may end up on the defensive and face an uphill battle trying to limit the damage. Many of the same techniques used to deliver bad news personally are useful when organizations face a crisis or must deliver bad news to various stakeholders. Smart organizations involved in a crisis prefer to communicate the news openly to employees and stockholders. A crisis might involve serious performance problems, a major relocation, massive layoffs, a management shakeup, or public controversy. Instead of letting rumors distort the truth, managers ought to explain the organization's side of the story honestly and promptly.

Morale can be destroyed when employees learn of major events affecting their jobs through the grapevine or from news accounts—rather than from management. When bad news must be delivered to individual employees, management may want to deliver the news personally. With large groups, however, this is generally impossible. Instead, organizations deliver bad news through multiple channels ranging from hard-copy memos, which are formal and create a permanent record, to digital media. Such electronic messages can take the form of intranet posts, e-mails, videos, webcasts, internal as well as external blogs, and voice mail.

The draft of the intranet blog post shown in Figure 9.13 announces a substantial increase in the cost of employee health-care benefits. However, the message suffers from many problems. It announces jolting news bluntly in the first sentence. Worse, it offers little or no explanation for the steep increase in costs. It also sounds insincere (*We did everything possible . . .*) and arbitrary. In a final miscue, the writer fails to give credit to the company for absorbing previous health-care cost increases.

The revision of this bad-news message uses the indirect strategy and improves the tone considerably. Notice that it opens with a relevant, upbeat buffer regarding health care—but says nothing about increasing costs. For a smooth transition, the second paragraph begins with a key idea from the opening (*comprehensive package*). The reasons section discusses rising costs with explanations and figures. The bad news (*you will be paying $119 a month*) is clearly presented but embedded within the paragraph. Throughout, the writer strives to show the fairness of the company's position. The ending, which does not refer to the bad news, emphasizes how much the company is paying and what a wise investment it is.

Ethics Check

An Abrupt Exit Is Bad News

A barista working for a large coffee chain walked in one Monday morning and without warning bluntly announced to the shift manager, whom she disliked, that she was leaving. Then she walked out. She had found a better-paying job. Because the chain had a relatively high turnover, a barista's departure wasn't usually taken personally. Could the barista's dropping the bomb on her boss and coworkers have negative consequences, and is it fair to leave the way she did?

Figure 9.13 **Announcing Bad News to Employees**

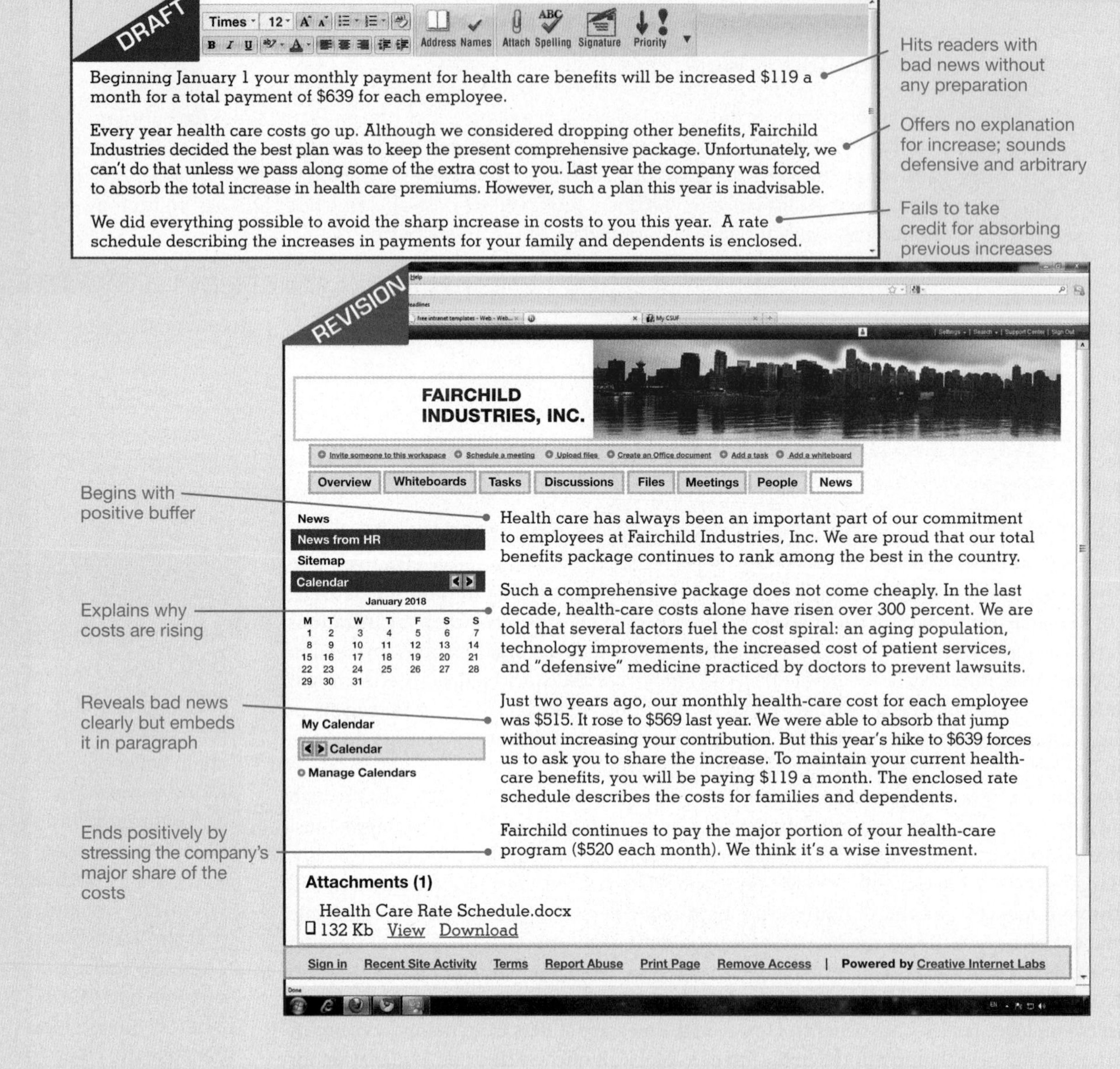

DRAFT
Beginning January 1 your monthly payment for health care benefits will be increased $119 a month for a total payment of $639 for each employee.
Every year health care costs go up. Although we considered dropping other benefits, Fairchild Industries decided the best plan was to keep the present comprehensive package. Unfortunately, we can't do that unless we pass along some of the extra cost to you. Last year the company was forced to absorb the total increase in health care premiums. However, such a plan this year is inadvisable.
We did everything possible to avoid the sharp increase in costs to you this year. A rate schedule describing the increases in payments for your family and dependents is enclosed.
Hits readers with bad news without any preparation
Offers no explanation for increase; sounds defensive and arbitrary
Fails to take credit for absorbing previous increases
REVISION
FAIRCHILD INDUSTRIES, INC.
Overview
Whiteboards
Tasks
Discussions
Files
Meetings
People
News
News
News from HR
Sitemap
Calendar
January 2018
My Calendar
Calendar
Manage Calendars
Health care has always been an important part of our commitment to employees at Fairchild Industries, Inc. We are proud that our total benefits package continues to rank among the best in the country.
Such a comprehensive package does not come cheaply. In the last decade, health-care costs alone have risen over 300 percent. We are told that several factors fuel the cost spiral: an aging population, technology improvements, the increased cost of patient services, and "defensive" medicine practiced by doctors to prevent lawsuits.
Just two years ago, our monthly health-care cost for each employee was $515. It rose to $569 last year. We were able to absorb that jump without increasing your contribution. But this year's hike to $639 forces us to ask you to share the increase. To maintain your current health-care benefits, you will be paying $119 a month. The enclosed rate schedule describes the costs for families and dependents.
Fairchild continues to pay the major portion of your health-care program ($520 each month). We think it's a wise investment.
Attachments (1)
Health Care Rate Schedule.docx
132 Kb View Download
Sign in Recent Site Activity Terms Report Abuse Print Page Remove Access | Powered by Creative Internet Labs
Begins with positive buffer
Explains why costs are rising
Reveals bad news clearly but embeds it in paragraph
Ends positively by stressing the company's major share of the costs

Notice that the entire message demonstrates a kinder, gentler approach than that shown in the first draft. Of prime importance in breaking bad news to employees is providing clear, convincing reasons that explain the decision. Parallel to this internal blog post, the message was also sent by e-mail. In smaller companies in which some workers do not have company e-mail, a hard-copy memo would be posted prominently on bulletin boards and in the lunchroom.

Saying *No* to Job Applicants

Being refused a job is one of life's major rejections. Tactless letters intensify the blow (*Unfortunately, you were not among the candidates selected for . . .*).

You can reduce the receiver's disappointment somewhat by using the indirect strategy—with one important variation. In the reasons section, it is wise to be vague in explaining why the candidate was not selected. First, giving concrete reasons may be painful to the receiver (*Your grade point average of 2.7 was low compared with the GPAs of other candidates*). Second, and more important, providing extra information may prove fatal in a lawsuit. Hiring and firing decisions generate considerable litigation today. To avoid charges of discrimination or wrongful actions, legal advisors warn organizations to keep employment rejection letters general, simple, and short.

The job refusal letter shown in Figure 9.14 is tactful but intentionally vague. It implies that the applicant's qualifications don't match those needed for the position, but the letter doesn't reveal anything specific. The writer could have included this alternate closing: *We wish you every success in finding a position that exactly fits your qualifications.*

Figure 9.14 **Saying *No* to Job Candidates**

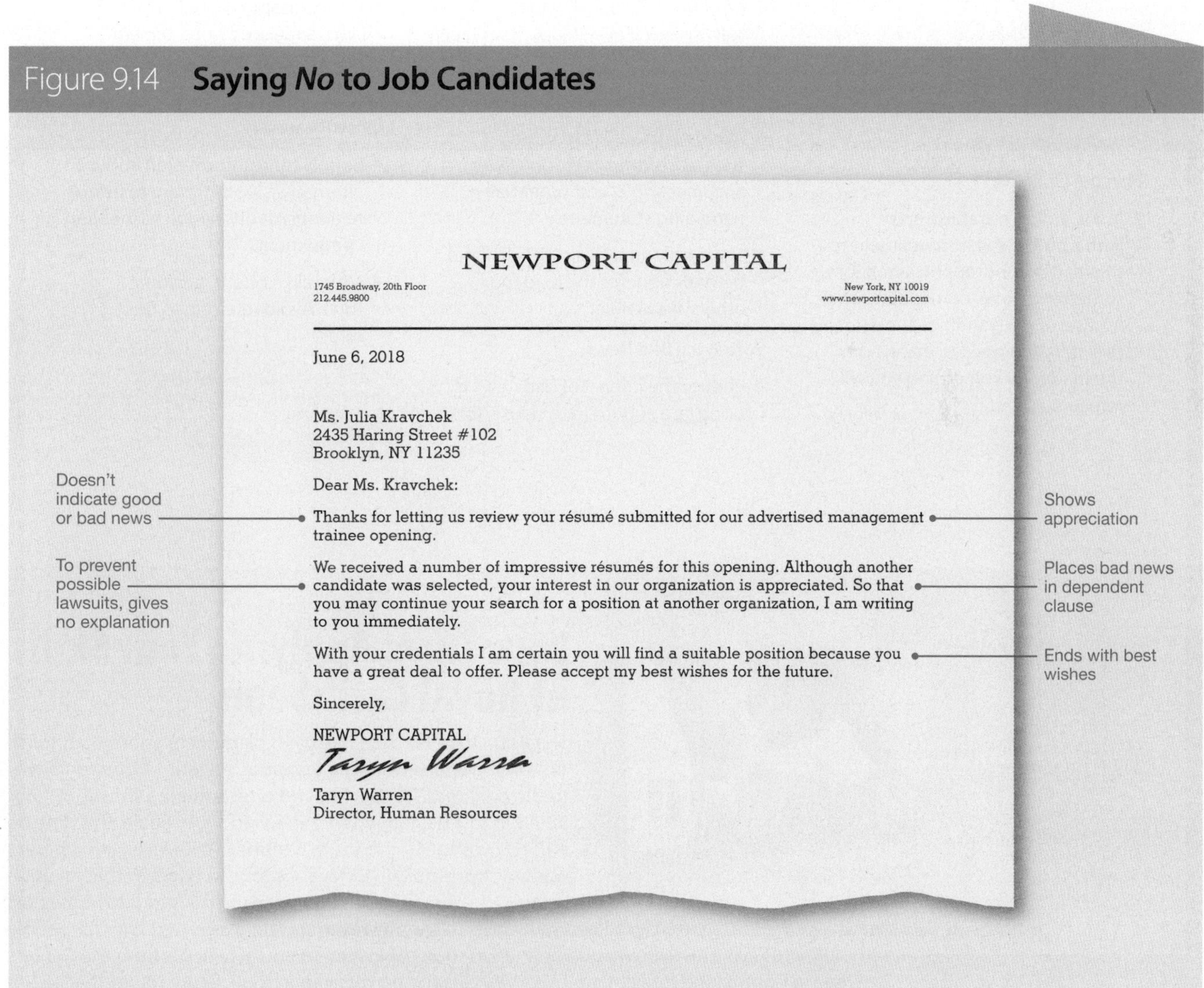

NEWPORT CAPITAL

1745 Broadway, 20th Floor
212.445.9800

New York, NY 10019
www.newportcapital.com

June 6, 2018

Ms. Julia Kravchek
2435 Haring Street #102
Brooklyn, NY 11235

Dear Ms. Kravchek:

Thanks for letting us review your résumé submitted for our advertised management trainee opening.

We received a number of impressive résumés for this opening. Although another candidate was selected, your interest in our organization is appreciated. So that you may continue your search for a position at another organization, I am writing to you immediately.

With your credentials I am certain you will find a suitable position because you have a great deal to offer. Please accept my best wishes for the future.

Sincerely,

NEWPORT CAPITAL

Taryn Warren

Taryn Warren
Director, Human Resources

The following checklist summarizes tips on how to communicate negative news inside and outside your organization.

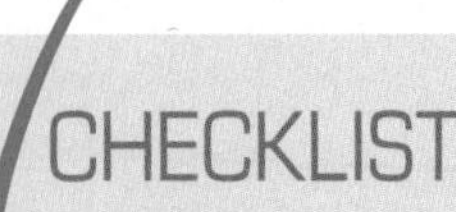

CHECKLIST

Conveying Negative News

Prewrite

- Decide whether to use the direct or indirect strategy. If the bad news is minor and will not upset the receiver, open directly. If the message is personally damaging and will upset the receiver, consider techniques to reduce its pain.
- Think through the reasons for the bad news.
- Remember that your primary goal is to make the receiver understand and accept the bad news as well as to maintain a positive image of you and your organization.

Plan the Opening

- In the indirect strategy, start with a buffer. Pay a compliment to the reader, show appreciation for something done, or mention some mutual understanding. Avoid raising false hopes or thanking the reader for something you will refuse.
- In the direct strategy, begin with a straightforward statement of the bad news.

Provide Reasons in the Body

- Except in credit and job refusals, explain the reasons for the negative message.
- In customer mishaps, clarify what went wrong, what you are doing to resolve the problem, and how you will prevent it from happening again.
- Use objective, nonjudgmental, and nondiscriminatory language.
- Avoid negativity (e.g., words such as *unfortunately, unwilling,* and *impossible*) and potentially damaging statements.
- Show how your decision is fair and perhaps benefits the reader or others, if possible.

Soften the Bad News

- Reduce the impact of bad news by using (a) a subordinate clause, (b) the passive voice, (c) a long sentence, or (d) a long paragraph.
- Consider implying the refusal, but be certain it is clear.
- Suggest an alternative, such as a lower price, a different product, a longer payment period, or a substitute. Provide help in implementing an alternative.
- Offset disappointment by offering gifts, a reduced price, benefits, tokens of appreciation, or something appropriate.

Close Pleasantly

- Supply more information about an alternative, look forward to future relations, or offer good wishes and compliments.
- Maintain a bright, personal tone. Avoid referring to the refusal.

Yeamake/Shutterstock.com

Your Turn: Applying Your Skills at Royal Caribbean

The *Anthem of the Seas* has been plagued by more than hurricane-force winds during a ferocious Atlantic storm on its way to the Bahamas. Barely repaired after suffering mostly interior damage, just days later the ship sailed south again, this time on a 12-day voyage to the South Caribbean. However, this itinerary was cut short too. Why? Royal Caribbean tweeted that an unfavorable weather forecast forced the ship to return to home port two days ahead of schedule to keep passengers safe. However, travelers reported over 65 people with norovirus symptoms being quarantined in their cabins for 48 hours. Officials from the Centers for Disease Control and Prevention (CDC) who inspected the ship in New Jersey found that 132 of 4,061 passengers and 16 of 1,592 crew members[47] suffered from gastrointestinal illness, most likely after consuming contaminated food.

Royal Caribbean must disinfect the huge ship to rid it of the highly contagious norovirus. Sanitation efforts will be boosted. Workers will have to scrub tables, handrails, and any surface that can be washed.[48] Nevertheless, the very next voyage to Barbados on April 16 must be canceled. Thousands of customers must be dealt the disappointing news, offered refunds, and provided incentives to reschedule their trips.

Vacationers wishing to reschedule their trips must proceed to RoyalCaribbean.com immediately. They can choose to sail on the *Quantum of the Seas* to Mexico in April or on the *Anthem* at a later date, but must complete their voyage within 24 months after the original departure date. In both cases, the cruise rates will not increase. Travelers choosing to rebook can also take advantage of a 50 percent discount on any additional four- to nine-day RCL cruise within 24 months. Travelers can call Guest Services at 1-800-256-6649.

Your Task

Assume that you are a trainee at Royal Caribbean. The assistant to the vice president of Guest Services asks you to draft the bad-news message to 4,500 customers. Ponder your strategy. Will you use a direct or an indirect strategy in your e-mail? Decide whether you should apologize, but be sure to explain the options clearly to your disappointed readers.

Summary of Learning Outcomes

1 Understand the strategies of business communicators in conveying negative news, apply the 3-x-3 writing process, and avoid legal liability.

- Explain clearly and completely while projecting a professional image.
- Convey empathy, sensitivity, and fairness.
- Be a mindful communicator who avoids careless and abusive language, which is defined as actionable language that is false, damaging to a person's reputation, and published (i.e., spoken in the presence of others or written).

2 Distinguish between the direct and indirect strategies in conveying unfavorable news.

- Use the direct strategy, with the bad news first, when the news is not damaging, when the receiver may overlook it, when the organization or receiver prefers directness, or when firmness is necessary.
- Use the indirect strategy, with a buffer and explanation preceding the bad news, when the bad news is personally upsetting, when it may provoke a hostile reaction, when it threatens the customer relationship, and when the news is unexpected.
- To avoid being unethical, never use the indirect method to deceive or manipulate the truth.

3 Explain the components of effective negative messages, including opening with a buffer, apologizing, showing empathy, presenting the reasons, cushioning the bad news, and closing pleasantly.

- To soften bad news, start with a buffer such as the best news, a compliment, appreciation, agreement, facts, understanding, or an apology.
- Explain the reasons that necessitate the bad news, trying to cite benefits to the reader or others.
- If you apologize, do so promptly and sincerely. Accept responsibility, but don't admit blame without consulting a superior or company counsel. Strive to project empathy.
- Strive to cushion the bad news with strategic positioning by (a) sandwiching it between other sentences, (b) presenting it in a subordinating clause, (c) using passive-voice

verbs, (d) accentuating the positive, (e) implying the refusal, and (f) suggesting a compromise or an alternative.

- Close pleasantly by (a) suggesting a means of following through on an alternative, (b) offering freebies, (c) extending good wishes, (d) anticipating future business, or (e) offering resale information or sales promotion.

4 Apply effective techniques for refusing typical requests or claims as well as for presenting bad news to customers in print or online.

- In rejecting requests for money, information, and action, follow the bad-news strategy: (a) begin with a buffer, (b) present valid reasons, (c) explain the bad news and possibly an alternative, and (d) close with good feelings and a positive statement.
- To deal with a disappointed customer, (a) call or e-mail the individual immediately; (b) describe the problem and apologize (when the company is to blame); (c) explain why the problem occurred, what you are doing to resolve it, and how you will prevent it from happening again; and (d) promote goodwill with a follow-up message.
- To handle negative posts and reviews online, (a) verify the situation, (b) respond quickly and constructively, (c) consider giving freebies such as refunds or discounts, (d) learn from negative comments as though they were real-time focus group input, and (e) be prepared to accept the inevitable and move on.
- To deny claims, (a) use the reasons-before-refusal strategy, (b) don't blame customers (even when they are at fault), (c) use neutral objective language to explain why the claim must be refused, and (d) consider offering resale information to rebuild the customer's confidence in your products or organization.
- When refusing credit, avoid language that causes hard feelings, strive to retain the customer on a cash basis, and avoid disclosures that could cause a lawsuit.

5 Describe and apply effective techniques for delivering bad news within organizations.

- To deliver workplace bad news in person, (a) gather all the information; (b) prepare and rehearse; (c) explain the past, present, and future; (d) consider taking a partner; (e) think about timing; and (f) be patient with the reaction.
- In announcing bad news to employees and to the public, strive to keep the communication open and honest, choose the best communication channel, and consider applying the indirect strategy, but give clear, convincing reasons.
- Be positive, but don't sugarcoat the bad news; use objective language.
- In refusing job applicants, keep messages short, general, and tactful.

Critical Thinking

1. Robert Bies, professor of management at Georgetown University, believes that an important ethical guideline in dealing with bad news within organizations is not to shock the recipient: "Bad news should never come as a surprise. Failure to warn senior leadership of impending bad news, such as poor sales or a loss of a major client, is a cardinal sin. So is failure to warn subordinates about mistakes in their performance and provide an opportunity for them to make corrections and improve."[49] Discuss the motivation of people who keep quiet and struggle with dispensing bad news. (L.O. 1–3)

2. Respected industry analyst Gartner Research issued a report naming social networking as one of the top ten disruptive (i.e., innovative) influences shaping information technology in the next five years.[50] Should organizations fear websites where consumers post negative messages about products and services? What actions can companies take in response to this disruptive influence? (L.O. 1–4)

3. Consider times when you have been aware that others were using the indirect strategy in writing or speaking to you. How did you react? (L.O. 2)

4. Living in Pittsburgh, Lauren Bossers worked virtually by e-mail and phone for a supply chain management software company in Dallas. She was laid off by phone. Bossers' manager had given her one day's notice; however, the news was still "shocking," and she responded with just *yes* or *no* to the HR officer who called: "I wasn't rude, but I didn't think it was my job to make them feel better," Bossers said. Software developer Jeff Langr was fired during a teleconference on Skype.[51] What might be some advantages and disadvantages to being let go remotely, if any? Why might it be a good idea to rein in one's frustration and anger? (L.O. 1, 5)

5. **Ethical Issue:** You work for a large corporation with headquarters in a small town. Recently, you received shoddy repair work and a huge bill from a local garage. Your car's transmission has the same problems that it did before you took it in for repair. You know that a complaint letter written on your corporation's stationery would be much more authoritative than one written on plain stationery. Should you use corporation stationery?

Writing Improvement Exercises

9.1 Organizational Strategies (L.O. 1–3)

YOUR TASK Identify which organizational strategy you would use for the following messages: direct or indirect.

a. A message from health-care provider CareFirst BlueCross BlueShield in which it must tell its 1.1 million members that their information in the form of names, birth dates, e-mail addresses, and subscriber information was compromised by hackers who obtained access to the company's website. The only good news is that member encryption prevented the cybercriminals from gaining access to social security numbers; medical claims; and employment, credit card, and other financial data.

b. A letter from a theme park refusing the request of a customer who wants free tickets. The customer was unhappy that she and her family had to wait in line a very long time to ride the new Delirium thrill roller coaster.

c. An announcement to employees that a financial specialist has canceled a scheduled lunchtime talk and cannot reschedule.

d. A message from a car insurance company that it will no longer insure family members who drive the family car. Customers may expand their policies with more comprehensive coverage at a higher cost.

e. An announcement from Amazon that it will begin charging state taxes on purchases, as mandated by law.

f. A memo from the manager denying an employee's request for special parking privileges. The employee works closely with the manager on many projects.

g. A memo from an executive refusing a manager's proposal to economize by purchasing refurbished computers. The executive and the manager both appreciate efficient, straightforward messages.

9.2 Employing Passive-Voice Verbs (L.O. 3)

YOUR TASK Revise the following sentences to present the bad news with passive-voice verbs.

a. Because management now requires more stringent security, we are postponing indefinitely requests for company tours.

b. We cannot offer free shipping after January 1. Act now!

c. Our retail stores will no longer be accepting credit cards for purchases under $5.

d. As manager, I cannot grant you the three-week vacation period you request because others have already reserved that period.

e. We do not examine patients until we have verified their insurance coverage.

f. Your car rental insurance coverage does not cover large SUVs.

g. Company policy prevents us from offering health and dental benefits until employees have been on the job for 12 months.

9.3 Subordinating Bad News (L.O. 3)

YOUR TASK Revise the following sentences to position the bad news in a subordinate clause. (**Hint:** Consider beginning the clause with *Although.*) Use passive-voice verbs for the bad news.

a. We regret that we cannot replace the cabinet hinge you need. The manufacturer no longer offers it. A new hinge should work for you, and we are sending it to you.

b. State law does not allow smoking within 5 feet of a state building. But the college has set aside 16 outdoor smoking areas.

c. We now offer all our catalog choices at our website, which is always current. Unfortunately, we no longer print or mail a complete print catalog. Our sustainability goals made it impossible for us to continue that practice.

d. We are sorry to report that we are unable to ship your complete order at this point in time. However, we are able to send two corner workstations now, and you should receive them within five days.

e. We appreciate your interest in our organization, but we cannot extend an employment offer to you at this time.

9.4 Implying Bad News (L.O. 3)

YOUR TASK Revise the following statements to *imply* the bad news. If possible, use passive-voice verbs and subordinate clauses to further de-emphasize the bad news.

DIRECT REFUSAL: We cannot send you a price list, nor can we sell our lawn mowers directly to customers. We sell only through authorized dealers, and your dealer is HomeCo.

IMPLIED REFUSAL: Our lawn mowers are sold only through authorized dealers, and your dealer is HomeCo.

a. We are sorry to tell you that we cannot ship our hand-dipped chocolate-covered fresh strawberries c.o.d. Your order was not accompanied by payment, so we are not shipping it. We have it ready, though, and will rush it to its destination as soon as you call us with your credit card number.

b. Unfortunately, we find it impossible to contribute to your excellent and worthwhile fund-raising campaign this year. At present all the funds of our organization are needed to lease equipment and offices for our new branch in Scottsdale. We hope to be able to support this commendable endeavor in the future.

c. Because of the holiday period, all our billboard space was used this month. Therefore, we are sorry to say that we could not give your charitable group free display space. However, next month, after the holidays, we hope to display your message as we promised.

Activities

Note: All Documents for Analysis are provided at **www.cengagebrain.com** for you to download and revise.

9.5 Document for Analysis: Request Refusal—Bitter Taste of the Beach (L.O. 1–4)

The following blunt refusal from a restaurant owner rejects a previously agreed-to favor. To avoid endangering a friendship and losing community goodwill, the writer needs to revise this message.

YOUR TASK List at least five weaknesses and suggest ways to improve this message. If your instructor directs, revise.

Current date

Ms. Diane Hinchcliffe
Taste of the Beach
310 Ocean Avenue, Suite 304
Carmel-by-the-Sea, CA 93521

Dear Ms. Hinchcliffe:

Unfortunately, we cannot participate in this summer's Taste of the Beach event. This may be particularly disappointing to you because, merely as a friendly gesture, I had earlier agreed to provide a selection of tasty hors d'oeuvres from my restaurant, The Zodiac. I'm sorry to let you down like this. We have participated in the past, but we just can't do it this year because our aging kitchen facilities require major and extensive remodeling.

I heard that this year's Taste of the Beach is really going to be a blast with new and old food, wine, music, and artistic offerings. How did you get so many prized vintners and all those well-known chefs, artists, and music groups to participate and perform?

This is probably quite disappointing to you (and to me) because the event supports Big Brothers Big Sisters of America. I know that BBBSA is simply the very best as a youth mentoring organization.

Let me repeat—I'm sorry we can't participate. Don't bother to beg me. But for your silent raffle we can offer you a coupon for a dinner for two. Of course, this could not be used until October when our renovations are completed.

Sincerely,

9.6 Document for Analysis: Bad News to Customers—Security Breach at Westport Payment Systems (L.O. 1–4)

E-Mail

The following poorly written e-mail tells customers that their e-mail addresses have been hacked. However, the message is clumsy and fails to include essential information in revealing security breaches to customers.

YOUR TASK Analyze the message and list at least seven weaknesses. If your instructor directs, revise it using the suggestions you learned in this chapter about security breach messages.

To: Dane Burgess <dane.burgess@premier.net>
From: Sierra Schneider <sschneider@westportpayment.org>
Subject: Security Incident at Westport Payment Systems

Companies and individuals across the country are experiencing more and more security breaches. This is just to let you know that you are receiving this e-mail because of a recent unfortunate security breach at Westport Payment Systems. Rest assured, however, that as a customer of Westport, your privacy was never at risk. We promise to guard your privacy around the clock.

Hackers last week were able to maliciously exploit a new function that we were trying to use to make the customer log-in process faster for you and our other customers. The hackers were ingenious and malicious, going to extreme lengths to gain access to some customer addresses at Westport. You should now beware of scams that may result from your address being used in phishing scams. To learn more, go to http://www.fdic.gov/consumers/consumer/alerts/phishing.html.

To provide even more information about this incident, the U.S. Postal Service will bring you a letter with more information. Taking your privacy very seriously, e-mail addresses are heavily protected here at Westport. Within hours of the hacker break-in, the log-in mechanism was disabled and a new procedure was established. The user is now required to enter their e-mail address and their password before they can log in successfully. E-mail addresses were the only information the hackers got. Other information such as account information and other personal information were never risked.

We appreciate you being a Westport customer.

Sincerely,

9.7 Document for Analysis: Claim Denial—Warranty Does Not Mean a New Device

(L.O. 1–4)

Following is a letter to a customer who demanded a brand-new replacement smartphone under her wireless phone protection plan.

YOUR TASK Analyze the message. List at least five weaknesses. If your instructor directs, revise the message.

Current date

Ms. Mia Tranquillo
501 Westhampton Way
Richmond, VA 23173

Dear Ms. Tranquillo:

This letter is being sent to you to inform you that warranty repairs or replacements are not available for damage caused by operator fault. The dot inside your smartphone indicates in bright red that the device suffered prolonged exposure to liquid. The phone also shows signs of heavy external abuse—quite rightly excluded from coverage under your protection plan.

Your phone retailer, Westhampton Wireless, at 422 Pleasant Valley Road, forwarded your device to us. Our service technician made an inspection. That's when he discovered that your Zero Plus handset had not been treated with proper caution and care. He said he had never seen such a gunky phone interior, and that without a doubt the gadget was subjected to blunt force on top of that! You are lucky that the touch screen did not crack or break and that you didn't lose all your data irretrievably since you apparently didn't bother to arrange for a backup. Today's smartphones are sophisticated high-tech devices. They must be handled with utmost respect. You wouldn't believe how many users accidentally drop their phones into the toilet.

The Peace of Mind Plan that you have purchased gets rave reviews from users. They love the protection their expensive equipment enjoys at a low monthly cost of $9.99. However, this plan plus the manufacturer's warranty on your Zero Plus covers only this one thing: manufacturing defects. Your warranty has expired by now, but it wouldn't cover neglect and abuse anyway. Your Peace of Mind Plan is in effect but only covers you for theft, loss, and malfunction. It explicitly excludes liquid and physical damage. In any case, there is always a deductible of $99. We can't replace the Zero Plus at no charge, as you request. But we could sell you a remanufactured model, at a cost of $149 plus tax. Your other option is to purchase a new device at full retail cost. Furthermore, since you have a two-year contract, you will be eligible for an upgrade as you are nearing month 20. You could go to www.westhamptonwireless.com to browse new calling plans and see current smartphones and perhaps order a product or service online.

Let us know what you want to do. We pride ourselves on our unparalleled customer service.

Sincerely,

9.8 Document for Analysis: Shooting Down Request for Salary Star Info (L.O. 1–4)

E-Mail

The following e-mail responds to an e-mail request from a well-known online writer seeking content for her industry blog. She requests salary and commission information of the star salespeople at MSI Laboratories, a large pharmaceutical firm.

YOUR TASK Revise the blunt message written by a senior executive. Yes, the request must be denied, but it can be done more tactfully so that it maintains the goodwill of this important writer.

To: Avalon Carrera <avalon.carrera@inthepipeline.net>
From: Ralph Freedman <rfreedman@msilaboratories.org>
Subject: Your Request
Attached: MSI Salespeople Fact Sheet

Dear Ms. Carrera:

I am writing in response to your request for salary information for our top sales reps. We cannot release such information because that disclosure would violate our employees' privacy and lead to lawsuits. However, the article you are researching for your blog In the Pipeline about comparative salaries and commissions sounds fascinating and will be most interesting to your readers. As a matter of fact, we are flattered that you wish to include MSI Laboratories. You may be interested to know that we have many outstanding young salespeople—some are male and some are female—who command top salaries.

I cannot reveal private employee information because each of our salespeople operates under an individual salary contract. This is a result of salary negotiations several years ago. During those negotiations an agreement was reached that both sales staff members and management agreed to keep the terms of these individual contracts confidential. For obvious reasons we cannot release specific salaries and commission rates. It has been suggested, however, that we can provide you with a list with the names of our top salespeople for a period of the past five years (see attached). As a matter of fact, three of the top salespeople are currently under the age of thirty-five.

Best wishes,

9.9 Request Refusal: Pink Phoenix Team Sinks Application (L.O. 1–4)

Web

Adobe Systems Incorporated prides itself on its commitment to employees who receive generous benefits and enjoy a supportive corporate culture. This core value may have contributed to the company's ranking among the top 50 of *Fortune* magazine's 100 Best Companies to Work For. The software giant is also known for its community involvement and corporate social responsibility efforts. This is why, like most large companies, Adobe receives many requests for sponsorships of charity events and community projects. True to its innovative spirit, the software company has streamlined the application process by providing an online sponsorship request form at its website.

You work in Corporate Affairs/Community Relations at Adobe and periodically help decide which nonprofits obtain support. Just yesterday you received an e-mail from Pink Phoenix of Portland, Oregon, a dragon boat racing team of breast cancer survivors. The ancient Chinese sport has spread around the globe with competitions held not only in Asia but also in many Western countries. Dragon boat racing has gained popularity in North America among breast cancer patients who bond with fellow survivors, engage in healthy competition, and exercise regularly on the water. Synchronicity and technique are more important than brute strength, which is the main reason even recreational paddlers enjoy this fast-growing water sport.

The survivor team would like Adobe to sponsor a dragon boat festival in Portland in less than a month, an event potentially drawing at least 20 survivor teams that would compete against each other. Your company is already funding several cancer charities and has a policy of sponsoring many causes. Naturally, no corporate giving program has infinite funds, nor can it green-light every request. Adobe steers clear of religious, political, and "pornographic" events. The team judging the sponsorship entries wants to ensure that each proposal reaches audiences affiliated with Adobe. Most important, applicants must submit their requests at least six weeks before the event.

YOUR TASK As a junior staff member in Corporate Affairs/Community Relations, write an e-mail to Pink Phoenix captain Jenny Johnson (*jjohnson@pinkphoenix.org*) refusing her initial request and explaining the Adobe sponsorship philosophy and submission rules.

9.10 Request Refusal: Sorry to Be Unable to Help Neglected Children (L.O. 1–4)

As a vice president of a financial services company, you serve many clients, and they sometimes ask your company to contribute to their favorite charities. You recently received a letter from Elliana Larios asking for a substantial contribution to the National Court Appointed Special Advocate (CASA) Association. On visits to your office, she has told you about its programs to recruit, train, and support volunteers in their work with abused children. She herself is active in your town as a CASA volunteer, helping neglected children find safe, permanent homes. She told you that children with CASA volunteers are more likely to be adopted and are less likely to reenter the child welfare system.

You have a soft spot in your heart for children and especially for those who are mistreated. You sincerely want to support CASA and its good work. But times are tough, and you can't be as generous as you have been in the past. Ms. Larios wrote a special letter to you asking you to become a Key contributor, with a pledge of $2,000.

YOUR TASK Write a refusal letter that maintains good relations with your client. Address it to Ms. Elliana Larios, 8569 East 39th Street, Phoenix, AZ 85730.

9.11 Bad News to Customers: Putting the Brakes on Bakery Deliveries (L.O. 1–4)

As the owner of La Boulangerie Bakery in Baton Rouge, Louisiana, you have a devoted clientele savoring your delicacies. Your salty caramel cupcakes offer an irresistible salty-sweet flavor combination using fleur de sel crystals hand harvested from the pristine seas off Brittany, France. These salt granules complement the sweet buttery caramel that flavors both the cake and frosting. Although your cupcakes are a trendy hit, you also feature delicious cakes, squares, cookies, croissants, and breads. Your bakery has a medium-sized storefront; however, most of your business comes from supplying local restaurants and coffee shops with your tantalizing treats. You own two trucks that make deliveries to customers throughout the Baton Rouge metropolitan area.

Although La Boulangerie is financially successful, rising costs have severely undercut your profits over the past few months. You know that you are not the only business owner dealing with rising prices. Many of your suppliers have raised their prices over the past year. Specifically, the higher prices of wheat and sugar have resulted in a drastic increase in your production costs. Previously, you did not charge for deliveries made to your wholesale clients. However, you now feel that you have no choice but to add a delivery charge for each order to cover your increased costs and the price of gas.

YOUR TASK As the owner of La Boulangerie Bakery, write a letter to your wholesale clients in which you announce a $20 charge per delivery. Try to think of a special offer to soften the blow. Address the first letter to Mr. Emil Broussard, Café Broussard, 2013 West Lee Drive, Baton Rouge, LA 70820.

9.12 Bad News to Customers: Blunder in Scheduling Fairytale Cottage Wedding (L.O. 1–4)

As the wedding planner at Sea Island Resort in Georgia, you just discovered a terrible mistake. Two weddings have been scheduled for the same Saturday in June. How could this happen? You keep meticulous records, but six months ago, you were away for two weeks. Another employee filled in for you. She apparently didn't understand the scheduling system and lined up two weddings for the Cloister Chapel on June 14. The month of June, of course, is the busiest month of the year. Weddings in the popular fairytale cottage Cloister Chapel are usually booked for two years in advance, and it can handle only one wedding a day.

It's now January, and Kellie Singer, one of the brides-to-be called to check on her arrangements. That's when you discovered the mistake. However, you didn't reveal the blunder to Kellie on the telephone. From experience, you know how emotional brides can be when their plans go awry. Now you must decide what to do. Your manager has given you complete authority in scheduling weddings, and you know he would back nearly any decision you make to rectify the mistake. Unfortunately, all of your Sea Island wedding venues are booked for June Saturdays. However, you do have some midweek openings for the Cloister Chapel in early June. If one of the brides could change to midweek, you might offer one free night in a sumptuous bridal suite to smooth ruffled feathers.

Sea Island offers dreamlike settings for unforgettable wedding celebrations. Brides, grooms, and their guests can enjoy five-star resort services, five miles of private coastline, glittering ballrooms, custom banquets, and alluringly wooded and landscaped strolling areas.

YOUR TASK Decide what course of action to take. The two brides-to-be are Kellie Singer, 3201 Peachtree Lane, Cumming, GA 30016, and Julie Brehm, 240 Lakeview Avenue, Atlanta, GA 30305. In a memo to your instructor, explain your response strategy. If you plan a phone call, outline what you plan to say. If your instructor requests, write a letter and copy your instructor.

9.13 Claim Denial: Whining on the Web
(L.O. 1–4)

E-Mail Social Media 

The growth of social networking has also spawned many websites dedicated to customer reviews and complaints—for example, Angie's List, which profiles local service companies, contractors, and professionals. More specifically, companies such as Cruise Critic focus solely on vacation travel by ship. Visit Complaints.com, Ripoff Report, or another complaint site. Study ten or more complaints about products or companies (e.g., iPhone, Starbucks, Delta Air Lines).

YOUR TASK Select one complaint and, as a company employee, respond to it employing some of the techniques presented in this chapter. Submit a copy of the complaint along with your response to your instructor. Your instructor may request that you write an e-mail or a letter.

9.14 Claim Denial: Pricey Prescription Eyewear Left on Plane (L.O. 1–4)

Pacific Southern Airlines (PSA) had an unhappy customer. Cynthia Mercier-Walters flew from Philadelphia, Pennsylvania, to Phoenix, Arizona. The flight stopped briefly at Hartsfield-Jackson Atlanta International Airport, where she got off the plane for half an hour. When she returned to her seat, her $400 prescription reading glasses were gone. She asked the flight attendant where the glasses were, and the attendant said they probably were thrown away since the cleaning crew had come in with big bags and tossed everything in them. Ms. Mercier-Walters tried to locate the glasses through the airline's lost-and-found service, but she failed.

Then she wrote a strong letter to the airline demanding reimbursement for the loss. She felt that it was obvious that she was returning to her seat. The airline, however, knows that an overwhelming number of passengers arriving at hubs switch planes for their connecting flights. The airline does not know who is returning. What's more, flight attendants usually announce that the plane is continuing to another city and that passengers who are returning should take their belongings. Cabin cleaning crews speed through planes removing newspapers, magazines, leftover foods, and trash. Airlines feel no responsibility for personal items left in cabins.[52]

YOUR TASK As a staff member of the customer relations department of Pacific Southern Airlines, deny the customer's claim but retain her goodwill using techniques learned in this chapter. The airline never refunds cash, but it might consider travel vouchers for the value of the glasses. Remember that apologies cost nothing. Write a claim denial to Ms. Cynthia Mercier-Walters, 8400 S 51st Avenue, Glendale, AZ 85301.

9.15 Bad News to Customers: Selecting Sturdy Stepper for Snap Fitness Gym (L.O. 1–4)

You are delighted to receive a large order from Lawrence Holder at Snap Fitness Gym. This order includes two Lifecycle Trainers (at $1,295 each), four Pro Abdominal Boards (at $295 each), three Tunturi Muscle Trainers (at $749 each), and three Dual-Action StairClimbers (at $1,545 each).

You could ship immediately except for one problem. The Dual-Action StairClimber is intended for home use, not for gym or club use. Customers like it because they say it is more like scaling a mountain than climbing a flight of stairs. With each step, users exercise their arms to pull or push themselves up. Its special cylinders absorb shock so that no harmful running impact results. However, this model is not what you would recommend for gym use. You feel Mr. Holder should order your premier stair climber, the LifeStep (at $2,395 each). This unit has sturdier construction and is meant for heavy use. Its sophisticated electronics provide a selection of customer-pleasing programs that challenge muscles progressively with a choice of workouts. It also quickly multiplies workout gains with computer-controlled interval training. Electronic monitors inform users of step height, calories burned, elapsed time, upcoming levels, and adherence to fitness goals. For gym use the LifeStep is clearly better than the Dual-Action StairClimber. The bad news is that the LifeStep is considerably more expensive.

You get no response when you try to call Mr. Holder to discuss the problem. Should you ship what you can, or hold the entire order until you learn whether he wants the Dual-Action StairClimber or the LifeStep? Or perhaps you should substitute the LifeStep and send only two of them.

YOUR TASK Decide what to do and write a letter to be faxed to Lawrence Holder, Snap Fitness Gym, 1212 Bahama Drive, Richmond, KY 40475.

9.16 Bad News to Customers: Glitch Admits Rejected Student Applicants (L.O. 1–4)

E-Mail

Johns Hopkins University recently made a big mistake. It inadvertently welcomed 293 rejected applicants to the Baltimore, Maryland, campus. The e-mail said, "Embrace the YES!" in the subject line. "Welcome to the Class of 2019! We can't wait for you to get to campus. Until then, as one of the newest members of the family, we hope you'll show your Blue Jay pride."[53]

That message was intended to be sent to the 3,065 students who had been accepted. Instead, it went to a subset of students who had applied but were denied. David Phillips, vice provost for admissions and financial aid at Hopkins, blamed human error for the mistake. A subcontractor that helps the prestigious university with electronic communication used the wrong list of e-mail addresses, the vice provost explained. "We apologize to the students affected and to their families," Phillips said. "Admissions decision days are stressful enough. We very much regret having added to the disappointment felt by a group of very capable and hard-working students, especially ones who were so committed to the idea of attending Johns Hopkins that they applied early decision."[54]

One applicant, who had already received a rejection from Hopkins, Sam Stephenson, was confused, his mother said. What could the university do to correct this massive slip-up?

YOUR TASK For David Phillips, vice provost for admissions and financial aid, write an appropriate bad-news message to the students who received the message in error. Many applicants will be wondering what their real admission status is.

9.17 Bad News to Customers: Pick a Price Hike (L.O. 1–4)

Select a product or service that you now use (e.g., newspaper, Internet service, water or electricity, propane or natural gas, cell or landline phone, car insurance). Assume that the provider must raise its rates and that you are the employee who must notify customers. Should you use a letter, e-mail, company website, or blog? Decide whether you should use the direct or indirect strategy. Gather as much information as you can about the product or service. What, if anything, justifies the increase? What benefits can be cited?

YOUR TASK Prepare a rate increase announcement. Submit it along with a memo explaining your rationale for the strategy you chose.

9.18 Disappointed Customers: J. Crew Cashmere for a Song? (L.O. 1–4)

E-Mail

Who wouldn't want a cashmere zip turtleneck sweater for $28? At the J. Crew website, many delighted shoppers scrambled to order the bargain cashmere. Unfortunately, the price should have been $228! Before J. Crew officials could correct the mistake, several hundred e-shoppers had bagged the bargain sweater for their digital shopping carts.

When the mistake was discovered, J. Crew immediately sent an e-mail to the soon-to-be disappointed shoppers. The subject line shouted "Big Mistake!" A J. Crew executive began her message with this statement: "I wish we could sell such an amazing sweater for only $28. Our price mistake on your new cashmere zip turtleneck probably went right by you, but rather than charge you such a large difference, I'm writing to alert you that this item has been removed from your recent order."

As an assistant in the communication department at J. Crew, you saw the e-mail that was sent to customers and you tactfully suggested that the bad news might have been broken differently. Your boss says, "OK, hot stuff. Give it your best shot."

YOUR TASK Although you have only a portion of the message, analyze the customer bad-news message sent by J. Crew. Using the principles suggested in this chapter, write an improved e-mail. In the end, J. Crew decided to allow customers who ordered the sweater at $28 to reorder it for $128 to $140, depending on the size. Customers were given a special website to go to, to reorder (make up an address). Remember that J. Crew customers are youthful and hip. Keep your message upbeat.[55]

9.19 Disappointed Customers: No Checks, No Pay (L.O. 1–4)

Team

Ethan Alexander, a printing company sales manager, must tell one of his clients that the payroll checks her company ordered are not going to be ready by the date Alexander had promised. The printing company's job scheduler overlooked the job and didn't get the checks into production in time to meet the deadline. As a result, Alexander's client, a major insurance company, is going to miss its pay run.

Alexander meets with internal department heads. They decide on the following plan to remedy the situation: (a) move the check order to the front of the production line; (b) make up for the late production date by shipping some of the checks—enough to meet their client's immediate payroll needs—by air freight; (c) deliver the remaining checks by truck.[56]

YOUR TASK Form groups of three or four students. Discuss the following issues about how to present the bad news to Mia Madison, Alexander's contact person at the insurance company.

a. Should Alexander call Madison directly or delegate the task to his assistant?
b. When should Madison be informed of the problem?
c. What is the best procedure for delivering the bad news?
d. What follow-up would you recommend to Alexander?

Be prepared to share your group's responses during a class discussion. Your instructor may ask two students to role-play the presentation of the bad news.

9.20 Credit Refusal: Cash Rules at Crunch Gym (L.O. 1–4)

As manager of Crunch Gym, you must refuse the application of Ava Koenig for an Extended Membership. This is strictly a business decision. You liked Ava very much when she applied, and she seems genuinely interested in fitness and a healthy lifestyle. However, your Extended Membership plan qualifies the member for all your testing, exercise, recreation, yoga, and aerobics programs. This multiservice program is expensive for the club to maintain because of the large staff required. Applicants must have a solid credit rating to join. To your disappointment, you learned that Ava's credit rating is decidedly negative. Her credit report indicates that she is delinquent in payments to four businesses, including Total Body Fitness Center, your principal competitor.

You do have other programs, including your Drop In and Work Out plan, which offers the use of available facilities on a cash basis. This plan enables a member to reserve space on the racquetball and handball courts. The member can also sign up for yoga and exercise classes, space permitting. Since Ava is far in debt, you would feel guilty allowing her to plunge in any more deeply.

YOUR TASK Refuse Ava Koenig's credit application, but encourage her cash business. Suggest that she make an inquiry to the credit-reporting company Experian to learn about her credit report. She is eligible to receive a free credit report if she mentions this application. Write to Ava Koenig, 20 S Broadway, Apt. 4, Billings, MT 59101.

9.21 Bad News to Employees: Saying Goodbye to Gourmet Meals and Perks (L.O. 1–3, 5)

Communication Technology

When high-tech start-up Minx first hit the technology scene, it created a big splash. Its music streaming and voice control technology promised to revolutionize the field. It attracted $500,000 in seed money, suggesting that it could hire the best talent and create amazing new products. But Minx quickly fell off the fast track. It spent nearly $400,000 on a Bluetooth product that sold only 28 units. In addition, a botched security update resulted in the company's having to conduct a nationwide recall of one of its smart products. Yet, other products have been successful, and the company is not facing bankruptcy.

Initially, Minx offered amazing perks to attract the best and brightest talent. It provided an in-house chef with free gourmet meals, unlimited snacks, on-site acupuncture, and free yoga classes. Its offices were pet-friendly, and new employees received a $10,000 cash signing bonus. To counter the long hours that the tech world notoriously demands of its workers, Minx offered relaxation areas with table tennis and foosball tables.

Unfortunately, bad times have made it necessary for Minx to pull back on its employee perks. Although no staff people are being released, the in-house chef has to go, along with on-site acupuncture, yoga classes, and the $10,000 signing bonus. However, it's still a good place to work, and camaraderie is high.

YOUR TASK As a communications trainee in the CEO's office, you have been asked to draft an intranet post or a memo to employees announcing the bad news. Explain the cutbacks that affect current employees. Employ the bad-news techniques taught in this chapter. What could soften this bad news?

9.22 Bad News to Employees: Nixing Social Media at Work (L.O. 1–5)

E-Mail

Web

Your boss at MarketingMatters, a hip midsized public relations agency, is concerned that the youngest employee generation may be oversharing on Facebook. Two supervisors have complained that they spotted inappropriate photos on Facebook posted by a small group of millennials on the company payroll. This group of twentysomethings is close-knit. Its members maintain friendships outside the office and in cyberspace. They are smart and plugged in, but they seem to have trouble recognizing boundaries of age and authority. They party every weekend, which is code for a lot of drinking, marijuana use, and even salacious escapades—all of which the young workers generously document with smartphone cameras on the spot and occasionally in real time. Sometimes they share snarky comments about their workplace, such as *Rough day at work* or *Talked to the most idiotic client ever!* On top of that, the young people think nothing of friending their colleagues and supervisors. Their friends rank in the hundreds; some in the group have exceeded 1,000 friends on Facebook.

MarketingMatters has embraced cutting-edge technology because the management believes that information sharing and collaboration tools can lead to networking opportunities and, if used correctly, to increased productivity. The company maintains a permissive stance toward Internet use, but concern is growing that the young people are headed for trouble. The abuses continue despite the company's comprehensive Internet and social media use policy, which was widely disseminated. Probably the biggest risk MarketingMatters fears is the leaking of confidential information on social networking sites. The managers also complain that the millennials spend too much time on Facebook during office hours. Your boss is becoming impatient. After several meetings, the management decides to disallow social media use during work hours and to caution all employees against dangerous breaches of company policy and social media netiquette.

YOUR TASK Draft a message to be distributed by e-mail for the signature of your boss, Darcy M. Diamond, Director, Human Resources. Your message should remind all employees about the existing social networking policy and tactfully yet clearly announce the end of personal social media use at the office. The prohibition is effective immediately. Your message should also warn about the pitfalls of oversharing online.

Test Your Etiquette IQ

New communication platforms and casual workplace environments have blurred the lines of appropriateness, leaving workers wondering how to navigate uncharted waters. Indicate whether the following statements are true or false. Then see if you agree with the responses on p. R-1.

1. You panic when you can't remember the name of someone you have met before. The best strategy is to pretend you remember the person and try to engage in small talk while searching for clues to the person's identity.

   ________ True ________ False

2. You are taking a new employee, Meredith Lee, around introducing her to the office staff. The vice president shows up in the hallway. You should introduce him by saying, "Meredith, I'd like you to meet Mr. Richmond, our vice president."

   ________ True ________ False

3. When a woman is introduced to a man, he should wait for her to extend her hand first.

   ________ True ________ False

Chat About It

In each chapter you will find five discussion questions related to the chapter material. Your instructor may assign these topics for you to discuss in class, in an online chat room, or on an online discussion board. Some of the discussion topics may require outside research. You may also be asked to read and respond to postings made by your classmates.

TOPIC 1: Discuss your own examples of effective and ineffective apologies. Which elements determine whether we find an apology credible and sincere?

TOPIC 2: Many people say they prefer the direct approach when receiving bad news. What situational factors might cause you to use the indirect approach with these people?

TOPIC 3: Which strategies have you used to soften the blow of significant bad news with your family and friends? If you haven't, imagine situations in which such strategic thinking might be wise.

TOPIC 4: A flyer at a city bus stop announced a fare increase with the title *Rate Changes*. Was this title effective? If not, what title might have worked better?

TOPIC 5: You are an executive at a company that suddenly has to lay off 400 employees within three days or risk financial disaster. You have to make the cuts quickly, but you don't want to be impersonal by announcing the cuts by e-mail. How would you announce the bad news?

Grammar and Mechanics | *Review 9*

Number Usage

Review Guides 47 through 50 about number usage in Appendix D, Grammar and Mechanics Guide, beginning on page D-16. On a separate sheet, revise the following sentences to correct errors in number usage. For each error you locate, write the guide number that reflects this usage. Sentences may have more than one error. If a sentence is correct, write *C*. When you finish, check your answers on page Key-2.

EXAMPLE: We have 9 donors who are willing to contribute 200 dollars to the charity drive.

REVISION: We have **nine** donors who are willing to contribute **$200** to the charity drive. [Guides 47, 49]

1. 23 call centers in India will be switching from customer service to mortgage processing.
2. Faced with a 522 million dollar deficit, the mayor sent pink slips to fifteen thousand city employees.
3. UPS deliveries are expected before ten AM and again at four thirty PM.
4. Consumers find that sending a one hundred forty character tweet is easier than writing a complaint letter.
5. Fewer than ½ of the stockholders submitted their ballots before the June 15th deadline.
6. In the first 2 weeks of the year, we expect to hire at least 10 new employees.
7. On April 15th our attorney notified all 4 managers of the lawsuit.
8. You can burn one hundred fifty calories by walking as little as thirty minutes..
9. A 5-year loan for a twenty-five thousand dollar new car with 20% down would have monthly payments of three hundred fifty-six dollars.
10. Although he expected to spend fifty dollars or less, Jake spent sixty-five dollars for the gift.

References

[1] Almasy, S., & Machado, A. (2016, February 11). Royal Caribbean apologizes to Anthem ship passengers battered by storm. CNN. Retrieved from http://www.cnn.com/2016/02/10/us/new-jersey-anthem-of-seas-cruise-ship-extreme-storm

[2] Sloan, G., & Rice, D. (2016, February 9). Meteorologists: Royal Caribbean blew it by sailing into storm. *USA Today*. Retrieved from http://www.usatoday.com/story/news/nation/2016/02/09/royal-caribbean-anthem-cruise-storm/80051782; Sloan, G. (2016, February 9). Giant Royal Caribbean ship damaged in "extreme" storm will return to port. *USA Today*. Retrieved from http://www.usatoday.com/story/news/nation/2016/02/08/anthem-cruise-ship-storm/79997114

[3] Number of cruise passengers carried worldwide from 2007 to 2019 (in millions). (2016). Statista. Retrieved from http://www.statista.com/statistics/270605/cruise-passengers-worldwide; Revenue of the cruise industry worldwide from 2008 to 2015 (in billion U.S. dollars). (2016). Statista. Retrieved from http://www.statista.com/statistics/204572/revenue-of-the-cruise-line-industry-worldwide-since-2008

[4] Klein, R. (2016). Events at sea. Cruise Junkie. Retrieved from http://www.cruisejunkie.com/Overboard.html

[5] Spagat, E. (2010, November 11). Stricken cruise ship reaches San Diego amid cheers. Associated Press. Retrieved from http://www.deseretnews.com/article/700080738/Stricken-cruise-ship-reaches-San-Diego-amid-cheers.html; Passengers back on land after "nightmare" sea cruise. (2010, November 11). CTV News. http://www.ctvnews.ca/passengers-back-on-land-after-nightmare-sea-cruise-1.573498

[6] Golden, F., & Lenhart, M. (2012, February 27). Carnival Corp. besieged by bad news. *Travel Market Report*. Retrieved from http://www.travelmarketreport.com/tmrarticledisplay?aid=6968

[7] Number of cruise passengers carried worldwide from 2007 to 2019 (in millions). (2016). Statista. Retrieved from http://www.statista.com/statistics/270605/cruise-passengers-worldwide

[8] Based on Strom, S. (2015, December 21). Chipotle e.coli cases rise, with 5 more ill in Midwest. *The New York Times*. Retrieved from http://www.nytimes.com/2015/12/22/business/chipotle-e-coli-cases-rise-with-5-more-ill-in-midwest.html?_r=1

[9] Smith, B. (2015, January 29). Sorry wasn't enough. Here's what we're doing now. LinkedIn. Retrieved from https://www.linkedin.com/pulse/sorry-wasnt-enough-heres-what-were-doing-now-brad-smith

[10] Goodarzi, S. (2015, January 22). An apology to our TurboTax desktop customers. Intuit TurboTax Blog. Retrieved from http://blog.turbotax.intuit.com/uncategorized/an-apology-to-our-turbotax-desktop-customers-18817

[11] Chow, E. K. (2014, April 1). Why Courtney Love's "Twibel" lawsuit is good for the Internet. *The Huffington Post*. Retrieved from http://www.huffingtonpost.com/eugene-k-chow/why-courtney-love-twibel_b_4688426.html

[12] Gardner, E. (2015, August 27). Courtney Love ends defamation row with $350K settlement. *The Hollywood Reporter*. Retrieved from http://www.hollywoodreporter.com/thr-esq/courtney-love-ends-defamation-row-818025

[13] Stratton, B. J., & Becker, S. J. (2013, December 23). Inappropriate e-mail use by employees can constitute cause for dismissal. Bennett Jones Thought Network. Retrieved from http://blog.bennettjones.com/2013/12/23/inappropriate-e-mail-use-by-employees-can-constitute-cause-for-dismissal

[14] McCord, E. A. (1991, April). The business writer, the law, and routine business communication: A legal and rhetorical analysis. *Journal of Business and Technical Communication*, 183.

[15] Ibid.

[16] Creelman, V.(2012). The case for "living" models. *Business Communication Quarterly, 75*(2), 181.

[17] Veltsos, J. (2012). An analysis of data breach notifications as negative news. *Business Communication Quarterly, 75*(2), 198. doi:10.1177/1080569912443081

[18] Canavor, N. (2012). *Business writing in the digital age*. Thousand Oaks, CA: Sage, p. 62.

[19] Joyce, C. (2012, November). The impact of direct and indirect communication. International Ombudsman Association. Retrieved from https://www.ombudsassociation.org/Resources/IOA-Publications/The-Independent-Voice/November-2012/The-Impact-of-Direct-and-Indirect-Communication.aspx

[20] Canavor, N. (2012). *Business writing in the digital age*. Thousand Oaks, CA: Sage, p. 61.

[21] Bousis, G. Quoted in Young Entrepreneur Council. (2014, October 1). 9 (polite) ways to reject a customer. Inc. Retrieved from http://www.inc.com/young-entrepreneur-council/9-polite-ways-to-reject-a-customer.html

[22] Based on Shontel, A. (2015, October 13.) Here's the e-mail Jack Dorsey sent all Twitter employees on Tuesday morning about 336 of them being laid off. Business Insider. Retrieved from http://www.businessinsider.com/jack-dorseys-layoff-letter-to-twitters-staff-2015-10

[23] Kashtan, M. (2013, May 20). Saying "no" without saying "no": How to say "no" to someone so they know they still matter to us. *Psychology Today*. Retrieved from https://www.psychologytoday.com/blog/acquired-spontaneity/201305/saying-no-without-saying-no

[24] Green Coffee Bean extract marketer to refund customers. (2015, January 27). Truth in Advertising. Retrieved from https://www.truthinadvertising.org/green-coffee-bean-extract-marketer-refund-customers; Oz watch: TV host pulls curtain on phony endorsements. (2013, May 31). Truth in Advertising. Retrieved from https://www.truthinadvertising.org/oz-watch-tv-host-pulls-curtain-on-phony-endorsements

[25] Hollis, L. (2014, February 27). Sorry seems to be the hardest word. *Management Today UK*. Retrieved from http://www.managementtoday.co.uk/news/1281578/sorry-seems-hardest-word

[26] Schweitzer, M. (2006, December). Wise negotiators know when to say "I'm sorry." *Negotiation*, 4. Retrieved from Business Source Complete database.

[27] Chance, D., Cicon, J., & Ferris, S. P. (2016, January). Poor performance and the value of corporate honesty. *Journal of Corporate Finance, 33*. doi:10.1016/j.jcorpfin.2015.04.008. Retrieved from http://search.proquest.com

[28] ten Brinke, L., & Adams, G. S. (2015). Saving face? When emotion displays during public apologies mitigate damage to organizational performance. *Organizational Behavior and Human Decision Processes, 133*. doi:10.1016/j.obhdp.2015.05.003. Retrieved from http://search.proquest.com

[29] Cited in Canavor, N. (2012). *Business writing in the digital age*. Thousand Oaks, CA: Sage, p. 62.

[30] Glinton, S. (2016, January 11). "We didn't lie," Volkswagen CEO says of emission scandal. NPR. Retrieved from http://www.npr.org/sections/thetwo-way/2016/01/11/462682378/we-didnt-lie-volkswagen-ceo-says-of-emissions-scandal

[31] Parmar, B. (2015, January 8). Corporate empathy is not an oxymoron. *Harvard Business Review*. Retrieved from https://hbr.org/2015/01/corporate-empathy-is-not-an-oxymoron

[32] Ibid.

[33] Ibid.

[34] Letters to Lands' End. (1991, February). 1991 Lands' End Catalog. Dodgeville, WI: Lands' End, p. 100.

[35] Mowatt, J. (2002, February). Breaking bad news to customers. *Agency Sales*, p. 30; Dorn, E. M. (1999, March). Case method instruction in the business writing classroom. *Business Communication Quarterly, 62*(1), 51-52.

[36] Guliani, B. K. (2016, February 15). Twitter's greater revenue is due to its faster responses. Digital Vidya Blog. Retrieved from http://www.digitalvidya.com/blog/twitters-greater-revenue-is-due-to-its-faster-responses; Kapner, S. (2012, October 5). Citi won't sleep on customer tweets. *The Wall Street Journal*, p. 1.

[37] Vaughan, P. (2014, July 23). 72% of people who complain on Twitter expect a response within an hour. Hubspot Blogs. Retrieved from http://blog.hubspot.com/marketing/twitter-response-time-data

[38] Morin, A. (2015, November 28). Waiting for a reply? Study explains the psychology behind e-mail response time. *Forbes*. Retrieved from http://www.forbes.com/sites/amymorin/2015/11/28/waiting-for-a-reply-study-explains-the-psychology-behind-email-response-time/#598ffa3e4ec0

[39] Taylor, J. (2016, January 22). Customer service response time down 12% on Facebook and Twitter. Our Social Times. Retrieved from http://oursocialtimes.com/social-customer-service-response-times-down-12

[40] Wagner, S. (2012, September 11). CEO addresses Sept. 10 service outage. Retrieved from http://www.pcworld.com/article/262317/godaddy_apologizes_for_outage_with_30_discounts.html

[41] Ngak, C. (2012, September 10). GoDaddy goes down, Anonymous claims responsibility. CBSNews.com Retrieved from http://www.cbsnews.com/8301-501465_162-57509744-501465/godaddy-goes-down-anonymous-claims-responsibility

[42] Forbes, M. (1999). How to write a business letter. In K. Harty (Ed.), *Strategies for business and technical writing*. Boston: Allyn & Bacon, p. 108.

[43] Browning, M. (2003, November 24). Work dilemma: Delivering bad news a good way. *Government Computer News*, p. 41; Mowatt, J. (2002, February). Breaking bad news to customers. *Agency Sales*, p. 30.

[44] Ensall, S. (2007, January 30). Delivering bad news. *Personnel Today*, p. 31. Retrieved from Business Source Premier database; Lewis, B. (1999, September 13). To be an effective leader, you need to perfect the art of delivering bad news. *InfoWorld*, p. 124.

[45] Ziglar, Z. (2011, January 18). Dad, you do choose your daughter's husband. Retrieved from http://www.ziglar.com/newsletter/?p=949

[46] Livingston, J. (2008, September 17). Author Holly Weeks talks communication. [Interview]. Human Resources iQ. Retrieved from http://www.humanresourcesiq.com/business-strategies/articles/author-holly-weeks-talks-communication

[47] Anthem of the Seas: Norovirus cruise illness outbreaks. (2016). Retrieved from http://www.cruiseminus.com/anthem-of-the-seas/#position

[48] "Anthem of the Seas" cuts latest trip short due to severe weather, norovirus. CBS New York. Retrieved from http://newyork.cbslocal.com/2016/02/28/anthem-of-the-seas-severe-weather-norovirus

[49] Bies, R. (2012, May 30). The 10 commandments for delivering bad news. *Forbes*. Retrieved from http://www.forbes.com/sites/forbesleadership forum/2012/05/30/10-commandments-for-delivering-bad-news/#73d795c21df9

[50] Gartner identifies top ten disruptive technologies for 2008-2012. (n.d.). [Press release]. Gartner. Retrieved from https://www.gartner.com/it/page.jsp?id=681107

[51] Fired by email or phone? Here's how to deal with it. (2012, January 5). Reuters. Retrieved from http://www.reuters.com/article/email-firing-idUSN1E80406420120105

[52] Based on Burbank, L. (2007, June 8). Personal items can be swept away between flights. *USA Today*, p. 3D.

[53] Anderson, N. (2014, December 16). Johns Hopkins mistakenly says "yes" to hundreds of rejected applicants. *The Washington Post*. Retrieved from https://www.washingtonpost.com/local/education/johns-hopkins-mistakenly-says-yes-to-hundreds-of-rejected-applicants/2014/12/16/20b5f9f4-8575-11e4-b9b7-b8632ae73d25_story.html

[54] Ibid.

[55] Sorkin, A. R. (1999, November). J. Crew web goof results in discount. *The New York Times*, p. D3.

[56] Mishory, J. (2008, June). Don't shoot the messenger: How to deliver bad news and still keep customers satisfied. *Sales and Marketing Management*, p. 18.

Chapter 10 Persuasive and Sales Messages

Phovoir/Shutterstock.com

LEARNING OUTCOMES

After studying this chapter, you should be able to

1 Explain digital age persuasion, identify time-proven persuasive techniques, and apply the 3-x-3 writing process to persuasive messages in print and online.

2 Describe the traditional four-part AIDA strategy for creating successful persuasive messages, and apply the four elements to draft effective and ethical business messages.

3 Craft persuasive messages that request actions, make claims, and deliver complaints.

4 Understand interpersonal persuasion at work, and write persuasive messages within organizations.

5 Create effective and ethical direct-mail and e-mail sales messages.

6 Apply basic persuasive techniques in developing compelling press releases.

Yeamake/Shutterstock.com

ōlloclip: Smartphone Lenses That Sell Themselves

"If I had to explain trade show life in three words, it would be: exciting, exhausting, and educational," says Lena Galasko, a young, charismatic sales & channel marketing representative at ōlloclip of Huntington Beach, California. The tech startup sells mobile photography accessories—small, wearable lenses that clip onto smartphones and dramatically increase users' creative photography options.

Despite long hours at times, Lena seems to have the life many college graduates dream of. She promotes products that are functional and well made, as she tells it. She travels to trade shows and hip events, such as CES in Las Vegas and SXSW in Austin, Texas. Within 12 recent months, Lena visited ten cities in five countries on two continents. Of course, she documents her trips with her own ōlloclip-enhanced photography on Instagram, Facebook, and other social media.

Lena Galasko

Lena Galasko

Lena Galasko

Lena took a huge gamble when she joined fledgling ōlloclip after graduating with a degree in international business. She was the first official hire—a "first born" or "No. 1"—as the joke goes within the company. ōlloclip was founded in 2011 by the UK-born amateur photographer Patrick O'Neill. The expat successfully used the crowdfunding platform Kickstarter to launch his company literally in his kitchen. He persuaded 1,300 backers from 50 countries to fork over almost $70,000 on his original funding goal of $15,000.

"As a European myself, I was intrigued by a small company with a promising global brand building future," Lena says. Her good instinct has served her well. Once ōlloclip secured retail placement in all North American Apple stores and at Best Buy, its brand of mobile photography began to thrive. In 2013 Patrick O'Neill was named Entrepreneur of the Year by *Entrepreneur* magazine. In December 2014 the company sold its millionth lens and now offers macro, wide-angle, fisheye, ultra-wide, and telephoto lenses as well as other accessories. Most recently, ōlloclip was featured in the History Channel's *Million Dollar Genius* show.

Like many smart marketers, Lena listens to customers and tailors the product demonstration to fit their needs. A dermatologist interested in a macro lens might not view a quirky fisheye lens as a huge priority. Because Lena is actively using ōlloclip lenses, she is able to showcase their features and sell without actually selling, as the puts it. "Customers love real!" she says. "Ours is very much a soft sell, but we make every effort to tell our story." Public relations is key to ōlloclip's strategy. Six agencies on four continents are telling this story—for example, by offering photo contests. Journalists are listening. Rave reviews are pouring in by the likes of *Wired*, *PC Word*, and *Mashable*.[1] You will learn more about this case later in this chapter.

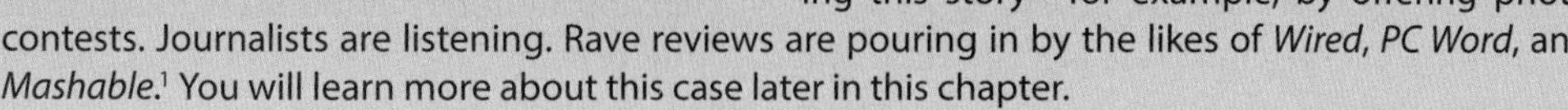

Critical Thinking

- Why is using a gentle, soft-sell approach so important to persuasion?
- What are some critical take-aways from Lena's story and her views of persuasion?
- What factors influenced ōlloclip's success?

LEARNING OUTCOME 1

Explain digital age persuasion, identify time-proven persuasive techniques, and apply the 3-x-3 writing process to persuasive messages in print and online.

Persuading Effectively and Ethically in the Contemporary Workplace

Contemporary businesses have embraced leaner corporate hierarchies, simultaneously relying on teams, eliminating division walls, and blurring the lines of authority. As teams and managers are abandoning the traditional command structure, sophisticated persuasive skills are becoming ever more important at work. Businesspeople must try to influence others.[2] Pushy hard-sell techniques are waning because today's consumers have many choices and can be fickle. At ōlloclip, marketers opt for soft-sell approaches; they emphasize user benefits and let their products speak for themselves, aided by spectacular stills and videos shot with ōlloclip smartphone lenses. Unlike the pros at ōlloclip, however, many of us are poor persuaders, or we don't always recognize subtle persuasive tactics directed at us.[3]

Although we are subjected daily to a barrage of print and electronic persuasive messages, we often fail to recognize the techniques of persuasion. To be smart consumers, we need to be alert to persuasive practices and how they influence behavior. Being informed is our best defense. Yet more than ever in today's digital world, we should also realize that persuasion has the power "to change attitudes and behaviors on a mass scale," as persuasion guru B. J. Fogg at Stanford puts it. Social networks enable individuals or groups to reach virtually limitless audiences and practice what Fogg calls "mass interpersonal persuasion."[4] This puts a lot of power into the hands of many.

You have already studied techniques for writing routine request messages that require minimal persuasion. However, this chapter focuses on messages that require deliberate and skilled persuasion in the workplace. This chapter also addresses selling, both offline and online.

What Is Persuasion?

As communication scholar Richard M. Perloff defines it, persuasion is "a symbolic process in which communicators try to convince other people to change their attitudes or behaviors regarding an issue through the transmission of a message in an atmosphere of free choice."[5] Helping us understand how persuasion works, this definition has five components, which are outlined in the following sections.

Persuasion Is a Symbolic Process. Symbols are meaningful words, signs, and images infused with rich meaning—for example, words such as *liberty*, signs such as national flags, and images such as the red cross for rescue or the apple for computers. An ethical persuader understands the power of symbols and does not use them to trick others. Because people's attitudes change slowly, persuasion takes time.

Persuasion Involves an Attempt to Influence. Persuasion involves a conscious effort to influence another person with the understanding that change is possible. For instance, when you ask your boss for permission to telecommute, you intend to achieve a specific outcome and assume that your boss can be swayed.

Persuasion Is Self-Persuasion. Ethical communicators give others the choice to accept their arguments by making compelling, honest cases to support them. They plant the seed but do not coerce. They leave it to others to "self-influence"—that is, to decide whether to make the change. In the case of telecommuting, you would want to present to your boss clear benefits of working from home but definitely not push hard.

Persuasion Involves Transmitting a Message. Persuasive messages can be verbal or nonverbal, and they can be conveyed face-to-face or via the Internet, TV, radio, and other media. Persuasive messages are not always rational. They often appeal to our emotions. Consider the car commercial playing your favorite tune and showing pristine landscapes, not a gridlocked interstate during rush hour.

Persuasion Requires Free Choice. Although *free* is a difficult term to define, we can perhaps agree that people are free when they are not forced to comply, when they can refuse the idea suggested to them, and when they are not pressured to act against their own preferences.

Many smart thinkers have tried to explain how savvy persuaders influence others. One classic model illustrating persuasion is shown in Figure 10.1. In the definitive book *Influence*,[6] Robert B. Cialdini outlined six psychological triggers that prompt us to act and to believe: reciprocation, commitment, social proof, liking, authority, and scarcity. Each "weapon of automatic influence" motivates us to say *yes* or *no* without much thinking or awareness. Our complex world forces us to resort to these shortcuts. Needless to say, such automatic responses make us vulnerable to manipulation.

If you become aware of these gut-level mechanisms that trigger decisions, you will be able to resist unethical and manipulative persuasion more easily. Conversely, this knowledge might make you a successful persuader.

Figure 10.1 **Six Basic Principles That Direct Human Behavior**

Reciprocation
"The Old Give and Take ... and Take"

Humans seem to be hardwired to give and take. If someone does us a favor, most of us feel obligated to return the favor. This rule is so binding that it may lead to a *yes* to a request we might otherwise refuse. This explains the "gifts" that accompany requests for money.

Commitment
"Hobgoblins of the Mind"

We believe in the correctness of a difficult choice once we make it. We want to keep our thoughts and beliefs consistent with what we have already decided. Fund-raisers may ask for a small amount at first, knowing that we are likely to continue giving once we start.

Social Proof
"Truths Are Us"

To determine correct behavior, we try to find out what other people think is correct. We see an action as more acceptable when others are doing it. Advertisers like to tell us that a product is "best-selling"; the message is that it must be good because others think so.

Liking
"The Friendly Thief"

We are more likely to accept requests of people we know and like or those who say they like us. Tupperware capitalizes on this impulse to buy from a friend. Strangers are persuasive if they are likable and attractive. Also, we favor people who are or appear to be like us.

Authority
"Directed Deference"

We tend to obey authority because we learn that a widely accepted system of authority is beneficial to the orderly functioning of society. People exuding authority, even con artists, can trigger our mechanical, blind compliance. Testimonials bank on this response to authority.

Scarcity
"The Rule of the Few"

We tend to regard opportunities as more valuable when their availability is restricted. Scarce items seem more appealing to us. The idea of potential loss greatly affects our decisions. Marketers may urge customers not to miss out on a "limited-time offer."

Ethics Check

Subtle Use of Persuasion in an Age of Social Media and Information Overload

Professional persuaders try to generate "a distinct kind of automatic, mindless compliance" in people, a "willingness to say yes without thinking first," believes psychologist Robert B. Cialdini. The best-selling author of *Influence* cautions: "The ever-accelerating pace and informational crush of modern life will make . . . unthinking compliance more and more prevalent in the future. It will be increasingly important for the society, therefore, to understand the how and why of automatic influence." What does this mean for you as a consumer and participant in social media?[7]

How Has Persuasion Changed in the Digital Age?

The preoccupation with persuasion is not new. From the days of Aristotle in ancient Greece and Machiavelli in Renaissance Italy, philosophers, politicians, and businesspeople have longed to understand the art of influencing others. However, persuasion in the twenty-first century is different from persuasion in previous historic periods in distinct ways.[8] The most striking developments are less than three decades old.

The Volume and Reach of Persuasive Messages Have Exploded. Although the exact numbers are difficult to establish, experts estimate that the average American adult endures approximately 300 "ad impressions" and other persuasive appeals a day.[9] TV, radio, the Internet, and mobile phones blast myriad messages to the far corners of the earth. A Pew Research study shows that the United States continues to be seen favorably by people around the globe despite a complex post-9/11 political climate,[10] due, perhaps in part, to its pervasive popular culture.

Persuasive Messages Spread at Warp Speed. Popular U.S. TV shows such as *The Big Bang Theory,* the action drama *NCIS,* and the *Crime Scene Investigation* series are global phenomena.[11] Popular music and social media engage fans halfway around the world. Furthermore, election year campaign buzz also travels at dizzying speed.

Organizations of All Stripes Are in the Persuasion Business. Companies, ad agencies, PR firms, social activists, lobbyists, marketers, and more, spew persuasive messages. Although outspent by corporations that can sink millions into image campaigns, activists use social networks to galvanize their followers.

Persuasive Techniques Are More Subtle and Misleading. Instead of a blunt, pushy hard-sell approach, persuaders play on emotions by using flattery, empathy, nonverbal cues, and likability appeals. They are selling an image or a lifestyle, not a product.[12] In this age of spin, the news media are increasingly infiltrated by partisan interests and spread messages masquerading as news.

Persuasion Is More Complex and Impersonal. American consumers are more diverse and don't necessarily think alike. To reach them, marketers carefully study target groups and customize their appeals. Technology has increased the potential for distortion. People can "mash up" content, give it meanings the original source never intended, and blast it into the world in seconds.

You probably recognize how important it is not only to become a skilled persuader, but also to identify devious messages and manipulation attempts directed at you. When you want your ideas to prevail, start thinking about how to present them. Listeners and readers will be more inclined to accept what you are offering if you focus on important strategies, outlined in Figure 10.2 and further discussed throughout the chapter.

wavebreakmedia/Shutterstock.com

Reality Check

Authenticity Wins

"You must be genuinely respectful and authentic—people are very intuitive and will sense any effort to manipulate them. Be sensitive to their frames of reference and speak in a language they will understand."[13]

—Susan Dowell, *psychotherapist*

Applying the 3-x-3 Writing Process to Persuasive Messages

Changing people's views and overcoming their objections are difficult tasks. Pulling it off demands planning and being perceptive. The 3-x-3 writing process provides a helpful structure for laying a foundation for persuasion. Of particular importance here are (a) analyzing the purpose, (b) adapting to the audience, (c) collecting information, and (d) organizing the message.

Analyzing the Purpose: Knowing What You Want to Achieve. The goal of a persuasive message is to convert the receiver to your ideas and motivate action. To accomplish this feat in the age of social media, persuaders seek to build relationships with their audiences. Even so, a message without a clear purpose is doomed. Too often, inexperienced writers reach the end of the first draft of a message before discovering exactly what they want the receiver to think or do.

Meet Chef James Barry. The owner of Wholesome2Go, an organic-food home-delivery service, understands contemporary persuasive techniques. A former personal chef for celebrities, Chef James is convinced that all his customers want to feel special. He knows that to achieve success today, he must cultivate relationships, not just push products.[14] He engages his clients by maintaining a website, tweeting updates, and posting on his Facebook, Instagram, and Pinterest pages. Wholesome2Go also has a YouTube channel. Frequently, Chef James sends persuasive e-mails such as the one shown in Figure 10.3 that spreads holiday cheer and creates buzz about an upcoming special offer.

Adapting to the Audience to Make Your Message Heard. In addition to identifying the purpose of a persuasive message, you also need to concentrate on the receiver. Zorba the Greek wisely observed, "You can knock forever on a deaf man's door." A persuasive message is futile unless it meets the needs of its audience. In a broad sense, you want to show how your request helps the receiver achieve some of life's major goals or fulfills key needs: money, power, comfort, confidence, importance, friends, peace of mind, and recognition, to name a few.

On a more practical level, you want to show how your request solves a problem, achieves a personal or work objective, or just makes life easier for your audience. Chef James is planning his sugar detox offer for early January to help his established customers recover from the excesses of the holiday season. The health benefits and lower prices will appeal to his audience. When adapting persuasive requests to your audience, consider these questions that receivers will very likely be asking themselves:

Why should I?
What's in it for me?
What's in it for you?
Who cares?

Figure 10.2 Effective Persuasion Techniques

Establish credibility

- Show that you are truthful, experienced, and knowledgeable.
- Use others' expert opinions and research to support your position.

Make a reasonable, specific request

- Make your request realistic, doable, and attainable.
- Be clear about your objective. Vague requests are less effective.

Tie facts to benefits

- Line up plausible support such as statistics, reasons, and analogies.
- Convert the supporting facts into specific audience benefits.

Recognize the power of loss

- Show what others stand to lose if they don't agree.
- Know that people dread losing something they already possess.

Expect and overcome resistance

- Anticipate opposition from conflicting beliefs, values, and attitudes.
- Be prepared to counter with well-reasoned arguments and facts.

Share solutions and compromise

- Be flexible and aim for a solution that is acceptable to all parties.
- Listen to people and incorporate their input to create buy-in.

Figure 10.3 How Wholesome2Go Engages the Audience

Chef James The Books

Order Meals
Fill in the intake form to start receiving our delicious, healthy meals.

Questions? Simply reply to this email.

Hi, Irene!

Happy Holidays from all of us at Wholesome2Go! We've got exciting news to share with you for the New Year.

As you know, we are the premier food company providing the most healthy, effective, and sustainable detox in Los Angeles: The 14-day Sugar Control Detox

Normally this detox costs $71 a day for food and nutritional support.

Get ready for **a very special three-day sale of the 14-Day Sugar Control Detox** from our nutritional partner, Eat Naked, happening on January 7th, 8th, and 9th.

You will have the opportunity to have Wholesome2Go provide you with sugar control meals for only $50 a day! **That's over $200 in savings from our normal program.**

Eat Naked hasn't revealed all the details for this super sale yet, so consider this a little taste of what's to come. Learn more here and make sure to sign up to receive this special offer.

This week, enjoy our thank you holiday video from the Wholesome2Go team. We are grateful for all your support.

Much health and happiness this holiday season. Wishing you the best New Year's ever!

Cheers,

Chef James and Team W2G
Wholesome2Go

If you wish to stop receiving our e-mails or to change your options, please go to Manage Your Subscription.
Wholesome2Go, PO Box 801, Culver City, CA 90232

Personalizes the letter to connect with customers

Captures attention with holiday greetings and teaser announcement

Makes it easy to order the meals and share the information on social media

Announces benefit of savings and uses graphic highlighting for emphasis

Builds excitement by not revealing the full news

Invites action to sign up for special offer and view holiday video

Employs *you* view throughout

Provides opt-out statement

Contemporary persuaders understand that their audiences want to feel special and wish to have their needs met. Consumers today are savvy and know that they have many choices. Chef James uses all popular social networks to engage his customers and to build a sincere relationship with them.

Adapting to your audience means learning about audience members and analyzing why they might resist your proposal. It means searching for ways to connect your purpose with their needs. If completed before you begin writing, such analysis goes a long way toward overcoming resistance and achieving your goal.

UPPA/ZUMApress/Newscom

Reality Check

Leaping Into the Future: Dancing to Persuade

Vineet Nayar dramatically turned around his ailing company to triple its annual revenues and earn it the ranking as India's best employer. Once Nayar even danced to a popular Bollywood song to rally his troops and build rapport. He credits his 55,000 employees for the transformation: "How did I persuade them to do it? I spoke the truth as I saw it, offered ideas, told stories, asked questions, and even danced. Most important, I made the leap myself."[15]

—Vineet Nayar, *former CEO of HCL Technologies, author, philanthropist*

Researching and Organizing Persuasive Data. Once you have analyzed the audience and considered how to adapt your message to its needs, you are ready to collect data and organize it. You might brainstorm and prepare cluster diagrams to provide a rough outline of ideas. Chef James studies the competition and sets his sustainable whole food prices lower than most. However, he knows that price is not the first concern of his clients, who love the value and convenience of receiving tasty, healthy meals. Social media networks provide him with feedback. Chef James understands that New Year's resolutions to eat healthy food and lose weight might reduce resistance to his offer.

The next step in a persuasive message is organizing data into a logical sequence. If you are asking for something that you know will be approved, little persuasion is required. In that case, you would make a direct request, as you studied in Chapter 8. However, when you expect resistance or when you need to educate the receiver, the indirect strategy often works better. The classic indirect strategy known by the acronym AIDA works well for many persuasive requests, not just in selling. Figure 10.4 summarizes this four-part strategy for

Figure 10.4 **The AIDA Strategy for Persuasive Messages**

STRATEGY	CONTENT	SECTION
Attention	Captures attention, creates awareness, makes a sales proposition, prompts audience to read on	Opening
Interest	Describes central selling points, focuses not on features of product/service but on benefits relevant to the reader's needs	Body
Desire	Reduces resistance, reassures the reader, elicits the desire for ownership, motivates action	Body
Action	Offers an incentive or gift, limits the offer, sets a deadline, makes it easy for the reader to respond, closes the sale	Closing

From Guffey/Loewy, Essentials of Business Communication (with www.meguffey.com Printed Access Card), 9E. © 2013 Cengage Learning.

overcoming resistance and crafting successful persuasive messages. Chef James uses AIDA to create goodwill as he persuades his readers to view his cheerful holiday video and to consider an upcoming discounted offer.

LEARNING OUTCOME 2

Describe the traditional four-part AIDA strategy for creating successful persuasive messages, and apply the four elements to draft effective and ethical business messages.

Blending Four Major Elements in Successful Persuasive Messages

Although AIDA, the indirect strategy, appears to contain separate steps, successful persuasive messages actually blend the four steps into a seamless whole. Also, the sequence of the steps may change depending on the situation and the emphasis. Regardless of where they are placed, the key elements in persuasive requests are (a) gaining your audience's attention, (b) building interest by convincing your audience that your proposal is worthy, (c) eliciting desire for the offer and reducing resistance, and (d) prompting action. Figure 10.5 summarizes the tools writers use when following the AIDA strategy.

Gaining Attention in Persuasive Messages

To grab attention, the opening statement in a persuasive request should be brief, relevant, and engaging. When only mild persuasion is necessary, the opener can be low-key and factual. If, however, your request is substantial and you anticipate strong resistance, provide a thoughtful, provocative opening. Following are some examples.

- **Problem description.** In a recommendation to hire temporary employees: *Last month legal division staff members were forced to work 120 overtime hours, costing us $6,000 and causing considerable employee unhappiness.* With this opener you have presented a capsule of the problem your proposal will help solve.
- **Unexpected statement.** In a memo to encourage employees to attend an optional sensitivity seminar: *Men and women draw the line at decidedly different places in identifying what behavior constitutes sexual harassment.* Note how this opener gets readers thinking immediately.
- **Reader benefit.** In a letter promoting Clear Card, a service that helps employees make credit card purchases without paying interest: *The average employee carries nearly $13,000 in revolving debt and pays $2,800 in interest and late fees. The Clear Card charges zero percent interest.* Employers immediately see the benefit of this offer to employees.

Figure 10.5 **Applying the Four-Part AIDA Strategy to Persuasive Documents**

Attention	Interest	Desire	Action
Summary of problem	Facts, figures	Reduce resistance	Describe specific request
Unexpected statement	Expert opinions	Anticipate objections	Sound confident
Reader benefit	Examples	Offer counterarguments	Make action easy to take
Compliment	Specific details	Use *What if?* scenarios	Offer incentive or gift
Related facts	Direct benefits	Demonstrate competence	Don't provide excuses
Stimulating question	Indirect benefits	Show value of proposal	Repeat main benefits

- **Compliment.** In a letter inviting a business executive to speak: *Because our members admire your success and value your managerial expertise, they want you to be our speaker.* In offering praise or compliments, however, be careful to avoid obvious flattery. Be sincere and don't exaggerate.
- **Related facts.** In a message to company executives who are considering restricting cell phone use by employee drivers: *A recent study revealed that employers pay an average of $16,500 each time an employee is in a traffic accident.* This relevant fact sets the scene for the interest-building section that follows.
- **Stimulating question.** In a plea for funds to support environmental causes: *What do golden tortoise beetles, bark spiders, flounders, and Arctic foxes have in common?* Readers will be curious to find the answer to this intriguing question. (They all change color depending on their surroundings.)

Building Interest in Persuasive Messages

After capturing attention, a persuasive request must retain that attention and convince the audience that the request is reasonable. To justify your request, be prepared to invest in a few paragraphs of explanation. Persuasive requests are likely to be longer than direct requests because the audience must be convinced rather than simply instructed. You can build interest and conviction through the use of the following:

- Facts, statistics
- Examples
- Expert opinion
- Specific details
- Direct benefits
- Indirect benefits

Showing how your request can benefit the audience directly or indirectly is a key factor in persuasion. If you were asking alumni to contribute money to a college foundation, for example, you might promote *direct benefits* such as listing the donor's name in the college magazine or sending a sweatshirt with the college logo. Another direct benefit is a tax write-off for the contribution. An *indirect benefit* might be feeling good about "paying it forward," thus helping the college and knowing that students will benefit from the gift. Nearly all charities rely in large part on indirect benefits to promote their causes.

Helga Esteb/Shutterstock.com

Reality Check

Feed a Cookie to the Monster

When Terry Tietzen, a developer of customer loyalty software, has a big idea that meets resistance, he imagines that the resistance is a monster. He must feed the monster cookies so that it will start liking the idea and not feel overwhelmed. "So I have to break it down into smaller steps," he explains. His feed-the-monster-a-cookie approach coaxes people to buy in to a new idea with little nibbles.[16]

—Terry Tietzen, *founder and CEO, Edatanetworks*

Eliciting Desire and Reducing Resistance in Persuasive Requests

The best persuasive requests anticipate audience resistance. How will the receiver object to the request? When brainstorming, try *What if?* scenarios. Let's say you want to convince management that the employees' cafeteria should switch from disposable to ceramic dishes. What if managers say the change is too expensive? What if they argue that they recycle paper and plastic? What if they contend that ceramic dishes would increase cafeteria labor and energy costs? What if they protest that ceramic is less hygienic? For each of these *What if?* scenarios, you need a counterargument.

Countering resistance and prompting desire in the receiver is important, but you must do it with finesse (*Although ceramic dishes cost more at first, they actually save money over time*). You can minimize objections by presenting your counterarguments in sentences that emphasize benefits: *Ceramic dishes may require a little more effort in cleaning, but they bring warmth and graciousness to meals. Most important, they help save the environment by requiring fewer resources and eliminating waste.* However, don't dwell on counterarguments, thus making them overly important. Finally, avoid bringing up outlandish objections that may never have occurred to the receiver in the first place.

Another factor that reduces resistance and elicits desire is credibility. Receivers are less resistant if your request is reasonable and if you are believable. When the receiver does not know you, you may have to establish your expertise, refer to your credentials, or demonstrate your competence. Even when you are known, you may have to establish your knowledge in a given area. If you are asking your manager for a flashy tablet, you might have to establish your credibility by providing information from reputable sources about the latest tablet models, their portability, memory, cost, battery life, and so on.

Some charities establish their credibility by displaying on their stationery the names of famous people who serve on their boards. The credibility of speakers making presentations is usually outlined by someone who introduces them.

Prompting Action in Persuasive Messages

After gaining attention, building interest, eliciting desire, and reducing resistance, you will want to inspire the newly receptive audience to act. Knowing exactly what action you favor before you start to write enables you to point your arguments toward this important final paragraph. Here you make your recommendation as specifically and confidently as possible—without seeming pushy. A proposal from one manager to another might conclude with, *So that we can begin using the employment assessment tests by May 1, please send a return e-mail immediately.* In making a request, don't sound apologetic (*I'm sorry to have to ask you this, but . . .*), and don't supply excuses (*If you can spare the time, . . .*). Compare the following persuasive e-mail closings recommending training seminars in communication skills.

Too General

We are certain we can develop a series of training sessions that will improve the communication skills of your employees.

Too Timid

If you agree that our training proposal has merit, perhaps we could begin the series in June.

Too Pushy

Because we are convinced that you will want to begin improving the skills of your employees immediately, we have scheduled your series to begin in June.

Effective

You will see significant improvement in the communication skills of your employees. Please call me at 469-439-2201 by May 1 to give your approval so that training sessions may start in June, right after the completion of your internal restructuring.

Note how the last opening suggests a specific and easy-to-follow action. It also provides a deadline and a reason for that date.

Figure 10.6 exemplifies the AIDA persuasive strategy just discussed. Writing for her research firm, Danuta Hajek seeks to persuade other companies to complete a questionnaire revealing

Figure 10.6 **Persuasive Request**

1 Prewriting

Analyze: The purpose of this letter is to persuade the reader to complete and return a questionnaire.

Anticipate: Although the reader is busy, he may respond to appeals to his professionalism and to his need for salary data in his own business.

Adapt: Because the reader may be uninterested at first and require persuasion, use the indirect strategy.

2 Drafting

Research: Study the receiver's business and find ways to relate this request to company success.

Organize: Gain attention by opening with relevant questions. Build interest by showing how the reader's compliance will help his company and others. Reduce resistance by promising confidentiality and offering free data.

Draft: Prepare a first draft with the intention to revise.

3 Revising

Edit: Revise to show direct and indirect benefits more clearly. Make sure the message is as concise as possible.

Proofread: In the first sentence, spell out *percent* rather than using the symbol. Check the use of all question marks. Start all lines at the left for a block-style letter.

Evaluate: Will this letter convince the reader to complete and return the questionnaire?

HERRON & HOGAN RESEARCH
435 N Tampa Street, Tampa, FL 33602, www.hhresearch.com
PH 813.878.2300
FAX 813.878.4359

May 18, 2018

Mr. Gregory S. Janssen
Mellon Wealth Management
444 1st Street S, Suite 450
St. Petersburg, FL 33701

Dear Mr. Janssen:

Would you like access to more reliable salary data than Glassdoor has to offer? Has your company ever lost a valued employee to another organization that offered 20 percent more in salary for the same position?

To remain competitive in hiring and to retain qualified workers, companies rely on survey data showing current salaries. Herron & Hogan Research has been collecting business data for a quarter century and has been honored by the American Management Association for its accurate data. We need your help in collecting salary data for today's workers. Information from the enclosed questionnaire will supply companies like yours with such data.

Your information, of course, will be treated confidentially. The questionnaire takes but a few moments to complete, and it can provide substantial dividends for professional organizations just like yours that need comparative salary data.

To show our gratitude for your participation, we will send you free comprehensive salary surveys for your industry and your metropolitan area. Not only will you find basic salaries, but you will also learn about bonus and incentive plans, special pay differentials, expense reimbursements, and perquisites such as a company car and credit card.

Comparative salary data are impossible to provide without the support of professionals like you. Please complete the questionnaire and return it in the prepaid envelope before June 1, our spring deadline. Participating in this survey means that you will no longer be in the dark about how much your employees earn compared with others in your industry.

Sincerely yours,

HERRON & HOGAN RESEARCH

Danuta Hajek

Danuta Hajek
Director, Survey Research

Enclosures

Left annotations:
- Poses two short questions related to the reader
- Presents reader benefit tied to request explanation; establishes credibility
- Anticipates and counters resistance to confidentiality and time/effort objections
- Offers free salary data as a direct benefit
- Provides deadline and a final benefit to prompt action

Right annotations:
- Gains attention
- Builds interest
- Elicits desire and reduces resistance
- Appeals to professionalism, an indirect benefit
- Motivates action

salary data. To most organizations, salary information is strictly confidential. What can she do to convince strangers to part with such private information?

To gain attention, Danuta poses two short questions that spotlight the need for salary information. To build interest and establish trust, she states that Herron & Hogan Research has been collecting business data for a quarter century and has received awards. She ties her reasonable request to audience benefits.

Being an Ethical Persuader

A persuader is effective only when he or she is believable. If receivers suspect that they are being manipulated or misled, or if they find any part of the argument untruthful, the total argument fails. Fudging on the facts, exaggerating a point, omitting something crucial, or providing deceptive emphasis may seem tempting to some business communicators, but such schemes usually backfire. Consider the case of a manager who sought to persuade employees to accept a change in insurance benefits. His memo emphasized a small perk (easier handling of claims) but de-emphasized a major reduction in total coverage. Some readers missed the main point—as the manager intended. Others recognized the deception, however, and before long the manager's credibility was lost.

Persuasion becomes unethical when facts are distorted, overlooked, or manipulated with an intent to deceive. Applied to language that manipulates, such distortion and twisting of the meaning is called *doublespeak*. Of course, persuaders naturally want to put forth their strongest case. However, that argument must be based on truth, objectivity, and fairness.

Consumers complain in blogs, tweets, and online posts about businesses resorting to aggressive sales tactics, manipulation, and downright lies.[17] Many such complaints point to car buying. The Federal Trade Commission recently stepped in to prevent two Las Vegas–area car dealers from falsely promising tempting purchase and lease offers that were revoked in small-print disclaimers.[18] Honest business communicators would not sacrifice their good reputation for short-term gain. Once lost, credibility is difficult to regain.

Rido/Shutterstock.com

Reality Check

Ethical Persuaders Embrace Clear Language

"Talk show pundits and boardroom hotshots are fond of using obscure terms and acronyms to signal their sophistication, but in fact by doing so they often lose meaning. Confusion serves no one except those who intend to deceive."[19]

—Greg Satell, *consultant and public speaker*

LEARNING OUTCOME 3

Craft persuasive messages that request actions, make claims, and deliver complaints.

Writing Persuasive Requests, Making Claims, and Delivering Complaints

Convincing someone to change a belief or to perform an action when that person is reluctant requires planning and skill—and sometimes a little luck. A written, rather than face-to-face, request may require more preparation but can be more effective. For example, you may ask a businessperson to make a presentation to your club. You might ask a company to encourage its employees to participate in a charity drive. Another form of persuasion involves claims or complaints. All of these messages require skill in persuasion. Persuasion is often more precise and controlled when you can think through your purpose and prepare a thoughtful message in writing. AIDA, the indirect strategy, gives you an effective structure.

Writing Persuasive Requests

Persuading someone to do something that largely benefits you may not be the easiest task. Fortunately, many individuals and companies are willing to grant requests for time, money, information, cooperation, and special privileges. They comply for a variety of reasons. They may just happen to be interested in your project, or they may see goodwill potential for themselves. Professionals sometimes feel obligated to contribute their time or expertise to "give back." Often, though, businesses and individuals comply because they see that others will benefit from the request.

The persuasive request shown in Figure 10.6 incorporates many of the techniques that are effective in persuasion: establishing credibility, making a reasonable and precise request, tying facts to benefits, and eliciting desire while overcoming resistance in the receiver.

Writing Persuasive Claims

Persuasive claims may involve damaged products, mistaken billing, inaccurate shipments, warranty problems, limited return policies, insurance snafus, faulty merchandise, and so on. Generally, the direct strategy is best for requesting straightforward adjustments (see Chapter 8). When you feel your request is justified and will be granted, the direct strategy is most efficient. However, if a past request has been refused or ignored, or if you anticipate reluctance, then the indirect strategy is appropriate.

Developing a Logical Persuasive Argument. Strive for logical development in a claim message. You might open with sincere praise, an objective statement of the problem, a point of agreement, or a quick review of what you have done to resolve the problem. Then you can explain precisely what happened or why your claim is legitimate. Don't provide a blow-by-blow chronology of details; just hit the highlights. Be sure to enclose copies of relevant invoices, shipping orders, warranties, and payments. Close with a clear statement of what you want done: a refund, replacement, credit to your account, or other action. Be sure to think through the possibilities and make your request reasonable.

Using a Moderate Tone. The tone of your message is important. Don't suggest that the receiver intentionally deceived you or intentionally created the problem. Rather, appeal to the receiver's sense of responsibility and pride in the company's good name. Calmly express your disappointment in view of your high expectations of the product and of the company. Communicating your feelings without rancor is often your strongest appeal.

Composing Effective Complaints

As their name suggests, complaints deliver bad news. Some complaint messages just vent anger. However, if the goal is to change something (and why bother to write except to motivate change?), then persuasion is necessary. An effective claim message makes a reasonable and valid request, presents a logical case with clear facts, and has a moderate tone. Anger and emotion are not effective persuaders.

Denise Blanchard's e-mail, shown in Figure 10.7, follows the persuasive pattern as she seeks credit for two VoIP (voice over Internet protocol) office systems. Actually, she was quite upset because her company was counting on these new Internet systems to reduce its phone bills. Instead, the handsets produced so much static that incoming and outgoing calls were all but impossible to hear. The full setup also proved to be too complex for the small business.

What's more, Denise was frustrated that the Return Merchandise Authorization form she filled out at the company's website seemed to sink into a dark hole in cyberspace. She had reason to be angry! However, she resolved to use a moderate tone in writing her complaint e-mail because she knew that a calm, unemotional tone would be more effective. She opted for a positive opening, a well-documented claim, and a request for specific action in the closing.

Ethics Check

Complaint Bullying

As any salesperson will tell you, some customers seem to believe that if they vent their anger and make a scene at the store, bullying and intimidating a fearful sales representative, they are more likely to get their way. Indeed, some sales staff may cave in, wishing to defuse the ruckus. Is it fair to resort to such tactics to get what one wants? Does the end justify the means?

Figure 10.7 Persuasive Claim (Complaint) E-Mail

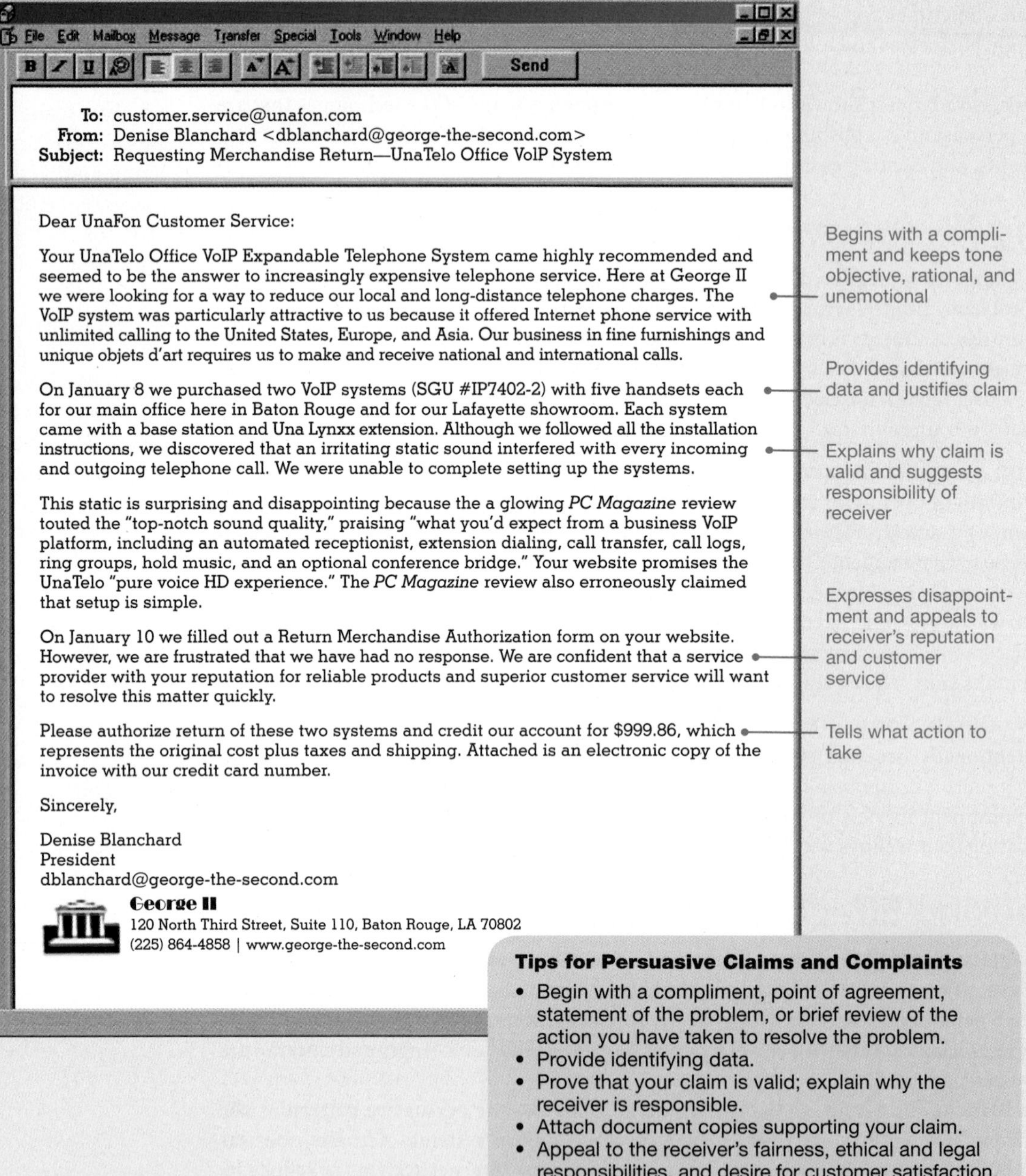

To: customer.service@unafon.com
From: Denise Blanchard <dblanchard@george-the-second.com>
Subject: Requesting Merchandise Return—UnaTelo Office VoIP System

Dear UnaFon Customer Service:

Your UnaTelo Office VoIP Expandable Telephone System came highly recommended and seemed to be the answer to increasingly expensive telephone service. Here at George II we were looking for a way to reduce our local and long-distance telephone charges. The VoIP system was particularly attractive to us because it offered Internet phone service with unlimited calling to the United States, Europe, and Asia. Our business in fine furnishings and unique objets d'art requires us to make and receive national and international calls.

On January 8 we purchased two VoIP systems (SGU #IP7402-2) with five handsets each for our main office here in Baton Rouge and for our Lafayette showroom. Each system came with a base station and Una Lynxx extension. Although we followed all the installation instructions, we discovered that an irritating static sound interfered with every incoming and outgoing telephone call. We were unable to complete setting up the systems.

This static is surprising and disappointing because the a glowing *PC Magazine* review touted the "top-notch sound quality," praising "what you'd expect from a business VoIP platform, including an automated receptionist, extension dialing, call transfer, call logs, ring groups, hold music, and an optional conference bridge." Your website promises the UnaTelo "pure voice HD experience." The *PC Magazine* review also erroneously claimed that setup is simple.

On January 10 we filled out a Return Merchandise Authorization form on your website. However, we are frustrated that we have had no response. We are confident that a service provider with your reputation for reliable products and superior customer service will want to resolve this matter quickly.

Please authorize return of these two systems and credit our account for $999.86, which represents the original cost plus taxes and shipping. Attached is an electronic copy of the invoice with our credit card number.

Sincerely,

Denise Blanchard
President
dblanchard@george-the-second.com

George II
120 North Third Street, Suite 110, Baton Rouge, LA 70802
(225) 864-4858 | www.george-the-second.com

File Edit Mailbox Message Transfer Special Tools Window Help
Send
Begins with a compliment and keeps tone objective, rational, and unemotional
Provides identifying data and justifies claim
Explains why claim is valid and suggests responsibility of receiver
Expresses disappointment and appeals to receiver's reputation and customer service
Tells what action to take

Tips for Persuasive Claims and Complaints

- Begin with a compliment, point of agreement, statement of the problem, or brief review of the action you have taken to resolve the problem.
- Provide identifying data.
- Prove that your claim is valid; explain why the receiver is responsible.
- Attach document copies supporting your claim.
- Appeal to the receiver's fairness, ethical and legal responsibilities, and desire for customer satisfaction.
- Describe your feelings and your disappointment.
- Avoid sounding angry, emotional, or irrational.
- Close by telling exactly what you want done.

Using the AIDA Strategy to Request Actions, Make Claims, and Deliver Complaints

Prewrite

- Determine your purpose. Know exactly what you want to achieve.
- Anticipate the reaction of your audience. Remember that the receiver is thinking, *Why should I? What's in it for me? What's in it for you? Who cares?*

Gain Attention

- Use the indirect strategy rather than blurting out the request immediately.
- Begin with a problem description, unexpected statement, reader benefit, compliment, related facts, or stimulating question to grab attention.

Build Interest

- Convince the audience that your request is reasonable.
- Develop interest by using facts, statistics, examples, testimonials, and specific details.
- Establish your credibility, if necessary, by explaining your background and expertise. Use testimonials, expert opinion, or research if necessary.
- Support your request by tying facts to direct benefits (increased profits, more efficient operations, better customer relations, money savings, a returned favor) or indirect benefits (improving the community, giving back to the profession, helping the environment).
- In claims and complaints, be objective but prove the validity of your request.

Elicit Desire and Reduce Resistance

- Anticipate objections to your request by using *What if?* scenarios and provide compelling counterarguments.
- Demonstrate credibility and competence.
- In claims and complaints, use a moderate, unemotional tone.

Motivate Action

- Make a precise request that spells out exactly what you want done. Add a deadline if necessary.
- Repeat a key benefit, provide additional details, or offer an incentive. Express appreciation.
- Be confident without seeming pushy.

Writing Persuasive Messages in Digital Age Organizations

LEARNING OUTCOME 4

Understand interpersonal persuasion at work, and write persuasive messages within organizations.

As noted earlier, the lines of authority are blurry in information age workplaces, and the roles of executives are changing. Technology has empowered rank-and-file employees who can turn to their companies' intranets and don't need their managers to be information providers—formerly a crucial managerial role. "Instead of being controllers or hoarders of knowledge," one top executive said, most contemporary managers "viewed themselves as collaborators and mentors, trusted for their experience—not their gigabytes of memory."[20]

As a recent company memo shows, Starbucks CEO Howard Schultz customarily calls his employees *partners*, suggesting equality, at least in attitude.[21] Amazon-owned Internet shoe seller Zappos is experimenting with *holacracy*, a boss-less self-management experiment. Zappos has taken the flattening of hierarchies to an extreme by replacing teams and managers with fully empowered employee *circles*.[22] The jury is still out on whether holacracy is a success. Nevertheless, at tech company Evernote, the structure is open and flat, too. "Nobody has an office. In fact, there are no perks that are signs of seniority. Obviously, there are differences in compensation, but there are no status symbols," says CEO Phil Libin.[23]

This shift in authority is affecting the writing strategies and the tone of workplace persuasive messages. You may still want to be indirect if you hope to persuade your boss to do something he or she will be reluctant to do; however, your boss, in turn, will be less likely to rely on the power of position and just issue commands. Rather, today's executives increasingly bank on persuasion to achieve buy-in from subordinates.[24]

This section focuses on messages flowing downward and upward within organizations. Horizontal messages exchanged among coworkers resemble those discussed earlier in requesting actions.

© Frank Sonnenberg

Reality Check

Leading With Character

"Leaders with character are highly effective. They have no need to pull rank or resort to command and control to get results. Instead, they're effective because they're knowledgeable, admired, trusted, and respected. This helps them secure buy-in automatically, without requiring egregious rules or strong oversight designed to force compliance."[25]

—Frank Sonnenberg, *author of* Follow Your Conscience

Persuading Employees: Messages Flowing Downward

Employees traditionally expect to be directed in how to perform their jobs; therefore, instructions or directives moving downward from superiors to subordinates usually required little persuasion. Messages such as information about procedures, equipment, or customer service still use the direct strategy, with the purpose immediately stated.

However, employees are sometimes asked to volunteer for projects such as tutoring disadvantaged children or helping at homeless shelters. Some organizations encourage employees to join programs to stop smoking, lose weight, or start exercising. Organizations may ask employees to participate in capacities outside their work roles—such as spending their free time volunteering for charity projects. In such cases, the four-part indirect AIDA strategy provides a helpful structure.

Because many executives today rely on buy-in instead of exercising raw power, messages flowing downward require attention to tone. Warm words and a conversational tone convey a caring attitude. Persuasive requests coming from trusted superiors are more likely to be accepted than requests from dictatorial executives who rely on threats and punishments to secure compliance. The proverbial carrot has always been more persuasive than the stick. Because the words *should* and *must* sometimes convey a negative tone, be careful in using them.

Figure 10.8 shows a memo e-mailed by Gabriela Marrera, director of HR Staffing and Training at a large bank. Her goal is to persuade employees to participate in HandsOn Miami Day, a fund-raising and community service event that the bank sponsors. In addition to volunteering their services for a day, employees also have to pay $30 to register! You can see that this is no small persuasion task for Gabriela.

Gabriela decides to follow the AIDA four-part indirect strategy beginning with gaining attention. Notice, for example, that she strives to capture attention by describing specific benefits of volunteering in Miami. The second paragraph of this persuasive message builds interest by listing examples of what volunteers have accomplished during previous HandsOn Miami events. To reduce resistance, the third paragraph explains why the $30 fee makes sense. To motivate action in the closing, Gabriela saved a strong indirect benefit. The bank will chip in $30 for every employee who volunteers before the deadline. This significant indirect benefit along with the direct benefits of having fun and joining colleagues in a community activity combine to create a strong persuasive message.

Persuading the Boss: Messages Flowing Upward

Convincing management to adopt a procedure or invest in a product or new equipment requires skillful communication. Managers are just as resistant to change as others are. Providing facts, figures, and evidence is critical when submitting a recommendation to your boss. When selling an idea to management, strive to make a strong dollars-and-cents case.[26] A request that emphasizes how the proposal saves money or benefits the business is more persuasive than one that simply announces a good deal or tells how a plan works.

Figure 10.8 Persuasive Organizational Message Flowing Downward

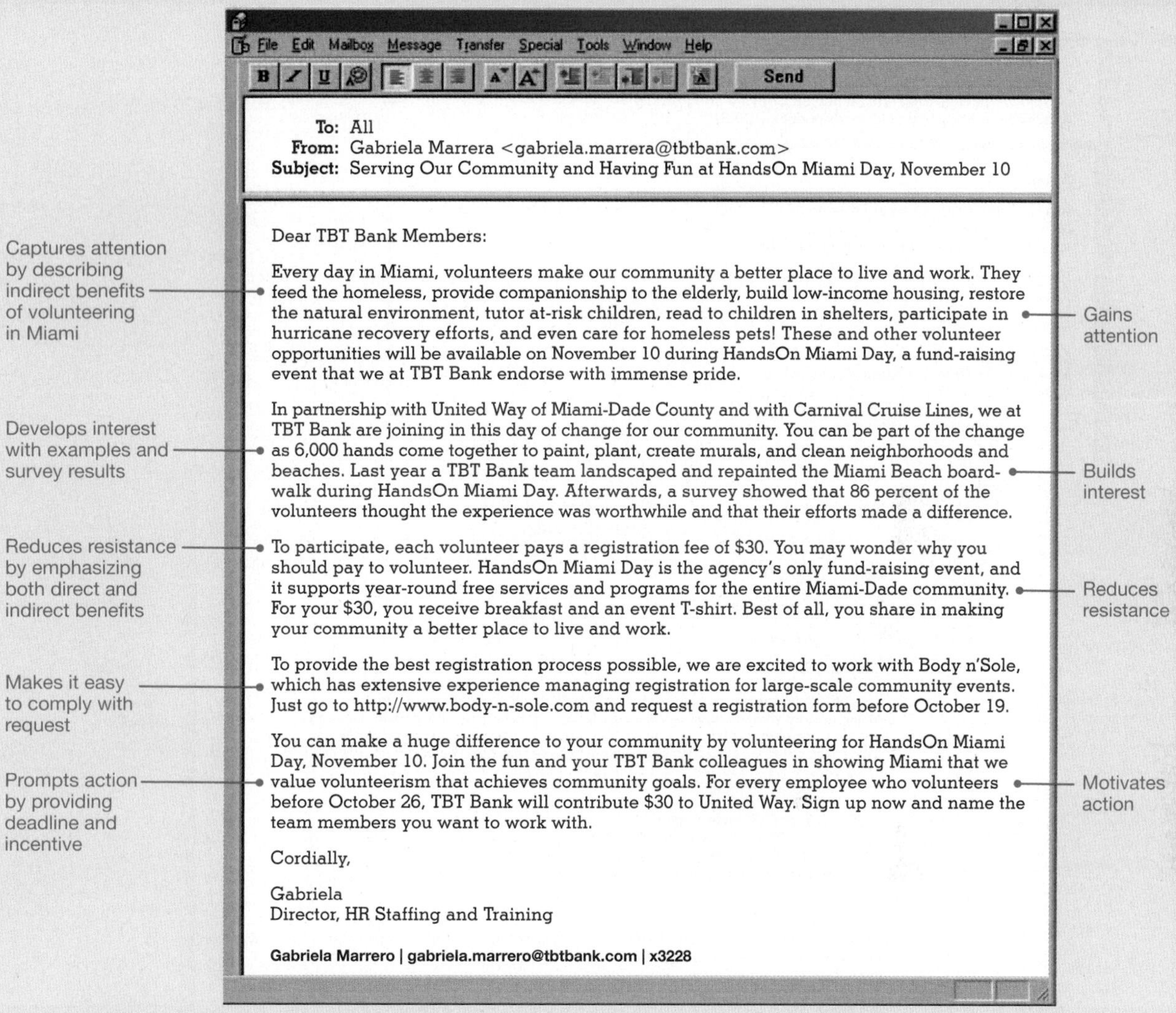

File Edit Mailbox Message Transfer Special Tools Window Help

Send

To: All
From: Gabriela Marrera <gabriela.marrera@tbtbank.com>
Subject: Serving Our Community and Having Fun at HandsOn Miami Day, November 10

Dear TBT Bank Members:

Every day in Miami, volunteers make our community a better place to live and work. They feed the homeless, provide companionship to the elderly, build low-income housing, restore the natural environment, tutor at-risk children, read to children in shelters, participate in hurricane recovery efforts, and even care for homeless pets! These and other volunteer opportunities will be available on November 10 during HandsOn Miami Day, a fund-raising event that we at TBT Bank endorse with immense pride.

Captures attention by describing indirect benefits of volunteering in Miami

Gains attention

In partnership with United Way of Miami-Dade County and with Carnival Cruise Lines, we at TBT Bank are joining in this day of change for our community. You can be part of the change as 6,000 hands come together to paint, plant, create murals, and clean neighborhoods and beaches. Last year a TBT Bank team landscaped and repainted the Miami Beach boardwalk during HandsOn Miami Day. Afterwards, a survey showed that 86 percent of the volunteers thought the experience was worthwhile and that their efforts made a difference.

Develops interest with examples and survey results

Builds interest

To participate, each volunteer pays a registration fee of $30. You may wonder why you should pay to volunteer. HandsOn Miami Day is the agency's only fund-raising event, and it supports year-round free services and programs for the entire Miami-Dade community. For your $30, you receive breakfast and an event T-shirt. Best of all, you share in making your community a better place to live and work.

Reduces resistance by emphasizing both direct and indirect benefits

Reduces resistance

To provide the best registration process possible, we are excited to work with Body n'Sole, which has extensive experience managing registration for large-scale community events. Just go to http://www.body-n-sole.com and request a registration form before October 19.

Makes it easy to comply with request

You can make a huge difference to your community by volunteering for HandsOn Miami Day, November 10. Join the fun and your TBT Bank colleagues in showing Miami that we value volunteerism that achieves community goals. For every employee who volunteers before October 26, TBT Bank will contribute $30 to United Way. Sign up now and name the team members you want to work with.

Prompts action by providing deadline and incentive

Motivates action

Cordially,

Gabriela
Director, HR Staffing and Training

Gabriela Marrero | gabriela.marrero@tbtbank.com | x3228

In describing an idea to your boss, state it confidently and fairly. Don't undermine your suggestions with statements such as *This may sound crazy* or *I know we tried this once before but* . . . . Show that you have thought through the suggestion by describing the risks involved as well as the potential benefits. You may wonder whether you should even mention the downside of a suggestion. Most bosses will be relieved and impressed to know that you have considered the risks as well as the benefits to a proposal.[27] Two-sided arguments are generally more persuasive because they make you sound credible and fair. Presenting only one side of a proposal reduces its effectiveness because such a proposal seems biased, subjective, and flawed.

Persuasive messages traveling upward require a special sensitivity to tone. When asking superiors to change views or take action, use phrases such as *we suggest* and *we recommend* rather than *you must* and *we should.* Avoid sounding pushy or argumentative. Strive for a conversational, yet professional tone that conveys warmth, competence, and confidence.

When Marketing Assistant Leonard Oliver wanted his boss to authorize the purchase of a multifunction color laser copier, he knew he had to be persuasive. His memo, shown in Figure 10.9, illustrates an effective approach.

Figure 10.9 Persuasive Message Flowing Upward

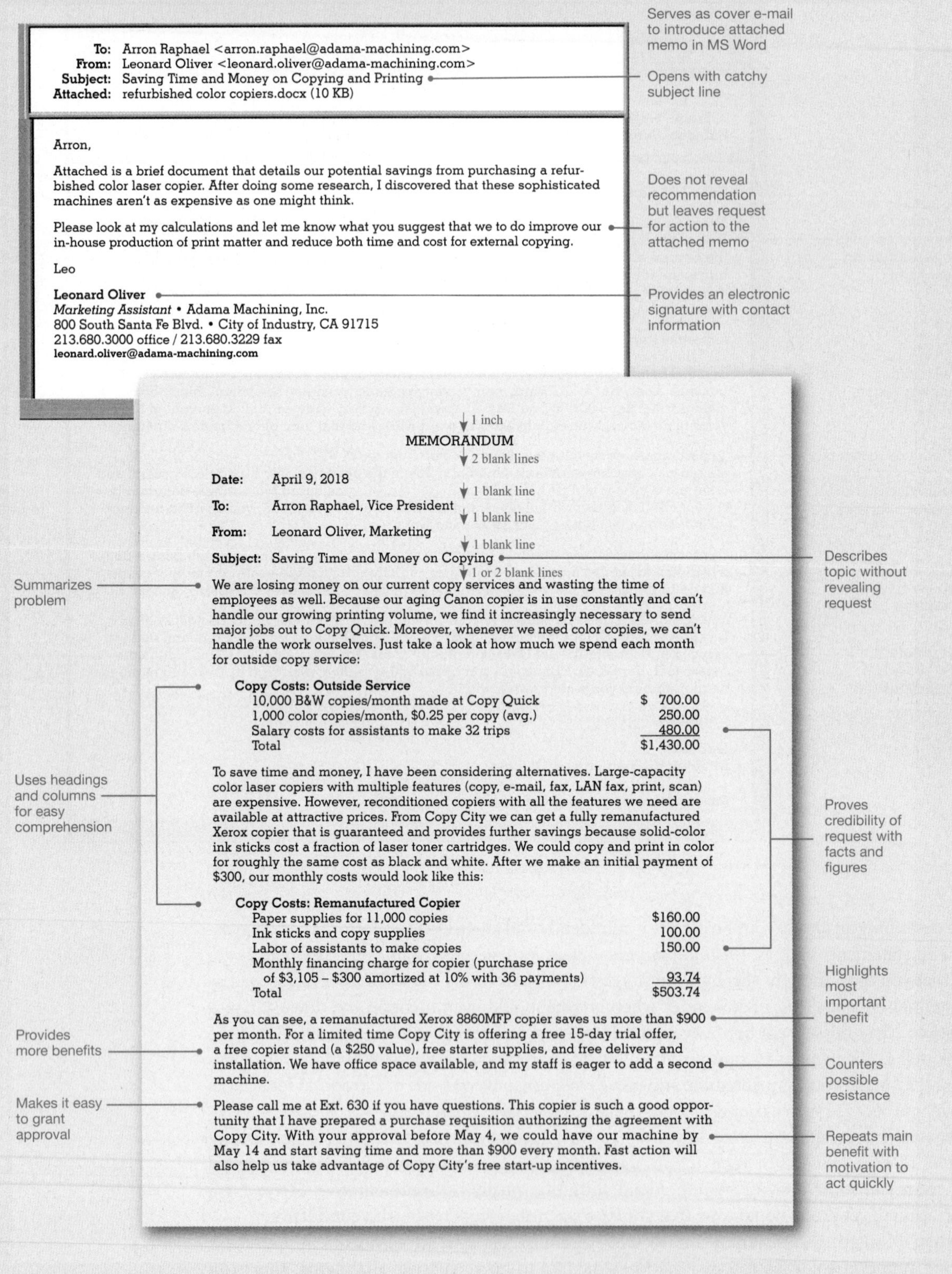

To: Arron Raphael <arron.raphael@adama-machining.com>
From: Leonard Oliver <leonard.oliver@adama-machining.com>
Subject: Saving Time and Money on Copying and Printing
Attached: refurbished color copiers.docx (10 KB)

Arron,

Attached is a brief document that details our potential savings from purchasing a refurbished color laser copier. After doing some research, I discovered that these sophisticated machines aren't as expensive as one might think.

Please look at my calculations and let me know what you suggest that we to do improve our in-house production of print matter and reduce both time and cost for external copying.

Leo

Leonard Oliver
Marketing Assistant • Adama Machining, Inc.
800 South Santa Fe Blvd. • City of Industry, CA 91715
213.680.3000 office / 213.680.3229 fax
leonard.oliver@adama-machining.com

1 inch

MEMORANDUM

2 blank lines

Date: April 9, 2018

1 blank line

To: Arron Raphael, Vice President

1 blank line

From: Leonard Oliver, Marketing

1 blank line

Subject: Saving Time and Money on Copying

1 or 2 blank lines

We are losing money on our current copy services and wasting the time of employees as well. Because our aging Canon copier is in use constantly and can't handle our growing printing volume, we find it increasingly necessary to send major jobs out to Copy Quick. Moreover, whenever we need color copies, we can't handle the work ourselves. Just take a look at how much we spend each month for outside copy service:

Copy Costs: Outside Service

10,000 B&W copies/month made at Copy Quick	$ 700.00
1,000 color copies/month, $0.25 per copy (avg.)	250.00
Salary costs for assistants to make 32 trips	480.00
Total	$1,430.00

To save time and money, I have been considering alternatives. Large-capacity color laser copiers with multiple features (copy, e-mail, fax, LAN fax, print, scan) are expensive. However, reconditioned copiers with all the features we need are available at attractive prices. From Copy City we can get a fully remanufactured Xerox copier that is guaranteed and provides further savings because solid-color ink sticks cost a fraction of laser toner cartridges. We could copy and print in color for roughly the same cost as black and white. After we make an initial payment of $300, our monthly costs would look like this:

Copy Costs: Remanufactured Copier

Paper supplies for 11,000 copies	$160.00
Ink sticks and copy supplies	100.00
Labor of assistants to make copies	150.00
Monthly financing charge for copier (purchase price of $3,105 – $300 amortized at 10% with 36 payments)	93.74
Total	$503.74

As you can see, a remanufactured Xerox 8860MFP copier saves us more than $900 per month. For a limited time Copy City is offering a free 15-day trial offer, a free copier stand (a $250 value), free starter supplies, and free delivery and installation. We have office space available, and my staff is eager to add a second machine.

Please call me at Ext. 630 if you have questions. This copier is such a good opportunity that I have prepared a purchase requisition authorizing the agreement with Copy City. With your approval before May 4, we could have our machine by May 14 and start saving time and more than $900 every month. Fast action will also help us take advantage of Copy City's free start-up incentives.

Serves as cover e-mail to introduce attached memo in MS Word
Opens with catchy subject line
Does not reveal recommendation but leaves request for action to the attached memo
Provides an electronic signature with contact information
Describes topic without revealing request
Summarizes problem
Uses headings and columns for easy comprehension
Proves credibility of request with facts and figures
Highlights most important benefit
Provides more benefits
Counters possible resistance
Makes it easy to grant approval
Repeats main benefit with motivation to act quickly

Notice that Leo's memo isn't short. A successful persuasive message typically takes more space than a direct message because proving a case requires evidence. In the end, Leo chose to send his memo as an e-mail attachment accompanied by a polite, short e-mail because he wanted to keep the document format in MS Word intact. He also felt that the message was too long to paste into his e-mail program. The subject line announces the purpose of the message but without disclosing the actual request. The strength of the persuasive document in Figure 10.9 is in the clear presentation of comparison figures showing how much money the company can save by purchasing a remanufactured copier.

Creating Effective Sales Messages in Print and Online

LEARNING OUTCOME 5

Create effective and ethical direct-mail and e-mail sales messages.

The best sales messages, whether delivered by direct mail or by e-mail, have much in common. They use persuasion to promote specific products and services. In our coverage we are most concerned with sales messages delivered by postal mail or by e-mail. In this section we look at how to apply the 3-x-3 writing process to sales messages. We also present techniques developed by experts to draft effective sales messages, in print and online.

wavebreakmedia/Shutterstock.com

Reality Check

When Selling, Keep It Real

"My advice to salespeople is this: represent products or services you genuinely respect; be well informed about the design and benefits of the products or service; be curious and sensitive towards the customer's needs; and if appropriate, use your knowledge to help the customer take concrete steps towards understanding and purchasing the product or service."[28]

—Lisa Robin Marks, *former real estate developer, investor, environmental activist*

Applying the 3-x-3 Writing Process to Sales Messages

Marketing professionals analyze and perfect every aspect of a sales message to encourage consumers to read and act on the message. Like the experts, you will want to pay close attention to analysis and adaptation before writing the actual message.

Analyzing the Product. Prior to sitting down to write a sales message promoting a product, you must study the item carefully. What can you learn about its design, construction, raw materials, and manufacturing process? What can you learn about its ease of use, efficiency, durability, and applications? Be sure to consider warranties, service, price, premiums, exclusivity, and special appeals. At the same time, evaluate the competition so that you can compare your product's strengths with the competitor's weaknesses.

Now you are ready to identify your central selling point, the main theme of your appeal. In one of its marketing campaigns, the U.S. Marine Corps chose "chaos" as its central selling point. Dramatic footage focuses on Marines providing humanitarian aid in unstable regions around the world because many millennials find such service appealing.[29] In its latest campaign, the Corps is also targeting its core audience: "This advertisement is evolutionary for Marine Corps advertising because it depicts a more modern, Millennial-driven interpretation of America," said Master Sgt. Bryce Piper.[30] Analyzing your product and studying the competition help you determine what to emphasize in your sales message.

Determining the Purpose of a Sales Message. Equally as important as analyzing the product is determining the specific purpose of your message. Do you want the reader to call for a free video and brochure? Listen to a podcast at your website? Fill out an order form? Send a credit card authorization? Before you write the first word of your message, know what response you want and what central selling point you will emphasize to achieve that purpose.

Adapting a Sales Message to Its Audience. Despite today's predominance of e-mail marketing over direct-mail letters, in terms of response rates, sales letters win by a mile. Direct mail achieves a 3.7 percent response rate compared with e-mail's paltry 0.1 percent. Even all digital channels *combined* achieve a response rate of 0.62 percent.[31] Overall, though, despite its effectiveness, direct mail is used less and less; only half of respondents in a study said they are using this channel, primarily because of its cost and the effort it demands.[32] The response rate can be increased dramatically by targeting the audience through selected database mailing lists. Let's say you are selling fitness equipment. A good mailing list might come from subscribers to fitness or exercise magazines, whom you would expect to have similar interests, needs, and demographics (age, income, and other characteristics). With this knowledge you can adapt the sales message to a specific audience.

Axsimen/Shutterstock.com

Reality Check

Direct Mail: Alive and Well

"Direct mail continues to be a very strong and successful channel, both in terms of response rates and cost-per-acquisition. It may be more expensive on a 'per piece' basis than digital channels, but it packs a punch that cannot be replicated with a digital channel alone."[33]

—Debora Haskel, *VP marketing, IWCO Direct, a multichannel marketing firm*

Crafting Successful Sales Messages

Direct mail is usually part of multichannel marketing campaigns. These messages are a powerful means to make sales, generate leads, boost retail traffic, solicit donations, and direct consumers to websites. Direct mail is a great channel for personalized, tangible, three-dimensional messages that are less invasive than telephone solicitations and less reviled than unsolicited e-mail. A recent study shows that tangible direct mail appears to have a greater emotional impact than virtual mail. Brain scans suggest that physical materials "engage a different (and presumably more retentive) part of the brain."[34] Figure 10.10 juxtaposes the most relevant features of traditional direct-mail and online sales messages.

Betting on Highly Targeted, Relevant Direct Mail

Although not as flashy as social media campaigns, direct mail still works as long as it is personalized and relevant.[35] Experts know that most recipients do look at their direct mail and respond to it; in fact, 79 percent of consumers act on direct mail immediately, whereas only 45 percent deal with e-mail right away.[36] The ever-increasing spending on digital and mobile advertising reflects the channels where the eyeballs are. Now more money goes to digital and interactive marketing ($60 billion) than to traditional direct-mail marketing ($46 billion), and digital spending is forecast to reach 103 billion by 2019.[37] Nevertheless, savvy marketers keep direct mail, "the golden child of the print media family,"[38] in their marketing mix.

Professionals who specialize in traditional direct-mail services have made it a science. They analyze a market, develop an effective mailing list, study the product, prepare a sophisticated campaign aimed at a target audience, and motivate the reader to act. You have probably received

Figure 10.10 **Characteristics of Traditional Versus Online Sales Messages**

Characteristics of Traditional Versus Online Sales Messages

Traditional Direct Mail (Sales Letter)	E-Commerce (E-Mail, Social Media Messages)
Creating static content (hard copy)	Creating dynamic digital content
Anticipating a single response (inquiry, sale)	Creating engagement instead of selling overtly
Resorting to "spray-and-pray" approach	Building one-to-one relationships and communities around brands
Single communication channel	Multiple communication channels
Limited response	Potentially unlimited responses
Monologue	Dialogue, potential for mass diffusion
Private response	Public, shared response
Asynchronous (delayed) response	Instant, real-time response possible
Passive	Interactive, participatory
Promoter-generated content	User-generated content
The needs of target groups must be anticipated and met in advance.	Consumers expect that brands understand their unique needs and deliver.
Direct mail is preferred for information about insurance, financial services, and health care; excellent channel for offline customers.	**Savvy brands respond nimbly to customer participation; today's sophisticated consumers dislike "hard sell."**

many direct-mail packages, often called junk mail. These packages typically contain a sales letter, a brochure, a price list, illustrations of the product, testimonials, and other persuasive appeals. Chances are they will keep coming, but they will be a lot more relevant to you and your spending habits.

Considering the Value of Sales Letters

Because sales letters are generally written by specialists, you may never write one on the job. Why learn how to write a sales letter? Learning the techniques of sales writing will help you be more successful in any communication that requires persuasion and promotion. What's more, you will recognize sales strategies directed at you, which will make you a more perceptive consumer of ideas, products, and services.

Your primary goal in writing a sales message is to get someone to devote a few moments of attention to it. You may be promoting a product, a service, an idea, or yourself. In each case the most effective messages will follow the AIDA strategy and (a) gain attention, (b) build interest, (c) elicit desire and reduce resistance, and (d) motivate action. This is the same recipe we studied earlier, but the ingredients are different.

Gaining Attention in Sales Messages. One of the most critical elements of a sales message is its opening paragraph. This opener should be short (one to five lines), honest, relevant, and stimulating. Marketing pros have found that eye-catching typographical arrangements or provocative messages, such as the following, can hook a reader's attention:

- **Offer:** *Subscribe now and get a free iPad to enjoy your programming on the go!*
- **Promise:** *Now you can raise your sales income by 50 percent or even more with the proven techniques found in . . . .*
- **Question:** *Why wait in the Starbucks line for a pitiful paper cup when for $20 you can have the Chiseled Chrome Coffee Cup, a handsome stylish tumbler of your own to refill every morning?*
- **Quotation or proverb:** *Necessity is the mother of invention.*
- **Fact:** *The Greenland Eskimos ate more fat than anyone in the world. And yet . . . they had virtually no heart disease.*
- **Product feature and its benefit:** *The Atlas sock is made from cotton, polyester, and carbonized coffee. Yup! Coffee helps filter odor, but equally important, we use pressure mapping and thermal imaging to create a ridiculously comfortable sock!*
- **Startling statement:** *Bigger houses cost less.*
- **Personalized action setting:** *It's 4:30 p.m. and you've got to make a decision. You need everybody's opinion, no matter where they are. Before you pick up your phone to call them one at a time, pick up this card: WebEx Teleconference Services.*

Other openings calculated to capture attention include a solution to a problem, an anecdote, a personalized statement using the receiver's name, and a relevant current event.

Building Interest With Rational and Emotional Appeals. In this phase of your sales message, you should describe clearly the product or service. In simple language emphasize the central selling points that you identified during your prewriting analysis. Those selling points can be developed using rational or emotional appeals.

Rational appeals are associated with reason and intellect. They translate selling points into references to making or saving money, increasing efficiency, or making the best use of resources. In general, rational appeals are appropriate when a product is expensive, long-lasting, or important to health, security, or financial success.

Emotional appeals relate to status, ego, and sensual feelings. Appealing to the emotions is sometimes effective when a product is inexpensive, short-lived, or nonessential. Many clever sales messages, however, combine emotional and rational strategies for a dual appeal. Consider these examples:

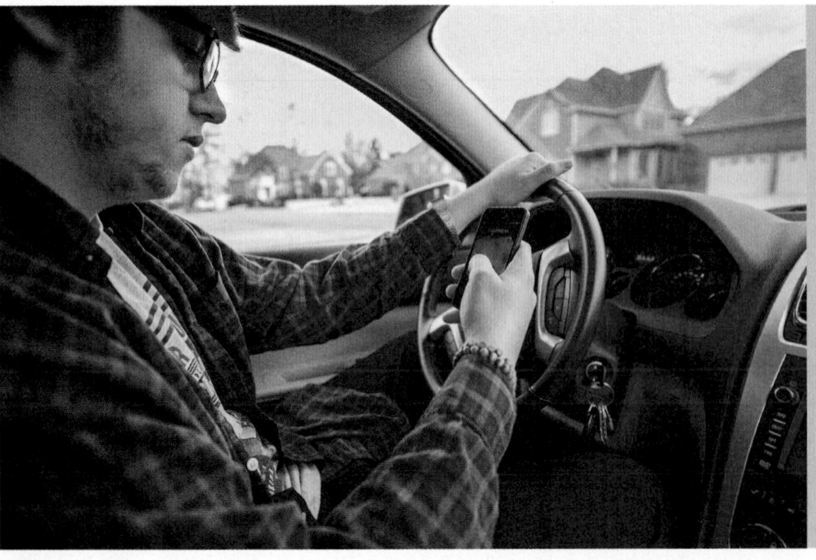

Leigh J/Shutterstock.com

Public service announcements (PSAs) about distracted driving use different strategies in their messages. Some PSAs cite statistics as a rational appeal; others show horrific accidents as a scare tactic. Recently, a New Zealand advertising agency used humor in its PSA to discourage using a phone while driving. As a cover of Lionel Richie's "Hello" plays, a series of young drivers reach for their phones but are blocked when the front seat passenger grabs the driver's hand. The driver appears shocked as the passenger looks on with adoring eyes. The tag line reads: "Put me first. Drive phone free." Is humor an effective strategy for a PSA aimed at distracted drivers?

Rational Appeal

You can buy the things you need and want, pay household bills, and pay off higher-cost loans and credit cards—as soon as you are approved and your ChoiceCredit card account is opened.

Emotional Appeal

Leave the urban bustle behind and escape to sun-soaked Bermuda! To recharge your batteries with an injection of sun and surf, all you need is your bathing suit, a little suntan lotion, and your ChoiceCredit card.

Dual Appeal

New ChoiceCredit cardholders are immediately eligible for a $200 travel certificate and additional discounts at fun-filled resorts. Save up to 40 percent while lying on a beach in picturesque, sun-soaked Bora-Bora, the year-round resort.

A physical description of your product is not enough, however. Zig Ziglar, thought by some to be America's greatest salesperson, pointed out that no matter how well you know your product, no one is persuaded by cold, hard facts alone. In the end, people buy because of product benefits.[39] Your job is to translate those cold facts into warm feelings and reader

Ethics Check

Scare Tactics

Direct marketers sometimes resort to scare tactics—for example, to make us purchase alarm systems or subscribe to monitoring services. They may also appeal to our compassion and guilt before the holidays in soliciting money for the less fortunate. Are such emotional appeals ethical?

PLUGGED IN

The Role of Social Media in Persuading People and Prompting Sales

Self-improvement legend Dale Carnegie believed that humans are not rational beings, as is commonly believed. Rather, he wrote in one of his best-selling books: "We are dealing with creatures of emotion, creatures bristling with prejudices and motivated by pride and vanity."[40] Similarly, salesmanship guru Zig Ziglar claimed, "People don't buy for logical reasons. They buy for emotional reasons."[41] This is hardly news to veteran salespeople; however, until recently, modern economic theory assumed that humans make logical decisions based on rational calculations. The influence of emotions on decision making was largely overlooked.[42]

Emotions Guide Decision Making. Neurological research supports the view that human decision making is a process guided by emotions. As Robert Cialdini and others have argued, people seem to make nearly automated, split-second decisions that they then justify with logical reasoning. We are not aware of our biases and influences and sometimes rationalize or even fictionalize our past behavior.[43] Human beings are also more likely to be persuaded by people or entities they like and know. These two insights have important implications for social media marketing. They explain why so much emphasis today is placed on customer *engagement*, mostly carried out through social networks.

Social Media Are for Engagement and Branding. Adobe CEO Shantanu Narayen calls engagement "the new business mandate." He believes that "the health of a company relies on the extent to which it creates meaningful and sustainable interactions" with customers.[44] Engaged customers are more loyal and willing to recommend products. Social media success depends on creating an emotional connection.[45] One expert likens social media to a cocktail party at which one mingles and networks but does not rudely hawk products and services.[46] Social media are for branding, not selling, claims another expert.[47] Yet even consumers who are fans don't necessarily want to be friends with brands.[48]

Social Media Don't Drive Sales Much (Yet). Although people use social networks to connect with friends, find jobs, and evaluate brands, they tell researchers that social media fail to provide prompt and effective customer service.[49] Consumers also don't go to social media sites to shop.[50] Only 1.5 percent of e-commerce Web traffic represents referrals from social media, although social-driven retail sales are rising.[51] Still, just 5 percent of online retail revenue stems from social commerce.[52] At the same time, shopping with mobile devices has exceeded purchases made on desktop computers.[53] Reaching consumers via social media is a holy grail for many marketers but remains elusive. Although retailers and brands are going where their most likely customers are congregating online, this doesn't mean that consumers welcome sales pitches on their favorite social media sites.

When It Comes to Sales, E-Mail and Direct-Mail Marketing Rule. A much-cited channel preference study found that 65 percent of people who received direct mail (i.e., postal mail) made a purchase or engaged in a different marketing channel prompted by the direct-mail sender. Direct mail is second only to e-mail marketing, which induces 66 percent of recipients to make purchases.[54] Even in the digital age, direct mail is going strong, despite the uncertain future of the U.S. Postal Service. In terms of triggering sales, e-mail and sales letters still outperform social media.[55] Marketers today understand that to send seamless messages, they must use multiple channels, online and offline.

Figure 10.11 HealthSelect Sales Letter

1 Prewriting

Analyze: The purpose is to persuade the reader to respond by calling, chatting with a representative online, or returning a reply card to obtain information.

Anticipate: The audience is individuals and families who may be interested in health insurance. The central selling point is the value and flexibility of the various health plans.

Adapt: Because readers will be reluctant, use the indirect pattern, AIDA.

2 Drafting

Research: Gather facts to promote your product and its benefits.

Organize: Gain attention by addressing the cost of health insurance. Emphasize that insurance protects assets, and focus on reader benefits. Motivate action by promising a no-obligation quote. Encourage a response with a toll-free number and an easy-reply card.

Draft: Prepare a first draft for a pilot study.

3 Revising

Edit: Use short paragraphs and short sentences. Replace *bankrupt you* with *break the bank.*

Proofread: Use bulleted list for features and benefits description. Set headings boldface, and underscore other important information. Hyphenate *easy-to-understand*. Check for any medical or bureaucratic jargon.

Evaluate: Monitor the response rate to this letter to assess its effectiveness.

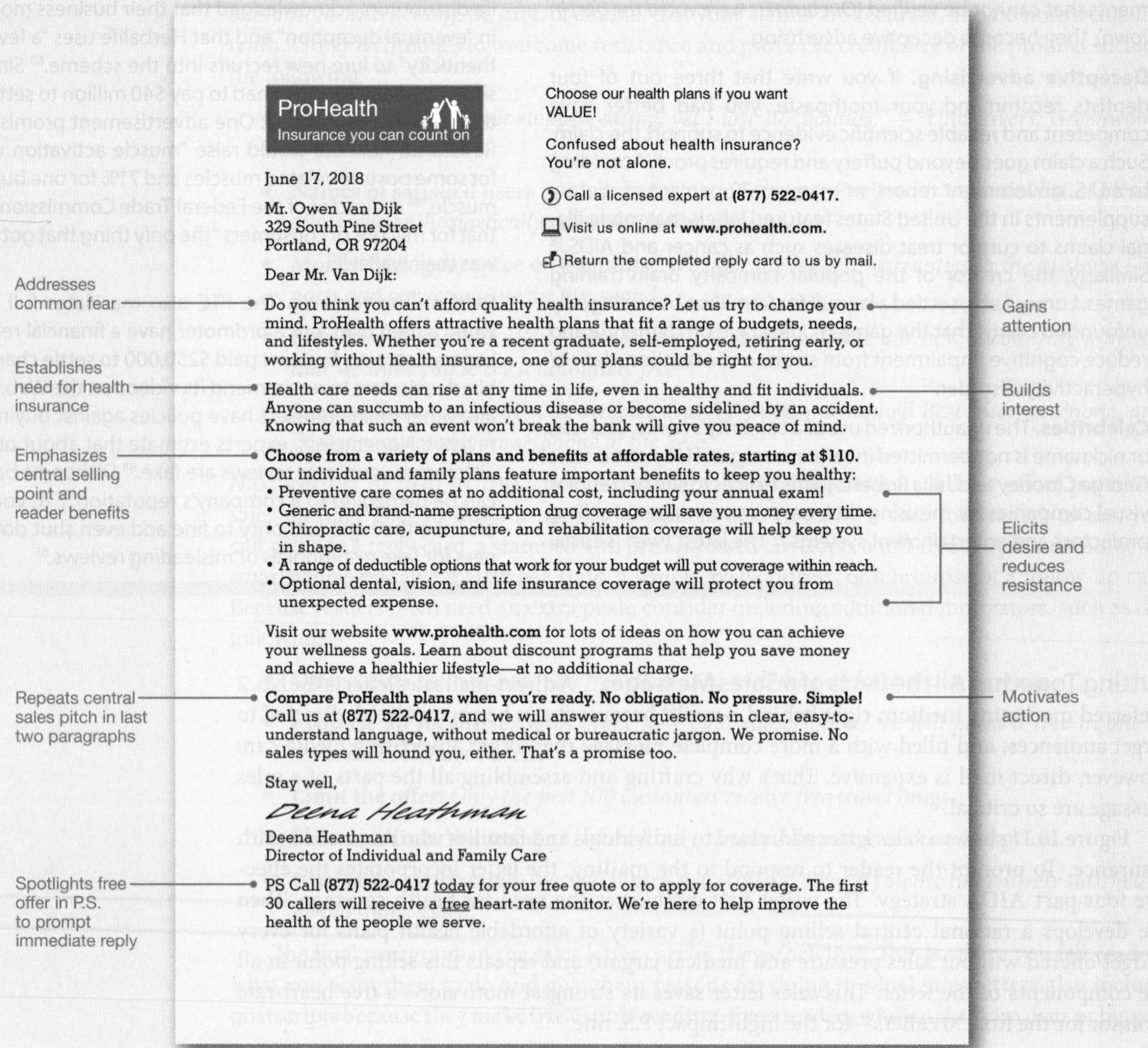

ProHealth
Insurance you can count on

Choose our health plans if you want VALUE!

Confused about health insurance? You're not alone.

Call a licensed expert at **(877) 522-0417.**

Visit us online at **www.prohealth.com.**

Return the completed reply card to us by mail.

June 17, 2018

Mr. Owen Van Dijk
329 South Pine Street
Portland, OR 97204

Dear Mr. Van Dijk:

Do you think you can't afford quality health insurance? Let us try to change your mind. ProHealth offers attractive health plans that fit a range of budgets, needs, and lifestyles. Whether you're a recent graduate, self-employed, retiring early, or working without health insurance, one of our plans could be right for you.

Health care needs can rise at any time in life, even in healthy and fit individuals. Anyone can succumb to an infectious disease or become sidelined by an accident. Knowing that such an event won't break the bank will give you peace of mind.

Choose from a variety of plans and benefits at affordable rates, starting at $110. Our individual and family plans feature important benefits to keep you healthy:

- Preventive care comes at no additional cost, including your annual exam!
- Generic and brand-name prescription drug coverage will save you money every time.
- Chiropractic care, acupuncture, and rehabilitation coverage will help keep you in shape.
- A range of deductible options that work for your budget will put coverage within reach.
- Optional dental, vision, and life insurance coverage will protect you from unexpected expense.

Visit our website **www.prohealth.com** for lots of ideas on how you can achieve your wellness goals. Learn about discount programs that help you save money and achieve a healthier lifestyle—at no additional charge.

Compare ProHealth plans when you're ready. No obligation. No pressure. Simple! Call us at (877) 522-0417, and we will answer your questions in clear, easy-to-understand language, without medical or bureaucratic jargon. We promise. No sales types will hound you, either. That's a promise too.

Stay well,

Deena Heathman

Deena Heathman
Director of Individual and Family Care

PS Call (877) 522-0417 <u>today</u> for your free quote or to apply for coverage. The first 30 callers will receive a <u>free</u> heart-rate monitor. We're here to help improve the health of the people we serve.

Addresses common fear
Establishes need for health insurance
Emphasizes central selling point and reader benefits
Repeats central sales pitch in last two paragraphs
Spotlights free offer in P.S. to prompt immediate reply
Gains attention
Builds interest
Elicits desire and reduces resistance
Motivates action

Writing Successful E-Mail Sales Messages

E-mail remains the primary channel for brand communication today. Seventy percent of consumers favor e-mail when interacting with brands—over direct mail, SMS, and other marketing messages.[67] E-mail is the most used digital channel for customer communication (51 percent),[68] and 77 percent of consumers prefer permission-based marketing through e-mail.[69] E-mails cost between $11 and $15 per consumer response versus about $19 per response for traditional direct mail.[70]

Much like traditional direct mail, e-mail marketing can attract new customers, keep existing ones, encourage future sales, cross-sell, and cut costs. However, e-marketers can create and send a promotion in half the time it takes to print and distribute a traditional message. To reach today's consumer, marketers must target their e-mails well if they wish to even get their messages opened. "In order for your email program to be truly effective, your messages must be relevant, targeted and engaging to the people who receive them," says one marketing specialist.[71]

Selling by E-Mail. If you will be writing online sales messages for your organization, try using the following techniques gleaned from the best-performing e-mail marketers. Although much e-marketing dazzles receivers with colorful graphics, we focus on the words involved in persuasive sales messages. Earlier in the chapter, Figure 10.3 showing an e-mail sales message from Wholesome2Go demonstrates many of the principles discussed here.

The first rule of e-marketing is to communicate only with those who have given permission. By sending messages only to opt-in folks, you greatly increase your open rate—e-mails that will be opened. E-mail users detest spam. However, receivers are surprisingly receptive to offers tailored specifically to them. Remember that today's customer is somebody—not just anybody. Following are a few guidelines that will help you create effective e-mail sales messages:

- **Craft a catchy subject line.** Include an audience-specific location (*Emporium in Vegas Opens Soon!*); ask a meaningful question (*What's Your Dream Vacation?*); and use no more than 50 characters. Promise realistic solutions. Offer discounts or premiums.
- **Keep the main information "above the fold."** E-mails should be top heavy. Primary points should appear early in the message (before the first fold in a letter) so that they capture the reader's attention.
- **Make the message short, conversational, and focused.** Because on-screen text is taxing to read, be brief. Focus on one or two central selling points only.
- **Sprinkle testimonials throughout the copy.** Consumers' own words are the best sales copy. These comments can serve as callouts or be integrated into the copy.
- **Provide a means for opting out.** It's polite and a good business tactic to include a statement that tells receivers how to be removed from the sender's mailing database.

Writing Short Persuasive Messages Online

Increasingly, writers are turning to social network posts to promote their businesses, further their causes, and build their online personas. As we have seen, social media are not primarily suited for overt selling; however, tweets and other online posts can be used to influence others and to project a professional, positive social online presence.

Typically, organizations and individuals with followers post updates of their events, exploits, thoughts, and experiences. In persuasive tweets and posts, writers try to pitch offers, prompt specific responses, or draw the attention of their audiences to interesting events and media links. Figure 10.12 displays a sampling of persuasive tweets.

Note that the compact format of a tweet requires extreme conciseness and efficiency. Don't expect the full four-part AIDA strategy to be represented in a 140-character Twitter message. Instead, you may see attention getters and calls for action, both of which must be catchy and intriguing. Regardless, many of the principles of persuasion apply even to micromessages.

Figure 10.12 **Analyzing Persuasive Tweets**

Tweet promoting professional services by offering the reader a general benefit

Sandra Zimmer @sandrazimmer
Coaching for authentic presentations, public speaking & **persuasive messages** to help you shine. tinyurl.com/m5hrrx
Expand Reply Retweet Favorite

Tweet offering a freebie to promote a book and urging action by restricting the availability of the freebie

Jessica Brody @JessicaBrody
5 autographed copies of UNREMEMBERED (UK edition) are up for grabs on Free Book Friday teens this week! Check it out! ow.ly/k5k6M

Delta @Delta
Be sure to enter our Kick It in NYC contest before the curtain closes. Enter now! oak.ctx.ly/r/1nwv pic.twitter.com/CRHxOwKe
View photo Reply Retweet Favorite

An airline creating urgency by suggesting that time to enter a contest is running out

James Barry @ChefJamesBarry
The Sugar Control Detox is coming and at an insanely low price! This opportunity is available to everyone, no... fb.me/S2XDfTXB
View media Reply Retweet Favorite

Teaser tweet by a small business owner announcing an upcoming promotion

A nonprofit organization requesting political action of advocacy for a popular cause

Army of Women @ArmyofWomen
Think #breastcancer should be a Nat. priority? Tell the president HERE:ow.ly/dnMd3
Expand Reply Retweet Favorite

Prominent philanthropist tweeting to motivate giving by reassuring followers of charities' merit

Bill Gates @BillGates
Make your donations count. @CharityNav provides great information on the impact non-profits are actually having. b-gat.es/ThLBLJ
Expand

Mike Bloomberg @MikeBloomberg
I've joined @Instagram. Follow me here: instagram.com/mikebloomberg
Expand

Tweet by a notable public figure announcing his new social network account and inviting followers along

Guy Kawasaki @GuyKawasaki
Are you a writer? Here are some fantastic resources available free today as a download on the APE website.... fb.me/10bBh8apK
Expand Reply Retweet Favorite

Tweet by well-known businessperson offering a free resource using an attention-getter

Whether you actually write sales messages on the job or merely receive them, you will better understand their organization and appeals by reviewing this chapter and the tips in the following checklist:

LEARNING OUTCOME 6

Apply basic persuasive techniques in developing compelling press releases.

Developing Persuasive Press Releases

Press (news) releases announce important information to the media, whether traditional or digital. Such public announcements can feature new products, new managers, new facilities, sponsorships, participation in community projects, awards given or received, joint ventures, donations, or seminars and demonstrations. Naturally, organizations hope that the media will pick up this news and provide good publicity. However, purely self-serving or promotional information is not appealing to magazine and newspaper editors or to TV producers. To get them to read beyond the first sentence, press release writers follow these principles:

- Open with an attention-getting lead or a summary of the important facts.
- Include answers to the five *Ws* and one *H* (*who, what, when, where, why,* and *how*) in the article—but not all in the first sentence!

CHECKLIST

Preparing Persuasive Direct-Mail and E-Mail Sales Messages

Prewrite

- Analyze your product or service. What makes it special? What central selling points should you emphasize? How does it compare with the competition?
- Profile your audience. How will this product or service benefit this audience?
- Decide what you want the audience to do at the end of your message.
- For e-mails, send only to those who have opted in.

Gain Attention

- Describe a product feature, present a testimonial, make a startling statement, or show the reader in an action setting.
- Offer something valuable, promise the reader a result, or pose a stimulating question.
- Suggest a solution to a problem, offer a relevant anecdote, use the receiver's name, or mention a meaningful current event.

Build Interest

- Describe the product or service in terms of what it does for the reader. Connect cold facts with warm feelings and needs.
- Use rational appeals if the product or service is expensive, long-lasting, or important to health, security, or financial success. Use emotional appeals to suggest status, ego, or sensual feelings.
- Explain how the product or service can save or make money, reduce effort, improve health, produce pleasure, or boost status.

Elicit Desire and Reduce Resistance

- Counter anticipated reluctance with testimonials, money-back guarantees, attractive warranties, trial offers, or free samples.
- Build credibility with results of performance tests, polls, or awards.
- If price is not a selling feature, describe it in small units (*only 99 cents an issue*), show it as savings, or tell how it compares favorably with that of the competition.

Motivate Action

- Close by repeating a central selling point and describing an easy-to-take action.
- Prompt the reader to act immediately with a gift, incentive, limited offer, deadline, or guarantee of satisfaction.
- Put the strongest motivator in a postscript.
- In e-mails include an opportunity to opt out.

- Appeal to the audience of the target media. Emphasize reader benefits written in the style of the focus publication or newscast.
- Present the most important information early, followed by supporting information. Don't put your best ideas last because they may be chopped off or ignored.
- Insert intriguing and informative quotations of chief decision makers to lend the news release credibility.
- Make the document readable and visually appealing. Limit the text to one or two double-spaced pages with attractive formatting.
- Look and sound credible—no typos, no imaginative spelling or punctuation, no factual errors.

The most important ingredient of a press release, of course, is *news*. Articles that merely plug products end up in the circular file, or they languish unread on a company website. The press release in Figure 10.13 announced the launch of a unique breast cancer research study conducted by two reputable medical organizations, Dr. Susan Love Research Foundation and City of Hope. The announcement provides an appealing headline and describes the purpose as well as the process of the massive, long-term research. The Health of Women Study is unusual in that it employs crowdsourcing and actively involves huge numbers of subjects online and by mobile devices. Moreover, data will be shared with all interested researchers and the participants themselves.

Figure 10.13 **Press Release With a Broad Appeal**

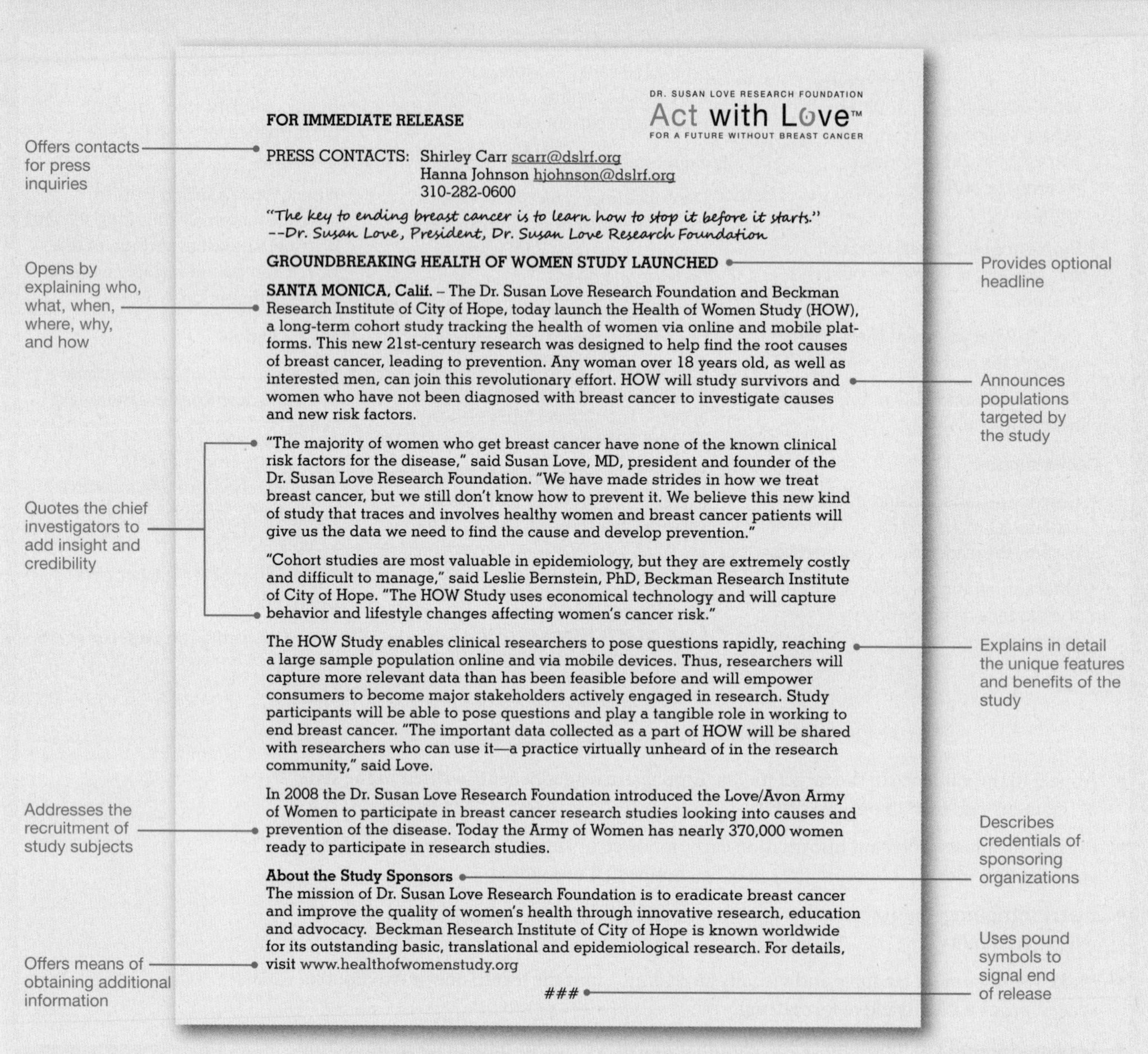
DR. SUSAN LOVE RESEARCH FOUNDATION
Act with Love™
FOR A FUTURE WITHOUT BREAST CANCER

FOR IMMEDIATE RELEASE

PRESS CONTACTS: Shirley Carr scarr@dslrf.org
Hanna Johnson hjohnson@dslrf.org
310-282-0600

"The key to ending breast cancer is to learn how to stop it before it starts."
--Dr. Susan Love, President, Dr. Susan Love Research Foundation

GROUNDBREAKING HEALTH OF WOMEN STUDY LAUNCHED

SANTA MONICA, Calif. – The Dr. Susan Love Research Foundation and Beckman Research Institute of City of Hope, today launch the Health of Women Study (HOW), a long-term cohort study tracking the health of women via online and mobile platforms. This new 21st-century research was designed to help find the root causes of breast cancer, leading to prevention. Any woman over 18 years old, as well as interested men, can join this revolutionary effort. HOW will study survivors and women who have not been diagnosed with breast cancer to investigate causes and new risk factors.

"The majority of women who get breast cancer have none of the known clinical risk factors for the disease," said Susan Love, MD, president and founder of the Dr. Susan Love Research Foundation. "We have made strides in how we treat breast cancer, but we still don't know how to prevent it. We believe this new kind of study that traces and involves healthy women and breast cancer patients will give us the data we need to find the cause and develop prevention."

"Cohort studies are most valuable in epidemiology, but they are extremely costly and difficult to manage," said Leslie Bernstein, PhD, Beckman Research Institute of City of Hope. "The HOW Study uses economical technology and will capture behavior and lifestyle changes affecting women's cancer risk."

The HOW Study enables clinical researchers to pose questions rapidly, reaching a large sample population online and via mobile devices. Thus, researchers will capture more relevant data than has been feasible before and will empower consumers to become major stakeholders actively engaged in research. Study participants will be able to pose questions and play a tangible role in working to end breast cancer. "The important data collected as a part of HOW will be shared with researchers who can use it—a practice virtually unheard of in the research community," said Love.

In 2008 the Dr. Susan Love Research Foundation introduced the Love/Avon Army of Women to participate in breast cancer research studies looking into causes and prevention of the disease. Today the Army of Women has nearly 370,000 women ready to participate in research studies.

About the Study Sponsors
The mission of Dr. Susan Love Research Foundation is to eradicate breast cancer and improve the quality of women's health through innovative research, education and advocacy. Beckman Research Institute of City of Hope is known worldwide for its outstanding basic, translational and epidemiological research. For details, visit www.healthofwomenstudy.org

###

Offers contacts for press inquiries
Opens by explaining who, what, when, where, why, and how
Quotes the chief investigators to add insight and credibility
Addresses the recruitment of study subjects
Offers means of obtaining additional information
Provides optional headline
Announces populations targeted by the study
Explains in detail the unique features and benefits of the study
Describes credentials of sponsoring organizations
Uses pound symbols to signal end of release

The best press releases focus on information that appeals to a targeted audience. A breast cancer study focusing on the potential causes and prevention of the disease is likely to generate keen and wide-ranging interest. The credibility of the study's sponsors discourages sensationalist coverage. Indirectly, the nonprofit organizations may also attract more research subjects and donations. Figure 10.13 illustrates many useful techniques for creating effective press releases.

Newspapers, magazines, and digital media are more likely to publish a press release that is informative, interesting, and helpful. The websites of many organizations today provide readily available media information including press releases and photos.

Your Turn: Applying Your Skills at ōlloclip

Early on, ōlloclip defined its mission as follows: "To create mobile photography accessories that excite the inner artist in everyone and help capture and share those spontaneous moments simply and efficiently." Besides convenience, ōlloclip lenses promise to turn even average hobbyists into exceptional photographers. The company's Instagram presence reflects the ōlloclip motto that "images speak louder."

To identify its key target audience, ōlloclip defined four sets of users: digital youth who largely point the camera at themselves; the general population (i.e., people who want to up their social media game); action sports and outdoor enthusiasts who want portability and who hunt for *the* shot; and professional photographers who recognize smartphones as a terrific medium to capture great content.

As a photography company, ōlloclip heavily relies on Instagram. The company's other main social media platforms are Facebook, Twitter, YouTube, Snapchat, and Periscope, a new video app. Staff members also communicate by e-mail, Skype, and Trello, a new project management tool. Like most tech companies, ōlloclip encourages informal, but respectful interaction "with a Silicon Valley feel," says Lena Galasko, ōlloclip sales rep. She and her coworkers can be "serious and formal when necessary within the team or with customers."

Your Task

You hope to be chosen to intern at ōlloclip, where you may be asked to help with the monthly e-newsletter Lena sends to retailers and distributors. You may also be assigned to assist the social media team. Some writing tasks include writing tweets, photo captions, and short news items from the world of photography. As a writing sample, Lena asks you to send her a professional e-mail message describing your background, education, and career plans. She wants you to explain why you wish to intern at ōlloclip, what you like about the company, and what you hope to learn.

Summary of Learning Outcomes

1 Explain digital age persuasion, identify time-proven persuasive techniques, and apply the 3-x-3 writing process to persuasive messages in print and online.

- Persuasion is the ability to use words and other symbols to influence an individual's attitudes and behaviors.
- Six psychological triggers prompt us to act and to believe: reciprocation, commitment, social proof, liking, authority, and scarcity.
- Digital age persuasion is prolific, widespread, far-reaching, and fast-moving.
- Persuasive techniques today are more subtle and misleading than those used in the past, as well as more complex and impersonal.
- Effective persuaders establish credibility, make a specific request, tie facts to benefits, recognize the power of loss, expect and overcome resistance, share solutions, and compromise.
- Before writing, communicators decide what they want the receiver to do or think; they adapt their message to their audience; and they collect information and organize it into an appropriate strategy. They are indirect if the audience might resist the request.

2 Describe the traditional four-part AIDA strategy for creating successful persuasive messages, and apply the four elements to draft effective and ethical business messages.

- Include four major elements to craft a persuasive message: gain attention, build interest, elicit desire while reducing resistance, and motivate action.
- Gain attention by opening with a problem, unexpected statement, reader benefit, compliment, related fact, or stimulating question.
- Build interest with facts, expert opinions, examples, details, and direct and indirect reader benefits.
- Elicit desire and reduce resistance by anticipating objections and presenting counterarguments.
- Conclude by motivating a specific action and making it easy for the reader to respond.
- As an ethical persuader, avoid distortion, exaggeration, and doublespeak when making persuasive arguments.

3 Craft persuasive messages that request actions, make claims, and deliver complaints.

- Think through your purpose and prepare a thoughtful message.
- Assume that receivers comply because they want to "give back" and because others may benefit.
- Understand that persuasive claims involve damaged products, billing mistakes, warranty problems, and similar issues.
- Make a logical argument, adopt an objective, unemotional tone, and prove that your request has merit.
- Open claims with sincere praise, an objective statement of the problem, a point of agreement, or a quick review of what you have done to resolve the problem.
- Elicit desire and reduce resistance by anticipating objections and providing counterarguments.
- Motivate action by stating exactly what is to be done; add a deadline if necessary, and express appreciation.

4 Understand interpersonal persuasion at work, and write persuasive messages within organizations.

- Executives rely on persuasion and employee buy-in, not so much on the power of their position.
- When asking subordinates to volunteer for projects or to make lifestyle changes, organizations may use the AIDA strategy to persuade.
- In messages flowing downward, good writers use a conversational tone and warm words; they focus on direct and indirect benefits.
- In messages flowing upward, such as recommendations from subordinates to supervisors, providing evidence is critical; making a strong dollars-and-cents appeal whenever appropriate strengthens the argument.
- Two-sided arguments are more persuasive because they make writers sound credible and fair.

5 Create effective and ethical direct-mail and e-mail sales messages.

- Sales messages must be preceded by careful analysis of the product or service until the central selling point can be identified.

- Effective sales messages begin with a short, honest, and relevant attention getter.
- Simple language describing appropriate appeals builds interest.
- Testimonials, money-back guarantees, or free trials can reduce resistance and elicit desire.
- A gift, incentive, or deadline can motivate action.
- E-marketing messages should be sent only to opt-in receivers; such messages begin with a catchy subject line, keep the main information "above the fold," are short and focused, convey urgency, include testimonials if available, and provide a means for unsubscribing.
- Tweets and other short persuasive social media posts can influence others and can project a professional presence; even brief posts may contain AIDA components.

6 Apply basic persuasive techniques in developing compelling press releases.

- Open with an attention-getting lead or summary of the important facts.
- Answer the questions *who, what, when, where, why,* and *how.*
- Write carefully to appeal to the audience of the target media.
- Present the most important information early, make your press release visually appealing, and make sure it looks and sounds credible.

Critical Thinking

1. Many consumers rely on product reviews posted online, presumably by ordinary citizens describing their authentic experiences. Unfortunately, though, Amazon and Yelp, the most prominent of the many Internet review sites, have been called out for fake and paid-for reviews. Amazon has threatened to sue people posting fake public reviews.[72] Why is it important that online reviews be trustworthy? Which of Robert B. Cialdini's six psychological triggers applies to persuasion resulting from reading about other people's experiences with products and services?
2. What are some of the underlying motivations that prompt individuals to agree to requests that do not directly benefit themselves or their organizations? (L.O. 3)
3. How are direct-mail sales letters and e-mail sales messages similar, and how are they different? (L.O. 5)
4. Why are magazine and newspaper editors or TV producers wary of press (news) releases from businesses and reluctant to turn them into articles? (L.O. 6)
5. **Ethical Issue:** Los Angeles–based clothing company Barabas seized the moment after Sean Penn's notorious *Rolling Stone* interview with brutal Mexican drug kingpin Joaquin "El Chapo" Guzmán. The clothier used the name and likeness of the drug lord on its website, flanked by photos of attractive male models wearing the same distinctive cotton shirts of the Fantasy and Crazy Paisley lines. The all-caps announcement read: "EL CHAPO GUZMAN WEARING BARABAS SHIRT!"[73] The Internet exploded with astonishment and bafflement after Penn's interview with the crime boss. Barabas' excitement about its infamous customer also met with criticism, but the company couldn't keep the $128 shirts on the shelves.[74] At one point Internet traffic crashed the Barabas website. Yet public outrage ultimately prompted the clothier to remove overt references to El Chapo and his photos. However, if one types *El Chapo* into the search window on the main page of the Barabas site, the shirts pop right up. Is it ethical to resort to such extreme means to drive sales?

Activities

Note: All Documents for Analysis are provided at **www.cengagebrain.com** for you to download and revise.

10.1 Document for Analysis: Poor Persuasive Request Inviting Speaker to Discuss Seven Cardinal Sins in Food Service (L.O. 1–3)

The following letter from a program chair strives to persuade a well-known chef to make a presentation before a local restaurant association. But the letter is not very persuasive. How could this message be more persuasive? What reader benefits could it offer? What arguments could be made to overcome resistance? How should a persuasive message conclude?

YOUR TASK Analyze the following invitation and list its weaknesses. If your instructor directs, revise the letter.

Current date

Ms. Danielle Watkins
The Beverly Hills Hotel
9641 Sunset Boulevard
Beverly Hills, CA 90210

Dear Ms. Watkins:

We know you are a very busy hospitality professional as chef at the Beverly Hills Hotel, but we would like you to make a presentation to the San Francisco chapter of the National Restaurant Association. I was asked to write you since I am program chair.

I heard that you made a really good presentation at your local chapter in Los Angeles recently. I think you gave a talk called "Avoiding the Seven Cardinal Sins in Food Service" or something like that. Whatever it was, I'm sure we would like to hear the same or a similar presentation. All restaurant operators are interested in doing what we can to avoid potential problems involving discrimination, safety at work, how we hire people, etc. As you well know, operating a fast-paced restaurant is frustrating—even on a good day. We are all in a gigantic rush from opening the door early in the morning to shutting it again after the last customer has gone. It's a rat race and easy to fall into the trap with food service faults that push a big operation into trouble.

Enclosed please find a list of questions that our members listed. We would like you to talk in the neighborhood of 45 minutes. Our June 10 meeting will be in the Oak Room of the Westin St. Francis Hotel in San Francisco and dinner begins at 7 p.m.

How can we get you to come to San Francisco? We can only offer you an honorarium of $200, but we would pay for any travel expenses. You can expect a large crowd of restaurateurs who are known for hooting and hollering when they hear good stuff! As you can see, we are a rather informal group. Hope you can join us!

Sincerely,

10.2 Document for Analysis: Persuasive Message Flowing Upward Re: Importing T-Shirts From China (L.O. 1–3)

E-Mail

In the following message, Luke tries to convince his boss, the vice president of marketing, that their organization could save money by importing T-shirts from China. However, his message could be improved by employing several strategies for persuasion.

YOUR TASK Analyze the following e-mail and list its weaknesses. If your instructor directs, revise the message.

To: Bryanna Mazzetta <bryanna@worldclasstrainer.com>
From: Luke Downey <luke@worldclasstrainer.com>
Subject: Possible Chance for Saving Money

We always try our best to meet customers and sell Worldclass Trainer equipment at numerous trade shows. But instead of expanding our visits to these trade shows, the company continues to cut back the number that we attend. And we have fewer staff members attending. I know that you have been asking us to find ways to reduce costs, but I don't think we are going about it right.

With increased airfare and hotel costs, my staff has tried to find ways to live within our very tight budget. Yet, we are being asked to find other ways to reduce our costs. I'm currently thinking ahead to the big Las Vegas trade show coming up in September.

One area where we could make a change is in the gift that we give away. In the past we have presented booth visitors with a nine-color T-shirt that is silk-screened and gorgeous. But it comes at a cost of $23 for each and every one of these beauties from a top-name designer.

To save money, I suggest that we try a $6 T-shirt made in China, which is reasonably presentable. It's got our name on it, and, after all, folks just use these shirts for workouts. Who cares if it is a fancy silk-screened T-shirt or a functional Chinese one that has "Worldclass Trainer" plastered on the chest? Because we give away 2,000 T-shirts at our largest show, we could save big bucks by dumping the designer shirt. But we have to act quickly. I'm sending a cheap one for you to see.

Let me know what you think.

Luke
[Full contact information]

10.3 Document for Analysis: Favor Request—Facebook Flub? (L.O. 1–3)

E-Mail Social Media

A student chose Facebook to request a recommendation from his professor. The following message suffers from many writing faults, including poor tone and flawed persuasive strategy.

YOUR TASK Analyze the Facebook message and list at least five weaknesses. If your instructor directs, revise the message. Decide whether to use Facebook, of which the receiver is a member, or a conventional e-mail to make this request.

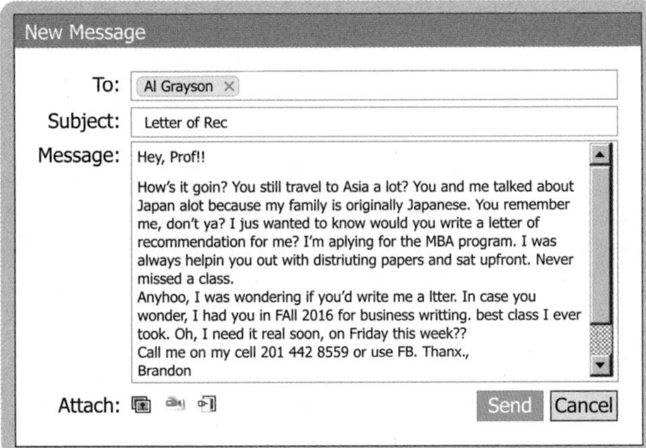
New Message

To: Al Grayson

Subject: Letter of Rec

Message: Hey, Prof!!

How's it goin? You still travel to Asia a lot? You and me talked about Japan alot because my family is originally Japanese. You remember me, don't ya? I jus wanted to know would you write a letter of recommendation for me? I'm aplying for the MBA program. I was always helpin you out with distriuting papers and sat upfront. Never missed a class.
Anyhoo, I was wondering if you'd write me a ltter. In case you wonder, I had you in FAll 2016 for business writting. best class I ever took. Oh, I need it real soon, on Friday this week??
Call me on my cell 201 442 8559 or use FB. Thanx.,
Brandon

Attach: Send Cancel

10.4 Analyzing Tweets: Finding Persuasive Techniques in Micromessages (L.O. 1, 2, and 5)

Communication Technology E-Mail Social Media Web

As you have learned in this chapter, the time-tried AIDA sales technique is alive and well even in 140-character Twitter messages. Of course, we can't expect to find all four parts in a single tweet.

YOUR TASK Study the following tweets and describe the persuasive techniques they employ. **HINT**: You may find that Twitter users rely on attention getters, calls for action, emotional appeals, incentives, and testimonials. They may also create urgency to stoke readers' interest. Chat about your findings in class or on your favorite course-management platform. Your instructor may ask you to collect your own examples of persuasive tweets or other social media posts and discuss their frequency as well as effectiveness. After you have collected a sample large enough to allow you to generalize, compose an e-mail or post about your observations.

10.5 The Art of Persuasion—Understanding Aristotle's Rhetoric (L.O. 1)

Social Media

Besides the persuasive models introduced in this chapter, many more exist. One of the oldest and best-known modes of persuasion comes from Aristotle (384–322 BC). The Greek philosopher identified three components of persuasion: *ethos, pathos,* and *logos*.

Ethos describes the merit, character, and expertise of a speaker. Persuasion is possible when the audience believes that the persuader is credible and has a good reputation. For instance, we tend to believe a successful coach speaking about training methods. Testimonials in advertising are an example of ethos.

Pathos describes an emotional appeal. It means the style of delivery—for example, when a speaker exhibits passion and uses colorful metaphors, language, attention getters, and more. When successful, pathos triggers feelings in the audience intended by the speaker, such as empathy or outrage.

Logos describes a rational appeal. It is the persuasive technique of an argument based in logic and appealing to the audience's intellect. Logos requires us to support our ideas with sound reasons, relevant statistics, and other solid evidence.

As experts point out, most persuaders skillfully weave all three tactics into a seamless, effective persuasive message.[75] In reputable publications such as *The Wall Street Journal* and *The New York Times*, and mainstream news media such as CBS, ABC, and CNN, expect logos to dominate the generally "civilized" debate. Contributors featured in these media generally rank high on ethos. On the political fringes, however, be they left- or right-leaning, pathos dominates over logos. Similarly, expect a lot more pathos than logos in advertising.

YOUR TASK Look for persuasive messages: speeches on YouTube or opinion pieces such as editorials or blog entries. Examine them for ethos, pathos, and logos. The discussion of rational and emotional appeals in this chapter might be helpful. Jot down your observations, and bring your notes to class. If your instructor directs, submit a written interpretation discussing the ethos, pathos, and logos of a speech, an ad, or an opinion piece.

10.6 The Strategies of Persuasion—Testing Hugh Rank's Model (L.O. 1)

Theorist Hugh Rank created a relatively simple model of persuasion. He believed that persuaders resort to two main strategies to reach their goals. Figure 10.14 illustrates Rank's model. Simply put, persuaders intensify their own strong points and the weaknesses of their opponent or a competing idea. Second, they downplay their own weak points and the strengths of their opponent or a competing idea.

Figure 10.14 **Hugh Rank's Persuasive Model**

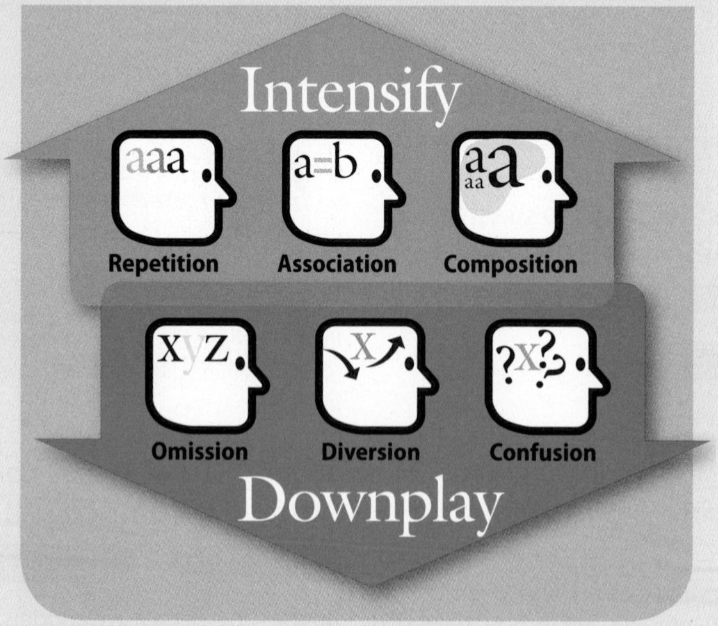

Intensify
Repetition
Association
Composition
Omission
Diversion
Confusion
Downplay

Intensifying is achieved by repetition, association, and composition. Words and visual patterns of a key ingredient of a persuasive message are repeated to become memorable. Think jingles, recurring images, key phrases, or slogans—"The Ultimate Driving Machine" (BMW), for example. Association works by linking the idea or product with something that has emotional appeal; for example, attractive, youthful people in their pristine kitchen. Composition can also enhance the message by contrasting it with an opposite (e.g., a cleaning product shown to work wonders on very dirty floors or clothes).

Downplaying is achieved with omission, diversion, and confusion. Omission means leaving out information that might contradict the positive message (e.g., ignoring high purchase and maintenance costs). Diversion is a tactic to cause the audience to overlook a certain negative aspect of the product or idea—for example, by pointing out fuel economy gear in a snazzy vehicle to reduce attention to its poor gas mileage overall. Confusion is used to cover up known weaknesses in one's own argument, idea, or product. In the case of a giant gas guzzler, the persuader might emphasize performance data, racing wins, and so on, to gloss over poor buyer satisfaction and a poor safety record.

YOUR TASK Look for examples to test Rank's model. Find advertising, opinion pieces, speeches, and other persuasive messages to illustrate the intensify–downplay model. In a class discussion or an e-mail to your instructor, discuss whether it is unethical to intensify or downplay, and give examples.

10.7 Persuasive Request: Inviting an Alumna to Speak (L.O. 1–3)

E-Mail

As public relations director for the Business and Accounting Association on your campus, you have been asked to find a keynote speaker for the first meeting of the school year. The owner of a successful local firm, TempHelp4You, is an alumna of your university. You think not only that many students would enjoy learning about how she started her business, but also that some might like to sign up with her temporary help agency. She would need to prepare a 30-minute speech and take questions after the talk. The event will be held from noon until 1:30 p.m. on a date of your choosing in Branford Hall. You can offer her lunch at the event and provide her with a parking permit that she can pick up at the information kiosk at the main entrance to your campus. You need to have her response by a deadline you set.

YOUR TASK Write a direct-approach e-mail to Marion Minter in which you ask her to speak at your club's meeting. Send it to *mminter@temphelp4you.com*.

10.8 Persuasive Request: Providing Suitable Suits to Interviewees (L.O. 1–3)

You saw an interesting article describing a Suitable Suits program at Barnard College. Its College of Career Development kept a closet filled with 21 crisp black suits that students could borrow for job interviews. Students made an appointment with the office and agreed to dry clean the suits before returning them. At Barnard the program was paid for with a grant from a prominent financial firm. You think that a Suitable Suits program is worth exploring with your dean.

YOUR TASK Write a persuasive message requesting an appointment with your dean to discuss a Suitable Suits program at your school. You don't have all the answers and you are not sure how such a program would operate, but you think the idea is worth discussing. Can you convince the dean to see you? Should you write an e-mail or a letter?

10.9 Persuasive Request: Please Write Me a Letter of Recommendation (L.O. 1–3)

E-Mail

As a student, you will need letters of recommendation to find a job, to apply for a scholarship or grant, or to enter graduate school. Naturally, you will consider asking one or several of your college instructors. You talk to a senior you know to find out how to get a busy professor to write you an effective letter. Your friend Paul has the following basic advice for you:

Ask only instructors who have had the opportunity to observe your performance and who may still remember you fondly. Two to five years after you attended a course of 20 to 40 students, your teachers may not recall you at all. Second, contact only professors who can sing your praises. If your grades were lackluster, don't expect a glowing endorsement. Some teachers may flatly refuse to write a recommendation that they cannot make wholeheartedly. Last, make it easy for them to agree to your request and to write a solid letter promptly by following these guidelines:

If possible, make the first request in person. This way, your former instructor will be more likely to remember you. Introduce yourself by name and try to point out something memorable you have done to help your professor recall your performance. Have a copy of the job description, scholarship information, grant requirements, or graduate school application ready. Carry a copy of a recent polished résumé. Alternatively, promise to e-mail these documents and any other information that will help your recommender recall you in a professional setting and understand the nature of the application process. Confirm any agreement by e-mail promptly, and set a firm yet reasonable deadline by which the letter must be received. Don't expect to get a letter if you ask at the last minute. On the other hand, if you give your instructor too much time, he or she may forget. In that case, don't be afraid to nudge gently by e-mail to remind the recommender when the deadline draws closer.

YOUR TASK Write a persuasive request by e-mail asking your instructor (or supervisor or manager) to write you a letter of recommendation for a job application, grant, scholarship, or graduate school application. Provide all relevant information to make it easy for your reader to write a terrific letter. Explain any potential attachments.

10.10 Persuasive Claim: Waikiki Beach Country Club Gets Scammed by Phony Toner Phoner (L.O. 1–3)

Melody was new to her job as administrative assistant at the Waikiki Beach Country Club in Honolulu. Alone in the office one morning, she answered a phone call from Nick, who said he was the country club's copier contractor. "Hey, look, Babydoll," Nick purred, "the price on the toner you use is about to go way up. I can offer you a great price on this toner if you order right now." Melody knew that the copy machine regularly needed toner, and she thought she should go ahead and place the order to save the country club some money. Ten days later two bottles of toner arrived, and Melody was pleased at the perfect timing. The copy machine needed it right away. Three weeks later Maureen, the bookkeeper, called to report a bill from Copy Machine Specialists for $960.43 for two bottles of toner. "What's going on here?" asked Maureen. "We don't purchase supplies from this company, and this price is totally off the charts!"

Melody spoke to the manager, Dan Yamamoto, who immediately knew what had happened. He blamed himself for not training Melody. "Never, never order anything from a telephone solicitor, no matter how fast-talking or smooth he sounds," warned Dan. He outlined an office policy for future supplies purchases. Only certain people can authorize or finalize a purchase, and purchases require a confirmed price including shipping costs settled in advance. But what to do about this $960.43 bill? The country club had already begun to use the toner, although the current copies were looking faint and streaked.

YOUR TASK As Dan Yamamoto, decide how to respond to this obvious scam. Should you pay the bill? Should you return the unused bottle? Write a persuasive claim to Copy Machine Specialists, 4320 Admiralty Way, Honolulu, HI 96643. Supply any details necessary.

10.11 Persuasive Claim: No Champagne for Breakfast (L.O. 3)

As regional manager for an electronics parts manufacturer, you and two other employees attended a conference in Charleston, South Carolina. You stayed at the Spring Hill Inn because your company recommends that employees use this hotel. Generally, your employees have liked their accommodations, and the rates have been within your company's budget.

Now, however, you are unhappy with the charges you see on your company's credit card statement from Spring Hill Inn. When your department's administrative assistant made the reservations, she was assured that you would receive the weekend rates and that a hot breakfast—in the hotel restaurant, the Clarion—would be included in the rate. You hate those cold sweet rolls and instant coffee "continental" breakfasts, especially when you have to leave early and won't get another meal until afternoon. So you and the other two employees went to the restaurant and ordered a hot meal from the menu.

When you received the credit card statement, though, you saw a charge for $132 for three champagne buffet breakfasts in the Clarion. You hit the ceiling! For one thing, you didn't have a buffet breakfast and certainly no champagne. The three of you got there so early that no buffet had been set up. You ordered pancakes and sausage, and for this you were billed $44 each. You are outraged! What's worse, your company may charge you personally for exceeding the expected rates.

In looking back at this event, you remember that other guests on your floor were having a "continental" breakfast in a lounge on your floor. Perhaps that's where the hotel expected all guests on the weekend rate to eat. However, your administrative assistant had specifically asked about this matter when she made the reservations, and she was told that you could order breakfast from the menu at the hotel's restaurant.

YOUR TASK You want to straighten out this problem, and you can't do it by telephone because you suspect that you will need a written record of this entire mess. Write a persuasive claim to Customer Service, Spring Hill Inn, 115 Lady Street, Charleston, SC 29401. Should you include a copy of the credit card statement showing the charge?

10.12 Persuasive Claim: Mysterious Legal Costs (L.O. 3)

Originally a shipbuilding village, the town of Mystic, Connecticut, captures the spirit of the nineteenth-century seafaring era. But it is best known for Mystic Pizza, a bustling local pizzeria featured in a movie that launched the film career of Julia Roberts. Today, customers line the sidewalk waiting to taste its pizza, called by some "a slice of heaven."

Assume that you are the business manager for Mystic Pizza's owners. They were approached by an independent vendor who wants to use the Mystic Pizza name and secret recipes to distribute frozen pizza through grocery and convenience stores. As business manager, you worked with a law firm, Peabody, Conn, Manges & Traurig. This firm was to draw up contracts regarding the use of Mystic Pizza's name and quality standards for the product. When you received the bill from Harry Peabody, you were flabbergasted. It itemized 38 hours of attorney preparation, at $400 per hour, and 55 hours of paralegal assistance, at $100 per hour. The bill also showed $415 for telephone calls, which might be accurate because Mr. Peabody had to talk with the owners, who were vacationing in Italy at the time. You seriously doubt, however, that an experienced attorney would require 38 hours to draw up the contracts in question. When you began checking, you discovered that excellent legal advice could be obtained for $200 an hour.

YOUR TASK Decide what you want to request, and then write a persuasive request to Harry Peabody, Attorney at Law, Peabody, Conn, Manges & Traurig, 252 Broad Street, Boston, MA 02109. Include an end date and a reason for it.

10.13 Persuasive Organizational Message Flowing Downward: Supporting Project H.E.L.P. (L.O. 4)

E-Mail

As employee relations manager of Prudential Financial, one of your tasks is to promote Project H.E.L.P. (Higher Education Learning Program), an on-the-job learning opportunity. Project H.E.L.P. is a combined effort of major corporations and the Newark Unified School District. You must recruit 12 employees who will volunteer as instructors for 50 or more students. The students will spend four hours a week at the Prudential Newark facility earning an average of five units of credit a semester.

This semester the students will be serving in the Claims, Word Processing, Corporate Media Services, Marketing, Communications, Library, and Administrative Support departments. Your task is to convince employees in these departments to volunteer. They will be expected to supervise and instruct the students. In return, employees will receive two hours of release time per week to work with the students. The program has been very successful thus far. School officials, students, and employees alike express satisfaction with the experience and the outcomes.

YOUR TASK Write a persuasive memo or e-mail with convincing appeals that will bring you 12 volunteers to work with Project H.E.L.P. Add any necessary information.

10.14 Persuasive Organizational Request Flowing Downward: Please Dump Your Own Trash (L.O. 4)

E-Mail

In offices across the country, employees are being asked to empty their own desk trash cans instead of having custodial staff empty them. Sure, it sounds like a small thing, but it could make a big difference in custodial fees.

"One of the really labor-intensive parts of custodial work is walking to people's desks and emptying the trash," said Dana Williams, director of facilities for a commission that manages buildings for more than 100 state agencies in Texas. Having employees empty their own waste baskets is expected to save at least $825,000 annually in labor costs in Texas.

In addition to saving money, employees who empty their own trash cans could become more conscious of recycling. At the University of Washington, employees have been emptying their own trash cans for over a decade. The program was started as part of an environmental initiative, but now it is recognized as a money saver. Gene Woodard, the director of building services at the university, admitted that the program was not always enthusiastically welcomed. He said that some employees complained about "stinky trash cans they forgot to empty before a vacation." He noted, however, that such mistakes were made only once.

Dartmouth College recently launched a similar program as part of a sustainability initiative. Psychology professor Catherine Cramer said that she already was recycling nearly all the targeted items. "The only real change will be that I am expected to haul it to some central place myself instead of having custodial staff pick it up. The real goals here, however prettily wrapped in sustainability rhetoric, are rather obvious," she wrote on a university website. Professor Cramer questioned the economics of transferring work from the school's lowest-paid workers to higher-paid employees. "While I am certainly not above emptying my own trash," she said, "it's less clear to me that it's a good use of my professional time, especially to make the frequent trips necessitated by a tiny bucket."

In the private sector, companies are also saving money and enhancing recycling by having employees handle their own trash cans. Brewer Science, a semiconductor supplier in Missouri, has had some employees empty their trash cans for many years. Its custodial staff is now a quarter of its original size, and its costs for hauling waste remained the same even as the company doubled in size.

The Business Division at your university has been singled out for a pilot program to determine whether the entire campus will implement a trash-can-emptying program. The primary goal is saving money in the midst of campus-wide budget cuts of 25 percent in every division. The busy dean of the Business Division asks you, his executive assistant, to draft a message for him. He knows that he could simply announce a new trash mandate and demand that faculty members comply. However, he wants to persuade them to buy in to this program so that they comply willingly. He also would like to see his division cited as an example for the entire university.[76]

YOUR TASK For the signature of Dean Michael Ravera, draft a persuasive e-mail addressed to Business Division faculty members. Ask them to begin emptying their own desk trash cans weekly into the large dumpsters in the basement. Supply additional plausible details to enhance this persuasive message.

10.15 Persuasive Organizational Message Flowing Downward: Become an Urban Farming Volunteer (L.O. 4)

E-Mail Web

As employee relations manager of Paychex of San Francisco, one of your tasks is to promote Urban Farming, a global organization that has established almost 60,000 gardens in nearly 40 cities. Originating in the Detroit area, Urban Farming is a combined effort of major corporations. You must recruit 12 coworkers who will volunteer to plant gardens and teach community families about healthy eating.

Your task is to find volunteers in your company to start a community garden and in turn recruit other Paychex volunteers. San Francisco offers more than 5,000 vacant lots to choose from, and the city already manages 40 gardens. Paychex volunteers will be expected to attend training sessions and then to supervise and instruct participating members of the community. In return, employees will receive two hours of release time per week to work on their Urban Farming projects. The program has been very successful thus far, and the interest in community gardens is growing.

YOUR TASK Learn more about Urban Farming by searching the Web. Then write a persuasive memo or e-mail with convincing appeals that will bring you 12 volunteers to work with Urban Farming.

10.16 Persuasive Message Flowing Upward: We Want a Four-Day Workweek (L.O. 4)

E-Mail Team Web

Some companies and municipalities are switching to a four-day workweek to reduce traffic congestion, air pollution, and stressed employees. Compressing the workweek into four 10-hour days sounds pretty good to you. You would much prefer having Friday free to schedule medical appointments and take care of family business, in addition to leisurely three-day weekends.

As a manager at Skin Essentials, a mineral-based skin care products and natural cosmetics company, you are convinced that the company's 200 employees could switch to a four-day workweek with many resulting benefits. For one thing, they would save on gasoline and commute time. You know that many cities and companies have already implemented a four-day workweek with considerable success. You took a quick poll of immediate employees and managers and found that 80 percent thought that a four-day workweek was a good idea. One said, "This would be great! Think of what I could save on babysitting and lunches!"

YOUR TASK With a group of other students, conduct research on the Web and discuss your findings. What are the advantages of a four-day workweek? What organizations have already tried it? What appeals could be used to persuade management to adopt a four-day workweek? What arguments could be expected, and how would you counter them? Individually or as a group, prepare a one-page persuasive e-mail or memo addressed to the Skin Essentials Management Council. Decide on a goal. Do you want to suggest a pilot study? Should you meet with management to present your ideas? How about starting a four-day workweek immediately?

10.17 Persuasive Organizational Message Flowing Upward: No Free Fruit? (L.O. 4)

E-Mail

Always seeking out efficiencies, Omni Hotels looked for ways to slice expenses. Omni operates 43 luxury hotels and resorts in leading business gateways and leisure destinations across North America. From exceptional golf and spa retreats to dynamic business settings, each Omni showcases the local flavor of the destination while featuring four-diamond services.

Omni Hotels ranks at the top in "Highest in Guest Satisfaction Among Upscale Hotel Chains," according to J. D. Power. One signature amenity it has offered for years is a bowl of free apples in its lobbies. However, providing apples costs hundreds of thousands of dollars a year. They have to cut costs somewhere, and executives are debating whether to cut out apples as a way to save money with minimal impact on guests.

Omni Hotels prides itself on delivering superior service through The Power of One, a service program that provides associates the training and authority to make decisions that exceed the expectations of guests. The entire culture of the hotel creates a positive, supportive environment that rewards associates through the Omni Service Champions program. As an Omni associate, you are disturbed that the hotel is considering giving up its free apples. You hope that executives will find other ways to cut expenses, such as purchasing food in smaller amounts or reducing the hours of its lobby cafes.[77]

YOUR TASK In the true sense of The Power of One, you decide to express your views to management. Write a persuasive message to Richard Johnson (*rjohnson@omni.com*), Vice President, Operations, Omni Hotels, 420 Decker Drive, Irving, TX 75062. Should you write a letter or an e-mail? In a separate note to your instructor, explain your rationale for your channel choice and your message strategy.

10.18 Persuasive Organizational Message Flowing Upward: Counting on Tips (L.O. 4)

Team

Perched high atop a granite cliff overlooking the rugged Big Sur coastline sits Pacific's Edge Restaurant, where migrating whales may be seen from every table in the dining room. Sunsets here are so spectacular that the entire dining room often breaks out in spontaneous applause. You truly enjoy working in this magical Big Sur resort setting—except for one thing. You have occasionally been "stiffed" by a patron who left no tip. You know your service is excellent, but some customers just don't get it. They seem to think that tips are optional, a sign of appreciation. For servers, however, tips are 80 percent of their income.

In a recent *New York Times* article, you learned that some restaurants—such as the famous Coach House Restaurant in New York—automatically add a 15 percent tip to the bill. In Santa Monica the Lula restaurant prints gratuity guidelines on checks, showing customers what a 15 or 20 percent tip would be. You also know that American Express displays a gratuity calculation on its terminals. This means that diners don't even have to do the math!

YOUR TASK Because they know you are studying business communication, your fellow servers have asked you to write a serious letter to Constantine Delmonico, General Manager, Big Sur Properties, 48130 California Highway 1, Big Sur, CA 93920. They think a letter will be more effective than a conversation. Persuade him to adopt mandatory tipping guidelines in the restaurant. Talk with fellow servers (your classmates) to develop logical persuasive arguments.

10.19 Taking Aim at Puffery in Advertising (L.O. 5)

Communication Technology | Social Media | Web

As you have seen in this chapter, puffery in advertising may be tacky, but it is not illegal. Few of us take claims seriously that shout, *the best pizza in town, largest selection of electronics, the ultimate fresh breath, the world's juiciest hamburgers, the biggest pie money can buy,* or *coldest beer.* After all, such exaggerated claims cannot be proven and do not fool anyone.

Serious, quantifiable claims, however, must be backed up with evidence, or they could mean litigation: "Our chicken has less fat than a hamburger. It's better for you."[78] This bold claim was investigated, and the fried chicken restaurant had to stop using it in its advertising. Yes, the fried chicken had a little less total fat than a hamburger, but it contained more harmful transfat, sodium, and cholesterol, making it higher in calories—a decidedly unhealthy alternative. As the FTC points out, a restaurant can compare itself to others, but it must tell the truth.

YOUR TASK Look for examples of puffery and find ads that would need to prove their claims. How can you tell which is which? Discuss examples in class or in an online forum set up for your class.

10.20 Using Reader Benefits to Sell (L.O. 1, 5)

Web

Audience benefits sell. People are more likely to be persuaded when they see a direct or indirect benefit of a product, service, idea, or cause. Features may describe a product or service, but they don't tell a story. To be persuasive, writers must convert features into benefits. They must tell the audience how they can best use the item to benefit from it.

YOUR TASK Online or offline find a product or service that you admire. Be sure to locate a detailed description of the item's unique features. Create a table and in the left column list the item's features. In the right column, convert the features into benefits by matching them to the needs of your target audience.

10.21 Direct-Mail Sales Letter: Pitaya—Selling a "Superfruit" (L.O. 5)

E-Mail

Eric Helms is the founder and CEO of Juice Generation, a chain of juice and smoothie bars in New York City. He bought the exclusive rights to a year's supply of pitaya, a little-known softball-sized fruit of a cactus found in Nicaragua. The Vietnamese dragonfruit is the pitaya's Asian cousin. To prevent agricultural pests from entering the United States, only the fruit's frozen pulp may be shipped from Central America. The pitaya reportedly tastes like a cross between strawberries and wheatgrass and is said to contain an antioxidant believed to protect from cancer-causing free radicals. David Wolfe, author of *Superfoods*, is enthusiastic: "It's one of my favorite fruits of all time. It's superhigh in vitamin

C and superhydrating." Yet even within health food circles, the fruit is still largely unknown.

The "superpremium" juice business that focuses on healthy, exotic nectars (such as pomegranate and, most recently, the açaí berry) is a multibillion-dollar enterprise. The big players all have their brands—for example, Odwalla (Coca-Cola), Naked (PepsiCo), and Jamba Juice. Celebrities such as Russell Simmons and Gwyneth Paltrow have endorsed juicing. Salma Hayek, a longtime juicer, cofounded the Cooler Cleanse juice brand with Helms.

The term *superfruit* is a marketing term, referring to fruits heavy in antioxidants, but without any scientific or regulatory definition, says Jeffrey Blumberg, director of the U.S. Department of Agriculture's antioxidants research laboratory. "As most natural fruits contain one or more positive nutrient attributes," Blumberg explains, "any one might be considered by someone 'super' in its own way." An industry primer is blunt: "Superfruits are the product of strategy, not something you find growing on a tree."[79] POM Wonderful lost a lawsuit to the FTC for deceptive advertising of its pomegranate juice.

Helms' Juice Generation partnered with a factory in Nicaragua that employs only single mothers who scoop and blend the fruit. The women pour the pulp into 3.5-ounce packets that are frozen for shipping. The Pink Pitaya Coco Blend, a mix of coconut, banana, and pitaya, costs $8.45. "You have to give people what they want, but also what they should be trying," Helms believes.[80]

YOUR TASK Write a sales letter or a marketing e-mail promoting the Pink Pitaya Coco Blend. Your audience in this campaign will probably be gyms with in-house juice bars. Introduce the exotic pitaya fruit and explain its benefits. Cull information from the scenario to include a testimonial. Make sure your claims are ethical and legal.

10.22 Sales Message: Subscribing to Organic Greens (L.O. 5)

E-Mail

Many consumers worry about what's in their food. They fear conventional factory farming, wish to be good stewards of the environment, and desire a sustainable lifestyle. Wholesome, organic food can increasingly be found on the shelves of mainstream supermarkets. Even big-box stores such as Costco—not just health food stores such as Mother's Market, Sprouts Farmers Market, and Whole Foods Market—are capitalizing on the farm-to-table trend. Weekly farmers' markets selling local produce and fruit are common across America.

But even busy urbanites who don't like to travel to shop can embrace healthier fare by subscribing to farm fresh veggies and fruit online for home delivery. Services such as Farm Fresh to You in California, themselves organic farmers since 1976, partner with other organic farms to offer customizable boxes with several service and delivery options. Because these co-op-type outfits benefit from economies of scale, their prices, although higher than those of conventional markets, are not exorbitant. The delivery services also offer priceless convenience. Subscribers can customize their boxes on the Fair & Fresh Farming website, or they can let the farmers select the content for them.

The advantages of receiving weekly boxes filled with healthy seasonal produce include fresh, delicious taste, wholesome food that's free from herbicides and pesticides, and less traffic by ordering a custom box online each week or less frequently. In addition, subscribers are supporting small family farms that supply local, in-season fruit and veggies instead of buying greens that are flown halfway around the world. Depending on location, subscribers receive their boxes on Tuesday or Wednesday if they order a box by 10 a.m. on Sunday. For Thursday or Friday delivery, orders must be placed by 10 a.m. on Tuesday. New members receive 20 percent off their first order.

YOUR TASK Write a sales message—a letter or an e-mail—for the signature of "Marketer-in-Chief" Martina Sabatini, Fair & Fresh Farming, 513 E Valentine Road, Glendive, MT 59330. Provide an enticing but accurate explanation of the service, and invite your reader to subscribe. Focus on audience benefits.

10.23 Sales Message: Promoting Products and Services (L.O. 5)

E-Mail

Identify a situation in your current job or a previous one in which a sales message is or was needed. Using suggestions from this chapter, write an appropriate sales message that promotes a product or service. Use actual names, information, and examples. If you have no work experience, imagine a business you would like to start: word or data processing, pet grooming, car detailing, cleaning, tutoring, specialty knitting, balloon decorating, delivery service, child or elder care, gardening, lawn care, or something else.

YOUR TASK Write a sales letter or an e-mail marketing message selling your product or service to be distributed to your prospective customers. Be sure to tell them how to respond.

You don't need to know HTML or have a Constant Contact account to craft a concise and eye-catching online sales message. Try designing it in Microsoft Word and saving it as a Web page (go to the **File** tab and select **Save As**; then in the **Save as type** line, select **Web Page**). Consider adding graphics or photos—either your own or samples borrowed from the Internet. As long as you use them for this assignment and don't publish them online, you are not violating copyright laws.

10.24 Micromessages: Analyzing Twitter Feeds for AIDA Components (L.O. 1, 2, and 5)

Communication Technology | Social Media | Web

People are increasingly sharing persuasive and promotional social media posts. Most of the persuasive micromessages incorporate some elements of sales techniques—individual AIDA components. Naturally, few of us would buy something solely on the basis of a tweet, but such micromessages are teasers or alerts, directing receivers to websites, video clips, and other media sites.

Tip: To find persuasive posts fast, view the ultra-brief LinkedIn member ads visible on the right side of most LinkedIn screens. Alternatively, visit the sponsored links at *Bloomberg Businessweek*. Determine whether tweets and posts ask questions, favor the "you" view, and use other features that are hallmarks of persuasion. Share your results in class. Analyze and critique each other's findings.

Examples:

Consider these LinkedIn posts and the commentaries that follow:

> ***Spruce up Business Events. "Frank is fantastic." Skilled, fun, interactive musical entertainment.*** *Opts for vivid language and attracts attention with a benefit in the opening; includes a claim resembling a testimonial.*
>
> ***Senior Women Executives. Apply now to the Association of Women in Business. Register free.*** *Calls on a specific audience; uses "you" view; free registration encourages compliance.*
>
> ***Masters in Counseling. Earn a Chapman M.A. and jumpstart your career. Apply by Jan. 31.*** *Advertises graduate program as beneficial to career advancement; uses limited-time offer.*

Consider these tweets and the accompanying comments as models:

> ***With our updated Android app, share collections of photos with friends and family. Enjoy! http://wo.ly/gLknQ*** *Offers a benefit; conveys warmth* (Enjoy!)*; provides a useful hyperlink.*
>
> ***Enjoy easier, smarter access to Delta with the new http://delta.com and Fly Delta apps for smartphones and iPad: http://oka.xtr.ly/m/1umh*** *Employs "you" view; offers a benefit* (easier, smarter access)*; prompts a response with convenient hyperlinks.*
>
> ***Please donate to @RedCrossAU Tasmanian Bushfires Appeal http://bit.ly/Xs4l7g All donations over $2 are tax deductible #redcross #tasfires*** *Starts with a direct call for action; points out the benefit that contributions are tax deductible.*

YOUR TASK Examine a Twitter feed or other social media (e.g., LinkedIn) for persuasive micromessages that feature AIDA components such as attention getters, reader benefits, calls for action, limited-time offers, and freebies. Arrange them in categories as shown in Figure 10.12.

10.25 Writing Persuasive Tweets and Posts (L.O. 1, 5)

Communication Technology | Social Media | Web

Being able to compose effective and concise micromessages and posts will positively contribute to your professional online persona.

YOUR TASK Brainstorm to identify a special skill you have, an event you want others to attend, a charitable cause dear to your heart, or a product you like. Applying what you have learned about short persuasive messages online, write your own 140-character persuasive tweet or post. Use Figure 10.12 as a starting point and model.

10.26 Creating Newsy Press Releases (L.O. 6)

Web

You have been interviewed for a terrific job in corporate communications at an exciting organization. To test your writing skills, the organization asks you to rewrite one of its press releases for possible submission to your local newspaper. This means revising the information you find into a new press release that your local newspaper would be interested in publishing.

YOUR TASK Select an organization and study its press releases. For example, search the Web for *Amazon Media Room: Press Releases, FBI press release, Ben & Jerry's press release, Mars Candy press release, World Honda news release, Screen Actors Guild press release*, or an organization of your choice. Select one event or product that you think would interest your local newspaper. Although you can use the information from current press releases, don't copy the exact wording because the interviewer wants to see how you would present that information. Use the organization's format, and submit the press release to your instructor with a cover note identifying the newspaper or other publication in which you would like to see your press release published.

10.27 Press Release: Here's the Scoop! (L.O. 6)

YOUR TASK For a company where you now work or an organization you belong to, identify a product or service that could be publicized and write a press release. You could announce a new course at your college, a new president, new equipment, or a campaign to raise funds. The press release is intended for your local newspaper or online publication.

Test Your Etiquette IQ

New communication platforms and casual workplace environments have blurred the lines of appropriateness, leaving workers wondering how to navigate uncharted waters. Indicate whether the following statements are true or false. Then see if you agree with the responses on p. R-2.

1. At a business networking function, you should wait until the end of a conversation to pass out your business card.

   ________ True ________ False

2. Although you should never take home company equipment or major supplies, most employees are entitled to take home small items such as paper, folders, and pens.

   ________ True ________ False

3. In interacting with superiors, you should support your boss's decisions even though you think you might have made a better decision.

   ________ True ________ False

Chat About It

In each chapter you will find five discussion questions related to the chapter material. Your instructor may assign these topics for you to discuss in class, in an online chat room, or on an online discussion board. Some of the discussion topics may require outside research. You may also be asked to read and respond to postings made by your classmates.

TOPIC 1: Many users resent advertising pop-ups and banner ads on social media sites. They go to Facebook, Instagram, Pinterest, and Twitter to socialize virtually, not to shop. How do you feel about sales pitches on your favorite social media sites?

TOPIC 2: Consider your vast experience with TV and other advertising. Can you think of commercials or ads that seem to fall in the category of puffery or could even be considered deceptive? How do you know the difference between the two?

TOPIC 3: When have you had to persuade someone (a boss, parent, instructor, friend, or colleague) to do something or change a belief? What strategies did you use? Were they successful? How could you improve your technique?

TOPIC 4: When have you had to complain to a company, organization, or person about something that went wrong or that offended you? Share your experience. What channel did you use for your complaint? How effective was your channel choice and strategy? What would you change in your method for future complaints?

TOPIC 5: Think of a product you have used and like. If you were trying to sell that product, what rational appeals would you use? What emotional appeals would you use? Try to sell that product to your classmates.

Grammar and Mechanics | *Review 10*

Confusing Words and Frequently Misspelled Words

Review the lists of confusing words and frequently misspelled words in Appendix D, Grammar and Mechanics Guide, beginning on page D-17. On a separate sheet, revise the following sentences to correct word usage errors. Sentences may have more than one error. If a sentence is correct, write *C*. When you finish, check your answers on page Key-2.

EXAMPLE: He complained that his capitol investments had been aversely effected.

REVISION: He complained that his **capital** investments had been **adversely affected.**

1. The principle part of the manager's persuasive message contained a complement and valuable advise.
2. Did you allready analyse the product's major and miner appeals before writing the sales message?

3. In responding to the irate customer, Carmen made a conscience effort to show patients and present creditable facts.
4. Even in every day business affairs, we strive to reach farther and go beyond what is expected.
5. Before you procede with the report, please check those suprising statistics.
6. It's usally better to de-emphasize bad news then to spotlight it.
7. Incidently, passive-voice verbs can help you make a statement less personnel when neccessary.
8. Customers are more excepting of disapointing news if they are ensured that there requests were heard and treated fairly.
9. The customer's complaint illicited an immediate response that analized the facts carefully but was not to long.
10. When delivering bad news, try to acomodate a disatisfied customer with a plausible alternative.

References

[1] Based on Galasko, L., & Muttram, S. M., CEO, ōlloclip (personal communication with Dana Loewy, March 20, 2016).

[2] White, E. (2008, May 19). The art of persuasion becomes key. *The Wall Street Journal.* Retrieved from http://online.wsj.com/article/SB121115784262002373.html; McIntosh, P., & Luecke, R. A. (2011). *Increase your influence at work.* New York: American Management Association, p. 4.

[3] Hamilton, C. (2011). *Communicating for results* (9th ed.). Boston: Wadsworth, Cengage Learning, p. 373.

[4] Fogg, B. J. (2008). Mass interpersonal persuasion: An early view of a new phenomenon. Stanford Persuasive Tech Lab. Retrieved from http://captology.stanford.edu/wp-content/uploads/2014/03/MIP_Fogg_Stanford.pdf

[5] Perloff, R. M. (2013). *The dynamics of persuasion: Communication and attitudes in the 21st century* (5th ed.). New York: Routledge, pp. 12–19.

[6] Cialdini, R. B. (2009). *Influence: The psychology of persuasion.* New York: HarperCollins, p. xiv.

[7] Ibid., p. x.

[8] Discussion based on Perloff, R. M. (2013). *The dynamics of persuasion: Communication and attitudes in the 21st century* (5th ed.). New York: Routledge.

[9] Raab, D. (2015, September 29). How many ads do you see each day? Fewer than it seems (I think). Customer Experience Matrix. Retrieved from http://customerexperiencematrix.blogspot.de/2015/09/how-many-ads-per-day-do-you-see-fewer.html

[10] Wike, R., Stokes, B., & Poushter, J. (2015, June 23). Global Attitudes & Trends: America's global image. Pew Research Center. Retrieved from http://www.pewglobal.org/2015/06/23/1-americas-global-image

[11] Adalian, J. (2015, December 2). The most popular U.S. TV shows in 18 countries around the world. Vulture. Retrieved from http://www.vulture.com/2015/12/most-popular-us-tv-shows-around-the-world.html?mid=facebook_nymag

[12] Perloff, R. M. (2013). *The dynamics of persuasion: Communication and attitudes in the 21st century* (5th ed.). New York: Routledge, p. 9.

[13] Canavor, N. (2012). *Business writing in the digital age.* Thousand Oaks, CA: Sage, p. 169.

[14] Patel, S. (2016, January 4). 5 easy ways to build more business relationships as an entrepreneur. *Entrepreneur.* Retrieved from https://www.entrepreneur.com/article/254465

[15] Nayar, V. (2010, June). How I did it: A maverick CEO explains how he persuaded his team to leap into the future. *Harvard Business Review.* Retrieved from http://hbr.org/2010/06/how-i-did-it-a-maverick-ceo-explains-how-he-persuaded-his-team-to-leap-into-the-future/ar/1

[16] Bryant, A. (2012, March 25). Want to innovate? Feed a cookie to the monster. *The New York Times.* Retrieved from http://www.nytimes.com/2012/03/25/business/terry-tietzen-of-edatanetworks-on-promoting-innovation.html

[17] Young Entrepreneur Council. (2014, November 24). 8 pushy sales tactics that could harm your business. *Inc.* Retrieved from http://www.inc.com/young-entrepreneur-council/8-pushy-sales-tactics-that-could-harm-your-business.html; James, G. (2010, March 11). Enterprise Rent-A-Car: When sales tactics backfire. CBSNews.com/Moneywatch. Retrieved from http://www.cbsnews.com/8301-505183_162-28548988-10391735/enterprise-rent-a-car-when-sales-tactics-backfire; Strauss, S. (2010, May 24). Ask an expert: Do us a favor and avoid the hard sell, it's bad for business. USAToday.com. Retrieved from http://usatoday30.usatoday.com/money/smallbusiness/columnist/strauss/2010-05-23-hard-sell-tactics_N.htm; Salmon, J. (2010, May 12). Barclays hard sell tactics exposed. This is MONEY.co.uk. Retrieved from http://www.thisismoney.co.uk/money/saving/article-1693952/Barclays-hard-sell-tactics-exposed.html

[18] Tressler, C. (2015, June 29). FTC curbs auto dealers' deceptive advertising. Federal Trade Commission. Retrieved from https://www.consumer.ftc.gov/blog/ftc-curbs-auto-dealers-deceptive-advertising

[19] Satell, G. (2014, June 8). How a genius thinks. Digital Tonto. Retrieved from http://www.digitaltonto.com/2014/how-a-genius-thinks

[20] Nayar, V. (2011, August 8). The manager's new role. HBR Blog Network. Retrieved from http://blogs.hbr.org/hbr/nayar/2011/08/the-manager-new-role.html

[21] Harwell, D. (2015, August 24). Starbucks' CEO sent this bizarre memo telling baristas to be nicer because of the stock turmoil. *The Washington Post.* Retrieved from https://www.washingtonpost.com/news/business/wp/2015/08/24/starbucks-chief-sent-a-bizarre-memo-telling-baristas-to-be-nicer-because-of-the-stock-market

[22] Feloni, R. (2016, January 14). Zappos CEO Tony Hsieh explains why 18% of employees quit during the company's radical management experiment. *Business Insider.* Retrieved from http://www.businessinsider.com/zappos-ceo-tony-hsieh-on-holacracy-transition-2016-1; Silverman, R. E. (2015, May 20). At Zappos, banishing the bosses brings confusion. *The Wall Street Journal.* Retrieved from http://www.wsj.com/articles/at-zappos-banishing-the-bosses-brings-confusion-1432175402

[23] Bryant, A. (2012, April 7). The phones are out, but the robot is in. *The New York Times.* Retrieved from http://www.nytimes.com/2012/04/08/business/phil-libin-of-evernote-on-its-unusual-corporate-culture.html

[24] McIntosh, P., & Luecke, R. A. (2011). *Increase your influence at work.* New York: AMACOM, p. 2.

[25] Brandon, J. (2014, December 12). 20 leadership experts share their best leadership tip. *Inc.* Retrieved from http://www.inc.com/john-brandon/20-leadership-experts-share-their-best-leadership-tip.html

[26] Pollock, T. (2003, June). How to sell an idea. *SuperVision*, p. 15. Retrieved from http://search.proquest.com

[27] Communicating with the boss. (2006, May). *Communication Briefings*, p. 8.
[28] Personal communication with Mary Ellen Guffey, March 28, 2016.
[29] Dao, J. (2012, March 9). Ad campaign for Marines cites chaos as job perk. *The New York Times*. Retrieved from http://www.nytimes.com/2012/03/10/us/marines-marketing-campaign-uses-chaos-as-a-selling-point.html?_r=0
[30] Perkins, D. (2015, March 18). Corps times release of new ad with March Madness. *Marine Corps Times*. Retrieved from http://www.marinecorpstimes.com/story/military/2015/03/16/march-madness-marine-corps-advertisements/24866553
[31] Haskel, D. (2015, April 14). 2015 DMA response rate report: Direct mail outperforms all digital channels combined by nearly 600%. IWCO Direct. Retrieved from http://www.iwco.com/blog/2015/04/14/dma-response-rate-report-and-direct-mail
[32] Ibid.
[33] Ibid.
[34] Lee, K. (2015, May 22). Seven reasons to make direct mail part of your digital marketing. ClickZ. Retrieved from https://www.clickz.com/clickz/column/2409287/seven-reasons-to-make-direct-mail-part-of-your-digital-marketing-plan; Millward Brown. (2009). Using neuroscience to understand the role of direct mail, p. 2. Retrieved from http://www.millwardbrown.com/Insights/CaseStudies/NeuroscienceDirectMail.aspx
[35] Compton, J. (2015, March 4). Direct mail goes digital. Direct Marketing. Retrieved from http://www.dmnews.com/direct-mail/direct-mail-goes-digital/article/400201; Direct mail statistics show B2B mailings are still effective. (2011, March 8). The Ballantine Corporation. Retrieved from https://www.ballantine.com/direct-mail-statistics; Hartong, B. (2011, March). Revitalize your direct mail strategy. *Customer Interaction Solutions*, p. 10. Retrieved from http://proquest.umi.com
[36] Ward, S. (2016, January 4). The B2B marketing mix: Direct mail campaigns. Pardot. Retrieved from http://www.pardot.com/blog/the-b2b-marketing-mix-direct-mail-campaigns; Macleod, I. (2013, October). Infographic: Consumers more likely to deal with direct mail immediately compared to email. The Drum. Retrieved from http://www.thedrum.com/news/2013/10/23/infographic-consumers-more-likely-deal-direct-mail-immediately-compared-email; DMA releases 2010 response rate trend report. (2010, June 15). Direct Marketing Association. Retrieved from http://www.the-dma.org/cgi/dispannouncements?article=1451; Hartong, B. (2011, March). Revitalize your direct mail strategy. Customer Interaction Solutions, p. 10. Retrieved from http://proquest.umi.com
[37] Direct mail marketing spending in the United States from 2009 to 2014 (in billion U.S. dollars). (2016). Statista. Retrieved from http://www.statista.com/statistics/289174/direct-mail-marketing-spending-us; Jones, R. (2013, October 31). Data quality news: Direct mail is still a relevant marketing strategy in 2013. Experian. Retrieved from http://www.qas.com/data-quality-news/direct_mail_is_still_a_relevant_marketing_strategy_in_2013_9721.htm; Statistical Fact Book. (2011). The Direct Marketing Association. Retrieved from http://www.the-dma.org/cgi/disppressrelease?article=1474+++++
[38] Tinz, M. (2015, August 4). 4 ways to integrate direct mail into your digital marketing landscape. *Entrepreneur*. Retrieved from http://www.entrepreneur.com/article/249119
[39] McLaughlin, K. (1990, October). Words of wisdom. *Entrepreneur*, p. 101. See also Wastphal, L. (2001, October). Empathy in sales letters. *Direct Marketing*, p. 55.
[40] Carnegie, D. (2009). *How to win friends and influence people*. New York: Simon & Schuster, p. 14.
[41] Kruse, K. (2012, November 28). Zig Ziglar: 10 quotes that can change your life. *Forbes*. Retrieved from http://www.forbes.com/sites/kevinkruse/2012/11/28/zig-ziglar-10-quotes-that-can-change-your-life
[42] Bechara, A. (2004). The role of emotion in decision-making: Evidence from neurological patients with orbitofrontal damage. *Brain and Cognition*, 55, 30-40. doi:10.1016/j.bandc.2003.04.001
[43] Nahmias, E. (2012, August 13). Does contemporary neuroscience support or challenge the reality of free will? Big Questions Online. Retrieved from https://www.bigquestionsonline.com/content/does-contemporary-neuroscience-support-or-challenge-reality-free-will
[44] Wolfe, R. (2011, November 2). 5 tales of customer engagement: Brands connecting with buyers. Business 2 Community. Retrieved from http://www.business2community.com/branding/5-tales-of-customer-engagement-brands-connecting-with-buyers-071205#XIHT0r1lm0iIJp2T.97
[45] Huy, Q., & Shipilov, A. (2012, November 29). Use social media to build emotional capital. HBR Blog Network. Retrieved from http://blogs.hbr.org/cs/2012/11/use_social_media_to_build_emot.html
[46] Scott, D. M. (2011). *The new rules of marketing & PR* (3rd ed.). Hoboken, NJ: John Wiley & Sons, p. 39.
[47] Kendall, J. C. (2012, December 2). Facebook: Waste of time for most advertisers. Retrieved from http://www.socialmediatoday.com/content/facebook-waste-time-most-advertisers
[48] ExactTarget. (2012). The 2012 channel preference survey. Retrieved from http://www.exacttarget.com/subscribers-fans-followers/sff14.aspx
[49] Morrison, K. (2015, June 10). Report: Social media is the slowest way to resolve customer service issues. *Adweek*. Retrieved from http://www.adweek.com/socialtimes/report-social-media-is-the-slowest-way-to-resolve-customer-service-issues/621548
[50] Elkind, J. (2016, February 15). Making the most of social media, even when it's not driving sales. Marketing Land. Retrieved from http://marketingland.com/making-social-media-even-not-driving-sales-163234
[51] Smith, C. (2015, June 30). It's time for retailers to start paying close attention to social media. *Business Insider*. Retrieved from http://www.businessinsider.com/social-commerce-2015-report-2015-6; Delzio, S. (2015, May 27). Social media marketing trends gaining traction in 2015: New research. Social Media Examiner. Retrieved from http://www.socialmediaexaminer.com/social-media-marketing-trends-gaining-traction-in-2015-new-research
[52] O'Hara, J. (2015, March 27). How your small business can use social media to boost sales. *Entrepreneur*. Retrieved from http://www.entrepreneur.com/article/244383
[53] Black Friday Report 2015. IBM Watson Trend Hub. Retrieved from http://www-01.ibm.com/software/marketing-solutions/benchmark-reports/black-friday-report-2015.pdf
[54] Peel, M. B. (2015, March 9). 4 reasons direct mail should be part of your plan to acquire new customers. *Insurance Journal*. Retrieved from http://www.insurancejournal.com/magazines/features/2015/03/09/359395.htm; ExactTarget. (2012). The 2012 channel preference survey. Retrieved from http://www.exacttarget.com/subscribers-fans-followers/sff14.aspx
[55] Haskel, D. (2015, April 14). 2015 DMA response rate report: Direct mail outperforms all digital channels combined by nearly 600%. IWCO Direct. Retrieved from http://www.iwco.com/blog/2015/04/14/dma-response-rate-report-and-direct-mail; Peel, M. B. (2015, March 9). 4 reasons direct mail should be part of your plan to acquire new customers. *Insurance Journal*. Retrieved from http://www.insurancejournal.com/magazines/features/2015/03/09/359395.htm
[56] Weeks, J. (2015, October 30). Dietary supplements: Is regulation of the industry too lax? CQ Researcher. Retrieved from http://library.cqpress.com/cqresearcher/document.php?id=cqresrre2015103000; Wagner, L. (2015, November 17). Justice Department announces criminal charges against dietary supplement firms. NPR. Retrieved from http://www.npr.org/sections/thetwo-way/2015/11/17/456396714/justice-department-announces-criminal-charges-against-dietary-supplement-firms
[57] Robbins, R. (2016, January 5). Lumosity will pay $2 million to settle "deceptive" brain training claims. *Business Insider*. Retrieved from http://mobile.businessinsider.com/lumosity-pays-ftc-2-million-brain-training-claims-2016-1
[58] Anand, S. (2012, June 19). George Clooney and Julia Roberts sue for unauthorized use of their names and images. Retrieved from http://www.lfirm.com/blog/2012/06/george-clooney-and-julia-roberts-sue-for-unauthorized-use-of-their-names-and-images.shtml
[59] Boggs, S. P. (2014, June 2). Celebrity tweets can cost you millions. Lexology. Retrieved from http://www.lexology.com/library/detail.aspx?g=6b07fee7-a280-4e16-a9a6-430f6d34e111
[60] Investment companies: Video released by Pershing Square Capital Management exposes senior distributors admitting that Herbalife uses a "level of inauthenticity," leading to "eventual deception." (2015, January 3). *Investment Weekly News*, p. 534.
[61] O'Donnell, J. (2012, May 17). Sketchers to pay $40M over ad claims. *USA Today*, p. 1B.
[62] Ibid.
[63] Streitfeld, D. (2012, January 26). For $2 a star, an online retailer gets 5-star reviews. *The New York Times*. Retrieved from http://www.nytimes.com/2012/01/27/technology/for-2-a-star-a-retailer-gets-5-star-reviews.html
[64] Streitfeld, D. (2012, August 25). The best book reviews money can buy. *The New York Times*. Retrieved from http://www.nytimes.com/2012/08/26/business/book-reviewers-for-hire-meet-a-demand-for-online-raves.html?pagewanted=all&_r=0
[65] Warner, D. (2015, April 10). The legal lowdown on fake or paid reviews. Tech.Co. Retrieved from http://tech.co/legal-lowdown-fake-paid-reviews-2015-04

[66] Haskel, D. (2015, April 14). 2015 DMA response rate report: Direct mail outperforms all digital channels combined by nearly 600%. IWCO Direct. Retrieved from http://www.iwco.com/blog/2015/04/14/dma-response-rate-report-and-direct-mail

[67] Email vastly preferred by consumers for brand communications. (2016, March 30). MarketingCharts. Retrieved from http://www.marketingcharts.com/online/email-vastly-preferred-by-consumers-for-brand-communications-66661

[68] Colwyn, S. (2015, January 15). State of the art digital marketing 2015. Smart Insights. Retrieved from http://www.smartinsights.com/managing-digital-marketing/marketing-innovation/state-of-digital-marketing/attachment/stateoftheartdigitalmarketingsmartinsights

[69] Arno, C. (2015, February 9). How companies can engage with email marketing. TotalRetail. Retrieved from http://www.mytotalretail.com/article/how-companies-can-engage-with-email-marketing/3

[70] Haskel, D. (2015, April 14). 2015 DMA response rate report: Direct mail outperforms all digital channels combined by nearly 600%. IWCO Direct. Retrieved from http://www.iwco.com/blog/2015/04/14/dma-response-rate-report-and-direct-mail

[71] Ibid.

[72] Dvorak, J. C. (2015, October 21). Write an Amazon review, go to jail. *PC Magazine*. Retrieved from http://www.pcmag.com/article2/0,2817,2493493,00.asp

[73] Domonoske, C. (2016, January 13). You, too, can dress like "El Chapo." NPR. Retrieved from http://www.npr.org/sections/thetwo-way/2016/01/13/462901056/you-too-can-dress-like-el-chapo

[74] Nicks, D. (2016, January 12). El Chapo's shirts are flying off the shelves. *Money*. Retrieved from http://time.com/money/4177540/el-chapo-shirts-barabas; Masunaga, S. (2016, January 27). As seen on "El Chapo": There's a mad rush for this L.A. clothing company's shirts. *The Los Angeles Times*. Retrieved from http://www.latimes.com/business/la-fi-el-chapo-shirtmaker-20160127-story.html

[75] Larson, C. U. (2013). *Persuasion: Reception and responsibility* (13th ed.). Boston: Wadsworth, Cengage Learning, p. 17.

[76] Based on Reddy, S. (2010, November 1). Memo to all staff: Dump your trash. *The Wall Street Journal*, p. A4.

[77] Based on Yu, R. (2009, 13 March). Hotels take action to pare down food, restaurant expenses. *USA Today*, p. 3D.

[78] Scenario based on Federal Trade Commission. (n.d.). FTC fact sheet: It looks good . . . but is it true? Retrieved from https://www.consumer.ftc.gov/sites/default/files/games/off-site/youarehere/pages/pdf/FTC-Ad-Marketing_Looks-Good.pdf

[79] Scenario based on Rubin, C. (2012, September 6). Pitaya: The selling of a superfruit. *Bloomberg Businessweek*. Retrieved from http://www.businessweek.com/articles/2012-09-06/pitaya-the-selling-of-a-superfruit

[80] Ibid.

[81] Don't buy this jacket, Black Friday and the New York Times. (2011, November). The Cleanest Line. [Blog]. Retrieved from http://patagonia.typepad.com/files/nyt_11-25-11.pdf

UNIT 4

Reports, Proposals, and Presentations

Minerva Studio/Shutterstock.com

Chapter 11 Reporting in the Digital Age Workplace

LEARNING OUTCOMES

After studying this chapter, you should be able to

1 Explain informational and analytical report functions, organizational strategies, and writing styles as well as typical report formats.

2 Apply the 3-x-3 writing process to contemporary business reports to create well-organized documents that show a firm grasp of audience and purpose.

3 Locate and evaluate secondary sources such as databases and Internet resources, and understand how to conduct credible primary research.

4 Identify the purposes and techniques of citation and documentation in business reports, and avoid plagiarism.

5 Generate, use, and convert numerical data to visual aids, and create meaningful and attractive graphics.

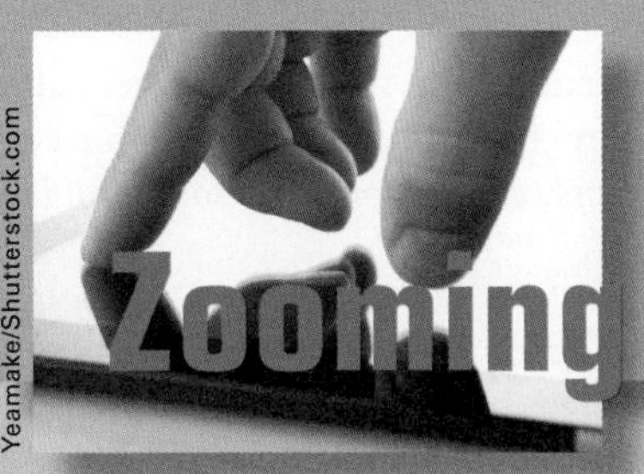

Yeamake/Shutterstock.com

Research for the Public Good at Pew

Reports are vital to organizations both large and small. They allow supervisors to stay informed about projects. They provide data that help management answer questions and make decisions. They synthesize information so that leaders can solve problems. Creating these important documents requires critical thinking as well as the ability to write clearly and correctly.

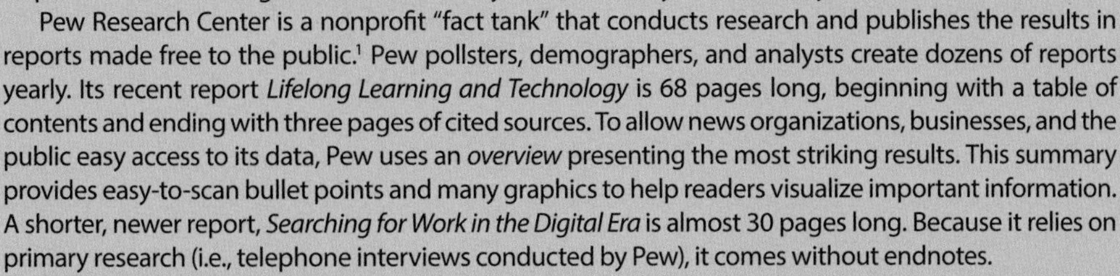

Pew Research Center is a nonprofit "fact tank" that conducts research and publishes the results in reports made free to the public.[1] Pew pollsters, demographers, and analysts create dozens of reports yearly. Its recent report *Lifelong Learning and Technology* is 68 pages long, beginning with a table of contents and ending with three pages of cited sources. To allow news organizations, businesses, and the public easy access to its data, Pew uses an *overview* presenting the most striking results. This summary provides easy-to-scan bullet points and many graphics to help readers visualize important information. A shorter, newer report, *Searching for Work in the Digital Era* is almost 30 pages long. Because it relies on primary research (i.e., telephone interviews conducted by Pew), it comes without endnotes.

Reports such as these may differ from the documents you write in your classes because they provide fact-based chunks of data to an information-hungry world; on the other hand, they are also conceived as in-depth explorations backed by solid scientific research for those who wish to dig deeper. Regardless of format, Pew reports are the result of a series of steps the writing team takes to complete the task, including (a) analyzing the problem, (b) conducting the research, (c) illustrating the data, (d) writing, and (e) revising and proofreading. Pew's polished products, which reach thousands of readers across the globe, are easy to read and aesthetically pleasing. They show that the authors have a firm grasp of their audience and purpose.

It is not surprising that Pew demands excellence of its report writers. Team members must possess "excellent writing and editing skills"[2] and "strong quantitative skills, including an ability to use various statistical programs to organize and analyze data."[3] Such skills are valued not just by Pew but by all organizations that must communicate in reports, both informal and formal.

Whether a report is seen by only a few key members of an organization or by thousands of readers around the world, good report-writing skills are essential for any business writer.

Critical Thinking

- Why are reports so important to organizations?
- Why do nonprofit organizations such as Pew Research Center provide their data free to the public?
- Why do reports such as *Searching for Work in the Digital Era* contain graphics?

Reporting in the Digital Age Workplace

Learning Outcome 1

Explain informational and analytical report functions, organizational strategies, and writing styles as well as typical report formats.

Digital age organizations compete in a world of constant change facilitated by innovative technology and the ability to generate and share vast amounts of data. Efficient reporting plays a critical role in helping organizations sift through data and make major decisions. Whether a company decides to launch a new product, expand into new markets, reduce expenses, improve customer service, or increase its social media presence, the decisions are usually based on information submitted in reports. Routine reports keep managers informed about work in progress. Focused, in-depth reports help managers analyze the challenges they face before recommending solutions. As we have seen, Pew Research Center generates reputable, accurate reports on important topics; however, it leaves policy decisions and advocacy to others.

Business reports range widely in length, purpose, and delivery mode. Some are short, informal bulleted lists with status updates. Others are formal 100-page financial forecasts. Sometimes they must follow a standard format as prescribed by law; for example, audit reports must conform to generally accepted accounting principles adopted by the U.S. Securities and Exchange Commission. Routine reports may be generated weekly or monthly, whereas reports generated irregularly, as needed, may cover specific problems or situations. Report findings may be presented orally in a meeting or shared online. Many reports today are delivered digitally in e-mail messages, PDF (portable document format) files, or slide decks. These files can then be accessed on a company's intranet, posted on the Internet, or saved on cloud servers off-site.

This chapter examines the functions, organizational strategies, writing style, and formats of typical business reports. It also introduces the report-writing process and discusses methods of collecting, documenting, and illustrating data. Some reports provide information only; others analyze and make recommendations. Although reports vary greatly in length, content, form, and formality level, they all have one or more of the following purposes: *to convey information, answer questions,* and *solve problems.*

Basic Report Functions

In terms of what they do, most reports fit into one of two broad categories: informational reports and analytical reports.

Informational Reports. Reports that present data without analysis or recommendations are primarily informational. For such reports, writers collect and organize facts, but they do not analyze the facts for readers. A trip report describing an employee's visit to a trade show, for example, presents information. Weekly bulleted status reports distributed by e-mail to a team record the activities of each group member and are shared with supervisors. Other reports that present information without analysis are monthly sales reports, progress reports, and government compliance reports.

Analytical Reports. Reports that provide data or findings, analyses, and conclusions are analytical. If requested, writers also supply recommendations. Analytical reports may intend to persuade readers to act or change their beliefs. For example, if you were writing a yardstick report that compares several potential manufacturing locations for a new automobile plant, you would compare the locations using the same criteria and then provide a recommendation. Other reports that provide recommendations are feasibility studies (e.g., for expansion opportunities) and justification reports (e.g., for buying equipment or changing procedures).

To distinguish among findings, conclusions, and recommendations, consider the example of an audit report. The auditor compiles facts and figures—the findings of the report—to meet the purpose or objective of the audit. Drawing inferences from the findings, the auditor arrives at conclusions. With the audit objectives in mind, the auditor may then propose corrective steps or actions as part of the recommendations.

maxuser/Shutterstock.com

Reality Check

Everything but the Kitchen Sink

"[Annual report] authors are unsure about what to include in their reports (or indeed where to put it) so they throw everything in. Consequently, such reports are often bursting to the gunnels with the minutiae of every forensic detail, no stone is left unturned, no waffle spared - the result, reams and reams of paper. And the reward, for all this toil? Ninety percent of readers will just read the summary."[4]

—Julie Wales, *senior training consultant, Lines of Communication*

Organizational Strategies

Like other business messages, reports may be organized directly or indirectly. The reader's anticipated reaction and the content of a report determine its organizational strategy, as illustrated in Figure 11.1. In long reports, such as corporate annual reports, some parts may be developed directly, whereas other parts are arranged indirectly.

Direct Strategy. When you place the purpose for writing close to the beginning of a report, the organizational strategy is direct. Informational reports, such as the short report shown in Figure 11.2, are usually arranged directly. They open with an introduction, which

Figure 11.1 **Audience Analysis and Report Organization**

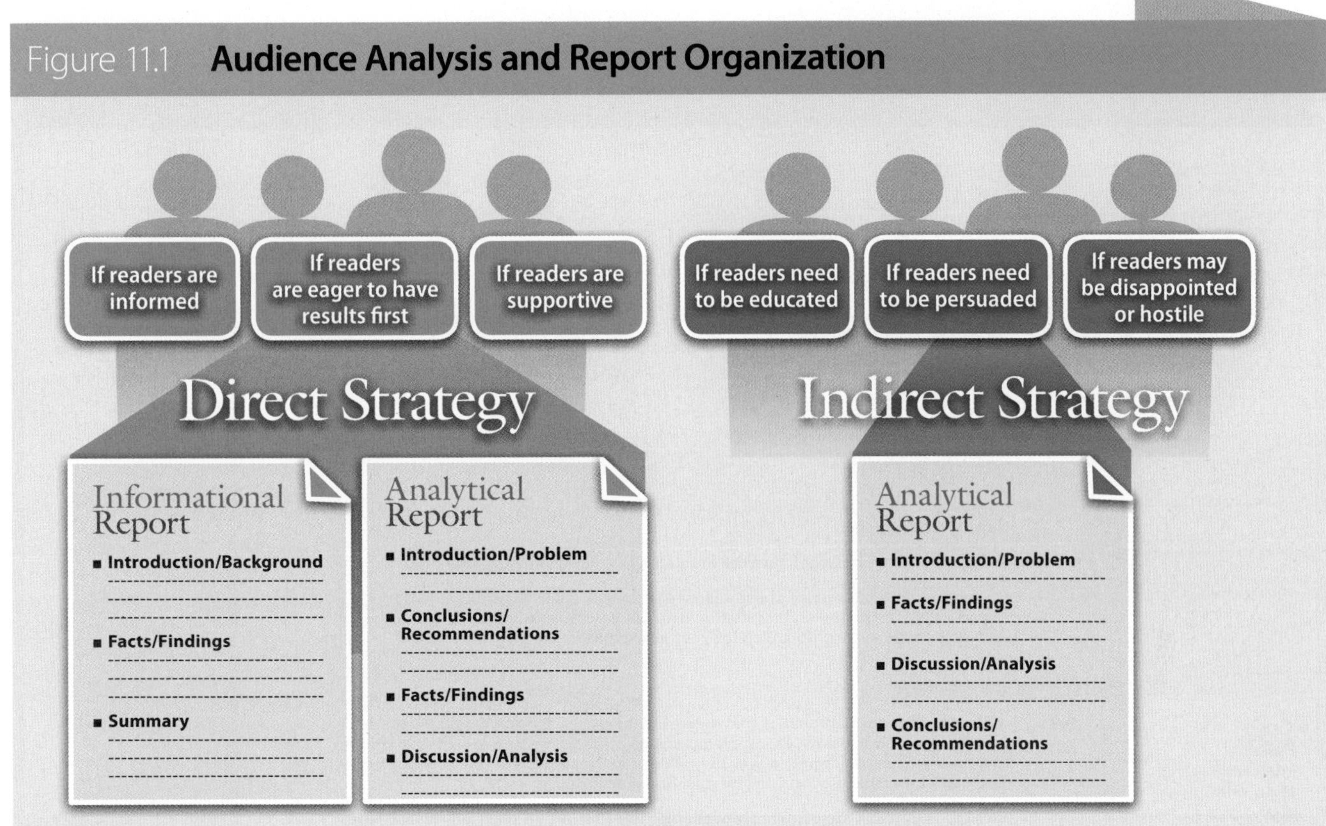

is followed by the facts and a summary. In Figure 11.2 the writer responds to a request for information about a legal services plan. The report opens with an introduction that provides details about the available plans. The facts about the plans' benefits, divided into three subtopics and identified by descriptive headings, follow. The report ends with a summary and a complimentary close.

Analytical reports may also be organized directly, especially when readers are supportive of or familiar with the topic. Many busy executives prefer this strategy because it gives them the results of the report immediately. They don't have to spend time wading through the facts, findings, discussion, and analyses to get to the two items they are most interested in—the conclusions and recommendations. Figure 11.3 illustrates such an arrangement. This short analytical report describes environmental hazards of a property that a realtor has just listed. The realtor is familiar with the investigation and eager to learn the recommendations. Therefore, the memo is organized directly. You should be aware, though, that unless readers are familiar with the topic, they may find the direct strategy confusing. Many readers prefer the indirect strategy because it seems logical and mirrors the way they solve problems.

Indirect Strategy. The organizational strategy is indirect when the conclusions and recommendations, if requested, appear at the end of the report. Such reports usually begin with an introduction or description of the problem, followed by facts and interpretations from the writer. They end with conclusions and recommendations. This strategy is helpful when readers are unfamiliar with the problem. This strategy is also useful when readers must be persuaded or when they may be disappointed in or hostile toward the report's findings. The writer is more likely to retain the reader's interest by first explaining, justifying, and analyzing the facts and then making recommendations. This strategy also seems most rational to readers because it follows the normal thought process: problem, alternatives (facts), solution.

Figure 11.2 Short Informational Report

Shield Legal Services

P.O. Box 465
Round Rock, TX 78664

(512) 248-8931
www.shieldlegal.com

Uses letterhead stationery for an informal report addressed to an outsider

September 17, 2018

Ms. Ava Hammond, Office Manager
Lake Austin Homeowners
3902 Oak Hill Drive
Austin, TX 78134

Dear Ms. Hammond:

Subject: Request for Legal Services Plan for a Homeowners' Association

Thank you for your inquiry about a legal services plan for your homeowners' association. The following information describes our available plans and gives instructions for setting up a plan for your association.

Presents introduction and facts without analysis or recommendations

Introduction

A legal services plan promotes preventive law by letting members talk to attorneys whenever problems arise. Prompt legal advice often prevents expensive litigation. Because groups can supply a flow of business to the plan's attorneys, groups can negotiate free consultations, follow-ups, and discounts.

Two types of plans are commonly available. The first, a free plan, offers free legal consultations and discounts for services when the participating groups are large enough to generate business for the plan's attorneys. The second type is the prepaid plan. Prepaid plans provide more benefits, but members must pay annual fees, usually $200 or more a year.

Because you inquired about a free plan for your homeowners' association, the following information describes how to set up such a program.

Arranges steps for setting up a plan into sections with descriptive headings

Determine What Benefits Your Group Needs

The first step in establishing a free legal services plan is to meet with the members of your group to decide what benefits you want. Typical benefits include:

Emphasizes benefits in paragraph headings

Free consultations. Members may consult a participating attorney—by phone or in the attorney's office—to discuss any matter. The number of consultations is unlimited, provided that each is about a separate matter. Consultations are generally limited to 30 minutes, but they include substantive analysis and advice.

Free document review. Important papers—such as leases, insurance policies, and installment sales contracts—may be reviewed with legal counsel. Members may ask questions and receive an explanation of terms.

Tips for Short Informational Reports

- Use letter format for short informal reports sent to outsiders.
- Organize the facts section into logical divisions identified by consistent headings.
- Single-space the body.
- Double-space between paragraphs.
- Leave 2 blank lines above each side heading.
- Create side margins of 1 to 1.25 inches.
- Add a second-page heading, if necessary, consisting of the addressee's name, the date, and the page number.

Figure 11.2 **(Continued)**

Identifies second page with a header

Ms. Ava Hammond   Page 2   September 17, 2018

Discount on additional services. For more complex matters, participating attorneys charge members 75 percent of the attorney's normal fee. However, some attorneys choose to charge a flat fee for commonly needed services.

Uses parallel headings for consistency and readability

Select the Attorneys for Your Plan

Groups with geographically concentrated memberships have an advantage in forming legal plans. These groups can limit the number of participating attorneys and yet provide adequate service. Generally, smaller panels of attorneys are advantageous.

Assemble a list of candidates, inviting them to apply. The best way to compare prices is to have candidates submit their fees. Your group can then compare fee schedules and select the lowest bidder, if price is important. Arrange to interview attorneys in their offices.

After selecting an attorney or a panel, sign a contract. The contract should include the reason for the plan, what the attorney agrees to do, what the group agrees to do, how each side can end the contract, and the signature of both parties. You may also wish to include references to malpractice insurance, assurance that the group will not interfere with the attorney–client relationship, an evaluation form, a grievance procedure, and responsibility for government filings.

Publicize the Plan to Your Members

Members will not use a plan if they don't know about it, and a plan will not be successful if it is unused. Publicity must be vocal and ongoing. Announce it at the association's website, in newsletters, and at meetings.

Persistence is the key. All too frequently, leaders of an organization assume that a single announcement is all that's needed. They expect members to see the value of the plan and remember that it is available. Most organization members, though, are not as involved as the leadership. Therefore, it takes more publicity than the leadership usually expects to reach and maintain the desired level of awareness.

Summary

A successful free legal services plan involves designing a program, choosing the attorneys, and publicizing the plan. To learn more about these steps or to order a $45 how-to manual, call me at (512) 248-9282.

Includes complimentary close and signature

Sincerely,

Gary T. Rodriguez

Gary T. Rodriguez, Esq.
Executive Director

Informal and Formal Writing Styles

Like other business messages, reports can range from informal to formal, depending on their purpose, audience, and setting. Research reports from consultants to their clients tend to be rather formal. Such reports must project objectivity, authority, and impartiality. However, depending on the industry, a report to your boss describing a trip to a conference is normally informal.

Figure 11.3 Short Analytical Report

Applies memo format for short, informal internal report

Presents recommendations first (direct pattern) because reader is supportive and familiar with topic

Combines findings and analyses in short report

Uses first paragraph as introduction

Diamond Environmental, Inc.

Interoffice Memo

DATE: March 7, 2018
TO: Paul Gregory, President
FROM: Izzie Edwards, Environmental Engineer I.E.
SUBJECT: Investigation of Mountain Park Commercial Site

For New River Realty, Inc., I've completed a preliminary investigation of its Mountain Park property listing. The following recommendations are based on my physical inspection of the site, official records, and interviews with officials and persons knowledgeable about the site.

Recommendations

To reduce its potential environmental liability, New River Realty should take the following steps in regard to its Mountain Park listing:

- Conduct an immediate asbestos survey at the site, including inspection of ceiling insulation material, floor tiles, and insulation around a gas-fired heater vent pipe at 2539 Mountain View Drive.
- Prepare an environmental audit of the generators of hazardous waste currently operating at the site, including Mountain Technology.
- Obtain lids for the dumpsters situated in the parking areas and ensure that the lids are kept closed.

Findings and Analyses

My preliminary assessment of the site and its immediate vicinity revealed rooms with damaged floor tiles on the first and second floors of 2539 Mountain View Drive. Apparently, in recent remodeling efforts, these tiles had been cracked and broken. Examination of the ceiling and attic revealed further possible contamination from asbestos. The insulation for the hot-water tank was in poor condition.

Located on the property is Mountain Technology, a possible hazardous waste generator. Although I could not examine its interior, this company has the potential for producing hazardous material contamination.

In the parking area, large dumpsters collect trash and debris from several businesses. These dumpsters were uncovered, thus posing a risk to the general public.

In view of the construction date of the structures on this property, asbestos-containing building materials might be present. Moreover, this property is located in an industrial part of the city, further prompting my recommendation for a thorough investigation. New River Realty can act immediately to eliminate one environmental concern: covering the dumpsters in the parking area.

Tips for Short Analytical Reports

- Use memo format for most short (ten or fewer pages) informal reports within an organization.
- Leave side margins of 1 to 1.25 inches.
- Sign your initials on the *From* line.
- Use an informal, conversational style.
- For direct analytical reports, put recommendations first.
- For indirect analytical reports, put recommendations last.

Figure 11.4 Report-Writing Styles

	Informal Writing Style	Formal Writing Style
Appropriate Use	• Short, routine reports • Reports for familiar audiences • Noncontroversial reports • Internal use reports • Internal announcements and invitations	• Lengthy, formal reports and proposals • Research studies • Controversial or complex reports • External use reports • Formal invitations
Overall Effect	• Friendly tone • Relationship building • Casual	• Objectivity and accuracy • Sense of professionalism and fairness • Professional distance between writer and reader
Writing Style Characteristics	• Use of first-person pronouns (*I, we, me, my, us, our*) • Use of contractions (*can't, don't*) • Emphasis on active-voice verbs (*I conducted the study*) • Shorter sentences • Familiar words • Conversational language	• Use of third person (*the researcher, the writer*, depending on the circumstances) • Absence of contractions (*cannot, do not*) • Use of passive-voice verbs (*the study was conducted*) • Professional, respectful language • Absence of humor and figures of speech • Elimination of "editorializing" (author's opinions and perceptions)

An office worker once called a grammar hotline service with this problem: "We've just sent a report to our headquarters, and it was returned with this comment, 'Put it in the third person.' What do they mean?" The hotline experts explained that management apparently wanted a more formal writing style, using third-person constructions (*the company* or *the researcher* instead of *we* or *I*). Figure 11.4, which compares the characteristics of formal and informal report-writing styles, can help you decide which style is appropriate for your reports. Note that, increasingly, formal report writers use contractions and active-voice verbs. Today, report writers try to avoid awkward third-person references to themselves as *the researchers* or *the authors* because it sounds stilted and outdated.

Typical Report Formats

Reporting in organizations remains a key need in business today. Many types of reports coexist and vary greatly by sector or industry. The format of a report depends on its length, topic, audience, and purpose. After considering these elements, you will probably choose from among the following formats.

Digital Formats and PDF Files. Writers routinely save and distribute reports as portable document format (PDF) files. This file type, invented by Adobe, condenses documents while preserving the formatting and graphics. A report created with Microsoft Word, Excel, or PowerPoint can easily be saved as a PDF file. A PDF report might include links to external websites, a nice advantage over printed reports. Web-based reports may feature engaging multimedia effects, such as interactive charts and video.

Digital Slide Decks. Many business writers deliver their report information in digital slideshows, also called slide decks. These slides can be sent by e-mail, embedded on the Web, or posted on a company intranet. When used in reporting, slide decks may have more text

Figure 11.5 **Informal Reports Delivered as Slide Decks**

Source: http://www.exacttarget.com/resource-center/digital-marketing/infographics/sff-german-digital-republic

than typical presentation slides. Photographs, tables, charts, and other visuals make slide decks more inviting to read than print pages of dense report text. Not surprisingly, communicators in marketing, technology, media, entertainment, and consulting are fond of using slide deck reports to summarize their statistics and other findings. Figure 11.5 shows several slides from global marketing company ExactTarget analyzing the Internet market in Germany.

Infographics. Infographics, short for information graphics, are visual representations of data or information. They can display complex information quickly and clearly, and they are easier to understand than written text. Infographics are also affordable and easily shared on social media platforms. In fact, good infographics can go viral when viewers embed and spread the word about them in their blogs and on their social media networks. Infographics can tell compelling stories that help all types of businesses attract and inform consumers.

E-Mail and Memo Formats. Many reports are attached to e-mails, posted online, or, if short, embedded in the body of e-mails. For short informal reports that stay within organizations, the memo format may still be appropriate. Memo reports begin with essential background information, using standard headings: *Date, To, From,* and *Subject*, as shown in Figure 11.3. Memo reports differ from regular memos in length, use of headings, and deliberate organization.

Today, memo reports are rarely distributed in hard copy; more likely they are shared electronically as PDF files.

Forms and Templates. Office workers use digital forms that are usually made available on the company intranet or the Internet. Such electronic templates are suitable for repetitive data, such as monthly sales reports, performance appraisals, merchandise inventories, and personnel and financial reports. Employees can customize and fill in the templates and forms. Then they distribute them electronically or print them. Using standardized formats and headings saves a writer time and ensures that all necessary information is included.

Letter Format. The letter format for short informal reports (usually eight or fewer pages) addressed outside an organization can still be found in government agencies, real estate, and accounting firms. Prepared on office stationery, a letter report contains a date, inside address, salutation, and complimentary close, as shown in Figure 11.2. Although they may carry information similar to that found in correspondence, letter reports usually are longer and show more careful organization than typical letters. They also include headings to guide the reader through the content and may come with attachments. Like memo reports, letter reports are also likely to be sent to clients as PDF files.

Manuscript Format. For longer, more formal reports, business writers use the manuscript format. These reports are usually printed on plain paper without letterhead or memo forms. They too can be shared digitally as PDF files. They begin with a title followed by systematically displayed headings and subheadings. You will see examples of proposals and formal reports using the manuscript format in Chapter 13.

Applying the 3-x-3 Writing Process to Contemporary Reports

LEARNING OUTCOME 2

Apply the 3-x-3 writing process to contemporary business reports to create well-organized documents that show a firm grasp of audience and purpose.

Because business reports are systematic attempts to compile often complex information, answer questions, and solve problems, the best reports are developed methodically. In earlier chapters the 3-x-3 writing process was helpful in guiding the writing of short projects such as e-mails, memos, and letters. That same process is even more necessary when writers are preparing longer projects such as reports and proposals. After all, an extensive project poses a greater organizational challenge than a short one and, therefore, requires a rigorous structure to help readers grasp the message. Let's channel the writing process into seven steps:

Step 1: Analyze the problem and purpose.

Step 2: Anticipate the audience and issues.

Step 3: Prepare a work plan.

Step 4: Conduct research.

Step 5: Organize, analyze, interpret, and illustrate the data.

Step 6: Compose the first draft.

Step 7: Edit, proofread, and evaluate.

How much time you spend on each step depends on your report task. A short informational report on a familiar topic might require a brief work plan, little research, and no data analysis. A complex analytical report, on the other hand, might demand a comprehensive work plan, extensive research, and careful data analysis. In this section we consider the first three steps in the process—analyzing the problem and purpose, anticipating the audience and issues, and preparing a work plan.

To illustrate the planning stages of a report, we will watch Emily Mason develop a report she's preparing for her boss, Joshua Nichols, at Pharmgen Laboratories. Joshua asked Emily to investigate the problem of transportation for sales representatives. Currently, some Pharmgen reps visit customers (mostly doctors and hospitals) using company-leased cars. A few reps drive their own cars, receiving reimbursements for use. In three months Pharmgen's leasing agreements for 14 cars will expire, and Joshua is considering a major change. Emily's task is to investigate the choices and report her findings to Joshua.

Analyzing the Problem and Purpose

The first step in writing a report is understanding the problem or assignment clearly. For complex reports, prepare a written problem statement to clarify the task. In analyzing her report task, Emily had many questions: Is the problem that Pharmgen is spending too much money on leased cars? Does Pharmgen wish to invest in owning a fleet of cars? Is Joshua unhappy with the paperwork involved in reimbursing sales reps when they use their own cars? Does he suspect that reps are submitting inflated mileage figures? Before starting research for the report, Emily talked with Joshua to define the problem. She learned several dimensions of the situation and wrote the following statement to clarify the problem—both for herself and for Joshua.

> ***Problem statement:*** *The leases on all company cars will be expiring in three months. Pharmgen must decide whether to renew them or develop a new policy regarding transportation for sales reps. Expenses and paperwork for employee-owned cars seem excessive.*

Emily further defined the problem by writing a specific question that she would try to answer in her report:

> ***Problem question:*** *What plan should Pharmgen follow in providing transportation for its sales reps?*

Now Emily was ready to concentrate on the purpose of the report. Again, she had questions: Exactly what did Joshua expect? Did he want a comparison of costs for buying and leasing cars? Should she conduct research to pinpoint exact reimbursement costs when employees drive their own cars? Did he want her to do all the legwork, present her findings in a report, and let him make a decision? Or did he want her to evaluate the choices and recommend a course of action? After talking with Joshua, Emily was ready to write a simple purpose statement for this assignment.

> ***Simple statement of purpose:*** *To recommend a plan that provides sales reps with cars to be used in their calls.*

Preparing a written purpose statement is a good idea because it defines the focus of a report and provides a standard that keeps the project on target. In writing useful purpose statements, choose action verbs telling what you intend to do: *analyze, choose, investigate, compare, justify, evaluate, explain, establish, determine,* and so on. Notice that Emily's statement begins with the action verb *recommend.*

Some reports require only a simple statement of purpose: *to investigate expanded teller hours, to select a manager from among four candidates, to describe the position of accounts supervisor.* Many assignments, though, demand additional focus to guide the project. An expanded statement of purpose considers three additional factors: scope, limitations, and significance.

Scope and Limitations. What issues or elements will be investigated? The scope statement prepares the audience by clearly defining which problem or problems will be analyzed and solved. To determine the scope, Emily brainstormed with Joshua and others to pin down her task. She learned that Pharmgen currently has enough capital to consider purchasing a fleet of cars outright. Joshua also told her that employee satisfaction is almost as important as cost-effectiveness. Moreover, he disclosed his suspicion that employee-owned cars cost Pharmgen more than leased cars. Emily had many issues to sort out in setting the boundaries of her report.

What conditions affect the generalizability and utility of a report's findings? As part of the scope statement, the limitations further narrow the subject by focusing on constraints or exclusions. For this report Emily realized that her conclusions and recommendations might apply only to reps in her Kansas City sales district. Her findings would probably not be appropriate for reps in Seattle, Phoenix, or Atlanta. Another limitation for Emily was time. She had to complete the report in four weeks, thus restricting the thoroughness of her research.

Significance. Why is the topic worth investigating at this time? Some topics, after initial examination, turn out to be less important than originally thought. Others involve problems that cannot be solved, making a study useless. For Emily and Joshua, the problem had significance because Pharmgen's leasing agreement would expire shortly and decisions had to be made about a new policy for the transportation of sales reps.

Emily decided to expand her statement of purpose to define the scope, describe the limitations of the report, and explain the significance of the problem.

> ***Expanded statement of purpose:*** *The purpose of this report is to recommend a plan that provides sales reps with cars to be used in their calls. The report will compare costs for three plans: outright ownership, leasing, and compensation for employee-owned cars. It will also measure employee reactions to each plan. The report is significant because Pharmgen's current leasing agreement expires March 31 and an improved plan could reduce costs and paperwork. The study is limited to costs for sales reps in the Kansas City district.*

After expanding her statement of purpose, Emily checked it with Joshua to be sure she was on target.

© Marianne Elliott

Reality Check

I Love Writing, Even Report Writing

"My years at the United Nations made me the Grand Mistress of report writing. We wrote daily, weekly, monthly and annual reports. A couple of years in the UN and you can write reports in your sleep. Because I cared so deeply about the people I was writing about, I wanted to be sure the people in Kabul or New York who read my reports were paying attention. So I taught myself to tell a good story in every report. People pay attention and keep reading for a good story."[5]

—Marianne Elliott, *writer and human rights advocate*

Anticipating the Audience and Issues

After defining the purpose of a report, a writer must think carefully about who will read it. Concentrating solely on a primary reader is a major mistake. Although one individual may have solicited the report, others within the organization may eventually read it, including people in upper management and in other departments. A report to an outside client may first be read by someone who is familiar with the problem and then be distributed to others less familiar with it. Moreover, candid statements to one audience may be offensive to another audience. Emily could make a major blunder, for instance, if she mentioned Joshua's suspicion that sales reps were padding their mileage statements. If the report were made public—as it probably would be to explain a new policy—the sales reps could feel insulted that their integrity was questioned.

As Emily considered her primary and secondary readers, she asked herself these questions:

- *What do my readers need to know about this topic?*
- *What do they already know?*
- *What is their education level?*
- *How will they react to this information?*
- *Which sources will they trust?*
- *How can I make this information readable, believable, and memorable?*

Answers to these questions help writers determine how much background material to include, how much detail to add, whether to include jargon, what method of organization and presentation to follow, and what tone to use.

In the planning stages, a report writer must also break the major investigative problem into subproblems. This process, sometimes called *factoring*, identifies issues to be investigated or possible solutions to the main problem. In this case Pharmgen must figure out the best way to transport sales reps. Each solution or issue that Emily considers becomes a factor or subproblem to be investigated. Emily came up with three tentative solutions to provide transportation to sales reps: (a) purchase cars outright, (b) lease cars, or (c) compensate employees for using their own cars. These three factors formed the outline of Emily's study.

Emily continued to factor these main points into the following subproblems for investigation: What plan should Pharmgen use to transport its sales reps?

I. Should Pharmgen purchase cars outright?
   A. How much capital would be required?
   B. How much would it cost to insure, operate, and maintain company-owned cars?
   C. Do employees prefer using company-owned cars?

II. Should Pharmgen lease cars?
   A. What is the best lease price available?
   B. How much would it cost to insure, operate, and maintain leased cars?
   C. Do employees prefer using leased cars?

III. Should Pharmgen compensate employees for using their own cars?
   A. How much has it cost in the past to compensate employees who used their own cars?
   B. How much paperwork is involved in reporting expenses?
   C. Do employees prefer being compensated for using their own cars?

Each subproblem would probably be further factored into additional subproblems. These issues may be phrased as questions, as Emily's are, or as statements. In factoring a complex problem, prepare an outline showing the initial problem and its breakdown into subproblems. Make sure your divisions are consistent (don't mix issues), exclusive (don't overlap categories), and complete (don't skip significant issues).

Preparing a Work Plan

After analyzing the problem, anticipating the audience, and factoring the problem, you are ready to prepare a work plan. A good work plan includes the following:

- Statement of the problem (based on key background/contextual information)
- Statement of the purpose including the scope with limitations and significance
- Research strategy including a description of potential sources and methods of collecting data
- Tentative outline that factors the problem into manageable chunks
- Work schedule

Preparing a plan encourages you to evaluate your resources, set priorities, outline a course of action, and establish a schedule. Having a plan keeps you on track and provides management a means of measuring your progress.

A work plan gives a complete picture of a project. Because the usefulness and quality of any report rest primarily on its data, you will want to develop a clear research strategy, which includes allocating plenty of time to locate sources of information. For firsthand information you might interview people, prepare a survey, or even conduct a scientific experiment. For secondary information you will probably search electronic materials on the Internet and printed materials such as books and magazines. Your work plan describes how you expect to generate or collect data. Because data collection is a major part of report writing, the next section of this chapter treats the topic more fully.

Figure 11.6 shows a complete work plan for a proposal pitched by social marketing company BzzAgent's advertising executive Dave Balter to his client Lee Jeans. A work plan is useful because it outlines the issues to be investigated. Notice that considerable thought and discussion and even some preliminary research are necessary to be able to develop a useful work plan.

Although this tentative outline guides the investigation, it does not determine the content or order of the final report. You may, for example, study five possible solutions to a problem. If two prove to be useless, your report may discuss only the three winners. Moreover, you will

Figure 11.6 Work Plan for a Formal Report

Statement of Problem

Many women between the ages of 22 and 35 have trouble finding jeans that fit. Lee Jeans hopes to remedy that situation with its One True Fit line. We want to demonstrate to Lee that we can create a word-of-mouth campaign that will help it reach its target audience.

Statement of Purpose

Defines purpose, scope, limits, and significance of report

The purpose of this report is to secure an advertising contract from Lee Jeans. We will examine published accounts about the jeans industry and Lee Jeans in particular. In addition, we will examine published results of Lee's current marketing strategy. We will conduct focus groups of women in our company to generate campaign strategies for our pilot study of 100 BzzAgents. The report will persuade Lee Jeans that word-of-mouth advertising is an effective strategy to reach women in this demographic group and that BzzAgent is the right company to hire. The report is significant because an advertising contract with Lee Jeans would help our company grow significantly in size and stature.

Research Strategy (Sources and Methods of Data Collection)

Describes primary and secondary data

We will gather information about Lee Jeans and the product line by examining published marketing data and conducting focus group surveys of our employees. In addition, we will gather data about the added value of word-of-mouth advertising by examining published accounts and interpreting data from previous marketing campaigns, particularly those targeted toward similar age groups. Finally, we will conduct a pilot study of 100 BzzAgents in the target demographic.

Tentative Outline

Factors problem into manageable chunks

I. How effectively has Lee Jeans marketed to the target population (women ages 22 to 35)?
  A. Historically, who has typically bought Lee Jeans products? How often? Where?
  B. How effective are the current marketing strategies for the One True Fit line?
II. Is this product a good fit for our marketing strategy and our company?
  A. What do our staff members and our sample survey of BzzAgents say about this product?
  B. How well does our pool of BzzAgents correspond to the target demographic in terms of age and geographic distribution?
III. Why should Lee Jeans engage BzzAgent to advertise its One True Fit line?
  A. What are the benefits of word of mouth in general and for this demographic in particular?
  B. What previous campaigns have we engaged in that demonstrate our company's credibility?
  C. What are our marketing strategies, and how well did they work in the pilot study.

Work Schedule

Estimates time needed to complete report tasks

Investigate Lee Jeans and One True Fit line's current marketing strategy — July 15–25
Test product using focus groups
Create campaign materials for BzzAgents
Run a pilot test with a selected pool of 100 Bzz
Evaluate and interpret findings
Compose draft of report
Revise draft
Submit final report

Tips for Preparing a Work Plan

- Start early; allow plenty of time for brainstorming and preliminary research.
- Describe the problem motivating the report.
- Write a purpose statement that includes the report's scope, significance, and limitations.
- Describe the research strategy including data collection sources and methods.
- Divide the major problem into subproblems stated as questions to be answered.
- Develop a realistic work schedule citing dates for the completion of major tasks.
- Review the work plan with whoever authorized the report.

organize the report to accomplish your goal and satisfy the audience. A busy executive who is familiar with a topic may prefer to read the conclusions and recommendations before a discussion of the findings. If someone authorizes the report, be sure to review the work plan with that person (your manager, client, or professor, for example) before proceeding with the project.

LEARNING OUTCOME 3

Locate and evaluate secondary sources such as databases and Internet resources, and understand how to conduct credible primary research.

Identifying Secondary Sources and Conducting Primary Research

Research, or the gathering of information, is one of the most important steps in writing a report. As the philosopher Goethe once said: "The greater part of all mischief in the world arises from the fact that men do not sufficiently understand their own aims. They have undertaken to build a tower, and spend no more labor on the foundation than would be necessary to erect a hut." Think of your report as a tower. Because a report is only as good as its foundation—the questions you ask and the data you gather to answer those questions—the remainder of this chapter describes the fundamental work of finding, documenting, and illustrating data.

As you analyze a report's purpose and audience and prepare your research strategy, you will identify and assess the data you need to support your argument or explain your topic. As you do, you will answer questions about your objectives and audience: Will the audience need a lot of background or contextual information? Will your readers value or trust statistics, case studies, or expert opinions? Will they want to see data from interviews or surveys? Will summaries of focus groups be useful? Should you rely on organizational data? Figure 11.7 lists five forms of data and provides questions to guide you in making your research accurate and productive.

Figure 11.7 **Gathering and Selecting Report Data**

Form of Data	Questions to Ask
Background or historical	How much do my readers know about the problem? Has this topic/issue been investigated before? Are those sources current, relevant, and/or credible? Will I need to add to the available data?
Statistical	What or who is the source? How recent are the data? How were the figures derived? Will this data be useful in this form?
Expert opinion	Who are the experts? What are their biases? Are their opinions in print? Are they available for interviewing? Do we have in-house experts?
Individual or group opinion	Whose opinion(s) would the readers value? Have surveys or interviews been conducted on this topic? If not, do questionnaires or surveys exist that I can modify and/or use? Would focus groups provide useful information?
Organizational	What are the proper channels for obtaining in-house data? Are permissions required? How can I learn about public and private companies?

Locating Secondary Sources

Data fall into two broad categories: primary and secondary. Primary data result from first-hand experience and observation. Secondary data come from reading what others have experienced or observed and written down. Illustrating primary research, the U.S. Food and Drug Administration investigated Garden of Life Raw Meal Organic Shakes & Meal Replacements. It discovered a salmonella outbreak afflicting at least 33 people in 23 states. Lab tests conducted by the government agency found the culprit: contaminated organic moringa leaf powder.[6] These same sets of data become secondary after they have been published and, let's say, a newspaper reporter uses them in an article about food safety. Secondary data are easier and cheaper to gather than primary data, which might involve interviewing large groups or sending out questionnaires.

We discuss secondary data first because that is where nearly every research project should begin. Often, something has already been written about your topic. Reviewing secondary sources can save time and effort and prevent you from reinventing the wheel. Most secondary material is available either in print or electronically.

Toria/Shutterstock.com

Reality Check

Modern Librarians as Information Curators

"In the nonstop tsunami of global information, librarians provide us with floaties and teach us to swim."[7]

—Linton Weeks, *national correspondent, NPR Digital News*

Print Resources. Although we are seeing a steady movement away from print data and toward electronic data, print sources are still the most visible part of most libraries. Much information is available only in print.

By the way, if you are an infrequent library user, begin your research by talking with a reference librarian about your project. Librarians won't do your research for you, but they will steer you in the right direction. Many librarians help you understand their computer, cataloging, and retrieval systems by providing advice, brochures, handouts, and workshops.

Books. Although quickly outdated, books provide excellent historical, in-depth data. Like most contemporary sources, books can be located through online listings.

- **Online catalogs.** Most libraries today have digitized their card catalogs, allowing users to learn whether a book is located in the library and currently available. Moreover, online catalogs can help you trace and borrow items from other area libraries through interlibrary loan if your college doesn't own them.
- **Card catalogs.** Very few libraries still maintain card catalogs with all books indexed on 3-by-5 cards alphabetized by author, title, and subject.

Periodicals. Magazines, pamphlets, and journals are called *periodicals* because of their recurrent, or periodic, publication. Journals are compilations of scholarly articles. Articles in journals and other periodicals are extremely useful because they are concise, limited in scope, and current and can supplement information in books. Current publications are digitized and available in full text online, often as PDF documents.

Indexes. University libraries today offer online access to *The Readers' Guide to Periodical Literature*, an index now offered by EBSCO, a major provider of online databases. Contemporary business writers rely almost totally on electronic indexes and research databases to locate references, abstracts, and full-text articles from magazines, journals, and newspapers, such as *The New York Times*.

When using Web-based online indexes, follow the on-screen instructions or ask for assistance from a librarian. Beginning with a subject search such as *manufacturers' recalls* is helpful because it generally turns up more relevant citations than keyword searches—especially when searching for names of people (*Akio Toyoda*) or companies (*Toyota*). Once you locate usable references, print a copy of your findings, save them to a flash drive or in a cloud-based storage location such as Dropbox, or send them to your e-mail address.

Research Databases. As a writer of business reports today, you will probably begin your secondary research with electronic resources. Online databases have become the staple of secondary research. Most writers turn to them first because they are fast and easy to use. You can conduct detailed searches without ever leaving your office, home, or dorm room.

A *database* is a collection of information stored digitally so that it is accessible by computer or mobile electronic devices and searchable. Databases provide bibliographic information (titles of documents and brief abstracts) and full-text documents. Databases contain a rich array of magazine, newspaper, and journal articles, as well as newsletters, business reports, company profiles, government data, reviews, and directories. The five databases most useful to business writers are ABI/INFORM Complete (ProQuest), Business Source Premier (EBSCO), JSTOR Business, Factiva (Dow Jones), and LexisNexis Academic. Figure 11.8 shows the ABI/INFORM Complete search menu.

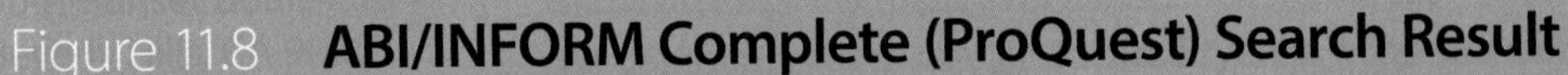

Figure 11.8 **ABI/INFORM Complete (ProQuest) Search Result**

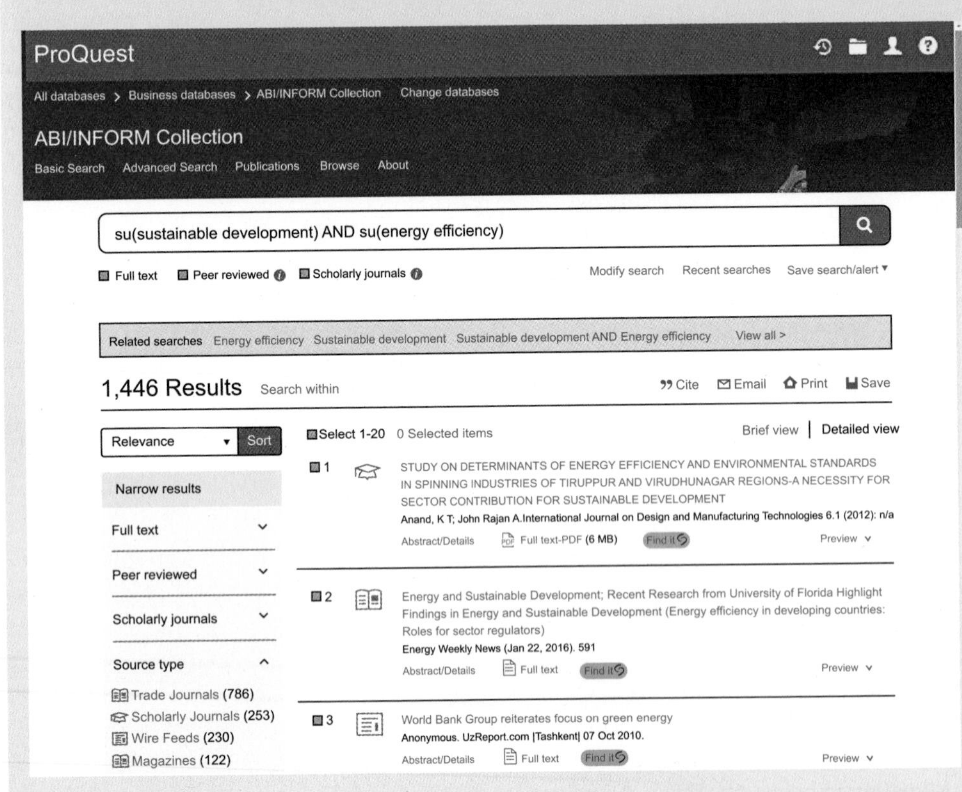

ABI/INFORM (ProQuest) indexes over 4,000 journals and features more than 3,000 full-text documents about business topics. Users can access newspapers, magazines, reports, dissertations, book reviews, scholarly journals, and trade publications. Figure 11.8 shows that the search terms *sustainable development* and *energy efficiency* brought up 181 full-text search results. When retrieving too many results, savvy researchers further narrow their search to retrieve a more manageable number.

Developing a search strategy and narrowing your search can save time. Think about the time frame for your search, the language of publication, and the types of materials you will need. Most databases enable you to focus a search easily. For example, if you were researching the Great Recession and wanted to look at articles published in a specific year, most search tools would enable you to limit your search to that period. All databases and search engines allow you to refine your search and increase the precision of your hits.

Efficient search strategies take time to master. Therefore, before wasting time and retrieving lots of useless material, talk to a university librarian. College and public libraries as well as some employers offer free access to several commercial databases, sparing you the high cost of individual subscriptions.

The Web

If you are like most adults today, you probably use the Web for entertainment and work every day. Chances are you have a Facebook or Instagram page, and perhaps you play one of the countless free online games. You have probably looked up directions on Google Maps and may have bid on or sold items on eBay. You are likely to download ringtones for your smartphone, and perhaps you listen to music streaming on Spotify or Pandora. In short, you rely on the Internet daily for information and entertainment. In this section we examine the Web as an effective research tool.

Web Search Tools. Finding what you are looking for on the Web is hopeless without powerful, specialized search tools, such as Google, Bing, Yahoo Search, and Ask. These search tools can be divided into two types: subject (or Web) directories and search engines. In addition, some search engines (e.g., Dogpile and Search.com), also called *aggregators*, specialize in metasearching. This means that they combine several powerful search engines into one.

Search engines differ in the way they trawl the vast amount of data on the Web. Google uses automated software, called bots, that regularly collect and index the information from each Web location visited. To get the most from Google, try the Advanced search feature. It resembles the query fields in research databases and allows you to narrow your searches more effectively than you can when you rely on a simple search and thus obtain only the most popular results that Google displays first. Some search tools (e.g., Ask) use natural-language-processing technology to enable you to ask questions to gather information. BizNar is another sophisticated, comprehensive business search engine and portal. To compare the quality of results, or hits, try the same keyword or query using various search sites.

Applying Internet Search Strategies and Techniques. To conduct a thorough search for the information you need, build a (re)search strategy by understanding the tools available. Figure 11.9 outlines several effective search techniques.

To improve your odds of discovering more relevant sources, try these additional research strategies used by successful Internet sleuths:

- Learn basic Boolean search strategies. You can save yourself a lot of time and frustration by narrowing your search with the following Boolean operators:

  AND Identifies only documents containing all of the specified words: **employee AND productivity AND morale**

  OR Identifies documents containing at least one of the specified words: **employee OR productivity OR morale**

  NOT Excludes documents containing the specified word: **employee productivity NOT morale**

  NEAR Finds documents containing target words or phrases within a specified distance, for instance, within ten words: **employee NEAR productivity**.

Ethics Check

The High Cost of Fraudulent Research

Over two decades, the Japanese anesthesiologist Yoshitaka Fujii fabricated 172 papers. An investigating panel found no records of patients or of any medication given. Among the 172 bogus papers, authorities discovered 126 studies of randomized, double-blind, controlled trials that were total fabrications. Fujii parlayed his high productivity into new jobs, research funding, and speaking fees. He even applied for prizes, although he never won. Discuss this case.

Figure 11.9 **Useful Internet Search Techniques**

USE TWO OR THREE SEARCH TOOLS.
• Conduct a topic search using a subject directory such as ipl2, Internet Public Library, INFOMINE, or the WWW Virtual Library.
• Switch to a search engine or metasearch engine once you have narrowed your topic.
KNOW YOUR SEARCH TOOL.
• Always read the description of each new search site you visit, including the FAQs, Help, and How to Search sections.
• Take advantage of special features (e.g., the News, Images, Videos, Books, and other categories) on Google, that can speed up your Search.
USE NOUNS AS SEARCH WORDS.
The right keywords, up to eight words in a query, can narrow the search effectively.
COMBINE KEYWORDS INTO PHRASES.
Phrases, marked by the use of quotation marks (e.g., *business ethics*), will limit results to specific matches.
USE WILD CARDS.
Try wildcards, such as asterisks, because most search engines support them. The search term *cent** will retrieve cents, whereas *cent*** will retrieve both *center* and *centre*.

- **Keep trying.** If a search produces no results, check your spelling. If you are using Boolean operators, check the syntax of your queries. Try synonyms and variations on words. Try to be less specific in your search term. If your search produces too many hits, try to be more specific. Use the Advanced feature of your search engine to narrow your search. Think of words that uniquely identify what you are looking for. Use as many relevant keywords as possible.
- **Repeat your search a week later.** For the best results, return to your search a couple of days or a week later. The same keywords will probably produce additional results. That's because millions of new pages are being added to the Web every day. The ranking of hits can also change depending on how often a link is accessed by Internet users.

Credibility of Internet Sources. Most Internet users tend to assume that any information turned up by a search engine has somehow been evaluated as part of a valid selection process. Wrong! Unlike library-based research, information at many sites has not undergone the editing or scrutiny of scholarly publication procedures. The information we read in journals and most reputable magazines is reviewed, authenticated, and evaluated.

Information on the Web is much less reliable than information from traditional sources. Blogs and discussion forum entries illustrate this problem. They change constantly and may disappear fast, so that your source can't be verified. Many don't provide any references or reveal sources that are either obscure or suspect. Academic researchers prefer lasting, scholarly sources.

PLUGGED IN

Staying on Top of Research Data

In collecting search results, you can easily lose track of websites and articles you quoted. To document Web data that may change, as well as to manage all your other sources, you need a plan for saving the information. At the very least, you will want to create a *working bibliography* or list of *references* in which you record the URL of each electronic source. These techniques can help you stay in control of your data:

- **Saving sources to a local drive or USB flash drive** has advantages, including being able to open the document in a browser even if you don't have access to the Internet. More important, saving sources to disk or memory stick preserves information that may not be available later. Using either the **File** and **Save As** or the **File** and **Save Page As** menu command in your browser, you can store the information permanently. Save images and other kinds of media by either right-clicking or command-clicking on the item, and selecting **Save** Picture As or Save Image As.
- **Copying and pasting** information you find on the Web into MS Word is an easy way to save and store it. Copy and paste the URL into the file as well, and record the URL in your working bibliography. You can save most files as PDFs simply by choosing the **Print** command and selecting Adobe PDF in the Printer window of the Print menu. You can keep your PDF documents as electronic files or print paper copies later.
- **Printing** pages is a handy way to gather and store information. Doing so enables you to have copies of important data that you can annotate or highlight. Make sure the URL prints with the document (usually on the bottom of the page). If not, write it on the page.
- **Bookmarking favorites** is an option within browsers to enable you to record and store the URLs of important sources. The key to using this option is creating folders with relevant names and choosing concise and descriptive names for bookmarks.
- **Cloud storage and e-mailing** documents, URLs, or messages to yourself are also useful strategies. Many databases and online magazines permit you to e-mail information and sometimes the entire article to your account. A cloud storage account such as Dropbox or iCloud lets you access your files from any electronic device.

Wikipedia and Other Encyclopedias. College-level research requires you to use general encyclopedia information only as a starting point for more in-depth research. That means you will not cite Wikipedia, Ask, general encyclopedias, search engines, or similar reference works in your writing. Their information is too fluid and too general. However, these information-packed sites often provide their own references (bibliographies) that you can employ in your research. Locate the original sources of information rather than the condensed reference articles.

To use the Internet meaningfully, you must scrutinize what you find and check who authored and published it. Here are specific criteria to consider as you examine a site:

- **Currency.** What is the date of the Web page? Is some of the information obviously out-of-date? If the information is time sensitive and the site has not been updated recently, the site is probably not reliable.
- **Authority.** Who publishes or sponsors this Web page? What makes the presenter an authority? Is information about the author or creator available? Is a contact address available for the presenter? Learn to be skeptical about data and assertions from individuals and organizations whose credentials are not verifiable.
- **Content.** Is the purpose of the page to entertain, inform, convince, or sell? How would you classify this page (e.g., news, personal, advocacy, reference)? Who is the intended audience, based on content, tone, and style? Can you judge the overall value of the content compared with the other resources on this topic?
- **Accuracy.** Do the facts seem reliable? Are there errors in spelling, grammar, or usage? Do you see any evidence of bias? Are references provided? Errors and missing references should alert you that the data may be questionable.

DREAMWORKS PICTURES/Album/Newscom

New York is the Big Apple and Santa Fe is the City Different, but what is Glendale, California? Boring! The nondescript Los Angeles suburb hired a municipal branding firm to come up with a way for Glendale to siphon off visitors from the adjacent, better-known cities of Pasadena and Burbank. After a year's worth of research, the firm differentiated dowdy Glendale by highlighting its glitziest firms, the animation studios DreamWorks and Walt Disney Imagineering. Using the tagline "Glendale: Your Life. Animated." leverages the city's unique advantage over its nearby competitors. What kinds of primary and secondary research would need to be collected to analyze a city's appeal to tourists?[8]

Conducting Primary Research

Although you will start nearly every business report assignment by sifting through secondary sources, you may sometimes need primary data to give a complete picture. Business reports that solve specific current problems typically rely on primary, firsthand data. If, for example, management wants to discover the cause of increased employee turnover in its Seattle office, it must investigate conditions in Seattle by collecting recent information. Providing answers to business problems often means generating primary data through surveys, interviews, observation, or experimentation.

Surveys. Surveys collect data from groups of people. Before developing new products, for example, companies often survey consumers to learn their needs. The advantages of surveys are that they gather data economically and efficiently. Increasingly, consumers are asked to fill out online questionnaires and are taken either to a proprietary website or the popular survey platform SurveyMonkey. Snail-mailed or e-mailed surveys too reach big groups nearby or at great distances. Moreover, people responding to mailed or e-mailed surveys have time to consider their answers, thus improving the accuracy of the data.

Mailed or e-mailed surveys, of course, have disadvantages. Because most of us rank them with junk mail or spam, response rates may be low. Furthermore, respondents may not represent an accurate sample of the overall population, thus invalidating generalizations from the group. Let's say, for example, that an insurance company sends out a questionnaire asking about provisions in a new policy. If only older people respond, the questionnaire data cannot be used to generalize what people in other age groups might think. If a survey is only e-mailed, it may miss small audiences that do not use the Internet.

A final problem with surveys has to do with truthfulness. Some respondents exaggerate their incomes or distort other facts, thus causing the results to be unreliable. Nevertheless, surveys may be the best way to generate data for business and student reports. In preparing print or electronic surveys, consider these pointers:

- **Select the survey population carefully.** Many surveys question a small group of people (a sample) and project the findings to a larger population. Let's say that a survey of your class reveals that the majority prefer cheese pizza. Can you then say that all students on your campus (or in the nation) prefer cheese pizza? To be able to generalize from a survey, you need to make the sample large enough. In addition, you need to determine whether the sample represents the larger population. For important surveys you will want to learn sampling techniques. As for college eating habits, a recent study found that American students make decidedly unhealthy choices among take-out food—in this order: frozen yogurt, waffle fries, chicken souvlaki pita, chocolate chip brownies, and hibachi chicken. (Cheese pizza is among the top ten.)[9]

- **Explain why the survey is necessary.** In a cover letter or an opening paragraph, describe the need for the survey. Suggest how someone or something other than you will benefit. If appropriate, offer to send recipients a copy of the findings.
- **Consider incentives.** If the survey is long, persuasive techniques may be necessary. Response rates can be increased by offering money (such as a $1 bill), coupons, gift certificates, books, or other gifts.
- **Limit the number of questions.** Resist the temptation to ask for too much. Request only information you will use. Don't, for example, include demographic questions (income, gender, age, and so forth) unless the information is necessary to evaluate responses.
- **Use questions that produce quantifiable answers.** Check-off, multiple-choice, yes–no, and scale (or rank-order) questions, illustrated in Figure 11.10, provide quantifiable data that are easily tabulated. Low-cost Web-based applications such as SurveyMonkey help automate the output of the data. Responses to open-ended questions (*What should the bookstore do about plastic bags?*) reveal interesting, but difficult-to-quantify perceptions.[10] To obtain workable data, give interviewees a list of possible responses, as shown in items 5 through 8 of Figure 11.10. For scale and multiple-choice questions, try to present all the possible answer choices. To be safe, add an *Other* or *Don't know* category in case the choices seem insufficient to the respondent. Many surveys use scale questions because they capture degrees of feelings. Typical scale headings are *Agree strongly, Agree somewhat, Neutral, Disagree somewhat,* and *Disagree strongly.*
- **Avoid leading or ambiguous questions.** The wording of a question can dramatically affect responses to it.[11] When respondents were asked, "Are we spending too much, too little, or about the right amount on *assistance to the poor?*" 13 percent responded *Too much.* When the same respondents were asked, "Are we spending too much, too little, or about the right amount on *welfare?*" 44 percent responded *Too much.* Because words have different meanings for different people, you must strive to use objective language and pilot test your questions with typical respondents. Ask neutral questions (*Do CEOs earn too much, too little, or about the right amount?*). Also, avoid queries that really ask two or more things (*Should the salaries of CEOs be reduced or regulated by government legislation?*). Instead, break them into separate questions (*Should the salaries of CEOs be reduced by government legislation? Should the salaries of CEOs be regulated by government legislation?*).
- **Make it easy for respondents to return the survey.** Researchers often provide prepaid self-addressed envelopes or business-reply envelopes. Survey software such as SurveyMonkey helps users develop simple, template-driven questions and allows survey takers to follow a link to take the survey.
- **Conduct a pilot study.** Try the questionnaire with a small group so that you can remedy any problems. In the survey shown in Figure 11.10, female students generally favored cloth bags and were willing to pay for them. Male students opposed purchasing cloth bags. By adding a gender category, researchers could verify this finding. The pilot study also revealed the need to ensure an appropriate representation of male and female student in the survey.

Interviews. Some of the best report information, particularly on topics about which little has been written, comes from individuals. These individuals are usually experts or veterans in their fields. Consider both in-house and outside experts for business reports. Tapping these sources will call for in-person, telephone, or online interviews. To elicit the most useful data, try these techniques:

- **Locate an expert.** Ask managers and individuals who are considered to be most knowledgeable in their areas. Check membership lists of professional organizations, and consult articles about the topic. Most people enjoy being experts or at least recommending them. You could also *crowdsource* your question in social media; that is, you could pose the query to your network to get input from your contacts.

Figure 11.10 **Preparing a Survey Using SurveyMonkey**

1 Prewriting

Analyze: The purpose is to help the bookstore decide whether it should replace plastic bags with cloth bags for customer purchases.

Anticipate: The audience will be busy students who will be initially uninterested.

Adapt: Because students will be unwilling to participate, the survey must be short and simple. Its purpose must be significant and clear. It must be easy to access online.

2 Drafting

Research: Ask students how they would react to cloth bags. Use their answers to form response choices.

Organize: Open by explaining the survey's purpose and importance. In the body ask clear questions that produce quantifiable answers. Conclude with appreciation and instructions.

Draft: Write the first version of the online questionnaire.

3 Revising

Edit: Try out the questionnaire with a small representative group. Revise unclear questions.

Proofread: Read for correctness. Be sure that answer choices do not overlap and that they are complete. Provide an *Other* category if appropriate (as in Question 9).

Evaluate: Is the survey clear, attractive, and easy to complete?

Greendale College Bookstore

STUDENT SURVEY

The Greendale College Bookstore wants to do its part in protecting the environment. Each year we give away 45,000 plastic bags for students to carry off their purchases. We are considering changing from plastic to cloth bags or some other alternative, but we need your views.

1. What is your gender?

○ Female
○ Male

2. How many units are you currently carrying?

○ 15 or more units
○ 9 to 14 units
○ 8 to fewer units

3. How many times have you visited the bookstore this semester?

○ 0 times
○ 1 time
○ 2 times
○ 3 times
○ 4 or more times

4. Indicate your concern for the environment.

○ Very concerned
○ Concerned
○ Unconcerned

5. To protect the environment, would you be willing to change to another type of bag when buying books?

○ Yes
○ No

6. Indicate your feeling about the following alternatives.

For major purchases the bookstore should:

	Agree	Undecided	Disagree
Continue to provide plastic bags.	○	○	○
Provide no bags; encourage students to bring their own bags.	○	○	○
Provide no bags; offer cloth bags at reduced price (about $3).	○	○	○

- **Prepare for the interview.** Learn about the individual you are interviewing, and make sure you can pronounce the interviewee's name. Research the background and terminology of the topic. Let's say you are interviewing a corporate communication expert about producing an in-house newsletter. You ought to be familiar with terms such as *font* and software such as PagePlus and Xara Page & Layout Designer. In addition, be prepared by making a list of questions that pinpoint your focus on the topic. Ask the interviewee if you may record the talk. Familiarize yourself with the recording device beforehand.
- **Maintain a professional attitude.** Call before the interview to confirm the arrangements, and then arrive on time. Be prepared to take notes if your recorder fails (and remember to ask permission beforehand if you want to record). Use your body language to convey respect.
- **Make your questions objective and friendly.** Adopt a courteous and respectful attitude. Don't get into a debating match with the interviewee, and don't interrupt. Remember that you are there to listen, not to talk! Use open-ended questions to draw experts out.
- **Watch the time.** Tell interviewees in advance how much time you expect to need for the interview. Don't overstay your appointment. If your subject rambles, gently try to draw him or her back to the topic; otherwise, you may run out of time before asking all your questions.
- **End graciously.** Conclude the interview with a general question, such as *Is there anything you would like to add?* Express your appreciation, and ask permission to telephone later if you need to verify points.

Neilson Barnard/Getty Images

Reality Check

Analyzing Primary and Secondary Data to Win

Experts such as Tom Peters recognize the value of ongoing primary and secondary research to gain a competitive advantage: "Even gross indicators, such as market share by segment, relative revenue, and relative earnings, can give you a good start on competitive analysis. These are crude measures, yet I am surprised at how few (1) collect the data, (2) update them regularly, and (3) share them widely within the firm. Every person in the company should have ready, visible access to the numbers on market share—yours and your competitors'—updated weekly."[12]

—Tom Peters, *management consultant and best-selling author*

Observation and Experimentation. Some kinds of primary data can be obtained only through firsthand observation and investigation. If you determine that you need observational data, then you need to plan carefully. Most important is deciding what or whom you are observing and how often those observations are necessary. For example, if you want to learn more about an organization's telephone customer service, you probably need to conduct an observation (along with interviews and perhaps even surveys). You will want to answer questions such as *How long does a typical caller wait before a customer service rep answers the call?* and *Is the service consistent?* Recording 60-minute periods at various times throughout a week will give you a better picture than just observing for an hour on a Friday before a holiday.

To observe, arrive early enough to introduce yourself and set up any equipment. If you are recording, secure permissions beforehand. In addition, take notes, not only of the events or actions but also of the settings. Changes in environment often have an effect on actions. Starbucks chief Howard Schultz long resisted research, advertising, and customer surveys. Instead of relying on sophisticated marketing research, Schultz would visit 25 Starbucks locations a week to learn about his customers. Amidst a huge Starbucks expansion in China and India, the CEO continues his hands-on strategy, visiting stores and talking to baristas.[13]

Ethics Check

Cribbing From References?

Doing last-minute research for a class or work project, you are in a hurry; therefore, you decide to copy some sources from the list of references that you found in an article on your topic to boost your number of works cited. Is it unethical to list sources you have not actually read?

Experimentation produces data suggesting causes and effects. Informal experimentation might be as simple as a pretest and posttest in a college course. Did students learn in the course? Scientists and professional researchers undertake more formal experimentation. They control variables to test their effects. Assume, for example, that Hershey's wants to test the hypothesis (a tentative assumption) that chocolate provides an emotional lift. An experiment testing the hypothesis would separate depressed people into two groups: the chocolate eaters (the experimental group) and the chocolate deprived (the control group). Such experiments are not done haphazardly, however. Valid experiments require sophisticated research designs.

LEARNING OUTCOME 4

Identify the purposes and techniques of citation and documentation in business reports, and avoid plagiarism.

Documenting Information

In writing business reports, you will often build on the ideas and words of others. In Western culture, whenever you borrow the ideas of others, you must give credit to your information sources. This is called *documentation*.

The Purposes of Documentation

As a careful writer, you should take pains to document report data properly for the following reasons:

- **To strengthen your argument.** Including good data from reputable sources will convince readers of your credibility and the logic of your reasoning.
- **To protect yourself against charges of plagiarism.** Acknowledging your sources keeps you honest. *Plagiarism*, which is unethical and in some cases illegal, is the act of using others' ideas without proper documentation.
- **To instruct the reader.** Citing references enables readers to pursue a topic further and make use of the information themselves.
- **To save time.** The world of business moves so quickly that words and ideas must often be borrowed—which is very acceptable when you give credit to your sources.

Intellectual Theft: Plagiarism

Plagiarism of words or ideas is a serious offense and can lead to loss of a job. Famous historians, several high-level journalists, and even college professors[14] have suffered grave consequences for copying from unnamed sources. Your instructor may use a commercial plagiarism detection service such as Turnitin, which cross-references much of the information on the Web, looking for documents with identical phrasing. The result, an "originality report," shows the instructor whether you have been accurate and honest.

You can avoid charges of plagiarism as well as add clarity to your work by knowing what to document and by developing good research habits. First, however, let's consider the differences between business and academic writing with respect to documentation.

Academic Documentation and Business Practices

In the academic world, documentation is critical. Especially in the humanities and sciences, students are taught to cite sources by using quotation marks, parenthetical citations, footnotes, and bibliographies. College term papers require full documentation to demonstrate that a student has become familiar with respected sources and can cite them properly in developing an argument. Giving credit to the authors is extremely important. Students who plagiarize risk a failing grade in a class and even expulsion from school.

In business, however, documentation and authorship are sometimes viewed differently. Business communicators on the job may find that much of what is written does not follow the standards they learned in school. In many instances, individual authorship is unimportant.

For example, employees may write for the signature of their bosses. The writer receives no credit. Similarly, teams turn out documents for which none of the team members receive individual credit. Internal business reports, which often include chunks of information from previous reports, also don't give credit. Even information from outside sources may lack detailed documentation. However, if facts are questioned, business writers must be able to produce their source materials.

Although both internal and external business reports are not as heavily documented as school assignments or term papers, business communication students are well advised to learn proper documentation methods. In the workplace, stealing the ideas of others and passing them off as one's own can be corrosive to the business because it leads to resentment and worse. One writer suggests that in addition to causing businesses to lose the public's trust, unethical practices undermine free markets and free trade.[15]

© Carrie Marcinkevage

Reality Check

Plagiarizing Admissions Essays?!

About 40 business schools in the United States—Duke, Penn State, and UCLA among them—use anticheating software to weed out plagiarized applications essays before even reading college applications. Thus, cheaters are largely screened out of the classroom. "If you stop it at the door, there is less plagiarism in the classroom, and hopefully, less plagiarism in the workplace."[16]

—Carrie Marcinkevage, *MBA managing director, Smeal College of Business, Penn State*

What to Document

When you write reports, especially in college, you are continually dealing with other people's ideas. You are expected to conduct research, synthesize ideas, and build on the work of others. But you are also expected to give proper credit for borrowed material. To avoid plagiarism, you must give credit whenever you use the following:[17]

- Another person's ideas, opinions, examples, or theory
- Any facts, statistics, graphs, and drawings that are not common knowledge
- Quotations of another person's actual spoken or written words
- Paraphrases of another person's spoken or written words
- Visuals, images, and any kind of electronic media

Information that is common knowledge requires no documentation. For example, the statement *The Wall Street Journal is a popular business newspaper* would require no citation. Statements that are not common knowledge, however, must be documented. For example, the following statement would require a citation because most people do not know these facts: *Austin, Texas, has been the nation's fastest-growing city for five of the past six years. Austin's projected 3.15 percent population growth rate is the highest among 100 metro areas.*[18] More important, someone went through the trouble and expense of assembling this original work and now *owns* it. Cite sources for such proprietary information—in this case, statistics reported by a newspaper or magazine. You probably know to use citations to document direct quotations, but you must also cite ideas that you summarize in your own words.

When in doubt about common knowledge, check to see whether the same piece of information is available in at least three sources in your topic's specific field and appears without citation. If what you borrow doesn't fall into one of the five categories listed earlier, for which you must give credit, you are safe in assuming it is common knowledge. Copyright and intellectual property are discussed in greater detail later in this chapter.

Good Research Habits

As they gather sources, report writers have two methods available for recording the information they find. The time-honored manual method of notetaking works well because information is recorded on separate cards, which can then be conveniently arranged in the order needed to develop a thesis or argument. Today, however, writers prefer to do their research online. Traditional notetaking may seem antiquated and laborious in comparison. Let's explore both methods.

Paper Note Cards. To make sure you know whose ideas you are using, train yourself to take excellent notes. If possible, know what you intend to find before you begin your research so that you won't waste time on unnecessary notes. Here are some pointers on taking good notes:

- Record all major ideas from various sources on separate note cards.
- Include all publication information (author, date, title, and so forth) along with precise quotations.
- Consider using one card color for direct quotes and a different color for your paraphrases and summaries.
- Put the original source material aside when you are summarizing or paraphrasing.

Digital Records. Instead of recording facts on note cards, savvy researchers take advantage of digital media tools, as noted in the accompanying Plugged In box. Beware, however, of the risk of cutting and pasting your way into plagiarism. Here are some pointers on taking good virtual notes:

- Begin your research by setting up a folder on your local drive or cloud-based storage site. On the go, you can access these files with any mobile electronic device, or you can use a USB flash drive to carry your data.
- Create subfolders for major sections, such as introduction, body, and closing.
- When you find facts on the Web or in research databases, highlight the material you want to record, copy it, and paste it into a document in an appropriate folder.
- Be sure to include all publication information in your references or works-cited lists.
- As discussed in the section on managing research data, consider archiving on a USB flash drive or external disk drive those Web pages or articles used in your research in case the data must be verified.

The Fine Art of Paraphrasing

In writing reports and using the ideas of others, you will probably rely heavily on *paraphrasing*, which means restating an original passage in your own words and in your own style. To do a good job of paraphrasing, follow these steps:

1. Read the original material intently to comprehend its full meaning.
2. Write your own version without looking at the original.
3. Avoid repeating the grammatical structure of the original and merely replacing words with synonyms.
4. Reread the original to be sure you covered the main points but did not borrow specific language.

To better understand the difference between plagiarizing and paraphrasing, study the following passages. Notice that the writer of the plagiarized version uses the same grammatical construction as the source and often merely replaces words with synonyms. Even the acceptable version, however, requires a reference to the source author.

Source
We have seen, in a short amount of time, the disappearance of a large number of household brands that failed to take sufficient and early heed of the software revolution that is upending traditional brick-and-mortar businesses and creating a globally pervasive digital economy.[19]

Plagiarized version
Many trusted household name brands disappeared very swiftly because they did not sufficiently and early pay attention to the software revolution that is toppling traditional physical businesses and creating a global digital economy. (Saylor, 2012)

Acceptable paraphrase
Digital technology has allowed a whole new virtual global economy to blossom and very swiftly wipe out some formerly powerful companies that responded too late or inadequately to the disruptive force that has swept the globe. (Saylor, 2012)

When and How to Quote

On occasion, you will want to use the exact words of a source, but beware of overusing quotations. Documents that contain pages of spliced-together quotations suggest that writers have few ideas of their own. Wise writers and speakers use direct quotations for three purposes only:

- To provide objective background data and establish the severity of a problem as seen by experts
- To repeat identical phrasing because of its precision, clarity, or aptness
- To duplicate exact wording before criticizing

When you must use a long quotation, try to summarize and introduce it in your own words. Readers want to know the gist of a quotation before they tackle it. For example, to introduce a quotation discussing the shrinking staffs of large companies, you could precede it with your words: *In predicting employment trends, Charles Waller believes the corporation of the future will depend on a small core of full-time employees.* To introduce quotations or paraphrases, use wording such as the following:

According to Waller, ...

Waller argues that . . . .

In his recent study, Waller reported . . . .

Use quotation marks to enclose exact quotations, as shown in the following: *"The current image," says Charles Waller, "of a big glass-and-steel corporate headquarters on landscaped grounds directing a worldwide army of tens of thousands of employees may soon be a thing of the past" (2013, p. 51).*

Copyright Information

The U.S. Copyright Act of 1976 protects authors—literary, dramatic, and artistic—of published and unpublished works. The word *copyright* refers to "the right to copy," and a key provision is *fair use.* Under fair use, individuals have limited use of copyrighted material without needing to acquire permission. These uses are for criticism, comment, news reporting, teaching, scholarship, and research. Unfortunately, the distinctions between fair use and infringement are not clearly defined.

Four-Factor Test to Assess Fair Use. What is fair use? Actually, it is a shadowy territory with vague and often disputed boundaries—now even more so with the addition of cyberspace. Courts use four factors as a test in deciding disputes over fair use:

- **Purpose and character of the use, particularly whether for profit.** Courts are more likely to allow fair use for nonprofit educational purposes than for commercial ventures.

- **Nature of the copyrighted work.** When information is necessary for the public good—such as medical news—courts are more likely to support fair use.
- **Amount and substantiality of portion used.** Copying a 200-word passage from a 200,000-word book might be allowed, but not 200 words from a 1,000-word article or a substantial part of a shorter work. A total of 300 words is mistakenly thought by many to be an acceptable limit for fair use, but courts have not upheld this figure. Don't rely on it.
- **Effect of the use on the potential market.** If use of the work may interfere with the author's potential profit from the original, fair use copying would not be allowed.

How to Avoid Copyright Infringement. Whenever you borrow words, charts, graphs, photos, music, and other media—in short, any *intellectual property*—be sure you know what is legal and acceptable. The following guidelines will help:

- **Assume that all intellectual property is copyrighted.** Nearly everything created privately and originally after 1989 is copyrighted and protected whether or not it has a copyright notice.
- **Realize that Internet items and resources are NOT in the public domain.** No modern intellectual or artistic creation is in the public domain (free to be used by anyone) unless the owner explicitly says so.
- **Observe fair-use restrictions.** Be aware of the four-factor test. Avoid appropriating large amounts of outside material.
- **Ask for permission.** You are always safe if you obtain permission. Write to the source, identify the material you wish to include, and explain where it will be used. Expect to pay for permission.
- **Don't assume that a footnote is all that is needed.** Including a footnote to a source prevents plagiarism but not copyright infringement. Anything copied beyond the boundaries of fair use requires permission.

For more information about *copyright law, fair use, public domain,* and *work for hire,* you can search the Web with these keywords.

Citation Formats

You can direct readers to your sources with parenthetical notes inserted into the text and with bibliographies. The most common citation formats are those presented by the Modern Language Association (MLA) and the American Psychological Association (APA). Learn more about how to use these formats in Appendix B.

Robert Gauthier/Los Angeles Times/Getty Images

Reality Check

Clarity and Simplicity in Information Design

"The interior decoration of graphics generates a lot of ink that does not tell the viewer anything new. The purpose of decoration varies—to make the graphic appear more scientific and precise, to enliven the display, to give the designer an opportunity to exercise artistic skills. Regardless of its cause, it is all non-data-ink or redundant data-ink, and it is often chartjunk."[26]

—Edward Tufte, *statistician and pioneer of data visualization*

PLUGGED IN

Telling a Story With Infographics

Although infographics seem to have burst onto the scene within the last decade, Edward Tufte, a pioneer of data visualization, has introduced brilliant nineteenth-century examples. One strikingly depicts Napoleon's ill-fated Russian campaign of 1812—the diminishing numbers of soldiers, their movements, and even the temperatures during their retreat.[20] Pictograms and ideograms (images and symbols visualizing an idea or action) date back thousands of years to cave paintings, hieroglyphs, and other writing systems.[21]

Contemporary infographics gurus include Ryan Case and Nicholas Felton, known for turning ordinary details of everyday life into strikingly expressive charts. Felton is credited with inspiring Facebook's Timeline feature.[22] An information design wiz, Felton once charted a year of his life in an annual report format. With Case, he created Daytum, an app that allows users to visualize their own personal statistics.

Purpose. Good infographics tell a story and allow the reader to make sense of ever-growing amounts of data. The purpose of the best infographics, it has been said, is to "add intelligence and insight to the digital noise buzzing around us every day."[23] Information design master Francesco Franchi claims that "infographic thinking" is not just pretty images; rather, it means creating a new, nonlinear reading experience and encouraging critical thought. Franchi believes that the best infographic design is informative and entertaining. It invites the reader to participate in the process of interpretation, he says.[24] Well-executed infographics illustrate often complex topics and data almost at one glance. Substituted for ho-hum, conventional visuals, good infographics can be stunning.

Infographics Software. Today even amateur designers can create captivating infographics. Any software that can merge text and visuals can help create infographics. However, no single piece of software is the ultimate tool.[25] Some come with a steep learning curve (e.g., Adobe Illustrator and Adobe Photoshop), whereas others are easier to use (Apple iWork and MS Office). Some are cloud-based; others can be downloaded. Try out Google Public Data Explorer, StatSilk, Visualize Free, Hohli, or Creately.

Popular Uses. A few innovative companies have turned some reports and executive summaries into infographics. Résumés, advocacy documents such as white papers, decision trees, maps, flowcharts, instructions, rankings, brand messages, and more have been presented as infographics. Although infographics can tell a story with images and entertain while doing so, they can take up a lot of space and, therefore, are most appropriate online. There, viewers and readers can scroll unconstrained by the printed page. Not all businesses have embraced the sometimes whimsical infographics. Apple Inc. sticks with a plain-vanilla Form 10-K and does not produce a glossy annual report, but many corporations do. Smartphone apps allow users to track and share the numbers in their lives by creating personal infographics.

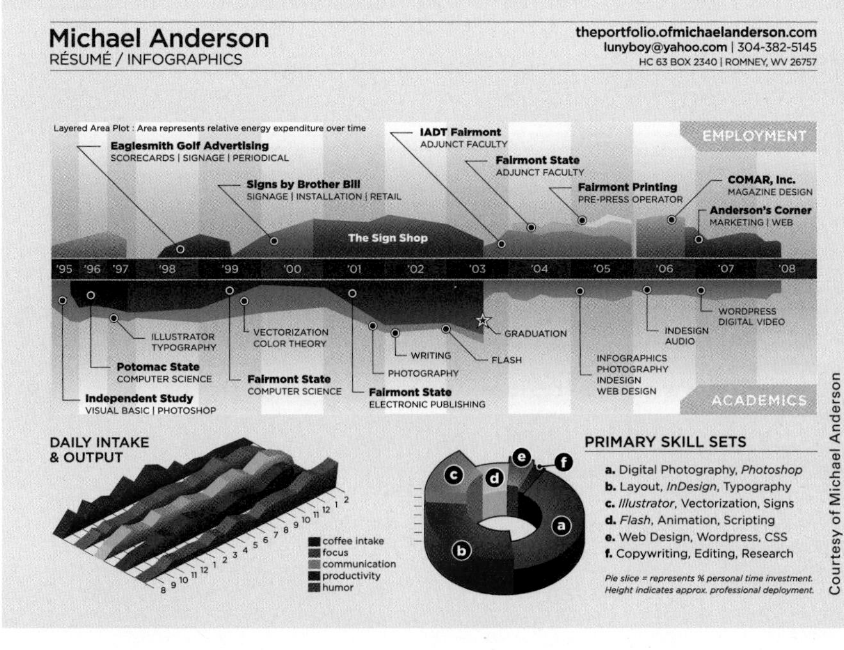

Courtesy of Michael Anderson

The key to infographics is to present a concise and compelling story through images and graphical elements that encourages the reader or viewer to actively participate in the interpretation. One newly popular application of infographics is visual résumés.

LEARNING OUTCOME 5

Generate, use, and convert numerical data to visual aids, and create meaningful and attractive graphics.

Creating Effective Graphics

After collecting and interpreting information, you need to consider how best to present it. If your report contains complex data and numbers, you may want to consider graphics such as tables and charts. These graphics clarify data, create visual interest, and make numerical data meaningful. By simplifying complex ideas and emphasizing key data, well-constructed graphics make key information easier to remember. However, the same data can be shown in many forms; for example, in a chart, table, or graph. That's why you need to know how to match the graphic with your objective and how to incorporate it into your report.

Matching Graphics and Objectives

In developing the best graphics, you must decide what data you want to highlight and which graphics are most appropriate given your objectives. Tables? Bar charts? Pie charts? Line charts? Surface charts? Flowcharts? Organization charts? Pictures? Figure 11.11 summarizes appropriate uses for each type of graphic. The following sections discuss each type in more detail.

Tables. Probably the most frequently used graphic in reports is the table. Because a table presents quantitative or verbal information in systematic columns and rows, it can clarify large quantities of data in small spaces. The disadvantage is that tables do not readily display trends. You may have made rough tables to help you organize the raw data collected from questionnaires or interviews. In preparing tables for your readers or listeners, however, you need to pay more attention to clarity and emphasis. Here are tips for making good tables, one of which is provided in Figure 11.12:

- Place titles and labels at the top of the table.
- Arrange items in a logical order (alphabetical, chronological, geographical, highest to lowest), depending on what you need to emphasize.
- Provide clear headings for the rows and columns.

Figure 11.11 **Matching Graphics to Objectives**

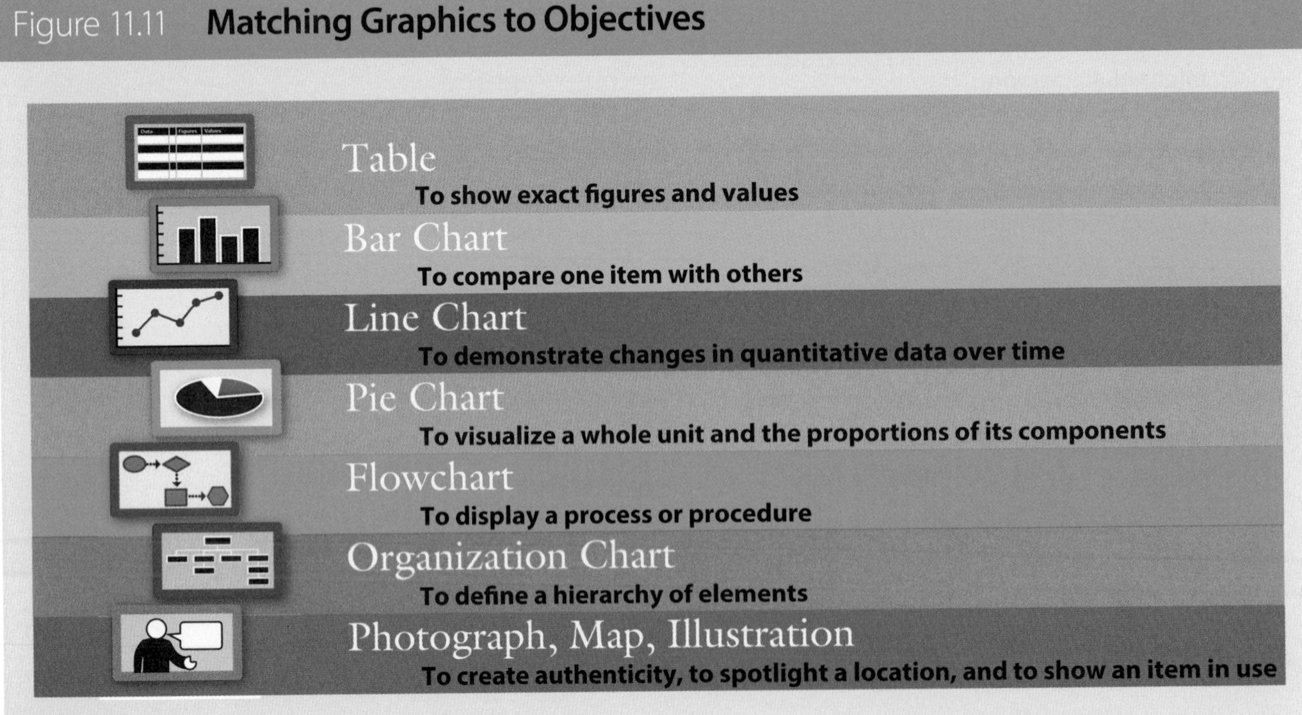

Table
To show exact figures and values
Bar Chart
To compare one item with others
Line Chart
To demonstrate changes in quantitative data over time
Pie Chart
To visualize a whole unit and the proportions of its components
Flowchart
To display a process or procedure
Organization Chart
To define a hierarchy of elements
Photograph, Map, Illustration
To create authenticity, to spotlight a location, and to show an item in use

Figure 11.12 Table Summarizing Precise Data

Figure 1 MPM ENTERTAINMENT COMPANY Income by Division (in millions of dollars)				
	Theme Parks	Motion Pictures	DVDs & Blu-ray Discs	Total
2014	$15.8	$39.3	$11.2	$66.3
2015	18.1	17.5	15.3	50.9
2016	23.8	21.1	22.7	67.6
2017	32.2	22.0	24.3	78.5
2018 (projected)	35.1	21.0	26.1	82.2

Source: *Industry Profiles* (New York: DataPro, 2017) 225.

- Identify the units in which figures are given (percentages, dollars, units per worker hour) in the table title, in the column or row heading, with the first item in a column, or in a note at the bottom.
- Use *N/A* (*not available*) for missing data.
- Make long tables easier to read by shading alternate lines or by leaving a blank line after groups of five.
- Place tables as close as possible to the place where they are mentioned in the text.

Figure 11.11 shows the purposes of various graphics. Tables, as illustrated in Figure 11.12, are especially suitable for illustrating exact figures in systematic rows and columns. The table in our figure is particularly useful because it presents data about the MPM Entertainment Company over several years, making it easy to compare several divisions. Figures 11.13 through 11.16 highlight some of the data shown in the MPM Entertainment Company table, illustrating four types of bar charts: vertical, horizontal, grouped, and segmented 100 percent bar charts, each of which creates a unique effect.

Bar Charts. Although they lack the precision of tables, bar charts enable you to make emphatic visual comparisons by using horizontal or vertical bars of varying lengths. Bar charts are useful for comparing related items, illustrating changes in data over time, and showing segments as a part of the whole. Note how the varied bar charts present information in differing ways.

Many techniques for constructing tables also hold true for bar charts. Here are a few additional tips:

- Keep the length and width of each bar and segment proportional.
- Include a total figure in the middle or at the end of the bar if the figure helps the reader and does not clutter the chart.
- Start dollar or percentage amounts at zero.
- Place the first bar at some distance (usually half the amount of space between bars) from the *y*-axis.
- Avoid showing too much information, to avoid clutter and confusion.
- Place each bar chart as close as possible to the place where it is mentioned in the text.

Line Charts. The major advantage of line charts is that they show changes over time, thus indicating trends. The vertical axis is typically the dependent variable; and the horizontal axis,

Figure 11.13 **Vertical Bar Chart**

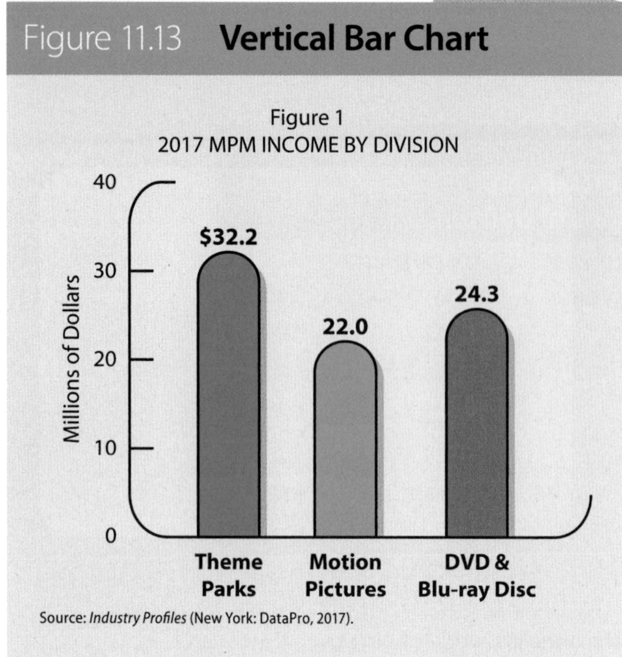

Figure 11.14 **Horizontal Bar Chart**

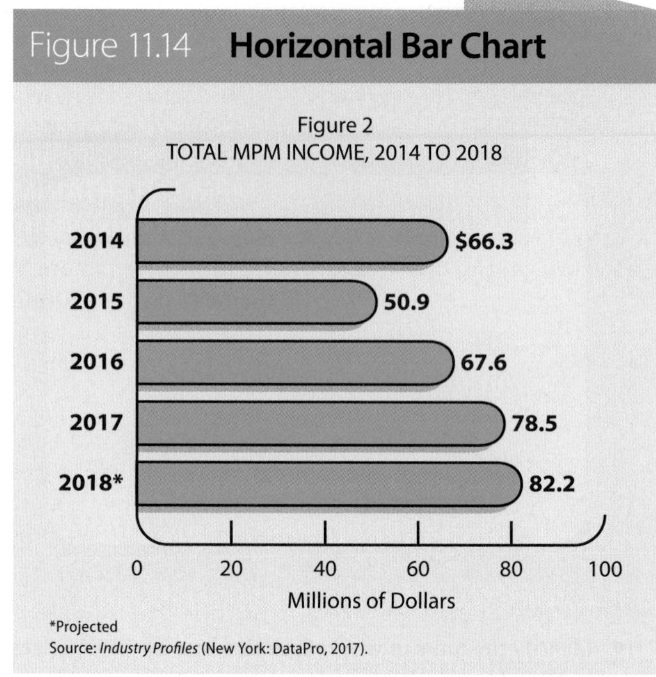

Figure 11.15 **Grouped Bar Chart**

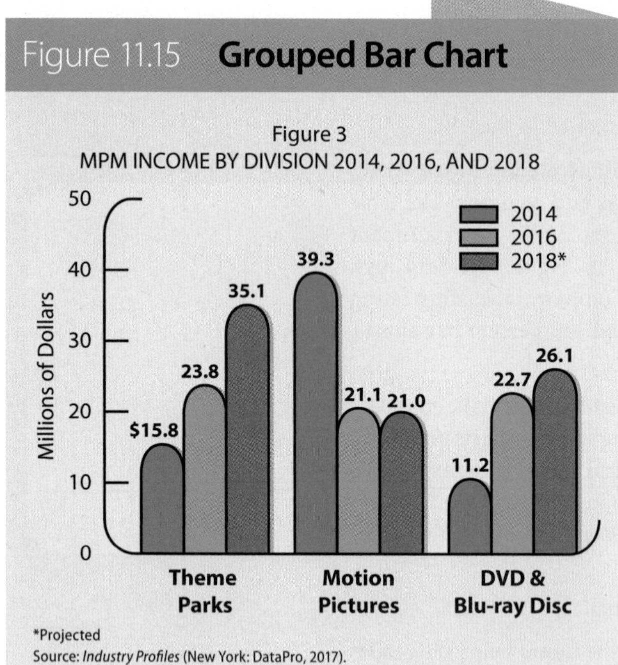

Figure 11.16 **Segmented 100 Percent Bar Chart**

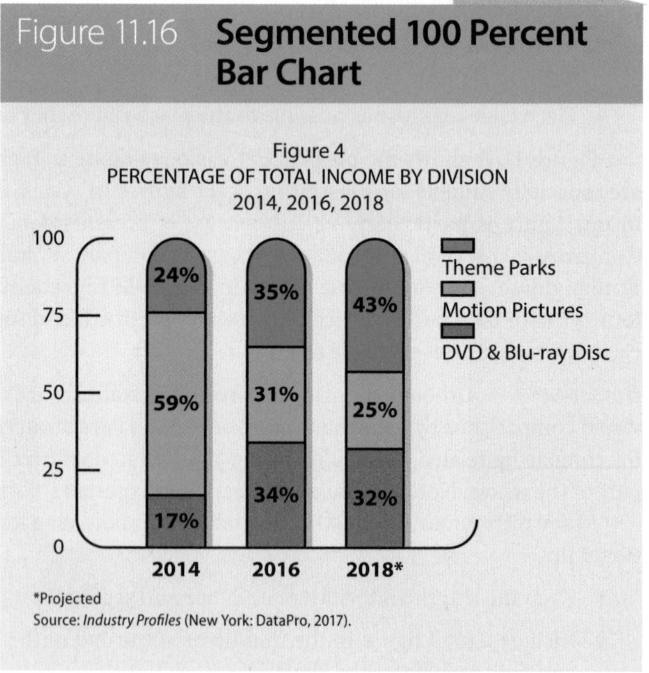

the independent one. Simple line charts (Figure 11.17) show just one variable. Multiple line charts compare items, such as two or more data sets, using the same variable (Figure 11.18). Segmented line charts (Figure 11.19), also called surface charts, illustrate how the components of a whole change over time. To prepare a line chart, remember these tips:

- Begin with a grid divided into squares.
- Arrange the time component (usually years) horizontally across the bottom; arrange values for the other variable vertically.

- Draw small dots at the intersections to indicate each value at a given year.
- Connect the dots and add color if desired.
- To prepare a segmented (surface) chart, plot the first value (say, DVD and Blu-ray disc income) across the bottom; add the next item (say, motion picture income) to the first figures for every increment; for the third item (say, theme park income), add its value to the total for the first two items. The top line indicates the total of the three values.

Pie Charts. Pie charts, or circle graphs, enable readers to see a whole and the proportion of its components, or wedges. Although less flexible than bar or line charts, pie charts are useful for showing percentages, as Figure 11.20 illustrates. They are very effective for lay, or nonexpert,

Figure 11.17 **Simple Line Chart**

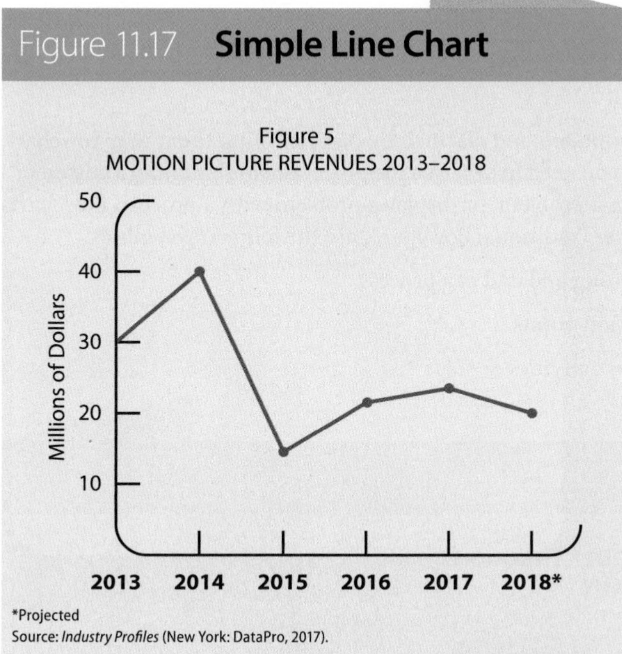

Figure 11.18 **Multiple Line Chart**

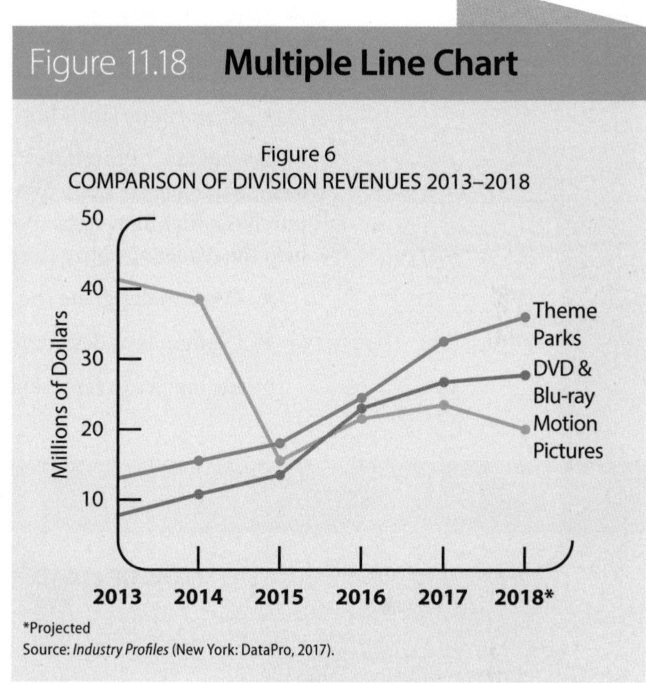

Figure 11.19 **Segmented Line (Area) Chart**

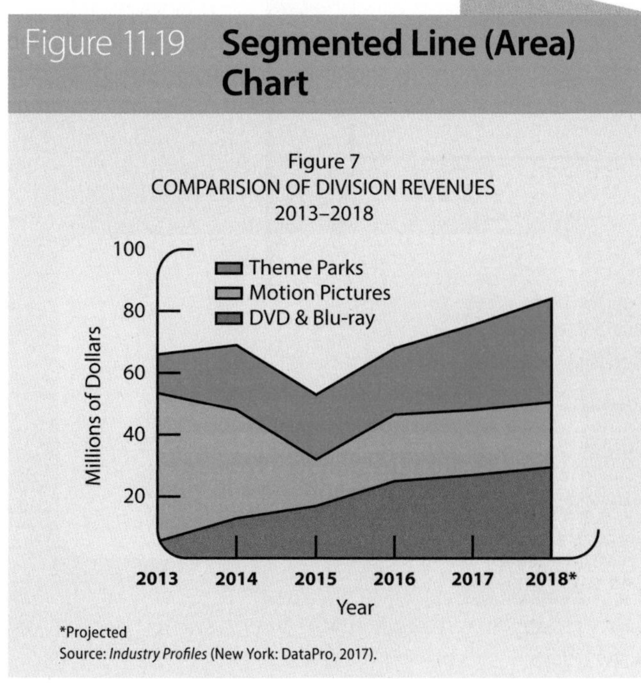

Figure 11.20 **Pie Chart**

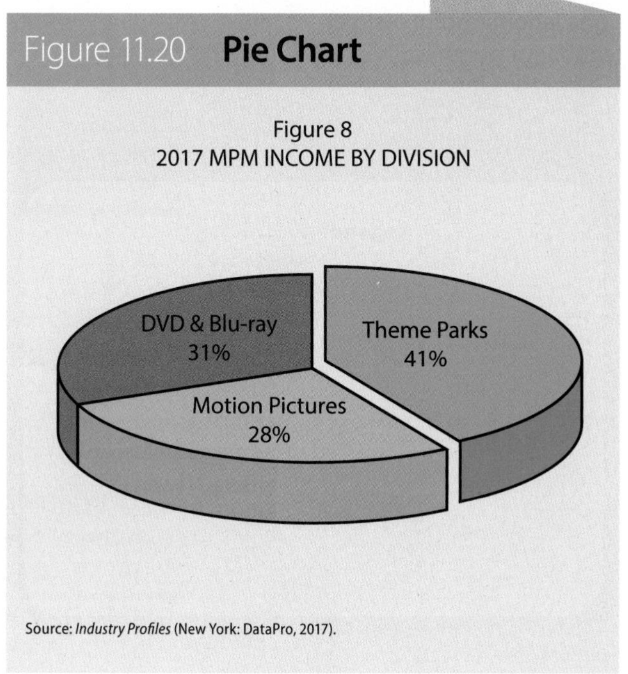

audiences. Notice that a wedge can be exploded, or popped out, for special emphasis, as seen in Figure 11.20. MS Excel and other spreadsheet programs provide a selection of three-dimensional pie charts. For the most effective pie charts, follow these suggestions:

- Make the biggest wedge appear first. Computer spreadsheet programs correctly assign the biggest wedge first (beginning at the 12 o'clock position) and arrange the others in order of decreasing size as long as you list the data representing each wedge on the spreadsheet in descending order.
- Include, if possible, the actual percentage or absolute value for each wedge.
- Use four to six segments for best results; if necessary, group small portions into a wedge called *Other.*
- Draw radii from the center.
- Distinguish wedges with color, shading, or cross-hatching.
- Keep all the labels horizontal.

Flowcharts. Procedures are simplified and clarified by diagramming them in a flowchart, as shown in Figure 11.21. Whether you need to describe the procedure for handling a customer's purchase, highlight steps in solving a problem, or display a problem with a process, flowcharts help the reader visualize the process. Traditional flowcharts use the following symbols:

- Ovals to designate the beginning and end of a process
- Diamonds to designate decision points
- Rectangles to represent major activities or steps

Figure 11.21 **Flowchart**

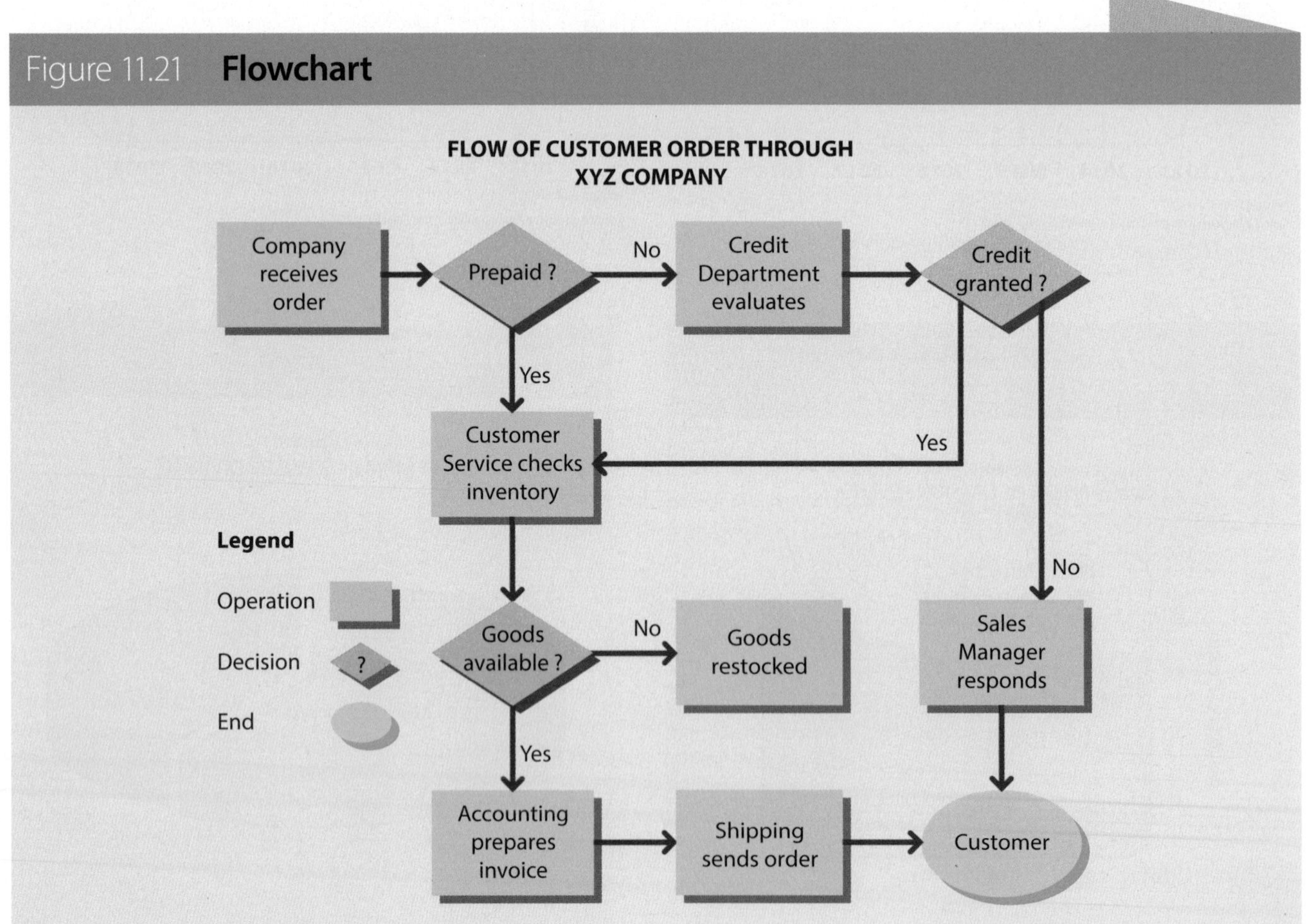

Organization Charts. Many large organizations are so complex that they need charts to show the chain of command, from the boss down to the line managers and employees. Organization charts provide such information as who reports to whom, how many subordinates work for each manager (the span of control), and what channels of official communication exist. These charts may illustrate a company's structure—for example, by function, customer, or product. They may also be organized by the work being performed in each job or by the hierarchy of decision making.

Photographs, Maps, and Illustrations. Some business reports include photographs, maps, and illustrations to serve specific purposes. Photos, for example, add authenticity and provide a visual record. An environmental engineer may use photos to document hazardous waste sites. Maps enable report writers to depict activities or concentrations geographically, such as dots indicating sales reps in states across the country. Illustrations and diagrams are useful in indicating how an object looks or operates. A drawing showing the parts of a printer with labels describing their functions, for example, is more instructive than a photograph or verbal description.

With today's smart visualization tools as described in the Plugged In box, high-resolution photographs, maps, and illustrations can be inserted into business reports, or accessed through hyperlinks within electronically delivered documents. Online they can be animated or appear in clusters as they do in infographics.

Incorporating Graphics in Reports

Used appropriately, graphics make reports more interesting and easier to understand. In putting graphics into your reports, follow these suggestions for best effects:

- **Evaluate the audience.** Consider the reader, the content, your schedule, and your budget. Graphics take time and can be costly to print in color, so think carefully before deciding how many graphics to use. Six charts in an internal report to an executive may seem like overkill; however, in a long technical report to outsiders, six may be too few.
- **Use restraint.** Don't overuse color or decorations. Although color can effectively distinguish bars or segments in charts, too much color can be distracting and confusing. Remember, too, that colors themselves sometimes convey meaning: red suggests deficits or negative values; blue suggests calmness and authority; and yellow may suggest warning.
- **Be accurate and ethical.** Double-check all graphics for accuracy of figures and calculations. Be certain that your visuals aren't misleading—either accidentally or intentionally. Manipulation of a chart scale can make trends look steeper and more dramatic than they really are. Moreover, be sure to cite sources when you use someone else's facts. The Ethical Insight box discusses in more detail how to make ethical charts and graphs.
- **Introduce a graph meaningfully.** Refer to every graphic in the text, and place the graphic close to the point where it is mentioned. Most important, though, help the reader understand the significance of the graphic. You can do this by telling your audience what to look for or by summarizing the main point of the graphic. Don't assume the reader will automatically reach the same conclusions you reached from a set of data. Instead of saying, *The findings are shown in Figure 3,* tell the reader what to look for: *Two thirds of the responding employees, as shown in Figure 3, favor a flextime schedule.* The best introductions for graphics interpret them for readers.
- **Choose an appropriate caption or title style.** Like reports, graphics may use talking titles or generic, descriptive titles. Talking titles are more persuasive; they tell the reader what to think. Descriptive titles describe the facts more objectively.

Talking Title	Descriptive Title
Rising Workplace Drug Testing Unfair and Inaccurate	Workplace Drug Testing Up 277 Percent
College Students' Diets Clogged With Fat	College Students and Nutrition

Ethical Insight

Making Ethical Charts and Graphics

Business communicators must present graphical data in the same ethical, honest manner required for all other messages. Remember that the information shown in your charts and graphics will be used to inform others or help them make decisions. If this information is not represented accurately, the reader will be incorrectly informed; any decisions based on the data are likely to be faulty. In addition, mistakes in interpreting such information may have serious and long-lasting consequences.

Chart data can be distorted in many ways. Figure 1 shows advertising expenses displayed on an appropriate scale. Figure 2 shows the same information, but the horizontal scale, from 2010 to 2015, has been lengthened. Notice that the data have not changed, but the increases and decreases are smoothed out, so changes in expenses appear to be slight. In Figure 3 the vertical scale is taller and the horizontal scale is shortened, resulting in what appear to be sharp increases and decreases in expenses.

To avoid misrepresenting data, keep the following pointers in mind when designing your graphics:

- Use an appropriate type of chart or graphic for the message you wish to convey.
- Design the chart so that it focuses on the appropriate information.
- Include all relevant or important data; don't arbitrarily leave out necessary information.
- Don't hide critical information by including too much data in one graphic.
- Use appropriate scales with equal intervals for the data you present.

Career Application

Locate one or two graphics in a newspaper, magazine article, or annual report. Analyze the strengths and weaknesses of each graphic. Is the information presented accurately? Select a bar or line chart. Sketch the same chart but change the vertical or horizontal scales on the graphic. How does the message of the chart change?

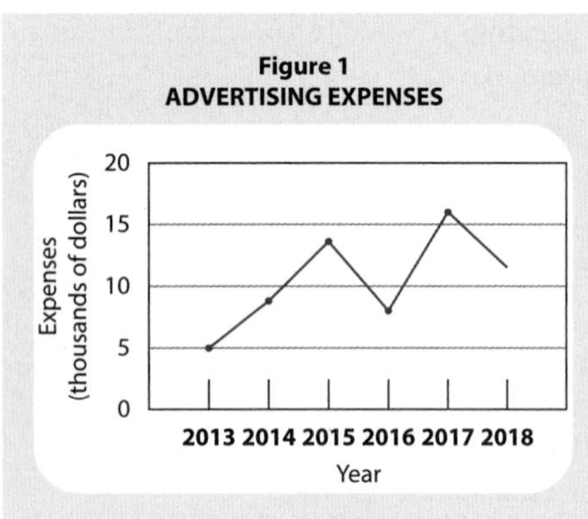

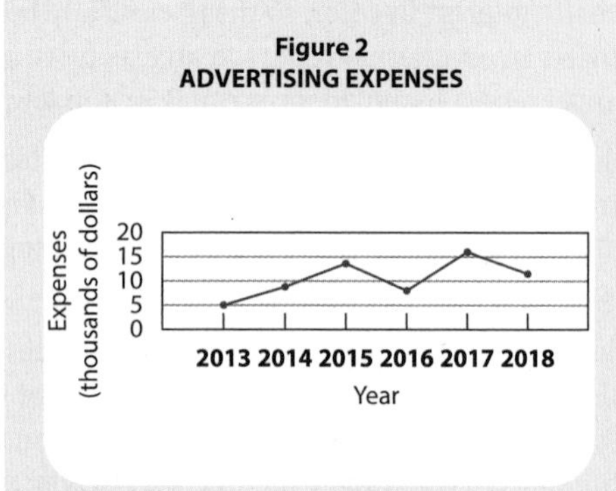

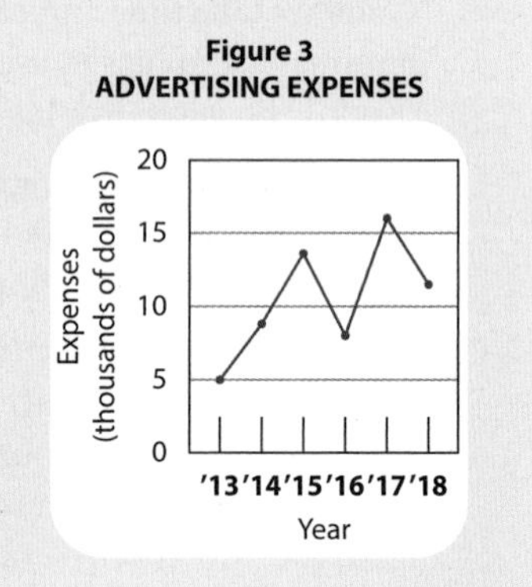

Your Turn: Applying Your Skills at Pew

You are excited about the possibility of becoming an intern for the Pew Financial Security and Mobility project, a division of the Pew Charitable Trusts, parent organization to the Pew Research Center. The project is devoted to studying the health and status of family finances. Most recently, the organization produced research and analysis titled *What Your Household Type Reveals About Your Financial Security.*

Although you cannot find evidence that Pew is looking for interns, you decide to send a letter to show your interest in obtaining an internship. You know that successful persuasive writing is genuine and sincere and uses the AIDA organizational strategy discussed in Chapter 10. You also think your letter should illustrate your knowledge of report writing as well as your skill as a writer.

Your Task

Visit the Pew Charitable Trusts' website (**http://www.pewtrusts.org**) to learn more about the organization and read *What Your Household Type Reveals About Your Financial Security.* Write an unsolicited job request letter that uses the AIDA persuasive organizational strategy and ask to be considered for an internship. Address the letter to Ms. Erin Currier, Director, Financial Security and Mobility, Pew Charitable Trusts, 901 E Street NW, Washington, DC 20004-2008.

Summary of Learning Outcomes

1 Explain informational and analytical report functions, organizational strategies, and writing styles as well as typical report formats.

- Informational reports—such as monthly sales reports, status updates, and compliance reports—present data without analysis or recommendations.
- Analytical reports provide findings, analyses, conclusions, and recommendations when requested. Examples include justification, recommendation, feasibility, and yardstick reports.
- Audience reaction and content determine whether a report is organized directly or indirectly.
- Reports organized directly reveal the purpose and conclusions immediately; reports organized indirectly place the conclusions and recommendations last.
- Reports written in a formal style use third-person constructions, avoid contractions, and may include passive-voice verbs. Informal reports use first-person constructions, contractions, shorter sentences, familiar words, and active-voice verbs.
- Reports may appear in various formats: e-mail, letter, memo, manuscript, template, infographic, or electronic slide deck. They may be shared electronically or in hard copy.

2 Apply the 3-x-3 writing process to contemporary business reports to create well-organized documents that show a firm grasp of audience and purpose.

- Report writers begin by clarifying a problem and writing a problem statement, which may include the scope, significance, and limitations of the project.
- After analyzing the audience and defining major issues, report writers prepare a work plan, including a tentative outline and work schedule.
- Next, data must be collected, organized, interpreted, and illustrated.
- After composing the first draft, report writers edit (often many times), proofread, and evaluate.

3 Locate and evaluate secondary sources such as databases and Internet resources, and understand how to conduct credible primary research.

- Secondary data may be located by searching for books, periodicals, and newspapers, mostly through electronic indexes and online research databases.
- Popular Internet search tools include Google, Bing, and Yahoo Search, but the retrieved information must be scrutinized for currency, authority, content, and accuracy.
- Researchers generate firsthand, primary data through surveys (in-person, online, and print), interviews, observation, and experimentation.
- Surveys are most efficient for gathering information from large groups of people.
- Interviews are useful when working with experts in the field.
- Firsthand observation can produce rich data, but it must be objective.
- Experimentation produces data suggesting cause and effect; valid experiments require sophisticated research designs and careful matching of experimental and control groups.

notice and focused on cell phone use in general and texting in particular as major causes of distracted driving. Several states have issued handheld cell phone bans.

d. Cities around the country enacted strict regulations banning trans fats in restaurant fare. Food processors nationwide are wondering whether they need to make changes before being forced to switch to nonhydrogenated fats by law. Food and Drug Administration regulations have already changed the definitions of common terms such as *fresh, fat free, low in cholesterol,* and *light.* The Old World Bakery worries that it may have to change its production process and rewrite all its package labels. Old World doesn't know whether to hire a laboratory or a consultant for this project.

e. Customers placing telephone orders for outdoor clothing and leisure wear with Eddie Bauer typically order only one or two items. The company wonders whether it can train telephone service reps to motivate customers to increase the number of items ordered per call.

11.5 Problem and Purpose Statements (L.O. 2)

YOUR TASK Identify a problem in your current job or a previous job, such as inadequate use of technology, inefficient procedures, spotty customer service, poor product quality, low morale, or a personnel problem. Assume that your boss agrees with your criticism and asks you to prepare a report. Write (a) a two- or three-sentence statement describing the problem, (b) a problem question, and (c) a simple statement of purpose for your report.

11.6 Plagiarism, Paraphrasing, and Citing Sources (L.O. 4)

One of the biggest challenges for student writers is paraphrasing secondary sources correctly to avoid plagiarism.

YOUR TASK For each of the following, read the original passage. Analyze the paraphrased version. List the weaknesses in relation to what you have learned about plagiarism and the use of references. Then write an improved version.

a. Original Passage

When the Tesla Model S launched four years ago, the all-electric luxury sedan certainly had its critics. Many of them were executives at German luxury carmakers, quick to dismiss the upstart American carmaker as a quixotic but doomed effort. But as the Model S won plaudits, achieved respectable sales, and captured the public's imagination, that attitude has changed. And that was before Tesla racked up nearly 400,000 reservations for its Model 3 sedan, which is expected to compete with German mainstays like the Audi A4 and BMW 3-Series. Now, Audi, BMW, Mercedes-Benz, and Porsche are downright worried about Tesla. "Tesla has promised a lot but has also delivered most of it," Dieter Zetsche—chairman of Mercedes parent Daimler—said earlier this month.[30]

Paraphrased Passage

Upon the launch of its Model S, Tesla had many detractors; most were executives at German car companies selling luxury cars. They dismissed the new California-based carmaker as a doomed effort. That attitude has changed as the Model S won praise, racked up considerable sales, and impressed the general public. Most recently, Tesla secured 400,000 early reservations for its Model 3, which will compete with German luxury cars such as the Audi A4 and the BMW 3-Series. Now that Tesla has promised a lot but has also delivered most of it, said Daimler chairman Dieter Zetsche, the German carmakers Audi, Mercedes-Benz, Porsche, and BMW are pretty worried about Tesla.

b. Original Passage

Lurking behind chartjunk is contempt both for the information and for the audience. Chartjunk promoters imagine that numbers and details are boring, dull, and tedious, requiring ornament to enliven. Cosmetic decoration, which frequently distorts the data, will never salvage an underlying lack of content. If the numbers are boring, then you've got the wrong numbers. Credibility vanishes in clouds of chartjunk; who would trust a chart that looks like a video game?[31]

Paraphrased Passage

Chartjunk creators hold the information they are conveying and their audience in contempt because they believe that statistical details are dull, unimaginative, and tedious and need to be spruced up with decorations. Purely ornamental design elements distort the data and cannot cover up a lack of content. If the statistics are boring, then they are the wrong statistics. Chartjunk kills credibility. Readers cannot trust a chart that looks like a video game.

c. Original Passage

Developing casual online game titles can be much less risky than trying to create a game that runs on a console such as an Xbox. Casual games typically cost less than $200,000 to produce, and production cycles are only six months to a year. There's no shelf space, packaging, or CD production to pay for. Best of all, there's more room for innovation.[32]

Paraphrased Passage

The development of casual online games offers less risk than creating games running on Xbox and other consoles. Usually, casual games are cheaper, costing under $200,000 to create and 6 to 12 months to produce. Developers save on shelf space, packaging, and CD production too. Moreover, they have more freedom to innovate.

11.7 Factoring and Outlining a Problem (L.O. 2)

Virgin America has asked your company, Connections International, to prepare a proposal for a training school for tour operators. Virgin America wants to know whether Burbank,

California, would be a good spot for its school. Burbank interests Virgin America, but only if nearby entertainment facilities can be used for tour training. The airline also needs an advisory committee consisting, if possible, of representatives of the travel community and perhaps executives of other major airlines. The real problem is how to motivate these people to cooperate with Virgin America.

You have heard that NBC Studios in Burbank offers training seminars, guest speakers, and other resources for tour operators. You wonder whether Magic Mountain in Valencia would also be willing to cooperate with the proposed school. Moreover, you remember that Griffith Park is nearby and might make a good tour training spot. Before Virgin America will settle on Burbank as its choice, it wants to know whether access to air travel is adequate. Virgin America's management team is also concerned about available school building space. Moreover, the carrier wants to know whether city officials in Burbank would be receptive to this tour training school proposal.

YOUR TASK To guide your thinking and research, factor this problem into an outline with several areas to investigate. Further divide the problem into subproblems, phrasing each entry as a question. For example, *Should the Virgin America tour training program be located in Burbank?* (See the work plan model in Figure 11.6.)

11.8 Preparing a Work Plan (L.O. 2)

Any long report project requires a structured work plan.

YOUR TASK Select a report topic from activities presented at the ends of Chapters 12 and 13 or from a comprehensive list of report topics at **www.cengagebrain.com.** For that report prepare a work plan that includes the following:

a. Statement of the problem
b. Expanded statement of purpose (including scope, limitations, and significance)
c. Research strategy to answer the questions
d. Tentative outline of key questions to answer
e. Work schedule (with projected completion dates)

11.9 Experimenting With Secondary Sources (L.O. 3)

Web

Secondary sources can provide quite different information depending on your mode of inquiry.

YOUR TASK Use Google or another search engine that supports Boolean searches to investigate a topic such as carbon footprint or sustainability, or any other business topic of interest to you. Explore the same topic using (a) keywords and (b) Boolean operators. Which method produces more relevant hits? Save two relevant sources from each search using two or more of the strategies presented in this chapter. Remember to include the URL for each article. Alternatively, compare your Google search results with those from a metasearch site such as Dogpile or Search.com.

In a memo to your instructor, list the bibliographical information from all sources and explain briefly which method was most productive.

11.10 Exploring Campus Food Preferences With SurveyMonkey (L.O. 3)

Communication Technology   E-Mail

Team

Your University Business Club (UBC) is abuzz about a GrubHub study that analyzed the ordering habits of American college students attending more than 100 schools in 47 states. Not unexpectedly perhaps, the campus favorites would not qualify as health food. In addition, students tend to order late at night, order almost 50 percent more than nonstudents do, and tip 5 percent less than nonstudents do.[33] The current top three late-night snacks are frozen yogurt, waffle fries, and chicken souvlaki pita, followed by brownies, hibachi chicken, vegetarian spring rolls, sweet and sour chicken, and the obligatory cheese pizza. Buffalo chicken wings and spicy California rolls round out the top ten.

Your UBC wants to advocate for a new, small student-run restaurant in the campus food court. But what food should it dish out? Is it true that college students overwhelmingly prefer food high in salt, sugar, and fat? Your club colleagues have chosen you to create an online survey to poll fellow students, staff, and faculty about their preferences. You hope to generate data that will support the feasibility of the eatery and help UBC create winning menu choices.

The main provider of online survey software, SurveyMonkey, makes creating questionnaires fast, fun, and easy. After signing up for the free no-frills basic plan, you can create brief online questionnaires and e-mail the links to your targeted respondents. The programs analyze and display the results for you—at no charge.

YOUR TASK In pairs or teams of three, design a basic questionnaire to survey students on your campus about food options in the campus cafeteria. Visit SurveyMonkey and sign up for the basic plan. After creating the online survey, e-mail the survey link to as many members of the campus community as possible. For a smaller sample, start by polling students in your class. Interpret the results. As a team, write a memo that you will e-mail to the campus food services administrator advocating for a student-run eatery featuring the top-scoring national or regional foods.

Your instructor may ask you to complete this activity as a report or proposal assignment after you study Chapter 12.

If so, write a feasibility report or proposal for the campus food services administrator and support your advocacy with the survey results.

11.11 Studying Teen and Young Adult Media Use (L.O. 3)

Communication Technology | E-Mail | Web

You know what you do online or how much TV you watch, but what does everybody else do? We tend to judge others by our own preferences and by behaviors we observe among our family, friends, and acquaintances. In marketing, however, hunches are not enough.

Your boss, Quinn Kaur, doesn't believe in stereotyping. She encourages her market researchers to be wary of all data. She asked you to explore so-called niche marketing opportunities in targeting teens, a notoriously fickle consumer group. Primarily, Ms. Kaur wants to know how teenagers communicate and, more specifically, how they use social media and e-mail. Understanding teen behavior is invaluable for the success of any promotional or ad campaign.

For a full picture to emerge, you will need to consult several recent studies. The best candidates for your research are surveys by the Nielsen Company, Pew Research Center's Internet, Science & Tech topics, Common Sense Media, and similar reputable sources of data. While Nielsen is a for-profit global market research company, Pew Research Center and Common Sense Media are nonprofit organizations.

YOUR TASK Ms. Kaur requested a brief informational e-mail report summarizing your main findings. Paraphrase correctly and don't just copy from the online source. Ms. Kaur may ask you later to analyze more comprehensive data in an analytical report and create a media use profile of American teens and young adults. You may be called on to create graphs to illustrate your findings.

11.12 Gathering Data: Target Aiming at a New Charitable Focus (L.O. 3, 4, and 5)

Communication Technology | E-Mail | Team | Web

Affectionately known as *Tar-jay*, Minneapolis-based Target Corporation takes corporate social responsibility seriously. The company has been praised for giving back to the community with higher-than-usual charitable contributions. At 3.2 percent of the retailer's profits, Target's annual donations amount to $149 million a year. The retailer ranks No. 8 among Forbes' top ten most generous companies.[36]

In the course of two decades, Target has donated over $432 million to more than 100,000 local schools under its Take Charge of Education program.[37] The company gave away 1 percent of shoppers' REDcard purchases to the education initiative, but it found over time that only 10 percent of REDcard holders enrolled in the program. The retailer also supported library makeovers and other school-based grants. It will continue to fund meal programs for schoolchildren and money for field trips. In all, Target has recently met its goal of giving away $1 billion to education within a mere five years.[38]

The new CEO, Brian Cornell, has instituted many changes, including a reorientation in charitable giving. As shoppers have shifted their attention from education to health as their main concern, the retailer has followed suit and is putting its money where its customers are most likely to appreciate it.

YOUR TASK Select one of the following tasks.

a. As a summer intern at Walmart, you are asked to prepare an informational memo about Target's charitable practices to send to your boss, Martin Chavez. Walmart is seeking greater community involvement to boost its public image. What types of projects does the Target Corporation fund? What other policies set this company apart from its competitors when it comes to giving back to the community? Write an individual informational e-mail or memo or one collaborative e-mail or memo as a team of summer interns. Alternatively, Martin Chavez could ask you to write an e-mail or memo describing how Target has handled controversies and what its actions say about the company's management and philosophy.

b. As a team of summer interns for Walmart, research the charitable giving of Target and other major corporations. Prepare an informational memo comparing and contrasting corporate practices. Target ranks fourth behind Walmart, Home Depot, and Lowe's in size. How much of their pretax earnings are these and other big chain stores spending on philanthropy? What types of causes do they embrace, and why? Do their policies seem consistent and purposeful over the long term? How do they justify charitable giving to their shareholders?

In each case, compile a bibliography of sources you used. Whenever appropriate, display numbers visually by creating charts, graphs, and tables.

You may want to start by viewing company mission statements and annual reports for discussions of corporate social responsibility, charitable giving, and worthy causes companies support. Then, go to independent sources for a more detached, objective perspective.

11.13 Gathering Data: *Fortune* Magazine's 100 Best Companies to Work For (L.O. 3, 4)

E-Mail

Some companies spend lavishly on unusual employee perks such as massages, in-house chefs, and sauna visits and offer generous compensation and benefits in the hope of attracting superior talent. At the same time, they remain profitable. Chances are that you haven't heard of at least two among the top five of *Fortune*'s 100 Best Companies to Work For—ACUITY Insurance headquartered in Wisconsin (No. 2) and New York–based Wegmans Food Market (No. 4). The perennial favorite, Google, now a subsidiary of holding company Alphabet, has again clinched the top spot. The Boston Consulting Group ranks third, and Quicken Loans is in fifth place. Formerly ranked among the top ten, outdoor powerhouse REI has slipped to No. 26. However, it still attracts active types who may bring their dogs to work, go on a midday bike ride, and test the products they sell. Sound nice? Just as companies have their distinctive corporate cultures, they also differ in why they are perceived as ideal employers.

YOUR TASK Visit the *Fortune* magazine website for the most current 100 Best Companies to Work For list. Examine the information about the top 20 or 25 highest-ranked companies. Watch the short video clips profiling each business. After studying the information, identify factors that attract and please workers. Take note of features shared across the board, but don't overlook quirky, unusual benefits. Summarize these trends in an informational e-mail or memo report. Alternatively, prepare an analytical report investigating employee satisfaction gleaned from the secondary data obtained on the *Fortune* site.

11.14 Who Gets Hurt? Examining Infamous Plagiarism Scandals (L.O. 4)

Team 

Have you ever wondered who gets hurt when students, teachers, journalists, scientists, and other authors are dishonest researchers and writers? Occasionally we read about people who plagiarize their work, try to cheat their way through college, invent news features, copy from others, or fabricate research results. Earlier in the chapter you learned about anesthesiologist Yoshitaka Fujii, who wrote 172 bogus scientific papers, 126 of which were based on imaginary research studies. Two shocking cases in medical research rival Fujii's fabrications in gravity and scope.

Former British surgeon Andrew Wakefield published an article in the reputable medical journal *The Lancet* that seemed to provide evidence that a common immunization against measles, mumps, and rubella (MMR) could cause autism. Wakefield had fabricated evidence and was found guilty of professional misconduct. He lost his license to practice as a medical doctor. His fraudulent research, however, caused a precipitous drop in vaccinations in the United Kingdom and Ireland. In the words of one pediatrician, "That paper killed children."[39] Many American parents still refuse to vaccinate their kids and are causing the spread of diseases that had been eradicated in the United States.[40]

A Harvard researcher's purposely nonsensical research paper, consisting of randomly generated text accompanied by two fake authors, was accepted by 17 of 37 medical journals. Journals publishing such bogus research are called predatory publishers. A prominent bioethicist calls such practices "publication pollution."[41]

YOUR TASK If your instructor directs, individually or as a team, investigate the cases of Andrew Wakefield, Joachim Boldt, Stephen Ambrose, Jayson Blair, Doris Kearns Goodwin, Jonah Lehrer, Kaavya Viswanathan, or other infamous plagiarists. Alternatively, you could focus on the case of 200 professors from 50 universities implicated in a massive publishing scam in South Korea.[42] Consider the authors' transgressions, their excuses, and the consequences of their actions. As a team, gather your individual research results, compare notes, and summarize your insights in a memo report to your instructor. This assignment could also be turned into a long report as presented in Chapter 12 if the investigation is expanded to include more detailed discussions and more cases.

11.15 Selecting Graphics (L.O. 5)

YOUR TASK Identify the best graphics forms to illustrate the following data.

a. Potential new residential development project
b. Annual restaurant industry sales figures
c. Government unemployment data by industry and sector, in percentages
d. Figures showing the distribution of the H3N2 strain of type A flu virus in humans by state
e. Figures showing the process of delivering water to a metropolitan area
f. LTE and 4G coverage in the United States, Canada, and Mexico
g. Figures showing what proportion of every state tax dollar is spent on education, social services, transportation, debt, and other expenses
h. Academic, administrative, and operation divisions of a college, from the president to department chairs and division managers
i. Figures comparing the sales of smartphones, tablets, and laptops over the past five years

11.16 Creating a Bar Chart (L.O. 5)

The ability to create appropriate and relevant graphics is a sought-after skill in today's information age workplace. Spreadsheet programs such as Excel make it easy to generate appealing visuals.

YOUR TASK Based on the statistics that follow, prepare (a) a bar chart comparing the latest tax rates in eight industrial countries and (b) a bar chart that shows the change from the previous year to the current year. The past-year data follow the current statistics in parentheses: Canada, 37 (39) percent; France, 52 (52) percent; Germany, 45 (45) percent; Japan, 35 (34) percent; Netherlands, 45 (46) percent; Sweden, 52 (52) percent; United Kingdom, 38 (41) percent; United States, 18 (22) percent. These figures represent a percentage of the gross domestic product for each country. The current figures are largely estimates by the U.S. Central Intelligence Agency. What should you emphasize in the chart and title? What trends do you recognize?

11.17 Creating a Line Chart (L.O. 5)

YOUR TASK Prepare a line chart showing the sales of Sidekick Athletic Shoes, Inc., for these years: 2017, $6.7 million; 2016, $5.4 million; 2015, $3.2 million; 2014, $2.1 million; 2013, $2.6 million; 2012, $3.6 million. In the chart title, highlight the trend you see in the data.

11.18 Searching for Data Visualization and Infographics in Annual Reports (L.O. 5)

Annual reports are infamous for being anything but fascinating reading even for the most ardent investors.

E-Mail Web

YOUR TASK Search annual reports filed by Fortune 500 companies, and examine to what extent they have embraced infographics. Critique their readability, clarity, and effectiveness in visualizing data. How were the visuals introduced in the text? What suggestions would you make to improve them? Can you detect any effort to present financials and other data in visually appealing, unconventional ways? In an e-mail or memo to your instructor, evaluate the use and effectiveness of graphics in three to five corporate annual reports.

11.19 Seeking Business Infographics (L.O. 1, 4, and 5)

Web

YOUR TASK. On the Web or in print, find an infographic that visualizes intriguing business-relevant data. Look for sources within or below the infographic. Are they indicated? If yes, are they credible? How much hard statistical information is provided in relation to the space the infographic occupies? Does the infographic meet its objective: is the information clearly presented, easy to read, and insightful? Report your findings orally or in writing. Be prepared to show your chosen infographic to the class. **Tip:** In Google or a similar search engine, type the keyword *infographic* and among the search categories, select *Images*.

11.20 College Students and Credit Card Debt (L.O. 3, 4)

E-Mail Web

Credit card companies used to woo college students with tempting offers of credit and sweetened the deal with free T-shirts and other small perks. As a result, many college kids found themselves deep in credit card debt fast without the means of repaying it. The U.S. Credit CARD Act of 2009 put an end to the lure of easy credit. Banks could no longer issue cards to people under age twenty-one unless they could prove they had their own income or a cosigner.[43] Today, issuers are much stingier about granting credit cards to all consumers, and Americans carry fewer cards than ever.[44]

Credit cards are a factor when students graduate with an average of $35,000 in loan debt. Because they can't buy cars, rent homes, or purchase insurance, graduates with substantial debt see a bleak future for themselves. This worrisome trend is likely to continue, experts believe, because today's college students are already the most indebted graduates in history.[45]

A local newspaper plans to run a self-help story about college students and credit cards. The editor asks you, a young part-time reporter, to prepare a memo with information that could be turned into an article. The article would focus on parents of students who are about to leave for college. What can parents do to help students avoid sinking deeply into credit card debt?

YOUR TASK Using ABI/INFORM Complete, EBSCO, Factiva, or LexisNexis and the Web, locate basic information about student credit card options. In an e-mail or memo, discuss shared credit cards and other options. Your goal is to be informative, not to reach conclusions or make recommendations. Use one or more of the techniques discussed in this chapter to track your sources. Address your memo to Paula Parks, editor.

Test Your Etiquette IQ

New communication platforms and casual workplace environments have blurred the lines of appropriateness, leaving workers wondering how to navigate uncharted waters. Indicate whether the following statements are true or false. Then see if you agree with the responses on p. R-2.

1. It's considered poor manners to wear your headphones in workplace elevators or in hallways.

   ________ True ________ False

2. If you have been invited to attend a meeting of a group you have never met before, you should enter the room and take an empty seat without causing a fuss.

   ________ True ________ False

3. Giving a personal gift to your boss is acceptable if the gift is expensive and tasteful.

   ________ True ________ False

Chat About It

In each chapter you will find five discussion questions related to the chapter material. Your instructor may assign these topics for you to discuss in class, in an online chat room, or on an online discussion board. Some of the discussion topics may require outside research. You may also be asked to read and respond to postings made by your classmates.

TOPIC 1: Research suggests that colleges with strong, explicit ethics codes and zero tolerance of cheating have the lowest incidence of academic dishonesty. Find the student handbook on your portal (or check the university catalog) for rules of conduct regarding cheating. Are they clear? Does your school make students pledge not to cheat? How do you feel about such efforts?

TOPIC 2: What are some business topics that you would like to research and perhaps would even enjoy writing about? Explain and compare notes with your peers.

TOPIC 3: The Internet has brought the paper mills to the masses. Some students pay to have their papers written by shady authors online. Discuss the views in your class regarding this practice and how it could be harmful to honest students. Is any harm done to colleges and universities? Society?

TOPIC 4: Why is it important for a nonexpert on a topic to use professional journals as report sources?

TOPIC 5: Is plagiarism worth the risk of being caught? Why or why not?

Grammar and Mechanics | *Review 11*

Total Review

The first nine chapters reviewed specific guides from Appendix D, Grammar and Mechanics Guide. The exercises in this and the remaining chapters are total reviews, covering all of the grammar and mechanics guides plus confusing words and frequently misspelled words.

Each of the following sentences has **three** errors in grammar, punctuation, capitalization, usage, or spelling. On a separate sheet, write a correct version. Avoid adding new phrases, starting new sentences, or rewriting in your own words. When finished, compare your responses with the key beginning on page Key-2.

EXAMPLE: Many jobs in todays digital workplace are never advertised, there part of the hidden job market.

REVISION: Many jobs in **today's** digital workplace are never **advertised; they're** part of the hidden job market.

1. One creditable study revealed that thirty percent of jobs go to companies inside candidates.
2. Networking is said to be the key to finding a job, however, its easier said then done.
3. Some job seekers were paid five hundred dollars each to attend twelve sessions that promised expert job-searching advise.
4. To excel at networking an easy to remember e-mail address is a must for a candidate.

5. My friend asked me if I had all ready prepared a thirty second elevator speech?

6. When Lucy and myself were collecting data for the report we realized that twitter and Facebook could be significant.

7. Todays workers must brush up their marketable skills otherwise they may not find another job after being laid off.

8. Being active on LinkedIn and building an impressive internet presence is important, but the looseness of these connections mean you shouldn't expect much from them.

9. Just between you and I, one of the best strategys in networking are distributing business cards with your personal tagline.

10. On February 1st our company President revealed that we would be hiring thirty new employees, which was excellent news for everyone.

References

[1] About Pew Research Center. http://www.pewresearch.org/about

[2] Communications Assistant. Pew Research Center. Retrieved from http://www.pewresearch.org/about/careers/communications-assistant

[3] Research Associate, Journalism. Pew Research Center. Retrieved from https://jobs-prc.icims.com/jobs/4561/research-associate%2c-journalism/job

[4] Wales, J. (n.d.). Most people hate official reports—Effective report writing and creative business writing. Impact Factory. Retrieved from http://www.impactfactory.com/p/official_effective_report_writing_skills_training_development/wisdom_1712-2110-2613.html

[5] Elliott, M. (2010-2013). Writing. Retrieved from http://marianne-elliott.com/writing

[6] Investigation ends; Garden of Life powders pose ongoing threat. (2016, April 22). Food Safety News. Retrieved from http://www.foodsafetynews.com/2016/04/investigation-ends-garden-of-life-powders-pose-ongoing-threat/#.Vx6jPWNiDzl

[7] Weeks, L. (n. d.). 50 thought-provoking quotes about libraries and librarians. Ebook Friendly. Retrieved from http://ebookfriendly.com/best-quotes-about-libraries-librarians

[8] Based on Glendale, California, city branding study. North Star. Retrieved from http://www.northstarideas.com/case-studies/glendale-california

[9] Ledbetter, C. (2015, September 9). The 10 foods college students order the most. *The Huffington Post*. Retrieved from http://www.huffingtonpost.com/entry/foods-college-students-order-the-most_us_55f0443be4b093be51bce93f

[10] Giorgetti, D., & Sebastiani, F. (2003, December). Automating survey coding by multiclass text categories. *Journal of the American Society for Information Science and Technology, 54*(14), 1269. Retrieved from http://search.proquest.com

[11] Goldsmith, B. (2002, June). The awesome power of asking the right questions. *OfficeSolutions*, 52; Bracey, G. W. (2001, November). Research-question authority. *Phi Delta Kappan*, 191.

[12] Peters, T. (1991). *Thriving on chaos*. New York: HarperCollins, pp. 281-282.

[13] Burkitt, L. (2016, January 12). Starbucks to add thousands of stores in China. *The Wall Street Journal*. Retrieved from http://www.wsj.com/articles/starbucks-plans-thousands-of-new-stores-in-china-1452580905; Berfield, S. (2009, August 17). Howard Schultz versus Howard Schultz. *BusinessWeek*, p. 31.

[14] Stuart, E. (2016, January 19). ASU professor resigns amid plagiarism accusations. *Phoenix New Times*. Retrieved from http://www.phoenixnewtimes.com/news/asu-professor-resigns-amid-plagiarism-accusations-7980419; Iyengar, R. (2015, November 25). 200 South Korean professors charged in massive plagiarism scam. *Time*. Retrieved from http://time.com/4126853/south-korea-professors-books-plagiarism-authors-publishers; McCabe, F. (2014, December 2). UNLV fires professor accused of "serial plagiarism." *Review Journal*. Retrieved from http://www.reviewjournal.com/news/education/unlv-fires-professor-accused-serial-plagiarism

[15] Kuratko, D. F. (2016). *Entrepreneurship: Theory, Process, and Practice*. 10th ed. Boston, MA: Cengage Learning, pp. 45-46.

[16] Groden, C. (2015, November 19). MBA applicants are still cheating on essays. *Fortune*. Retrieved from http://fortune.com/2015/11/19/business-school-plagiarism

[17] Writing Tutorial Services, Indiana University. Plagiarism: What it is and how to recognize and avoid it. Retrieved from http://www.indiana.edu/~wts/pamphlets/plagiarism.shtml

[18] Carlyle, E. (2016, March 8). America's fastest-growing cities 2016. *Forbes*. Retrieved from http://www.forbes.com/sites/erincarlyle/2016/03/08/americas-fastest-growing-cities-2016/#59c2e0d77056

[19] Saylor, M. (2012). *The mobile wave: How mobile intelligence will change everything*. New York: Vanguard Press, p. ix.

[20] Tufte, E. (n.d.) Poster: Napoleon's march. Retrieved from http://www.edwardtufte.com/tufte/posters

[21] Arafah, B. (2010, May 21). Huge infographics design resources: Overview, principles, tips and examples. Onextrapixel.com. Retrieved from http://www.onextrapixel.com/2010/05/21/huge-infographics-design-resources-overview-principles-tips-and-examples

[22] Labarre, S. (2012, January). How infographics guru Nicholas Felton inspired Facebook's Timeline. Co.DESIGN. Retrieved from http://www.fastcodesign.com/1665062/how-infographics-guru-nicholas-felton-inspired-facebooks-timeline

[23] Kuang, C. (2011, December). 2 GE infographics offer hints about the future of data-driven management. Co.DESIGN. Retrieved from http://www.fastcodesign.com/1669049/2-infographics-from-ge-offer-hints-about-future-of-data-driven-management#1

[24] Pavlus, J. (2011, December). Why "infographic thinking" is the future, not a fad. Co.DESIGN. Retrieved from http://www.fastcodesign.com/1668987/why-infographic-thinking-is-the-future-not-a-fad

[25] Visually, Inc. (2012). Infographics software. Retrieved from http://visual.ly/learn/infographics-software

[26] Tufte, E. R. (1983). *The visual display of quantitative information*. Cheshire, CT: Graphics Press, p. 107.

[27] Gallo, C. (2016, March 23). The best perk at America's best employers is the one you don't see. *Forbes*. Retrieved from http://www.forbes.com/sites/carminegallo/2016/03/23/the-best-perk-at-americas-best-employers-is-the-one-you-dont-see/#642b3a2e3a4f

[28] Ibid.

[29] Reasons students hate writing essays or term papers. (n.d.) CustomPapers.com. Retrieved from http://custompapers.com/essay-not

[30] Edelstein, S. (2016, April 27). Now, finally, the Germans are getting scared of Tesla? Green Car Reports. Retrieved from http://www.greencarreports.com/news/1103623_now-finally-the-germans-are-getting-scared-of-tesla

[31] Tufte, E. (1990). *Envisioning information*. Cheshire, CT: Graphics Press, p. 34.

[32] Reena, J. (2006, October 16). Enough with the shoot-'em-ups. *Businessweek*, p. 92.

[33] Based on Ledbetter, C. (2015, September 9). The 10 foods college students order the most. *The Huffington Post*. Retrieved from http://www.huffingtonpost.com/entry/

foods-college-students-order-the-most_us_55f0443be4b093be51bce93f

[34] Jones, H., & Luscombe, B. (2015, November 3). 5 myths about how teens use technology. *Time*. Retrieved from http://time.com/4096797/teens-media-phone-use-myths-truths/?xid=time_socialflow_twitter

[35] Anderson, M. (2015, August 20). How having smartphones (or not) shapes the way teens communicate. Pew Research Center. Retrieved from http://www.pewresearch.org/fact-tank/2015/08/20/how-having-smartphones-or-not-shapes-the-way-teens-communicate

[36] Adams, S. (2014, July 15). America's most generous companies. *Forbes*. Retrieved from http://www.forbes.com/pictures/mkl45egeik/8-target-3/#702ba7b4236f

[37] Kumar, K. (2015, September 14). Target will end school charity program, shift giving focus to wellness. *Star Tribune*. Retrieved from http://www.startribune.com/target-will-end-school-charity-program-shift-giving-focus-to-wellness/327423181

[38] Ibid.

[39] Park, A. (2011, January 6). Study linking vaccines to autism is "fraudulent." *Time*. Retrieved from http://healthland.time.com/2011/01/06/study-linking-vaccines-to-autism-is-fraudulent

[40] Haberman, C. (2015, February 1). A discredited vaccine study's continuing impact on public health. *The New York Times*. Retrieved from http://www.nytimes.com/2015/02/02/us/a-discredited-vaccine-studys-continuing-impact-on-public-health.html

[41] Perry, S. (2015, April 7). "Plagiarism, fraud, and predatory publishing" are polluting science, says bioethicist Arthur Caplan. *Minnpost*. Retrieved from https://www.minnpost.com/second-opinion/2015/04/plagiarism-fraud-and-predatory-publishing-are-polluting-science-says-bioethic

[42] Iyengar, R. (2015, November 25). 200 South Korean professors charged in massive plagiarism scam. *Time*. Retrieved from http://time.com/4126853/south-korea-professors-books-plagiarism-authors-publishers

[43] Williams, G. (2015, August 11). Should your college kid get a credit card? *U.S. News & World Report*. Retrieved from http://money.usnews.com/money/personal-finance/articles/2015/08/11/should-your-college-kid-get-a-credit-card

[44] Holmes, T. E. (2014, November 6). Credit card ownership statistics. CreditCards.com. Retrieved from http://www.creditcards.com/credit-card-news/ownership-statistics-charts-1276.php

[45] Sparshott, J. (2015, May 8). Congratulations, class of 2015. You're the most indebted ever (for now). *The Wall Street Journal*. Retrieved from http://blogs.wsj.com/economics/2015/05/08/congratulations-class-of-2015-youre-the-most-indebted-ever-for-now

Chapter 12 Informal Business Reports

LEARNING OUTCOMES

After studying this chapter, you should be able to

1 Analyze, sort, and interpret statistical data and other information using tables, measures of central tendency (mean, median, and mode), and decision matrices.

2 Draw meaningful conclusions and make practical report recommendations after sound and valid analysis.

3 Organize report data logically, and provide reader cues to aid comprehension.

4 Write short informational reports that describe routine tasks.

5 Prepare short analytical reports that solve business problems.

Starbucks: Innovate or Die! The Global Chain That Wants to Remain Local

Zooming In

Amid fierce global competition, Starbucks is reinventing itself with innovative store concepts, constant expansion, and new beverages. The company continues to reign as the world's largest coffee shop chain by number of outlets and revenue, having soared to more than 24,000 retail locations in 70 countries.[1] The specialty coffee roaster and retailer has bolstered its presence in China, its second-largest and fastest-growing market.[2] The company has also entered India, a traditionally tea-loving country. In its own words, Starbucks set out to be "a different kind of company"[3] by providing a unique experience to customers and trying to create a connection "one person, one cup, and one neighborhood at a time."[4] Yet the global behemoth serves a whopping 60 million customers a week and employs almost 240,000 people.[5] With annual sales of $20.2 billion and a market capitalization of $85.3 billion, the company is "firing on all cylinders," according to *The Wall Street Journal,* even when its stock dips, as it has lately.[6]

Adding to its accolades, Starbucks consistently ranks among the top ten in the *Fortune* magazine list of the World's Most Admired Companies. It is known for its social responsibility initiatives such as fair-trade coffee sourcing, energy conservation, farmer loans, and ethical employment practices. Moreover, the retailer is regularly named among the top 100 on the *Forbes* list of America's Best Employers, not least because Starbucks gives health insurance and stock options to all employees, whom it calls partners.[7]

Howard Schultz successfully bucked traditional retail wisdom, for example, by locating stores so densely together that they cannibalized each other's sales. The New York metro area alone has 430 locations.[8] Schultz famously relied on his entrepreneurial instinct and scorned conventional market research. Although he is one of the most admired corporate executives of our time, Howard Schultz suffered a few flops, too. His headlong introduction of Sorbetto failed miserably, and Starbucks had to abandon the sugary beverage.[9] The company also has had mixed results with its music and film offerings. Moreover, Schultz admitted that he misread the depth of the Great Recession and its impact on his business. However, he scored a winner with Via, Starbucks' instant coffee, because this time he embraced focus groups and listened to his executives, who advocated a slow, methodical introduction.

The CEO's latest promising ventures are the opening of the coffee chain's first store in South Africa[10] and a foray into a new high-end ready-made chilled coffee as iced coffee is booming in the United States.[11] The company is expanding its mobile ordering and payment options and tweaking a new customer loyalty rewards system. You will learn more about Starbucks and be asked to complete a relevant task later in this chapter.

Critical Thinking

- Howard Schultz is betting on constant reinvention of his company. He said, "Innovation is in our DNA."[12] What kind of information should Starbucks gather to help it decide whether and how to introduce a new product to avoid pitfalls such as the failed Sorbetto beverage?
- How could Howard Schultz test his assumption that the intimate communal coffee-drinking experience is intact at Starbucks?
- How can collected information be transmitted to Starbucks' decision makers?

Analyzing Digital Age Data

Much of the information that allows decision makers to run their organizations efficiently in this digital age comes to them in the form of reports. To respond nimbly to changing economic times, Starbucks and other businesses need information to stay abreast of what is happening inside and outside of their firms. This chapter focuses on analyzing and organizing data, drawing conclusions, providing reader cues, and writing informal business reports.

Given the easy access to research databases, the Web, and other sources of digitized information, collecting information is nearly effortless today. However, making sense of the massive amounts of data you may collect is much harder. You may feel overwhelmed as you look at a jumble of digital files, printouts, articles, interview notes, questionnaire results, and statistics. Unprocessed data become meaningful information through skillful and accurate sorting, analysis, combination, and recombination. You will be examining each item to see what it means by itself and what it means when connected with other data. You are looking for meanings, relationships, and answers to the research questions posed in your work plan.

Learning Outcome 1

Analyze, sort, and interpret statistical data and other information using tables, measures of central tendency (mean, median, and mode), and decision matrices.

Stefano Cavoretto/Shutterstock.com

Reality Check

Have a Plan and Do Research

"Failure to do market research before you begin a business venture or during its operation is like driving a car from Texas to New York without a map or street signs. You have to know which direction to travel and how fast to go. A good market research plan indicates where and who your customers are. It will also tell you when they are most likely and willing to purchase your goods or use your services."[13]

—William Bill, *Wealth Design Group LLC*

Tabulating and Analyzing Data

After collecting numerical data and other information, you must tabulate and analyze them. Fortunately, several techniques can help you simplify, summarize, and classify large amounts of data. The most helpful summarizing techniques are tables, statistical concepts (mean, median, and mode), correlations, grids, and decision matrices.

Tables. Tables usually help researchers summarize and simplify data. Using columns and rows, tables make quantitative information easier to comprehend. After assembling your data, you will want to prepare preliminary tables to enable you to see what the information means. Here is a table summarizing the response to one question from a campus survey about student parking:

Question: Should student fees be increased to build parking lots?

	Number	Percentage	
Strongly agree	76	11.5	**To simplify the table, combine these items. 50 percent support the proposal**
Agree	255	38.5	
No opinion	22	3.3	
Disagree	107	16.1	**To simplify the table, combine these items. 46.7 (nearly 47) percent oppose the proposal**
Strongly disagree	203	30.6	
Total	**663**	**100.0**	

Notice that this preliminary table includes a total number of responses and a percentage for each response. (To calculate a percentage, divide the figure for each response by the total number of responses and then multiply the result by 100.)

Sometimes data become more meaningful when cross-tabulated. This process allows us to analyze two or more variables together. By breaking down our student survey data into male and female responses, shown in the following table, we make an interesting discovery.

Question: Should student fees be increased to build parking lots?

	Total		Male			Female		
	Number	Percentage	Number	Percentage		Number	Percentage	
Strongly agree	76	11.5	8	2.2	**= 17.5 percent**	68	22.0	**= 87 percent SUPPORT**
Agree	255	38.5	54	15.3		201	65.0	
No opinion	22	3.3	12	3.4		10	3.2	
Disagree	107	16.1	89	25.1	**= 79.1 percent**	18	5.8	**= 9.8 percent OPPOSE**
Strongly disagree	203	30.6	191	54.0		12	4.0	
Total	**663**	**100.0**	**354**	**100.0**		**309**	**100.0**	

Although 50 percent of all student respondents supported the proposal, among females the approval rating was much higher. You naturally wonder why such a disparity exists. Are female students unhappier than male students with the current parking situation? If so, why? Is safety a reason? Are male students more concerned with increased fees than female students are?

By cross-tabulating the findings, you sometimes uncover data that may help answer your problem question or that may prompt you to explore other possibilities. Do not, however, undertake cross-tabulation unless it serves more than merely satisfying your curiosity. Tables also help you compare multiple data collected from questionnaires and surveys. Figure 12.1 shows, in raw form, responses to several survey items. To convert these data into a more usable form, you need to calculate percentages for each item. Then you can arrange the responses in some rational sequence, such as largest percentage to smallest.

Once the data are displayed in a table, you can more easily draw conclusions. As Figure 12.1 shows, Westside College students apparently are not interested in public transportation or shuttle buses from satellite lots. They want to park on campus and restrict visitor parking; and only half are willing to pay for new parking lots.

Figure 12.1 **Converting Survey Data Into Finished Tables**

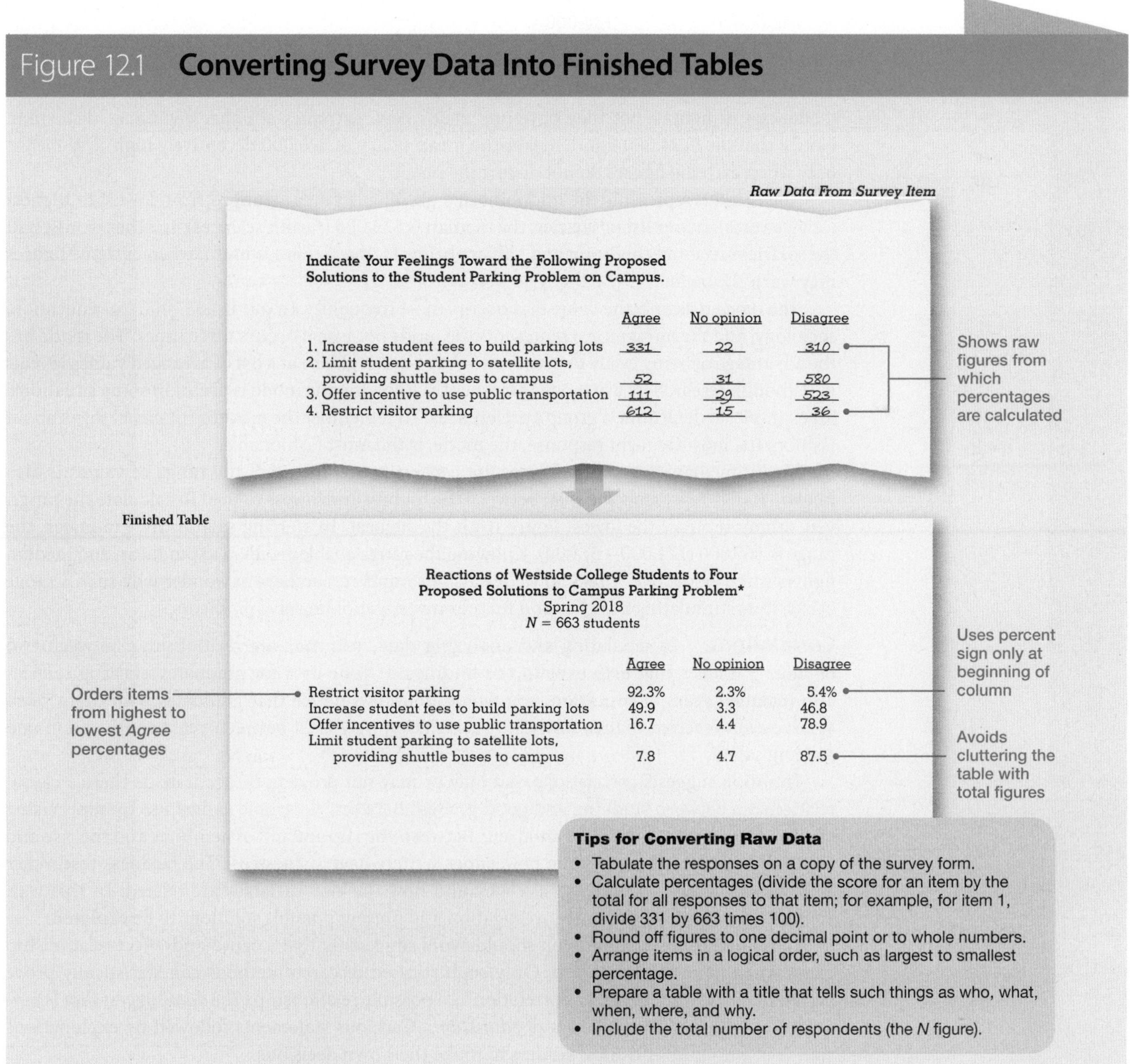

Raw Data From Survey Item

Indicate Your Feelings Toward the Following Proposed Solutions to the Student Parking Problem on Campus.

	Agree	No opinion	Disagree
1. Increase student fees to build parking lots	331	22	310
2. Limit student parking to satellite lots, providing shuttle buses to campus	52	31	580
3. Offer incentive to use public transportation	111	29	523
4. Restrict visitor parking	612	15	36

Shows raw figures from which percentages are calculated

Finished Table

Reactions of Westside College Students to Four Proposed Solutions to Campus Parking Problem*
Spring 2018
N = 663 students

	Agree	No opinion	Disagree
Restrict visitor parking	92.3%	2.3%	5.4%
Increase student fees to build parking lots	49.9	3.3	46.8
Offer incentives to use public transportation	16.7	4.4	78.9
Limit student parking to satellite lots, providing shuttle buses to campus	7.8	4.7	87.5

Orders items from highest to lowest *Agree* percentages

Uses percent sign only at beginning of column

Avoids cluttering the table with total figures

Tips for Converting Raw Data

- Tabulate the responses on a copy of the survey form.
- Calculate percentages (divide the score for an item by the total for all responses to that item; for example, for item 1, divide 331 by 663 times 100).
- Round off figures to one decimal point or to whole numbers.
- Arrange items in a logical order, such as largest to smallest percentage.
- Prepare a table with a title that tells such things as who, what, when, where, and why.
- Include the total number of respondents (the N figure).

Measures of Central Tendency. Tables help you organize data, and the three Ms—mean, median, and mode—help you describe data. These statistical terms are all occasionally used loosely to mean "average." To be safe, though, you should learn to apply these statistical terms precisely.

When people say *average*, they usually intend to indicate the *mean*, or arithmetic average. Let's say that you are studying the estimated starting salaries of graduates from disciplines ranging from education to medicine:

Education	$ 57,000	*Mode (figure occurring most frequently)*
Sociology	57,000	
Humanities	57,000	
Biology	63,000	
Health sciences	73,000	*Median (middle point in continuum)*
Business	76,000	*Mean (arithmetic average)*
Law	84,000	
Engineering	92,000	
Medicine	124,000	

To find the mean, you simply add all the salaries and divide by the total number of items. Therefore, the mean salary is $75,888 (almost $76,000). Means are very useful to indicate central tendencies of figures, but they have one major flaw: extremes at either end cause distortion. Notice that the $124,000 figure makes the mean salary of $76,000 deceptively high. Use means only when extreme figures do not distort the result.

The *median* represents the midpoint in a group of figures arranged from lowest to highest (or vice versa). In our list of salaries, the median is $73,000 (health sciences). In other words, half the salaries are above this point and half are below it. The median is useful when extreme figures may warp the mean.

The *mode* is simply the value that occurs most frequently. In our list $57,000 (for education, sociology, and the humanities) represents the mode because it occurs three times. The mode has the advantage of being easily determined—just a quick glance at a list of arranged values reveals it. Although researchers use mode infrequently, knowing the mode is useful in some situations; for example, to determine a group's preferences. To remember the meaning of *mode*, think about fashion: the most frequent response, the mode, is the most fashionable.

Mean, median, and mode figures are especially helpful when the range of values is also known. Range represents the span between the highest and lowest values. To calculate the range, you simply subtract the lowest figure from the highest. In starting salaries for graduates, the range is $67,000 (124,000 – 57,000). Knowing the range enables readers to put mean and median figures into perspective. This knowledge also prompts researchers to wonder why such a range exists, thus stimulating hunches and further investigation to solve problems.

Correlations. In tabulating and analyzing data, you may see relationships between two or more variables that help explain the findings. If your data for graduates' starting salaries also included years of education, you would doubtless notice that graduates with more years of education received higher salaries. A correlation may exist between years of education and starting salary.

Intuition suggests correlations that may or may not prove to be accurate. Is there a causal relationship between studying and good grades? Between electronic gadget use by supervising adults and increased injuries of children? Between the rise and fall of hemlines and the rise and fall of the stock market (as some newspaper writers have suggested)? The business researcher who sees a correlation needs to ask why and how the two variables are related. In this way, apparent correlations stimulate investigation and present possible solutions to be explored.

In reporting correlations, you should avoid suggesting that a cause-and-effect relationship exists when none can be proved. Only sophisticated research methods can statistically prove correlations. Instead, present a correlation as a possible relationship (*The data suggest that beginning salaries are related to years of education*). Cautious statements followed by explanations gain you credibility and allow readers to make their own decisions.

Sergey Nivens/Shutterstock.com

Researchers live by the principle that "correlation does not imply causation." However, the two concepts are often mistakenly interchanged. Recently, several studies found a link—or a correlation—between long-term use of over-the-counter antihistamines and dementia later in life. Although direct cause-and-effect was never stated, sensationalist headlines blurred the subtle difference between correlation and causation. The ensuing confusion drove many users of the common medications to panic unnecessarily. Researchers have no control over how the media report data; but when composing reports, business writers have tools to ensure a clear distinction between correlation and causation. How can business writers accurately present correlations in reports?[14]

Grids. Another technique for analyzing raw data—especially verbal data—is the grid. Let's say you have been asked by the CEO to collect opinions from all vice presidents about the CEO's four-point plan to build cash reserves. The grid shown in Figure 12.2 enables you to summarize the vice presidents' reactions to each point. Notice how this complex verbal information is transformed into concise, manageable data; readers can see immediately which points are supported and which are opposed. Imagine how long you could have struggled to comprehend the meaning of this verbal information without a grid.

Arranging data in a grid also works for projects such as feasibility studies and yardstick reports that compare many variables. *Consumer Reports* often uses grids to show information. In addition, grids help classify employment data. For example, suppose your boss asks you to recommend one individual from among many job candidates. You could arrange a grid with names across the top and distinguishing characteristics—experience, skills, education, and

Figure 12.2 Grid to Analyze Complex Verbal Data About Building Cash Reserves

	Point 1	Point 2	Point 3	Point 4	Overall Reaction
Vice President 1	Disapproves. "Too little, too late."	Strong support. "Best of all points."	Mixed opinion. "Must wait and see market."	Indifferent.	Optimistic, but "hates to delay expansion for six months."
Vice President 2	Disapproves. "Creates credit trap."	Approves.	Strong disapproval.	Approves. "Must improve receivable collections."	Mixed support. "Good self-defense plan."
Vice President 3	Strong disapproval.	Approves. "Key to entire plan."	Indifferent.	Approves, but with "caveats."	"Will work only with sale of unproductive fixed assets."
Vice President 4	Disapproves. "Too risky now."	Strong support. "Start immediately."	Approves, "but may damage image."	Approves. "Benefits far outweigh costs."	Supports plan. Suggests focus on Pacific Rim markets.

other employment interests—down the left side. Summarizing each candidate's points offers a helpful tool for drawing conclusions and writing a report.

Decision Matrices. A decision matrix is a special grid that helps managers make the best choice among complex options. Designed to eliminate bias and poor judgment, decision matrices are helpful in many fields. Assume you need to choose the most appropriate laptop for your sales representatives. You are most interested in weight, battery life, price, and hard drive size. You want to compare these features in four highly rated business laptop models. Figure 12.3 shows a simple decision matrix to help you make the choice. In Table 1, you evaluate each of the desired features on a scale of 1 to 5. Because the Apple MacBook Air weighs in at a very light 2.60 pounds,

Figure 12.3 Decision Matrix Used to Choose a Business Laptop for Sales Reps

Unweighted Decision Matrix—Table 1

Features:	Weight	Battery Life	Price	Hard Drive	Total
Laptop Options					
Dell Precision: 2.8 GHz, 4.98 lbs, 5 hrs, $1,500, 1.5 TB	1	2	2	5	
Lenovo ThinkPad: 2.3 GHz, 3.5 lbs, 9:10 hrs, $1,300, 256 GB	2	4	4	3	
Apple MacBook Air: 1.6 GHz, 2.6 lbs, 17:36 hrs, $1,400, 128 GB	5	5	3	1	
Acer TravelMate: 2.6 GHz, 3.31 lbs, 7:30 hrs, $1,200, 265 GB	3	3	5	3	

Weighted Decision Matrix—Table 2

Features:	Weight	Battery Life	Price	Hard Drive	Total
Laptop Options **Weights:**	**5**	**10**	**5**	**7**	
Dell Precision: 2.8 GHz, 4.98 lbs, 5 hrs, $1,500, 1.5 TB	5	20	10	35	70
Lenovo ThinkPad: 2.3 GHz, 3.5 lbs, 9:10 hrs, $1,300, 256 GB	10	40	20	21	91
Apple MacBook Air: 1.6 GHz, 2.6 lbs, 17:36 hrs, $1,400, 128 GB	25	50	15	7	97
Acer TravelMate: 2.6 GHz, 3.31 lbs, 7:30 hrs, $1,200, 265 GB	15	30	25	21	91

Tips for Creating a Decision Matrix

- **Select the most important criteria.** For a laptop computer, the criteria were weight, battery life, price, and hard drive size.
- **Create a matrix.** List each laptop model (Apple, Dell, and others) down the left side. Place the features across the top of the columns.
- **Evaluate the criteria.** Use a scale of 1 (lowest) to 5 (highest). Rate each feature for each option, as shown in Table 1.
- **Assign relative weights.** Decide how important each feature is, and give it a weight.
- **Multiply the scores.** For each feature in Table 1, multiply by the weights in Table 2 and write the score in the box.
- **Total the scores.** The total reveals the best choice.

you give it a score of 5 for weight. However, its hard drive capacity is much less desirable, and you give it a score of 1 for hard drive.

After you have evaluated all of the laptop models in Table 1, you assign relative weights to each feature. You decide to assign a factor of 5 to weight as well as to unit price because these two aspects are of average importance. However, your field sales reps want laptops with batteries that last. Therefore, battery life is twice as important; you assign it a factor of 10. You assign a factor of 7 to the size of the hard drive because this option is slightly more important than price, but somewhat less important than battery life. Then you multiply the scores in Table 1 with the weights and total them, as shown in Table 2. According to the weighted matrix and the rating system used, the Apple MacBook Air should be purchased for the sales reps because it received the highest score of 97 points, closely followed by the Lenovo ThinkPad and Acer TravelMate with 91 points.

Drawing Conclusions and Making Recommendations

LEARNING OUTCOME 2

Draw meaningful conclusions and make practical report recommendations after sound and valid analysis.

The sections devoted to conclusions and recommendations are the most widely read portions of a report. Knowledgeable readers go straight to the conclusions to see what the report writer thinks the data mean. Because conclusions summarize and explain the findings, they represent the heart of a report.

Your value in an organization rises considerably if you can analyze information logically, draw conclusions, and show how the data answer questions and solve problems. Responding to a growing demand for sustainable electronics, Dutch entrepreneur Bas van Abel has developed the Fairphone, a fair-trade device. This easy-to-fix, upgradable modular smartphone is now carried by 100,000 European users who are drawn to Fairphone's sustainability and ethics. Smartphone manufacturers have incurred criticism for sourcing conflict metals extracted under dangerous, toxic working conditions frequently by children. With its rapid obsolescence cycles, the industry is generating huge amounts of electronic waste, mainly because the units cannot be easily upgraded and repaired.[15] Solving such problems requires research. Drawing logical conclusions from data is crucial to business success.

Analyzing Data to Arrive at Conclusions

Any set of data can produce a variety of meaningful conclusions. Always bear in mind, though, that the audience for a report wants to know how these data relate to the problem being studied. What do the findings mean in terms of solving the original report problem?

For example, the Marriott Corporation recognized a serious problem among its employees. Conflicting home and work requirements seemed to be causing excessive employee turnover and decreased productivity. To learn the extent of the problem and to consider solutions, Marriott hired Hospitality Consultants to survey its staff. The hotel chain learned, among other things, that nearly 35 percent of its employees had children under age twelve, and 15 percent had children under age five. Other findings, shown in Figure 12.4, indicated that one third of its staff with young children took time off because of child-care difficulties. Moreover, many current employees left previous jobs because of work and family conflicts. The survey also showed that managers did not consider child-care or family problems to be appropriate topics for discussion at work.

A sample of possible conclusions that a writer might draw from these findings is shown in Figure 12.4. Notice that each conclusion relates to the initial report problem. Although only a few possible findings and conclusions are shown here, you can see that the conclusions try to explain the causes for the home/work conflict among employees. Many report writers would expand the conclusion section by explaining each item and citing supporting evidence. Even for simplified conclusions, such as those shown in Figure 12.4, you will want to list each item separately and use parallel construction (balanced sentence structure).

Figure 12.4 **Report Conclusions and Recommendations in Intranet Screen View**

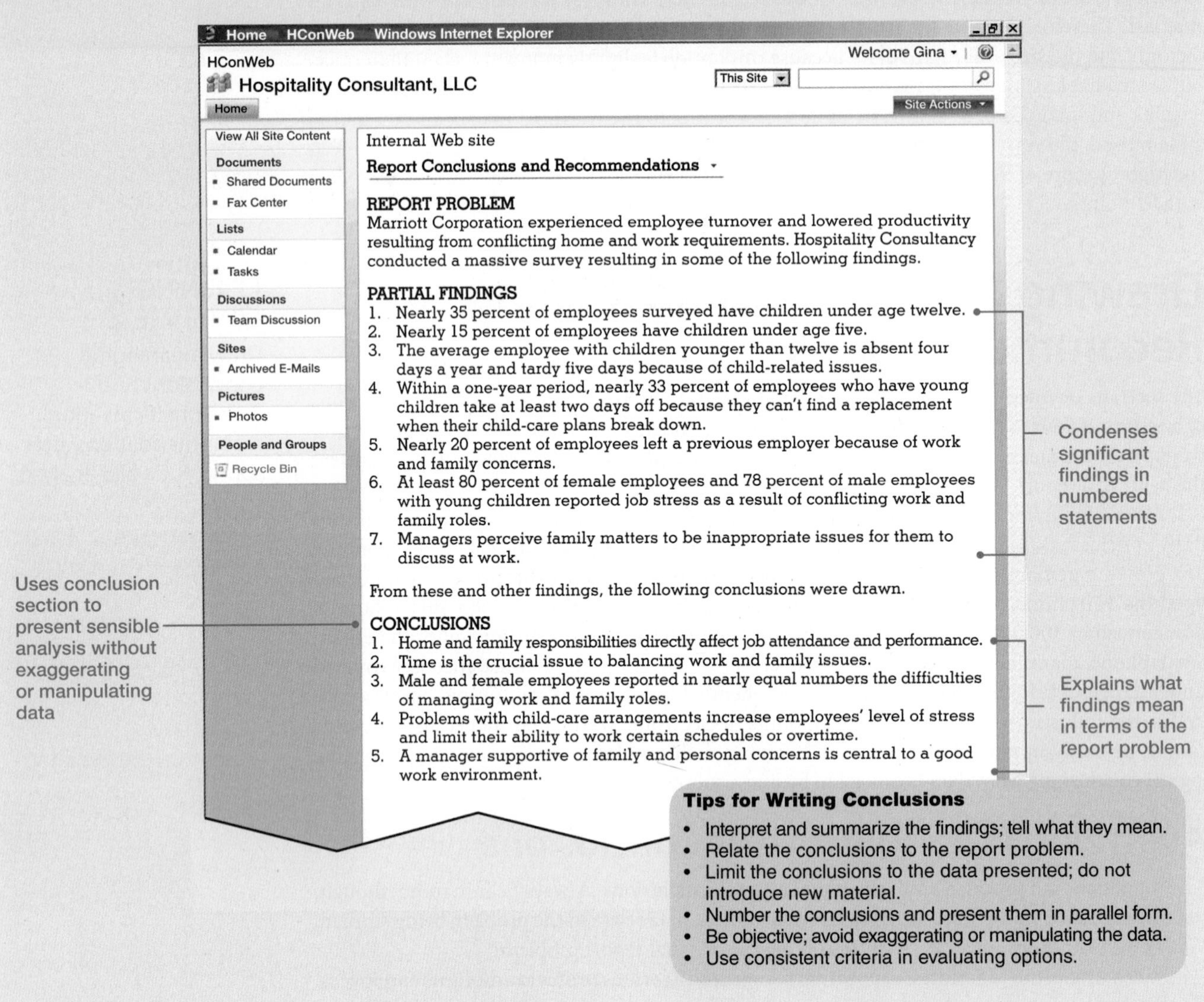

Although your goal is to remain objective, drawing conclusions naturally involves a degree of subjectivity. Your goals, background, and frame of reference all color the inferences you make. All writers interpret findings from their own perspectives, but they should not manipulate them to achieve a preconceived purpose. You can make your report conclusions more objective by using consistent evaluation criteria. Let's say you are comparing computers for an office equipment purchase. If you evaluate each by the same criteria (such as price, specifications, service, and warranty), your conclusions are more likely to be bias-free.

You also need to avoid the temptation to sensationalize or exaggerate your findings or conclusions. Be careful of words such as *many, most,* and *all.* Instead of *many of the respondents felt . . . ,* you might more accurately write *some of the respondents felt . . . .* Examine your motives before drawing conclusions. Do not let preconceptions or wishful thinking color your reasoning.

Figure 12.4 **Continued**

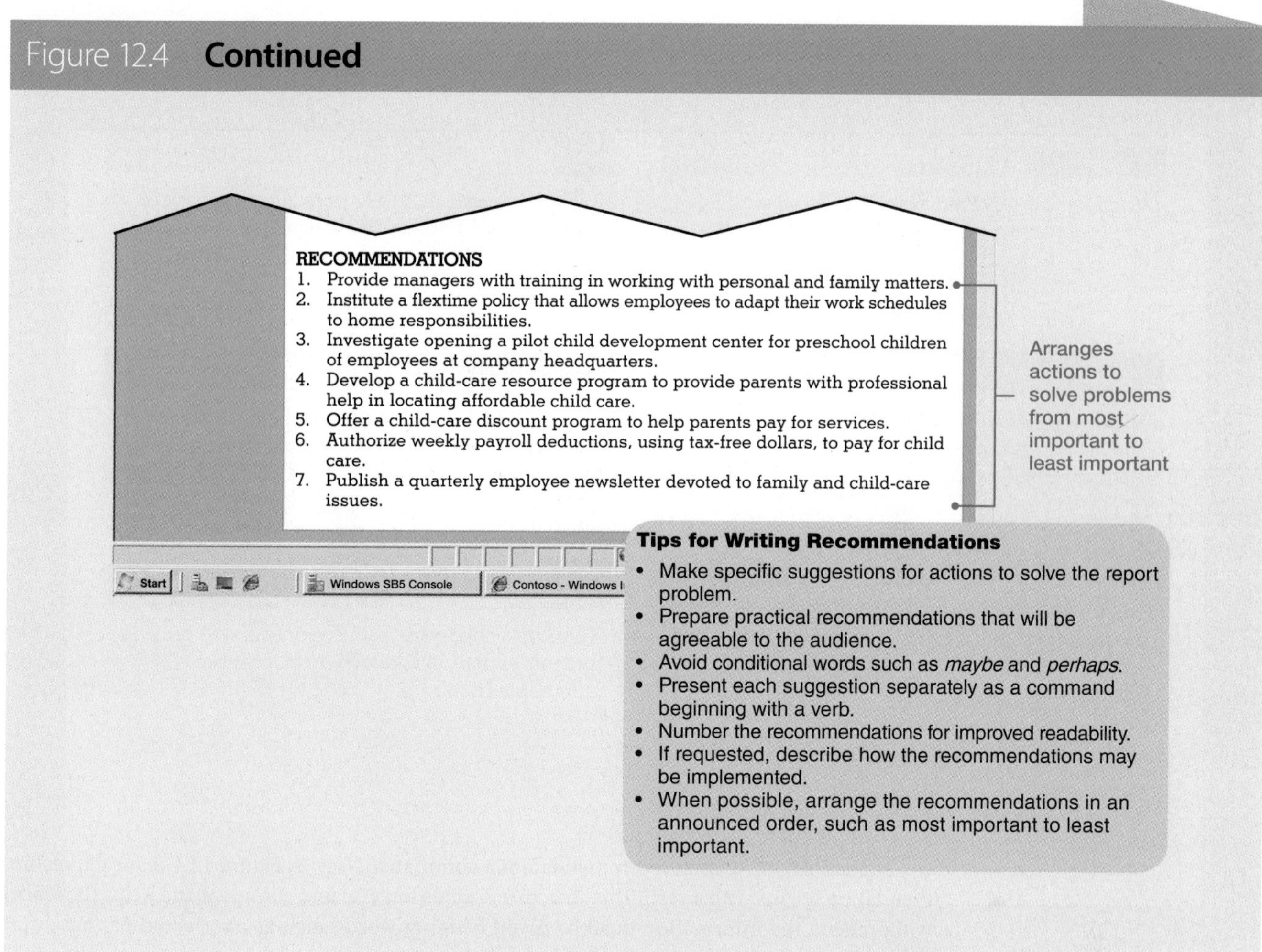

RECOMMENDATIONS
1. Provide managers with training in working with personal and family matters.
2. Institute a flextime policy that allows employees to adapt their work schedules to home responsibilities.
3. Investigate opening a pilot child development center for preschool children of employees at company headquarters.
4. Develop a child-care resource program to provide parents with professional help in locating affordable child care.
5. Offer a child-care discount program to help parents pay for services.
6. Authorize weekly payroll deductions, using tax-free dollars, to pay for child care.
7. Publish a quarterly employee newsletter devoted to family and child-care issues.
Arranges actions to solve problems from most important to least important
Start
Windows SB5 Console
Contoso - Windows I
Tips for Writing Recommendations
• Make specific suggestions for actions to solve the report problem.
• Prepare practical recommendations that will be agreeable to the audience.
• Avoid conditional words such as *maybe* and *perhaps*.
• Present each suggestion separately as a command beginning with a verb.
• Number the recommendations for improved readability.
• If requested, describe how the recommendations may be implemented.
• When possible, arrange the recommendations in an announced order, such as most important to least important.

Preparing Report Recommendations

Conclusions explain what the problem is, whereas recommendations tell how to solve it. Typically, business readers prefer specific, practical recommendations. They want to know exactly how to implement the suggestions. The specificity of your recommendations depends on your authorization. What are you commissioned to do, and what does the reader expect? In the planning stages of your report project, you anticipate what the reader wants in the report. Use your intuition and your knowledge of the audience to determine how comprehensive your recommendations should be.

In the recommendations section of the Marriott employee survey, shown in Figure 12.4, the consultants summarized their recommendations. In the actual report, the consultants would back up each recommendation with specifics and ideas for implementing them. For example, the child-care resource recommendation would be explained: it provides parents with the names of agencies and professionals who specialize in locating child care across the country.

A good report provides practical recommendations that are agreeable to the audience. In the Marriott survey, for example, the consulting company knew that the company wanted to help employees cope with conflicts between family and work obligations. As a result, the report's conclusions and recommendations focused on ways to resolve the conflict. If Marriott's goal had been merely to save money by reducing employee absenteeism, the recommendations would have been quite different.

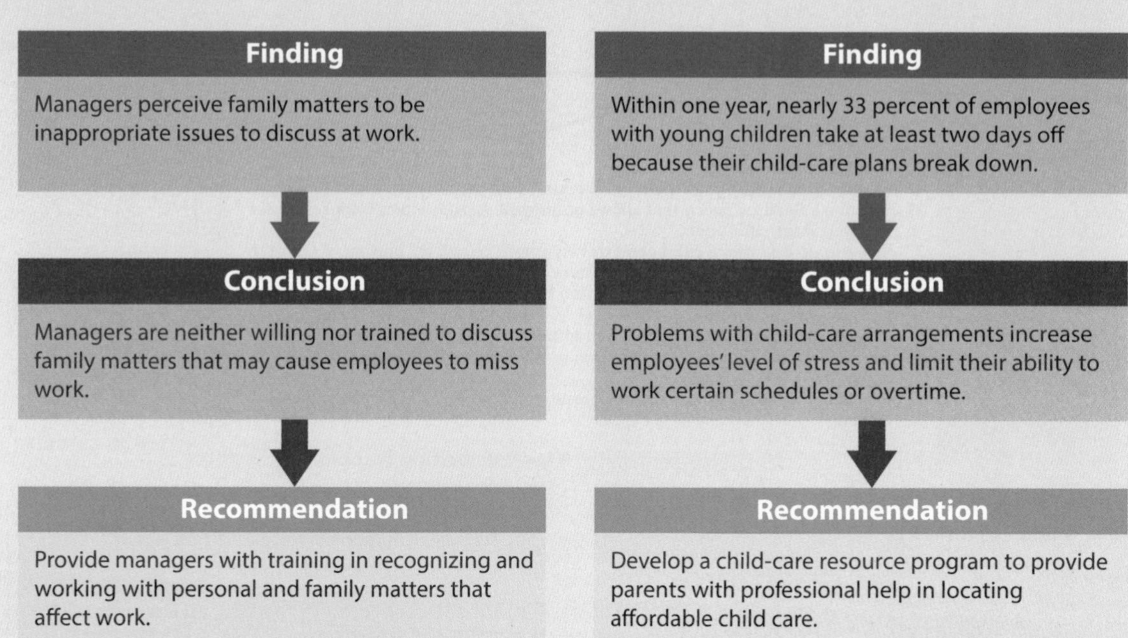

Finding
Managers perceive family matters to be inappropriate issues to discuss at work.
Conclusion
Managers are neither willing nor trained to discuss family matters that may cause employees to miss work.
Recommendation
Provide managers with training in recognizing and working with personal and family matters that affect work.
Finding
Within one year, nearly 33 percent of employees with young children take at least two days off because their child-care plans break down.
Conclusion
Problems with child-care arrangements increase employees' level of stress and limit their ability to work certain schedules or overtime.
Recommendation
Develop a child-care resource program to provide parents with professional help in locating affordable child care.

Figure 12.5 **Understanding Findings, Conclusions, and Recommendations**

If possible, make each recommendation a command. Note in Figure 12.4 that each recommendation begins with a verb. This structure sounds forceful and confident and helps the reader comprehend the information quickly. Avoid hedging words such as *maybe* and *perhaps*; they reduce the strength of recommendations.

Experienced writers may combine recommendations and conclusions. In short reports writers may omit conclusions and move straight to recommendations. An important point about recommendations is that they include practical suggestions for solving the report problem. Furthermore, they are always the result of logical analysis.

Moving From Findings to Recommendations

Recommendations evolve from the interpretation of the findings and conclusions. Consider the examples from the Marriott survey summarized in Figure 12.5.

LEARNING OUTCOME 3

Organize report data logically, and provide reader cues to aid comprehension.

Organizing Data

After collecting sets of data, interpreting them, drawing conclusions, and thinking about the recommendations, you are ready to organize the parts of the report into a logical framework. Poorly organized reports lead to frustration. Readers will not understand, remember, or be persuaded. Wise writers know that reports rarely "just organize themselves." Instead, the report author must impose organization on the data and provide cues so the reader can follow the logic of the writer.

Informational reports, as you learned in Chapter 11, generally present data without interpretation. As shown in Figure 12.6, informational reports typically consist of three parts. Analytical reports, which generally analyze data and draw conclusions, typically contain four parts. However, the parts in analytical reports do not always follow this

Figure 12.6 Organizational Strategies for Informational and Analytical Reports

Informational Reports	Analytical Reports	
Direct Strategy	**Direct Strategy**	**Indirect Strategy**
I. Introduction/background	I. Introduction/problem	I. Introduction/problem
II. Facts/findings	II. Conclusions/recommendations	II. Facts/findings
III. Summary/conclusion	III. Facts/findings	III. Discussion/analysis
	IV. Discussion/analysis	IV. Conclusions/recommendations

sequence. For readers who know about the project, are supportive, or are eager to learn the results quickly, the direct strategy is appropriate. Conclusions and recommendations, if requested, appear up front. For readers who must be educated or persuaded, the indirect strategy works better. Conclusions and recommendations appear last, after the findings have been presented and analyzed.

Although every report is unique, the overall organizational strategies described here generally hold true. The real challenge, though, lies in (a) organizing the facts/findings and discussion/analysis sections and (b) providing reader cues.

Ordering Information Logically

Whether you are writing informational or analytical reports, you must structure the data you have collected. Five common organizational methods are by time, component, importance, criteria, and convention. Regardless of the method you choose, be sure that it helps the reader understand the data. Reader comprehension, not writer convenience, should govern organization. Additional examples of organizational principles are presented in Chapter 14.

Time. Ordering data by time means establishing a chronology of events. Agendas, minutes of meetings, progress reports, and procedures are usually organized by time. For example, a report describing an eight-week training program would most likely be organized by weeks. A plan for the step-by-step improvement of customer service would be organized by steps. A monthly trip report submitted by a sales rep might describe customers visited during Week 1, Week 2, and so on.

Beware of overusing chronologies (time) as an organizing method for reports, however. Although this method is easy and often mirrors the way data are collected, chronologies—like the sales rep's trip report—tend to be boring, repetitious, and lacking in emphasis. Readers cannot always pick out what is important.

Component. Especially for informational reports, data may be organized by components such as location, geography, division, product, or part. For instance, a report detailing company expansion might divide the plan into West Coast, East Coast, and Midwest expansion. The report could also be organized by divisions: personal products, consumer electronics, and household goods. A report comparing profits among makers of athletic shoes might group the data by company: Nike, Adidas, New Balance, ASICS, and so forth. Organization by component works best when the classifications already exist.

Importance. Organization by importance involves beginning with the most important item and proceeding to the least important—or vice versa. For example, a report discussing the reasons for declining product sales would present the most important reason first followed by less important ones. The Marriott consultants' report describing work/family conflicts might begin by discussing child care, if the writer considered it the most important issue. Using importance to structure findings involves a value judgment. The writer must decide what is most important, always keeping in mind the readers' priorities and expectations. Busy readers appreciate seeing important points first; they may skim or skip other points.

On the other hand, building to a climax by moving from least important to most important enables the writer to focus attention at the end. Thus, the reader is more likely to remember the most important item. Of course, the writer also risks losing the reader's attention along the way.

Criteria. Establishing criteria by which to judge helps writers to treat topics consistently. Let's say your report compares health plans A, B, and C. For each plan you examine the same standards: cost per employee, amount of deductible, and patient benefits. The resulting data could then be organized either by plans or by criteria, as Figure 12.7 illustrates:

Although you might favor organizing the data by plans (because that is the way you collected the data), the better way is by criteria. When you discuss patient benefits, for example, you would examine all three plans' benefits together. Organizing a report around criteria helps readers make comparisons, instead of forcing them to search through the report for similar data.

Convention. Many operational and recurring reports are structured according to convention. That is, they follow a prescribed plan that everyone understands. For example, an automotive parts manufacturer might ask all sales reps to prepare a weekly report with these headings: *Competitive observations* (competitors' price changes, discounts, new products, product problems, distributor changes, product promotions), *Product problems* (quality, performance, needs), and *Customer service problems* (delivery, mailings, correspondence, social media, Web traffic). Management gets exactly the information it needs in an easy-to-read form.

Like operating reports, proposals are often organized conventionally. They might use such groupings as background, problem, proposed solution, staffing, schedule, costs, and authorization. As you might expect, reports following these conventional, prescribed structures greatly simplify the task of organization. Proposals and long reports are presented in Chapter 13.

Providing Reader Cues

When you finish organizing a report, you probably see a neat outline in your mind: major points supported by subpoints and details. Readers, however, do not know the material as well as you do; they cannot see your outline. To guide them through the data, you need to provide the equivalent of a map and road signs. For both formal and informal reports, devices such as introductions, transitions, and headings prevent readers from getting lost.

Figure 12.7 **Ordering Information Logically by Using Criteria**

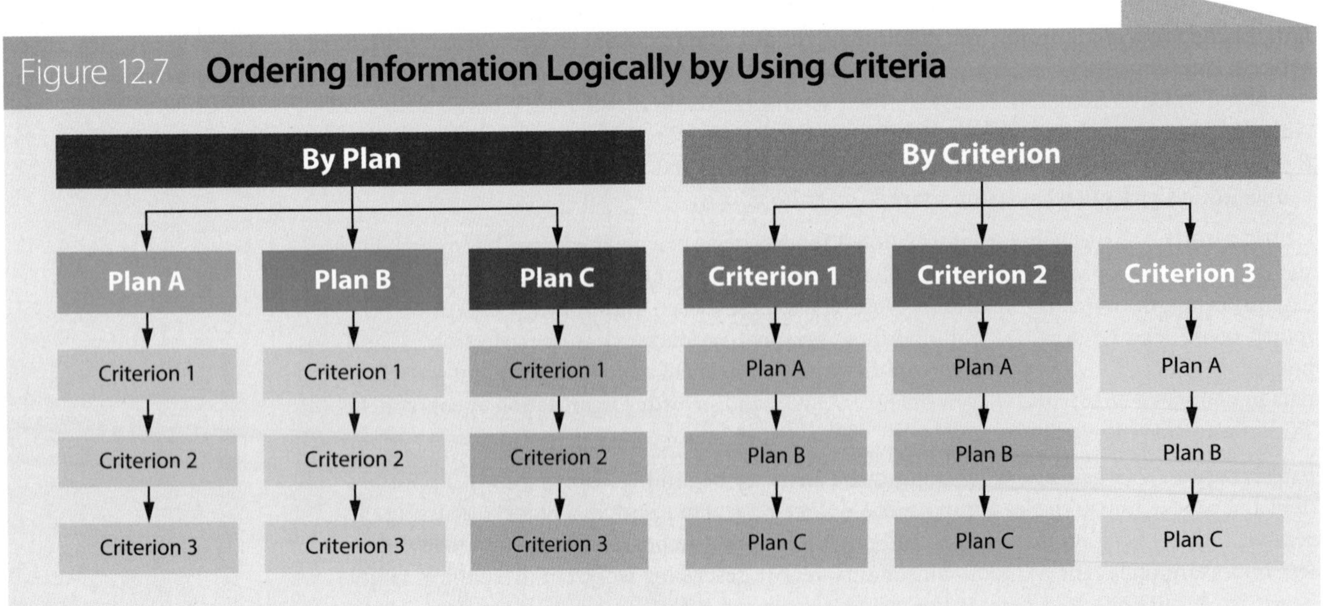

Introduction. One of the best ways to point a reader in the right direction is to provide a report introduction that does three things:

- Tells the purpose of the report
- Describes the significance of the topic
- Previews the main points and the order in which they will be developed

The following paragraph includes all three elements in introducing a report on computer security:

> *This report examines the security of our current computer operations and presents suggestions for improving security. Lax computer security could mean loss of information, loss of business, and damage to our equipment and systems. Because many former employees released during recent downsizing efforts know our systems, we must make major changes. To improve security, I will present three recommendations: (a) begin using dongles that limit access to our computer system, (b) alter log-on and log-off procedures, and (c) move central computer operations to a more secure area.*

This opener tells the purpose (examining computer security), describes its significance (loss of information and business, damage to equipment and systems), and outlines how the report is organized (three recommendations). Good openers in effect set up a contract with the reader. The writer promises to cover certain topics in a specified order. Readers expect the writer to fulfill the contract. They want the topics to be developed as promised—using the same wording and presented in the order mentioned. For example, if in your introduction you state that you will discuss the use of *dongles* (USB security devices), do not change the heading for that section to *security keys.* Remember that the introduction provides a map to a report; switching the names on the map will ensure that readers get lost. To maintain consistency, delay writing the introduction until you have completed the report. Long, complex reports may require introductions, brief internal summaries, and previews for each section.

Transitions. Expressions such as *on the contrary, at the same time*, and *however* show relationships and help reveal the logical flow of ideas in a report. These transitional expressions enable writers to tell readers where ideas are headed and how they relate. Notice how abrupt the following three sentences sound without any transition: *The iPad was the first mainstream tablet. [In fact] Reviewers say the iPad with Retina Display is still the best. [However] The display of the Google Nexus tablet trumps even the iPad's stunning screen.*

The following transitional expressions (see Chapter 5, Figure 5.6, for a complete list) enable you to show readers how you are developing your ideas:

To present additional thoughts: *additionally, again, also, moreover, furthermore*

To suggest cause and effect: *accordingly, as a result, consequently, therefore*

To contrast ideas: *at the same time, but, however, on the contrary, though, yet*

To show time and order: *after, before, first, finally, now, previously, then, to conclude*

To clarify points: *for example, for instance, in other words, that is, thus*

In using these expressions, recognize that they do not have to sit at the head of a sentence. Listen to the rhythm of the sentence, and place the expression where a natural pause occurs. If you are unsure about the placement of a transitional expression, position it at the beginning of the sentence. Used appropriately, transitional expressions serve readers as guides; misused or overused, they can be as distracting and frustrating as too many road signs on a highway.

Headings. Good headings are another structural cue that assists readers in comprehending the organization of a report. They highlight major ideas, allowing busy readers to see the big picture at a glance. Moreover, headings provide resting points for the mind and for the eye, breaking up large chunks of text into manageable and inviting segments.

Report writers may use functional or talking headings (see examples in Figure 12.8). Functional headings show the outline of a report but provide little insight for readers. Functional

Figure 12.8 **Distinguishing Among Functional, Talking, and Combination Headings**

Functional Headings	Talking Headings	Combination Headings
• Background • Findings • Personnel • Production Costs	• Lack of Space and Cost Compound Parking Program • Survey Shows Support for Parking Fees	• Introduction: Lack of Parking Reaches Crisis Proportions • Parking Recommendations: Shuttle and New Structures

headings are useful for routine reports. They are also appropriate for sensitive topics that might provoke emotional reactions. By keeping the headings general, experienced writers hope to minimize reader opposition or reaction to controversial subjects.

Talking headings provide more information and spark interest. Unless carefully written, however, talking headings can fail to reveal the organization of a report. With some planning, though, headings can combine the best attributes of both functional and talking, as Figure 12.8 shows.

The best strategy for creating helpful talking headings is to write a few paragraphs first and then generate a talking heading that covers both paragraphs. To create the most effective headings, follow a few basic guidelines:

- **Use appropriate heading levels.** The position and format of a heading indicate its level of importance and relationship to other points. Figure 12.9 illustrates and discusses a commonly used heading format for business reports. For an overview of alphanumeric and decimal outlines, see Figures 5.3 and 5.4.
- **Capitalize and emphasize carefully**. Most writers use all capital letters (without underlines) for main titles, such as report, chapter, and unit titles. For first- and second-level headings, they capitalize only the first letter of main words such as nouns, verbs, adjectives, adverbs, names, and so on. Articles (*a, an, the*), conjunctions (*and, but, or, nor*), and prepositions with three or fewer letters (*in, to, by, for*) are not capitalized unless they appear at the beginning or end of the heading. For additional emphasis, most writers use a bold font, as shown in Figure 12.9.
- **Try to balance headings within levels.** Although it may not be always possible, attempt to create headings that are grammatically similar at a given level. For example, *Developing Product Teams* and *Presenting Plan to Management* are balanced, but *Development of Product Teams* and *Presenting Plan to Management* are not.
- **For short reports use first-level or first- and second-level headings.** Many business reports contain only one or two levels of headings. For such reports use first-level headings (centered, bolded) and, if needed, second-level headings (flush left, bolded). See Figure 12.9.
- **Include at least one heading per report page, but don't end the page with a heading.** Headings increase the readability and attractiveness of report pages. Use at least one per page to break up blocks of text. Move a heading that is separated from the text that follows from the bottom of the page to the top of the following page.
- **Apply punctuation correctly.** Omit end punctuation in first- and second-level headings. End punctuation is required in third-level headings because they are capitalized and punctuated like sentences. Proper nouns (names) are capitalized in third-level headings as they would be in a sentence.

Figure 12.9 **Styles for Heading Levels**

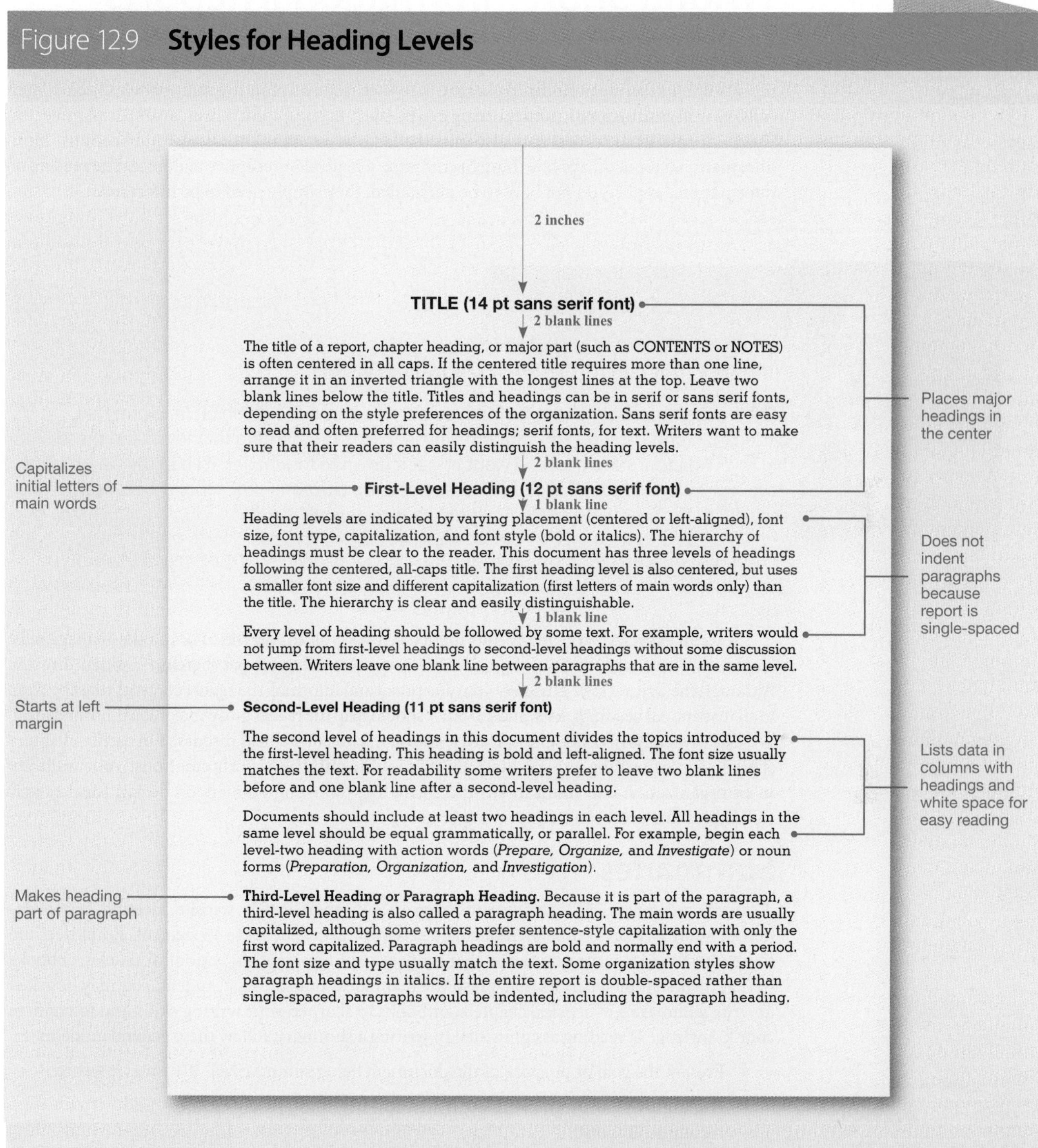

2 inches
TITLE (14 pt sans serif font)
2 blank lines
The title of a report, chapter heading, or major part (such as CONTENTS or NOTES) is often centered in all caps. If the centered title requires more than one line, arrange it in an inverted triangle with the longest lines at the top. Leave two blank lines below the title. Titles and headings can be in serif or sans serif fonts, depending on the style preferences of the organization. Sans serif fonts are easy to read and often preferred for headings; serif fonts, for text. Writers want to make sure that their readers can easily distinguish the heading levels.
2 blank lines
First-Level Heading (12 pt sans serif font)
1 blank line
Heading levels are indicated by varying placement (centered or left-aligned), font size, font type, capitalization, and font style (bold or italics). The hierarchy of headings must be clear to the reader. This document has three levels of headings following the centered, all-caps title. The first heading level is also centered, but uses a smaller font size and different capitalization (first letters of main words only) than the title. The hierarchy is clear and easily distinguishable.
1 blank line
Every level of heading should be followed by some text. For example, writers would not jump from first-level headings to second-level headings without some discussion between. Writers leave one blank line between paragraphs that are in the same level.
2 blank lines
Second-Level Heading (11 pt sans serif font)
The second level of headings in this document divides the topics introduced by the first-level heading. This heading is bold and left-aligned. The font size usually matches the text. For readability some writers prefer to leave two blank lines before and one blank line after a second-level heading.
Documents should include at least two headings in each level. All headings in the same level should be equal grammatically, or parallel. For example, begin each level-two heading with action words (Prepare, Organize, and Investigate) or noun forms (Preparation, Organization, and Investigation).
Third-Level Heading or Paragraph Heading. Because it is part of the paragraph, a third-level heading is also called a paragraph heading. The main words are usually capitalized, although some writers prefer sentence-style capitalization with only the first word capitalized. Paragraph headings are bold and normally end with a period. The font size and type usually match the text. Some organization styles show paragraph headings in italics. If the entire report is double-spaced rather than single-spaced, paragraphs would be indented, including the paragraph heading.
Places major headings in the center
Capitalizes initial letters of main words
Does not indent paragraphs because report is single-spaced
Starts at left margin
Lists data in columns with headings and white space for easy reading
Makes heading part of paragraph

- **Keep headings short but clear.** One-word headings are emphatic but not always clear. For example, the heading *Budget* does not adequately describe figures for a summer project involving student interns for an oil company in Texas. Try to keep your headings brief (no more than eight words), but make sure they are understandable. Experiment with headings that concisely tell who, what, when, where, and why.

LEARNING OUTCOME 4

Write short informational reports that describe routine tasks.

Writing Short Informational Reports

Now that you are familiar with the basics of gathering, interpreting, and organizing data, you are ready to enter that information into short informational or analytical reports. Informational reports often describe periodic, recurring activities (such as monthly sales or weekly customer calls) as well as situational, nonrecurring events (such as trips, conferences, and special projects). Short informational reports may also take the form of summaries of longer publications. Most informational reports have one thing in common: a neutral or receptive audience. The readers of informational reports do not have to be persuaded; they simply need to be informed.

© Liz Farmer

Reality Check

Making Financial Information Reader Friendly

"[T]he government has a responsibility to tell citizens what's going on in a form that citizens can understand. [You shouldn't] have to learn accounting to understand these big thick financial statements—I want to get it down to four pages. If I had my way, I'd have legislation to require all federal agencies to do citizen-centric reports because, if they did them, the state and locals would have to as well."[16]

—Relmond Van Daniker, *former CEO of the Association of Government Accountants (AGA)*

You can expect to write many informational reports as an entry-level or middle-management employee. These reports generally deliver nonsensitive data and are therefore written directly. Although the writing style is usually conversational and informal, the report contents must be clear to all readers. All headings, lists, and graphics should help the reader grasp major ideas immediately.

The principles of conciseness, clarity, courtesy, and correctness discussed in earlier chapters apply to report writing as well. Your ability to write effective reports can boost your visibility in an organization and result in advancement. The following pointers on design features and techniques can assist you in improving your reports.

Summaries

A summary compresses the main points from a book, report, article, website, meeting, or convention. A summary saves time by reducing a report or article by 85 to 95 percent. Employees are sometimes asked to write summaries that condense technical reports, periodical articles, or books so that their staff or superiors may grasp the main ideas quickly. As a student, you may be asked to write summaries of articles, chapters, or books to sharpen your writing skills and to confirm your knowledge of reading assignments. In writing a summary, follow these general guidelines:

- Present the goal or purpose of the document being summarized. Why was it written?
- Highlight the research methods (if appropriate), findings, conclusions, and recommendations.
- Omit illustrations, examples, and references.
- Organize for readability by including headings and bulleted or enumerated lists.
- Include your reactions or an overall evaluation of the document if asked to do so.

An *executive summary* summarizes a long report, proposal, or business plan. It concentrates on what management needs to know from a longer report. How to prepare an executive summary is covered in Chapter 13.

Figure 12.10 **The Top Ten Tips for Designing Better Documents**

1 Analyze your audience.
Give readers what they need. Avoid flashiness in traditional documents. Use headings and lists to suit a busy audience.

2 Avoid amateurish effects.
Strive for simple, clean, and forceful effects. Do not overwhelm readers with cluttered documents.

3 Choose an appropriate font size.
Use body text that is 11 to 12 points tall. Larger type looks amateurish. Smaller type is hard to read.

4 Use a consistent type font.
Stay with a single family of type within one document. For emphasis and contrast, vary the font size and weight with bold, italic, and other selections.

5 Do not justify right margins.
Opt for ragged-right margins to add white space. Slower readers find ragged-right text more legible.

6 Separate paragraphs and sentences properly.
Skip a line between single-spaced paragraphs. Indent five spaces in double-spaced text. Don't skip a line. Be consistent.

7 Design readable headings.
For high readability, show most headings in upper- and lowercase and choose sans-serif type such as Arial or Calibri.

8 Strive for an attractive page layout.
Balance print and white space. Provide a focal point three lines above the center of the page. Expect readers to scan a page in a Z pattern.

9 Use graphics and clip art with restraint.
You can import, copy, or scan charts, drawings, photos, and clip art into documents. Use only images that are well drawn, relevant, and appropriately sized.

10 Develop expertise.
Use the desktop publishing features of your current word processing program, or learn software such as PagePlus or Adobe InDesign.

Effective Document Design

Desktop publishing packages, sophisticated word processing programs, and high-quality laser printers now make it possible for you to turn out professional-looking documents and promotional materials. Resist the temptation, however, to overdo it by incorporating too many features in one document. The top ten design tips summarized in Figure 12.10 will help you apply good sense and solid design principles in "publishing" your documents.

Periodic (Activity) Reports

Most businesses—especially larger ones—require *periodic reports* (sometimes called *activity reports*) to keep management informed of operations. These recurring reports are written at regular intervals—weekly, monthly, yearly—so that management can monitor business strategies and, if necessary, remedy any problems. Some periodic reports simply contain figures, such as sales volume, the number and kind of customer service calls, shipments delivered, accounts payable, and personnel data. More challenging periodic reports require descriptions and discussions of activities. In preparing a narrative description of their activities, employees writing periodic reports usually do the following:

- Summarize regular activities and events performed during the reporting period
- Describe irregular events deserving the attention of management
- Highlight special needs and problems

Managers naturally want to know that routine activities are progressing normally. Employees today enjoy a great deal of independence and shoulder much responsibility as a result of flattened hierarchies on the job. They often work flexible hours in far-flung locations. Keeping track of their activities and the tasks they were assigned is crucial in such an environment. Routine reports are typically sent by e-mail and may take the form of efficient bulleted lists without commentary.

Figure 12.11 shows a weekly activity report prepared by Jack Tang, a senior Web producer at the information technology firm Argyl Macro in Silicon Valley. Jack is responsible for his firm's Web presence in Asian countries or territories, mainly Japan, China, Hong Kong, and Vietnam. In his weekly reports to his supervisor, Virat Sharma, Jack neatly divides his projects into three categories: *completed*, *in progress*, and *ongoing*. *In progress* means the task is not yet completed, or pending. *Ongoing* refers to continuous tasks such as regular maintenance. Virat, the manager,

Figure 12.11 **Periodic (Activity) Report**

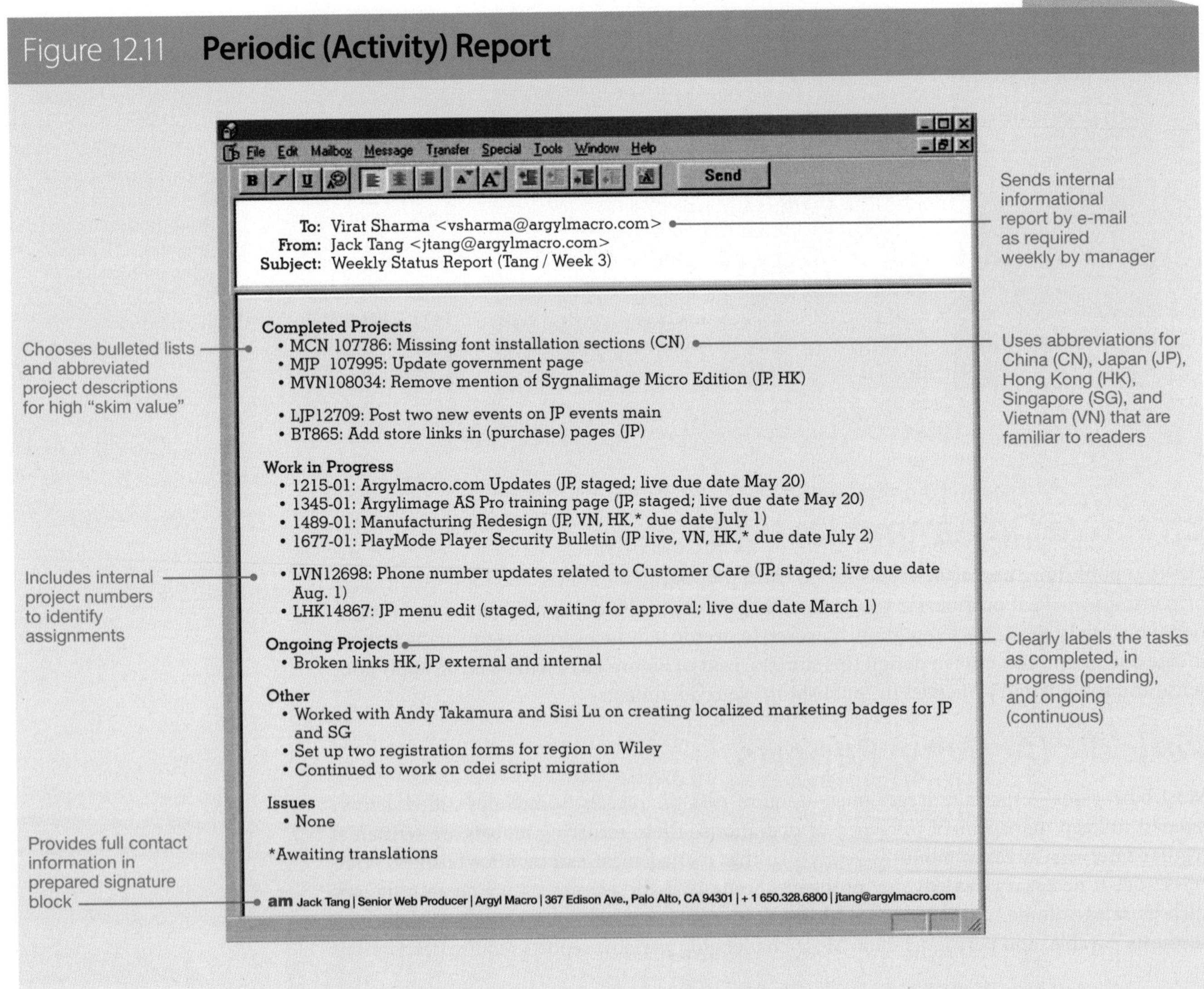

To: Virat Sharma <vsharma@argylmacro.com>
From: Jack Tang <jtang@argylmacro.com>
Subject: Weekly Status Report (Tang / Week 3)

Completed Projects
- MCN 107786: Missing font installation sections (CN)
- MJP 107995: Update government page
- MVN108034: Remove mention of Sygnalimage Micro Edition (JP, HK)

- LJP12709: Post two new events on JP events main
- BT865: Add store links in (purchase) pages (JP)

Work in Progress
- 1215-01: Argylmacro.com Updates (JP, staged; live due date May 20)
- 1345-01: Argylimage AS Pro training page (JP, staged; live due date May 20)
- 1489-01: Manufacturing Redesign (JP, VN, HK,* due date July 1)
- 1677-01: PlayMode Player Security Bulletin (JP live, VN, HK,* due date July 2)

- LVN12698: Phone number updates related to Customer Care (JP, staged; live due date Aug. 1)
- LHK14867: JP menu edit (staged, waiting for approval; live due date March 1)

Ongoing Projects
- Broken links HK, JP external and internal

Other
- Worked with Andy Takamura and Sisi Lu on creating localized marketing badges for JP and SG
- Set up two registration forms for region on Wiley
- Continued to work on cdei script migration

Issues
- None

*Awaiting translations

am Jack Tang | Senior Web Producer | Argyl Macro | 367 Edison Ave., Palo Alto, CA 94301 | + 1 650.328.6800 | jtang@argylmacro.com then combines the activity reports from all his subordinates into a separate periodic report detailing the department's activities to send to his superiors.

Jack justifies the use of jargon, the lack of a salutation and complimentary close, and ultra-short bulleted items as follows: "We e-mail our reports internally, so some IT jargon can be expected. The readers will understand it. Virat and upper management all want reporting to be brief and to the point. Bullets fit us just fine." Periodic reports ensure that information within the company flows steadily and that supervisors know the status of current and pending projects. This efficient information flow is all the more important because Jack works at home two days a week to spend time with his young children. Several of his coworkers also telecommute.

Trip, Convention, and Conference Reports

Employees sent on business trips or to conventions and conferences typically must submit reports when they return. Organizations want to know that their money was well spent in funding the travel. These reports inform management about new procedures, equipment, and laws as well as supply information affecting products, operations, and service.

The hardest parts of writing these reports are selecting the most relevant material and organizing it coherently. Generally, it is best not to use chronological sequencing (*in the morning we did X, at lunch we heard Y, and in the afternoon we did Z*). Instead, you should focus on three to five topics in which your reader will be interested. These items become the body of the report. Then simply add an introduction and a closing, and your report is organized. Here is a general outline for trip, conference, and convention reports:

- Begin by identifying the event (exact date, name, and location) and previewing the topics to be discussed.
- Summarize in the body three to five main points that might benefit the reader.
- Itemize your expenses, if requested, on a separate sheet.
- Close by expressing appreciation, suggesting action to be taken, or synthesizing the value of the trip or event.

Madison Gardner was recently hired as marketing specialist in the Marketing Department of a wireless devices and consumer electronics store in Seattle, Washington. Recognizing her lack of experience in online customer service, the marketing manager gave her permission to attend a two-day training conference titled Social Customer Service. Her boss, Bryce Corliss, encouraged Madison to attend, saying, "We are serious about increasing our social media involvement, and we want to build solid relationships with our customers while promoting our products. Come back and tell us what you learned." When she returned, Madison wrote the conference report shown in Figure 12.12. Here is how she described its preparation: "I know my boss values brevity, so I worked hard to make my report no more than a page. The conference saturated me with great ideas, far too many to cover in one brief report. So, I decided to discuss two topics that would most benefit our staff. By the third draft, I had compressed my ideas into a manageable size without sacrificing any of the meaning."

Progress and Interim Reports

Continuing projects often require progress or interim reports to describe their status. These reports may be external (advising customers about the headway of their projects) or internal (informing management of the status of activities). Progress reports typically follow this pattern of development:

- Specify in the opening the purpose and nature of the project.
- Provide background information if the audience requires filling in.
- Describe the work completed.
- Explain the work currently in progress, including personnel, activities, methods, and locations.
- Describe current problems and anticipate future problems and possible remedies.
- Discuss future activities and provide the expected completion date.

Figure 12.12 Conference Report

Date: February 25, 2018

To: Bryce Corliss, Marketing Manager *BC*

From: Madison Gardner, Marketing Specialist

Subject: Conference on Social Customer Service–January 2018

I attended the Social Customer Service conference in Bellevue, Washington, on January 28-29, sponsored by Social Solutions Inc. The conference emphasized the importance of delivering excellent customer service in social spaces (social media gathering places). As we prepare to increase our social media involvement, this report summarizes two topics that would benefit our employees: (a) the rising expectations of customers in social media networks, and (b) the role of customer service specialists.

Identifies the topic and previews the report's contents

The Rising Expectations of Customers in Social Spaces

Conference presenters emphasized the following customer service expectations:

- Customers expect social business connections to be helpful and friendly—always.
- Online customers expect that you're listening and will remember what they said to you last time.
- Before buying, customers are powerfully influenced by user reviews, Facebook comments, Twitter feeds, and forum messages.
- Customers expect honest and prompt responses when they have questions and complaints.

Sets off major topics with bold headings in the same font

The Role of Customer Service Specialists

Whether a company hires a social media management service or uses in-house personnel, the responsibilities of social customer service specialists are the same:

- Monitor customer feedback and respond promptly to questions and complaints.
- Check social media platforms for mention of their businesses. Send text message responses to the right people immediately.
- Examine the company's Facebook activity and create dialogue on Twitter.
- When problems occur, own up to them and explain publicly what you're doing to make things right.

Covers the main ideas that will benefit the reader

Sharing Conference Highlights

Companies realize the importance of communicating with customers promptly and personally, especially in social spaces. Since our company is heavily invested in social media platforms, the conference topics seemed especially relevant. I would be happy to share highlights from the conference at our next management meeting. Let me know what date and time work best.

Concludes with an offer to share information

As a location manager for Angel City Productions, Ellie Harper frequently writes progress reports, such as the one shown in Figure 12.13. Producers want to know what she is doing, and a phone call does not provide a permanent record. Here is how she described the reasoning behind her progress report: "I usually include background information in my reports because a director does not always know or remember exactly what specifications I was given for a location search. Then I try to hit the high points of what I have completed and what I plan to do next, without getting bogged down in tiny details. Although it would be easier to skip them, I have learned to be up front with any problems I anticipate. I do not tell how to solve the problems, but I feel duty-bound to at least mention them."

Figure 12.13 **Progress Report**

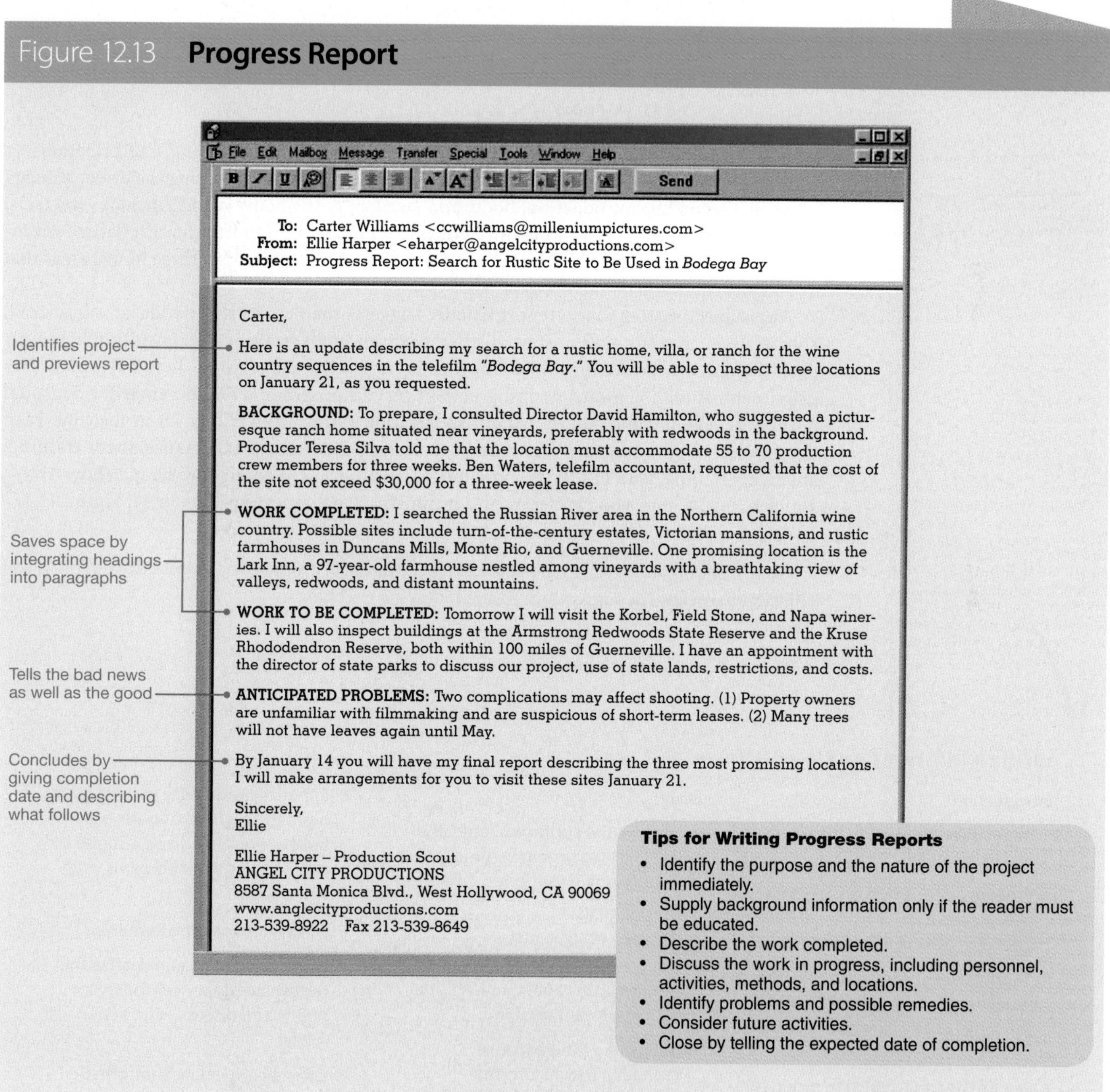

To: Carter Williams <ccwilliams@milleniumpictures.com>
From: Ellie Harper <eharper@angelcityproductions.com>
Subject: Progress Report: Search for Rustic Site to Be Used in *Bodega Bay*

Carter,

Here is an update describing my search for a rustic home, villa, or ranch for the wine country sequences in the telefilm "*Bodega Bay*." You will be able to inspect three locations on January 21, as you requested.

BACKGROUND: To prepare, I consulted Director David Hamilton, who suggested a picturesque ranch home situated near vineyards, preferably with redwoods in the background. Producer Teresa Silva told me that the location must accommodate 55 to 70 production crew members for three weeks. Ben Waters, telefilm accountant, requested that the cost of the site not exceed $30,000 for a three-week lease.

WORK COMPLETED: I searched the Russian River area in the Northern California wine country. Possible sites include turn-of-the-century estates, Victorian mansions, and rustic farmhouses in Duncans Mills, Monte Rio, and Guerneville. One promising location is the Lark Inn, a 97-year-old farmhouse nestled among vineyards with a breathtaking view of valleys, redwoods, and distant mountains.

WORK TO BE COMPLETED: Tomorrow I will visit the Korbel, Field Stone, and Napa wineries. I will also inspect buildings at the Armstrong Redwoods State Reserve and the Kruse Rhododendron Reserve, both within 100 miles of Guerneville. I have an appointment with the director of state parks to discuss our project, use of state lands, restrictions, and costs.

ANTICIPATED PROBLEMS: Two complications may affect shooting. (1) Property owners are unfamiliar with filmmaking and are suspicious of short-term leases. (2) Many trees will not have leaves again until May.

By January 14 you will have my final report describing the three most promising locations. I will make arrangements for you to visit these sites January 21.

Sincerely,
Ellie

Ellie Harper – Production Scout
ANGEL CITY PRODUCTIONS
8587 Santa Monica Blvd., West Hollywood, CA 90069
www.anglecityproductions.com
213-539-8922 Fax 213-539-8649

File Edit Mailbox Message Transfer Special Tools Window Help
Send
Identifies project and previews report
Saves space by integrating headings into paragraphs
Tells the bad news as well as the good
Concludes by giving completion date and describing what follows
Tips for Writing Progress Reports
• Identify the purpose and the nature of the project immediately.
• Supply background information only if the reader must be educated.
• Describe the work completed.
• Discuss the work in progress, including personnel, activities, methods, and locations.
• Identify problems and possible remedies.
• Consider future activities.
• Close by telling the expected date of completion.

EMMANUEL DUNAND/AFP/Getty Images

Music-streaming service Spotify is part of the industry trend of providing both free and paid access to a huge inventory of music. Unlike Internet radio app Pandora, however, Spotify allows listeners to choose an unlimited number of songs to share with friends or to listen to at any time. The Swedish-based service partners with broadcasters, festivals, blogs, and NGOs to bring music to their constituents. As a privately held company, Spotify must issue monthly financial reports to its board of directors. What types of information would business communicators need to include in these reports?[17]

Investigative Reports

Investigative reports deliver data for specific situations—without offering interpretations or recommendations. These nonrecurring reports are generally arranged using the direct strategy with three segments: introduction, body, and summary. The body—which includes the facts, findings, or discussion—may be organized by time, component, importance, criteria, or convention. What is important is dividing the topic into logical segments—say, three to five areas that are roughly equal and do not overlap.

The subject matter of the report usually suggests the best way to divide or organize it. Abby Gabriel, an information specialist for a Minneapolis health-care consulting firm, was given the task of researching and writing an investigative report for St. John's Hospital. Her assignment: study the award-winning patient service program at Good Samaritan Hospital and report how it improved its patient satisfaction rating from 6.2 to 7.8 in just one year. Abby collected data and then organized her findings into four parts: management training, employee training, patient services, and follow-up program. Although we do not show Abby's complete report here, you can see a similar informational report in Chapter 11, Figure 11.2.

Whether you are writing a periodic, trip, conference, progress, or investigative report, you will want to review the suggestions in the following checklist.

Writing Informational Reports

Introduction

- **Begin directly.** Identify the report and its purpose.
- **Provide a preview.** If the report is over a page long, give the reader a brief overview of its organization.
- **Supply background data selectively.** When readers are unfamiliar with the topic, briefly fill in the necessary details.
- **Divide the topic.** Strive to group the facts or findings into three to five roughly equal segments that do not overlap.

Body

- **Arrange the subtopics logically.** Consider organizing by time, component, importance, criteria, or convention.
- **Use clear headings.** Supply functional or talking headings (at least one per page) that describe each important section.
- **Determine the degree of formality.** Use an informal, conversational writing style unless the audience expects a more formal tone.
- **Enhance readability with graphic highlighting.** Make liberal use of bullets, numbered and lettered lists, headings, underlined items, and white space.

Summary/Concluding Remarks

- **When necessary, summarize the report.** Briefly review the main points and discuss what action will follow.
- **Offer a concluding thought.** If relevant, express appreciation or a willingness to provide further information.

© Rob Ashton

Reality Check

Love It or Hate It, Skillful Report Writing Is Essential

"Report writing skills are crucial to communicating your research, ideas, and recommendations. Losing the gems of months of research in confusing, convoluted prose helps neither you nor your readers. The way you write can be more important than what you write. An instantly readable report will usually have more impact than one that is difficult to decipher."[18]

—Rob Ashton, *CEO of Emphasis, report-writing expert and coach*

Preparing Short Analytical Reports

LEARNING OUTCOME 5

Prepare short analytical reports that solve business problems.

You may recall that informational reports generally provide data only. This section describes three common types of analytical business reports: (a) justification/recommendation reports, (b) feasibility reports, and (c) yardstick reports. These reports involve collecting and analyzing data, evaluating the results, drawing conclusions, and making recommendations.

Analytical reports differ significantly from informational reports. Although both seek to collect and present data clearly, analytical reports also evaluate the data and typically try to persuade the reader to accept the conclusions and act on the recommendations. Informational reports emphasize facts; analytical reports emphasize reasoning and conclusions.

For some situations you may organize analytical reports directly with the conclusions and recommendations near the beginning. Directness is appropriate when the reader has confidence in the writer, based on either experience or credentials. Frontloading the recommendations also works when the topic is routine or familiar and the reader is supportive.

Directness can backfire, though. If you announce the recommendations too quickly, the reader may immediately object to a single idea. Once the reader has an unfavorable mind-set, changing it may be difficult. A reader may also believe that you have oversimplified or overlooked something significant if you provide your recommendations first. When you must lead the reader through the process of discovering the solution, use the indirect strategy: present conclusions and recommendations last.

Most analytical reports answer questions about specific problems and aid in decision making (e.g., *How can we use social media most effectively? Should we close the El Paso plant? Should we buy or lease company cars?*). Analytical reports provide conclusions that help management answer these questions.

Justification/Recommendation Reports

Both managers and employees must occasionally write reports that justify or recommend actions, such as buying equipment, changing a procedure, hiring an employee, consolidating departments, or investing funds. These reports may also be called *internal proposals* because their persuasive nature is similar to that of external proposals (presented in Chapter 13). Large organizations sometimes prescribe how these reports should be organized and formatted; they often use forms with conventional headings. When you are free to select an organizational plan yourself, however, let your audience and topic determine your choice of the direct or indirect strategy.

Direct Strategy. For nonsensitive topics and recommendations that will be agreeable to readers, you can organize directly according to the following sequence:

- Identify the problem or need briefly.
- Announce the recommendation, solution, or action concisely and with action verbs.

- Explain more fully the benefits of the recommendation or steps necessary to solve the problem.
- Include a discussion of pros, cons, and costs.
- Conclude with a summary specifying the recommendation and necessary action.

Indirect Strategy. When a reader may oppose a recommendation or when circumstances suggest caution, do not rush to reveal your recommendation. Consider using the following sequence for an indirect approach to your recommendations:

- Refer to the problem in general terms, not to your recommendation, in the subject line.
- Describe the problem or need your recommendation addresses. Use specific examples, supporting statistics, and authoritative quotes to lend credibility to the seriousness of the problem.
- Discuss alternative solutions, beginning with the least likely to succeed.
- Present the most promising alternative (your recommendation) last.
- Show how the advantages of your recommendation outweigh its disadvantages.
- Summarize your recommendation. If appropriate, specify the action it requires.
- Ask for authorization to proceed, if necessary.

Cheyenne St. Marie, an executive assistant at a large petroleum and mining company in Fairbanks, Alaska, received a challenging research assignment. Her boss, the director of Human Resources, asked her to investigate ways to persuade employees to quit smoking. Here is how she described her task: "We banned smoking many years ago inside our buildings and on the premises, but we never tried very hard to get smokers to actually kick their habits. My job was to gather information about the problem and learn how other companies have helped workers stop smoking. The report would go to my boss, but I knew he would pass it along to the management council for approval."

Continuing her explanation, Cheyenne said, "If the report were just for my boss, I would put my recommendation right up front, because I'm sure he would support it. But the management council is another story. They need persuasion because of the costs involved—and because some of them are smokers. Therefore, I put the alternative I favored last. To gain credibility, I cited my sources. I had enough material for a ten-page report, but I kept it to two pages in keeping with our company report policy." Cheyenne chose MLA style to document her sources. A long report that uses the APA style is shown in Chapter 13.

Cheyenne single-spaced her report, shown in Figure 12.14, because her company prefers this style. Some companies prefer the readability of double-spacing. Be sure to check with your organization for its preference before printing your reports.

Feasibility Reports

Feasibility reports examine the practicality and advisability of following a course of action. They answer this question: Will this plan or proposal work? Feasibility reports typically are internal reports written to advise on matters such as consolidating departments, offering a wellness program to employees, or hiring an outside firm to handle a company's accounting or social media presence. These reports may also be written by consultants called in to investigate a problem. The focus of these reports is on the decision: rejecting or proceeding with the proposed option. Because your role is not to persuade the reader to accept the decision, you will want to present the decision immediately. In writing feasibility reports, consider these suggestions:

- Announce your decision immediately.
- Provide a description of the background and problem necessitating the proposal.
- Discuss the benefits of the proposal.

Ethics Check

Must Workers Enthusiastically Use Their Company's Products and Services?

PayPal president David Marcus is fed up with PayPal workers who don't use the global online payment system that employs them. His strongly worded e-mail to his company's San Jose, California, staff of 2,000 people made the rounds in Silicon Valley and triggered a lively debate. Marcus reacted to reports that employees at headquarters refused to download their company's app or forgot their PayPal passwords. The PayPal chief bluntly demanded to show passion or pack up: [D]o yourself a favor, go find something that will connect with your heart and mind elsewhere. A life devoid of purpose, and passion for what you do everyday [*sic*] is a waste of the precious time you have on this earth to make it better."[19] Do you agree with Marcus?

Figure 12.14 Justification/Recommendation Report, MLA Style

DATE: October 11, 2018

TO: Austin Sebastian, Director, Human Resources

FROM: Cheyenne St. Marie, Executive Assistant *C.S.M.*

SUBJECT: Smoking Cessation Programs for Employees

At your request, I have examined measures that encourage employees to quit smoking. As company records show, approximately 23 percent of our employees still smoke, despite the antismoking and clean-air policies we adopted in 2016. To collect data for this report, I studied professional and government publications; I also inquired at companies and clinics about stop-smoking programs.

Introduces purpose of report, tells method of data collection, and previews organization

Avoids revealing recommendation immediately

This report presents data describing the significance of the problem, three alternative solutions, and a recommendation based on my investigation.

Uses headings that combine function and description

Significance of Problem: Health Care and Productivity Losses

Employees who smoke are costly to any organization. The following statistics show the effects of smoking for workers and for organizations:

- Absenteeism is 40 to 50 percent greater among smoking employees.
- Accidents are two to three times greater among smokers.
- Bronchitis, lung and heart disease, cancer, and early death are more frequent among smokers (Arhelger 4).

Documents data sources for credibility, uses MLA style citing author and page number in the text

Although our clean-air policy prohibits smoking in the building, shop, and office, we have done little to encourage employees to stop smoking. Many workers still go outside to smoke at lunch and breaks. Other companies have been far more proactive in their attempts to stop employee smoking. Many companies have found that persuading employees to stop smoking was a decisive factor in reducing their health insurance premiums. Below is a discussion of three common stop-smoking measures tried by other companies, along with a projected cost factor for each (Rindfleisch 4).

Discusses least effective alternative first

Alternative 1: Literature and Events

The least expensive and easiest stop-smoking measure involves the distribution of literature, such as "The Ten-Step Plan" from Smokefree Enterprises and government pamphlets citing smoking dangers. Some companies have also sponsored events such as the Great American Smoke-Out, a one-day occasion intended to develop group spirit in spurring smokers to quit. "Studies show, however," says one expert, "that literature and company-sponsored events have little permanent effect in helping smokers quit" (Mendel 108).

Cost: Negligible

- Describe the problems that may result.
- Calculate the costs associated with the proposal, if appropriate.
- Show the time frame necessary for implementing the proposal.

Cora Hidalgo, human resources manager for a large public accounting firm in Philadelphia, wrote the feasibility report shown in Figure 12.15. Because she discovered that the company was

Figure 12.14 (Continued)

Austin Sebastian October 11, 2018 Page 2

Alternative 2: Stop-Smoking Programs Outside the Workplace

Local clinics provide treatment programs in classes at their centers. Here in Fairbanks we have the Smokers' Treatment Center, ACC Motivation Center, and New-Choice Program for Stopping Smoking. These behavior-modification stop-smoking programs are acknowledged to be more effective than literature distribution or incentive programs. However, studies of companies using off-workplace programs show that many employees fail to attend regularly and do not complete the programs.

Cost: $1,200 per employee, three-month individual program (New-Choice Program)
$900 per employee, three-month group session

Highlights costs for easy comparison

Alternative 3: Stop-Smoking Programs at the Workplace

Many clinics offer workplace programs with counselors meeting employees in company conference rooms. These programs have the advantage of keeping a firm's employees together so that they develop a group spirit and exert pressure on each other to succeed. The most successful programs are on company premises and also on company time. Employees participating in such programs had a 72 percent greater success record than employees attending the same stop-smoking program at an outside clinic (Honda 35). A disadvantage of this arrangement, of course, is lost work time—amounting to about two hours a week for three months.

Arranges alternatives so that most effective is last

Cost: $900 per employee, two hours per week of release time for three months

Conclusions and Recommendation

Summarizes findings and ends with specific recommendation

Smokers require discipline, counseling, and professional assistance in kicking the nicotine habit, as explained at the American Cancer Society Web site ("Guide to Quitting Smoking"). Workplace stop-smoking programs on company time are more effective than literature, incentives, and off-workplace programs. If our goal is to reduce health care costs and lead our employees to healthful lives, we should invest in a workplace stop-smoking program with release time for smokers. Although the program temporarily reduces productivity, we can expect to recapture that loss in lower health care premiums and healthier employees.

Therefore, I recommend that we begin a stop-smoking treatment program on company premises with two hours per week of release time for participants for three months.

Reveals recommendation only after discussing all alternatives

Page 3

Works Cited

Magazine — Arhelger, Zack. "The End of Smoking." *The World of Business*, 5 Nov. 2017, pp. 3-8.

Website article — "Guide to Quitting Smoking." *The American Cancer Society.org*, 27 Oct. 2017, http://www.cancer.org/healthy/stayawayfromtobacco/guidetoquittingsmoking/guide-to-quitting-smoking-toc.

Journal article — Honda, Emeline M. "Managing Anti-Smoking Campaigns: The Case for Company Programs." *Management Quarterly*, vol. 32, 2016, pp. 29-47.

Book — Mendel, I. A. *The Puff Stops Here.* Science Publications, 2016.

Newspaper article — Rindfleisch, Terry. "Smoke-Free Workplaces Can Help Smokers Quit, Expert Says." *Evening Chronicle*, 4 Dec. 2017, pp. 4+.

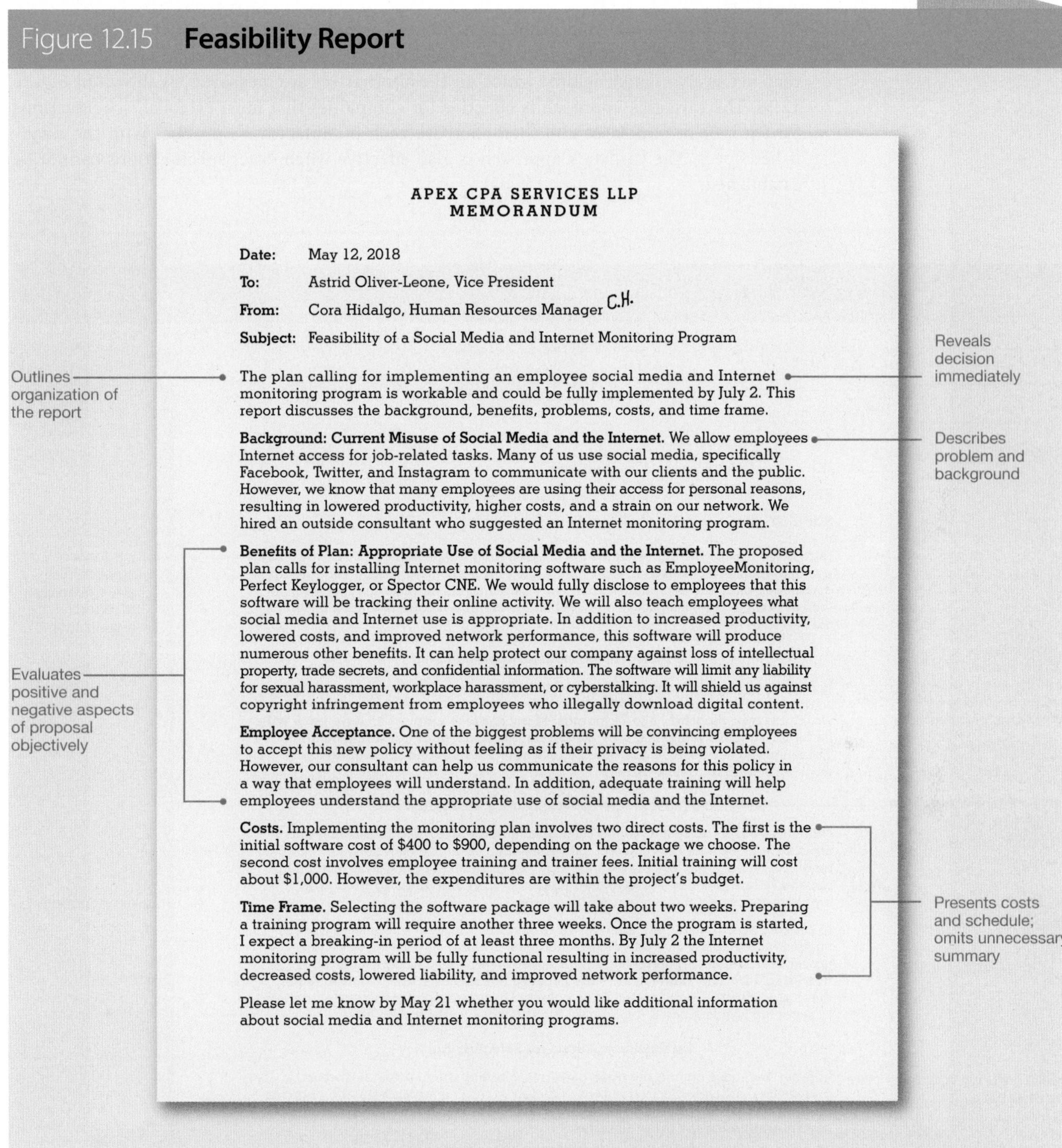
Outlines organization of the report
Evaluates positive and negative aspects of proposal objectively
Reveals decision immediately
Describes problem and background
Presents costs and schedule; omits unnecessary summary

APEX CPA SERVICES LLP
MEMORANDUM

Date: May 12, 2018

To: Astrid Oliver-Leone, Vice President

From: Cora Hidalgo, Human Resources Manager C.H.

Subject: Feasibility of a Social Media and Internet Monitoring Program

The plan calling for implementing an employee social media and Internet monitoring program is workable and could be fully implemented by July 2. This report discusses the background, benefits, problems, costs, and time frame.

Background: Current Misuse of Social Media and the Internet. We allow employees Internet access for job-related tasks. Many of us use social media, specifically Facebook, Twitter, and Instagram to communicate with our clients and the public. However, we know that many employees are using their access for personal reasons, resulting in lowered productivity, higher costs, and a strain on our network. We hired an outside consultant who suggested an Internet monitoring program.

Benefits of Plan: Appropriate Use of Social Media and the Internet. The proposed plan calls for installing Internet monitoring software such as EmployeeMonitoring, Perfect Keylogger, or Spector CNE. We would fully disclose to employees that this software will be tracking their online activity. We will also teach employees what social media and Internet use is appropriate. In addition to increased productivity, lowered costs, and improved network performance, this software will produce numerous other benefits. It can help protect our company against loss of intellectual property, trade secrets, and confidential information. The software will limit any liability for sexual harassment, workplace harassment, or cyberstalking. It will shield us against copyright infringement from employees who illegally download digital content.

Employee Acceptance. One of the biggest problems will be convincing employees to accept this new policy without feeling as if their privacy is being violated. However, our consultant can help us communicate the reasons for this policy in a way that employees will understand. In addition, adequate training will help employees understand the appropriate use of social media and the Internet.

Costs. Implementing the monitoring plan involves two direct costs. The first is the initial software cost of $400 to $900, depending on the package we choose. The second cost involves employee training and trainer fees. Initial training will cost about $1,000. However, the expenditures are within the project's budget.

Time Frame. Selecting the software package will take about two weeks. Preparing a training program will require another three weeks. Once the program is started, I expect a breaking-in period of at least three months. By July 2 the Internet monitoring program will be fully functional resulting in increased productivity, decreased costs, lowered liability, and improved network performance.

Please let me know by May 21 whether you would like additional information about social media and Internet monitoring programs.

Figure 12.15 **Feasibility Report**

losing time and money as a result of personal e-mail and Internet use by employees, she talked with the vice president, Astrid Oliver-Leone, about the problem. Astrid didn't want Cora to take time away from her job to investigate what other companies were doing to prevent this problem. Instead, she suggested that they hire a consultant to investigate what other companies were doing to prevent or limit personal e-mail and Internet use. The vice president then wanted to know whether the consultant's plan was feasible. Although Cora's report is only one page long, it provides all the necessary information: background, benefits, employee acceptance, costs, and time frame.

Yardstick Reports

Yardstick reports examine problems with two or more solutions. To determine the best solution, the writer establishes criteria by which to compare the alternatives. The criteria then act as a yardstick against which all the alternatives are measured, as shown in Figure 12.16. The yardstick approach is effective for companies that must establish specifications for equipment purchases and then compare each manufacturer's product with the established specs. The yardstick approach is also effective when exact specifications cannot be established.

Figure 12.16 **Yardstick Report**

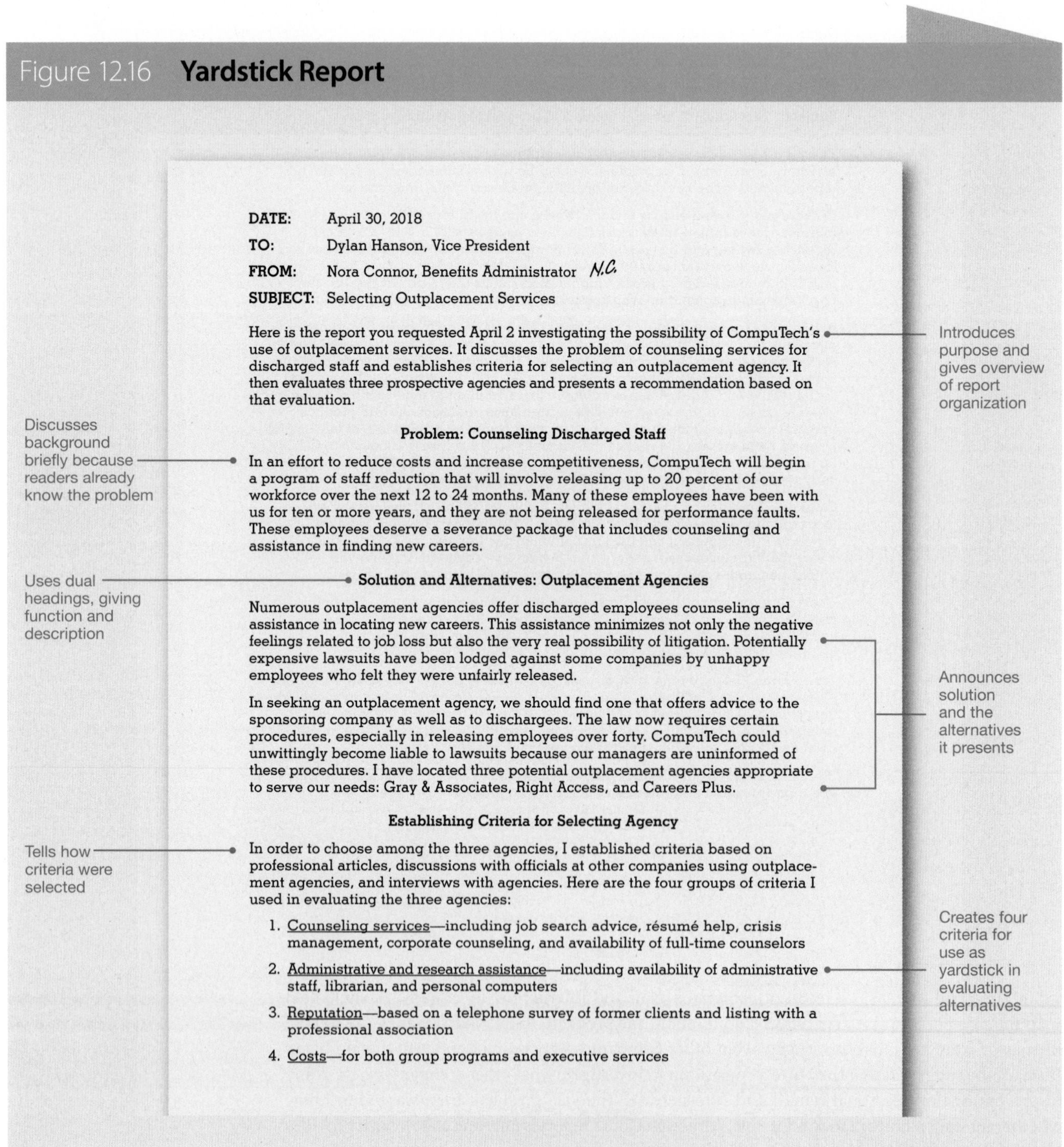

DATE: April 30, 2018
TO: Dylan Hanson, Vice President
FROM: Nora Connor, Benefits Administrator *N.C.*
SUBJECT: Selecting Outplacement Services

Here is the report you requested April 2 investigating the possibility of CompuTech's use of outplacement services. It discusses the problem of counseling services for discharged staff and establishes criteria for selecting an outplacement agency. It then evaluates three prospective agencies and presents a recommendation based on that evaluation.

Problem: Counseling Discharged Staff

In an effort to reduce costs and increase competitiveness, CompuTech will begin a program of staff reduction that will involve releasing up to 20 percent of our workforce over the next 12 to 24 months. Many of these employees have been with us for ten or more years, and they are not being released for performance faults. These employees deserve a severance package that includes counseling and assistance in finding new careers.

Solution and Alternatives: Outplacement Agencies

Numerous outplacement agencies offer discharged employees counseling and assistance in locating new careers. This assistance minimizes not only the negative feelings related to job loss but also the very real possibility of litigation. Potentially expensive lawsuits have been lodged against some companies by unhappy employees who felt they were unfairly released.

In seeking an outplacement agency, we should find one that offers advice to the sponsoring company as well as to dischargees. The law now requires certain procedures, especially in releasing employees over forty. CompuTech could unwittingly become liable to lawsuits because our managers are uninformed of these procedures. I have located three potential outplacement agencies appropriate to serve our needs: Gray & Associates, Right Access, and Careers Plus.

Establishing Criteria for Selecting Agency

In order to choose among the three agencies, I established criteria based on professional articles, discussions with officials at other companies using outplacement agencies, and interviews with agencies. Here are the four groups of criteria I used in evaluating the three agencies:

1. Counseling services—including job search advice, résumé help, crisis management, corporate counseling, and availability of full-time counselors
2. Administrative and research assistance—including availability of administrative staff, librarian, and personal computers
3. Reputation—based on a telephone survey of former clients and listing with a professional association
4. Costs—for both group programs and executive services

Introduces purpose and gives overview of report organization
Discusses background briefly because readers already know the problem
Uses dual headings, giving function and description
Announces solution and the alternatives it presents
Tells how criteria were selected
Creates four criteria for use as yardstick in evaluating alternatives

For example, long before Nissan Motor Company decided to produce its Altima, Rogue, and Leaf models and a new Infiniti luxury SUV in its existing plant in Smyrna (Tennessee), the auto manufacturer had conducted an internal competition to find a suitable location. The No. 8 global carmaker evaluated several sites, including one in Japan. Nissan considered important criteria such as manufacturing costs (including currency fluctuations), the potential for high product quality, and the proximity to the market in the United States. Today, the Smyrna location is one of the top-producing plants in the world, employing almost 8,000 workers.[20]

Figure 12.16 **(Continued)**

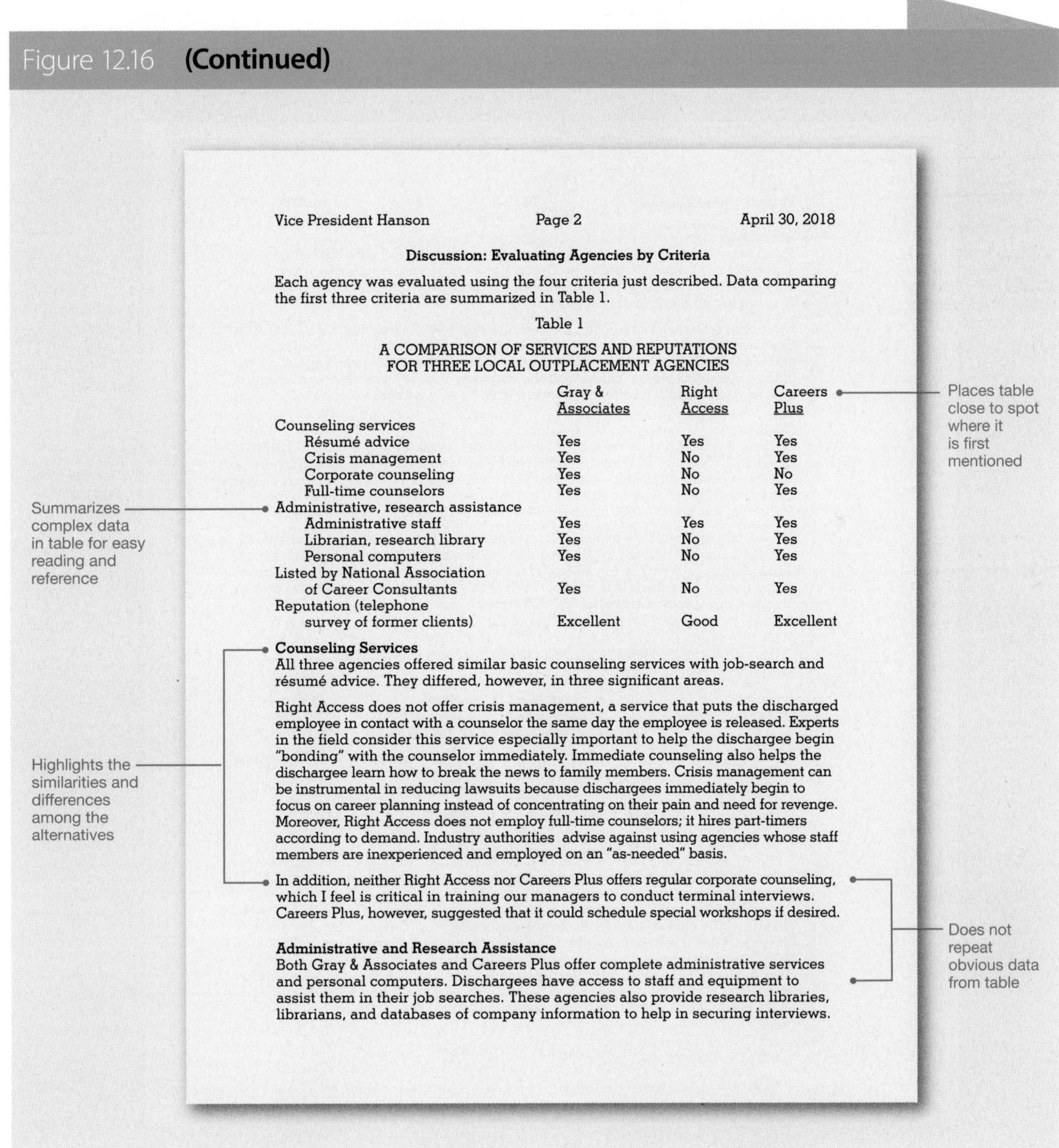

Vice President Hanson　　Page 2　　April 30, 2018

Discussion: Evaluating Agencies by Criteria

Each agency was evaluated using the four criteria just described. Data comparing the first three criteria are summarized in Table 1.

Table 1

A COMPARISON OF SERVICES AND REPUTATIONS FOR THREE LOCAL OUTPLACEMENT AGENCIES

	Gray & Associates	Right Access	Careers Plus
Counseling services			
Résumé advice	Yes	Yes	Yes
Crisis management	Yes	No	Yes
Corporate counseling	Yes	No	No
Full-time counselors	Yes	No	Yes
Administrative, research assistance			
Administrative staff	Yes	Yes	Yes
Librarian, research library	Yes	No	Yes
Personal computers	Yes	No	Yes
Listed by National Association of Career Consultants	Yes	No	Yes
Reputation (telephone survey of former clients)	Excellent	Good	Excellent

Counseling Services
All three agencies offered similar basic counseling services with job-search and résumé advice. They differed, however, in three significant areas.

Right Access does not offer crisis management, a service that puts the discharged employee in contact with a counselor the same day the employee is released. Experts in the field consider this service especially important to help the dischargee begin "bonding" with the counselor immediately. Immediate counseling also helps the dischargee learn how to break the news to family members. Crisis management can be instrumental in reducing lawsuits because dischargees immediately begin to focus on career planning instead of concentrating on their pain and need for revenge. Moreover, Right Access does not employ full-time counselors; it hires part-timers according to demand. Industry authorities advise against using agencies whose staff members are inexperienced and employed on an "as-needed" basis.

In addition, neither Right Access nor Careers Plus offers regular corporate counseling, which I feel is critical in training our managers to conduct terminal interviews. Careers Plus, however, suggested that it could schedule special workshops if desired.

Administrative and Research Assistance
Both Gray & Associates and Careers Plus offer complete administrative services and personal computers. Dischargees have access to staff and equipment to assist them in their job searches. These agencies also provide research libraries, librarians, and databases of company information to help in securing interviews.

Places table close to spot where it is first mentioned
Summarizes complex data in table for easy reading and reference
Highlights the similarities and differences among the alternatives
Does not repeat obvious data from table

The real advantage to yardstick reports is that alternatives can be measured consistently using the same criteria. Writers using a yardstick approach typically do the following:

- Begin by describing the problem or need.
- Explain possible solutions and alternatives.
- Establish criteria for comparing the alternatives; tell how the criteria were selected or developed.

Figure 12.16 **(Continued)**

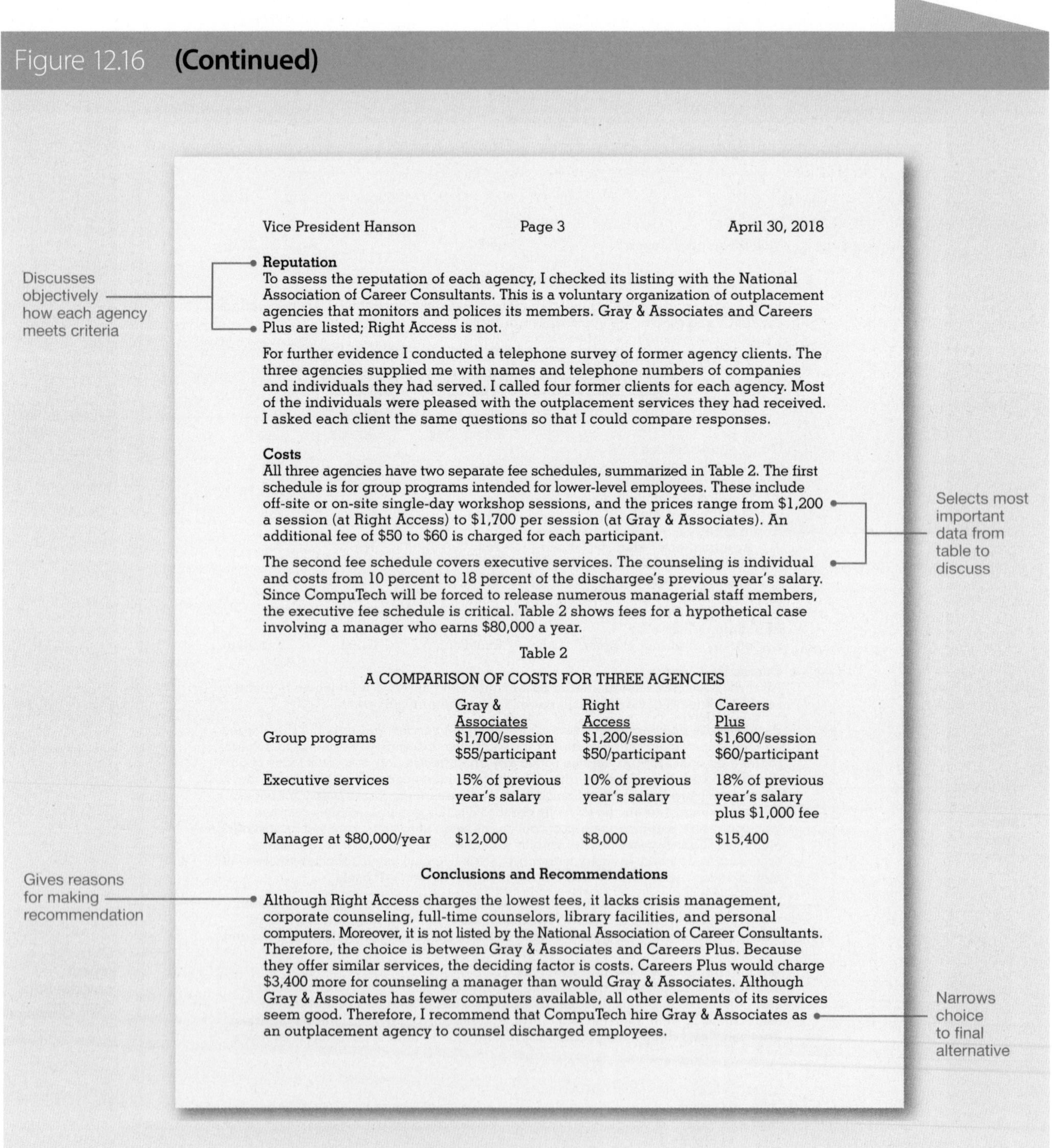

Vice President Hanson — Page 3 — April 30, 2018

Reputation

To assess the reputation of each agency, I checked its listing with the National Association of Career Consultants. This is a voluntary organization of outplacement agencies that monitors and polices its members. Gray & Associates and Careers Plus are listed; Right Access is not.

For further evidence I conducted a telephone survey of former agency clients. The three agencies supplied me with names and telephone numbers of companies and individuals they had served. I called four former clients for each agency. Most of the individuals were pleased with the outplacement services they had received. I asked each client the same questions so that I could compare responses.

Costs

All three agencies have two separate fee schedules, summarized in Table 2. The first schedule is for group programs intended for lower-level employees. These include off-site or on-site single-day workshop sessions, and the prices range from $1,200 a session (at Right Access) to $1,700 per session (at Gray & Associates). An additional fee of $50 to $60 is charged for each participant.

The second fee schedule covers executive services. The counseling is individual and costs from 10 percent to 18 percent of the dischargee's previous year's salary. Since CompuTech will be forced to release numerous managerial staff members, the executive fee schedule is critical. Table 2 shows fees for a hypothetical case involving a manager who earns $80,000 a year.

Table 2

A COMPARISON OF COSTS FOR THREE AGENCIES

	Gray & Associates	Right Access	Careers Plus
Group programs	$1,700/session $55/participant	$1,200/session $50/participant	$1,600/session $60/participant
Executive services	15% of previous year's salary	10% of previous year's salary	18% of previous year's salary plus $1,000 fee
Manager at $80,000/year	$12,000	$8,000	$15,400

Conclusions and Recommendations

Although Right Access charges the lowest fees, it lacks crisis management, corporate counseling, full-time counselors, library facilities, and personal computers. Moreover, it is not listed by the National Association of Career Consultants. Therefore, the choice is between Gray & Associates and Careers Plus. Because they offer similar services, the deciding factor is costs. Careers Plus would charge $3,400 more for counseling a manager than would Gray & Associates. Although Gray & Associates has fewer computers available, all other elements of its services seem good. Therefore, I recommend that CompuTech hire Gray & Associates as an outplacement agency to counsel discharged employees.

Discusses objectively how each agency meets criteria
Selects most important data from table to discuss
Gives reasons for making recommendation
Narrows choice to final alternative

- Discuss and evaluate each alternative in terms of the criteria.
- Draw conclusions and make recommendations.

Nora Connor, benefits administrator for computer manufacturer CompuTech, was called on to write the report in Figure 12.16 comparing outplacement agencies. These agencies counsel discharged employees and help them find new positions; fees are paid by the former employer. Nora knew that times were bad for CompuTech and that extensive downsizing would take place in the next two years. Her task was to compare outplacement agencies and recommend one to CompuTech.

After collecting information, Nora found that her biggest problem was organizing the data and developing a system for making comparisons. All the outplacement agencies she investigated seemed to offer the same basic package of services.

With the information she gathered about three outplacement agencies, she made a big grid listing the names of the agencies across the top. Down the side she listed general categories—such as services, costs, and reputation. Then she filled in the information for each agency. This grid, which began to look like a table, helped her organize all the pieces of information. After studying the grid, she saw that all the information could be grouped into four categories: counseling services, administrative and research assistance, reputation, and costs. She made these the criteria she would use to compare agencies.

Next, Nora divided her grid into two parts, which became Table 1 and Table 2. In writing the report, she could have made each agency a separate heading, followed by a discussion of how it measured up to the criteria. Immediately, though, she saw how repetitious that would become. Therefore, she used the criteria as headings and discussed how each agency met each criterion—or failed to meet it. Making a recommendation was easy once Nora had made the tables and could see how the agencies compared.

Writing Direct Requests and Responses

Introduction

- **Identify the purpose of the report.** Explain why the report is being written.
- **Describe the significance of the topic.** Explain why the report is important.
- **Preview the organization of the report.** Especially for long reports, explain how the report will be organized.
- **Summarize the conclusions and recommendations for receptive audiences.** Use the direct strategy only if you have the confidence of the reader.

Findings

- **Discuss pros and cons.** In recommendation/justification reports, evaluate the advantages and disadvantages of each alternative. For unreceptive audiences consider placing the recommended alternative last.
- **Establish criteria to evaluate alternatives.** In yardstick reports, create criteria to use in measuring each alternative consistently.
- **Support the findings with evidence.** Supply facts, statistics, expert opinion, survey data, and other proof from which you can draw logical conclusions.
- **Organize the findings for logic and readability.** Arrange the findings around the alternatives or the reasons leading to the conclusion. Use headings, enumerations, lists, tables, and graphics to focus emphasis.

Conclusions/Recommendations

- **Draw reasonable conclusions from the findings.** Develop conclusions that answer the research question. Justify the conclusions with highlights from the findings.
- **Make recommendations, if asked.** For multiple recommendations prepare a list. Use action verbs. Explain fully the benefits of the recommendation or steps necessary to solve the problem or answer the question.

Your Turn: Applying Your Skills at Starbucks

Starbucks understands that it has to innovate by introducing new products and creating unique store concepts to secure its continued growth at home and around the world. The company designs all store locations strictly in-house, employing high-level designers. Starbucks has successfully experimented with reclaimed materials and prefabricated components, at one point repurposing old shipping containers. Concurrently with building three new roasting megastores, Starbucks has also created highly profitable mini drive-through and walk-up outlets that feature limited beverage and food choices but provide faster service and show above-average sales growth.[21]

Although the materials are standardized and recycled in the new mini outlets, the exterior materials are intended to blend into each particular environment. At approximately 500 square feet, the diminutive buildings are bound to sprout up at a location near you; drive-throughs account for more than 40 percent of company-operated stores.[22] Best of all, they are LEED-certified. LEED, short for Leadership in Energy and Environmental Design, was established by the U.S. Green Building Council and applied originally to energy-efficient office buildings. Starbucks seems bent on leading the field in environmental stewardship.

Aside from these stand-alone, small-footprint outlets, Starbucks is expanding on this hyperlocal express format.[23] The company is betting on tiny urban locations that offer a limited menu built on speed and convenience for that quick caffeine fix busy commuters in high-traffic areas crave. Mobile ordering and digital payment speed up the customer experience.

Your Task

As assistant to Howard Schultz, you are asked to form a research team. Its purpose is to study the feasibility of new prefabricated LEED-certified Starbucks stores across the United States. Prepare a feasibility report addressed to Howard Schultz that analyzes the suitability of a modular mini Starbucks in your town, city, or region. You would want to consider how such a new type of Starbucks could fit into a neighborhood you know well. The small, modular stores could help Starbucks save power and decrease its carbon footprint. Some have speculated that the company might eventually be able to move off the power grid in some locations.[24] Alternatively, you could explore Starbucks' Shared Planet initiatives and write an informational report that focuses on the company's environmental record.

Summary of Learning Outcomes

1 Analyze, sort, and interpret statistical data and other information using tables, measures of central tendency (mean, median, and mode), and decision matrices.

- To make sense of report information, writers sort it into tables or analyze it by mean (the arithmetic average), median (the midpoint in a group of figures), and mode (the most frequent response); range represents a span between the highest and lowest figures.
- Grids help organize complex data into rows and columns.
- A decision matrix, a special grid with weights, assists decision makers in choosing objectively among complex options.
- Writers need to maintain accuracy in applying statistical techniques to gain and maintain credibility with their readers.

2 Draw meaningful conclusions and make practical report recommendations after sound and valid analysis.

- Writers explain what the survey data mean in a conclusion—especially in relation to the original report problem; they interpret key findings and may attempt to explain what caused the problem.
- Reports that call for recommendations require writers to make specific suggestions for actions that can solve the report problem.
- Recommendations should be feasible, practical, and potentially agreeable to the audience; they should relate to the initial report problem.
- Recommendations may be combined with conclusions.

3 Organize report data logically, and provide reader cues to aid comprehension.

- Reports may be organized in many ways, including by (a) time (establishing a chronology), (b) component (discussing a problem by geography, division, or product), (c) importance (arranging data from most important to least important, or vice versa), (d) criteria (comparing items by standards), or (e) convention (using an already established grouping).
- To help guide the reader through the text, introductions, transitions, and headings serve as cues.

4 Write short informational reports that describe routine tasks.

- Typical informational reports include periodic, trip, convention, progress, and investigative reports.
- The introduction in informational reports previews the purpose and supplies background data, if necessary.
- The body of an informational report is generally divided into three to five segments that may be organized by time, component, importance, criteria, or convention; clear headings make the body easy to scan. Unless formality is expected, an informal, conversational style is used.
- In the conclusion writers review the main points and discuss actions that will follow; the report may conclude with a final thought, appreciation, or an offer to provide more information.
- Like all professional documents, a well-written report cements the writer's credibility with the audience; writers need to apply all the writing techniques addressed in Chapters 4, 5, and 6.

5 Prepare short analytical reports that solve business problems.

- Typical analytical reports include justification/recommendation reports, feasibility reports, and yardstick reports.
- Justification/recommendation reports organized directly identify a problem, immediately announce a recommendation or solution, discuss its merits, and explain the action to be taken.
- Justification/recommendation reports organized indirectly describe a problem, discuss alternative solutions, prove the superiority of one solution, and ask for authorization to proceed with that solution.
- Feasibility reports, generally organized directly, study the advisability of following a course of action; they describe the background of, advantages and disadvantages of, costs of, and time frame for implementing the proposal.
- Yardstick reports compare two or more solutions to a problem by measuring each against a set of established criteria, thus ensuring consistency. Yardstick reports usually describe a problem, explain possible solutions, establish criteria for comparing alternatives, evaluate each alternative in terms of the criteria, draw conclusions, and make recommendations.

Critical Thinking

1. What technology trends do you think will affect business reporting and delivery in the future? (L.O. 1-5)
2. When tabulating and analyzing data, you may discover relationships between two or more variables that help explain the findings. Can you trust these correlations and assume that their relationship is one of cause and effect? (L.O. 1)
3. How can you increase your chances that your report recommendations will be implemented? (L.O. 2)
4. What are the major differences between informational and analytical reports? (L.O. 4, 5)
5. **Ethical Issue:** As *The New York Times* reported, "Every day, on average, a scientific paper is retracted because of misconduct." Two percent of scientists are willing to admit that they have manipulated their data to suit their purposes. Considering that researchers publish about 2 million articles each year, 2 percent is not a negligible number. The Office of Research Integrity within the U.S. Department of Health and Human Services has cracked down on at least a dozen researchers for irregularities such as plagiarism and fabrication of results.[25] What might motivate such misconduct, and why is it a serious offense? (L.O. 2)

Activities

12.1 Minding the Three Ms (L.O. 1)

Nine homes recently sold in your community in the following order and for these amounts: $360,000; $460,000; $360,000; $380,000; $360,000; $420,000; $380,000; $520,000; and $360,000. Your boss, Andrew Santoso, a realtor with Hagen & Associates, wants you to compute the mean, median, and mode for this real estate market.

YOUR TASK Compute the mean, median, and mode for the recently sold homes. Explain your analysis as well as the characteristics of each type of "average."

12.2 Interpreting Survey Results (L.O. 1)

Team

Your business communication class at Westside College was asked by the college bookstore manager, Craig Daniels, to conduct a survey. Concerned about the environment, Daniels wants to learn students' reactions to eliminating plastic bags, of which the bookstore gives away 45,000 annually. Students answered questions about a number of proposals, resulting in the following raw data:

For major purchases the bookstore should:

	Agree	Undecided	Disagree
1. Continue to provide plastic bags	132	17	411
2. Provide no bags; encourage students to bring their own bags	414	25	121
3. Provide no bags; offer cloth bags at a reduced price (about $3)	357	19	184
4. Give a cloth bag with each major purchase, the cost to be included in registration fees	63	15	482

YOUR TASK In groups of four or five, do the following:

a. Convert the data into a table (see Figure 12.1) with a descriptive title. Arrange the items in a logical sequence.

b. How could these survey data be cross-tabulated? Would cross-tabulation serve any purpose?

c. Given the conditions of this survey, name at least three conclusions that researchers could draw from the data.

d. Prepare three to five recommendations to be submitted to Mr. Daniels. How could the bookstore implement them?

e. Role-play a meeting in which the recommendations and implementation plan are presented to Mr. Daniels. One student plays the role of Mr. Daniels; the remaining students play the role of the presenters.

12.3 Distinguishing Conclusions From Recommendations (L.O. 2)

A study led by psychologists at Kent State University examined empirical research on ten common studying techniques, such as highlighting text with markers and taking practice tests. For each technique, the researchers explored the assumptions underlying the strategy. They studied what empirical research has to teach us about actual effectiveness. They found that despite the prevalence of various study techniques such as highlighting text and writing summaries, many of these student-preferred strategies do not work very well.[26]

YOUR TASK Based on the preceding facts, indicate whether the following statements are conclusions or recommendations:

a. Many instructors rightly assume that their students don't have the necessary study skills.

b. Although it is a common learning technique, imitating the style of famous writers is not always an effective study tool.

c. Instructors need to teach study skills to help students maximize their use of time and outcomes.

d. Highlighting text has little to offer in the way of subsequent performance.

e. Students should identify the main ideas in the text *before* highlighting to benefit from this technique.

f. Researchers found that many typical student study techniques are ineffective.

g. Students should consider techniques they have never tried before; for example, interleaved practice, which mixes different types of material or problems in a single study session.

12.4 Picking the Best Laptop With a Decision Matrix (L.O. 1, 2)

You want to buy a low-cost laptop for your college work and consider price the most important feature. The sheer number of options in countless laptops overwhelms you.

YOUR TASK Study Figure 12.3 and change the weights in Table 2 to reflect your emphasis on low price, to which you will assign a factor of 10 because it is twice as important to you as unit weight, which receives a factor of 5. The hard drive size is likewise secondary to you, so you give it a 5 also. Last, you change battery life to a factor of 7 from 10 because it is less important than price, but more important than unit weight and hard drive size. Calculate the new scores. Which low-budget computer wins this time?

12.5 Using a Decision Matrix to Buy a Car (L.O. 1, 2)

Alan, an outrigger canoe racer, needs to buy a new car. He wants a vehicle that will carry his disassembled boat and outrigger. At the same time, he will need to travel long distances on business. His passion is soft-top sports cars, but he is also concerned about gas mileage. These four criteria are impossible to find in one vehicle. Alan has the following choices:

- Station wagon
- SUV with or without a sunroof
- Four-door sedan, a high-miles-per-gallon family car
- Sports car, convertible

He wants to consider the following criteria:

- Price
- Ability to carry cargo such as a canoe
- Fuel efficiency
- Comfort over long distances
- Good looks and fun
- Quality build/manufacturer's reputation

YOUR TASK Follow the steps outlined in Figure 12.3 to determine an assessment scale and to assign a score to each feature. Then, consider which weights are probably most important to Alan, given his needs. Calculate the totals to find the vehicle that's most suitable for Alan.

12.6 Organizing Data (L.O. 3)

Team

YOUR TASK In groups of three to five, discuss how the findings in the following reports could be best organized (i.e., by time, component, importance, criteria, or convention).

a. A set of drill guidelines for businesses described in a recommendation report detailing four levels of emergency response to earthquakes

b. A city's building division website reporting permits issued during a specific date range

c. A report comparing the benefits of buying or leasing a fleet of electric vehicles. The report presents data on depreciation, upfront cost, maintenance, battery life, range on one charge, and other factors.

d. A progress report written by a team of researchers to keep their supervisor informed at each of the five project stages

e. A report comparing the sales volumes of the agents of a large national realtor based on the number of listings taken, number of listings sold, total sales in the agents' market areas, and more.

f. A recommendation report to be submitted to management presenting four building plans to improve access to your building, in compliance with federal regulations. The plans range considerably in feasibility and cost.

g. An investigative report describing a company's expansion plans in South America, Europe, Australia, and Southeast Asia

h. An employee performance appraisal submitted annually

12.7 What's in a Name? Identify Heading Types (L.O. 3)

YOUR TASK Identify the following report headings and titles as *functional, talking,* or *combination.* Discuss the usefulness and effectiveness of each.

a. Project Costs
b. How to Prevent Identity Theft
c. Disadvantages
d. Balancing Worker Productivity and Social Media Use
e. Case Study: America's Most Sustainable Company
f. Recommendations: Solving Our Applicant-Tracking Problem
g. Comparing Costs of Hiring Exempt and Nonexempt Employees
h. Budget

12.8 Executive Summary: Briefing the Boss (L.O. 4)

Web

Like many executives, your boss is too rushed to read long journal articles. However, she is eager to keep up with developments in her field. She asks you to submit to her one summary every month on an article of interest to help her stay abreast of research in her field.

YOUR TASK In your field of study, select a professional journal, such as the *Journal of Management*. Using an electronic database search or a Web search, look for articles in your target journal. Select an interesting article that is at least five pages long, and write an executive summary in memo format. Include an introduction that might begin with *As you requested, I am submitting this executive summary of . . . .* Identify the author, article title, journal, and date of publication. Explain what the author intended to do in the study or article. Summarize three or four of the most important findings of the study or article. Use descriptive rather than functional headings. Your boss would also like a concluding statement indicating your response to the article. Address your memo to Karen James.

12.9 Periodic Report: Checking in With the Boss (L.O. 4)

E-Mail

You work hard at your job, but you rarely see your boss. He or she has asked to be informed of your activities and accomplishments and any problems you are encountering.

YOUR TASK For a job that you currently hold or a previous one, describe your regular activities, discuss irregular events that management should be aware of, and highlight any special needs or problems you are having. If you don't have a job, communicate to your instructor your weekly or monthly activities as they are tied to your classes, homework, and writing assignments. Establish components or criteria such as those in the bulleted e-mail in Figure 12.11. Use the memo format, or write an e-mail report in bullet form as shown in Figure 12.11. Address the memo or the e-mail report to your boss or, alternatively, to your instructor.

12.10 Progress Report: Providing a Project Update (L.O. 4)

E-Mail

If you are writing a long report either for another course or for the long report assignment in Chapter 13, you will want to keep your instructor informed of your progress.

YOUR TASK Write a progress report informing your instructor of your work. Briefly describe the project (its purpose, scope, limitations, and methodology), work completed, work yet to be completed, problems encountered, future activities, and expected completion date. Address the e-mail report to your instructor. If your instructor allows, try your hand at the bulleted e-mail report in Figure 12.11.

12.11 Progress Report: When Will You Reach Your Objective? (L.O. 4)

You have made an agreement with your parents (or spouse, partner, relative, or friend) that you would submit a progress report at this time.

YOUR TASK Prepare a progress report in letter format in which you do the following: (a) describe your headway toward your educational goal (such as employment, degree, or certificate); (b) summarize the work you have completed thus far; (c) discuss the work currently in progress, including your successes and anticipated obstacles; and (d) outline what you have left to complete.

12.12 Investigative Report: Seeking New Riders (L.O. 4)

Web

As a junior sales associate working for Chicago BMW Motorcycles, you are very happy that bike sales are bouncing back in a big way, along with the recovering economy. In fact, BMW Motorrad USA is breaking sales records in the United States and around the world.[27] BMW relies on a well-heeled clientele consisting mostly of middle-aged men. However, the German motorcycle manufacturer is struggling to capture a share of the market larger than the 5 percent it has in the United States, as opposed to 25 percent in Germany. BMW Motorrad's latest strategy is to build smaller and less expensive motorbikes under 500 cc in emerging markets such as China, India, and Brazil.[28]

Sales of the ever-popular Harley-Davidson motorcycles are up, too, and the quintessential American brand is holding on to a 51 percent domestic market share.[29] The manufacturer's core target audience has likewise traditionally been white, male, and middle-aged. This is why Harley-Davidson is now trying to appeal to women riders and to a younger generation of would-be bikers. You bring up this topic with your boss, Bryan Smiley, and he asks you to find out what exactly Harley-Davidson is doing.

YOUR TASK Visit the Harley-Davidson USA website and study how the legendary motorcycle manufacturer is targeting females and younger riders. Write an informational report in memo form addressed to Bryan Smiley. Which of its motorcycles does your competitor promote as ideal for women, and why? How about apparel? What other ways has Harley-Davidson found to attract female riders and younger bikers?

12.13 Investigative Report: Minding Your Manners Abroad (L.O. 4)

Intercultural Team Web

Your boss, Marian Yang, wants to know more about intercultural and international business etiquette. Today, most managers recognize that they need to be polished and professional to earn the respect of diverse audiences. Assume that your boss will assign different countries to several interns and recent hires. Choose a country that interests you and conduct a Web search. For example, in a Google search, input terms such as *business etiquette*, *business etiquette abroad*, and *intercultural communication*. You could visit websites such as the popular, informative etiquette and business guides for specific countries by Kwintessential Ltd. Also consider CountryWatch and the Central Intelligence Agency's (CIA) *The World Factbook*.

YOUR TASK As an intern or a new-hire, write a memo report about one country that is considerably different from the United States and that offers new business opportunities. Address your report to Marian Yang, president of WorldTech. Confine your research to what U.S. managers need to know about business etiquette in that culture. You should investigate social customs such as greetings, attire, gift giving, formality, business meals, attitudes toward time, and communication styles to help your boss avoid etiquette blunders. The purpose of your report is to promote business, not tourism. Compare your results with those of other students and, if directed, compile them in an informational team report.

12.14 Informational or Analytical Report: Examining Tweets and Other Social Media Posts (L.O. 4, 5)

E-Mail

Web

Select a Fortune 500 company that appeals to you, and search recent tweets and Facebook posts about it. Soon you will recognize trends and topic clusters that may help you organize the report content by criteria. For example, if you use the hashtag to conduct a subject search on Coca-Cola (i.e., *#Coca-Cola*), you will obtain a huge number of tweets about the company and brand. They will range from fan posts, buying tips, exhortations to recycle plastic, and specious cleaning tips involving Coke all the way to urban legends (e.g., the acid in Coke will completely dissolve a T-bone steak in two days). Many returned tweets will be only marginally interesting because they show up just because *#Coca-Cola* is mentioned.

If you explore Facebook, you will mostly find official pages and fan sites, most of which display favorable posts. You would have to look hard to find negative posts, partly because companies moderate discussions and often remove offensive posts according to their user agreements.

YOUR TASK Write either an informational or analytical report about the company you chose. In an informational report to your instructor, you could summarize your findings in memo form or as an e-mail. Describe how the tweets about the company are trending. Are they overwhelmingly positive or negative? Organize the report around the subject areas you identify (criteria). Alternatively, you could write an analytical report detailing the strategies your chosen company adopts in responding to tweets and Facebook posts. Your analytical report would evaluate the organization's social media responses and provide specific examples to support your claims.

12.15 Informational Report: Prospecting for Potential Employers (L.O. 4)

Web

You are considering jobs with a Fortune 500 company, and you want to learn as much as possible about it.

YOUR TASK Select a Fortune 500 company and collect information about it on the Web. If available, use your library's ProQuest subscription to access Hoover's company records for basic facts. Then take a look at the company's website; check its background, news releases, and annual report. Learn about its major product, service, or emphasis. Find its Fortune 500 ranking, its current stock price (if listed), and its high and low range for the year. Look up its profit-to-earnings ratio. Track its latest marketing plan, promotion, or product. Identify its home office, major officers, and number of employees. In a memo report to your instructor, summarize your research findings. Explain why this company would be a good or bad employment choice.

12.16 Justification/Recommendation Report: Money to Burn for a Good Cause (L.O. 5)

Web

Great news! MegaTech, the startup company where you work, has become enormously successful. Now the owner

additional staff costs, and miscellaneous expenses are estimated at $7,000. Isabel believes the budget balance could be used for a videographer to film and edit the show for $20,000, which the company can later use to generate more sales.

Although the showroom is small, not having to pay for the space is a plus, and garments and dressing rooms are available before the event. The smaller space could create an intimate setting. In the showroom, Robert could give more attention to the most promising guests. Guests could see where the designer's vision is conceived, view the designer's other collections, and meet company employees.

YOUR TASK In the role of Isabel Diaz, write a memo report to Robert Smith with your analysis and recommendations.

12.23 Feasibility Report: Heavenly Scents Considers a Social Media Consultant (L.O. 5)

You are the vice president of marketing for Heavenly Scents, a manufacturer and distributor of scented flameless candles and candle warmers. The president, Andrea Matos, feels that the company could do a better job of building relationships with its customers—current and future. Andrea knows the company's two main competitors are gaining ground in brand awareness and sales. While she also knows that Heavenly Scents has created a Facebook page, she wants the company to build a broader social media strategy. Andrea thinks it might be wise to hire a social media consultant to help in this effort, and she wants your advice.

To provide Andrea with an informed recommendation, you decide to conduct research to answer the following questions:

1. Is the company collecting social media data (e.g., tracking number of likes, number of followers, product reviews), and is the company using the data?
2. Does the Marketing Department have employees with the skills to implement this strategy without a consultant's help?
3. If the company has this talent, do employees have the time to implement this strategy?
4. How long will it take to implement this strategy?
5. What social media tools should the company use? What services do consultants provide?
6. What is the cost of hiring a social media consultant?
7. What are the disadvantages of hiring a consultant?
8. What could go wrong if the company hires a consultant?

As vice president of marketing, you already know the answers to many of these questions, but Andrea, understandably, does not.

You conduct internal research and learn that the company collects data from Facebook, but it doesn't analyze that data for decision making. Two of the Marketing Department's 12 employees have some social media knowledge and skills, but neither has the knowledge, experience, or time to implement a social media strategy. A consultant would have skills and time to do this, and to uncover the social media tools and strategies other companies are using.

The estimated implementation time for a social media strategy is two months. Many social media consultants recommend using a wide range of networking sites in this time frame, including Facebook, Twitter, Pinterest, Instagram, Snapchat, and blogging. The average fees for social media consulting services appear in the following table.

Average Fees for Social Media Consulting Services

Platform	Setup Charge	Monthly Charges
Facebook	$1,000 for initial page setup	$1,550 for monthly content management
Twitter, Pinterest, Snapchat, and Instagram (charge for each)	$900 for account setup	$950 for monthly account management
Blogging	$2,150 for design and template creation	$1,990 per month for writing and editing content for the blog (one post per week)

You have identified two main disadvantages of hiring a social media consultant. First, the consultant will not be an expert in your company or its products. You'll have to combine the consultant's knowledge of social media channels with your knowledge of the scented candle business. Second, it's impossible to accurately predict the return on investment of these services. The best you can do is monitor costs and make sure you receive the contracted services.

Reading about the Smucker's and LG social media fiascos taught you that remaining silent in a Twitter conversation, not planning for problems, and removing negative Facebook comments are major social media blunders. Smucker's received much criticism for its stance against labeling genetically modified organisms (GMOs), and people turned to its Facebook page to complain. In response, Smucker's tried to take control of the situation by deleting the comments—and made the situation far worse. LG tried to make fun of Apple by tweeting, "Our smartphones don't bend; they are naturally curved ;)." The big problem was that the tweet was sent from an iPhone. In contrast, learning about Marc Jacobs' success in debuting his fragrance line through pop-up shops that used social media communication as currency for prizes and gifts showed you how effective these media channels can be. To avoid problems, the company could make one employee responsible for monitoring social media content, participating in Twitter conversations, and posting daily on Facebook, Instagram, and Snapchat—if all are selected.

YOUR TASK Write a three-page memo report to the president. Make clear your decision regarding whether to hire a consultant, leaving which social media channels to add to the person chosen to direct this strategy. Include all the results of your research in the report, condensing it to stay within the page-length limit. Format the report for easy reading.

12.24 Yardstick Report: Comparing Fashion Trunk Show Options (L.O. 5)

Based in New York City, Elizabeth Wilson is the designer and owner of a contemporary women's dress company, Add Dress. She is interested in building her brand and increasing sales revenue through a promotional strategy new to her company, the trunk show. In a trunk show, the designer brings the line to a retailer for a special in-store showing for the store's customers. The designer works with individual customers, educating them about the collection and providing personal fashion consultations. Customers view the full line, rather than the limited number of styles the retail buyer selects within the constraints of an inventory budget.

Although customers will not find every size and color available in each garment style, they can try on garments to find their correct sizes and place orders for the styles that fit their needs. Customers prepay orders and receive the items weeks later. The division of sales revenues in a trunk show is fairly standard. The vendor receives the wholesale price, and the retailer receives the markup, usually double the wholesale price. For example, if a dress retails for $200, Add Dress earns $100, and the store receives $100 when it sells. Costs associated with putting on a trunk show can be large—from mailing invitations to providing refreshments. With costs in mind, Elizabeth evaluates three location options for her first trunk show.

Option 1: A boutique that currently carries the line

Samantha's is a high-end boutique in Dallas, Texas, with a large customer following and sales volume. The store sells Add Dress very well. After asking the owners of Samantha's about their experiences in trunk shows, Elizabeth learned that they have had great success with them, averaging $15,000 in retail sales for two 3-hour trunk showings, afternoon and evening.

Samantha's owners indicate that they cover all in-store costs associated with trunk shows, such as invitations, refreshments, and additional staff. Samantha's also pays half the cost of advertising the trunk show event (e.g., newspaper, magazine, and radio)—which is usually $5,000 in total. The company featured in the trunk show pays the other half. The store owners mention that items from the line used as trunk show "freebies," costing about $500 at wholesale for Add Dress, significantly affect sales. These giveaways can be used to motivate sales associates to bring in their personal clientele, and to entice customers to attend the show and participate in drawings for free merchandise. Finally, the store owners discuss travel expenses. They let Elizabeth know that she is welcome as a guest in one of their homes, eliminating the cost of a hotel. She would, however, pay approximately $500 in airfare through her company to travel to and from Dallas, and another $500 to ship the sample line back and forth. Based on their experience with trunk shows, Samantha's owners estimate that sales would be about $15,000 retail, or $7,500 wholesale.

Option 2: A major specialty store chain that is currently not carrying the line

From the day she opened her company, Elizabeth envisioned her line in Nordstrom, but she has been unable to break into its dress department. A trunk show may open the door. Elizabeth draws up a proposal to sell the trunk show concept to the Nordstrom dress buyer for the fashion retailer's new store opening in New York City. She makes an introductory call, and the buyer is interested in her concept. She learns, however, that the merchandising manager must approve new vendors before Nordstrom can add the line. Elizabeth proposes that, in exchange for a $10,000 wholesale order from Nordstrom, she will present a three-hour Add Dress trunk show. Add Dress will cover all costs of the trunk show: $3,000 for advertising; $1,000 for wholesale giveaway dresses as incentives to draw customers and motivate sales personnel; and $500 for sales associates from her showroom. The trunk show line will incur no shipping costs because the new Nordstrom store is in New York. Elizabeth conservatively estimates that the show will generate $8,000 in retail sales, or $4,000 wholesale.

Option 3: Designer Debut, multiple trunk shows at a retailer

Henri's, a well-known women's apparel store in New York, sponsors an eight-hour Designer Debut at the start of each season. The designers show and sell their lines in booths set up by Henri's in every department of the store. Here Elizabeth could reach new customers, and Henri's may decide to carry the line. Customers order items at designers' booths and prepay at Henri's cash terminals, providing Henri's with an overview of best-selling lines. After the event, designers are paid for the wholesale total of their lines' sales. Elizabeth would incur costs for this event. Designers pay a fee for the booths based on size ($1,000 on average). She will need to pay her showroom personnel for working this weekend event, which would amount to about $1,000. Henri's advertises Designer Debut in a big way; however, Elizabeth wants to purchase a $350 half-page advertisement for Add Dress in the directory handed to each customer who attends. After discussion with the coordinator of Designer Debut, Elizabeth estimates that the show will result in $17,000 in retail sales, or $8,500 wholesale.

YOUR TASK Prepare a decision matrix such as the following. Write a three- to five-page report with your analysis and recommendations, and include your decision matrix in the report.

Decision Matrix

Variables	Samantha's	Nordstrom	Designer Debut at Henri's
Costs a. Booth rental			
b. Advertising			
c. Personnel			
d. Giveaways (wholesale)			
e. Travel and shipping			
TOTAL COSTS			
Sales (wholesale) a. Guaranteed			
b. Estimated			

12.25 Yardstick Report: Selecting the Best Social Media Manager Candidate (L.O. 5)

You have worked long and hard to become the chief marketing officer (CMO) of a global retailer, Fast Fashion, with revenues of over $5 billion. Fast Fashion offers casual and career apparel and accessories at value prices for women ages twenty-five to thirty-five. It operates approximately 3,800 stores in the United States, Europe, Puerto Rico, and Canada.

Because you recognize the growth and future impact of social media, you work with the chief executive officer (CEO) and human resources (HR) director to fund and develop a new position for the company, social media manager. Your goal is to find the perfect candidate to promote the company brand and—as all businesses hope—build customer engagement through social media. With HR, you develop the job description and advertise the job, screen applications, and select three candidates to interview. Although their strengths and weaknesses differ, all three meet the job requirements, have excellent references, and are impressive interviewees. With résumés, interview notes, and the job description in hand, you sit down at your desk to develop a decision matrix and list the pros and cons of each candidate in order to write a report for the CEO, concluding with your recommendation.

Job Description

At Fast Fashion, talented people are our greatest asset. We offer a competitive compensation package and excellent benefits.

Job Title and Overview:

Manager, Social Media—Fast Fashion. The Social Media Manager is responsible for the content and communication strategy across all social platforms—driving brandawareness, increasing product purchases, and promoting the company's image.

Required Qualifications and Functions (Weighted):

- Bachelor's degree in marketing, communication, computer systems, or a related field
- Three years or more of social media marketing work in a multiunit retail company, preferably in apparel (20%)
- Experienced in building an audience on relevant social media channels through daily publishing and recommending of social content and trends based on social listening (40%)
- Demonstrated superb written, verbal, and visual communication; positive, energetic personality; and ability to direct cross-functional teams and juggle multiple projects (20%)
- Strong analytical, organizational, and creative problem-solving skills; able to work with the internal teams on postevent and return-on-investment (ROI) analyses (20%)

Candidate 1: Shawna Jackson

Shawna has a BS degree in mass communication from a state university. She earned a 3.0/4.0 cumulative GPA, worked part-time as night manager in women's apparel at WalMart while in college, and participated in extracurricular volunteer activities in the community provided by student organizations in her major. Since graduating three years ago, Shawna has worked as assistant to the social media director of a national home furnishings retail chain. In the interview Shawna appeared a bit nervous and shy, but warmed up when she showed her portfolio. Her portfolio includes samples of work in a wide range of social media channels, including Facebook, Pinterest, Snapchat, and Instagram. It illustrates her strong written, visual, and technological skills.

Candidate 2: John Andrews

John graduated at the top of his class with a BS degree in computer information systems from a private college. While in college, he worked 30 hours a week in the campus Computer Services Department. Upon graduation, he worked for a major electronics retailer for three years, starting as the technology department manager and moving up to store manager. He left this management position to start his own company, in which he oversaw the marketing of products and services through websites, social media, and text messages. For two years John built his entrepreneurial business and recently sold it. Ready to use his business knowledge in a large corporation, he wants to focus on social media in a corporation that offers opportunities for promotion and growth, and fulfill his desire to run a business. During the interview, John shared his salary history, revealing that he made much more than this position offers. He seems to be a confident and extroverted interviewee.

Candidate 3: Lauren Chin

Lauren earned a BS degree in fashion merchandising from a state university, graduating with a 3.5/4.0 cumulative GPA. She worked in Nordstrom's Executive Trainee Program for two years in apparel merchandising at corporate headquarters. While there, she recognized that she loved her social time online as much as she disliked her time developing and analyzing quantitative merchandising reports. Ready for a change, she returned to college to complete a master's degree in digital media. Lauren worked part-time in apparel retailing chains while in college. For three years she has operated a blog with a growing number of followers. Lauren is active on Facebook, Pinterest, and Instagram. In the interview she appeared relaxed and well versed in using new and growing social media channels.

YOUR TASK Write a memo report of three to five pages. Complete the decision matrix with the weights provided, and include it in your report. No weight is necessary for education, as all candidates fulfill this requirement. For each criterion in the decision matrix, provide one of three rankings for each candidate with a score of 3 as the highest, 2 as the second highest, and 1 for the candidate who ranks the lowest. For example, if you believe Shawna has the highest level of social media marketing experience and Lauren has the lowest level, you would post 3 for Shawna, 2 for John, and 1 for Lauren. Multiply each weight by the ranking, repeat for the other criteria, and then add the results to compute a total. From your decision matrix, draw conclusions and then make recommendations in your yardstick report. Overall, which candidate is best for the position, and why?

Decision Matrix

Candidates	Demonstrated ability to lead teams and to juggle multiple projects (20%)	Quality and quantity of knowledge and work experience in social media (40%)	Strong analytical, organizational, and creative problem-solving skills (20%)	Social media marketing experience with a multiunit retail company (20%)	Total
Shawna Jackson					
John Andrews					
Lauren Chin					

Test Your Etiquette IQ

New communication platforms and casual workplace environments have blurred the lines of appropriateness, leaving workers wondering how to navigate uncharted waters. Indicate whether the following statements are true or false. Then see if you agree with the responses on p. R-2.

1. You're sick and must miss work tomorrow. Because you don't feel well, it's acceptable to text your boss to say you won't be in.

   ________ True ________ False

2. You know that Marisa is out of the office, but you just had a brilliant idea to share with her. You should call and leave a voice-mail message so that she can hear it when she returns.

   ________ True ________ False

3. As a manager, you are upset because your employee Mike is habitually late for meetings. You would like to reprimand him in front of everyone to serve as a lesson, but the better plan is to speak to him privately.

   ________ True ________ False

Grammar and Mechanics | *Review 12*

Total Review

The first nine chapters reviewed specific guides from Appendix D, Grammar and Mechanics Guide. The exercises in this and the remaining chapters are total reviews, covering all of the grammar and mechanics guides plus confusing words and frequently misspelled words.

Each of the following sentences has **three** errors in grammar, punctuation, capitalization, usage, or spelling. On a separate sheet, write a correct version. Avoid adding new phrases, starting new sentences, or rewriting in your own words. When finished, compare your responses with the key beginning on page Key-3.

EXAMPLE: The auditors report, which my boss and myself read closely, contained the following three main flaws, factual inaccuracies, omissions, and incomprehensible language.

REVISION: The **auditor's** report, which my boss and I read closely, contained the following three main **flaws:** factual inaccuracies, omissions, and incomprehensible language.

1. After our supervisor and her returned from their meeting at 2:00 p.m., we were able to sort the customers names more quickly.
2. 6 of the 18 workers in my department were released, as a result we had to work harder to achieve our goals.
3. Toyota, the market-leading japanese carmaker continued to enjoy strong positive ratings despite a string of much publicized recalls.
4. Michaels presentation to a nonprofit group netted him only three hundred dollars, a tenth of his usual honorarium but he believes in pro bono work.
5. To reflect our guiding principals and our commitment to executive education we offer financial support to more than sixty percent of our current MBA candidates.
6. Our latest press release which was written in our Corporate Communication Department announces the opening of three asian offices.
7. In his justification report dated September first, Justin argued that expansion to twelve branch offices could boost annual revenue to 22 million dollars.

8. The practicality and advisability of opening 12 branch offices is what will be discussed in the consultants feasability report.
9. The President, who had went to a meeting in the Midwest, delivered a report to Jeff and I when he returned.
10. Because some organizations prefer single spaced reports be sure to check with your organization to learn it's preference.

References

[1] Starbucks coffee international. (2016). Retrieved from http://www.starbucks.com/business/international-stores; Revenue of selected leading coffeehouse chains worldwide in 2015 (in million U.S. dollars). (2016). Statista. Retrieved from http://www.statista.com/statistics/270091/coffee-house-chains-ranked-by-revenue

[2] Yan, S. (2016, January 12). Starbucks adding 1,400 new shops in China. *CNN Money.* Retrieved from http://money.cnn.com/2016/01/12/investing/starbucks-china-expansion

[3] Kapur, M. (2012, November 9). Interview with Starbucks CEO Howard Schultz. [Transcript of video]. CNN.com. Retrieved from http://transcripts.cnn.com/TRANSCRIPTS/1211/09/ta.01.html

[4] Our mission. (2016). Retrieved from http://www.starbucks.com/about-us/company-information/mission-statement

[5] Krishna, S. (2012, October 25). India's coffee market competition is ferocious: Howard Schultz, Starbucks. *The Economic Times.* Retrieved from http://articles.economictimes.indiatimes.com/2012-10-25/news/34729911_1_starbucks-howard-schultz-tatas

[6] The world's biggest public companies. (2016, May). #389 Starbucks. *Forbes.* Retrieved from http://www.forbes.com/companies/starbucks; Kingsbury, K. (2016, April 22). Starbucks firing on all cylinders, even if its stock isn't. *The Wall Street Journal.* Retrieved from http://blogs.wsj.com/moneybeat/2016/04/22/starbucks-firing-on-all-cylinders-even-if-its-stock-isnt

[7] Dill, K. (2016, March 23). America's best employers 2016. *Forbes.* Retrieved from http://www.forbes.com/sites/kathryndill/2016/03/23/americas-best-employers-2016/#67a96af32d07; Kapur, M. (2012, November 9). Interview with Starbucks CEO Howard Schultz. [Transcript of video]. CNN.com. Retrieved from http://transcripts.cnn.com/TRANSCRIPTS/1211/09/ta.01.html

[8] Morris, K. (2016, April 5). Starbucks to open its largest store in the world in Manhattan. *The Wall Street Journal.* Retrieved from http://www.wsj.com/articles/starbucks-to-open-its-largest-store-in-the-world-in-manhattan-1459884905

[9] Miller, C. C. (2011, March 13). A changed Starbucks. A changed C.E.O. *The New York Times.* Retrieved from http://www.nytimes.com

[10] Wexler, A. (2016, April 21). Starbucks opens first store in South Africa. *The Wall Street Journal.* Retrieved from http://www.wsj.com/articles/starbucks-opens-first-store-in-south-africa-1461239313

[11] Kaplan, J. (2016, May 23). Cold coffee is booming in the U.S. *Bloomberg.* Retrieved from http://www.bloomberg.com/news/articles/2016-05-23/cold-coffee-is-booming-in-the-u-s-now-everyone-is-piling-in

[12] Pritanjali, R. (2014, November 17). What makes Starbucks CEO Howard Schultz so successful? The Motley Fool. Retrieved from http://www.fool.com/investing/general/2014/11/17/what-makes-starbucks-ceo-howard-schultz-so-success.aspx

[13] Pyle, L. S. (2010, September 23). How to do market research—the basics. *Entrepreneur.* Retrieved from https://www.entrepreneur.com/article/217345

[14] Based on Goldin, R. (2015, August 19.) Causation vs correlation. Stats.org. Retrieved from http://www.stats.org/causation-vs-correlation

[15] Cequa, A. (2016, May 14). Fairphone is the ethical smartphone that wants you to rethink mobile technology. *The Huffington Post.* Retrieved from http://www.huffingtonpost.com/the-love-summit/fairphone-is-the-ethical_b_9971666.html; Rigg, J. (2015, September 25). Fairphone delivers on its ethical, modular smartphone. Endgadget. Retrieved from http://www.engadget.com/2015/09/25/fairphone-2; Lütticke, M. (2013, January 24). FairPhone—A smartphone for a good conscience. DW.de. Retrieved from http://www.dw.de/fairphone-a-smartphone-for-a-good-conscience/a-16544455

[16] Quoted in Farmer, L. (2014, October 30). Exit interview with AGA's Relmond Van Daniker. Governing.com. Retrieved from http://www.governing.com/topics/finance/interview-association-government-accountants-relmond-daniker.html

[17] Sisario, B. (2015, May 8). Spotify's revenue is growing, but so are its losses. *The New York Times.* Retrieved from http://www.nytimes.com/2015/05/09/business/media/as-spotify-expands-revenue-rises-and-losses-deepen.html?_r=0

[18] Ashton, R. (n.d.). Top ten writing tips for scientists. Sciencebase. Retrieved from http://www.sciencebase.com/science-blog/writing-tips-for-scientists

[19] Novet, J. (2014, February 11). PayPal chief reams employees: Use our app or quit. VentureBeat. Retrieved from http://venturebeat.com/2014/02/11/paypal-chief-reams-employees-use-our-app-or-quit

[20] Williams, G. C. (2014, June 4). Could Nissan's Smyrna plant become world's largest auto plant? *The Tennessean.* Retrieved from http://www.tennessean.com/story/money/cars/2014/06/04/nissans-smyrna-plant-become-worlds-largest/9955033; Vlasic, B., Tabuchi, H., & Duhigg, C. (2012, August 4). Pursuit of Nissan, a jobs lesson for the tech industry? *The New York Times.* Retrieved from http://www.nytimes.com; Infiniti game on for big 2012. (2012, February 20). Nissan Reports. Retrieved from http://reports.nissan-global.com/EN/?p=3320

[21] Lanks, B. (2015, September 5). Starbucks plans three new kinds of stores. *Bloomberg.* Retrieved from http://www.bloomberg.com/news/articles/2014-09-05/starbucks-will-open-more-drive-throughs-more-high-end-coffeeshops; Ledbetter, C. (2015, April 30). Starbucks launches "express format" for impatient customers. *The Huffington Post.* Retrieved from http://www.huffingtonpost.com/2015/04/30/starbucks-express-shops_n_7182038.html; Wilson, M. (2012, October 8). An experimental new Starbucks store: Tiny, portable, and hyper local. Yahoo Finance. Retrieved from http://finance.yahoo.com/news/an-experimental-new-starbucks-store--tiny--portable--and-hyper-local.html?page=all

[22] Lanks, B. (2015, September 5). Starbucks plans three new kinds of stores. *Bloomberg.* Retrieved from http://www.bloomberg.com/news/articles/2014-09-05/starbucks-will-open-more-drive-throughs-more-high-end-coffeeshops

[23] Rhodes, M. (2015, April 30). Need a quick fix? First express Starbucks lands in NYC. *Wired.* Retrieved from http://www.wired.com/2015/04/need-quick-fix-first-express-starbucks-lands-nyc

[24] Wilson, M. (2012, October 8). An experimental new Starbucks store: Tiny, portable, and hyper local. Yahoo Finance. Retrieved from http://finance.yahoo.com/news/an-experimental-new-starbucks-store--tiny--portable--and-hyper-local.html?page=all

[25] Marcus, A., & Oransky, I. (2015, May 22). What's behind big science frauds? *The New York Times.* Retrieved from http://www.nytimes.com/2015/05/23/opinion/whats-behind-big-science-frauds.html?_r=0

[26] Based on Sommers, S. (2013, January 31). Highlight this blog post at your own risk. *The Huffington Post.* Retrieved from http://www.huffingtonpost.com/sam-sommers/highlight-this-blog-post-_b_2587017.html?utm_hp_ref=education

[27] Fleming, W. (2016, January 10). BMW Motorrad USA posts record sales for 2015. BMW Motorcycle Owners of America. Retrieved from http://www.bmwmoa.org/news/268738/BMW-Motorrad-USA-posts-record-sales-for-2015.htm; BMW Motorrad sets third quarter sales record. *Cycle World.* Retrieved from http://www.cycleworld.com/2015/10/08/bmw-motorrad-sets-third-quarter-sales-record

[28] BMW Motorrad rolls boldly into the future. (n.d.). SIS International Research. Retrieved from https://www.sisinternational.com/bmw-motorrad-future

[29] Harley-Davidson reports fourth quarter and full-year 2015 results. (2016, January 28). PR Newswire. Retrieved from http://www.prnewswire.com/news-releases/harley-davidson-reports-fourth-quarter-and-full-year-2015-results-300211052.html

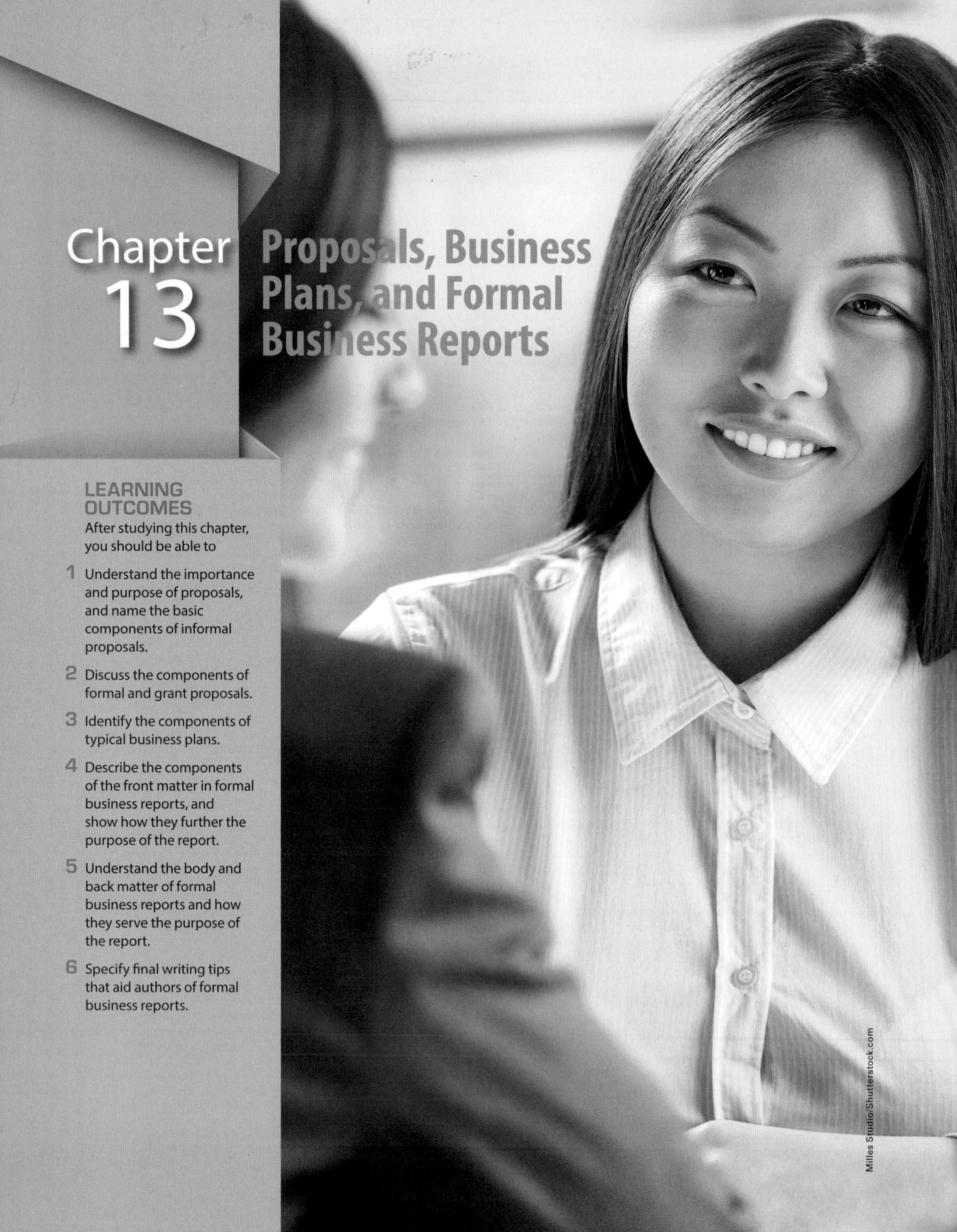

Chapter 13 Proposals, Business Plans, and Formal Business Reports

LEARNING OUTCOMES

After studying this chapter, you should be able to

1. Understand the importance and purpose of proposals, and name the basic components of informal proposals.
2. Discuss the components of formal and grant proposals.
3. Identify the components of typical business plans.
4. Describe the components of the front matter in formal business reports, and show how they further the purpose of the report.
5. Understand the body and back matter of formal business reports and how they serve the purpose of the report.
6. Specify final writing tips that aid authors of formal business reports.

Milles Studio/Shutterstock.com

SpaceX Soars on the Wings of its Proposals

Yeamake/Shutterstock.com

Founded in 2002, Space Exploration Technologies Corporation, known simply as SpaceX, has quickly become a nimble player in the challenging and capital-intensive aerospace industry. With only 4,000 employees, the Hawthorne, California–based company has in some respects surged ahead of much larger competitors such as Boeing, winning government contracts with NASA worth billions.[1] Led by its charismatic founder, Elon Musk, SpaceX has secured the most missions to resupply the International Space Station (ISS) at least through 2024. Several U.S. commercial contractors are vying for a NASA budget for ISS missions of $14 billion over the next decade.

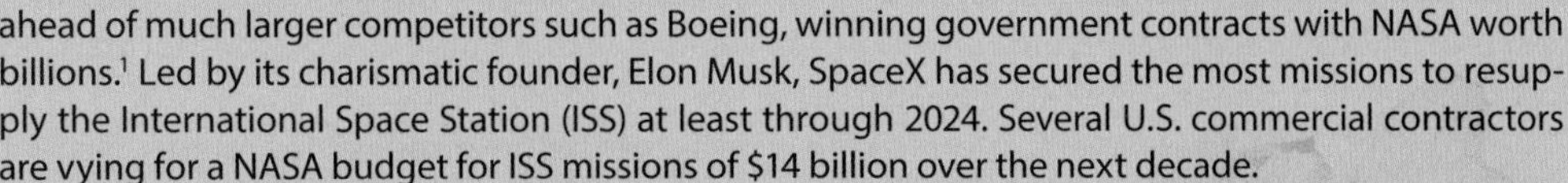

Elon Musk, who also cofounded PayPal and Solar City and simultaneously runs Tesla Motors, is a relentless, hard-driving boss. An extraordinary mind, Musk is infamous for putting in 100+ work hours a week and sleeping in his office when his company must solve problems or meet deadlines. He exhibits a fierce, crushing temper and expects unflagging commitment from his many brilliant engineers. He famously said to his employees who routinely work 80-hour weeks: "Not enough of you are working on Saturdays."[2] Considered by many a real-life Iron Man, Musk is an inventor and business magnate known for his bold vision of the future, most prominently of space travel to Mars to establish a presence on the Red Planet.

One of the greatest triumphs for SpaceX came when the company secured a groundbreaking deal to develop a spacecraft to ferry astronauts to the ISS again, thus ending the sole reliance of the United States on Russian launches. Boeing was awarded $4.2 billion and SpaceX received $2.6 billion, each to develop what NASA calls a "differently redundant" space taxi to lower technical risk and keep a lid on costs with fixed-price deals. SpaceX is known for being an efficient, low-cost supplier.[3] But how was SpaceX able to win such well-funded contracts? Certainly, the company's breakthrough technical expertise is one factor. However, its strict adherence to the space agency's rigorous RFP standards and killer proposals have clinched the lucrative deals.

Such success is the culmination of lengthy, intense effort, as one of the many NASA requests for proposals makes clear: "Each task has milestones with specified amounts and performance dates. Each mission requires complex preparation and several years of lead time."[4]

Critical Thinking

- Why are proposals vitally important to a company such as SpaceX?
- How are proposals at SpaceX similar to and different from proposals or long reports written by students?
- How can team members maintain consistency and meet deadlines when writing important, time-constrained, multivolume documents such as formal proposals?

Writing Informal Proposals

LEARNING OUTCOME 1
Understand the importance and purpose of proposals, and name the basic components of informal proposals.

Proposals can mean life or death for an organization. Why are they so important? Let's begin by defining what they are. A *proposal* may be defined as a written offer to solve a problem, provide a service, or sell equipment. Profit-making organizations, such as SpaceX, depend on proposals to compete for business. A well-written proposal can generate millions of dollars of income. Smaller organizations also depend on proposals to sell their products and services. Equally dependent on proposals are many nonprofit organizations. Their funding depends on grant proposals, to be discussed shortly.

Some proposals are internal, often taking the form of justification and recommendation reports. You learned about these persuasive reports in Chapter 12. Most proposals, however, are external, such as those written at SpaceX. These proposals respond to requests for proposals (RFPs). When government organizations or businesses know exactly what they want, they prepare a *request for proposals* (RFP), specifying their requirements. Government agencies such as NASA as well as private businesses use RFPs to solicit competitive bids from vendors. RFPs ensure that bids are comparable and that funds are awarded fairly, using consistent criteria.

Proposals may be further divided into two categories: solicited and unsolicited. Most proposals are solicited. For example, the city of Philadelphia published an 87-page RFP seeking proposal bids for 24/7 audio and video programming at its international airport, PHL. Applicants were to submit plans for installing equipment and providing content.[5] Enterprising companies looking for work or a special challenge might submit an unsolicited proposal. For example, the Center for the Advancement of Science in Space (CASIS), which runs the International Space

Station U.S. National Laboratory, welcomes innovative unsolicited proposals to develop groundbreaking technologies and products.[6] Although many kinds of proposals exist, we'll focus on informal, formal, and grant proposals.

Components of Informal Proposals

Informal proposals may be presented in manuscript format (usually no more than ten pages) with a cover page, or they may take the form of short (two- to four-page) letters. Sometimes called *letter proposals*, they usually contain six principal components: introduction, background, proposal, staffing, budget, and authorization. As you can see in Figure 13.1, both informal and formal proposals contain these six basic parts.

Figure 13.2 illustrates a letter proposal to a Texas dentist who sought to improve patient satisfaction. Notice that it contains all six components of an informal proposal.

Introduction. Most proposals begin by briefly explaining the reasons for the proposal and highlighting the writer's qualifications. To make your introduction more persuasive, you should strive to provide a hook, such as the following:

- Hint at extraordinary results with details to be revealed shortly.
- Promise low costs or speedy results.
- Mention a remarkable resource (well-known authority, new computer program, well-trained staff) available exclusively to you.
- Identify a serious problem (worry item) and promise a solution, to be explained later.
- Specify a key issue or benefit that you feel is the heart of the proposal.

Figure 13.1 **Components of Informal and Formal Proposals**

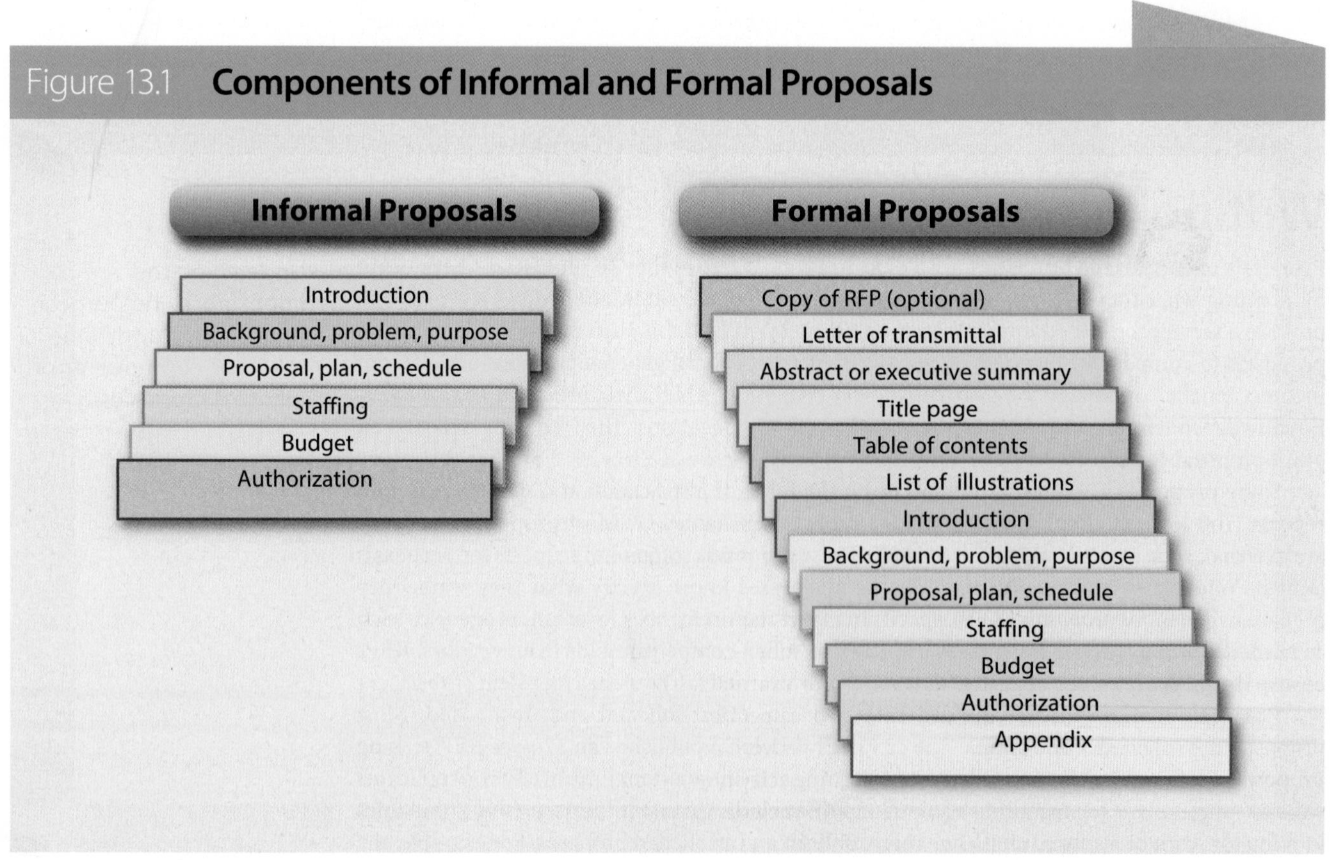

Reality Check

Combating Writer's Block

"To conquer writer's block, begin with a bulleted list of what the customer is looking for. The list is like a road map; it gets you started and keeps you headed in the right direction."[7]

—Mary Piecewicz, *former Hewlett-Packard proposal manager*

Although writers may know what goes into the proposal introduction, many face writer's block before they get started. Proposal expert Tom Sant recommends a method he calls *cognitive webbing* to overcome the paralyzing effects of writer's block and arrive at a proposal writing plan. Dr. Sant tells proposal writers to (a) identify the outcome the client seeks, (b) brainstorm by writing down every idea and detail that will help the client achieve that objective, and (c) prioritize by focusing on the client's most pressing needs.[8] You may have brainstormed using a similar technique, sometimes called *mind mapping*, to generate ideas for your papers. Like brainstorming, mind mapping involves generating ideas around a single word and grouping those ideas into major and minor categories, thus creating a web of relationships.

In the proposal introduction shown in Figure 13.2, Ronald Bridger focused on what the customer wanted. The researcher analyzed the request of Texas dentist Louisa Canto and decided that she was most interested in specific recommendations for improving service to her patients. However, Ron did not hit on this hook until he had written a first draft and had come back to it later. It's not a bad idea to put off writing the proposal introduction until after you have completed other parts. In longer proposals the introduction also describes the scope and limitations of the project, as well as outlining the organization of the material to come.

Background, Problem, and Purpose. The background section identifies the problem and discusses the goals or purposes of the project. In an unsolicited proposal, your goal is to convince the reader that a problem exists. Therefore, you must present the problem in detail, discussing such factors as revenue losses, failure to comply with government regulations, or loss of customers. In a solicited proposal, your aim is to persuade the reader that you understand the problem completely and that you have a realistic solution. If you are responding to an RFP, follow the requirements precisely, and use the company's language in your description of the problem. For example, if the RFP asks for the *design of a maintenance program for wireless communication equipment*, don't call it a *customer service program for wireless products*. The background section might include segments titled *Statement of Need, Basic Requirements, Most Critical Tasks*, or *Important Secondary Problems*.

Proposal, Plan, and Schedule. In the proposal section itself, you should discuss your plan for solving the problem. In some proposals this is tricky because you want to disclose enough of your plan to secure the contract without giving away so much information that your services aren't needed. Without specifics, though, your proposal has little chance, so you must decide how much to reveal.

The proposal section often includes the implementation plan. If research is involved, state what methods you will use to gather the data. Remember to be persuasive by showing how your methods and products will benefit the reader. For example, show how the initial investment will pay off later. The proposal might even promise specific *deliverables*—tangible items your project will produce for the customer. A proposal deliverable might be a new website design or an online marketing plan. To add credibility, also specify how the project will be managed and how its progress will be audited. Most writers also include a schedule or timetable of activities showing the proposal's benchmarks for completion.

Figure 13.2 Informal Letter Proposal

1 Prewriting

Analyze: The purpose of this letter proposal is to persuade the reader to accept this proposal.

Anticipate: The reader expects this proposal but must be convinced that this survey project is worth its hefty price.

Adapt: Because the reader will be resistant at first, use a persuasive approach that emphasizes benefits.

2 Drafting

Research: Collect data about the reader's practice and other surveys of patient satisfaction.

Organize: Identify four specific purposes (benefits) of this proposal. Specify the survey plan. Promote the staff, itemize the budget, and ask for approval.

Draft: Prepare a first draft, expecting to improve it later.

3 Revising

Edit: Revise to emphasize benefits. Improve readability with functional headings and lists. Remove jargon and wordiness.

Proofread: Check spelling of client's name. Verify dates and calculation of budget figures. Recheck all punctuation.

Evaluate: Is this proposal convincing enough to sell the client?

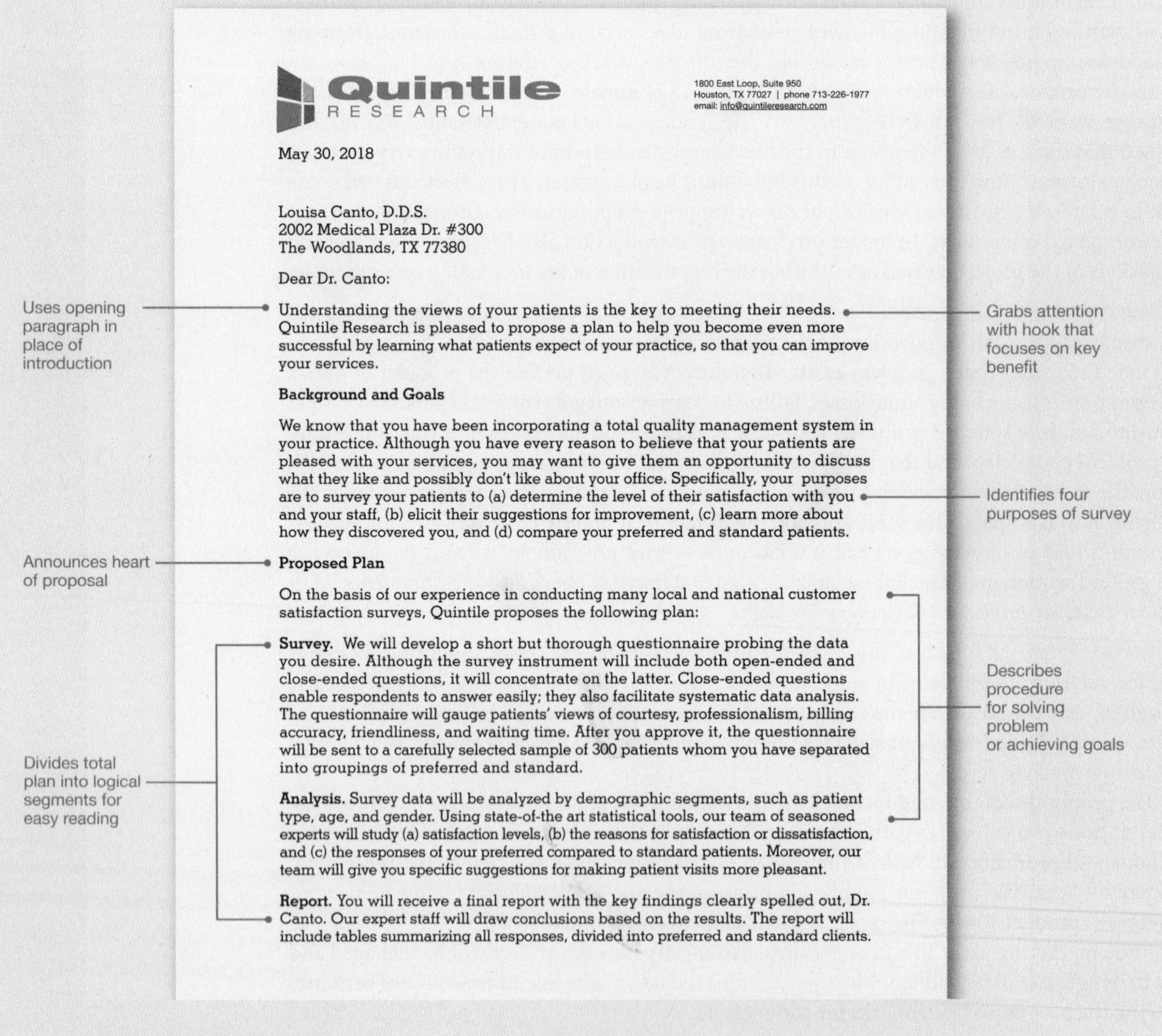

Quintile RESEARCH

1800 East Loop, Suite 950
Houston, TX 77027 | phone 713-226-1977
email: info@quintileresearch.com

May 30, 2018

Louisa Canto, D.D.S.
2002 Medical Plaza Dr. #300
The Woodlands, TX 77380

Dear Dr. Canto:

Understanding the views of your patients is the key to meeting their needs. Quintile Research is pleased to propose a plan to help you become even more successful by learning what patients expect of your practice, so that you can improve your services.

Background and Goals

We know that you have been incorporating a total quality management system in your practice. Although you have every reason to believe that your patients are pleased with your services, you may want to give them an opportunity to discuss what they like and possibly don't like about your office. Specifically, your purposes are to survey your patients to (a) determine the level of their satisfaction with you and your staff, (b) elicit their suggestions for improvement, (c) learn more about how they discovered you, and (d) compare your preferred and standard patients.

Proposed Plan

On the basis of our experience in conducting many local and national customer satisfaction surveys, Quintile proposes the following plan:

Survey. We will develop a short but thorough questionnaire probing the data you desire. Although the survey instrument will include both open-ended and close-ended questions, it will concentrate on the latter. Close-ended questions enable respondents to answer easily; they also facilitate systematic data analysis. The questionnaire will gauge patients' views of courtesy, professionalism, billing accuracy, friendliness, and waiting time. After you approve it, the questionnaire will be sent to a carefully selected sample of 300 patients whom you have separated into groupings of preferred and standard.

Analysis. Survey data will be analyzed by demographic segments, such as patient type, age, and gender. Using state-of-the art statistical tools, our team of seasoned experts will study (a) satisfaction levels, (b) the reasons for satisfaction or dissatisfaction, and (c) the responses of your preferred compared to standard patients. Moreover, our team will give you specific suggestions for making patient visits more pleasant.

Report. You will receive a final report with the key findings clearly spelled out, Dr. Canto. Our expert staff will draw conclusions based on the results. The report will include tables summarizing all responses, divided into preferred and standard clients.

Uses opening paragraph in place of introduction
Grabs attention with hook that focuses on key benefit
Identifies four purposes of survey
Announces heart of proposal
Describes procedure for solving problem or achieving goals
Divides total plan into logical segments for easy reading

Figure 13.2 (Continued)

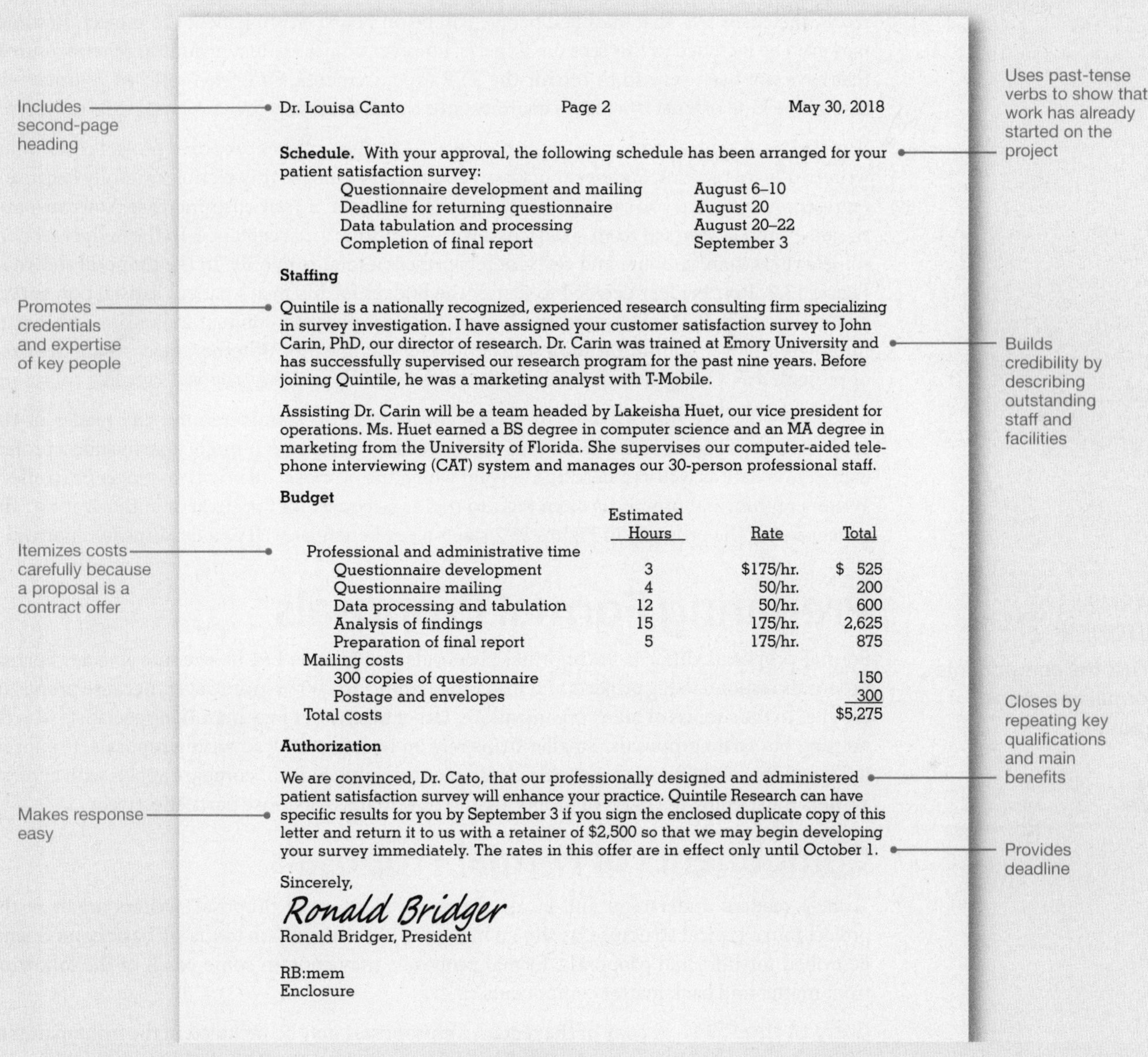
Includes second-page heading
Uses past-tense verbs to show that work has already started on the project
Promotes credentials and expertise of key people
Builds credibility by describing outstanding staff and facilities
Itemizes costs carefully because a proposal is a contract offer
Closes by repeating key qualifications and main benefits
Makes response easy
Provides deadline

Dr. Louisa Canto Page 2 May 30, 2018

Schedule. With your approval, the following schedule has been arranged for your patient satisfaction survey:

Questionnaire development and mailing	August 6–10
Deadline for returning questionnaire	August 20
Data tabulation and processing	August 20–22
Completion of final report	September 3

Staffing

Quintile is a nationally recognized, experienced research consulting firm specializing in survey investigation. I have assigned your customer satisfaction survey to John Carin, PhD, our director of research. Dr. Carin was trained at Emory University and has successfully supervised our research program for the past nine years. Before joining Quintile, he was a marketing analyst with T-Mobile.

Assisting Dr. Carin will be a team headed by Lakeisha Huet, our vice president for operations. Ms. Huet earned a BS degree in computer science and an MA degree in marketing from the University of Florida. She supervises our computer-aided telephone interviewing (CAT) system and manages our 30-person professional staff.

Budget

	Estimated Hours	Rate	Total
Professional and administrative time			
Questionnaire development	3	$175/hr.	$ 525
Questionnaire mailing	4	50/hr.	200
Data processing and tabulation	12	50/hr.	600
Analysis of findings	15	175/hr.	2,625
Preparation of final report	5	175/hr.	875
Mailing costs			
300 copies of questionnaire			150
Postage and envelopes			300
Total costs			$5,275

Authorization

We are convinced, Dr. Cato, that our professionally designed and administered patient satisfaction survey will enhance your practice. Quintile Research can have specific results for you by September 3 if you sign the enclosed duplicate copy of this letter and return it to us with a retainer of $2,500 so that we may begin developing your survey immediately. The rates in this offer are in effect only until October 1.

Sincerely,

Ronald Bridger

Ronald Bridger, President

RB:mem
Enclosure

Reality Check

What About Intellectual Theft?

"You may fear that revealing your ideas about how to solve a problem during the proposal process could result in clients taking those ideas and completing the project themselves. In rare cases, that may happen. But you'll have more success if you don't hoard your ideas."[9]

—Michael W. McLaughlin, *consultant and coauthor of* Guerilla Marketing for Consultants

13Imagery/Shutterstock.com

Staffing. The staffing section of a proposal describes the staff qualifications for implementing the proposal as well as the credentials and expertise of the project leaders. In other words, it attests to the size and qualifications of the staff. The staffing section is a good place to endorse and promote your staff and to demonstrate to the client that your company can do the job. As a result, the client sees that qualified people will be on board to implement the project. Résumés may even be included in this section. Experts, however, advise against including generic résumés that have not been revised to mirror the RFP's requirements. Only well-tailored résumés will inspire the kind of trust in a team's qualifications that is necessary for a proposal to be accepted.[10]

Budget. A central item in most proposals is the budget, a list of proposed project costs. Some writers title this section *Statement of Costs*. You need to prepare this section carefully because it represents a contract; you cannot raise the price later—even if your costs increase. You can—and should—protect yourself from rising costs with a deadline for acceptance. In the budget section, some writers itemize hours and costs; others present a total sum only. In the proposal shown in Figure 13.2, Ron Bridger decided to justify the budget for his firm's patient satisfaction survey by itemizing the costs. However, the budget for a proposal to conduct a one-day seminar to improve employee communication skills might be a lump sum. Whether the costs are itemized or presented as a lump sum depends on the reader's needs and the proposal's goals.

Conclusion and Authorization. The closing section should remind the reader of the proposal's key benefits and make it easy for the reader to respond. It might also include a project completion date as well as a deadline beyond which the proposal offer will no longer be in effect. Writers of informal proposals often refer to this as a request for approval or authorization. The conclusion of the proposal in Figure 13.2 states a key benefit as well as a deadline for approval.

LEARNING OUTCOME 2

Discuss the components of formal and grant proposals.

Preparing Formal Proposals

Formal proposals differ from informal proposals not in style but in size and format. Formal proposals respond to big projects and may range from 5 to 200 or more pages. Because proposals are vital to the success of many organizations, larger businesses may maintain specialists who do nothing but write proposals. Smaller firms rely on in-house staff to write proposals. Proposals use standard components that enable companies receiving bids to "compare apples with apples." Writers must know the parts of proposals and how to develop those parts effectively.

Components of Formal Proposals

To help readers understand and locate the parts of a formal proposal, writers organize the project into a typical structure, as shown in Figure 13.1. In addition to the six basic components described for informal proposals, formal proposals may contain some or all of the following front matter and back matter components.

Copy of the RFP. A copy of the request for proposals may be included in the front matter of a formal proposal. Large organizations may have more than one RFP circulating, in which case identification is necessary.

Letter of Transmittal. A letter of transmittal, usually bound inside formal proposals, addresses the person who is designated to receive the proposal or who will make the final decision. The letter describes how you learned about the problem or confirms that the proposal responds to the enclosed RFP. This persuasive letter briefly presents the major features and benefits of your proposal. Here, you should assure the reader that you are authorized to make the bid and mention the time limit for which the bid stands. You may also offer to provide additional information and ask for action, if appropriate.

Abstract or Executive Summary. An abstract is a brief summary (typically one page) of a proposal's highlights intended for specialists or technical readers. An executive summary also reviews the proposal's highlights, but it is written for managers and should be less technically oriented. An executive summary tends to be longer than an abstract, up to 10 percent of the original text. In reports and proposals, the executive summary typically represents a nutshell version of the entire document and addresses all its sections or chapters. Formal proposals may contain either an abstract or an executive summary, or both. For more information about writing executive summaries and abstracts, use a search engine such as Google.

Title Page. The title page includes the following items, generally in this order: title of proposal, name of client organization, RFP number or other announcement, date of submission, and the authors' names and/or the name of their organization.

Table of Contents. Because most proposals don't contain an index, the table of contents becomes quite important. A table of contents should include all headings and their beginning page numbers. Items that appear before the contents (copy of RFP, letter of transmittal, abstract, and title page) typically are not listed in the contents. However, any appendixes should be listed.

List of Illustrations. Proposals with many tables and figures often contain a list of illustrations. This list includes each figure or table title and its page number. If you have just a few figures or tables, however, you may omit this list.

Appendix(es). Ancillary material of interest to only some readers goes in appendixes. Appendix A might include résumés of the principal investigators or testimonial letters. Appendix B might include examples or a listing of previous projects. Other appendixes could include audit procedures, technical graphics, or professional papers cited in the body of the proposal.

Grant Proposals

A *grant proposal* is a formal proposal submitted to a government or civilian organization that explains a project, outlines its budget, and requests money in the form of a grant. Every year the U.S. government, private foundations, and public corporations make available billions of dollars in funding for special projects. These funds, or grants, require no repayment, but the funds must be used for the purposes outlined in the proposal. Grants are often made to charities, educational facilities, and especially to nonprofits. Securing funding can mean life or death for nonprofits and other organizations.

Organizations such as McDonald's offer millions of dollars in grants to support health care. This past year some of the many grants from Ronald McDonald House Charities focused on medical projects in Burma, Vietnam, Cambodia, and Uganda as well as other African countries, but also on kindergarten readiness and mental health benefiting children in the United States. The Burma Humanitarian Mission provided training and equipment for backpack medics who administer health care services to 14,000 children annually in conflict zones.[11]

Stephane Bidouze/Shutterstock.com

Ronald McDonald House Charities provided a grant to Seva Foundation to prevent blindness in and restore sight to 32,000 Cambodian children through community-based eye care education and medical eye services.

Many of the parts of a grant proposal are similar to those of a formal proposal. A grant proposal includes an abstract and a needs statement that explains a problem or situation that the grant project proposes to address. The body of the proposal explains that the problem is significant enough to warrant funding and that the proposal can solve the problem. The body also describes short- and long-term goals, which must be reasonable, measurable, and attainable within a specific time frame. An action plan tells what will be done by whom and when. The budget outlines how the money will be spent. Finally, a grant proposal presents a plan for measuring progress toward completion of its goal.

Skilled grant writers are among the most in-demand professionals today. A grant writer is the vital connecting link between a funder and the grant seeker. Large projects may require a team of writers to produce various sections of a grant proposal. Then one person does the final editing and proofreading. Effective grant proposals require careful organization, planning, and writing. Skillful writing is particularly important because funding organizations may receive thousands of applications for a single award.

Well-written proposals win contracts and sustain the business life of many companies, individuals, and nonprofit organizations. The following checklist summarizes key elements to remember in writing proposals.

CHECKLIST

Writing Proposals

Introduction

- **Indicate the purpose.** Specify why you are making the proposal.
- **Develop a persuasive hook.** Suggest excellent results, low costs, or exclusive resources. Identify a serious problem, or name a key issue or benefit.

Background, Problem, and Purpose

- **Provide the necessary background.** Discuss the significance of the proposal and the goals or purposes that matter to the client.
- **Introduce the problem.** For unsolicited proposals convince the reader that a problem exists. For solicited proposals show that you fully understand the customer's problem and its ramifications.

Proposal, Plan, and Schedule

- **Explain the proposal.** Present your plan for solving the problem or meeting the need.
- **Discuss plan management and evaluation.** If appropriate, tell how the plan will be implemented and evaluated.
- **Outline a timetable.** Furnish a schedule showing what will be done and when.

Staffing

- **Promote the qualifications of your staff.** Explain the specific credentials and expertise of the key personnel for the project.
- **Mention special resources and equipment.** Show how your support staff and resources are superior to those of the competition.

Budget

- **Show project costs.** For most projects itemize costs. Remember, however, that proposals are contracts.
- **Include a deadline.** Here or in the conclusion, present a date beyond which the bid figures are no longer valid.

Authorization

- **Ask for approval.** Make it easy for the reader to authorize the project (for example, *Sign and return the enclosed duplicate copy*).

LEARNING OUTCOME 3

Identify the components of typical business plans.

Creating Effective Business Plans

Another form of proposal is a business plan. Let's say you want to start your own business. Unless you can count on the Bank of Mom and Dad, you will need financial backing such as a bank loan, seed money from an individual angel investor, or funds supplied by venture capitalists. A business plan is critical for securing financial support of any kind. Such a plan also ensures that you have done your homework and know what you are doing in launching your business. It provides you with a detailed road map to chart a course to success.

Creating a business plan for an entirely new concept takes time. Estimates range from 100 to 200 hours.[12] Consultants can probably do it in less time, but they may be pricey with hourly rates ranging from $50 to $150 or more; some professional writers offer flat rates starting at $400 to $1,000, but the cost can add up to as much as $15,000.[13] Budding entrepreneurs often prefer to save the cash and do it themselves. Classic software such as Business Plan Pro or top-rated LivePlan can help those who have done their research and assembled the relevant data, and just want formatting help. Enloop, a free business plan app, makes it quick and easy to provide a financial forecast for bankers and investors.[14] However, no business plan app can provide a cookie-cutter plan that works for everyone.

Components of Typical Business Plans

For people who are serious about starting a business, the importance of a comprehensive, thoughtful business plan cannot be overemphasized, says the Small Business Administration. A *business plan* may be defined as a description of a proposed company that explains how it expects to achieve its marketing, financial, and operational goals. If you are considering becoming an entrepreneur, your business plan is more likely to secure the funds it needs if it is carefully written and includes the following elements.

Stephen Nellis/Business Times photo

Every year, young entrepreneurs participating in the New Venture Competition offered at the University of California, Santa Barbara, work with local business mentors in the hope of winning up to $40,000 in cash and the chance to launch their business. Students make 60- to 90-second elevator pitches and write comprehensive business plans. Using persuasive writing techniques reinforced with research and data, the business plans include sections that describe the idea, analyze the market situation, and project income. Past competition winners have started successful companies including Phone Halo, which produces a tracking device, and Inogen, a firm that created and markets a compact oxygen delivery system. Why is the executive summary often the most important section of a business plan?[15]

Letter of Transmittal. A letter of transmittal provides contact information for all principals and explains your reason for writing. If you are seeking venture capital or an angel investor, the transmittal letter may become a pitch letter. In that case you would want to include a simple description of your idea and a clear statement of what's in it for the investor. The letter should include a summary of the market, a brief note about the competition, and an explanation of why your business is worthy of investment.

Mission Statement. A business plan mission statement explains the purpose of your business and why it will succeed. Because potential investors will be looking for this mission statement, consider highlighting it with a paragraph heading (*Mission Statement*) or use bolding or italics. Some consultants say that you should be able to write your mission statement in eight or fewer words.[16] Others think that one or two short paragraphs might be more realistic. Many Fortune 500 companies have created mission statements that are both inspirational and concrete. For example, Starbucks states its mission simply but graphically: "To inspire and nurture the human spirit—one person, one cup and one neighborhood at a time." As illustrated in Figure 13.3, mission statements should be simple, concise, memorable, and unique.

© Tim Berry

Reality Check

Why You Need to Write Your Own Business Plan

"The best business plan is one you do yourself. . . . Consider hiring somebody from the outside only if you have the budget for it. . . . Cheap business plan writing strikes me as about as good an idea as cheap surgery, cheap dentistry, or discount sushi."[17]

—Tim Berry, *founder and chairman of Palo Alto Software, maker of Business Plan Pro*

Executive Summary. Your executive summary, which is written last, highlights the main points of your business plan and should not exceed two pages. It should conclude by introducing the parts of the plan and asking for financial backing. Some business plans combine the mission statement and executive summary.

Figure 13.3 Creating Winning Mission Statements

Definition

A mission statement describes the reason an organization or program exists.

GOALS should be:

- Easily understood
- Free of complex words and buzz words
- Concise, memorable, and simple
- Unique in distinguishing a business or program

QUESTIONS TO PONDER

What do we do?

Why and how do we serve our clients?

What image do we want to convey?

Why did we start this business?

What is the broadest way to describe our work?

EXAMPLES

Nonprofit Organizations

Wounded Warrior Project: To honor and empower wounded warriors

The Humane Society: Celebrating Animals, Confronting Cruelty

Charity Water: We're a nonprofit organization bringing clean, safe drinking water to people in developing countries.

Make-A-Wish: We grant the wishes of children with life-threatening medical conditions to enrich the human experience with hope, strength and joy.

Fortune 500 Companies

Nike: To bring inspiration and innovation to every athlete in the world

ADM: To unlock the potential of nature to improve the quality of life

Gap, Inc. is a brand-builder. We create emotional connections with customers around the world through inspiring product design, unique store experiences, and compelling marketing.

Amazon: To be the most customer-centric company in the world, where people can find and discover anything they want to buy online

Table of Contents and Company Description. List the page numbers and topics included in your plan. Identify the form of your business (proprietorship, partnership, or corporation) and its type (merchandising, manufacturing, or service). For existing companies, describe the company's founding, growth, sales, and profit.

Product or Service Description. In jargon-free language, explain what you are providing, how it will benefit customers, and why it is better than existing products or services. For startups, explain why the business will be profitable. Investors aren't always looking for a unique product or service. Instead, they are searching for a concept whose growth potential distinguishes it from others competing for funds.

Market Analysis. Discuss market characteristics, trends, projected growth, customer behavior, complementary products and services, and barriers to entry. Identify your customers and how you will attract, hold, and increase your market share. Discuss the strengths and weaknesses of your direct and indirect competitors.

Operations and Management. Explain specifically how you will run your business, including location, equipment, personnel, and management. Highlight experienced and well-trained members of the management team and your advisors. Many investors consider this the most important factor in assessing business potential. Can your management team implement this business plan?

Financial Analysis. Outline a realistic startup budget that includes fees for legal and professional services, occupancy, licenses and permits, equipment, insurance, supplies, advertising and promotions, salaries and wages, accounting, income, and utilities. Also present an operating budget that projects costs for personnel, insurance, rent, depreciation, loan payments, salaries, taxes, repairs, and so on. Explain how much money you have, how much you will need to start up, and how much you will need to stay in business.

Appendixes. Provide necessary extras such as managers' résumés, promotional materials, and product photos in appendixes. Most appendixes contain tables that exhibit the sales forecast, a personnel plan, anticipated cash flow, profit and loss, and a balance sheet.

Ethics Check

Honesty Is Key

A business plan's purpose is to help manage a company and raise capital; hence, it is a persuasive document that must be accurate and honest. Whether the goal is to persuade a lender or investors or whether it is the blueprint for running operations, the business plan must be realistic. What are the risks of fudging numbers or sugarcoating potential challenges?

Sample Business Plans on the Web

Writing a business plan is easier if you can see examples and learn from experts' suggestions. On the Web you will find many sites devoted to business plans. Some sites want to sell you something; others offer free advice. One of the best sites, that of Palo Alto Software (**http://www.bplans.com/samples/sba.php**), does try to sell business plans and software. However, in addition to useful advice and blogs from experts, the site provides over 100 free samples of business plans ranging from aircraft rental to wedding consultant businesses. These simple but helpful plans illustrate diverse business startups.

At the Small Business Administration (SBA) site (**http://www.sba.gov/business-plan/1**), you will find more business plan advice. By registering with the SBA, you can access an eight-step plan for building a business plan. The SBA site provides helpful business startup information about financing, marketing, employees, taxes, and legal matters. Regardless of how good your business plan ends up being, experts emphasize that business plans are living documents and must be revised periodically or they become "old and useless."[18]

Writing Formal Business Reports

LEARNING OUTCOME 4

Describe the components of the front matter in formal business reports, and show how they further the purpose of the report.

A *formal report* may be defined as a document in which a writer analyzes findings, draws conclusions, and makes recommendations intended to solve a problem. Formal business reports are similar to formal proposals in length, organization, and tone. Instead of making an offer, however, formal reports represent the product of thorough investigation and analysis. They present ordered information to decision makers in business, industry, government, and education. In many ways formal business reports are extended versions of the analytical business reports presented in Chapter 12. If you are preparing a formal business report, be sure to review the work plan that appears in Figure 11.6 in Chapter 11.

Informal and formal business reports have similar components, as shown in Figure 13.4, but, as might be expected, formal reports have more sections.

Front Matter Components of Formal Business Reports

A number of front matter and back matter items lengthen formal reports but enhance their professional tone and serve their multiple audiences. Formal reports may be read by many

Figure 13.4 **Components of Informal and Formal Reports**

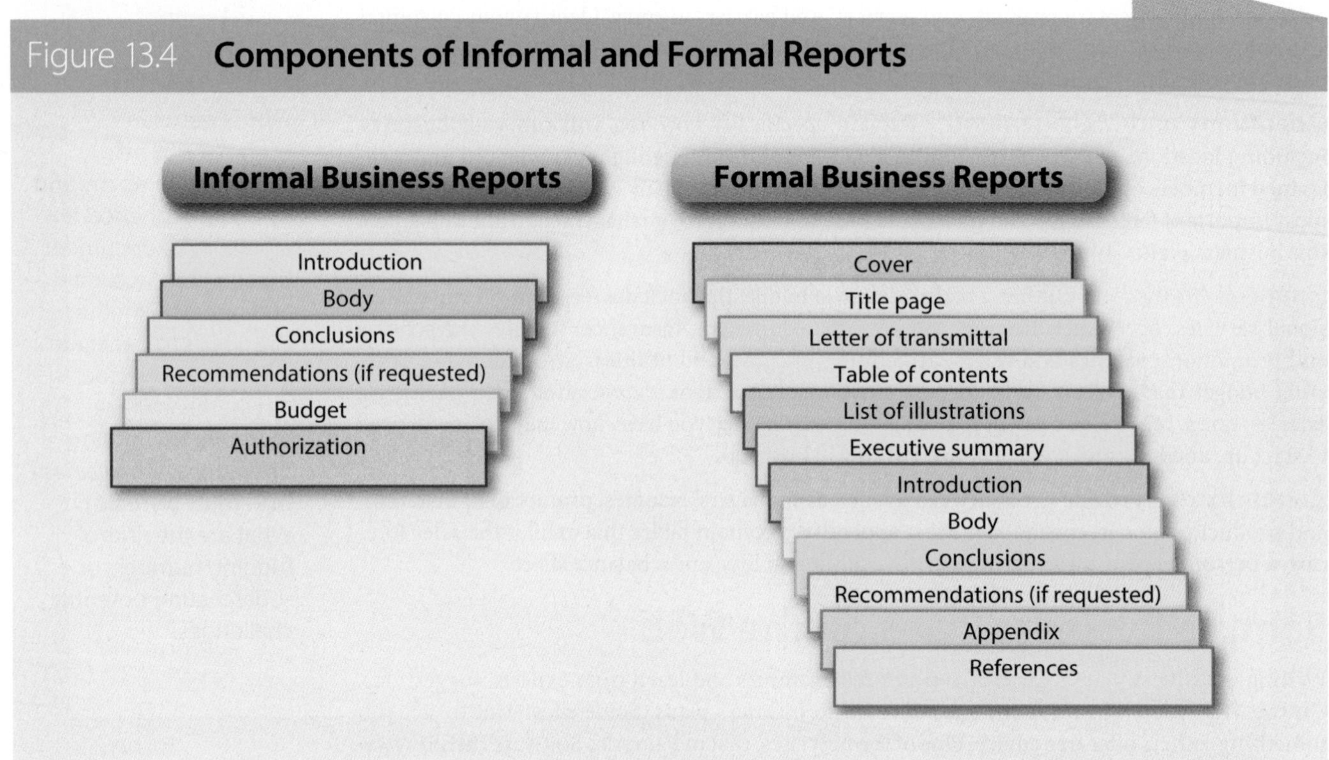

levels of managers, along with technical specialists and financial consultants. Therefore, breaking a long, formal report into small segments makes its information more accessible and easier to understand for all readers. The segments in the front of the report, called front matter or preliminaries, are discussed in this section. They are also illustrated in Figure 13.5, the model formal report shown later in the chapter. This analytical report studies the economic impact of an industrial park on Flagstaff, Arizona, and recommends increasing the city's revenues.

Cover. Traditional formal reports are usually enclosed in vinyl or heavy paper binders to protect the pages and to create a professional, finished appearance. Some companies have binders imprinted with their name and logo. The title of the report may appear through a cut-out window or may be applied with an adhesive label. Formal reports provided digitally may present an attractive title with the company logo.

Title Page. A report title page, as illustrated in the Figure 13.5 model report, begins with the name of the report typed in uppercase letters (no underscore and no quotation marks). Next comes *Presented to* (or *Submitted to*) and the name, title, and organization of the individual receiving the report. Lower on the page is *Prepared by* (or *Submitted by*) and the author's name plus any necessary identification. The last item on the title page is the date of submission. All items after the title are typed in a combination of upper- and lowercase letters.

Letter or Memo of Transmittal. Generally written on organization stationery, a letter or memorandum of transmittal introduces a formal report. You will recall that letters are sent to external audiences; and memos, to internal audiences. A transmittal letter or memo uses the direct strategy and is usually less formal than the report itself (for example, the letter or memo may use contractions and the first-person pronouns *I* and *we*). The transmittal letter or memo typically (a) announces the topic of the report and tells how it was authorized; (b) briefly describes the project; (c) highlights the report's findings, conclusions, and recommendations, if the reader is expected to be supportive; and (d) closes with appreciation for the assignment, instruction for the reader's follow-up actions, acknowledgement of help from others, or offers of assistance in answering questions. If a report is going to various readers, a special transmittal letter or memo should be prepared for each, anticipating how each reader will use the report.

Table of Contents. The table of contents shows the headings in the report and their page numbers. It gives an overview of the report topics and helps readers locate them. You should wait to prepare the table of contents until after you have completed the report. For short reports you should include all headings. For longer reports you might want to list only first- and second-level headings. Leaders (spaced or unspaced dots) help guide the eye from the heading to the page number. Items may be indented in outline form or typed flush with the left margin.

List of Illustrations. For reports with several figures or tables, you may wish to include a list to help readers locate them. This list may appear on the same page as the table of contents, space permitting. For each figure or table, include a title and page number. Some writers distinguish between tables and all other illustrations, which they call figures. If you make the distinction, you should prepare separate lists of tables and figures. Because the model report in Figure 13.5 has few illustrations, the writer labeled them all *figures*, a method that simplifies numbering.

Executive Summary. The purpose of an executive summary is to present an overview of a longer report to people who may not have time to read the entire document. Generally, an executive summary is prepared by the author of the report. However, occasionally you may be asked to write an executive summary of a published report or article written by someone else. In either case, your goal is to summarize the important points. The best way to prepare an executive summary is to do the following:

- **Look for strategic words and sentences.** Read the completed report carefully. Pay special attention to the first and last sentences of paragraphs, which often contain summary statements. Look for words that enumerate (*first, next, finally*) and words that express causation (*therefore, as a result*). Also, look for words that signal essentials (*basically, central, leading, principal, major*) and words that contrast ideas (*however, consequently*).
- **Prepare an outline with headings.** At a minimum, include headings for the purpose, findings, and conclusions/recommendations. What kernels of information would your reader want to know about these topics?
- **Fill in your outline.** Some writers cut and paste important parts of the text. Then they condense with careful editing. Others find it more efficient to create new sentences as they prepare the executive summary.
- **Begin with the purpose.** The easiest way to begin an executive summary is with the words *The purpose of this report is to* . . . . Experienced writers may be more creative.
- **Follow the report sequence.** Present all your information in the order in which it is found in the report.
- **Eliminate nonessential details.** Include only main points. Do not include anything not in the original report. Use minimal technical language.
- **Control the length.** An executive summary is usually no longer than 10 percent of the original document. Thus, a 100-page report might require a 10-page summary. A 10-page report might need only a 1-page summary—or no summary at all. The executive summary for a long report may also include graphics to highlight main points.

To see a representative executive summary, look at Figure 13.5. Although it is only one page long, this executive summary includes headings to help the reader see the main divisions immediately. Let your organization's practices guide you in determining the length and format of an executive summary.

Introduction. Formal reports begin with an introduction that sets the scene and announces the subject. Because they contain many parts that serve different purposes, formal reports are somewhat redundant. The same information may be included in the letter of transmittal, summary, and introduction. To avoid sounding repetitious, try to present the data slightly differently. However, do not skip the introduction because you have included some of its information elsewhere. You cannot be sure that your reader saw the information earlier. A good report introduction typically covers the following elements, although not necessarily in this order:

- **Background.** Describe events leading up to the problem or need.
- **Problem or purpose.** Explain the report topic, and specify the problem or need that motivated the report.
- **Significance.** Tell why the topic is important. You may wish to quote experts or cite newspapers, journals, books, Web resources, and other secondary sources to establish the importance of the topic.
- **Scope.** Clarify the boundaries of the report, defining what will be included or excluded.
- **Organization.** Orient readers by giving them a road map that previews the structure of the report.

Beyond these minimal introductory elements, consider adding any of the following information that may be relevant to your readers:

- **Authorization.** Identify who commissioned the report. If no letter of transmittal is included, also tell why, when, by whom, and to whom the report was written.
- **Literature review.** Summarize what other authors and researchers have published on this topic, especially for academic and scientific reports.
- **Sources and methods.** Describe your secondary sources (periodicals, books, databases). Also explain how you collected primary data, including the survey size, sample design, and statistical programs you used.
- **Definitions of key terms.** Define words that may be unfamiliar to the audience. Also define terms with special meanings, such as *small businesses* when it specifically means businesses with fewer than 30 employees.

LEARNING OUTCOME 5

Understand the body and back matter of formal business reports and how they serve the purpose of the report.

Body and Back Matter Components of Formal Business Reports

The body of a formal business report is the "meat" of the document. In this longest and most substantive section of the text, the author or team discusses the problem and findings, before reaching conclusions and making recommendations. Extensive and bulky materials that don't fit in the text belong in the appendix. Although some very long reports may have additional components, the back matter usually concludes with a list of sources. Figure 13.4 shows the parts of typical reports, the order in which they appear, and elements usually found only in formal reports.

Because formal business reports can be long and complex, they usually include more sections than routine informal business reports do. These components are standard and conventional; that is, the audience expects to see them in a professional report. Documents that conform to such expectations are easier to read and deliver their message more effectively. You will find most of the components addressed here in the model report in Figure 13.5, the formal analytical report studying the economic impact of an industrial park on Flagstaff, Arizona.

Body. The principal section in a formal report is the body. It discusses, analyzes, interprets, and evaluates the research findings or solution to the initial problem. This is where you show the evidence that justifies your conclusions. Organize the body into main categories following your original outline or using one of the organizational methods described in Chapter 12 (i.e., time, component, importance, criteria, or convention).

Although we refer to this section as the body, it does not carry that heading. Instead, it contains clear headings that explain each major section. Headings may be functional or talking. Functional heads (such as *Results of the Survey, Analysis of Findings,* or *Discussion*) help readers identify the purpose of the section but do not reveal what is in it. Such headings are useful for routine reports or for sensitive topics that may upset readers. Talking heads (for example, *Anatomy of a Market Crash* or *Your Money as a Force for Good*) are more informative and interesting, but they do not help readers see the organization of the report. The model report in Figure 13.5 uses combination headings; as the name suggests, they combine functional heads for organizational sections (*Introduction, Conclusions and Recommendations*) with talking heads that reveal the content. The headings divide the body into smaller parts.

Conclusions. This important section tells what the findings mean, particularly in terms of solving the original problem. Some writers prefer to intermix their conclusions with the analysis of the findings—instead of presenting the conclusions separately. Other writers place the conclusions before the body so that busy readers can examine the significant information immediately. Still others combine the conclusions and recommendations. Most writers, though, present the conclusions after the body because readers expect this structure. In long reports this section may include a summary of the findings. To improve comprehension, you may present the conclusions in a numbered or bulleted list. See Chapter 12 for more suggestions on drawing conclusions.

Recommendations. When asked, you should submit recommendations that make precise suggestions for actions to solve the report problem. Recommendations are most helpful when they are practical, reasonable, feasible, and ethical. Naturally, they should evolve from the findings and conclusions. Do not introduce new information in the conclusions or recommendations sections. As with conclusions, the position of recommendations is somewhat flexible. They may be combined with conclusions, or they may be presented before the body, especially when the audience is eager and supportive. Generally, though, in formal reports they come last.

Recommendations require an appropriate introductory sentence, such as *The findings and conclusions in this study support the following recommendations.* When making many recommendations, number them and phrase each as a command, such as *Begin an employee fitness program with a workout room available five days a week.* If appropriate, add information describing how to implement each recommendation. Some reports include a timetable describing the who, what, when, where, why, and how for putting each recommendation into operation. Chapter 12 provides more information about writing recommendations.

Appendix(es). Incidental or supporting materials belong in appendixes at the end of a formal report. These materials are relevant to some readers but not to all. They may also be too bulky to include in the text. Appendixes may include survey forms, copies of other reports, tables of data, large graphics, and related correspondence. If multiple appendixes are necessary, they are named *Appendix A, Appendix B,* and so forth.

Works Cited or References. If you use the MLA (Modern Language Association) referencing format, list all sources of information alphabetically in a section titled *Works Cited.* If you use the APA (American Psychological Association) format, your list is called *References.* Your listed sources must correspond to in-text citations in the report whenever you are borrowing words or ideas from published and unpublished resources.

Regardless of the documentation format, you must include the author, title, publication, date of publication, page number, and other significant data for all ideas or quotations used in your report. For electronic references include the preceding information plus the Internet address, or URL, leading to the citation. For model electronic and other citations, examine the list of references at the end of Figure 13.5. Appendix B of this textbook contains documentation models and information.

Ethics Check

Cheater on the Team

If one of your teammates cowriting a formal report with you has been found to have plagiarized a portion of your writing project, typically the instructor will punish the entire group, assuming ownership by the entire team. After all, researchers are expected to deliver a product that they have jointly prepared. Is this fair?

Final Writing Tips

LEARNING OUTCOME 6

Specify final writing tips that aid authors of formal business reports.

Formal business reports are not undertaken lightly. They involve considerable effort in all three phases of writing, beginning with analysis of the problem and anticipation of the audience (as discussed in Chapter 4). Researching the data, organizing it into a logical presentation, and composing the first draft (Chapter 5) make up the second phase of writing. Editing, proofreading, and evaluating (Chapter 6) are completed in the third phase. Although everyone approaches the writing process somewhat differently, the following tips offer advice in problem areas faced by most writers of formal reports:

- **Allow sufficient time.** The main reason given by writers who are disappointed with their reports is "I just ran out of time." Develop a realistic timetable and stick to it.
- **Finish data collection.** Do not begin writing until you have collected all the data and drawn the primary conclusions. Starting too early often results in having to backtrack. For reports based on survey data, complete the tables and figures first.
- **Work from a good outline.** A big project such as a formal report needs the order and direction provided by a clear outline, even if the outline has to be revised as the project unfolds.
- **Create a proper writing environment.** You will need a quiet spot where you can spread out your materials and work without interruption. Formal reports demand blocks of concentration time.
- **Use the features of your computer wisely.** Your word processor enables you to keyboard quickly; revise easily; and check spelling, grammar, and synonyms readily. A word of warning, though: save your document often and keep backup copies in the cloud, on disks, or on other devices. Print out important materials so that you have a hard copy. Take these precautions to guard against the grief caused by lost files, power outages, and computer malfunctions.
- **Write rapidly; revise later.** Some experts advise writers to record their ideas quickly and save revision until after the first draft is completed. They say that quick writing avoids wasted effort spent in polishing sentences or even sections that may be cut later. Moreover, rapid writing encourages fluency and creativity. However, a quick-and-dirty first draft does not work for everyone. Many business writers prefer a more deliberate writing style, so consider this advice selectively and experiment to find the method that works best for you.
- **Save difficult sections.** If some sections are harder to write than others, save them until you have developed confidence and a rhythm from working on easier topics.
- **Be consistent in verb tense.** Use past-tense verbs to describe completed actions (for example, *the respondents said* or *the survey showed*). Use present-tense verbs, however, to explain current actions (*the purpose of the report is, this report examines, the table shows*). When citing references, use past-tense verbs (*Jones reported that*). Do not switch back and forth between present- and past-tense verbs in describing related data.
- **Generally avoid *I* and *we*.** To make formal reports seem as objective and credible as possible, most writers omit first-person pronouns. This formal style sometimes results in the overuse of passive-voice verbs (for example, *periodicals were consulted* and *the study was conducted*). Look for alternative constructions (*periodicals indicated* and *the study revealed*). It is also possible that your organization may allow first-person pronouns, so check before starting your report.
- **Let the first draft sit.** After completing the first version, put it aside for a day or two. Return to it with the expectation of revising and improving it. Don't be afraid to make major changes.
- **Revise for clarity, coherence, and conciseness.** Read a printed copy out loud. Do the sentences make sense? Do the ideas flow together naturally? Can wordiness and flabbiness be cut out? Make sure that your writing is so clear that a busy manager does not have to reread any part. See Chapter 6 for specific revision suggestions.
- **Proofread the final copy three times.** First, read a printed copy slowly for word meanings and content. Then read the copy again for spelling, punctuation, grammar, and other mechanical errors. Finally, scan the entire report to check its formatting and consistency (page numbering, indenting, spacing, headings, and so forth).

Putting It All Together

Formal reports in business generally aim to study problems and recommend solutions. Sophia Silva, senior research consultant with Red Rock Development Company, was asked to study the economic impact of a local industrial park on the city of Flagstaff, Arizona, resulting in the formal report shown in Figure 13.5.

The city council hired the consultants to evaluate Coconino Industrial Park and to assess whether future commercial development would stimulate further economic growth. Sophia Silva subdivided the economic impact into three aspects: Revenues, Employment, and Indirect Benefits. The report was compiled from survey data as well as from secondary sources that Sophia consulted.

Sophia's report illustrates many of the points discussed in this chapter. Although it is a good example of the typical report format and style, it should not be viewed as the only way to present a report. Wide variation exists in business and academic reports.

Figure 13.5 **Model Formal Report With APA Citation Style**

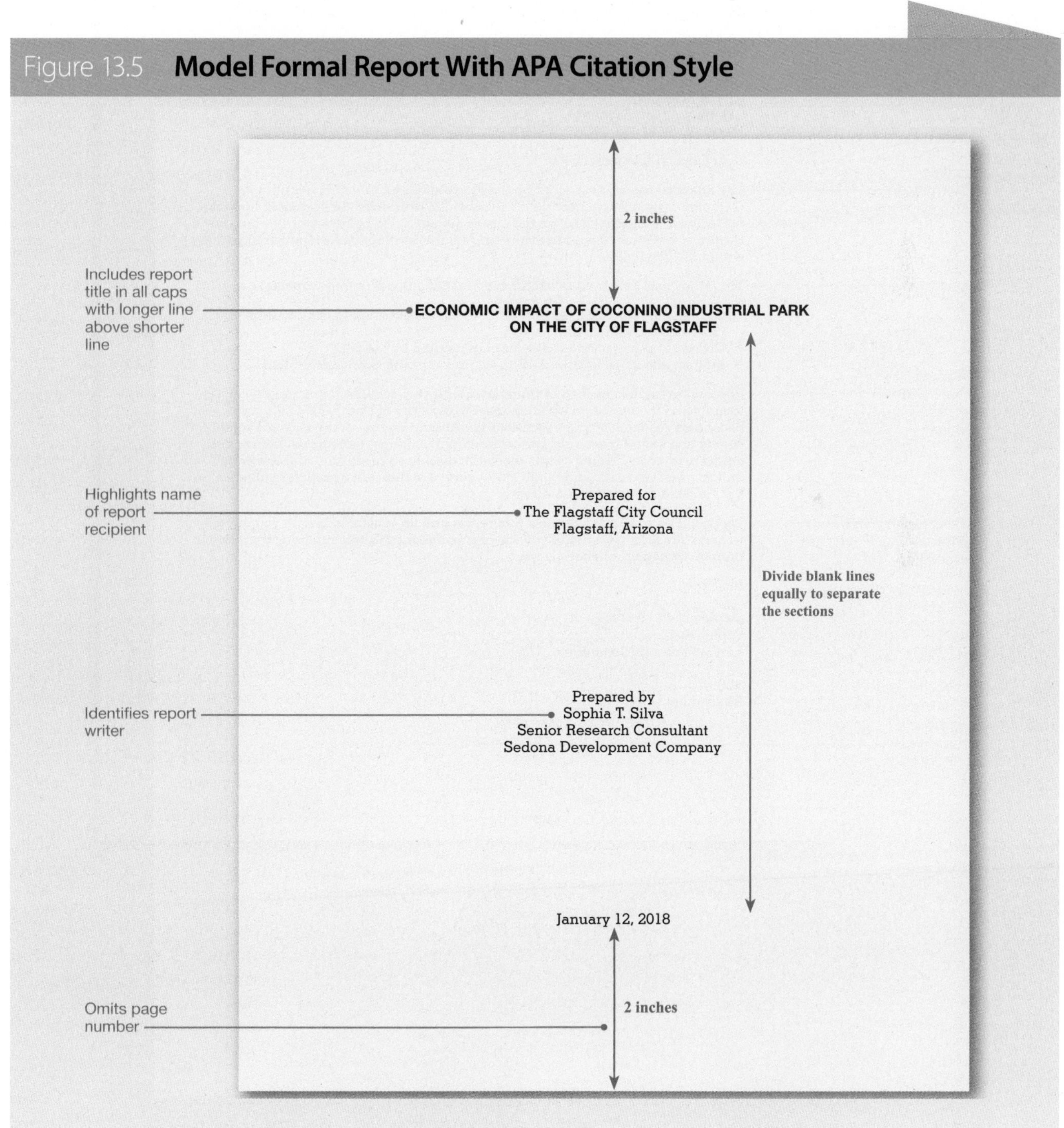

Figure 13.5 (Continued)

RED ROCK DEVELOPMENT COMPANY

426 Saddle Rock Circle
Sedona, Arizona 86340

www.redrockdevco.com
928.450.3348

January 12, 2018

City Council
City of Flagstaff
211 West Aspen Avenue
Flagstaff, AZ 86001

Dear Council Members:

Announces report and identifies authorization

The attached report, requested by the Flagstaff City Council in a letter to Goldman-Lyon & Associates dated October 20, describes the economic impact of Coconino Industrial Park on the city of Flagstaff. We believe you will find the results of this study useful in evaluating future development of industrial parks within the city limits.

Gives broad overview of report purposes

This study was designed to examine economic impact in three areas:

- Current and projected tax and other revenues accruing to the city from Coconino Industrial Park
- Current and projected employment generated by the park
- Indirect effects on local employment, income, and economic growth

Describes primary and secondary research

Primary research consisted of interviews with 15 Coconino Industrial Park (CIP) tenants and managers, in addition to a 2016 survey of over 5,000 CIP employees. Secondary research sources included the Annual Budget of the City of Flagstaff, county and state tax records, government publications, periodicals, books, and online resources. Results of this research, discussed more fully in this report, indicate that Coconino Industrial Park exerts a significant beneficial influence on the Flagstaff metropolitan economy.

Offers to discuss report; expresses appreciation

We would be pleased to discuss this report and its conclusions with you at your request. My firm and I thank you for your confidence in selecting our company to prepare this comprehensive report.

Sincerely,

Sophia E. Silva
Sophia E. Silva
Senior Research Consultant

SES:mef
Attachment

Uses Roman numerals for prefatory pages

ii

Figure 13.5 **(Continued)**

Uses leaders to guide eye from heading to page number

Indents secondary headings to show levels of outline

Includes tables and figures in one list for simplified numbering

TABLE OF CONTENTS

LIST OF FIGURES

iii

Figure 13.5 **(Continued)**

Opens directly with major research findings

Identifies data sources

Summarizes organization of report

Condenses recommendations

EXECUTIVE SUMMARY

The city of Flagstaff can benefit from the development of industrial parks like the Coconino Industrial Park. Both direct and indirect economic benefits result, as shown by this in-depth study conducted by Red Rock Development Company. The study was authorized by the Flagstaff City Council when Goldman-Lyon & Associates sought the City Council's approval for the proposed construction of a G-L industrial park. The City Council requested evidence demonstrating that an existing development could actually benefit the city.

Our conclusion that the city of Flagstaff benefits from industrial parks is based on data supplied by a survey of 5,000 Coconino Industrial Park employees, personal interviews with managers and tenants of CIP, city and state documents, and professional literature.

Analysis of the data revealed benefits in three areas:

- **Revenues.** The city of Flagstaff earned over $3 million in tax and other revenues from the Coconino Industrial Park in 2016. By 2025 this income is expected to reach $5.4 million (in constant 2016 dollars).
- **Employment.** In 2016, CIP businesses employed a total of 7,035 workers, who earned an average wage of $56,579. By 2025, CIP businesses are expected to employ directly nearly 15,000 employees who will earn salaries totaling over $998 million.
- **Indirect benefits.** Because of the multiplier effect, by 2025 Coconino Industrial Park will directly and indirectly generate a total of 38,362 jobs in the Flagstaff metropolitan area.

On the basis of these findings, it is recommended that development of additional industrial parks be encouraged to stimulate local economic growth. The city would increase its tax revenues significantly, create much-needed jobs, and thus help stimulate the local economy in and around Flagstaff.

iv

Figure 13.5 **(Continued)**

Uses a bulleted list for clarity and ease of reading

Lists three problem questions

Describes authorization for report and background of study

Includes APA citation with author name and date

INTRODUCTION: COCONINO AND THE LOCAL ECONOMY

This study was designed to analyze the direct and indirect economic impact of Coconino Industrial Park on the city of Flagstaff. Specifically, the study seeks answers to these questions:

- What current tax and other revenues result directly from this park? What tax and other revenues may be expected in the future?
- How many and what kinds of jobs are directly attributable to the park? What is the employment picture for the future?
- What indirect effects has Coconino Industrial Park had on local employment, incomes, and economic growth?

BACKGROUND: THE ROLE OF CIP IN COMMERCIAL DEVELOPMENT

The development firm of Goldman-Lyon & Associates commissioned this study of Coconino Industrial Park at the request of the Flagstaff City Council. Before authorizing the development of a proposed Goldman-Lyon industrial park, the city council requested a study examining the economic effects of an existing park. Members of the city council wanted to determine to what extent industrial parks benefit the local community, and they chose Coconino Industrial Park as an example.

For those who are unfamiliar with it, Coconino Industrial Park is a 400-acre industrial park located in the city of Flagstaff about 4 miles from the center of the city. Most of the land lies within a specially designated area known as Redevelopment Project No. 2, which is under the jurisdiction of the Flagstaff Redevelopment Agency. Planning for the park began in 2002; construction started in 2004.

The original goal for Coconino Industrial Park was development for light industrial users. Land in this area was zoned for uses such as warehousing, research and development, and distribution. Like other communities, Flagstaff was eager to attract light industrial users because such businesses tend to employ a highly educated workforce, are relatively quiet, and do not pollute the environment (Cohen, 2017). The city of Flagstaff recognized the need for light industrial users and widened an adjacent highway to accommodate trucks and facilitate travel by workers and customers coming from Flagstaff.

1

Figure 13.5 **(Continued)**

The park now contains 14 building complexes with over 1.25 million square feet of completed building space. The majority of the buildings are used for office, research and development, marketing and distribution, or manufacturing uses. Approximately 50 acres of the original area are yet to be developed.

Provides specifics for data sources

Data for this report came from a 2016 survey of over 5,000 Coconino Industrial Park employees; interviews with 15 CIP tenants and managers; the annual budget of the city of Flagstaff; county and state tax records; and current books, articles, journals, and online resources. Projections for future revenues resulted from analysis of past trends and "Estimates of Revenues for Debt Service Coverage, Redevelopment Project Area 2" (Miller, 2016, p. 79).

Uses combination heads

DISCUSSION: REVENUES, EMPLOYMENT, AND INDIRECT BENEFITS

Previews organization of report

The results of this research indicate that major direct and indirect benefits have accrued to the city of Flagstaff and surrounding metropolitan areas as a result of the development of Coconino Industrial Park. The research findings presented here fall into three categories: (a) revenues, (b) employment, and (c) indirect benefits.

Revenues

Coconino Industrial Park contributes a variety of tax and other revenues to the city of Flagstaff, as summarized in Figure 1. Current revenues are shown, along with projections to the year 2025. At a time when the economy is unstable, revenues from an industrial park such as Coconino can become a reliable income stream for the city of Flagstaff.

Places figure close to textual reference

Figure 1

REVENUES RECEIVED BY THE CITY OF FLAGSTAFF
FROM COCONINO INDUSTRIAL PARK

Current Revenues and Projections to 2025

	2016	2025
Sales and use taxes	$1,966,021	$3,604,500
Revenues from licenses	532,802	962,410
Franchise taxes	195,682	220,424
State gas tax receipts	159,420	211,134
Licenses and permits	86,213	201,413
Other revenues	75,180	206,020
Total	$3,015,318	$5,405,901

Source: Arizona State Board of Equalization Bulletin. Phoenix: State Printing Office, 2017, p. 28.

2

Figure 13.5 **(Continued)**

Sales and Use Revenues

Continues interpreting figures in table

As shown in Figure 1, the city's largest source of revenues from CIP is the sales and use tax. Revenues from this source totaled $1,966,021 in 2016, according to figures provided by the Arizona State Board of Equalization (2017, p. 28). Sales and use taxes accounted for more than half of the park's total contribution to the total income of $3,015,318.

Other Revenues

Other major sources of city revenues from CIP in 2016 include alcohol licenses, motor vehicle in lieu fees, trailer coach licenses ($532,802), franchise taxes ($195,682), and state gas tax receipts ($159,420). Although not shown in Figure 1, other revenues may be expected from the development of recently acquired property. The U.S. Economic Development Administration has approved a grant worth $975,000 to assist in expanding the current park eastward on an undeveloped parcel purchased last year. Revenues from leasing this property may be sizable.

Projections

Includes ample description of electronic reference

Total city revenues from CIP will nearly double by 2025, producing an income of $5.4 million. This estimate is based on an annual growth rate of 0.65 percent, as projected by the Bureau of Labor Statistics.

Employment

Sets stage for next topic to be discussed

One of the most important factors to consider in the overall effect of an industrial park is employment. In Coconino Industrial Park the distribution, number, and wages of people employed will change considerably in the next six years.

Distribution

A total of 7,035 employees currently work in various industry groups at Coconino Industrial Park. The distribution of employees is shown in Figure 2. The largest number of workers (58 percent) is employed in manufacturing and assembly operations. The next largest category, computer and electronics, employs 24 percent of the workers. Some overlap probably exists because electronics assembly could be included in either group. Employees also work in publishing (9 percent), warehousing and storage (5 percent), and other industries (4 percent).

Although the distribution of employees at Coconino Industrial Park shows a wide range of employment categories, it must be noted that other industrial parks would likely generate an entirely different range of job categories.

3

Your Task

Select one of the suggested tasks. For Task 1, in a two- or three-person team, plan the report and have each team member prepare an outline of his or her assigned section. As a team, review and improve the outlines with written comments and annotations. For Task 2, individually research, plan, and write a one- to two-page memo.

Summary of Learning Outcomes

1 Understand the importance and purpose of proposals, and name the basic components of informal proposals.

- Proposals are important to organizations because they generate business or funding.
- A proposal is a written offer to solve problems, provide services, or sell equipment.
- Requests for proposals (RFPs) specify what a proposal should include.
- Standard parts of informal proposals include (a) a persuasive introduction explaining the purpose of the proposal; (b) background identifying the problem and project goals; (c) a proposal, plan, or schedule outlining the project; (d) a section describing staff qualifications; (e) expected costs; and (f) a request for approval or authorization.

2 Discuss the components of formal and grant proposals.

- Formal proposals may include additional parts not found in informal proposals: (a) a copy of the RFP (request for proposals); (b) a letter of transmittal; (c) an abstract or executive summary; (d) a title page; (e) a table of contents; (f) a list of illustrations; and (g) an appendix.
- A grant proposal is a formal document submitted to a government agency or funding organization that explains a project, outlines its budget, and requests grant money that requires no repayment.
- Grants are made to charities, educational facilities, and especially to nonprofits.

3 Identify the components of typical business plans.

- A business plan describes a proposed business and explains how it expects to achieve its marketing, financial, and operational goals.
- Typical business plans include a letter of transmittal, mission statement, executive summary, table of contents, company description, product or service description, market analysis, description of operations and management, financial analysis, and appendixes.
- Startup businesses seeking financial backing must pay particular attention to the product or service description as well as the operations and management analyses. Startups must prove growth potential and present a team capable of implementing the business plan.

4 Describe the components of the front matter in formal business reports, and show how they further the purpose of the report.

- In a formal report, the author analyzes findings, draws conclusions, and makes recommendations intended to solve a problem.
- The front matter may include a cover, title page, letter or memo of transmittal, table of contents, list of illustrations, and an executive summary that explains key points.
- In the introduction the writer typically discusses the significance, scope, and organization of the report as well as its authorization, relevant literature, sources, methods of research, and definitions of key terms.

5 Understand the body and back matter of formal business reports and how they serve the purpose of the report.

- The body of the report discusses, analyzes, interprets, and evaluates the research findings or solution to a problem.
- The conclusion states what the findings mean and how they relate to the report's purpose.
- The recommendations explain how to solve the report problem.
- The last portions of a formal report are the appendix(es) and references or works cited.

6 Specify final writing tips that aid authors of formal business reports.

- Before writing, develop a realistic timetable and collect all necessary data.
- While writing, work from a good outline, compose in a quiet environment, and use the features of your computer wisely.
- Remember that some writers like to write rapidly, intending to revise later; other writers prefer a more deliberate writing style, perfecting their prose as they go.
- As you write, use verb tenses consistently and generally avoid *I* and *we*.
- After completing the first draft, wait a few days before you edit to improve clarity, coherence, and conciseness; proofread the final copy three times.

Critical Thinking

1. In what ways is a proposal similar to a persuasive sales message? (L.O. 1, 2)
2. Some people say that business reports shouldn't contain footnotes. If you were writing your first business report and did considerable research, what would you do about documenting your sources? (L.O. 5)
3. Which category of proposal, solicited or unsolicited, is more likely to succeed, and why? (L.O. 1)
4. If you were about to launch a new business, would you write your business plan from scratch or use a software program? What are the pros and cons of each method? (L.O. 3)
5. **Ethical Issue:** How can a team of writers ensure that each member shoulders an equal or fair amount of the work on an extensive writing project, such as a formal proposal or business report?

Activities

13.1 Proposal: Social Media Bound (L.O. 1)

E-Mail Social Media Web

Businesses both large and small are flocking to social media platforms to engage consumers in conversations and also to drive sales through deals and coupons. Small businesses have found that social media and the Internet help them to level the playing field. They can foster closer relationships with clients and identify potential customers. Flirty Cupcakes owner Tiffany Kurtz says that Facebook and Twitter greatly helped her with product innovation, market expansion, and customer service.[19] Many other entrepreneurs are using social media to launch and expand their businesses.

YOUR TASK Using the Internet, search for small businesses that have used social media to start a business or expand their market share. Select four businesses to study. Analyze their use of social media. What do they have in common? When these companies were first launched, most of them probably needed to borrow money to get started. How might these companies have described the social media potential in writing a proposal seeking funding? In which of the proposal components would this information be best placed? In an e-mail or memo to your instructor, describe briefly the four companies you selected. Then, for one company write a portion of the proposal in which the entrepreneur explains how he or she plans to use social media to promote the business. How much time do you think the entrepreneur would need to devote to social media weekly? What platforms would be most useful?

13.2 Proposal: Pinpoint That Workplace Problem (L.O. 1)

The ability to spot problems before they turn into serious risks is prized by most managers. Drawing on your internship and work experience, can you identify a problem that could be solved with a small to moderate financial investment? Look for issues such as a lack of lunch or break rooms for staff; badly needed health initiatives such as gyms or sport club memberships; low-gas-mileage, high-emission company vehicles; or a lack of recycling efforts.

YOUR TASK Discuss with your instructor the workplace problem you have identified. Make sure you choose a relatively weighty problem that can be lessened or eliminated with a minor expenditure. Be sure to include a cost–benefit analysis. Address your unsolicited letter or memo proposal to your current or former boss and copy your instructor.

13.3 Proposal: Calling All Budding Entrepreneurs (L.O. 1)

Web

Perhaps you have fantasized about one day owning your own company, or maybe you have already started a business. Proposals are offers to a very specific audience whose business you are soliciting. Think of a product or service that you like or know something about. On the Web or in research databases, study the market so that you understand going rates, prices, and costs. Search the Small Business Administration's website for valuable tips on how to launch and manage a business.

YOUR TASK Choose a product or service you would like to offer to a particular audience, such as a dating consulting service, a window cleaning business, a bakery specializing in your favorite cakes, an online photography business, or a new Asian or European hair care line. Discuss products and services as well as target audiences with your instructor. Write an informal letter proposal promoting your chosen product or service.

13.4 Proposal: Lending a Hand with Proposal Writing (L.O. 1, 2)

Web

Many new companies with services or products to offer would like to land corporate or government contracts. However, they are intimidated by the proposal and RFP processes. Your friend Clara, who has started her own designer uniform company, has asked you for help. Her goal is to offer her colorful yet functional uniforms to hospitals and clinics. Before writing a proposal, however, she wants to see examples and learn more about the process.

YOUR TASK Use the Web to find at least two examples of business proposals. Don't waste time on sites that want to sell templates or books. Find actual examples. Try **http://www.bplans.com/samples/sba.cfm**. Then prepare a memo to Clara in which you do the following:

a. Identify two sample business proposals.

b. Outline the parts of each proposal.

c. Compare the strengths and weaknesses of each proposal.

d. Draw conclusions. What can Clara learn from these examples?

13.5 Proposal: Healing With Linda Vista Sports Medicine (L.O. 1)

Team

Sports medicine is increasingly popular, especially in university towns. A new medical clinic, Linda Vista Sports Medicine, is opening its doors in your community. A friend recommended your small business to the administrator of the clinic, and you received a letter asking you to provide information about your service. The new medical clinic specializes in sports medicine, physical therapy, and cardiac rehabilitation services. It is interested in retaining your company, rather than hiring its own employees to perform the service your company offers.

YOUR TASK Working in teams, first decide what service you offer. It could be landscaping, uniforms, uniform laundering, general cleaning, a cloud-based filing system, online medical supplies, patient transportation, supplemental hospice care, temporary office support, social media guidance, or food service. As a team, develop a letter proposal outlining your plan, staffing, and budget. Use persuasion to show why contracting your services is better than hiring in-house employees. In the proposal letter, request a meeting with the administrative board. In addition to a written proposal, you may be expected to make an oral presentation that includes visual aids and/or handouts. Send your proposal to Dr. Carl Strohmayer, Director, Linda Vista Sports Medicine. Supply a local address.

13.6 Grant Writing: Learning From Nonprofits (L.O. 1, 2)

Web

Nonprofit organizations are always seeking grant writers, and you would like to gain experience in this area. You've heard that they pull down good salaries, and one day you might even decide to become a professional grant/proposal writer. However, you first need experience. You saw a Web listing from The Actors Theatre Workshop advertising for a grant writer to "seek funding for general operating expenses and program-related funding." A grant writer would "develop proposals, generate boilerplates for future applications, and oversee a writing team." This listing sounds good, but you need a local position.

YOUR TASK Search the Web for local nonprofits. Alternatively, your instructor may already know of local groups seeking grant writers, such as a United Way member agency, an educational institution, or a faith-based organization. Talk with your instructor about an assignment. Your instructor may ask you to submit a preliminary memo report outlining ten or more guidelines you expect to follow when writing proposals and grants for nonprofit organizations.

13.7 Service Learning: Write Away! (L.O. 1, 2, 4, and 5)

E-Mail Web

Your school may be one that encourages service learning, a form of experiential learning. You could receive credit for a project that bridges academic and nonacademic communities. Because writing skills are in wide demand, you may have an opportunity to simultaneously apply your skills, contribute to the community, and expand your résumé. The National Service-Learning Clearinghouse describes service learning as "a teaching and learning strategy that integrates meaningful community service with instruction and reflection to enrich the learning experience, teach civic responsibility, and strengthen communities."[20] The Web offers many sites devoted to examples of students engaging in service-learning projects.

YOUR TASK Research possible service-learning projects in this class or another. Your instructor may ask you to submit a memo or e-mail message analyzing your findings. Describe at least four completed service-learning projects that you found on the Web. Draw conclusions about what made them successful or beneficial. What kinds of similar projects might be possible for you or students in your class? Your instructor may use this as a research project or turn it into a hands-on project by having you find a service organization in your community that needs trained writers.

13.8 Business Plans: Homing in on Mission Statements (L.O. 3)

E-Mail

Large and small businesses develop mission statements to explain their purposes. Some statements are excellent; others, less so.

YOUR TASK Analyze the following selection of Fortune 500 company descriptions and mission statements.[21] In a class discussion or an e-mail to your instructor, (a) list four goals of mission statements (see Figure 13.3), (b) list five questions to be answered in preparing mission statements, (c) explain which of the following statements fulfill the goals of winning mission statements discussed in Figure 13.3, and (d) tell how the following statements could be improved.

Company	Mission Statement
1. AGCO manufactures and distributes agricultural equipment such as replacement parts, tractors, hay tools, and implements.	Profitable growth through superior customer service, innovation, quality, and commitment.
2. Dover Corporation manufactures equipment such as garbage trucks and electronic equipment such as ink-jet printers and circuit board assemblies.	To be the leader in every market we serve, to the benefit of our customers and our shareholders.
3. Eaton Corporation supplies parts for fluid power, electrical systems, automobiles, and trucks.	We are committed to attracting, developing, and keeping a diverse workforce that reflects the nature of our global business.
4. Graybar Electric Company acquires, stores, and distributes electrical, data, and communication components such as wire, cable, and lighting products.	We are a vital link in the supply chain, adding value with efficient and cost-effective service and solutions for our customers and our suppliers.
5. Harley-Davidson, Inc., manufactures motorcycles with over 32 models of touring and custom Harleys plus motorcycle accessories, motorcycle clothing apparel, and engines.	We fulfill dreams through the experience of motorcycling, by providing to motorcyclists and to the general public an expanding line of motorcycles and branded products and services in selected market segments.
6. IBM provides computer hardware such as mainframes, servers, storage systems, printing systems, and semiconductors, as well as software related to business integration, networking, operating systems, systems management, and so forth.	Operating a safe and secure government.

13.9 Business Plan: Would You Survive the Shark Tank? (L.O. 3)

Team  Web

Business plans at many schools are more than classroom writing exercises. They have won regional, national, and worldwide prizes. Although some contests are part of MBA programs, other contests are available for undergraduates. As part of a business plan project, you and your team are challenged to come up with an idea for a new business or service. For example, you might want to offer a lunch service with fresh sandwiches or salads delivered to office workers' desks. You might propose building a better website for an organization. You might want to start a document preparation business that offers production, editing, and printing services. You might have a terrific idea for an existing business to expand with a new product or service.

YOUR TASK Working in teams, explore entrepreneurial ventures based on your experience and expertise. Conduct team meetings to decide on a product or service, develop a work plan, assign responsibilities, and create a schedule. Your goal is to write a business plan that will convince potential investors (sometimes your own management) that you have an excellent business idea and that you can pull it off. Check out sample business plans on the Web. The two deliverables from your project will be your written business plan and an oral presentation. Your written plan should include a cover, transmittal document (letter or memo), title page, table of contents, executive summary, proposal (including introduction, body, and conclusion), appendix items, glossary (optional), and sources. In the body of the document, be sure to explain your mission and vision, the market, your marketing strategy, operations, and financials. Address your business plan to your instructor.

13.10 Executive Summary: Reviewing Articles (L.O. 2, 5)

E-Mail  Web

Many managers and executives are too rushed to read long journal articles, but they are eager to stay current in their fields. Assume that your boss has asked you to help him stay abreast of research in his field. He asks you to submit to him one executive summary every month on an article of interest.

YOUR TASK In your field of study, select a professional journal, such as the *Journal of Management*. Using ProQuest, Factiva, EBSCO, or some other database, look for articles in your target journal. Select an interesting article that is at least five pages long. Write an executive summary in a memo format. Include an introduction that might begin with *As you requested, I am submitting this executive summary of....* Identify the author, article title, journal, and date of publication. Explain what the author intended to do in the study or article. Summarize three or four of the most important findings of the study or article. Use descriptive, or talking, headings rather than functional headings. Summarize any recommendations made. Your boss would also like a concluding statement indicating your reaction to the article. Address your memo to Sam Beimer. Alternatively, your instructor may ask you to e-mail your executive summary in the body of a properly formatted message or as an MS Word attachment in correct memo format.

13.11 Unsolicited Proposal: Your Campus Business Organization Needs Cash (L.O. 1)

Team

Let's say you are a member of a campus business club, such as the Society for the Advancement of Management (SAM), the American Marketing Association (AMA), the American Management Association (AMA), the Accounting Society (AS), the Finance Association (FA), or the Association of Information Technology Professionals (AITP). Your organization has managed its finances well, and therefore, it is able to fund monthly activities. However, membership dues are insufficient to cover any extras. Identify a need such as a hardware or software purchase, a special one-time event that would benefit a great number of students, or officer training.

YOUR TASK Request one-time funding to cover what you need by writing an unsolicited letter or memo proposal to your assistant dean, who oversees student business clubs. Identify your need or problem, show the benefit of your request, support your claims with evidence, and provide a budget (if necessary).

13.12 Unsolicited Proposal: Keeping Gizmos Safe in Residence Halls (L.O. 1, 2)

Team Web

As an enterprising college student, you recognized a problem as soon as you arrived on campus. Dorm rooms filled with pricey digital doodads were very attractive to thieves. Some students move in with more than $3,000 in gear, including laptops, tablets, flat-screen TVs, digital cameras, MP3 players, video game consoles, smartphones, and hoards of other digital delights. You solved the problem by buying an extra-large steel footlocker in which to stash your valuables. However, shipping the footlocker was expensive (nearly $100), and you had to wait for it to arrive from a catalog company. Your bright idea is to propose to the Associated Student Organization (ASO) that it allow you to offer these steel footlockers to students at a reduced price and with campus delivery. Your footlocker, which you found by searching the Web, is extremely durable and works great as a coffee table, nightstand, or card table. It comes with a smooth interior liner and two compartments.

YOUR TASK Working individually or with a team, imagine that you have made arrangements with a manufacturer to act as an intermediary selling footlockers on your campus at a reduced price. Consult the Web for manufacturers and make up your own figures. How can you get the ASO's permission to proceed? Give that organization a cut? Use your imagination in deciding how this plan might work on a college campus. Then prepare an unsolicited proposal to your ASO. Outline the problem and your goals of protecting students' valuables and providing convenience. Check the Web for statistics regarding on-campus burglaries. Such figures should help you develop one or more persuasive hooks. Then explain your proposal, project possible sales, discuss a timetable, and describe your staffing. Submit your proposal to Anthony Johnson, president, Associated Student Organization.

13.13 Formal Business Report: Gathering Data for International Expansion (L.O. 4–6)

Intercultural Team Web

U.S. businesses are expanding into foreign markets with manufacturing plants, sales offices, and branches abroad. Many Americans, however, have little knowledge of or experience with people from other cultures. To prepare for participation in the global marketplace, you are to collect information for a report focused on an Asian, Latin American, European, or African country where English is not regularly spoken. Before selecting the country, though, consult your campus international student program for volunteers who are willing to be interviewed. Your instructor may make advance arrangements with international student volunteers.

YOUR TASK In teams of three to five, collect information about your target country from electronic databases, the Web, and other sources. Then invite an international student representing your target country to be interviewed by your group. Alternatively, you could interview a faculty member who hails from another country. Prepare and know your interview questions and be courteous; people like to talk about themselves, but no one wants to waste time.

As you conduct primary and secondary research, investigate the topics listed in Figure 13.6. Confirm what you learn in your secondary research by talking with your interviewee. When you complete your research, write a report for the CEO of your company (make up a name and company).

Figure 13.6 Intercultural Interview Topics and Questions

Social Customs

- How do people react to strangers? Are they generally friendly? Hostile? Reserved?
- How do people greet each other?
- What are the appropriate manners when you enter a room? Bow? Nod? Shake hands with everyone?
- How are names used for introductions? Is it appropriate to inquire about one's occupation or family?
- What are the attitudes toward touching?
- How does one express appreciation for an invitation to another's home? Bring a gift? Send flowers? Write a thank-you note? Are any gifts taboo?
- Are there any customs related to how or where one sits?
- Are any facial expressions or gestures considered rude?
- How close do people stand when talking?
- What is the attitude toward punctuality in social situations? In business situations?
- What are acceptable eye contact patterns?
- What gestures indicate agreement? Disagreement?

Family Life

- What is the basic unit of social organization? Basic family? Extended family?
- Do women work outside of the home? In what occupations?

Housing, Clothing, and Food

- Are there differences in the kinds of housing used by different social groups? Differences in location? Differences in furnishings?
- What occasions require special clothing?
- Are some types of clothing considered taboo?
- What is appropriate business attire for men? For women?
- How many times a day do people eat?
- What types of places, food, and drink are appropriate for business entertainment? Where is the seat of honor at a table?

Class Structure

- Into what classes is society organized?
- Do racial, religious, or economic factors determine social status?
- Are there any minority groups? What is their social standing?

Political Patterns

- Are there any immediate threats to the political survival of the country?
- How is political power manifested?
- What channels are used for expressing political opinions?
- What information media are important?
- Is it appropriate to talk politics in social situations?

Religion and Folk Beliefs

- To which religious groups do people belong? Is one predominant?
- Do religious beliefs influence daily activities?
- Which places are considered sacred? Which objects? Which events?
- How do religious holidays affect business activities?

Economic Institutions

- What are the country's principal products?
- Are workers organized in unions?
- How are businesses owned? By family units? By large public corporations? By the government?
- What is the standard work schedule?
- Is it appropriate to do business by telephone? By computer?
- How has technology affected business procedures?
- Is participatory management used?
- Are there any customs related to exchanging business cards?
- How is status shown in an organization? Private office? Secretary? Furniture?
- Are businesspeople expected to socialize before conducting business?

Value Systems

- Is competitiveness or cooperation more prized?
- Is thrift or enjoyment of the moment more valued?
- Is politeness more important than honesty?
- What are the attitudes toward education?
- Do women own or manage businesses? If so, how are they treated?
- What are your people's perceptions of Americans? Do Americans offend you? What has been hardest for you to adjust to in the United States? How could Americans make this adjustment easier for you?

Assume that your company plans to expand its operations abroad. Your report should advise the company's executives of the social customs, family life, attitudes, religions, education, and values of the target country. Remember that your company's interests are business oriented; do not dwell on tourist information. Write your report individually or in teams.

13.14 Report Topics for Proposals, Business Plans, and Formal Reports (L.O. 1-6)

Team 

A list of nearly 100 report topics is available at **www.cengagebrain.com**. The topics are divided into the following categories: accounting, finance, personnel/human resources, marketing, information systems, management, and general business/education/campus issues. You can collect information for many of these reports by using electronic databases and the Web. Your instructor may assign them as individual or team projects. All involve critical thinking in organizing information, drawing conclusions, and making recommendations. The topics are appropriate for proposals, business plans, and formal business reports. Also, a number of self-contained report activities that require no additional research are provided at the end of Chapter 12.

YOUR TASK As directed by your instructor, select a topic from the report list at **www.cengagebrain.com.**

Test Your Etiquette IQ

New communication platforms and casual workplace environments have blurred the lines of appropriateness, leaving workers wondering how to navigate uncharted waters. Indicate whether the following statements are true or false. Then see if you agree with the responses on p. R-2.

1. Office casual means you can be comfortable and wear your Saturday clothes to work.

   _______ True _______ False

2. If a group of businesspeople is approaching a door, the first male should hold the door for any woman in the group.

   _______ True _______ False

3. In your office you rarely drink the coffee or eat the pastries that are often available. Although everyone is expected to contribute to these office treats, you are justified in refusing because you seldom partake of the goodies and you feel that it is not your obligation to support the snacking habits of others.

   _______ True _______ False

Chat About It

In each chapter you will find five discussion questions related to the chapter material. Your instructor may assign these topics for you to discuss in class, in an online chat room, or on an online discussion board. Some of the discussion topics may require outside research. You may also be asked to read and respond to postings made by your classmates.

TOPIC 1: Why do experts refer to a business plan as a living document? Some have said that a business plan needs constant review and adjustment. What might account for such a short shelf life?

TOPIC 2: If you had control over a big company's philanthropic budget, which causes would you support and why? What kind of appeal in a grant proposal would you consider persuasive?

TOPIC 3: Some consulting firms use experienced managers, but they also employ inexperienced, lower-paid staff to lower costs. How would you write the staffing section of a proposal with experienced managers but inexperienced staff?

TOPIC 4: Discuss the pros and cons of the following two methods for completing the outline of the executive summary of a formal report: (a) cutting and pasting existing report sentences, or (b) creating new sentences.

TOPIC 5: Is it ethical for a student team to substantially revise a report from a team that wrote about the same topic during the previous semester? What does your school say about such a practice?

Total Review

Each of the following sentences has **three** errors in grammar, punctuation, capitalization, usage, or spelling. On a separate sheet, write a correct version. Avoid adding new phrases, starting new sentences, or rewriting in your own words. When finished, compare your responses with the key beginning on page Key-3.

EXAMPLE: If you face writers block you should review your 3 main reasons for writing.

REVISION: If you face **writer's block,** you should review your **three** main reasons for writing.

1. Our Manager and CEO both worked on the thirty page proposal. Which was due immediately.
2. Supervisors in 2 departments' complained that there departments should have been consulted.
3. The RFP and it's attachments arrived to late for my manager and I to complete the necessary research.
4. Although we worked everyday on the proposal, we felt badly that we could not meet the May 15th deadline.
5. If the program and staff is to run smooth we must submit an effective grant proposal.
6. Although short a successful mission statement should capture the businesses goals and values. In a few succinct sentences.
7. A proposal budget cannot be changed if costs raise later, consequently, it must be written careful.
8. A good eight-word mission statement is a critical tool for funding, it helps startup company's evolve there big idea without being pulled off track.
9. Entrepreneur Stephanie Rivera publisher of a urban event callendar, relies on social media to broadcast her message.
10. Stephanie asked Jake and myself to help her write a business plan. That would guide her new company and garner perminent funding.

References

[1] Based on Grush, L. (2016, February 24). NASA awards SpaceX with five more cargo mission to the International Space Station. The Verge. Retrieved from http://www.theverge.com/2016/2/24/11109566/spacex-nasa-contract-additional-cargo-missions-2018; Gebhardt, C., & Bergin, C. (2016, January 14). NASA awards CRS2 contracts to SpaceX, Orbital ATK, and Sierra Nevada. NASA Spaceflight.com. Retrieved from https://www.nasaspaceflight.com/2016/01/nasa-awards-crs2-spacex-orbital-atk-sierra-nevada; Schierholz, S., & Huot, D. (2014, September 26). NASA expands commercial space program, requests proposals for second round of cargo resupply contracts for International Space Station. NASA.gov. Retrieved from http://www.nasa.gov/press/2014/september/nasa-expands-commercial-space-program-requests-proposals-for-second-round-of

[2] Anonymous. (2014, June 22). What is it like to work with Elon Musk? Quora.com. Retrieved from https://www.quora.com/What-is-it-like-to-work-with-Elon-Musk/answers/5559684

[3] Pasztor, A. (2014, September 16). Boeing and SpaceX share $6.8 billion in NASA space taxi contracts. *The Wall Street Journal*. Retrieved from http://www.wsj.com/articles/boeing-and-spacex-share-6-8-billion-in-nasa-space-taxi-contracts-1410904245

[4] Warner, C., Schierholz, S., & Huot, D. (2016, January 14). NASA awards International Space Station cargo transport contracts. NASA.gov. Retrieved from http://www.nasa.gov/press-release/nasa-awards-international-space-station-cargo-transport-contracts

[5] Request for proposals for network programming for the City of Philadelphia. (2016, April 28). The City of Philadelphia, Philadelphia International Airport. Retrieved from http://www.phila.gov/rfp/Documents/Network%20RFP%20-%20Final.pdf

[6] Center for the Advancement of Science in Space. (n.d.). Unsolicited proposals. Retrieved from http://www.iss-casis.org/Opportunities/UnsolicitedProposals.aspx

[7] Piecewicz, Mary. Former proposal manager, Hewlett-Packard (personal communication with Mary Ellen Guffey).

[8] Sant, T. (2012). *Persuasive business proposals* (3rd ed.). New York: AMACOM, p. 114.

[9] McLaughlin, M. W. (n.d.). 12 tips for writing a winning proposal. Retrieved from http://c-nsc.org/tips-writing-a-winning-proposal

[10] Greenwood, G., & Greenwood, J. (2008). SBIR proposal writing basics: Resumes must be written well. Greenwood Consulting Group. Retrieved from http://www.g-jgreenwood.com/sbir-proposal-writing-articles

[11] What we do. (n.d.) Ronald McDonald House Charities. Retrieved from http://www.rmhc.org/grants

[12] How long does it take to create a business plan? (n.d.). SCORE Association. Retrieved from https://youngstown.score.org/node/834797

[13] Berry, T. (n.d.). What to pay that business plan consultant, Part 2. Bplans. Retrieved from http://timberry.bplans.com/what-to-pay-that-business-planning-consultant-part-2.html

[14] Schindler, E. (2016, January 29). The best business plan software of 2016. *PC Magazine.* Retrieved from http://www.pcmag.com/article2/0,2817,2492624,00.asp; Lewis, H. (2013, January 5). Hassle-free business plans. *New York Post.* Retrieved from http://www.nypost.com/p/news/business/hassle_free_business_plans_4tqWOfXU9hmWrsLUKgFECO

[15] Based on Acebu, E. (2015, December 16). Everything but the elevator. UCSB. Retrieved from http://www.tmp.ucsb.edu/mtm/everything-elevator

[16] Starr, K. (2012, September 18). The eight-word mission statement. *Stanford Social Innovation Review.* Retrieved from http://www.ssireview.org/blog/entry/the_eight_word_mission_statement

[17] Berry, T. (2014, June 25). True story: Why you don't want a business plan writer. U.S. Small Business Administration. Retrieved from https://www.sba.gov/blogs/true-story-why-you-dont-want-business-plan-writer

[18] Ibid.

[19] Ratner, H. M. (2012, March 1). 9 businesses that social media built. *Today's Chicago Woman.* Retrieved from http://www.tcwmag.com/9-businesses-social-media-built

[20] Office of Civic Engagement & Service. (n.d.). Definition of service learning. Fayetteville State University. Retrieved from http://www.uncfsu.edu/civic-engagement/service-learning/definition-of-service-learning

[21] Partially based on McKeown, G. (2012, October 4). If I read one more platitude-filled mission statement, I'll scream. HBR Blog Network. Retrieved from http://blogs.hbr.org/cs/2012/10/if_i_read_one_more_platitude_filled_mission_statement.html. Also partially based on Missionstatements.com. Ideas and inspirations for defining your own mission statement. (n.d.). Retrieved from http://www.missionstatements.com/fortune_500_mission_statements.html

Chapter 14 Business Presentations

LEARNING OUTCOMES

After studying this chapter, you should be able to

1. Recognize various types of business presentations, and discuss two important first steps in preparing for any of these presentations.
2. Explain how to organize your business presentation, understand contemporary visual aids, and know how to build audience rapport.
3. Create an impressive, error-free multimedia presentation that shows a firm grasp of basic visual design principles.
4. Specify delivery techniques for use before, during, and after a presentation to keep the audience engaged.
5. Organize presentations for intercultural audiences and in teams.
6. List techniques for improving telephone skills to project a positive image.

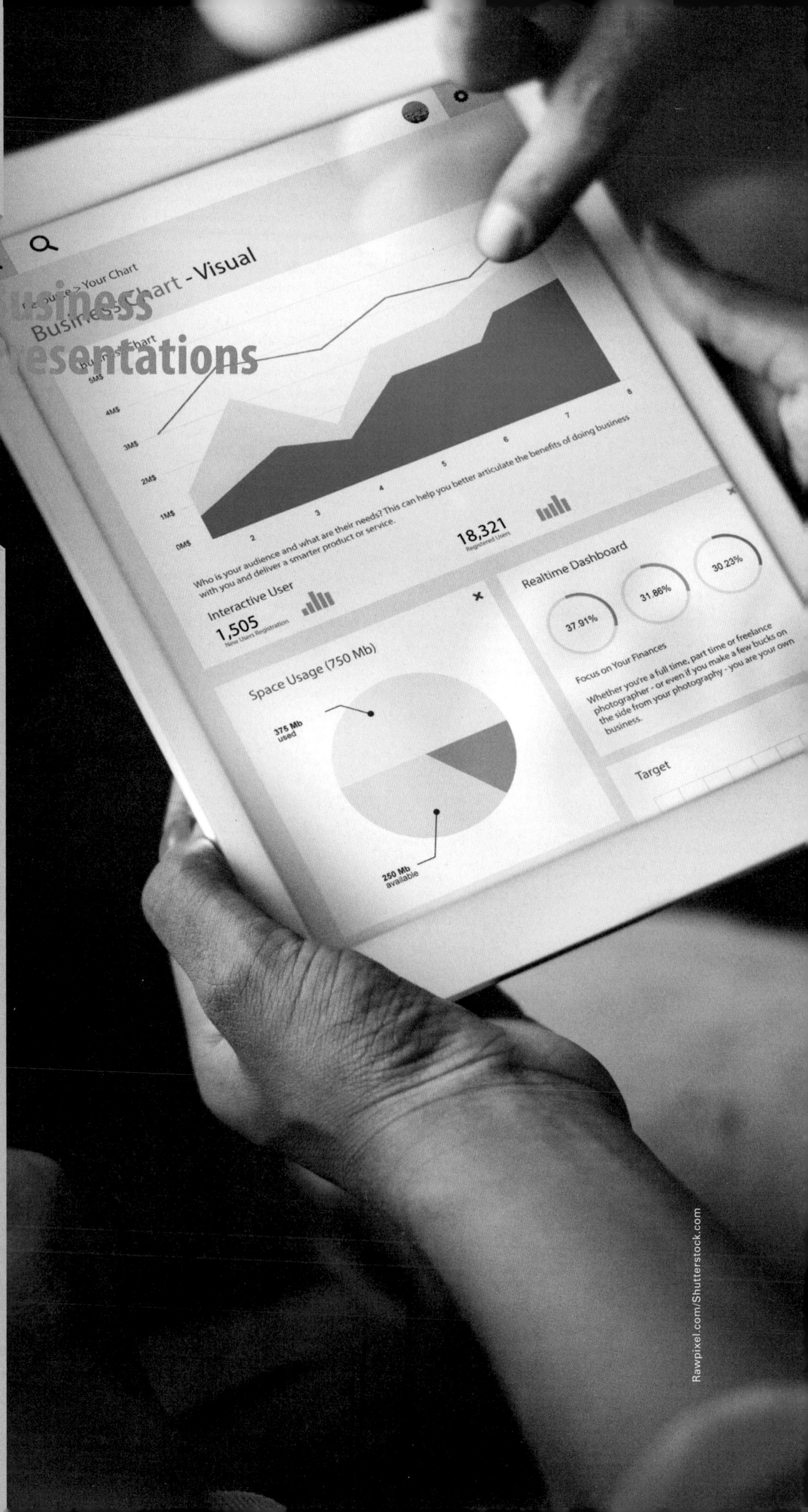

Rawpixel.com/Shutterstock.com

Jean-luc Doumont: Engineering Effective Presenting Skills Worldwide

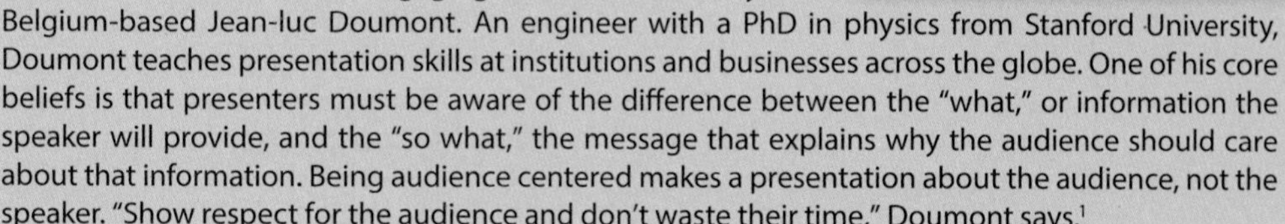

Yeamake/Shutterstock.com

Hooking an audience and capturing its attention is crucial to effective presentations. To do so, presenters must be clear, understandable, and engaging from the onset, says Belgium-based Jean-luc Doumont. An engineer with a PhD in physics from Stanford University, Doumont teaches presentation skills at institutions and businesses across the globe. One of his core beliefs is that presenters must be aware of the difference between the "what," or information the speaker will provide, and the "so what," the message that explains why the audience should care about that information. Being audience centered makes a presentation about the audience, not the speaker. "Show respect for the audience and don't waste their time," Doumont says.[1]

Photographee.eu/Shutterstock.com

Doumont divides presentation preparation into five steps. *Planning* defines the presentation's purpose and audience as well as any time and space constraints. *Designing* concentrates on developing content with an introduction, body, and conclusion. An introduction must go beyond the attention-grabbing hook and preview three to five main points that will be discussed later. The body should contain support for these points and smooth transitions between them. The talk should conclude by recapping key points and then reminding the audience of the main take-away.

The *creating slides* step is optional, Doumont says. "Do your slides right . . . or don't do slides at all," he advises.[2] Limit each slide to one message that you make verbally. *Delivering* the presentation is key to its success. Doumont considers delivery a performance that requires practice. He recommends against reciting an entire presentation from memory to avoid sounding canned. Instead, he suggests memorizing an outline and recreating the words spoken during practice sessions to sound extemporaneous. Look at everyone in the audience, move from behind the podium, and make deliberate gestures. Project confidence by controlling your body.

Some speakers consider the last element of delivering effective presentations intimidating. *Answering questions*, however, is essential to a successful presentation. Be honest and remain calm and professional. Repeat or rephrase the question while addressing the answer to the entire audience. By following these steps and remembering your audience at all times, you will give your listeners what they need to act on the information you have delivered.[3]

Critical Thinking

- Why is the "so what" of a presentation so important?
- Why does Jean-luc Doumont say, "Do your slides right . . . or don't do them at all"?
- How can you build rapport with your audience?

Creating Effective Business Presentations

Learning Outcome 1

Recognize various types of business presentations, and discuss two important first steps in preparing for any of these presentations.

Unlike motivational expert Tony Robbins, activist Martin Luther King Jr., or the late Apple founder Steve Jobs, few of us will ever talk to an audience of millions—whether face-to-face or aided by technology. We won't be invited to give a TED talk, motivate millions, or introduce a spectacular new product. At some point, however, all businesspeople have to inform others or sell an idea. Such informative and persuasive presentations are often conveyed in person and involve audiences of various sizes. If you are like most people, you have some apprehension when speaking in public. That's normal. Good speakers are made, not born. The good news is that you can conquer the fear of public speaking and hone your skills with instruction and practice.

Speaking Skills and Your Career

The savviest future businesspeople take advantage of opportunities in college to develop their speaking skills. Such skills often play an important role in a successful career. In a recent PayScale survey, 39 percent of managers found new graduates lacking in public speaking;

46 percent would like to see better overall communication skills.[4] Speaking skills are useful at every career stage. You might, for example, have to make a sales pitch before customers, speak to a professional gathering, or describe your company's expansion plans to your banker.

When you are in the job market, remember that speaking skills rank high on recruiters' wish lists. According to an annual survey of career services professionals, 67 percent of the respondents named verbal communication as a key attribute they seek in an applicant's résumé; being well-spoken ranks among the top ten employability skills.[5] A recent Harris poll for presentation software service Prezi revealed that 70 percent of professionals who give presentations consider them "critical to their success at work."[6]

This chapter prepares you to use speaking skills in making professional oral presentations, whether alone or as part of a team, whether face-to-face or virtually. Before we dive into the specifics of how to become an excellent presenter, the following section addresses the types of business presentations you may encounter in your career.

Reality Check

Why Fear of Speaking Is Not an Option

"Poor presentation skills mean that leaders fail to inspire their teams, products fail to sell, entrepreneurs fail to attract funding, and careers fail to soar. That seems like a big price to pay for neglecting such a basic skill that anyone can improve upon."[7]

—Carmine Gallo, *communication coach, keynote speaker, author*

Understanding Presentation Types

A common part of a business professional's life is making presentations. Some presentations are informative, whereas others are persuasive. Some are face-to-face; others, virtual. Some are performed before big audiences, whereas others are given to smaller groups. Some presentations are elaborate; others are simple. Figure 14.1 shows a sampling of business presentations you may encounter in your career.

Knowing Your Purpose

Regardless of the type of presentation, you must prepare carefully to ensure that it is effective. The most important part of your preparation is deciding what you want to accomplish. Do you want to sell a health-care program to a prospective client? Do you want to persuade management to increase the marketing budget? Whether your goal is to persuade or to inform, you must have a clear idea of where you are going. At the end of your presentation, what do you want your listeners to remember or do?

Linda DeZube, a loan officer at Main Street Trust, faced such questions as she planned a talk for a class in small business management. Linda's former business professor had asked her to return to campus and give the class advice about borrowing money from banks in order to start new businesses. Because Linda knew so much about this topic, she found it difficult to extract a specific purpose statement for her presentation. After much thought she narrowed her purpose to this: *To inform potential entrepreneurs about three important factors that loan officers consider before granting start-up loans to launch small businesses.* Her entire presentation focused on ensuring that the class members understood and remembered three principal ideas.

Figure 14.1 **Types of Business Presentations**

- Overview or summary of an issue, proposal, or problem
- Delivery of information, discussion of questions, collection of feedback

- Oral equivalent of business reports and proposals
- Informational or persuasive oral account, simple or elaborate

- Online, prerecorded audio clip delivered over the Web
- Opportunity to launch products, introduce and train employees, and sell products and services

- Collaboration facilitated by technology (telepresence or Web)
- Real-time meeting online with remote colleagues

- Web-based presentation, lecture, workshop, or seminar
- Digital transmission with or without video to train employees, interact with customers, or promote products

Knowing Your Audience

As in any type of communication, a second key element in preparation is analyzing your audience, anticipating the reactions of audience members, and adjusting to their needs if necessary. Audiences may fall into four categories, as summarized in Figure 14.2. By anticipating your audience, you have a better idea of how to organize your presentation. A friendly audience, for example, will respond to humor and personal experiences. A hostile audience requires an even, controlled delivery style with objective data and expert opinion. Whatever type of audience you will face, remember to plan your presentation so that it focuses on audience benefits. People in your audience will want to know what's in it for them.

Other elements, such as age, gender, education level, experience, and the size of the audience, will affect your style and message. Analyze the following questions to determine your organizational pattern, delivery style, and supporting material.

- How will this topic appeal to this audience?
- How can I relate this information to my listeners' needs?
- How can I earn respect so that they accept my message?
- What would be most effective in making my point? Facts? Statistics? Personal experiences? Expert opinion? Humor? Cartoons? Graphic illustrations? Demonstrations? Case histories? Analogies?
- What measures must I take to ensure that this audience remembers my main points?

If you have agreed to speak to an audience with which you are unfamiliar, ask for the names of a half dozen people who will be in the audience. Contact them and learn about their backgrounds and expectations for the presentation. This information can help you answer questions about what they want to hear and how deeply you should explore the subject. You will want to thank these people when you start your talk. Doing this kind of homework will impress the audience.

Figure 14.2 Succeeding With Four Audience Types

Audience Members	Organizational Pattern	Delivery Style	Supporting Material
Friendly			
They like you and your topic.	Use any pattern. Try something new. Involve the audience.	Be warm, pleasant, and open. Use lots of eye contact and smiles.	Include humor, personal examples, and experiences.
Neutral			
They are calm, rational; their minds are made up, but they think they are objective.	Present both sides of the issue. Use pro/con or problem/solution patterns. Save time for audience questions.	Be controlled. Do nothing showy. Use confident, small gestures.	Use facts, statistics, expert opinion, and comparison and contrast. Avoid humor, personal stories, and flashy visuals.
Uninterested			
They have short attention spans; they may be there against their will.	Be brief—include no more than three points. Avoid topical and pro/con patterns that seem lengthy to the audience.	Be dynamic and entertaining. Move around. Use large gestures.	Use humor, cartoons, colorful visuals, powerful quotations, and startling statistics.
	Avoid darkening the room, standing motionless, passing out handouts, using boring visuals, or expecting the audience to participate.		
Hostile			
They want to take charge or to ridicule the speaker; they may be defensive, emotional.	Organize using a noncontroversial pattern, such as a topical, chronological, or geographical strategy.	Be calm and controlled. Speak evenly and slowly.	Include objective data and expert opinion. Avoid anecdotes and humor.
	Avoid a question-and-answer period, if possible; otherwise, use a moderator or accept only written questions.		

Reality Check

Telling Stories to Be Memorable

"Stories and punchlines pack power. Humor anchors key points. Humor makes your message memorable."[8]

—Dianna Booher, *communication consultant and author*

Connecting With Audiences by Organizing Content and Using Visual Aids

LEARNING OUTCOME 2

Explain how to organize your business presentation, understand contemporary visual aids, and know how to build audience rapport.

After determining your purpose and analyzing the audience, you are ready to collect information and organize it logically. Good organization and intentional repetition are the two most powerful keys to audience comprehension and retention. In fact, many speech experts recommend the following admittedly repetitious, but effective, plan:

- **Step 1:** Tell them what you are going to tell them.
- **Step 2:** Tell them.
- **Step 3:** Tell them what you have told them.

In other words, repeat your main points in the introduction, body, and conclusion of your presentation. Although it is redundant, this strategy is necessary in oral presentations. Let's examine how to construct the three parts of an effective presentation: introduction, body, and conclusion.

Capturing Attention in the Introduction

How many times have you heard a speaker begin with *It's a pleasure to be here,* or *I'm honored to be asked to speak*, or the all-too-common *Today I'm going to talk about*. . . . Boring openings such as these get speakers off to a dull start. Avoid such banalities by striving to accomplish three goals in the introduction to your presentation:

- Capture listeners' attention and get them involved.
- Identify yourself and establish your credibility.
- Preview your main points.

If you are able to appeal to listeners and involve them in your presentation right from the start, you are more likely to hold their attention until the finish. Consider some of the same techniques that you used to open sales letters: a question, a startling fact, a joke, a story, or a quotation. Some speakers achieve involvement by opening with a question or command that requires audience members to raise their hands or stand up. Additional techniques to gain and keep audience attention are presented in the accompanying Career Coach box.

To establish your credibility, you need to describe your position, knowledge, education, or experience—whatever qualifies you to speak. The way you dress, the self-confidence you display, and your direct eye contact can also build credibility. In addition, try to connect with your audience. Listeners respond particularly well to speakers who reveal something of themselves and identify with them. A consultant addressing office workers might reminisce about how she started as an administrative assistant; a CEO might tell a funny story in which the joke is on him. Use humor if you can pull it off (not everyone can); self-effacing humor may work best for you.

After capturing your audience's attention and effectively establishing your credibility, you will want to preview the main points of your topic, perhaps with a visual aid.

Take a look at Linda DeZube's introduction, shown in Figure 14.3, to see how she integrated all the elements necessary for a good opening.

Organizing the Body of the Presentation

The most effective oral presentations focus on a few principal ideas. Therefore, the body of your short presentation (20 minutes or shorter) should include a limited number of main points—say, two to four. Develop each main point with adequate, but not excessive, explanation and details. Too many details can obscure the main message, so keep your presentation simple and logical. Remember, listeners have no pages to refer to should they become confused.

Career Coach

Gaining and Keeping Audience Attention

Experienced speakers know how to capture the attention of an audience and how to maintain that attention throughout a presentation. You can spruce up your presentations by trying these twelve proven techniques.

- **A promise.** Begin with a realistic promise that keeps the audience expectant (for example, *By the end of this presentation, you will know how you can increase your sales by 50 percent!*).
- **Drama.** Open by telling an emotionally moving story or by describing a serious problem that involves the audience. Throughout your talk include other dramatic elements, such as a long pause after a key statement. Change your vocal tone or pitch. Professionals use high-intensity emotions such as anger, joy, sadness, and excitement.
- **Eye contact.** As you begin, command attention by surveying the entire audience to take in all listeners. Give yourself two to five seconds to linger on individuals to avoid fleeting, unconvincing eye contact. Don't just sweep the room and the crowd.
- **Movement.** Leave the lectern area whenever possible. Walk around the conference table or down the aisles of the presentation room. Try to move toward your audience, especially at the beginning and end of your talk.
- **Questions.** Keep listeners active and involved with rhetorical questions. Ask for a show of hands to get each listener thinking. The response will also give you a quick gauge of audience attention.
- **Demonstrations.** Include a member of the audience in a demonstration (for example, *I'm going to show you exactly how to implement our four-step customer courtesy process, but I need a volunteer from the audience to help me*).
- **Samples/props.** If you are promoting a product, consider using items to toss out to the audience or to award as prizes to volunteers. You can also pass around product samples or promotional literature. Be careful, though, to maintain control.
- **Visuals.** Give your audience something to look at besides yourself. Use a variety of visual aids in a single session. Also consider writing the concerns expressed by audience members on a flipchart or on a whiteboard or Smart Board as you go along.
- **Dress.** Enhance your credibility with your audience by dressing professionally for your presentation. Professional attire will help you look competent and qualified, making your audience more likely to listen and take you seriously.
- **Current events/statistics.** Mention a current event or statistic (the more startling, the better) that is relevant to your topic and to which the audience can relate.
- **A quote.** Quotations, especially those made by well-known individuals, can be powerful attention-getting devices. The quotation should be pertinent to your topic, short, and interesting.
- **Self-interest.** Review your entire presentation to ensure that it meets the critical *What's-in-it-for-me* audience test. Remember that people are most interested in things that benefit them.

wavebreakmedia/Shutterstock.com

When Linda DeZube began planning her presentation, she realized immediately that she could talk for hours on her topic. She also knew that listeners are not good at separating major and minor points. Therefore, instead of drowning her listeners in information, she sorted out a few main ideas. In the banking industry, loan officers generally ask the following three questions of each budding entrepreneur: (a) Are you ready to hit the ground running in starting your business? (b) Have you done your homework? and (c) Have you made realistic projections of sales, cash flow, and equity investment? These questions would become her main points, but Linda wanted to streamline them further so that her audience would be sure to remember them. She encapsulated the questions in three words: *experience, preparation,* and *projection*. As you can see in Figure 14.3, Linda prepared a sentence outline showing these three main ideas. Each is supported by examples and explanations.

How to organize and sequence main ideas may not be immediately obvious when you begin working on a presentation. The following methods, which review and amplify those discussed in Chapter 12, provide many possible strategies and examples to help you organize a presentation:

- **Chronology.** A presentation describing the history of a problem, organized from the first sign of trouble to the present.
- **Geography/space.** A presentation about the changing diversity of the workforce, organized by regions in the country (East Coast, West Coast, and so forth).

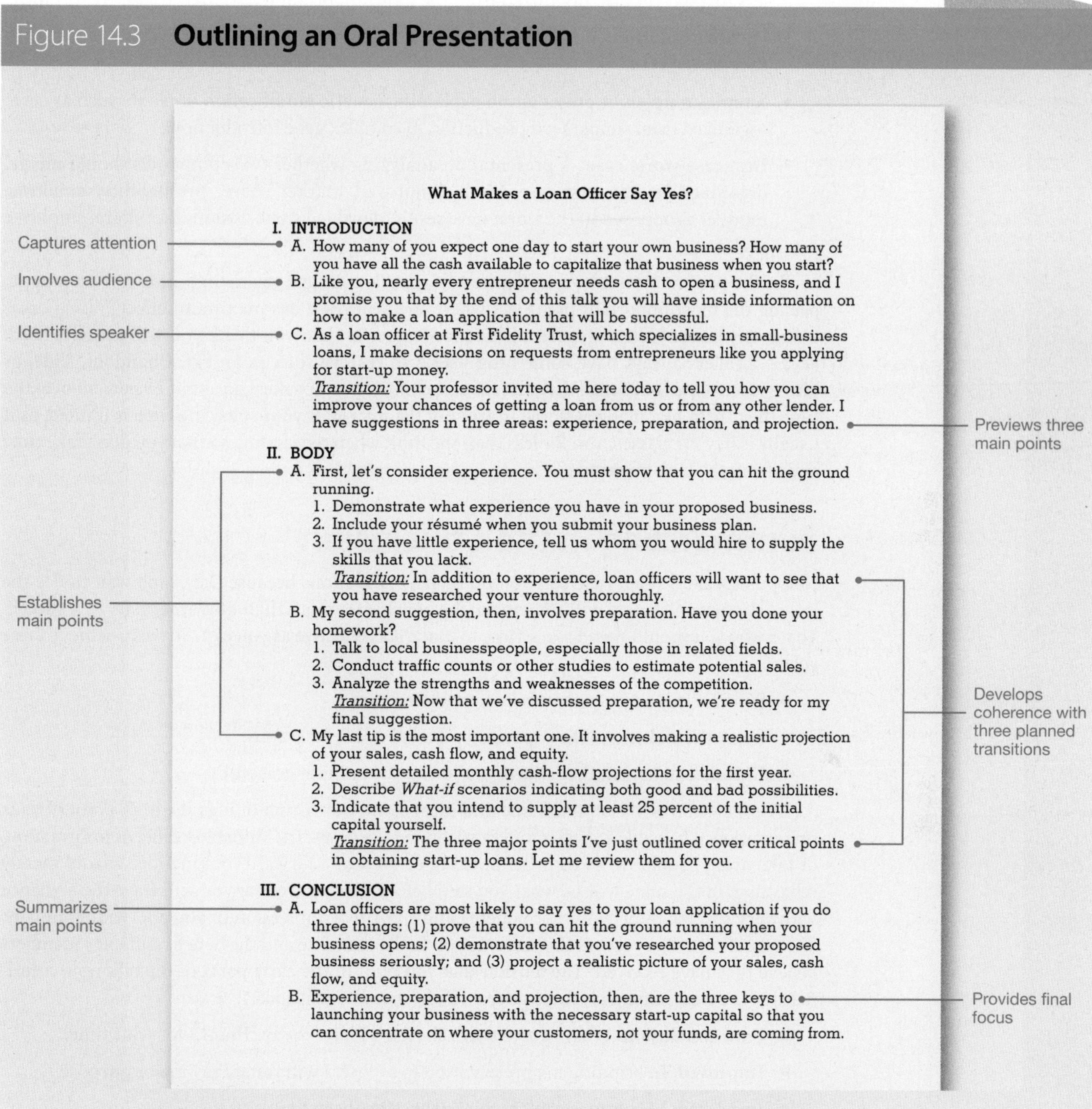

Figure 14.3 Outlining an Oral Presentation

- **Topic/function/conventional grouping.** A presentation discussing mishandled airline baggage, organized by names of airlines.
- **Comparison/contrast (pro/con).** A presentation comparing e-marketing with traditional direct mail.
- **Journalistic pattern (the six Ws).** A presentation describing the prevention of identity theft and how to recover after identity thieves strike. Organized by *who, what, when, where, why,* and *how.*
- **Value/size.** A presentation describing fluctuations in housing costs, organized by home prices.

- **Importance.** A presentation describing five reasons a company should move its headquarters to a specific city, organized from the most important reason to the least important.
- **Problem/solution.** A presentation offering a solution to a problem of declining sales, such as reducing staff.
- **Simple/complex.** A presentation explaining genetic modification of plants such as corn, organized from simple seed production to complex gene introduction.
- **Best case/worst case.** A presentation analyzing whether two companies should merge, organized by the best-case result (improved market share, profitability, employee morale) as opposed to the worst-case result (devalued stock, lost market share, employee malaise).

In the presentation shown in Figure 14.3, Linda arranged the main points by importance, placing the most important point last where she believes it has maximum effect. When organizing any presentation, prepare a little more material than you think you will actually need. Savvy speakers always have something useful in reserve such as an extra handout, slide, or idea—just in case they finish early. At the same time, most speakers go about 25 percent over the time they spent practicing at home in front of the mirror. If your speaking time is limited, as it usually is in your classes, aim for less than the limit when rehearsing, so that you don't take time away from the next presenters.

Summarizing in the Conclusion

Nervous speakers often rush to wrap up their presentations because they can't wait to flee the stage. However, listeners will remember the conclusion more than any other part of a speech. That's why you should spend some time to make it as effective as you can. Strive to achieve three goals:

- Summarize the main themes of the presentation.
- Leave the audience with a specific and memorable take-away.
- Include a statement that allows you to exit the podium gracefully.

A conclusion is like a punch line and must stand out. Think of it as the high point of your presentation, a valuable kernel of information to take away. The valuable kernel of information, or take-away, should tie in with the opening or present a forward-looking idea. Avoid merely rehashing, in the same words, what you said before, but ensure that you will leave the audience with very specific information or benefits and a positive impression of you and your company. The take-away is the value of the presentation to the audience and the benefit audience members believe they have received. The tension that you built in the early parts of the talk now culminates in the close. Compare these poor and improved conclusions:

- **Poor conclusion:** Well, I guess that's about all I have to say. Thanks for your time.
- **Improved:** In bringing my presentation to a close, I will restate my major purpose . . . .
- **Improved:** In summary, my major purpose has been to . . . .
- **Improved:** In conclusion, let me review my three major points. They are . . . .

Notice how Linda DeZube, in the conclusion shown in Figure 14.3, summarized her three main points and provided a final focus to listeners.

If you are promoting a recommendation, you might end as follows: *In conclusion, I recommend that we retain Matrixx Marketing to conduct a telemarketing campaign beginning September 1 at a cost of X dollars. To do so, I suggest that we (a) finance this campaign from our operations budget, (b) develop a persuasive message describing our new product, and (c) name Lisa Beck to oversee the project.*

In your conclusion you could use an anecdote, an inspiring quotation, or a statement that ties in the opener and offers a new insight. Whatever you choose, be sure to include a closing thought that indicates you are finished.

Establishing Audience Rapport

Good speakers are adept at building audience rapport. They form a bond with the audience, often entertaining as well as informing. How do they do it? From observations of successful and unsuccessful speakers, we have learned that the good ones use a number of verbal and nonverbal techniques to connect with the audiences. Their helpful techniques include providing effective imagery, supplying verbal signposts, and using body language strategically.

imtmphoto/Shutterstock.com

Reality Check

What Is Rapport?

"Take any relationship between two people and you'll find the first thing that created their bond was something they had in common. . . . Rapport is created by a feeling of commonality. Rapport is power."

—Tony Robbins, *entrepreneur, best-selling author, philanthropist*

Effective Imagery. You will lose your audience quickly if you fill your talk with abstractions, generalities, and dry facts. To enliven your presentation and enhance comprehension, try using some of the techniques shown in Figure 14.4. However, beware of exaggeration or distortion. Keep your imagery realistic and credible.

Verbal Signposts. Speakers must remember that listeners, unlike readers of a report, cannot control the rate of presentation or read back through pages to review main points. As a result, listeners get lost easily. Knowledgeable speakers help the audience recognize the organization and main points in an oral message with verbal signposts. They keep listeners on track by including helpful previews, summaries, and transitions such as these:

- **Previewing**

  The next segment of my talk presents three reasons for. . . .
  Let's now consider the causes of. . . .

- **Summarizing**

  Let me review with you the major problems I have just discussed. . . .
  You see, then, that the most significant factors are. . . .

- **Switching directions**

  Thus far we have talked solely about . . . ; now let's move to. . . .
  I have argued that . . . and . . . , but an alternate view holds that. . . .

You can further improve any oral presentation by including appropriate transitional expressions such as *first, second, next, then, therefore, moreover, on the other hand, on the contrary,* and *in conclusion.* These transitional expressions, which you learned about in Chapter 5 (see Figure 5.6), build coherence, lend emphasis, and tell listeners where you are headed. Notice in Linda DeZube's outline in Figure 14.3 the specific transitional elements designed to help listeners recognize each new principal point.

Nonverbal Messages. Although what you say is most important, the nonverbal messages you send can also have a powerful effect on how well your audience receives your message. How you look, how you move, and how you speak can make or break your presentation. The following suggestions focus on nonverbal tips to ensure that your verbal message resonates with your audience.

Figure 14.5 Pros and Cons of Visual Aid Options

Medium	Pros	Cons
Medium: High Tech		
Multimedia slides	Create professional appearance with many color, art, graphic, and font options. Allow users to incorporate video, audio, and hyperlinks. Offer ease of use and transport via removable storage media, Web download, or e-mail attachment. Are inexpensive to update.	Present potential incompatibility issues. Require costly projection equipment and practice for smooth delivery. Tempt user to include razzle-dazzle features that may fail to add value. Can be too one-dimensional and linear.
Zoom presentations	Enable presenter to zoom in on and out of content to show the big picture or specific details in nonlinear, 3D quality. Provide attractive templates. Allow users to insert rich media. Offer an interactive, cinematic, and dynamic experience.	Require Internet access because they are cloud based. Don't allow editing of images. Offer limited font choices. Can be difficult to operate for some presenters used to individual slides; can make moving around the canvas challenging. Zooming can be distracting and even nauseating.
Video	Gives an accurate representation of the content; strongly indicates forethought and preparation.	Creates potential for compatibility issues related to computer video formats. Is generally expensive to create and update.
Medium: Low Tech		
Handouts	Encourage audience participation. Are easy to maintain and update. Enhance recall because audience keeps reference material.	Increase risk of unauthorized duplication of speaker's material. Can be difficult to transport. May cause speaker to lose audience's attention.
Flipcharts or whiteboards	Provide inexpensive option available at most sites. Enable users to (a) create, (b) modify or customize on the spot, (c) record comments from the audience, and (d) combine with more high-tech visuals in the same presentation.	Require graphics talent. Can be difficult for larger audiences to see. Can be cumbersome to transport. Easily wear with use.
Props	Offer a realistic reinforcement of message content. Increase audience participation with close observation.	Lead to extra work and expense in transporting and replacing worn objects. Are of limited use with larger audiences.

Andrey Yurlov/Shutterstock.com; Elena Elisseeva/Shutterstock.com; HotVector/Shutterstock.com; Marko Rupena/Shutterstock.com; Mykola Komarovskyy/Shutterstock.com; Andrey_Popov/Shutterstock.com

presentation software often prepare a set of their slides along with notes to hand out to viewers. Timing the distribution of any handout, though, is tricky. To avoid distractions and to keep control, announce and discuss handouts during the presentation, but delay distributing them until after you finish.

Zoom Presentations. Many business presenters feel limited by multimedia slides, which tend to be linear. As a result, some communicators prefer more dynamic visual aids. Using software such as Prezi, a cloud-based presentation and storytelling tool, businesspeople can design 3D presentations. These 3D presentations allow the speaker to zoom in on and out of images to help the audience understand and remember content, details, and relationships.[11] Zoom presentations allow presenters to communicate their ideas in a more exciting, creative way. Audience

Figure 14.6 Prezi Zoom Presentation

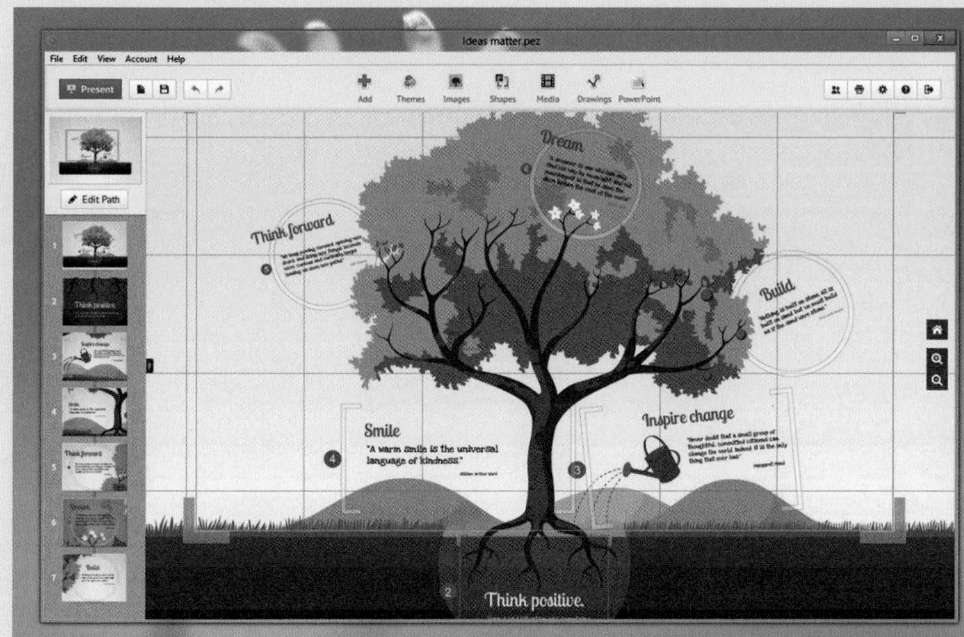

Prezi uses one canvas for a presentation rather than individual slides. Here is an example of the main canvas of a zoom presentation. Clicking on any section of this canvas will zoom in on detailed information. For example, if you click on the area around the tree roots, you will zoom in on a quote about thinking positively, as shown in the thumbnail images in the left pane.

Source: http://prezi-a.akamaihd.net/presskit/Prezi%20Desktop/PreziDesktop_Windows.png

members also seem to appreciate the cinematic, interactive quality of these presentations. Figure 14.6 shows what a typical Prezi canvas looks like during the design process.

Moving Beyond PowerPoint Bullets Electronic slideshows, created using PowerPoint in particular, are a staple of business presentations. However, overuse or misuse may be the downside of the ever-present PowerPoint slideshow. Over more than two decades of the software program's existence, millions of poorly created and badly delivered presentations have tarnished PowerPoint's reputation as an effective communication tool. Tools are helpful only when used properly.

In the last few years, several communication consultants have tried to show businesspeople how they can move beyond bullet points. The experts recommend creating slideshows that tell a story and send a powerful message with much less text and more images.[12] Presentation guru Garr Reynolds urges readers to unleash their creativity: "Do not rely on Microsoft or Apple or anyone else to dictate your choices. Most of all, do not let mere habit—and the habits of others—dictate

Rawpixel.com/Shutterstock.com

The best way to foster engagement during a presentation is to involve the audience, and software developers have created new programs that do exactly that. Glisser, an online platform that integrates audience responses into presentations, connects the speaker to members of the audience, who use their own mobile devices to provide immediate feedback via polls, surveys, and social media. The platform also allows audience members to access presentation slides in real time and to electronically make notes to keep for future reference. Why do good presenters strive for more audience participation? [13]

Figure 14.7 **SlideRocket Presentation**

SlideRocket is a cloud-based presentation software. Like PowerPoint, it allows users to create slides, but it takes the emphasis off bullet points. Instead, SlideRocket offers numerous tools to help users create visually rich slides: stock photos, flash animation, 2D and 3D transitional effects, tables, and charts.

Source: http://www.sliderocket.com/product/

your decisions on how you prepare and design and deliver your presentations."[14] However, before breaking with established rules and expectations, you first need to understand design basics.

Even much-touted alternatives to PowerPoint, such as Prezi, emaze, and SlideRocket, require some knowledge of the sound design principles covered in the next section. Figure 14.7 shows some of the tools that SlideRocket provides to create a visually rich presentation. The goal is to abandon boring bulleted lists.

LEARNING OUTCOME 3

Create an impressive, error-free multimedia presentation that shows a firm grasp of basic visual design principles.

Preparing Engaging Multimedia Presentations

When operated by proficient designers and skillful presenters, PowerPoint, Keynote, or Prezi can add visual impact to any presentation. In the sections that follow, you will learn to create an impressive multimedia presentation with the most widely used presentation software program, PowerPoint. You will also learn about Prezi zoom presentations as an alternative to PowerPoint or SlideRocket slides. With any software program, of course, gaining expertise requires an investment of time and effort. You could take a course, or you could teach yourself through an online tutorial. Another way to master PowerPoint or Prezi is to read a book such as Faithe Wempen's *PowerPoint Bible* or Russell Anderson-Williams's *Mastering Prezi for Business Presentations*, now in its second edition.

Applying the 3-x-3 Writing Process to Multimedia Presentations

Some presenters prefer to create their visuals first and then develop the narrative around their visuals. Others prefer to prepare their content first and then create the visual component. The risk associated with the first approach is that you may be tempted to spend too much time making your visuals look good and not enough time preparing your content. Remember that great-looking slides never compensate for thin content.

The following sections explain how to adjust your visuals to the situation and your audience. We review the three phases of the writing process and show how they can help you develop a visually appealing PowerPoint, SlideRocket, or Prezi presentation. In the first phase (prewriting), you analyze, anticipate, and adapt. In the second phase, you research, organize, compose, and design. In the third phase, you edit, proofread, and evaluate.

Analyzing the Situation and Purpose

Making the best design choices for your presentation depends greatly on your analysis of the situation and the purpose of your slideshow. Will your slides be used during a live presentation? Will they be part of a self-running presentation such as in a store kiosk? Will they be saved on a server so that users can watch the presentation online at their convenience? Will they be sent as a PowerPoint show or a PDF slide deck to a client instead of a hard-copy report? Will your presentation mainly run on smartphones or tablets?

If you are e-mailing the presentation or posting it online as a self-contained file or slide deck, it should feature more text than one that you would deliver orally. If, on the other hand, you are creating slides for a live presentation, you will likely rely more on images than on text.

Adjusting Slide Design to Your Audience

Think about how you can design your presentation to get the most positive response from your audience. Audiences respond, for example, to the colors, images, and special effects you use. Primary ideas are generally best conveyed with bold colors such as blue, green, and purple. Because the messages that colors convey can vary from culture to culture, presenters must choose colors and other design elements carefully.

The Meaning of Color. In the United States, blue is the color of credibility, tranquility, conservatism, and trust. Therefore, it is the background color of choice for many business presentations and social media sites. Green relates to interaction, growth, money, and stability. It can work well as a background or an accent color. Purple can also work as a background or accent color. It conveys spirituality, royalty, dreams, and humor.[15] As for text, adjust the color to provide high contrast so that it is readable. White or yellow, for example, usually works well on dark backgrounds.

Adapt the slide colors based on where you will give the presentation. Use light text on a dark background for presentations in darkened rooms. Use dark text on a light background for presentations in lighted rooms. Avoid using a dark font on a dark background, such as red text on a dark blue background. In the same way, avoid using a light font on a light background, such as white text on a pale blue background.

The Power of Images. Adapt the amount of text on your slide to how your audience will use the slides. As a general guideline, most graphic designers encourage *the 6-x-6 rule*: "Six bullets per screen, max; six words per bullet, max."[16] You may find, however, that breaking this rule is sometimes necessary, particularly when your users will be viewing the presentation on their own with no speaker assistance. For most purposes, though, strive to break free from bulleted lists whenever possible and minimize the use of text.

When using presentation software such as PowerPoint, try to avoid long, boring bulleted lists. You can alter layouts by repositioning, resizing, or changing the fonts for the placeholders in which your title, bulleted list, organization chart, video clip, photograph, or other elements appear. Figure 14.8 shows how to make your slides visually more appealing and memorable even with relatively small changes.

Notice that the bulleted items on the Before Revision slide in Figure 14.8 are not parallel. The wording looks as if the author had been brainstorming or freewriting a first draft. The second and sixth bullet points express the same thought, that shopping online is convenient and easy for customers. Some bullet points are too long. On the After Revision slide, the former bullets have become captions that accompany illustrations. The captions are short and well within the 6-x-6 rule, although they are complete sentences. The illustrations in the revised slide add interest and highlight the message. You may use icons and stock photos that you download from the Internet for personal or school use without penalty, or consider taking your own digital pictures.

You can also use other PowerPoint features, such as SmartArt, to add variety and pizzazz to your slides. Converting pure text and bullet points to graphics, charts, and other images will keep your audience interested and help them retain the information you are presenting.

Figure 14.8 Using Images and Illustrations for Greater Impact

Before Revision

Reasons for Selling Online

- Your online business can grow globally.
- Customer convenience.
- You can conduct your business 24/7.
- No need for renting a retail store or hiring employees.
- Reduce inquiries by providing policies and a privacy statement.
- Customers can buy quickly and easily.

After Revision

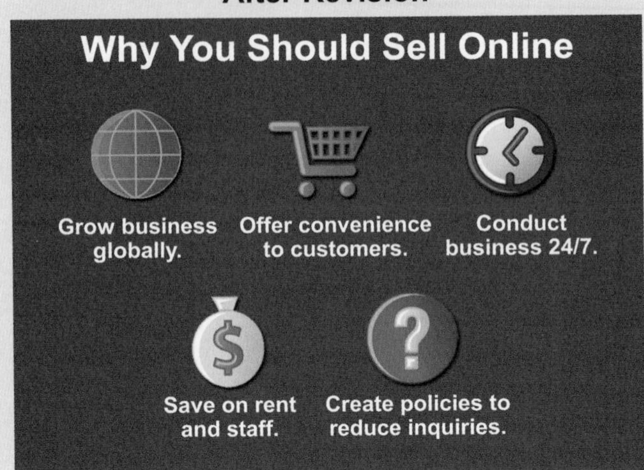

Why You Should Sell Online
Grow business globally.
Offer convenience to customers.
Conduct business 24/7.
Save on rent and staff.
Create policies to reduce inquiries.

The slide on the left contains bullet points that are not parallel and that overlap in meaning. The second and sixth bullet points say the same thing. Moreover, some bullet points are too long. After revision, the slide on the right has a more convincing title illustrating the "you" view. The bullet points are shorter, and each begins with a verb for parallelism and an emphasis on action. The illustrations add interest.

The Impact of Special Effects. Just as you anticipate audience members' reactions to color, you can usually anticipate their reactions to special effects. Using animation and sound effects—flying objects, swirling text, clashing cymbals, and the like—only because they are available is not a good idea. Special effects distract your audience, drawing attention away from your main points. You should add animation features only if doing so helps convey your message or adds interest to the content. When your audience members leave, they should be commenting on the ideas you conveyed—not on the wild swivels and sound effects. The zooming effect of Prezi presentations can add value to your presentation as long as it helps your audience understand connections and remember content. The motion should not make your listeners dizzy.

Building Your Business Presentation

After considering design principles and their effects, you are ready to start putting together your presentation. In this section you will learn how to organize and compose your presentation, which templates to choose, and how to edit, proofread, and evaluate your work.

Organizing Your Presentation. When you prepare your presentation, translate the major headings in your outline into titles for slides. Then build bullet points using short phrases. In Chapter 5 you learned to improve readability by using graphic highlighting techniques, including bullets, numbers, and headings. In preparing a PowerPoint, SlideRocket, or Prezi presentation, you will use those same techniques.

The slides (or canvas) you create to accompany your spoken ideas can be organized with visual elements that will help your audience understand and remember what you want to communicate. Let's say, for example, that you have three points in your presentation. You can create a blueprint slide that captures the three points in a visually appealing way, and then you can use that slide several times throughout your presentation. Near the beginning, the blueprint slide provides an overview of your points. Later, it provides transitions as you move from point to point. For transitions, you can direct your audience's attention by highlighting the next point you will be talking about. Finally, the blueprint slide can be used near the end to provide a review of your key points.

Composing Your Presentation. During the composition stage, many users fall into the trap of excessive formatting and programming. They fritter away precious time fine-tuning their slides or canvas and don't spend enough time on what they are going to say and how they will say it. To avoid this trap, set a limit for how much time you will spend making your slides or canvas visually appealing. Your time limit will be based on how many "bells and whistles" (a) your audience expects and (b) your content requires to make it understandable.

Remember that not every point and not every thought requires a visual. In fact, it's smart to switch off the presentation occasionally and direct the focus to yourself. Darkening the screen while you discuss a point, tell a story, give an example, or involve the audience will add variety to your presentation.

Create a slide or canvas only if it accomplishes at least one of the following purposes:

- Generates interest in what you are saying and helps the audience follow your ideas
- Highlights points you want your audience to remember
- Introduces or reviews your key points
- Provides a transition from one major point to the next
- Illustrates and simplifies complex ideas

Consider perusing the Help articles built into your presentation software or purchasing one of many inexpensive guides to electronic slide presentations. Your presentations will be more appealing, and you will save time if you know, for example, how to design with master slides and how to create your own templates. In a later section of this chapter, you will find very specific steps to follow as you create your presentation.

Working With Templates. All presentation programs require you to (a) select or create a template that will serve as the background for your presentation and (b) make each individual slide by selecting a layout that best conveys your message. Novice and even advanced users often use existing templates because they are designed by professionals who know how to combine harmonious colors, borders, bullet styles, and fonts for pleasing visual effects. If you prefer, you can alter existing templates so they better suit your needs. Adding a corporate logo, adjusting the color scheme to better match the colors used on your organization's website, or selecting a different font are just some of the ways you can customize existing templates. One big advantage of templates is that they get you started quickly.

Be careful, though, of what one expert calls visual clichés.[17] Overused templates and clip art that come preinstalled with PowerPoint, SlideRocket, and Prezi can weary viewers who have seen them repeatedly in presentations. Instead of using a standard template, search for *PowerPoint template, SlideRocket template*, or *Prezi template* in your favorite search tool. You will see hundreds of templates available as free downloads. Unless your employer requires that presentations all have the same look, your audience will appreciate fresh templates that complement the purpose of your presentation and provide visual variety.

Revising and Proofreading Your Presentation. Use the PowerPoint slide sorter view to rearrange, insert, and delete slides during the revision process. You can use the Prezi editor to make any necessary changes to your canvas. This is the time to focus on making your presentation as clear and concise as possible. If you are listing items, be sure they all use parallel grammatical form. Figure 14.9 shows how to revise a PowerPoint slide to improve it for conciseness, parallelism, and other features. Study the design tips described in the first slide and determine which suggestions the author did not follow. Then compare it with the revised slide.

As you are revising, check carefully to find spelling, grammar, punctuation, and other errors. Use the PowerPoint, SlideRocket, or Prezi spell-check feature, but don't rely on it solely. Careful proofing, preferably from a printed copy of the slideshow, is a must. Nothing is as embarrassing as projecting errors on a huge screen in front of an audience. Also, check for consistency in how you capitalize and punctuate points throughout the presentation.

Evaluating Your Presentation. The final stage in applying the 3-x-3 writing process to developing a PowerPoint, SlideRocket, or Prezi presentation involves evaluation. Is your message presented in a visually appealing way? Have you tested your slides on the equipment and in the room you will be using during your presentation? Do the colors you selected work in this new setting? Are the font styles and sizes readable from the back of the room? Figure 14.10 shows examples of PowerPoint slides that incorporate what you have learned in this discussion.

Figure 14.9 **Designing More Effective Slides**

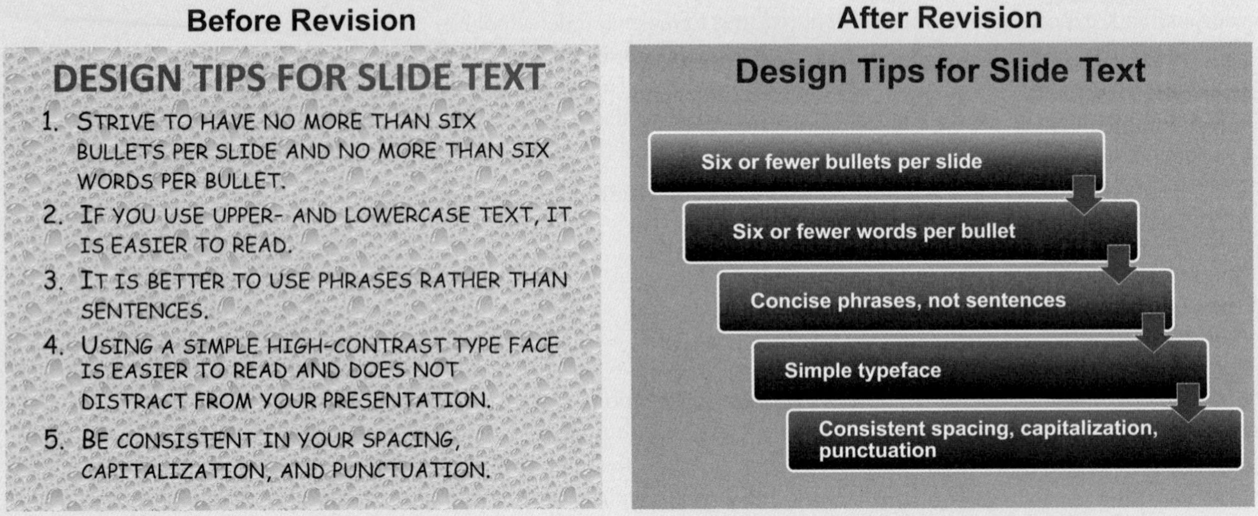

Before Revision

DESIGN TIPS FOR SLIDE TEXT
1. STRIVE TO HAVE NO MORE THAN SIX BULLETS PER SLIDE AND NO MORE THAN SIX WORDS PER BULLET.
2. IF YOU USE UPPER- AND LOWERCASE TEXT, IT IS EASIER TO READ.
3. IT IS BETTER TO USE PHRASES RATHER THAN SENTENCES.
4. USING A SIMPLE HIGH-CONTRAST TYPE FACE IS EASIER TO READ AND DOES NOT DISTRACT FROM YOUR PRESENTATION.
5. BE CONSISTENT IN YOUR SPACING, CAPITALIZATION, AND PUNCTUATION.

After Revision

The slide on the left uses a difficult-to-read font style. In addition, the slide includes too many words per bullet and violates most of the slide-making rules it covers. After revision, the slide on the right provides an appealing color combination, uses short bullet points in a readable font style, and creates an attractive list using PowerPoint SmartArt features.

The dark purple background and the matching hues in the slideshow shown in Figure 14.10 are standard choices for many business presentations. With an unobtrusive dark background, white fonts are a good option for maximum contrast and, hence, readability. The creator of the presentation varied the slide design to break the monotony of bulleted or numbered lists. Images and animated diagrams add interest and zing to the slides.

Preparing and Anticipating

Solid preparation and anticipating your talk are crucial. One expert advises presenters to rehearse, record themselves on video, critique the recording, and then repeat this process until they are satisfied with their performance.[18] Solid preparation will boost your confidence. Allow plenty of time before your presentation to set up and test your equipment. Confirm that the places you plan to stand are not in the line of the projected image. Audience members don't appreciate having part of the slide displayed on your body. Make sure that all video or Web links are working and that you know how to operate all features the first time you try.

No matter how much time you put into preshow setup and testing, you still have no guarantee that all will go smoothly. Therefore, always bring backups of your presentation. Overhead transparencies and handouts of your presentation provide good substitutes. Transferring your presentation to a CD or a USB flash drive that could run from any available computer might prove useful as well. Copying your digital file to the cloud (e.g., Dropbox or Google Drive) or sending it to yourself as an e-mail attachment can also prove beneficial.

Some presenters allow their PowerPoint slides, SlideRocket slides, or Prezi canvases to steal their thunder. Advertising mogul David Ogilvy once observed, "Most people use PowerPoint like a drunk uses a lamppost—for support rather than for illumination."[19] Although multimedia presentations can supply terrific sizzle, they cannot replace the steak. In developing a presentation, don't expect your visuals to carry the show. You can avoid being upstaged by not relying totally on your slides or canvas. Remember that you are still the main attraction!

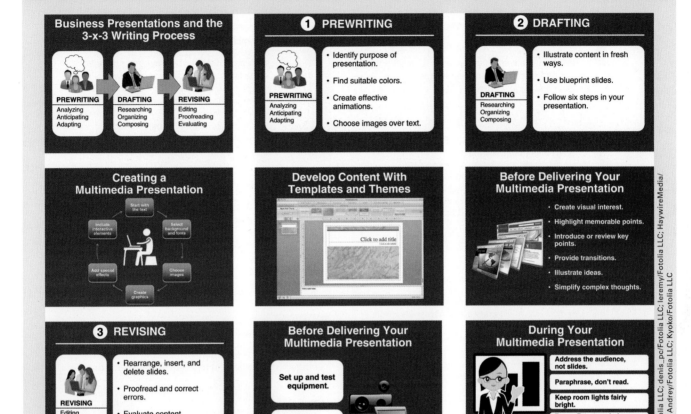

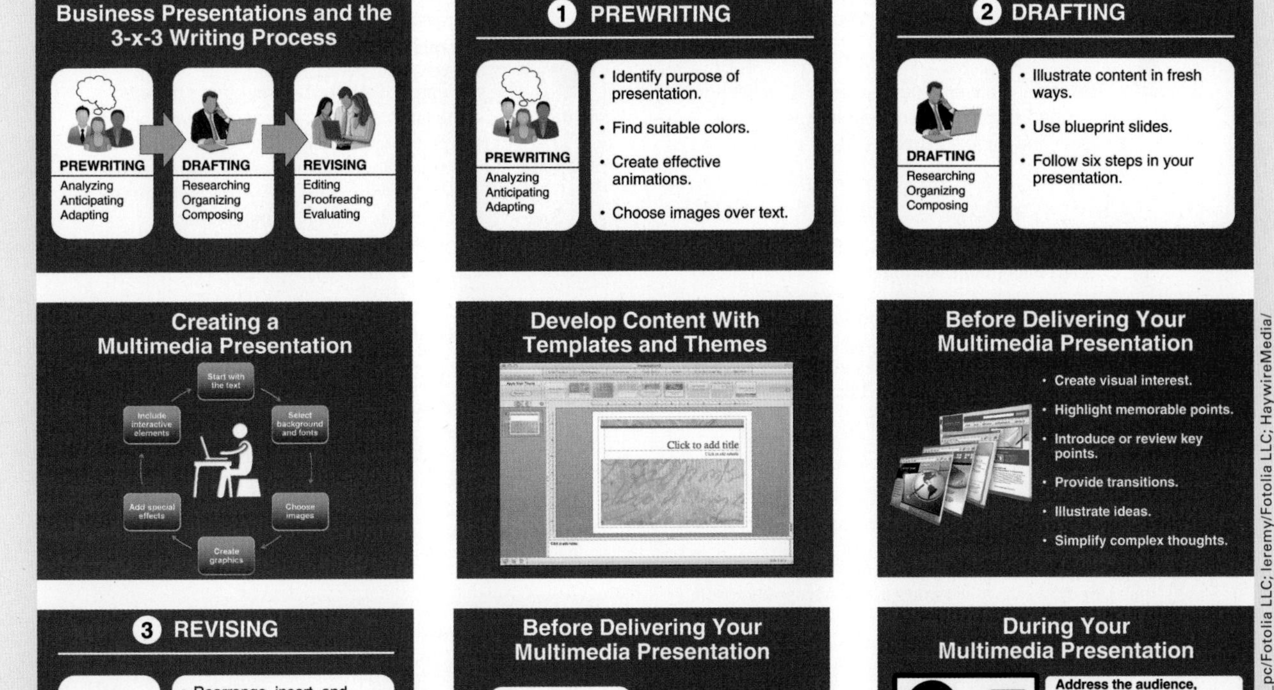

Figure 14.10 **PowerPoint Slides That Illustrate Multimedia Presentations**

iadams/Fotolia LLC; denis_pc/Fotolia LLC; leremy/Fotolia LLC; HaywireMedia/Fotolia LLC; Andrey/Fotolia LLC; Kyoko/Fotolia LLC

Seven Steps to a Powerful Multimedia Presentation

We have now discussed many suggestions for making effective PowerPoint, SlideRocket, and Prezi presentations, but you may still be wondering how to put it all together. Figure 14.11 presents a step-by-step process for creating a powerful multimedia presentation:

Polishing Your Delivery and Following Up

Once you have organized your presentation and prepared visuals, you are ready to practice delivering it. You will feel more confident and appear more professional if you know more about various delivery methods and techniques to use before, during, and after your presentation.

LEARNING OUTCOME 4

Specify delivery techniques for use before, during, and after a presentation to keep the audience engaged.

Choosing a Delivery Method

Inexperienced speakers often hold on to myths about public speaking. They may believe that they must memorize an entire presentation or read from a manuscript to be successful. Let's debunk the myths and focus on effective delivery techniques.

Figure 14.11 Seven Steps to a Powerful Multimedia Presentation

1 Start with the text.

What do you want your audience to believe, do, or remember? Organize your ideas into an outline with major and minor points.

2 Select background and fonts.

Choose a template or create your own. Focus on consistent font styles, sizes, colors, and backgrounds. Try to use no more than two font styles in your presentation. The point size should be between 24 and 36, and title fonts should be larger than text font.

3 Choose images that help communicate your message.

Use relevant clip art, infographics, photographs, maps, or drawings to illustrate ideas. Access Microsoft Office Online in PowerPoint and choose from thousands of images and photographs, most of which are in the public domain and require no copyright permissions. Before using images from other sources, determine whether permission from the copyright holder is required.

4 Create graphics.

Use software tools to transform boring bulleted items into appealing graphics and charts. PowerPoint's SmartArt feature can be used to create organization charts, cycles and radials, time lines, pyramids, matrixes, and Venn diagrams. Use PowerPoint's Chart feature to develop types of charts including line, pie, and bar charts. But don't overdo the graphics!

5 Add special effects.

To keep the audience focused, use animation and transition features to control when text or objects appear. With motion paths, 3D, and other animation options, you can move objects to various positions on the slide and zoom in on and out of images and text on your canvas. To minimize clutter, you can dim or remove them once they have served their purpose.

6 Create hyperlinks.

Make your presentation more interactive and intriguing by connecting to videos, spreadsheets, or websites.

Viorel Sima/Shutterstock.com

7 Move your presentation online.

Make your presentation available by posting it to the Internet or an organization's intranet. Even if you are giving a face-to-face presentation, attendees appreciate these electronic handouts. The most complex option for moving your multimedia presentation to the Web involves a Web conference or broadcast. To discourage copying, convert your presentations to PDF documents—with a watermark and in black and white, if needed. SlideRocket presentations can be embedded in a website or blog to be viewed by anyone who visits the site

Avoid Memorizing Your Presentation. Unless you are an experienced performer, you will sound robotic and unnatural if you try to recite your talk by heart. What's more, forgetting your place can be disastrous! That is why we don't recommend memorizing an entire oral presentation. However, memorizing significant parts—the introduction, the conclusion, and perhaps a meaningful quotation—can make your presentation dramatic and impressive.

Don't Read From Your Notes. Reading your business presentation to an audience from notes or a manuscript is boring, and listeners will quickly lose interest. Because reading suggests that you don't know your topic well, the audience loses confidence in your expertise. Reading

Grigvovan/Shutterstock.com

When the founders of the microlending nonprofit organization Kiva make business presentations around the world, audiences respond with enthusiastic applause and even tears. Kiva's online lending platform connects personal lenders with poverty-stricken individuals in developing nations, enabling villagers to start tomato farms, carpet kiosks, and other small ventures that improve their lives. Kiva's presentations include heartwarming stories and videos about village entrepreneurs to show that small loans can make a big difference. What tips can communicators follow to deliver powerful, inspirational presentations?

also prevents you from maintaining eye contact. You can't see audience reactions; consequently, you can't benefit from feedback.

Deliver Your Presentation Extemporaneously. The best plan for delivering convincing business presentations, by far, is to speak *extemporaneously,* especially when you are displaying a multimedia presentation such as a PowerPoint slideshow, SlideRocket slideshow, or Prezi canvas. Extemporaneous delivery means speaking freely, generally without notes, after preparing and rehearsing. You comment on the multimedia visuals you have prepared. Reading from notes or a manuscript in addition to a PowerPoint slideshow, SlideRocket slides, or a Prezi canvas will damage your credibility.

Know When Notes Are Appropriate. If you give a talk without multimedia technology, you may use note cards or an outline containing key sentences and major ideas, but beware of reading from a script. By preparing and then practicing with your notes, you can use them while also talking to your audience in a conversational manner. Your notes should be neither entire paragraphs nor single words. Instead, they should contain a complete sentence or two to introduce each major idea. Below the topic sentence(s), outline subpoints and illustrations. Note cards will keep you on track and prompt your memory, but only if you have rehearsed the presentation thoroughly.

Rich Polk/Getty Images Entertainment/Getty Images

Reality Check

Is Any Speaker Ever 100 Percent Comfortable?

"You're never really comfortable. Even though you may think you are . . . you really aren't." But in time, "you learn how to open, how to sustain, how to pace . . ." and you will get more comfortable.[20]

—Jerry Seinfeld, *comedian, actor, writer, producer*

Combating Stage Fright

Nearly everyone experiences some stage fright when speaking before a group. Rarely, though, will the fear of public speaking lead to freezing completely, as happened to Hollywood filmmaker Michael Bay. The director of big-budget action movies (*Transformers*) literally fled soon after walking on stage at CES, the big consumer electronics show in Las Vegas, in front of cameras and a huge audience.[21]

Being afraid is quite natural and results from actual physiological changes occurring in your body. Faced with a frightening situation, your body responds with the fight-or-flight response, discussed more fully in the accompanying Career Coach box. You can learn to control and reduce stage fright, as well as to incorporate techniques for effective speaking, by using the following strategies and techniques before, during, and after your presentation.

Career Coach

How to Avoid Stage Fright

Ever get nervous before making a presentation? Everyone does! And it's not all in your head, either. When you face something threatening or challenging, your body reacts in what psychologists call the fight-or-flight response. This physical reflex provides your body with increased energy to deal with threatening situations. It also creates those sensations—dry mouth, sweaty hands, increased heartbeat, and stomach butterflies—that we associate with stage fright. The fight-or-flight response arouses your body for action—in this case, making a presentation.

Because everyone feels some form of apprehension before speaking, it's impossible to eliminate the physiological symptoms altogether. However, you can reduce their effects with the following techniques:

- **Breathe deeply.** Use deep breathing to ease your fight-or-flight symptoms. Inhale to a count of ten, hold this breath to a count of ten, and exhale to a count of ten. Concentrate on your counting and your breathing; both activities reduce your stress.
- **Convert your fear.** Don't view your sweaty palms and dry mouth as evidence of fear. Interpret them as symptoms of exuberance, excitement, and enthusiasm to share your ideas.
- **Know your topic and come prepared.** Feel confident about your topic. Select a topic that you know well and that is relevant to your audience. Prepare thoroughly and practice extensively.
- **Use positive self-talk.** Remind yourself that you know your topic and are prepared. Tell yourself that the audience is on your side—because it is! Moreover, most speakers appear to be more confident than they feel. Make this apparent confidence work for you.
- **Take a sip of water.** Drink some water to alleviate your dry mouth and constricted voice box, especially if you're talking for more than 15 minutes.
- **Shift the spotlight to your visuals.** At least some of the time the audience will be focusing on your slides, transparencies, handouts, or whatever you have prepared—and not totally on you.
- **Ignore any stumbles.** If you make a mistake, ignore the stumble and keep going. Don't apologize or confess your nervousness. The audience will forget any mistakes quickly.
- **Feel proud when you finish.** You will be surprised at how good you feel when you finish. Take pride in what you have accomplished, and your audience will reward you with applause and congratulations. Your body, of course, will call off the fight-or-flight response and return to normal!

Before Your Presentation

Speaking in front of a group will be less daunting if you allow for adequate preparation, sufficient practice, and rehearsals. Interacting with the audience and limiting surprises such as malfunctioning equipment will also enhance your peace of mind. Review the following tips for a smooth start:

Prepare Thoroughly. One of the most effective strategies for reducing stage fright is knowing your subject thoroughly. Research your topic diligently and prepare a careful sentence outline. Those who try to wing it usually suffer the worst butterflies—and give the worst presentations.

Rehearse Repeatedly. When you rehearse, practice your entire presentation. In PowerPoint you may print out speaker's notes, an outline, or a handout featuring miniature slides, which are excellent for practice. If you don't use an electronic slideshow, place your outline sentences on separate note cards. You may also wish to include transitional sentences to help you move to the next topic as you practice. Rehearse alone or before friends and family. Also consider making an audio or video recording of your rehearsals so you can evaluate your effectiveness.

Time Yourself. Most audiences tend to get restless during longer talks. Therefore, try to complete your presentation in 20 minutes or less. If you have a time limit, don't go over it. Set a simple kitchen timer during your rehearsal to keep track of time. Better yet, use the PowerPoint function Rehearse Timings in the Slide Show tab to measure the length of your talk as you practice. Other presentation software packages offer similar features.

Dress Professionally. Dressing professionally for a presentation will make you look more credible to your audience. You will also feel more confident. If you are not used to professional attire, practice wearing it so that you appear comfortable during your presentation.

Check the Room and the Equipment. If you are using a computer, a projector, or sound equipment, be certain they are operational. Before you start, check electrical outlets and the position of the viewing screen. Ensure that the seating arrangement is appropriate to your needs.

Greet Members of the Audience. Try to make contact with a few members of the audience when you enter the room, while you are waiting to be introduced, or when you walk to the podium. Your body language should convey friendliness, confidence, and enjoyment.

Practice Stress Reduction. If you feel tension and fear while you are waiting your turn to speak, use stress-reduction techniques, such as deep breathing. Additional techniques to help you conquer stage fright are presented in the accompanying Career Coach box.

During Your Presentation

To stay in control during your talk, to build credibility, and to engage your audience, follow these time-tested guidelines for effective speaking:

Start with a Pause and Present Your First Sentence From Memory. When you first approach the audience, take a moment to make yourself comfortable. Establish your control of the situation. By memorizing your opening, you can immediately develop rapport with the audience through eye contact. You will also sound confident and knowledgeable.

Maintain Eye Contact. If the size of the audience overwhelms you, pick out two individuals on the right and two on the left. Talk directly to these people. Don't ignore listeners in the back of the room. Even when presenting to a large audience, try to make genuine, not fleeting eye contact with as many people as possible during your presentation.

Control Your Voice and Vocabulary. This means speaking in moderated tones but loudly enough to be heard. Eliminate verbal static, such as *ah, er, like, you know,* and *um*. Silence is preferable to meaningless fillers when you are thinking of your next idea.

Show Enthusiasm. If you are not excited about your topic, how can you expect your audience to be? Show passion for your topic through your tone, facial expressions, and gestures. Adding variety to your voice also helps to keep your audience alert and interested.

Skip the Apologies. Avoid weak openings, such as *I know you have heard this before, but we need to review it anyway.* Or: *I had trouble with my computer and the slides, so bear with me.* Unless the issue is blatant, such as not being able to load the presentation or make the projector work, apologies are counterproductive. Focus on your presentation.

Slow Down and Know When to Pause. Many novice speakers talk too rapidly, displaying their nervousness and making it very difficult for audience members to understand their ideas. Put the brakes on and listen to what you are saying. Pauses give the audience time to absorb an important point. Silence can be effective especially when you are transitioning from one point to another.

Move Naturally. If you have a lectern, don't hide behind it. Move about casually and naturally. Avoid fidgeting with your clothing, hair, or items in your pockets. Do not roll up your sleeves or put your hands in your pockets. Learn to use your body to express a point.

Control Visual Aids With Clickers, Pointers, and Blank Screens. Discuss and interpret each visual aid for the audience. Move aside as you describe it so that people can see it fully. Learn to use a clicker to advance your slides remotely. Use a laser pointer if necessary, but steady your hand if it is shaking. Dim the slideshow when not discussing the slides. In Slide Show view in PowerPoint, press *B* on the keyboard to blacken the screen or *W* to turn the screen white. In Prezi, remember to zoom back out when necessary.

Avoid Digressions. Stick to your outline and notes. Don't suddenly include clever little anecdotes or digressions that occur to you on the spot. If it is not part of your rehearsed material, leave it out so you can finish on time.

Summarize Your Main Points and Drive Home Your Message. Conclude your presentation by reiterating your main points or by emphasizing what you want the audience to think or do. Once you have announced your conclusion, proceed to it directly.

After Your Presentation

As you are concluding your presentation, handle questions and answers competently and provide handouts, if appropriate. Try the following techniques:

Distribute Handouts. If you prepared handouts with data the audience will not need during the presentation, pass them out when you finish to prevent any distraction during your talk.

Encourage Questions but Keep Control. If the situation permits a question-and-answer period, announce it at the beginning of your presentation. Then, when you finish, ask for questions. Set a time limit for questions and answers. If you don't know the answer to a question, don't make one up or panic. Instead offer to find the answer within a day or two. If you make such a promise, be sure to follow through. Don't allow one individual to dominate the Q & A period. Keep the entire audience involved.

Repeat Questions. Although you may have heard the question, some audience members may not have. Begin each answer by repeating the question. This also gives you thinking time. Then, direct your answer to the entire audience.

Reinforce Your Main Points. You can use your answers to restate your primary ideas (*I'm glad you brought that up because it gives me a chance to elaborate on . . .*). In answering questions, avoid becoming defensive or debating the questioner.

Avoid *Yes, but* Answers. The word *but* immediately cancels any preceding message. Try replacing it with *and*. For example, *Yes, X has been tried. And Y works even better because . . . .*

End With a Summary and Appreciation. To signal the end of the session before you take the last question, say something like *We have time for just one more question.* As you answer the last question, try to work it into a summary of your main points. Then, express appreciation to the audience for the opportunity to talk with them.

CHECKLIST

Preparing and Organizing Oral Presentations

Getting Ready to Speak

- **Identify your purpose.** Decide what you want your audience to believe, remember, or do when you finish. Aim all parts of your talk toward this purpose.
- **Analyze the audience.** Consider how to adapt your message (its organization, appeals, and examples) to your audience's knowledge and needs.

Organizing the Introduction

- **Connect with the audience.** Capture the audience's attention by opening with a promise, story, startling fact, question, quote, relevant problem, or self-effacing joke.
- **Establish your authority.** Demonstrate your credibility by identifying your position, expertise, knowledge, or qualifications.
- **Preview your main points.** Introduce your topic and summarize its principal parts.

Organizing the Body

- **Develop two to four main points.** Streamline your topic so that you can concentrate on its major issues.
- **Arrange the points logically.** Sequence your points chronologically, from most important to least important, by comparison and contrast, or by some other strategy.
- **Prepare transitions.** Between major points write bridge statements that connect the previous item to the next one. Use transitional expressions as verbal signposts (*first, second, then, however, consequently, on the contrary,* and so forth).
- **Have extra material ready.** Be prepared with more information and visuals in case you have additional time to fill.

Organizing the Conclusion

- **Review your main points.** Emphasize your main ideas in the closing so your audience will remember them.
- **Provide a strong, final focus.** Tell how your listeners can use this information, why you have spoken, or what you want them to do. End with a specific audience benefit or thought-provoking idea (a take-away), not just a lame rehash.

Designing Visual Aids

- **Select your medium carefully.** Consider the pros and cons of each alternative.
- **Highlight main ideas.** Use visual aids to illustrate major concepts only. Keep them brief and simple.

- **Try to replace bullets whenever possible.** Use flowcharts, diagrams, time lines, images, and so forth, to substitute for bulleted lists when suitable.
- **Use visual aids skillfully.** Talk to the audience, not to the visuals. Paraphrase their content.

Developing Multimedia Presentations

- **Learn to use your software program.** Study template and layout designs to see how you can adapt them to your purposes.
- **Select colors based on the light level in the room.** Consider how mixing light and dark fonts and backgrounds affects their visibility. Use templates and preset layouts if your presentation software is new to you.
- **Use bulleted points for major ideas.** Make sure your points are parallel, and observe the 6-x-6 rule.
- **Include multimedia options that will help you convey your message.** Use moderate animation features and hyperlinks to make your talk more interesting and to link to files with related content in the same document, in other documents, or on the Internet. Use Prezi's zooming feature to help audience members narrow in on details.
- **Make speaker's notes.** Jot down the narrative supporting each visual, and use these notes to practice your presentation. Do not read from notes while speaking to an audience, however.
- **Maintain control.** Don't let your slides or canvas upstage you. Engage your audience by using additional techniques to help them visualize your points.

Developing Intercultural and Team Presentations

LEARNING OUTCOME 5

Organize presentations for intercultural audiences and in teams.

Most of the information presented thus far assumes you are a single presenter before a traditional audience. However, in this digital global world of work, presentations take on myriad forms and purposes. Now we'll explore effective techniques for adapting presentations to intercultural audiences and participating in team presentations.

Adapting Presentations to Intercultural Audiences

Every good speaker adapts to the audience, and intercultural presentations call for special adjustments and sensitivity. Most people understand that they must speak slowly, choose simple English, avoid jargon and clichés, use short sentences, and pause frequently when communicating with nonnative speakers of English.

Beyond these basic language adaptations, however, more fundamental sensitivity is often necessary. In organizing a presentation for an intercultural audience, you may need to anticipate and adapt to various speaking conventions, values, and nonverbal behaviors. You may also need to contend with limited language skills and a reluctance to voice opinions openly.

© Rana Sinha

Presenting Internationally

"When the audience is international, you'll need to step out of your own frame of reference and focus on making communication relevant for your target group. The aim is to 'localize.' By focusing on the audiences' own frames of reference, you acknowledge their importance and pave the way for them to come closer to you."[22]

—Rana Sinha, *cross-cultural trainer, consultant*

Understanding Different Values and Nonverbal Behaviors. In addressing intercultural audiences, anticipate expectations and perceptions that may differ significantly from what you may consider normal. Remember, for example, that the North American emphasis on getting to the point quickly is not equally prized across the globe. Therefore, think twice about delivering your main idea up front. Many people (notably those in Japanese, Latin American, and Arabic cultures) consider such directness to be brash and inappropriate. Remember that others may not share our cultural emphasis on straightforwardness.

When working with an interpreter or speaking before individuals whose English is limited, you must be very careful about your language. For example, you will need to express ideas in small chunks to give the interpreter time to translate. You may need to slow down as you speak and stop after each thought to allow time for the translation that will follow. Even if your presentation or speech is being translated simultaneously, remember to speak slowly and to pause after each sentence to ensure that your message is rendered correctly in the target language.

The same advice is useful in organizing presentations. You may want to divide your talk into distinct topics, developing each separately and encouraging a discussion period after each one. Such organization enables participants to ask questions and digest what has been presented. This technique is especially effective in cultures in which people communicate in "loops." In the Middle East, for example, Arab speakers "mix circuitous, irrelevant (by American standards) conversations with short dashes of information that go directly to the point." Presenters who are patient, tolerant, and "mature" (in the eyes of the audience) will make the sale or win the contract. Trust must be earned.[23]

Match your presentation and your nonverbal messages to the expectations of your audience. In Germany, for instance, successful presentations tend to be dense with facts and precise statistics. Americans might say "around 30 percent," whereas a German presenter might say "30.4271 percent." Similarly, constant smiling is not as valued in Europe as it is in North America. Many Europeans distrust a speaker who is cracking jokes, smiling, or laughing in a business presentation. Rather, many expect a rational—that is, serious—fact-based delivery.

American-style enthusiasm is often interpreted abroad as hyperbolic exaggeration or, worse, as dishonesty and can lead to misunderstandings. If an American says "Great job!" to offer praise, a Spanish counterpart might believe that the American has approved the project. "When Europeans realize there's no commitment implied," warned an intercultural consultant, "they might feel deceived or that the American is being superficial."[24]

Remember, too, that some cultures prefer greater formality than Americans exercise. When communicating with people from such cultures, instead of first names, use only honorifics (*Mr.* or *Ms.*) and last names, as well as academic or business titles—such as *Doctor* or *Director*. Writing on a flipchart or transparency seems natural and spontaneous in this country. Abroad, though, such informal techniques may suggest that the speaker does not value the audience enough to prepare proper visual aids in advance.[25]

Adjusting Visual Aids to Intercultural Audiences. Although you may have to exercise greater caution with culturally diverse audiences, you still want to use visual aids to help communicate your message. Find out from your international contact whether you can present in English or will need an interpreter. In many countries listeners are too polite or too proud to speak up when they don't understand a speaker. One expert advises explaining important concepts in several ways using different words and then requesting members of the audience to relay their understanding of what you have just said back to you. Another expert suggests packing more text on PowerPoint slides and staying closer to its literal meaning. After all, most nonnative speakers of English understand written text much better than spoken English. In the United States, presenters may spend 90 seconds on a slide, whereas in other countries they may need to slow down to two minutes per slide.[26]

To ensure clarity and show courtesy, provide handouts in both English and the target language. Never use numbers without projecting or writing them out for all to see. If possible, say numbers in both languages, but only if you can pronounce or even speak the target language well enough to avoid embarrassment. Distribute translated handouts, summarizing your important information, when you finish.

Ethics Check

The Robot Presenter

In one of your courses, you are witnessing a PowerPoint presentation, during which it becomes obvious that the speaker has completely memorized her talk. However, she stumbles badly a few times, struggling to remember her lines. Worse yet, you perceive her accent as nearly impenetrable. How should the instructor and the class handle the evaluation of such a presentation?

Preparing Collaborative Presentations With Teams

For many reasons increasing numbers of organizations are using teams, as discussed in Chapter 2. The goal of some teams is an oral presentation to pitch a new product or to win a high-stakes contract. Before Apple CEO Tim Cook and his team roll out one of their hotly anticipated new electronic gadgets, you can bet that team members spend months preparing so that the presentation flows smoothly. The same is true of most new product launches or major announcements. Teams collaborate to make sure the presentation meets its objectives.

Other teams form as needed to tackle challenges efficiently and fast. Spanish clothing chain Zara is famous for bringing leading-edge, yet inexpensive fashion trends to the consumer within weeks, not months like its competitors. Nimble cross-functional teams "can quickly innovate across organizational boundaries," making the company a lot more responsive than traditional organizations.[27] The outcome of any team effort is often (a) a written report, (b) a multimedia slideshow or presentation, or (c) an oral presentation delivered live. The boundaries are becoming increasingly blurred between flat, two-dimensional hard-copy reports and multimedia, hyperlinked slideshows and zoom presentations. Both hard-copy reports and multimedia presentations are delivered to clients in business today.

Whether your team produces written reports, multimedia presentations, or oral presentations, you generally have considerable control over how each project is organized and completed. If you have been part of any team efforts before, you also know that such projects can be very frustrating—particularly when some team members don't carry their weight or when members cannot resolve conflict. On the other hand, team projects can be harmonious and productive when members establish ground rules and follow guidelines related to preparing, planning, and collecting information as well as for organizing, rehearsing, and evaluating team projects.

Preparing to Work Together. Before any group begins to talk about a specific project, members should get together and establish basic ground rules. One of the first tasks is naming a leader to conduct meetings, a recorder to keep a record of group decisions, and an evaluator to determine whether the group is on target and meeting its goals. The group should decide whether it will be governed by consensus (everyone must agree), by majority rule, or by some other method.

When teams first organize, they should also consider the value of conflict. By bringing conflict into the open and encouraging confrontation, teams can prevent personal resentment and group dysfunction. Confrontation can actually create better final products by promoting new ideas and avoiding groupthink. Conflict is most beneficial when team members can air their views fully. Another important topic to discuss during team formation is how to deal with team members who are not pulling their share of the load. Teams should decide whether they will "fire" members who are not contributing or take some other action in dealing with slackers.

The most successful teams make meetings a top priority. They compare schedules to set up the best meeting times, and they meet often, either in person or virtually. They avoid other responsibilities that might disrupt these meetings. Today's software and mobile apps make collaborating online efficient and productive. Team members can use tools such as Google Drive, Dropbox, or SlideRocket to jointly create and edit documents and presentations in the cloud. Prezi offers a tool called Meeting that allows team members to collaborate live on a Prezi canvas. Team members can work on presentations with others from anywhere in the world at any time of day, synchronously or asynchronously.

Planning and Preparing the Document or Presentation. Once teams have established ground rules, members are ready to discuss the target document or presentation. During these discussions, they must be sure to keep a record of all decisions. They should establish the specific purpose for the document or presentation and identify the main issues involved. They must decide on the final format. For a collaborative business report, they should determine what parts to include, such as an executive summary, figures, and an appendix.

Team members should consider how the report or presentation will be delivered—in person, online, or by e-mail. For a team oral presentation, they should decide on its parts, length, and graphics. For either written or oral projects, they should profile the audience and focus on the questions audience members would want answered. If the report or presentation involves persuasion, they must decide what appeals would achieve the team's purpose.

Next, the team should develop a work plan (see Chapter 11), assign jobs, and set deadlines. If time is short, members should work backward from the due date. For oral presentations, teams must schedule time for content and creative development as well as for a series of rehearsals. The best-planned presentations can fall apart if they are poorly rehearsed.

For oral presentations, all team members should have written assignments. These assignments should detail each member's specific responsibilities for researching content, producing visuals, developing handouts, building transitions between segments, and showing up for rehearsals. For written reports, members must decide how the final document will be composed: individuals working separately on assigned portions, one person writing the first draft, the entire group writing the complete document together, or some other method. Team members will be responsible for collecting information; organizing, writing, and revising; and editing, rehearsing, and evaluating the document or presentation.

Collecting Information. One of the most challenging jobs for team projects is generating and collecting information. Unless facts are accurate, the most beautiful report or the most high-powered presentation will fail. Team members should brainstorm for ideas, assign topics, and decide who will be responsible for gathering what information. Establishing deadlines for collecting information is important if a team is to remain on schedule. Team members should also discuss ways to ensure the accuracy of the information collected.

Organizing, Writing, and Revising. When a project progresses into the organizing and writing stages, a team may need to modify some of its earlier decisions. Members may review the proposed organization of the document or presentation and adjust it if necessary. In composing the first draft of a written report or presentation, team members will probably write separate segments. As they work on these segments, they should use the same version of a word processing or presentation graphics program to facilitate combining files. They can also use Google Drive, Dropbox, or SlideRocket to edit documents.

As individuals work on separate parts of a written report, the team should decide on one person (probably the best writer) to coordinate all the parts. The writer strives for a consistent style, format, and feel in the final product. For oral presentations, team members must try to make logical connections between segments. Each presenter builds a bridge to the next member's topic to create a smooth transition. Team members should also agree to use the same template, and they should allow only one person to make global changes in color, font, and other formatting on the slide and title masters.

Reality Check

© Joan Ford Photography

Presenting as a Team

"Anytime you present with another person, you need to plan for at least double—and perhaps even triple—the time it normally takes to prepare and practice a presentation you deliver on your own. When presenting as a team, every team member should at least understand all of the material and possibly even be able to present ALL of the material —and that takes time!"[28]

—Lisa B. Marshall, *consultant, author, host and creator of The Public Speaker podcast*

Editing, Rehearsing, and Evaluating. The last stage in a collaborative project involves editing, rehearsing, and evaluating. For a written report, one person should assume the task of merging the various files, running a spell-checker, and examining the entire document for consistency of design, format, and vocabulary. That person is responsible for finding and correcting grammatical and mechanical errors. Then the entire group meets as a whole to evaluate the final document. Does it fulfill its purpose and meet the needs of the audience?

For oral presentations, one person should also merge all the files and be certain that they are consistent in design, format, and vocabulary. Teams making presentations should practice together several times. If that is not feasible, experts say that teams must schedule at least one full real-time rehearsal with the entire group.[29] Whenever possible, the team should practice in a room that is similar to the location of the talk. Video recording one of the rehearsals will give each presenter the opportunity to critique his or her own performance. Scheduling a dress rehearsal with an audience at least two days before the actual presentation is helpful. Team members should also practice fielding questions.

Successful group documents emerge from thoughtful preparation, clear definitions of contributors' roles, commitment to a group-approved plan, and a willingness to take responsibility for the final product. More information about writing business reports appeared in previous chapters of this book.

Improving Speaking Skills for Effective Phone Calls

LEARNING OUTCOME 6

List techniques for improving telephone skills to project a positive image.

One form of business presentation involves presenting yourself on the telephone, a skill that is still very important in today's workplace. Despite the continuing reliance on e-mail, the telephone remains an extremely important piece of equipment in offices. With today's wireless technology, it doesn't matter whether you are in or out of the office—you can always be reached by phone. This section focuses on traditional telephone techniques as well as cell phone use and voice mail—all opportunities for making a good impression. As a business communicator, you can be more productive, efficient, and professional by following some simple suggestions.

Making Telephone Calls Professionally

Before making a telephone call, decide whether the intended call is really necessary. Could you find the information yourself? If you wait a while, will the problem resolve itself? Perhaps your message could be delivered more efficiently by some other means. Some companies have found that telephone calls are often less important than the work they interrupt. Alternatives to telephone calls include instant messaging, texting, e-mail, memos, and calls to automated voice mail systems. If you must make a telephone call, consider using the following suggestions to make it fully productive:

- **Plan a mini-agenda.** Have you ever been embarrassed when you had to make a second telephone call because you forgot an important point the first time? Before placing a call, jot down notes regarding all the topics you need to discuss.
- **Use a three-point introduction.** When placing a call, immediately (a) name the person you are calling, (b) identify yourself and your affiliation, and (c) give a brief explanation of your reason for calling. For example: *May I speak to Larry Lopez? This is Hillary Dahl of Sebastian Enterprises, and I'm seeking information about a software program called ZoneAlarm Internet Security.*
- **Be brisk if you are rushed.** For business calls when your time is limited, avoid questions such as *How are you?* Instead, say, *Lisa, I knew you would be the only one who could answer these two questions for me.* Another efficient strategy is to set a contract with the caller: *Look, Lisa, I have only ten minutes, but I really wanted to get back to you.*
- **Be cheerful and accurate.** Let your voice show the same kind of animation that you radiate when you greet people in person. In your mind try to envision the individual answering the telephone. A smile can certainly affect the tone of your voice, so smile at that person.
- **Be professional and courteous.** Remember that you are representing yourself and your company when you make phone calls. Use professional vocabulary and courteous language. Say *thank you* and *please* during your conversations. Don't eat, drink, or chew gum while talking on the phone, which can often be heard on the other end.

- **Bring it to a close.** The responsibility for ending a call lies with the caller. This is sometimes difficult to do if the other person rambles on. You may need to use suggestive closing language, such as the following: (a) *I have certainly enjoyed talking with you;* (b) *I have learned what I needed to know, and now I can proceed with my work;* (c) *Thanks for your help;* (d) *I must go now, but may I call you again in the future if I need . . . ?* or (e) *Should we talk again in a few weeks?*
- **Avoid telephone tag.** If you call someone who's not in, ask when it would be best to call again. State that you will call at a specific time—and do it. If you ask a person to call you, give a time when you can be reached—and then be sure you are available at that time.
- **Leave complete voice mail messages.** Always enunciate clearly and speak slowly when giving your telephone number or spelling your name. Be sure to provide a complete message, including your name, your telephone number, and the time and date of your call. Explain your purpose so that the receiver can be ready with the required information when returning your call.

Receiving Telephone Calls Professionally

With a little forethought you can project a professional image and make your telephone a productive, efficient work tool. Developing good telephone manners and techniques, such as the following, will also reflect well on you and on your organization.

- **Identify yourself immediately.** In answering your telephone or someone else's, provide your name, title or affiliation, and, possibly, a greeting. For example, *Larry Lopez, Digital Imaging Corporation. How may I help you?* Force yourself to speak clearly and slowly. Remember that the caller may be unfamiliar with what you are saying and fail to recognize slurred syllables.
- **Be responsive and helpful.** If you are in a support role, be sympathetic to callers' needs. Instead of *I don't know,* try *That's a good question; let me investigate.* Instead of *We can't do that,* try *That's a tough one; let's see what we can do.* Avoid *No* at the beginning of a sentence. It sounds especially abrasive and displeasing because it suggests total rejection.
- **Practice telephone confidentiality.** When answering calls for others, be courteous and helpful, but don't give out confidential information. Better to say, *She's away from her desk* or *He's out of the office* than to report a colleague's exact whereabouts. Also, be tight-lipped about sharing company information with strangers.
- **Take messages carefully.** Few things are as frustrating as receiving a potentially important phone message that is illegible. Repeat the spelling of names and verify telephone numbers. Write messages legibly and record their time and date. Promise to give the messages to intended recipients, but don't guarantee return calls.
- **Leave the line respectfully.** If you must put a call on hold, let the caller know and give an estimate of how long you expect the call to be on hold. Give the caller the option of holding (e.g., *Would you prefer to hold, or would you like me to call you back?*).

Ethics Check

Telling White Lies

Obviously, you wouldn't want to tell callers that your colleague went to the restroom or that your boss is responding to e-mail from a golf course in Hilo, Hawaii. But what about people who, for instance, hide behind voice mail and want you to lie about it? When is it acceptable to tell white lies on the phone to maintain confidentiality and decorum, and when is lying for others wrong?

Reality Check

blackzheep/Shutterstock.com

Have We Lost All Decency?

"It's a matter of priorities. When you have your phone on the table, you're communicating to the person in front of you that they are important, until something more important, whether it's a text message or a Twitter notification, comes up on your phone."[30]

—Mindy Lockard, *etiquette consultant (aka, The Gracious Girl)*

Using Smartphones for Business

The smartphone has become an essential part of communication in the workplace. The number of U.S. cell phone users has by far outpaced the number of landline telephone users, and the number of people using mobile electronic devices and tablet computers keeps growing.[31] Approximately 92 percent of Americans now own a cell phone, 68 percent of U.S. adults have a smartphone,[32] and almost half of wireless customers live without landlines.[33]

Constant connectivity is posing new challenges in social settings and is perceived as distracting to group dynamics, a Pew study found.[34] However, people's views on acceptable cell phone use vary. More than three quarters don't object to using a cell phone while walking down the street, on public transport, and when waiting in line. Even in restaurants, smartphone use is acceptable to 38 percent. However, respondents strongly condemned cell phone use during meetings, in movie theaters, and in places of worship. Although Americans view cell phones as distracting and annoying, many do access their own devices in group settings.

Because so many people depend on their smartphones, it is important to understand proper use and etiquette. Most of us have experienced thoughtless and rude cell phone behavior. Researchers say that the rampant use of mobile electronic devices has increased workplace incivility. Most employees consider texting and compulsive e-mail checking while working and during meetings disruptive, even insulting. To avoid offending, smart business communicators practice professional cell phone etiquette, as outlined in Figure 14.12.

Figure 14.12 **Adopting Courteous and Responsible Cell Phone Practices**

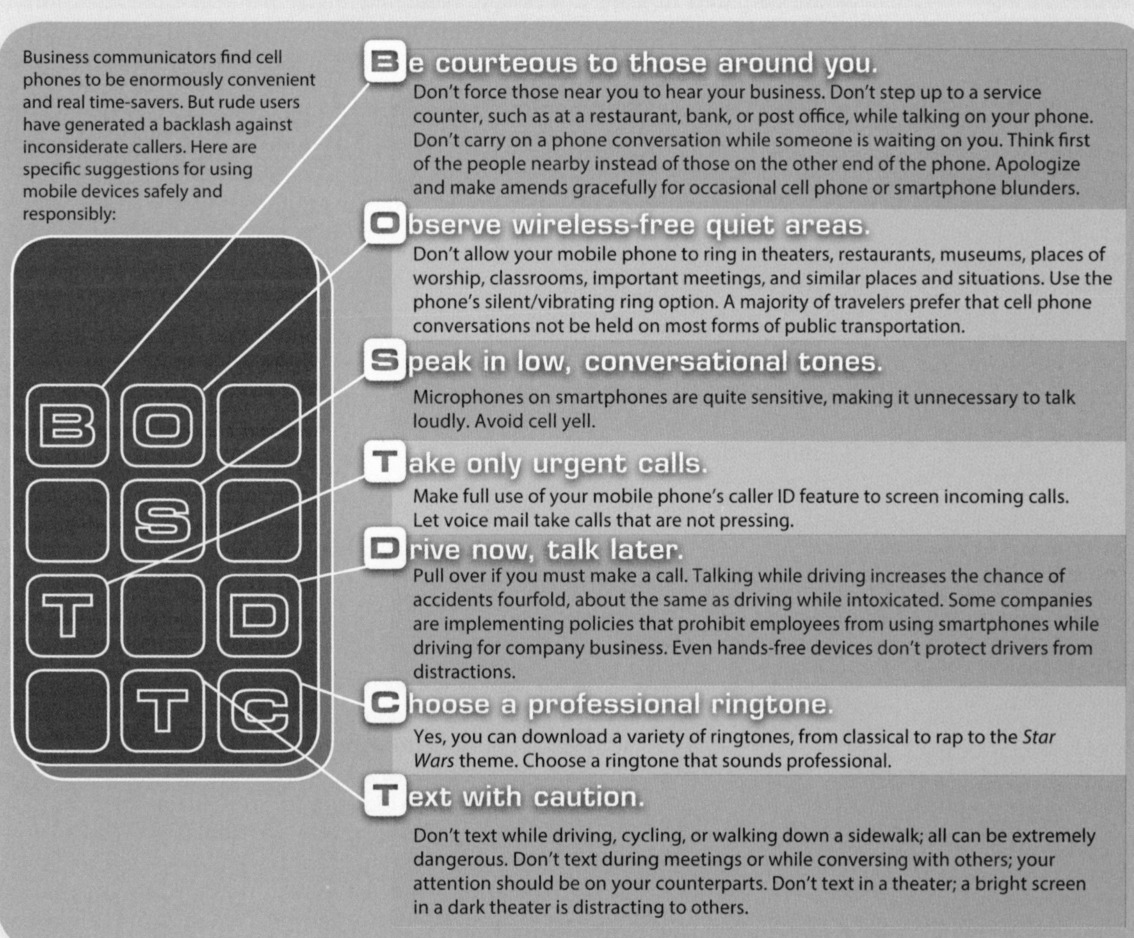

Business communicators find cell phones to be enormously convenient and real time-savers. But rude users have generated a backlash against inconsiderate callers. Here are specific suggestions for using mobile devices safely and responsibly:
B O S T D T C
Be courteous to those around you.
Don't force those near you to hear your business. Don't step up to a service counter, such as at a restaurant, bank, or post office, while talking on your phone. Don't carry on a phone conversation while someone is waiting on you. Think first of the people nearby instead of those on the other end of the phone. Apologize and make amends gracefully for occasional cell phone or smartphone blunders.
Observe wireless-free quiet areas.
Don't allow your mobile phone to ring in theaters, restaurants, museums, places of worship, classrooms, important meetings, and similar places and situations. Use the phone's silent/vibrating ring option. A majority of travelers prefer that cell phone conversations not be held on most forms of public transportation.
Speak in low, conversational tones.
Microphones on smartphones are quite sensitive, making it unnecessary to talk loudly. Avoid cell yell.
Take only urgent calls.
Make full use of your mobile phone's caller ID feature to screen incoming calls. Let voice mail take calls that are not pressing.
Drive now, talk later.
Pull over if you must make a call. Talking while driving increases the chance of accidents fourfold, about the same as driving while intoxicated. Some companies are implementing policies that prohibit employees from using smartphones while driving for company business. Even hands-free devices don't protect drivers from distractions.
Choose a professional ringtone.
Yes, you can download a variety of ringtones, from classical to rap to the *Star Wars* theme. Choose a ringtone that sounds professional.
Text with caution.
Don't text while driving, cycling, or walking down a sidewalk; all can be extremely dangerous. Don't text during meetings or while conversing with others; your attention should be on your counterparts. Don't text in a theater; a bright screen in a dark theater is distracting to others.

Making the Best Use of Voice Mail

Because telephone calls can be disruptive, many businesspeople make extensive use of voice mail to intercept and screen incoming calls on their landlines and smartphones. Here are some ways to make voice mail work most effectively for you.

On the Receiver's End.

Your voice mail should project professionalism and provide an easy way for your callers to leave messages for you. Here are some voice mail etiquette tips:

- **Don't overuse voice mail.** Don't use voice mail to avoid taking phone calls. It is better to answer calls yourself than to let voice mail messages build up.
- **Prepare a professional, concise, friendly greeting.** Make your voice mail greeting sound warm and inviting, both in tone and content. Identify yourself, thank the caller, and briefly explain that you are unavailable. Invite the caller to leave a message or, if appropriate, to call back. Here's a typical voice mail greeting: *Hi! This is Larry Lopez of Proteus Software, and I appreciate your call. I'm either working with customers or talking on another line at the moment. Please leave your name, number, and reason for calling so that I can be prepared when I return your call.*
- **Respond to messages promptly.** Check your messages regularly, and try to return all voice mail messages within one business day.
- **Plan for vacations and other extended absences.** If you will not be picking up voice mail messages for an extended period, let callers know how they can reach someone else if needed.

On the Caller's End.

When leaving a voice mail message, you should follow these tips:

- **Be prepared to leave a message.** Before calling someone, be prepared for voice mail. Decide what you are going to say and what information you will include in your message. If necessary, write your message down before calling.
- **Leave a concise, thorough message.** When leaving a message, always identify yourself using your complete name and affiliation. Mention the date and time you called and a brief explanation of your reason for calling. Always leave a complete phone number, including the area code. Tell the receiver the best time to return your call. Don't ramble.
- **Speak slowly and articulate.** You want to make sure that your receiver will be able to understand your message. Speak slowly and pronounce your words carefully, especially when providing your phone number. The receiver should be able to write information down without having to replay your message.
- **Be careful with confidential information.** Don't leave confidential or private information in a voice mail message. Remember that anyone could gain access to this information.

Your Turn: Applying Your Skills

You love your new internship planning special projects for an NGO (nongovernmental organization) that sends medical supplies to the needy in developing countries. At a recent staff meeting, many account representatives expressed the desire to learn how to make better presentations to donors. Your supervisor has asked you to find someone who can give the staff members a workshop designed to teach presentation skills. You recently heard Jean-luc Doumont speak at your college and think he'd be a perfect fit for your NGO. To illustrate what you learned from Doumont as a way to persuade your boss to hire him, you decide to create a PowerPoint presentation instead of a written document.

Your Task

In teams of three or four, research Jean-luc Doumont at **http://www.principiae.be** and peruse a YouTube video featuring Doumont discussing effective slides at **https://www.youtube.com/watch?v=meBXuTIPJQk.** With your group, create a short presentation geared to your audience—your supervisor—that will convince her to hire Doumont.

Summary of Learning Outcomes

1 Recognize various types of business presentations, and discuss two important first steps in preparing for any of these presentations.

- Speaking skills rank high on employers' wish lists and are crucial to career success.
- Presentations can be informative or persuasive, face-to-face or virtual, performed in front of big audiences or smaller groups, and elaborate or simple.
- Business professionals give a variety of business presentations including briefings, reports, podcasts, virtual presentations, and webinars.
- Once speakers know what they want to accomplish with their presentation, they must identify the purpose and the audience, so that they can aim the entire presentation toward their goal and adjust their message and style to the audience's knowledge and needs.

2 Explain how to organize your business presentation, understand contemporary visual aids, and know how to build audience rapport.

- The introduction should capture the listener's attention, identify the speaker, establish credibility, and preview the main points.
- The body should discuss two to four main points, with appropriate explanations, details, and verbal signposts to guide listeners.
- The conclusion should review the main points, provide a memorable take-away, and allow the speaker to leave the podium gracefully.
- Speakers establish rapport with their audiences by using effective imagery, useful verbal signposts or transitions, and appropriate nonverbal behavior.
- Contemporary visual aids—such as multimedia slides, handouts, and zoom presentations—illustrate and emphasize main points, draw audience interest, and make the presenter look more professional, better prepared, and more persuasive.
- Whenever possible, savvy speakers move beyond boring bulleted text and choose vivid images.

3 Create an impressive, error-free multimedia presentation that shows a firm grasp of basic visual design principles.

- Before creating a presentation, effective speakers analyze its purpose, delivery, and distribution.
- Expert presenters adjust their slide design to their audiences and demonstrate that they understand the meaning of color, the power of images, and the impact of special effects.
- When composing a talk, presenters organize their work by translating the major headings in the outline into slide titles and avoid formatting and fine-tuning their slides prematurely.

- For a quick start, speakers use templates, but they avoid visual clichés—that is, overused visuals.
- The final stage of creating a slideshow requires revising and proofreading as well as evaluating.
- Presenters must anticipate potential technical difficulties, rehearse, and create backups of their presentations.

4 Specify delivery techniques for use before, during, and after a presentation to keep the audience engaged.

- Effective public speaking techniques include avoiding memorizing, refraining from reading from notes, and delivering the presentation extemporaneously (speaking freely, without notes).
- When speaking without slides, presenters may use note cards or rough outlines to stay on track.
- Stage fright is lessened by breathing deeply, converting fear, preparing well, using positive self-talk, sipping water, shifting focus to the visuals, ignoring stumbles, and feeling proud at the end.
- Before the talk, speakers prepare a sentence outline, rehearse repeatedly, time themselves, dress professionally, check the room, greet audience members, and practice stress reduction.
- During the talk, speakers present the first sentence from memory, maintain eye contact, control their voice, show enthusiasm, skip apologies, pace themselves, use pauses, move naturally, control visuals competently, avoid digressions, and summarize their main points.
- After the talk, savvy presenters distribute handouts and answer questions; they repeat questions, reinforce main points, avoid *yes, but* answers; and end with a summary and appreciation.

5 Organize presentations for intercultural audiences and in teams.

- Businesspeople adapt language to intercultural audiences and understand different conventions.
- In nonnative environments, presenters speak slowly, use simple English, avoid directness, break the presentation into short chunks, respect formality, and adapt visuals to their audiences.
- Teams of presenters should name a leader; discuss decision making; work out a schedule; consider the value of conflict; determine how to rein in uncooperative members; and decide on the purpose, form, and procedures for preparing the final document or presentation.
- Teams collect information, brainstorm ideas, assign topics, establish deadlines, and plan meetings to discuss drafts.
- Teams coordinate their assigned contributions and edit, rehearse, and evaluate their presentations.

6 List techniques for improving telephone skills to project a positive image.

- Efficient callers plan a mini-agenda, use a three-point introduction (name, affiliation, and purpose), practice sounding cheerful and courteous, and use closing language.
- Savvy businesspeople avoid telephone tag by leaving complete voice mail messages.
- In answering calls, workers identify themselves immediately, show a helpful attitude, don't give out confidential information when answering for others, and take careful messages.

- Workers need to follow proper etiquette when using their smartphones for business.
- Skilled businesspeople prepare a concise, friendly voice mail greeting, respond to messages promptly, and plan for extended absences.
- Callers should be prepared to leave a concise message, speak slowly and clearly, and not reveal confidential information.

Critical Thinking

1. Most people never address large audiences and live in fear of public speaking. Why then should you hone your presentation skills? (L.O. 1)
2. Communication expert Dianna Booher claims that enthusiasm is infectious and "boredom is contagious."[35] What does this mean for you as a presenter? How can you avoid being a boring speaker? (L.O. 2, 3)
3. Why do many communication consultants encourage businesspeople to move beyond bullet points? What do they recommend instead, and why? (L.O. 2, 3)
4. How can speakers prevent multimedia presentation software from stealing their thunder? (L.O. 3)
5. Discuss effective techniques for reducing stage fright. (L.O. 4)
6. **Ethical Issue:** General Motors CEO Mary Barra inherited a mess when she ascended to the top post in her beleaguered company. Several GM car models had exhibited problems with their ignition switches, which turned off engines at highway speeds, causing 124 deaths and 275 injuries. As early as 2001, company insiders knew about the problem, but ultimately took no action. Even as the scandal broke, GM first underreported the casualties.[36] Mary Barra pulled no punches. In a town hall meeting, she unflinchingly addressed a global audience.[37] How should a chief executive respond to such a scandal? What could Barra say to restore trust in the company? (L.O. 1–3)

Activities

14.1 Learning From the Best: Analyzing a Famous Speech (L.O. 1–3)

Web

YOUR TASK Search online for a speech by a significant businessperson or a well-known public figure. Consider watching the following iconic political speeches, thought to be among the best in the twentieth century: Martin Luther King Jr.'s "I Have a Dream" speech, President Kennedy's inaugural address, and Franklin Delano Roosevelt's Pearl Harbor address.[38] If you prefer business tycoons dispensing advice, search for the best-known commencement speeches—for example, Steve Jobs's "Stay Hungry, Stay Foolish" Stanford address, Salman Khan's "Live Your Life Like It's Your Second Chance" speech, or Sheryl Sandberg's "Rocketship" commencement speech at Harvard. Transcripts of these and other well-known speeches are also available online.[39] Write a memo report or give a short presentation to your class critiquing the speech in terms of the following:

a. Effectiveness of the introduction, body, and conclusion
b. Evidence of effective overall organization
c. Use of verbal signposts to create coherence
d. Emphasis on two to four main points
e. Effectiveness of supporting facts (use of examples, statistics, quotations, and so forth)
f. Focus on audience benefits
g. Enthusiasm for the topic
h. Body language and personal mannerisms

14.2 Sizing Up Your Audience (L.O. 1, 2)

YOUR TASK Select a recent issue of *Fortune, The Wall Street Journal, Fast Company, Bloomberg Businessweek, The Economist,* or another business periodical approved by your instructor. Based on an analysis of your classmates, select an article that will appeal to them and that you can relate to their needs. Submit to your instructor a one-page summary that includes (a) the author, article title, source, issue date, and page reference; (b) a one-paragraph article summary; (c) a description of why you believe the article will appeal to your classmates; and (d) a summary of how you can relate the article to their needs. Your instructor may make this a topic for a class presentation.

14.3 Hiring a Famous Motivational Speaker (L.O. 1)

Communication Technology | Social Media | Team | Web

Have you ever wondered why famous business types, politicians, athletes, and other celebrities can command high speaking fees? How much are they really making per appearance, and what factors may justify their sometimes exorbitant fees? You may also wonder how a motivational speaker or corporate trainer might benefit you and your class or your campus community. Searching for and selecting an expert is easy online with several commercial speaker bureaus vying for clients. All bureaus provide detailed speaker bios, areas of expertise, and fees. One even features video previews of its clients.

The preeminent agencies for booking talent are All American Speakers Bureau, BigSpeak Speakers Bureau, Speakerpedia, and Brooks International Speakers & Entertainment Bureau. Speakerpedia represents the likes of economist Nouriel Roubini, Jack Welch, Richard Branson, and Suze Orman. BigSpeak standouts are Deepak Chopra, Dr. Susan Love, and distance swimmer Diana Nyad. Brooks International features financier and philanthropist Mike Milken and TV commentator and personal finance expert Terry Savage, among others.

YOUR TASK Imagine that you have a budget of up to $100,000 to hire a well-known public speaker. In teams or individually, select a business-related category of speaker by visiting one of the speaker bureaus online. For example, choose several prominent personal finance gurus (Orman, Savage, and others) or successful entrepreneurs and venture capitalists (e.g., Elon Musk, Richard Branson, Jack Welch). Other categories are motivational speakers, philanthropists, and famous economists. Study their bios for clues about their expertise and accomplishments.

Comparing at least three speakers, come up with a set of qualities that apparently make these individuals sought-after speakers. Consider how those qualities could enlighten you and your peers. To enrich your experience and enhance your knowledge, watch videos of your chosen speakers on YouTube or the TED website, if available. Check talent agencies, personal websites, and Facebook for further information. Write a memo report about your speaker group, or present your findings orally, with or without a slide presentation. If your instructor directs, recommend your favorite speaker and give reasons for your decision.

14.4 Follow Your Favorite Business Personality on Twitter (L.O. 1)

Communication Technology | Social Media | Web

YOUR TASK On Twitter, in the Search window on top of the page, enter the name of the businessperson whose tweets you wish to follow. Elon Musk, Guy Kawasaki, Richard Branson, Suze Orman, and other well-known businesspeople are avid Twitter users. Over the course of a few days, read the tweets of your favorite expert. After a while, you should be able to discern some trends and areas of interest. Note whether and how your subject responds to queries from followers. What are his or her favorite topics? Report your findings to the class, verbally with notes or using PowerPoint or Prezi. If you find particularly intriguing tweets and links, share them with the class.

14.5 Taming Stage Fright (L.O. 4)

E-Mail | Team

What scares you the most about making a presentation in front of your class? Being tongue-tied? Fearing all eyes on you? Messing up? Forgetting your ideas and looking unprofessional?

YOUR TASK Discuss the previous questions as a class. Then, in groups of three or four, talk about ways to overcome these fears. Your instructor may ask you to write a memo, an e-mail, or a discussion board post (individually or collectively) summarizing your suggestions, or you may break out of your small groups and report your best ideas to the entire class.

14.6 How Much Speaking Can You Expect in Your Field? (L.O. 1, 4)

Team

YOUR TASK Interview one or two individuals in your professional field. How is oral communication important in this profession? Does the need for oral skills change as one advances? What suggestions can these people make to newcomers to the field for developing proficient oral communication skills? Discuss your findings with your class.

14.7 Creating an Outline for an Oral Presentation (L.O. 1, 2)

One of the hardest parts of preparing an oral presentation is developing the outline.

YOUR TASK Select an oral presentation topic from the list in **Activity 14.15**, or suggest an original topic. Prepare an outline for your presentation using the following format:

Title	
Purpose	
	I. INTRODUCTION
State your name	A.
Gain attention and involve audience	B.
Establish credibility	C.
Preview main points	D.
Transition	
	II. BODY
Main point	A.
Illustrate, clarify, contrast	1.
	2.
	3.
Transition	
Main point	B.
Illustrate, clarify, contrast	1.
	2.
	3.
Transition	
Main point	C.
Illustrate, clarify, contrast	1.
	2.
	3.
Transition	
	III. CONCLUSION
Summarize main points	A.
Provide final focus or take-away	B.
Encourage questions	C.

14.8 Critiquing a Satirical Clip Lampooning PowerPoint (L.O. 1–3)

Web

YOUR TASK Watch Don McMillan's now famous YouTube classic "Life After Death by PowerPoint." Which specific PowerPoint ills is McMillan satirizing? Write a brief summary of the short clip for discussion in class. With your peers discuss whether the bad habits the YouTube video parodies correspond with design principles introduced in this chapter.

14.9 Observing and Outlining a TED Talk (L.O. 1–3)

Communication Technology | E-Mail | Web

To learn from the presentation skills of the best speakers today, visit the TED channel on YouTube or the TED website. Watch one or more of the 2,400+ TED talks (motto: Ideas worth spreading) available online. Standing at over one billion views worldwide, the presentations cover topics from the fields of technology, entertainment, and design (TED).

YOUR TASK If your instructor directs, select and watch one of the TED talks and outline it. You may also be asked to focus on the speaker's presentation techniques based on the guidelines you have studied in this chapter. Jot down your observations either as notes for a classroom discussion or to serve as a basis for an informative memo or e-mail. If directed by your instructor, compose a concise yet informative tweet directing Twitter users to your chosen TED talk and commenting on it.

14.10 Talking About Your Job (L.O. 1–3)

Communication Technology

What if you had to create a presentation for your classmates and instructor, or perhaps a potential recruiter, that describes the multiple tasks you perform at work? Could you do it in a five-minute PowerPoint, SlideRocket, or Prezi presentation?

Your instructors, for example, may wear many hats. Most academics (a) teach; (b) conduct research to publish; and (c) provide services to the department, college, university, and community. Can you see how those aspects of their profession lend themselves to an outline of primary slides (teaching, publishing, service) and second-level slides (instructing undergraduate and graduate classes, presenting workshops, and giving lectures under the teaching label)?

YOUR TASK Now it's your turn to introduce the duties you perform (or performed) in a current or past job, volunteer activity, or internship in a brief, simple, yet well-designed PowerPoint or Prezi presentation. Your goal is to inform your audience of your job duties in a three- to five-minute talk. Use animation features and graphics where appropriate.

14.11 Perfecting the Art of the Elevator Pitch (L.O. 1–3)

"Can you pass the elevator test?" asks presentation whiz Garr Reynolds in a new twist on the familiar scenario.[40] He suggests that this technique will help you sharpen your core message. In this exercise, you need to pitch your idea in a few brief moments instead of the 20 minutes you had been granted with your vice president of product marketing. You arrive at her door for your appointment as she is leaving, coat and briefcase in hand. Something has come up. This meeting is a huge opportunity for you if you want to get the OK from the executive team. Could you sell your idea during the elevator ride and the walk to the parking lot? Reynolds asks. Although this scenario may never happen, you will possibly be asked to shorten a presentation, say, from an hour to 30 minutes or from 20 minutes to 5 minutes. Could you make your message tighter and clearer on the fly?

YOUR TASK Take a business idea you may have, a familiar business topic you care about, or a promotion or raise you wish to request. Create an impromptu two- to five-minute speech making a good case for your core message. Even though you won't have much time to think about the details of your speech, you should be sufficiently familiar with the topic to boil it down and yet be persuasive.

14.12 Improving Telephone Skills by Role-Playing (L.O. 6)

YOUR TASK Your instructor will divide the class into pairs. For each scenario take a moment to read and rehearse your role silently. Then play the role with your partner. If time permits, repeat the scenarios, changing roles.

Partner 1	Partner 2
a. You are the personnel manager of Megatronics, Inc. Call Kathy Gemma, office manager at ComputersRUs. Inquire about a job applicant, Summer Ochoa, who listed Ms. Gemma as a reference. Respond to Partner 2.	a. You are the receptionist for ComputersRUs. The caller asks for Kathy Gemma, who is home sick today. You don't know when she will be able to return. Answer the call appropriately.
b. Call Ms. Gemma again the following day to inquire about the same job applicant, Summer Ochoa. Ms. Gemma answers today, but she talks on and on, describing the applicant in great detail. Tactfully end the conversation.	b. You are now Ms. Gemma, office manager. Describe Summer Ochoa, an imaginary employee. Think of someone with whom you have worked. Include many details, such as her ability to work with others, her appearance, her skills at computing, her schooling, her ambition, and so forth.
c. You are now the receptionist for Gordon Lee, of Lee Imports. Answer a call for Mr. Lee, who is working in another office, at Extension 134, where he will accept calls.	c. You are now an administrative assistant for attorney Jonathan Sullivan. Call Gordon Lee to verify a meeting date Mr. Sullivan has with Mr. Lee. Use your own name in identifying yourself.
d. You are now Gordon Lee, owner of Lee Imports. Call your attorney, Jonathan Sullivan, about a legal problem. Leave a brief, incomplete message.	d. You are now the receptionist for attorney Jonathan Sullivan. Mr. Sullivan is skiing in Aspen and will return in two days, but he doesn't want his clients to know where he is. Take a message.
e. Call Mr. Sullivan again. Leave a message that will prevent telephone tag.	e. Take a message again as the receptionist for attorney Jonathan Sullivan.

14.13 Presenting Yourself Professionally on the Telephone and in Voice Mail (L.O. 6)

YOUR TASK Practicing the phone skills you learned in this chapter, leave your instructor a professional voice mail message. Prepare a mini-agenda before you call. Introduce yourself. If necessary, spell your name and indicate the course and section. Speak slowly and clearly, especially when leaving your phone number. Think of a comment you could make about an intriguing fact, a peer discussion, or your business communication class.

14.14 Presenting Yourself Professionally When Texting (L.O. 6)

Communication Technology

Your phone skills extend not only to voice mail but also to the brief text messages you send to your boss and coworkers. Such professional texts are often markedly different in style and tone from the messages you may be exchanging with friends.

YOUR TASK Send a professional text message to your instructor or to another designated partner in class responding to one of the following scenarios: (a) Explain why you must be late to an important meeting; (b) request permission to purchase a piece of important equipment for the office; or (c) briefly summarize what you have learned in your latest staff development seminar (use a key concept from one of your business classes). Use the recipient's e-mail address to send your text. Do not use abbreviations or smiley faces.

14.15 Something to Talk About: Topics for an Oral Presentation (L.O. 1–5)

Team

YOUR TASK Select a topic from the following list or from the report topics in the activities at the ends of Chapters 11 and 12. An expanded list of report topics is available at your Student Companion Website. Individually or as a team, prepare a short oral presentation. Consider yourself an expert or a team of experts called in to explain some aspect of the topic before a group of interested people. Because your time is limited, prepare a concise yet forceful presentation with effective visual aids.

If this is a group presentation, form a team of three or four members and conduct thorough research on one of the following topics, as directed by your instructor. Follow the tips on team presentations in this chapter. Divide the tasks fairly, meet for discussions and rehearsals, and crown your achievement with a 10- to 15-minute presentation to your class. Make your multimedia presentation interesting and dynamic.

a. How can businesses benefit from Facebook, Instagram, Twitter, or LinkedIn? Cite specific examples in your chosen field.

b. Which is financially more beneficial to a business, leasing or buying company cars?

c. Tablet computers and other mobile devices are eroding the market share previously held by laptops and netbooks. Which brands are businesses embracing, and why? Which features are a must-have for businesspeople?

d. What kind of marketing works best with students on college campuses? Word of mouth? Internet advertising? Free samples? How do students prefer to get information about goods and services?

e. How can your organization appeal to its members to prevent them from texting while driving or from driving under the influence?

f. Companies usually do not admit shortcomings. However, some admit previous failures and use them to strategic advantage. For example, Domino's Pizza ran a commercial in which its customers said that its pizza tasted like ketchup and cardboard. Find three or more examples of companies admitting weaknesses, and draw conclusions from their strategies. Would you recommend this as a sound marketing ploy?

g. How can students and other citizens contribute to conserving gasoline and other fossil fuel to save money and help slow global climate change?

h. What is the career outlook in a field of your choice? Consider job growth, compensation, and benefits. What kind of academic or other experience is typically required in your field?

i. What is the economic outlook for a given product, such as electric cars, laptop computers, digital cameras, fitness equipment, or a product of your choice?

j. What is telecommuting, and for what kinds of workers is it an appropriate work alternative?

k. What are the Webby Awards, and what criteria do the judges use to evaluate websites?

l. What franchise would offer the best investment opportunity for an entrepreneur in your area?

m. What should a guide to proper smartphone etiquette include?

n. Why should a company have a written e-mail, Web use, and social media policy?

o. Where should your organization hold its next convention?

p. What is the outlook for real estate (commercial or residential) investment in your area?

q. What do the personal assistants for celebrities do, and how does one become a personal assistant? (Investigate the Association of Celebrity Personal Assistants.)

r. What kinds of gifts are appropriate for businesses to give clients and customers during the holiday season?

s. What scams are on the Federal Trade Commission's list of top ten consumer scams, and how can consumers avoid falling for them?

t. How can your organization or institution improve its image?

u. What are the pros and cons of using Prezi zoom presentations? Would they be appropriate in your field?

v. How can consumers protect themselves against identity theft?

w. What franchise would offer the best investment opportunity for an entrepreneur in your area?

x. What are the differences among casual, business casual, and business formal attire?

y. What is a sustainable business? What can companies do to become sustainable?

z. What smartphone apps are available that will improve a businessperson's productivity?

Test Your Etiquette IQ

New communication platforms and casual workplace environments have blurred the lines of appropriateness leaving workers wondering how to navigate uncharted waters. Indicate whether the following statements are true or false. Then see if you agree with the responses on p. R-2.

1. If a man has been invited to a business lunch by a businesswoman, he should offer to pay for his own lunch even if the host has made it clear that she is paying.

   ________ True ________ False

2. As an invited guest at a business dinner, you should not order beer, wine, appetizers, or desserts unless the host does.

   ________ True ________ False

3. At a business lunch, it is permissible to discuss topics such as sex, politics, or religion only if you know the other guests very well.

   ________ True ________ False

Chat About It

In each chapter you will find five discussion questions related to the chapter material. Your instructor may assign these topics for you to discuss in class, in an online chat room, or on an online discussion board. Some of the discussion topics may require outside research. You may also be asked to read and respond to postings made by your classmates.

TOPIC 1: Remember some of the speeches or oral presentations you have witnessed. What were some of the elements that made them stand out, whether positively or negatively?

TOPIC 2: How would you classify your classmates as an audience for student presentations: friendly, neutral, uninterested, or hostile? Why?

TOPIC 3: Why do some presenters avoid making steady eye contact? What might these individuals do to correct this problem?

TOPIC 4: Do your own informal tally in your class to find out what you and your classmates consider acceptable cell phone use in various settings—when walking down the street, in a restaurant, in a place of worship, in class, on a date, and more.

TOPIC 5: When is it acceptable not to return a call when a callback was requested?

Grammar and Mechanics | *Review 14*

Total Review

Each of the following sentences has a total of **three** errors in grammar, punctuation, capitalization, usage, or spelling. On a separate sheet, write a correct version. Avoid adding new phrases, starting new sentences, or rewriting in your own words. When finished, compare your responses with those in the key beginning on page Key-3.

EXAMPLE: My accountant and me are greatful to be asked to make a short presentation, however, we may not be able to cover the entire budget.

REVISION: My accountant and I are grateful to be asked to make a short presentation; however, we may not be able to cover the entire budget.

1. The CEOs assistant scheduled my colleague and I for a twenty minute presentation to explain the new workplace sustainability initiative.
2. PowerPoint presentations, claims one expert should be no longer then twenty minutes and have no more than ten slides.
3. The introduction to a presentation should accomplish 3 goals, (a) capture attention, (b) establish credibility and (c) preview main points.
4. In the body of a short presentation speakers should focus on no more than 3 principle points.
5. A poll of two thousand employees revealed that 4/5 of them said they feared giving a presentation more then anything else they could think of.
6. A list with forty tips for inexperienced speakers are found in the article titled "Quick Tips For Speakers."
7. The Director of operations made a fifteen-minute presentation giving step by step instructions on achieving our sustainability goals.
8. In the Spring our companies stock value is expected to raise at least 10 percent.
9. The appearance and mannerisms of a speaker definately effects a listeners evaluation of the message.
10. Because the bosses daughter was a dynamic speaker who had founded a successful company she earned at least twenty thousand dollars for each presentation.

References

[1] Doumont, J. (2016, April 15). Lecture on presentation skills for UCSB Writing Program.

[2] Doumont, J. (2009). Effective oral presentations. Retrieved from http://www.treesmapsandtheorems.com/pdfs/TM&Th-3.0-summary.pdf and adapted from Doumont, J. (2009). *Trees, maps, and theorems*. Kraainem, Belgium: Principiae.

[3] Doumont, J. (2009). Effective oral presentations. Retrieved from http://www.treesmapsandtheorems.com/pdfs/TM&Th-3.0-summary.pdf

[4] Leveling up: How to win in the skills economy. (2016). PayScale. Retrieved from http://www.payscale.com/data-packages/job-skills

[5] Job outlook 2015 survey. (2014, November 12). National Association of Colleges and Employers. Retrieved from http://www.naceweb.org/s11122014/job-outlook-skills-qualities-employers-want.aspx

[6] Gallo, C. (2014, September 25). New survey: 70 percent say presentation skills are critical for career success. *Forbes*. Retrieved from http://www.forbes.com/sites/carminegallo/2014/09/25/new-survey-70-percent-say-presentation-skills-critical-for-career-success/#3681690410c9

[7] Ibid.

[8] Booher, D. (2012). On speaking. *Quotations on communication and other quips*. AudioInk.

[9] Dr. John J. Medina as quoted by Reynolds, G. (2013). *Presentation zen design* (2nd ed.). Berkeley, CA: New Riders, p. 97.

[10] Howder, R. (n.d.). About Prezi. Retrieved from http://prezi.com/about

[11] The Basics. (2016). Prezi. Retrieved from http://prezi.com/the-basics

[12] Atkinson, C. (2011). *Beyond bullet points* (3rd ed.). Redmond, WA: Microsoft Press.

[13] Based on Cross, B. (2015, May 28). Glisser: Event slide sharing tool [Review]. EventMB. Retrieved from http://www.eventmanagerblog.com/glisser-event-slidesharing-tool#dWYGRQbmHI1ZV2mm.97

[14] Reynolds, G. (2008). *Presentation Zen*. Berkeley, CA: New Riders, p. 220. See also Reynolds, G. (2010). *Presentation Zen design*. Berkeley, CA: New Riders.

[15] Booher, D. (2003). *Speak with confidence: Powerful presentations that inform, inspire, and persuade*. New York: McGraw-Hill Professional, p. 126; see also Ciotti, G. (2016, April 13). The psychology of color in marketing and branding. *Entrepreneur*. Retrieved from https://www.entrepreneur.com/article/233843

[16] Bates, S. (2005). *Speak like a CEO: Secrets for commanding attention and getting results*. New York: McGraw-Hill Professional, p. 113.

[17] Sommerville, J. (n.d.). The seven deadly sins of PowerPoint presentations. About.com. Retrieved from http://entrepreneurs.about.com/cs/marketing/a/7sinsofppt.htm; Avoid visual clichés when presenting. (2013, April 19). HBR.org. Retrieved from http://business.time.com/2013/04/19/avoid-visual-cliches-when-presenting

[18] Walker, T. J. (2011, June 7). Should I rehearse, and for how long? – Presentation training. *Forbes*. Retrieved from http://www.forbes.com/sites/tjwalker/2011/06/07/should-i-rehearse-and-for-how-long-presentation-training/#3e678c3166a1

[19] Hedges, K. (2014, November 14). Six ways to avoid death by PowerPoint. *Forbes*. Retrieved from http://www.forbes.com/sites/work-in-progress/2014/11/14/six-ways-to-avoid-death-by-powerpoint/#79137f5f34cb

[20] Quoted in Reynolds, G. (2014, January 20). Coping with presentation anxiety & "stage fright." Presentation Zen. Retrieved from http://www.presentationzen.com/presentationzen/2014/01/dealing-with-presentation-anxiety-stage-fright.html

[21] Reynolds, G. (2014, January 20). Coping with presentation anxiety & "stage fright." Presentation Zen. Retrieved from http://www.presentationzen.com/presentationzen/2014/01/dealing-with-presentation-anxiety-stage-fright.html

[22] Sinha, R. (n.d.). Making a presentation in front of international audiences. Dot-Connect. Retrieved from http://www.dot-connect.com/Making_a_presentation_in_front_of_international_audiences.html

[23] Aslani, S., Brett, J. M., Ramirez-Marin, J. Y., Tinsley, C. H., & Weingart, L. R. (2013, September 2). Doing business in the Middle East. Kellogg Insight. Retrieved from http://insight.kellogg.northwestern.edu/article/doing_business_in_the_middle_east. See also Wunderle, W. (n.d.). Through the lens of cultural awareness. Combat Studies Institute Press. Retrieved from http://usacac.army.mil/cac2/cgsc/carl/download/csipubs/wunderle.pdf; see also Marks, S. J. (2001, September). Nurturing global workplace connections. *Workforce*, p. 76.

[24] Brandel, M. (2006, February 20). Sidebar: Don't be the ugly American. *Computerworld*. Retrieved from http://www.computerworld.com/s/article/108772/Sidebar_Don_t_Be_the_Ugly_American

[25] Dulek, R. E., Fielden, J. S., & Hill, J. S. (1991, January/February). International communication: An executive primer. *Business Horizons*, p. 22.

[26] Davidson, R., & Rosen, M. Cited in Brandel, M. (2006, February 20). Sidebar: Don't be the ugly American. *Computerworld*. Retrieved from http://www.computerworld.com/s/article/108772/Sidebar_Don_t_Be_the_Ugly_American

[27] Letting go of efficiency can accelerate your company—Here's how. (2015). First Round Review. Retrieved from http://firstround.com/review/Responsiveness-New-Efficiency

[28] Marshall, L. B. (2010, April 23). How to present with another speaker. Quick and Dirty Tips. Retrieved from http://publicspeaker.quickanddirtytips.com/How-To-Present-With-Another-Speaker.aspx

[29] Peterson, R. (n.d.). Presentations: Are you getting paid for overtime? Presentation Coaching Institute. Retrieved from http://www.passociates.com/getting_paid_for_overtime.shtml; The sales presentation: The bottom line is selling. (2001, March 14). Marken Communications. Retrieved from http://www.markencom.com/docs/01mar14.htm

[30] Lockard, M. (2012, May 11) Smartphone etiquette: Have we lost all decency? Retrieved from https://blogs.windows.com/devices/2012/05/11/smartphone-etiquette-have-we-lost-all-decency

[31] Anderson, M. (2015, October 29). Technology device ownership: 2015. Pew Research Center. Retrieved from http://www.pewinternet.org/2015/10/29/technology-device-ownership-2015

[32] Ibid.

[33] Keeter, S., & McGeeney, K. (2015, January 7). Pew Research will call more cellphones in 2015. Pew Research Center. Retrieved from http://www.pewresearch.org/fact-tank/2015/01/07/pew-research-will-call-more-cellphones-in-2015

[34] Rainie, L., & Zickuhr, K. (2015, August 26). Americans' views on mobile etiquette. Pew Research Center. Retrieved from http://www.pewinternet.org/2015/08/26/americans-views-on-mobile-etiquette

[35] Booher, D. (2011). Speak with confidence. AudioInk.

[36] Korosec, K. (2015, August 24). Ten times more deaths linked to faulty switch than GM first reported. *Fortune*. Retrieved from http://fortune.com/2015/08/24/feinberg-gm-faulty-ignition-switch

[37] Text, video of GM CEO Mary Barra on switch report. *USAToday*. Retrieved from http://www.usatoday.com/story/money/cars/2014/06/05/gm-ceo-mary-barra-speech-switch-recall-report/10012715

[38] Search YouTube or search the top 100 speeches at American Rhetoric: http://www.americanrhetoric.com/top100speechesall.html

[39] Nisen, M., & Guey, L. (2013, May 15). 23 of the best pieces of advice ever given to graduates. *Business Insider*. Retrieved from http://www.businessinsider.com/best-commencement-speeches-of-all-time-2013-5

[40] Reynolds, G. (2008). *Presentation Zen*. Berkeley, CA: New Riders, pp. 64 ff.

UNIT 5

Employment Communication

Chapter 15
The Job Search, Résumés, and Cover Letters in the Digital Age

Chapter 16
Interviewing and Following Up

Nicotombo/Shutterstock.com

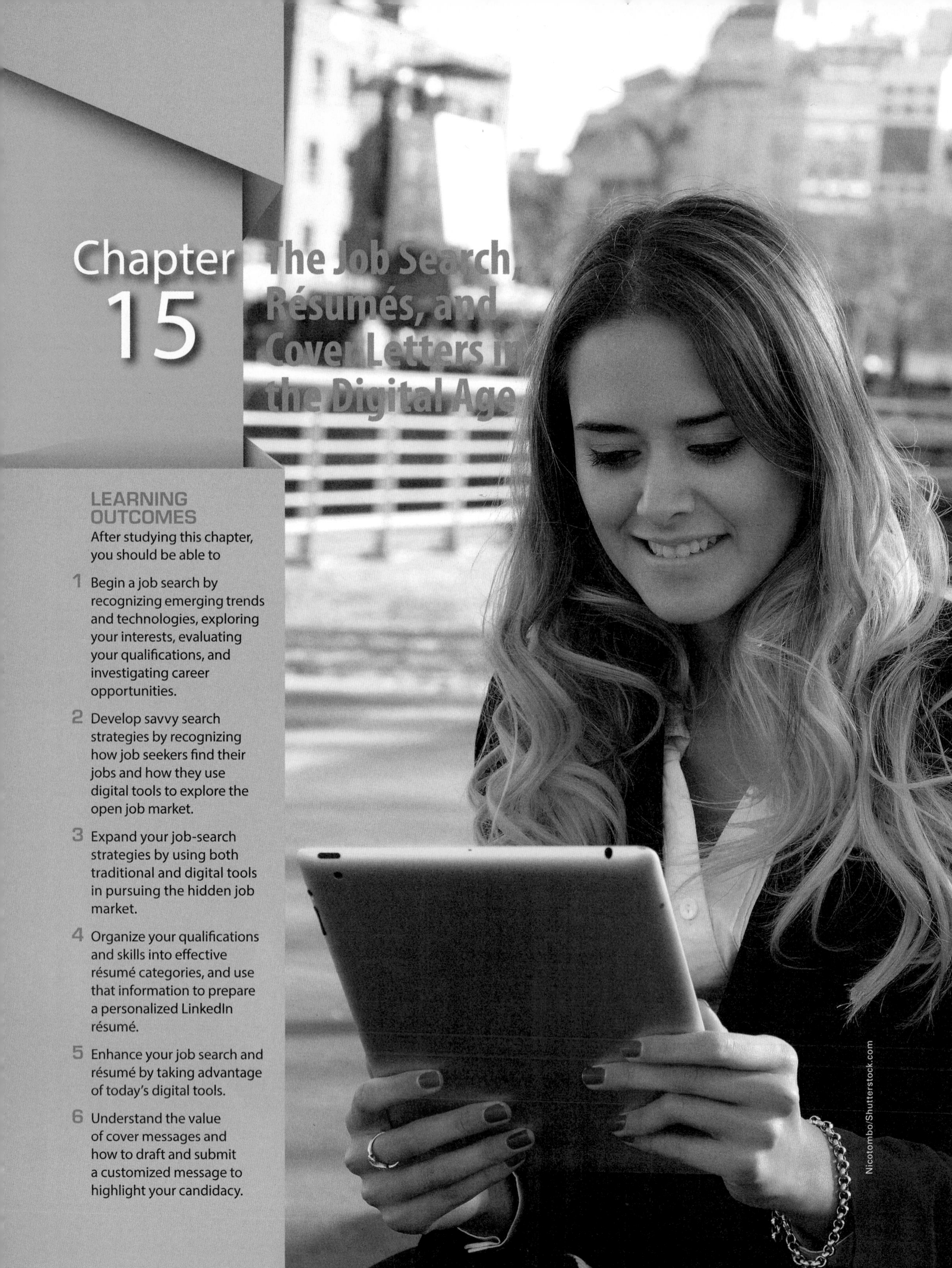

Chapter 15 The Job Search, Résumés, and Cover Letters in the Digital Age

LEARNING OUTCOMES

After studying this chapter, you should be able to

1 Begin a job search by recognizing emerging trends and technologies, exploring your interests, evaluating your qualifications, and investigating career opportunities.

2 Develop savvy search strategies by recognizing how job seekers find their jobs and how they use digital tools to explore the open job market.

3 Expand your job-search strategies by using both traditional and digital tools in pursuing the hidden job market.

4 Organize your qualifications and skills into effective résumé categories, and use that information to prepare a personalized LinkedIn résumé.

5 Enhance your job search and résumé by taking advantage of today's digital tools.

6 Understand the value of cover messages and how to draft and submit a customized message to highlight your candidacy.

Nicotombo/Shutterstock.com

Graduating From Classroom to Career

Yeamake/Shutterstock.com

You've been in school for a long time, but the end is in sight. Now, however, you begin to worry about the job market and how to land a dream job.

"Hiring managers expect young professionals to be job-hunting experts," observes career expert and experienced hiring manager Heather Huhman in her ebook *#ENTRYLEVELtweet: Taking Your Career From Classroom to Cubicle*.[1] The truth is, however, that most college students and recent grads don't know how to search for a job or what to expect. It's easy to be misled by misconceptions and myths.

One myth is that all job openings are posted on job boards.[2] This is definitely not true, she says. Many hiring managers refuse to post job openings because they fear receiving too many applications from unqualified candidates. Instead, large numbers of positions become part of the hidden job market, which is why Huhman passionately encourages recent grads to network vigorously. She agrees with other job-search experts who claim that as many as 80 percent of jobs are found through networking.[3] Another myth is that simply applying for jobs will land an interview. In the current tough job market, however, candidates must actively network and maintain a positive presence online.[4]

As technology continues to transform our world, Huhman notes that mobile technology is changing the way people—especially millennials—search and apply for jobs. Using mobile apps, job seekers today have fun searching for jobs from anywhere. One study reported that 47 percent of candidates use their mobile devices to search for jobs from bed.[5] To be ready to capitalize on an opening, she recommends creating a mobile-friendly résumé and cover letter.[6]

Alexander Raths/Shutterstock.com

Just as technology expands and transforms the job search, it also enables candidates to thoroughly research targeted companies. Probably the most helpful advice Huhman gives to new grads concerns researching each targeted company. Find out all you can, and then tailor your résumé to that company. "Think of it this way," she says. "Why would an organization want to invest time in you if you haven't invested any time in them? Small details like personalized résumés, cover letters, and thank-you notes can go a long way."[7]

Critical Thinking

- You are still in college, and the world of work may be way off in the future. Why, then, is it important to research the job market and even prepare a résumé if you are not in the market at this time?
- What do you know about the hidden job market, and how does networking help a new grad find a job in this elusive market?
- How many résumés should a recent grad prepare? What format is preferable?

Job Searching in the Digital Age

LEARNING OUTCOME 1

Begin a job search by recognizing emerging trends and technologies, exploring your interests, evaluating your qualifications, and investigating career opportunities.

Good news! For the third year in a row, college graduates can look forward to an uptick in hiring.[8] Whether you are actively looking for a position now or hope to do so later, becoming aware of job trends and requirements is important so that you can tailor your education to be successful when you enter the market. This chapter presents cutting-edge advice regarding job searching, résumé writing, and cover messages to give you an advantage in a labor market that is more competitive, more mobile, and more dependent on technology than ever before.

A successful job search today requires a blend of old and new job-hunting skills. Traditional techniques are still effective, but savvy job candidates must also be ready to act on emerging trends, some of which are presented in Figure 15.1. Job boards, social networks, and mobile technologies have all become indispensable tools in hunting for a job. Surprisingly, however, even in this digital age, personal networking, referrals, and who you know continue to be primary routes to hiring.

If you are fearful of entering a highly competitive job market, think of the many advantages you have. "Organizations are very interested in hiring young people because they have a lot of energy and are willing to do whatever it takes to get the job done," says one career specialist.[9] Think about your recent training, current skills, and enthusiasm. Remember, too, that you are less expensive to hire than older, experienced candidates. In addition, you have this book with the latest research, invaluable advice, and perfect model documents to guide you in your job search. Think positively!

Figure 15.1 **Looking at the Latest Trends in Job Searching and Résumés**

Mobile technologies are on the rise.

Candidates use apps to apply for jobs, and recruiters use mobile devices to post jobs, contact candidates, and forward résumés to colleagues.

Networking— it's who you know.

Recruiters say their best job candidates come from referrals. Now, more than ever, you need to be proactive in making professional connections.

Communication and interpersonal skills are in high demand.

Sales and marketing careers are booming, and these careers demand writing, speaking, and team skills.

Social media presence is a must.

Those who haven't developed a social media presence may be left in the dust.

It's all digital.

Today candidates e-mail their résumés, post them to Internet job boards, or publish them on their own Web pages.

Résumés must please scanners and skimmers.

Overwhelmed with candidates, recruiters hurriedly skim résumés preselected by scanning devices.

Using Technology to Aid Your Job Search

Technology is increasingly an integral part of the job-search process. Nearly every job hunter today has at least one mobile device, and the number of apps for these devices is overwhelming. You can download apps to plan your career, organize the job-search process, scour numerous job boards, receive immediate job alerts, and even arrange lunch dates to network and meet others in your field. Working from a smartphone, you can create, store, and send a résumé at the beach, on the train, or whenever a terrific opening pops up.

Organizations Bet on Technology. Beyond mobile devices, technology has greatly affected the way organizations announce jobs, select candidates, screen résumés, and conduct interviews. Big (and increasingly medium-sized) companies tend to use applicant tracking systems (ATS) to automatically post openings, select résumés, rank candidates, and generate interview requests. In this chapter you'll learn to craft your job search and résumé to take advantage of tracking systems and other technologies flooding the job-search market.

It's an Employers' Market. At the same time that a tsunami of technology is revolutionizing the job scene, other significant changes in the labor market will affect your job search and subsequent employment. In years past the emphasis was on what the applicant wanted. Today it's on what the employer wants.[10] Employers are most interested in how candidates will add value to their organizations. That's why today's most successful candidates customize their résumés to highlight their qualifications for each opening. In addition, career paths are no longer linear; most new-hires will not begin a job and steadily rise through the ranks. Jobs are more short-lived, and people are constantly relearning and retraining.

The Résumé Is Not Dead. The résumé is still important, but it may not be the document that introduces the job seeker these days. Instead, the résumé may come only after the candidate has established a real-world relationship. What's more, chances are that your résumé and cover message will be read digitally rather than in print. Although some attention-grabbing publications scream that the print résumé is dead, the truth is that every job hunter needs one. Whether offered online or in print, your résumé should be always available and current.

It's natural to think that the first step in finding a job is writing a résumé. However, that's a mistake. The job-search process actually begins long before you are ready to prepare your résumé. Regardless of the kind of employment you seek, you must invest time and effort in getting ready. Your best plan for completing a successful job search involves a four-step process: (1) analyzing yourself, (2) developing a job-search strategy, (3) preparing a résumé, and (4) knowing the hiring process, as illustrated in Figure 15.2.

Figure 15.2 **4 Steps in a Successful Job Search**

1
Analyze Yourself
▪ Identify your interests and goals.
▪ Assess your qualifications.
▪ Explore career opportunities.
2
Develop a Job-Search Strategy
▪ Search the open job market.
▪ Pursue the hidden job market.
▪ Cultivate your online presence.
▪ Build your personal brand.
▪ Network, network, network!
3
Create a Customized Résumé
▪ Choose a résumé style.
▪ Organize your info concisely.
▪ Tailor your résumé to each position.
▪ Optimize for digital technology.
4
Know the Hiring Process
▪ Submit a résumé, application, or e-portfolio.
▪ Undergo screening and hiring interviews.
▪ Accept an offer or reevaluate your progress.

Launching Your Job Search With Self-Analysis

The first step in a job search is analyzing your interests and goals and evaluating your qualifications. This means looking inside yourself to explore what you like and dislike so that you can make good employment choices. For guidance in choosing a career that eventually proves to be satisfying, ask yourself the following questions:

- What are you passionate about? Can you turn this passion into a career?
- Do you enjoy working with people, data, or things?
- How important are salary, benefits, technology support, and job stimulation?

> **Ethics Check**
>
> **Millennials Accused of Job Hopping**
>
> "Changing jobs every couple of years is the new norm and it might even benefit your career. Just ask a millennial," asserts a headline in *Fortune*. Are millennials getting a bad rap? How is changing jobs good or bad for your career?

- Must you work in a specific city, geographic area, or climate?
- Are you looking for security, travel opportunities, money, power, or prestige?
- How would you describe the perfect job, boss, and coworkers?

Evaluating Your Qualifications

In addition to analyzing your interests and goals, take a good look at your qualifications. Remember that today's job market is not so much about what you want, but what the employer wants. What assets can you offer? Your responses to the following questions will target your thinking as well as prepare a foundation for your résumé. Always keep in mind, though, that employers seek more than empty assurances; they will want proof of your qualifications.

- What technology skills can you present? What specific software programs are you familiar with, what Internet experience do you have, and what social media skills can you offer?
- Do you communicate well in speech and in writing? Do you know another language? How can you verify these talents?
- What other skills have you acquired in school, on the job, or through activities? How can you demonstrate these skills?
- Do you work well with people? Do you enjoy teamwork? What proof can you offer? Consider extracurricular activities, clubs, class projects, and jobs.
- Are you a leader, self-starter, or manager? What evidence can you offer? What leadership roles have you held?
- Do you learn quickly? Can you think critically? How can you demonstrate these characteristics?

Investigating Career Opportunities

The job picture in the United States is extraordinarily dynamic and flexible. On average, workers between ages eighteen and thirty-eight in the United States will have ten different employers over the course of their careers. The median job tenure of wage earners and salaried workers is 4.4 years with a single employer.[11] Although you may frequently change jobs in the future (especially before you reach age forty), you still need to train for a specific career. In exploring job opportunities, you will make the best decisions when you can match your interests and qualifications with the requirements and rewards of specific careers. Where can you find the best career data? Here are some suggestions:

- **Visit your campus career center.** Most campus career centers have literature, inventories, career-related software programs, and employment or internship databases that allow you to explore such fields as accounting, finance, office technology, information systems, and hotel management.
- **Search for apps and online help.** Many job-search sites—such as Indeed, Monster, and CareerBuilder—offer career-planning information and resources. One popular app is iPQ Career Planner, a free tool with a 52-question assessment test to zero in on your strengths and weaknesses.
- **Use your library.** Print and online resources in your library are especially helpful. Consult *O*NET Occupational Information Network, Dictionary of Occupational Titles, Occupational Outlook Handbook,* and *Jobs Rated Almanac* for information about job requirements, qualifications, salaries, and employment trends.
- **Take a summer job, internship, or part-time position in your field.** Nothing is better than trying out a career. Many companies offer internships and temporary or part-time jobs to begin training college students and to develop relationships with them. An amazing number of interns are hired into full-time positions—57 percent in one recent study.[12]

- **Interview someone in your chosen field.** People are usually flattered when asked to describe their careers. Inquire about needed skills, required courses, financial and other rewards, benefits, working conditions, future trends, and entry requirements.
- **Volunteer with a nonprofit organization.** Many colleges and universities encourage service learning. In volunteering their services, students gain valuable experience, and nonprofits appreciate the expertise and fresh ideas that students bring.
- **Monitor the classified ads.** Early in your college career, begin monitoring want ads and the websites of companies in your career area. Check job availability, qualifications sought, duties, and salary ranges. Don't wait until you are about to graduate to explore the job market.

Developing a Job-Search Strategy Focused on the Open Job Market

LEARNING OUTCOME 2

Develop savvy search strategies by recognizing how job seekers find their jobs and how they use digital tools to explore the open job market.

Once you have analyzed what you want in a job and what you have to offer, you are ready to focus on a job-search strategy. You're probably most interested in how job seekers today are finding their jobs. What methods did they use? A study by staffing firm Jobvite, summarized in Figure 15.3, reveals how 1,303 employed U.S. workers found their "best"

Figure 15.3 **How Did Job Seekers Find Their Best Jobs?**

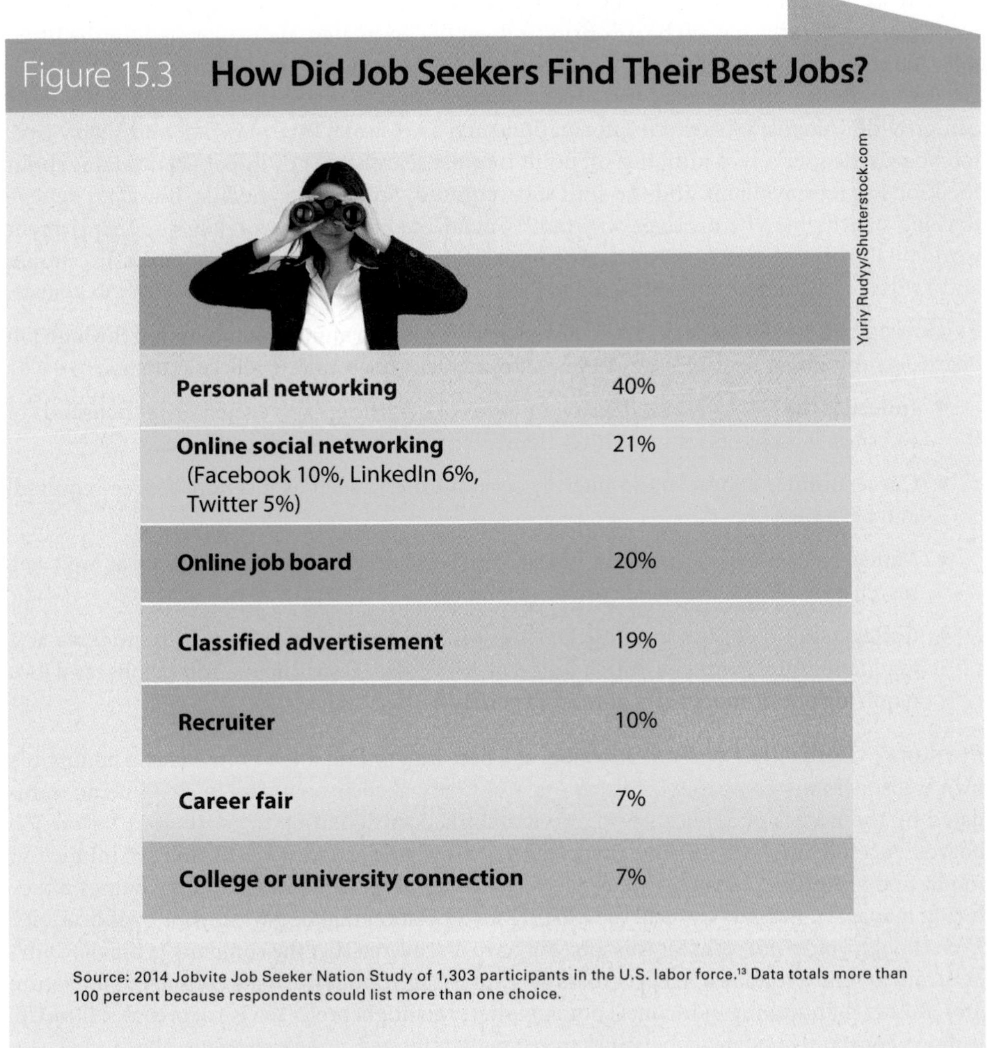

Personal networking	40%
Online social networking (Facebook 10%, LinkedIn 6%, Twitter 5%)	21%
Online job board	20%
Classified advertisement	19%
Recruiter	10%
Career fair	7%
College or university connection	7%

Source: 2014 Jobvite Job Seeker Nation Study of 1,303 participants in the U.S. labor force.[13] Data totals more than 100 percent because respondents could list more than one choice.

jobs. When the first two categories are combined, you see that a resounding 61 percent of respondents used some form of networking, whether person-to-person or online, to locate their best jobs.

Despite the explosion of digital job-search apps and online job boards, networking remains the No. 1 tool for finding a desirable position. Technology, however, plays an increasingly weighty role in the job search. As that happens, the line between online and traditional networking blurs. Explaining this trend, one executive said: "Online social networking may not always be separate from traditional networking since one so often leads to the other. A job seeker uses the Internet to track down former associates or acquaintances and then reaches out to them in person."[14]

Both networking and online searching are essential tools in locating jobs, but where are those jobs? The *open job market* consists of jobs that are advertised or listed. The *hidden job market* consists of jobs that are never advertised or listed. Some analysts and authors claim that between 50 and 80 percent of all jobs are filled before they even make it to online job boards or advertisements.[15] Those openings are in the hidden job market, which we will explore shortly. First, let's start where most job seekers start—in the open job market.

Searching the Open Job Market

The open job market consists of positions that are advertised or listed publicly. Most job seekers start searching by using Google to look for positions in their fields and within their commute areas. Sadly, searching online is a common, but not always rewarding, approach. Both recruiters and job seekers complain about online job boards, such as Monster and Indeed. Corporate recruiters say that the big job boards bring a flood of candidates, many unsuited for the listed jobs. Job candidates grumble that listings are frequently outdated and fail to produce leads.

Although the Internet may seem like a giant swamp that swallows résumés, job boards can provide valuable job-search information such as résumé, interviewing, and salary tips. Job boards also serve as a jumping-off point in most searches. They inform candidates about the kinds of jobs available and the skill sets required. Some professionals, however, believe that job boards may be on their way out.[16] Social media sites have taken the recruitment world by storm, and savvy millennials and others are eagerly turning to LinkedIn, Facebook, and Twitter to search for jobs. Still, many job seekers will begin their search with job boards.

Exploring the Big Boards. As Figure 15.3 indicates, the number of jobs found through job boards is substantial. Four of the most popular job sites are useful for college students:

- **Indeed** is the No. 1 job site, offering millions of job listings aggregated from thousands of websites. It accounts for more hires than all the other job boards combined.
- **CareerBuilder** allows you to filter by several criteria such as location, degree required, and pay range.
- **Monster** permits you to upload your résumé and offers networking boards as well as a search alert service that sends you targeted posts.
- **CollegeGrad** describes itself as the "number one entry-level job site" for students and graduates. Applicants can search for entry-level jobs, internships, summer jobs, and jobs requiring one or more years of work experience.

Pursuing Company Leads. Probably the best way to find a job online is at a company's own website. Many companies post job openings only at their own sites to avoid being inundated by the hordes of applicants—many unqualified—responding to postings at online job boards. A company's website is the first place to go if you have a specific employer in mind. You might find vision and mission statements, a history of the organization, and the names of key hiring managers. Possibly you will see a listing for a position that doesn't fit your qualifications. Even though you're not right for this job, you have discovered that the company is hiring. Don't be afraid to send a résumé and cover message expressing your desire to be considered for future jobs. Rather than seeking individual company sites, you might prefer to visit aggregator **LinkUp**. It shows constantly updated job listings from small, midsized, and large companies.

Checking Niche Sites. If you seek a job in a specialized field, look for a niche site, such as **Dice** for technology jobs, **Advance Healthcare Network** for jobs in the medical field, and **Accountemps** for temporary accounting positions. Niche websites also exist for job seekers with special backgrounds or needs, such as **GettingHired** for disabled workers and **Workforce50** for older workers. If you are looking for a short-term job, check out **CoolWorks**, which specializes in seasonal employment. If you yearn for a government job, try **USAJOBS**, a website for students and recent graduates interested in federal service.

Taking Advantage of Mobile Apps. Job seekers are eagerly embracing smartphone apps to gain an edge in the job search. With many of the following mobile apps, you can access and vet job openings as soon as they are listed—even when you are on the go.[17] Like its full website, the **Indeed Job Search** app lets you filter your search results based on your field, desired salary, and location. The app **Hidden Jobs** lists nearly 2 million unpublicized jobs by tracking company job announcements so you don't have to. **Intro** is an app that connects you to people in your field or in your social media network. **JobAware** allows you to integrate all your Internet job-search activity including LinkedIn. **JobCompass** helps you narrow the search to your zip code. **LinkedUp Job Search Engine, Monster, Reach, Simply Hired, Snagajob,** and **Switch** all offer mobile links to job listings from a variety of sources.

Checking Newspapers, Career Fairs, and Other Sources. Despite the rush to mobile technology, some organizations still list openings in newspapers. Don't overlook this possibility, especially for local jobs. Plenty of jobs can also be found through career fairs and university and college alumni contacts.

When posting job-search information online, it's natural to want to put your best foot forward and openly share information that will get you a job. The challenge is to strike a balance between supplying enough information and protecting yourself. To avoid some of the risks involved, see the cautions described in Figure 15.4

Figure 15.4 Protecting Yourself When Posting at Online Job Boards

- **Use reputable, well-known sites** and never pay to post your résumé.
- **Don't divulge personal data** such as your date of birth, social security number, or home address. Use your city and state or region in place of your home address.
- **Set up a separate e-mail account** with a professional-sounding e-mail address for your job search.
- **Post privately** if possible. Doing so means that you can control who has access to your e-mail address and other information.
- **Keep careful records** of every site on which you posted. At the end of your job search, remove all posted résumés.
- **Don't include your references** or reveal their contact information without permission.
- **Don't respond to blind job postings** (those without company names or addresses). Unfortunately, scammers use online job boards to post fake job ads to gather your personal information.

LEARNING OUTCOME 3

Expand your job-search strategies by using both traditional and digital tools in pursuing the hidden job market.

Unlocking the Hidden Job Market With Networking

Not all available positions are announced or advertised in the open job market. As mentioned earlier, between 50 and 80 percent of jobs are estimated to be in the hidden job market.[18] Companies prefer to avoid publicizing job announcements openly for a number of reasons. They don't welcome the deluge of unqualified candidates. What's more, companies dislike hiring unknown quantities. Career coach Donald Asher, author of *Cracking the Hidden Job Market*, sets this scene: Imagine you are a hiring manager facing hundreds of résumés on your desk and a coworker walks in with the résumé of someone she vouches for. Which résumé do you think hits the top of the stack?[19] Companies prefer known quantities.

The most successful job candidates seek to transform themselves from unknown into known quantities through networking. More jobs today are found through referrals and person-to-person contacts than through any other method. That's because people trust what they know. Therefore, your goal is to become known to a large network of people, and this means going beyond close friends.

Building a Personal Network

Because most candidates find jobs today through networking, be prepared to work diligently to build your personal networks. This effort involves meeting people and talking to them about your field or industry so that you can gain information and locate job vacancies. Not only are many jobs never advertised, but some positions aren't even contemplated until the right person appears. One recent college grad underwent three interviews for a position, but the company hired someone else. After being turned down, the grad explained why he thought he was perfect for this company but perhaps in a different role. Apparently, the hiring manager agreed and decided to create a new job (in social media) because of the skills, personality, and perseverance of this determined young grad. Traditional networking pays off, but it requires dedication. Here are three steps that will help you establish your own network:

Step 1. Develop a contact list. Make a list of anyone who would be willing to talk with you about finding a job. Figure 15.5 suggests possibilities. Even if you haven't talked with people in years, reach out to them in person or online. Consider asking your campus career center for alumni willing to talk with students. Also dig into your social networking circles, which we will discuss shortly.

Step 2. Make contacts in person and online. Call the people on your list or connect online. To set up a meeting in person, say, *Hi,_______. I'm looking for a job and I wonder if you could help me out. When could I come over to talk about it?* During your visit be friendly, well organized, polite, and interested in what your contact has to say. Provide a copy of your résumé, and try to keep the conversation centered on your job search. Your goal is to get two or more referrals. In pinpointing your request, ask, *Do you know of anyone who might have an opening for a person with my skills?* If the person does not, ask, *Do you know of anyone else who might know of someone?*

Step 3. Follow up on your referrals. Call or contact the people on your list. You might say something like, *Hello. I'm Stacy Rivera, a friend of Jason Tilden. He suggested that I ask you for help. I'm looking for a position as a marketing trainee, and he thought you might be willing to spare a few minutes and steer me in the right direction.* Don't ask for a job. During your referral interview, ask how the individual got started in this line of work, what he or she likes best (or least) about the work, what career paths exist in the field, and what problems a newcomer must overcome. Most important, ask how a person with your background and skills might get started in the field. Send an informal thank-you note to anyone who helps you in your job search, and stay in touch with the most promising people. Ask whether you could stay in contact every three weeks or so during your job search.

Unfortunately, many new grads are reluctant to engage in traditional person-to-person networking because it feels pushy, and it definitely requires considerable effort. They are much more comfortable with networking through social media sites.

Figure 15.5 **Whom to Contact in Networking**

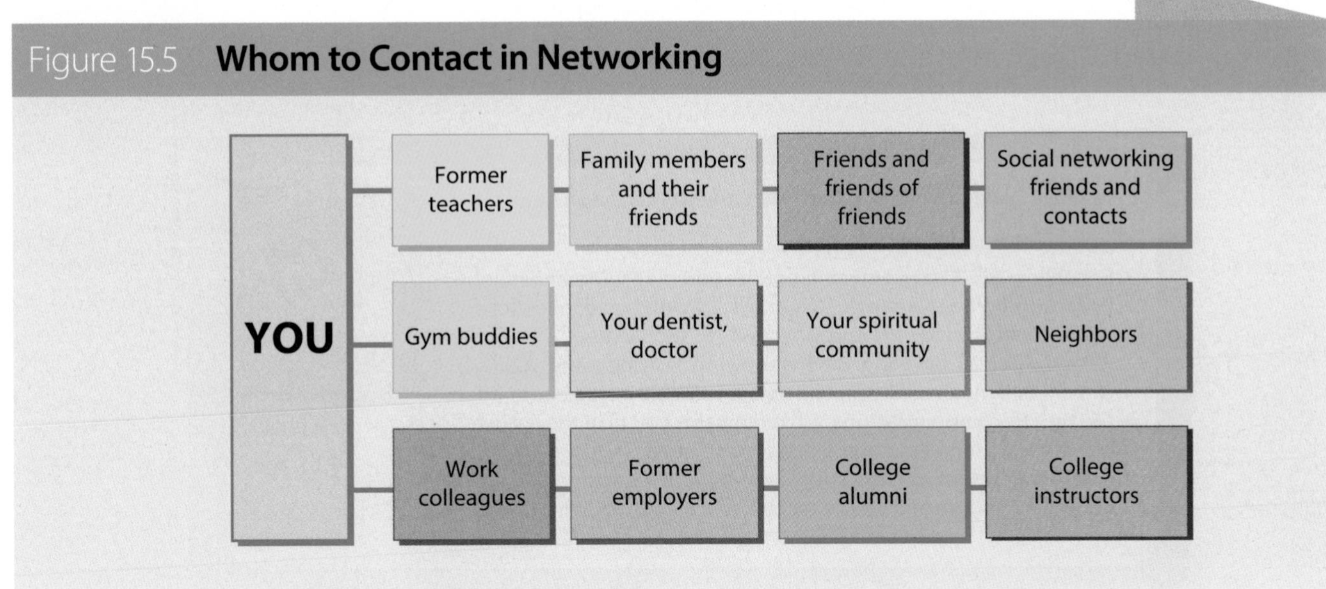

Targeting Social Media in a Job Search

As digital technology continues to change our lives, job candidates have powerful new tools at their disposal: social media networks. These networks have become critical in a job search. If you just send out your résumé blindly, not much will happen. However, if you have a referral, your chances of landing an interview multiply. Today's expansion of online networks has produced an additional path to developing those coveted referrals.

Letting LinkedIn Help You Find a Job. If you are seriously looking for a job, it's extremely important that you list yourself at LinkedIn. This social media site dominates the world of job searching and recruiting. In a recent poll of 1,855 recruiting and staffing professionals, 95 percent said that they used LinkedIn as a recruiting tool.[20] It's truly the place to find and be found, especially for new grads. It lists well over a million and a half student jobs and internships in addition to millions of full-time jobs.[21] Developing an online presence at LinkedIn enables you to post information about yourself in one central place where it's available to potential employers, graduate schools, future colleagues, and people you will want to stay connected to. A LinkedIn page tells the working world that you are a professional, and it remains significant even after you obtain a position.

JuliusKielaitis/Shutterstock.com

Reality Check

Without LinkedIn, You Don't Exist

"Think of LinkedIn as your résumé that never sleeps. But a lot more. It's your professional brand in the world. It's the result you actually *want* up top when someone Googles you. . . . If you're not on LinkedIn, you simply don't exist in the working world."[22]

—Omar Garriott, *director of product marketing, Salesforce; former senior product marketing manager, LinkedIn*

Figure 15.6 Harnessing the Power of LinkedIn

Five Ways College Students Can Use LinkedIn to Help Them Find a Job

1. **Receiving Job Alerts.** LinkedIn notifies you of recommended jobs.
2. **Leveraging Your Network.** You may start with two connections, but you can leverage those connections to thousands.
3. **Researching a Company.** Before applying to a company, you can check it out on LinkedIn and locate valuable inside information.
4. **Getting Recommendations.** LinkedIn helps you take the awkwardness out of asking for recommendations. It's so easy!
5. **Helping Companies Find You.** Many companies are looking for skilled college grads, and your strong profile on LinkedIn can result in inquiries.

Roman Pyshchyk/Shutterstock.com

One of the best ways to use LinkedIn is to search for a company in which you are interested. Try to find company employees who are connected to other people you know. Then use that contact as a referral when you apply. You can also send an e-mail to everyone in your LinkedIn network asking for help or for people they could put you in touch with. Don't be afraid to ask an online contact for advice on getting started in a career and for suggestions to help a newcomer break into that career. Another excellent way to use a contact is to have that person look at your résumé and help you tweak it. Like Facebook, LinkedIn has status updates, and it's a good idea to update yours regularly so that your connections know what is happening in your career search and afterward.

Although some young people have the impression that LinkedIn is for old fogies, that perception is changing as more and more college students and grads sign up. LinkedIn can aid your job search in at least five ways, as shown in Figure 15.6. Because LinkedIn functions in many ways as a résumé, you will find tips for preparing your LinkedIn page in our discussion of résumés in the next pages.

Enlisting Other Social Networks in a Job Hunt. In addition to LinkedIn, job seekers can join Facebook, Twitter, and Google+ to find job opportunities, market themselves to companies, showcase their skills, highlight their experience, and possibly land that dream job. Because organizations may post open jobs to their Facebook or Twitter pages prior to advertising them elsewhere, you might gain a head start on submitting an application by following them on these sites. If you have a Facebook account, examine your profile and decide what you want prospective employers to see—or not see. Create a simple profile with minimal graphics, widgets, and photos. Post only content relevant to your job search or career, and choose your friends wisely.

Employers often use these social media sites to check the online presence of a candidate. One report revealed that nine out of ten recruiters use social media to search, keep tabs on, and vet candidates before the interview.[23] Make sure your social networking accounts represent you professionally. You can make it easy for your potential employer to learn more about you by including an informative bio in your Twitter or Facebook profile that has a link to your LinkedIn profile. You can also make yourself more discoverable by posting thoughtful blog posts and tweets on topics related to your career goal.

sebastiano volponi/MARKA/Alamy Stock Photo

Employers routinely refer to job applicants' social media sites to discover indiscretions. Perhaps less commonly known, however, is that Facebook is increasingly used as a tool to recruit employees. Savvy job seekers know to use the social networking platform to expand their professional connections, illustrate their social media know-how, and craft their profiles to accentuate work history. When using Facebook as part of a job search, candidates must be extremely careful to separate personal friends from professional contacts. The professional contacts list becomes a way for job seekers to reach out by posting industry-related content and personal work-related status updates. How can you build your personal brand on Facebook?[24]

Creating Your Personal Brand

A large part of your job-search strategy involves building a brand for yourself. You may be thinking, *Who me? A brand?* Yes, absolutely! Even college grads should seriously consider branding because finding a job in a competitive market is tough. Before you get into the thick of the job hunt, focus on developing your brand so that you know what you want to emphasize.

Personal branding involves deciding what makes you special and desirable in the job market. What is your unique selling point? What special skill set makes you stand out among all job applicants? What would your instructors or employers say is your greatest strength? Think about your intended audience. What are you promoting about yourself?

Experts suggest that you create a tagline that describes what you do, who you are, and what's special about you. A nurse wrote this fetching tagline:

> *Tireless, caring Registered Nurse who helps pediatric cancer patients and their families feel at ease throughout treatment and recovery*

If you prefer a shorter tagline for your business card, consider the sample taglines for new grads in Figure 15.7. It's OK to shed a little modesty and strut your stuff. However, do keep your tagline simple, short, and truthful so that it's easy to remember.

Once you have a tagline, prepare a professional-looking business card with your name and tagline. Include an easy-to-remember e-mail address such as *firstname.lastname@ domain.com.* Consider using CardDrop, an app that creates a digital business card to use to connect with new contacts and help you be remembered.

Now that you have your tagline and business card, work on an elevator speech. This is a pitch that you can give in 60 seconds or less describing who you are and what you can offer. Tweak your speech for your audience, and practice until you can say it naturally. Here are suggestions to help you prepare your own authentic elevator speech depending on your situation:

> *Hi, my name is ___________, and I am about to graduate from __________ with a major in____________. I'm looking to ____________ because I enjoy __________. Recently I ____________ where I was able to develop skills such as ___________. I'm most confident about my skills in __________. I'm inspired by the field (or position) of __________ because ___________ . My ultimate aim is to ___________. I'm looking for a position in __________. Do you have any suggestions or advice on how I can __________?*

Figure 15.7 **Branding YOU**

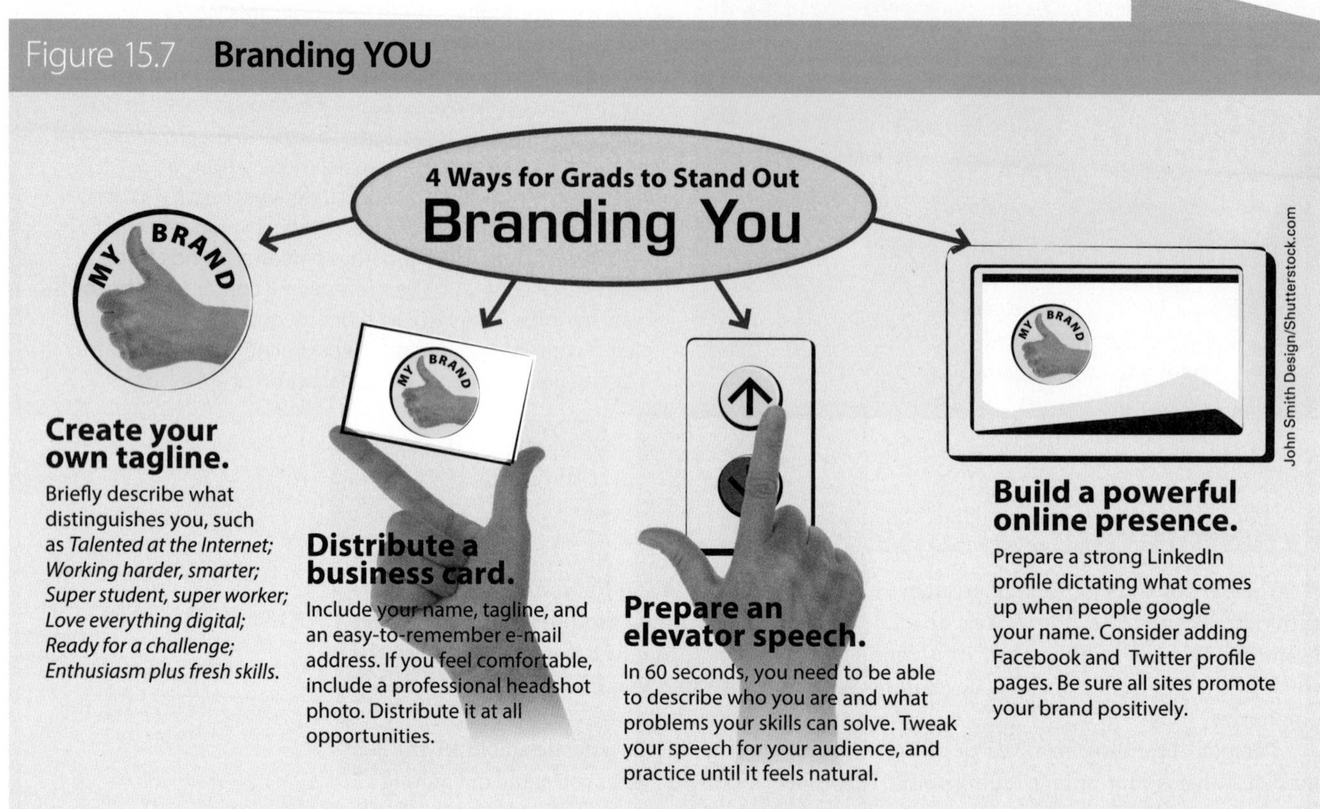

4 Ways for Grads to Stand Out
Branding You
MY BRAND
Create your own tagline.
Briefly describe what distinguishes you, such as *Talented at the Internet; Working harder, smarter; Super student, super worker; Love everything digital; Ready for a challenge; Enthusiasm plus fresh skills.*
Distribute a business card.
Include your name, tagline, and an easy-to-remember e-mail address. If you feel comfortable, include a professional headshot photo. Distribute it at all opportunities.
Prepare an elevator speech.
In 60 seconds, you need to be able to describe who you are and what problems your skills can solve. Tweak your speech for your audience, and practice until it feels natural.
Build a powerful online presence.
Prepare a strong LinkedIn profile dictating what comes up when people google your name. Consider adding Facebook and Twitter profile pages. Be sure all sites promote your brand positively.
John Smith Design/Shutterstock.com

LEARNING OUTCOME 4

Organize your qualifications and skills into effective résumé categories, and use that information to prepare a personalized LinkedIn page.

Customizing Your Résumé

In today's highly competitive job market, the focus is not so much on what you want but on what the employer needs. That's why you must customize your résumé for every position you seek. The competition is so stiff today that you cannot get by with a generic, one-size-fits-all résumé. Although you can start with a basic résumé, you should customize it to fit each company and position if you want it to stand out from the crowd.

The Internet has made it so simple to apply for jobs that recruiters are swamped with applications. As a job seeker, you have between 5 and 20 seconds to catch the recruiter's eye—if your résumé is even read by a person. It may very well first encounter an *applicant tracking system* (ATS). This software helps businesses automatically post openings, screen résumés, rank candidates, and generate interview requests. These automated systems make writing your résumé doubly challenging. Although your goal is to satisfy a recruiter or hiring manager, that person may never see your résumé unless it is selected by the ATS. Because so many organizations are using ATS software today, this chapter provides you with the latest advice on how to get your résumé ranked highly—so that it will then proceed to a real human being who will call you for an interview.

Choosing a Résumé Style

The first step in preparing a winning, customized résumé that appeals to both the human reader and the ATS screening device is to decide what style to use. Résumés usually fall into two categories: chronological and functional. This section presents basic information as well as insider tips on how to choose an appropriate résumé style, determine its length, and arrange its parts. You will also learn about adding a summary of qualifications, which many busy recruiters welcome. Models of the résumé styles discussed in the following sections are shown in our comprehensive Résumé Gallery.

What Is a Chronological Résumé? The most popular résumé format is the chronological format, shown in Figures 15.11, 15.12, and 15.14 in our Résumé Gallery. The chronological résumé lists work history job by job but in reverse order, starting with the most recent position. Recruiters favor the chronological format because they are familiar with it and because it quickly reveals a candidate's education and experience. The chronological style works well for candidates who have experience in their field of employment and for those who show steady career growth, but it is less helpful for people who have changed jobs frequently or who have gaps in their employment records. For college students and others who lack extensive experience, the functional résumé format may be preferable.

What Is a Functional Résumé? The functional résumé, shown in Figure 15.13, focuses on a candidate's skills rather than on past employment. Like a chronological résumé, a functional résumé begins with the candidate's name, contact information, job objective, and education. Instead of listing jobs, though, the functional résumé groups skills and accomplishments in special categories, such as Supervisory and Management Skills or Retailing and Marketing Experience. This résumé style highlights accomplishments and can de-emphasize a negative employment history.

People who have changed jobs frequently, who have gaps in their employment records, or who are entering an entirely different field may prefer the functional résumé. Recent graduates with little or no related employment experience often find the functional résumé useful. Older job seekers who want to downplay a long job history and job hunters who are afraid of appearing overqualified may also prefer the functional format. Be aware, though, that online job boards may insist on the chronological format. In addition, some recruiters are suspicious of functional résumés, thinking the candidate is hiding something.

How Long Should a Résumé Be? Experts disagree on how long a résumé should be. Conventional wisdom has always held that recruiters prefer one-page résumés. However, recruiters who are serious about candidates often prefer the kind of details that can be provided in a two-page or longer résumé. What's more, with today's digital résumés, length is no longer restricted. The best advice is to make your résumé as long as needed to present your skills to recruiters and hiring managers. Individuals with more experience will naturally have longer résumés. Those with fewer than ten years of experience, those making a major career change, and those who have had only one or two employers will likely have one-page résumés. Those with ten years or more of related experience may have two-page résumés. Finally, some senior-level managers and executives with a lengthy history of major accomplishments might have résumés that are three pages or longer.[25]

Organizing Your Information Into Effective Résumé Categories

Although résumés have standard categories, their arrangement and content should be strategically planned. A customized résumé emphasizes skills and achievements aimed at a particular job or company. It shows a candidate's most important qualifications first, and it de-emphasizes weaknesses. In organizing your qualifications and information, try to create as few headings as possible; more than six looks cluttered. No two résumés are ever exactly alike, but most writers include all or some of these categories: Main Heading, Career Objective, Summary of Qualifications, Education, Experience, Capabilities and Skills, and Awards and Activities.

Main Heading. Your résumé, whether chronological or functional, should start with an uncluttered and simple main heading. The first line should always be your name; add your middle initial for an even more professional look. Format your name so that it stands out on the page. Following your name, list your contact information, including your address, area code and phone number, and e-mail address. Some candidates are omitting their street addresses to protect their privacy and for safety reasons. Your telephone should be one where you can receive messages. The outgoing message at this number should be in your voice, it should state your full name, and it should be concise and professional. If you include your cell phone number and are expecting an important call from a recruiter, pick up only when you are in a quiet environment and can concentrate.

For your e-mail address, be sure it sounds professional instead of something like *toosexy4you@gmail.com* or *sixpackguy@yahoo.com.* Also be sure that you are using a personal e-mail address. Putting your work e-mail address on your résumé announces to prospective employers that you are using your current employer's resources to look for another job. If you have a LinkedIn profile or a website where an e-portfolio or samples of your work can be viewed, include the links in the main heading.

Alexander Raths/Shutterstock.com

Reality Check

Make Your Résumé Reveal What You Want

"Hiring managers are busy folks who can't afford to waste any time trying to figure out what your career goals are. They won't take the time to do this; they'll just move on to the next resume. . . . If you're targeting a particular position, add a formal objective statement and reference the job opening. The hiring manager will see you took time to customize your resume and that the opportunity is important to you."[26]

—Kim Isaacs, *author and Monster résumé expert*

Career Objective. Although experts don't agree on whether to include an objective on a résumé, nearly all agree that if you do, it should be very specific. A well-written objective—customized for the job opening—makes sense, especially for new grads with fresh training and relevant skills. Strive to include strategic keywords from the job listing because these will help tracking systems select your résumé. Focus on what you can contribute to the organization, not on what the organization can do for you.

> **Poor objective:** *To obtain a position with a well-established organization that will lead to a lasting relationship in the field of marketing.* (Sounds vague and self-serving.)
>
> **Improved objective:** *To obtain a position that capitalizes on my recent training in business writing and marketing to boost customer contacts and expand brand penetration using my social media expertise.* (Names specific skills and includes many nouns that might snag the attention of an applicant tracking system.)

Instead of an objective, one résumé expert recommends listing the job title of the position for which you are applying, including the words *Target Job Title* as shown here:

> *Target Job Title: Medical Administrative Assistant*

Using a customized objective or a job title makes it clear that you have taken the time and made the effort to prepare your résumé for the position.[27] If you decide to omit a career objective, be sure to discuss your career goals in your cover message.

Optional Summary of Qualifications. Over the past decade, the biggest change in résumés has been a switch from a career objective to a summary of qualifications at the top.[28] Once a job is advertised, a hiring manager may receive hundreds or even thousands of résumés.

A summary ensures that your most impressive qualifications are not overlooked by a recruiter who is skimming résumés quickly. A summary also enables you to present a concentrated list of many relevant keywords for a tracking system to pick up, thus boosting your chance of selection.[29] Additionally, because résumés today may be viewed on tablets and smartphones, the summary spotlights your most compelling qualifications in a highly visible spot.

A summary of qualifications (also called Career Profile, Job Summary, or Professional Highlights) may be a short summary statement or a list of three to eight bulleted statements that prove that you are the ideal candidate for the position. When formulating these statements, consider your experience in the field, your education, your unique skills, awards you have won, certifications you hold, and any other accomplishments. Strive to quantify your achievements wherever possible. Target the most important qualifications an employer will be looking for in the person hired for this position. Focus on nouns that might be selected as keywords by a tracking system. Examples of qualifications summaries appear in Figures 15.11 and 15.14.

Education. The next component in a chronological résumé is your education—if it is more noteworthy than your work experience. In this section you should include the name and location of schools, dates of attendance, major fields of study, and degrees received. By the way, once you have attended college, you don't need to list high school information on your résumé.

Your grade point average (GPA) and/or class ranking may be important to prospective employers. One way to enhance your GPA is to calculate it in your major courses only (for example, *3.6/4.0 in major*). Doing so is not unethical as long as you clearly show that your GPA is in the major only. Looking to improve their hiring chances, some college grads are now offering an unusual credential: their scores on the Graduate Record Examination. Large companies and those specializing in computer software and financial services reportedly were most interested in applicants' GRE scores.[30]

Under Education you might be tempted to list all the courses you took, but such a list makes for dull reading and consumes valuable space. Include a brief list of courses only if you can relate them to the position sought. When relevant, include certificates earned, seminars attended, workshops completed, scholarships awarded, and honors earned. If your education is incomplete, include such statements as *BS degree expected 6/18* or *80 units completed in 120-unit program*. Title this section Education, Academic Preparation, or Professional Training. If you are preparing a functional résumé, you will probably put the Education section below your skills summary, as in Figure 15.13.

Work Experience or Employment History. When your work or volunteer experience is significant and relevant to the position sought, this information should appear before your education. List your most recent employment first and work backward, including only those jobs that you think will help you win the targeted position. A job application form may demand a full employment history, but your résumé may be selective. Be aware, though, that time gaps in your employment history will probably be questioned in the interview. For each position show the following:

- Employer's name, city, and state
- Dates of employment (month and year)
- Most important job title
- Significant duties, activities, accomplishments, and promotions

Be sure to include relevant volunteer work. A survey conducted by LinkedIn revealed that 41 percent of LinkedIn hiring managers consider volunteer work experience as respectable as paid work experience when evaluating candidates.[31]

Your employment achievements and job duties will be easier to read if you place them in bulleted lists. Rather than list every single thing you have done, customize your information so that it relates to the targeted job. Your bullet points should be concise but not complete sentences, and they usually do not include personal pronouns (*I, me, my*). Strive to be specific:

Poor: *Worked with customers*

Improved: *Developed superior customer service skills by successfully interacting with 40+ customers daily*

Whenever possible, quantify your achievements:

Poor: *Did equipment study and report*

Improved: *Conducted research and wrote final study analyzing equipment needs of 100 small businesses in Houston*

Poor: *Was successful in sales*

Improved: *Personally generated orders for sales of $90,000 annually*

In addition to technical skills, employers seek individuals with communication, management, and interpersonal capabilities. This means you will want to select work experiences and achievements that illustrate your initiative, dependability, responsibility, resourcefulness, flexibility, and leadership. Employers also want people who can work in teams.

Poor: *Worked effectively in teams*

Improved: *Enjoyed collaborating with five-member interdepartmental team in developing ten-page handbook for temporary workers*

Poor: *Joined in team effort on campus*

Improved: *Headed 16-member student government team that conducted the most successful voter registration in campus history*

Statements describing your work experience should include many nouns relevant to the job you seek. These nouns may match keywords sought by the applicant tracking system. To appeal to human readers, your statements should also include action verbs, such as those in Figure 15.8. Starting each of your bullet points with an action verb helps ensure that your bulleted lists are parallel.

Figure 15.8 **Action Verbs for a Powerful Résumé**

Communication Skills	Teamwork, Supervision Skills	Management, Leadership Skills	Research Skills	Clerical, Detail Skills	Creative Skills
clarified	advised	analyzed	assessed	activated	acted
collaborated	coordinated	authorized	collected	approved	conceptualized
explained	demonstrated	coordinated	critiqued	classified	designed
interpreted	developed	directed	diagnosed	edited	fashioned
integrated	evaluated	headed	formulated	generated	founded
persuaded	expedited	implemented	gathered	maintained	illustrated
promoted	facilitated	improved	interpreted	monitored	integrated
resolved	guided	increased	investigated	proofread	invented
summarized	motivated	organized	reviewed	recorded	originated
translated	set goals	scheduled	studied	streamlined	revitalized
wrote	trained	strengthened	systematized	updated	shaped

Courtesy of Roberta Chinsky Matuson

Reality Check

Forget Vague Generalities

"Many résumé writers tend to aim for vague generalities and abstract attributes, focusing on their communication skills and ability to work as a team player. In a tough market, you need to move beyond these kinds of generic claims and focus on specifics. List each of your pertinent skills and responsibilities, and then back them up with fact-based bullets that explicitly prove your point."[32]

—Roberta Chinsky Matuson, *job-search consultant and president, Matuson Consulting*

Capabilities and Skills. Recruiters want to know specifically what you can do for their companies. List your special skills, including many nouns that relate to the targeted position. Talk about your ability to use the Internet, search engines, software programs, social media, office equipment, and communication technology tools. Use expressions such as *proficient in, competent in, experienced in,* and *ability to,* as illustrated in the following:

Poor: *Have payroll experience*

Improved: *Proficient in preparing federal, state, and local payroll tax returns as well as franchise and personal property tax returns*

Poor: *Trained in computer graphics*

Improved: *Certified in graphic design including infographics through an intensive 350-hour classroom program*

Poor: *Have writing skills*

Improved: *Competent in writing, editing, and proofreading reports, tables, letters, memos, e-mails, manuscripts, and business forms*

You will also want to highlight exceptional aptitudes, such as working well under stress, learning computer programs quickly, and interacting with customers. If possible, provide details and evidence that back up your assertions. Include examples of your writing, speaking, management, organizational, interpersonal, and presentation skills—particularly those that are relevant to your targeted job. For recent graduates, this section can be used to give recruiters evidence of your potential and to highlight successful college projects.

Awards, Honors, and Activities. If you have three or more awards or honors, highlight them by listing them under a separate heading. If not, put them in the Education or Work Experience section, if appropriate. Include awards, scholarships (financial and other), fellowships, dean's list, honors, recognition, commendations, and certificates. Be sure to identify items clearly. Your reader may be unfamiliar, for example, with Greek organizations, honoraries, and awards; tell what they mean.

Poor: *Recipient of Star award*

Improved: *Recipient of Star award given by Pepperdine University to outstanding graduates who combine academic excellence and extracurricular activities*

It's also appropriate to include school, community, volunteer, and professional activities. Employers are interested in evidence that you are a well-rounded person. This section provides an opportunity to demonstrate leadership and interpersonal skills. Strive to use action statements.

Poor: *Treasurer of business club*

Improved: *Collected dues, kept financial records, and paid bills while serving as treasurer of 35-member business management club*

Personal Data. Résumés in the United States omit personal data, such as birth date, marital status, height, weight, national origin, health, disabilities, and religious affiliation. Such information doesn't relate to genuine occupational qualifications, and recruiters are legally barred from asking for such information. Some job seekers do, however, include hobbies or interests (such as skiing or photography) that might grab the recruiter's attention or serve as conversation starters. For example, let's say you learn that your hiring manager enjoys distance running. If you have run a marathon, you may want to mention it. Many executives play tennis or golf, two sports highly suitable for networking. You could also indicate your willingness to travel or to relocate, since many companies will be interested.

Include References? Listing references directly on a résumé takes up valuable space. Moreover, references are not normally instrumental in securing an interview—few companies check them before the interview. Instead, recruiters prefer that you bring to the interview a list of individuals willing to discuss your qualifications. Therefore, you should prepare a separate list, such as that in Figure 15.9, when you begin your job search. Consider three to five individuals, such as instructors, your current employer or previous employers, colleagues or subordinates, and other professional contacts. Ask whether they would be willing to answer inquiries regarding your qualifications for employment. Be sure, however, to provide them with

Figure 15.9 **Sample Reference List**

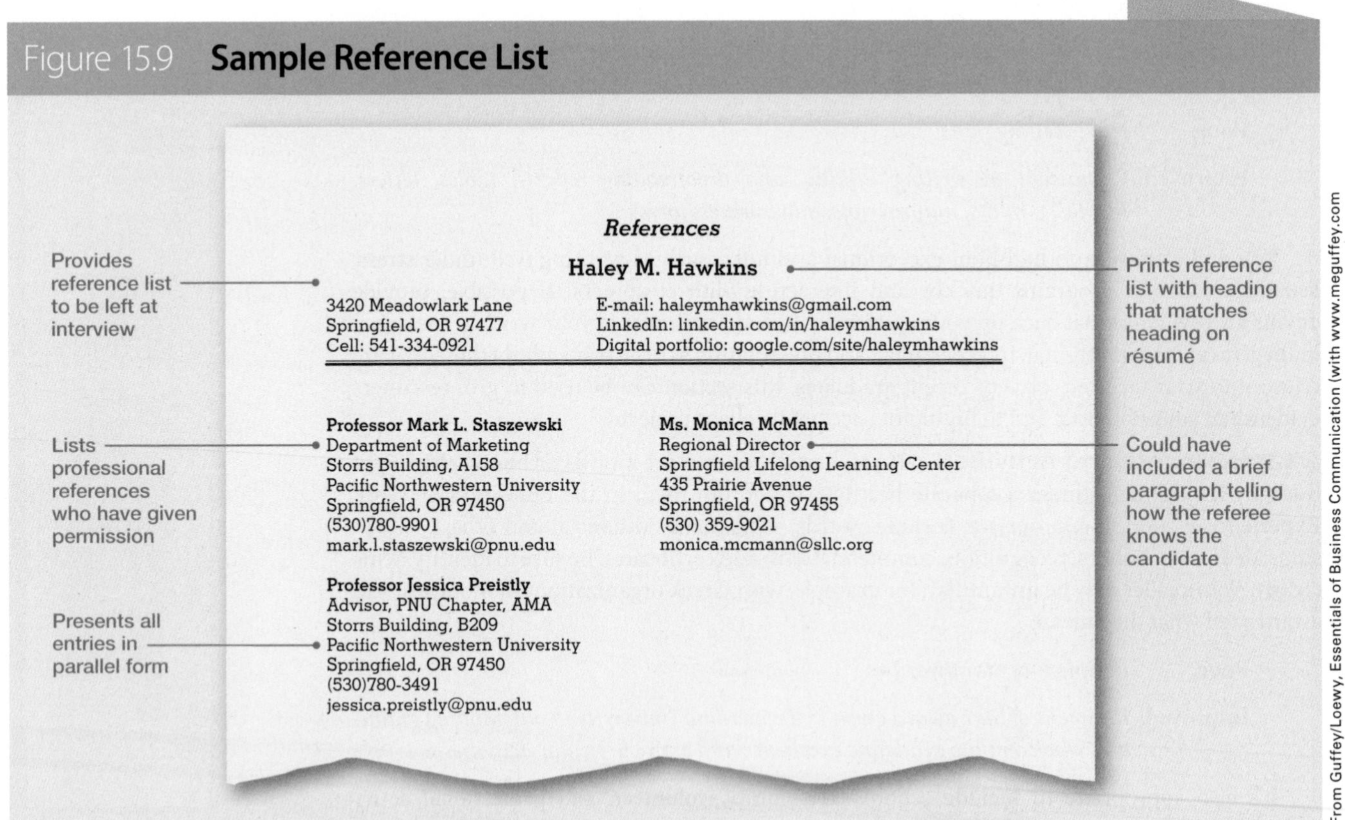

From Guffey/Loewy, Essentials of Business Communication (with www.meguffey.com Printed Access Card), 9E.

an opportunity to refuse. No reference is better than a negative one. Better yet, to avoid rejection and embarrassment, ask only those contacts who you are confident will give you a glowing endorsement.

Do not include personal or character references, such as friends, family, or neighbors, because recruiters rarely consult them. One final note: Most recruiters see little reason for including the statement *References furnished upon request.* It is unnecessary and takes up precious space.

Preparing a LinkedIn Résumé

Because it's usually the first place hiring managers and recruiters go to look for candidates online, be sure to prepare a LinkedIn profile/résumé. It takes a little effort, but it's well worth the investment. LinkedIn provides a template with standard résumé categories in which you fill in your qualifications. Compared with a print résumé, LinkedIn has many advantages. You have ample space to expand the description of your skills and qualifications. Your LinkedIn page also allows you to be more conversational and personal than you can be within the confines of a restricted résumé. You can even use the pronoun *I* to tell your story more naturally and passionately.

Headline. To stand out, prepare an informative headline that appears below your name. It should include keywords in your field and a brief description of what you want, such as the following:

Marketing Grad and Social Media Branding Specialist Seeking Internship

Recent Grad With Billing and Coding Training in Medical Insurance Field

Seeking Recruiter/Human Resources Assistant Position in Health Services Field

Finance and Management Grad Looking for Position as Analyst Trainee

Some experts suggest that you write an even longer headline that takes full advantage of the 120-character LinkedIn space to sell yourself. Check out this recent grad's headline:

Communication Graduate, Specializing in Millennials, Mobile Marketing. Interested in Survey Research and Data Analysis

If you fail to insert anything in the headline space, LinkedIn defaults to whatever you insert in Current Position. Don't let that happen! Use the headline to promote your most enticing expertise.

Photo. To increase your chance of being selected, definitely include a photo. Profiles with photos are known to score 14 times more views than those without. Your photo should be a head-and-shoulder shot in work-appropriate attire. Should you smile? A recent study by New York University researchers revealed that people who looked a "little" happy in their photos made the best impression.[33]

Profile. In your profile/summary, use keywords and phrases that might appear in job descriptions. Include quantifiable achievements and specifics that reveal your skills. Unsurprisingly, listing your skills at LinkedIn makes you 13 times more likely to be viewed.[34] You can borrow much of this information from your résumé. In the Work Experience and Education fields, include all of your experience, not just your current position. Follow the tips presented earlier for presenting information in these résumé fields.

Recommendations. Encourage your instructors and employers to recommend you. Having recommendations in your profile makes you look more credible, trustworthy, and reliable. Career coach Susan Adams even encourages job seekers to offer to write the draft for the recommender; in the world of LinkedIn, she says, this is perfectly acceptable.[35] Figure 15.10 shows a portion of a new graduate's LinkedIn page.

Figure 15.10 LinkedIn Profile/Résumé for New Grad

At LinkedIn Haley Hawkins is able to present a more personal description of her background, education, and experience than on her résumé. She includes a photo and a headline, "Honors graduate in e-marketing with social expertise." Her summary briefly describes her skills and experience, but one expert warns candidates not to cut corners on the summary statement. Describe what motivates you and use first-person pronouns, unlike what you would do on a résumé. LinkedIn gives you a chance to be more conversational than you can be in a résumé. You may be asked to present this same kind of personalized résumé information at job boards.

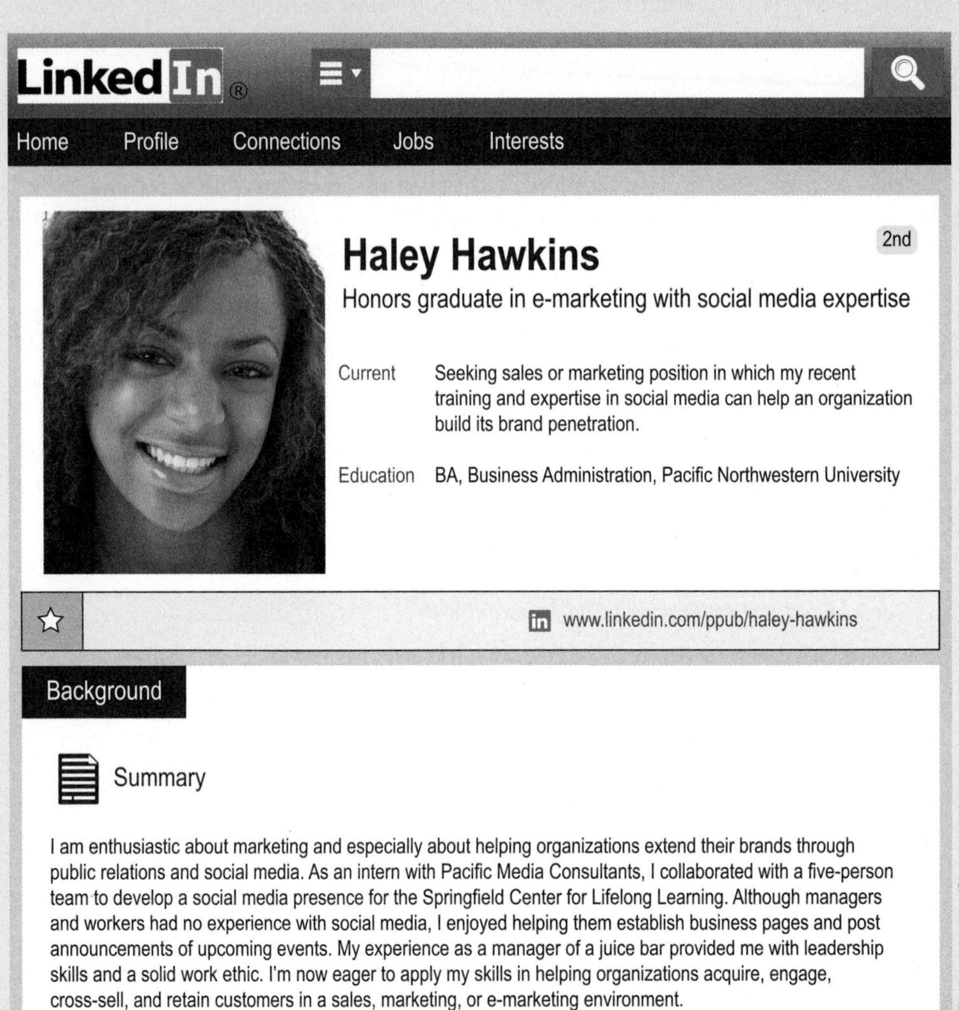

LinkedIn
Home
Profile
Connections
Jobs
Interests
Haley Hawkins
2nd
Honors graduate in e-marketing with social media expertise
Current
Seeking sales or marketing position in which my recent training and expertise in social media can help an organization build its brand penetration.
Education
BA, Business Administration, Pacific Northwestern University
www.linkedin.com/ppub/haley-hawkins
Background
Summary
I am enthusiastic about marketing and especially about helping organizations extend their brands through public relations and social media. As an intern with Pacific Media Consultants, I collaborated with a five-person team to develop a social media presence for the Springfield Center for Lifelong Learning. Although managers and workers had no experience with social media, I enjoyed helping them establish business pages and post announcements of upcoming events. My experience as a manager of a juice bar provided me with leadership skills and a solid work ethic. I'm now eager to apply my skills in helping organizations acquire, engage, cross-sell, and retain customers in a sales, marketing, or e-marketing environment.

Monkey Business Images/Shutterstock.com

wavebreakmedia/Shutterstock.com

Reality Check

The Fastest Way to Lose a Job

"If you lie on your résumé, land the job, and your employer later discovers you can't actually maneuver an Excel sheet or code in JavaScript, there is a good chance that they'll be within their legal right to terminate your employment."[36]

—Lauren Kreps, *e-mail marketing consultant, Shake Law, Inc.*

Figure 15.11 Chronological Résumé: Recent University Graduate With Limited Experience

Haley Hawkins used Microsoft Word to design a traditional chronological résumé that she plans to give to recruiters at campus job fairs or during interviews. The two-column formatting enables recruiters and hiring managers to immediately follow the chronology of her education and experience. This formatting is easy to create by using the Word table feature and removing the borders so that no lines show.

Haley includes an objective that is specific in describing what she seeks but broad enough to encompass many possible positions. Her summary of qualifications emphasizes the highlights of her experience and education. Because she has so little experience, she includes a brief list of related courses to indicate her areas of interest and training. Although she has limited paid experience that relates to the position she seeks, she is able to capitalize on her intern experience by featuring accomplishments and transferable skills.

Haley M. Hawkins

3420 Meadowlark Lane
Springfield, OR 97477
Cell: 541-334-0921

E-mail: haleymhawkins@gmail.com
LinkedIn: linkedin.com/in/haleymhawkins
Digital portfolio: google.com/site/haleymhawkins

OBJECTIVE

Position in sales, marketing, or e-marketing in which my marketing, communication, and social media expertise helps an organization expand its brand penetration.

SUMMARY OF QUALIFICATIONS

- Graduated with honors in e-marketing from Pacific Northwestern University
- Applied e-marketing and public relations training as a successful intern
- Experienced in posting to Twitter, Facebook, YouTube, and other platforms
- Keep up-to-date with constantly evolving technologies in online social networking
- Developed strong work ethic with part-time jobs that financed more than 50 percent of my education
- Honed leadership skills as vice president of award-winning chapter of American Marketing Association

EDUCATION AND RELATED COURSE WORK

BA in Business Administration, Pacific Northwestern University, Cum Laude — May, 2018
Major: Business Administration with e-marketing emphasis.
Minor: Organizational Communication
GPA: Major, 3.7; overall 3.5 (A = 4.0)

Marketing Research and Analysis — Marketing Communication
Social Relations in the Workplace — Professional Public Relations
Writing for the Web and Social Media — Organizational Behavior

PROFESSIONAL EXPERIENCE

Social Media Intern — 09/2017–02/2018
Pacific Media Consultants, Springfield, Oregon

- Collaborated with 5-person team to develop social media presence for Center for LifeLong Learning
- Introduced clients to LinkedIn and established Facebook and Twitter accounts for LifeLong Learning staff
- Demonstrated how to boost social media presence with announcements and tweets of upcoming activities
- Prepared brochure, handouts, name tags, and press kit to promote one Saturday event
- Handled over 40 client calls with the account management team, ranging from project check-ins to inbound client inquiries in a professional and personable manner

Manager — 06/2015–08/2017
Juice Zone, Eugene, Oregon

- Developed management skills in assuming all responsibilities in absence of store owners including finances, scheduling, and oversight
- Supervised daily store operations, maintained store security, and managed a team of 5 to 10 employees to ensure productivity and profitability

HONORS ACTIVITIES

- Received Brooks Award as the outstanding graduate in marketing based on academic excellence and service to the community
- Served as vice president of Pacific Northwestern University chapter of the American Marketing Association, providing monthly marketing forums, events, and competitions, helping our chapter earn national recognition

Figure 15.14 Chronological Résumé: University Graduate With Substantial Experience

Because Rachel has many years of experience and seeks executive-level employment, she highlighted her experience by placing it before her education. Her summary of qualifications highlighted her most impressive experience and skills. This chronological two-page résumé shows the steady progression of her career to executive positions, a movement that impresses and reassures recruiters.

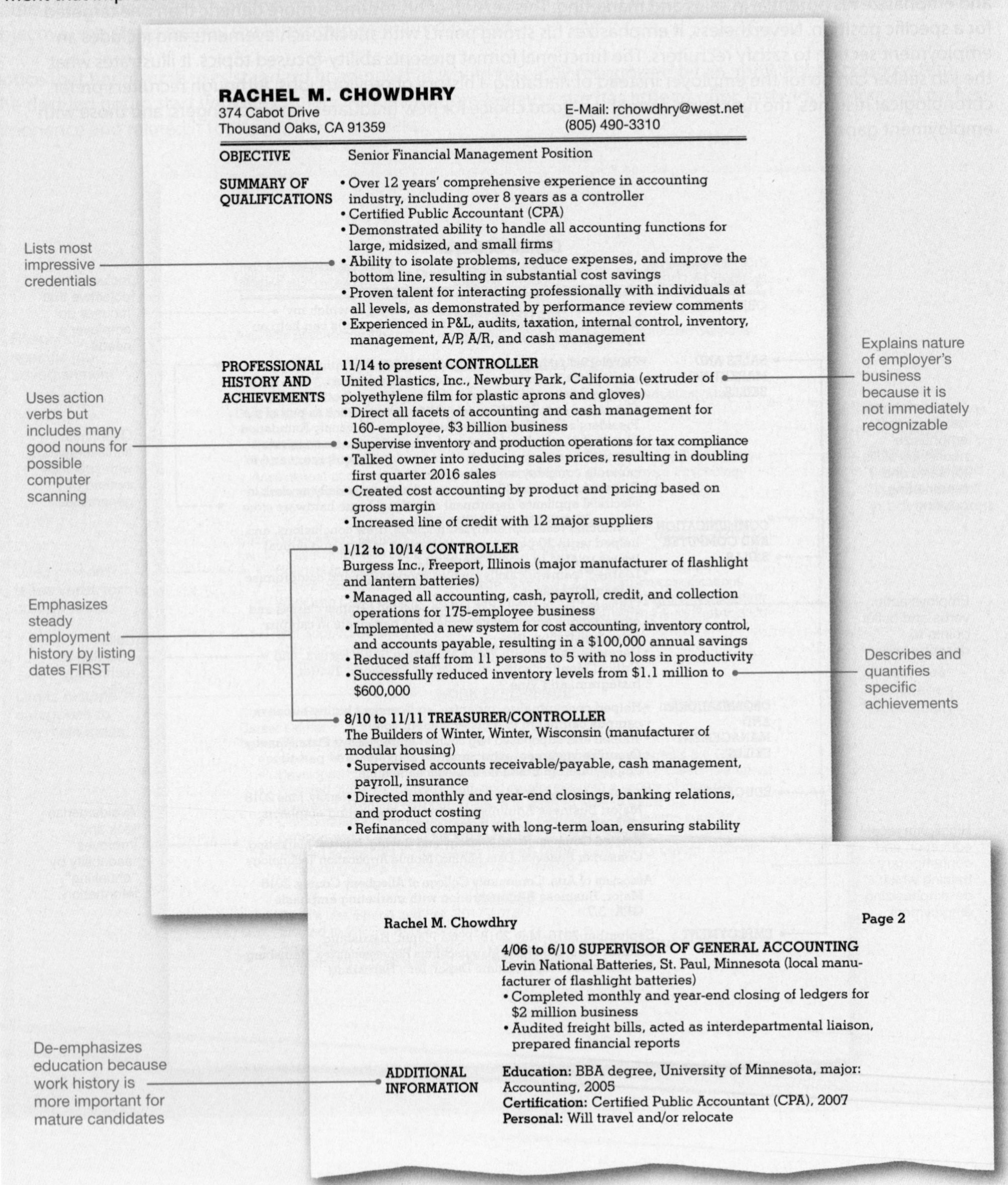

RACHEL M. CHOWDHRY
374 Cabot Drive
Thousand Oaks, CA 91359
E-Mail: rchowdhry@west.net
(805) 490-3310

OBJECTIVE Senior Financial Management Position

SUMMARY OF QUALIFICATIONS
- Over 12 years' comprehensive experience in accounting industry, including over 8 years as a controller
- Certified Public Accountant (CPA)
- Demonstrated ability to handle all accounting functions for large, midsized, and small firms
- Ability to isolate problems, reduce expenses, and improve the bottom line, resulting in substantial cost savings
- Proven talent for interacting professionally with individuals at all levels, as demonstrated by performance review comments
- Experienced in P&L, audits, taxation, internal control, inventory, management, A/P, A/R, and cash management

PROFESSIONAL HISTORY AND ACHIEVEMENTS

11/14 to present CONTROLLER
United Plastics, Inc., Newbury Park, California (extruder of polyethylene film for plastic aprons and gloves)
- Direct all facets of accounting and cash management for 160-employee, $3 billion business
- Supervise inventory and production operations for tax compliance
- Talked owner into reducing sales prices, resulting in doubling first quarter 2016 sales
- Created cost accounting by product and pricing based on gross margin
- Increased line of credit with 12 major suppliers

1/12 to 10/14 CONTROLLER
Burgess Inc., Freeport, Illinois (major manufacturer of flashlight and lantern batteries)
- Managed all accounting, cash, payroll, credit, and collection operations for 175-employee business
- Implemented a new system for cost accounting, inventory control, and accounts payable, resulting in a $100,000 annual savings
- Reduced staff from 11 persons to 5 with no loss in productivity
- Successfully reduced inventory levels from $1.1 million to $600,000

8/10 to 11/11 TREASURER/CONTROLLER
The Builders of Winter, Winter, Wisconsin (manufacturer of modular housing)
- Supervised accounts receivable/payable, cash management, payroll, insurance
- Directed monthly and year-end closings, banking relations, and product costing
- Refinanced company with long-term loan, ensuring stability

Rachel M. Chowdhry Page 2

4/06 to 6/10 SUPERVISOR OF GENERAL ACCOUNTING
Levin National Batteries, St. Paul, Minnesota (local manufacturer of flashlight batteries)
- Completed monthly and year-end closing of ledgers for $2 million business
- Audited freight bills, acted as interdepartmental liaison, prepared financial reports

ADDITIONAL INFORMATION
Education: BBA degree, University of Minnesota, major: Accounting, 2005
Certification: Certified Public Accountant (CPA), 2007
Personal: Will travel and/or relocate

Lists most impressive credentials
Uses action verbs but includes many good nouns for possible computer scanning
Emphasizes steady employment history by listing dates FIRST
De-emphasizes education because work history is more important for mature candidates
Explains nature of employer's business because it is not immediately recognizable
Describes and quantifies specific achievements

Polishing Your Résumé and Keeping It Honest

As you continue to work on your résumé, look for ways to improve it. For example, consider consolidating headings. By condensing your information into as few headings as possible, you will produce a clean, professional-looking document. Study other résumés for valuable formatting ideas. Ask yourself what graphic highlighting techniques you can use to improve readability: capitalization, underlining, indenting, and bulleting. Experiment with headings and styles to achieve a pleasing, easy-to-read message. Moreover, look for ways to eliminate wordiness. For example, instead of *Supervised two employees who worked at the counter*, try *Supervised two counter employees*. Review Chapter 4 for more tips on writing concisely.

A résumé is expected to showcase a candidate's strengths and minimize weaknesses. For this reason, recruiters expect a certain degree of self-promotion. Some résumé writers, however, step over the line that separates honest self-marketing from deceptive half-truths and flat-out lies. Distorting facts on a résumé is unethical; lying may be illegal. Most important, either practice can destroy a career. In the accompanying Ethical Insight feature, learn more about how to keep your résumé honest and about the consequences of fudging the facts.

Ethical Insight

Fudging the Facts on Résumés: Worth the Risk?

Given today's competitive job market, it might be tempting to puff up your résumé. You certainly wouldn't be alone in telling fibs or outright whoppers. A recent CareerBuilder survey of 2,532 hiring and human resources managers revealed that 56 percent have caught a lie on a résumé.[37]

Candidates may embellish their skills or background information to qualify for a position, but it's a risky game. Background checks are much easier now with the Internet and professionals who specialize in sniffing out untruths. What's more, puffing up your qualifications may be unnecessary. The same CareerBuilder survey revealed that 42 percent of employers would consider a candidate who met only three out of five key qualifications for a job.[38]

After they have been hired, candidates may think they are safe—but organizations often continue the checking process. If hiring officials find a discrepancy in a GPA or prior experience and the error is an honest mistake, they meet with the new-hire to hear an explanation. If the discrepancy wasn't a mistake, they will likely fire the person immediately.

No job seeker wants to be in the unhappy position of explaining résumé errors or defending misrepresentation. Avoiding the following actions can keep a job candidate off the hot seat:

- **Enhancing education, grades, or honors.** Some job candidates claim degrees from colleges or universities when in fact they merely attended classes. Others increase their grade point averages or claim fictitious honors. Any such dishonest reporting is grounds for dismissal when discovered.
- **Inflating job titles and salaries.** Wishing to elevate their status, some applicants misrepresent their titles or increase their past salaries. For example, one technician called himself a programmer when he had actually programmed only one project for his boss. A mail clerk who assumed added responsibilities conferred upon herself the title of supervisor.
- **Puffing up accomplishments.** Job seekers may inflate their employment experience or achievements. One clerk, eager to make her photocopying duties sound more important, said that she assisted the *vice president in communicating and distributing employee directives*. Similarly, guard against taking sole credit for achievements that required many people. When recruiters suspect dubious claims on résumés, they nail applicants with specific—and often embarrassing—questions during their interviews.
- **Altering employment dates.** Some candidates extend the dates of employment to hide unimpressive jobs or positions they lost. Others try to hide periods of unemployment and illness. Although their employment histories have no gaps, their résumés are dishonest and represent potential booby traps.

If you do get a job based on dishonesty, you could find yourself over your head in completing the required tasks, and the fear of being discovered would be a constant burden. It's simply not worth the risk.

Proofreading Your Résumé

After revising your résumé, you must proofread, proofread, and proofread again for spelling, grammar, mechanics, content, and format. Then have a knowledgeable friend or relative proofread it yet again. This is one document that must be perfect. Because the job market is so competitive, one typo, one misspelled word, or a single grammatical error could eliminate you from consideration.

By now you may be thinking that you'd like to hire someone to write your résumé. Don't! First, you know yourself better than anyone else could know you. Second, you will end up with either a generic or a one-time résumé. A generic résumé in today's highly competitive job market will lose out to a customized résumé nine times out of ten. Equally useless is a one-time résumé aimed at a single job. What if you don't get that job? Because you will need to revise your résumé many times as you seek a variety of jobs, be prepared to write (and rewrite) it yourself.

LEARNING OUTCOME 5
Enhance your job search and résumé by taking advantage of today's digital tools.

Enhancing Your Job Search With Today's Digital Tools

Just as electronic media have changed the way candidates seek jobs, these same digital tools are transforming the way employers select qualified candidates. As discussed earlier, the first reader of your résumé may very well be an applicant tracking system (ATS). As many as 90 percent of large companies and scores of smaller companies are now employing these systems. Why have they become so popular? In this digital era, the process of applying for jobs has become so effortless that organizations are flooded with résumés. Screening systems whittle down the cumbersome applicant pool to just a handful of qualified applicants for the human hiring managers to review more closely. The sad truth for applicants, however, is that up to 75 percent of résumés don't make it past the ATS screening.[39]

Maximizing the Rank of Your Résumé

The higher your résumé ranks when it is evaluated by an applicant tracking system, the more likely it will be reviewed by a recruiter or hiring manager. In the past candidates tried to game the system by stuffing their résumés with keywords. Newer screening systems are not so easily fooled. Although keywords are important, "the system looks for relevance of the keyword to your work history and education," advises job-search authority Quint Careers.[40] In addition to including the right keywords in context, your résumé must qualify in other ways to be selected. The following techniques, in addition to those cited earlier, can boost the probability that your résumé will rank high enough to qualify for review by a human reader.

- **Include specific keywords or phrases in context.** Study carefully any advertisements and job descriptions for the position you want. Describe your experience, education, and qualifications in terms associated with the job advertisement or job description for this position. However, don't just plop a keyword into your résumé; use it in context to ensure ATS recognition (e.g., *collaborated within four-member team to create a pilot business plan*).
- **Focus on nouns.** Although action verbs will make your résumé appeal to a recruiter, the applicant tracking system will often be looking for nouns in three categories: (a) a job title, position, or role (e.g., *accountant, Web developer, team leader*); (b) a technical skill or specialization (e.g., *Javascript, e-newsletter editor*); and (c) a certification, a tool used, or specific experience (e.g., *Certified Financial Analyst, Chartered Financial Analyst*).
- **Use variations of the job title.** Tracking systems may seek a slightly different job title from what you list. To be safe, include variations and abbreviations (e.g., *occupational therapist, certified occupational therapist,* or *COTA*). If you don't have experience in your targeted area, use the job title you list in your objective.
- **Concentrate on the Skills section.** A majority of keywords sought by employees relate to specialized or technical skill requirements. Therefore, be sure the Skills section of your résumé is loaded with nouns that describe your skills and qualifications.
- **Keep the formatting simple.** Stay away from logos, pictures, symbols, and shadings.
- **Use conventional headings.** Include familiar headings such as *Skills, Qualifications,* and *Education.* ATS software may not recognize headings such as *Professional Engagement* or *Core Competencies.*

Showcasing Your Qualifications in a Career E-Portfolio

With the workplace becoming increasingly digital, you have yet another way to display your qualifications to prospective employers—the career e-portfolio. This is a collection of digital files that can be navigated with the help of menus and hyperlinks much like a personal website.

What Goes in a Career E-Portfolio? An e-portfolio provides viewers with a snapshot of your talents, accomplishments, and technical skills. In this digital age, it can become one of the top hits in an Internet search for your name.[41] It may include a copy of your career-specific résumé, reference letters, commendations for special achievements, awards, certificates, work samples, a complete list of your courses, thank-you letters, and other items that tout your accomplishments. An e-portfolio could also offer links to digital copies of your artwork, film projects, videos, blueprints, documents, photographs, multimedia files, and blog entries that might otherwise be difficult to share with potential employers.

Because e-portfolios offer a variety of resources in one place, they have many advantages, as seen in Figure 15.15. When they are posted on websites, they can be viewed at an employer's convenience. Let's say you are talking on the phone with an employer in another city who wants to see a copy of your résumé. You can simply refer the employer to the website where your résumé resides. E-portfolios can also be seen by many individuals in an organization without circulating a paper copy. However, the main reason for preparing an e-portfolio is to show off your talents and qualifications more thoroughly than you can in a print résumé.

Some recruiters may be skeptical about e-portfolios because they fear that such presentations will take more time to view than paper-based résumés do. As a result, nontraditional job applications may end up at the bottom of the pile or be ignored. That's why some applicants submit a print résumé in addition to an e-portfolio.

How Are E-Portfolios Accessed? E-portfolios are generally accessed at websites, where they are available around the clock to employers. If the websites are not password protected, however, you should remove personal information. Some colleges and universities make website space available for student e-portfolios. In addition, institutions may provide instruction and

Figure 15.15 **Making a Career E-Portfolio**

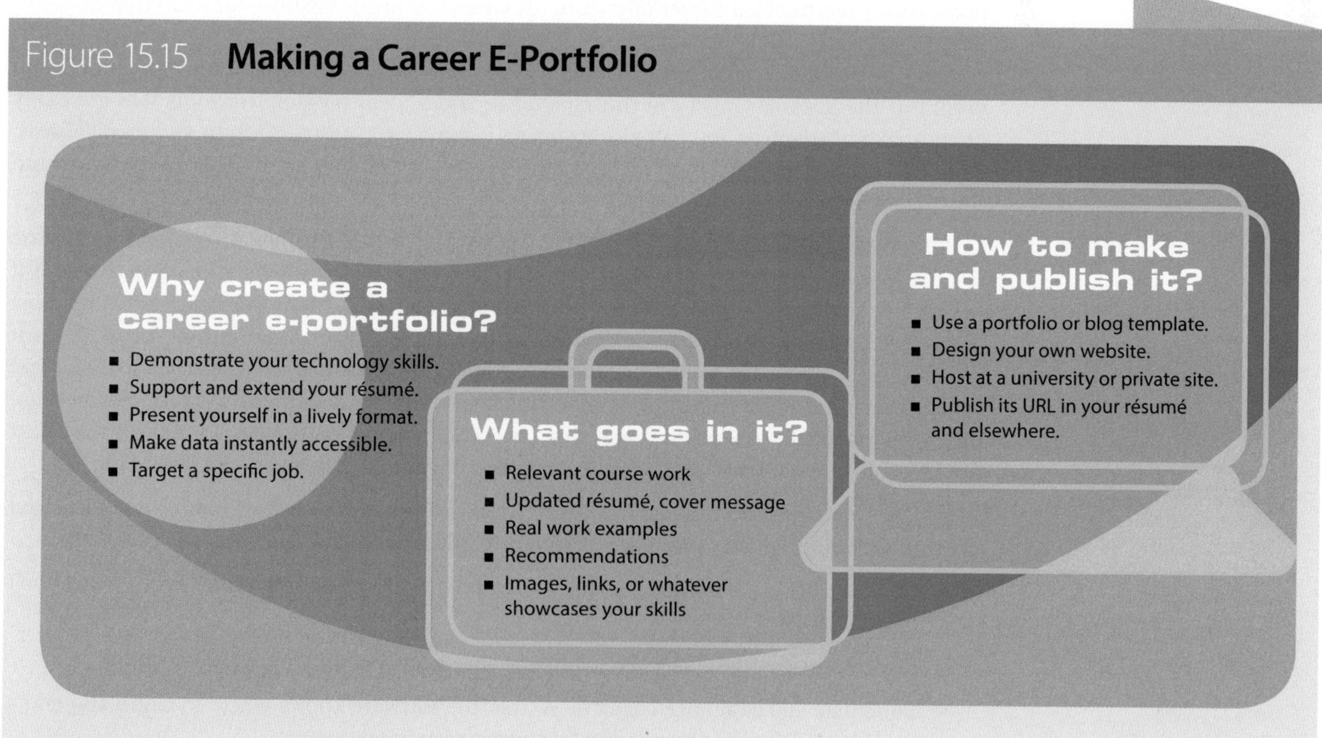
Why create a career e-portfolio?
▪ Demonstrate your technology skills.
▪ Support and extend your résumé.
▪ Present yourself in a lively format.
▪ Make data instantly accessible.
▪ Target a specific job.
What goes in it?
▪ Relevant course work
▪ Updated résumé, cover message
▪ Real work examples
▪ Recommendations
▪ Images, links, or whatever showcases your skills
How to make and publish it?
▪ Use a portfolio or blog template.
▪ Design your own website.
▪ Host at a university or private site.
▪ Publish its URL in your résumé and elsewhere.

resources for scanning photos, digitizing images, and preparing graphics. E-portfolios may also be burned onto CDs and DVDs to be mailed to prospective employers.

Expanding Your Employment Chances With a Video Résumé

Still another way to expand your employment possibilities is with a video résumé. Video résumés enable job candidates to present their experience, qualifications, and interests in video form. This format has many benefits. It allows candidates to demonstrate their public speaking, interpersonal, and technical skills more impressively than they can in traditional print résumés. Both employers and applicants can save recruitment and travel costs by using video résumés. Instead of flying distant candidates to interviews, organizations can see them digitally.

Video résumés are becoming more prevalent with the popularity of YouTube, inexpensive webcams, and widespread broadband. With simple edits on a computer, you can customize a video message to a specific employer and tailor your résumé for a particular job opening. In making a video résumé, dress professionally in business attire, just as you would for an in-person interview. Keep your video to three minutes or less. Explain why you would be a good employee and what you can do for the company that hires you.

Before committing time and energy to a video résumé, decide whether it is appropriate for your career field. Such presentations make sense for online, media, social, and creative professions. Traditional organizations, however, may be less impressed. Done well, a video résumé might give you an edge. Done poorly, however, it could bounce you from contention.

How Many Résumés and What Format?

At this point you may be wondering how many résumés you should make, and what format they should follow. The good news is that you need only one basic résumé that you can customize for various job prospects and formats.

Preparing a Basic Print-Based Résumé. The one basic résumé you should prepare is a print-based traditional résumé. It should be attractively formatted to maximize readability. This résumé is useful (a) during job interviews, (b) for person-to-person networking situations, (c) for recruiters at career fairs, and (d) when you are competing for a job that does not require an electronic submission.

You can create a basic, yet professional-looking résumé by using your word processing program. The Résumé Gallery in this chapter provides ideas for simple layouts that are easily duplicated and adapted. You can also examine résumé templates for design and format ideas. Their inflexibility, however, may be frustrating as you try to force your skills and experience into a predetermined template sequence.

Converting to a Plain-Text Résumé for Digital Submission. After preparing a basic résumé, you can convert it to a plain-text résumé so that it is ready for e-mailing. Parts of it will also be available for uploading to online submission forms. Many job-board sites and most government employers require job candidates to complete official application forms. Even if your résumé contains the same information, an application form is often required for legal and data processing as well as for employer convenience. Plain-text documents are preferred because they avoid possible e-mail viruses and word processing incompatibilities. To make a plain-text résumé, convert your basic résumé into a new document in which you do the following:

- Use basic fonts such as Helvetica or Arial. Eliminate the use of italics, boldface, and underlining, which cause some scanners to glitch or choke.
- Consider using capital letters rather than boldface type to emphasize words—but don't overdo the caps.
- Remove images, designs, colors, and any characters not on a standard keyboard.
- Punctuate and capitalize correctly so that the software knows where to begin and end a field. Avoid lowercase expression frequently seen in texting.

- If you use a header or footer feature to place your name at the top of your résumé, be sure that your name and contact information also appear in the body of the résumé.
- In Microsoft Word, save the document with *Plain Text (*.txt)* as the file type.
- Send yourself a copy embedded within an e-mail message to check its appearance. Also send it to a friend to try it out.

Submitting Your Résumé

The format you choose for submitting your résumé depends on what is required. If you are responding to a job advertisement, be certain to read the listing carefully to learn how the employer wants you to submit your résumé. Not following the prospective employer's instructions can eliminate you from consideration before your résumé is even reviewed. If you have any doubt about what format is desired, send an e-mail inquiry to a company representative, or call and ask. Most organizations request one of the following submission formats:

- **Word document.** Some organizations ask candidates to send their résumés and cover messages by surface mail. Others request that résumés be submitted as Word documents attached to e-mail messages, despite the fear of viruses.
- **Plain-text document.** As discussed earlier, many employers expect applicants to submit résumés and cover letters as plain-text documents. This format is also widely used for posting to an online job board or for sending by e-mail. Plain-text résumés may be embedded within or attached to e-mail messages.
- **PDF document.** For safety reasons some employers prefer PDF (portable document format) files. A PDF résumé looks exactly like the original and cannot be altered. Most computers have Adobe Acrobat Reader installed for easy reading of PDF files. Converting your résumé to a PDF file can be easily done by saving it as a PDF file, which preserves all formatting.
- **Company database.** Larger organizations and the government may prefer that you complete an online form with your résumé information. This enables them to plug your data into their template categories for rapid searching. You might be able to cut and paste the information from your résumé into the form; however, uploading the information is less likely to choke a scanning device.[42]

Because your résumé is probably the most important message you will ever write, you will revise it many times. With so much information in concentrated form and with so much riding on its outcome, your résumé demands careful polishing, proofreading, and critiquing. The following checklist will help you review the primary steps in creating and submitting a customized résumé.

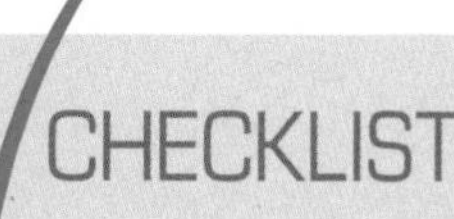

Creating and Submitting a Customized Résumé

Preparation

- **Analyze your strengths.** Determine what aspects of your education, experience, and personal characteristics will be assets to prospective employers.
- **Research job listings.** Learn about available jobs, common qualifications, and potential employers. The best résumés are customized for specific jobs with specific companies.

Heading, Objective, and Summary of Qualifications

- **Identify yourself.** List your name, address, telephone numbers, and possibly links to your e-portfolio and LinkedIn profile.
- **Include a career objective for a targeted job.** Use an objective only if it is intended for a specific job (*Objective: Junior cost accountant position in the petroleum industry*).
- **Prepare a summary of qualifications.** Include a list of three to eight bulleted statements that highlight your qualifications for the targeted position.

Education

- **Name your degree, date of graduation, and institution.** Emphasize your education if your experience is limited.

(Continued)

- **List your major and GPA.** Give information about your studies, but don't inventory all your courses.

Work Experience

- **Itemize your jobs.** Start with your most recent job. Give the employer's name and city, dates of employment (month, year), and most significant job title.
- **Describe your experience.** Use action verbs and keyword nouns to summarize achievements and skills relevant to your targeted job.
- **Promote your soft skills.** Give evidence of communication, management, and interpersonal talents. Employers want more than empty assurances; try to quantify your skills and accomplishments (*Developed teamwork skills while collaborating within six-member task force in producing 20-page mission statement*).

Special Skills, Achievements, and Awards

- **Highlight your technology skills.** Remember that nearly all employers seek employees who are proficient in using the Internet, e-mail, word processing, social media, spreadsheets, and presentation programs.
- **Show that you are a well-rounded individual.** List awards, experiences, and extracurricular activities—particularly if they demonstrate leadership, teamwork, reliability, loyalty, industry, initiative, efficiency, and self-sufficiency.

Final Tips

- **Look for ways to condense your data.** Omit all street addresses except your own. Consolidate your headings. Study models and experiment with formats to find the most readable and efficient groupings.
- **Omit references.** Have a list of references available for the interview, but don't include them or refer to them on your résumé unless you have a reason to do so.
- **Resist the urge to inflate your qualifications.** Be accurate in listing your education, grades, honors, job titles, employment dates, and job experience.
- **Proofread, proofread, proofread! Make this important document perfect by proofreading at least three times.** Ask a friend to check it, too.

Submitting

- **Follow instructions for submitting.** Learn whether the employer wants candidate information in a print résumé, e-mail résumé, plain-text version, PDF file, company database, or some other format.
- **Practice sending a plain-text résumé.** Before submitting a plain-text résumé, try sending it to yourself or friends. Perfect your skill in achieving an attractive format.

LEARNING OUTCOME 6

Understand the value of cover messages and how to draft and submit a customized message to highlight your candidacy.

Cover Messages–Do They Still Matter?

A cover message, also known as a *cover letter* or *letter of application*, has always been a graceful way of introducing your résumé. However, with the steady movement toward online recruiting and digitized applicant tracking systems, cover letters are losing significance for recruiters. A recent survey by JobVite revealed that 63 percent of the 1,404 recruiter respondents thought that cover messages were unimportant.[43] Employment counselors, such as Jen H. Luckwaldt at PayScale, were quick to point out that JobVite's core business is helping recruiters find candidates through social networks, thus possibly slanting the findings.[44]

Other critics of the JobVite survey explained that recruiters may skip over cover messages because they are involved only with initial screening. Hiring managers present a different story. They often seek as much information as they can obtain to avoid expensive bad hires, and cover letters reveal writing skills as well as key evidence missing in a résumé.[45]

Adam Gregor/Shutterstock.com

Reality Check

When Cover Letters Matter, They Matter a Lot

In responding to reports that cover messages are no longer important, one hiring manager said, "You see, there are still a significant amount of employers who put a very high emphasis on the cover letter. While this amount might be less than the number of employers ignoring your cover letters, it's still a significant enough number that not submitting the document could be highly damaging to your application. In other words: *Keep writing cover letters!*"[46]

—Jeff Lareau, *program manager, Workforce Development, CompTIA*

Although some recruiters may not value cover letters, these messages still play an important role in the job application process—especially to hiring managers. Given the stiff competition for jobs today, candidates can set themselves apart with well-written cover messages. If you are required to apply via software that limits your input, how can you get your cover message and résumé to key decision makers? Use LinkedIn or the company website to learn the names of those involved with hiring, and send your résumé and cover letter directly to these individuals calling attention to your candidacy.

Creating a Customized Cover Message

Especially in today's competitive employment scene, candidates must make themselves stand out. Cover messages reveal to employers your ability to put together complete sentences and to sound intelligent. In addition, many employers still prefer that you e-mail a résumé and a cover letter because it's more convenient for them than going online.[47] A cover message also can be more personal, and it showcases your special talents without relying on a chronology of your education and employment.

Although many hiring managers favor cover messages, they disagree about their length. Some prefer short messages with no more than two paragraphs embedded in an e-mail message. Other recruiters desire longer messages that supply more information, thus giving them a better opportunity to evaluate a candidate's qualifications and writing skills. These recruiters argue that hiring and training new employees is expensive and time consuming; therefore, they welcome extra data to guide them in making the best choice the first time. Follow your judgment in writing a brief or a longer cover message.

Regardless of its length, a cover message should have three primary parts: (a) an opening that captures attention, introduces the message, and identifies the position; (b) a body that sells the candidate and focuses on the employer's needs; and (c) a closing that requests an interview and motivates action. When putting your cover message together, remember that the biggest mistake job seekers make when writing cover messages is being too generic. You should, therefore, write a personalized, customized cover message for every position that interests you.

Gaining Attention in the Opening

Your cover message will be more appealing—and more likely to be read—if it begins by addressing the reader by name. Rather than sending your letter to the *Hiring Manager* or *Human Resources Department*, try to identify the name of the appropriate individual by studying the company's website. You could also call the human resources department and ask the name of the person in charge of hiring. Another possibility is using LinkedIn to find someone working in the same department as the position in the posted job. This person may know the name of the hiring manager. If you still cannot find the name of any person to address, you might replace the salutation of your letter with a descriptive subject line such as *Application for Marketing Specialist Position.*

How you open your cover message depends largely on whether the application is solicited or unsolicited. If an employment position has been announced and applicants are being solicited, you can use a direct approach. If you do not know whether a position is open and you are prospecting for a job, use an indirect approach. Whether direct or indirect, the opening should attract the attention of the reader. Strive for openings that are more imaginative than *Please consider this letter an application for the position of* . . . or *I would like to apply for* . . . .

Openings for Solicited Jobs. When applying for a job that has been announced, consider some of the following techniques to open your cover message:

- **Refer to the name of an employee in the company.** Remember that employers always hope to hire known quantities rather than complete strangers.

Jacob Benoit, a member of your Customer Service Department, told me that Alliance Resources is seeking a customer service trainee. The enclosed summary of my qualifications demonstrates my preparation for this position.

At the suggestion of Abigail Freed, in your Legal Services Department, I submit my qualifications for the position of staffing coordinator.

Melanie Cervantes, placement director at Southwest University, told me that Dynamic Industries has an opening for a technical writer with knowledge of Web design and graphics.

- **Refer to the source of your information precisely.** If you are answering an advertisement, include the exact position advertised and the name and date of the publication. If you are responding to a position listed on an online job board, include the website name and the date the position was posted.

  From your company's website, I learned about your need for a sales representative for the Ohio, Indiana, and Illinois regions. I am very interested in this position and am confident that my education and experience are appropriate for the opening.

  My talent for interacting with people, coupled with more than five years of customer service experience, make me an ideal candidate for the director of customer relations position you advertised on the CareerJournal website on August 3.

- **Refer to the job title, and describe how your qualifications fit the requirements.** Hiring managers are looking for a match between an applicant's credentials and the job needs.

  Ceradyne Company's marketing assistant opening is an excellent match with my qualifications. As a recent graduate of Western University with a major in marketing, I offer solid academic credentials as well as industry experience gained from an internship at Flotek Industries.

  Will an honors graduate with a degree in recreation and two years of part-time experience organizing social activities for a convalescent hospital qualify for your position of activity director?

  Because of my specialized training in finance and accounting at Michigan State University, I am confident that I have the qualifications you described in your advertisement for a staff accountant trainee.

Openings for Unsolicited Jobs. If you are unsure whether a position actually exists, you might use a more persuasive opening. Because your goal is to convince this person to read on, try one of the following techniques:

- **Demonstrate an interest in and knowledge of the reader's business.** Show the hiring manager that you have done your research and that this organization is more than a mere name to you.

  Because Signa HealthNet, Inc., is organizing a new information management team for its recently established group insurance division, could you use the services of a well-trained information systems graduate who seeks to become a professional systems analyst?

  I read with great interest the article in Forbes announcing the upcoming launch of US Bank. Congratulations on this new venture and its notable $50 million in loans precharter! The possibility of helping your bank grow is exciting, and I would like to explore a potential employment match that I am confident will be mutually beneficial.

- **Show how your special talents and background will benefit the company.** Human resources managers need to be convinced that you can do something for them.

  Could your rapidly expanding publications division use the services of an editorial assistant who offers exceptional language skills, an honors degree from the University of Mississippi, and two years' experience in producing a campus literary publication?

In applying for an advertised job, Sophia Williams wrote the solicited cover letter shown in Figure 15.16. Notice that her opening identifies the position advertised on the company's website so that the reader knows exactly what advertisement Sophia means. Using features on her word processing program, Sophia designed her own letterhead that uses her name and looks like professionally printed letterhead paper.

Figure 15.16 **Solicited Cover Letter**

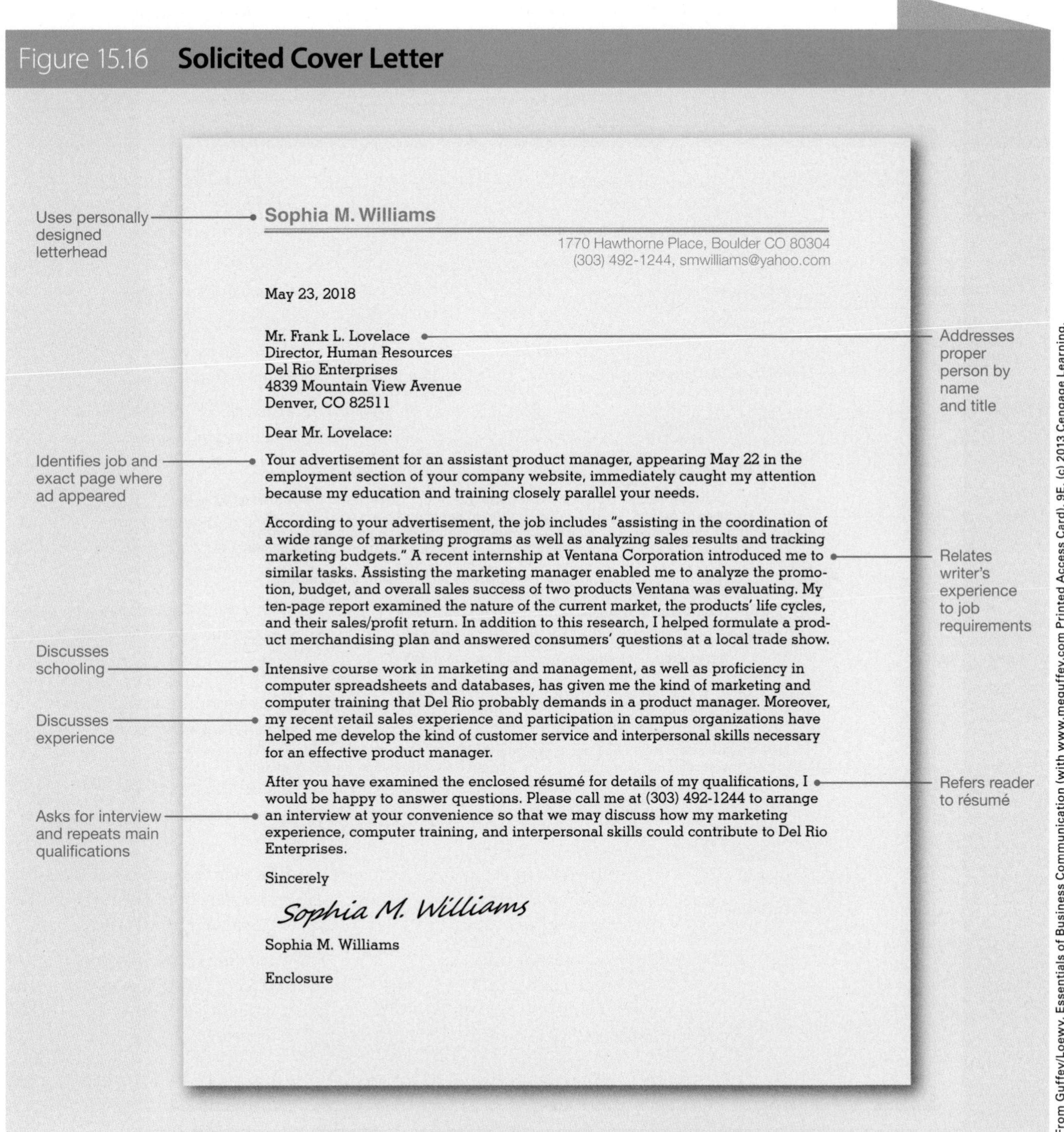

Sophia M. Williams

1770 Hawthorne Place, Boulder CO 80304
(303) 492-1244, smwilliams@yahoo.com

May 23, 2018

Mr. Frank L. Lovelace
Director, Human Resources
Del Rio Enterprises
4839 Mountain View Avenue
Denver, CO 82511

Dear Mr. Lovelace:

Your advertisement for an assistant product manager, appearing May 22 in the employment section of your company website, immediately caught my attention because my education and training closely parallel your needs.

According to your advertisement, the job includes "assisting in the coordination of a wide range of marketing programs as well as analyzing sales results and tracking marketing budgets." A recent internship at Ventana Corporation introduced me to similar tasks. Assisting the marketing manager enabled me to analyze the promotion, budget, and overall sales success of two products Ventana was evaluating. My ten-page report examined the nature of the current market, the products' life cycles, and their sales/profit return. In addition to this research, I helped formulate a product merchandising plan and answered consumers' questions at a local trade show.

Intensive course work in marketing and management, as well as proficiency in computer spreadsheets and databases, has given me the kind of marketing and computer training that Del Rio probably demands in a product manager. Moreover, my recent retail sales experience and participation in campus organizations have helped me develop the kind of customer service and interpersonal skills necessary for an effective product manager.

After you have examined the enclosed résumé for details of my qualifications, I would be happy to answer questions. Please call me at (303) 492-1244 to arrange an interview at your convenience so that we may discuss how my marketing experience, computer training, and interpersonal skills could contribute to Del Rio Enterprises.

Sincerely

Sophia M. Williams

Sophia M. Williams

Enclosure

Uses personally designed letterhead
Addresses proper person by name and title
Identifies job and exact page where ad appeared
Relates writer's experience to job requirements
Discusses schooling
Discusses experience
Refers reader to résumé
Asks for interview and repeats main qualifications

More challenging are unsolicited cover messages, such as the letter of Jared Chen shown in Figure 15.17. Because he hopes to discover or create a job, his opening must grab the reader's attention immediately. To do that, he capitalizes on company information appearing in an online article. Jared purposely kept his cover letter short and to the point because he anticipated that a busy executive would be unwilling to read a long, detailed letter. Jared's unsolicited letter prospects for a job. Some job candidates feel that such letters may be even more productive than efforts to secure advertised jobs because prospecting candidates face less competition and show initiative. Notice that Jared's letter uses a personal business letter format with his return address above the date.

Figure 15.17 **Unsolicited Cover Letter**

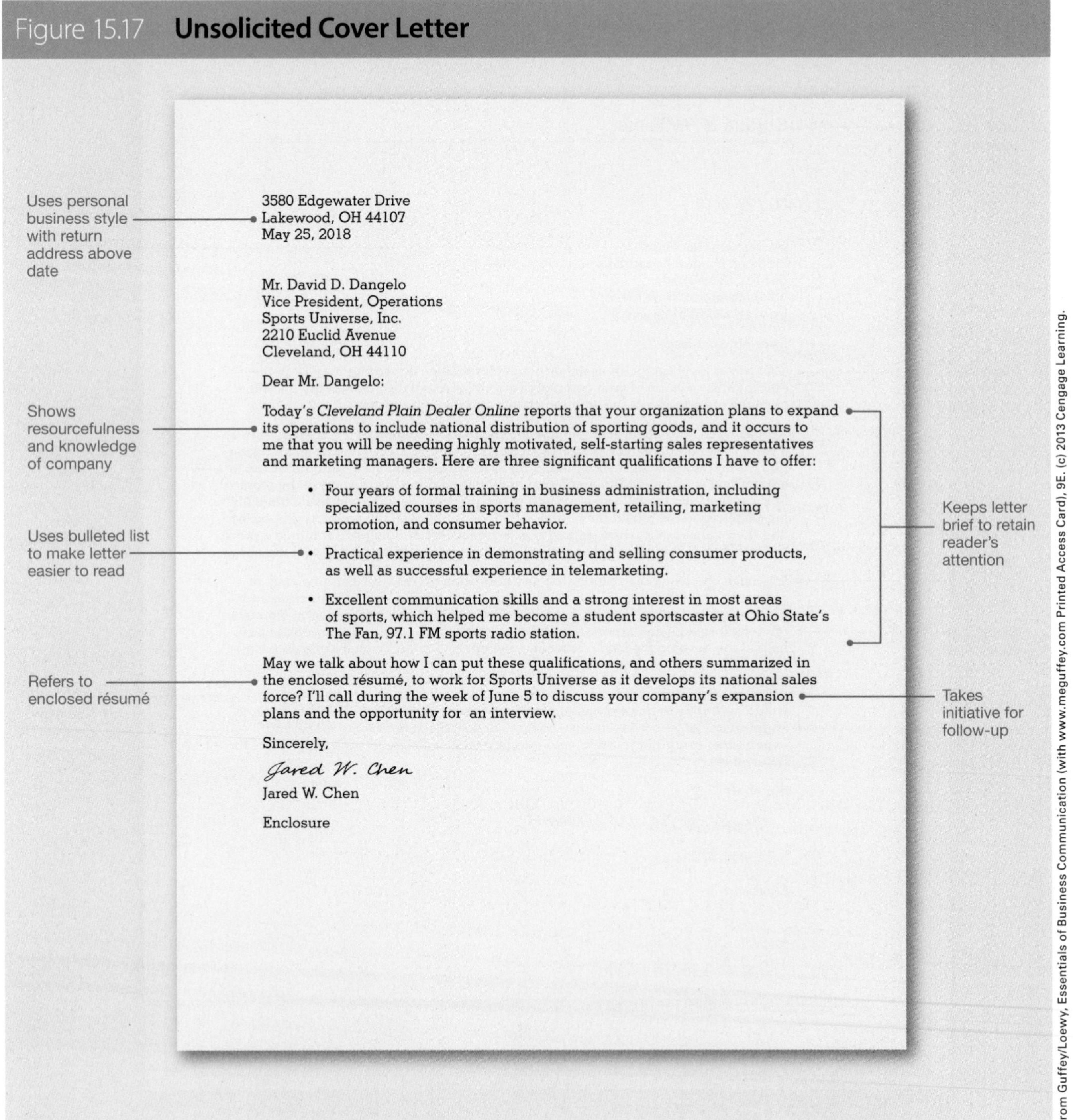

3580 Edgewater Drive
Lakewood, OH 44107
May 25, 2018

Mr. David D. Dangelo
Vice President, Operations
Sports Universe, Inc.
2210 Euclid Avenue
Cleveland, OH 44110

Dear Mr. Dangelo:

Today's *Cleveland Plain Dealer Online* reports that your organization plans to expand its operations to include national distribution of sporting goods, and it occurs to me that you will be needing highly motivated, self-starting sales representatives and marketing managers. Here are three significant qualifications I have to offer:

- Four years of formal training in business administration, including specialized courses in sports management, retailing, marketing promotion, and consumer behavior.
- Practical experience in demonstrating and selling consumer products, as well as successful experience in telemarketing.
- Excellent communication skills and a strong interest in most areas of sports, which helped me become a student sportscaster at Ohio State's The Fan, 97.1 FM sports radio station.

May we talk about how I can put these qualifications, and others summarized in the enclosed résumé, to work for Sports Universe as it develops its national sales force? I'll call during the week of June 5 to discuss your company's expansion plans and the opportunity for an interview.

Sincerely,

Jared W. Chen

Jared W. Chen

Enclosure

Uses personal business style with return address above date
Shows resourcefulness and knowledge of company
Uses bulleted list to make letter easier to read
Refers to enclosed résumé
Keeps letter brief to retain reader's attention
Takes initiative for follow-up

Promoting Your Strengths in the Message Body

Once you have captured the attention of the reader and identified your purpose in the letter opening, you should use the body of the letter to plug your qualifications for this position. If you are responding to an advertisement, you will want to explain how your preparation and experience fulfill the stated requirements. If you are prospecting for a job, you may not know the exact requirements. Your employment research and knowledge of your field, however, should give you a reasonably good idea of what is expected for the position you seek.

It is also important to stress reader benefits. In other words, you should describe your strong points in relation to the needs of the employer. Hiring officers want you to tell them what you can do for their organizations. This is more important than telling what courses you took in college or what duties you performed in your previous jobs.

Poor: *I have completed courses in business communication, report writing, and technical writing,*

Improved: *Courses in business communication, report writing, and technical writing have helped me develop the research and writing skills required of your technical writers.*

In the body of your letter, you may choose to discuss relevant personal traits. Employers are looking for candidates who, among other things, are team players, take responsibility, show initiative, and learn easily. Don't just list several personal traits, though; instead, include documentation that proves you possess these traits. Notice how the following paragraph uses action verbs to paint a picture of a promising candidate:

In addition to developing technical and academic skills at Florida Central University, I have gained interpersonal, leadership, and organizational skills. As vice president of the business students' organization, Gamma Alpha, I helped organize and supervise two successful fund-raising events. These activities involved conceptualizing the tasks, motivating others to help, scheduling work sessions, and coordinating the efforts of 35 diverse students. I enjoyed my success with these activities and look forward to applying my experience in your management trainee program.

Finally, in this section or the next, refer the reader to your résumé. Do so directly or as part of another statement.

Direct reference to résumé: *Please refer to the attached résumé for additional information regarding my education, experience, and skills.*

Part of another statement: *As you will notice from my enclosed résumé, I will graduate in June with a bachelor's degree in business administration.*

Motivating Action in the Closing

After presenting your case, you should conclude by asking confidently for an interview. Don't ask for the job. To do so would be presumptuous and naïve. In requesting an interview, you might suggest reader benefits or review your strongest points. Sound sincere and appreciative. Remember to make it easy for the reader to agree by supplying your telephone number and the best times to call you. In addition, keep in mind that some hiring officers prefer that you take the initiative to call them. Avoid expressions such as *I hope*, which weaken your closing. Here are possible endings:

Poor: *I hope to hear from you soon.*

Improved: *This brief description of my qualifications and the additional information on my résumé demonstrate my readiness to put my accounting skills to work for McLellan and Associates. Please call me at (405) 488-2291 before 10 a.m. or after 3 p.m. to arrange an interview.*

Poor: *I look forward to a call from you.*

Improved: *To add to your staff an industrious, well-trained administrative assistant with proven Internet and communication skills, call me at (350) 492-1433 to arrange an interview. I look forward to meeting with you to discuss further my qualifications.*

Poor: *Thanks for looking over my qualifications.*

Improved: *I look forward to the opportunity to discuss my qualifications for the financial analyst position more fully in an interview. I can be reached at (213) 458-4030.*

Sending Your Résumé and Cover Message

How you submit your résumé depends on the employer's instructions, which usually involve one of the following methods:

- Submit both your cover message and résumé in an e-mail message. Convert both to plain text.
- Send your cover message in an e-mail and attach your résumé (plain text, Word document, or PDF).
- Send a short e-mail message with both your cover message and résumé attached.
- Send your cover message and résumé as printed Word documents by U.S. mail.

Serious job candidates will take the time to prepare a professional cover message. If you are e-mailing your résumé, use the same cover message you would send by surface mail, but shorten it a bit, as illustrated in Figure 15.18. Just below your name, include your address, e-mail address, and phone number. For résumés submitted as PDF files, send the cover message as a PDF also.

Figure 15.18 **E-Mail Cover Message**

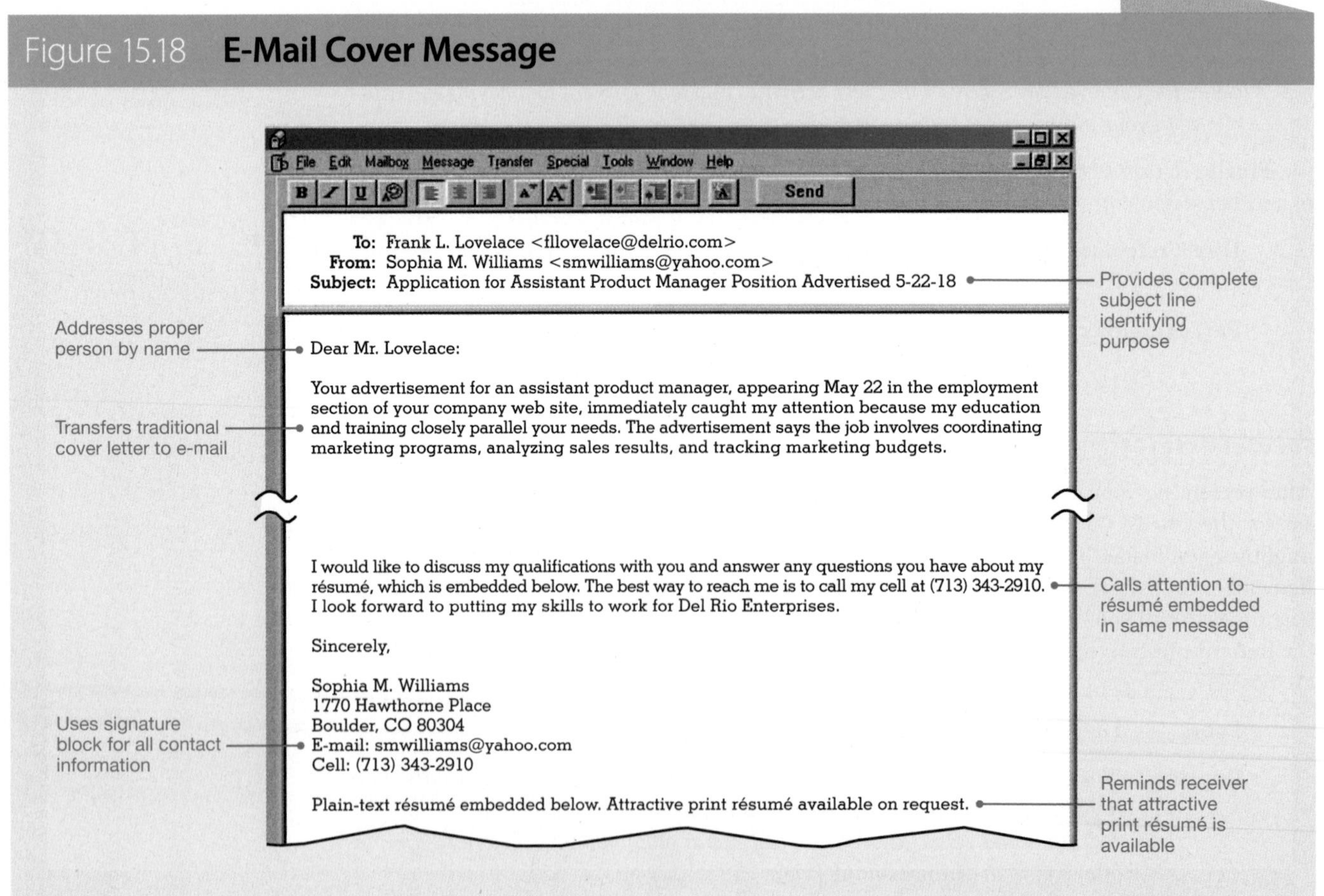

Final Tips for Successful Cover Messages

As you revise your cover message, notice how many sentences begin with *I*. Although it is impossible to talk about yourself without using *I*, you can reduce "I" domination with a number of thoughtful techniques. Make activities and outcomes, and not yourself, the subjects of sentences. Sometimes you can avoid "I" domination by focusing on the "you" view. Another way to avoid starting sentences with *I* is to move phrases from within the sentence to the beginning.

Poor: *I took classes in business communication and computer applications.*

Improved: *Classes in business communication and computer applications prepared me to* . . . . (Make activities the subject.)

Poor: *I enjoyed helping customers, which taught me to* . . . .

Improved: *Helping customers was a real pleasure and taught me to* . . . . (Make outcomes the subject.)

Poor: *I am a hardworking team player who* . . . .

Improved: *You are looking for a hardworking team player who* . . . . (Use the "you" view.)

Poor: *I worked to support myself all through college, thus building* . . . .

Improved: *All through college, I worked to support myself, thus building* . . . . (Move phrases to the beginning.)

However, strive for a comfortable style. In your effort to avoid sounding self-centered, don't write unnaturally.

Like your résumé, your cover message must look professional and suggest quality. This means using a traditional letter style, such as block format. Also, be sure to print it on the same quality paper as your résumé. As with your résumé, proofread it several times yourself; then have a friend read it for content and mechanics. Don't rely on spell-check to find all the errors. Like your résumé, your cover message must be perfect.

Your Turn: Applying Your Skills With Heather Huhman

Yeamake/Shutterstock.com

As a new assistant to career advisor Heather Huhman, you are a good source of information about how first-time job seekers view the job search. She wants your input for an article she plans to write that targets recent college graduates, both young and more mature. She wonders about the following: Do students give much thought to job searching and résumé writing before they graduate and enter the job market? How do students view networking in general and social networking sites in particular as they relate to finding jobs? Ms. Huhman suggests that you query your current and former classmates and get back to her. She would like to use the information you develop to write a meaningful article with advice for new grads.

Your Task

In groups of three to four, address the topics Ms. Huhman has brought up. Ask each student to contribute at least two responses. Individually or as a group, summarize your findings in an e-mail report addressed to <*hhuhman@xxx.xxx*> but delivered to your instructor. Treat this message as a short report, dividing it into logical sections with headings.

Summary of Learning Outcomes

1 Begin a job search by recognizing emerging trends and technologies, exploring your interests, evaluating your qualifications, and investigating career opportunities.

- Recognize that searching for a job in this digital age now includes such indispensable tools as job boards, social networks, and mobile technologies.
- Start the process by learning about yourself, your field of interest, and your qualifications. How do your skills match what employers seek?
- To investigate career opportunities, visit a campus career center, search for apps and online help, take a summer job, interview someone in your field, volunteer, or join professional organizations.
- Identify job availability, the skills and qualifications required, duties, and salaries.

2 Develop savvy search strategies by recognizing how job seekers find their jobs and how they use digital tools to explore the open job market.

- Research reveals that job seekers found their best jobs through personal networking, online social networking, online job boards, classified advertisements, recruiters, college fairs, and other connections.
- In searching the open job market—that is, jobs that are listed and advertised—explore the big job boards, such as Indeed, CareerBuilder, Monster, and CollegeGrad.
- To find a job with a specific company, go directly to that company's website and check its openings and possibilities.
- For jobs in specialized fields, search some of the many niche sites, such as Dice for technology positions or CoolWorks for seasonal employment.
- Take advantage of mobile apps to access and vet job openings as soon as they are listed.
- Protect yourself when using online job boards by posting privately, not revealing personal information, keeping careful records, and avoiding blind job postings.

3 Expand your job-search strategies by using both traditional and digital tools in pursuing the hidden job market.

- Estimates suggest that as many as 80 percent of jobs are in the hidden job market—that is, never advertised. Successful job candidates find jobs in the hidden job market through networking.
- An effective networking procedure involves (a) developing a contact list, (b) reaching out to these contacts in person and online in search of referrals, and (c) following up on referrals.
- Because electronic media and digital tools continue to change our lives, savvy candidates use social media networks—especially LinkedIn—to extend their networking efforts.
- Invaluable in a job search, LinkedIn enables candidates to receive job alerts, leverage their networks, research companies, get recommendations, and help companies locate them online.
- Effective networking strategies include building a personal brand, preparing a professional business card with a tagline, composing a 60-second elevator speech that describes what you can offer, and building a powerful online presence.

4 Organize your qualifications and skills into effective résumé categories, and use that information to prepare a personalized LinkedIn résumé.

- Because of intense competition, you must customize your résumé to appeal to an applicant tracking system (ATS) as well as to a human reader.
- Chronological résumés, which list work and education by dates, rank highest with recruiters. Functional résumés, which highlight skills instead of jobs, may be helpful for people with little experience, those changing careers, and those with negative employment histories.
- Arrange your skills and achievements to aim at a particular job or company.
- Study models to effectively arrange the résumé main heading and the optional career objective, summary of qualifications, education, work experience, capabilities, awards, and activities sections.
- The most effective résumés include action verbs to appeal to human readers and job-specific nouns that become keywords selected by applicant tracking systems.
- Prepare a LinkedIn page with a headline, photo, profile, and information about your education, skills, and experience. Encourage your instructors and employers to post recommendations.

5 Enhance your job search and résumé by taking advantage of today's digital tools.

- To maximize the rank of your résumé when it is evaluated by an automated tracking system, include specific keywords such as nouns that name job titles, technical skills, and tools used or specific experience.
- Consider preparing a career e-portfolio to showcase your qualifications. This collection of digital files can feature your talents, accomplishments, and technical skills. It may include examples of academic performance, photographs, multimedia files, and other items beyond what can be shown in a résumé.
- A video résumé enables you to present your experience, qualifications, and interests in video form.
- Start with a basic print-based résumé from which you can make a plain-text résumé stripped of formatting to be embedded within e-mail messages and submitted online.
- Decide whether you should submit your résumé as a Word, plain-text, or PDF document. You may also be asked to enter your information into a company database.

6 Understand the value of cover messages and how to draft and submit a customized message to highlight your candidacy.

- Although applicant tracking systems may accept only a résumé, cover messages still play an important role in the job application process, especially to hiring managers.
- Cover messages help recruiters make decisions, and they enable candidates to set themselves apart from others.
- In the opening of a cover message, gain attention by addressing the receiver by name and identifying the job. You might also identify the person who referred you.
- In the body of the message, build interest by stressing your strengths in relation to the stated requirements. Explain what you can do for the targeted company.
- In the body or closing, refer to your résumé, request an interview, and make it easy for the receiver to respond.
- If you are submitting your cover message by e-mail, shorten it a bit and include your complete contact information in the signature block.

Critical Thinking

1. The way candidates search for jobs and the way they are hired has changed dramatically in the digital age. Name some of the changes that have taken place. In your opinion, have the changes had a positive or a negative effect? Why? (L.O. 1)
2. Why do you think some businesses avoid advertising job openings? If jobs are unlisted, how can candidates locate them? (L.O. 3)
3. Some employment authors claim that the paper résumé is dead or dying. What's behind this assertion, and how should current job candidates respond? (L.O. 4)
4. Why might it be more effective to apply for unsolicited jobs than for advertised jobs? Discuss the advantages and disadvantages of letters that prospect for jobs. (L.O. 6)
5. **Ethical Issue:** Some jobs are advertised even when a leading candidate has the position nailed down. The candidate could be an internal applicant or someone else with an inside track. Although not required by law, management policies and human resources departments at many companies demand that hiring managers list all openings on job boards or career sites. Often, hiring managers have already selected candidates for these phantom jobs. Do you believe it is ethical to advertise jobs that are not really available?[48]

Activities

15.1 Document for Analysis: Poorly Written Résumé (L.O. 4)

One effective way to improve your writing skills is to critique and edit the résumé of someone else.

YOUR TASK Analyze the following poor résumé. List at least eight weaknesses. Your instructor may ask you to revise sections of this résumé before showing you an improved version.

Résumé
Camille Elena Montano
1340 East Phillips Ave., Apt. D Littleton, CO 80126
Phone 455-5182 | E-Mail: Hotchilibabe@gmail.com | LinkedIn

OBJECTIVE
I'm dying to become an accounting associate in the "real world" with a big profitable company that will help me get the experience I need to become a CPA.

SKILLS
Microsoft Word, MS Outlook, Powerpoint, Excel, spreadsheets Excel; experienced with QuickBooks, great composure in stressful situations; 3 years as leader and supervisor and 4 years in customer service

EDUCATION
Arapahoe Community College, Littleton, Colorado. AA degree, Fall 2015

Now I am pursuing a BA in Accounting at CSU-Pueblo, majoring in Accounting; my minor is Finance. Completed 64 units of upper-level units. My expected degree date is June 2018; I recieved a Certificate of Completion in Entry Level Accounting in December 2015. My overall GPA is 3.5 on a 4.0 = A system.

I graduated East High School, Denver, CO in 2011.

Highlights:

- Named Line Manger of the Month at Target, 10/2014 and 03/2015
- Obtained a Certificate in Entry Level Accounting, June 2015
- Chair of Accounting Society, Spring and fall 2017
- Dean's Honor List, Fall 2017
- Financial advisor training completed through Primerica (May 2016)
- Webmaster for M.E.Ch.A, Spring 2017

Part-Time Employment

Financial Consultant, 2016 to present I worked only part-time (January 2016-present) for Primerica Financial Services, Pueblo, CO to assist clients in refinancing a mortgage or consolidating a current mortgage loan and also to advice clients in assessing their need for life insurance.

Target, Littleton, CO. As line manager, from September 2014 - August 2015, I supervised 12 cashiers and front-end associates. I helped to write schedules, disciplinary action notices, and performance appraisals. I also kept track of change drawer and money exchanges; occasionally was manager on duty for entire store. Named line manager of the month August 2014 and March 2015.

Mr. K's Floral Design of Denver. I taught flower design from August, 2013 to September, 2014. I supervised 5 florists, made floral arrangements for big events like weddings, send them to customers, and restocked flowers.

15.2 Document for Analysis: Poor Cover Letter (L.O. 6)

The following cover letter accompanies Camille Montano's résumé (**Activity 15.1**).

YOUR TASK Analyze each section of the following cover letter and list its weaknesses. Your instructor may ask you to revise this letter before showing you an improved version.

To Whom It May Concern:

I saw your accounting associate position listing yesterday and would like to apply right away. It would be so exiting to work for your esteemed firm! This position would really give me much needed real-world experience and help me become a CPA.

I have all the qualifications you require in your add and more. I am a senior at Colorado State University-Pueblo and an Accounting major (with a minor in Finance) and have completed 64 units of upper-level course work. Accounting and Finance are my passion and I want to become a CPA and a financial advisor. I have taken eight courses in accounting and now work as a part-time financial advisor with Primerica Financial Services in Pueblo. I should also tell you that I was at Target for four years. I learned alot, but my heart is in accounting and finance.

I am a team player, a born leader, motivated, reliable, and I show excellent composure in stressful situations, for example, when customers complain. I put myself through school and always carry at least 12 units while working part time.

You will probably agree that I am a good candidate for your accounting position, which I understand should start about July 1. I feel that my motivation, passion, and strong people skills will serve your company well.

Sincerely,

15.3 Beginning Your Job Search With Self-Analysis (L.O. 1)

E-Mail

YOUR TASK In an e-mail or a memo addressed to your instructor, answer the questions in the earlier section titled "Launching Your Job Search With Self-Analysis." Draw a conclusion from your answers. What kind of career, company, position, and location seem to fit your self-analysis?

15.4 Evaluating Your Qualifications (L.O. 1–3)

YOUR TASK Prepare four worksheets that inventory your qualifications in these areas: employment; education; capabilities and skills; and awards, honors, and activities. Use active verbs when appropriate and specific nouns that describe job titles and skills.

a. **Employment.** Begin with your most recent job or internship. For each position list the following information: employer; job title; dates of employment; and three to five duties, activities, or accomplishments. Emphasize activities related to your job goal. Strive to quantify your achievements.

b. **Education.** List degrees, certificates, and training accomplishments. Include courses, seminars, and skills that are relevant to your job goal. Calculate your grade point average in your major.

c. **Capabilities and skills.** List all capabilities and skills that qualify you for the job you seek. Use words and phrases such as *skilled, competent, trained, experienced*, and *ability to*. Also list five or more qualities or interpersonal skills necessary for success in your chosen field. Write action statements demonstrating that you possess some of these qualities. Empty assurances aren't good enough; try to show evidence (*Developed teamwork skills by working on a committee of eight to produce a . . .*).

d. **Awards, honors, and activities.** Explain any awards so that the reader will understand them. List campus, community, and professional activities that suggest you are a well-rounded individual or possess traits relevant to your target job.

15.5 Choosing a Career Path (L.O. 1)

Web

Many people know amazingly little about the work done in various occupations and the training requirements.

YOUR TASK Use the online *Occupational Outlook Handbook* at **http://www.bls.gov/ooh**, prepared by the Bureau of Labor Statistics (BLS), to learn more about an occupation of your choice. This is the nation's premier source for career information. The career profiles featured cover hundreds of occupations and describe what people in these occupations do, the work environment, how to get these jobs, how much they earn, and more. Each profile also includes BLS employment projections for the 2010–2020 decade.

Find the description of a position for which you could apply in two to five years. Learn about what workers do on the job, working conditions, training and education needed, earnings, and expected job prospects. Print the pages from the *Occupational Outlook Handbook* that describe employment in the area in which you are interested. If your instructor directs, attach these copies to the cover letter you will write in **Activity 15.10**.

15.6 Locating Salary Information (L.O. 1)

Web

What salary can you expect in your chosen career?

YOUR TASK Visit **http://www.salary.com** and select an occupation based on the kind of employment you are seeking now or will be seeking after you graduate. Skip any advertisements that pop up. Click Free Salary Info, and use your current geographic area or the location where you would like to work after graduation. What wages can you expect in this occupation? Click to learn more about this occupation. Take notes on three or four interesting bits of information you uncovered about this career. Bring a printout of the wage information to class, and be prepared to discuss what you learned.

15.7 Searching the Job Market (L.O. 1)

Web

Where are the jobs? Even though you may not be in the market at the moment, become familiar with the kinds of available positions because job awareness should be an important part of your education.

YOUR TASK Clip or print a job advertisement or announcement from (a) the classified section of a newspaper, (b) a job board on the Web, (c) a company website, or (d) a professional association listing. Select an advertisement or announcement describing the kind of employment you are seeking now or plan to seek when you graduate. Save this advertisement or announcement to attach to the résumé you will write in **Activity 15.9.**

15.8 Posting a Résumé on the Web (L.O. 2)

Team Web

Learn about the procedure for posting résumés at job boards on the Web.

YOUR TASK Prepare a list of three websites where you could post your résumé. In a class discussion or in an e-mail to your instructor, describe the procedures involved in posting a résumé and the advantages for each site.

15.9 Writing Your Résumé (L.O. 4)

YOUR TASK Using the data you developed in **Activity 15.4**, write your résumé. Aim it at the full-time job, part-time position, or internship that you located in **Activity 15.7**. Attach the job listing to your résumé. Also prepare a list of references. Revise your résumé until it is perfect.

15.10 Preparing Your Cover Message (L.O. 6)

E-Mail

YOUR TASK Using the job listing you found for **Activity 15.7**, write a cover message introducing your résumé. Decide whether it should be a letter or an e-mail. Again, revise until it is perfect.

15.11 Using LinkedIn in Your Job Search (L.O. 2)

Social Media 

LinkedIn is the acknowledged No. 1 site for job seekers and recruiters. It's free and easy to join. Even if you are not in the job market yet, becoming familiar with LinkedIn can open your eyes to the kinds of information employers seek and also give you practice in filling in templates such as those that applicant tracking systems employ.

YOUR TASK To become familiar with LinkedIn, set up an account and complete a profile. This consists of a template with categories to fill in. The easiest way to begin is to view a LinkedIn video taking you through the steps of creating a profile. Search for *LinkedIn Profile Checklist.* It discusses how to fill in information in categories such as the following:

- **Photo.** Have a friend or a professional take a photo that shows your head and shoulders. No selfies! Wear work-appropriate attire and a smile.
- **Headline.** Use a tagline to summarize your professional goals.
- **Summary.** Explain what motivates you, what you are skilled at, and where you want to go in the future.
- **Experience.** List the jobs you have held and be sure to enter the information precisely in the template categories. You can even include photos and videos of your work.

You can fill in other categories such as Organizations, Honors, and Publications. After completing a profile, discuss your LinkedIn experience with classmates. If you already have an account set up, discuss how it operates and your opinion of its worth. How can LinkedIn help students now and in the future?

15.12 Tweeting to Find a Job (L.O. 5)

Social Media Team 

Twitter résumés are a new twist on job hunting. While most job seekers struggle to contain their credentials on one page, others are tweeting their credentials in 140 characters or fewer! Here is an example from TheLadders.com:

RT #Susan Moline seeks a LEAD/SR QA ENG JOB http://bit.ly/1ThaW @TalentEvolution - http://bit.ly/QB5DC @TweetMyJobs.com #résumé #QA-Jobs-CA

Are you scratching your head? Let's translate: (a) RT stands for retweet, allowing your Twitter followers to repeat this message to their followers. (b) The hashtag (#) always means *subject;* prefacing your name, it makes you easy to find. (c) The uppercase abbreviations indicate the job title, here *Lead Senior Quality Assurance Engineer.* (d) The first link is a tiny URL, a short Web address or alias provided free by

TinyURL.com and other URL-shrinking services. The first short link reveals the job seeker's Talent Evolution profile page; the second directs viewers to a job seeker profile created on TweetMyJobs.com. (e) The hashtags indicate the search terms used as seen here: name, quality assurance jobs in California, and the broad term *résumé*. When doing research from within Twitter, use the @ symbol with a specific Twitter user name or the # symbol for a subject search.

YOUR TASK As a team or individually, search the Web for *tweet résumé*. Pick one of the sites offering to tweet your résumé for you—for example, TweetMyJobs.com or Tweet My Résumé. Describe to your peers the job-search process via Twitter presented on that website. Some services are free, whereas others come with charges. If you select a commercial service, critically evaluate its sales pitch and its claims. Is it worthwhile to spend money on this service? Do clients find jobs? How does the service try to demonstrate that? As a group or individually, share the results with the class.

15.13 Analyzing and Building Student E-Portfolios (L.O. 5)

Communication Technology | Team | Web

Take a minute to conduct a Google search on your name. What comes up? Are you proud of what you see? If you want to change that information—and especially if you are in the job market—think about creating a career e-portfolio. Building such a portfolio has many benefits. It can give you an important digital tool to connect with a large audience. It can also help you expand your technology skills, confirm your strengths, recognize areas in need of improvement, and establish goals for improvement. Many students are creating e-portfolios with the help of their schools.

YOUR TASK No. 1. Before attempting to build your own career e-portfolio, take a look at those of other students. Use the Google search term *student career e-portfolio* to see lots of samples. Your instructor may assign you individually or as a team to visit specific digital portfolio sites and summarize your findings in a memo or a brief oral presentation. You could focus on the composition of the site, page layout, links provided, software tools used, colors selected, or types of documents included.

YOUR TASK No. 2. Next, examine websites that provide tutorials and tips on how to build career e-portfolios. One of the best sites can be found by searching for *career e-portfolios San Jose State University.* Your instructor may have you individually or as team write a memo summarizing tips on how to create an e-portfolio and choose the types of documents to include. Alternatively, your instructor may ask you to actually create a career e-portfolio.

Test Your Etiquette IQ

New communication platforms and casual workplace environments have blurred the lines of appropriateness, leaving workers wondering how to navigate uncharted waters. Indicate whether the following statements are true or false. Then see if you agree with the responses on p. R-2.

1. To be sure your résumé gets maximum exposure, you should apply to the same job multiple times in the same week to guarantee that your name keeps popping up on the company's radar.

   ________ True ________ False

2. You're currently employed but have decided to move on. As you begin the job search, you should share your decision only with coworkers who can help you find another position and who promise to keep your goal secret.

   ________ True ________ False

3. The safest way to avoid a cell phone blunder during a job interview is to not take your phone with you at all. If you leave it locked in your car, you will not be tempted to look at it. Remember that you may be observed from the moment you walk into the building, and being glued to your phone could present a less-than-favorable impression.

   ________ True ________ False

Chat About It

In each chapter you will find five discussion questions related to the chapter material. Your instructor may assign these topics for you to discuss in class, in an online chat room, or on an online discussion board. Some of the discussion topics may require outside research. You may also be asked to read and respond to postings made by your classmates.

TOPIC 1: A study by career website The Ladders found that candidates need to apply to a job within 72 hours after it has been posted online. After that, chances of being hired drop by more than 50 percent. Does this sound reasonable to you? How could job candidates apply so quickly?

TOPIC 2: A friend has been on the job market for many months without success. She's applied at a few job boards, but she's depressed and claims that her résumé has dropped into a black hole. What advice could you give to improve her job search?

TOPIC 3: Why do you think it is so important to customize your résumé for each employer and each job for which you apply? How do you think employers will respond to a customized résumé versus a generic résumé? Is creating a customized résumé for each position worth your time and effort? Share your opinions with your classmates.

TOPIC 4: In your opinion, what is the difference between honest self-marketing and deception? What are some examples from your experience?

TOPIC 5: A blogger recently wrote that "cover letters probably don't matter, but you still need one." How can you justify cover letters?

Grammar and Mechanics | *Review 15*

Total Review

Each of the following sentences has **three** errors in grammar, punctuation, capitalization, usage, or spelling. On a separate sheet, write a correct version. Avoid adding new phrases or rewriting sentences in your own words. When finished, compare your responses with the key beginning on page Key-3.

EXAMPLE: If you have 10 or fewer years' of experience, its customary to prepare a one-page résumé.

REVISION: If you have **ten** or fewer **years** of experience, **it's** customary to prepare a one-page résumé.

1. To conduct a safe online job search, you should: (a) Use only reputable job boards, (2) keep careful records, and (c) limit the number of sites on which you post your résumé.
2. Todays employers use sights such as Facebook to learn about potential employees. Which means that a job seeker must maintain a professional online presence.
3. When searching for jobs candidates discovered that the résumé is more likely to be used to screen candidate's then for making hiring decisions.
4. If I was you I would shorten my résumé to 1 page and include a summary of qualifications.
5. Mitchell wondered whether it was alright to ask his professor for employment advise?
6. At last months staff meeting team members examined several candidates résumés.
7. Rather then schedule face to face interviews the team investigated video-conferencing.
8. 11 applicants will be interviewed on April 10th, consequently, we may need to work late to accommodate them.
9. Although as many as twenty-five percent of jobs are found on the Internet the principle source of jobs still involves networking.
10. If Troy had went to the companies own website he might have seen the position posted immediately.

References

[1] *#ENTRYLEVELtweet: Taking Your Career From Classroom to Cubicle.* (2010). Silicon Valley: Thinkhaha ebook.

[2] Huhman, H. (2013). Five hiring process myths you need to know. Careerealism. Retrieved from http://www.careerealism.com/hiring-process-myths

[3] Huhman, H. (n.d.). Networking 360: Coming full circle with networking. Careerealism. Retrieved from http://www.careerealism.com/networking-360-coming-full-circle-networking

[4] Huhman, H. (2013). Five hiring myths you need to know. Careerealism. Retrieved from http://www.careerrealism.com/hiring-process-myths

[5] Ibid.

[6] Huhman, H. (2015, February 23). 5 tips for your mobile job search. Glassdoor. Retrieved from https://www.glassdoor.com/blog/5-tips-mobile-job-search

[7] Huhman, H. (2009, March 12). Guest post from Heather Huhman: Impressing hiring managers to get your dream job. Awesome and Unemployed. Retrieved from http://awesomeandunemployed.wordpress.com/2009/12/03/impress-hiring-mgrs

[8] Gellman, L. (2016, April 26). Job outlook brightens for new college grads. *The Wall Street Journal,* p. B6. See also Lidgett, A. (2015, October 8). More jobs for new grads? Employers want to hire 15 percent more college graduates in 2015-16 academic year: Report. International Business Times. Retrieved from http://www.ibtimes.com/more-jobs-new-grads-employers-want-hire-15-percent-more-college-graduates-2015-16-2132711.

[9] Chan, A. quoted in Purdy, C. (n.d.). 10 job search mistakes of new college grads. Monster. Retrieved from http://career-advice.monster.com/job-search/getting-started/ten-jobsearch-mistakes-of-new-college-grads/article.aspx

[10] Waldman, J. (2014, February 16). 10 things you need to know about today's job search. Careerrealism. Retrieved from http://www.careerealism.com/todays-job-search

[11] Bureau of Labor Statistics. (2015, March). National longitudinal surveys: Number of jobs held in a lifetime. Bureau of Labor Statistics. Retrieved from http://www.bls.gov/nls/nlsfaqs.htm#anch41. See also Bureau of Labor Statistics. (2014, September 18). Economic news release: Employee tenure summary. Bureau of Labor Statistics. Retrieved from http://www.bls.gov/news.release/tenure.nr0.htm; Kimmit, R. M. (2007, January 23). Why job churn is good. *The Washington Post,* p. A17. Retrieved from http://www.washingtonpost.com/wp-dyn/content/article/2007/01/22/AR2007012201089.html

[12] National Association of Colleges and Employers. (2015). 2015 internship and co-op survey. NACE. Retrieved from https://www.naceweb.org/uploadedFiles/Content/static-assets/downloads/executive-summary/2015-internship-co-op-survey-executive-summary.pdf

[13] Jobvite. (2014). Jobvite job seeker nation study. Jobvite. Retrieved from http://web.jobvite.com/rs/jobvite/images/2014%20Job%20Seeker%20Survey.pdf

[14] Adams, S. (2011, June 7). Networking is still the best way to find a job, survey says. *Forbes.* Retrieved from http://www.forbes.com/sites/susanadams/2011/06/07/networking-is-still-the-best-way-to-find-a-job-survey-says/#5820cbce2754

[15] Laumeister, G. (2015, June 2). How to navigate the hidden job market. DailyWorth. Retrieved from https://www.dailyworth.com/posts/3611-the-hidden-job-market-and-what-to-do-about-it-laumeister. See also Collamer, N. (2013, August 12). 6 ways to crack the 'hidden' job market. *Forbes.* Retrieved from http://www.forbes.com/sites/nextavenue/2013/08/12/6-ways-to-crack-the-hidden-job-market/#3c9bbc1c5e99

[16] Stewart, R. (2015, November 25). 4 reasons why job boards are still a useful tool for employers. TalentCulture. Retrieved from http://www.talentculture.com/4-reasons-why-job-boards-are-still-a-useful-tool-for-employers

[17] Nuckles, B. (2015, January 8). 12 best job search apps. Business News Daily. Retrieved from http://www.businessnewsdaily.com/5992-best-job-search-apps.html

[18] Collamer, N. (2013, August 12). 6 ways to crack the 'hidden' job market. *Forbes.* Retrieved from http://www.forbes.com/sites/nextavenue/2013/08/12/6-ways-to-crack-the-hidden-job-market/#1491d5c95e99. See also Mathison, D., & Finney, M. I. (2009). *Unlock the hidden job market: 6 steps to a successful job search when times are tough.* Upper Saddle River, NJ: Pearson Education, FI Press.

[19] Richardson, V. (2011, March 16). Five ways inside the 'hidden job market.' Daily Finance. Retrieved from http://www.dailyfinance.com/2011/03/16/five-ways-inside-the-hidden-job-market

[20] Jobvite. (2014). 2014 Social recruiting survey. Jobvite. Retrieved from https://www.jobvite.com/wp-content/uploads/2014/10/Jobvite_SocialRecruiting_Survey2014.pdf

[21] Garriott, O. (2015, February 6). 10 LinkedIn tips for students and new grads. LinkedIn Pulse. Retrieved from https://www.linkedin.com/pulse/10-tips-students-new-grads-linkedin-omar-garriott

[22] Ibid.

[23] Singer, M. (2015, September 22). Welcome to the 2015 recruiter nation, formerly known as the social recruiting survey. Jobvite. Retrieved from http://www.jobvite.com/blog/welcome-to-the-2015-recruiter-nation-formerly-known-as-the-social-recruiting-survey

[24] Sundberg, J. (2016, February 8.) The rise of Facebook recruitment. Link Humans [Blog]. Retrieved from http://linkhumans.com/blog/rise-facebook-recruitment

[25] Isaacs, K. (n.d.). How long should my résumé be? Monster. Retrieved from http://career-advice.monster.com/resumes-cover-letters/resume-writing-tips/how-to-decide-on-resume-length/article.aspx

[26] Isaacs, K. (n.d.). Career advice: Résumé help and job interview tips. Monster. Retrieved from http://career-advice.monster.com/resumes-cover-letters/resume-writing-tips/whats-your-resume-objective/article.aspx

[27] Joyce, S. P. (2014, April 8). How to quickly and easily customize your résumé for each opportunity. Work Coach Café. Retrieved from http://www.workcoachcafe.com/2014/04/08/customize-your-resume

[28] Korkki, P. (2007, July 1). So easy to apply, so hard to be noticed. *The New York Times.* Retrieved from http://www.nytimes.com/2007/07/01/business/yourmoney/01career.html

[29] Slack, M. (n.d.). How to write a qualifications summary. Résumé Genius. Retrieved from https://resumegenius.com/how-to-write-a-resume/qualifications-summary-writing-guide

[30] Berrett, D. (2013, January 25). My GRE score says I'm smart. Hire me. *The Chronicle of Higher Education,* p. A4.

[31] Linkedin for Volunteers. (n.d.). Use your skills to make a positive impact. Retrieved from https://volunteer.linkedin.com

[32] Matuson, R. C. (n.d.). Recession-proof your résumé. HCareers. Retrieved from http://www.hcareers.com/us/resourcecenter/tabid/306/articleid/522/default.aspx

[33] Hehman, E., Flake, J. K., & Freeman, J. B. (2015). Static and dynamic facial cues differentially affect the consistency of social evaluations. *Personality and Social Psychology Bulletin,* 1-12. doi:10.1177/0146167215591495

[34] Fisher, C. (2015, January 21). Brand YOU year: How to brand yourself without sounding like everyone else. LinkedIn Official Blog. Retrieved from http://blog.linkedin.com/2015/01/21/brand-you-year-how-to-brand-yourself-without-sounding-like-everyone-else

[35] Adams, S. (2015, April 23). Seven ways to make LinkedIn help you find a job. *Forbes.* Retrieved from http://www.forbes.com/sites/susanadams/2015/04/23/seven-ways-to-make-linkedin-help-you-find-a-job/#15325a752079

[36] Kreps, L. (2015, June 25). The legal risks of lying on your résumé. Shake Law.com [Blog]. Retrieved from http://www.shakelaw.com/blog/lying-on-your-resume

[37] CareerBuilder. (2015, December 31). Employers reveal biggest résumé blunders in annual CareerBuilder survey. CareerBuilder. Retrieved from http://www.careerbuilder.com/share/aboutus/pressreleasesdetail.aspx?sd=8/13/2015&id=pr909&ed=12/31/2015

[38] Ibid.

[39] Skillings, P. (2015, March 1). How to get the applicant tracking system to pick your résumé. Big Interview [Blog]. Retrieved from http://biginterview.com/blog/2015/03/applicant-tracking-system.html

[40] Quint Careers. (n.d.). Applicant tracking systems 101 for job-seekers: Understanding the ATS technology that dominates online job search. Retrieved from http://www.quintcareers.com/understanding-applicant-tracking-systems

[41] National Association of Colleges and Employers. (2015, April 1). Tips for helping students create an effective career eportfolio. Retrieved from http://www.naceweb.org/s04012015/students-create-career-eportfolio.aspx

[42] Vaas, L. (n.d.). Résumé, meet technology: Making your résumé format machine-friendly. The Ladders. Retrieved from http://www.theladders.com/career-advice/resume-technology-resume-format-machine-friendly

[43] JobVite. (2015, July). The JobVite recruiter national survey 2015. Retrieved from https://www.jobvite.com/wp-content/uploads/2015/09/jobvite_recruiter_nation_2015.pdf

[44] Luckwaldt, J. H. (2015, September 28). Cover letters probably don't matter, but you still need one. PayScale. Retrieved from http://www.payscale.com/career-news/2015/09/cover-letters-probably-dont-matter-but-you-still-need-one#pageTop

[45] Crispo, V. (2015, April 22). So . . . do cover letters matter? Idealist Careers. Retrieved from http://idealistcareers.org/so-do-cover-letters-matter

[46] Quoted in Luckwaldt, J. H. (2015, September 28). Cover letters probably don't matter, but you still need one. Payscale. Retrieved from http://www.payscale.com/career-news/2015/09/cover-letters-probably-dont-matter-but-you-still-need-one#pageTop

[47] Cavazos, N. (2014, April 15). Do cover letters matter? ZipRecruiter. Retrieved from https://www.ziprecruiter.com/blog/do-cover-letters-still-matter

[48] Weber, L., & Kwoh, L. (2013, January 9). Beware the phantom job listing. *The Wall Street Journal*, pp. B1 and B6.

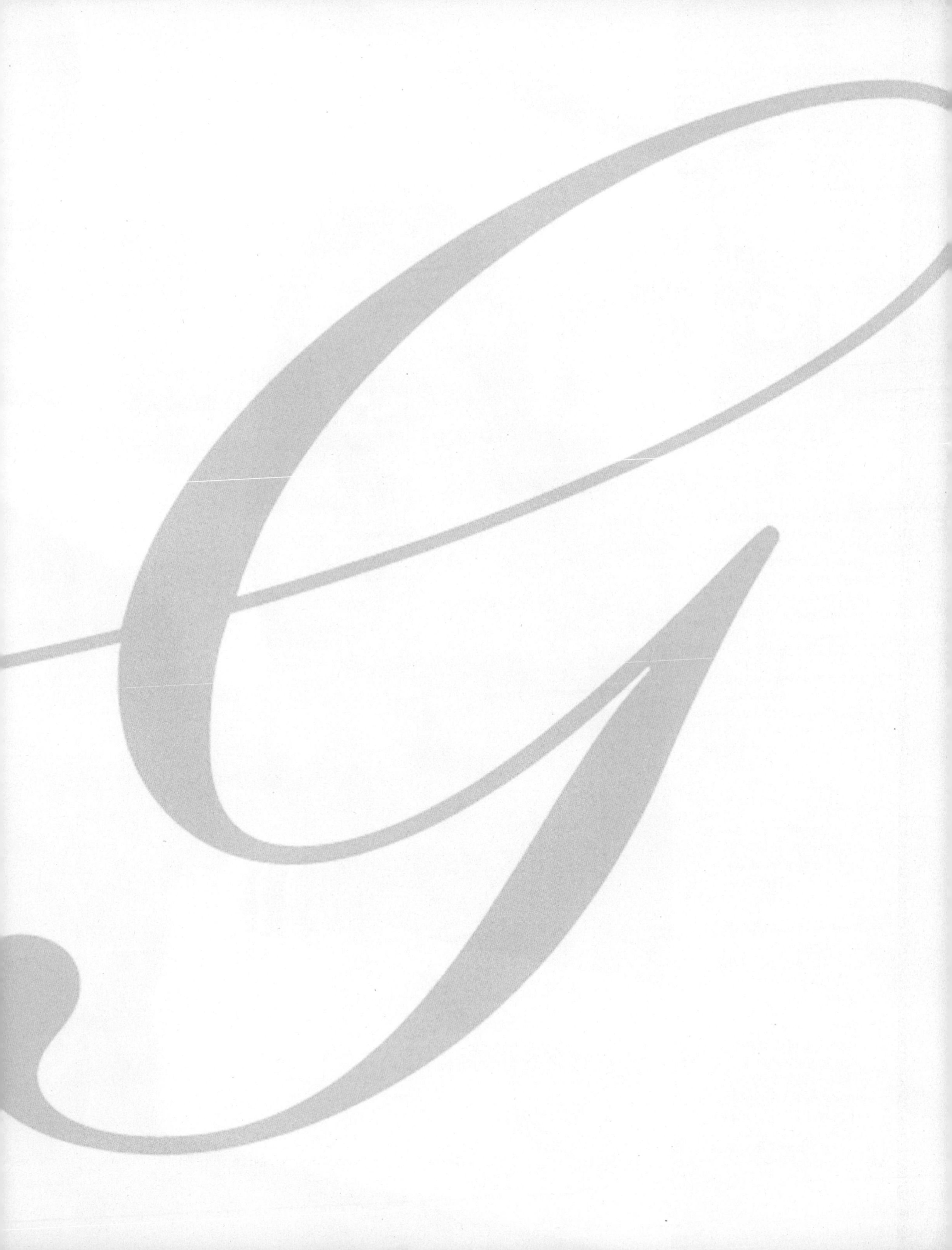

Chapter 16 Interviewing and Following Up

goodluz/Shutterstock.com

LEARNING OUTCOMES

After studying this chapter, you should be able to

1 Explain the purposes, sequence, and types of job interviews, including screening, one-on-one, panel, group, sequential, and video interviews.

2 Describe what to do *before* an interview, including ensuring professional phone techniques, researching the target company, rehearsing success stories, cleaning up digital dirt, dressing properly, and fighting fear.

3 Describe what to do *during* an interview, including controlling nonverbal messages and answering typical interview questions.

4 Describe what to do *after* an interview, including thanking the interviewer, contacting references, and writing follow-up messages.

5 Prepare additional employment documents such as applications, rejection follow-up messages, acceptance messages, and resignation letters.

Yeamake/Shutterstock.com

Zooming In

Achieving Interview Success in Today's Competitive Job Market

The job market has become remarkably complicated and competitive, especially for recent grads. If you are new to the job market or changing careers, career coach Don Georgevich offers practical advice. A leading authority in job interviewing and résumé writing, Georgevich helps job candidates cut through the red tape of interviews so that they are hired for the jobs they want. The author of three top-selling career books plus e-tools, blogs, YouTube videos, and Internet articles, Georgevich shares special advice for those who are new to the job-search process.

"For new grads, being aware of recent trends and preparing diligently for the interview is crucial," he stressed in an e-mail message to Mary Ellen Guffey. "The more you study the company and the job description, combined with how you believe your skills and experiences fit in, the more prepared you will be. You can even predict what to expect in a typical interview because interviewers tend to repeat common questions."

Courtesy of Don Georgevich

When asked how new grads and career changers can gain traction in a highly competitive job market, Georgevich stressed demonstrating transferable skills. For example, candidates can say, "I have [blank] skills and I can use them to do [blank] for you." Job seekers need to connect the dots for employers and show how their qualifications fit the targeted position. "All too often," he said, "job seekers leave it up to the interviewer to figure out what they are good at doing instead of taking a proactive stance."

A recent trend is video interviewing, either for initial screening or to choose among final candidates. "Keep in mind," Georgevich said, "that an employer will be reviewing videos from many candidates. To make yours stand out, start off with an eye-opening statement, such as 'In this video I'm going to show why I'm the only person you need to consider for this position.' Then proceed to show that you understand the company, its products, and its pains."

Companies today are putting candidates through many layers of interviewing to avoid a bad hire. Because the hiring process is more stretched out, it's more important than ever to follow up with the hiring manager to avoid being forgotten. Your goal is to stay in close contact without being a pest. To follow up, call about once every seven to ten days after your interview. Recent graduates, Georgevich said, seem to prefer only e-mail or text follow-ups, but he highly recommends a phone call to make a personal connection and achieve greater authenticity. From the beginning to the end of the process, the hiring manager wants to discover whether you are a good culture fit and whether you are truly invested in the company.[1] You will learn more about working with Don Georgevich and be asked to complete a relevant task later in this chapter.

Critical Thinking

- Can novice job seekers predict what a job interview will involve?
- How is interviewing a two-way street? What does this mean for job candidates?
- How can job seekers show recruiters or hiring managers that they are invested in a position during the job interview?

Interviewing Effectively in Today's Competitive Job Market

Learning Outcome 1

Explain trends, purposes, sequence, and types of job interviews, including screening, one-on-one, panel, group, sequential, and video interviews.

Just as searching for a job has changed dramatically in this digital age, so has interviewing. The good news is that employers are hiring. However, competition is stiff, as career coach Don Georgevich pointed out in the Zooming In feature. Whether you are completing your education and searching for your first serious position or are in the workforce and striving to change jobs—a job interview can be life changing. Because employment is a major part of everyone's life, the job interview takes on enormous importance.

Most people consider job interviews extremely stressful, eliciting as much or more anxiety than making a speech or going on a first date. However, the more you learn about the process and the more prepared you are, the less stress you will feel. Moreover, a job interview is a two-way street. It is not just about being judged by the employer. You, the applicant, will be using the job interview to evaluate the employer. Do you really want to work for this organization?

To be successful in a highly competitive market, you must keep up with the latest trends and techniques that recruiters use to choose the very best candidates. Figure 16.1 illustrates six hot trends in today's employment scene. To help you respond to these trends, this chapter presents the latest tips as well as other traditional techniques that will improve your interviewing skills and boost your confidence.

You will learn how to gather information about a prospective employer, how to project a professional image, how to reduce nervousness during an interview, and how to prepare for video interviews. Because today's recruiters regularly check social media and the Internet to vet applicants, this chapter presents valuable advice on using social media safely and skillfully. Additionally, you will find typical interview questions, possible responses, and advice on how to cope with illegal inquiries and salary matters. Moreover, you will receive pointers on significant questions you can ask during an interview. Finally, you will learn how to follow up successfully after an interview.

Yes, job interviews can be intimidating and stressful. However, you can expect to ace an interview when you know what's coming and prepare thoroughly. Remember, preparation often determines who gets the job. First, though, you need to know the purposes of employment interviews, the typical sequence of events, and the types of interviews you might encounter in your job search.

Figure 16.1 **Latest Trends in Interviewing**

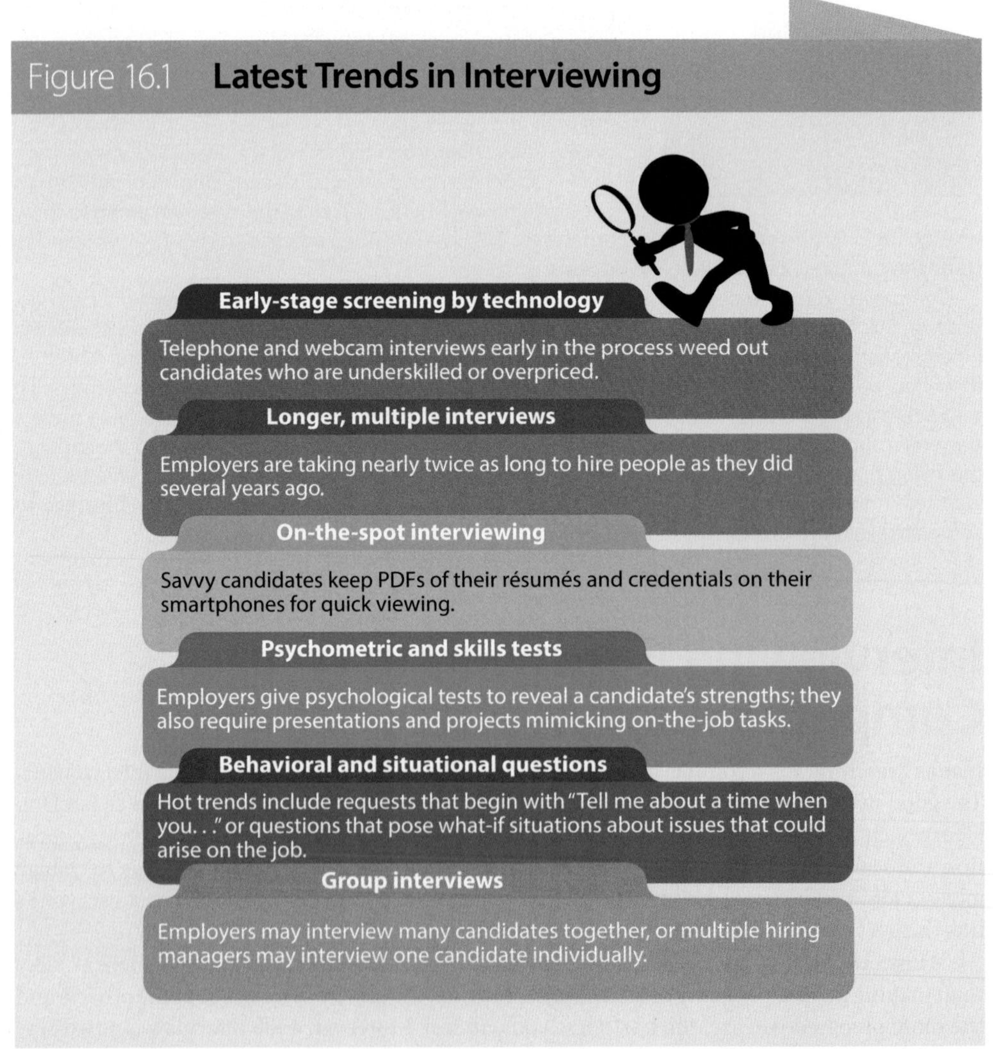

Early-stage screening by technology
Telephone and webcam interviews early in the process weed out candidates who are underskilled or overpriced.
Longer, multiple interviews
Employers are taking nearly twice as long to hire people as they did several years ago.
On-the-spot interviewing
Savvy candidates keep PDFs of their résumés and credentials on their smartphones for quick viewing.
Psychometric and skills tests
Employers give psychological tests to reveal a candidate's strengths; they also require presentations and projects mimicking on-the-job tasks.
Behavioral and situational questions
Hot trends include requests that begin with "Tell me about a time when you. . ." or questions that pose what-if situations about issues that could arise on the job.
Group interviews
Employers may interview many candidates together, or multiple hiring managers may interview one candidate individually.

Purposes and Sequencing of Employment Interviews

An interview has several purposes for you as a job candidate. It is an opportunity to (a) convince the employer of your potential, (b) learn more about the job and the company, and (c) expand on the information in your résumé. This is the time for you to gather information to determine whether you would fit into the company culture. You should also be thinking about whether this job suits your career goals.

From the employer's perspective, the interview is an opportunity to (a) assess your abilities in relation to the requirements for the position; (b) discuss your training, experience, knowledge, and abilities in more detail; (c) see what drives and motivates you; and (d) decide whether you would fit into the organization.

The hiring process often follows a six-stage sequence, as illustrated in Figure 16.2. Following the application, interviews proceed from screening interviews to hiring interviews.

Screening Interviews

Screening interviews do just that—they screen candidates to eliminate those who fail to meet minimum requirements. Companies use screening interviews to save time and money by weeding out lesser-qualified candidates before scheduling final face-to-face or video interviews. Although initial screening interviews may be conducted during job fairs or on college campuses, they usually take place by telephone or video.

During an initial screening interview, the interviewer will probably ask you to provide details about the education and experience listed on your résumé; therefore, you must be prepared to promote your qualifications. If you do well on the initial interview, you may be invited to a secondary screening interview. This interview may be conducted by a human resources specialist with more specific questions relating to the open position. It could be a telephone or a video interview scheduled on Skype. The interviewer is trying to decide whether you are a strong enough candidate to be interviewed by a hiring manager.

Hiring/Placement Interviews

The most promising candidates selected from screening interviews are invited to hiring/placement interviews. Hiring managers want to learn whether candidates are motivated, qualified, and a good fit for the position. Their goal is to learn how the candidate would fit into their organization. Conducted in depth, hiring/placement interviews take many forms.

One-on-One Interviews. In one-on-one interviews, which are most common, you can expect to sit down with a company representative and talk about the job and your qualifications. If the representative is the hiring manager, questions will be specific and job related. If the representative is from human resources, the questions will probably be more general.

Figure 16.2 **Six Stages of the Hiring Process**

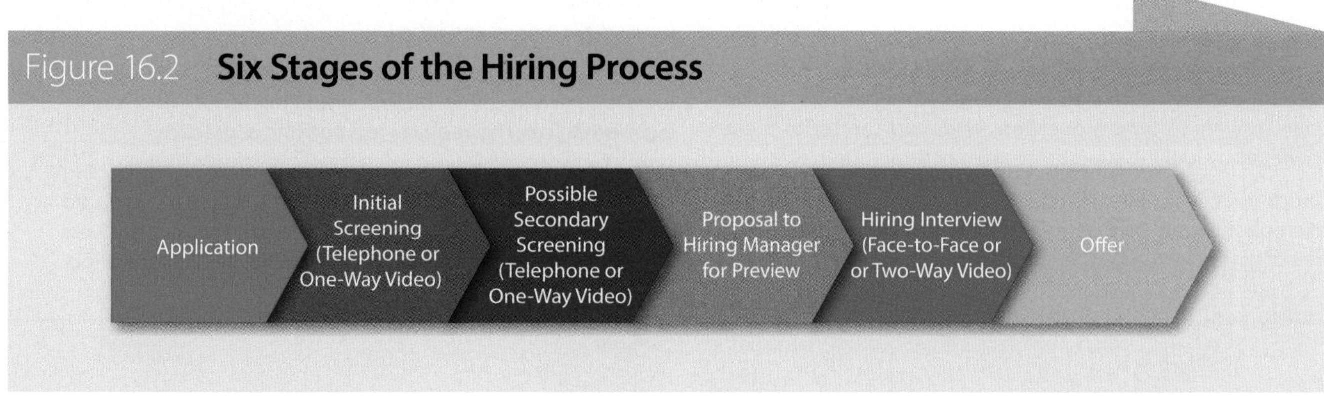

Panel Interviews. Panel interviews are typically conducted by people who will be your supervisors and colleagues. Usually seated around a table, interviewers take turns asking questions. Panel interviews are advantageous because they save the company time and money, and they show you how the staff works together. If possible before these interviews, try to gather basic biographical information about each panel member. This information may be available on the company website or LinkedIn. When answering questions, maintain eye contact with the questioner as well as with the others. Expect to repeat information you may have given in earlier interviews. Try to take paper-and-pen notes during the interview so that you can remember each person's questions and what was important to that individual. Don't take notes on a laptop or other digital device as interviewers may think you are checking incoming texts.

Group Interviews. Group interviews occur when a company interviews several candidates for the same position at the same time. Some employers use this technique to evaluate leadership skills and communication styles. During a group interview, stay focused on the interviewer, and treat the other candidates with respect. Even if you are nervous, try to remain calm, take your time when responding, and express yourself clearly. The key during a group interview is to make yourself stand out from the other candidates in a positive way.

Sequential Interviews. In a sequential interview, you meet individually with two or more interviewers one-on-one over the course of several hours or days. For example, you may meet with human resources representatives, your hiring manager, and potential future supervisors and colleagues in your division or department. You must listen carefully and respond positively to all interviewers. Promote your qualifications to each one; don't assume that any interviewer knows what was said in a previous interview. Keep your responses fresh, even when repeating yourself many times over. Subsequent interviews also tend to be more in-depth than first

PLUGGED IN

Preparing for a Video Job Interview

Both one-way and two-way video interviews enable job seekers to connect with potential employers without traveling. However, because video interviews present many potential pitfalls, preparation is essential. The following tips can help you make sure you are ready.

Do your homework. Using the Internet, learn all that you can about the target company including its competitors, its products, and its goals.

Plan your answers. For one-way interviews, you have the questions in advance giving you a marvelous opportunity to prepare perfect responses. For two-way interviews, practice your answers to typical questions until you can recite them flawlessly by looking straight into the camera.

Check your tech. Be sure you know how your webcam and microphone work so that your audio and video are clear and free of glitches. Position the camera at eye level.

Look at your lighting. Place a light behind your computer so that your face is not in the shadows.

Control your surroundings. The room you sit in should be neat, attractive, and quiet. Avoid distractions such as barking dogs, crying children, flushing toilets, or ringing cell phones.

Dress to impress. Just as you would prepare for a face-to-face interview, be well groomed. If you are interviewing for a professional position, wear a suit. Avoid distracting prints, disturbingly bright colors, and loud jewelry.

Practice, practice, practice. Know your answers well enough to be natural and comfortable in saying them, but avoid sounding mechanical. This requires lots and lots of practice.

Be the best you can be. Sit up straight, look interested by leaning forward slightly, and don't let your eyes drop, suggesting you are reading from a script. Don't mumble or fidget. Focus on answers and stories that demonstrate why you are the best fit for the job.

interviews, which means that you need to be even more prepared and know even more about the company.

Video Interviews. Perhaps the hottest trend in interviewing is the rush to video interviews. One-way (asynchronous) video interviewing enables a candidate to respond to a list of prescripted questions prepared by the hiring organization. When convenient, the candidate creates a video recording of the answers. The interviewer can view the job seeker, but the job seeker cannot see the interviewer. One-way interviewing benefits employers by cutting the time needed to meet lots of candidates; it benefits candidates by enabling them to be interviewed at their leisure without traveling to distant locations. Candidates also can practice and perfect their responses by rerecording.

Two-way video interviewing is similar to regular face-to-face interviewing, but it is typically conducted through video chat. A key advantage of two-way interviewing is that it provides an interactive forum enabling hiring companies to better assess a candidate's communication skills, body language, and personality. Preparing for either a one-way or a two-way video interview is extremely important; check out the accompanying Plugged In for tips to help you succeed.

No matter what interview structure you encounter, you will feel more comfortable if you know what to do before, during, and after the interview.

Before the Interview

LEARNING OUTCOME 2

Describe what to do *before* an interview, including ensuring professional phone techniques, researching the target company, rehearsing success stories, cleaning up digital dirt, dressing properly, and fighting fear.

Once you have sent out at least one résumé or filled out at least one job application, you must consider yourself an active job seeker. Being active in the job market means that you should be prepared to be contacted by potential employers. As discussed earlier, employers often use screening interviews to narrow the list of candidates. If you do well in the screening interview, you will be invited to an in-person or video meeting.

Ensuring Professional Phone Techniques

Even with the popularity of e-mail, most employers contact job applicants by phone to set up interviews. Employers can judge how well applicants communicate by hearing their voices and expressions over the phone. Therefore, once you are actively looking for a job, anytime the phone rings, it could be a potential employer. Don't make the mistake of letting an unprofessional voice mail message or a lazy roommate or a sloppy cell phone manner ruin your chances. To make the best impression, try these tips:

- On your answering machine device, make sure that your outgoing message is concise and professional, with no distracting background sounds. It should be in your own voice and include your full name for clarity. You can find more tips for creating professional telephone messages in Chapter 14.
- Tell those who might answer your phone at home about your job search. Explain to them the importance of acting professionally and taking complete messages. Family members or roommates can affect the first impression an employer has of you.
- If you have children, prevent them from answering the phone during your job search. Children of all ages are not known for taking good messages!
- If you have put your cell phone number on your résumé, don't answer unless you are in a good location to carry on a conversation with an employer. It is hard to pay close attention when you are driving down the highway or eating in a noisy restaurant!
- Use voice mail to screen calls. By screening incoming calls, you can be totally in control when you return a prospective employer's call. Organize your materials and ready yourself psychologically for the conversation.

Making the First Conversation Impressive

Whether you answer the phone directly or return an employer's call, make sure you are prepared for the conversation. Remember that this is the first time the employer has heard your voice. How you conduct yourself on the phone will create a lasting impression. To make that first impression a positive one, follow these tips:

- Keep a list on your cell phone or near the telephone of positions for which you have applied.
- Treat any call from an employer just like an interview. Use a professional tone and businesslike language. Be polite and enthusiastic, and sell your qualifications.
- If caught off guard by the call, ask whether you can call back in a few minutes. Take that time to organize your materials and yourself.
- Have a copy of your résumé available so that you can answer any questions that come up. Also have your list of references, a calendar, and a notepad handy.
- Be prepared for a screening interview. As discussed earlier, this might occur during the first phone call.
- Take good notes during the phone conversation. Obtain accurate directions, and verify the spelling of your interviewer's name. If you will be interviewed by more than one person, get all of their names.
- If given a chance, ask for an interview on Tuesday at 10:30 a.m. This is considered the most opportune time. Avoid the start of the day on Monday and the end of the day on Friday.[2]
- Before you hang up, reconfirm the date and time of your interview. You could say something like *I look forward to meeting with you next Wednesday at 2 p.m.*

Pan_kung/Shutterstock.com

Reality Check

Interviewing Success Requires More Than Just Showing Up

"Whoever said 80 percent of success is just showing up wasn't thinking about job interviews. Thoroughly preparing for an interview makes a huge difference in how well you do. And it can also make you a lot less nervous."[3]

—Alison Green, *management consultant and blogger*

Researching the Target Company

Once you have scheduled an in-person or video interview, you need to start preparing for it. One of the most important steps in effective interviewing is gathering detailed information about a prospective employer. Never enter an interview cold. Recruiters are impressed by candidates who have done their homework.

Scouring the Internet for Important Company Data. Search the potential employer's website, news sources, trade journals, and industry directories. Unearth information about the job, the company, and the industry. Learn all you can about the company's history, mission and goals, size, geographic locations, and number of employees. Check out its customers, competitors, culture, management structure, reputation in the community, financial condition, strengths and weaknesses, and future plans, as well as the names of its leaders. A good place to check is the About Us section on its website.

Analyzing the Company's Advertising. In addition to its online presence, examine the company's ads and promotional materials, including sales and marketing brochures. One candidate, a marketing major, spent a great deal of time poring over brochures from an aerospace contractor. During his initial interview, he shocked and impressed the recruiter with his knowledge of the company's guidance systems. The candidate had, in fact, relieved the interviewer of his least-favorite task—explaining the company's complicated technology.

Locating Inside Information. To locate inside information, use social media sources such as LinkedIn and Twitter. Like the company on Facebook and comment shrewdly on the organization's status updates and other posts. Beyond these sites, check out employee review websites such as Glassdoor to get the inside scoop on what it's like to work there.[4] Online tools such as LinkedIn's JobsInsider toolbar can help you discover whether you know someone who already works at the company.

Try to connect with someone who is currently employed by the company—but not working in the immediate area where you wish to be hired. Be sure to seek out someone who is discreet. Blogs are also excellent sources for insider information and company research. In addition, don't forget to google the interviewer.

As you learn about a company, you may uncover information that convinces you that this is not the company for you. It is always better to learn about negatives early in the process. More likely, though, the information you collect will help you tailor your interview responses to the organization's needs. You know how flattered you feel when an employer knows about you and your background. That feeling works both ways. Employers are pleased when job candidates take an interest in them.

Rehearsing Success Stories

To feel confident and be ready to sell your qualifications, prepare and practice success stories. These stories are specific examples of your educational and work-related experience that demonstrate your qualifications and achievements. Look over the job description and your résumé to determine what skills, training, personal characteristics, and experience you want to emphasize during the interview. Then prepare a success story for each one. Incorporate numbers, such as dollars saved or percentage of sales increased, whenever possible. Your success stories should be detailed but brief. Think of them as 30-second sound bites.

Practice telling your success stories until they fluently roll off your tongue and sound natural. Then in the interview, be certain to find places to insert them. Tell stories about (a) dealing with a crisis, (b) handling a tough interpersonal situation, (c) successfully juggling many priorities, (d) changing course to deal with changed circumstances, (e) learning from a mistake, (f) working on a team, and (g) going above and beyond expectations.

David J. Green - lifestyle themes/Alamy Stock Photo

Preparing for an interview is essential to making a good impression, and an excellent way to prepare is to visit Glassdoor.com. A job and recruiting website, Glassdoor contains company reviews, salary ranges, and interview information—all from former or current employees. The website recently created a list of companies that received top ratings for providing "positive interview experiences." Glassdoor even posts sample interview questions submitted by candidates who have been interviewed at a given company. Being armed with inside knowledge about an organization can help candidates feel more confident during an interview. Why is it important to prepare questions to ask at an interview?[5]

Cleaning Up Digital Dirt

Potential employers definitely screen candidates' online presence using Google and social media sites such as Facebook, LinkedIn, and Twitter. A recent CareerBuilder survey revealed that 49 percent of hiring managers who screen candidates via social networks said they had found information that caused them not to hire a candidate. What turned them off? The top reasons cited were (a) provocative or inappropriate photographs, videos, or information; (b) content about drinking or doing drugs; (c) discriminatory comments related to race, religion, and other protected categories; (d) criticism of previous employers or colleagues; and (e) poor communication skills.[6] Teasing photographs and provocative comments about drinking, drug use, and sexual exploits make students look immature and unprofessional. Think about cleaning up your online presence by following these steps:

- **Remove questionable content.** Remove any incriminating, provocative, or distasteful photos, content, and links that could make you look unprofessional to potential employers.
- **Stay positive.** Don't complain about things in your professional or personal life online. Even negative reviews you have written on sites such as Amazon can turn employers off.
- **Be selective about who is on your list of friends.** You don't want to miss out on an opportunity because you seem to associate with negative, immature, or unprofessional people. Your best bet is to make your personal social networking pages private. Monitor your settings because they often change.
- **Don't discuss your job search if you are still employed.** Employees can find themselves in trouble with their current employers by writing status updates or sending tweets about their job searches.

Dressing for, Traveling to, and Arriving at Your Interview

The big day has arrived! Ideally, you are fully prepared for your interview. Now you need to make sure that everything goes smoothly. On the day of your interview, give yourself plenty of time to groom and dress.

Deciding What to Wear. What to wear may worry you because business attire today ranges from ultracasual to formal suits. The best plan is to ask your interviewer what is appropriate, advises career counselor Liz Ryan.[7] Ask this when the interview is arranged, and you will be greatly relieved. Here's what you definitely should not wear, according to Monster.com:[8](a) ill-fitting clothes; (b) overly casual attire, such as jeans, tennis shoes, shorts, T-shirts, hats, flip-flops, and any item promoting messages or brands; (c) distracting items; (d) excessive accessories; or (e) something very different from what the interviewer suggested.

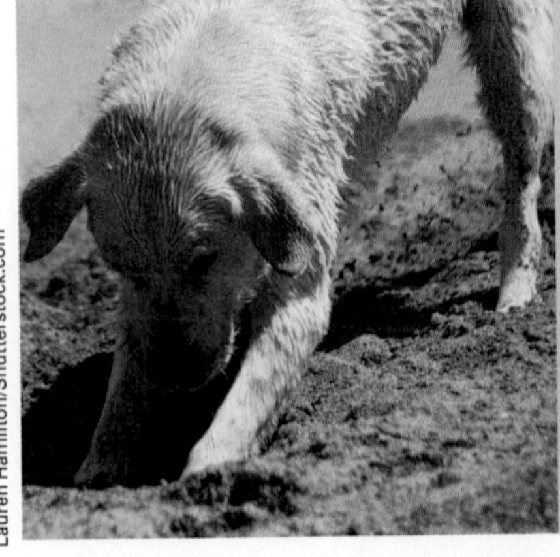

Lauren Hamilton/Shutterstock.com

Removing questionable content from social media sites should be the first step of any job search. Unsuitable material may include your own photos or posts. However, inappropriate content is just as likely to come from someone else's comments about you or photos of you posted on another page. Remember to view your social media presence the same way a future employer would, and ask yourself whether the personal information you share would be embarrassing if it were publicly known. Never rely on your own privacy settings: Anyone following you can capture a screen image and repost it. Why is a good idea to google yourself?[9]

Make sure you can arrive at the employer's office without being rushed. If something unexpected happens that will to cause you to be late, such as an accident or bridge closure, call the interviewer right away to explain what is happening. Most interviewers will be understanding, and your call will show that you are responsible. On the way to the interview, don't smoke, don't eat anything messy or smelly, and don't load up on perfume or cologne. Arrive at the interview five or ten minutes early, but not earlier. If you are very early, wait in the car or in a café nearby. If possible, check your appearance before going in.

Being Polite and Pleasant. When you enter the office, be courteous and congenial to everyone. Remember that you are being judged not only by the interviewer but also by the receptionist and anyone else who sees you before and after the interview. They will notice how you sit, what you read, and how you look. Introduce yourself to the receptionist, and wait to be invited to sit. You may be asked to fill out a job application while you are waiting. You will find tips for doing this effectively later in this chapter.

Greeting the Interviewer and Making a Positive First Impression. Greet the interviewer confidently, and don't be afraid to initiate a handshake. Doing so exhibits professionalism and confidence. Extend your hand, look the interviewer directly in the eye, smile pleasantly, and say, *I'm pleased to meet you, Mr. Thomas. I am Constance Ferraro.* In this culture a firm, not crushing, handshake sends a nonverbal message of poise and assurance. Once introductions have taken place, wait for the interviewer to offer you a chair. Make small talk with upbeat comments such as *This is a beautiful headquarters* or *I'm very impressed with the facilities you have here.* Don't immediately begin rummaging in your briefcase for your résumé. Being at ease and unrushed suggests that you are self-confident.

Fighting Fear

Expect to be nervous before and during the interview. It's natural! One survey revealed that job interviews are more stressful than going on a blind date, being pulled over by the police, or taking a final exam without studying.[10] One of the best ways to overcome fear is to know what happens in a typical interview. You can further reduce your fears by following these suggestions:

- **Practice interviewing.** Try to get as much interviewing practice as you can—especially with real companies. The more times you experience the interview situation, the less nervous you will be. However, don't schedule interviews unless you are genuinely interested in the organization. If offered, campus mock interviews also provide excellent practice, and the interviewers will offer tips for improvement.
- **Prepare thoroughly.** Research the company. Know how you will answer the most frequently asked questions. Be ready with success stories. Rehearse your closing statement. Knowing that you have done all you can to be ready for the interview is a tremendous fear preventive.
- **Understand the process.** Find out ahead of time how the interview will be structured. Will you be meeting with an individual, or will you be interviewed by a panel? Is this the first of a series of interviews? Don't be afraid to ask about these details before the interview so that an unfamiliar situation won't catch you off guard.
- **Dress appropriately.** If you have checked with the interviewer in advance and know that you are dressed properly, you will feel more confident. When in doubt, tend toward more conservative, professional attire.
- **Breathe deeply.** Plan to take deep breaths, particularly if you feel anxious while waiting for the interviewer. Deep breathing makes you concentrate on something other than the interview and also provides much-needed oxygen.
- **Know that you are not alone.** Everyone feels some anxiety during a job interview. Interviewers expect some nervousness, and a skilled interviewer will try to put you at ease.
- **Remember that an interview is a two-way street.** The interviewer isn't the only one who is gleaning information. You have come to learn about the job and the company. In fact, during some parts of the interview, you will be in charge. This should give you courage.

LEARNING OUTCOME 3

Describe what to do *during* an interview, including controlling nonverbal messages and answering typical interview questions.

During the Interview

Throughout the interview you will be answering questions and asking your own questions. Your demeanor, body language, and other nonverbal cues will also be on display. The interviewer will be trying to learn more about you, and you should be learning more about the job and the organization. Although you may be asked some unique questions, many interviewers ask standard, time-proven questions, which means that you can prepare your answers ahead of time. You can also prepare by learning techniques to control those inevitable butterflies in the tummy.

Sending Positive Nonverbal Messages and Acting Professionally

You have already sent nonverbal messages to your interviewer by arriving on time, being courteous, dressing appropriately, and greeting the receptionist confidently. You will continue to send nonverbal messages throughout the interview. Remember that what comes out of your mouth and what is written on your résumé are not the only messages an interviewer receives from you. Nonverbal messages also create powerful impressions. You can send positive nonverbal messages during face-to-face and online interviews by following these tips:

- **Control your body movements.** Keep your hands, arms, and elbows to yourself. Don't lean on a desk. Keep your feet on the floor. Don't cross your arms in front of you. Keep your hands out of your pockets.
- **Exhibit good posture.** Sit erect, leaning forward slightly. Don't slouch in your chair; at the same time, don't look too stiff and uncomfortable. Good posture demonstrates confidence and interest.
- **Practice appropriate eye contact.** A direct eye gaze, at least in North America, suggests interest and trustworthiness. If you are being interviewed by a panel, remember to maintain eye contact with all interviewers.
- **Use gestures effectively.** Nod to show agreement and interest. Gestures should be used as needed, but not overused.
- **Smile enough to convey a positive attitude.** Have a friend give you honest feedback on whether you generally smile too much or not enough.
- **Listen attentively.** Show the interviewer you are interested and attentive by listening carefully to questions. This will also help you answer questions appropriately.
- **Turn off your cell phone or other electronic devices.** Avoid the embarrassment of having your device ring, or even as much as buzz, during an interview. Turn off your electronic devices completely; don't just switch them to vibrate.
- **Don't chew gum.** Chewing gum during an interview is distracting and unprofessional.
- **Sound enthusiastic and interested—but sincere.** The tone of your voice has an enormous effect on the words you say. Avoid sounding bored, frustrated, or sarcastic during an interview. Employers want employees who are enthusiastic and interested.
- **Avoid empty words.** Filling your answers with verbal pauses such as *um*, *uh*, *like*, and *basically* communicates that you are not prepared. Also avoid annoying distractions such as clearing your throat repeatedly or sighing deeply.
- **Be confident, but not cocky.** Most recruiters want candidates who are self-assured but not too casual or even arrogant. Let your body language, posture, dress, and vocal tone prove your confidence. Speak at a normal volume and enunciate words clearly without mumbling.

Naturally, hiring managers make subjective decisions based on intuition, but they need to ferret out pleasant people who fit in. To that end, some recruiters apply the airport test to candidates by asking themselves the following: Would I want to be stuck in the airport for 12 hours with this person if my flight were delayed?[11]

Recruiters may apply the airport test.

Monkey Business Images/
Shutterstock.com

Reality Check

Practice Out Loud Because You Won't Get a Second Chance

"Practice interviewing out loud with mentors, adult fans, or even in the mirror. Most students have not done many (if any) job interviews—and definitely not when under pressure. It's important to hear the words you intend to speak, including the tone, emphasis, inflections and facial impressions, so that you don't blow it when it really counts. It's rare to get a second chance."[12]

—Andy Chan, *vice president for Personal & Career Development, Wake Forest University*

Preparing to Answer Interview Questions

One way you can compensate for lack of experience is to have carefully prepared and well-rehearsed responses to typical interview questions. In addition, the way you answer questions can be almost as important as what you say. Use the interviewer's name and title from time to time when you answer. *Yes, Ms. Luna, I would be pleased to tell you about . . . .* People like to hear their own names, but don't overuse this technique. Avoid answering questions with a simple *yes* or *no*; elaborate on your answers to better promote yourself and your assets. Keep your answers positive; don't criticize anything or anyone.

During the interview it may be necessary to occasionally refocus and clarify vague questions. Some interviewers are inexperienced and ill at ease in the role. You may even have to ask your own question to understand what was asked: *By ____, do you mean _____?* Consider closing out some of your responses with *Does that answer your question?* or *Would you like me to elaborate on any particular experience?*

Always aim your answers at the key characteristics interviewers seek: expertise, competence, motivation, interpersonal skills, decision-making skills, enthusiasm for the company and the job, and a pleasing personality. Remember to stay focused on your strengths. Don't reveal weaknesses, even if you think they make you look human. You won't be hired for your weaknesses, only for your strengths.

As you respond, be sure to use good English and enunciate clearly. Avoid slurred words such as *gonna* and *din't*, as well as slangy expressions such as *yeah, like*, and *ya know.* As you practice answering expected interview questions, it is always a good idea to make an audio or video recording. Is your speech filled with verbal static?

You can't expect to be perfect in an employment interview. No one is. But you can avert sure disaster by avoiding certain topics and behaviors such as those described in Figures 16.3 and 16.4.

The following sections present questions that may be asked during employment interviews. To get you thinking about how to respond, we have provided an answer for, or a discussion of, one or more of the questions in each group. As you read the remaining questions in each group, think about how you could respond most effectively. For additional questions, contact your campus career center, or consult one of the career websites discussed in Chapter 15.

Questions to Get Acquainted

After opening introductions, recruiters generally try to start the interview with personal questions designed to put you at ease. They are also striving to gain an overview to see whether you will fit into the organization's culture. When answering these questions, keep the employer's needs in mind and try to incorporate your success stories.

1. Tell me about yourself.
   Experts agree that you must keep this answer short (one to two minutes tops) but on target. Use this chance to promote yourself. Stick to educational, professional, or business-related

Figure 16.3 Ten Interview Actions to Avoid

1. Don't be late or too early. Arrive five to ten minutes before your scheduled interview.

2. Don't be rude or annoying. Treat everyone you come into contact with warmly and respectfully. Avoid limp handshakes, poor eye contact or staring, and verbal ticks such as *like, you know,* and *um*.

3. Don't criticize anyone or anything. Avoid saying anything negative about your previous employer, supervisors, colleagues, or job. The tendency is for interviewers to wonder if you would speak about their companies similarly.

4. Don't act unprofessionally. Don't discuss controversial subjects, and don't use profanity. Don't answer your cell phone or fiddle with it. Silence all electronic devices so that they don't even buzz, or turn them off completely. Don't bring food or coffee.

5. Don't emphasize salary or benefits. Don't address salary, vacation, or benefits early in an interview. Let the interviewer set the pace; win him or her over first.

6. Don't focus on your imperfections. Never dwell on your liabilities or talk negatively about yourself.

7. Don't interrupt. Interrupting is not only impolite but also prevents you from hearing a complete question or remark. Don't talk too much or too little. Answer interview questions to the best of your ability, but avoid rambling as much as terseness.

8. Don't bring someone along. Don't bring a friend or relative with you to the interview. If someone must drive you, ask that person to drop you off and come back later.

9. Don't appear impatient or bored. Your entire focus should be on the interview. Don't glance at your watch, which can imply that you are late for another appointment. Be alert and show interest in the company and the position.

10. Don't act desperate. A sure way to turn off an interviewer is to act too desperate. Don't focus on why you need the job; focus instead on how you will add value to the organization.

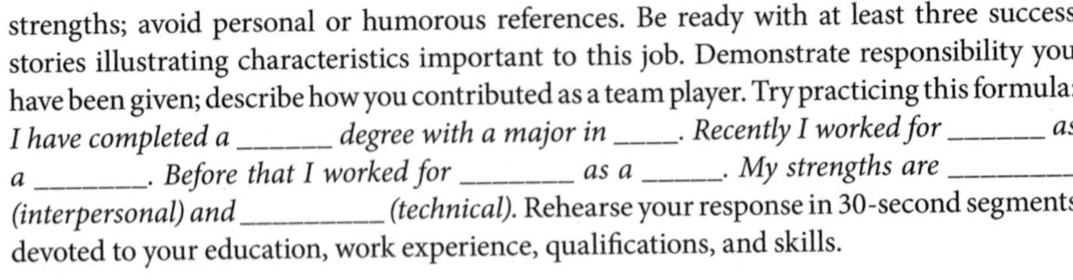

strengths; avoid personal or humorous references. Be ready with at least three success stories illustrating characteristics important to this job. Demonstrate responsibility you have been given; describe how you contributed as a team player. Try practicing this formula: *I have completed a ______ degree with a major in ____. Recently I worked for _______ as a ________. Before that I worked for ________ as a _____. My strengths are _________ (interpersonal) and __________ (technical).* Rehearse your response in 30-second segments devoted to your education, work experience, qualifications, and skills.

2. What are your greatest strengths?
Reread your résumé and cover letter to review what you want to promote. Stress your strengths that are related to the position, such as *I am well organized, thorough, and attentive to detail.* Tell success stories and give examples that illustrate these qualities: *My supervisor says that my research is exceptionally thorough. For example, I recently worked on a research project in which I . . . .*

Figure 16.4 How to Bomb a Job Interview

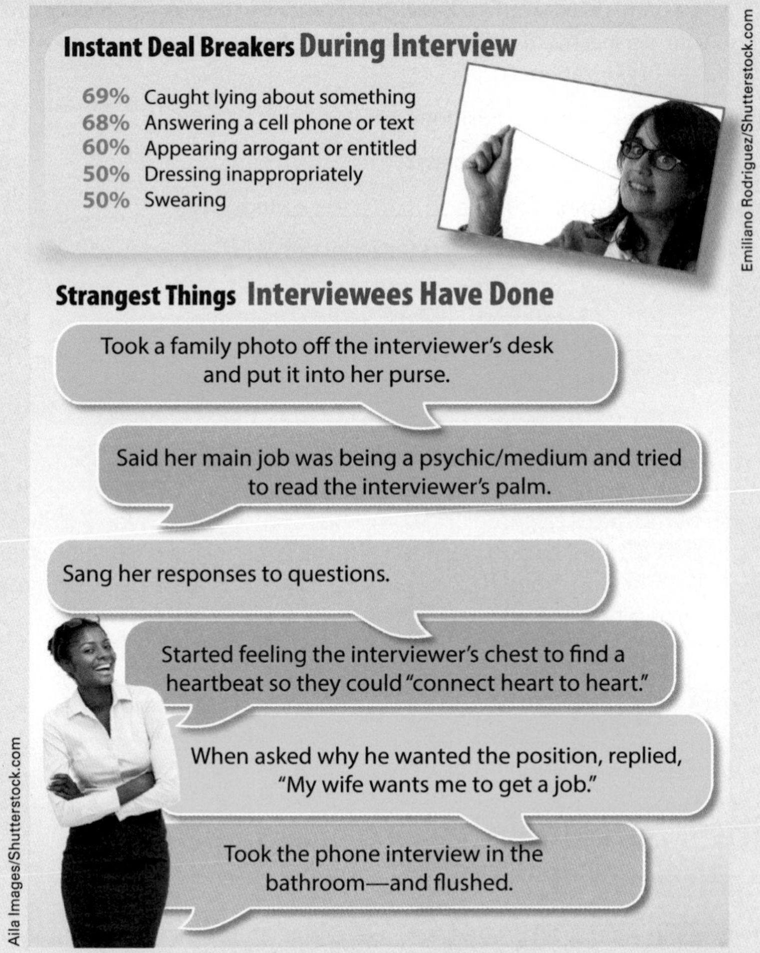

Instant Deal Breakers During Interview

- 69% Caught lying about something
- 68% Answering a cell phone or text
- 60% Appearing arrogant or entitled
- 50% Dressing inappropriately
- 50% Swearing

Emiliano Rodriguez/Shutterstock.com

Strangest Things Interviewees Have Done

Took a family photo off the interviewer's desk and put it into her purse.

Said her main job was being a psychic/medium and tried to read the interviewer's palm.

Sang her responses to questions.

Started feeling the interviewer's chest to find a heartbeat so they could "connect heart to heart."

When asked why he wanted the position, replied, "My wife wants me to get a job."

Took the phone interview in the bathroom—and flushed.

Aila Images/Shutterstock.com

Source: Based on 2015 CareerBuilder survey of more than 2,500 hiring and human resource managers. Retrieved from http://www.careerbuilder.com/share/aboutus/pressreleasesdetail.aspx?sd=1%2F14%2F2016&id=pr929&ed=12%2F31%2F2016

3. Do you prefer to work by yourself or with others? Why?
   This question can be tricky. Provide a middle-of-the-road answer that not only suggests your interpersonal qualities but also reflects an ability to make independent decisions and work without supervision.
4. What was your major in college, and why did you choose it?
5. What are some things you do in your spare time?

Questions to Gauge Your Interest

Interviewers want to understand your motivation for applying for a position. Although they will realize that you are probably interviewing for other positions, they still want to know why you are interested in this particular position with this organization. These types of questions help them determine your level of interest.

1. Why do you want to work for [name of company]?
   Questions like this illustrate why you must research an organization thoroughly before the interview. The answer to this question must prove that you understand the company and its culture. This is the perfect place to bring up the company research you did before the interview. Show what you know about the company, and discuss why you want to become a part of this organization. Describe your desire to work for this organization not only from your perspective but also from its point of view. What do you have to offer that will benefit the organization?
2. Why are you interested in this position?
3. What do you know about our company?
4. Why do you want to work in the _______________ industry?
5. What interests you about our products (or services)?

Bloomberg/Getty Images

Reality Check

Stretching the Truth

"Occasionally you bump into a talented and competent candidate . . . who's so lacking in the EQ components of humility and realness that you can't take a chance. This young man had a lot of the right stuff, but when he started telling us that he had never made a mistake in his life and didn't expect to, we knew we'd heard enough."[13]

—Jack and Suzy Welch, *management consultants and authors*

Questions About Your Experience and Accomplishments

After questions about your background and education and questions that measure your interest, the interview generally becomes more specific with questions about your experience and accomplishments. Remember to show confidence when you answer these questions. If you are not confident in your abilities, why should an employer be?

1. Why should we hire you when we have applicants with more experience or better credentials?
   In answering this question, remember that employers often hire people who present themselves well instead of others with better credentials. Emphasize your personal strengths that could be an advantage with this employer. Are you a hard worker? How can you demonstrate it? Have you had recent training? Some people have had more years of experience but actually have less knowledge because they have done the same thing over and over. Stress your experience using the latest methods and equipment. Be sure to mention your computer training and Internet savvy. Emphasize that you are open to new ideas and learn quickly. Above all, show that you are confident in your abilities.
2. Describe the most rewarding experience of your career so far.
3. How have your education and professional experiences prepared you for this position?
4. What were your major accomplishments in each of your past jobs?
5. What was a typical workday like?
6. What job functions did you enjoy most? Least? Why?

7. Tell me about your technical skills.
8. Who was the toughest boss you ever worked for and why?
9. What were your major achievements in college?
10. Why did you leave your last position? *OR:* Why are you leaving your current position?

Questions About the Future

Questions that look into the future tend to stump some candidates, especially those who have not prepared adequately. Employers ask these questions to see whether you are goal oriented and to determine whether your goals are realistic.

1. Where do you expect to be five (or ten) years from now?
   Formulate a realistic plan with respect to your present age and situation. The important thing is to be prepared for this question. It is a sure kiss of death to respond that you would like to have the interviewer's job! Instead, show an interest in the current job and in making a contribution to the organization. Talk about the levels of responsibility you would like to achieve. One employment counselor suggests showing ambition but not committing to a specific job title. Suggest that you hope to have learned enough to have progressed to a position in which you will continue to grow. Keep your answer focused on educational and professional goals, not personal goals.
2. If you got this position, what would you do to be sure you fit in?
3. This is a large (or small) organization. Do you think you would like that environment?
4. Do you plan to continue your education?
5. What do you predict for the future of the ______________ industry?
6. How do you think you can contribute to this company?
7. What would you most like to accomplish if you get this position?
8. How do you keep current with what is happening in your profession?

© Carole Martin

Reality Check

The Most Dreaded Interview Question

Job candidates fear being asked about their greatest weakness. "The best way to handle this question is to minimize the trait and emphasize the positive. Select a trait and come up with a solution to overcome your weakness. Stay away from personal qualities and concentrate more on professional traits."[14]

—Carole Martin, *veteran career coach and Monster.com writer*

Challenging Questions

The following questions may make you uncomfortable, but the important thing to remember is to answer truthfully without dwelling on your weaknesses. As quickly as possible, convert any negative response into a discussion of your strengths.

1. What is your greatest weakness?
   It is amazing how many candidates knock themselves out of the competition by answering this question poorly. Actually, you have many choices. You can present a strength as a weakness (*Some people complain that I'm a workaholic or that I'm too attentive to details*).

However, hiring managers have heard that cliché too often. Instead, mention a corrected weakness (*Because I was terrified of making presentations, I took a college course and also joined a speakers' club*). You could cite an unrelated skill (*I really need to brush up on my Spanish*). You can cite a learning objective (*One of my long-term goals is to learn more about coding and programming*). Another possibility is to reaffirm your qualifications (*I have no weaknesses that would affect my ability to do this job*).

2. What type of people do you have no patience for?
   Avoid letting yourself fall into the trap of sounding overly critical. One possible response is, *I have always gotten along well with others. But I confess that I can be irritated by complainers who don't accept responsibility.*
3. If you could live your life over, what would you change and why?
4. How would your former (or current) supervisor describe you as an employee?
5. What do you want the most from your job?
6. What is your grade point average, and does it accurately reflect your abilities?
7. Have you ever used drugs?
8. Who in your life has influenced you the most and why?
9. What are you reading right now?
10. Describe your ideal work environment.
11. Is the customer always right?
12. How do you define success?

Questions About Salary

Nearly all salaries are negotiable, depending on your qualifications. Knowing the typical salary range for the target position is very important in this negotiation. The recruiter can tell you the salary ranges—but you will have to ask. If you have had little experience, you will probably be offered a salary somewhere between the low point and the midpoint in the range. With more experience, you can negotiate for a higher figure. A word of caution, though. One personnel manager warns that candidates who emphasize money are suspect because they may leave if offered a few thousand dollars more elsewhere. See the accompanying Career Coach box for dos and don'ts in negotiating a starting salary. Here are typical salary-related questions:

1. What salary are you looking for?
   One way to handle salary questions is to ask politely to defer the discussion until it is clear that a job will be offered to you (*I'm sure when the time comes, we will be able to work out a fair compensation package. Right now, I'd rather focus on whether we have a match*). If salary comes up and you are not sure whether the job is being offered to you, it's time to be blunt. Ask, "Are you making me a job offer?" Another possible response to a salary question is to reply candidly that you can't know what to ask until you know more about the position and the company. If you continue to be pressed for a dollar figure, give a salary range with an annual dollar amount. Be sure to do research before the interview so that you know what similar jobs are paying in your geographic region. As an expert negotiator said, "In business as in life, you don't get what you deserve, you get what you negotiate."[15] See the accompanying Career Coach box for more tips on discussing salary.
2. How much are you presently earning?
3. How much do you think you are worth?
4. How much money do you expect to earn within the next ten years?
5. Are you willing to take a pay cut from your current (or previous) job?

wavebreakmedia/Shutterstock.com

Career Coach

Let's Talk Money: Salary Negotiation Dos and Don'ts

Nearly all salaries are negotiable. The following dos and don'ts can guide you to a better starting salary.

- **Do** make sure you have done your research on the salary you should expect for the position you are seeking. **Do** understand how geographic location affects salary ranges.
- **Don't** bring up salary before the employer does. **Do** delay salary negotiations until you know exactly what the position entails.
- **Do** be aware of your strengths and achievements. **Do** be sure to demonstrate the value you will bring to the employer.
- **Don't** tell the employer the salary you need to pay your bills or meet personal obligations.
- **Do** let the employer make the first salary offer. **Do**, if asked, say you expect a salary that is competitive with the market, or give a salary range that you find acceptable.
- **Don't** inflate your current earnings just to get a higher salary offer.
- **Don't** feel obligated to accept the first salary offer. **Do** negotiate salary if the offer made is inadequate.
- **Do** thank the employer for the offer when it is made. **Don't** try to negotiate right after the offer is made. **Do** take the time to consider all factors before making any job offer decisions.
- **Don't** be overly aggressive in negotiating the salary you want.
- **Don't** focus solely on salary. **Do** consider the entire compensation package.
- **Do** try to obtain other concessions (shorter review time, better title, better workspace) or benefits (bonuses, vacation time) if you aren't successful at negotiating a salary you want.
- **Don't** enter salary negotiations as part of an ego trip or game.
- **Don't** agree to the first acceptable salary offer you receive if you are not sure about the job or the company.
- **Do** get the offer in writing.

Situational Questions

Questions related to situations help employers test your thought processes and logical thinking. When using situational questions, interviewers describe a hypothetical situation and ask how you would handle it. Situational questions are based on the type of position for which you are interviewing. Knowledge of the position and the company culture will help you respond favorably to these questions. Even if the situation sounds negative, keep your response positive. Here are a few examples with possible responses to the first two:

1. How would you respond if your fellow team members strongly resisted a proposal you made in a meeting?
   You might explain the rationale behind your proposal with specific examples of the benefits that the recommendation could bring to the team. If the team continues to oppose your proposal, you should let it go and move on.
2. What would you do if you knew that your boss gave your team data that was totally wrong?
   Let's say, for example, that in a team meeting your boss provided data that had not been updated, and you recognized the error immediately. Before responding, you should confirm that your figures are correct. Then you might tactfully share the correct data in a private conversation with your boss. You could suggest that the error was an oversight perhaps caused by figures that were released after an initial report, and say that you know that your boss would want to base the team project on accurate data. You would not correct your boss in front of the team, and you would try to understand why the mistake was made.
3. Your supervisor has just told you that she is dissatisfied with your work, but you think it is acceptable. How would you resolve the conflict?
4. Your supervisor has told you to do something a certain way, and you think you know a far better way to complete the task. What would you do?

Ethics Check

As businesses increasingly emphasize workplace ethics, you may be asked to tell about a time when you were challenged ethically. One workplace compliance officer advised candidates not to respond that you have never faced an ethical challenge. "You want a candidate," he said, "who avoids misconduct, not someone who lies and says they've never done anything wrong."[16] Do you agree?

–Tim Mazur, COO of the Ethics and Compliance Officer Association

5. Assume that you are hired for this position. You soon learn that one of the staff members is extremely resentful because she applied for your position and was turned down. As a result, she is being unhelpful and obstructive. How would you handle the situation?
6. A colleague has told you in confidence that she suspects another colleague of stealing. What would your actions be?
7. You have noticed that communication between upper management and first-level employees is eroding. How would you address this problem?

Behavioral Questions

Instead of traditional interview questions, you may be asked to tell stories. The interviewer may say, *Describe a time when . . .* or *Tell me about a time when . . . .* To respond effectively, learn to use the storytelling, or STAR, technique, as illustrated in Figure 16.5. Ask yourself what the Situation or Task was, what Action you took, and what the Results were.[17] Practice using this method to recall specific examples of your skills and accomplishments. To be fully prepared, develop a coherent and articulate STAR narrative for every bullet point on your résumé. When answering behavioral questions, describe only educational and work-related situations or tasks, and try to keep them as current as possible. Here are a few examples of behavioral questions:

1. Tell me about a time when you solved a difficult problem.
   Tell a concise story explaining the situation or task, what you did, and the result. For example, *When I was at Ace Products, we continually had a problem of excessive back orders. After analyzing the situation, I discovered that orders went through many unnecessary steps. I suggested that we eliminate much paperwork. As a result, we reduced back orders by 30 percent.* Go on to emphasize what you learned and how you can apply that learning to this job. Practice your success stories in advance so that you will be ready.
2. Describe a situation in which you were able to use persuasion to convince someone to see things your way.
   The recruiter is interested in your leadership and teamwork skills. You might respond as follows: *I have learned to appreciate the fact that the way you present an idea is just as*

Figure 16.5 **Using the STAR Technique to Answer Behavioral Interview Questions**

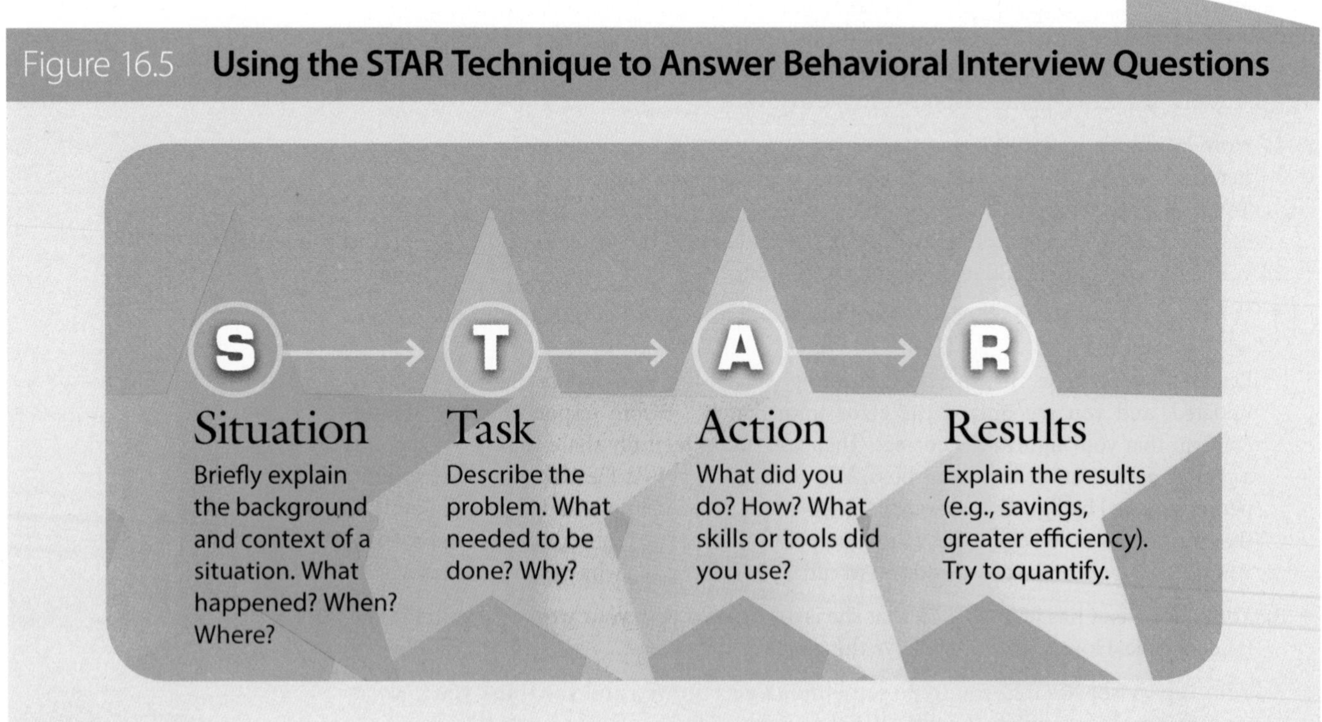

S
T
A
R
Situation
Briefly explain the background and context of a situation. What happened? When? Where?
Task
Describe the problem. What needed to be done? Why?
Action
What did you do? How? What skills or tools did you use?
Results
Explain the results (e.g., savings, greater efficiency). Try to quantify.

important as the idea itself. When trying to influence people, I put myself in their shoes and find some way to frame my idea from their perspective. I remember when I . . . .

3. Describe a time when you had to analyze information and make a recommendation.
4. Describe a time that you worked successfully as part of a team.
5. Tell me about a time that you dealt with confidential information.
6. Give me an example of a time when you were under stress to meet a deadline.
7. Tell me about a time when you had to go above and beyond the call of duty to get a job done.
8. Tell me about a time you were able to deal with another person successfully even though that individual did not like you personally (or vice versa).
9. Give me an example of when you showed initiative and took the lead.
10. Tell me about a recent situation in which you had to deal with an upset customer or coworker.

Illegal and Inappropriate Questions

U.S. federal law states that "it is illegal to discriminate against someone (applicant or employee) because of that person's race, color, religion, sex (including gender identity, sexual orientation, and pregnancy), national origin, age (40 or older), disability or genetic information."[18] Therefore, it is inappropriate for interviewers to ask any question related to these areas. These questions become illegal, though, only when a court of law determines that the employer is asking them with the intent to discriminate.[19]

Many illegal interview questions are asked innocently by inexperienced interviewers. A recent survey revealed that 20 percent of interviewers admitted that they had unknowingly asked an illegal question.[20] Some interviewers are only trying to be friendly when they inquire about your personal life or family. Regardless of the intent, how should you react? If you find the question harmless and if you want the job, go ahead and answer it. If you think that answering it would damage your chance to be hired, try to deflect the question tactfully with a response such as *Could you tell me how my marital status relates to the responsibilities of this position?* or *I prefer to keep my personal and professional lives separate.*

If you are uncomfortable answering a question, try to determine the reason behind it; you might answer, *I don't let my personal life interfere with my ability to do my job,* or, *Are you concerned with my availability to work overtime?* Another option, of course, is to respond to any inappropriate or illegal question by confronting the interviewer and threatening a lawsuit or refusing to answer. However, you could not expect to be hired under these circumstances. In any case, you might wish to reconsider working for an organization that sanctions such procedures.

Here are selected inappropriate and illegal questions that you may or may not want to answer:[21]

1. What is your marital status? Are you married? Do you live with anyone? Do you have a boyfriend (or girlfriend)? (However, employers can ask your marital status after hiring for tax and insurance forms.)
2. Do you have any disabilities? Have you had any recent illnesses? (But it is legal to ask if the person can perform specific job duties, such as *Can you carry a 50-pound sack up a 10-foot ladder five times daily?*)
3. I notice you have an accent. Where are you from? What is the origin of your last name? What is your native language? (However, it is legal to ask what languages you speak fluently if language ability is related to the job.)
4. Have you ever filed a workers' compensation claim or been injured on the job?
5. Have you ever had a drinking problem or been addicted to drugs? (But it is legal to ask if a person uses illegal drugs.)
6. Have you ever been arrested? (But it is legal to ask, *Have you ever been convicted of ____________?* when the crime is related to the job.)

7. How old are you? What is your date of birth? When did you graduate from high school? (But it is legal to ask, *Are you 16 years [or 18 years or 21 years] old or older?* depending on the age requirements for the position.)
8. Of what country are you a citizen? Are you a U.S. citizen? Where were you born? (But it is legal to ask, *Are you authorized to work in the United States?*)
9. What is your maiden name? (But it is legal to ask, *What is your full name?* or, *Have you worked under another name?*)
10. Do you have any religious beliefs that would prevent you from working weekends or holidays? (An employer can, however, ask you if you are available to work weekends and holidays or otherwise within the company's required schedule.)
11. Do you have children? Do you plan to have children? Do you have adequate child-care arrangements? (However, employers can ask for dependent information for tax and insurance purposes after you are hired. Also, they can ask if you would be able to travel or work overtime on occasion.)
12. How much do you weigh? How tall are you? (However, employers can ask you about your height and weight if minimum standards are necessary to safely perform a job.)
13. Are you in debt?
14. Do you drink socially or smoke?

Asking Your Own Questions

At some point in the interview, usually near the end, you will be asked whether you have any questions. The worst thing you can do is say *No,* which suggests that you are not interested in the position. Instead, ask questions that will help you gain information and will impress the interviewer with your thoughtfulness and interest in the position. Remember that this interview is a two-way street. You must be happy with the prospect of working for this organization. You want a position that matches your skills and personality. Use this opportunity to learn whether this job is right for you. Be aware that you don't have to wait for the interviewer to ask you for questions. You can ask your own questions throughout the interview to learn more about the company and position. Here are some questions you might ask:

1. What will my duties be (if not already discussed)?
2. Tell me what it is like working here in terms of the people, management practices, workloads, expected performance, and rewards.
3. What training programs are available from this organization? What specific training will be given for this position?
4. Who would be my immediate supervisor?
5. What is the organizational structure, and where does this position fit in?
6. Is travel required in this position?
7. How and by whom will my job performance be evaluated?
8. Assuming my work is excellent, where do you see me in five years?
9. How long do employees generally stay with this organization?
10. What are the major challenges for a person in this position?
11. What do you see in the future of this organization?
12. May I have a tour of the facilities?
13. This job seems to be exactly what I'd really like to do. Do we have a fit here?
14. What is the next step in the hiring process?
15. When do you expect to make a decision?

Ending Positively

After you have asked your questions, the interviewer will signal the end of the interview, usually by standing up or by expressing appreciation that you came. If not addressed earlier, you should at this time find out what action will follow. Career coach Don Georgevich recommends asking the interviewer when a decision will be made and whether you may follow up. "Interviewers always say yes," he reports, "and now you have permission to call them. In fact, they will expect your call."[22] This is not the time to be shy. Too many candidates leave the interview without knowing their status or when they will hear from the recruiter.

Before you leave, summarize your strongest qualifications, show your enthusiasm for obtaining this position, and thank the interviewer for a constructive interview and for considering you for the position. Ask the interviewer for a business card, which will provide the information you need to write a thank-you message.

Shake the interviewer's hand with confidence, and acknowledge anyone else you see on the way out. Be sure to thank the receptionist. Departing gracefully and enthusiastically will leave a lasting impression on those responsible for making the final hiring decision.

After the Interview

LEARNING OUTCOME 4

Describe what to do *after* an interview, including thanking the interviewer, contacting references, and writing follow-up messages.

After leaving the interview, immediately make notes of what was said in case you are called back for a second interview. Write down key points that were discussed, the names of people you spoke with, and other details of the interview. Ask yourself what went really well and what you could improve. Note your strengths and weaknesses during the interview so that you can work to improve in future interviews.

Sending a Thank-You Message

After a job interview, you should always send a thank-you message. Why? This courtesy sets you apart from other applicants, most of whom will not bother. In addition, more than one in five hiring managers say they are *less* likely to hire a candidate who *doesn't* follow up an interview with a message.[23] Your message also reminds the interviewer of your visit and shows your good manners and genuine enthusiasm for the job.

Generally, you have three options for your message: a handwritten note card, a word-processed letter on bond paper, or an e-mail. No texts. Handwritten cards are always impressive. However, 89 percent of the managers in one survey said that sending a thank-you note in the form of an e-mail was altogether acceptable.[24] Your preparation and knowledge of the company culture will help you determine whether a traditional thank-you letter sent by mail or an e-mail is more appropriate. If you choose e-mail, make sure that you use professional language, standard capitalization, and proper punctuation.

© Jenny Foss

Reality Check

Wowing the Interviewer With a Thank-You From the Parking Lot

"Thank-you notes matter: They give you a terrific opportunity to follow up with the decision-maker right away. I encourage job seekers to get thank-you notes out (to each individual they've met in the interview process) immediately after the interview. Same day. From your laptop in the parking lot, if you really want to wow them."[25]

—Jenny Foss, *job search strategist, career coach*

Your message will be most effective if sent immediately after your interview. In your message, refer to the date of the interview, the exact title of the job for which you were interviewed, and specific topics discussed. Try to mention something you liked about the interview such as *Job interviews can be stressful, but you made me feel comfortable, and I am grateful for that.* Avoid worn-out phrases such as *Thank you for taking the time to interview me.* Be careful, too, about overusing *I*, especially to begin sentences. Most important, show that you really want the job and that you are qualified for it. Notice how the letter in Figure 16.6 conveys enthusiasm and confidence.

If you have been interviewed by more than one person, send a separate thank-you message to each interviewer.

Figure 16.6 **Interview Follow-Up Message**

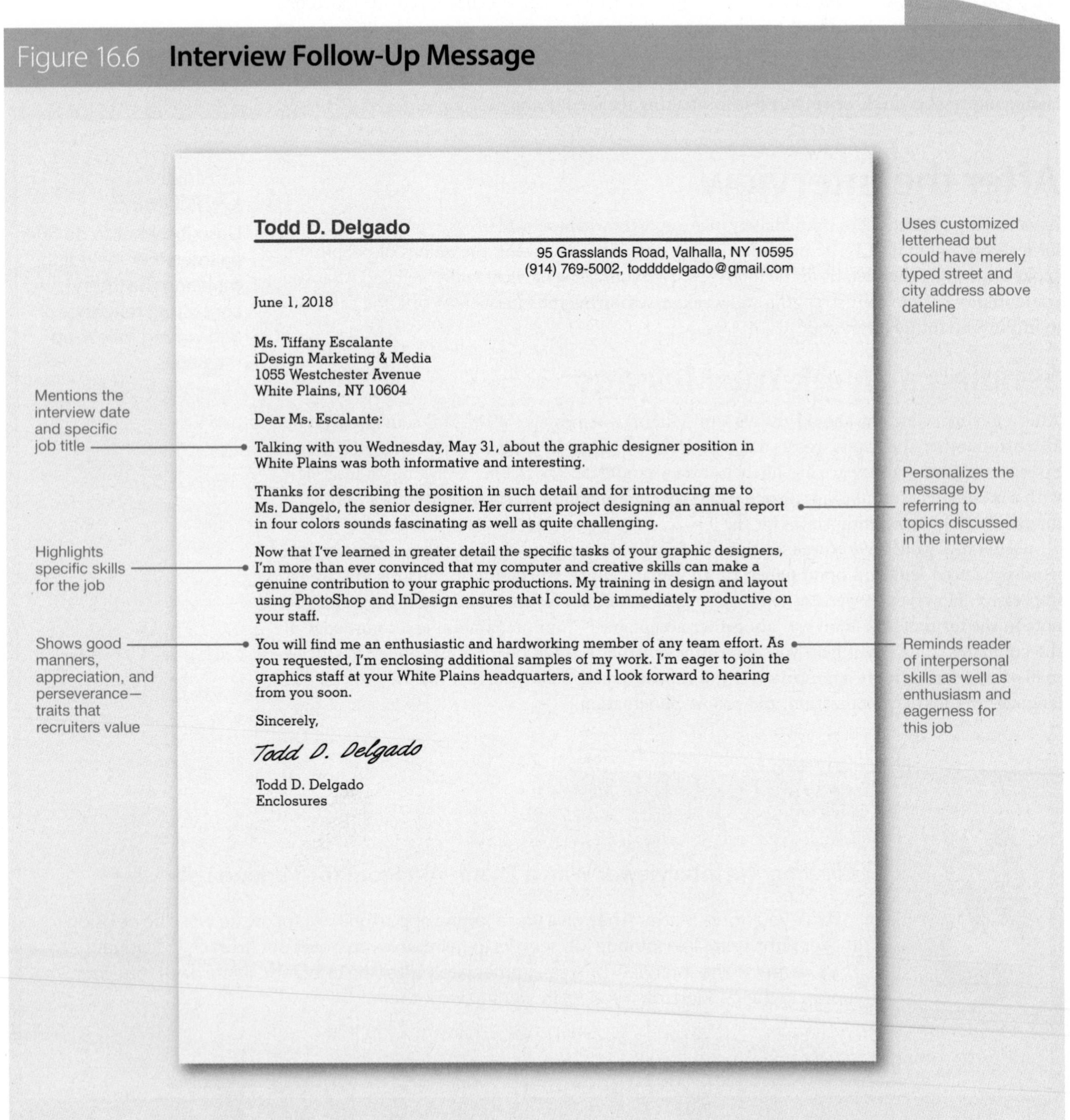
Todd D. Delgado

95 Grasslands Road, Valhalla, NY 10595
(914) 769-5002, toddddelgado@gmail.com

June 1, 2018

Ms. Tiffany Escalante
iDesign Marketing & Media
1055 Westchester Avenue
White Plains, NY 10604

Dear Ms. Escalante:

Talking with you Wednesday, May 31, about the graphic designer position in White Plains was both informative and interesting.

Thanks for describing the position in such detail and for introducing me to Ms. Dangelo, the senior designer. Her current project designing an annual report in four colors sounds fascinating as well as quite challenging.

Now that I've learned in greater detail the specific tasks of your graphic designers, I'm more than ever convinced that my computer and creative skills can make a genuine contribution to your graphic productions. My training in design and layout using PhotoShop and InDesign ensures that I could be immediately productive on your staff.

You will find me an enthusiastic and hardworking member of any team effort. As you requested, I'm enclosing additional samples of my work. I'm eager to join the graphics staff at your White Plains headquarters, and I look forward to hearing from you soon.

Sincerely,

Todd D. Delgado

Todd D. Delgado
Enclosures

Uses customized letterhead but could have merely typed street and city address above dateline
Mentions the interview date and specific job title
Personalizes the message by referring to topics discussed in the interview
Highlights specific skills for the job
Shows good manners, appreciation, and perseverance—traits that recruiters value
Reminds reader of interpersonal skills as well as enthusiasm and eagerness for this job

Contacting Your References

Once you have thanked your interviewer, it is time to alert your references that they may be contacted by the employer. You might also have to request a letter of recommendation to be sent to the employer by a certain date. As discussed in Chapter 15, you should have already asked permission to use these individuals as references, and you should have supplied them with a copy of your résumé and information about the types of positions you are seeking

To provide the best possible recommendation, your references need information. What position have you applied for with what company? What should they stress to the prospective employer? Let's say you are applying for a specific job that requires a letter of recommendation. Professor Patel has already agreed to be a reference for you. To get the best letter of recommendation from Professor Patel, help her out. Write an e-mail or letter telling her about the position, its requirements, and the recommendation deadline. Include copies of your résumé, college transcript, and, if applicable, the job posting or ad with detailed information about the opening. You might remind her of a positive experience with you that she could use in the recommendation. Remember that recommenders need evidence to support generalizations. Give them appropriate ammunition, as the student has done in the following request:

Dear Professor Patel:

Recently I interviewed for the position of administrative assistant in the Human Resources Department of Host International. Because you kindly agreed to help me, I am now asking you to write a letter of recommendation to Host.

In a reference request letter, tell immediately why you are writing. Identify the target position and company.

The position calls for good organizational, interpersonal, and writing skills, as well as computer experience. To help you review my skills and training, I enclose my résumé. As you may recall, I earned an A in your business communication class last fall; and you commended my long report for its clarity and organization.

Specify the job requirements so that the recommender knows what to stress.

Please send your letter to Mr. Marquis Jones at Host International before July 1 in the enclosed stamped, addressed envelope. I'm grateful for your support and promise to let you know the results of my job search.

Provide a stamped, addressed envelope.

Sincerely,

Following Up

If you don't hear from the interviewer within five days, or at the specified time, consider following up. Of course, if you have remembered to ask the interviewer when a decision is expected and whether you may follow up, you are all set. Otherwise, the standard advice to job candidates is to contact the interviewer with a follow-up e-mail or phone call.

An e-mail to find out how the decision process is going may be your best bet because such a message is less intrusive than a phone call. An e-mail message also gives the interviewer time to look up your status information, leaves a paper trail, and eliminates annoying phone tag.[26] The following follow-up e-mail message would impress the interviewer:

Dear Ms. Escalante:

I enjoyed my interview with you last Wednesday for the graphic designer position. You should know that I'm very interested in this opportunity with iDesign Marketing & Media. Because you mentioned that you might have an answer this week, I'm eager to know how your decision process is coming along. I look forward to hearing from you.

Inquire courteously; don't sound demanding or desperate.

Sincerely,

If you follow up by phone, say something like, *I'm calling to find out the status of your search for the ____________ position.* Or you could say, *I'm wondering what else I can do to convince you that I'm the right person for this job.* It's important to sound professional and courteous. Sounding desperate, angry, or frustrated that you have not been contacted can ruin your chances.

Depending on the response you get to your first follow-up request, you may have to follow up additional times. Keep in mind, though, that some employers won't tell you about their hiring decision unless you are the one hired. Don't harass the interviewer, and don't force a decision. If you don't hear back from an employer within several weeks after following up, it is best to assume that you didn't get the job, and you should continue your job search.

LEARNING OUTCOME 5

Prepare additional employment documents such as applications, rejection follow-up messages, acceptance messages, and resignation letters.

Preparing Additional Employment Documents

Although the résumé and cover letter are your major tasks, other important documents and messages are often required during the job-search process. You may need to complete an employment application form and write follow-up letters. You might also have to write a letter of resignation when leaving a job. Because each of these tasks reveals something about you and your communication skills, you will want to put your best foot forward. These documents often subtly influence company officials to offer a job.

Application Form

Some organizations require job candidates to fill out application forms instead of, or in addition to, submitting résumés. This practice permits them to gather and store standardized data about each applicant. Whether the application is on paper or online, follow the directions carefully and provide accurate information. The following suggestions can help you be prepared:

- Carry a card summarizing vital statistics not included on your résumé. If you are asked to fill out an application form in an employer's office, you will need a handy reference to the following data: graduation dates; beginning and ending dates of all employment; salary history; full names, titles, and present work addresses of former supervisors; full addresses and phone numbers of current and previous employers; and full names, occupational titles, occupational addresses, and telephone numbers of people who have agreed to serve as references.
- Look over all the questions before starting.
- If filling out a paper form, write neatly using blue or black ink. Many career counselors recommend printing your responses; cursive handwriting can be difficult to read.
- Answer all questions honestly. Write *Not applicable* or *N/A* if appropriate. Don't leave any sections blank.
- Use accurate spelling, grammar, capitalization, and punctuation.
- If asked for the position desired, give a specific job title or type of position. Don't say, *Anything* or *Open*. These answers make you look unfocused; moreover, they make it difficult for employers to know what you are qualified for or interested in.
- Be prepared for a salary question. Unless you know what comparable employees are earning in the company, the best strategy is to suggest a salary range or to write *Negotiable* or *Open*.
- Be prepared to explain the reasons for leaving previous positions. Use positive or neutral phrases such as *Relocation, Seasonal, To accept a position with more responsibility, Temporary position, To continue education,* or *Career change*. Avoid words or phrases such as *Fired, Quit, Didn't get along with supervisor,* and *Pregnant*.
- Look over the application before submitting to make sure it is complete and that you have followed all instructions.

Application or Résumé Follow-Up Message

If your résumé or application generates no response within a reasonable time, you may decide to send a short follow-up e-mail or letter such as the following. Doing so (a) jogs the memory of the personnel officer, (b) demonstrates your serious interest, and (c) allows you to emphasize your qualifications or to add new information.

Dear Ms. Gutierrez:

Please know I am still interested in becoming an administrative support specialist with Quad, Inc.

Open by reminding the reader of your interest.

Since submitting an application [or résumé] in May, I have completed my degree and have been employed as a summer replacement for office workers in several downtown offices. This experience has honed my word processing and communication skills. It has also introduced me to a wide range of office procedures.

Review your strengths or add new qualifications.

Please keep my application in your active file and let me know when my formal training, technical skills, and practical experience can go to work for you.

Close positively; avoid accusations that make the reader defensive.

Sincerely,

Rejection Follow-Up Message

If you didn't get the job and you think it was perfect for you, don't give up. Employment specialists encourage applicants to respond to a rejection. The candidate who was offered the position may decline, or other positions may open up. In a rejection follow-up e-mail or letter, it is OK to admit that you are disappointed. Be sure to add, however, that you are still interested and will contact the company again in a month in case a job opens up. Then follow through for a couple of months—but don't overdo it. You should be professional and persistent, not annoying. Here is an example of an effective rejection follow-up message:

Dear Mr. O'Leary:

Although disappointed that someone else was selected for your accounting position, I appreciate your promptness and courtesy in notifying me.

Subordinate your disappointment to your appreciation at being notified promptly and courteously.

Because I am confident that you would benefit from my technical and interpersonal skills in your fast-paced environment, please consider keeping my résumé in your active file. My desire to become a productive member of your Transamerica staff remains strong.

Emphasize your continuing interest.

Our interview on ______ was very enjoyable, and I especially appreciate the time you and Ms. Goldstein spent describing your company's expansion into international markets. To enhance my qualifications, I have enrolled in a course in international accounting at CSU.

Refer to specifics of your interview.

Should you have an opening for which I am qualified, you may reach me at (818) 719-3901. In the meantime, I will call you in a month to discuss employment possibilities.

Take the initiative; tell when you will call for an update.

Sincerely,

Job Acceptance and Rejection Message

When all your hard work pays off, you will be offered the position you want. Although you will likely accept the position over the phone, it is a good idea to follow up with an acceptance e-mail or letter to confirm the details and to formalize the acceptance. Your acceptance message might look like this:

Dear Ms. Reed:

Confirm your acceptance of the position with enthusiasm.

It was a pleasure talking with you earlier today. As I mentioned, I am delighted to accept the position of project manager with Innovative Creations, Inc., in your Seattle office. I look forward to becoming part of the IC team and starting work on a variety of exciting and innovative projects.

Review salary and benefits details.

As we agreed, my starting salary will be $46,000, with a full benefits package including health and life insurance, retirement plan, and two weeks of vacation per year.

Include the specific starting date.

I look forward to starting my position with Innovative Creations on September 15, 2018. Before that date I will send you the completed tax and insurance forms you need. Thanks again for this opportunity, Ms. Reed.

Sincerely,

If you must turn down a job offer, show your professionalism by writing a sincere letter. This letter should thank the employer for the job offer and explain briefly that you are turning it down. Taking the time to extend this courtesy could help you in the future if this employer has a position you really want. Here's an example of a job rejection letter:

Dear Mr. Rosen:

Thank the employer for the job offer and decline the offer without giving specifics.

Thank you very much for offering me the position of sales representative with Bendall Pharmaceuticals. It was a difficult decision to make, but I have accepted a position with another company.

Express gratitude and best wishes for the future.

I appreciate your taking the time to interview me, and I wish Bendall much success in the future.

Sincerely,

Resignation Letter

After you have been in a position for a period of time, you may find it necessary to leave. Perhaps you have been offered a better position, or maybe you have decided to return to school full-time. Whatever the reason, you should leave your position gracefully and tactfully. Although you will likely discuss your resignation in person with your supervisor, it is a good idea to document your resignation by writing a formal letter. Some resignation letters are brief, while others contain great detail. Remember that many resignation letters are placed in personnel files; therefore, you should format and write yours using the professional business letter–writing techniques you learned earlier. Here is an example of a basic letter of resignation:

Dear Ms. Byrne:

Confirm the exact date of resignation. Remind the employer of your contributions.

This letter serves as formal notice of my resignation from Allied Corporation, effective Friday, August 15. I have enjoyed serving as your project manager for the past two years, and I am grateful for everything I have learned during my employment with Allied.

Offer assistance to prepare for your resignation.

Please let me know what I can do over the next two weeks to help you prepare for my departure. I would be happy to help with finding and training my replacement.

End with thanks and a forward-looking statement.

Thanks again for providing such a positive employment experience. I will long remember my time here.

Sincerely,

Although the employee who wrote the preceding resignation letter gave the standard two-week notice, you may find that a longer notice is necessary. The higher your position and the greater your responsibility, the longer the notice you give your employer should be. You should, however, always give some notice as a courtesy.

Writing job acceptance, job rejection, and resignation letters requires effort. That effort, however, is worth it because you are building bridges that may carry you to even better jobs in the future.

Your Turn: Applying Your Skills

Yeamake/Shutterstock.com

You have begun to apply for internships in your chosen field and want to be prepared if one of the organizations contacts you for an interview. You decide to begin thinking about transferable skills you have developed in school. You also think you should develop success stories or illustrations of the three basic skills that career coach Don Georgevich says all employers want: communication skills, computer skills, and people skills.

Your Task

List two or more anecdotes that illustrate each of the following: your communication skills, your computer skills, and your people skills. Think about experiences you have had at jobs, while volunteering, or in school that show you possess each characteristic. Remember that even entry-level and low-wage jobs such as babysitting and waiting tables provide opportunities to develop career-related skills. Then practice with a classmate until you can retell each story in an articulate and confident manner. Revise your list, improving the content and delivery. Your instructor may have you submit your list or recite your success stories in class.

Summary of Learning Outcomes

1 Explain trends, purposes, sequence, and types of job interviews, including screening, one-on-one, panel, group, sequential, and video interviews.

- Current trends in interviewing include (a) early-stage screening by technology; (b) longer, multiple interviews; (c) on-the-spot interviewing; (d) psychometric and skills tests; (e) behavioral and situational questions; and (f) group interviews.
- As a job candidate, you have the following purposes in an interview: (a) convince the employer of your potential, (b) learn more about the job and the company, and (c) expand on the information in your résumé.
- From the employer's perspective, the interview is an opportunity to (a) assess your abilities in relation to the requirements for the position; (b) discuss your training, experience, knowledge, and abilities in more detail; (c) see what drives and motivates you; and (d) decide whether you would fit into the organization.
- Screening interviews, conducted by telephone or video, seek to eliminate less qualified candidates.
- Hiring/placement interviews may be one-on-one, panel, group, sequential, or video.

2 **Describe what to do *before* an interview, including ensuring professional phone techniques, researching the target company, rehearsing success stories, cleaning up digital dirt, dressing properly, and fighting fear.**

- Prepare for telephone screening interviews by ensuring professional answering techniques and screening incoming calls.
- Make the first conversation impressive by using professional, businesslike language, and having your résumé, a calendar, and a list of your references handy.
- Research the target company by scouring the Internet and the company's advertising to learn about its products, history, mission, goals, size, geographic locations, employees, customers, competitors, culture, management structure, reputation in the community, finances, strengths, weaknesses, and future plans.
- Strive to locate inside information through social media.
- Rehearse 30-second success stories that demonstrate your qualifications and achievements.
- Check your online presence and strive to clean up any digital dirt.
- Decide what to wear to the interview by asking the interviewer what is appropriate.
- To reduce fear before an interview, remind yourself that you are thoroughly prepared and that interviewing is a two-way street.

3 **Describe what to do *during* an interview, including controlling nonverbal messages and answering typical interview questions.**

- During your interview send positive nonverbal messages by controlling body movements, showing good posture, maintaining eye contact, using gestures effectively, and smiling enough to convey a positive, professional attitude.
- Listen attentively, turn off your cell phone or other electronic devices, don't chew gum, and sound enthusiastic and sincere.
- Be prepared to respond to traditional inquiries such as *Tell me about yourself.*
- Practice answering typical questions such as why you want to work for the organization, why you should be hired, how your education and experience have prepared you for the position, where you expect to be in five or ten years, what your greatest weaknesses are, and how much money you expect to earn.
- Be ready for situational questions that ask you to respond to hypothetical situations. Expect behavioral questions that begin with *Tell me about a time when you* . . . .
- Think about how you would respond to illegal or inappropriate questions, as well as questions you would ask about the job.
- End the interview positively by summarizing your strongest qualifications, showing enthusiasm for obtaining the position, thanking the interviewer, asking what the next step is, and requesting permission to follow up.

4 **Describe what to do *after* an interview, including thanking the interviewer, contacting references, and writing follow-up messages.**

- After leaving the interview, immediately make notes of the key points discussed.
- Note your strengths and weaknesses during the interview so that you can work to improve in future interviews.
- Write a thank-you letter, card, or e-mail including the date of the interview, the exact job title for which you were interviewed, specific topics discussed, and gratitude for the interview.
- Alert your references that they may be contacted.
- If you don't hear from the interviewer when expected, call or send an e-mail to follow up. Sound professional, not desperate, angry, or frustrated.

5 Prepare additional employment documents such as applications, rejection follow-up messages, acceptance messages, and resignation letters.

- When filling out an application form, look over all the questions before starting.
- If asked for a salary figure, provide a salary range or write *Negotiable* or *Open*.
- If you don't get the job, consider writing a letter that expresses your disappointment but also your desire to be contacted in case a job opens up.
- If you are offered a job, write a letter that confirms the details and formalizes your acceptance.
- When refusing a position, write a sincere letter turning down the job offer.
- Upon resigning from a position, write a letter that confirms the date of resignation, offers assistance to prepare for your resignation, and expresses thanks.

Critical Thinking

1. Online psychometric and skills tests with multiple-choice questionnaires have become a hot trend in interviewing today. Employers may ask not only how applicants would handle tricky situations, but also how happy they are or how much they have stolen from their previous employer. The multiple-choice format poses a dilemma for applicants because they don't know whether to be truthful or say what the employer might want to hear. Is this practice fair? What are some advantages and disadvantages of this practice? (L.O. 1, 2)
2. Like criminal background checks and drug tests, social media background checks have become commonplace in today's recruiting. What are the pros and cons of conducting such checks as a primary or sole means of screening applicants?[27]
3. If you are asked an illegal interview question, why is it important to first assess the intentions of the interviewer?
4. Why is it a smart strategy to thank an interviewer, to follow up, and even to send a rejection follow-up message? Are any risks associated with this strategy?
5. **Ethical Issue:** A recruiter for an organization has an outstanding prospect for a position. As part of his screening process, the recruiter checks the online presence of the candidate and discovers from her social networks that she is 18 weeks pregnant—and happily so. He knows that the target position involves a big project that will go live just about the time she will be taking maternity leave. He decides not to continue the hiring process with this candidate. Is his action legal? Ethical? What lesson could be learned about posting private information online?

Activities

Note: All Documents for Analysis are provided at **www.cengagebrain.com** for you to download and revise.

16.1 Document for Analysis: Camille's Poor Interview Follow-Up Letter (L.O. 4)

Team

YOUR TASK Study the following poorly written interview follow-up letter. In teams or in a class discussion, list at least five weaknesses. It has problems with punctuation, wordiness, proofreading, capitalization, sentence structure, and other writing techniques you have studied.

1340 East Phillips Avenue
Apartment D
Littleton, CO 80126
June 17, 2018

Ms. Michelle Genovese
High Country Accounting
2810 East Sixth Avenue
Denver, CO 80218-3453

Dear Ms. Genovese:

It was altogether extremely enjoyable to talk with you about the open position at High Country Accounting. The position as you presented it seems to be a excellent match for my training and skills. The creative approach to Account Management that you described, confirmed my desire to work in a imaginative firm such as High County Accounting.

I would bring to the position strong organizational skills, and I have the ability to encourage others to work cooperatively within the department. My training in analysis and application of accounting data and financial reporting; as well as my experience as a financial consultant in the mortgage industry would enable me to help with the backlog of client projects that you mentioned.

I certainly understand your departments need for strong support in the administrative area. I am definitely attentive to details and my organizational skills will help to free you to deal with more pressing issues in the management area. I neglected to emphasize during our very interesting interview that I also have a minor in finance despite the fact that it was on my résumé.

Thanks for taking the time to interview me, and explain the goals of your agency along with the dutys of this position. As I am sure you noticed during the interview I am very interested in working for High Country Accounting because I need to get a job to start paying off my student loans, and look forward to hearing from you about this position. In the event that you might possibly need additional information from me or facts about me, all you need to do is shoot me an e-mail.

Sincerely,

Camille Montano

16.2 What Social Media Info Turns Interviewers On or Off? (L.O. 1, 2)

E-Mail Social Media

Team

Hiring managers are increasingly searching social media sites to research job candidates. A recent CareerBuilder survey reveals that most hiring managers aren't intentionally looking for digital dirt. Six in ten employers say they are merely looking for information about candidates "that supports their qualifications for the job."[28]

Surprisingly, it may not be what they find but what is missing that matters. More than four in ten hiring managers say "they are less likely to interview job candidates if they are unable to find information about that person online." Hiring managers who did find social media information online revealed that the following negative items turned them off:

Social Media Behavior Hurting Job Seekers

Provocative or inappropriate photographs, videos, or information	46 percent
Information about candidate drinking or using drugs	43 percent
Discriminatory comments related to race, religion, gender, etc.	33 percent
Complaints about previous company or fellow employees	31 percent
Poor communication skills	29 percent

Conversely, social media behavior that impresses recruiters includes the following positive impressions: candidate's background information supported job qualifications (44 percent), candidate's site conveyed a professional image (44 percent), candidate's personality came across as a good fit with company culture (43 percent), candidate was well-rounded and showed a wide range of interests (40 percent), and candidate had great communication skills (36 percent).

YOUR TASK Conduct a social media audit in your course. Armed with the knowledge acquired in this chapter and the information in this activity, critically evaluate fellow students' social media sites such as Facebook, Instagram, Google+, Twitter, and LinkedIn. In pairs or larger groups, look for positive attributes as well as negative qualities that may repel hiring managers. Report your findings orally or compile them in an e-mail or memo. If you identify negative behavior, discuss remedies such as how to remove offensive material.

16.3 Employing Social Media to Investigate Jobs (L.O. 2)

Social Media

Blogs and social media sites such as Facebook, Twitter, and LinkedIn are becoming important tools in the job-search process. By accessing blogs, company Facebook pages, LinkedIn pages, and Twitter feeds, job seekers can locate much insider information about a company's culture and day-to-day activities.

YOUR TASK Using the Web, locate a blog that is maintained by an employee of a company where you might like to work. Monitor the blog for at least a week. Also, access the company's Facebook and Instagram pages, check its LinkedIn presence, and monitor any Twitter feeds for at least a week. Prepare a short report summarizing what you learned about the company through reading the blog postings, status updates, and tweets. Include a statement of whether this information would be valuable during your job search.

16.4 Digging for Digital Dirt: Keeping a Low Profile Online (L.O. 2)

Social Media

Before embarking on your job hunt, you should find out what employers might find if they searched your personal life in cyberspace, specifically on Facebook, Instagram, Twitter, and so forth. Running your name through Google and other search engines, particularly enclosed in quotation marks to lower the number of hits, is usually the first step. To learn even more, try some of the people-search sites such as 123people, Snitch.name, and PeekYou. They collect information from a number of search engines, websites, and social networks.

YOUR TASK Use Google, 123people, and another search tool to explore the Web for your full name, enclosed in quotation marks. In Google, don't forget to run an *Images* search at **http://www.google.com/images** to find any photos of questionable taste. If your instructor requests, share your insights with the class—not the salacious details, but general observations—or write a short memo summarizing the results.

16.5 Using Glassdoor to Prepare for Interviews and Find Salary Data (L.O. 1, 2)

E-Mail | Social Media | Web

You may be familiar with LinkedIn, the social network devoted to all things career. Perhaps you have a profile on LinkedIn. However, did you know that Glassdoor is another superb source of job-search information, postings, and reviews? In anonymous posts, Glassdoor dishes on company reviews, salary comparisons, CEO approval ratings, interviews, and more. If you want authentic insider data about job interviews and other invaluable information, check out Glassdoor.

Let's say you wish to know what LinkedIn is like as an employer and how happy applicants are with LinkedIn's interview process. You would search on the company by name and could refine your search by targeting a specific job title and location. You would see that at 4.6, the career network has a high rating overall and that its CEO Jeff Weiner has achieved a stellar 98 percent approval rating.

YOUR TASK At the Glassdoor site, search for your dream employer. You can select from industries or search for companies by name. Examine the reviews and the interview modalities. How happy are interviewees and current workers with their employer? Share your results with the class and, if asked, report your findings in a document—a memo, e-mail, or informal report.

16.6 Yes, You Can Interview People in Fewer Than 140 Characters! (L.O. 1, 3)

Social Media | Team | Web

Digital marketing strategist, angel investor, and best-selling author Jay Baer published an e-book, *The Best of Twitter 20* that presents 22 Twitter interviews (twitterviews) he conducted with social media luminaries. The experts, to whom Baer posed 20 questions in no more than 140 characters within approximately 90 minutes, include Joseph Jaffe, Gary Vaynerchuk, Spike Jones, and Amber Naslund.

YOUR TASK Search for a phrase such as *Baer and The Twitter 20*. Visit Baer's blog Convince & Convert, download the free e-book, or read it online. You can also access the individual links on Baer's website, taking you directly to the social media expert of your choice. Study the twitterviews. Then, if your instructor directs, team up for a role-play, in which one student acts as the interviewer and the other plays the interviewee. The roles can be switched after a while. Prepare at least five concise career-related questions that you will convert into tweets. In turn, your counterpart will tweet back his or her answers. If you don't want to use a live Twitter feed, type up your tweets in a word processing program that will allow you to count characters. You can model your list of tweets on Baer's transcript format.

16.7 Building Interview Skills With Worksheets (L.O. 3)

Successful interviews require diligent preparation and repeated practice. To be well prepared, you need to know what skills are required for your targeted position. In addition to computer and communication skills, employers generally want to know whether you work well with a team, accept responsibility, solve problems, are efficient, meet deadlines, show leadership, save time and money, and are a hard worker.

YOUR TASK Consider a position for which you are eligible now or one for which you will be eligible when you complete your education. Identify the skills and traits necessary for this position. If you prepared a résumé in Chapter 15, be sure that it addresses these targeted areas. Now prepare interview worksheets listing at least ten technical and other skills or traits you think a recruiter will want to discuss in an interview for your targeted position.

16.8 Telling Success Stories (L.O. 3)

You can best showcase your talents if you are ready with your own success stories that illustrate how you have developed the skills or traits required for your targeted position.

YOUR TASK Using the worksheets you prepared in **Activity 16.7**, prepare success stories that highlight the required skills or traits. Select three to five stories to develop into answers to potential interview questions. For example, here is a typical question: *How does your background relate to the position we have open?* A possible response: *As you know, I have just completed an intensive training program in ____________. In addition, I have over three years of part-time work experience in a variety of business settings. In one position I was selected to manage a small business in the absence of the owner. I developed responsibility and customer service skills in filling orders efficiently, resolving shipping problems, and monitoring key accounts. I also inventoried and organized products worth over $200,000. When the owner returned from a vacation to Florida, I was commended for increasing sales and was given a bonus in recognition of my efforts.* People relate to and remember stories. Try to shape your answers into memorable stories.

16.9 Talent Assessments: Evaluating Job Scenarios (L.O. 1, 2)

Web

What do Macy's, PetSmart, Radio Shack, Walmart, and Burger King have in common? They use preemployment testing to identify applicants who will fit into the organization. Unlike classical aptitude tests that began in the military, today's online multiple-choice tests assess integrity, collegiality, and soft skills in general.

To give you a flavor of these talent assessments, here are three typical scenarios:

1. You have learned that eye contact is important in communication. How much eye contact should you have when conversing with someone in a professional environment?

A At all times. You want to make sure the person knows you are paying attention.

B About 60-70 percent of the time

C Every now and then. You don't want to make the other person uncomfortable.

D About half the time

2. You are attending an important meeting with colleagues who are more senior than you are. How much should you speak at the meeting?

A You should look very interested but not speak at all unless they request it.

B You should speak only when the topic is in your area of expertise.

C You should try to talk as much as possible to show your knowledge.

D You should speak in the beginning of the meeting and every now and then.

3. You just found out that people at work are spreading a bad rumor about you that is untrue. How would you respond?

A Tell everybody that it is not true. You need to clear your name.

B Don't react to it at all. It'll blow over eventually.

C Find out who started it so you talk to them to make sure that they will never do it again.

D Talk to others about another coworker's rumor so people will forget about yours.

YOUR TASK Answer the questions; then compare your answers with those of your classmates. Discuss the scenarios. What specific skills or attributes might each question be designed to measure? Do you think such questions are effective? What might be the best way to respond to the scenarios? Your instructor may share the correct answers with you. If your instructor directs, search the Web for more talent assessment questions. Alternatively, your instructor might ask you to create your own workplace (or college) scenarios to help you assess an applicant's soft skills. As a class you could compare questions/scenarios and quiz each other.

16.10 Getting Ready to Wear Interview Attire (L.O. 2, 3)

Web

As you prepare for your interview by learning about the company and the industry, don't forget a key component of interview success: creating a favorable first impression by wearing appropriate business attire. Job seekers often have nebulous ideas about proper interview wear. Some wardrobe mishaps include choosing a conservative power suit but accessorizing it with beat-up casual shoes or a shabby bag. Grooming glitches include dandruff on dark suit fabric, dirty fingernails, and mothball odor. Women sometimes wrongly assume that any black clothing items are acceptable, even if they are too tight, revealing, sheer, or made of low-end fabrics. Most image consultants agree that workplace attire falls into three main categories: business formal, business casual, and casual. Only business formal is considered proper interview apparel.

YOUR TASK To prepare for your big day, search the Web for descriptions and images of *business formal*. You may research *business casual* and *casual* styles, but for an interview, always dress on the side of caution—conservatively. Compare prices and look for suit sales to buy one or two attractive interview outfits. Share your findings (notes, images, and price range for suits, solid shoes, and accessories) with the class and your instructor.

16.11 Rehearsing Answers to Interview Questions (L.O. 3)

Team

Practice makes perfect in interviewing. The more often you rehearse responses to typical interview questions, the closer you are to getting the job.

YOUR TASK Select three questions from each of the following question categories discussed in this chapter: questions to get acquainted, questions to gauge your interest, questions about your experience and accomplishments, questions about the future, and challenging questions. Write your answers to each set of questions. Try to incorporate skills and traits required for the targeted position, and include success stories where appropriate. Polish these answers and your delivery technique by practicing in front of a mirror or by making an audio or video recording. Your instructor may choose this assignment as a group activity in class.

16.12 Anticipating Situational Interview Questions (L.O. 3)

Team Web

Situational interview questions can vary widely from position to position. You should know enough about a position to understand some of the typical situations you would encounter on a regular basis.

YOUR TASK Use your favorite search tool to locate typical descriptions of a position in which you are interested. Based on these descriptions, develop a list of six to eight typical situations someone in this position would face; then write situational interview questions for each of these scenarios. In pairs, role-play interviewer and interviewee, alternating with each question.

16.13 Examining Behavioral Interview Questions (L.O. 3)

Team 

Behavioral interview questions are increasingly popular, and you will need a little practice before you can answer them easily.

YOUR TASK Use your favorite search tool to locate lists of behavioral questions on the Internet. Select five skill areas such as communication, teamwork, and decision making. For each skill area, find three behavioral questions that you think would be effective in an interview. In pairs, role-play interviewer and interviewee, alternating with each question. You goal is to answer effectively in one or two minutes. Remember to use the STAR method when answering.

16.14 Negotiating a Salary (L.O. 3)

Team

Negotiating a *salary can be* tricky. You want to get what you're worth, but you don't want to offend or scare off the recruiter—especially in a competitive job market. Worse yet, negotiating doesn't come naturally to Americans. "Most people in our country are not used to bargaining," says salary expert Matthew Deluca. "But if you don't bargain, you're not going to get all you should."[29]

YOUR TASK To build your negotiating skills, reread the Career Coach box in this chapter. Then, role-play a situation in which a hiring manager offers a candidate a starting salary of $44,500. The candidate wants $48,000 to start. The candidate responds to preliminary questions and negotiates the salary offer.

16.15 Creating a Digital or Paper Interview Cheat Sheet (L.O. 3)

Even the best-rehearsed applicants sometimes forget to ask the questions they prepared, or they fail to stress their major accomplishments in job interviews. Sometimes applicants are so rattled they even forget the interviewer's name. To help you keep your wits during an interview, make a cheat sheet—either paper or digital—that summarizes key facts, answers, and questions. Review it before the interview and again as the interview is ending to be sure you have covered everything that is critical.

YOUR TASK Prepare a cheat sheet with the following information:

Day and time of interview:
Meeting with: [name(s) of interviewer(s), title, company, city, state, zip, telephone, cell, video, e-mail]
Major accomplishments (four to six):
Management or work style (four to six):
Things you need to know about me (three or four items):
Reason I left my last job:
Answers to difficult questions (four or five answers):
Questions to ask interviewer:
Things I can do for you:

16.16 Responding to Inappropriate and Illegal Interview Questions (L.O. 3)

Although some questions are considered inappropriate and potentially illegal by the government, many interviewers ask them anyway—whether intentionally or unknowingly. Being prepared is important.

YOUR TASK Assume you are being interviewed at one of the top companies on your list of potential employers. The interviewing committee consists of a human resources manager and the supervising manager of the department in which you would work. At various times during the interview, the supervising manager asks questions that make you feel uncomfortable. For example, he asks whether you are married. You know this question is inappropriate, but you see no harm in answering it. Then, however, he asks how old you are. Because you started college early and graduated in three and a half years, you are worried that you may not be considered mature enough for this position. However, you have most of the other qualifications required, and you are convinced you could succeed on the job. How should you answer this question?

16.17 Asking Your Own Questions (L.O. 3)

When it is your turn to ask questions during the interview process, be ready.

YOUR TASK Decide on three to five questions that you would like to ask during an interview. Write them down and practice asking them so that you sound confident and sincere.

16.18 Embracing Mock Interviews (L.O. 3)

Team

One of the best ways to understand interview dynamics and to develop confidence is to role-play the parts of interviewer and candidate in a mock interview.

YOUR TASK Choose a partner for this activity. Each partner makes a list of two interview questions for each of the eight interview question categories presented in this chapter. In team sessions you and your partner role-play an actual interview. One acts as interviewer; the other is the candidate. Prior to the interview, the candidate tells the interviewer the job he or she is applying for and the name of the company. For the interview, the interviewer and candidate should dress appropriately and sit in chairs facing each other. The interviewer greets the candidate and makes the candidate comfortable. The candidate gives the interviewer a copy of his or her résumé. The interviewer asks three questions (or more, depending on your instructor's time schedule) from the candidate's list. The interviewer may also ask follow-up questions, if appropriate. When finished, the interviewer ends the meeting graciously. After one interview, partners reverse roles and repeat.

16.19 YouTube: Critiquing Interview Skills (L.O. 3)

Web

The adage *Practice makes perfect* is especially true for interviewing. The more you confront your fears in mock or real interviews, the calmer and more confident you will be when your dream job is on the line. Short of undergoing your own interview, you can also learn from observation. YouTube and other video sites offer countless video clips showing examples of excellent, and poor, interviewing techniques.

YOUR TASK Visit YouTube or search the Internet for other interview videos. Select a clip that you find particularly entertaining or informative. Watch it multiple times and jot down your observations. Then summarize the scenario in a paragraph or two. Provide examples of interview strategies that worked and those that didn't, applying the information you learned in this chapter. If required, share your insights about the video with the class.

16.20 Minding Your Table Manners (L.O. 3)

Web

Although they are less likely for entry-level candidates, interviews over business meals are a popular means to size up the social skills of a job seeker, especially in second and subsequent interviews. Candidates coveting jobs with a lot of face-to-face contact with the public may be subjected to the ultimate test: table manners. Interviews are nerve-racking and intimidating enough, but imagine having to juggle silverware, wrangle potentially messy food, and keep your clothing stain free—all this while listening carefully to what is being said around the table and giving thoughtful, confident answers.

YOUR TASK Researching tips can help you avoid the most common pitfalls associated with interviews over meals. Use your favorite search engine and try queries such as *interview dining tips*, *interviewing over meals*, and so forth. Consider the credibility of your sources. Are they authorities on the subject? Compile a list of tips and jot down your sources. Share the list with your peers. If your instructor directs, discuss the categories of advice provided. Then, as a class assemble a universal list of the most common interview tips.

16.21 Thanking the Interviewer (L.O. 4)

You have just completed an exciting employment interview, and you want the interviewer to remember you.

YOUR TASK Write a follow-up thank-you letter to Ronald T. Ranson, Human Resources Development, Electronic Data Sources, 1328 Peachtree Plaza, Atlanta, GA 30314 (or a company of your choice). Make up any details needed.

16.22 Following Up After Submitting Your Résumé (L.O. 4)

E-Mail

A month has passed since you sent your résumé and cover letter in response to a job advertisement. You are still interested in the position and would like to find out whether you still have a chance.

YOUR TASK Write a follow-up e-mail or letter to an employer of your choice that does not offend the reader or damage your chances of employment.

16.23 Refusing to Take *No* for an Answer (L.O. 5)

After an excellent interview with Electronic Data Sources (or a company of your choice), you are disappointed to learn that someone else was hired. However, you really want to work for EDS.

YOUR TASK Write a follow-up message to Ronald T. Ranson, Human Resources Development, Electronic Data Sources, 1328 Peachtree Plaza, Atlanta, GA 30314 (or a company of your choice). Indicate that you are disappointed but still interested.

16.24 Accepting a Job Offer (L.O. 5)

Your dream has come true: you have just been offered an excellent position. Although you accepted the position on the phone, you want to send a formal acceptance letter.

YOUR TASK Write a job acceptance letter to an employer of your choice. Include the job title, your starting date, and details about your compensation package. Make up any necessary details.

16.25 Evaluating Your Course

Let's assume your boss has paid your tuition for this course. As you complete the course, he or she asks you for a letter about your experience in the course.

YOUR TASK Write a letter to a boss in a real or imaginary organization explaining how this course made you more valuable to the organization.

Test Your Etiquette IQ

New communication platforms and casual workplace environments have blurred the lines of appropriateness, leaving workers wondering how to navigate uncharted waters. Indicate whether the following statements are true or false. Then see if you agree with the responses on p. R-2.

1. To make the best impression in a job interview, walk around the side of the table or desk to shake hands. Try not to have a barrier between you and the person you are meeting.

_______ True _______ False

2. You practiced perfecting your handshake before your job interview, and you know that you should squeeze assertively but not painfully and shake three or four times. However, in your first interview, the handshake did not go well. To save face, you should immediately apologize to the interviewer.

_______ True _______ False

3. During a job interview, it's perfectly acceptable to jot down a few notes in a professional-looking binder or notepad—but not on an iPad or other electronic device.

_______ True _______ False

Chat About It

In each chapter you will find five discussion questions related to the chapter material. Your instructor may assign these topics for you to discuss in class, in an online chat room, or on an online discussion board. Some of the discussion topics may require outside research. You may also be asked to read and respond to postings made by your classmates.

TOPIC 1: A hiring manager gave this advice to candidates interviewing for jobs: In advance of an interview, check the LinkedIn profiles of the people you will be meeting. LinkedIn generally makes users aware of who has been viewing their profiles, and it will give the hiring manager the appearance that you are doing your homework. Does this sound like snooping to you? Is this good or bad advice?

TOPIC 2: What is your greatest fear of what you might do or what might happen to you during an employment interview? How can you overcome your fears?

TOPIC 3: If you are interviewing for a company where most of the employees are dressed very casually, should you wear similar clothes to a job interview with that company? Why or why not?

TOPIC 4: You confide in a friend that you don't feel confident about going to job interviews. She tells you that you need more practice, and she suggests that you apply for jobs that you know you don't want and accept interviews with companies in which you are not genuinely interested just so you can develop your interviewing skills. She says that interviewers expect some *shopping.* Do you agree? Should you take her advice? Why or why not?

TOPIC 5: Should job candidates be required to give their social media passwords to recruiters when asked? Explain your view. What does your state allow in this regard?

Grammar and Mechanics | *Review 16*

Total Review

Each of the following sentences has **three** errors in grammar, punctuation, capitalization, usage, or spelling. On a separate sheet, write a correct version. Avoid adding new phrases, starting new sentences, or rewriting in your own words. When finished, compare your responses with those in the key beginning on page Key-3.

1. Most interviews usualy cover the same kinds of questions, therefore smart candidates prepare for them.
2. Rodney wondered how many companys use social media to check candidates backgrounds?
3. Despite the heavy use of e-mail many employers' use the telephone to reach candidates and set up there interviews.
4. In interviewing job candidates recruiters have the following three purposes, assessing their skills, discussing their experience and deciding whether they are a good fit for the organization.
5. If your job history has gaps in it be prepared to explain what you did during this time, and how you kept up to date in your field.
6. Interviewing is a two way street and candidates should be prepared with there own meaningful questions.
7. Kadence was asked whether she had a bachelors degree, and whether she had three years experience.
8. If you are consentious and want to create a good impression be sure to write a thank you message after a job interview.
9. When Marias interview was over she told friends that she had done good.
10. Maria was already to send a thank-you message, when she realized she could not spell the interviewers name.

References

[1] Georgevich, D., career coach (personal communication with Mary Ellen Guffey, June 10, 2016).

[2] Zhang, L. (n.d.) The best (and worst) times to schedule an interview. The Muse. Retrieved from https://www.themuse.com/advice/the-best-and-worst-times-to-schedule-an-interview

[3] Green, A. (2011, February 7). How to prepare for a job interview. *U.S. News & World Report*. Retrieved from http://money.usnews.com/money/blogs/outside-voices-careers/2011/02/07/how-to-prepare-for-a-job-interview

[4] Huhman, H. (2014, August 29). 7 things to research before any job interview. Glassdoor. Retrieved from https://www.glassdoor.com/blog/7-research-job-interview

[5] Adams, S. (2015, September 15). The companies that give the best job interviews. Forbes. Retrieved from http://www.forbes.com/sites/susanadams/2015/09/15/the-companies-that-give-the-best-job-interviews/#3bc8a91f1048

[6] CareerBuilder. (2016, April 28). Number of employers using social media to screen candidates has increased 500 percent over the last decade. CareerBuilder. Retrieved from http://www.careerbuilder.com/share/aboutus/pressreleases-detail.aspx?ed=12%2F31%2F2016&id=pr945&sd=4%2F28%2F2016

[7] Ryan, L. (2015, March 21). What to wear to a job interview. Forbes. Retrieved from http://www.forbes.com/sites/lizryan/2015/03/21/what-to-wear-to-a-job-interview/#325cf0117605

[8] Conlan, C. (n.d.). The 6 worst things to wear to a job interview. Monster.com. Retrieved from http://www.monster.com/career-advice/article/worst-things-to-wear-to-job-interview

[9] George Washington University. Himmelfarb Health Sciences Library. (2015, December 8.) E-professionalism: Social media resources: Cleaning up your digital dirt. Retrieved from http://libguides.gwumc.edu/c.php?g=27787&p=170414

[10] Active listening for interview success: How your ears can help you land the job. (2007, September 25). Hcareers.com. Retrieved from http://www.hcareers.com/us/resourcecenter/tabid/306/articleid/250/default.aspx

[11] Susan L. Hodas cited in Korkki, P. (2009, September 13). Subtle cues can tell an interviewer "pick me." *The New York Times*. Retrieved from http://www.nytimes.com/2009/09/13/jobs/13search.html?_r=0

[12] Chan, A. (2013, June 14). Top 10 interview tips for new college graduates. *The Huffington Post*. Retrieved from http://www.huffingtonpost.com/andy-chan/new-graduates-interview-tips_b_3443514.html

[13] Welch, S., & Welch, J. (2008, July 7). Hiring is hard work. *BusinessWeek*, p. 80.

[14] Martin, C. (n.d.). List of strengths and weaknesses: What to say in your interview. Monster.com. Retrieved from http://www.monster.com/career-advice/article/greatest-strengths-and-weaknesses

[15] Karrass, C. L. (n.d.). *In business as in life, you don't get what you deserve, you get what you negotiate.* Beverly Hills, CA: Stanford St. Press.

[16] Mazur, T. quoted in Dezube, D. (n.d.). How to interview to uncover a candidate's ethical standards. Monster. Retrieved from http://hiring.monster.com/hr/hr-best-practices/recruiting-hiring-advice/interviewing-candidates/interview-questions-to-ask-candidates.aspx

[17] Tyrell-Smith, T. (2011, January 25). Tell a story that will get you hired. *U.S. News & World Report*. Retrieved from http://money.usnews.com/money/blogs/outside-voices-careers/2011/01/25/tell-a-story-that-will-get-you-hired

[18] U.S. Equal Employment Opportunity Commission. (2016). Prohibited employment policies/practices. Retrieved from https://www.eeoc.gov/laws/practices

[19] Doyle, A. (n.d.). Illegal interview questions. About.com. Retrieved from http://jobsearchtech.about.com/od/interview/l/aa022403.htm

[20] 1 in 5 employers has unknowingly asked an illegal interview question. (2015, April 15). CareerBuilder. Retrieved from http://www.careerbuilder.com/share/aboutus/pressreleasesdetail.aspx?sd=4%2F9%2F2015&id=pr877&ed=12%2F31%2F2015

[21] Common interview questions: What you can ask and when it is legal. (n.d.). Monster.com. Retrieved from http://hiring.monster.com/hr/hr-best-practices/small-business/conducting-an-interview/common-interview-questions.aspx. See also 1 in 5 employers has unknowingly asked an illegal interview question. (2015, April 9). CareerBuilder. Retrieved from http://www.careerbuilder.com/share/aboutus/pressreleases-detail.aspx?sd=4%2F9%2F2015&id=pr877&ed=12%2F31%2F2015

[22] Georgevich, D. (2016, June 10). Career coach. Personal communication with Mary Ellen Guffey.
[23] More than one-in-five hiring managers say they are less likely to hire a candidate who didn't send a thank-you note, finds new CareerBuilder survey. (2011, December 31). CareerBuilder. Retrieved from http://www.careerbuilder.com/share/aboutus/pressreleasesdetail.aspx?id=pr631&sd=4/14/2011&ed=12/31/2011
[24] Ibid.
[25] Foss, J. (2012, May 12). 4 non-annoying ways to follow up after an interview. Forbes. Retrieved from http://www.forbes.com/sites/dailymuse/2012/05/30/4-non-annoying-ways-to-follow-up-after-an-interview/2
[26] Owens, Y. (n.d.). 3 rules for following up with a recruiter. The Muse. Retrieved from https://www.themuse.com/advice/3-rules-for-following-up-with-a-recruiter
[27] Klazema, M. (2016, February 10). The pros and cons to strictly doing a background check on social media. Social Media Today. Retrieved from http://www.socialmediatoday.com/social-business/pros-and-cons-strictly-doing-background-check-social-media
[28] Number of employers using social media to screen candidates has increased 500 percent over the last decade. (2016, April 28). CareerBuilder. Retrieved from http://www.careerbuilder.com/share/aboutus/pressreleasesdetail.aspx?ed=12%2F31%2F2016&id=pr945&sd=4%2F28%2F2016
[29] Quoted in DeZube, D. (n.d.). Ten questions to ask when negotiating a salary. Monster.com. Retrieved from http://career-advice.monster.com/salary-benefits/negotiation-tips/10-salary-negotiation-questions/article.aspx

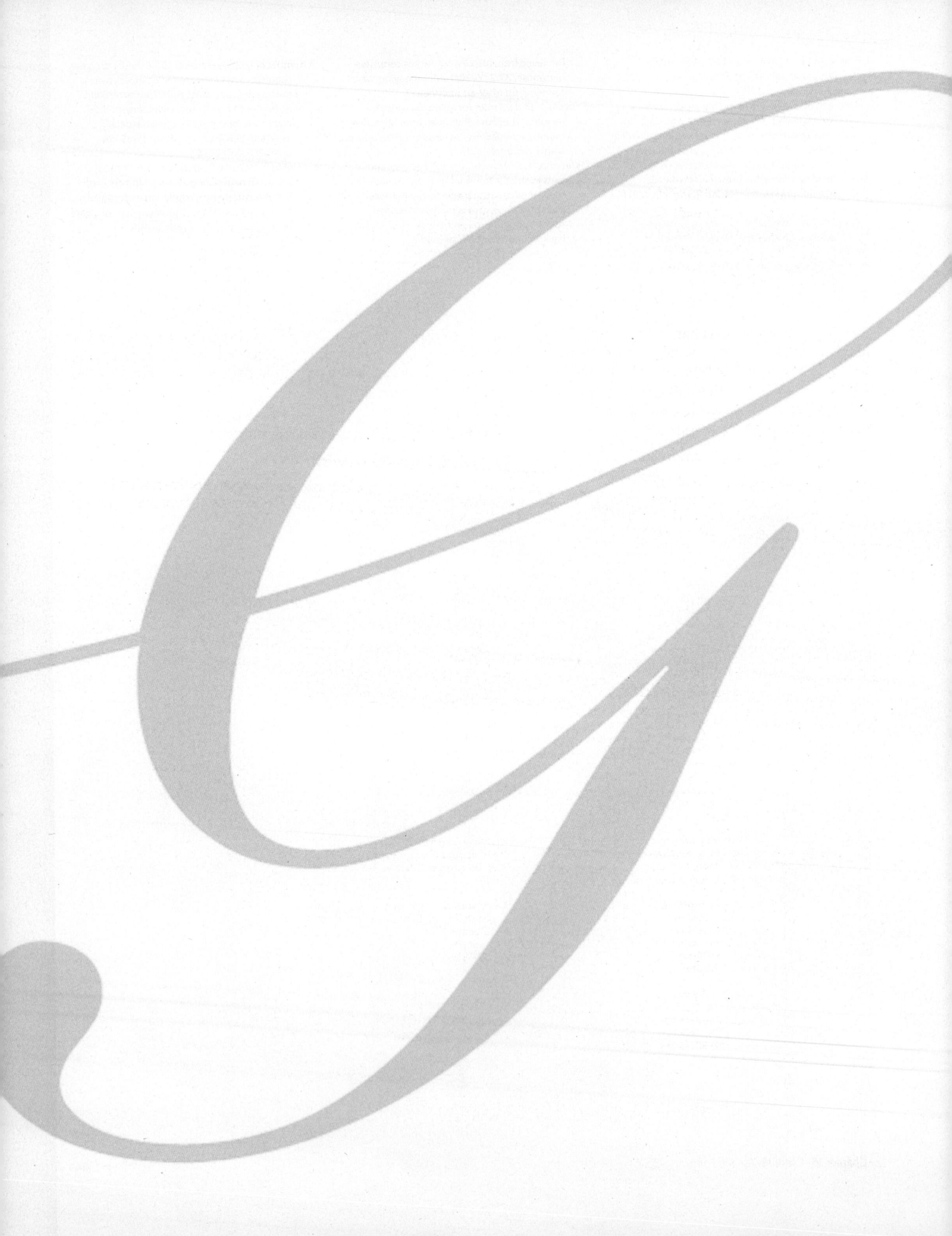

Appendix A

Document Format Guide

Business communicators produce numerous documents that have standardized formats. Becoming familiar with these formats is important because business documents actually carry two kinds of messages. Verbal messages are conveyed by the words chosen to express the writer's ideas. Nonverbal messages are conveyed largely by the appearance of a document and its adherence to recognized formats. To ensure that your documents carry favorable nonverbal messages about you and your organization, you will want to give special attention to the appearance and formatting of your e-mails, letters, envelopes, memos, and résumés.

E-Mail Messages

E-mail is an appropriate channel for short messages. Usually, e-mails do not replace business letters or memos that are lengthy, require permanent records, or transmit confidential or sensitive information. This section describes formats and usage. The following suggestions, illustrated in Figure A.1, may guide you in setting up the parts of any e-mail. Always check, however, with your organization to ensure that you follow its practices.

***To* Line.** Include the receiver's e-mail address after *To*. If the receiver's address is recorded in your address book, you just have to click it. Be sure to enter all addresses very carefully since one mistyped letter prevents delivery.

***From* Line.** Most mail programs automatically include your name and e-mail address after *From*.

***Cc* and *Bcc*.** Insert the e-mail address of anyone who is to receive a copy of the message. *Cc* stands for carbon copy or courtesy copy. Don't be tempted, though, to send needless copies just because it is easy. *Bcc* stands for blind carbon

Figure A.1 **Typical E-Mail**

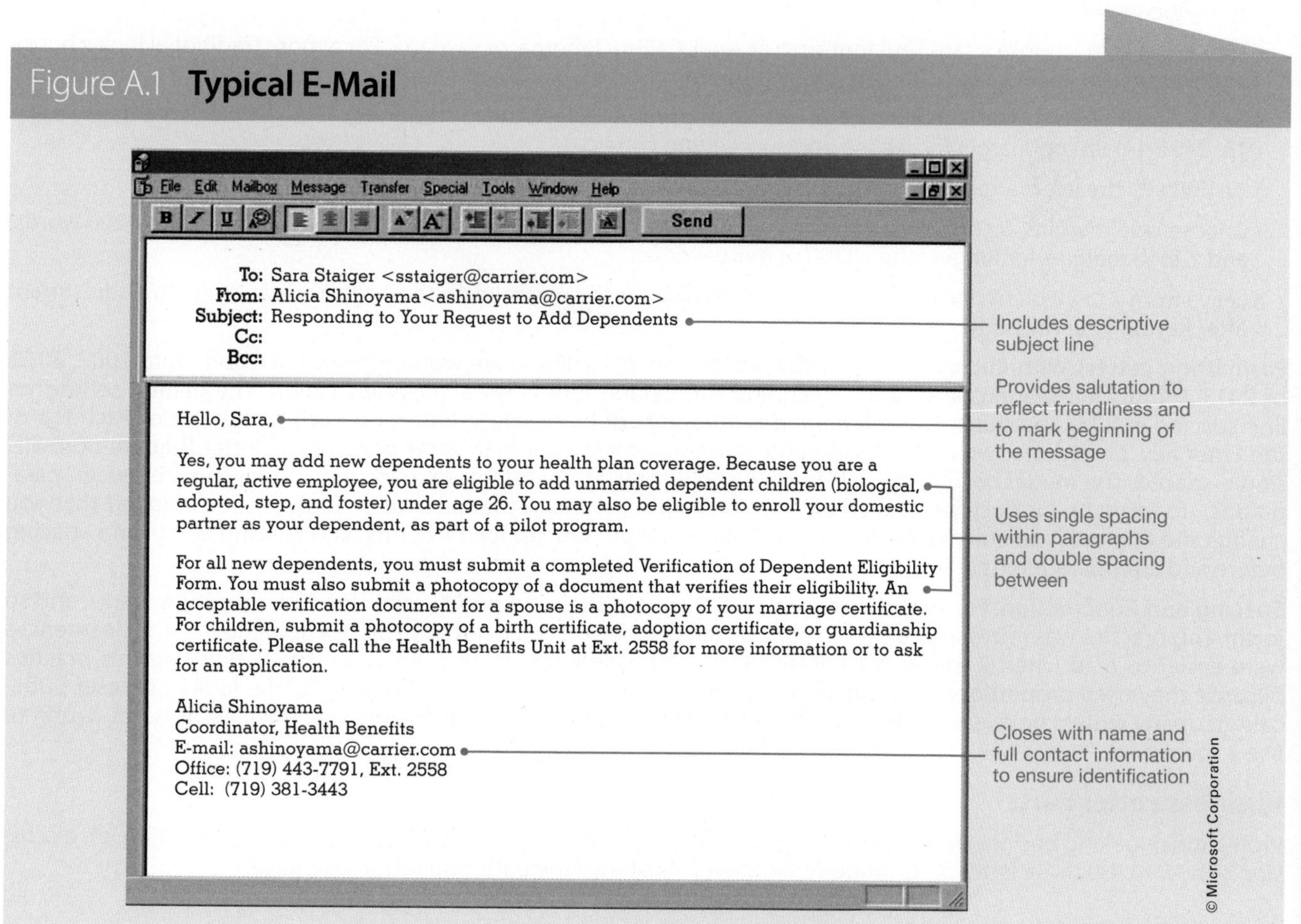
To: Sara Staiger <sstaiger@carrier.com>
From: Alicia Shinoyama<ashinoyama@carrier.com>
Subject: Responding to Your Request to Add Dependents
Cc:
Bcc:

Hello, Sara,

Yes, you may add new dependents to your health plan coverage. Because you are a regular, active employee, you are eligible to add unmarried dependent children (biological, adopted, step, and foster) under age 26. You may also be eligible to enroll your domestic partner as your dependent, as part of a pilot program.

For all new dependents, you must submit a completed Verification of Dependent Eligibility Form. You must also submit a photocopy of a document that verifies their eligibility. An acceptable verification document for a spouse is a photocopy of your marriage certificate. For children, submit a photocopy of a birth certificate, adoption certificate, or guardianship certificate. Please call the Health Benefits Unit at Ext. 2558 for more information or to ask for an application.

Alicia Shinoyama
Coordinator, Health Benefits
E-mail: ashinoyama@carrier.com
Office: (719) 443-7791, Ext. 2558
Cell: (719) 381-3443

File Edit Mailbox Message Transfer Special Tools Window Help
Send
Includes descriptive subject line
Provides salutation to reflect friendliness and to mark beginning of the message
Uses single spacing within paragraphs and double spacing between
Closes with name and full contact information to ensure identification
© Microsoft Corporation

copy. Some writers use *bcc* to send a copy of the message without the addressee's knowledge. Writers also use the *bcc* line for mailing lists. When a message is sent to a number of people and their e-mail addresses should not be revealed, the *bcc* line works well to conceal the names and addresses of all receivers.

Subject. Identify the subject of the e-mail with a brief but descriptive summary of the topic. Be sure to include enough information to be clear and compelling. Capitalize the initial letters of main words. Main words are all words except (a) the articles *a, an,* and *the*; (b) prepositions containing two or three letters (such as *at, to, on, by, for*); (c) the word *to* in an infinitive (*to work, to write*); and (d) the word *as*—unless any of these words are the first or last word in the subject line.

Salutation. Include a brief greeting, if you like. Some writers use a salutation such as *Dear Erica* followed by a comma or a colon. Others are more informal with *Hi, Erica; Hello, Erica; Good morning*; or *Greetings*.

Message. Ideally, cover just one topic in your message, and try to keep your total message under three screens in length. Single-space and be sure to use both upper- and lowercase letters. Double-space between paragraphs.

Closing. If you choose to conclude an e-mail with a closing, you might use *Cheers, Best wishes,* or *Warm regards,* followed by your name and complete contact information. Some people omit their e-mail address because they think it is provided automatically. However, programs and routers do not always transmit the address. Therefore, always include it along with other identifying information in the closing.

Attachment. Use the attachment window or button to select the name of any file you wish to send with your e-mail. You can also attach a Web page to your message.

Business Letters

Business communicators write business letters primarily to correspond with people outside the organization. Letters may go to customers, vendors, other businesses, and the government. The following information will help you format your letters following conventional guidelines.

Conventional Letter Placement, Margins, and Line Spacing. The following are conventional guidelines for setting up business documents:

- For a clean look, choose a sans serif font such as Arial, Calibri, Tahoma, or Verdana. For a more traditional look, choose a serif font such as Times New Roman. Use a 10-point, 11-point, or 12-point size.
- Use a 2-inch top margin for the first page of a letter printed on letterhead stationery. This will place the date on line 13. Use a 1-inch top margin for second and succeeding pages.
- Justify only the left margin. Set the line spacing to single.
- Choose side margins according to the length of your letter. Set 1.5-inch margins for short letters (under 200 words) and 1-inch margins for longer letters (200 or more words).
- Leave from 2 to 10 blank lines following the date to balance the message on the page. You can make this adjustment after keying your message.

Formatting Letters With Microsoft Word 2007, 2010, and 2013. If you are working with Microsoft Word 2007, 2010, or 2013, the default margins are set at 1 inch and the default font is set at 11-point Calibri. The default setting for line spacing is 1.15, and the paragraph default is 10 points of blank space following each paragraph or each tap of the Enter key. Many letter writers find this extra space excessive, especially after parts of the letter that are normally single-spaced. The model documents in this book show conventional single-spacing with 1 blank line between paragraphs. To format your documents with conventional spacing and yet retain a clean look, we recommend that you change the Microsoft defaults to the following: Arial or Calibri font set for 11 points, line spacing at 1.0, and spacing before and after paragraphs at 0.

Spacing and Punctuation. For some time typists left 2 spaces after end punctuation (periods, question marks, and so forth). This practice was necessary, it was thought, because typewriters did not have proportional spacing and sentences were easier to read when 2 spaces separated them. Professional typesetters, however, never followed this practice because they used proportional spacing, and readability was not a problem. Influenced by the look of typeset publications, many writers now leave only 1 space after end punctuation. As a practical matter, however, it is not wrong to use 2 spaces.

Business Letter Parts

Professional-looking business letters are arranged in a conventional sequence with standard parts. Following is a discussion of how to use these letter parts properly. Figure A.2 illustrates the parts of a block style letter.

Figure A.2 Block and Modified Block Letter Styles

Letterhead

Island Graphics
893 Dillingham Boulevard
Honolulu, HI 96817-8817
(808) 493-2310
http://www.islandgraphics.com

↓ Dateline is 2 inches from the top or 1 blank line below letterhead

Dateline — September 13, 2018

↓ 1 to 9 blank lines

Inside address — Mr. T. M. Wilson, President
Visual Concept Enterprises
1901 Kaumualii Highway
Lihue, HI 96766

↓ 1 blank line

Salutation — Dear Mr. Wilson:

↓ 1 blank line

Subject line — Subject: Block Letter Style

↓ 1 blank line

Body —

This letter illustrates block letter style, about which you asked. All typed lines begin at the left margin. The date is usually placed 2 inches from the top edge of the paper or 1 blank line below the last line of the letter head, whichever position is lower.

This letter also shows mixed punctuation. A colon follows the salutation, and a comma follows the complimentary close. Open punctuation requires no colon after the salutation and no comma following the close, however, open punctuation is seldom seen today.

If a subject line is included, it appears 1 blank line below the salutation. The word *Subject* is optional. Most readers will recognize a statement in this position as the subject without an identifying label. The complimentary close appears 1 blank line below the end of the last paragraph.

↓ 1 blank line

Complimentary close — Sincerely,

↓ 3 blank lines

Mark H. Wong

Signature block — Mark H. Wong
Graphic Designer

↓ 1 blank line

Reference initials — MHW:pil

Modified block style, mixed punctuation

In the modified block style letter shown at the left, the date is centered or aligned with the complimentary close and signature block, which start at the center. Mixed punctuation includes a colon after the salutation and a comma after the complimentary close, as shown above and at the left.

Letterhead. Most business organizations use 8½ x 11-inch paper printed with a letterhead displaying their official name, street address, Web address, e-mail address, and telephone and fax numbers. The letterhead may also include a logo and an advertising message.

Dateline. On letterhead paper you should place the date 1 blank line below the last line of the letterhead or 2 inches from the top edge of the paper (line 13). On plain paper place the date immediately below your return address. Because the date goes on line 13, start the return address an appropriate number of lines above it. The most common dateline format is as follows: *June 9, 2018*. Don't use *th* (or *rd, nd,* or *st*) when the date is written this way. For European or military correspondence, use the following dateline format: *9 June 2018*. Notice that no commas are used.

Addressee and Delivery Notations. Delivery notations such as *VIA U.S. MAIL AND E-MAIL, FAX TRANSMISSION, FEDEX, MESSENGER DELIVERY, CONFIDENTIAL,* and *CERTIFIED MAIL* are typed in all capital letters between the dateline and the inside address.

Inside Address. Type the inside address—that is, the address of the organization or person receiving the letter—single-spaced, starting at the left margin. The number of lines between the dateline and the inside address depends on the size of the letter body, the type size (point or pitch size), and the length of the typing lines. Generally, 1 to 9 blank lines are appropriate.

Be careful to duplicate the exact wording and spelling of the recipient's name and address on your documents. Usually, you can copy this information from the letterhead of the correspondence you are answering. If, for example, you are responding to *Jackson & Perkins Company*, do not address your letter to *Jackson and Perkins Corp.*

Always be sure to include a courtesy title such as *Mr., Ms., Mrs., Dr.,* or *Professor* before a person's name in the inside address—for both the letter and the envelope. Although many women in business today favor *Ms.*, you should use whatever title the addressee prefers.

Generally spell out *Avenue, Street,* and *Company* unless they appear as abbreviations in the printed letterhead of the document being answered.

Attention Line. An attention line allows you to send your message officially to an organization but to direct it to a specific individual, officer, or department. However, if you know an individual's complete name, it is always better to use it as the first line of the inside address and avoid an attention line. Placing an attention line first in the address block enables you to paste it directly onto the envelope:

> Attention Marketing Director
> The MultiMedia Company
> 931 Calkins Avenue
> Rochester, NY 14301

Salutation. For most letter styles, place the letter greeting, or salutation, 1 blank line below the last line of the inside address or the attention line (if used). If the letter is addressed to an individual, use that person's courtesy title and last name (*Dear Ms. Davis*). Even if you are on a first-name basis (*Dear Dana*), be sure to add a colon (not a comma or a semicolon) after the salutation. Do not use an individual's full name in the salutation (not *Dear Ms. Dana Davis*) unless you are unsure of gender (*Dear Dana Davis*).

It's always best to address messages to people. However, if a message is addressed to an organization, consider these salutations: an organization of men (*Gentlemen*), an organization of women (*Ladies*), an organization of men and women (*Ladies and Gentlemen*). If a message is addressed to an undetermined individual, consider these salutations: a woman (*Dear Madam*), a man (*Dear Sir*), a title (*Dear Customer Service Representative*).

Subject and Reference Lines. Although experts suggest placing the subject line 1 blank line below the salutation, many businesses actually place it above the salutation. Use whatever style your organization prefers. Reference lines often show policy or file numbers; they generally appear 1 blank line above the salutation. Use initial capital letters for the main words or all capital letters.

Body. Most business letters and memorandums are single-spaced, with double-spacing between paragraphs. Very short messages may be double-spaced with indented paragraphs.

Complimentary Close. Typed 1 blank line below the last line of the letter, the complimentary close may be formal (*Very truly yours*) or informal (*Sincerely* or *Cordially*).

Signature Block. In most letter styles, the writer's typed name and optional identification appear 3 or 4 blank lines below the complimentary close. The combination of name, title, and organization information should be arranged to achieve a balanced look. The name and title may appear on the same line or on separate lines, depending on the length of each. Use commas to separate categories within the same line, but not to conclude a line.

Sincerely yours,

Jeremy M. Wood

Jeremy M. Wood, Manager
Technical Sales and Services

Cordially yours,

Casandra Baker-Murillo

Casandra Baker-Murillo
Executive Vice President

Some organizations include their names in the signature block. In such cases the organization name appears in all caps 1 blank line below the complimentary close, as shown here:

Cordially,

LIPTON COMPUTER SERVICES

Shelina A. Simpson

Shelina A. Simpson
Executive Assistant

Reference Initials. If used, the initials of the typist and writer are typed 1 blank line below the writer's name and title. Generally, the writer's initials are capitalized and the typist's are lowercased, but this format varies.

Enclosure Notation. When an enclosure or attachment accompanies a document, a notation to that effect appears 1 blank line below the reference initials. This notation reminds the typist to insert the enclosure in the envelope, and it reminds the recipient to look for the enclosure or attachment. The notation may be spelled out (*Enclosure, Attachment*), or it may be abbreviated (*Enc., Att.*). It may indicate the number of enclosures or attachments, and it may also identify a specific enclosure (*Enclosure: Form 1099*).

Copy Notation. If you make copies of correspondence for other individuals, you may use *cc* to indicate courtesy copy, *pc* to indicate photocopy, or merely *c* for any kind of copy. A colon following the initial(s) is optional.

Second-Page Heading. When a letter extends beyond one page, use plain paper of the same quality and color as the first page. Identify the second and succeeding pages with a heading consisting of the name of the addressee, the page number, and the date. Use the following format or the one shown in Figure A.3:

Ms. Sara Hendricks 2 May 3, 2018

Both headings appear 6 blank lines (1 inch) from the top edge of the paper followed by 2 blank lines to separate them from the continuing text. Avoid using a second page if you have only 1 line or the complimentary close and signature block to fill that page.

Plain-Paper Return Address. If you prepare a personal or business letter on plain paper, place your address immediately above the date. Do not include your name; you will type (and sign) your name at the end of your letter. If your return address contains 2 lines, begin typing so that the date appears 2 inches from the top. Avoid abbreviations except for a two-letter state abbreviation.

580 East Leffels Street
Springfield, OH 45501
December 14, 2018

Ms. Ellen Siemens
Escrow Department
TransOhio First Federal
1220 Wooster Boulevard
Columbus, OH 43218-2900

Dear Ms. Siemens:

For letters in the block style, type the return address at the left margin. For modified block style letters, start the return address at the center to align with the complimentary close.

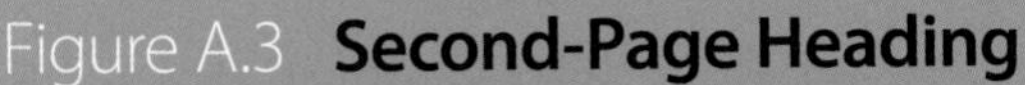

Figure A.3 **Second-Page Heading**

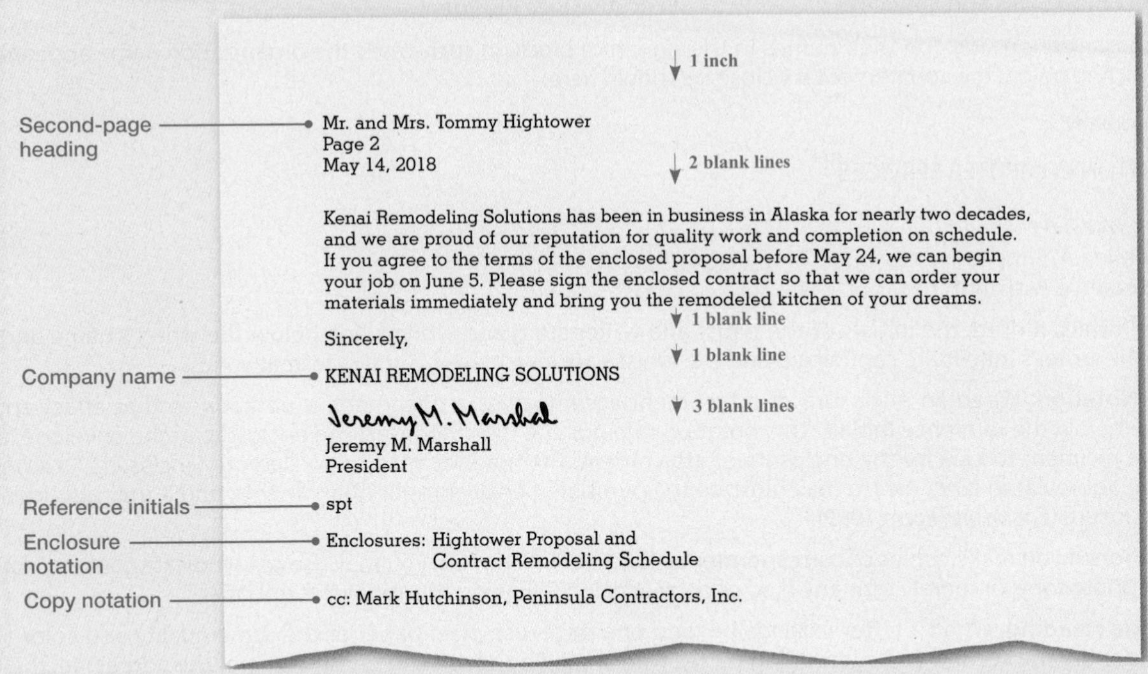

Letter and Punctuation Styles

Most business letters today are prepared in either block or modified block style, and they generally use mixed punctuation.

Block Style. In the block style, shown in Figure A.2, all lines begin at the left margin. This style is a favorite because it is easy to format.

Modified Block Style. The modified block style differs from the block style in that the date and closing lines appear in the center, as shown at the bottom of Figure A.2. The date may be (a) centered, (b) begun at the center of the page (to align with the closing lines), or (c) backspaced from the right margin. The signature block—including the complimentary close, writer's name and title, or organization identification—begins at the center. The first line of each paragraph may begin at the left margin or may be indented 5 or 10 spaces. All other lines begin at the left margin.

Mixed Punctuation Style. Most businesses today use mixed punctuation, shown in Figure A.2. It requires a colon after the salutation and a comma after the complimentary close. Even when the salutation is a first name, a colon is appropriate.

Envelopes

An envelope should be of the same quality and color of stationery as the letter it carries. Because the envelope introduces your message and makes the first impression, you need to be especially careful in addressing it. Moreover, how you fold the letter is important.

Return Address. The return address is usually printed in the upper left corner of an envelope, as shown in Figure A.4. In large companies some form of identification (the writer's initials, name, or location) may be typed above the company name and address. This identification helps return the letter to the sender in case of nondelivery.

On an envelope without a printed return address, single-space the return address in the upper left corner. Beginning on line 3 on the fourth space (½ inch) from the left edge, type the writer's name, title, company, and mailing address. On a word processor, select the appropriate envelope size and make adjustments to approximate this return address location.

Mailing Address. On legal-sized No. 10 envelopes (4⅛ x 9½ inches), begin the address on line 13 about 4¼ inches from the left edge, as shown in Figure A.4. For small envelopes (3⅝ x 6½ inches), begin typing on line 12 about 2½ inches from the left edge. On a word processor, select the correct envelope size and check to be sure your address falls in the desired location.

The U.S. Postal Service recommends that addresses be typed in all caps without any punctuation. This Postal Service style, shown in the small envelope in Figure A.4, was originally developed to facilitate scanning by optical character

Figure A.4 Envelope Formats

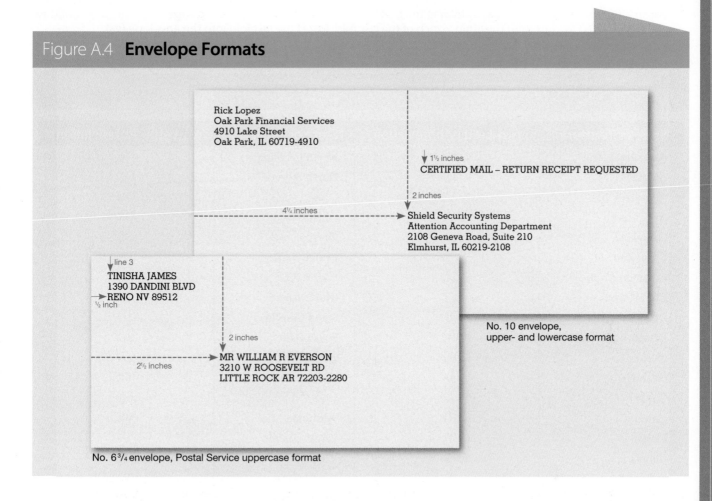

Rick Lopez
Oak Park Financial Services
4910 Lake Street
Oak Park, IL 60719-4910

1½ inches

CERTIFIED MAIL – RETURN RECEIPT REQUESTED

2 inches

4¼ inches

Shield Security Systems
Attention Accounting Department
2108 Geneva Road, Suite 210
Elmhurst, IL 60219-2108

No. 10 envelope, upper- and lowercase format

line 3

TINISHA JAMES
1390 DANDINI BLVD
RENO NV 89512

½ inch

2 inches

2½ inches

MR WILLIAM R EVERSON
3210 W ROOSEVELT RD
LITTLE ROCK AR 72203-2280

No. 6¾ envelope, Postal Service uppercase format

readers. Today's OCRs, however, are so sophisticated that they scan upper- and lowercase letters easily. Many companies today do not follow the Postal Service format because they prefer to use the same format for the envelope as for the inside address. If the same format is used, writers can take advantage of word processing programs to copy the inside address to the envelope, thus saving keystrokes and reducing errors. Having the same format on both the inside address and the envelope also looks more professional and consistent. For those reasons you may choose to use the familiar upper- and lowercase combination format. But you will want to check with your organization to learn its preference.

In addressing your envelopes for delivery in this country or in Canada, use the two-letter state and province abbreviations shown in Figure A.5. Notice that these abbreviations are in capital letters without periods.

Folding. The way a letter is folded and inserted into an envelope sends additional nonverbal messages about a writer's professionalism and carefulness. Most businesspeople follow the procedures shown here, which produce the least number of creases to distract readers.

For large No. 10 envelopes, begin with the letter face up. Fold slightly less than one third of the sheet toward the top, as shown in the following diagram. Then fold down the top third to within ⅓ inch of the bottom fold. Insert the letter into the envelope with the last fold toward the bottom of the envelope.

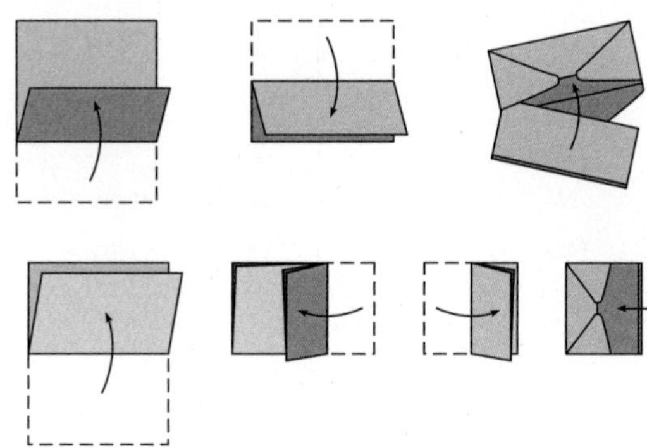

For small No. 6¾ envelopes, begin by folding the bottom up to within ⅓ inch of the top edge. Then fold the right third over to the left. Fold the left third to within ⅓ inch of the last fold. Insert the last fold into the envelope first.

Figure A.5 **Abbreviations of States, Territories, and Provinces**

State or Territory	Two-Letter Abbreviation	State or Territory	Two-Letter Abbreviation
Alabama	AL	North Carolina	NC
Alaska	AK	North Dakota	ND
Arizona	AZ	Ohio	OH
Arkansas	AR	Oklahoma	OK
California	CA	Oregon	OR
Canal Zone	CZ	Pennsylvania	PA
Colorado	CO	Puerto Rico	PR
Connecticut	CT	Rhode Island	RI
Delaware	DE	South Carolina	SC
District of Columbia	DC	South Dakota	SD
Florida	FL	Tennessee	TN
Georgia	GA	Texas	TX
Guam	GU	Utah	UT
Hawaii	HI	Vermont	VT
Idaho	ID	Virgin Islands	VI
Illinois	IL	Virginia	VA
Indiana	IN	Washington	WA
Iowa	IA	West Virginia	WV
Kansas	KS	Wisconsin	WI
Kentucky	KY	Wyoming	WY
Louisiana	LA	**Canadian Province**	
Maine	ME	Alberta	AB
Maryland	MD	British Columbia	BC
Massachusetts	MA	Labrador	LB
Michigan	MI	Manitoba	MB
Minnesota	MN	New Brunswick	NB
Mississippi	MS	Newfoundland	NF
Missouri	MO	Northwest Territories	NT
Montana	MT	Nova Scotia	NS
Nebraska	NE	Ontario	ON
Nevada	NV	Prince Edward Island	PE
New Hampshire	NH	Quebec	PQ
New Jersey	NJ	Saskatchewan	SK
New Mexico	NM	Yukon Territory	YT
New York	NY		

Appendix B
Documentation Formats

For many reasons business writers are careful to properly document report data. Citing sources strengthens a writer's argument, as you learned in Chapter 11, while also shielding the writer from charges of plagiarism. Moreover, good references help readers pursue further research. As a business writer, you can expect to routinely borrow ideas and words to show that your ideas are in synch with the rest of the business world, to gain support from business leaders, or simply to save time in developing your ideas. To be ethical, however, you must show clearly what you borrowed and from whom.

Source notes tell where you found your information. For quotations, paraphrases, graphs, drawings, or online images you have borrowed, you need to cite the original authors' names, full titles, and the dates and facts of publication. The purpose of source notes, which appear at the end of your report, is to direct your readers to the complete references. Many systems of documentation are used by businesses, but they all have one goal: to provide clear, consistent documentation.

Rarely, business writers use content notes, which are identified with a raised number at the end of the quotation. At the bottom of the page, the number is repeated with a remark, clarification, or background information.

During your business career, you may use a variety of documentation systems. The two most common systems in the academic world are those of the American Psychological Association (APA) and the Modern Language Association (MLA). Each organization has its own style for text references and bibliographic lists. This textbook uses a modified APA style. However, business organizations may use their own documentation systems.

Before starting any research project, whether for a class or in a business, inquire about the preferred documentation style. For school assignments ask about specifics. For example, should you include URLs and dates of retrieval for Web sources? For workplace assignments ask to see a previous report either in hard-copy version or as an e-mail attachment.

In your business and class writing, you will usually provide a brief citation in parentheses that refers readers to the complete reference that appears in a references or works-cited section at the end of your document. Following is a summary of APA and MLA formats with examples.

American Psychological Association Format

First used primarily in the social and physical sciences, the American Psychological Association (APA) documentation format uses the author-date method of citation. This method, with its emphasis on current information, is especially appropriate for business. Within the text, the date of publication of the referenced work appears immediately after the author's name (Rivera, 2016), as illustrated in the brief APA example in Figure B.1. At the end of the report, all references appear alphabetically on a page labeled References. The APA format does not require a date of retrieval for online sources, but you should check with your instructor or supervisor about the preferred format for your class or organization. For more information about the APA format, see the *Publication Manual of the American Psychological Association,* Sixth Edition (Washington, DC: American Psychological Association, 2009).

APA In-Text Format. Within your text, document each text, figure, or personal source with a short description in parentheses. Following are selected guidelines summarizing the important elements of APA style.

- For a direct quotation, include the last name of the author(s), if available, and the year of publication; for example, *(Meadows, 2016, p. 32).* If no author is shown in the text or on a website, use a shortened title or a heading that can be easily located on the References page; for example, *(History, n.d.).*
- If you mention the author in the text, do not use the name again in the parenthetical reference. Just cite the date; for example, *According to Meadows (2016).*
- Search for website dates on the home page or at the bottom of Web pages. If no date is available for a source, use *n.d.*

APA References Format. At the end of your report, in a section called References, list all references alphabetically by author, or by title if no author is available. To better understand the anatomy of an APA scholarly journal article reference, see Figure B.2.

Figure B.1 Portions of APA Text Page and References

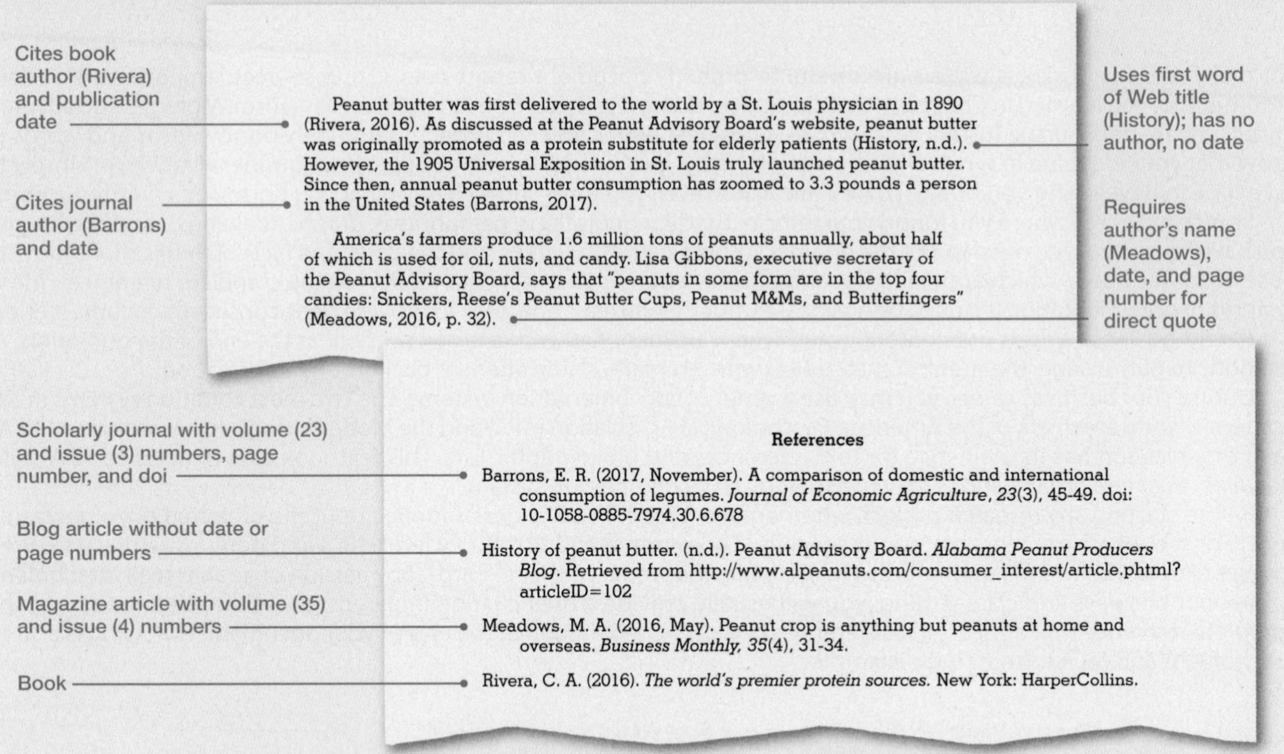
Cites book author (Rivera) and publication date

Cites journal author (Barrons) and date

Uses first word of Web title (History); has no author, no date

Requires author's name (Meadows), date, and page number for direct quote

Peanut butter was first delivered to the world by a St. Louis physician in 1890 (Rivera, 2016). As discussed at the Peanut Advisory Board's website, peanut butter was originally promoted as a protein substitute for elderly patients (History, n.d.). However, the 1905 Universal Exposition in St. Louis truly launched peanut butter. Since then, annual peanut butter consumption has zoomed to 3.3 pounds a person in the United States (Barrons, 2017).

America's farmers produce 1.6 million tons of peanuts annually, about half of which is used for oil, nuts, and candy. Lisa Gibbons, executive secretary of the Peanut Advisory Board, says that "peanuts in some form are in the top four candies: Snickers, Reese's Peanut Butter Cups, Peanut M&Ms, and Butterfingers" (Meadows, 2016, p. 32).

Scholarly journal with volume (23) and issue (3) numbers, page number, and doi

Blog article without date or page numbers

Magazine article with volume (35) and issue (4) numbers

Book

References

Barrons, E. R. (2017, November). A comparison of domestic and international consumption of legumes. *Journal of Economic Agriculture, 23*(3), 45-49. doi: 10-1058-0885-7974.30.6.678

History of peanut butter. (n.d.). Peanut Advisory Board. *Alabama Peanut Producers Blog*. Retrieved from http://www.alpeanuts.com/consumer_interest/article.phtml?articleID=102

Meadows, M. A. (2016, May). Peanut crop is anything but peanuts at home and overseas. *Business Monthly, 35*(4), 31-34.

Rivera, C. A. (2016). *The world's premier protein sources.* New York: HarperCollins.

Figure B.2 Anatomy of an APA Journal Article Reference

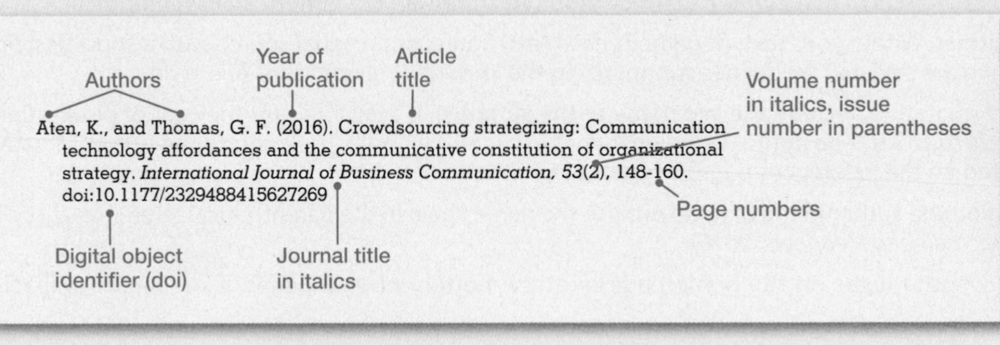

Aten, K., and Thomas, G. F. (2016). Crowdsourcing strategizing: Communication technology affordances and the communicative constitution of organizational strategy. *International Journal of Business Communication, 53*(2), 148-160. doi:10.1177/2329488415627269

Figure credit

As with all documentation methods, APA has specific capitalization, punctuation, and sequencing rules, some of which are summarized here:

- Include the last name of the author(s) followed by initials. APA is gender neutral, so first and middle names are not spelled out; for example, *(Aten, K.)*.
- Show the date of publication in parentheses immediately after the author's name. A magazine citation will also include the month and day in the parentheses.
- Use sentence-style capitalization for all titles except journal titles. Do not use quotation marks for article or journal titles.

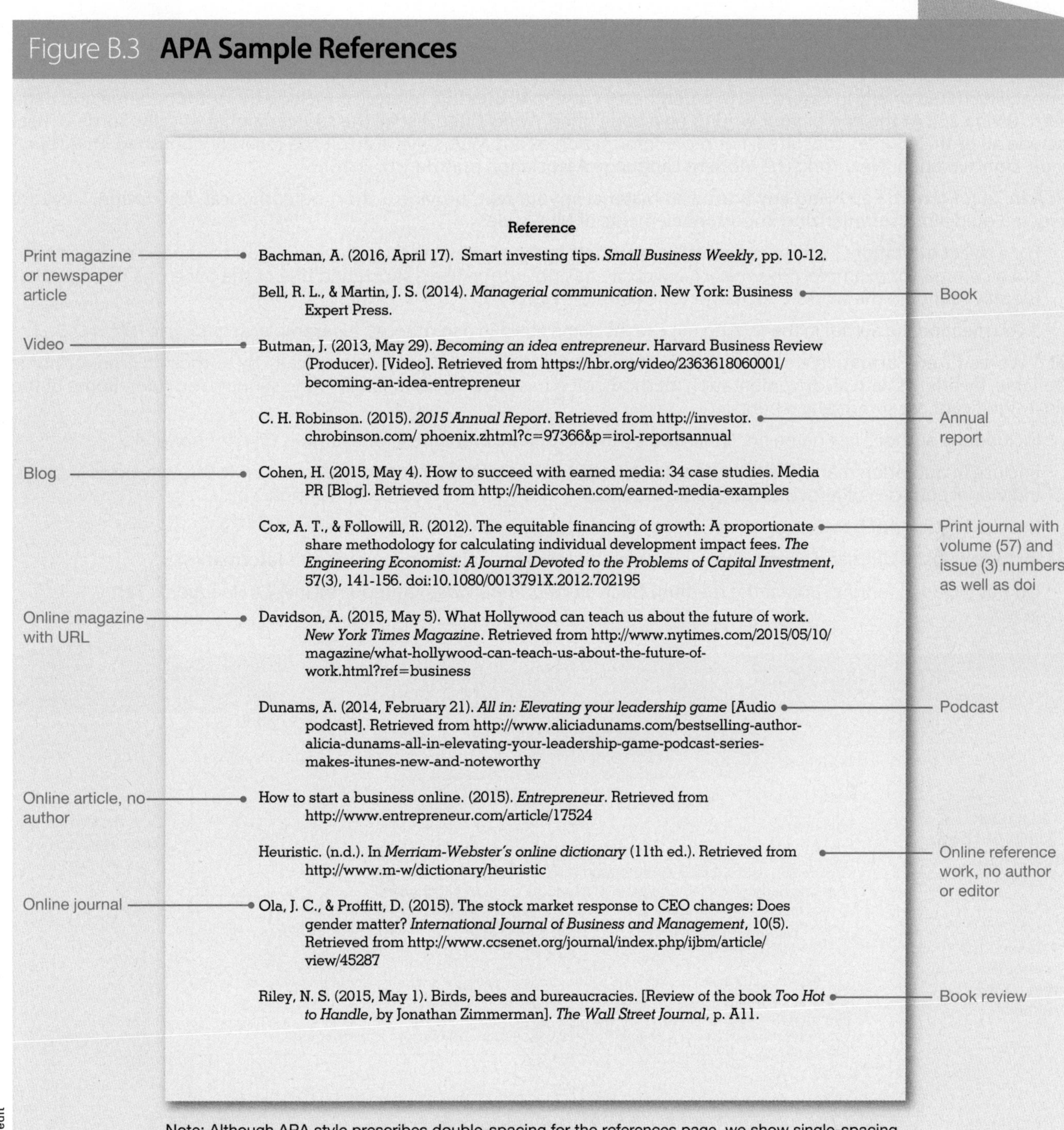

Reference
Print magazine or newspaper article
Bachman, A. (2016, April 17). Smart investing tips. *Small Business Weekly*, pp. 10-12.
Bell, R. L., & Martin, J. S. (2014). *Managerial communication*. New York: Business Expert Press.
Book
Video
Butman, J. (2013, May 29). *Becoming an idea entrepreneur*. Harvard Business Review (Producer). [Video]. Retrieved from https://hbr.org/video/2363618060001/becoming-an-idea-entrepreneur
C. H. Robinson. (2015). *2015 Annual Report*. Retrieved from http://investor.chrobinson.com/ phoenix.zhtml?c=97366&p=irol-reportsannual
Annual report
Blog
Cohen, H. (2015, May 4). How to succeed with earned media: 34 case studies. Media PR [Blog]. Retrieved from http://heidicohen.com/earned-media-examples
Cox, A. T., & Followill, R. (2012). The equitable financing of growth: A proportionate share methodology for calculating individual development impact fees. *The Engineering Economist: A Journal Devoted to the Problems of Capital Investment*, 57(3), 141-156. doi:10.1080/0013791X.2012.702195
Print journal with volume (57) and issue (3) numbers as well as doi
Online magazine with URL
Davidson, A. (2015, May 5). What Hollywood can teach us about the future of work. *New York Times Magazine*. Retrieved from http://www.nytimes.com/2015/05/10/magazine/what-hollywood-can-teach-us-about-the-future-of-work.html?ref=business
Dunams, A. (2014, February 21). *All in: Elevating your leadership game* [Audio podcast]. Retrieved from http://www.aliciadunams.com/bestselling-author-alicia-dunams-all-in-elevating-your-leadership-game-podcast-series-makes-itunes-new-and-noteworthy
Podcast
Online article, no author
How to start a business online. (2015). *Entrepreneur*. Retrieved from http://www.entrepreneur.com/article/17524
Heuristic. (n.d.). In *Merriam-Webster's online dictionary* (11th ed.). Retrieved from http://www.m-w/dictionary/heuristic
Online reference work, no author or editor
Online journal
Ola, J. C., & Proffitt, D. (2015). The stock market response to CEO changes: Does gender matter? *International Journal of Business and Management*, 10(5). Retrieved from http://www.ccsenet.org/journal/index.php/ijbm/article/view/45287
Riley, N. S. (2015, May 1). Birds, bees and bureaucracies. [Review of the book *Too Hot to Handle*, by Jonathan Zimmerman]. *The Wall Street Journal*, p. A11.
Book review
Note: Although APA style prescribes double-spacing for the references page, we show single-spacing to conserve space and to represent preferred business usage.
Figure credit

Figure B.3 APA Sample References

- Italicize titles of books, journals, magazines, and newspapers.
- Include the digital object identifier (doi) when available for online periodicals. If no doi is available, include the home page URL unless the source is difficult to retrieve without the entire URL.
- Break a URL or doi only before a mark of punctuation such as a slash.
- If the website content may change, as in a wiki, include a retrieval date; for example, Retrieved *7 July 2017 from http://www.encyclopediaofmath.org/index.php/MainPage.* Please note, however, that many instructors require that all Web references be identified by their URLs.

For an expanded list of contemporary APA documentation format examples, see Figure B.3.

Modern Language Association Format

Writers in the humanities and the liberal arts frequently use the Modern Language Association (MLA) documentation format, illustrated briefly in Figure B.4. In parentheses close to the textual reference, include the author's name and page cited (Rivera 25). At the end of your writing on a page titled Works Cited, list all the sources alphabetically. Some writers include all of the sources consulted. For more information about MLA style, consult the recently published *MLA Handbook*, Eighth Edition (New York: The Modern Language Association of America, 2016).

MLA In-Text Format. Following any borrowed material in your text, provide a short parenthetical description. Here are selected guidelines summarizing important elements of MLA style:

- For a direct quotation, enclose in parentheses the last name of the author(s), if available, and the page number without a comma; for example, *(Rivera 25)*. If a website has no author, use a shortened title of the page or a heading that is easily found on the works-cited page; for example, *("History")*.
- If you mention the author in the text, do not use the name again in parentheses; for example, *According to Rivera (27) . . .*

MLA Works-Cited Format. In a section called Works Cited, list all references alphabetically by author or, if no author is available, by title. As with all documentation methods, MLA has specific capitalization and sequencing rules. Some of the most significant are summarized here:

- Include the author's last name first, followed by the first name and initial; for example, *Rivera, Charles A.*
- Enclose in quotation marks the titles of articles, essays, stories, chapters of books, pages in websites, articles in blogs, individual episodes of television and radio broadcasts, and short musical compositions.
- Italicize the titles of books, magazines, newspapers, websites, blogs, and journals.
- Include website URLs and access dates if your instructor or organization requests this information.
- Do not include identification of the medium (such as *Web, Print, Video*) as required in *MLA Handbook*, 7e.

Figure B.4 **Portions of MLA Text Page and Works Cited**

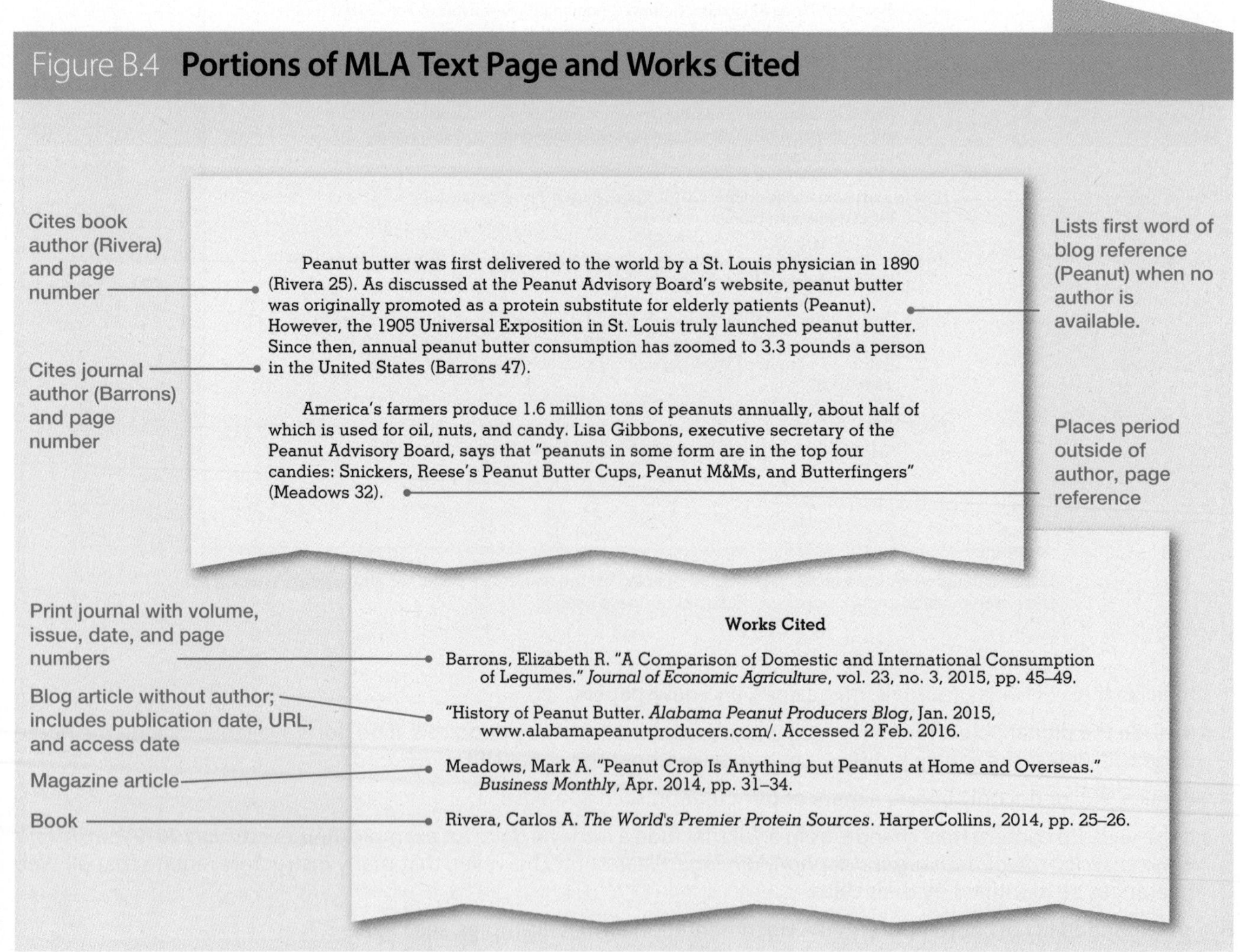

Cites book author (Rivera) and page number
Cites journal author (Barrons) and page number
Lists first word of blog reference (Peanut) when no author is available.
Places period outside of author, page reference
Peanut butter was first delivered to the world by a St. Louis physician in 1890 (Rivera 25). As discussed at the Peanut Advisory Board's website, peanut butter was originally promoted as a protein substitute for elderly patients (Peanut). However, the 1905 Universal Exposition in St. Louis truly launched peanut butter. Since then, annual peanut butter consumption has zoomed to 3.3 pounds a person in the United States (Barrons 47).
America's farmers produce 1.6 million tons of peanuts annually, about half of which is used for oil, nuts, and candy. Lisa Gibbons, executive secretary of the Peanut Advisory Board, says that "peanuts in some form are in the top four candies: Snickers, Reese's Peanut Butter Cups, Peanut M&Ms, and Butterfingers" (Meadows 32).
Print journal with volume, issue, date, and page numbers
Blog article without author; includes publication date, URL, and access date
Magazine article
Book
Works Cited
Barrons, Elizabeth R. "A Comparison of Domestic and International Consumption of Legumes." *Journal of Economic Agriculture*, vol. 23, no. 3, 2015, pp. 45–49.
"History of Peanut Butter. *Alabama Peanut Producers Blog*, Jan. 2015, www.alabamapeanutproducers.com/. Accessed 2 Feb. 2016.
Meadows, Mark A. "Peanut Crop Is Anything but Peanuts at Home and Overseas." *Business Monthly*, Apr. 2014, pp. 31–34.
Rivera, Carlos A. *The World's Premier Protein Sources*. HarperCollins, 2014, pp. 25–26.

Figure credit

Figure B.5 Anatomy of an MLA Journal Article Reference

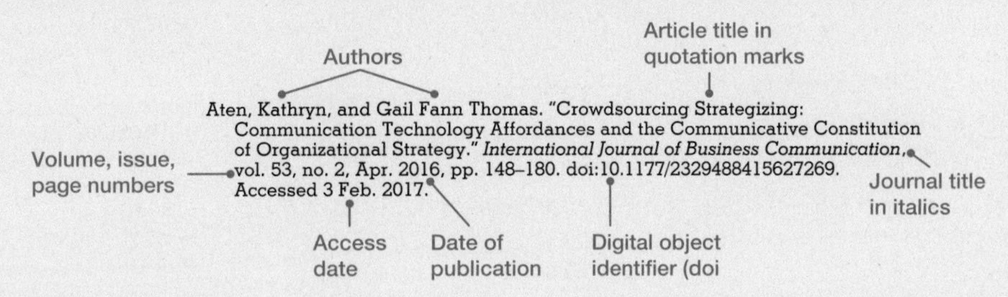

Figure credit

Figure B.6 MLA Sample References

Works Cited

Print magazine or newspaper article	Bachman, Alicia. "Smart Investing Tips." *Small Business Weekly*, 17 Apr. 2016, pp. 10–12.	
	Bell, Reginald L., and Jeanette S. Martin. *Managerial Communication*. Business Expert Press, 2014.	Book
Online video. Note: MLA style omits *http://* in URLs	Butman, John. "Becoming an Idea Entrepreneur." *Harvard Business Review*, 29 May 2013, hbr.org/video/2363618060001/becoming-an-idea-entrepreneur. Accessed 19 Aug. 2017.	
	C. H. Robinson. *2015 Annual Report*, 22 Dec. 2015, media.corporate-ir.net/media_files/IROL/97/97366 /AnnualReport/index.html. Accessed 12 Sep. 2017.	Annual report from website
Blog	Cohen, Heidi. "How to Succeed With Earned Media: 34 Case Studies." *Media PR*, 4 May 2015, heidicohen.com/earned-media-examples. Accessed 26 Sep. 2016.	
	Cox, Arthur T., and Robert Followill. "The Equitable Financing of Growth: A Proportionate Share Methodology for Calculating Individual Development Impact Fees." *The Engineering Economist: A Journal Devoted to the Problems of Capital Investment*, vol. 57, no. 3, 2012, pp. 141–156.	Print journal with volume (57) and issue (3) numbers
Online magazine	Davidson, Adam. "What Hollywood Can Teach Us About the Future of Work." *New York Times Magazine*, 5 May 2015, www.nytimes.com/2015/05/10/magazine/what-hollywood-can-teach-us-about-the-future-of-work.html?ref=business. Accessed 9 July 2015.	
	Dunams, Alicia. "All In: Elevating Your Leadership Game." 21 Feb. 2014, www.aliciadunams.com/bestselling-author-alicia-dunams-all-in elevating-your-leadership-game-podcast-series-makes-itunes-new-and-noteworthy. Accessed 5 Mar. 2016.	Podcast
Online article, no author	"How to Start a Business Online." *Entrepreneur*, 2015, www.entrepreneur.com/article/17524. Accessed 23 May 2017.	
	Hunter, Douglas. "Re: CEOs' exorbitant salaries." Received by Hector Sotomeyor, 23 June 2017.	E-mail message
Online journal with volume (10) and issue (5) numbers as well as doi	Ola, J. Christian, and Dennis Proffitt. "The Stock Market Response to CEO Changes: Does Gender Matter?" *International Journal of Business and Management*, vol. 10, no. 5, 2015, www.ccsenet.org/journal/index.php/ijbm/article/view/45287. Accessed 10 Apr. 2017, doi:10.5539/ijbm.v10n5p1.	
	Riley, Naomi Schaefer. "Birds, Bees and Bureaucracies." *The Wall Street Journal*. Review of *Too Hot to Handle* by Jonathan Zimmerman, 1 May 2015, p. 11.	Book review

Note: Check with your instructor or organization about whether to cite URLs and date of access.

Figure credit

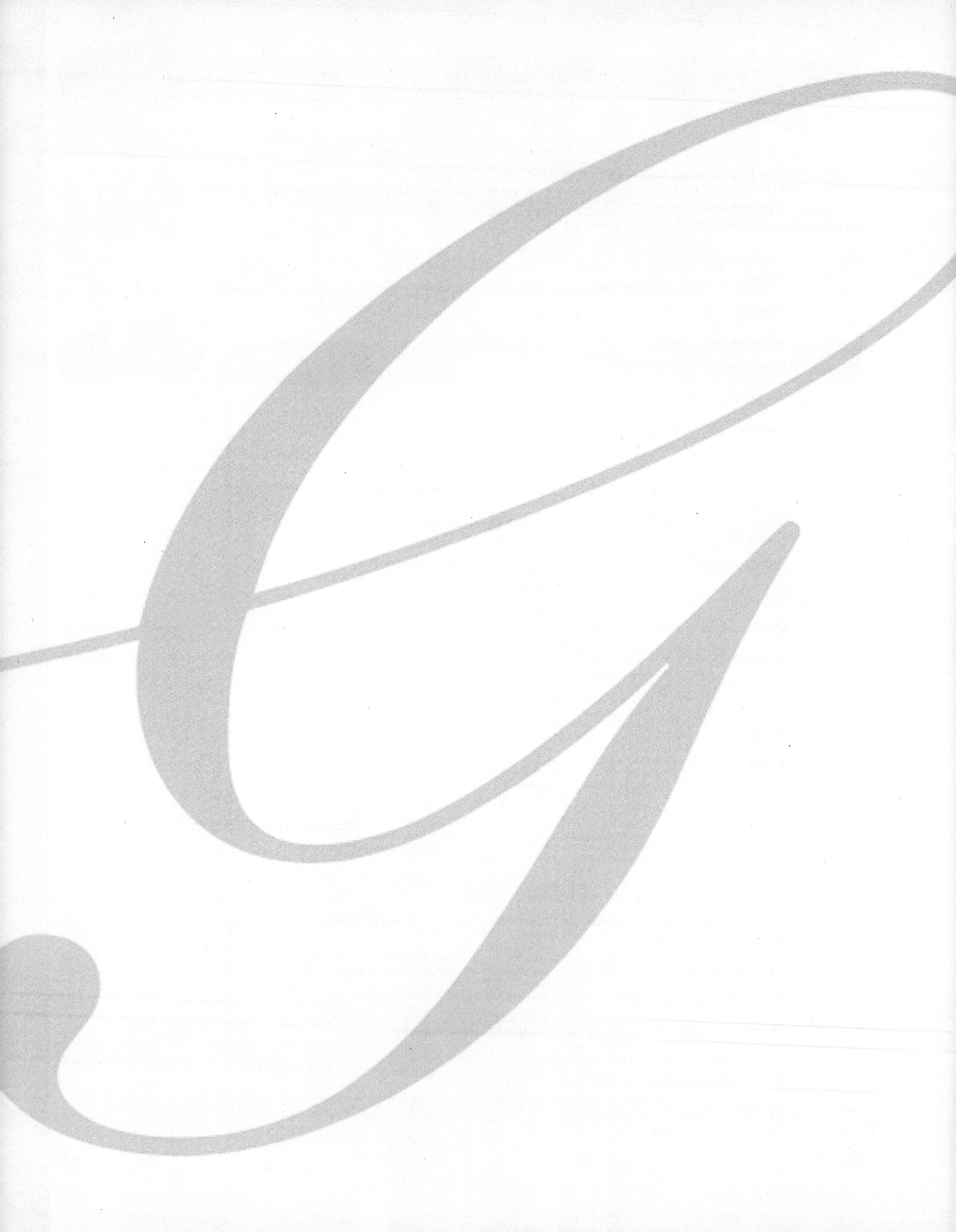

Appendix C

Correction Symbols and Proofreading Marks

In marking your papers, your instructor may use the following symbols or abbreviations to indicate writing weaknesses. Studying these symbols and suggestions will help you understand your instructor's remarks. Knowing this information can also help you evaluate and improve your own e-mails, memos, letters, reports, and other writing. These symbols are keyed to your Grammar and Mechanics Guide and to the text.

Adj Hyphenate two or more adjectives that are joined to create a compound modifier before a noun. See G/M Guide 20.

Adv Use adverbs, not adjectives, to describe or limit the action. See G/M Guide 19.

Apos Use apostrophes to show possession. See G/M Guides 31–33.

Assgn Follow the assignment instructions.

Awk Recast to avoid awkward expression.

Bias Use inclusive, bias-free language. See Chapter 4.

Cap Use capitalization appropriately. See G/M Guides 39–46.

CmConj Use a comma before the coordinating conjunction in a compound sentence. See G/M Guide 23.

CmDate Use commas appropriately in dates, addresses, geographical names, degrees, and long numbers. See G/M Guide 24.

CmIn Use commas to set off internal sentence interrupters. See G/M Guide 25.

CmIntr Use commas to separate introductory clauses and certain phrases from independent clauses. See G/M Guide 22.

CmSer Use commas to separate three or more items (words, phrases, or short clauses) in a series. See G/M Guide 21.

Coh Improve coherence between ideas. Repeat key ideas, use pronouns, or use transitional expressions. See Chapter 5.

Cl Improve the clarity of ideas or expression so that the point is better understood. See Chapter 6.

CS Avoid comma-splice sentences, Do not use a comma to splice (join) two independent clauses. See G/M Guide 3 and Chapter 5.

CmUn Avoid unnecessary commas. See G/M Guide 26.

: Use a colon after a complete thought that introduces a list of items. Use a colon in business letter salutations and to introduce long quotations. See G/M Guides 29 and 30.

Direct Use the direct strategy by emphasizing the main idea. See Chapter 5.

Dash Use a dash to set off parenthetical elements, to emphasize sentence interruptions, or to separate an introductory list from a summarizing statement. See G/M Guide 36.

DD Use document design (white space, margins, typefaces, bullets, lists, indentions, or headings) to enhance readability. See Chapter 6.

DM Avoid dangling modifiers by placing modifiers close to the words they describe or limit. See Chapter 5.

Filler Avoid fillers such as *there are* or long lead-ins such as *this is to inform you that*. See Chapter 6.

Format Choose an appropriate format for this document. See Appendix A.

Frag Avoid fragments by expressing ideas in complete sentences. A fragment is a broken-off part of a sentence. See Chapter 5 and G/M Guide 1.

MM Avoid misplaced modifiers by placing modifiers close to the words they describe or limit. See Chapter 5.

Num	Use number or word form appropriately. See G/M Guides 47–50.
Ob	Avoid stating the obvious.
Org	Improve organization by grouping similar ideas.
Par	Express ideas in parallel form. See Chapter 5.
Paren	Use parentheses to set off nonessential sentence elements such as explanations, directions, questions, or references. See G/M Guide 37.
Period	Use one period to end a statement, command, indirect question, or polite request. See G/M Guide 34.
Pos	Express an idea positively rather than negatively. See Chapter 4.
PosPro	Use possessive-case pronouns to show ownership. See G/M Guide 33.
Pro	Use nominative-case pronouns as subjects of verbs and as subject complements. Use objective-case pronouns as objects of prepositions and verbs. See G/M Guides 11–13.
ProAgr	Make pronouns agree in number and gender with the words to which they refer (their antecedents). See G/M Guide 17.
ProVag	Be sure that pronouns such as *it, which, this*, and *that* refer to clear antecedents. See G/M Guide 18.
?	Use a question mark after a direct question and after statements with questions appended. See G/M Guide 35.
Quo	Use quotation marks to enclose the exact words of a speaker or writer; to distinguish words used in a special sense; or to enclose titles of articles, chapters, or other short works. Words used in a special sense may also be shown with italics. See G/M Guide 38.
Redun	Avoid expressions that repeat meaning or include unnecessary words. See Chapter 6.
RunOn	Avoid run-on (fused) sentences. A sentence with two independent clauses must be joined by a coordinating conjunctions (*and, or, nor, but*) or by a semicolon (;). See Chapter 5 and G/M Guide 2.
Self	Use *self*-ending pronouns only when they refer to previously mentioned nouns or pronouns. See G/M Guide 15.
;	Use a semicolon to join closely related independent clauses or to separate items in a series when one or more of the items contains internal commas. See G/M Guides 27 and 28.
Shift	Avoid a confusing shift in verb tense, mood, or voice. See G/M Guides 4 and 5.
Sp	Check misspelled words.
Trans	Use an appropriate transition. See Chapter 5 and Chapter 12.
Tone	Use a conversational, positive, and courteous tone that promotes goodwill. See Chapter 4.
You	Focus on developing the "you" view. See Chapter 4.
VbAgr	Make verbs agree with subjects. See G/M Guides 6–10.
VbMood	Use the subjunctive mood to express hypothetical (untrue) ideas. See G/M Guide 5.
VbTnse	Use present-tense, past-tense, and part-participle forms correctly. See G/M Guide 4.
VbVce	Use active- and passive-voice verbs appropriately. See Chapter 5.
WC	Focus on precise word choice. See Chapter 4.
Wordy	Avoid wordiness including flabby expressions, long lead-ins, unnecessary *there is/are* fillers, redundancies, and trite business phrases. See Chapter 6.

Proofreading Marks

Proofreading Mark	Draft Copy	Final Copy
Align horizontally	TO: Rick Munoz	TO: Rick Munoz
Align vertically	166.32 132.45	166.32 132.45
Capitalize	Coca-cola sending a pdf file	Coca-Cola sending a PDF file
Close up space	meeting at 3 p. m.	meeting at 3 p.m.
Center	Recommendations	Recommendations
Delete	in my final judgement	in my judgment
Insert apostrophe	our companys product	our company's product
Insert comma	you will of course	you will, of course,
Insert hyphen	tax free income	tax-free income
Insert period	Ms Holly Hines	Ms. Holly Hines
Insert quotation mark	shareholders receive a bonus.	shareholders receive a "bonus."
Insert space	wordprocessing program	word processing program
Lowercase (remove capitals)	the Vice President HUMAN RESOURCES	the vice president Human Resources
Move to left	I. Labor costs	I. Labor costs
Move to right	A. Findings of study	A. Findings of study
Spell out	aimed at 2 depts	aimed at two departments
Start new paragraph	Keep the screen height of your computer at eye level.	Keep the screen height of your computer at eye level.
Stet (don't delete)	officials talked openly	officials talked openly
Transpose	accounts recievable	accounts receivable
Use boldface	Conclusions bf	**Conclusions**
Use italics	The Perfect Résumé ital	*The Perfect Résumé*

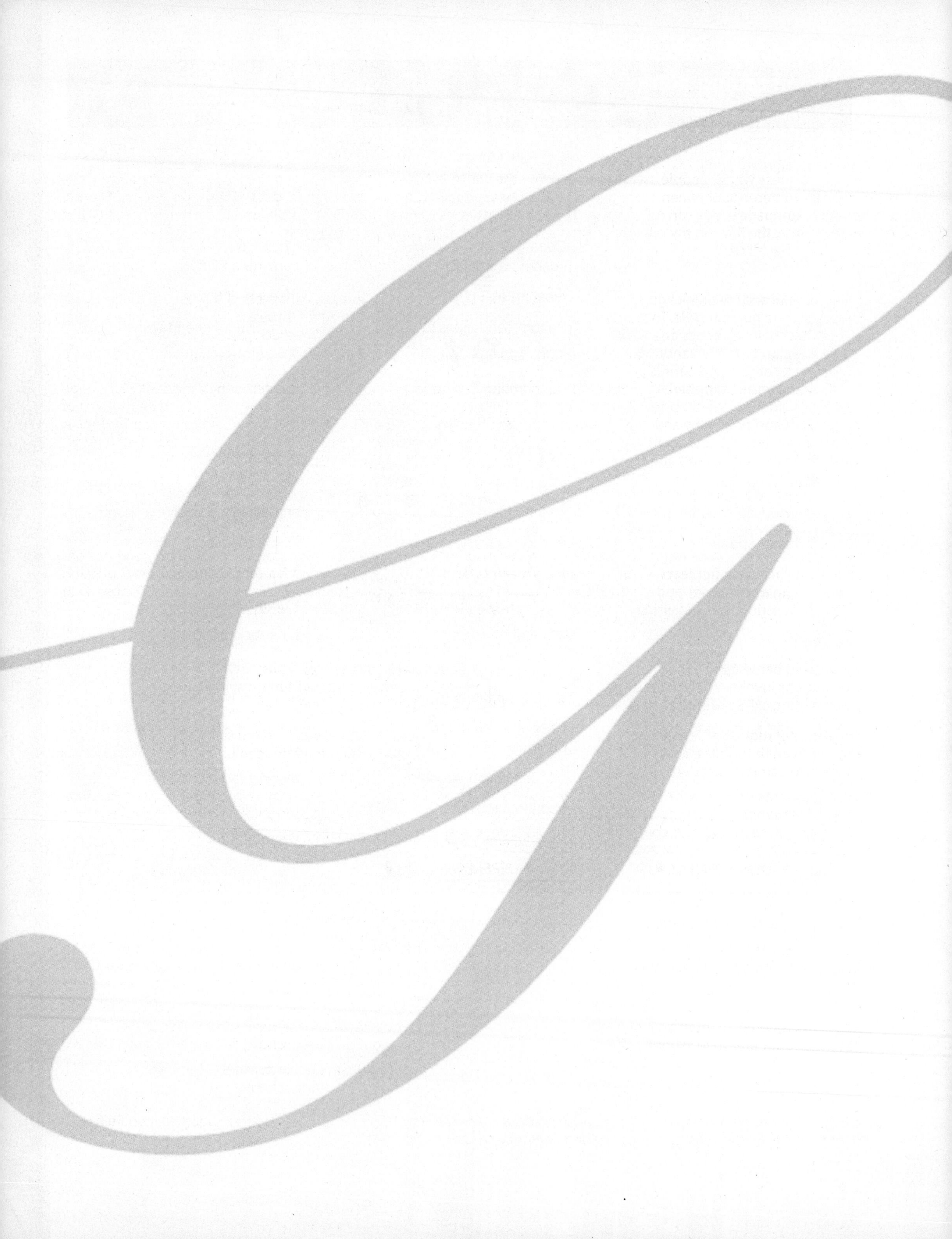

Appendix D

Grammar and Mechanics Guide

In the business world, people are often judged by the way they speak and write. Using the language competently can mean the difference between success and failure. Speakers may sound accomplished, but when they put ideas in print, errors in language usage can destroy their credibility. One student observed, "When I talk, I get by on my personality, but when I write, the flaws in my communication show through. That's why I'm in this class."

How This Grammar and Mechanics Guide Can Help You

This grammar and mechanics guide contains 50 guidelines covering sentence structure, grammar, usage, punctuation, capitalization, and number style. These guidelines focus on the most frequently used—and abused—language elements. Frequent checkpoint exercises enable you to try your skills immediately. When you finish, check your answers on page Key-1.

In addition to the 50 language guides in this appendix, you will find a list of 160 frequently misspelled words plus a quick review of selected confusing words.

The concentrated materials in this guide help novice business communicators focus on the major areas of language use. This guide focuses on principal language guidelines and troublesome words. Your objective should be mastery of these language principles and words, which represent a majority of the problems encountered by business writers. A more comprehensive treatment of grammar and punctuation guidelines can be found in Clark and Clark's *HOW: A Handbook for Office Professionals* and Guffey and Seefer's *Business English*.

Grammar and Mechanics Guidelines

Sentence Structure

GUIDE 1: Avoid sentence fragments. A fragment is an incomplete sentence. You can recognize a complete sentence because it (a) includes a subject (a noun or pronoun that interacts with a verb), (b) includes a verb (a word expressing action or describing a condition), and (c) makes sense (comes to a closure). A complete sentence is an independent clause. One of the most serious errors a writer can make is punctuating a fragment as if it were a complete sentence.

Fragment	Improved
Because 90 percent of all business transactions involve written messages. Good writing skills are critical.	Because 90 percent of all business transactions involve written messages, good writing skills are critical.
The recruiter requested a writing sample. Even though the candidate seemed to communicate well.	The recruiter requested a writing sample, even though the candidate seemed to communicate well.

Tip: Fragments often can be identified by the words that introduce them—words such as *although, as, because, even, except, for example, if, instead of, since, so, such as, that, which,* and *when*. These words introduce dependent clauses. Make sure such clauses are always connected to independent clauses.

DEPENDENT CLAUSE | INDEPENDENT CLAUSE

Since she became supervisor, she had to write more memos and reports.

GUIDE 2: Avoid run-on (fused) sentences. A sentence with two independent clauses must be joined by a coordinating conjunction (*and, or, nor, but*) or by a semicolon (;). Without a conjunction or a semicolon, a run-on sentence results.

Run-On	Improved
Rachel considered an internship she also thought about graduate school.	Rachel considered an internship, and she also thought about graduate school. Rachel considered an internship; she also thought about graduate school.

GUIDE 3: Avoid comma-splice sentences. A comma splice results when a writer joins (splices together) two independent clauses—without using a coordinating conjunction (*and, or, nor, but*).

Comma Splice	Improved
Disney World operates in Orlando, EuroDisney serves Paris.	Disney World operates in Orlando; EuroDisney serves Paris.
	Disney World operates in Orlando, and EuroDisney serves Paris.
Visitors wanted a resort vacation, however they were disappointed.	Visitors wanted a resort vacation; however, they were disappointed.

Tip: In joining independent clauses, beware of using a comma and words such as *consequently, furthermore, however, therefore, then,* and *thus*. These conjunctive adverbs require semicolons.

Note: Sentence structure is also covered in Chapter 5.

✓Checkpoint

Revise the following to rectify sentence fragments, comma splices, and run-ons.

1. Although it began as a side business for Disney. Destination weddings now represent a major income source.
2. About 2,000 weddings are held yearly. Which is twice the number just ten years ago.
3. Weddings may take place in less than one hour, however the cost may be as much as $5,000.
4. Limousines line up outside Disney's wedding pavilion, they are scheduled in two-hour intervals.
5. Most couples prefer a traditional wedding, others request a fantasy experience.

For all the Checkpoint sentences, compare your responses with the answers at the end of Appendix D.

Verb Tense

GUIDE 4: Use present-tense, past-tense, and past-participle verb forms correctly.

Present Tense	Past Tense	Past Participle
(Today I ______)	(Yesterday I ______)	(I have ______)
am	was	been
begin	began	begun
break	broke	broken
bring	brought	brought
choose	chose	chosen
come	came	come
do	did	done
give	gave	given
go	went	gone
know	knew	known
pay	paid	paid
see	saw	seen
steal	stole	stolen
take	took	taken
write	wrote	written

The package *came* yesterday, and Kevin *knew* what it contained.

If I *had seen* the shipper's bill, I *would have paid* it immediately.

I *know* the answer now; I wish I *had known* it yesterday.

Tip: Probably the most frequent mistake in tenses results from substituting the past-participle form for the past tense. Notice that the past-participle tense requires auxiliary verbs such as *has, had, have, would have,* and *could have.*

Faulty	Correct
When he *come* over last night, he *brung* pizza.	When he *came* over last night, he *brought* pizza.
If he *had came* earlier, we *could have saw* the video.	If he *had come* earlier, we *could have seen* the video.

Verb Mood

GUIDE 5: Use the subjunctive mood to express hypothetical (untrue) ideas. The most frequent misuse of the subjunctive mood involves using *was* instead of *were* in clauses introduced by *if* and *as though* or containing *wish.*

If I *were* (not *was*) you, I would take a business writing course.

Sometimes I wish I *were* (not *was*) the manager of this department.

He acts as though he *were* (not *was*) in charge of this department.

Tip: If the statement could possibly be true, use *was.*

If I *was* to blame, I accept the consequences.

✓Checkpoint

Correct faults in verb tense and mood.

6. If I was you, I would have went to the ten o'clock meeting.
7. Kevin could have wrote a better report if he had began earlier.
8. When the project manager seen the report, he immediately come to my office.
9. I wish the project manager was in my shoes for just one day.
10. If the manager had knew all that we do, I'm sure he would have gave us better reviews.

Verb Voice

For a discussion of active- and passive-voice verbs, see Chapter 5.

Verb Agreement

GUIDE 6: Make subjects agree with verbs despite intervening phrases and clauses. Become a detective in locating true subjects. Don't be deceived by prepositional phrases and parenthetic words that often disguise the true subject.

Our study of annual budgets, five-year plans, and sales proposals *is* (not *are*) progressing on schedule. (The true subject is *study.*)

The budgeted item, despite additions proposed yesterday, *remains* (not *remain*) as submitted. (The true subject is *item.*)

A vendor's evaluation of the prospects for a sale, together with plans for follow-up action, *is* (not *are*) what we need. (The true subject is *evaluation.*)

Tip: Subjects are nouns or pronouns that control verbs. To find subjects, cross out prepositional phrases beginning with words such as *about, at, by, for, from, of,* and *to.* Subjects of verbs are not found in prepositional phrases. Also, don't be tricked by expressions introduced by *together with, in addition to,* and *along with.*

GUIDE 7: With subjects joined by *and*, use plural verbs. Watch for true subjects joined by the conjunction *and.* They require plural verbs.

The CEO and one of his assistants *have* (not *has*) ordered a limo.

Considerable time and money *were* (not *was*) spent on remodeling.

Exercising in the gym and jogging every day *are* (not *is*) how he keeps fit.

Tip: Subjects joined by *or* or *nor* may require singular or plural verbs. The verb should agree with the closer subject.

Either the software or the printer *is* (not *are*) causing the glitch. (The verb is controlled by the closer subject, *printer.*)

Neither St. Louis nor Chicago *has* (not *have*) a chance of winning. (The verb is controlled by *Chicago.*)

Tip: In joining singular and plural subjects with *or* or *nor,* place the plural subject closer to the verb. Then, the plural verb sounds natural. For example, *Either the manufacturer or the distributors are responsible.*

GUIDE 8: Use singular verbs for most indefinite pronouns. The following pronouns all take singular verbs: *anyone, anybody, anything, each, either, every, everyone, everybody, everything, neither, nobody, nothing, someone, somebody,* and *something.*

Everyone in both offices *was* (not *were*) given a bonus.

Each of the employees *is* (not *are*) being interviewed.

GUIDE 9: Use singular or plural verbs for collective nouns, depending on whether the members of the group are operating as a unit or individually. Words such as *faculty, administration, class, crowd,* and *committee* are considered *collective* nouns. If the members of the collective are acting as a unit, treat them as singular subjects. If they are acting individually, it is usually better to add the word *members* and use a plural verb.

Correct

The Finance Committee *is* working harmoniously. (*Committee* is singular because its action is unified.)

The Planning Committee *are* having difficulty agreeing. (*Committee* is plural because its members are acting individually.)

Improved

The Planning Committee members *are* having difficulty agreeing. (Add the word *members* if a plural meaning is intended.)

Tip: In the United States, collective nouns are generally considered singular. In Britain collective nouns are generally considered plural.

✓Checkpoint

Correct the errors in subject–verb agreement.

11. The time and talent of Instagram was spent developing a blockbuster ad campaign.
12. Your e-mail message, along with both of its attachments, were not delivered to my computer.
13. Each of the Fortune 500 companies are being sent a survey regarding women in management.
14. A full list of names and addresses are necessary before we can begin.
15. Either the judge or the attorney have asked for a recess.

Plural Nouns

GUIDE 10: For nouns ending in *s, x, z, ch,* or *sh,* form the plural by adding *es*.

All *businesses* must pay their *taxes.*

The *Lopezes* purchased two *watches* as graduation gifts.

Nouns ending in *y* form the plural in two ways. When the letter before *y* is a vowel (*a, e, i, o, u*), form the plural by adding *s* only. When the letter before *y* is a consonant (all letters other than vowels), form the plural by changing the *y* to *ie* and adding *s.*

Several *attorneys* worked on the privacy cases.

Both *cities* provided extensive *libraries* for citizens.

Pronoun Case

GUIDE 11: Learn the three cases of pronouns and how each is used. Pronouns are substitutes for nouns. Every business writer must know the following pronoun cases.

Subjective (Nominative) Case	Objective Case	Possessive Case
Used for subjects of verbs and subject complements	Used for objects of prepositions and objects of verbs	Used to show possession
we		
I	me	my, mine
us	our, ours	
you	you	you, yours
he	him	his
she	her	her, hers

Subjective (Nominative) Case	Objective Case	Possessive Case
Used for subjects of verbs and subject complements	Used for objects of prepositions and objects of verbs	Used to show possession
it	it	its
they	them	their, theirs
who, whoever	whom, whomever	whose

GUIDE 12: Use subjective-case pronouns as subjects of verbs and as complements. Complements are words that follow linking verbs (such as *am, is, are, was, were, be, being,* and *been*) and rename the words to which they refer.

> *She* and *I* (not *her* and *me*) will be collaborating. (Use a subjective-case pronoun as the subject of the verb phrase *will be collaborating.*)
>
> We hope that Marci and *he* (not *him*) will join our team. (Use a subjective-case pronoun as the subject of the verb phrase *will join.*)
>
> It must have been *she* (not *her*) who called last night. (Use a subjective-case pronoun as a subject complement.)

Tip: If you feel awkward using subjective pronouns after linking verbs, rephrase the sentence to avoid the dilemma. Instead of *It is she who is the boss,* say, *She is the boss.*

GUIDE 13: Use objective-case pronouns as objects of prepositions and verbs.

> Send the e-mail to *her* and *me* (not *she* and *I*). (The pronouns *her* and *me* are objects of the preposition *to.*)
>
> The CEO appointed Rick and *him* (not *he*) to the committee. (The pronoun *him* is the object of the verb *appointed.*)

Tip: When a pronoun appears in combination with a noun or another pronoun, ignore the extra noun or pronoun and its conjunction. Then, the case of the pronoun becomes more obvious.

> Jason asked Jennifer and *me* (not *I*) to lunch. (Ignore *Jennifer and.*)
>
> The waiter brought hamburgers to Jason and *me* (not *I*). (Ignore *Jason and.*)

Tip: Be especially alert to the following prepositions: *except, between, but,* and *like.* Be sure to use objective pronouns as their objects.

> Just between you and *me* (not *I*), that mineral water comes from the tap.
>
> Everyone except Robert and *him* (not *he*) responded to the invitation.

GUIDE 14: Use possessive pronouns to show ownership. Possessive pronouns (such as *hers, yours, whose, ours, theirs,* and *its*) require no apostrophes.

> All reports except *yours* (not *your's*) have to be rewritten.
>
> The apartment and *its* (not *it's*) contents are *hers* (not *her's*) until June.

Tip: Don't confuse possessive pronouns and contractions. Contractions are shortened forms of subject–verb phrases (such as *it's* for *it is, there's* for *there is, who's* for *who is,* and *they're* for *they are*).

✓Checkpoint

Correct errors in pronoun case.

16. My partner and me have looked at many apartments, but your's has the best location.
17. We thought the car was her's, but it's license plate does not match.
18. Just between you and I, do you think the companies will merge?
19. Neither the boss nor me knows whether its broken, but its condition should have been reported to him or I earlier.
20. We received several applications, but your's and her's were missing

GUIDE 15: Use pronouns ending in *self* only when they refer to previously mentioned nouns or pronouns.

The president *himself* ate all the M&Ms.

Send the chocolates to Mike or *me* (not *myself*).

Tip: Trying to sound less egocentric, some radio and TV announcers incorrectly substitute *myself* when they should use *I* (*Jimmy and* I [not *myself*] *are cohosting the tournament*).

GUIDE 16: Use *who* or *whoever* for subjective-case constructions and *whom* or *whomever* for objective-case constructions. In determining the correct choice, it is helpful to substitute *he* for *who* or *whoever* and *him* for *whom* or *whomever.*

For *whom* was this software ordered? (The software was ordered for *him.*)

Who did you say called? (You did say *he* called)

Give the supplies to *whoever* asked for them. (In this sentence the clause *whoever asked for them* functions as the object of the preposition *to.* Within the clause *whoever* is the subject of the verb *asked.* Again, try substituting *he: he asked for them.*)

✓Checkpoint

Correct any errors in the use of *self*-ending pronouns and *who/whom.*

21. The manager herself is willing to call whoever we decide to honor.
22. Who have you hired to investigate the data breach?
23. I have a pizza for whomever placed the online order.
24. The meeting is set for Wednesday; however, Matt and myself cannot attend.
25. Incident reports must be submitted by whomever experiences a personnel problem.

Pronoun Reference

GUIDE 17: Make pronouns agree in number and gender with the words to which they refer (their antecedents). When the gender of the antecedent is obvious, pronoun references are simple.

One of the men failed to fill in *his* (not *their*) name on the application. (The singular pronoun *his* refers to the singular *One.*)

Each of the female nurses was escorted to *her car* (not *their cars*). (The singular pronoun *her* and singular noun *car* are necessary because they refer to the singular subject *Each.*)

Somebody on the girls' team left *her* (not *their*) headlights on.

When the gender of the antecedent could be male or female, sensitive writers today have a number of options.

Faulty	Improved
Every employee should receive *their* check Friday. (The plural pronoun *their* does not agree with its singular antecedent *employee.*)	All employees should receive *their* checks Friday. (Make the subject plural so that the plural pronoun *their* is acceptable. This option is preferred by many writers today.)
	All employees should receive checks Friday. (Omit the possessive pronoun entirely.)
	Every employee should receive *a* check Friday. (Substitute *a* for a pronoun.)
	Every employee should receive *his or her* check Friday. (Use the combination *his or her.* However, this option is wordy and should be avoided.)

GUIDE 18: Be sure that pronouns such as *it, which, this,* and *that* refer to clear antecedents. Vague pronouns confuse the reader because they have no clear single antecedent. The most troublesome are *it, which, this,* and *that.* Replace vague pronouns with concrete nouns, or provide these pronouns with clear antecedents.

Faulty	Improved
Our office recycles as much paper as possible because *it* helps the environment. (Does *it* refer to *paper, recycling,* or *office?*)	Our office recycles as much paper as possible because *such an effort* helps the environment. (*Effort* supplies a concrete noun for the vague pronoun *it.*)
The disadvantages of some mobile apps can offset their advantages. *That* merits further evaluation. (What merits evaluation: advantages, disadvantages, or the offsetting of one by the other?)	The disadvantages of some mobile apps can offset their advantages. That fact merits further evaluation. (*Fact* supplies a concrete noun for the vague pronoun *that.*)
Negotiators announced an expanded wellness program, reductions in dental coverage, and a proposal to move child-care facilities off site. *This* ignited employee protests. (What exactly ignited employee protests?)	Negotiators announced an expanded wellness program, reductions in dental coverage, and a proposal to move child-care facilities off site *This change in child-care facilities* ignited employee protests. (The pronoun *This* now has a clear reference.)

Tip: Whenever you use the words *this, that, these,* and *those* by themselves, a red flag should pop up. These words are dangerous when they stand alone. Inexperienced writers often use them to refer to an entire previous idea, rather than to a specific antecedent, as shown in the preceding examples. You can usually solve the problem by adding another idea to the pronoun (such as *this change*).

✓Checkpoint

Correct the faulty and vague pronoun references in the following sentences. Numerous remedies exist.

26. Every employee must wear their picture identification badge.
27. Flexible working hours may mean slower career advancement, but it appeals to many workers.
28. Any renter must pay his rent by the first of the month.
29. Someone in this office reported that his computer had a virus.
30. Obtaining agreement on job standards, listening to coworkers, and encouraging employee suggestions all helped to open lines of communication. This is particularly important in team projects.

Adjectives and Adverbs

GUIDE 19: Use adverbs, not adjectives, to describe or limit the action of verbs. Use adjectives after linking verbs.

Andrew said he did *well* (not *good*) on the exam. (The adverb *well* describes how he did.)

After its tune-up, the engine is running *smoothly* (not *smooth*). (The adverb *smoothly* describes the verb phrase *is running.*)

Don't take the manager's criticism *personally* (not *personal*). (The adverb *personally* tells how to take the criticism.)

She finished her homework *more quickly* (not *quicker*) than expected. (The adverb *more quickly*) explains how she finished her homework.)

Liam felt *bad* (not *badly*) after he heard the news. (The adjective *bad* follows the linking verb *felt*.)

GUIDE 20: Hyphenate two or more adjectives that are joined to create a compound modifier before a noun.

You need an *easy-to-remember* e-mail address and a *one-page* résumé.

Person-to-person networking continues to be the best way to find a job.

Tip: Don't confuse adverbs ending in *-ly* with compound adjectives: *newly enacted* law and *highly regarded* CEO would not be hyphenated.

✓Checkpoint

Correct any problems in the use of pronouns, adjectives, and adverbs.

31. My manager and me could not resist the once in a lifetime opportunity.
32. Because John and him finished their task so quick, they made a fast trip to the recently opened snack bar.
33. If I do good on the exam, I qualify for many part time jobs and a few full time positions.
34. The vice president told him and I not to take the announcement personal.
35. In the not too distant future, we may enjoy more practical uses of robots and drones.

Commas

GUIDE 21: Use commas to separate three or more items (words, phrases, or short clauses) in a series. (Comma Series: CmSer)

Downward communication delivers job instructions, procedures, and appraisals.

In preparing your résumé, try to keep it brief, make it easy to read, and include only job-related information.

The new ice cream flavors include cookie dough, chocolate raspberry truffle, cappuccino, and almond amaretto.

Tip: Some professional writers omit the comma before *and*. However, most business writers prefer to retain that comma because it prevents misreading the last two items as one item. Notice in the previous example how the final two ice cream flavors could have been misread if the comma had been omitted.

GUIDE 22: Use commas to separate introductory clauses and certain phrases from independent clauses. (Comma Introductory: CmIntro) This guideline describes the comma most often omitted by business writers. Sentences that open with dependent clauses (frequently introduced by words such as *since, when, if, as, although,* and *because*) require commas to separate them from the main idea. The comma helps readers recognize where the introduction ends and the big idea begins. Introductory phrases of four or more words, and phrases containing verbal elements, also require commas.

If you recognize introductory clauses, you will have no trouble placing the comma. (A comma separates the introductory dependent clause from the main clause.)

When you have mastered this rule, half the battle with commas will be won.

As expected, additional explanations are necessary. (Use a comma even if the introductory clause omits the understood subject: *As we expected.*)

In the spring of last year, we opened our franchise. (Use a comma after a phrase containing four or more words.)

Having considered several alternatives, we decided to invest. (Use a comma after an introductory verbal phrase.)

To invest, we needed $100,000. (Use a comma after an introductory verbal phrase, regardless of its length.)

Tip: Short introductory prepositional phrases (three or fewer words) require no commas. Don't clutter your writing with unnecessary commas after introductory phrases such as *by 2020, in the fall,* or *at this time.*

GUIDE 23: Use a comma before the coordinating conjunction in a compound sentence. (Comma Conjunction: CmConj) The most common coordinating conjunctions are *and, or, nor,* and *but.* Occasionally, *for, yet,* and *so* may also function as coordinating conjunctions. When coordinating conjunctions join two independent clauses, commas are needed.

The investment sounded too good to be true, *and* many investors were dubious about it. (Use a comma before the coordinating conjunction *and* in a compound sentence.)

Southern California is the financial fraud capital of the world, *but* some investors refuse to heed warning signs.

Tip: Before inserting a comma, test the two independent clauses. Can each of them stand alone as a complete sentence? If either is incomplete, skip the comma.

Promoters said the investment offer was for a limited time and could not be extended even one day. (Omit a comma before *and* because the second part of the sentence is not a complete independent clause.)

Lease payments are based largely on your down payment and on the value of the car at the end of the lease. (Omit a comma before *and* because the second half of the sentence is not a complete independent clause.)

✓Checkpoint

Add appropriate commas.

36. Before she enrolled in this class Erin used to sprinkle her writing with commas semicolons and dashes.
37. After studying punctuation she learned to use commas more carefully and to reduce her reliance on dashes.
38. At this time Erin is engaged in a serious yoga program but she also finds time to enlighten her mind.
39. Next fall Erin may enroll in communication and merchandising courses or she may work for a semester to earn money.
40. When she completes her junior year she plans to apply for an internship in Los Angeles Burbank or Long Beach.

GUIDE 24: Use commas appropriately in dates, addresses, geographical names, degrees, and long numbers. (Comma Date: CmDate)

September 30, 1993, is his birthday. (For dates use commas before and after the year.)

Send the application to James Kirby, 20045 45th Avenue, Lynnwood, WA 98036, as soon as possible. (For addresses use commas to separate all units except the two-letter state abbreviation and the zip code.)

Lisa expects to move from Cupertino, California, to Sonoma, Arizona, next fall. (For geographical areas use commas to enclose the second element.)

Karen Munson, CPA, and Richard B. Larsen, PhD, were the speakers. (Use commas to enclose professional designations and academic degrees following names.)

The latest census figures show the city's population to be 342,000. (In figures use commas to separate every three digits, counting from the right.)

GUIDE 25: Use commas to set off internal sentence interrupters. (Comma Internal: CmIn) Sentence interrupters may be verbal phrases, dependent clauses, contrasting elements, or parenthetical expressions (also called transitional phrases). These interrupters often provide information that is not grammatically essential.

Harvard researchers, working steadily for 18 months, developed a new cancer therapy. (Use commas to set off an internal interrupting verbal phrase.)

The new therapy, which applies a genetically engineered virus, raises hopes among cancer specialists. (Use commas to set off nonessential dependent clauses.)

Dr. James C. Morrison, who is one of the researchers, made the announcement. (Use commas to set off nonessential dependent clauses.)

It was Dr. Morrison, not Dr. Arturo, who led the team effort. (Use commas to set off a contrasting element.)

This new therapy, by the way, was developed from a herpes virus. (Use commas to set off a parenthetical expression.)

Tip: Parenthetical (transitional) expressions are helpful words that guide the reader from one thought to the next. Here are typical parenthetical expressions that require commas:

as a matter of fact	in addition	of course
as a result	in the meantime	on the other hand
consequently	nevertheless	therefore
for example		

Tip: Always use *two* commas to set off an interrupter, unless it begins or ends a sentence.

✓Checkpoint

Insert necessary commas.

41. James listed 1805 Martin Luther King Street San Antonio Texas 78220 as his forwarding address.
42. This report is not however one that must be classified.
43. Employment of paralegals which is expected to decrease 12 percent next year is contracting because of the slow economy and automation.
44. The contract was signed May 15 2012 and remains in effect until May 15 2018.
45. As a matter of fact the average American drinks enough coffee to require 12 pounds of coffee beans annually.

GUIDE 26: Avoid unnecessary commas (Comma Unnecessary: CmNo). Do not use commas between sentence elements that belong together. Do not automatically insert commas before every *and* or at points where your voice might drop if you were saying the sentence out loud.

Faulty

Growth will be spurred by the increasing complexity of business operations, and by large employment gains in trade and services. (A comma unnecessarily precedes *and.*)

All students with high grades, are eligible for the honor society. (A comma unnecessarily separates the subject and verb.)

One of the reasons for the success of the business honor society is, that it is very active. (A comma unnecessarily separates the verb and its complement.)

Our honor society has, at this time, over 50 members. (Commas unnecessarily separate a prepositional phrase from the sentence.)

✓Checkpoint

Remove unnecessary commas. Add necessary ones.

46. Car companies promote leasing because it brings customers back into their showrooms sooner, and gives dealers a steady supply of late-model used cars.
47. When shopping for a car you may be offered a fantastic leasing deal.
48. The trouble with many leases is, that the value of the car at the end of the lease may be less than expected.
49. We think on the other hand, that you should compare the costs of leasing and buying, and that you should talk to a tax advisor.
50. American and Japanese automakers are, at this time, offering intriguing lease deals.

Semicolons, Colons

GUIDE 27: Use a semicolon to join closely related independent clauses. Experienced writers use semicolons to show readers that two thoughts are closely associated. If the ideas are not related, they should be expressed in separate sentences. Often, but not always, the second independent clause contains a conjunctive adverb (such as *however, consequently, therefore,* or *furthermore*) to show the relation between the two clauses. Use a semicolon before a conjunctive adverb of two or more syllables (such as *however, consequently, therefore*, or *furthermore*) and a comma after it.

Learning history is easy; learning its lessons is almost impossible. (A semicolon joins two independent clauses.)

He was determined to complete his degree; consequently, he studied diligently. (A semicolon precedes the conjunctive adverb, and a comma follows it.)

Serena wanted a luxury apartment located near campus; however, she couldn't afford the rent. (A semicolon precedes the conjunctive adverb, and a comma follows it.)

Tip: Don't use a semicolon unless each clause is truly independent. Try the sentence test. Omit the semicolon if each clause could not stand alone as a complete sentence.

Faulty	Improved
There is no point in speaking; unless you can improve on silence. (The second half of the sentence is a dependent clause. It could not stand alone as a sentence.)	There is no point in speaking unless you can improve on silence.
Although I cannot change the direction of the wind; I can adjust my sails to reach my destination. (The first clause could not stand alone.)	Although I cannot change the direction of the wind, I can adjust my sails to reach my destination.

GUIDE 28: Use a semicolon to separate items in a series when one or more of the items contains internal commas.

Representatives from as far away as Blue Bell, Pennsylvania; Bowling Green, Ohio; and Phoenix, Arizona, attended the conference.

Stories circulated about Henry Ford, founder, Ford Motor Company; Lee Iacocca, former CEO, Chrysler Motor Company; and Shoichiro Toyoda, founder, Toyota Motor Company.

GUIDE 29: Use a colon after a complete thought that introduces a list of items. Words such as *these, the following,* and *as follows* may introduce the list or they may be implied.

The following cities are on the tour: Louisville, Memphis, and New Orleans.

An alternate tour includes several West Coast cities: Seattle, San Francisco, and San Diego.

Tip: Be sure that the statement before a colon is grammatically complete. An introductory statement that ends with a preposition (such as *by, for, at,* and *to*) or a verb (such as *is, are,* or *were*) is incomplete. The list following a preposition or a verb actually functions as an object or as a complement to finish the sentence.

Faulty	Improved
Three Big Macs were ordered by: Pam, Jim, and Lee. (Do not use a colon after an incomplete statement.)	Three Big Macs were ordered by Pam, Jim, and Lee.
Other items that they ordered were: fries, Cokes, and salads. (Do not use a colon after an incomplete statement.)	Other items that they ordered were fries, Cokes, and salads.

GUIDE 30: Use a colon after business letter salutations and to introduce long quotations.

Dear Mr. Duran: Dear Lisa:

In discussing social media conversations, the consultant said: "Finding the right balance will take time, if it is ever achieved. Unlike face-to-face conversations, there's really no good way yet for people to let one another know when they are revealing too much."

Tip: Use a comma to introduce short quotations. Use a colon to introduce long one-sentence quotations and quotations of two or more sentences.

✓Checkpoint

Add appropriate semicolons and colons.

51. Marco's short-term goal is an entry-level job his long-term goal however is a management position.
52. Speakers included the following professors Kathy Hill Sam Houston State University Lora Lindsey Ohio University and Michael Malone Central Florida College.

53. The recruiter was looking for three qualities loyalty initiative and enthusiasm.
54. Microsoft seeks experienced individuals however it will hire recent graduates who are skilled.
55. South Florida is an expanding region therefore many business opportunities are available.

Apostrophe

GUIDE 31: If an ownership word does NOT end in an *s* sound, add an apostrophe and *s*, whether the word is singular or plural.

We hope to show a profit in one year's time. (Add *'s* because the ownership word *year* is singular and does not end in *s*.)

The children's teacher allowed free time on the computer. (Add *'s* because the ownership word *children*, although it is plural, does not end in *s*.)

GUIDE 32: If an ownership word does end in an *s* sound and is singular, add an apostrophe and *s*.

The witness's testimony was critical. (Add *'s* because the ownership word *witness* is singular and ends in an *s*.)

The boss's cell phone rang during the meeting. (Add *'s* because the ownership word *boss* is singular and ends in an *s*.)

If the ownership word ends in an *s* sound and is plural, add only an apostrophe.

Both investors' portfolios showed diversification. (Add only an apostrophe because the ownership word *investors* is plural and ends in an *s*.)

Some workers' benefits will cost more. (Add only an apostrophe because the ownership word *workers* is plural and ends in an *s*.)

Tip: To determine whether an ownership word ends in an *s*, use it in an *of* phrase. For example, *one month's salary* becomes *the salary of one month*. By isolating the ownership word without its apostrophe, you can decide whether it ends in an *s*.

GUIDE 33: Use a possessive pronoun or add an apostrophe and *s* to make a noun possessive when it precedes a gerund (a verb form used as a noun).

We all protested *Laura's* (not *Laura*) smoking. (Add an apostrophe and *s* to the noun preceding the gerund.)

His (not *Him*) talking on his cell phone angered moviegoers. (Use a possessive pronoun before the gerund.)

I appreciate *your* (not *you*) answering the telephone while I was gone. (Use a possessive pronoun before the gerund.)

✓Checkpoint

Correct any problems with possessives.

56. Both companies executives received huge bonuses, even when employees salaries were falling.
57. In just one weeks time, we promise to verify all members names and addresses.
58. The manager and I certainly appreciate you bringing this matter to our CPAs attention.
59. All beneficiaries names must be revealed when insurance companies write policies.
60. Is your sister-in-laws job downtown?

Other Punctuation

GUIDE 34: Use one period to end a statement, command, indirect question, or polite request. Never use two periods.

Matt worked at BioTech, Inc. (Statement. Use only one period.)

Deliver it before 5 p.m. (Command. Use only one period.)

Stacy asked whether she could use the car next weekend. (Indirect question)

Will you please send me an employment application. (Polite request)

Tip: Polite requests often sound like questions. To determine the punctuation, apply the action test. If the request prompts an action, use a period. If it prompts a verbal response, use a question mark.

Faulty	Improved
Could you please correct the balance on my next statement? (This polite request prompts an action rather than a verbal response.)	Could you please correct the balance on my next statement.

Tip: To avoid the punctuation dilemma with polite requests, do not phrase the request as a question. Phrase it as a command: *Please correct the balance on my next statement*. It still sounds polite, and the punctuation problem disappears.

GUIDE 35: Use a question mark after a direct question and after statements with questions appended.

Are they hiring at BioTech, Inc.?

Most of their training is in-house, isn't it?

GUIDE 36: Use a dash to (a) set off parenthetical elements containing internal commas, (b) emphasize a sentence interruption, or (c) separate an introductory list from a summarizing statement. The dash has legitimate uses. However, some writers use it whenever they know that punctuation is necessary, but they are not sure exactly what. The dash can be very effective, if not misused.

Three top students—Gene Engle, Donna Hersh, and Mika Sato—won awards. (Use dashes to set off elements with internal commas.)

Executives at Apple—despite rampant rumors in the stock market—remained quiet regarding dividend earnings. (Use dashes to emphasize a sentence interruption.)

Japan, Taiwan, and Turkey—these were areas hit by recent earthquakes. (Use a dash to separate an introductory list from a summarizing statement)

GUIDE 37: Use parentheses to set off nonessential sentence elements, such as explanations, directions, questions, and references.

Researchers find that the office grapevine (see Chapter 1 for more discussion) carries surprisingly accurate information.

Only two dates (February 15 and March 1) are suitable for the meeting.

Tip: Careful writers use parentheses to de-emphasize and the dash to emphasize parenthetical information. One expert said, "Dashes shout the news; parentheses whisper it."

GUIDE 38: Use quotation marks to (a) enclose the exact words of a speaker; (b) enclose the titles of articles, chapters, or other short works; and (c) enclose specific definitions of words or expressions.

"If you make your job important," said the consultant, "it's quite likely to return the favor." (Quotation marks enclose the exact words of a speaker.)

The recruiter said that she was looking for candidates with good communication skills. (Omit quotation marks because the exact words of the speaker are not quoted.)

In *The Wall Street Journal,* I saw an article titled "Communication for Global Markets." (Quotation marks enclose the title of an article. Italics identify the names of newspapers, magazines, and books.)

The term *tweet* refers to "a post made on the microblogging site Twitter." (Quotation marks enclose the definition of a word.)

For jargon, slang, words used in a special sense such as humor or irony, and words following *stamped* or *marked,* some writers use italics. Other writers use quotation marks.

Computer criminals are often called *hackers* (or "hackers"). (Jargon)

My teenager said that the film *The Hunger Games* is *sick* (or "sick"). (Slang)

Justin claimed that he was *too ill* (or "too ill") to come to work yesterday. (Irony)

The package was stamped *Fragile* (or "Fragile"). (Words following *stamped*)

Tip: Never use quotation marks arbitrarily, as in *Our "spring" sale starts April 1.*

✓Checkpoint

Add appropriate punctuation.

61. Will you please send your print catalog as soon as possible
62. (Direct quotation) Our Super Bowl promotion said the CEO will cost nearly $500,000
63. (De-emphasize) Two kinds of batteries see page 16 of the instruction booklet may be used in this camera
64. Tim wondered whether sentences could end with two periods
65. Stephanie plans to do a lot of chillaxing during her vacation

Capitalization

GUIDE 39: Capitalize proper nouns and proper adjectives. Capitalize the *specific* names of persons, places, institutions, buildings, religions, holidays, months, organizations, laws, races, languages, and so forth. Do not capitalize seasons, and do not capitalize common nouns that make *general* references.

Proper Nouns	Common Nouns
Michelle Deluca	the manufacturer's rep
Everglades National Park	the wilderness park
College of the Redwoods	the community college
Empire State Building	the downtown building
Environmental Protection Agency	the federal agency
Persian, Armenian, Hindi	modern foreign languages
Annual Spring Festival	in the spring

Proper Adjectives	
Hispanic markets	Italian dressing
Xerox copy	Japanese executives
Swiss chocolates	Reagan economics

GUIDE 40: Capitalize only specific academic courses and degrees.

Professor Donna Hernandez, PhD, will teach Accounting 121 next spring.

James Barker, who holds bachelor's and master's degrees, teaches marketing.

Jessica enrolled in classes in management, English, and business law.

GUIDE 41: Capitalize courtesy, professional, religious, government, family, and business titles when they precede names.

Mr. Jameson, Mrs. Alvarez, and Ms. Robinson (Courtesy titles)

Professor Andrews, Dr. Lee (Professional titles)

Rabbi Cohen, Pastor Williams, Pope Francis (Religious titles)

Senator Tom Harrison, Mayor Jackson (Government titles)

Uncle Edward, Mother Teresa, Cousin Vinney (Family titles)

Vice President Morris, Budget Director Lopez (Business titles)

Do not capitalize a title when it is followed by an appositive (that is, when the title is followed by a noun that renames or explains it).

Only one professor, Jonathan Marcus, favored a tuition hike.

Local candidates counted on their governor, Lee Jones, to help raise funds.

Do not capitalize titles following names unless they are part of an address:

Mark Yoder, president of Yoder Enterprises, hired all employees.

Paula Beech, director of Human Resources, interviewed all candidates.

Send the package to Amanda Lopez, Advertising Manager, Cambridge Publishers, 20 Park Plaza, Boston, MA 02116. (Title in an address)

Generally, do not capitalize a title that replaces a person's name.

Only the president, his chief of staff, and one senator made the trip.

The director of marketing and the sales manager will meet at 1 p.m.

Do not capitalize family titles used with possessive pronouns.

my mother, his father, your cousin

GUIDE 42: Capitalize the main words in titles, subject lines, and headings. *Main* words are all words except (a) the articles *a, an,* and *the*; (b) the conjunctions *and, but, or,* and *nor*; (c) prepositions containing two or three letters (e.g., *of, for, in, on, by*); (d) the word *to* in infinitives (such as *to work, to write,* and *to talk*); and (e) the word *as*—unless any of these words are the first or last words in the title, subject line, or heading.

I enjoyed the book *A Customer Is More Than a Name.* (Book title)

Team Meeting to Discuss Deadlines Rescheduled for Friday (Subject line)

We liked the article titled "Advice From a Pro: How to Say It With Pictures." (Article)

Check the Advice and Resources link at the CareerBuilder website.

(Note that the titles of books are italicized, but the titles of articles are enclosed in quotation marks.)

GUIDE 43: Capitalize names of geographic locations. Capitalize *north, south, east, west,* and their derivatives only when they represent specific geographic regions.

from the Pacific Northwest	heading northwest on the highway
living in the West	west of the city
Midwesterners, Southerners	western Oregon, southern Ohio
peace in the Middle East	a location east of the middle of the city

GUIDE 44: Capitalize the main words in the specific names of departments, divisions, or committees within business organizations. Do not capitalize general references.

All forms are available from our Department of Human Resources.

The Consumer Electronics Division launched an upbeat marketing campaign.

We volunteered for the Employee Social Responsibility Committee.

You might send an application to their personnel department.

GUIDE 45: Capitalize product names only when they refer to trademarked items. Do not capitalize the common names following manufacturers' names.

Dell laptop computer	Skippy peanut butter	NordicTrack treadmill
Eveready Energizer	Norelco razor	Canon color copier
Coca-Cola	Panasonic plasma television	Big Mac sandwich

GUIDE 46: Capitalize most nouns followed by numbers or letters (except in page, paragraph, line, and verse references).

Room 14	Exhibit A	Flight 12, Gate 43
Figure 2.1	Plan No. 1	Model Z2010

✓Checkpoint

Capitalize all appropriate words.

66. vice president moore bought a new droid smartphone before leaving for the east coast.
67. when you come on tuesday, travel west on highway 5 and exit at mt. mckinley street.
68. The director of our human resources department called a meeting of the company's building security committee.
69. our manager and president are flying on american airlines flight 34 leaving from gate 69 at the dallas/fort worth international airport.
70. my father read a businessweek article titled can you build loyalty with bricks and mortar?

Number Usage

GUIDE 47: Use word form to express (a) numbers *ten* and under and (b) numbers beginning sentences. General references to numbers *ten* and under should be expressed in word form. Also use word form for numbers that begin sentences. If the resulting number involves more than two words, however, recast the sentence so that the number does not fall at the beginning.

We received *six* text messages from *four* sales reps.

Fifteen customers responded to our *three* cell phone ads today.

A total of 155 smartphones were awarded as prizes. (Avoid beginning the sentence with a long number such as *one hundred fifty-five.*)

GUIDE 48: Use figures to express most references to numbers 11 and over.

Over *150* people from *53* companies attended the two-day workshop.

A four-ounce serving of Haagen-Dazs toffee crunch ice cream contains *300* calories and *19* grams of fat.

GUIDE 49: Use figures to express money, dates, clock time, decimals, and percentages.

One item costs only *$1.95*; most, however, were priced between *$10* and *$35*. (Omit the decimals and zeros in even sums of money.)

We scheduled a meeting for May 12. (Notice that we do NOT write May 12th.)

We expect deliveries at 10:15 a.m. and again at 4 p.m. (Use lowercase *a.m.* and *p.m.*)

All packages must be ready by 4 o'clock. (Do NOT write 4:00 o'clock.)

When U.S. sales dropped *4.7* percent, net income fell *9.8* percent. (In contextual material use the word *percent* instead of the symbol %.)

GUIDE 50: Use a combination of words and figures to express sums of 1 million and over. Use words for small fractions.

Orion lost *$62.9 million* in the latest fiscal year on revenues of *$584 million*. (Use a combination of words and figures for sums of 1 million and over.)

Only *one half* of the registered voters turned out. (Use words for small fractions.)

Tip: To ease your memory load, concentrate on the numbers normally expressed in words: numbers *ten* and under, numbers at the beginning of a sentence, and small fractions. Nearly everything else in business is generally written with figures.

✓Checkpoint

Correct any inappropriate expression of numbers or abbreviations.

71. Although he budgeted fifty dollars, Jake spent 94 dollars and 34 cents for supplies.
72. Is the meeting on November 7th or November 14th?
73. UPS deliveries arrive at nine AM and again at four fifteen PM.
74. The company applied for a fifty thousand dollar loan at six%.
75. The U.S. population is just over 300,000,000, and the world population is estimated to be about 7,100,000,000.

Confusing Words

accede:	to agree or consent
exceed:	over a limit
accept:	to receive
except:	to exclude; (prep) but
adverse:	opposing; antagonistic
averse:	unwilling; reluctant
advice:	suggestion, opinion
advise:	to counsel or recommend
affect:	to influence
effect:	(n) outcome, result; (v) to bring about, to create
all ready:	prepared
already:	by this time
all right:	satisfactory
alright:	unacceptable variant spelling
altar:	structure for worship
alter:	to change
appraise:	to estimate
apprise:	to inform
ascent:	(n) rising or going up
assent:	(v) to agree or consent
assure:	to promise
ensure:	to make certain
insure:	to protect from loss
capital:	(n) city that is seat of government; wealth of an individual; (adj) chief
capitol:	building that houses state or national lawmakers
cereal:	breakfast food
serial:	arranged in sequence
cite:	to quote; to summon
site:	location
sight:	a view; to see
coarse:	rough texture
course:	route; part of a meal; unit of learning
complement:	that which completes
compliment:	(n) praise or flattery; (v) to praise or flatter
conscience:	regard for fairness
conscious:	aware
council:	governing body
counsel:	(n) advice, attorney, consultant; (v) to give advice
credible:	believable
creditable:	good enough for praise or esteem; reliable
desert:	(n) arid land; (v) to abandon
dessert:	sweet food
device:	invention or mechanism
devise:	to design or arrange
disburse:	to pay out
disperse:	to scatter widely
elicit:	to draw out
illicit:	unlawful
envelop:	(v) to wrap, surround, or conceal
envelope:	(n) a container for a written message
every day:	each single day
everyday:	ordinary
farther:	a greater distance
further:	additional
formally:	in a formal manner
formerly:	in the past
grate:	(v) to reduce to small particles; to cause irritation; (n) a frame of crossed bars blocking a passage
great:	(adj) large in size; numerous; eminent or distinguished
hole:	an opening
whole:	complete
imply:	to suggest indirectly
infer:	to reach a conclusion
lean:	(v) to rest against; (adj) not fat
lien:	(n) legal right or claim to property
liable:	legally responsible
libel:	damaging written statement
loose:	not fastened
lose:	to misplace
miner:	person working in a mine
minor:	(adj) lesser; (n) person under age
patience:	calm perseverance
patients:	people receiving medical treatment
personal:	private, individual
personnel:	employees
plaintiff:	(n) one who initiates a lawsuit
plaintive:	(adj) expressive of suffering or woe

populace:	(n) the masses; population of a place	*than:*	conjunction showing comparison
populous:	(adj) densely populated	*then:*	adverb meaning "at that time"
precede:	to go before	*their:*	possessive form of *they*
proceed:	to continue	*there:*	at that place or point
precedence:	priority	*they're:*	contraction of *they are*
precedents:	events used as an example	*to:*	preposition; sign of the infinitive
principal:	(n) capital sum; school official; (adj) chief	*too:*	adverb meaning "also" or "to an excessive extent"
principle:	rule of action	*two:*	a number
stationary:	immovable	*waiver:*	abandonment of a claim
stationery:	writing material	*waver:*	to shake or fluctuate

160 Frequently Misspelled Words

absence
accommodate
achieve
acknowledgment
across
adequate
advisable
analyze
annually
appointment
argument
automatically
bankruptcy
becoming
beneficial
budget
business
calendar
canceled
catalog
changeable
column
committee
congratulate
conscience
conscious
consecutive
consensus
consistent
control
convenient
correspondence
courteous
criticize
decision
deductible
defendant
definitely
dependent
describe
desirable
destroy
development
disappoint
dissatisfied
division
efficient
embarrass
emphasis
emphasize
employee
envelope
equipped
especially
evidently
exaggerate
excellent
exempt
existence
extraordinary
familiar
fascinate
feasible
February
fiscal
foreign
forty
fourth
friend
genuine
government
grammar
grateful
guarantee
harass
height
hoping
immediate
incidentally
incredible
independent
indispensable
interrupt
irrelevant
itinerary
judgment
knowledge
legitimate
library
license
maintenance
manageable
manufacturer
mileage
miscellaneous
mortgage
necessary
nevertheless
ninety
ninth
noticeable
occasionally
occurred
offered
omission
omitted
opportunity
opposite
ordinarily
paid
pamphlet
permanent
permitted
pleasant
practical
prevalent
privilege
probably
procedure
profited

prominent
quality
quantity
questionnaire
receipt
receive
recognize
recommendation
referred
regarding
remittance
representative
restaurant
schedule
secretary
separate
similar
sincerely
software
succeed
sufficient
supervisor
surprise
tenant
therefore
thorough
though
through
truly
undoubtedly
unnecessarily
usable
usage
using
usually
valuable
volume
weekday
writing
yield

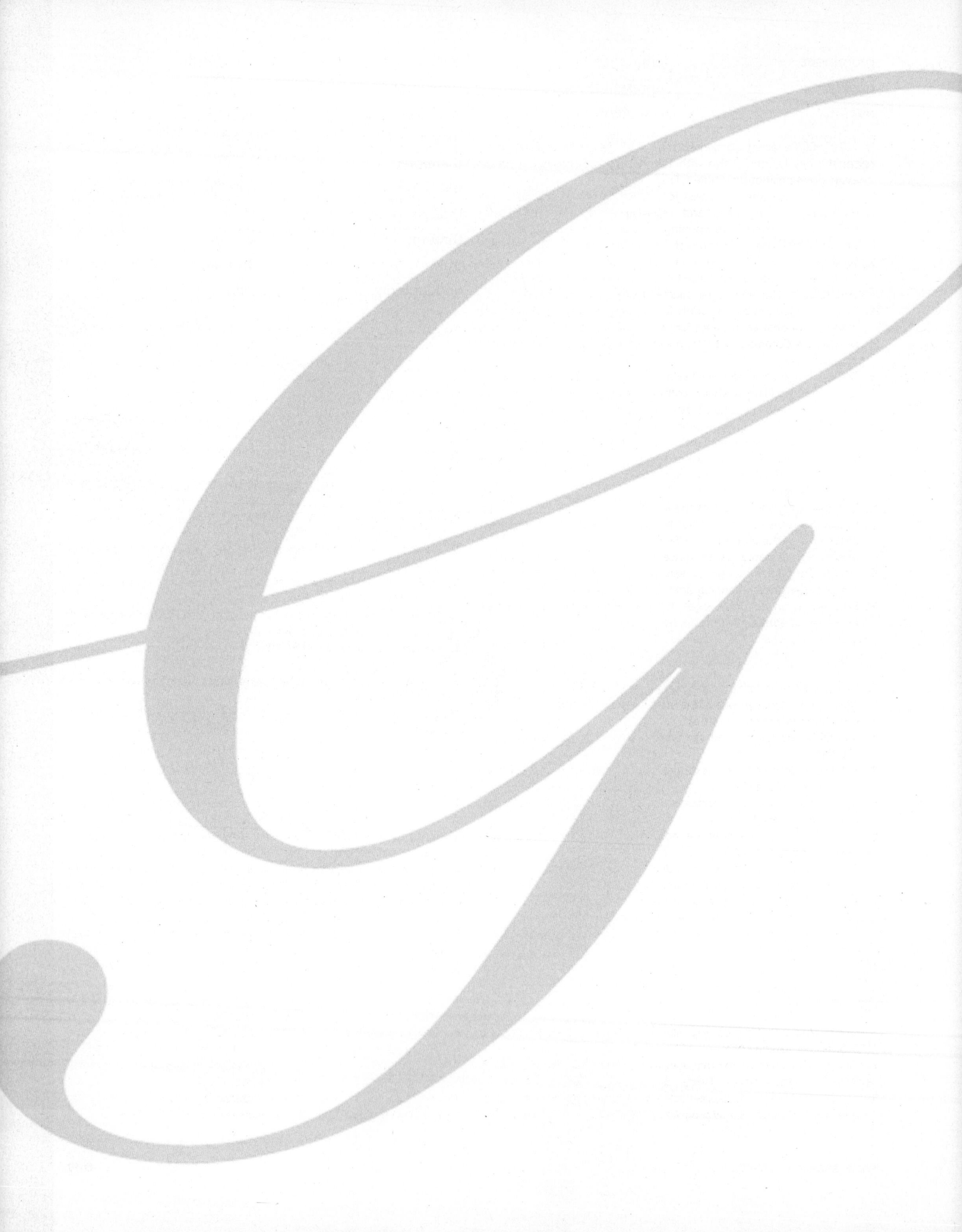

Key to Grammar and Mechanics

Chapter 1

1. Although the recent job market for new college graduates is **brighter, it's** still highly competitive with 1.5 unemployed workers vying for every open position. [b, Guide 1, Fragment]
2. Economists say this is the best job market in nearly a **decade; the** improving U.S. economy and accelerating retirements of baby boomers are creating job openings across many fields. [c, Guide 3, Comma splice. Use a semicolon or start a new sentence with *However.*]
3. Because you are entering a fast-paced, competitive, and highly connected digital **environment, communication** and technology skills are critical to your career success. [b, Guide 1, Fragment]
4. Many qualified people will apply for **openings; however,** candidates with exceptional communication skills will immediately stand out. [c, Guide 3, Comma splice. Use a semicolon or start a new sentence with *However.*]
5. Nearly all potential employers said that being able to think critically, communicate clearly, and solve complex problems are more important than a candidate's undergraduate major. [a, Correctly punctuated]
6. The nine-to-five job may soon be a relic of the **past if** millennials have their way. [b, Guide 1, Fragment]
7. Knowledge workers must be able to explain their **decisions; they** must be critical thinkers. [d, Guide 2, Run-on sentence. Use a semicolon or start a new sentence with *They.*]
8. Approximately 75 percent of the information gathered through the grapevine turns out to be **true; however,** that means that at least 25 percent of the information is false. [c, Guide 3. Comma splice. Use a semicolon or start a new sentence with *However.*]
9. Ethical companies experience less litigation, and they also are the target of less government regulation. [a, Correctly punctuated]
10. Even when an action is **legal, it** may violate generally accepted principles of right and wrong. [b, Guide 1, Fragment]

Chapter 2

1. Have you **spoken** with the other members of the virtual team? [Guide 4]
2. During job interviews one of the most frequently requested soft skills **is** writing proficiency. [Guide 6]
3. Meredith said she wished she **were** team leader for just one day. [Guide 5]
4. Better decisions and faster response time **explain** why companies are using teams. [Guide 7]
5. Neither the speaker nor members of the team **were** bothered by the technical mishap. [Guide 7]
6. Conflict and disagreement **are** normal and should be expected in team interactions. [Guide 7]
7. Every piece of information including e-mails and texts **was** made public during the trial. [Guides 6 and 8]
8. A committee of faculty and students **is** examining strategies to improve campus conservation efforts. [Guide 9]
9. Each of the employees was given the opportunity to **choose** a team to join. [Guide 4]
10. *C*

Chapter 3

1. During the investigation two **attorneys** questioned all witnesses thoroughly. [Guide 10]
2. Please send texts to my manager and **me** so that she and I both understand the situation. [Guide 13]
3. Google encourages developers to create apps and games for families and children using **its** new program. [Guide 14]
4. **It's** a smart move on Google's part because it allows **us** consumers to select age-appropriate games for our children. [Guides 14 and 13]
5. Send the report to the administrative assistant or **me** when it's finished. [Guide 15]
6. Every online sales rep must improve **his or her** writing skills to handle chat sessions. *OR:* All online sales reps must improve their writing skills to handle chat sessions. [Guide 17]
7. The contract will be awarded to **whoever** submitted the lowest bid. [Guide 16]
8. Most applications were made in time, but **yours** and **hers** missed the deadline. [Guide 14]
9. Just between you and me, who do you think will be our new president? [*C*, Guide 13]
10. It must have been **she** who sent the e-mail to Jason and me. [Guide 12]

Chapter 4

1. The ability to prepare a purposeful, concise, and audience-centered message does not come **naturally** to most people. [Guide 19]
2. Samantha thought she had done **well** when she wrote her part of the team report. [Guide 19]
3. The team wiki enables everyone to see the most **up-to-the-minute** status information. [Guide 20]
4. All of our **newly created** team documents can be posted **quickly** to the wiki. [Guides 20 and 19]
5. We all felt **bad** when one member lost her laptop and had no backup. [Guide 19]
6. The 3-x-3 writing process provides **step-by-step** instructions for preparing messages. [Guide 20]
7. Kevin found it difficult to pass up the **once-in-a-lifetime** opportunity to travel worldwide. [Guide 20]
8. Our project ran **smoothly** after Jennifer reorganized the team. [Guide 19]
9. **Locally installed** online collaboration tools are **easy to use** and work well. [Guide 20]
10. **Well-written** business messages sound conversational but professional. [Guide 20]

Chapter 5

1. Informal research methods include looking in the **files,** talking with your **boss,** and interviewing the target audience. [Guide 21]
2. When we use company **e-mail,** we realize that our messages are monitored. [Guide 22]
3. By learning to distinguish between dependent and independent **clauses,** you will be able to avoid serious sentence faults. [Guide 22]
4. Active-voice verbs are best in most business **messages,** but passive-voice verbs are useful when sensitivity is required. [Guide 23]
5. We hired Gabriella **Lugo,** who was the applicant with the best **qualifications,** as our new social media manager. [Guide 25]
6. Although the letter was written on April 15, **2014,** it was not delivered until **June 30,** 2018. [Guide 24]
7. The new social media **business,** by the **way,** is flourishing and is expected to show a profit soon. [Guide 25]
8. After he **graduates,** Luke plans to move to Austin and find work there. [Guide 22]
9. Last fall our company introduced policies regulating the use of cell **phones, texting,** and e-mail on the job. [Guide 21]
10. The problem with many company telecommunication policies is that the policies are self-policed and never enforced. [*C*, Guide 26]

Chapter 6

1. Tech specialists created a snazzy new **app; however**, it lacked an exciting name. [Guide 27]
2. Companies find it difficult to name new **products; consequently**, they often hire specialists. [Guide 27]
3. New product names must be **interesting; however**, many of the best names are already taken. [Guide 27]
4. Branding a product is a creative **endeavor;** the name becomes a product's shorthand. [Guide 27]
5. Global names must be appealing in such faraway places as **Beijing, China; Toronto, Canada; and Dubai City,** United Arab Emirates. [Guide 28]
6. One naming expert warned companies with the following **comment:** "Be aware of global consequences. For example, Bimbo is the name of a Mexican baking conglomerate. However, the word in English has an unsavory meaning." [Guide 30]
7. Product and company names are developed by combining the following three linguistic **elements:** morphemes, phonemes, and syntax. [Guide 29]
8. One of the reasons company names such as Google and Apple work is that they are **catchy; however**, they are also backed by high-quality products. [Guide 27]
9. Some English sounds (such as L, V, F, and W) are considered **feminine;** others (such as X, M, and Z) are viewed as masculine. [Guide 27]
10. Among the company officers judging new names were Sierra Love, vice **president;** Rachel Lohr, **CFO;** and Megan Cervantes, manager. [Guide 28]

Chapter 7

1. In just one **year's** time, James increased the number of his blog followers by 50 percent. [Guide 31]
2. Many followers of **James's** blog commented on the overuse of the Reply All button. [Guide 32]
3. Even her friends resented **Rebecca's** smoking in the hallways. [Guide 33]
4. Our three top sales **reps**—Sam, Ashley, and **Noah**—received substantial bonuses. [Guide 36]
5. Success often depends on an **individual's** ability to adapt to change. [Guide 31]
6. You must replace the ink cartridge **(see** page 8 in the **manual)** before printing. [Guide 37]
7. Zeke wondered whether all sales **managers'** databases needed to be updated. [Guide 32]
8. (Direct quotation) **"The** death of **e-mail,"** said Mike Song, **"has** been greatly **exaggerated."** [Guide 38]
9. My friend recommended an article titled **"Ten** Tools for Building Your Own Mobile **App."** [Guide 38]
10. The staffing meeting starts at 10 a.m. sharp, doesn't **it?** [Guide 35]

Chapter 8

1. Our **sales manager** and **director of operations** thought that the **company** should purchase a new **Nordictrack** treadmill for the **fitness** room. [Guides 41, 39, 45]
2. All **American Airlines** passengers must exit the plane at **Gate** 2B in **Terminal** 4 when they reach **Seattle-Tacoma International Airport**. [Guides 39, 46]
3. The secretary of state of the **United States** urged members of the **European Union** to continue to seek peace in the **Middle East**. [Guides 41, 39, 43]
4. My **uncle**, who lives in the **Midwest**, has a **Big Mac** and a **Diet Coke** for **lunch** nearly every day. [Guides 41, 43, 45]
5. Our corporate **vice president** and **president** met with several **directors** on the **West Coast** to discuss how to develop **apps** for **Facebook**. [Guides 41, 43, 39]
6. The **world's highest tax rate** is in **Belgium,** said **Professor Du-Babcock**, who teaches at the **City University of Hong Kong**. [Guides 39, 41]
7. Alyson Davis, who heads our **Consumer Services Division**, has a **master's degree** in **marketing** from **California State University**. [Guides 44, 40, 39]
8. Please consult **Figure** 2.3 in **Chapter** 2 to obtain **U.S. Census Bureau** population figures for the **Northeast**. [Guides 46, 39, 43]
9. Last **summer** did you see the article titled "**The Global Consequences** of **Using Crops** for **Fuel**"? [Guides 39, 42]
10. Kahee plans to take courses in **management, economics**, and **history** in the **spring**. [Guides 40, 39]

Chapter 9

1. **Twenty-three** call centers in India will be switching from customer service to mortgage processing. [Guide 47]
2. Faced with a **$522 million** deficit, the mayor sent pink slips to **15,000** city employees. [Guides 50, 48]
3. UPS deliveries are expected before **10 a.m.** and again at **4:30 p.m.** [Guide 49]
4. Consumers find that sending a **140-character** tweet is easier than writing a complaint letter. [Guide 48]
5. Fewer than **one half** of the stockholders submitted their ballots before the **June 15** deadline. [Guides 50, 49]
6. In the first **two** weeks of the year, we expect to hire at least **ten** new employees. [Guide 47]
7. On **April 15** our attorney notified all **four** managers of the lawsuit. [Guides 49, 47]
8. You can burn **150** calories by walking as little as **30** minutes. [Guide 48]
9. A **five**-year loan for a **$25,000** new car with **20 percent** down would have monthly payments of **$356**. [Guides 47, 49]
10. Although he expected to spend **$50** or less, Jake spent **$65** for the gift.

Chapter 10

1. The **principal** part of the manager's persuasive message contained a **compliment** and valuable **advice**.
2. Did you **already analyze** the product's major and **minor** appeals before writing the sales message?
3. In responding to the irate customer, Carmen made a **conscious** effort to show **patience** and present **credible** facts.
4. Even in **everyday** business affairs, we strive to reach **further** and go beyond what is expected.
5. Before you **proceed** with the report, please check those **surprising** statistics.
6. It's **usually** better to de-emphasize bad news **than** to spotlight it.
7. **Incidentally**, passive-voice verbs can help you make a statement less **personal** when **necessary**.
8. Customers are more **accepting** of **disappointing** news if they are **assured** that **their** requests were heard and treated fairly.
9. The customer's complaint **elicited** an immediate response that **analyzed** the facts carefully but was not **too** long.
10. When delivering bad news, try to **accommodate** a **dissatisfied** customer with a plausible alternative.

Chapter 11

1. One **credible** study revealed that **30** percent of jobs go to **companies'** inside candidates.
2. Networking is said to be the key to finding a **job;** however, **it's** easier said **than** done.
3. Some job seekers were paid **$500** each to attend **12** sessions that promised expert job-searching **advice**.
4. To excel at **networking, a candidate** must have an **easy-to-remember** e-mail address.

5. My friend asked me if I had **already** prepared a **30-second** elevator **speech.**
6. When Lucy and **I** were collecting data for the **report,** we realized that **Twitter** and Facebook could be significant.
7. **Today's** workers must brush up their marketable **skills; otherwise,** they may not find another job after being laid off.
8. Being active on LinkedIn and building an impressive **Internet** presence **are** important, but the looseness of these connections **means** you shouldn't expect much from them.
9. Just between you and **me,** one of the best **strategies** in networking **is** distributing business cards with your personal tagline.
10. On **February 1** our company **president** revealed that we would be hiring **30** new employees, which was excellent news for everyone.

Chapter 12

1. After our supervisor and **she** returned from their meeting at **2 p.m.,** we were able to sort the **customers'** names more quickly.
2. **Six** of the 18 workers in my department were **released;** as a **result,** we had to work harder to achieve our goals.
3. Toyota, the market-leading **Japanese carmaker,** continued to enjoy strong positive ratings despite a string of **much-publicized** recalls.
4. **Michael's** presentation to a nonprofit group netted him only **$300,** a tenth of his usual **honorarium,** but he believes in pro bono work.
5. To reflect our guiding **principles** and our commitment to executive **education,** we offer financial support to more than **60** percent of our current MBA candidates.
6. Our latest press **release,** which was written in our Corporate Communication **Department,** announces the opening of three **Asian** offices.
7. In his justification report dated **September 1,** Justin argued that expansion to **12** branch offices could boost annual revenue to **$22 million.**
8. The practicality and advisability of opening 12 branch offices **are** what will be discussed in the **consultant's feasibility** report.
9. The **president,** who had **gone** to a meeting in the **Midwest,** delivered a report to Jeff and **me** when he returned.
10. Because some organizations prefer **single-spaced reports,** be sure to check with your organization to learn **its** preference.

Chapter 13

1. Our **manager** and CEO both worked on the **30-page proposal,** which was due immediately.
2. Supervisors in **two departments** [delete apostrophe] complained that **their** departments should have been consulted.
3. The RFP and **its** attachments arrived **too** late for my manager and **me** to complete the necessary research.
4. Although we worked **every day** on the proposal, we felt **bad** that we could not meet the **May 15** deadline.
5. If the program and staff **are** to run **smoothly,** we must submit an effective grant proposal.
6. Although **short,** a successful mission statement should capture the **business's** goals and values [delete period] **in** a few succinct sentences.
7. A proposal budget cannot be changed if costs **rise later;** consequently, it must be written **carefully.**
8. A good eight-word mission statement is a critical tool for **funding;** it helps startup **companies** evolve **their** big idea without being pulled off track.
9. Entrepreneur Stephanie **Rivera,** publisher of **an** urban event **calendar,** relies on social media to broadcast her message.
10. Stephanie asked Jake and **me** to help her write a business **plan that** would guide her new company and garner **permanent** funding.

Chapter 14

1. The **CEO's** assistant scheduled my colleague and **me** for a **20**-minute presentation to explain the new workplace sustainability initiative.
2. PowerPoint presentations, claims one **expert,** should be no longer **than 20** minutes and have no more than ten slides.
3. The introduction to a presentation should accomplish **three goals:** (a) capture attention, (b) establish **credibility,** and (c) preview main points.
4. In the body of a short **presentation,** speakers should focus on no more than **three principal** points.
5. A poll of **2,000** employees revealed that **four fifths** of them said they feared giving a presentation more **than** anything else they could think of.
6. A list with **40** tips for inexperienced speakers **is** found in the article titled "Quick Tips **for** Speakers."
7. The **director** of operations made a **15**-minute presentation giving **step-by-step** instructions on achieving our sustainability goals.
8. In the **spring** our **company's** stock value is expected to **rise** at least 10 percent.
9. The appearance and mannerisms of a speaker **definitely affect** a **listener's** evaluation of the message.
10. Because the **boss's** daughter was a dynamic speaker who had founded a successful **company,** she earned at least **$20,000** for each presentation.

Chapter 15

1. To conduct a safe online job search, you **should [delete colon]** (a) **use** only reputable job boards, (**b**) keep careful records, and (c) limit the number of sites on which you post your résumé.
2. **Today's** employers use **sites** such as Facebook to learn about potential **employees,** which means that a job seeker must maintain a professional online presence.
3. When searching for **jobs,** candidates discovered that the résumé is more likely to be used to screen **candidates than** for making hiring decisions.
4. If I **were you,** I would shorten my résumé to **one** page and include a summary of qualifications.
5. Mitchell wondered whether it was **all right** to ask his professor for employment **advice.**
6. At last **month's** staff **meeting,** team members examined several **candidates'** résumés.
7. Rather **than** schedule **face-to-face interviews,** the team investigated videoconferencing.
8. **Eleven** applicants will be interviewed on **April 10;** consequently, we may need to work late to accommodate them.
9. Although as many as **25** percent of jobs are found on the **Internet,** the **principal** source of jobs still involves networking.
10. If Troy had **gone** to the **company's** own **website,** he might have seen the position posted immediately.

Chapter 16

1. Most interviews **usually** cover the same kinds of **questions; therefore,** smart candidates prepare for them.
2. Rodney wondered how many **companies** use social media to check **candidates' backgrounds.**
3. Despite the heavy use of **e-mail,** many **employers** use the telephone to reach candidates and set up **their** interviews.
4. In interviewing job **candidates,** recruiters have the following three **purposes:** assessing their skills, discussing their **experience,** and deciding whether they are a good fit for the organization.
5. If your job history has gaps in **it,** be prepared to explain what you did during this **time** [delete comma] and how you kept **up-to-date** in your field.

6. Interviewing is a **two-way street,** and candidates should be prepared with **their** own meaningful questions.
7. Kadence was asked whether she had a **bachelor's degree** [delete comma] and whether she had three **years'** experience.
8. If you are **conscientious** and want to create a good **impression,** be sure to write a **thank-you** message after a job interview.
9. When **Maria's** interview was **over,** she told friends that she had done **well.**
10. Maria was **all ready** to send a thank-you **message** [omit comma] when she realized she could not spell the **interviewer's** name.

Key to Grammar and Mechanics Checkpoint Exercises in Appendix D

This key shows all corrections. If you marked anything else, double-check the appropriate guideline.

1. Disney, destination
2. yearly, which
3. hour; however,
4. pavilion;
5. wedding;
6. If I *were* you, I would have *gone*
7. could have *written* . . . had *begun* earlier.
8. project manager *saw* . . . immediately *came*
9. project manager *were*
10. manager had *known* . . . would have *given*
11. time and talent *were* spent (Note that two subjects require a plural verb.)
12. attachments, *was* (Note that the subject is *message.*)
13. Each of . . . companies *is* (Note that the subject is *Each.*)
14. list of names and addresses *is* (Note that the subject is *list.*)
15. attorney *has*
16. My partner and *I* . . . but *yours*
17. was *hers*, but *its*
18. you and *me*
19. Neither the boss nor *I* knows whether *it's* broken, but its condition should have been reported to him or *me* earlier.
20. but *yours* and *hers*
21. *whomever*
22. *Whom* have you hired
23. for *whoever*
24. Matt and *I*
25. by whoever
26. Every employee must wear *a* picture identification badge. *OR: All employees* must wear *picture identification badges.*
27. slower career advancement, but *flexible scheduling* appeals to many workers. (Revise to avoid the vague pronoun *it.*)
28. Any renter must pay *the* rent . . . . *OR: All renters* must pay *their* rent . . . .
29. reported that *a* computer . . . . *OR:* reported that *his or her* computer . . . .
30. communication. *These techniques are* particularly important . . . . (Revise to avoid the vague pronoun *This.*)
31. My manager and *I* could not resist the *once-in-a-lifetime* opportunity.
32. John and *he* finished their task so *quickly* (Do not hyphenate *recently opened.*)
33. do *well* . . . *part-time* jobs and a few *full-time*
34. told him and *me* . . . *personally.*
35. *not-too-distant* future
36. class, Erin . . . with commas, semicolons,
37. studying punctuation,
38. program,
39. merchandising courses,
40. junior year, . . . in Los Angeles, Burbank,
41. Street, San Antonio, Texas 78220,
42. not, however,
43. paralegals, . . . next year,
44. May 15, 2012, . . . May 15, 2018.
45. fact,
46. sooner [delete comma]
47. car,
48. is [delete comma]
49. think, on the other hand, . . . buying [delete comma]
50. automakers are [delete comma] at this time [delete comma]
51. entry-level job; his long-term goal, however,
52. professors: Kathy Hill, San Houston State University; Lora Lindsey, Ohio University; and Michael Malone, Central Florida College.
53. qualities: loyalty, initiative,
54. individuals; however,

55. region; therefore,
56. companies'... employees'
57. one week's time, ... members'
58. appreciate *your*... CPA's
59. beneficiaries'
60. sister-in-law's
61. possible.
62. "Our Super Bowl promotion," said the CEO, "will cost nearly $500,000."
63. Two kinds of batteries (see page 16 of the instruction booklet)
64. two periods.
65. *chillaxing* or "chillaxing"
66. Vice President Moore ... Droid ... East Coast
67. When . . .Tuesday, . . . Highway 5 . . . Mt. McKinley Street.
68. Human Resources Department ... Building Security Committee
69. Our ... American Airlines Flight 34 ... Gate 69 at the Dallas/Fort Worth International Airport
70. My . . . *Businessweek* article titled "Can You Build Loyalty With Bricks and Mortar?"
71. $50 ... $94.34
72. November 7 or November 14 [delete *th*]
73. 9 a.m.... 4:15 p.m. (Note only one period at the end of the sentence.)
74. $50,000 loan at 6 percent.
75. 300 million ... 7.1 billion

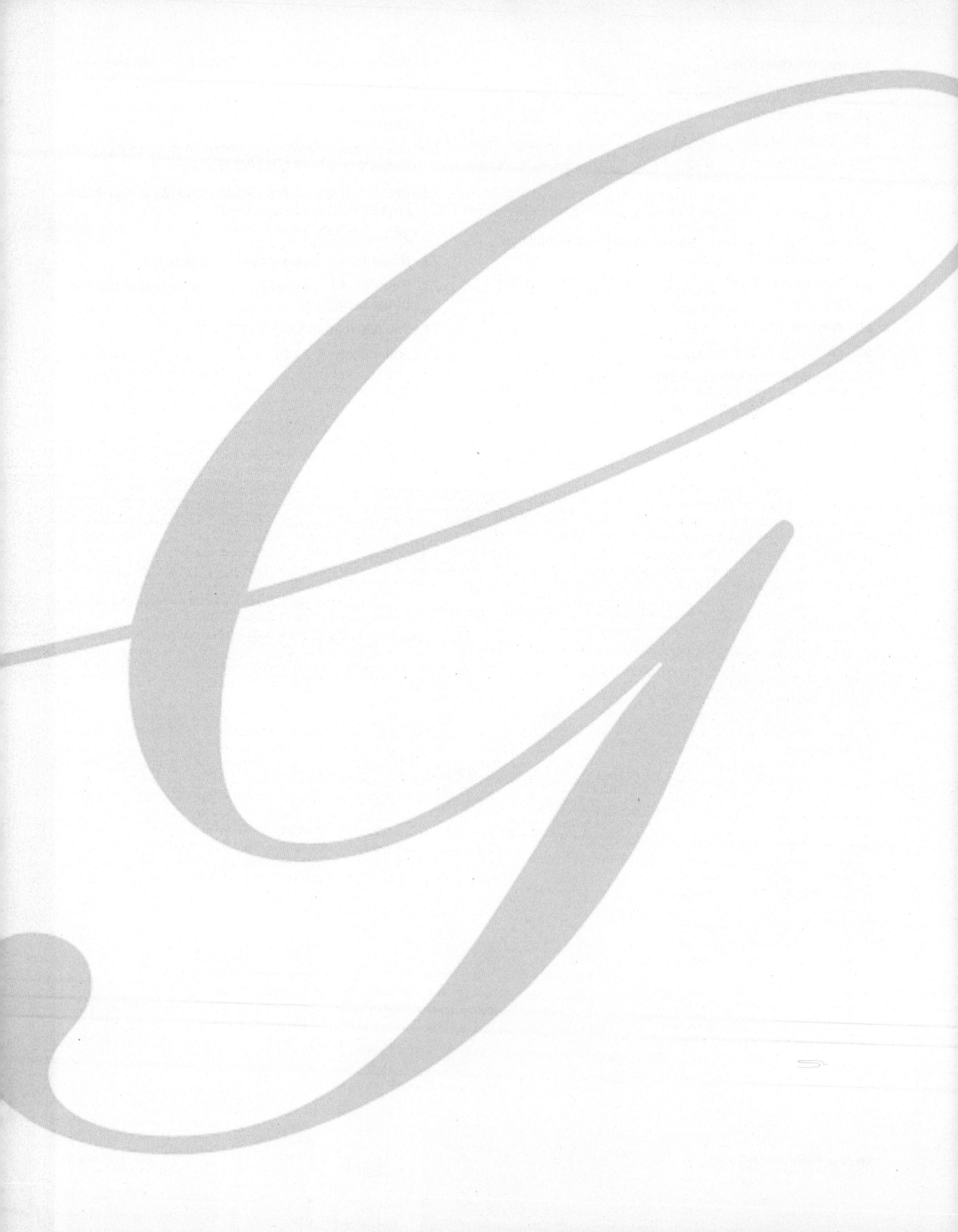

Etiquette IQ Responses

Chapter 1

1. **True.** Should you respond to your boss's e-mail or wait until Monday? Much depends on your relationship with your boss, but generally you can observe a common e-mail rule: Respond to e-mails within 24 hours. It's reasonable to set boundaries on your free time. If you are a boss, by the way, don't send demanding e-mails or texts to employees on weekends or after hours.
2. **False.** Should you phone your vacationing coworker with a work question? Certainly not! Everyone deserves a vacation. Get your information elsewhere. It's also considerate to avoid sending texts or e-mail requests that demand immediate responses after working hours. If at all possible, wait until regular work time to conduct your business unless you know your receiver works 24/7.
3. **False.** Don't make instant enemies by storing smelly food in a communal refrigerator. And certainly don't warm it up the next day in the office microwave. If you must store something smelly in the refrigerator, double-wrap it and remove it as soon as possible. On the topic of office food, if you didn't put food in the refrigerator, don't eat it.

Chapter 2

1. **False.** Never perform personal grooming tasks (such as combing your hair or clipping your fingernails) during a business meeting.
2. **False.** At a networking function, you should plan to spend about five to seven minutes with each person and then move on.
3. **True.** You should always respect the personal space and privacy of individuals. Never open the closed door of a coworker or superior. Decide whether your business is important enough to interrupt the person by knocking.

Chapter 3

1. **False.** When abroad, it's wise to remember that Americans are often accused of being too loud, informal, and overly expressive with body language. Show restraint.
2. **True.** Show respect in more formal environments by opening doors and allowing older businesspeople to enter and be seated first.
3. **False.** Americans tend to assume that others around the world do things as they do. Shaking hands and maintaining eye contact are accepted behavior in the United States, but in other parts of the world, people may not want to shake hands, and eye contact is offensive.

Chapter 4

1. **False.** Among the most offensive people in open offices are *speaker freakers,* those who take their calls with speaker on. This practice is especially disruptive in open offices or those with cubicles. If you must have your hands free, get a headset.
2. **False.** First, don't shout to anyone over the top of cubicles. Second, don't eavesdrop on conversations. Third, never give advice to a coworker about information you overheard on any call. It's difficult working in close surroundings, but try to observe others' privacy and personal space.
3. **False.** It's not wise to take even short personal calls at work. Before doing so, learn what your organization's policy is. Tell your friends and family your work hours, cautioning them not to call. Remember that how you act at work sends a message about your professionalism.

Chapter 5

1. **True.** Although it's wise to warn coworkers by texting that you will be late, it's even better to make sure you are on time with proper planning.
2. **False.** The person facing you should always take precedence over an incoming text.
3. **False.** Just because you can't hear doesn't mean the caller can't hear you. Always refrain from bellowing.

Chapter 6

1. **False.** It is good manners to simulate a knock by tapping lightly on the wall before entering a cubicle; even better is to call or e-mail in advance to ask about a good time for your visit.
2. **True.** Never divulge confidential information told to you by employees. As a general rule, whether you are a manager or an employee, it's better not to discuss your own personal affairs with colleagues.
3. **False.** Do not expect to be good buddies with your boss, regardless of any similarity in age or personality. Realize that your boss is in charge. Be friendly at business functions, but don't strive to socialize outside of business hours.

Chapter 7

1. **False.** Contrary to what some believe, e-mails should be held to the same standards as other workplace documents. Ditch the slang, use proper punctuation, and be sure to proofread before you hit Send.
2. **False.** Never forward e-mail messages without first seeking the permission of the sender. A message sent to you was meant for your eyes only. The writer may have used a totally different tone if the message were going to the secondary audience.
3. **False.** Never put cell phones, briefcases, or anything dirty on restaurant tables. Lots of people also consider it bad manners to accept cell phone calls in any public place.

Chapter 8

1. **True.** Etiquette authorities say that even though personal gifts may be prohibited within an organization, it is acceptable to show appreciation by sending a gourmet food basket or a subscription to a trade magazine for the entire office.
2. **True.** Business cards should be treated as gifts. After accepting a card, you should admire it and perhaps say something about it. Don't stuff it in your pocket or immediately write something on it.
3. **True.** Unless you have a close relationship with the caller, do not pick up a ringing phone and immediately identify the caller by using that person's first name. It startles the caller and might suggest that you are sneaky by screening incoming calls.

Chapter 9

1. **False.** You should calmly say, "I remember meeting you, but I can't remember your name." Don't try to bluff your way through your encounter. Because many people can't remember names, you should help others remember yours by announcing it when you greet someone who may have forgotten your name. Don't expect people to remember your name.

2. **False.** You should say, "Mr. Richmond, I would like to introduce Meredith Lee, a new office employee." The senior-ranking person should be mentioned first. However, when introducing a guest, client, or business partner, that person should always be the first to be introduced to coworkers and superiors, regardless of the peers' or supervisors' rank or seniority.
3. **False.** It is no longer necessary for a man to wait for a woman to extend her hand. Men and women are workplace equals today.

Chapter 10

1. **True.** Do not offer your business card immediately, and always pass each card out personally. Don't distribute cards as if they were flyers.
2. **False.** Never take home any office supplies. No matter how entitled you feel, it is thievery.
3. **True.** It is your responsibility to support your boss's decisions, even if you disagree with them. You can strive to make changes, but do so constructively and through the proper channels.

Chapter 11

1. **True.** Wearing headphones is like hanging a Do Not Disturb sign around your neck. In workplace elevators and hallways, take advantage of opportunities to connect socially with coworkers.
2. **False.** You should wait to sit down and ask where you may sit.
3. **False.** It is generally not a good idea to give personal or expensive gifts to your boss.

Chapter 12

1. **False.** Don't do it! As an employee, you have a responsibility to contact your employer regarding absence and lateness. If you text, it could give the impression that you have something to hide. It's better to make a phone call.
2. **False.** Many workers dislike voice-mail messages. If possible, wait until she returns to talk with her in person or on the phone. Sending an e-mail is also possible.
3. **True.** Delivering bad news such as a reprimand is better done privately. If your goal is to change behavior, private talks are more effective than humiliating public dress-downs.

Chapter 13

1. **False.** Even office casual has its boundaries (e.g., no bare midriffs, no sloppy jeans or sweatshirts, no flip-flops). If you are striving for a promotion, try to dress one or two notches above office casual.
2. **False.** The first person should hold the door for whomever follows, regardless of gender.
3. **False.** In an office environment, if everyone contributes and if you occasionally use the coffee or pastries, you are obligated to contribute. Always contribute your fair share toward group gifts, treats, or housekeeping.

Chapter 14

1. **False.** Expect the host, whether male or female, to pay for a meal. Don't offer to pay for your own meal.
2. **True.** You should not order liquor, appetizers, or desserts unless the host does, and your meal should not cost more than the host's. If unsure about the most appropriate selections, ask your host for recommendations.
3. **False.** Sex, politics, religions, and other sensitive topics are off limits no matter how well you think you know the others.

Chapter 15

1. **False.** Hiring managers, recruiters, and human resources professionals are busy people. Don't waste their time and risk angering them with multiple applications.
2. **False.** Sharing your decision to search for another job with coworkers may make you feel more comfortable, but doing so forces you into a position of weakness. A coworker could easily slip up, and your boss might hear of your decision long before you are ready to leave.
3. **True.** This seems extreme, but it is a recommendation that makes sense for anyone whose phone never leaves his or her side. Hiring managers may be reluctant to invest in those whose lives revolve around their phones.

Chapter 16

1. **True.** By all means, try to shake hands with members of the interviewing team without reaching over desks or tables.
2. **False.** Don't call attention to mishaps in an interview, including a weak handshake. Smile, ignore any flubs, and continue to project enthusiasm and confidence.
3. **True.** Taking a few notes during an interview conveys a sincere interest in what your interviewers have to say and gives you a chance to jot down a question to ask at the appropriate time. However, some hiring managers think negatively of an applicant who shows up and starts taking electronic notes. Doing so forces the interviewee to lose eye contact with the interviewer.

Index

Italic page numbers indicated illustrative information in figures

C

D

E

F

K

L

M

N

O

P

S

Y

Z